HANDBOOK OF COUNSELING PSYCHOLOGY

FOURTH EDITION

Edited by

Steven D. Brown

Robert W. Lent

WILEY

John Wiley & Sons, Inc.

Library of Congress Cataloging-in-Publication Data:

Handbook of counseling psychology / edited by Steven D. Brown,
Robert W. Lent.—4th ed.
    p.   cm.
Includes bibliographical references.
ISBN-13: 978-0-470-09622-2 (cloth)
1. Counseling psychology. 2. Psychology, Applied. I. Brown, Steven D.
(Steven Douglas), 1947– II. Lent, Robert W. (Robert William), 1953–
BF637.C6H315   2008
158′.3—dc22   2007026258

Printed in the United States of America.
10 9 8 7 6 5 4 3 2 1

To Linda Heath for years of love, friendship, and good humor; Zachary and Kathryn Brown for their support and myriad ways for keeping life interesting; Elma and Irvin Brown for always believing in me; René Dawis and Lloyd Lofquist for serving as exceptional scholarly role models early in my career; Suzette Speight and Liz Vera for being such professionally stimulating and supportive colleagues; and my students for their invaluable contributions to our work together.

S. D. B.

To Ellen and Jeremy, who taught me that work has its place but, at the end of the day (and all during the day), nothing beats family; Rich Russell, for being my advisor, mentor, "big brother," and friend; Ohio State's counseling psychology program, for being the graduate training powerhouse it was; my colleagues at Maryland, for continually inspiring me with their dedication to scholarship and practice; my advisees, for their infusion of curiosity and energy; and Howie Gresh, my Coney Island pal, for keeping me laughing for 50 years.

R. W. L.

Contributors

Saba Rasheed Ali, PhD
Psychological and Quantitative Foundations
The University of Iowa
Iowa City, Iowa

Consuelo Arbona, PhD
Department of Educational Psychology
University of Houston
Houston, Texas

Patrick Ian Armstrong, PhD
Department of Psychology
Iowa State University
Ames, Iowa

Rashanta A. Bledman, BA
Department of Educational, School, and
    Counseling Psychology
University of Missouri–Columbia
Columbia, Missouri

Nancy E. Betz, PhD
Department of Psychology
The Ohio State University
Columbus, Ohio

Kathleen J. Bieschke, PhD
Department of Counselor Education,
    Counseling Psychology, and
    Rehabilitation Services
Pennsylvania State University
University Park, Pennsylvania

Gary R. Brooks, PhD
Department of Psychology and
    Neurosciences
Baylor University
Waco, Texas

Steven D. Brown, PhD
Counseling Psychology Program
Loyola University Chicago
Chicago, Illinois

Hung Chiao, MEd
Department of Educational, School, and
    Counseling Psychology
University of Missouri–Columbia
Columbia, Missouri

Kathleen Chwalisz, PhD
Department of Psychology
Southern Illinois University
Carbondale, Illinois

Nicole Coleman, PhD
Department of Educational Psychology
University of Houston
Houston, Texas

Madonna G. Constantine, PhD
Department of Counseling and Clinical
    Psychology
Teachers College, Columbia
    University
New York, New York

James M. Croteau, PhD
Department of Counselor Education and
    Counseling Psychology
Western Michigan University
Kalamazoo, Michigan

Devon L. Cummings, MA
Department of Psychology
The University of Akron
Akron, Ohio

Steven J. Danish, PhD
Counseling Psychology Program
Virginia Commonwealth University
Richmond, Virginia

Lisa M. Edwards, PhD
Department of Counseling and Educational
    Psychology
Marquette University
Milwaukee, Wisconsin

Timothy R. Elliott, PhD
Department of Educational Psychology
Texas A& M University
College Station, Texas

Dorothy L. Espelage, PhD
Department of Educational Psychology
University of Illinois at Urbana-Champaign
Champaign, Illinois

Ruth E. Fassinger, PhD
Department of Counseling and Personnel
    Services
University of Maryland
College Park, Maryland

James Fauth, PhD
Center for Research on Psychological
    Practice
Antioch University New England
Keene, New Hampshire

Tanya Forneris, PhD
School of Kinesiology and
    Health Studies
Queens University
Kingston, Ontario, Canada

Nadya A. Fouad, PhD
Department of Educational Psychology
University of Wisconsin—Milwaukee
Milwaukee, Wisconsin

Debra L. Franko, PhD
Department of Counseling and Applied
    Educational Psychology
Northeastern University
Boston, Massachusetts

Charles J. Gelso, PhD
Department of Psychology
University of Maryland
College Park, Maryland

Diane Y. Genther, BA
Psychology and Research in
    Education
University of Kansas
Lawrence, Kansas

Lucia Albino Gilbert, PhD
Office of the Provost
University of Santa Clara
Santa Clara, California

Rodney K. Goodyear, PhD
Rossier School of Education
University of Southern California
Los Angeles, California

Paul A. Gore Jr., PhD
Department of Educational Psychology
University of Utah
Salt Lake City, Utah

Arpana Gupta, MEd
Department of Psychology
University of Tennessee
Knoxville, Tennessee

Emily Hamilton, MA
Department of Educational, School, and
    Counseling Psychology
University of Missouri–Columbia
Columbia, Missouri

Jeffrey A. Hayes, PhD
Department of Counselor Education,
    Counseling Psychology, and
    Rehabilitation Services
Pennsylvania State University
University Park, Pennsylvania

P. Paul Heppner, PhD
Department of Educational, School, and
    Counseling Psychology
University of Missouri–Columbia
Columbia, Missouri

Clara E. Hill, PhD
Department of Psychology
University of Maryland
College Park, Maryland

Jennifer M. Hill, BA
Psychological and Quantitative
    Foundations
The University of Iowa
Iowa City, Iowa

Arthur M. Horne, PhD
Department of Counseling and Human
    Development Services
University of Georgia
Athens, Georgia

Zac E. Imel, MA
Department of Counseling Psychology
University of Wisconsin–Madison
Madison, Wisconsin

Arpana G. Inman, PhD
Department of Education and Human
    Services
Lehigh University
Bethlehem, Pennsylvania

Neeta Kantamneni, MS
Department of Educational Psychology
University of Wisconsin–Milwaukee
Milwaukee, Wisconsin

Mai M. Kindaichi, MA, EdM
Department of Counseling and Clinical
    Psychology
Teachers College, Columbia University
New York, New York

Sarah Knox, PhD
Department of Educational and Counseling
    Psychology
Marquette University
Milwaukee, Wisconsin

Nicholas Ladany, PhD
Department of Education and Human
    Services
Lehigh University
Bethlehem, Pennsylvania

Michael J. Lambert, PhD
Department of Psychology
Brigham Young University
Provo, Utah

Christine M. Lee, PhD
Department of Psychiatry and Behavioral
    Sciences
University of Washington
Seattle, Washington

Robert W. Lent, PhD
Department of Counseling and Personnel
    Services
University of Maryland
College Park, Maryland

Frederick T. L. Leong, PhD
Department of Psychology
Michigan State University
East Lansing, Michigan

Wade C. Leuwerke, PhD
Department of Counselor
    Education
Drake University
Des Moines, Iowa

James W. Lichtenberg, PhD
Psychology and Research in
    Education
University of Kansas
Lawrence, Kansas

William Ming Liu, PhD
Psychological and Quantitative
    Foundations
The University of Iowa
Iowa City, Iowa

Shane J. Lopez, PhD
Psychology and Research in Education
University of Kansas
Lawrence, Kansas

Jessica L. Manning, MA
Department of Counselor Education and
    Counseling Psychology
Western Michigan University
Kalamazoo, Michigan

Matthew P. Martens, PhD
Department of Counseling, Educational
    Psychology, and Research
University of Memphis
Memphis, Tennessee

Matthew J. Miller, PhD
Division of Counseling Psychology
University at Albany, SUNY
Albany, New York

Laurie B. Mintz, PhD
Department of Educational, School,
    and Counseling Psychology
University of Missouri–Columbia
Columbia, Missouri

Marie L. Miville, PhD
Department of Counseling and Clinical
    Psychology
Teachers College, Columbia University
New York, New York

Clayton Neighbors, PhD
Department of Psychiatry and Behavioral
    Sciences
University of Washington
Seattle, Washington

Roberta L. Nutt, PhD
Association of State and
    Provincial Psychology Boards
Montgomery, Alabama

Ezemenari Obasi, PhD
Department of Psychology
Southern Illinois University
Carbondale, Illinois

David B. Peterson, PhD
Division of Special Education and
    Counseling
California State University Los
    Angeles
Los Angeles, California

Joseph G. Ponterotto, PhD
Division of Psychological and Educational
    Services
Fordham University at Lincoln Center
New York, New York

Jill Rader, PhD
Independent Practice
Austin, Texas

Daryn Rahardja, MS
W. W. Wright School of Education
Indiana University
Bloomington, Indiana

Lillian M. Range, PhD
Professional Programs Division
Our Lady of Holy Cross College
New Orleans, Louisiana

Christopher C. Rector, PhD
Counseling Psychology Program
Loyola University Chicago
Chicago, Illinois

James R. Rogers, PhD
Department of Psychology
The University of Akron
Akron, Ohio

James B. Rounds, PhD
Department of Educational
    Psychology
University of Illinois at Urbana-
    Champaign
Champaign, IL

Lisa Wallner Samstag, PhD
Department of Psychology
Long Island University
Brooklyn, New York

Hung-Bin Sheu, PhD
Division of Psychology in
    Education
Arizona State University
Tempe, Arizona

Suzette L. Speight, PhD
Counseling Psychology Program
Loyola University Chicago
Chicago, Illinois

Mindi N. Thompson, MA
Department of Psychology
The University of Akron
Akron, Ohio

Elizabeth M. Vera, PhD
Counseling Psychology Program
Loyola University Chicago
Chicago, Illinois

David A. Vermeersch, PhD
Department of Psychology
Loma Linda University
Loma Linda, California

Bruce E. Wampold, PhD
Department of Counseling Psychology
University of Wisconsin–Madison
Madison, Wisconsin

James L. Werth Jr., PhD
Department of Psychology
The University of Akron
Akron, Ohio

John S. Westefeld, PhD
Psychological and Quantitative
    Foundations
The University of Iowa
Iowa City, Iowa

Susan C. Whiston, PhD
W. W. Wright School of Education
Indiana University
Bloomington, Indiana

Elizabeth Nutt Williams, PhD
Department of Psychology
St. Mary's College of Maryland
St. Mary's, Maryland

Preface

This edition of the *Handbook of Counseling Psychology,* like all three prior editions, has three primary objectives: (1) to provide a scholarly review of important areas of counseling psychology inquiry, (2) to elaborate directions for future research, and (3) to draw specific suggestions for practice that derive from the scholarly literature in counseling psychology and related disciplines. Also, as in the third edition, we asked authors, as much as possible, to report effect sizes and to use these, and published meta-analyses, to draw inferences about the current state of knowledge in the field, to suggest questions for future investigation, and to derive practice implications. We are pleased to see that the research literature on topics addressed in this edition had advanced sufficiently so that, in many cases, our authors could use meta-analyses and report effect sizes to summarize their literature and draw implications. We are also pleased that many authors calculated and reported effect sizes when preexisting meta-analyses were not available.

Despite the broad continuities with prior editions, this edition departs from the others in significant ways. First, as readers of past editions will notice, there are more, but shorter, chapters in this edition. Our decision to include shorter chapters on more focused topics was solidified by an email survey we conducted with the membership of the Society of Counseling Psychology. Our goals were to capture advances in a wider range of the field while allowing authors to cover circumscribed topics in reasonable depth. We hope readers find this choice to be a good one. We thank our authors for trying so hard to follow length guidelines (not an easy task) and for their graciousness when difficult decisions had to be made to reduce their text to page limits.

The section topics and their ordering also depart from earlier editions. Part I of this edition, a *Handbook* mainstay, covers important current professional and scientific issues, but many of the topics in this edition are new and reflect important emerging professional trends. The coverage in this section was largely suggested to us by our survey of Division 17 members. Topics that were mentioned frequently included the new APA ethics code; managed care and prescription privileges; the growing use of technology in research, assessment, and counseling; the international growth of counseling psychology; social justice issues; and the growing attention to positive psychology. Each of these topics is covered in Part I.

The subsequent three sections cover important research in the most active areas of counseling psychology inquiry over the past 10 years. Brent Mallinckrodt, in response to our e-mail survey, kindly provided us with a content (key word) analysis of research published in the *Journal of Counseling Psychology* and *The Counseling Psychologist* since the publication of the third edition of this *Handbook.* The results revealed that the most active areas of counseling psychology research in this time frame were, in order, multicultural psychology, counseling and supervision process and outcome, and vocational psychology. These topics, therefore, are covered in Part II (multicultural psychology), Part III (counseling and supervision), and Part IV (vocational psychology) of this edition.

Part V covers topics on development and prevention. Although Brent Mallinckrodt's content analysis did not reveal that prevention per se engages the research attention of large numbers of counseling psychologists, it did show that many in our field are interested in health and disease, suicide, substance abuse, eating disorders, and school violence. Because we continue to believe that development and prevention are of historic and contemporary significance to counseling psychology, we decided to include chapters on each of the preceding topics, but to ask authors to take a preventive rather than remedial-treatment approach to them. These topics are complemented by two promotion-oriented chapters on resiliency interventions for at-risk youth and interventions to promote positive development and competencies. We hope the chapters in Part V will stimulate readers to give renewed thought to promoting positive development and resiliency and preventing (rather than only treating) psychological and health-related problems.

ACKNOWLEDGMENTS

We have many people to thank for their help throughout this project. First, we thank the many Division 17 members who responded to our email survey. Their suggestions were invaluable in helping us create a volume that spoke as much as possible to the current interests and concerns of those working in our field. Second, we thank Brent Mallinckrodt for going above and beyond what we had asked for in the survey. His content analysis gave us an excellent picture of contemporary counseling psychology research and provided us with an empirical basis for organizing this edition of the *Handbook*. Third, we are indebted to topic experts who took time out of their busy schedules to help us consider what to include in each Part. After deciding on the main sections and developing a preliminary set of chapter topics in each section, we emailed experts in each area (often multiple times) for input and suggestions about content and possible authors. The ultimate set of topics covered in each Part owes much to the thoughtful suggestions of Consuelo Arbona, Fred Borgen, Jean Carter, Ruth Fassinger, Nadya Fouad, Charlie Gelso, Paul Gore, Puncky Heppner, Clara Hill, Mary Ann Hoffman, Fred Leong, Jim Lichtenberg, Brent Mallinckrodt, Matt Miller, Laurie Mintz, Karen Multon, Karen O'Brien, Joe Ponterotto, Jim Rounds, Mark Savickas, Derald Wing Sue, Terry Tracey, Liz Vera, and Bruce Wampold.

We are also indebted to Tracey Belmont, who served as our editor in the beginning stages of this project, for getting us started and for her always helpful suggestions. We are equally indebted to Lisa Gebo, our editor at Wiley, who kept our noses to the grindstone and shepherded the project through to its completion. Lisa's graciousness and good humor are very much appreciated.

As always, we thank our families for their patience, support, and inspiration. We could not have completed this edition of the *Handbook* without them. Finally, we thank each other. Although a bit out of the ordinary for an acknowledgment, we've had, and continue to have, a heck of a professional run together based on mutual respect, complementary talents, and a long-lasting friendship—three characteristics that have sustained our professional collaborations and have, for each of us, enhanced our lives in innumerable ways.

STEVEN D. BROWN
ROBERT W. LENT

Contents

PART I: PROFESSIONAL AND SCIENTIFIC ISSUES

1. Legal and Ethical Issues Affecting Counseling Psychologists   3
   James L. Werth Jr., Devon L. Cummings, and Mindi N. Thompson

2. The Changing Landscape of Professional Practice in Counseling Psychology   21
   James W. Lichtenberg, Rodney K. Goodyear, and Diane Y. Genther

3. Technological Advances: Implications for Counseling Psychology Research, Training, and Practice   38
   Paul A. Gore Jr. and Wade C. Leuwerke

4. Social Justice and Counseling Psychology: A Challenge to the Profession   54
   Suzette L. Speight and Elizabeth M. Vera

5. A Growing Internationalization of Counseling Psychology   68
   P. Paul Heppner, Frederick T. L. Leong, and Hung Chiao

6. The Interface of Counseling Psychology and Positive Psychology: Assessing and Promoting Strengths   86
   Shane J. Lopez and Lisa M. Edwards

PART II: DIVERSITY AND MULTICULTURAL PSYCHOLOGY

7. Conceptual and Measurement Issues in Multicultural Psychology Research   103
   Matthew J. Miller and Hung-Bin Sheu

8. Theoretical and Empirical Advances in Multicultural Counseling and Psychology   121
   Joseph G. Ponterotto

9. Multicultural Competence in Counseling Psychology Practice and Training   141
   Madonna G. Constantine, Marie L. Miville, and Mai M. Kindaichi

10. Social Class and Classism: Understanding the Psychological Impact of Poverty
    and Inequality   159
    William Ming Liu and Saba Rasheed Ali

11. Psychology of Gender   176
    Roberta L. Nutt and Gary R. Brooks

12. Counseling Psychology and Sexual Orientation: History, Selective Trends, and Future
    Directions   194
    James M. Croteau, Kathleen J. Bieschke, Ruth E. Fassinger, and Jessica L. Manning

13. Advances in Conceptualizing and Studying Disability   212
    David B. Peterson and Timothy R. Elliott

PART III: COUNSELING AND SUPERVISION

14. Measuring and Improving Psychotherapy Outcome in Routine Practice   233
    Michael J. Lambert and David A. Vermeersch

15. The Importance of Treatment and the Science of Common Factors in Psychotherapy   249
    Zac E. Imel and Bruce E. Wampold

16. A Tripartite Model of the Therapeutic Relationship   267
    Charles J. Gelso and Lisa Wallner Samstag

17. Facilitating Insight in Counseling and Psychotherapy   284
    Clara E. Hill and Sarah Knox

18. Therapist Self-Awareness: Interdisciplinary Connections and Future Directions   303
    Elizabeth Nutt Williams, Jeffrey A. Hayes, and James Fauth

19. Culture and Race in Counseling and Psychotherapy: A Critical Review of
    the Literature   320
    Frederick T. L. Leong and Arpana Gupta

20. Developments in Counseling Skills Training and Supervision   338
    Nicholas Ladany and Arpana G. Inman

PART IV: CAREER DEVELOPMENT AND VOCATIONAL PSYCHOLOGY

21. Advances in Vocational Theories   357
    Nancy E. Betz

22. Vocational Psychology and Individual Differences   375
    Patrick Ian Armstrong and James B. Rounds

23. Conceptualizing and Diagnosing Problems in Vocational Decision Making   392
      Steven D. Brown and Christopher C. Rector

24. Contextual Factors in Vocational Psychology: Intersections of Individual, Group,
      and Societal Dimensions   408
      Nadya A. Fouad and Neeta Kantamneni

25. Work, Family, and Dual-Earner Couples: Implications for Research and Practice   426
      Lucia Albino Gilbert and Jill Rader

26. Vocational Counseling Process and Outcome   444
      Susan C. Whiston and Daryn Rahardja

27. Understanding and Promoting Work Satisfaction: An Integrative View   462
      Robert W. Lent

PART V: DEVELOPMENT AND PREVENTION

28. Risk and Resilience   483
      Consuelo Arbona and Nicole Coleman

29. Promoting Positive Development and Competency across the Life Span   500
      Steven J. Danish and Tanya Forneris

30. Promoting Health and Preventing and Reducing Disease   517
      Kathleen Chwalisz and Ezemenari Obasi

31. Suicide Prevention   535
      John S. Westefeld, Lillian M. Range, James R. Rogers, and Jennifer M. Hill

32. Substance Abuse Prevention and Treatment   552
      Matthew P. Martens, Clayton Neighbors, and Christine M. Lee

33. Preventing Eating and Weight-Related Disorders: Toward an Integrated Best
      Practices Approach   570
      Laurie B. Mintz, Emily Hamilton, Rashanta A. Bledman, and Debra L. Franko

34. School Violence and Bullying Prevention: From Research-Based Explanations to
      Empirically Based Solutions   588
      Dorothy L. Espelage and Arthur M. Horne

Author Index   607

Subject Index   629

PART I

Professional and Scientific Issues

CHAPTER 1

Legal and Ethical Issues Affecting Counseling Psychologists

JAMES L. WERTH JR.
DEVON L. CUMMINGS
MINDI N. THOMPSON

Many ethical and legal developments have affected the practice, research, and education of counseling psychologists since Kitchener and Anderson's (2000) chapter was written for the previous edition of the *Handbook*. Most notably, the American Psychological Association (APA, 2002) revised its Ethical Principles of Psychologists and Code of Conduct (Ethics Code). In addition, the implications of laws such as the Health Insurance Portability and Accountability Act (HIPAA) are significant. Further, such professional issues as competence and impairment have received widespread attention in psychology. This chapter provides an overview of a selected set of legal and ethical issues currently affecting counseling psychologists. We focus primarily on developments since the previous edition of the *Handbook,* but for the sake of comprehensiveness, we include reviews of areas that have continuing relevance.

We first discuss fundamental risk management considerations that psychologists or trainees should keep in mind regardless of their specific situation. Next there are two major sections, each with several subcomponents. Because of the significant energy invested in examining and defining professional competence, we highlight the movement to define competencies, issues related to professionals or students with competence problems, and self-care. We then review several potentially challenging ethical situations: (a) dealing with conflicts between professional ethics and the demands of employers, (b) fulfilling the duty to protect, (c) protecting the integrity of the assessment process, and (d) conducting action research and examining socially sensitive topics. However, although it is also important to consider the ethical and legal implications of recent advances in online therapy, assessment, and research, we do not include these activities here because they are discussed by Gore and Leuwerke (Chapter 3, this volume).

Because there are comprehensive sources that detail the revisions to the APA's (2002) new Ethics Code and the rationale for these revisions (e.g., Fisher, 2003; Knapp & VandeCreek, 2003), we do not discuss them here. However, we do want to note that several leading ethicists in counseling psychology contributed material that helped shape the current version of the Ethics Code, especially its aspirational General Principles. For example, although credit is rightfully given to Beauchamp and Childress (1979) for initially articulating the ethical metaprinciples of autonomy, beneficence, nonmaleficence, and justice, it was Karen Kitchener who, in a 1984 article in The *Counseling Psychologist* (*TCP*), brought the metaprinciples into psychology. Ideas present in Meara, Schmidt, and Day's (1996) *TCP* article on virtue ethics also are evident in the General Principles. Thus, counseling psychologists have played an important role in the conceptualization of psychology's ethical theory and practice.

RISK MANAGEMENT

No chapter on ethical and legal issues would be complete without a discussion of informed consent, documentation, consultation, and the use of an ethical decision-making model. Keeping these considerations in mind and following the suggestions in this chapter can help not only to protect the psychologist or trainee but to maximize the likelihood that the client, evaluee, or research participant receives the best possible treatment. Because most of the discussion has revolved around the relevance of these aspects to providing psychotherapy, we focus on this professional activity in the following discussion, but the points raised are just as relevant in other situations.

Informed Consent

One of the most essential things psychologists and graduate students can do to reduce the possibility of having ethical or legal charges filed against them is to provide thorough informed consent to clients (and their guardian(s) if the client is unable legally to make decisions for her- or himself). The importance of informed consent is underscored throughout the new APA (2002) Ethics Code. What to include in informed consent can be found in the Ethics Code as well as in commentaries on the code (e.g., Fisher, 2003), state regulations, and journal articles (e.g., Pomerantz & Handelsman, 2004; Talbert & Pipes, 1988). Informed consent should be seen as a process, instead of a one-time event at the outset of counseling, research, or assessment. Information should be provided and revisited when the context indicates it may be especially relevant (e.g., when discussing potential harm to self, others, or vulnerable persons). Not only does this approach assist individuals in making choices in the present, it also reduces the likelihood of future problems because people will have received information to help them make decisions about whether to participate or what to disclose during participation.

Although there are options for ways to discuss informed consent and what to include in these discussions, there also may be legal constraints related to managed care, state statutes, and federal laws such as HIPAA. For example, because of the current federal law related to disclosure of sexual orientation in the military ("Don't Ask, Don't Tell") and the fact that commanding officers may have access to mental health records, military psychologists must provide specific, ongoing informed consent with their clients regarding limits to confidentiality, what will be documented in mental health records, and other important information that could potentially affect a client's career (Johnson & Buhrke, 2006). Similarly, informed consent can be complicated when a psychologist is conducting an evaluation for a court. In these situations, informed consent related to the suitability and limitations of a given assessment tool, the implications of using the evaluation in the case, and alternative ways to gain the same data is essential for the defendant and defense counsel to understand, regardless of whether the psychologist was retained by the prosecution or the defense (Cunningham, 2006).

Further, given the proliferation of television and radio shows and Internet websites related to counseling, the public may have misconceptions about what will happen during therapy or assessment situations. In addition, clients may have drawn conclusions about their presenting concerns, have attempted to self-diagnose, or may have been exposed to inaccurate information about specific treatment approaches. It thus behooves psychologists to be proactive in providing information as well as in considering whether to give clients a set of questions they may want to ask, such as was developed by Pomerantz and Handelsman (2004).

Documentation

Several developments have underscored the crucial role of documentation. In particular, the APA (1993) has developed guidelines for record keeping; there is discussion of documentation in regulations and laws; and there is evidence of its role in judicial decision making in cases involving psychologists' provision of services (e.g., Soisson, VandeCreek, & Knapp, 1987). An illustration of how much more complicated record keeping has become in the past decade is that the APA recently finished revising its official record-keeping guidelines, and the new ones are several times longer than the earlier version. The old saying, "if it isn't written down, it didn't happen," may appear trite, but a complete, contemporaneous record is the psychologist's or trainee's best defense if something bad happens. By documenting what they did and why, and what they did not do and why not, professionals or students can demonstrate the thoroughness of their decision making.

A related issue is when notes and other documentation related to counseling can be released to other people. The passage of HIPAA has alleviated some of the concern about access to records. Specifically, a provision in this law allows for process notes to be kept in a separate part of a client's file and, therefore, to be inaccessible to managed care companies. The law states that companies cannot demand to see psychotherapy notes to authorize or pay for services. Under HIPAA, clients do not have access to these notes; however, state law preempts HIPAA in situations that are more empowering of clients, so in some states, clients may gain access to their entire file. Even though HIPAA states that companies do not have access to psychotherapy notes, companies still may try to obtain them. A provider who allows an insurance company access to psychotherapy notes without the client's consent is in violation of the law. Thus, therapists need to be familiar with all aspects of the law.

Consultation

Providing informed consent and keeping good records (including documenting the provision of informed consent) help show what one did with a client. A way to demonstrate that these actions were appropriate (met the "standard of care") is to consult with other professionals and then document the consultants' recommendations or the conclusions drawn from the consultation. By checking with someone else, providers demonstrate that decisions are based on more than just their own perceptions. This is especially important when values may be affecting clinical decisions, when there is a risk of possible harm to someone, and when the issues in the case are new to the provider. For example, if a practitioner working in a counseling center has a client who wants to address substance abuse issues and the provider has limited experience in this area, the practitioner should consult a colleague who is knowledgeable about substance abuse treatment to ensure that the client receives appropriate care. Consultation can also be helpful because each situation is context-dependent, and there may be few hard-and-fast rules for how to respond in a given situation. For instance, the cultural background of a client may significantly affect treatment planning or the course of counseling. Thus, practitioners should also consider consulting with others who have greater expertise working with clients from particular backgrounds.

Ethical Decision-Making Models

Because what psychologists and trainees have found effective or useful in the past when faced with a dilemma or difficult case may not apply in the present situation, it is imperative to consider the variety of issues that may affect responses to various situations (Barnett, Behnke, Rosenthal, & Koocher, 2007). Ethical decision-making models facilitate a comprehensive review of relevant considerations, and all models emphasize consultation, documentation, and informed consent. There are many such ethical decision-making models in the literature (e.g., Barret, Kitchener, & Burris, 2001; Hansen & Goldberg, 1999; for a review, see Cottone & Claus, 2000), including some that emphasize cultural factors (e.g., Garcia, Cartwright, Winston, & Borzuchowska, 2003).

Although there are several proposed models of ethical decision making, there are no data on how these models are used or how useful they are perceived to be. Cottone and Claus (2000) argued that this lack of empirical research indicates that the utility of these models is unknown. Thus, there is a need for research on how ethical dilemmas are actually resolved and what may interfere with the application of the published models (e.g., time pressure, lack of knowledge, fear of appearing incompetent, affective responses, practitioner biases). Until such data are collected, the primary value of the models may be in highlighting issues to take into account (and document, if necessary) when making decisions, especially when various ethical principles appear to be in conflict or when legal and ethical aspects seem incompatible (Knapp, Gottlieb, Berman, & Handelsman, 2007).

An Example of Risk Management

In closing this section, we briefly highlight the application of risk management to the assessment and treatment of suicidal clients as an example of how professionals can attempt to prevent negligence and maximize the likelihood of positive outcomes. Given that all practitioners will have a suicidal client at some point in their careers, psychologists and trainees can benefit from being aware of risk management strategies. However, following these suggestions does not guarantee that a suicide or lawsuit can be averted, but the recommendations should help in the event of a negative outcome.

As mentioned earlier, documentation, informed consent, and consultation are essential. In addition to these aspects, Packman, O'Connor Pennuto, Bongar, and Orthwein (2004) stated that to maximize adherence to risk management suggestions, psychologists should include procedures such as (a) knowing the risk factors for suicide; (b) obtaining risk assessment data throughout treatment (rather than only at an initial screening); (c) providing referrals when one is not competent to provide the care needed; (d) asking about historical information related to past suicide attempts and self-harming incidents, lethality of the attempts, and past suicidal ideation; (e) obtaining treatment records from previous treatment providers; (f) determining the diagnostic impression of the client; and (g) knowing one's legal and ethical responsibilities.

Berman (2006) offered even more specific recommendations, including (a) conducting risk assessments whenever the client's symptoms or circumstances change; (b) not relying on no-suicide contracts as the only means for intervention; (c) talking to family members when appropriate; (d) trying to limit access to the means for suicide; (e) collaborating with other professionals who are working with the client (e.g., psychiatrist, case manager, social worker); (f) asking about suicidal ideation and behaviors on a regular basis; (g) considering what circumstances could provoke suicidal behavior; and (h) conducting mental status exams at each session. Despite the reasonability of such risk management steps, it is notoriously difficult to predict suicide (see Westefeld, Range, Rogers, & Hill, Chapter 31, this volume).

In summary, a variety of issues should be addressed with all clients on an ongoing basis to ensure appropriate, ethical treatment. Although risk management may appear to involve many special strategies that psychologists and trainees should address, being thorough in the assessment and treatment of clients will help prevent professional negligence and increase the likelihood of providing appropriate treatment. Thus, we encourage psychologists and students to be aware of both the general and specific risk management strategies that apply in their specific areas of client care.

COMPETENCE

"Competency is generally understood to mean that a professional is qualified, capable, and able to understand and do certain things in an appropriate and effective manner" (Rodolfa et al., 2005, p. 348). There are several domains of competency, such as assessment and diagnosis. Because of the importance of these issues, we focus on the recent movement to define competencies, identifying and responding to persons with competence problems (both trainees and professionals), and promoting self-care as a way to develop and maintain competence. We envision that there will be continued emphasis on these areas; counseling psychology students and professionals will, therefore, want to remain aware of emerging developments.

Movement to Define Competencies

Concern about developing and defining student competence led the Association of Psychology Post-doctoral and Internship Centers (APPIC) to host a conference where participants broke into 10 work groups to develop state-of-the-art analyses of training in their respective areas of emphasis (Kaslow et al., 2004). Rodolfa et al. (2005) presented a "competency cube" that brings the various areas of emphasis together and shows their relationships. (A draft of benchmarks based on the competency cube can be viewed at http://www.psychtrainingcouncils.org/pubs/Comptency%20Benchmarks.pdf.) Three of these work groups appeared most relevant for this chapter: (a) ethical, legal, public policy/advocacy, and professional issues; (b) individual and cultural diversity; and (c) supervision. Consistent with counseling psychology's core values, we consider multicultural competence to be a part of all the other aspects of competence as well as a competency area of its own.

Ethics Competence

de las Fuentes, Willmuth, and Yarrow (2005) summarized the efforts of the group "charged with addressing the identification, training, and assessment of the development of competence in ethics, legal, public policy, advocacy, and professional issues" (p. 362). The group reached consensus that psychologists and graduate students needed four abilities (p. 362):

1. to appraise and adopt or adapt one's own ethical decision-making model and apply it with personal integrity and cultural competence in all aspects of professional activities;
2. to recognize ethical and legal dilemmas in the course of their professional activities (including the ability to determine whether a dilemma exists through research and consultation);
3. to recognize and reconcile conflicts among relevant codes and laws and to deal with convergence, divergence, and ambiguity; and
4. to raise and resolve ethical and legal issues appropriately.

The group also stated that trainees and professionals need knowledge and awareness of "the self in community as a moral individual and an ethical professional" (p. 362) and "the various professional ethical principles and codes; practice standards and guidelines; civil and criminal statutes; and regulations and case law relevant to the practice of psychology" (p. 363). The working group also maintained that, to facilitate ethics training, programs need to consider the student application/selection process and provide an environment that fosters ethical reflection and action (see Bashe, Anderson, Handelsman, & Klevansky, 2007, for ideas).

Multicultural Competence

Multicultural competence has received much attention over the past few years (e.g., see Constantine, Miville, & Kindaichi, Chapter 9, this volume). Multiculturalism emphasizes unique issues related to race, ethnicity, gender, sexual orientation, language, age, social class, disability, education, and religious and spiritual orientation that are specific to each individual (APA, 2003). Regarding multicultural competence, Sue, Arredondo, and McDavis (1992) stated that counselors must be aware of their biases, have an understanding of the worldview of their clients, and develop appropriate interventions for each client. As part of the APPIC competencies conference, the Individual and Cultural Differences work group focused on the first two components: (1) the counselors' awareness of their own assumptions and values, and (2) knowledge of issues experienced by culturally diverse clients (Henderson, Roysircar, Abeles, & Boyd, 2004). These authors focused on diversity based on racial and ethnic background, age, and sexual orientation, and they provided examples of how these variables can affect a therapist's perceptions and interventions.

Multiculturalism and multicultural competence has become such an important topic that the APA (2003) developed guidelines for multicultural education, training, research, practice, and organizational change for psychologists. Moreover, counseling psychologists have emphasized the importance of understanding how their own privileges and biases influence their work in practice, research, advocacy, and training (e.g., Goodyear et al., 2000; Neimeyer & Diamond, 2001; Vera & Speight, 2003). Given the emphasis and importance that counseling psychology has placed on multiculturalism, it is essential that counseling psychologists and students become aware of multicultural competencies and their implications for appropriate and ethical practice.

Faculty and Supervisor Competence

Research about the competence of faculty and supervisors is limited. In fact, research is essentially nonexistent about the competent practice of faculty members. The American Association of University Professors (2006), however, has a statement on professional ethics that explicitly addresses the responsibility of university professors to develop and maintain their competence.

Some work has been devoted to discussing ethical practices and issues related to supervision (e.g., J. M. Bernard & Goodyear, 2004). Much of the literature about supervision competence has focused on the supervisee's experiences (e.g., Nelson & Friedlander, 2001). For example, Ladany, Lehrman-Waterman, Molinaro, and Wolgast (1999) examined supervisees' perceptions of their supervisors, focusing on adherence to ethical practices, the working alliance, and the satisfaction of the supervisees. Over half of the respondents reported that their supervisors had violated one or more ethical guidelines. The two most common violations related to (1) performance evaluation and monitoring of supervisee activities and (2) violation of confidentiality related to supervision. Greater nonadherence to ethical principles on the part of the supervisor was related to a weaker supervisory alliance and lower levels of supervisee satisfaction. In interpreting the findings, the authors noted that supervisors may be unaware of the ethical guidelines, as this is still a developing aspect of supervision. Thus, supervisors should consult the literature, agency policies, relevant ethical guidelines, and colleagues when determining how to provide ethical supervision.

Although no specific competencies about supervision have been approved, there was a work group on supervision at the APPIC Competencies Conference. Falender et al. (2004) developed a framework to begin defining supervision competencies. First, they argued that *knowledge* is an important element. This would include knowledge of ethical and legal issues related to supervision; the area in which one is supervising; diversity; the developmental process of supervisees; aspects of evaluation; and theories, models, and research related to supervision. The second competency, *skills*, includes competencies such as balancing multiple roles, being flexible, using science to inform practice, performing self-assessments, and promoting the growth of the supervisee. The third area, *values,* refers to such aspects as the supervisor being respectful and empowering, adhering to ethical principles, engaging in self-education, and remaining aware of one's expertise and limitations. The fourth competency reflects the *social contexts* in which supervision occurs; the authors argued that the supervisor must be aware of the environment and how it may influence the supervision relationship. The fifth competency consists of the *need to train supervisors* through coursework as well as supervision of supervision and other related experiences that allow a supervisor to develop appropriate skills and knowledge. Finally, the authors argued *supervisor competence should be assessed* to determine that a person meets the minimum qualifications to be an effective supervisor.

Persons with Competence Problems

The work on competence development overlaps with concern about assessing and responding to what traditionally has been called student and professional *impairment,* which has been defined as "any physical, emotional, or educational deficiency that interferes with the quality of the professional performance, education, or family life" (Boxley, Drew, & Rangel, 1986, p. 50); an inability or unwillingness of the person to acquire and maintain professional standards, skills, and handle personal stress; and any clear pattern of behavior from the professional or supervisee that is harmful or deficient (e.g., Boxley et al., 1986; Forrest, Elman, Gizara, & Vacha-Haase, 1999; Gizara & Forrest, 2004). More recently, impairment has been referred to as "problematic students" or "trainees with competence problems" in discussions about training (e.g., Rosenberg, Getzelman, Arcinue, & Oren, 2005; L. Forrest, personal communication, September 2006) and providing "colleague assistance" to professionals. We discuss both student and professional competence problems in the following subsections.

Graduate Students with Competence Problems

Given the increased attention to competence and problems with competence, Johnson and Campbell (2002) argued that graduate programs need to begin to adopt some character (the honesty and integrity with which a person deals with others) and fitness (competence and ability) requirements to minimize the admittance of people who may experience competence problems in graduate school or afterward. They proposed six dimensions that they believe should be essential characteristics of all professional psychologists: (1) personality adjustment (open-mindedness, flexibility, and intellectual curiosity), (2) psychological stability, (3) responsible use of substances, (4) integrity (the person is incorruptible and would not perform actions for the wrong reasons), (5) prudence (being planful and appropriately cautious, exercising good judgment in decision making), and (6) caring (a pattern of respect and sensitivity to welfare and needs of others). There is some overlap between these components of character and fitness with virtue ethics (Meara et al., 1996). No information is available on the degree to which programs have actually used these ideas in admissions decisions.

It is not unusual for some students with problems to be admitted into a graduate program in counseling or clinical psychology. Although the data are limited, most programs deal frequently with at least one student who may have "competence problems" or is "impaired," with a majority of programs appearing to dismiss at least one student over a 3-year period (Vacha-Haase, Davenport, & Kerewsky, 2004) because of any combination of the following issues: deficient interpersonal skills, supervision difficulties, personality disorders, emotional problems, academic dishonesty, and inadequate clinical skills (Oliver, Bernstein, Anderson, Blashfield, & Roberts, 2004). However, professionals who understand that they have a role as gatekeepers for the profession often report difficulties acknowledging or acting on issues surrounding trainee impairment (J. M. Bernard & Goodyear, 2004; Oliver et al., 2004).

Once a student is determined to be at risk of having competence problems or is unable to perform adequately, the issue becomes how to respond appropriately. Data indicate that students perceive faculty to be unwilling to deal with such situations (Oliver et al., 2004), and faculty indicate that they are concerned about striking a balance between helping the student and fulfilling their gatekeeping responsibilities (Vacha-Haase et al., 2004). If a student is performing inadequately in formal classes, resolution may be relatively easy. But if the problem is more interpersonal and nebulous, then concern about appropriate assessment and documentation and fear of lawsuits may affect the responses of faculty and the university.

In their qualitative study with internship site training directors and supervisors, Gizara and Forrest (2004) highlighted complexities involved in dealing with trainee competence. Their data supported earlier reports that professionals often struggle with these issues because of the perceived incompatibility between identifying as a counseling psychologist and deciding that a trainee is experiencing competence problems. This complexity may be intensified when multiple roles exist among professionals and trainees (Schoener, 1999). To assist programs with developing appropriate responses, the Council of Chairs of Training Councils (2004) developed a consensus statement on competence that programs can adopt in whole or in part and include in the information they provide to new students. This is intended to provide informed consent regarding the extensiveness of the evaluation process to incoming students.

Students and interns also acknowledge both the prevalence and the complexity of the issues associated with trainee competence. For example, Mearns and Allen (1991) found that 91% of the students in their sample had dealt with at least one issue of impairment or ethical impropriety with a peer during graduate training. In another investigation, students reported emotional reactions to peer impairment including frustration, ambivalence, helplessness, and resentment toward peers or faculty. In addition to these emotional responses, students noted a sense of confusion, lost opportunities, and extra work stemming from faculty's apparent lack of response to the situation (Oliver et al., 2004). Further, of significant concern is that students believe that faculty members were aware of only some of their peers with problems (Oliver et al., 2004).

It is important to consider how students may respond to their peers who need assistance or are acting inappropriately and even unethically. Several studies have documented that students do not appear willing to confront their peers or go to faculty even when they recognize that there is a problem. Their reasons include guilt associated with reporting a friend, fear of incorrect judgment, and worry about how faculty will interpret their reports (J. L. Bernard & Jara, 1986; Betan & Stanton, 1999; Oliver et al., 2004). This is a significant concern because students may be more likely than faculty to witness or experience competence problems with their peers.

Professional Competence

Professional competence has received significant attention in the literature (e.g., APA, 2006; J. L. Bernard, Murphy, & Little, 1987). However, Herman (1993) argued that discussions of therapist competence have only focused on how much training and experience the person has had and that this is insufficient because research has demonstrated that these considerations have limited influence on treatment outcomes. Therefore, Herman stated that competence must also incorporate the personal characteristics of therapists, as well as their use of research in guiding practice.

Overholser and Fine (1990) also discussed professional competence, focusing on five areas of therapist incompetence. These authors maintained that there is incompetence resulting from lack of knowledge, which must be addressed through lifelong learning and a recognition of one's own limits. Second, incompetence can be because of inadequate clinical skills, such as an inability to provide informed consent and too much emphasis on giving advice and self-disclosure. The third area is incompetence as a result of deficient technical skills (e.g., assessment, specific therapy techniques) that require specific knowledge and expertise before a therapist can use such skills effectively with clients. Fourth, incompetence can stem from poor judgment, which may occur in case conceptualization and treatment planning with particular clients. Finally, incompetence can result from disturbing interpersonal attributes, such as poor social skills and impairment. Given these sources of incompetence, the authors argued that it is the responsibility of psychologists to maintain the integrity of the field by preventing and addressing incompetence as they become aware of it in students, colleagues, or themselves.

Addressing the unethical or incompetent behavior of other professionals deserves more attention. Although this may be uncomfortable and there may be many reasons not to confront such situations (e.g., Good, Thoreson, & Shaughnessy, 1995), psychologists have a responsibility to address such issues to maintain the professionalism of the field, the competency of psychologists in general, and the ethical principles of the profession. However, research indicates that professionals, like students, are unwilling to confront fellow psychologists who are acting inappropriately or unethically (J. L. Bernard et al., 1987; Overholser & Fine, 1990). The problem is so significant that the APA (2006) convened a group to discuss colleague assistance and developed an extensive monograph on the issue, with explicit directions about how to approach and help peers (see also Good et al., 1995).

Self-Care

There has been increasing attention to issues of competence, the inherent stresses involved in the profession, and the empirically documented level of distress among mental health practitioners (e.g., Gilroy, Carroll, & Murra, 2002; Sherman & Thelen, 1998; Thoreson, Miller, & Krauskopf, 1989). Barnett, Johnston, and Hillard (2005) said that devoting ongoing attention to self-care and wellness takes on ethical importance for mental health practitioners. These authors stated that an individual's distress may naturally progress toward problems with competence if the person does not recognize, attend to, and remedy personal and professional issues. They underscored the explicit connection between self-care and the general principles underlying the APA's (2002) code of ethics (e.g., "Psychologists strive to be aware of the possible effect of their own physical and mental health on their ability to help those with whom they work," p. 1062). They called for practitioners to monitor and be proactive in dealing with their own distress by practicing self-care.

Additionally, many authors have offered routine preventive and remedial strategies for practitioners and trainees. Barnett et al. (2005) suggested that awareness of one's own level of distress is critical in any effort to prevent or remediate distress. They provided self-assessment questionnaires to help practitioners and trainees engage in self-reflection and identified online resources to assist with preventing and responding to distress and burnout. Similarly, Norcross (2000) offered a compilation of "clinician recommended, research informed, and practitioner-tested" self-care strategies (p. 710). These practical recommendations for trainees and professionals to avoid burnout include embracing multiple strategies that draw from a variety of theoretical orientations, diversifying everyday experiences by finding a balance of personal and professional life, and taking the time to appreciate the rewards associated with one's work.

CHALLENGING ETHICAL SITUATIONS

There are situations and environments that lend themselves to ethical dilemmas and possible legal ramifications. Based on our review of the literature and our own experience, we selected four that have received attention in recent years and that we believe will continue to be the focus of future discussion and scholarship. In particular, we discuss (1) conflicts between professional ethics and the demands of employers, (2) the duty to protect, (3) maintenance of the integrity of the assessment situation, and (4) issues associated with conducting action research and examining socially sensitive topics.

Conflicts between Professional Ethics and the Demands of Employers

One of the topics receiving significant attention in psychology is the tension between a practitioner's ethics and the demands of an employer or supervisor (e.g., ranking officer, university administrator, warden). There has been much controversy over the appropriate role of psychologists in interrogations and other coercive situations (e.g., APA, 2005), the primary responsibilities of a corrections psychologist (e.g., Bonner, 2005), and appropriate ways for colleges and universities to respond to students who may be at risk of harming themselves (e.g., Westefeld et al., 2006).

Perhaps no recent topic has held the attention and galvanized the activism of psychologists and others as the war in Iraq and related issues, such as the detention and interrogation of people held in conjunction with the war or those suspected of being terrorists. The right of psychologists to protest or support policies and actions by the government has not been the source of the debate; rather, the possible involvement of psychologists in interrogations and the proper role, if any, of psychologists in situations where people are being held against their will (particularly by the military) has been controversial. The extent to which psychologists have been involved is a matter of speculation. However, in response to news reports and requests from psychologists involved in activities related to national security, the APA (2005) convened a task force that issued a report reviewing the ethics of involvement in interrogations. The Board of Directors adopted the report as APA policy and the Council of Representatives adopted the report's recommendations and several related items, including a statement that no circumstances ever justify a psychologist engaging in torture (S. Behnke, personal communication, February 19, 2007). Currently there is discussion on a closely related issue: whether the ethical standard in the APA (2002) Ethics Code regarding conflicts between ethics and law needs to be amended.

The overarching concern involves whether it is ethical for psychologists to be involved in interrogating people when coercive techniques may be involved (APA, 2005). A military psychologist's job may be to assist in gathering information from people being held against their will, but how far that assistance goes, where the line demarcating ethical from unethical behavior lies, and what the consequences are of crossing that line are at the crux of the matter. Some who are against any involvement of psychologists in coercive situations want it to be unethical for psychologists to assist in interrogations; others, regardless of their specific position regarding situations such as Guantanamo Bay, argue that such a position would make it unethical for some military (and possibly police) psychologists to do their jobs.

Those arguing for a change in the Ethics Code maintain that such a revision would allow psychologists who are against some tactics allegedly being used by the military to say that they cannot participate in those interrogations because they violate the Ethics Code. Although few psychologists may be directly involved in assisting the military in these cases, the possible dilemmas faced by psychologists illustrate the larger issues related to situations where a psychologist is being told to do something by a superior that may be contrary to the psychologist's conscience or beliefs about proper professional conduct.

Another environment where there may be conflicts between psychologists' perceptions of their roles and the demands of the employer is within correctional facilities. Given the high percentage of people in the criminal justice system who have mental health problems (James & Glaze, 2006), it is likely that more psychologists will be providing counseling and other services in such facilities. Here, limits to confidentiality and dual roles are often at the forefront of tension between a practitioner's ethics and employer demands. When an inmate discloses information to a psychologist that could potentially affect the security of the institution or the well-being of staff or other inmates, confidentiality may not be possible because the psychologist is often expected to disclose that information to the employer (i.e., institution officials; Bonner, 2005). Furthermore, psychologists are sometimes asked to act as if they were a correctional officer, which places them in dual roles with inmates because of having yet another form of power over their clients. Finally, psychologists may be placed in positions in which they are evaluating or treating individuals who have been sentenced to death and they cannot change the outcome, even though the APA (2001b) has a resolution against the death penalty.

Another relevant situation that may be even more common among counseling psychologists given their traditional work settings relates to how a college or university will respond to a student who may be at risk of self-harm. In some places, institutional policy may mandate notifying parents of students' suicidal ideation or attempts (Baker, 2005) or dismissing students who threaten or attempt suicide (Pavela, 2006). In other instances, an administrator may want information or access to records related to a student about whom there are safety concerns. Although both psychology faculty and counseling center psychologists may encounter students who disclose personal information such as suicidality, the situation for instructors has been discussed less often (Haney, 2004). The extent of confidentiality between a faculty member and a student is, in most situations, more ambiguous because these discussions are less governed by university policies, case law, and state statutes than are the revelations that take place in the context of a staff psychologist-client relationship.

Several recent court cases involving college students who have thought about, attempted, or died by suicide have led administrators to be concerned about their own and the school's liability if a student is harmed or dies (Baker, 2005; Pavela, 2006; Westefeld et al., 2006). Some of the policies that have been drafted in response to these cases have given the administration permission or direction to take fairly strong action; thus, an administrator may want access to as much information as possible to decide what to do. For example, a dean may request to see case files and talk to a student's counselor. In such instances, the provider may feel caught between the demands of the administrator and the confidentiality of the student. Concerns about rupturing the therapeutic alliance are naturally linked to the release of information without the client's permission.

This scenario has parallels with the reporting of child abuse, in that an external force is placing limits on the degree of confidentiality in the counseling relationship—and not following the directive (i.e., reporting abuse or giving information to an administrator) can have significant consequences for the therapist (and possibly the client). Supervisees have even less control in such situations in that they are bound not only by the university's policies and demands of administrators but also by the directions of their supervisors. Given these issues, counseling centers would be well served by having policies (and informed consent for clients) in place stating which administrators, if any, have access to records. Such policies also need to clarify how breaches of confidentiality should be managed and documented.

The current state of the world and the litigious nature of U.S. society suggest that these situations will not disappear. In fact, other situations involving therapist loyalties are likely to continue to garner attention. For example, staff in counseling centers that provide disability assessments to students may be pressed to reveal information to other campus representatives about students referred for testing or counseling; they may also be pressured to diagnose a student with a condition to help the student stay in good standing in school or to receive academic accommodations. Thus, counseling psychologists who work in such capacities need to be familiar with the Ethics Code as well as established ethical decision-making models and state-of-the art analyses of possible resolutions to such difficult situations. We anticipate that the APA and other official bodies will continue to provide information on these dilemmas.

Duty to Protect

Many professionals erroneously discuss the "duty to warn" in relation to the famous *Tarasoff v. Regents of the University of California* (1976) case. The justices in that decision actually said there was a *duty to protect,* which is an even broader mandate. Because there has been so much misinformation about *Tarasoff,* even in ethics articles and books, we urge readers to review the actual case. Suffice it to say that the duty to protect allows professionals many more ways to intervene in potential instances of harm to another than just warning the potential victim or authorities. Each jurisdiction has statutes and case law on this issue, and some of these may have specified that the only way to protect is by breaking confidentiality or attempting hospitalization. Counseling psychologists and students need to check the requirements in their respective locations (Werth, Welfel, & Benjamin, 2007).

The standard discussion of the duty to protect involves reviewing situations involving potential murder or suicide; however, it has been argued that the underlying issue is whether substantial harm may occur to the person or to another individual within a relatively short period and, therefore, a larger number of situations may lead to a duty to protect (Werth & Rogers, 2005; Werth et al., 2007). Using this more expansive view, we decided to focus on other areas where the duty to protect may be an issue with clients: HIV disease, driving, eating disorders, and end-of-life decisions. Of these four, the oldest and most discussed is the possible dilemma about what to do when a client who has HIV is engaging in risky behaviors (e.g., unprotected intercourse, sharing needles used to inject drugs). A book (Anderson & Barret, 2001) that has been written on this topic thoroughly discusses various dilemmas and ways of resolving them (e.g., breaking confidentiality by talking to the police, the health department, or other person(s) who may have been exposed). However, because states may have statutes or cases prescribing or limiting the psychologist's options in such settings, consultation with an attorney may be useful.

On the other hand, clients may present other types of situations where little guidance has been offered. Driving is an area that has been receiving more attention lately. As a result of the aging of the population, newspaper stories about elderly drivers are not uncommon, and data on numbers of accidents reveal that older adults have higher rates than most other age groups (Knapp & VandeCreek, 2005). The larger issue is operating potentially dangerous equipment, which is relevant to many more people and makes concerns about harm to self or others and, therefore, the potential duty to protect, directly relevant to counseling psychologists and trainees.

A person's ability to safely operate equipment, such as an automobile or truck, forklift, or assembly line, can be affected by reduced reflex speed, vision issues, medication side effects, medical conditions, and cognitive impairments. In some of these situations, a physician may have an obligation to intervene and discuss the potential need to reduce or eliminate the use of dangerous equipment. However, psychologists and trainees may also be considered to have a duty to protect the person and others who may be harmed if the professional or student knew (or should have known) that a person's ability to use equipment safely was impaired. Options may include getting the person voluntarily to stop operating the equipment, discussing the situation with the client's loved one, or reporting the situation to the police or employer.

Another example of a clinical situation that may involve the duty to protect but about which there has been little written is related to clients with disordered eating. There is the possibility that a client's behaviors may be so extreme that the therapist is concerned about the client's safety. To our knowledge, only one article has appeared providing some suggestions for what counseling psychologists may need to do with clients who have anorexia (the mortality data indicate that death from anorexia is a distinct possibility, whereas the data do not indicate a heightened risk related to bulimia) and the therapist has concerns about the client's risk of death (Werth, Wright, Archambault, & Bardash, 2003). In such cases, the counselor can meet the duty to protect in a variety of ways, including breaking confidentiality, trying to get the client to go into inpatient treatment voluntarily, or attempting to hospitalize the client involuntarily. Although the authors concluded that there may be times when the therapist has a duty to protect, they noted that the ethics literature also leaves open the possibility of letting the client's disease take its course and helping the client to die peacefully.

This latter option is related to the emerging literature on psychologists' responsibilities when clients make decisions that may affect the manner and timing of their death (e.g., what is the psychologist's role when a terminally ill client wants to overdose on medication, or when a clinically depressed client wants to discontinue dialysis?). Kitchener and Anderson (2000) discussed the more narrow but related issue of "rational suicide" in the previous edition of the *Handbook*. The American Counseling Association's (2005) new code of ethics has a section on working with terminally ill clients, but psychologists will need to extrapolate from the existing APA (2002) Ethics Code and related literature when faced with this issue. In 2000, the APA Working Group on Assisted Suicide and End-of-Life Decisions issued a comprehensive report, and resolutions on End-of-Life Issues and Care (APA, 2001c), and on Assisted Suicide (APA, 2001a) were subsequently passed by the Council of Representatives.

Werth and Rogers (2005) argued that the set of "Issues to Consider when Exploring End-of-Life Decisions" that was developed by the APA Working Group could be used to help satisfy the duty to protect with clients making decisions that may affect the manner and timing of death. These authors stated that the duty to protect did not mandate prevention of harm in all situations; rather, they indicated that the key issue involves whether the client has impaired judgment when making the decision. They maintained that if, after thoroughly reviewing the client's judgment and decision-making capacity, the therapist concluded that the client did not exhibit impaired judgment, then it could be ethically acceptable not to prevent the client from taking action that would likely lead to the client's death.

As can be seen from these examples, the duty to protect can be applied in a variety of situations and can lead to controversial decisions. We anticipate that the boundaries and nuances of the duty to protect and the options for discharging this duty will be discussed more thoroughly in the coming years.

Maintenance of the Integrity of the Assessment Situation

Changes to the standard on assessment apparently were among the most substantial and controversial of the 2002 revisions of the APA Ethics Code (Fisher, 2003; Knapp & VandeCreek, 2003). We provide a brief overview of issues involved in the release of test data and maintaining test security; we also highlight possible tensions between psychologists and attorneys regarding psychological assessment. Readers with a special interest in psychological testing are encouraged to consult more comprehensive sources.

In the 2002 Ethics Code, there is a distinction between *test data* and *test materials*. According to the code (Standard 9.04a), "The term *test data* refers to raw and scaled scores, client/patient responses to test questions or stimuli, and psychologists' notes and recordings concerning client/patient statements and behavior during an examination" (p. 1071). In addition, any written responses are considered test data. This part of the code goes on to state that if a client signs a release of information, test data can be given to other people (e.g., attorneys), not just other psychologists. The 1992 code prohibited releasing such information to unqualified individuals. There is a provision that psychologists may refuse to grant such release if they think a client may be harmed, but as with the earlier discussion of client access to records, HIPAA and state laws may preempt this part of the code. In Standard 9.11, the code defines *test materials* as "manuals, instruments, protocols, and test questions or stimuli and does not include *test data* as defined in Standard 9.04" (p. 1072). Something containing both test materials and test data (e.g., a Rorschach scoring sheet) is considered data, not materials, and therefore is accessible to clients and others to whom the client releases the information.

There has been extensive discussion of the implications of these definitions and the changes to this standard for psychologists and test publishers (e.g., see the *Journal of Personality Assessment, 82,* 23–47). The APA Committee on Legal Issues (2006) has offered some recommendations for psychologists facing requests to provide assessment-related material to attorneys or courts, but at this point, it does not appear as if psychologists or companies can prevent test data, or test materials that overlap, from being released to clients and others.

The release of test data has caused some concerns for psychologists in general and forensic psychologists in particular because of the different perspectives and roles psychologists and attorneys have in legal situations. Any psychologist may face a subpoena, so not specializing in court-related assessments does not make one immune from these issues. Victor and Abeles (2004) highlighted the tension here by noting that attorneys may consider it appropriate to coach clients how to respond to psychological assessments. Thus, if attorneys have access to test questions, scoring, or interpretation guides (i.e., assuming this information is considered test data), there is the potential that the integrity of assessments may be compromised.

A related issue being debated is whether attorneys (or other observers) have the right to be present when their clients are completing assessments. There has been some discussion of this in the neuropsychological literature (e.g., American Academy of Clinical Neuropsychology, 2001), and the APA has been examining the issue for several years although no policy positions have been endorsed thus far. However, we anticipate that there will continue to be discussion and debate about these issues in the future, even if the APA provides clear guidance.

Action Research and Examination of Socially Sensitive Topics

The detrimental effects of psychology's history of "misassumptions," "misadventures," and "misuses" have been well documented and have contributed to mistrust among community members and potential research participants (Strickland, 2000, p. 331; see also Darou, Hum, & Kurtness, 1993; Harris, Gorelick, Samuels, & Bempong, 1996). Given psychology's history, as well as the continuously changing demographics of the U.S. population, there has been increased attention to the ethical conduct of research with underrepresented populations in recent years. Specifically, theorists and researchers have focused on the role of ethics in community-based research approaches and socially sensitive research (i.e., research with potential social consequences or implications).

Potential challenges associated with action-oriented research approaches and socially sensitive research may be of particular concern for counseling psychologists and counseling psychology trainees because of the emphasis that the profession places on multiculturalism, science-practice integration, prevention, respect for all individuals, social justice, and a strengths-based, developmental perspective (e.g., Fouad et al., 2004; Neimeyer & Diamond, 2001). Indeed, because there have been numerous recent discussions related to the inclusion of social justice perspectives in training, research, and practice within counseling psychology (e.g., Fouad et al., 2004; Goodman et al., 2004; Toporek, Gerstein, Fouad, Roysircar, & Israel, 2006; Vera & Speight, 2003), it is critical to examine the ethical implications inherent in using these perspectives to inform research.

Some authors have proposed additional ethical considerations when conducting these types of research. Sieber and Stanley (1988) offered a taxonomy to guide researchers in their analysis of socially sensitive research. They suggested that ethical issues arise at several points in the research process (e.g., formulation of the research question, interpretation of findings) and that psychologists must consider 10 types of potential ethical issues (e.g., privacy, informed consent, risk/benefit ratio). Similarly, Fisher et al. (2002) argued that psychologists need to attend to additional considerations when conducting research with ethnic minority individuals. They encouraged researchers to apply a cultural perspective to the evaluation of research risks and benefits, engage in community consultation, and ensure that they have appropriate awareness and understanding of scientific, social, and political factors related to the groups represented in their research.

Koocher (2002) proposed a model containing six distinct domains (cognitive, affective, biological, legal, economic, and social and cultural risks) that should be examined to assess and minimize risk to research participants. He pointed to the need to consider the potential adverse effects for individuals participating in studies designed for at-risk youth, such as stigmatization and negative self-fulfilling prophecies (e.g., on the part of teachers); the possibility that researchers may collect data that would lead to mandatory reporting (e.g., child abuse or neglect); the possibility that participation in research might lead to litigation as a result of the participant's self-realization (e.g., the participant recalls negative emotions associated with specific experiences); and the potential for monetary compensation to increase the likelihood that low-income individuals would agree to potentially risky research participation or interruption of effective treatment for participation in experimental clinical trials.

Action-oriented research approaches (e.g., Participatory Action Research: Esposito & Murphy, 1999; Emancipatory Communitarian Approach: Prilleltensky, 1997) also lead to the need to reflect on challenging ethical issues as well as potential implications for participants, groups that the participants represent, and the general public. Although there are benefits to conducting such research, including working closely with participants and the possibility that research involvement will lead to participant empowerment, there is also the potential for harm as a result of misunderstanding roles, mistakes related to informed consent and confidentiality, and misinterpretation of results and their policy implications (see Kidd & Kral, 2005). Further, the inclusion of values and attention to issues of social importance in research may lead to a backlash from readers of scholarly journals, clients, policymakers, administrators, or the general public because of the controversial research.

A meta-analysis by Rind, Tromovitch, and Bauserman (1998) on sexual abuse—and the political and social backlash that stemmed from this study (for reviews see Garrison & Kober, 2002; Lilienfeld, 2002)—is an example of the need for researchers to consider the implications of their research when designing studies, gathering data, interpreting results, and disseminating information. Several authors dissected the controversy to raise awareness among researchers of the implications of their findings. These authors (e.g., Garrison & Kober, 2002; Lilienfeld, 2002) suggested ways for psychologists to avoid problems resulting from studying socially relevant and potentially controversial issues, including educating the public about sound research design, being knowledgeable about the policy-making process, emphasizing that one research study is not the final word, and acknowledging the potential misinterpretations of findings.

Psychologists need to carefully attend to multiple sides of issues (particularly controversial ones) when conceptualizing studies and their designs. For research that is socially sensitive to be viewed as credible, psychologists must acknowledge that their values are influencing their work and should actively seek to increase their own awareness of their biases, assumptions, and the potential misinterpretations of findings.

CONCLUSION

This chapter has highlighted significant ethical and legal issues that are relevant to counseling psychologists across their work settings and levels of experience. The APA Ethics Code, professional regulations, state statutes, and federal laws provide some direction for trainees and professionals, but no set of written guidelines can adequately cover all possible situations. The existing literature may provide assistance, and consultation with more experienced peers will also be helpful, but the beliefs and skills of the psychologist or trainee will influence the process of seeking out and interpreting information. Thus, to practice ethically, counseling psychologists and graduate students must continuously monitor their competence and biases in every professional situation.

REFERENCES

American Academy of Clinical Neuropsychology. (2001). Policy statement on the presence of third party observers in neuropsychological assessments. *Clinical Neuropsychologist, 14*, 433–439.

American Association of University Professors. (2006). *Policy documents and reports* (10th ed.). Baltimore: Johns Hopkins University Press.

American Counseling Association. (2005). *Code of ethics*. Alexandria, VA: Author. Retrieved July 1, 2006, from http://www.counseling.org/PDFs/ACA_2005_Ethical_Code10405.pdf.

American Psychological Association. (1993). Record keeping guidelines. *American Psychologist, 48*, 984–986.

American Psychological Association. (2001a). *Resolution on assisted suicide*. Retrieved January 12, 2006, from http://www.apa.org/pi/eol/activities.html#4.

American Psychological Association. (2001b). *Resolution on the death penalty in the United States*. Retrieved October 26, 2004, from http://www.apa.org/pi/deathpenalty.html.

American Psychological Association. (2001c). *Resolution on end-of-life issues and care*. Retrieved October 26, 2004, from http://www.apa.org/pi/eol/activities.html#3.

American Psychological Association. (2002). Ethical principles of psychologists and code of conduct. *American Psychologist, 57*, 1060–1073.

American Psychological Association. (2003). Guidelines on multicultural education, training, research, practice, and organizational change for psychologists. *American Psychologist, 58*, 377–402.

American Psychological Association. (2005). *Report of the Presidential Task Force on Psychological Ethics and National Security*. Washington, DC: Author. Retrieved November 10, 2006, from http://www.apa.org/releases/PENSTaskForceReportFinal.pdf.

American Psychological Association. (2006). *Advancing colleague assistance in professional psychology*. Washington, DC: Author. Retrieved November 10, 2006, from http://www.apa.org/practice/acca_monograph.pdf.

American Psychological Association Committee on Legal Issues. (2006). Strategies for private practitioners coping with subpoenas or compelled testimony for client records or test data. *Professional Psychology: Research and Practice, 37*, 215–222.

Anderson, J. R., & Barret, B. (Eds.). (2001). *Ethics in HIV-related psychotherapy: Clinical decision making in complex cases*. Washington, DC: American Psychological Association.

Baker, T. R. (2005). Notifying parents following a college student suicide attempt: A review of case law and FERPA, and recommendations for practice. *NASPA Journal, 42*, 513–533.

Barnett, J. E., Behnke, S. H., Rosenthal, S. L., & Koocher, G. P. (2007). In case of ethical dilemma, break glass: Commentary on ethical decision making in practice. *Professional Psychology: Research and Practice, 38*, 7–12.

Barnett, J. E., Johnston, L. C., & Hillard, D. (2005). Psychotherapist wellness as an ethical imperative. In L. VandeCreek & J. B. Allen (Eds.), *Innovations in clinical practice: Focus on health and wellness* (pp. 257–271). Sarasota, FL: Professional Resource Press.

Barret, B., Kitchener, K. S., & Burris, S. (2001). A decision model for ethical dilemmas in HIV-related psychotherapy and its application in the case of Jerry. In J. R. Anderson & B. Barret (Eds.), *Ethics in HIV-related psychotherapy: Clinical decision making in complex cases* (pp. 133–154). Washington, DC: American Psychological Association.

Bashe, A., Anderson, S. K., Hendelsman, M. M., & Klevansky, R. (2007). An acculturation model for ethics training: The ethics autobiography and beyond. *Professional Psychology: Research and Practice, 38*, 60–67.

Beauchamp, T. L., & Childress, J. F. (1979). *Principles of biomedical ethics*. New York: Oxford University Press.

Berman, A. L. (2006). Risk management with suicidal patients. *Journal of Clinical Psychology: In Session, 62*, 171–184.

Bernard, J. L., & Jara, C. S. (1986). The failure of clinical psychology graduate students to apply understood ethical principles. *Professional Psychology: Research and Practice, 17*, 313–315.

Bernard, J. L., Murphy, M., & Little, M. (1987). The failure of clinical psychologists to apply understood ethical principles. *Professional Psychology: Research and Practice, 18*, 489–491.

Bernard, J. M., & Goodyear, R. K. (2004). *Fundamentals of clinical supervision* (3rd ed.). Boston: Pearson.

Betan, E. J., & Stanton, A. L. (1999). Fostering ethical willingness: Integrating emotional and contextual awareness with rational analysis. *Professional Psychology: Research and Practice, 30*, 295–301.

Bonner, R. (2005). Ethical and professional issues for mental health providers in corrections. In L. VandeCreek & J. B. Allen, (Eds.), *Innovations in clinical practice: Focus on health and wellness* (pp. 273–286). Sarasota, FL: Professional Resource Press.

Boxley, R., Drew, C., & Rangel, D. (1986). Clinical trainee impairment in APA approved internship programs. *Clinical Psychologist, 39*, 49–52.

Cottone, R. R., & Claus, R. E. (2000). Ethical decision-making models: A review of the literature. *Journal of Counseling and Development, 78*, 275–283.

Council of Chairs of Training Councils. (2004). *The comprehensive evaluation of student-trainee competence in professional psychology programs.* Retrieved November 10, 2006, from http://www.appic.org/downloads/CCTC_Comprehensive_Ev82AA3.pdf.

Cunningham, M. D. (2006). Informed consent in capital sentencing evaluations: Targets and content. *Professional Psychology: Research and Practice, 37*, 452–459.

Darou, W. G., Hum, A., & Kurtness, J. (1993). An investigation of the impact of psychosocial research on a native population. *Professional Psychology: Research and Practice, 24*, 325–329.

de las Fuentes, C., Willmuth, M. E., & Yarrow, C. (2005). Competency training in ethics education and practice. *Professional Psychology: Research and Practice, 36*, 362–366.

Esposito, L., & Murphy, J. W. (1999). Desensitizing Herbert Bulmer's work on race relationship: Recent applications of his group position theory to the study of contemporary race prejudice. *Sociological Quarterly, 40*, 397–410.

Falender, C. A., Erickson Cornish, J. A., Goodyear, R., Hatcher, R., Kaslow, N. J., Leventhal, G., et al. (2004). Defining competencies in psychology supervision: A consensus statement. *Journal of Clinical Psychology, 60*, 771–785.

Fisher, C. B. (2003). *Decoding the ethics code: A practical guide for psychologists.* Thousand Oaks, CA: Sage.

Fisher, C. B., Hoagwood, K., Boyce, C., Duster, T., Frank, D. A., Grisso, T., et al. (2002). Research ethics for mental health science involving ethnic minority children and youths. *American Psychologist, 57*, 1024–1040.

Forrest, L., Elman, N., Gizara, S., & Vacha-Haase, T. (1999). Trainee impairment: Identifying, remediating, and terminating impaired trainees in psychology. *Counseling Psychologist, 27*, 627–686.

Fouad, N. A., McPherson, R. H., Gerstein, L., Blustein, D. L., Elman, N., Helledy, K. I., et al. (2004). Houston, 2001: Context and legacy. *Counseling Psychologist, 32*, 15–77.

Garcia, J. G., Cartwright, B., Winston, S. M., & Borzuchowska, B. (2003). A transcultural integrative model for ethical decision making in counseling. *Journal of Counseling and Development, 81*, 268–277.

Garrison, E. G., & Kober, P. C. (2002). Weathering a political storm: A contextual perspective on a psychological research controversy. *American Psychologist, 57*, 165–175.

Gilroy, P. J., Carroll, L., & Murra, J. (2002). A preliminary survey of counseling psychologists' personal experiences with depression and treatment. *Professional Psychology: Research and Practice, 33*, 402–407.

Gizara, S. S., & Forrest, L. (2004). Supervisors' experiences of trainee impairment and incompetence at APA-accredited internship sites. *Professional Psychology: Research and Practice, 35*, 131–140.

Good, G. E., Thoreson, R. W., & Shaughnessy, P. (1995). Substance use, confrontation of impaired colleagues, and psychological functioning among counseling psychologists: A national survey. *Counseling Psychologist, 23*, 703–721.

Goodman, L. A., Liang, B., Helms, J. E., Latta, R. E., Sparks, E., & Weintraub, S. R. (2004). Training counseling psychologists as social justice agents. *Counseling Psychologist, 32*, 793–837.

Goodyear, R. K., Cortese, J. R., Guzzardo, C. R., Allison, R. D., Claiborn, C. D., & Packard, T. (2000). Factors, trends, and topics in the evolution of counseling psychology training. *Counseling Psychologist, 28*, 603–621.

Haney, M. R. (2004). Ethical dilemmas associated with self-disclosure in student writing. *Teaching of Psychology, 31*, 167–171.

Hansen, N. D., & Goldberg, S. G. (1999). Navigating the nuances: A matrix of considerations for ethical-legal dilemmas. *Professional Psychology: Research and Practice, 30*, 495–503.

Harris, Y., Gorelick, P. B., Samuels, P., & Bempong, I. (1996). Why African Americans may not be participating in clinical trials. *Journal of the National Medical Center, 88*, 630–634.

Henderson, D. J., Roysircar, G., Abeles, N., & Boyd, C. (2004). Individual and cultural-diversity competency: Focus on the therapist. *Journal of Clinical Psychology, 60*, 755–770.

Herman, K. C. (1993). Reassessing predictors of therapist competence. *Journal of Counseling and Development, 72*, 29–32.

James, D. J., & Glaze, L. E. (2006). *Mental health problems of prison and jail inmates.* Washington, DC: Department of Justice. Retrieved January 22, 2007, from http://www.ojp.usdoj.gov/bjs/pub/pdf/mhppji.pdf.

Johnson, W. B., & Buhrke, R. A. (2006). Service delivery in a "don't ask, don't tell" world: Ethical care of gay, lesbian, and bisexual military personnel. *Professional Psychology: Research and Practice, 37*, 91–98.

Johnson, W. B., & Campbell, C. D. (2002). Character and fitness requirements for professional psychologists: Are there any? *Professional Psychology: Research and Practice, 33*, 46–53.

Kaslow, N. J., Borden, K. A., Collins, F. L., Jr., Forrest, L., Illfelder-Kaye, J., Nelson, P. D., et al. (2004). Competencies conference: Future directions in education and credentialing in professional psychology. *Journal of Clinical Psychology, 60*, 699–712.

Kidd, S. A., & Kral, M. J. (2005). Practicing participatory action research. *Journal of Counseling Psychology, 52*, 187–195.

Kitchener, K. S. (1984). Intuition, critical evaluation, and ethical principles: The foundation for ethical decisions in counseling psychology. *Counseling Psychologist, 12*(3), 43–55.

Kitchener, K. S., & Anderson, A. K. (2000). Ethical issues in counseling psychology: Old themes—new problems. In S. D. Brown & R. W. Lent (Eds.), *Handbook of counseling psychology* (3rd ed., pp. 50–82). New York: Wiley.

Knapp, S., Gottlieb, M., Berman, J., & Handelsman, M. M. (2007). When laws and ethics collide: What should psychologists do? *Professional Psychology: Research and Practice, 38*, 54–59.

Knapp, S., & VandeCreek, L. (2003). An overview of the major changes in the 2002 APA ethics code. *Professional Psychology: Research and Practice, 34*, 301–308.

Knapp, S., & VandeCreek, L. (2005). Ethical and patient management issues with older, impaired drivers. *Professional Psychology: Research and Practice, 36*, 197–202.

Koocher, G. P. (2002). Using the CABLES Model to assess and minimize risk in research: Control group hazards. *Ethics and Behavior, 12*, 75–86.

Ladany, N., Lehrman-Waterman, D., Molinaro, M., & Wolgast, B. (1999). Psychotherapy supervisor ethical practice: Adherence to guidelines, the supervisory working alliance, and supervisee satisfaction. *Counseling Psychologist, 27*, 443–475.

Lilienfeld, S. O. (2002). When worlds collide: Social science, politics, and the Rind et al. (1998) child sexual abuse meta-analysis. *American Psychologist, 57*, 176–188.

Meara, N. M., Schmidt, L. D., & Day, J. D. (1996). Principles and virtues: A foundation for ethical decisions, policies, and character. *Counseling Psychologist, 24*, 4–77.

Mearns, J., & Allen, G. J. (1991). Graduate students' experiences in dealing with impaired peers, compared with faculty predictions: An exploratory study. *Ethics and Behavior, 1*, 191–202.

Neimeyer, G. J., & Diamond, A. K. (2001). The anticipated future of counseling psychology in the United States: A Delphi poll. *Counseling Psychology Quarterly, 14*, 49–65.

Nelson, M., & Friedlander, M. L. (2001). A close look at conflictual supervisory relationships: The trainee's perspective. *Journal of Counseling Psychology, 48*, 384–395.

Norcross, J. C. (2000). Psychotherapist self-care: Practitioner-tested, research-informed strategies. *Professional Psychology: Research and Practice, 31*, 710–713.

Oliver, M. N. I., Bernstein, J. H., Anderson, K. G., Blashfield, R. K., & Roberts, M. C. (2004). An exploratory examination of students' attitudes toward "impaired" peers in clinical psychology training programs. *Professional Psychology: Research and Practice, 35*, 141–147.

Overholser, J. C., & Fine, M. A. (1990). Defining the boundaries of competence: Managing subtle cases of clinical incompetence. *Professional Psychology: Research and Practice, 21*, 462–469.

Packman, W. L., O'Connor Pennuto, T., Bongar, B., & Orthwein, J. (2004). Legal issues of professional negligence in suicide cases. *Behavioral Sciences and the Law, 22*, 697–713.

Pavela, G. (2006). Should colleges withdraw students who threaten or attempt suicide? *Journal of American College Health, 54*, 367–371.

Pomerantz, A. M., & Handelsman, M. M. (2004). Informed consent revisited: An updated written question format. *Professional Psychology: Research and Practice, 35*, 201–205.

Prilleltensky, I. (1997). Values, assumptions, and practices: Assessing the moral implications of psychological discourse and action. *American Psychologist, 52*, 517–535.

Rind, B., Tromovitch, P., & Bauserman, R. (1998). A meta-analytic examination of assumed properties of child sexual abuse using college samples. *Psychological Bulletin, 124*, 22–53.

Rodolfa, E., Bent, R., Euisman, E., Nelson, P., Rehm, L., & Ritchie, P. (2005). A cube model for competency development: Implications for psychology educators and regulators. *Professional Psychology: Research and Practice, 36*, 347–354.

Rosenberg, J. I., Getzelman, M. A., Arcinue, F., & Oren, C. Z. (2005). An exploratory look at students' experiences of problematic peers in academic professional psychology programs. *Professional Psychology: Research and Practice, 36*, 665–673.

Schoener, G. R. (1999). Practicing what we preach. *Counseling Psychologist, 27*, 693–701.

Sherman, M. D., & Thelen, M. H. (1998). Distress and professional impairment among psychologists in clinical practice. *Professional Psychology: Research and Practice, 29*, 79–85.

Sieber, J. E., & Stanley, B. (1988). Ethical and professional dimensions of socially sensitive research. *American Psychologist, 43*, 49–55.

Soisson, E. L., VandeCreek, L., & Knapp, S. (1987). Thorough record keeping: A good defense in a litigious era. *Professional Psychology: Research and Practice, 18*, 498–502.

Strickland, B. R. (2000). Misassumptions, misadventures, and the misuse of psychology. *American Psychologist, 55*, 331–338.

Sue, D. W., Arredondo, P., & McDavis, R. J. (1992). Multicultural counseling competencies and standards: A call to the profession. *Journal of Counseling and Development, 70*, 477–486.

Talbert, F. S., & Pipes, R. B. (1988). Informed consent for psychotherapy: Content analysis of selected forms. *Professional Psychology: Research and Practice, 19*, 131–132.

Tarasoff v. Regents of the University of California 551 P.2d 334 (1976).

Thoreson, R., Miller, M., & Krauskopf, C. (1989). The distressed psychologist: Prevalence and treatment considerations. *Professional Psychology: Research and Practice, 20*, 153–158.

Toporek, R. L., Gerstein, L. H., Fouad, N. A., Roysircar, G., & Israel, T. (2006). *Handbook for social justice in counseling psychology*. Thousand Oaks, CA: Sage.

Vacha-Haase, T., Davenport, D. S., & Kerewsky, S. D. (2004). Problematic students: Gatekeeping practices of academic professional psychology programs. *Professional Psychology: Research and Practice, 35*, 115–122.

Vera, E. M., & Speight, S. L. (2003). Multicultural competence, social justice, and counseling psychology: Expanding our roles. *Counseling Psychologist, 31*, 253–272.

Victor, T. L., & Abeles, N. (2004). Coaching clients to take psychological and neuropsychological tests: A clash of ethical obligations. *Professional Psychology: Research and Practice, 35*, 373–379.

Werth, J. L., Jr., & Rogers, J. R. (2005). Assessing for impaired judgment as a means of meeting the "duty to protect" when a client is a potential harm-to-self: Implications for clients making end-of-life decisions. *Mortality, 10*, 7–21.

Werth, J. L., Jr., Welfel, E. R., & Benjamin, G. A. H. (Eds.). (2007). *The duty to protect: Ethical, legal, and professional considerations in risk assessment and intervention*. Washington, DC: American Psychological Association.

Werth, J. L., Jr., Wright, K. S., Archambault, R. J., & Bardash, R. J. (2003). When does the "Duty to Protect" apply with a client who has anorexia nervosa? *Counseling Psychologist, 31*, 427–450.

Westefeld, J. S., Button, C., Haley, J. T., Kettmenn, J. J., MacConnell, J., Sandil, R., et al. (2006). College student suicide: A call to action. *Death Studies, 30*, 931–956.

Working Group on Assisted Suicide and End-of-Life Decisions. (2000). *Report to the American Psychological Association's Board of Directors*. Washington, DC: American Psychological Association Retrieved. January 2, 2007, from www.apa.org/pi/aseolf.html.

CHAPTER 2

The Changing Landscape of Professional Practice in Counseling Psychology

JAMES W. LICHTENBERG
RODNEY K. GOODYEAR
DIANE Y. GENTHER

Most counseling psychologists are engaged to some extent in providing professional services. Data from the most recent national survey of counseling psychologists showed that this was true of 68% of the members of the Society of Counseling Psychology (SCP) and 92% of counseling psychologists who were members of the APA but not of SCP (Goodyear et al., in press). The work of these practitioners has changed gradually over time, even as the specialty has retained many of its core values and its essential identity. These changes, which have been in response to changes in society, the marketplace, and the larger profession of psychology, have helped ensure that counseling psychology would remain a vital and relevant specialty.

This chapter focuses on three areas in which the evolution of counseling psychology has been particularly evident: managed care, prescriptive authority, and expanding practice roles for counseling psychologists. These issues have particular relevance to counseling psychologists in independent practice—23% of SCP members and 48% of counseling psychologist members of APA who were not SCP members (Goodyear et al., in press). But the issues are pervasive and so have some effect, however indirect, on almost all counseling psychologists, regardless of setting or role. We begin the chapter with a review of managed care and the ways it has affected the work of psychologists. This review sets the stage for the subsequent sections. Managed care has become a pervasive force that arguably has been a primary impetus for psychologists pursuing prescriptive authority and searching for alternative practice roles.

Each section is grounded in the conceptual and empirical literature. But because we wanted this chapter to accurately reflect current counseling psychology practice, we also conducted a brief, Web-based survey. We received responses from 234 (45% female; 55% male) members of SCP, with a mean age of 52.6 ($SD = 10.9$). They reported that their professional roles were academician (40.2%), clinical practitioner (39.7%), administrator (14.1%), and other (4.3%); 1.7% did not report professional roles. They were predominantly European American (83.8%), but also included African Americans (3.4%), Asian Americans (2.6%), bi/multiracial persons (1.7%), and others (4.3%). They were asked to respond to open-ended questions related to each of the three areas to be covered in this chapter. We quote some of their comments throughout the chapter.

MANAGED CARE AND COUNSELING PSYCHOLOGY

Fee-for-service (indemnity) insurance plans, such as Blue Cross/Blue Shield, were introduced in 1929 (Satcher, 1999), but until the early 1960s, psychologists had to receive their client referrals from, and be supervised by, psychiatrists to receive insurance reimbursement. This ended when states began to pass "freedom of choice" legislation that gave clients the option of receiving services directly from psychologists. Clinical psychologists, who were early entrants into the realm of independent practice, were the primary beneficiaries of this new legislation. Soon, though, some counseling psychologists began to move from the relative security of salaried, institutional positions to work as independent, fee-for-service professionals. Benjamin (2005, p. 22) observed that the freedom of choice legislation was responsible for enormous changes for these psychologists who, "with the exception of prescribing psychotropic medications and the obvious annual income differences, found themselves enjoying near parity with their psychiatrist colleagues in the mental health field. Psychologists now dominated the practice of psychotherapy; the golden age . . . had arrived."

But this golden age was short, ending in the early 1980s when managed mental health care became the norm. Cummings (1995) observed that passage to the new era was difficult for psychologists because they had "struggled for many years to attain autonomy only to see the rules of the game change just as it became the preeminent psychotherapy profession" (p. 12). These changes had an immediate, direct effect on psychologists in independent practice. But eventually almost all other practice settings were affected by managed care, even if only indirectly, and so the changes to professional psychology have been pervasive. The focus of this section is on the managed care era. We begin with an overview of managed behavioral health care and its evolution, and then address the sometimes profound effects that managed care has had on counseling psychologists and the clients they serve.

Managed Behavioral Health Care and Its Evolution

Prototypic managed care (MC) plans date back as far as the 1920s (Krieg, 1997), and Spiegel (1997) suggested that some MC concepts have their genesis much farther back, in a Babylonian code that Hammurabi imposed. But MC did not begin to have broad impact on health care delivery until the 1980s as a response to skyrocketing health care costs. Many explanations have been proposed for these dramatic cost increases (Brokowski, 1994; K. Davis, 1998): an aging U.S. population that is using more health care; an increase in medical malpractice suits; the public's greater expectations for health care availability; and the improvement of medical technology. But clinicians also were a factor. Cummings and Sayama (1995) noted, "As intrusive and arbitrary as managed care can be, when the practitioners had control there was no incentive within their ranks to reduce costs by increasing efficiency and effectiveness" (p. 29).

There have been a variety of cost containment strategies in the different forms that MC has assumed. The three most common are *health maintenance organizations* (HMOs), *preferred provider organizations* (PPOs), and *point of service plans* (POS). The HMOs either have practitioners on salary or in exclusive contractual arrangements. Members typically first see a primary care physician (PCP), the gatekeeper who arranges referrals to specialists and hospital admissions. These plans often are the most restrictive in terms of member choices, but also provide the greatest range of benefits for the lowest cost. The PPOs contract with a network of providers who are willing to accept lower reimbursement rates. Members can see providers outside the network, but pay higher deductible rates. The POS plans are HMO/PPO hybrids that are so-named because members choose which (HMO versus PPO) they will use each time they seek services. As with most HMOs, members typically initially see a PCP who makes referrals to providers in the plan's network. They can sidestep this option by seeing providers outside the network, though they will pay higher rates to exercise that option.

It is important to acknowledge this variety of management and cost containment strategies because discussions about MC too often have incorrectly implied that MC is monolithic, wielding a single blunt instrument to achieve its means. Related to this organizational diversity is that MC has affected—and been affected by—"two major concurrent trends in health care: the corporatization of private practice and the privatization of public services" (Belar, 2000, p. 239). The former trend is familiar to and much discussed by psychologists. The latter trend is evident in that by 2002, all but three states offered one or more forms of MC for the provision of Medicaid services and more than half (23.2 million) of Medicaid beneficiaries received at least some of their services through an MC organization (Kaye, 2005).

The result of these two trends has been that MC is responsible for the health care of burgeoning numbers of Americans. DeLeon, Bock, Richmond, Mays, and Cullen (2006) reported that 70.4 million Americans were covered by managed behavioral health organizations in 1993, but that number had more than doubled to 164.3 million by 2002. At the same time, the market has been consolidated so that a single company (Magellan Behavioral Health) covers approximately a third of these Americans, and over 56% of those enrolled in managed behavioral health plans are covered by one of only three managed behavioral health organizations (Magellan, ValueOptions, or United Behavioral Health).

As MC has permeated the market, it has changed. Belar (2000) used Goldsmith, Goran, and Nackel's (1996) model to describe these changes. In the first, cost-avoidant stage, MC companies compete with fee-for-service indemnity plans by decreasing inpatient stays and discounting fees. To accomplish these goals, MC organizations rely on preauthorizations, utilization reviews, and the substitution of ambulatory care for inpatient services. But as they cover more people, MC organizations begin to compete with one another rather than with fee-for-service providers.

This marks the second stage, during which value improvement replaces cost reduction as a differentiating feature of the services MC companies provide. Between-plan competition therefore begins to center on both client satisfaction and demonstrated outcomes. These trends are related as well to evidence-based practice and to integrated health services that optimize service to clients. The third stage occurs when MC companies pass a threshold of serving 70% to 80% of the population, including the poor and the elderly. At this point, the plans "discover that they are really in the public health business.... members' health problems mirror those found in the community, and health improvement through population-based strategies becomes increasingly important" (Belar, 2000, p. 240).

Indicators of Second Stage Functioning

It is unlikely that all MC organizations are functioning at the same stage. Some, such as Kaiser Permanente, seem to be at the third stage and so offer health promotion and community-based activities (Belar, 2000). In general, though, the following indicators suggest that most MC companies are functioning at the second stage.

Greater Integration of Health Services

One of those indicators is the movement toward greater integration of health services, with the corresponding elimination of carve-outs, that is,

> managed care arrangements in which a segment of health care (e.g., mental health) is given to a specialty organization to manage. Managed behavioral health care organizations (MBHOs) are carve-out firms that handle the mental health specialty arena. They were introduced in the 1980s to rein in mental health costs that were rapidly escalating. In short order MBHOs brought mental health costs under control. (Gray, Brody, & Johnson, 2005, p. 123)

Carve-outs unlink mental health services from broader health services. Gray et al. (2005) note, however, that because of important changes that have occurred during the past 2 decades (including the ascendancy of a biological model of psychiatry and the introduction of SSRIs; selective serotonin reuptake inhibitors—a type of antidepressant), the recent trend has been toward "carve-ins" that reintegrate mental health services into the broader health delivery system.

Emphasis on Accountability

Clarke, Lynch, Spofford, and DeBar (2006) cite MC organizations' increasing emphasis on improving the quality of care as one of the major trends shaping the delivery of mental health services.

Accountability for outcomes presently is focused primarily on the MC organizations. The *U.S. News and World Report,* in conjunction with the National Committee for Quality Assurance (NCQA), publishes an annual report that provides consumers with comparative information on more than 680 health plans. This accountability focus has had ripple effects in other practice settings as well. Williams and Edwardson (2000) found that university counseling center directors believed that MC was responsible for the increased levels of accountability they were experiencing.

A trend now is emerging, though, to extend accountability to practitioners. Speigel (1997) reminds us that holding health practitioners accountable for performance is not new and gave several examples from the Code of Hammurabi

> §218 If a physician operate on a man for a severe wound with a bronze lancet and cause the man's death, or open an abscess in the eye of a man with a bronze lancet and destroy the man's eye, they shall cut off his fingers.

The modern manifestation focuses on rewarding quality performance rather than only punishing inferior performance (e.g., Mallen, Vogel, & Rochlen, 2006; Trude, Au, & Christianson, 2006). This practice is not yet widespread, but is likely to become so. The Centers for Medicare and Medicaid Services now are working with at least 12 states to implement pay-for-performance (or quality-based purchasing) Medicaid programs. In fact, this is an international trend that is occurring in the United Kingdom and elsewhere. To reward quality is intuitively appealing. The problem is how to do so in a fair manner. This practice assumes that there is an accepted definition of quality and that client outcomes are assessed in a reliable and valid manner.

Each of the three primary methods of ensuring accountability has its own challenges. First, consumer satisfaction measures are probably the most common method. They focus on clients' subjective experience. Yet what clients need may be discrepant with what they desire and expect from therapy. Response rates also may be low (Lyons, Howard, O'Mahoney, & Lish, 1997). The second method, clinical outcome measures, includes change in symptoms. These can include self-report measures for high-functioning clients or clinician reports in cases of severely impaired clients (Lyons et al., 1997). The third method includes utilization measures that index a client's subsequent use of health care services. These have become a replacement for clinical outcome measures for two reasons: (1) utilization data are easier to gather than clinical outcome information, and (2) the use of services is the number one predictor of cost, a primary focus of MC. Historically, the assumption has been that the fewer services used, the better the client's level of functioning (Lyons et al., 1997).

Independent of this measurement issue, though, are several other pay-for-performance issues that, if left unresolved or poorly handled, could be detrimental to the public (Newman, 2005). "To the extent that the incented performance is made more difficult by sicker or less adherent patients, preselection of only healthier and compliant patients may result" (Newman, 2005, p. 2). Also, pay-for-performance may be unsuitable for small practice caseloads where a few extreme cases could significantly affect average quality measures. Additionally, some clinicians worry that the treatment they provide to certain clients is so complex that it will not be adequately reflected in typical quality measures.

Evidence-Based Practice

A third trend characteristic of the second phase of MC evolution has been its emphasis on evidence-based practice (EBP)—"the integration of the best available research with clinical expertise in the context of patient characteristics, culture, and preference" (APA Task Force on Evidence-Based Practice, 2006, p. 273). This is an area in which the goals of psychological scientists converge with those of MC; both are concerned with the delivery of the most effective treatments, albeit for different reasons.

The Effects of Managed Care: Challenges and Opportunities

While MC is a still-evolving phenomenon, it is having pervasive effects on psychological practice and, in so doing, is reshaping the very definition of that practice. We now consider some of the issues that MC has presented to psychologists. MC-imposed changes have been both positive and negative, although the judgment of the category into which a particular change belongs often is in the eye of the beholder. Because psychologists have had their incomes, autonomy, and even roles restricted, it is unsurprising that they tend to see the overall impact of MC as negative. This was the verdict of an overwhelming 85% of the independent practitioners in the Phelps, Eisman, and Kohout (1998) survey of 16,000 psychologists. That tone is reflected in much of the following discussion.

S. R. Davis and Meier (2001) identified nine major consequences of the managed care system that we have used to organize this discussion. We have, however, added a tenth consequence—the imposition of a medical model—and discuss this first.

Imposition of a Medical Model

Managed care requires that services be "medically necessary." Because this is not defined at the federal level, insurers typically impose their own definitions (Rosenbaum, Kamoie, Mauery, & Walitt, 2003). Common across those definitions is the assertion that "to qualify for payment, a service must be: For the treatment of sickness or injury; consistent with generally accepted medical practice; efficient, in the sense that a less expensive treatment works as well as a more expensive treatment, and not for the patient's or provider's convenience" (Ford, 1998, p. 183).

This medical model can be especially dissonant for counseling psychologists. One respondent to our survey noted, "I believe (and practice from) the orientation that many human difficulties are systemically and politically based." Others expressed frustration at being unable to receive reimbursement for the preventive and developmental interventions with which counseling psychologists are identified.

Types of Services and Who Delivers Them

Types of services have been substantially affected. It is difficult to get approval to provide assessment, a hallmark of psychology. One study found that brief crisis-intervention, drug counseling, and psychopharmacology are favored over more open-ended psychotherapy (Cypres, Landsberg, & Spellman, 1997). Another found that psychologists perceived MC companies as being more likely to support individual therapy over other treatment modalities (Keefe & Hall, 2001). Respondents to our survey complained about difficulties getting approvals to provide marital and family treatment as well as group therapy.

There also has been a shift in who is providing treatment. It is ironic that whereas the initial freedom of choice insurance laws provided psychologists the opportunity to displace psychiatrists as the primary providers of psychotherapy, the MC environment now is providing master's level practitioners the opportunity to displace psychologists from that role. Master's level social workers provided 56% of mental health services in 1998 compared with only 5% in 1991 (Clay, 1998). This situation is especially complicated for counseling psychology because so many of its doctoral programs have affiliated master's programs whose graduates then are figuratively disowned once they graduate and move into the marketplace as competitors.

Obsession with Cost

Cost containment was MC's raison d'être and one way it accomplished this has been through restricted reimbursement rates. Roughly two-thirds of the independent practitioners in the Phelps et al. (1998)

survey ranked low pay as one of their top five concerns about MC. One respondent to our survey articulated the issue succinctly: "I love doing therapy but the pay sucks."

Another cost containment strategy has been to emphasize brief treatments. Counseling psychologists are familiar with brief treatment, which fits with the work they often do in university counseling centers and elsewhere. But because MC organizations use their own algorithms, those limits often are inconsistent with what the practitioners believe is warranted for their clients. One respondent complained about time limits "for even very difficult issues, such as eating disorders." Another noted that it was difficult to "pace treatment, since I don't know if my 10 sessions (or whatever) will be extended." These treatment constraints often can place therapists in the role of advocate for the client to the MC company as they work to justify additional sessions.

Increase in Paperwork and Administrative Costs

S. R. Davis and Meier (2001) asserted, "The almost universal experience of clinicians is that managed care wastes a tremendous amount of their time" (p. 12). Many respondents to our survey complained about the extent and tone of their interactions with MC companies. Their complaints concerned extensive paperwork, phone calls to justify services, intrusiveness of utilization reviews, and the fact that clinical decisions were being made by lesser trained MC staff. There is also the ever-present threat of having services denied. One respondent noted, "While I have been questioned only a handful of times over the years and never had treatment denied, the threat of it is stressful." Finally, getting on a managed care insurance panel can be difficult, and once one is accepted, one must continually justify the treatment being provided and meet for periodic reviews.

Ethical and Legal Difficulties

Ethics have been much discussed in relationship to MC. About half of independent practitioners in the Phelps et al. (1998) survey ranked "ethical concerns created by managed care" as one of their top five concerns about MC. Yet it is interesting to consider Belar's (2000) comment: "Although mainstream psychology seems to view practice in a managed care environment as fraught with more ethical problems than an unmanaged, free-market environment, I am not certain that we can draw such conclusions" (p. 241).

Whether MC is ethically more challenging than the alternatives, it poses some unique ethical issues. In an MC environment, the clinician has a responsibility to argue for a longer period of treatment if an extension is in the client's best interest and if the purpose is to help the client find appropriate services once managed care will no longer provide reimbursement. The clinician must also decide what client information to disclose, and how, during utilization reviews. For further discussion of the legal and ethical aspects of MC, see Acuff et al. (1999) and Cooper and Gottlieb (2000).

Lack of Adequate Health Care

Tens of millions of Americans have no health insurance. Those who are fortunate enough to have some form of health insurance often have problems with the speed of service delivery or paying their portion of medical bills (Birenbaum & Cohen, 1998). One of our respondents who worked in a university counseling center commented, "We get . . . more students who have exhausted their (often limited) managed care eligibility [and] whose needs exceed the level of care we can provide as an 8–5 outpatient clinic, but they have nowhere else to go for affordable care." Another respondent asserted, "Some folks come to college just to access mental health services." Yet there also is evidence that for some populations, MC actually has increased service availability. Daley (2005) showed that a managed care mental health carve-out in Massachusetts improved access and continuity of care (i.e., use of a continuum of treatment services that decrease in intensity as the client prepares to live independently) for minorities. Across all racial and ethnic groups, access improved the most for Hispanics, whereas continuity of care increased the most for African Americans.

Training Opportunities and Emphases

Anecdotally, at least, training programs are giving more emphasis to brief treatments and greater attention to issues related to the delivery of treatments that are supported by evidence. MC also is affecting, to some extent, trainees' access to clients (because of rules requiring particular credentials for reimbursement). And students may also have difficulty finding sites that will provide instruction in the delivery of longer term psychological services (Donner, 1998).

Counseling psychology training directors reported to Daniels, Alva, and Olivares (2002) that their primary ways of adapting to an MC environment were to (a) address the ethical challenges this environment presents, (b) provide multicultural counseling skills for the diverse clientele students would serve, and (c) give greater attention to evidence-based treatments. They reported that they were not giving greater attention to business practices (e.g., marketing, financial strategies).

Agency Hardships

Many agencies providing psychological services are experiencing drastic cuts in government funding. Often the lag in reimbursement from the MC companies that increasingly manage those funds further complicates an agency's ability to survive financially, creating more work for those staff members that the agency can afford. Rankin (personal communication, October 1, 2006) also speculated that what seem to be deliberate delays in paying providers can cause resentment toward those clients for whom the delays occur. This is an area warranting research attention.

The Psychotherapy Factory

Cooper and Gottlieb (2000) noted that MC has forced private practitioners to merge the two cultures of psychology and business. That this merger has not always been easy is reflected in McWilliams's (2005) admonition to psychologists to "preserve their humanity" in this environment.

De-Emphasis on Psychiatric Hospitalization

Insurance companies' restrictions on the length of inpatient psychiatric hospital stays for which they will pay have "devastated the psychiatric hospital industry" (Kessler, 1998, p. 158). But it has affected practitioners as well. One respondent to our survey commented, "There have been situations in my state where insurance companies want to deny payment or admission for hospitalization but also do not want to take any responsibility for their decisions, which greatly increases the liability of the counselor."

Positive Aspects

While the 10 preceding points have mainly emphasized negative aspects of MC, we also want to note a few of its positive aspects. First, MC has created a mindfulness of scientific rigor that may have been lacking prior to its inception. McFall (2006) has asserted, "Unquestionably, the most powerful force behind improving the foundations of clinical psychology has been the advent of managed care in public health" (p. 6). Although clinicians may interpret the mandated provision of empirically supported treatments, as specified by MC companies, as restrictive and unnecessary, McFall argued that research should guide the delivery of mental health services and that this scientific direction will lead to better quality care than would a reliance on professed clinical expertise. Second, some practitioners also noted their improved access to clients. One respondent to our survey noted that MC companies refer clients who would not otherwise have heard of her.

In the next section, we discuss psychologists' movement toward prescriptive authority, which can be seen as one way in which they have attempted to create new roles and opportunities for themselves in the face of MC (Society for a Science of Clinical Psychology, 2001). In the final section, we consider new and emerging practice roles for psychologists. Although MC is not solely responsible for psychologists' search for new roles, it has been a primary force. The impetus may be negative, but the outcomes can be positive.

PRESCRIPTIVE AUTHORITY

The use of psychopharmacological agents to treat psychological disorders is not new. Although tranquilizers and antidepressant medication have been marketed since the 1950s, the use of psychopharmacological medications has increased substantially in recent years. There are several reasons for this increased (and some might suggest, almost routine) use of medications in the treatment of psychological disorders. These include advancements in knowledge of the structure and chemistry of the brain, the demands of managed care for shortened and empirically supported treatments for mental disorders, more favorable cultural attitudes toward mental health services, increased acceptance among mental health practitioners that medication can be an important component of a holistic approach, and the increasing numbers of therapists who work with primary care physicians or psychiatrists.

Benefits of Medication

Psychotherapy and psychopharmacological interventions have both been shown to yield beneficial effects for many psychological disorders, and it is generally believed (though not generally supported by research) that optimal treatment can be obtained through the combined use of psychotherapy and psychopharmacology (Westra, Eastwood, Bouffard, & Gerritsen, 2006). Research evidence suggests that psychotropic medications are a necessary component in the effective treatment of severe forms of chronic psychiatric disorders, such as bipolar mood (e.g., Kennedy, Lam, Nutt, & Thase, 2004; Yatham et al., 2005), and psychotic disorders (Gaudiano, 2005). However, the research findings for the treatment of depression and anxiety, which are among the most common mental disorders, are quite different. Meta-analyses commonly conclude that psychological and pharmacological interventions for depression and anxiety are equivalent in efficacy, and there is no consistent evidence to support the superiority of pharmacotherapy over psychotherapy for these disorders (Antonuccio, Danton, & DeNelsky, 1995; DeRubeis, Gelfand, Tang, & Simons, 1999; Otto, Smits, & Reese, 2005; Westra & Stewart, 1998).

The utility of drugs in the treatment of many psychological disorders does not preclude traditional psychotherapeutic interventions; psychotherapy appears to have important additive effects in the maintenance phase of treatment. In particular, relapse prevention intervention is associated with longer-term maintenance of treatment gains than is medication alone. Such relapse prevention effects have been shown to hold for depression (Hollon, 2003), anxiety (Otto et al., 2005), specific anxiety disorders (Gould, Otto, & Pollack, 1995; Gould, Otto, Pollack, & Yap, 1997), and eating disorders (Craighead & Agras, 1991).

To Prescribe or Not to Prescribe?

Despite the benefits of psychotropic medications for particular disorders, in all but a few jurisdictions prescription privileges are afforded only to medically trained practitioners, particularly psychiatrists. DeLeon, Fox, and Graham (1991) described the quest for prescription privileges for psychologists to be psychology's "next frontier." One justification for extending prescription privileges to other mental health professionals, specifically psychologists, is the limited availability of psychiatrists in many areas of the country (Heiby, DeLeon, & Anderson, 2004; Norfleet, 2002). Russ Newman (2001), the APA's Executive Director of Professional Practice, noted that the U.S. Surgeon General identified 444 counties in the United States as having no psychiatrists.

Not everyone is convinced that extending prescriptive authority to psychologists would fulfill unmet mental health needs. It has been argued that the psychiatrically underserved population is not especially large, and that the geographic distribution of psychologists is similar to that of psychiatrists, suggesting that there would not be a net gain in mental health coverage if psychologists could prescribe (Bush, 2001). Richard Harding, recent president of the American Psychiatric Association, has argued, "There is no societal need for more prescribing professionals. The needs of rural and other underserved patients can be met through collaboration between psychiatrists and other medical professionals" (Harding, 2001).

The debate over prescriptive authority for psychologists is not limited to disagreement between professional psychology and medicine. There is also ambivalence within psychology over whether psychologists want prescription privileges—with survey research suggesting that a reasonably high percentage (especially of more senior-level practitioners and academic psychologists) do not (deMayo, 2002; Fagan et al., 2004; Hayes, Walser, & Bach, 2002; Heiby et al., 2004; Luscher, Corbin, Bernat, Calhoun, & McNair, 2002; Stewart, Stewart, & Vogel, 2000; Walters, 2001).

Arguments in support of granting prescription privileges to psychologists have been summarized by the Task Force on Prescribing Privileges of the Society for the Science of Clinical Psychology (SSCP), a section within APA's Division 12 (Society of Clinical Psychology; also see Westra et al., 2006). Although the Task Force's report (Bush, 2001) ended by advocating *against* prescriptive authority for psychologists, its summary of key pro arguments is instructive.

First, psychotropic medications have become a major class of helpful interventions for clients. Although there is controversy over the actual degree of their efficacy, and over the biological and psychological mechanisms responsible for their apparent effects, such medications benefit a substantial percentage of the clients for whom they are prescribed. This includes people who lack access to psychosocial treatments, or who have refused or cannot be counted on to respond adequately to them. Second, as Fox (1988) has argued, the "use of medications is a logical extension of psychological practice" (p. 512). For many years, psychological science has recognized the role of biological factors in psychological and behavioral functioning, and accredited graduate programs in clinical and counseling psychology already offer at least some instruction in the biological bases of behavior.

Third, while most psychiatrists no longer offer psychotherapy or behavior therapy to their patients, they are legally permitted to do so. It is argued that, given appropriate training, applied psychologists should be able to join their psychiatric colleagues in providing the full spectrum of efficacious treatments. The precedent already exists for nonphysicians (nurses, optometrists, podiatrists) prescribing either with or without physician supervision (Westra et al., 2006).

Fourth, adequate prescription training can be accomplished in a time frame and at a financial cost accessible to many, if not most, psychologists. Indeed, it has been argued that there is precedent for such supplemental training in light of the prescriptive authority already given to several nonphysician groups, as noted (Heiby et al., 2004). In addition, a U.S. Department of Defense (DoD) study demonstrated that psychologists can prescribe safely and effectively. An independent evaluation of the DoD training program concluded that psychologists can be trained—using alternatives to traditional medical school— to prescribe medications safely (Newman, Phelps, Sammons, Dunivin, & Cullin, 2002).

Fifth, as mentioned earlier, many people lack access to psychiatrists and must look to general practitioners for psychotropic medications. Prescription privileges would help fill this gap. In addition, clients of prescribing psychologists would have a more complete array of treatment options available through a single practitioner. Finally, it has been argued that, as a group, applied psychologists cannot survive in today's competitive, oversupplied, managed care mental health context. Securing prescription privileges may be a matter of economic survival for practicing psychologists.

These pro arguments are balanced by arguments *against* granting prescriptive authority to psychologists. Physicians and many psychologists have both argued that safe and effective use of psychotropic medications requires extensive medical training and a thorough understanding of the brain and body. About half of all mentally ill patients also have other serious medical conditions requiring additional medications that psychologists are not trained to identify or diagnose (Harding, 2001).

It has also been argued that the addition of prescriptive authority will dilute the existing scope of psychological practice and skew the clinical contributions made by psychologists away from those areas (assessment and psychotherapy) in which they have traditionally made unique contributions. Thus the very foundations of psychology could be eroded, and the clinical practice of psychology might become indistinguishable from psychiatry (Bush, 2001; Heiby, 2002; Heiby et al., 2004). Yet another con argument is that adding prescriptive authority coursework to doctoral training programs would erode their ability to focus on what defines psychology in the first place—basic psychological science, research methodology, and empirically supported treatments (Bush, 2001; Heiby, 2002).

Counseling psychology's position on this matter is unclear. Although the APA is vigorously pursuing an agenda of securing prescription privileges for appropriately trained psychologists, SCP has yet to take a public position on this matter. A survey by Lichtenberg et al. (2001) showed little unanimity among counseling psychologists on the issue of prescriptive authority, although the differences in opinion appear most pronounced between those involved in professional practice and those involved in academic pursuits, a finding similar to the more informal survey we conducted prior to beginning this chapter.

Proposed Levels of Prescription Training

What amount of training and experience is appropriate and necessary to achieve competence at prescribing psychotropic medications? In 1996, the APA-approved curriculum guidelines for training in pharmacology that would lead to prescriptive authority for psychology. The curriculum, which was based on several earlier documents, including the Department of Defense Psychopharmacology Demonstration Project, involves three levels of training. Level 1, which can be completed during doctoral study, covers basic psychopharmacology education. Levels 2 and 3, which involve continued knowledge acquisition and supervised practical experience, require postdoctoral study. Levels 2 and 3 include courses in psychodiagnostics, pathophysiology, therapeutics, emergency treatment, substance abuse treatment, developmental psychopharmacology, and supervised clinical experience. Prescriptive authority would only be granted after completion of Level 3. Advancing from Level 1 to Levels 2 and 3 training requires a completed doctorate in psychology, a state license in psychology, and an active practice. Prerequisite knowledge of human biology, anatomy and physiology, biochemistry, neuroanatomy, and psychopharmacology is also required and can be completed as part of doctoral study.

At the time of this writing, a proposed revision of these recommended curricular guidelines is being circulated for review by the professional public. The revision, drafted by a task force of the APA's Board of Educational Affairs and Committee for the Advancement of Professional Practice, outlines revised recommended postdoctoral education and training in psychopharmacology for licensed psychologists who seek prescriptive authority (www.apa.org/ed/graduate/rev_curriculum.pdf).

Whether the preceding curriculum is sufficient to ensure competent prescriptive practice is a source of disagreement among professionals. But it is also a source of concern on another front, especially among graduate psychology faculty, that training for prescriptive authority would necessitate undergraduate-level prerequisites to entry into doctoral programs that would attract a different population of applicants into graduate programs and further diminish the emphasis on psychosocial/behavioral treatments (McFall, 2002). Further, the cost of training under this program, even if no undergraduate prerequisites are needed, would be considerable—estimated at $20,000 to $30,000 per student. This does not include income sacrificed to make time available for extended postdoctoral training. The impact of these financial costs may make such training unattainable for those with limited resources and this, in turn, would likely affect the diversity of those who could provide service.

No matter who prescribes psychotropic medications, practicing professionals must be aware of the medications their clients are taking, the type and impact of medical treatments being used, and who is providing this care. As counseling treatment plans are devised, pharmaceuticals can become a critically important element of care, and psychologists need to be aware of the side effects associated with medications that their clients may be taking. In addition, counseling psychologists must be informed about a client's medication practices, since they could conceivably make a recommendation to a primary care physician that would be in conflict with other medications being prescribed.

EXPANDING PRACTICE ROLES FOR COUNSELING PSYCHOLOGISTS

Interest now seems especially high among professional psychologists in creating new practice opportunities. Two interacting factors fueling that interest are (1) the impact that MC is having on the traditional practice of psychotherapy (e.g., restricted pay, competition by master's level practitioners) and (2) large increases in the supply of mental health practitioners due, at least in part, to free-standing schools of professional psychology, but also potentially attributable to increases in the licensing of master's-level providers. Even though the production of psychology PhDs remained essentially constant between 1988 and 2001, the number of PhDs increased by 169% (APA Research Office, 2005). In short, the search for new professional roles and activities is an issue of livelihood.

This search for new roles has been yielding creative results. In a survey of psychologists in independent practice, practitioners reported 180 specific fee-for-service activities in which they were engaged—all of which fell outside the purview of MC (Walfish, 2001). These services fell into several broad categories: (a) business psychology, (b) consultation to organizations, (c) forensic psychology, (d) group therapy, (e) health psychology, (f) psychoeducational services, (g) services to government, (h) teaching and supervision, and (i) miscellaneous other activities.

Factors Affecting Counseling Psychologists' Choice of New Roles and Settings

To those outside the field, the term *counseling psychology* might seem to anchor the work of its practitioners to the solitary role of counselor. But whereas the title of the specialty can serve as a role limitation, counseling psychologists actually have been resourceful in finding new roles for themselves.

A Sense of Broad Possibilities

For many years, counseling psychologists have tended to see themselves as relatively unconstrained in their role possibilities. It is instructive to consider discussions in the early 1980s of possible roles for counseling psychologists in consulting, mental health policy, HMOs, and design of job systems (Osipow, 1980; Tanney, 1982). In fact, entire issues of the *Counseling Psychologist* were devoted to prophecies about appropriate roles and settings for counseling psychologists (Whiteley, 1980, 1982).

Interest in alternative roles for counseling psychologists is not at all new. There has been for some time an encouragement toward what Neimeyer, Bowman, and Stewart (2001) have called "a plasticity in relation to the specialty's traditional identity moorings" (p. 776). That plasticity was implied when Ivey (1979) proclaimed counseling psychology to be:

> [the]most broadly based applied specialty.... Our practitioners focus on the broadest array of professional psychological activities of any specialty. The counseling psychologist has the greatest array of possible interventions to assist client development and works with populations from infants through seniors in an almost infinite array of settings. (p. 3)

Parenthetically, in exercising this freedom in role choice and enhancing their marketability, some counseling psychologists deny their professional identities. Tanney (1982) noted this some time ago and it was more recently confirmed by Goodyear et al. (in press) who found that whereas 43% of SCP members used the label "counseling psychologist" for themselves, that was true of only 23.8% of non-members of SCP (the corresponding proportions of those calling themselves simply a "psychologist" were 35% and 59% respectively). This trend was even more pronounced for those with a counseling psychology doctorate who were members of the APA, but not of SCP: only 24% used the label "counseling psychologist," while 60% called themselves "psychologist" and 9% used the term "clinical psychologist."

Scientist-Practitioner Training

Although not all counseling psychologists are being trained as scientist-practitioners, this model remains dominant in the field, and those trained in this model may have opportunities not available to psychologists trained simply as practitioners. Sanchez and Turner (2003) asserted:

> The scientist-practitioner may be best prepared to function in the managed care environment because this model, with its focus on integrating scientific and clinical knowledge, best prepares the doctoral-level clinician to educate utilization reviewers, evaluate effectiveness and efficiency of treatment through outcome research, design and manage integrated networks, develop and evaluate clinical practice guidelines, supervise nondoctoral providers, and deliver empirically based treatments. (p. 127)

These comments imply that some variant of clinical practice will remain central to the work of psychologists. However, it is not necessary that psychologists define themselves exclusively in terms of the provision of clinical practice. There are other possibilities, some of which may bear little surface similarity to what psychologists currently do in clinical settings. Some observers have suggested that psychology should look to law as a model. Although the market for attorneys is saturated, huge numbers graduate each year. New attorneys get jobs, even if not in traditional attorney roles. They often go directly into administration. It is not their specific legal competencies but rather their skills in critical thinking and problem solving that are gaining them entry to these positions.

Benjamin (2005) observed:

> One of the traditional strengths of doctoral education in psychology has been that students were trained as problem solvers, and were taught the methodological skills, including in critical thinking, to know how to conceptualize problems so that they could be solved. Evidence for this flexibility comes from the myriad places in which psychologists are found. They are in virtually any industry one can name (motion pictures, space exploration, police work, communications) and they hold a plethora of jobs that almost no one would have imagined a psychologist might pursue. . . . Psychotherapy, the brass ring for clinical psychologists [and many counseling psychologists], is not likely to disappear from their job description, but there seems little doubt that the position of preeminence in that arena is gone and will not return. (p. 25)

Training as a Barrier

A barrier to more widespread change in counseling psychology roles has been the training programs preparing current counseling psychology graduates. Various authors (e.g., McCrea et al., 2004; Osipow, 1980) have observed that core aspects of that training have remained virtually unchanged over the years. In response to a question about the preparation for our students to do what is now needed, either in the university-based or professional school graduate programs, Cummings (1996) commented, "No, no. We're training great psychologists for the 1980s! We're not prepared for the *90's* or the year 2000 whatsoever."

A reality of graduate training programs is that their faculty teach what they know, which in counseling psychology programs typically is psychotherapy. But it is also true that students typically enter their programs wanting to be psychotherapists, and there have been few reported systematic efforts to recruit students with less traditional interests. Those students who have other interests can feel pressured to conform. McCrea et al. (2004) noted, "When students take the path less traveled, they may feel undervalued . . . " (p. 80).

Training programs also exist as part of a larger training system, including training/curriculum expectations promulgated by the SCP the Council of Counseling Psychology Training Programs (CCPTP; Epperson, Fouad, Stoltenberg, & Murdock, 2005; Murdock, Alcorn, Heesacker, & Stoltenberg, 1998), and the APA's Committee on Accreditation (American Psychological Association, 2006); internship readiness expectations of member institutions of the Association of Psychology Postdoctoral and Internship Centers (APPIC); and competency expectations currently being discussed by the professional psychology training councils. Although these training expectations are not limited to clinical training, completing an internship nevertheless is a requirement for those in accredited training programs, and APA-accredited internships are primarily clinical in nature (Lichtenberg, 1987). Therefore, to be competitive for internship placement, students continue to take coursework and practica that will prepare them for a clinical internship and, in so doing, perpetuate traditional psychotherapy roles.

Whether counseling psychology is "the most broadly based applied specialty," as Ivey (1979) suggested almost 3 decades ago, may be debated. Certainly there is evidence to suggest that those trained as counseling psychologists have an array of professional practice options for which, by training, they may be well suited. Although surveys reveal that some counseling psychologists are branching into practice areas outside the traditional provision of psychotherapy, this remains the less common path. Establishing a practice niche "outside the box" is an option that relatively few counseling psychology practitioners have exercised, despite frustration with the demands and economic consequences of managed care, the competition from doctoral and subdoctoral independent practitioners, and the anticipated costs of prescriptive authority. This is not to say that the face of professional practice in counseling psychology is not changing. But the rethinking and realignment of the professional roles of counseling psychologists—encouraged as early as the mid-1980s—does not seem to have occurred in any significant fashion within the profession. Changes in the professional practice of counseling psychology, as may be true in other areas of professional psychology, have been more evolutionary than revolutionary.

SUMMARY

No profession exists apart from greater, macrocontextual influences. As an applied field, counseling psychology has evolved with the economic, societal, and professional demands of the times. In this chapter, we explored two major forces that are currently shaping our discipline: (1) managed health care and (2) the ongoing, often heated, discussion surrounding prescriptive authority for psychologists. We have illuminated the ways in which these and other issues have affected professional practice, closing with an examination of changing career roles counseling psychologists now occupy.

Managed care is the thread that runs through professional practice, as it influences not only the debate over prescription privileges but also the duties of psychologists in applied settings. Managed care companies dictate the duration of treatment and, to a great extent, the services rendered. Most psychologists believe that the policies imposed by managed care companies are inconvenient and restrictive, causing financial and ethical burdens. Nonetheless, it is important to acknowledge that managed care has positively affected some aspects of service delivery. Psychologists must now demonstrate that they are benefiting their clients and are accountable for the quality of the treatment they provide. These measures protect the public, ensure that psychologists are behaving ethically, and allow empirical research findings to inform practice.

A major implication of managed care has been the application of a medical model to the conceptualization and treatment of mental health issues. As a result, psychologists are more likely to consider pathology from a biological basis and view pharmacological interventions as appropriate. Some professionals refer to obtaining prescriptive authority as the next big step in applied psychology because it will allow psychologists parity with professionals in the medical field. Proponents of prescription privileges contend that obtaining such authority is necessary to ensure the survival of our field in the era of managed care.

As of this writing, two states (New Mexico and Louisiana) have granted psychologists prescription privileges, and the issue continues to be a primary focus of the APA and many state associations. Unanimity within professional psychology is lacking, with vocal, and at times strident, advocates arguing their positions for and against prescriptive authority. Counseling psychology, with its roots in a developmental as opposed to a medical model, finds itself torn, and there is a seeming silence within SCP about the specialty's position on the issue of prescriptive authority for counseling psychologists. It is uncertain how the debate over prescriptive authority will manifest itself in training and professional practice.

Issues of managed care and prescriptive authority are inevitably changing what it means to be a counseling psychologist and how professional roles are defined. Additionally, increasing numbers of students with doctoral degrees in professional psychology are graduating, nearly flooding the market with mental health service providers. Counseling psychologists thus find themselves in a unique position. For these reasons, it was necessary to include in this chapter a section describing the practice roles, both traditional and nontraditional, of professionals in the field.

The majority of counseling psychologists are engaged to some degree in the delivery of mental health services, and although the pervasive sentiment is one of broad marketability and numerous role opportunities, few counseling psychologists have ventured outside the realm of traditional academic and counselor positions. An explanation for this finding is that training over the years has remained unchanged, and thus students may feel as though there is little support for pursuing alternative career paths. It is essential to anticipate changes that will influence professional practice, including the implications of managed health care and prescriptive authority, as these changes provide counseling psychologists with new career roles and opportunities.

Counseling psychology has always been open to explore and challenge its identity. The landscape of professional practice is continually changing in response to internal and external pressures. Gelso and Fretz (2001) have described counseling psychology's changes and adaptations in terms of the field's stages of development. Similarly, Rude, Weissberg, and Gazda (1988), commenting on the evolving nature of our field, suggested, "Counseling psychology can be compared to an individual who pauses at various developmental junctures to reflect upon questions of identity, purpose, and means" (p. 424). It is uncertain how the practice of counseling psychology will change and what our practice will become. But what seems clear is that we are, or at least have been, an adaptable profession—capable of responding to social and financial exigencies, and to the evolving nature of psychological science. We expect this will continue to be the case.

REFERENCES

Acuff, C., Bennet, B. E., Bricklin, P., Canter, M., Knapp, S. J., Moldawsky, S., et al. (1999). Considerations for ethical practice in managed care. *Professional Psychology: Research and Practice, 30*, 563–575.

American Psychological Association. (1996). *Recommended postdoctoral training: Psychopharmacology for prescription privileges*. Washington, DC: Author.

American Psychological Association. (2006). *Guidelines and principles of program accreditation in professional psychology*. Washington, DC: Author.

American Psychological Association Research Office. (2005). *Research office index*. Available from http://research.apa.org/roindex.html.

APA Task Force on Evidence-Based Practice. (2006). Evidence-based practice in psychology. *American Psychologist, 61*, 271–285.

Antonuccio, D. O., Danton, W. G., & DeNelsky, G. Y. (1995). Psychotherapy versus medication for depression: Challenging the conventional wisdom with data. *Professional Psychology: Research and Practice, 26*, 574–585.

Belar, C. D. (2000). Ethical issues in managed care: Perspectives in evolution. *Counseling Psychologist, 28,* 237–241.

Benjamin, L. T., Jr. (2005). A history of clinical psychology as a profession in American (and a glimpse at its future). *Annual Review of Clinical Psychology, 1,* 1–30.

Birenbaum, A., & Cohen, H. J. (1998). Managed care and quality health services for people with developmental disabilities: Is there a future for UAPs? *Mental Retardation, 36,* 325–329.

Brokowski, A. (1994). Current mental health care environments: Why managed care is necessary. In R. Lowman & R. Resnick (Eds.), *The mental health professional's guide to managed care* (pp. 1–18). Washington, DC: American Psychological Association.

Bush, J. W. (2001, Winter). SSCP task force statement on prescription privileges. *Clinical Science,* 6–11.

Clarke, G., Lynch, F., Spofford, M., & DeBar, L. (2006). Trends influencing future delivery of mental health services in large healthcare systems. *Clinical Psychology: Science and Practice, 13,* 287–292.

Clay, R. (1998). Mental health professions vie for position in the next decade. *APA Monitor, 29*(10), 20–21.

Cooper, C. C., & Gottlieb, M. C. (2000). Ethical issues with managed care: Challenges facing counseling psychology. *Counseling Psychologist, 28,* 179–236.

Craighead, L. W., & Agras, W. S. (1991). Mechanisms of action in cognitive-behavioral and pharmacological interventions for obesity and bulimia nervosa. *Journal of Consulting and Clinical Psychology, 59*(1), 115–125.

Cummings, N. A. (1995). Impact of managed care on employment and training: A primer for survival. *Professional Psychology: Research and Practice, 26,* 10–15.

Cummings, N. A. (1996). Now we're facing the consequences. *Scientist-Practitioner, 6*(1), 9–13. Available from www.fenichel.com/Managed2.html.

Cummings, N. A., & Sayama, M. (1995). *Focused psychotherapy: A casebook of brief, intermittent psychotherapy throughout the life cycle.* New York: Brunner/Mazel.

Cypres, A., Landsberg, G., & Spellman, M. (1997). The impact of managed care on community mental health outpatient services in New York State. *Administration and Policy in Mental Health, 24,* 509–521.

Daley, M. C. (2005). Race, managed care, and the quality of substance abuse treatment. *Administration and Policy in Mental Health, 32,* 457–476.

Daniels, J., Alva, L. A., & Olivares, S. (2002). Graduate training for managed care: A national survey of psychology and social work programs. *Professional Psychology: Research and Practice, 33,* 587–590.

Davis, K. (1998). Managed health care: Forcing social work to make choices and changes. In G. Shamess & A. Lighburn (Eds.), *Humane managed care?* (pp. 409–429). Washington, DC: NASW Press.

Davis, S. R. & Meier, S. T. (2001). The causes and consequences of managed care. In J. Martinez, M. Stevens, T. Hyde, B. Kauser, & F. Banwarth (Eds.), *The elements of managed care: A guide for helping professionals* (pp. 1–14). Belmont, CA: Wadsworth.

DeLeon, P. H., Bock, P. S., Richmond, M. S., Mays, M., & Cullen, E. A. (2006). A perspective on the nation's antitrust policies: Implications for psychologists. *Professional Psychology: Research and Practice, 37,* 374–383.

DeLeon, P. H., Fox, R. E., & Graham, S. R. (1991). Prescription privileges: Psychology's next frontier? *American Psychologist, 46,* 384–393.

deMayo, R. A. (2002). Academic interests and experiences of doctoral students in clinical psychology: Implications for prescription privilege training. *Professional Psychology: Research and Practice, 33,* 499–501.

DeRubeis, R. J., Gelfand, L. A., Tang, T. Z., & Simons, A. D. (1999). Medications versus cognitive behavior therapy for severely depressed outpatients: Mega-analysis of four randomized comparisons. *American Journal of Psychiatry, 156,* 1007–1013.

Donner, S. (1998). Fieldwork crisis: Dilemmas, dangers, and opportunities. *Psychiatric Services, 49,* 183–184.

Epperson, D. L., Fouad, N. A., Stoltenberg, C. D., & Murdock, N. L. (2005). *Model training program in counseling psychology.* Retrieved May 12, 2007, from www.ccptp.org/model.htm.

Fagan, T. J., Ax, R. K., Resnick, R. J., Liss, M., Johnson, R. T., & Forbes, M. R. (2004). Attitudes among interns and directors of training: Who wants to prescribe, who doesn't, and why. *Professional Psychology: Research and Practice, 35,* 345–356.

Ford, W. E. (1998). Medical necessity: Its impact in managed mental health care. *Psychiatric Services, 49*(2), 183–184.

Fox, R. E. (1988). Prescription privileges: Their implications for the practice of psychology. *Psychotherapy, 25,* 501–507.

Gaudiano, B. A. (2005). Cognitive behavior therapies for psychotic disorders: Current empirical status and future directions. *Clinical Psychology: Science and Practice, 12*(1), 33–50.

Gelso, C., & Fretz, B. (2001). *Counseling psychology* (2nd ed.). Fort Worth, TX: Harcourt.

Goldsmith, J. G., Goran, M. M., & Nackel, J. G. (1996). New strategies for creating value. *Healthplan, 37*(3), 123–126.

Goodyear, R. K., Murdock, N., Lichtenberg, J. W., McPherson, R., Petren, S., & O'Byrne, K. K. (in press). Stability and change in counseling psychologists' identities, roles, functions, and career satisfaction across fifteen years. *Counseling Psychologist.*

Gould, R. A., Otto, M. W., & Pollack, M. H. (1995). A meta-analysis of treatment outcome for panic disorder. *Clinical Psychology Review, 15*, 819–844.

Gould, R. A., Otto, M. W., Pollack, M. H., & Yap, L. (1997). Cognitive behavioral and pharmacological treatment of generalized anxiety disorder: A preliminary meta-analysis. *Behavior Therapy, 28*, 285–305.

Gray, G. V., Brody, D. S., & Johnson, D. (2005). The evolution of behavioral primary care. *Professional Psychology: Research and Practice, 36*, 123–129.

Harding, R. K. (2001, October). Making the point on prescriptive authority: No. *Monitor on Psychology, 32*(9).

Hayes, S. C., Walser, R. D., & Bach, P. (2002). Prescription privileges for psychologists: Constituencies and conflicts. *Journal of Clinical Psychology, 58*, 697–708.

Heiby, E. M. (2002). Prescription privileges for psychologists: Can differing views be reconciles? *Journal of Clinical Psychology, 58*, 589–597.

Heiby, E. M., DeLeon, P. H., & Anderson, T. (2004). A debate on prescription privileges for psychologists. *Professional Psychology: Research and Practice, 35*, 336–344.

Hollon, S. D. (2003). Does cognitive therapy have an enduring effect? *Cognitive Therapy and Research, 27*(1), 71–75.

Ivey, A. E. (1979). Counseling psychology: The most broadly-based applied psychology specialty. *Counseling Psychologist, 8*(3), 3–6.

Kaye, N. (2005, June). *Medicaid managed care: Looking forward, looking back.* Portland, ME: National Academy for State Health Policy. Available on-line at http://www.nashp.org/Files/mmc_guide_final_draft_6-16.pdf.

Keefe, R. H., & Hall, M. L. (2001). Private practitioners' perceptions of the changes in their use of treatment modalities following participation in managed care panels. *Journal of Psychiatric Practice, 7*, 350–355.

Kennedy, S. H., Lam, R. W., Nutt, D. J., & Thase, M. E. (2004). *Treating depression effectively: Applying clinical guidelines.* Toronto: Martin Duniza, Taylor, & Francis Group.

Kessler, K. A. (1998). History of managed behavioral health care and speculations about its future. *Harvard Review of Psychiatry, 6*, 155–159.

Krieg, F. J. (1997, September). Managed care: A brief introduction. *Communique,* online newsletter of the National Association of School Psychologists. Available www.nasponline.org/publications/cq261mancare.html.

Lichtenberg, J. W. (1987). Research: A missing component in most internships. *Counseling Psychologist, 15*, 267–269.

Lichtenberg, J. W., Murdock, N., Petren, S., O'Byne, K. K., McPherson, R., & Goodyear, R. K. (2001, February). *A national survey of counseling psychologists: Contemporary roles, functions, and career satisfaction.* Presentation made to the National Conference on Counseling Psychology, Houston, TX.

Luscher, K. A., Corbin, W. R., Bernat, J. A., Calhoun, K. S., & McNair, L. D. (2002). Predictors of graduate student attitudes toward prescription privileges for psychologists. *Journal of Clinical Psychology, 58*, 783–792.

Lyons, J. S., Howard, K. I., O'Mahoney, M. T., & Lish, J. D. (1997). *The measurement and management of clinical outcomes in mental health.* New York: Wiley.

Mallen, M. J., Vogel, D. L., & Rochlen, A. B. (2006). Pay for performance in primary and specialty behavioral health care: Two "concept" proposals. *Professional Psychology: Research and Practice, 37*, 384–388.

McCrea, L. G., Bromley, J. L., McNally, C. J., O'Byrne, K. K., & Wade, K. A. (2004). Houston 2001: A student perspective on issues of identity, training, social advocacy, and the future of counseling psychology. *Counseling Psychologist, 32*, 78–88.

McFall, R. M. (2002). Training for prescriptions vs. prescriptions for training: Where are we now? Where should we be? How do we get there? *Journal of Clinical Psychology, 58*, 659–676.

McFall, R. M. (2006, Fall). The quest for a science of clinical psychology: A progress report. *Clinical Science,* 4–8.

McWilliams, N. (2005). Preserving our humanity as therapists. *Psychotherapy: Theory, Research, Practice, Training, 42*, 139–151.

Murdock, N. L., Alcorn, J., Heesacker, M., & Stoltenberg, C. (1998). Model training program in counseling psychology. *Counseling Psychologist, 26*, 658–672.

Neimeyer, G. J., Bowman, J., & Stewart, A. E. (2001). Internship and initial job placements in Counseling Psychology: A 26-year retrospective. *Counseling Psychologist, 29*, 763–780.

Newman, R. (2001, October). Making the point on prescriptive authority: Yes. *Monitor on Psychology, 32*(9).

Newman, R. (2005, October). Pay-for-performance: No panacea. *Monitor on Psychology, 36*(9), 30.

Newman, R., Phelps, R., Sammons, M. T., Dunivin, D. L., & Cullen, E. A. (2002). Evaluation of the Psychopharmacology Demonstration Project: A retrospective analysis. *Professional Psychology: Research and Practice, 31*(6), 598–603.

Norfleet, M. A. (2002). Responding to society's needs: Prescription privileges for therapists. *Journal of Clinical Psychology, 58*, 599–610.

Osipow, S. H. (1980). Toward counseling psychology in the year 2000. *Counseling Psychologist, 8*(4), 18–19.

Otto, M. W., Smits, J. A. J., & Reese, H. E. (2005). Combined psychotherapy and pharmacotherapy for mood and anxiety disorders in adults: Review and analysis. *Clinical Psychology: Science and Practice, 12*, 72–86.

Phelps, R., Eisman, E. J., & Kohout, J. (1998). Psychological practice and managed care: Results of the CAPP practitioner survey. *Professional Psychology: Research and Practice, 29*, 31–36.

Rosenbaum, S., Kamoie, B., Mauery, D. R., & Walitt, B. (2003, November). *Medical necessity in private health plans: Implications for behavioral health care* (DHHS Pub. No. SMA 03-3790). Rockville, MD: Center for Mental Health Services, Substance Abuse and Mental Health Services Administration. Available from http://mentalhealth.samhsa.gov/publications/allpubs/SMA03-3790/credits.asp.

Rude, S. S., Weissberg, M., & Gazda, G. M. (1988). Looking to the future: Themes from the Third National Conference for Counseling Psychology. *Counseling Psychologist, 16*, 423–430.

Sanchez, L. M., & Turner, S. M. (2003). Practicing psychology in the era of managed care: Implications for practice and training. *American Psychologist, 58*, 116–129.

Satcher, D. (1999). *Mental health: A report of the Surgeon General*. Rockville, MD: U.S. Dept of Health and Human Services. Available from www.surgeongeneral.gov/library/mentalhealth/home.html.

Spiegel, A. D. (1997, May). Hammurabi's managed health care—circa 1700 B.C. *Managed Care, 6*. Available from www.managedcaremag.com/archives/9705/9705.hammurabi.shtml.

Stewart, A. E., Stewart, E. A., & Vogel, D. L. (2000). A survey of interns' preferences and plans for postdoctoral training. *Professional Psychology: Research and Practice, 31*, 435–441.

Tanney, F. (1982). Counseling psychology in the marketplace. *Counseling Psychologist, 10*(2), 21–29.

Trude, S., Au, M., & Christianson, J. B. (2006). Health plan pay-for-performance strategies. *American Journal of Managed Care, 12*, 537–542.

Walfish, S. (2001). Developing a career in psychology. In A. Hess (Ed.), *Succeeding in graduate school: The career guide for psychology students* (pp. 385–398). Mahwah, NJ: Erlbaum.

Walters, G. D. (2001). A meta-analysis of opinion data on the prescription privilege debate. *Canadian Psychology, 42*, 119–125.

Westra, H. A., Eastwood, J. D., Bouffard, B. B., & Gerritsen, C. J. (2006). Psychology's pursuit of prescriptive authority: Would it meet the goals of Canadian health care reform? *Canadian Psychology, 47*, 77–95.

Westra, H. A., & Stewart, S. H. (1998). Cognitive-behavioral therapy and pharmacotherapy: Complementary or contradictory approaches to the treatment of anxiety. *Clinical Psychology Review, 18*(3), 307–340.

Whiteley, J. M. (Ed.). (1980). Counseling psychology in the year 2000 AD. *Counseling Psychologist, 8(4)*.

Whiteley, J. M. (Ed.). (1982). Counseling psychology: The next decade. *Counseling Psychologist, 10(2)*.

Williams, E. N., & Edwardson, T. L. (2000). Managed care and counseling centers: Training issues for the new millennium. *Journal of College Student Psychotherapy, 14*(3), 51–65.

Yatham, L. N., Kennedy, S. H., O'Donovan, C., Parikh, S., MacQueen, G., McIntyre, R., et al. (2005). Canadian Network for Mood and Anxiety Treatments (CANMAT) guidelines for the management of patients with bipolar disorder: Consensus and controversies. *Bipolar Disorders, 7*(Suppl. 3), 5–69.

CHAPTER 3

Technological Advances: Implications for Counseling Psychology Research, Training, and Practice

PAUL A. GORE JR.
WADE C. LEUWERKE

It is probably safe to assume that technological advances during the past 25 years have affected the work and leisure hours of every reader of this chapter. Personal computers (PCs), the Internet, email, personal digital assistants (PDAs), cellular telephones, and iPods have forever altered the way we work, communicate, and recreate. Professionals can get a sense of the relative impact technology is having on our discipline and society as a whole by noting the breadth and depth of the literature dealing with technology and human behavior. Psychologists are grappling with issues of Internet addiction (Chou, Condron, & Belland, 2005; Griffiths, 2003), the use of virtual reality in psychotherapy (Riva, 2005; Rothbaum, 2006), Web-delivered graduate education (Collins & Jerry, 2005), cybersupervision (Kanz, 2001; Miller, Miller, & Evans, 2002), computer-delivered assessment (Buchanan, 2003; Risko, Qu1ity, & Oakman, 2006), online psychotherapy (Mallen & Vogel, 2005), Internet research methods (Childress & Asamen, 1998; Kraut et al., 2004), telehealth interventions (Reed, McLaughlin, & Milholland, 2000), Internet infidelity (Hertlein & Piercy, 2006; Whitty & Carr, 2006), and the ethical and legal issues that can arise when using technology in psychological instruction, research, and practice (Keller & Lee, 2003; Koocher & Morray, 2000; Mallen, Vogel, & Rochlen, 2005).

As Mallen and Vogel (2005) aptly suggest, the future is now. Technology is currently an integral part of our clinical practice, graduate education, and research. Counseling psychologists and counseling psychology graduate students must familiarize themselves with the technological applications in our field as well as the unresolved issues that surround some of those applications. This discussion is not new. Many readers may have coped with the anxiety of using their first personal computer in the 1980s or confronted the nuances of email in the 1990s (e.g., when you hit "send" you better mean it). Literature discussing the use of these emerging technologies in research, teaching, and practice soon followed (e.g., Ben-Porath & Butcher, 1986; McCullough, Farrell, & Longabaugh, 1986). The discussion has simply intensified as technology has advanced and been applied to more fundamental practices (e.g., direct mental health service). Applications of technology in research, teaching, and practice have become so common that our students and clients now expect them.

A comprehensive review of the role of technology in counseling psychology is beyond the scope of this chapter. Many applications of technology, although interesting (e.g., self-help podcasts, virtual reality therapy), have not yet gained widespread application or attention in the psychological literature. In defining the scope of our chapter, we chose to concentrate on issues that are most important to counseling psychology educators, researchers, and practitioners. We address online counseling, the use of technology in graduate training and supervision, the use of the Internet in psychological research, and problematic behaviors resulting from technological advances and availability. When appropriate, ethical and legal issues in these areas are explored.

ONLINE COUNSELING

Online counseling, e-therapy, e-counseling, web-counseling, telehealth, telecounseling, and computer-mediated communication all refer to the provision of counseling or psychotherapy services at a distance for symptom amelioration or improvement of mental health (Alleman, 2002). Communication modalities include telephone, email, synchronous chat, videoconferencing (Mallen & Vogel, 2005), web logs (blogs) monitored by a therapist (Barak & Bloch, 2006), and voice-over IP (Internet Phone; Young, 2005). Although readers may be familiar with some of these technologies, many may be unfamiliar with chat, Internet videoconferencing, blogs, and IP technologies. Synchronous chat uses Web-based messaging or instant messaging programs for individuals to communicate in real time through text. Blogs allow individuals easily to post text, pictures, and videos on Web pages to be viewed by others. Voice-over IP is similar to the telephone except that audio is communicated through the Internet instead of through telephone lines. Videoconferencing uses the Internet to transmit both audio and video signals and most closely resembles face-to-face (FtF) counseling.

Online counseling is likely to continue growing in popularity and application (e.g., Alleman, 2002; Norcross, Hedges, & Prochaska, 2002). This growth will be driven by participants' comfort with online counseling, psychologists' technical expertise, and technological developments, particularly high-speed Internet access. It is critical that counseling psychologists become knowledgeable about the potential benefits, risks, and challenges that will accompany this growth (Suler, 2000).

Benefits and Risks of Online Counseling

Online counseling offers many benefits. It allows therapists to provide direct service to individuals who (a) are geographically isolated or homebound due to psychological problems (e.g., agoraphobia) or physical disability (Barnett & Scheetz, 2003; Shaw & Shaw, 2006), (b) traditionally do not seek FtF counseling services (Mallen, Vogel, Rochlen, & Day, 2005), (c) are more comfortable with the anonymity that online counseling provides (Liebert, Archer, Muson, & York, 2006), and (d) come from underserved or underrepresented populations. Clients who are currently seeing a counselor in person might also benefit from increased frequency of contact with their counselor via online communications (Castelnuovo, Gaggioli, Mantovani, & Riva, 2003).

Text-based online counseling may also be appropriate for individuals who feel embarrassed or ashamed talking about their concerns or for individuals more proficient at writing than speaking (e.g., English is a second language, communication is difficult because of cerebral palsy). Additionally, online counseling allows for more flexibility with respect to scheduling, can be provided at relatively low cost and, as some have suggested, promotes the therapeutic value of writing (Manhal-Baugus, 2001). Most online counseling occurs through the exchange of text (e.g., chat rooms, private instant messaging, and email); however, this is likely to change in the near future as high-speed Internet and Internet teleconferencing become more widely available.

There are also potential drawbacks and challenges to online counseling. First, the research on the therapeutic benefits of online counseling is in its infancy and its effectiveness has not been clearly demonstrated (Manhal-Baugus, 2001). Second, and as discussed in this chapter, unresolved legal issues are associated with providing online counseling services (Recupero & Rainey, 2005). Third, when providing text-based online counseling, the therapist has no access to important nonverbal information. (This concern may become moot as Internet video communication gains traction.) Fourth, not all treatment modalities (e.g., eye movement desensitization and reprocessing) are amenable to online counseling. Finally, graduate counseling training programs may not be prepared to provide instruction in issues related to technologically mediated services. Young (2005) found that consumers are aware of the pros and cons of online counseling. Clients identified anonymity, convenience, and access to qualified counselors as reasons for seeking online counseling; their top concerns related to privacy, security, and concern about being discovered by a friend or family member.

Research on Online Counseling

Mallen, Vogel, and Rochlen (2005) reviewed the emerging research related to online counseling. Their conclusions were generally supportive of online counseling in that both clients and counselors report positive therapy outcomes from online counseling experiences. Glueckauf, Fritz, et al. (2002) examined families who participated in counseling via videoconferencing, speakerphone, or FtF sessions and found positive and equivalent outcomes across all three modes of intervention. Teenage clients and their parents in this study reported improvement in specific family problems and gains on a measure of social skills ($\eta^2 = .25$ to .83). Another multiple modality study compared videoconferencing, two-way audio, and FtF counseling (Day & Schneider, 2002). Counseling outcome was assessed with a symptom checklist, global assessment of functioning, and a measure of specific problems. All three conditions were found to yield positive and equivalent gains when compared with a control group ($d = .73$ to 1.16). These findings are encouraging in that they demonstrate positive outcomes of online counseling as well as equivalency across different communication modalities.

Results from studies examining clients' attitudes toward, and satisfaction with, online counseling are also encouraging. According to Mallen, Vogel, Rochlen, and Day (2005), clients generally report online counseling as a helpful and positive experience. In a study of prison inmates receiving videoconference counseling, the vast majority (> 80%) of inmates claimed their videoconferencing sessions were positive, were as helpful or more helpful than FtF sessions, and that they would use these services again (Mageletta, Fagan, & Peyrot, 2000). In contrast, Leibert et al. (2006) reported that online counseling clients were satisfied, but not as satisfied as clients in FtF counseling. Several studies suggest the need for additional research on the use of online counseling with diverse client populations. One study found that Asian American and Asian international college students held less positive expectations of online counseling compared with FtF services (Chang & Chang, 2004). However, Chang, Yeh, and Krumboltz (2001) found a positive response to an online support group for Asian American male college students.

In addition to research on therapeutic outcomes and client satisfaction, several studies focus on the counseling process within the context of online counseling. Few would argue that the relationship between counselor and client is one of the most critical aspects of the counseling experience (see Gelso & Samstag, this volume). Although the literature in this area is in its infancy, Cook and Doyle (2002) reported that online clients developed a working alliance that was stronger than or equivalent to the alliance of clients receiving FtF counseling ($d = .60$). By contrast, Liebert et al. (2006) found that online clients could develop therapeutic relationships with their counselors, but mean ratings on a working alliance measure were lower than those observed in FtF counseling. In a study examining other psychotherapy processes in online counseling, Day and Schneider (2002) reported that clients were more verbally active during videoconferencing ($d = .62$) and audio interactions ($d = .57$) compared with FtF counseling. Similarly, Cohen and Kerr (1998) reported that clients found session depth, smoothness, and positivity to be equivalent across therapeutic modalities.

Legal and Ethical Issues Associated with Online Counseling

Concomitant with the proliferation of online counseling has been the recognition of the many ethical and legal issues associated with this practice. Chief among the concerns is whether direct psychological services should be provided online (Ragusea & VandeCreek, 2003). We are not alone in believing that online counseling has become a viable counseling modality and can be ethically provided with appropriate training and diligence. Online counseling is supported by a rapidly growing literature base, the inclusion of recommendations for Internet communication in the American Psychological Association (APA) Ethics Code (APA, 2002), experts in the counseling field (Norcross et al., 2002), and the articulation of principles for practice by the International Society for Mental Health Online (ISMHO, 2000).

Mallen and his colleagues (Mallen, Vogel, & Rochlen, 2005) offered a context for this ethical debate, noting that many concerns expressed about online counseling mirror those voiced about telephone counseling. A recent survey found that 98% of practitioners reported using the telephone in some manner, with 79% using the telephone for crisis work and 69% providing individual counseling over the phone. In contrast, only 2% of practitioners reported using the Internet to provide services (VandenBos & Williams, 2000). We anticipate that online counseling, like the telephone and email, will become commonplace in psychological practice.

Professional associations, including the National Board for Certified Counselors (2005) and ISMHO (2000), have articulated statements about the practice of online counseling. The APA (2002) Ethics Code specifically addresses distance electronic communications in four standards: informed consent, confidentiality, advertising, and media presentations. The Ethics Code acknowledges the potential limits to privacy and confidentiality when communications occur electronically. Fisher and Fried (2003) urge psychologists to pay particular attention to competence standard 2.01 and, when practicing in emerging areas for which training and standards do not yet exist, to take reasonable care to assure their own competence and the well-being of their clients.

There are many ethical concerns related to the practice of online counseling. Oravec (2000) argued that some presenting therapeutic issues (e.g., sexual abuse, violent relationships, and complicated bereavement) are inappropriate for online counseling. Another key concern is the maintenance of client confidentiality when transmitting information across the Internet (Barnett & Scheetz, 2003; Mallen, Vogel, & Rochlen, 2005). Conducting sessions via email is also problematic in that the security of emails during transmission cannot be guaranteed (Kanz, 2001; Ragusea & VandeCreek, 2003; Shapiro & Schulman, 1996), and anyone with access to the client's email account could read and send emails posing as the client.

Synchronous chat and videoconferencing are also problematic with respect to security and maintenance of confidentiality. Chat rooms are less secure than email, and encryption of video content for videoconferencing is uncommon (Ragusea & VandeCreek, 2003). Finally, psychologists must address the issues of session use and storage (Mallen, Vogel, & Rochlen, 2005). Vast amounts of electronically transmitted data can be stored cheaply and easily. Psychologists must carefully consider how they protect the security of electronic client communications.

The potential for miscommunication is another significant ethical concern for the provision of online counseling. Major obstacles in text-based communication include the inability to detect clients' nonverbal cues, emotional expression, or verbal emphases (Fisher & Fried, 2003; Mallen, Vogel, & Rochlen, 2005; Manhal-Baugus, 2001). These deficits of text-based communications may increase the risk of misdiagnosis (Recupero & Rainey, 2005). Synchronous chat offers some advantages over email as counselors may experience timing of responses and can elicit immediate feelings from clients. Videoconferencing most closely approximates FtF counseling, increasing the opportunity to assess nonverbal cues and emotions. However, videoconferencing is currently limited by connection speed, equipment quality, lighting difficulties, and restricted field of vision (Barnett & Scheetz, 2003).

Complete and accurate identification of practitioners and clients is another ethical concern. Shaw and Shaw (2006) examined ethical practices of online counseling websites and found sites that did not include the full name of the practitioner (12%), the state where the counselor was located (21%), evidence of licensure (33%), encryption software (72%), or the requirement that clients provide age or date of birth (54%). It is critical that online practitioners provide their full name, degree, licensure, and the professional organizations to which they belong. Practitioners should also obtain and attempt to verify every client's name, address, phone numbers, and age (Fisher & Fried, 2003; Ragusea & VandeCreek, 2003). In an emergency or crisis, practitioners must supply local service providers with accurate information to obtain appropriate care or to notify proper authorities in duty-to-warn situations (Barnett & Scheetz, 2003; Manhal-Baugus, 2001; Shapiro & Schulman, 1996). Ascertaining client age is critical as it may be unethical or illegal to provide services to a minor without parental permission, depending on circumstances and laws of the state where the client or counselor resides. Further, psychologists conducting online counseling must hold a license in each state where they practice. Providing services to clients residing in other states may jeopardize insurance coverage and conflict with state licensure laws (Barnett & Scheetz, 2003; Mallen, Vogel, & Rochlen, 2005).

Summary and Recommendations

Electronic delivery of direct therapeutic services is on the rise and will likely continue to grow in popularity. Although online counseling has numerous benefits, an equal number of legal and ethical issues must be resolved before those benefits can be fully realized. It is unclear how state licensure laws will be interpreted in situations where psychologists are providing online services to clients who reside outside the therapist's jurisdiction. Practitioners interested in starting or expanding their practice to include online counseling are strongly encouraged to consult with experienced colleagues, develop technical expertise, and review the growing literature related to online counseling (e.g., Glueckauf, Pickett, Ketterson, Loomis, & Rozensky, 2002). Many valuable resources have been developed with guidelines for practice (ISMHO, 2000) and comprehensive reviews of ethical issues involved in electronic practice (e.g., Shaw & Shaw, 2006).

Adoption of the following practices should reduce therapists' risk when providing online counseling: conduct a FtF meeting with clients (including an extensive intake assessment) before beginning online counseling; provide a comprehensive informed consent procedure (Recupero & Rainey, 2005); have an attorney review proposed procedures (Ragusea & VandeCreek, 2003); develop clear procedures for emergency situations (Koocher & Mooray, 2000) and technical failures (Fisher & Fried, 2003); and install an Internet firewall, virus protection software, intrusion detection software, and encryption software (Barnett & Scheetz, 2003). Technological advances and the growing acceptance of online counseling will open tremendous opportunities, but practitioners must be proactive and vigilant in following ethical standards of practice in this new medium.

Although preliminary research findings on the effectiveness of online counseling are promising, additional studies are needed to evaluate which clients and which online modalities are conducive to the development of a working alliance, whether online modalities are associated with positive therapeutic processes, and whether online counseling modalities are as or more effective than traditional FtF counseling. To establish the relative effectiveness of online counseling, researchers are encouraged not only to compare online counseling to FtF counseling, but also to evaluate the effectiveness of multiple online modalities. Finally, researchers are encouraged to employ designs that will permit the assessment of long-term client outcomes.

TRAINING AND SUPERVISION

Technological advances have also influenced the delivery of counseling training and supervision, yet compared with research on online therapy, considerably less attention has focused on the effectiveness, outcomes, and equivalency of online training and supervision. Technology has the potential to contribute positively to the training and supervision of professional psychologists. At the same time, individuals wishing to provide online training and supervision must attend to issues of confidentiality, security, informed consent, development of a working alliance, and effectiveness (Berger, 2004; Kanz, 2001; Oravec, 2000).

Examples of Online Training and Supervision Programs

Email, Web-based literature searches, and computer-based tutorial programs are now common applications in counseling psychology training programs (Berger, 2004). Advances in computer processing speed and Internet bandwidth have allowed educators to create more interactive and flexible training platforms. Jerry and Collins (2005) described an interactive website in which counseling students taking an online skills course can watch video demonstrations of counseling. Students indicate which skills are being used in the video by clicking in a counseling skills grid on the web site. These responses are available for later evaluation by the professor. The second author of this chapter uses chat software in a counseling methods class to afford additional skills practice time outside class. The text format also allows students to print a role-play transcript, make process comments, and submit these comments to the instructor for evaluation.

Other innovative educators have developed computer software programs for counselor training. *Counselor Assisted Supervision* (CAS) is a program that trainees can use to watch and critique tapes of their counseling sessions (Lehr, 2005). The program allows students to stop the tape after each counselor response and identify the intentions of their intervention as well as add process comments. Intentions can then be summarized and graphically displayed for use by the student and supervisor in supervision. Caspar, Berger, and Hautle (2004) described a case conceptualization program that presents a clinical case. Students enter a written case conceptualization and the program provides individualized feedback. The program uses latent semantic analysis to compare phrases from entered text with responses generated by multiple experts who reviewed the same case. Casper et al. described the program as being flexible because it can respond to trainee input and provide both a summary and comparison of the trainee's case conceptualization with that of experts.

Counselor training is being provided via the Internet in the form of individual courses and complete online programs (Collins & Jerry, 2005; Krieger & Stockton, 2004; Rudestam, 2004). Online course work may be offered in blended or entirely online formats. Blended classes provide some FtF instruction and supplement this with coursework conducted on the Internet, typically using a course management system (e.g., Blackboard). Online courses are presented entirely on the Internet and allow students and instructor to interact through asynchronous email and message boards as well as synchronous chat. Romano and Cikanek (2003) reported that students in an online course rated asynchronous discussion positively, whereas technical difficulties contributed to negative ratings of synchronous discussion. Jerry and Collins (2005) stressed the importance of providing an interactive and engaging experience with students because the FtF component of a classroom meeting is absent. These authors suggested regularly checking in with students, holding informal online chats, and quickly responding to email as mechanisms to increase the sense of connection for students.

In addition to individual courses, entire counseling program curricula are now being offered online. Collins and Jerry (2005) describe the development of the Campus Alberta Applied Psychology: Counseling Initiative (CAAP)—an online program that will award a master's degree in counseling psychology. Graduate training in counseling can also be found on the Internet through programs such as Capella University (PsyD in counseling psychology), Walden University (PhD in psychology, specialization in counseling psychology), and University of Phoenix (MS in counseling/mental health counseling).

Benefits and Risks of Online Training and Supervision

Email, synchronous chat, computer-assisted live supervision, and videoconferencing have all been identified as mechanisms to augment or replace FtF clinical supervision. Potential benefits to computer-based supervision include the ability to provide or receive supervision from a great distance (beneficial in supervising practitioners in rural areas), and the potential to receive supervision from experts in the field (Coursol, 2004; Gammon, Sorlie, Bergvik, & Hoifodt, 1998). Serious concerns remain, however, limiting the widespread application of technology to supervision. Many of the technologies proposed for use in clinical supervision lack sufficient security to assure anonymity and confidentiality of either trainee or clients. As with online counseling, online supervision may not result in the same supervisory dynamics as in FtF supervision (e.g., loss of nonverbal cues and opportunity to observe manifestations of transference and countertransference; Kanz, 2001). Finally, and perhaps most importantly, online supervision provided at a distance may make it difficult or impossible for supervisors to react appropriately in client crisis situations (Kanz, 2001; Oravec, 2000).

Research on Online Training and Supervision

The literature base on online supervision is sparse and tends to focus on supervisee reactions to text-based or videoconferencing supervision. Initial evidence and anecdotal reports suggests supervisees have a relatively positive reaction to distance supervision (Berger, 2004; Klitzke & Lombardo, 1991; Miller et al., 2002; Neukrug, 1991). However, distance supervision does not currently appear poised to replace FtF supervision. Coker, Jones, Staples, and Harbach (2002) reported that trainees found chat and chat-with-video as acceptable but less desirable than FtF supervision. Similarly, in examining supervisees' reactions to videoconferencing supervision, Gammon et al. (1998) reported that online supervision was viewed as an acceptable adjunct to, but not a replacement for, FtF supervision.

Summary and Recommendations

The computer and Internet hold great potential for the training and supervision of counseling psychologists. Technology is already influencing training modalities, from computer-based content tutorials to online counselor training programs. The profession will continue to grow in this direction as trainees and educators become more comfortable with distance communication, and as technology improves educators' ability to provide meaningful and engaging learning experiences. Online supervision appears to be a viable adjunct to traditional FtF supervision (Gammon et al., 1998; Kanz, 2001), although the field must continue to grapple with the ethical and technical challenges posed by conducting distance supervision.

The long-range impact of comprehensive online training programs remains to be seen. Distance education will likely make graduate training a possibility for more students. However, these programs will further strain an already burdened internship supply-and-demand situation. More distal outcomes will be assessed as graduates from online programs complete training and pursue licensure and employment.

Additional research on the effectiveness, outcomes, and equivalency of computer-assisted instruction and supervision is needed. Are students trained in counseling skills through the Internet prepared to provide services to clients in a traditional FtF setting? Is a different training and supervision paradigm necessary to properly equip online trainees with the skills to provide therapy? As with online counseling, researchers must examine which trainees, counseling courses, and therapy modalities are amenable and appropriate in an online format. It remains to be seen which model(s) of online training will emerge as effective and to what extent distance training and supervision will augment or replace traditional approaches.

Finally, although technology has found its way into the counseling psychology training environment, we found few resources to suggest that current counseling graduate students are receiving any formal training in the delivery of online counseling services. A complete set of recommendations for online counseling training is beyond the scope of this chapter, but the development of such guidelines seems prudent. They should include training in the use of different technologies as well as the modeling of online counseling behaviors by course instructors or supervisors, a discussion of special ethical and legal issues relevant to this practice, and a thorough review of the empirical literature examining the effectiveness of online counseling practices.

USING THE INTERNET TO CONDUCT RESEARCH

The widespread availability of personal computers in the 1980s revolutionized the role of technology in conducting psychological research (Grice, 1981; Noldus, Van de Loo, & Timmers, 1989). Computer use in psychological research grew exponentially with the advent of the Internet in the 1990s—unfortunately, so did concerns about using the Internet as a research tool. Literature on the use of technology in psychological research tends to focus on either (a) how technology is used as a methodological tool or (b) how technological advances influence the human condition. In this section, we restrict our discussion to the literature on the use of Internet technology as a methodological tool.

Benefits and Risks of the Internet as a Research Tool

Using the Internet as a research tool provides many benefits. One of the earliest recognized benefits was the potential to use the Internet to distribute and collect survey data (Hewson, Laurent, & Vogel, 1996). Granello and Wheaton (2004) noted that surveys delivered via the Internet (whether via the Web or email) are easily and inexpensively developed and distributed, can be widely distributed, and offer respondents a level of anonymity that may not be available with more traditional survey methods. If Web-delivered, survey responses are automatically recorded in a database, eliminating the potential for data entry and coding errors. Further, because of the way Internet communities have evolved, researchers interested in specific populations (e.g., lesbian, gay, bisexual, transgender [LGBT] persons, unemployed adults, persons seeking information about depression) can more effectively target their prospective participants by advertising the availability of their surveys on relevant web sites, through content or population-specific chat rooms, or through listservs (e.g., Liebert et al., 2006).

One way to judge the relative popularity of Internet-based survey research is to observe the proliferation of companies that offer online survey services. Companies such as SurveyMonkey and PollCat help researchers quickly develop and maintain online surveys and will export results on demand in common formats such as SPSS and Excel. Although the use of the Internet in psychological research may be on the rise, some authors note that publication biases may still exist among journal editors that restrict the overall number of published Internet studies (Mathy, Kerr, & Haydin, 2003).

The Internet also permits the unobtrusive study of human behavior. Because interpersonal interactions occurring online (e.g., via email or chat room conversations) are often archived on servers, there are opportunities to study social communication behavior by accessing archived (and transcribed) communication records (e.g., Barak & Bloch, 2006). A growing number of studies are exploring social interactions within Internet communities. In a study of racial/ethnic discourse among adolescents using chat rooms, Tynes, Reynolds, and Greenfield (2004) noted that participants were almost three times more likely to be exposed to a negative remark about race or ethnicity when participating in an unmoderated compared with a moderated chat room. Subrahmanyam, Smahel, and Greenfield (2006) noted that adolescents (a) compensate for the lack of visual cues available in chat rooms by providing identity information (most often gender), and (b) that sexual discourse varied as a function of participant gender and the type of chat room environment (moderated versus unmoderated).

Other researchers have described how the Internet can be used unobtrusively to observe the processes individuals engage in to acquire information. Gore and his colleagues (Gore, Bobek, Robbins, & Shayne, 2006; Gore & Leuwerke, 2000) used the Internet to study individuals' career exploratory and information-gathering behavior.

Not surprisingly, many of these potential benefits are also cause for concern. Mathy et al. (2003) and Granello and Wheaton (2004) provided excellent reviews of methodological issues that should be considered by those considering Internet-based research. Mathy and her colleagues noted that, while the Internet is becoming increasingly available to individuals from economically disadvantaged segments of the population, data collected online should not yet be considered truly representative of the U.S. population. Moreover, researchers should exercise caution in assuming that individuals using any particular type of Internet activity (e.g., email, chat room, Web browsing) are representative of the population at large or even the population of Internet users. Tuten and Bosnjak (2001) suggest that personality variables may be related to individuals' preference for different Internet activities (e.g., openness to experience correlated with viewing entertainment and product information web sites).

Concerns have also been raised about the psychometric properties of instruments delivered via the Internet versus more traditional survey methods. No clear answer exists about the equivalency of assessment using these two methods (Buchanan, 2003). Differences may be observed in reliability or validity estimates, factor structures, or mean scores. Joinson (1999) found that participants randomly assigned to complete an Internet survey had significantly lower levels of socially desirable responses compared with a similar group of students assigned to complete the same survey in paper-and-pencil format. As such, researchers are urged to continue to exercise caution in making assumptions of measurement equivalence, and to conduct research to establish the relationship between Internet and traditionally administered assessment instruments.

Researchers have also expressed concern about response rates from online surveys. Although some authors argue that Internet research response rates are considerably lower than mail surveys (Bachmann, Elfrink, & Vazzana, 1996; Granello & Wheaton, 2004), studies that have compared the response rates of participants randomly assigned to Internet or traditional mail response conditions (e.g., Lonsdale, Hodge, & Rose, 2006; Truell, Bartlett, & Alexander, 2002) reveal few differences in overall response rates. In general, researchers conducting Internet survey studies can expect response rates close to those obtained when soliciting participation through surface mail.

Ethical and Legal Issues in Using the Internet as a Research Tool

Several ethical and legal issues are related to the use of Internet and other technologies for research purposes. These issues involve the ethical principles of autonomy and nonmaleficence (Beauchamp & Childress, 2001). When conducting research, the ethical principle of autonomy is captured in the concept of informed consent and the right to withdraw consent at any time and for any reason. The informed consent process in Internet-based research requires special attention. Mathy et al. (2003) and others (Keller & Lee, 2003; Kraut et al., 2004; Michalak & Szabo, 1998) provide excellent reviews of this issue and possible strategies for maximizing participant autonomy in the research process. Two frequently used procedures have interested participants request a copy of the survey via email (with the email thus serving as consent) or use an introductory Web page to inform prospective participants of the risks and benefits and including a "consent" button that links participants to the survey instrument.

Informed consent becomes more complicated when investigators use in vivo research protocols, such as observing the communication patterns of individuals in an Internet chat room or studying the attitudes or behaviors of minors where the identity of a consenting parent may be difficult to verify. Researchers are also bound to inform their participants of the right to withdraw from participation, and investigators conducting Internet research must provide participants with a valid way of notifying them of a decision to withdraw from a study. Further, investigators need to establish a procedure for identifying data associated with participants who withdraw—an issue related to the concept of anonymity and confidentiality.

The protection of participant data is related to the ethical principle of nonmaleficence. As Mathy et al. (2003) noted, the Internet presents unprecedented risks for the breach of confidential client/participant information. Generally speaking, computer technologies such as email and the World Wide Web are not inherently secure and researchers must be mindful of data security. Investigators conducting clinical research may also be subject to the regulations included in the Health Insurance Portability and Accountability Act (HIPAA, 1996).

Summary and Recommendations

Most researchers can attest to the positive impact that computers and the Internet have had on conducting literature reviews, data collection and entry, and statistical analysis. The Internet is particularly useful in research as it supports (a) inexpensive development and dissemination of instruments,

(b) participant recruitment from specific populations, (c) increased participant anonymity, and (d) unobtrusive observation of participants. However, the expansion of technology as a research tool also raises methodological, ethical, and legal concerns.

Researchers who collect data through the Internet must be mindful of the representativeness of their sample, response rates, and the psychometric equivalence of online instruments compared with paper-and-pencil versions. All these issues must be considered when generalizing findings of Internet-based research to the larger population. Data security is a particularly critical ethical issue when collecting data online. Researchers are strongly encouraged to use physical safeguards such as backing up data, controlling access to the data through passwords, encrypting transmissions, and appropriately and thoroughly destroying data when necessary. In addition, psychologists conducting clinical research or gathering sensitive data should consult information technology and legal experts to maximize protection of participant data and to assure they are adhering to appropriate legal requirements.

Researchers must continue to examine and compare Internet and traditional research practices. Of particular interest are the equivalency of data collection methods and the psychometric properties of research instruments. Further, due to inequalities of Internet access and different patterns of Internet use, it may not be possible to generalize research findings to the population at large or even to other people who are online—an issue to which both researchers and research consumers should attend. As with many new research methodologies, widespread use of the process has preceded careful investigation of its validity and reliability. As evidence on the relative strengths and weaknesses of online research methods accumulates, researchers will be in a better position to apply these methods in an informed and responsible manner.

PROBLEM BEHAVIORS ASSOCIATED WITH INTERNET USE

Mitchell, Becker-Blease, and Finkelhor (2005) noted that "new technology tends to provoke new problems and new anxieties" (p. 498). The proliferation of the Internet and its infusion into mainstream life (home, work, leisure activities) has resulted in an increased incidence of Internet-related problem behaviors. Mitchell and her colleagues described results from a study of over 1,500 practitioners who worked with clients with Internet-related problems. The most frequently encountered problems were general overuse (e.g., excessive Web browsing), pornography and sexual exploitation, Internet infidelity, and gaming/gambling/role playing.

General Overuse of the Internet

Over 60% of clients identified as having an Internet-related problem express concerns related to general overuse (Mitchell et al., 2005). The exact definition of Internet overuse is still being debated. Some authors have defined it as Internet addiction using traditional dependence or tolerance criteria (Kandell, 1998), whereas others have suggested naming it pathological Internet use (PIU) and defining it as an impulse control disorder (Shapira, Goldsmith, Keck, Khosla, & McElroy, 2000; Young, 1996). According to Mitchell et al. (2005), clinicians' perspective on what constitutes overuse varies widely from 7 to 14 hours per week (18%) to over 28 hours per week (20%). Recent data released by Nielsen/Net Ratings suggests that U.S. home Internet usage averages nearly 30 hours per week per person (Nielsen/Net Ratings, 2006). Thus, a definition of overuse based on time alone may be inadequate. There appears to be agreement that any clinical definition of overuse must include an individual's desire to reduce the time spent using the Internet and must take into account the negative impact that use has on other life functions. Best estimates of the prevalence of general overuse in an Internet-using population (5%; Greenfield, 1999) suggest that most clinicians have encountered or soon will encounter this condition.

Pornography and Sexual Exploitation via the Internet

Perhaps more than any other aspect of the Internet, its use or misuse for the purposes of sexual gratification and exploitation has been at the forefront of popular media attention. This is partly the result of early media reports listing "sex" as the most frequently entered search engine term and stories describing the use of chat rooms as breeding grounds for pedophilic predators (Cooper, Delmonico, & Burg, 2000; Cooper, Griffen-Shelley, Delmonico, & Mathy, 2001). Although most counseling psychologists probably will not encounter the victims or perpetrators of Internet pedophilia, they are likely to have clients who engage in or are the victims of Internet infidelity, or who are concerned over their use of the Internet for sexual gratification.

Chief among the concerns of clients who report excessive use of the Internet is the excessive viewing of pornography. Exact figures on the prevalence of Internet pornography viewing are difficult, if not impossible, to gather given the inherently private and secret nature of this activity. Most authors agree that the prevalence of pornography use has dramatically increased relative to pre-Internet rates. Cooper and colleagues (Cooper et al., 2000, 2001) and others (e.g., Benotsch, Kalichman, & Cage, 2002) estimate that between 20% and 34% of adult Internet users have engaged in some form of online sexual activity such as searching for sexual partners, purchasing sexual material, or downloading erotica. Recent findings suggest the prevalence may be higher among some subgroups. Dew, Brubaker, and Hays (2006) reported that almost half of all male chat room respondents in their study had accessed sexually explicit web sites or exchanged sexually explicit photos with someone within 24 hours of responding to the survey. Data presented by Cooper et al. (2001) suggests that not all Internet users perceive their online sexual activity to be beyond their control.

Sexual exploitation via the Internet is another phenomenon that clinicians are likely to encounter. Sexual exploitation via the Internet was reported by 16% of clients in the Mitchell et al. (2005) study. These cases may involve unwanted or illegal seduction or inappropriate sexual involvement with children. Although media accounts suggest that Internet exploitation routinely involves strangers meeting on the Internet, Mitchell et al. noted that many cases involve exploitation by family members, friends, or coworkers. In such cases, the Internet is involved only superficially as might occur when one employee sends sexually suggestive and unwanted emails to another employee.

Internet Infidelity

Among men and women in committed sexual relationships, some forms of Internet activity may be perceived as infidelity. Mitchell et al. (2005) noted that 20% of clients in their study had concerns related to Internet infidelity. Although many therapists (and clients) struggle with the definition of Internet infidelity, most recent definitions include components of secrecy and sexual arousal. According to Cooper (2002), three aspects of Internet infidelity distinguish it from traditional infidelity: accessibility, affordability, and anonymity. With the widespread availability of Internet connections, Internet affairs can be carried out at any time and from virtually any location. In fact, a growing number of authors are discussing the phenomenon of workplace Internet sexual activity (Beard, 2002; Cooper, Safir, & Rosenmann, 2006; Davis, Flett, & Besser, 2002; Griffiths, 2002, 2003). Internet-based sexual affairs can be conducted entirely through cyberspace and remain anonymous, or they can be consummated through face-to-face meetings. The allure of anonymity was also noted by Mileham (2007) in her recent ethnographic study of Internet infidelity. Mileham noted three common characteristics among individuals who engage in extramarital chat room sexual discourse. Beyond the benefits of anonymity, many chat room participants convinced themselves that because their chat room behaviors did not involve physical contact, they did not constitute infidelity. Further, Mileham noted that many of her participants were using Internet liaisons to avoid the dynamics of their marital relationship.

Gaming, Gambling, and Role Playing on the Internet

Other forms of Internet excess are also drawing the attention of clinicians. For example, 15% of clients who report problematic Internet experiences do so as a result of gaming, gambling, or interactive role playing (Mitchell et al., 2005). Mitchell and colleagues categorized these behaviors into online gambling, solitary gaming, interpersonal or dynamic gaming, and fantasy role playing. Male clients outnumbered females in the frequency of these behaviors almost three to one. Some authors have suggested that college students may be particularly vulnerable to the temptations of Internet gambling and other forms of Internet addiction. The data suggest that less than 5% of college students engage in Internet gambling, with most doing so only a few times every month (LaBrie, Shaffer, LaPlante, & Wechsler, 2003; Rotunda, Kass, Sutton, & Leon, 2003). In contrast, almost 40% of college students in one study reported visiting interactive game sites (Rotunda et al., 2003).

Summary and Recommendations

The benefits associated with the growth of the Internet are not without their costs. Infidelity and gambling are age-old problems that have found new venues through the Internet. In contrast, general overuse and online role playing are phenomena created by the Internet. As with any evolving technology, it is difficult to predict what novel uses and abuses will subsequently emerge. We feel safe, however, in predicting an increased incidence of Internet-related problem behaviors as access and bandwidth increase. To prepare for this future, clinicians and researchers must grapple with basic issues such as how to conceptualize and define Internet-related problem behaviors, and how to effectively treat these conditions. It will also be necessary to incorporate these issues into the training and supervision of our graduate students.

We see an opportunity for specialty online practices to develop in the treatment of Internet-related problem behaviors. Given the secrecy and anonymity involved in this area, clients may prefer to work with a psychologist online. Further, specific Internet-based interventions could be developed to address problematic behaviors. A behavior modification program could be developed that tracks and reports an individual's Web viewing, providing an account of time on the Internet and the web sites viewed. Alternatively, an intervention could provide training in communication skills that clients could apply to in-person relationships to either increase interpersonal contact or improve relationships. Practitioners and researchers are encouraged to collaborate to develop and empirically examine new treatments.

Research is needed to more fully understand the development and expression of Internet-related problem behaviors. What are the long-term outcomes of relationships that have their origin on the Internet? What consequences are experienced by victims of online sexual exploitation or Internet infidelity? Further research is also needed to fully understand the extent to which these problems exist in the general population. It is possible that problems with online gambling or Internet infidelity are much more common than currently suspected but that clients are not seeking treatment. Finally, and ironically, research is needed to determine if Internet-based interventions are an effective way to treat individuals with problematic Internet use.

CONCLUSION

We have witnessed rapid technological advances during the past 25 years and will continue to experience new advances at an ever-increasing rate. These advances have shaped the way we work, play, and learn (Gore, Leuwerke, & Krumboltz, 2002) and thus the nature of our work as counseling psychologists. Our review of the literature and experience indicates that online counseling, Internet-based research, online training, and problematic behaviors are *current realities* for our clients and students. As we achieve equity in access and individuals become comfortable with new applications (e.g., videoconferencing), we expect *increased utilization* of online counseling, training, and Internet-based research, as well as more and new Internet-related problems. Counseling psychologists are encouraged to *embrace* these emerging technologies in their research, teaching, and practice and to ensure that technology is applied in helpful and responsible ways.

REFERENCES

Alleman, J. R. (2002). Online counseling: The internet and mental health treatment. *Psychotherapy: Theory, Research, Practice, Training, 39*, 199–209.

American Psychological Association. (2002). *Ethical principles of psychologists and code of conduct*. Retrieved January 24, 2007, from www.apa.org/ethics/code2002.html.

Bachmann, D., Elfrink, J., & Vazzana, G. (1996). Tracking the progress of e-mail vs. snail-mail. *Marketing Research, 8*(2), 31–35.

Barak, A., & Bloch, N. (2006). Factors related to perceived helpfulness in supporting highly distressed individuals through an online support chat. *CyberPsychology and Behavior, 9*, 60–68.

Barnett, J. E., & Scheetz, K. (2003). Technological advances and telehealth: Ethics, law, and the practice of psychotherapy. *Psychotherapy: Theory, Research, Practice, Training, 40*, 86–93.

Beard, K. W. (2002). Internet addiction: Current status and implications for employees. *Journal of Employment Counseling, 39*, 2–11.

Beauchamp, T. L., & Childress, J. F. (2001). *Principles of biomedical ethics* (5th ed.). Oxford: Oxford University Press.

Ben-Porath, Y. S., & Butcher, J. N. (1986). Computers in personality assessment: A brief past, an ebullient present, and an expanding future. *Computers in Human Behavior, 2*, 167–182.

Benotsch, E. G., Kalichman, S., & Cage, M. (2002). Men who have met sex partners via the internet: Prevalence, predictors, and implications for HIV prevention. *Archives of Sexual Behavior, 31*, 177–183.

Berger, T. (2004). Computer-based technological applications in psychotherapy training. *Journal of Clinical Psychology, 60*, 301–315.

Buchanan, T. (2003). Internet-based questionnaire assessment: Appropriate use in clinical contexts. *Cognitive Behavior Therapy, 32*, 100–109.

Caspar, F., Berger, T., & Hautle, I. (2004). The right view of your patient: A computer-assisted, individualized module for psychotherapy training. *Psychotherapy: Theory, Research, Practice, Training, 41*, 125–135.

Castelnuovo, G., Gaggioli, A., Mantovani, F., & Riva, G. (2003). New and old tools in psychotherapy: The use of technology for the integration of traditional clinical treatments. *Psychotherapy: Theory, Research, Practice, Training, 40*, 33–44.

Chang, T., & Chang, R. (2004). Counseling and the internet: Asian American and Asian international college students' attitudes toward seeking online professional psychological help. *Journal of College Counseling, 7*, 140–149.

Chang, T., Yeh, C. J., & Krumboltz, J. D. (2001). Process and outcome evaluation of an online-support group for Asian American male college students. *Journal of Counseling Psychology, 48*, 319–330.

Childress, C. A., & Asamen, J. K. (1998). The emerging relationship of psychology and the internet: Proposed guidelines for conducting internet intervention research. *Ethics and Behavior, 8*, 19–35.

Chou, C., Condron, L., & Belland, J. C. (2005). A review of the research on internet addiction. *Educational Psychology Review, 17*, 363–388.

Cohen, G. E., & Kerr, B. A. (1998). Computer-mediated counseling: An empirical study of a new mental health treatment. *Computers in Human Services, 15*, 13–26.

Coker, J. K., Jones, W. P., Staples, P. A., & Harbach, R. L. (2002). Cybersupervision in the first practicum: Implications for research and practice. *Guidance and Counseling, 18*, 33–38.

Collins, S., & Jerry, P. (2005). The Campus Alberta Applied Psychology Counseling Initiative: Web-based delivery of a graduate professional training program. *Journal of Technology in Human Services, 23*, 99–119.

Cook, J. E., & Doyle, C. (2002). Working alliance in online therapy as compared to face-to-face therapy: Preliminary results. *CyberPsychology and Behavior, 5*, 95–105.

Cooper, A. (2002). *Sex and the internet: A guidebook for clinicians*. New York: Brunner-Routledge.

Cooper, A., Delmonico, D. L., & Burg, R. (2000). Cybersex users, abusers, and compulsives: New findings and implications. *Sexual Addiction and Compulsivity, 7*, 5–29.

Cooper, A., Griffin-Shelley, E., Delmonico, D. L., & Mathy, R. M. (2001). Online sexual problems: Assessment and predictive variables. *Sexual Addiction and Compulsivity, 8*, 267–285.

Cooper, A., Safir, M. P., & Rosenmann, A. (2006). Workplace worries: A preliminary look at online sexually activities at the office—Emerging issues for clinicians and employers. *CyberPsychology and Behavior, 9*, 22–29.

Coursol, D. (2004). Cybersupervision: Conducting supervision on the information superhighway. In G. R. Walz & C. Kirkman (Eds.), *Cyberbytes: Highlighting compelling issues of technology in counseling* (pp. 7–16). Greensboro, NC: CAPS Press.

Davis, R. A., Flett, G. L., & Besser, A. (2002). Validation of a new scale for measuring problematic internet use: Implications for pre-employment screening. *CyberPsychlogy and Behavior, 5*, 331–345.

Day, S. X., & Schneider, P. L. (2002). Psychotherapy using distance technology: A comparison of face-to-face, video, and audio treatment. *Journal of Counseling Psychology, 49*, 499–503.

Dew, B., Brubaker, M., & Hays, D. (2006). From the alter to the internet: Married men and their online sexual behavior. *Sexual Addictions and Compulsivity, 13*, 195–207.

Fisher, C. B., & Fried, A. L. (2003). Internet-mediated psychological services and the American Psychological Association Ethics Code. *Psychotherapy: Theory, Research, Practice, Training, 40*, 103–111.

Gammon, D., Sorlie, T., Bergvik, S., & Hoifodt, T. S. (1998). Psychotherapy supervision conducted via videoconferencing: A qualitative study of users' experiences. *Nordic Journal of Psychiatry, 52*, 411–421.

Glueckauf, R. L., Fritz, S. P., Ecklund-Johnson, E. P., Liss, H. J., Dages, P., & Carney, P. (2002). Videoconferencing-based family counseling for rural teenagers with epilepsy: Phase 1 findings. *Rehabilitation Psychology, 47*, 49–72.

Glueckauf, R. L., Pickett, T. C., Ketterson, T. U., Loomis, J. S., & Rozensky, R. H. (2002). Preparation for the delivery of telehealth services: A self-study framework for expansion of practice. *Professional Psychology: Research and Practice, 34*, 159–163.

Gore, P. A., Jr., Bobek, B. L., Robbins, S. B., & Shayne, L. (2006). Computer-based career exploration: Usage patterns and a typology of users. *Journal of Career Assessment, 14*, 421–436.

Gore, P. A., Jr., & Leuwerke, W. C. (2000). Information technology for career assessment on the internet. *Journal of Career Assessment, 8*, 3–19.

Gore, P. A., Jr., Leuwerke, W. C., & Krumboltz, J. D. (2002). Technologically enriched and boundaryless lives: Time for a paradigm upgrade. *Counseling Psychologist, 30*, 847–857.

Granello, D. H., & Wheaton, J. E. (2004). Online data collection: Strategies for research. *Journal of Counseling and Development, 82*, 387–393.

Greenfield, D. N. (1999). Psychological characteristics of compulsive internet use: A preliminary analysis. *CyberPsychology and Behavior, 2*, 403–412.

Grice, G. R. (1981). Accurate reaction time research with the TRS-80 microcomputer. *Behavior Research Methods and Instrumentation, 13*, 674–676.

Griffiths, M. (2002). Occupational health issues concerning internet use in the workplace. *Work and Stress, 16*, 283–286.

Griffiths, M. (2003). Internet gambling: Issues, concerns, and recommendations. *CyberPsychology and Behavior, 6*, 557–568.

Health Insurance Portability and Accountability Act (1996). Retrieved January 24, 2007, from www.cms.hhs.gov/HIPAAGenInfo/.

Hertlein, K. M., & Piercy, F. P. (2006). Internet infidelity: A critical review of the literature. *Family Journal: Counseling and Therapy for Couples and Families, 14*, 366–371.

Hewson, C. M., Laurent, D., & Vogel, C. M. (1996). Proper methodologies for psychological and sociological studies conducted via the internet. *Behavior Research Methods, Instruments and Computers, 28*, 186–191.

International Society for Mental Health Online. (2000). *Suggested principles for the online provision of mental health services*. Retrieved January 24, 2007, from www.usd.edu/psyc/act/ismho.htm.

Jerry, P., & Collins, S. (2005). Web-based education in the human services: Use of web-based video clips in counseling skills training. *Journal of Technology in Human Services, 23*, 183–199.

Joinson, A. (1999). Social desirability, anonymity, and internet-based questionnaires. *Behavior Research Methods, Instruments, and Computers, 31*, 433–438.

Kandell, J. J. (1998). Internet addiction on campus: The vulnerability of college students. *CyberPsychology and Behavior, 1*, 11–17.

Kanz, J. E. (2001). Clinical-supervision.com: Issues in the provision of online supervision. *Professional Psychology: Research and Practice, 32*, 415–420.

Keller, H. E., & Lee, S. (2003). Ethical issues surrounding human participants research using the internet. *Ethics and Behavior, 13*, 211–219.

Klitzke, M. J., & Lombardo, T. W. (1991). A 'bug-in-the-eye' can be better than a 'bug-in-the-ear': A teleprompter technique for on-line therapy skills training. *Behavior Modification, 15*, 113–117.

Koocher, G. P., & Morray, E. (2000). Regulation of telepsychology: A survey of state attorneys general. *Professional Psychology: Research and Practice, 31*, 503–508.

Kraut, R., Olson, J., Banaji, M., Bruckman, A., Cohen, J., & Couper, M. (2004). Psychological research online: Report of Board of Scientific Affairs' advisory group on the conduct of research on the internet. *American Psychologist, 59*, 105–117.

Krieger, K. M., & Stockton, R. (2004). Technology and group leadership training: Teaching group counseling in an online environment. *Journal for Specialists in Group Work, 29*, 343–359.

LaBrie, R. A., Shaffer, H. J., LaPlante, D. A., & Wechsler, H. (2003). Correlates of college student gambling in the United States. *Journal of American College Health, 52*, 52–62.

Lehr, R. (2005). Using computer-assisted supervision in counselor education programs. *Canadian Journal of Counseling, 39*, 29–39.

Leibert, T., Archer, J., Jr., Munson, J., & York, G. (2006). An exploratory study of client perceptions of internet counseling and the therapeutic alliance. *Journal of Mental Health Counseling, 28*, 69–83.

Lonsdale, C., Hodge, K., & Rose, E. A. (2006). Pixels vs. paper: Comparing online and traditional survey methods in sport psychology. *Journal of Sport and Exercise Psychology, 28*, 100–108.

Magaletta, P. R., Fagan, T. J., & Peyrot, M. F. (2000). Telehealth in the Federal Bureau of Prisons: Inmates' perceptions. *Professional Psychology: Research and Practice, 31*, 497–502.

Mallen, M. J., & Vogel, D. L. (2005). Online counseling: A need for discovery. *Counseling Psychologist, 33*, 910–921.

Mallen, M. J., Vogel, D. L., & Rochlen, A. B. (2005). The practical aspects of online counseling: Ethics, training, technology, and competency. *Counseling Psychologist, 33*, 776–818.

Mallen, M. J., Vogel, D. L., Rochlen, A. B., & Day, S. X. (2005). Online counseling: Reviewing the literature from a counseling psychology framework. *Counseling Psychologist, 33*, 819–871.

Manhal-Baugus, M. (2001). E-therapy: Practical, ethical, and legal issues. *CyberPsychology and Behavior, 4*, 551–563.

Mathy, R. M., Kerr, D. L., & Haydin, B. M. (2003). Methodological rigor and ethical considerations in internet-mediated research. *Psychotherapy: Theory, Research, Practice, Training, 40*, 77–85.

McCullough, L., Farrell, A. D., & Longabaugh, R. (1986). The development of a microcomputer-based mental health information system: A potential tool for bridging the scientist-practitioner gap. *American Psychologist, 41*, 207–214.

Michalak, E. E., & Szabo, A. (1998). Guidelines for internet research: An update. *European Psychologist, 3*, 70–75.

Mileham, B. L. A. (2007). Online infidelity in internet chat rooms: An ethnographic exploration. *Computers in Human Behavior, 23*, 11–31.

Miller, K. L., Miller, S. M., & Evans, W. J. (2002). Computer-assisted live supervision in college counseling centers. *Journal of College Counseling, 5*, 187–192.

Mitchell, K. J., Becker-Blease, K. A., & Finkelhor, D. (2005). Inventory of problematic internet experiences encountered in clinical practice. *Professional Psychology: Research and Practice, 36*, 498–509.

National Board for Certified Counselors. (2005). *The practice of internet counseling.* Retrieved January 24, 2007, from www.nbcc.org/webethics2.

Neilsen/Net Ratings. (2006). *Internet audience metrics.* Retrieved December 15, 2006, from www.nielsen-netratings.com/.

Neukrug, E. S. (1991). Computer-assisted live supervision in counselor skills training. *Counselor Education and Supervision, 31*, 132–138.

Noldus, L. P., Van de Loo, E. L., & Timmers, P. H. (1989). Computers in behavioral research. *Nature, 341*(6244), 767–768.

Norcross, J. C., Hedges, M., & Prochaska, J. O. (2002). The face of 2010: A Delphi poll on the future of psychotherapy. *Professional Psychology: Research and Practice, 33*, 316–322.

Oravec, J. A. (2000). Internet and computer technology hazards: Perspectives for family counseling. *British Journal of Guidance and Counseling, 28*, 309–324.

Ragusea, A. S., & VandeCreek, L. (2003). Suggestions for the ethical practice of online psychotherapy. *Psychotherapy: Theory, Research, Practice, Training, 40*, 94–102.

Recupero, P. R., & Rainey, S. E. (2005). Informed consent to e-therapy. *American Journal of Psychotherapy, 59*, 319–331.

Reed, G. M., McLaughlin, C. J., & Milholland, K. (2000). Ten interdisciplinary principles for professional practice in telehealth: Implications for psychology. *Professional Psychology: Research and Practice, 31*, 170–178.

Risko, E. F., Quilty, L. C., & Oakman, J. M. (2006). Socially desirable responding on the web: Investigating the candor hypothesis. *Journal of Personality Assessment, 87*, 269–276.

Riva, G. (2005). Virtual reality in psychotherapy: Review. *CyberPsychology and Behavior, 8*, 220–230.

Romano, J. L., & Cikanek, K. L. (2003). Group work and computer applications: Instructional components for graduate students. *Journal for Specialists in Group Work, 28*, 23–34.

Rothbaum, B. O. (2006). Virtual reality exposure therapy. In B. O. Rothbaum (Ed.), *Pathological anxiety: Emotional processing in etiology and treatment* (pp. 227–244). New York: Guilford Press.

Rotunda, R. J., Kass, S. J., Sutton, M. A., & Leon, D. T. (2003). Internet use and misuse: Preliminary findings from a new assessment instrument. *Behavior Modification, 27*, 484–504.

Rudestam, K. E. (2004). Distributed education and the role of online learning in training professional psychologists. *Professional Psychology: Research and Practice, 35*, 427–432.

Shapira, N. A., Goldsmith, T. D., Keck, P. E., Khosla, U. M., & McElroy, S. L. (2000). Psychiatric features of individuals with problematic internet use. *Journal of Affective Disorders, 57*, 267–272.

Shapiro, D. E., & Schulman, C. E. (1996). Ethic and legal issues in e-mail therapy. *Ethics and Behavior, 6*, 107–124.

Shaw, H. E., & Shaw, S. F. (2006). Critical ethical issues in online counseling: Assessing current practices with an ethical intent checklist. *Journal of Counseling and Development, 84*, 41–53.

Subrahmanyam, K., Smahel, D., & Greenfield, P. (2006). Connecting developmental constructions to the internet: Identity presentation and sexual exploration in online teen chat rooms. *Developmental Psychology, 42*, 395–406.

Suler, J. R. (2000). Psychotherapy in cyberspace: A 5-dimensional model of online and computer-mediated psychotherapy. *CyberPsychology and Behavior, 3*, 151–159.

Truell, A. D., Bartlett, J. E., II, & Alexander, M. W. (2002). Response rate, speed, and completeness: A comparison of internet-based and mail surveys. *Behavior Research Methods, Instruments, and Computers, 34*, 46–49.

Tuten, T. L., & Bosnjak, M. (2001). Understanding differences in web usage: The role of need for cognition and the five factor model of personality. *Social Behavior and Personality, 29*, 391–398.

Tynes, B., Reynolds, L., & Greenfield, P. M. (2004). Adolescence, race, and ethnicity on the internet: A comparison of discourse in monitored vs. unmonitored chat rooms. *Journal of Applied Developmental Psychology, 25*, 667–684.

VandenBos, G. R., & Williams, S. (2000). The internet versus the telephone: What is telehealth anyway? *Professional Psychology: Research and Practice, 31*, 490–492.

Whitty, M. T., & Carr, A. N. (2006). *Cyberspace romance: The psychology of online relationships.* New York: Palgrave Macmillan.

Young, K. S. (1996). Internet addiction: The emergence of a new clinical disorder. *CyberPsychology and Behavior, 1*, 237–244.

Young, K. S. (2005). An empirical examination of client attitudes towards online counseling. *CyberPsychology and Behavior, 8*, 172–177.

CHAPTER 4

Social Justice and Counseling Psychology: A Challenge to the Profession

SUZETTE L. SPEIGHT
ELIZABETH M. VERA

Social justice is a rigorously debated concept in theology, philosophy, political science, and education. Social justice and injustice also have inextricable links to mental health and well-being. Historically in psychology, scholarship on psychologists' roles in combating injustice has been found primarily in community psychology (Rappaport, 1987; Sarason, 1981) and critical psychology literatures (D. Fox & Prilleltensky, 1997; Prilleltensky & Nelson, 2002). Counseling psychology's core principles and values are conceptually in line with social justice values and initiatives. An emphasis on person-environment interactions, valuing of diversity, and inclusion of prevention are theoretically aligned with a social justice agenda. Therefore, it is not surprising that counseling psychologists have made substantial contributions to the psychological literature on social justice practice and research.

In the past 7 years, counseling psychologists have published several major contributions, including literature on the application of a social justice agenda to the conceptualization of multicultural competence (Speight & Vera, 2004; Vera & Speight, 2003), teaching and training (Goodman et al., 2004), and vocational psychology (Blustein, McWhirter, & Perry, 2005). The *Handbook for Social Justice in Counseling Psychology* (Toporek, Gerstein, Fouad, Roysircar, & Israel, 2006), contains 35 chapters on applications of social justice research and practice.

Prior to these contributions, Atkinson, Thompson, and Grant (1993) and Lewis, Lewis, Daniels, and D'Andrea (1999) proposed important models of practice that included social justice-driven interventions. These models defined specific ways in which counseling professionals could expand their roles to include activities beyond the mainstays of psychotherapy and assessment. Arguments for the expansion of the roles of counseling psychologists were offered as early as the 1970s by Gottlieb (1975) who proposed the addition of the *advocate professional* to the scientist-practitioner training model. Counseling psychology's response to social injustice can be traced back to the early twentieth century when Parsons (1909) assisted urban, working-class populations in finding more satisfying vocations. As Fouad, Gerstein, and Toporek (2006) succinctly described, early counseling psychologists focused their social advocacy efforts on vocational issues for the poor, individuals with disabilities, women, veterans, and minorities. However, contemporary counseling psychology's commitment to issues of social justice has been described as "waxing and waning" over time (p. 12). Thus, although the majority of counseling psychology's explicit scholarship on social justice has been in the past decade, there is a rich history and tradition of responding to injustices.

DEFINING SOCIAL JUSTICE

Although various definitions of *social justice* exist in theological and philosophical writings, and have been debated since Plato and Aristotle, notions of equity and liberty are at the heart of the concept (Stevens & Wood, 1992). The goal of social justice is "full and equal participation of all groups in a society that is mutually shaped to meet their needs. Social justice includes a vision of society in which the distribution of resources is equitable and all members are physically and psychologically safe and secure" (Bell, 1997, p. 3). Early models of social justice included the Libertarian model that emphasized the connection between merit and liberty (Nozick, 1974). According to this model, the acquisition of resources need not be equitable, as long as equal opportunities exist and outcomes occur fairly, reflecting the sentiment "what one deserves." In theory, this position is consistent with capitalism and meritocracy.

A Liberal Reformist approach to justice builds on the Libertarian model but asserts that meritocracy cannot form the basis of justice and that inequity should not become structurally embedded in society (Rawls, 1971). In this theory, public policies would keep a "level playing field" by protecting the basic rights of those who have not benefited from the system. The Socialist approach to justice, commonly associated with Marx, posits that society should be structured in a way that guarantees equality, even at the expense of personal freedoms. Modern social justice theorists have criticized these models on the basis of their emphasis on outcome (i.e., the distribution of resources) rather than processes that guide decisions related to social equality (Young, 1990).

A more contemporary approach to social justice embraced by many scholars in psychology is referred to as a communitarian model of justice (Heller, 1987; Young, 1990). In this model of social justice, the process of decision making and interaction that occurs at both individual and systemic levels, as opposed to the actual distribution of resources, is the focus of interventions and policies. In Young's (1990) conceptualization of social justice, social organizations and processes are evaluated to elucidate practices of domination, privilege, and oppression. Thus, inequities are not solved by merely redistributing wealth or resources. Rather, the processes that facilitated unequal outcomes to begin with must be scrutinized and transformed.

Typically, marginalization is the main process by which social injustice is maintained. Young (1990) argues that in the United States a large proportion of the population is expelled from full participation in social life, including people of color, the elderly, the disabled, women, gay men, lesbians, bisexual people, and people who are involuntarily out of work. Thus, issues of social justice are important for the statistical majority of the population. Such a conceptualization of justice is logically related to issues of multiculturalism and diversity. Human diversity cannot flourish without notions of justice and equality (Albee, 2000; Helms & Cook, 1999; Martin-Baró, 1994; Ramirez, 1999; Vera & Speight, 2003).

SOCIAL JUSTICE IN COUNSELING PSYCHOLOGY

Isaac Prilleltensky has advocated for many years that social justice should be one of the main values guiding psychologists' work (Prilleltensky & Nelson, 2002). He argued, as did Martin-Baró (1994), that psychologists perpetuate injustice by overfocusing on individual factors to explain social behavior, which removes the individual from important sociohistorical contexts. In counseling psychology, some of the most recent scholarship has echoed this call to include larger contexts in both the conceptualization of human problems and the targets of interventions. Editor Robert Carter's initiation of the Social Justice Forum to feature articles that address social contexts as a recurring feature of the *Counseling Psychologist* has provided an essential outlet for scholarship on social justice and counseling psychology. This section reviews some of the major contributions to this literature by counseling psychologists.

Social Justice and Multicultural Counseling

Vera and Speight (2003) presented a critique of the existing multicultural counseling competencies that centered on the overrepresentation of therapy and assessment in these standards. To be truly committed to multiculturalism, the authors argued that social justice must be a grounding principle of all of our work, not just for the practice of therapy and assessment. Inevitably, identifying, examining, and combating the multiple forms of oppression (e.g., racism, classism) that adversely impact the lives of people of color must be central to our research and practice. The authors, drawing on the scholarship of both critical and community psychologists, recommended integrating systemic, proactive, and policy-focused interventions into direct-service work with multicultural populations. Outreach, prevention, and advocacy were cited as professional tools for combating oppression that affect culturally diverse populations. These activities have been affirmed as being important components of a social justice agenda by a host of scholars (Casas, 2005; Gerstein, 2006; Hage, 2003).

In addition to practice recommendations, Vera and Speight (2003) also offered suggestions for how research might better reflect a commitment to social justice. Specifically, a participatory-action research model was outlined as an approach to research that empowers participants to collaborate with investigators on projects that have social relevance to all involved. It was also recommended that the ultimate products of our research endeavors be reexamined. In addition to publishing findings in journals that are read primarily by other researchers, the authors suggested that informal outlets (e.g., newsletters, magazines) and presentations to the participants themselves be seen as highly regarded end-products of our scientific efforts. The article inspired a variety of reactions from important scholars in the field. Some of the reactions affirmed the concepts presented (e.g., M. Fox, 2003; Prilleltensky & Prilleltensky, 2003); and others criticized Vera and Speight for being ahistorical in their analysis by neglecting the gains of the multicultural movement in counseling psychology (Arredondo & Perez, 2003; Helms, 2003).

Social Justice and Counseling Psychology Training

Although the importance of social justice and systemic change are often endorsed by practitioners, there may be less agreement about who should be on the front lines of these efforts. Commonly, there is resistance from many professionals who are not accustomed to engaging in such efforts. Fortunately, there is an increasing literature that speaks to strategies for overcoming these potential barriers. In 2004, Goodman et al. presented an illuminating discussion on overcoming obstacles to social justice work with direct implications for training.

The authors extended feminist and multicultural counseling theories and described a set of principles that guide their social justice work. Among these principles were a commitment to (a) ongoing self-examination, (b) sharing power with constituents or clients, (c) giving voice to historically silenced populations, (d) raising the critical consciousness of clients, (e) focusing on strengths, and (f) empowering clients. One of the strengths of the Goodman et al. (2004) article is that the authors illustrated how the efforts of the faculty and students at Boston College are guided by these principles and how ethical dilemmas arise when applying these principles to real-world challenges. The authors discussed how there are instances when clients are truly not able to change systems of oppression and "although building on strengths highlights the power of individuals and communities, it may also conflict with the notion that the source of a particular problem resides outside the individual" (p. 825).

The article also illustrated the personal obstacles many students and professionals face when engaging in social justice endeavors, including the emotional costs of doing such work, structural obstacles (being untrained in community organization; current licensing and accreditation requirements), and the value system of academia (on which students and faculty members are dependent) that may not acknowledge or reward the time and energy necessary to sustain partnerships and provide service in the community. Addressing these very real dilemmas is important for counseling psychologists who truly value and wish to prioritize social justice endeavors in a professional world that may not equally prize the importance of this work.

Social Justice and Vocational Psychology

One of the domains in which social injustices are often most evident is the world of work (Blustein et al., 2005; Wilson, 1996). Thus, counseling psychologists, who are the leading scholars in vocational psychology, are well positioned to advocate for interventions aimed at combating injustices in educational and vocational opportunities and achievements. Blustein et al. (2005) provided a compelling critique of the traditional career development literature in which they argued that, historically, the field had been accused of developing theory and practice based on the experiences of "young, able-bodied, middle-class, White men in the United States" (p. 143). Fortunately, some of the most influential contemporary theories of career development have integrated the social context into their conceptualizations (Lent, Brown, & Hackett, 1994; Vondracek, Lerner, & Schulenberg, 1986). However, it is still typically the case that vocational interventions target individual clients or groups of clients to the exclusion of macro-level interventions that target systems that maintain educational and workplace inequities (Blustein, 2001; Blustein et al., 2005; O'Brien, 2001).

Blustein and colleagues (2005) presented an emancipatory communitarian approach to vocational psychology that integrated micro- and macro-level views of change. From this perspective, "individual difference factors presumed to help people actualize their vocational aspirations are viewed as naturally encountering systems that control how rewards and resources are dispersed, the distribution of which is often unfair and uneven" (p. 145). Their model closely examines the role that educational inequities play in setting the stage for future vocational injustice. At its heart, the emancipatory communitarian model requires activism to be an important component of responding to social injustices as "the concept of empowering disenfranchised people in their educational and working lives is limited as long as systems that reinforce and replicate their disempowerment remain untouched" (p. 152).

For practitioners, this model would require a combination of individual interventions that enhance self-efficacy and/or outcome expectations, with efforts that reduce oppressive practices in the workplace (Blustein et al., 2005). Among their recommendations for future research and practice in vocational psychology, Blustein et al. urged counseling psychologists to include community participants in all aspects of program building and evaluation, to instill critical consciousness in disenfranchised and privileged constituents, and to infuse social activism into our research and practice.

Adopting such an approach would result in confronting a variety of worker rights issues such as improving working conditions, establishing living wages, and challenging gender and racial inequities in income (Sloan, 2005). Many of these injustices are relevant in both U.S. and global contexts (Borgen, 2005), suggesting that broadening the scope of our interventions will also illuminate the need for an international framework and global partnerships. Although such an expansion would result in a new landscape for vocational psychology, the moral imperative to do so in many ways reaffirms the values of Parson's (1909) seminal efforts to respond to workplace inequities (Gainor, 2005).

Handbook of Social Justice in Counseling Psychology

There is renewed interest in issues of social justice among counseling psychologists. The publication of the *Handbook for Social Justice in Counseling Psychology: Leadership, Vision, and Action* (Toporek et al., 2006) represents a momentous event in the evolution of a social justice perspective in counseling psychology. Fouad et al. (2006) delineated the various constitutencies, conferences, initiatives, and publications that converged to set the stage for the publication of the *Handbook*. The *Handbook* is the best available compendium of the variety of social justice-driven efforts that counseling psychologists are making in training, schools, career development, health care, international, and legislative arenas. The *Handbook* provides practical illustrations, theoretical conceptualizations, and a blueprint for engaging in interdisciplinary interventions and research with marginalized communities. The contributors to the *Handbook* and its editors have made an outstanding contribution to the literature on social justice that will likely influence training, practice, and research in counseling psychology for years to come. Blustein (2006) heralded the *Handbook's* publication as evidence of counseling psychology's leadership "in professional psychology in advancing a perspective that is singularly unique, expansive, and visionary" (p. ix).

Current State of Social Justice in Counseling Psychology

A cursory review of recent publications related to issues of social justice in counseling psychology would lead to the conclusion that many counseling psychologists are indeed interested and involved in proactive, community-based, preventative interventions that address contextual or environmental difficulties of individuals and groups. Counseling psychologists can and do provide more than one-on-one remedial services to people and communities in need. Counseling psychologists are also challenged with how to educate graduate students and train interns in a range of interventions and roles as professional psychologists. Thus, a renewed social justice perspective can enhance and extend the field of counseling psychology and is entirely consistent with its core values. Helms (2003) stated that it is "difficult to quarrel with a [social justice] perspective that encourages counseling psychologists to do better by our sisters and brothers in marginalized communities" (p. 342).

However, it is hard to discern if the current renewed interest in social justice represents a wide, substantial movement in counseling psychology or if it is a specialized interest area promulgated by a few. Although it is too early to predict definitively the size and impact of the renewed interest in social justice per se among counseling psychologists, Baluch, Pieterse, and Bolden (2004) observed, "social action and social justice as integral aspects of how counseling psychologists conceptualize their work is not a new area of emphasis; however, it is yet to be a central aspect of how we see ourselves" (p. 91). Baluch et al.'s experiences as students caused them to conclude that social justice is "not currently a widely held identity" in the specialty (p. 92). Likewise, Fouad et al. (2006) stated, "it is clear that, as a field, we have a fair ways to go if, indeed, we want to embrace social justice as a central core identifying feature of our profession" (pp. 12–13).

Practical and ideological barriers hamper counseling psychologists' ability to embrace and implement a social justice perspective. As Helms (2003) asserted, managed care organizations pose obstacles to therapists' engagement in social justice work. When discussing with graduate students the need to expand our professional roles and repertoire of skills, we frequently hear real worry about the need to generate income and the doubt that prevention work, for instance, would be reimbursed by a third party payer. One student asked, "Yeah, that's good, Dr. Vera, but how am I going to get paid?" In a related vein, the idea of being knowledgeable about community resources and being able to link clients to such resources stirs up serious concerns in some trainees. Trainees have said, "Maybe I should have gone into social work instead" and "If I wanted to do that stuff, I would not have picked psychology for my career."

It would be a mistake summarily to dismiss these comments as only representing resistance to challenging the status quo. Instead, these comments accurately reflect our continued reliance on a mental health care delivery system in traditional settings that expects *DSM* diagnoses of mental illnesses for payment of psychological services. Psychology has been roundly criticized for "selling its soul to the devil;" namely the medical model (Albee, 2000). Recent gains in the quest for prescription privileges signal that a significant portion of psychologists will likely become even more closely aligned with the medical model. The current market dominance of the medical model and the potential expansion of psychology practice together appear to place counseling psychology in a somewhat uncomfortable position. Is the market pulling us in one direction while the call for social justice pulls us in another?

We could dramatize the tension as a battle between the specialty's foundational values on one hand and ambitious moneymaking on the other, but the tension is neither that simple nor static. Issues of social justice and issues of the marketplace both present challenges to our identities as individual counseling psychologists and collectively in psychology. A social justice perspective asks, "What type of counseling psychologist do you want to be"?

In many ways, a social justice orientation unsettles our identity as counseling psychologists. M. Fox (2003) talked about the trials of assistant professors who want to pursue their interests but need to answer to tenure committees and of graduate students who worry about traditional internships and poor job prospects for the type of work they really want to do. According to Fox, these professional and personal dilemmas arise from a desire for a greater integration of social justice issues into psychology and psychological education.

Many counseling psychologists may find it difficult to conduct "business as usual" once they become aware of the social forces restricting the life chances and choices of marginalized people. Clients frequently require a multidimensional approach. Unidimensional approaches—such as giving an Axis I diagnosis to, and conducting weekly psychotherapy with, a teenager who is involved in gang activity, living in poverty, and attending an under-resourced school—have obvious limitations. Such clients might need more than individual psychotherapy. However, counseling psychology training in the types of macro-level interventions many clients need lags far behind the desire to aid clients and communities.

ADVOCACY AND PUBLIC POLICY

Social Justice and Advocacy

Because advocacy and social action are recurring themes in existing counseling psychology scholarship on social justice, we include a review of this literature. Trusty and Brown (2005) and Field and Baker (2004) suggest that advocacy involves identifying unmet needs and taking actions to change the circumstances that contribute to problems or inequities that people experience. Advocates also plead the cause of another or defend causes. These observations suggest that advocacy involves working to change institutionalized policies and practices that impede the well-being of others so as to promote equity of opportunities for education, health, and other basic human rights. Kiselica and Robinson (2001) supported this idea with their definition of advocacy counseling as an approach to counseling in which the counselor goes beyond traditional verbal interventions to identify ways in which constituents voices are not heard or otherwise devalued.

Practitioners who serve as advocates are willing to challenge institutional barriers or policies that inhibit quality of life and help their clients to do so. Advocacy can take three forms: (1) helping clients advocate for themselves (empowerment), (2) advocating directly with institutions or policymakers on clients' behalf, and (3) advocating indirectly through training or educating professionals who work with underserved populations. Although most counselors feel comfortable working in partnership with their clients, directly confronting institutions or policymakers may represent "new ground," both personally and professionally. Grieger and Ponterrotto (1998) stated,

> advocacy and activism challenge us to take a moral and ethical stand with regard to the touchiest issues within our organizations, to publicly articulate our stand, and to risk the displeasure, if not the wrath, of those who hold power and authority. It may mean being unpopular, becoming a lightening rod for the anger and resistance of colleagues, and at times, it may mean being willing to put our jobs on the line in order to do the right thing. (p. 31)

Encouraging professionals to view themselves as advocates and social justice agents may, however, be easier said than done. There is confusion about the meaning of advocacy in counseling and the training that is necessary to promote competencies in advocacy (McCrae, Bromley, McNally, O'Byrne, & Wade, 2004). These authors state that rhetoric regarding social action will remain just that unless training efforts are mobilized. This is no doubt a reflection of the fact that few mental health and education training programs have coursework or practicum opportunities that prepare students for advocacy work.

Some findings suggest that even if such educational opportunities existed, there might not be widespread interest in advocacy work. Myers and Sweeney (2004) investigated counselors' attitudes about engaging in advocacy work for the counseling profession (e.g., increasing availability of counseling in schools and communities). Although the majority of counselors felt that advocacy for the profession of counseling was valuable, they preferred to see a paid lobbyist in the role. Thus, hiring others to advocate would be preferable to doing the work themselves. It is hard to know if these same individuals would agree that advocacy on behalf of marginalized groups should also be done by others, but the research that does exist (D'Andrea & Daniels, 1999) would suggest that less than 1% of mental health professionals include social activism as a part of their professional activities.

In a qualitative study, 1,200 White counselor educators, practitioners, and graduate students engaged in discussions about White racism in naturalistic settings. The authors sought to describe various dimensions of White racism and the dispositions that may give rise to these dimensions. The majority of participants fell into the *liberal disposition* category, which was described as a disposition in which a person is interested in multicultural issues and is relatively sophisticated in understanding the origins of racism, but not particularly motivated to take action to address these issues personally or professionally. The disposition most associated with social activism was termed the *principled activist disposition*; less than 1% of the sample was categorized in this group. These individuals were viewed as social-political activists who were consciously committed to empowering historically marginalized populations (D'Andrea & Daniels, 1999).

D'Andrea and Daniels's (1999) findings suggest that the professional community may have underestimated the difficulty of being able to "walk the walk" and to become advocates for social change. More scholarship is needed to clarify how it is that counseling psychologists become committed to this type of work. To date, there is only one published study that examined the characteristics of counseling professionals who become engaged in social justice work.

Nilsson and Schmidt (2005) investigated, via a survey methodology, characteristics that might be related to involvement in social activism among 134 counseling psychology graduate students. Predictor variables examined in this study included (a) desire for involvement in sociopolitical activism, (b) social interest (i.e., concern for the welfare of others), (c) problem-solving confidence, (d) approach-avoidance style, (e) personal control, (f) political ideology, (g) interest in politics, and (h) worldview. Although the full model accounted for 40% of the variance in social justice advocacy work, the authors found that having an interest in politics and having a desire to become involved in social activism were the best (and only) unique predictors of actual involvement in social activism.

Despite the lack of research investigating what leads counseling professionals to be involved in social justice work and the extent to which counseling professionals are interested in social justice work, there is a growing momentum to identify specific skills necessary for such work.

Advocacy Competencies

The National Association of School Counselors (NASC) has been active in identifying and promoting advocacy as a key aspect of school counselors' professional identities. Trusty and Brown (2005) along with Bemak and Chung (2005) defined the dispositions, knowledge, and skills necessary for competency in advocacy. Trusty and Brown (2005) argued that professionals must possess several types of dispositions to become interested in advocacy work. The first set of dispositions, called *advocacy dispositions*, or attitudes compatible with advocacy work, include altruistic motivation and willingness to take risks. Interestingly, Trusty and Brown argued that these dispositions are probably the least mutable to change, suggesting that people who have already developed these attitudes will be most likely to be interested in advocacy work, and that training people to acquire these dispositions may not be all that successful.

The second set of dispositions are *empowerment dispositions*, or attitudes acknowledging that clients or their families are often their best advocates, and that joining forces is more effective than speaking on behalf of clients. Third, *social advocacy dispositions*, in contrast to the previously mentioned advocacy dispositions, are attitudes recognizing that systemic-level change is necessary to the mental health and well-being of youth. Finally, *ethical dispositions* focus on an understanding of the ethics involved in engaging in advocacy work. Trusty and Brown argued that dispositions are critical to preparing yourself to engage in advocacy efforts.

Knowledge-based competencies involve a number of important content areas, including knowledge of (a) resources in the community and school, (b) relevant school policies and procedures, (c) dispute resolution tactics, (d) advocacy models (or the process by which we plan advocacy interventions), and (e) systems change strategies. Trusty and Brown (2005) argued that these knowledge sets are important to the logistics of engaging in advocacy.

Skills-based competencies involved in advocacy include basic counseling skills that would be applied in specific advocacy contexts. Some of the basic skills used include communication, collaboration, problem assessment, problem solving, and organizational skills. Being able to communicate with our constituents (e.g., parents in a school) as well as with policymakers (e.g., administrators) is an essential element of advocacy. Additionally, the ability to gather information to document needs is very important to effective policy work. Another critical skill is self-care. Self-care is essential because often advocacy and social justice work is long-term and successes are not guaranteed. Thus, being persistent, instilling hope in others, and avoiding burnout all require a strong set of self-care skills.

The aforementioned dispositions and competencies (Trusty & Brown, 2005) are very useful in conceptualizing training opportunities for future professionals. Field and Baker (2004) argue that because many formal training programs for mental health and education professionals do not yet have advocacy classes or field experiences, it is important to identify informal training opportunities for students to learn the process of engaging in advocacy work.

The American Counseling Association (ACA) is also developing advocacy competencies that are very similar to the aforementioned ones. The domains of competencies included in their list are client empowerment, community collaboration, public information, client advocacy, systems advocacy, and political advocacy. In the competencies for political advocacy, the ability to prepare convincing data and rationales for change, lobby legislators, and distinguish problems that are best resolved through political action are listed as required skills. At times, political action is clearly needed to improve the quality of life for many client populations, yet how professionals will go about gaining opportunities to engage in such activities is less clear.

Some caution against the use of professional-level advocacy efforts for fear that such interventions actually prevent clients from feeling empowered (because counselors are doing what clients should be learning to do for themselves). Additionally, there is a concern that advocacy work can overemphasize the importance of external factors in clients' lives. Parham and McDavis (1987) pointed out that by focusing on external factors alone we suggest that clients lack the mental fortitude to deal effectively with adverse conditions in society. An alternative position, however, is that advocacy can be an important additional tool that can help in diminishing the external stressors that affect marginalized clients. The goal of advocacy is ultimately self-empowerment of the client. Thus, if a counselor attends a school hearing or legal procedure with a client who feels intimidated by the system, the counselor can help to make sure that the client understands what decisions are being made and also can help the client protect his or her rights during the proceedings. Whether the counselor directly participates in the procedure or encourages the client to intervene on his or her own behalf, the counselor can model assertiveness skills and reinforce the client's sense of agency and expectation of fair treatment.

Beyond the advocacy interventions that may or may not include clients in the process, there is also an increasing call for psychologists to be active as public policy advocates who help to inform legislators about the mental health needs of communities. In the next section, we review the literature addressing the roles of counseling psychologists in the policy arena.

Social Justice and Public Policy

Is public policy advocacy a role that is compatible with the typical roles of counseling psychologists? Frost and Ouellette (2004) argued two important points in response to this question. The first point is that psychology has a history of lending its voice to policy debates on major social issues (e.g., APA, 2003; Benjamin & Crouse, 2002). Thus, such action has precedent. Second, psychologists have an ethical imperative to question the extent to which social policy is driven by science and whether science supports or contradicts social policy. This suggests that our skills as scientists or consumers of research are helpful to legislators who seek to build policy on best practice scholarship. Public policy advocacy efforts are well within our capabilities although they may not be common practices for counseling psychologists.

Becoming involved in public policy advocacy, however, involves an understanding of some of the inherent difficulties we encounter in doing such work. Choi et al. (2005) address these important dilemmas in their discussion of whether scientists and policymakers can effectively work together. These authors argued that there is a culture clash between the world of politics and the world of social scientists. Researchers have an agenda that includes publications and promotions, and they are usually trained to learn a great deal about delimited topics in their field. However, policymakers often live in a world that involves putting out fires, managing political crises, and knowing a little about a variety of topics. Policymakers prefer clear-cut answers and want the essence of an issue laid out for them in bullet points, whereas scientists are apt to equivocate and are often uncomfortable giving bottom-line recommendations. Furthermore, scientists obsess about the quality of evidence available about a particular research question, whereas policymakers are more comfortable using evidence generated more informally. Although this cultural clash may at first glance appear to be difficult to resolve, there have been several suggestions for how social scientists could position themselves to be received more readily by politicians.

Innvaer, Vist, and Trommald (2002) found that policymakers are most likely to use research in the development of legislation when (a) the research is timely, (b) there is a personal contact between the researcher and the policymaker, and (c) a clear summary of policy implications is stated in the research. Therefore, it behooves scientists to ask relevant, meaningful research questions, foster ongoing relationships with policymakers, and infuse policy implications into scholarly products. Additionally, McCartney and Rosenthal (2000) argued that social scientists need to be cognizant of the fact that real-life decisions that affect people are influenced by the papers we write, regardless of our intent, so it is essential for scholars to use methodologies and statistical tools that are comprehensible by and applicable to policymakers (e.g., reporting effect sizes, cost-benefit analyses).

FUTURE DIRECTIONS

Because interest in issues of social justice is experiencing a rebirth in recent years, future possibilities for research, theory, practice, education, and training appear boundless. In terms of research and theory, a particular research agenda focusing on issues of social justice has yet to be articulated. Any research agenda for social justice would need to prioritize community-based, interdisciplinary research that is meaningful to oppressed communities. Vera and Speight (2003) called for particular methodological approaches (e.g., participatory action research) that not only empower research participants but also lend themselves to investigating social problems. In addition to particular methodologies, the social justice perspective provokes compelling research questions.

Research

One exciting area of research is how to develop social justice advocates or allies. Social justice allies are members of dominant social groups who are working to end oppression. Broido (2000) interviewed six college student social justice allies to discover critical factors influencing their development as social justice allies. She found that the students held preexisting values supporting equality, sought out information about oppression, engaged in meaning-making strategies, developed self-confidence, and took advantage of opportunities to become involved in activism. Similarly, it would be important for doctoral programs and internships (especially those that purport to prepare their students or trainees for social justice work) to gain a fuller understanding of factors influential in the development of attributes (dispositions and competencies) that support a social justice perspective among their graduate students or trainees. Once identified, these factors can be built into a program and made available to students or trainees so that social justice dispositions and competencies can be cultivated and activism encouraged.

Ongoing program development, student or trainee assessment, and formative and summative evaluations could be linked to these social justice factors. Issues of fitness of current students and trainees would also be important to examine. What would fitness for social justice work look like? What are the critical attributes needed and how can they be developed in students who might be lacking them? The NASC and ACA standards, reviewed earlier, suggest some important attributes and skills and represent good starting points for program development and research efforts. How should training programs identify and manage students or trainees who are disinterested in issues of social justice, hold prejudicial views against certain groups, or have not developed the requisite attributes?

Thus, research on the development of social justice advocates and allies would be fundamental to training the next generation of counseling psychologists. A myriad of questions yet to be answered could become targets for research that has the potential to advance significantly our understanding of characteristics of social advocates and how these can be promoted. What sort of parental socialization practices and messages promote social justice attitudes? How do immersion, service learning, or study abroad experiences contribute to the development of social justice attitudes of graduate students? How do racial or ethnic identity attitudes relate to social justice attitudes and behaviors? What sort of educational experiences predict later social activism as a professional?

The answers to these and many other questions would allow for theory building about social justice attributes. The social and community psychology literatures might be instructive because both include theory and research on relevant concepts such as, just world beliefs (e.g., Lerner & Miller, 1978), sociopolitical development (Watts, Williams, & Jagers, 2003), and activist orientation (Corning & Myers, 2002). These lines of research and theory may provide starting points from which to formulate questions or to approach investigations relevant to the development of social justice attitudes and behaviors.

An area of research currently receiving attention from governmental funding agencies is mental health disparities. According to the Surgeon General's report on culture and mental health (U.S. Department of Health and Human Services, 2001), significant inequities exist between Whites and people of color regarding access to mental health services and the quality of mental health services received. The Surgeon General's report documents the existence of several specific disparities affecting the mental health care of racial and ethnic minorities compared with Whites: People of color (a) have less access to, and availability of, mental health services; (b) are less likely to receive needed mental health services; (c) often receive a poorer quality of mental health service; and (d) are underrepresented in mental health research.

For mental health professionals supporting a social justice agenda, mental health disparities is precisely the location where the proverbial "rubber meets the road." Members of oppressed groups in our society do not have sufficient access to mental health care, or receive substandard care, and because they are under-researched, the field does not know enough about their needs. These mental health disparities represent a critical social justice issue for professional psychology. Interventions designed to prevent or treat mental illness and to promote mental health are necessarily linked to issues of social inequities.

Thus, a wide range of unanswered questions remain. The Surgeon General's report (U.S. Department of Health and Human Services, 2001) concluded that the history of oppression and current instances of racism contribute negatively to the physical and mental health status of people of color. Research is needed that explores experiences of discrimination as pathways to mental illness. The influence of stress, coping, racial or ethnic identity, and acculturation on mental health outcomes should be examined.

The Surgeon General's report (U.S. Department of Health and Human Services, 2001) concludes that there is a lack of multicultural competence among medical professionals, contributing to the health disparities of people of color. Research into the experiences of consumers of mental health services is needed to determine the extent and effect of bias that they might encounter from professionals or institutions that prevents them from receiving appropriate services. The concept of multicultural competence, which counseling psychologists have been instrumental in defining, could be brought into the medical setting. The multicultural competence of health care professionals must first be operationalized so that needed educational interventions can be implemented to increase it. Utilizing the Sue, Arredondo, and McDavis (1992) tripartite model of multicultural competence—beliefs, knowledge, and skills—physicians could enhance their awareness of personal bias and prejudicial attitudes related to various ethnic or racial groups, increase their knowledge of various cultural dimensions underlying definitions of health and illness, and increase their skills in working with medical interpreters. The multicultural competence of health care professionals must be linked to how patients experience the medical encounter and, ultimately, to their health outcomes. Counseling psychology's leadership in multicultural competence makes the specialty uniquely qualified to forge new ground in health care delivery and medical education.

Moreover, given disparities in the quality of treatment received by people of color, empirically supported treatment options must be developed. Counseling psychologists could make significant contributions in the mental health disparities research arena.

Training

The million-dollar question remains: How do we go about educating counseling psychology students and trainees for the breadth of social justice work, from prevention to advocacy? What are the skills that students and trainees must develop to implement a social justice orientation in their professional work? "Despite the fact that awareness of oppressive environments has long been part of the counseling psychology domain, social justice remains only a small portion of our training and action" (Ivey & Collins, 2003, p. 293). Talleyrand, Chung, and Bemak (2006) described how the counseling masters and doctoral programs at George Mason University have been transformed to incorporate issues of social justice into current coursework, new courses, and field experiences. George Mason University is instructive due to the development and inclusion of unique training opportunities geared toward advocacy and public policy experiences. The program places students in internship positions with various governmental and professional organizations in the Washington, DC, area (e.g., Peace Corps) to give students a chance to practice their professional skills in the "real" world.

Given the sheer scope of social inequality in society, our students must be exposed to multiple disciplines to conceptualize problems and offer solutions. Baluch et al. (2004) suggested education in "public policy, public health, anthropology, history, and ethnic, gender, religious, and sexual orientation studies" (p. 95). The field has yet to delineate the needed skills, the curricular experiences, and educational outcomes associated with a social justice orientation. Yet, as Goodman et al. (2004) stated, the requisite curricular experiences or service learning opportunities have to be faculty-driven, not student-created. It may seem daunting to think about adding more to the already lengthy curricula of most counseling psychology doctoral programs. However, learning opportunities need not be part of classes. Many opportunities to learn advocacy skills could be part of service projects, partnerships with professional organizations, or continuing education programs. For example, the Illinois Psychological Association hosts a workshop that teaches the basic skills of lobbying in the state capital.

Moreover, our education and training efforts should be grounded in a critical examination of the various ethical considerations involved in embracing activism in our various roles as researchers, educators, consultants, and therapists (Kakkad, 2005). To advance a social justice perspective in counseling psychology, students and trainees must appreciate the social responsibility of our profession. "Educating future professionals in psychology to be more aware of and involved in issues of social justice is essential in a world increasingly plagued by the long-term and devastating effects of racism, discrimination, poverty, violence, and war" (Kakkad, p. 306).

CONCLUSION

Interest in social justice has been revitalized in counseling psychology. Although this is exciting, a social justice orientation for counseling psychologists requires an examination of our values and commitments and perhaps even a new a vision of ourselves as active agents for social change. Many counseling psychologists have the desire and interest to embrace a social justice orientation in their varied roles as clinicians, educators, and researchers. Being involved in communities, collaborating across disciplines, and engaging in multilevel interventions are strategies that allow counseling psychologists to participate in meaningful social justice work (Toporek et al., 2006).

Obviously, the myriad of injustices in our society cannot be solved by counseling psychologists alone. However, the core values, principles, and history of our specialty along with our unique knowledge base and skill set indicate that counseling psychologists can effectively address issues of justice and injustice. The current dialogue on social justice challenges counseling psychologists, individually and collectively, to reflect on our professional, moral, and ethical responsibilities for confronting social injustices in our society and promoting issues of social justice.

REFERENCES

Albee, G. W. (2000). The Boulder Model's fatal flaw. *American Psychologist, 55,* 247–248.

American Psychological Association. (2003). Amicus brief filed in the University of Michigan Affirmative Action Cases, Grutter v. Bollinger and Gratz v. Bollinger [Filed February 18, 2004].

Arredondo, P., & Perez, P. (2003). Expanding multicultural competence through social justice leadership. *Counseling Psychologist, 31,* 282–289.

Atkinson, D. R., Thompson, C. E., & Grant, S. K. (1993). A three-dimensional model for counseling racial/ethnic minorities. *Counseling Psychologist, 21,* 257–277.

Baluch, S. P., Pieterse, A. L., & Bolden, M. A. (2004). Counseling psychology and social justice: Houston . . . we have a problem. *Counseling Psychologist, 32*(1), 89–98.

Bell, L. A. (1997). Theoretical foundations for social justice education. In M. Adams, L. A. Bell, & P. Griffin (Eds.), *Teaching for diversity and social justice: A sourcebook* (pp. 3–15). New York: Routledge.

Bemak, F., & Chung, R. C. Y. (2005). Advocacy as a critical role for urban school counselors: Working toward equity and social justice. *Professional School Counseling, 8,* 196–202.

Benjamin, L. T., & Crouse, F. M. (2002). The American Psychological Association's response to Brown v. Board of Education: The case of Kenneth B. Clark. *American Psychologist, 57,* 38–50.

Blustein, D. L. (2001). Extending the reach of vocational psychology: Toward an integrative and inclusive psychology of work. *Journal of Vocational Behavior, 59,* 171–182.

Blustein, D. L. (2006). Forward. In R. L. Toporek, L. H. Gerstein, N. A. Fouad, G. Rosircar, & T. Israel (Eds.), *Handbook for social justice in counseling psychology: Leadership, vision, and action* (pp. ix–xi). Thousand Oaks, CA: Sage.

Blustein, D. L., McWhirter, E., & Perry, J. C. (2005). An emancipatory communitarian approach to vocational development theory, research, and practice. *Counseling Psychologist, 33,* 141–179.

Borgen, F. (2005). Advancing social justice in vocational theory, research, and practice. *Counseling Psychologist, 33,* 197–206.

Broido, E. M. (2000). The development of social justice allies during college: A phenomenological investigation. *Journal of College Student Development, 41*(1), 3–18.

Casas, J. M. (2005). Race and racism: The efforts of counseling psychology to understand and address the issues associated with these terms. *Counseling Psychologist, 33,* 501–512.

Choi, B. C. K., Pang, T., Lin, V., Puska, P., Sherman, G., Goddard, M., et al. (2005). Can scientists and policy makers work together? *Journal of Epidemiology and Community Health, 59,* 632–637.

Corning, A., & Myers, D. (2002). Individual orientation toward engagement in social action. *Political Psychology, 23*(4), 703–729.

D'Andrea, M., & Daniels, J. (1999). Exploring the psychology of White racism through naturalistic inquiry. *Journal of Counseling and Development, 77,* 93–101.

Field, J. E., & Baker, S. (2004). Defining and examining school counselor advocacy. *Professional School Counseling, 8,* 56–63.

Fouad, N. A., Gerstein, L. H., & Toporek, R. L. (2006). Social justice and counseling psychology in context. In R. L. Toporek, L. H. Gerstein, N. A. Fouad, G. Rosircar, & T. Israel (Eds.), *Handbook for social justice in counseling psychology: Leadership, vision, and action* (pp. 1–16). Thousand Oaks, CA: Sage.

Fox, D., & Prilleltensky, I. (1997). *Critical psychology: An introduction.* London: Sage.

Fox, M. D. R. (2003). Awareness is good, but action is better. *Counseling Psychologist, 31*(3), 299–304.

Frost, D. M., & Ouellette, S. C. (2004). Meaningful voices: How psychologists, speaking as psychologists, can inform social policy. *Analyses of Social Issues and Public Policy, 4,* 219–226.

Gainor, K. (2005). Social justice: The moral imperative of vocational psychology. *Counseling Psychologist, 33,* 180–188.

Gerstein, L. (2006). Counseling psychology's commitment to strengths: Rhetoric or reality? *Counseling Psychologist, 34,* 276–292.

Goodman, L., Liang, B., Helms, J., Latta, R., Sparks, E., & Weintraub, S. (2004). Training counseling psychologists as social justice agents: Feminist and multicultural principles in action. *Counseling Psychologist, 32,* 793–837.

Gottlieb, S. C. (1975). Psychology and the "Treatment Rights Movement." *Professional Psychology, 6*(3), 243–251.

Grieger, I., & Ponterrotto, J. (1998). Challenging intolerance. In C. Lee & G. Walz (Eds.), *Social action* (pp. 17–50). Alexandria, VA: American Counseling Association.

Hage, S. (2003). Reaffirming the unique identity of counseling psychology: Opting for the road less traveled by. *Counseling Psychologist, 31,* 555–563.

Heller, A. (1987). *Beyond justice.* New York: Basic Books.

Helms, J. E. (2003). A pragmatic view of social justice. *Counseling Psychologist, 31*(3), 305–313.

Helms, J. E., & Cook, D. A. (1999). *Using race and culture in counseling and psychotherapy: Theory and process.* Needleham Heights, MA: Allyn & Bacon.

Innvaer, S., Vist, J., & Trommald, M. (2002). Health policy makers' perceptions of their use of evidence: A systematic review. *Journal of Health Service, Research, and Policy, 7,* 239–244.

Ivey, A. E., & Collins, N. M. (2003). Social justice: A long-term challenge for counseling psychology. *Counseling Psychologist, 31*(3), 290–298.

Kakkad, D. (2005). A new ethical praxis: Psychologists' emerging responsibilities in issues of social justice. *Ethics and Behavior, 15*(4), 293–308.

Kiselica, M., & Robinson, M. (2001). Bringing advocacy counseling to life: The history, issues, and human dramas of social justice work in counseling. *Journal of Counseling and Development, 79,* 387–397.

Lent, R., Brown, S., & Hackett, G. (1994). Toward a unifying social cognitive theory of career and academic interest, choice, and performance [Monograph]. *Journal of Vocational Behavior, 45,* 79–122.

Lerner, M. J., & Miller, D. T. (1978). Just world research and the attribution process: Looking back and ahead. *Psychology Bulletin, 85,* 1030–1051.

Lewis, J. A., Lewis, M. D., Daniels, J. A., & D'Andrea, M. J. (1998). *Community counseling: Empowerment strategies for a diverse society.* Pacific Grove, CA: Brooks/Cole.

Martin-Baró, I. (1994). *Writings for a liberation psychology.* Cambridge, MA: Harvard University Press.

McCartney, K., & Rosenthal, R. (2000). Effect size, practical importance, and social policy for children. *Child Development, 71,* 173–180.

McCrea, L. G., Bromley, J. L., McNally, C. J., O'Byrne, K. K., & Wade, K. A. (2004). Houston 2001: A student perspective on issues of identity, training, social advocacy, and the future of counseling psychology. *Counseling Psychologist, 32,* 78–88.

Myers, J. E., & Sweeney, T. J. (2004). Advocacy for the counseling profession: Results of a national survey. *Journal of Counseling and Development, 82,* 466–471.

Nilsson, J., & Schmidt, C. (2005). Social justice advocacy among graduate students in counseling: An initial exploration. *Journal of College Student Development, 46,* 267–279.

Nozick, R. (1974). *Anarchy, state, and utopia.* New York: Basic Books.

O'Brien, K. (2001). The legacy of Parsons: Career counselors and vocational psychologists as agents of social change. *Career Development Quarterly, 50,* 66–76.

Parham, T. A., & McDavis, R. J. (1987). Black men, an endangered species: Who's really pulling the trigger? *Journal of Counseling and Development, 66,* 24–27.

Parsons, F. (1909). *Choosing a vocation.* Boston: Houghton-Mifflin.

Prilleltensky, I., & Nelson, G. (2002). *Doing psychology critically: Making a difference in diverse settings*. London: Palgrave MacMillan.

Prilleltensky, I., & Prilleltensky, O. (2003). Synergies for wellness and liberation in counseling psychology. *Counseling Psychologist, 31*, 273–281.

Ramirez, M. (1999). *Psychotherapy and counseling with minorities*. Boston: Allyn & Bacon.

Rappaport, J. (1987). Terms of empowerment/exemplars of prevention: Toward a theory for community psychology. *American Journal of Community Psychology, 15*, 121–144.

Rawls, J. (1971). *A theory of justice*. Cambridge, MA: Harvard University Press.

Sarason, S. B. (1981). An asocial psychology and a misdirected clinical psychology. *American Psychologist, 36*, 1072–1080.

Sloan, T. (2005). Global work-related suffering as a priority for vocational psychology. *Counseling Psychologist, 33*, 207–214.

Speight, S., & Vera, E. (2004). Social justice: Ready or not? *Counseling Psychologist, 32*, 109–118.

Stevens, E., & Wood, G. H. (1992). *Justice, ideology, and education: An introduction to the social foundations of education*. New York: McGraw-Hill.

Sue, D. W., Arredondo, P., & McDavis, R. J. (1992). Multicultural counseling competencies and standards: A call to the profession. *Journal of Counseling and Development, 70*, 477–486.

Talleyrand, R. M., Chung, R. C., & Bemak, F. (2006). Incorporating social justice in counselor training programs. In R. L. Toporek, L. H. Gerstein, N. A. Fouad, G. Rosircar, & T. Israel (Eds.), *Handbook for social justice in counseling psychology: Leadership, vision, and action* (pp. 44–58). Thousand Oaks, CA: Sage.

Toporek, R. L., Gerstein, L. H., Fouad, N. A., Roysircar, G., & Israel, T. (2006). Future directions for counseling psychology: Enhancing leadership, vision, and action in social justice. In R. L. Toporek, L. H. Gerstein, N. A. Fouad, G. Rosircar, & T. Israel (Eds.), *Handbook for social justice in counseling psychology: Leadership, vision, and action* (pp. 533–552). Thousand Oaks, CA: Sage.

Trusty, J., & Brown, D. (2005). Advocacy competencies for professional school counselors. *Professional School Counseling, 8*, 259–265.

U. S. Department of Health and Human Services, U. S. Public Health Service, Substance Abuse and Mental Health Services Administration. (2001). *Mental health: Culture, race, and ethnicity: A supplement to mental health—A report of the surgeon general*. Washington, DC: Author.

Vera, E., & Speight, S. L. (2003). Multicultural competence, social justice, and counseling psychology: Expanding our roles. *Counseling Psychologist, 31*, 253–272.

Vondracek, F., Lerner, R., & Schulenberg, J. (1986). *Career development: A life span developmental approach*. Hillsdale, NJ: Erlbaum.

Watts, R., Williams, N. C., & Jagers, R. (2003). Sociopolitical development. *American Journal of Community Psychology, 31*, 185–194.

Wilson, W. (1996). *When work disappears: The world of the new urban poor*. New York: Random House.

Young, I. M. (1990). *Justice and the politics of difference*. Princeton, NJ: Princeton University Press.

CHAPTER 5

A Growing Internationalization of Counseling Psychology

P. PAUL HEPPNER
FREDERICK T. L. LEONG
HUNG CHIAO

Counseling psychology in the United States has a long and distinguished history. Many scholars have documented and analyzed developments in various time periods (e.g., Heppner, Casas, Carter, & Stone, 2000), such as the founding of the Division of Counseling Psychology (e.g., Scott, 1980) and the major counseling journals (e.g., Blocher, 2000; Wrenn, 1966), and evolving research patterns (e.g., Borgen, 1984). Moreover, the stories and perceptions of some of the major pioneers and leaders of the field have been documented (Heppner, 1990; Heppner, Fouad, & Hansen, 2002). The profession evolved from a late-nineteenth-century vocational guidance movement into a strong and vibrant specialty within psychology. Perhaps for a variety of reasons, counseling psychology seems to have been an almost uniquely American discipline over the years. But we should not be mislead by this limited perspective.

As Pedersen (2005) noted, "the functions of counseling have been practiced for thousands of years and are not merely an invention of the last century or two" (p. xi). This chapter highlights the growing culturally sensitive voices and efforts to internationalize counseling psychology in the United States. A very different chapter with the same title as the one used here could be written by those in counseling and counseling psychology professions around the globe, with many other milestones being recorded. Moreover, very different concluding challenges and recommendations would be cited in such chapters. An understanding of our history and identity as U.S. counseling psychologists, including the journey to internationalize our specialty, allows us to become more aware of the contributions as well as limitations of our knowledge worldwide. Multicultural counseling is not only the fourth force of psychology (Pedersen, 1991), but an epochal school of knowledge that restructures the worldview of psychology so that we no longer live in a flat world, but a global multicultural village.

This chapter documents and analyzes the history of the growing internationalization of U.S. counseling psychology. By *internationalizing,* we refer to the inclusion of cross-national and cross-cultural perspectives in the predominant Western perspectives of counseling practice and research as traditionally operationalized in the United States. The first section of the chapter traces early events and forces leading to the internationalization of counseling psychology in the United States, beginning with international efforts in the 1940s when U.S. scholars provided consultation to promote the development of the counseling profession in other countries; the review ends with a discussion of current, collaborative efforts by U.S. and international colleagues to address important societal needs around the globe. The second section describes the growth of international psychological organizations, including recently evolving organizational structures to promote counseling psychology on an international level. The final section presents nine challenges that confront the internationalization movement in counseling psychology.

The authors would like to express their sincere gratitude to the following individuals for their helpful feedback on an earlier version of this chapter: Lawrence Gerstein, Paul Pedersen, Joseph Ponterotto, and Mark Savickas.

A few caveats are in order: Analyzing the history of a professional discipline is a difficult, subjective task, and it is influenced by personal biases and worldviews. Consequently, the first author selected coauthors who would provide expertise on different topics and from different worldviews. Nonetheless, because of the time span of this review, space limitations, and our own biases, there will undoubtedly be omissions of events, people, and developments.

HISTORY OF EFFORTS TO INTERNATIONALIZE U. S. COUNSELING PSYCHOLOGY

This review considers five categories of influence on the internationalization movement: (1) cultural, social, economic, political, and environmental events and forces; (2) the pioneering and persistent efforts of individual scholars to conceptualize and articulate the utility of internationalizing counseling psychology; (3) the growing number of voices with international experiences in U.S. counseling psychology; (4) structural changes in our professional organizations that promote cross-cultural perspectives; and (5) pioneering efforts of individuals in leadership positions to promote cultural perspectives in the specialty. Although the review generally follows a chronological pattern, the five categories of influence should not be conceptualized in a simple linear model. Rather, they are best depicted as a set of highly interactive and synergistic factors over time.

Early International Efforts

Although counseling psychology traces its roots to Frank Parsons and the vocational guidance movement of the early 1900s (e.g., Whiteley, 1980), it did not emerge as a recognized psychological specialty until the 1940s and 1950s when (a) the Veterans Administration created a new specialty called *counseling psychology* and (b) the field's pioneers established a formal professional organization (Division 17 of the American Psychological Association [APA], initially Personnel and Guidance, but now known as the Society of Counseling Psychology [SCP]). These two historic events subsequently led to the development of a general training model (the scientist-practitioner model) and a handful of accredited doctoral training programs (Blocher, 2000; Whiteley, 1980). Carl Rogers' influential book, *Counseling and Psychotherapy* (1942), and E. G. Williamson's book, *How to Counsel Students* (1939), were among the first textbooks on counseling. The members of the profession at that time were predominantly men of White European descent, which reflected the foundational values underlying the counseling profession.

Starting in the 1940s, U.S. counseling experts began to collaborate with counselors in other countries, and some of these countries fell under the influence of U.S. theorizing (Savickas, in press). There were also several early, government-aided efforts to export counseling from the United States to other countries. These efforts predated the awareness that counseling occurs in a particular cultural context. In the post-World War II reorganization of Japan's educational system, a number of U.S. counseling leaders (e.g., H. Borow, L. Brammer, W. Lloyd, D. Super, E. G. Williamson) served as consultants to the Japanese government. Similarly, in the 1960s, counseling psychology leaders (e.g., F. Robinson, C. G. Wrenn) were involved in establishing the counseling profession in England. Some of the earliest cross-national efforts in U.S. counseling psychology involved consulting with leaders in other countries to help our international colleagues develop a counseling profession.

In 1962, Gilbert Wrenn published a landmark book, *The Counselor in a Changing World,* which raised concerns about counselors' cultural insensitivity, cross-cultural competence, and cultural encapsulation (the inability to understand others from a different culture). Although Wrenn's message was clear about the importance of counselors' understanding of their own worldviews and how these may affect their work with clients from different cultures, it was not widely received. It would take another 40 years for these concerns to be more fully addressed. Other early efforts to increase cross-cultural communication in the counseling profession began in the mid-1960s with the creation of a new journal, the *International*

Journal for the Advancement of Counseling (IJAC). The journal provided a major international arena for the scholarly exchange of ideas on guidance and counseling. As of 2007, *IJAC*'s editorial board has counseling professionals from over 20 countries around the world.

By the early 1980s, a few counseling psychologists were granted Fulbright awards from the U.S. government in conjunction with various host countries. These awards allowed U.S. scholars to teach and conduct research abroad for 3 to 6 months, with the goal of increasing mutual understanding between the people of the United States and other countries (see www.cies.org). In 1986, McWhirter organized a group of Fulbright scholars to present their experiences at a symposium at the annual APA convention. Later versions of these presentations were subsequently published in the International Forum (IF) of The *Counseling Psychologist* (*TCP*; Hedlund, 1988; Heppner, 1988; McWhirter, 1988; Nugent, 1988; Skovholt, 1988). The IF was formalized by then-editor Fretz (1985), who wrote:

> The introduction of a periodic International Forum culminates an effort begun by John Whiteley to increase the involvement of our many international readers. Most welcome are descriptions of how the ideology of counseling psychology becomes actualized in diverse settings—what the continuities and discontinuities are between counseling psychology as presented in its traditional form and the unique needs of societies significantly different from the United States. Contributions are invited from both international readers and counseling psychologists who have provided professional services in international settings. (p. 6)

Although the IF represented a new professional structure to promote communication about international topics in a prominent counseling journal, most of its articles were about the experiences of Fulbright and other U.S. scholars visiting and working in other countries.

The Minnesota International Counseling Institute (MICI) was also created in the 1980s by counseling psychology faculty at the University of Minnesota (e.g., T. Skovholt, S. Hansen, J. Romano, K. Thomas). The MICI is a biennial gathering of international psychology and educational practitioners and scholars to advance the science and practice of cross-cultural counseling. The creation of the MICI provided a professional structure to promote scholarly exchanges among counseling professionals from around the world. By 2005, 152 international counseling and student development specialists from 40 countries had participated in the institute (Skovholt, Hansen, Goh, Romano, & Thomas, 2005).

Shrinking of Time and Space

The dawn of the twenty-first century witnessed tremendous social change. By way of contrast, consider the economic boom in the early 1960s. "An expanding economy, cheap energy, government subsidies, and a dominant position in the marketplace had made the hallmark of the 'good life' available to more Americans than ever" (Faragher, Buhle, Czitrom, & Armitage, 1997, p. 894). It was an era that saw the emergence of televisions as major sources of entertainment, telephones in most homes, and the advent of bulky mainframe computers the size of a room. Conversely, the recent advances in communication, transportation, manufacturing, and technology have created a much more economically, culturally, and socially interdependent world in which cross-cultural understanding is a key to success and survival. The Internet, in particular, has greatly facilitated communication around the globe. We have witnessed the inception of a "global village" that is "multicultural, multinational, and multiethnic" (Marsella, 1998, p. 1282). In essence, with the shrinking of time and space, our relationships as well as the way we work and play have been dramatically altered.

Changes in University Environments

The past few decades have also involved major changes in the scope of international commerce, growing economic interdependence, new challenges in higher education funding, and the September 11, 2001 terrorist attacks on the United States, which underscored the nonindependence of the United States as well as the interconnectedness of the world (Friedman, 2005). At the same time, more U.S. and international university leaders articulated the need for universities to prepare a new generation of graduates—students who would have relevant cultural skills to contribute to societal needs around the globe. The president of the National University of Singapore (NUS) wrote, "In a world of increasing cultural complexity, our students must learn to transcend boundaries of place, identity and norms, as well as bridge diverse cultures and perspectives . . . In this way, we can nurture global citizens who are able to contribute to a sustainable future for planet Earth." (Fong, 2006, p. 209). Many universities and colleges in the United States have become increasingly focused on building international connections, recruiting international students, and, in some disciplines, actively preparing graduates to work effectively in global communities and markets. As a result of a multitude of social and economic forces active at the beginning of the twenty-first century, faculty at many U.S. universities were encouraged and reinforced to extend their work into international contexts.

Articulation of the Pervasive Role of Culture in U.S. Counseling Psychology

During the 1990s and early 2000s, there was an increased focus on multicultural issues in the U.S. counseling psychology profession (Heppner et al., 2000). Although this focus primarily involved issues related to race/ethnicity, it broadened over time to include gender, sexual orientation, physical abilities, and social class. In addition to a broad array of research and scholarship, training and accreditation standards were revised, and there was increased diversity in journal editorial boards, professional organizations, and national leadership positions in counseling psychology. The specialty of counseling psychology contributed significantly to the multicultural movement in psychology and education; for example, by playing a major role in the development and adoption of the *Guidelines on Multicultural Education, Training, Research, Practice, and Organization Change for Psychologists* (APA, 2003). Despite such changes, many involved in the multicultural movement would argue that progress has been slow and that much remains to be done in this area.

Compared to the U.S. multicultural movement, change has been even less evident in the internationalization of U.S. counseling psychology. Several scholars noted that psychology and counseling psychology have been slow to incorporate cross-cultural perspectives in U.S. counseling psychology (e.g., Cheung, 2000; Gerstein & Ægisdóttir, 2005a; Heppner, 2006; Leong & Blustein, 2000; Leong & Ponterotto, 2003; Leung, 2003; Marsella, 1998; Pedersen & Leong, 1997). Some scholars characterized the discipline of U.S. psychology as a White middle-class enterprise "conceived in English, thought about in English, written about in English, and taking into account problems relevant to Anglo-Saxton culture" (Ardila, 1993, pp. 170–171). Moreover, Magrath (then president of the Association of State Universities and Land Grant Colleges; 1993) concluded that "Too many of our faculty, in all of disciplines, are far too insulated, and in fact and perception seen as indifferent to worlds other than their own" (p. 4). A number of surveys supported McGrath's conclusion (e.g., Altbach & Lewis, 1998).

There was, however, a small but growing number of counseling psychologists in the 1990s who saw the important impact of culture on counseling research and practice. Paul Pedersen guest edited a special issue of the *Journal of Counseling and Development* (*JCD*) devoted to "multiculturalism as a fourth force in counseling" in 1991. This special issue, while devoted to domestic multiculturalism, included many authors who were also committed to international multiculturalism. This special issue was followed by a volume edited by Pedersen (1999) on the same topic but with a more international set of authors. (*Note:* D'Andrea, Pedersen, and Foster are currently editing a major follow-up issue of *JCD*.)

In 1997, the incoming editor of *TCP* observed that the "increased internationalization of the world" was a major social force that necessitated a multitude of changes within the counseling psychology profession in the United States:

Counseling psychology can play an important role in building a global village that helps people improve their well-being, alleviate distress and maladjustment, resolve crises, modify maladaptive environments, and increase their ability to live more highly functioning lives. To do so, however, we must train counseling psychologists to be sensitive to, and skillful in, cross-cultural contexts with people who hold differing worldviews. (Heppner, 1997, p. 7)

In essence, Heppner not only suggested a change in the education and training of the next generation of U.S. counseling psychologists, but also a shift to viewing the counseling profession in the United States as part of a larger global movement, rather than as an insular enterprise. Thus, he indicated his desire to expand the IF in several ways; Heppner did so by (a) promoting an increased focus on international issues in the journal by recruiting leading scholars in the international movement in counseling psychology to serve as coeditors of the IF (F. T. L. Leong, P. Pedersen, J. Ponterotto, D. Blustein); (b) changing the editorial review process for international manuscripts to be sensitive to the worldviews of international scholars; and (c) appointing the first international scholar (S. A. Leung from Hong Kong) to serve as associate editor of *TCP*. During this time, Leong and Heppner also procured ongoing convention programming time at the annual convention of the APA to discuss international issues in counseling psychology.

As a result of these efforts, more international colleagues were encouraged to submit manuscripts, and a few more international scholars began to publish in *TCP* and in other counseling journals. On balance, there has been a slow increase in articles that (a) articulate a strong rationale for internationalizing counseling psychology, (b) discuss the pervasiveness of cultural affects on all aspects of counseling, (c) provide examples of the state of counseling professions in other countries, (d) articulate obstacles and challenges prohibiting change in the profession, and (e) recommend ways to internationalize U.S. counseling psychology (Cheung, 2000; Heppner, 2006; Leong & Blustein, 2000; Leong & Ponterotto, 2003; McWhirter, 2000; Nutt, 2006; Pederson & Leong, 1997). Cheung (2000) argued:

The meaning of counseling may seem obvious to American psychologists. The understanding of its meaning by American clients is assumed. In another cultural context, however, counseling may imply a different nature of relationship to both the provider and the recipient. Counseling needs to be deconstructed in the context of the culture in which it is offered. (p. 124)

Cheung indicated that culture defines what constitutes clients' problems, the cause of the problems (see Cheung, 1998), as well as the solutions and therapeutic interventions (see Sue & Sue, 1990).

Some articles have also discussed the need to examine the culturally encapsulated assumptions in prevailing theories and practices and to develop research models that would facilitate the move toward internationalizing counseling psychology (e.g., Gerstein, 2005; Heppner, 2006; Heppner et al., 2000; Leong & Blustein, 2000; Leong & Ponterotto, 2003; McWhirter, 2000; Norsworthy, 2005; Pedersen, 2003; Pedersen & Leong, 1997). Cheung (2000) highlighted the culturally encapsulated assumptions in U.S. counseling psychology:

Counseling psychology has been encapsulated in ethnocentric assumptions that are taken to be universal. The theories, research, and practice of counseling psychology, as a specialized profession, originate in the United States but are assumed to be universally applicable. When transported to other cultures where the field of psychology in general, and counseling psychology in particular, is fledging, it is simply transposed. There has often been little regard as to the applicability of the theories and practice. (p. 123)

A number of scholars identified other obstacles and challenges facing the U.S. counseling profession, and psychology in general, to becoming cross-culturally competent, such as: (a) short and superficial contacts with international colleagues, (b) few major U.S. institutions to support the internationalizing of the profession, (c) a tendency to believe our behaviors are typical of others, (d) feelings of superiority as a profession relative to other countries, (e) lack of exposure and knowledge to the work of international colleagues, (f) xenophobia, (g) difficulty in understanding and accepting others' worldviews, (h) inability to accept differences across cultures as simply differences, (i) an overemphasis on internal validity, and (j) psychological reactance, defensiveness, as well as other personality styles that contribute to the obstacles above (e.g., Gerstein & Ægisdóttir, 2005a; Heppner, 2006; Leong & Ponterotto, 2003; Leong & Santago-Riveria, 1999; Leung, 2003; Marsella, 1998; Segall, Lonner, & Berry, 1998).

Numerous scholars have articulated the need to attend to the cultural context in U.S. counseling psychology and abroad, and to be sensitive to potential problems when U.S. counseling constructs, methods, theories, and empirical findings are simply transported from one culture (i.e., the United States) to other cultures. Moreover, the emphasis on the cultural context in cross-national contexts is built on similar messages from within the U.S. multicultural movement. The early conceptualization of internationalization as "helping" our international colleagues has faded in many quarters and has been replaced by a new view of internationalization as a truly joint, collaborative enterprise designed to develop broader, culturally dependent psychological knowledge bases from around the world to help resolve societal problems across many cultural contexts (Heppner, 2006; Leong & Ponterotto, 2003).

A Growing Number of International Collaborations and Culturally Sensitive Voices

By the year 2000, approximately 50 counseling psychologists had received one or more Fulbright fellowships (McWhirter, 2000). Fulbright scholars have uniformly reported their experiences to be times of tremendous growth in cultural awareness and cross-cultural competence (e.g., McWhirter, 1988). The number of international students receiving graduate degrees in counseling psychology from U.S. training programs has also increased dramatically in recent years. Although such enrollments started slowly in the 1980s, by 2005 some programs reported that international students constituted from 20% to 50% of their doctoral programs (see Heppner, 2006). Some of these graduates found employment in the United States; others returned to work in their home countries. As a result, the number of counseling psychology voices with growing levels of cross-cultural sensitivity and competence has increased. All of these events represent a significant movement toward internationalizing U.S. counseling psychology.

In addition, counseling psychologists have developed a range of long-term collaborative projects. Rex Stockton has collaborated with colleagues to develop models of counselor training for those who work with HIV/AIDS in Botswana and Kenya. Norm Gysbers and his international colleagues are implementing and beginning to evaluate a comprehensive guidance program that was adapted for use in the primary and secondary schools of Hong Kong. A few U.S. training programs have developed programs aimed at promoting cross-cultural competencies in students and faculty. The University of Albany has developed a program to promote student exchanges and research collaboration with the Universidad de La Coruna (see Friedlander, Carranza, & Guzman, 2002). The Fordham Counseling Psychology Program offers a course on multicultural counseling in Orvieto, Italy every summer; the course includes lectures, experiential activities, small group exercises, and analysis of multicultural counseling cases (J. Fuertes, personal communication, March 5, 2007). The Ball State University Counseling Psychology and Guidance Services Program developed a 3-week International Immersion Practicum to promote counselors' cross-cultural competencies by pairing student supervisees with supervisors from the host country (see Alexander, Kruczek, & Ponterotto, 2005). A Bidirectional Cross-Cultural Immersion Program is a joint program developed between the National Taiwan Normal University and the University of Missouri-Columbia. Each university hosts students and faculty from the other university in a two week professional and cultural immersion experience (L. Wang & P. Heppner, personal communication, March 10, 2007).

There are other instances, not only of cross-national collaboration, but also long-term programmatic lines of research (e.g., applying social cognitive career theory to students' vocational development and to counselor training in Italy; Lent, Brown, Nota, & Soresi, 2003; Lent, Tracey, Brown, Soresi, & Nota,

2006; Soresi, Nota, & Lent, 2004; Tracey, Lent, Brown, Soresi, & Nota, 2006). Many others have been exposed to other cultures through an increasing number of invitations to interact with international colleagues and present keynote addresses, lectures, and workshops in a wide array of countries (e.g., Australia, Italy, Portugal, Taiwan, China, United Arab Emirates, Japan, South Korea, South Africa, Singapore, Iran). In the early part of the twenty-first century, multiple avenues of cross-national collaboration appeared between U.S. and international colleagues. These interactions began to create a critical mass of counseling psychologists around the globe with growing appreciation for the utility of cross-national collaboration to reach mutually beneficial goals.

Initiatives within Counseling Psychology Professional Organizations

Louise Douce chose globalization as her SCP presidential theme in 2003. Two of the succeeding presidents of SCP (P. Heppner & R. Nutt) also had a significant focus on international issues. One of Douce's projects was to invite a diverse group of counseling psychology scholars to brainstorm ideas to promote the globalization of counseling psychology. A second initiative, led by Stewart Cooper, Carolyn Enns, and Lawrence Gerstein, was to create a forum at the annual APA convention for counseling scholars interested in international issues to discuss common goals. Also in 2003, the Society of Vocational Psychology (SVP), a section within Division 17, held their first international conference in Coimbra, Portugal. Two years later, their second international conference was held in Vancouver, Canada. These and other SVP efforts have resulted in international scholars and students now comprising approximately 25% of the Society's membership. The efforts have also resulted in increased exposure of U.S. researchers to exciting new lines of research and practice, and placed their research and public policy in a global context (D. Blustein, personal communication, January 5, 2007).

As president of SCP in 2005, Heppner developed a number of initiatives to promote the internationalization of counseling psychology. Specifically, he (a) visited five countries to meet with leaders in the counseling profession to explore areas of international collaboration; (b) spearheaded, with Lawrence Gerstein, development of an International Section of SCP (www.international-counselingpsychology.org; after 18 months the Section had 189 members); (c) created, in conjunction with Y. Wang and O. Yakushko, an International Student Orientation to provide an orientation and mentoring for international students at the annual APA convention; (d) coordinated development of a new membership category in the SCP (international affiliate) and negotiated reduced membership fees for international affiliates (which significantly increased membership); and (e) developed an annual meeting of international leaders in counseling. As more structures are developed in our professional organizations to promote these types of discussions and collaborations, counseling psychology will be broadened and strengthened around the globe.

Other organizations, such as the Association for University and College Counseling Center Directors (AUCCCD), have increasingly addressed globalization issues through (a) deepening discussions about ways that counseling centers serve the needs of international students on their campuses and of study abroad students during all phases of their experiences, (b) increasing communication and collaboration with counseling center director colleagues in countries outside of North America, (c) establishing an AUCCCD listserv and an annual breakfast meeting dedicated to globalization interests, and (d) profiting from the presence of a small but growing number of AUCCCD directors from European, Arab, and Asian countries at its annual conferences (J. Resnick, personal communication, February 28, 2007).

GLOBAL GROWTH OF THE COUNSELING PROFESSION

The counseling profession is growing rapidly around the globe. However, there are cross-national differences in the identity and credentialing of counselors and counseling psychologists, and in the professional associations that represent them (Heppner & Gerstein, in press). To provide a context for international counseling psychology, we first describe the larger international psychology movement, focusing on four primary international psychological associations (see Davis, 2000). The International Association of Applied Psychology (IAAP) is the oldest international organization in psychology (founded in 1920 in Geneva, Switzerland).

Since 1974, it has held a professional conference every 4 years called the International Congress of Applied Psychology (ICAP). *Applied Psychology: An International Review* serves as the primary publication of IAAP. During his presidency of IAAP (1998 to 2002), Charles Spielberger published the *Encyclopedia of Applied Psychology*. Mike Frese, president (2002 to 2006), is in the process of producing a series of handbooks in applied psychology.

The second primary international association is the International Union of Psychological Sciences (IUPsyS), which was formally established in 1951 in Stockholm, Sweden. The IUPsyS is different from the other international organizations in that it functions somewhat like a United Nations of psychological associations. Its membership is composed of national psychological associations, with each country having representation. Like IAAP, IUPsyS holds a congress every 4 years. Its schedule is coordinated with that of the ICAP, which allows for a major international psychological congress to be held every 2 years. This staggering enables the executive committee of each of the associations to meet at each other's congress. The IUPsyS publishes the *International Journal of Psychology* (its primary journal) and the *International Handbook of Psychological Science* (Pawlik & Rosenweig, 2000).

The third major international association, the International Council of Psychologists, can be traced back to a group of U.S. women psychologists who organized the National Council of Women Psychologists (NCWP) in 1941 to contribute to the American war effort during World War II (Davis, 2000). The NCWP was almost terminated at the end of the war but a group of Canadian psychologists decided to reorganize it into the International Council of Women Psychologists. Memberships were extended to women psychologists from other countries. Eventually, in 1959, a number of male psychologists also began participating and the association dropped the term *women* from its title. Due to its small size, the ICP recently entered into a special affiliation agreement with IAAP, but it has maintained its autonomy.

The final major international association is the International Association for Cross-Cultural Psychology (IACCP). The IACCP held its first meeting in 1972 in Hong Kong and has since organized its congresses to coincide with that of the other major psychological congresses. The primary publication of IACCP is the *Journal of Cross-Cultural Psychology,* founded by Walter Lonner in 1970. The IACCP also publishes a newsletter called the *Cross-Cultural Psychology Bulletin.*

Of the four primary international psychology groups, the IAAP is most relevant to counseling psychology because of its applied focus. Surprisingly, until 2002, counseling psychologists had limited representation in IAAP. To be sure, individual counseling psychologists such as Donald Super, Mark Savickas, Beryl Hesketh, and Paul Pedersen had actively participated in IAAP, but through the activities and auspices of other divisions. Beginning with the ICAP in 1998, Frederick Leong began to organize several counseling colleagues (e.g., Savickas, Pedersen, Gati, Young) in the IAAP. With the help of these colleagues and the support of Charles Spielberger, then president of IAAP, Leong developed a proposal for the formation of a Counseling Psychology Division. This Division was formally recognized and given provisional status in 2002, becoming Division 16 of the IAAP.

After the inception of Division 16, an executive committee (EC) was formed. The founding EC included Savickas, Gati, and Young, with Leong as president. The group began working in the summer of 2004 on the infrastructure for the Division, with an electronic newsletter as the first order of business. Mark Leach served as the first newsletter editor, and Kevin Glavin developed a web site for the Division. Leong and the EC recruited counseling psychologists from over 15 countries to serve as national liaisons to the EC. The ICAP in Athens in July 2006 served as the Inaugural Congress for the Counseling Psychology Division. A full and successful program of symposia and poster sessions was presented in Athens, with significant attendance from counseling psychologists from many countries. The Division's first Distinguished Contributions to International Counseling Psychology Award was given to Paul Pedersen for his lifelong contributions.

Several descriptions of the history and current status of the counseling profession in a wide array of countries have been published in the past few years, and three journals have published special issues on this topic. The first is the major contribution of *TCP*, edited by Leong and Blustein (2000), with five articles from different countries and commentary articles by McWhirter and Cheung. Next, Gerstein and Ægisdóttir (2005a, 2005b) edited two special journal issues in the *Journal of Mental Health Counseling*. The first issue contained articles that described the history and current status of the counseling profession in China, Taiwan, Ghana, Japan, Fiji, Turkey, India, Ukraine, and Italy. The second issue described unique counseling programs and strategies employed in Brazil, Israel, Italy, and South Korea. Finally, Leong and Savickas (2007) published a special issue in *Applied Psychology: An International Review* devoted to international perspectives on counseling psychology to celebrate the founding of the Counseling Division in the IAAP. The issue focused on the current status of and future directions for counseling psychology in the Special Administrative Region (SAR) of Hong Kong and in 10 other countries (Australia, Canada, China, India, Israel, Japan, Korea, Portugal, France, South Africa). The U.S. counseling psychology's strengths, weaknesses, opportunities, and threats in each locale were analyzed, and objectives and strategies were offered for advancing counseling psychology over the next decade. These and other international articles published in *TCP* and other U.S. journals have significantly increased information available about the state of the counseling profession around the world.

Relevant developments for counselors have also occurred in the International Association for Educational and Vocational Guidance (IAEVG), which has its own journal, international conferences, and collaborative networks (see www.iaevg.org/iaevg/index.cfm?lang=2/). Several prominent U.S. (e.g., Savickas) and Canadian (e.g., Young) counseling psychologists are active in IAEVG. The next international meeting of SVP is set to take place in conjunction with an IAEVG conference in September 2007 in Italy due to the collaborative efforts of Paul Gore (SVP), Barry Chung (National Career Development Association), and Salvatore Soresi and Laura Nota (IAEVG).

Counseling and counseling psychology professions are vigorously growing around the world. However, until the inception of Division 16 of the IAAP in 2005, there had not been an organizational structure to represent the counseling psychology profession internationally. Many professionals are currently promoting counseling psychology in their own countries, and more professional organizations are being developed to promote counseling services around the world.

CHALLENGES AND OPPORTUNITIES

As noted earlier, although initiated in the 1940s, the movement to internationalize counseling psychology in the United States only began to pick up steam over the past decade. Many messages have been sent articulating the utility of cross-cultural competence, but it has taken some time for these messages to take root. Since 2000, there has been an accelerated interest in international perspectives in U.S. counseling psychology journals, a supportive infrastructure in U.S. professional associations, growing interest in training international students, and increased cross-national communication and collaborations. Moreover, counseling and counseling psychology professions are vigorously growing around the world, with a multiplicity of professional identities, training and credentialing standards, and professional service delivery models in evidence to address a broad range of societal needs. The final section presents concluding comments about the challenges and opportunities that face the counseling psychology profession.

Challenge 1: Overcoming our Ethnocentrism

Several authors have suggested that the biggest challenges for U.S. psychologists, including counseling psychologists, is overcoming our ethnocentrism (e.g., Cheung, 2000; Gerstein, 2005; Heppner, 2006;

Leong & Blustein, 2000; Leong & Ponterotto, 2003; Marsella, 1998; McWhirter, 2000; Norsworthy, 2005; Pedersen & Leong, 1997; Segal, Lonner & Berry, 1998). During the 1980s, some counseling psychologists questioned the value of such international experiences. McWhirter (2000) wrote that "my professional colleagues were supportive and happy for me, but many could not understand why a counseling psychologist would want to take his family to Turkey for anything other than a brief tourist trip, and some even questioned that" (p. 117). It was not uncommon for the motivations of counseling psychologists interested in international topics to be questioned, with the presumption that they are "only looking for an excuse for foreign travel" (McWhirter, 2000, p. 118). Undoubtedly, such attitudes and beliefs among U.S. counseling psychologist affected the development of the international movement in the counseling profession in the past.

When we are unaware of cultural issues, it is difficult to know what we do not know; this lack of awareness significantly restricts understanding, sensitivity, and appropriate responses. Based on the U.S. multicultural literature, exposure may be an important first step in breaking down ethnocentric walls. Qualitative and single-subject methods in conjunction with quantitative designs may be useful for scholars who choose to examine ethnocentrism and ways to reduce its limiting influences (see Morrow, Rakhsha, & Castaneda, 2001, regarding qualitative research designs that can be applied to studying cross-cultural ethnocentrism).

Challenge 2: Enhancing Cross-Cultural Competence

Our historical analysis of the past 60 years suggests that the U.S. counseling psychology profession has evolved from the notion of "helping" our international colleagues and moved toward building mutually beneficial, egalitarian cross-national collaborative relationships. However, building such relationships is often a complicated and challenging process that is not well understood. As Heppner (2006) noted, "it is all too easy to offend our international colleagues, and at the same time, all too easy for us to become anxious or feel offended as well" (p. 169). Such feelings often inhibit further development of cross-national collaborative relationships. Thus, a key issue for the future of the profession is enhancing cross-cultural competence (Heppner, 2006).

A number of scholars have written about various aspects of cross-cultural competence (e.g., Heppner, 2006; Leong & Ponterotto, 2003). Marsella and Pedersen (2004) provided a wide array of suggestions for internationalizing the counseling psychology curriculum. At this point, a major challenge for U.S. counseling psychologists is not only overcoming our ethnocentrism, but also deconstructing and thereby understanding the ambiguous construct of cross-cultural competence. Cross-cultural competence is so basic and fundamental to the internationalization movement, but also so ambiguous and overwhelming at the same time. The challenge is not only to define and assess cross-cultural competence (i.e., attitudes, knowledge, awareness, and skills), but also to learn how to promote it in the next generation of counseling psychologists. Given the dearth of information on this topic, qualitative methodologies and single-subject methodology may prove useful in promoting model building.

Challenge 3: Cultural Sensitivity versus Imposed Etics in Theory Development

A number of cross-cultural psychologists have warned of the dangers associated with the monopoly and hegemony of Western models of science (e.g., Gerstein, 2005; Leong, 2002; Marsella, 1998, 2006; Norsworthy, 2005). An important challenge is to recognize that our theoretical models may work in the United States but not necessarily in other countries. Cross-cultural psychologists have labeled this ethnocentric tendency in science as *imposed etics*—the assumption that the theories and models that apply to a person's cultural group are universal and can be easily applied to other cultural groups.

There are several approaches to including a cultural context in psychological theories (Heine et al., 2004; Leong, 2002). The first is the *universalism* approach where culture is considered to be an unimportant and nuisance variable that needs little or no attention. The cultural variable is essentially ignored. This universalism approach serves as the foundation for "imposed etics." The second is the *culture assimilation* approach wherein cultural differences are recognized but minimized based on the "melting pot" assumption that other racial or cultural groups will assimilate to mainstream American culture (Western European culture). To the extent that these groups assimilate, mainstream psychological theories and models will work equally well with them. In the international realm, this implies that Western models can be transported to other cultures and that globalization will make it relatively easy for these models to be assimilated into other countries.

Leong and colleagues (Leong & Lee, 2006; Leong & Serafica, 2001; Leong & Tang, 2002) have proposed another approach, the cultural accommodation model (CAM). This model aims to identify the missing cultural elements in the Western models from a cross-cultural perspective and potential culture-specific variables that can be used to address these cultural lacunae in Western models. This model involves three steps: (1) identifying the cultural gaps or blind spots of existing Western theories and models that restrict their cultural validity, (2) selecting current culturally specific concepts and models from cross-cultural and ethnic minority psychology to fill in the cultural gaps and modify or accommodate the theory to these cultural groups, and (3) testing the culturally accommodated theory to determine if it has incremental validity beyond the culturally unaccommodated theory. Most important, the CAM model strongly suggested that psychologists as scientists should test the theory or model with demonstrated incremental validity provided by the culture-specific variables (see Quintana, Troyano, & Taylor, 2001).

A significant amount of cross-cultural research is aimed at evaluating the cultural validity of Western models when applied to other cultures. In some instances, the Western models of psychology will be found to be culturally valid and more than adequate when directly applied to cultural groups in other countries or regions. In other instances, some of the cultural validity studies will find problems and inadequacies in Western models. It is important to note that although a Western model, or a modified Western model using the CAM or any other approach, might be able to predict or explain a particular phenomenon (e.g., psychological adjustment) in another culture outside the United States, it may not necessarily depict the most important constructs to explain a particular phenomenon in that culture. Although Western-based instruments have been appropriately translated, back-translated, and predict intended outcomes in other cultures, the cultural assumptions inherent in those inventories may not necessarily include the most important psychological constructs pertaining to that phenomenon in a non-Western culture. For example, U.S.-based applied problem solving and coping inventories have been utilized in many cultures around the world. But Heppner et al. (2006) found very different coping factors when Asian values and customs were utilized to create items; these East Asian coping factors depicted other psychological constructs that do not appear in U.S. models.

In short, the underlying cultural assumptions in *both* the Western models as well as the target culture must be adequately addressed in applying any psychological models from one culture to another. Thus, another approach is to first identify constructs and build theoretical models based on the cultural assumptions and customs of that particular culture, and then examine how Western-based constructs (and their underlying values) that have been particularly useful in the United States might add to a particular cultural model. This approach is more in line with the development of indigenous models to explain psychological phenomena in a particular culture (see next challenge) and similar to the derived etic method in cross-cultural psychology research (Berry, 1989). In short, identifying the match underlying the assumptions/cultural values of both cultures is a critical step to becoming culturally sensitive in cross-cultural theory development.

Just as we cannot assume that a Western theory of counseling is automatically going to work for other cultural groups, we cannot assume that certain culture-specific variables being added in any approach are automatically going to improve the cultural validity of the theory in question (Ægisdóttir, Gerstein, & Canel, in press). It is quite conceivable that different versions of a culturally sensitive model will have to be tested before the best set of variables can be found. The major foci and challenge for counseling psychology cross-cultural research is to develop knowledge bases and to interpret what we have observed in a culturally sensitive and appropriate way.

Challenge 4: Supporting and Extending Indigenous Psychologies

Related to the need to avoid imposed etics, there has been a movement in cross-cultural psychology that calls for the support of *indigenous psychologies* as a countervailing force to the wholesale exportation of Western models of psychology to other parts of the world (Kim & Berry, 1993). A quote from Durgan and Sinha (1993) in a chapter on indigenous psychology in India captures the essence of the problem quite well:

> When modern scientific psychology, based on the empirical, mechanistic, and materialistic orientations of the West, was imported into India as part of the general transfer of knowledge, it came in as a ready made intellectual package in the first decade of the century.... In fact, this transfer in a way constituted an element of the political domination of the West over the third world countries in the general process of modernization and Westernization.... Research conducted was by and large repetitive and replicative in character, the object being to supplement studies done in the West.... Thus, the discipline remained at best a pale copy of Western psychology, rightly designated as a Euro-American product with very little concern with social reality as it prevailed in India. (p. 31)

With the increasing internationalization of U.S. counseling psychology, it is incumbent on us not only to examine the cultural relevance of our models of counseling in other countries but also to support the identification, development, and evaluation of indigenous models of helping as potentially equally valid ways of healing. Indeed, many of these indigenous models predate Western models of counseling and psychotherapy. We also have much to gain by testing the generalizability of the knowledge and theories developed in other countries to U.S. populations. Our international colleagues have developed tremendous knowledge bases through their research and practice spanning hundreds and thousands of years. Ponterotto (Chapter 8, this volume) addresses the potential utility for U.S. counseling psychologists to apply knowledge on the *multicultural personality* that has been developed in the Netherlands. Moreover, the culturally related knowledge from other countries has the potential to help us conceptualize novel intervention strategies to address old problems. For example, the collectivistic-based school counseling program (Chao, Wang, & Yang, 2006) in Taiwan has tremendous potential for U.S. school counselors. Our challenge is to identify relevant knowledge bases developed in other countries and test their applicability to solving problems in the United States.

Challenge 5: Promoting the Integration of Multicultural and Cross-Cultural Foci

American counseling psychologists need to promote the integration and coexistence of multicultural and cross-cultural foci. In the past, there has been some tension between psychologists engaged in the U.S. multicultural movement and those engaged in cross-national activities. Sometimes the tension seems to result from the belief that a focus on cross-cultural issues will diminish or detract from a focus on multicultural issues, or vice versa. Henderson, Spigner-Littles, and Milhouse (2006) cited the necessity of understanding both indigenous and foreign cultures, "if practitioners are to understand traditional African Americans, Chinese Americans, Japanese Americans, and Mexican Americans, they must first understand traditional African, Chinese, Japanese, and Mexican cultures" (p. vii). A common goal of both foci is to promote the understanding of the role of culture in human behavior, and the absolute necessity of utilizing a cultural context in all aspects of our work as counseling psychologists. An increased sensitivity to the role of culture in understanding human behavior makes us better counseling psychologists. It is incumbent on scholars to demonstrate how multicultural and cross-cultural foci can build on and enrich one another in the service of common goals.

Challenge 6: Promoting Cross-National Research Collaborations

Time and space have shrunk, making communication and travel across national borders commonplace. At this time, U.S. counseling psychologists often travel to different countries; learn from others' models, worldviews, and experiences; and work collaboratively with international colleagues. It is more than abundantly clear that human beings' emotions, cognitive functions, motivations, reasoning, problem solving, and many other psychological constructs are learned, displayed, and interpreted in cultural contexts. Cross-cultural research has the potential to greatly enhance the knowledge bases in our specialty. Moreover, as responsible and culturally sensitive researchers, we need to obtain data from more international samples (Gerstein & Ægisdóttir, 2005a) to expand our knowledge bases.

It has been almost 30 years since the first call for diverse methodologies (Gelso, 1979), which has had a significant impact on counseling psychology (Heppner, Wampold, & Kivlighan, 2008). We envision another methodological revolution, one that will spark a fundamental change in the way we structure research questions and ideas, as well as conduct and evaluate research. Future researchers will constantly consult and collaborate with their international colleagues to exchange the latest research findings, formulate their research ideas in multinational research teams, collect data from many different countries, and discuss their results across various cultural contexts. Their papers will be reviewed by U.S. and international editors and reviewers.

The challenge for the counseling profession is how to promote and conduct meaningful cross-national research and create cross-cultural knowledge bases in counseling psychology. Two strategies to promote cross-cultural knowledge are by composing cross-national research teams and by conducting research on immigrant or international populations in the United States. The different cultural assumptions among members of international research teams can create obstacles and challenges (see Heppner, 2006). International research collaboration involves time, energy, and a good deal of relationship development. Research team members with different cultural perspectives may require more cross-cultural problem solving. As with domestic research teams, it is essential to start with networking and relationship building to get to know potential research collaborators.

There is a need for more information about what factors promote successful cross-national research. One strategy is to identify "best practices" by studying cross-national research teams that have been more and less effective. Another strategy is to study "best practices" in training the next generation of cross-national researchers in our graduate programs. It might also be useful to study successful cross-national researchers to identify effective coping strategies, communication styles, and personality variables. We need to know much more about the factors that promote successful cross-national research teams.

Challenge 7: Promoting Culturally Valid Practice around the Globe

Counseling practitioners worldwide often find inspiring new ideas from their foreign peers. Tai Chi and meditation are accepted as being therapeutic by a larger audience in the United States more now than 10 years ago. There is currently an active exchange of practical experiences with cohorts from different countries. There is a growing interest by U.S. researchers in the mental health and career needs in several Asian countries, most notably China. There is also interest in exporting U.S. counseling knowledge, philosophy, and techniques to China. However, we are responsible for ensuring that our knowledge, philosophy, and techniques are culturally relevant in different environments (see Leong & Lee, 2006 and also Challenge 3). Practice developments in counseling can greatly facilitate understanding of how culture affects the counseling process and outcomes across different cultures. A major challenge is not only to internationalize U.S. counseling practice, but also to validate, present, and publish research on the utility of cross-cultural practice.

Challenge 8: Enhancing and Promoting International Education

There are a number of unaddressed questions about the type of training that is best for international students. Most if not all of the APA-accredited doctoral programs train students in U.S.-based assessment models, counseling theories, and intervention strategies. Although the multicultural movement has broadened the U.S. training model overall, it remains a Western model based on Western values. Some colleagues maintain that international students enrolled in U.S. training programs should be able to counsel effectively in the United States and, indeed, some international graduates do seek employment in the United States. But should the mission of our training programs be bound to U.S. culture alone, or should it include the ability to work in other cultures? Should we have additional or different training goals for students intending to return to their home countries? Are these students expected to attain the same level of skill using Western counseling methods as U.S. students? Should an Asian international student who plans to return to his or her country also learn how to confront a client in ways that include relevant Asian values (e.g., interpersonal harmony)? One challenge facing the counseling profession pertains to the training goals for international students who plan to return to their home countries, or who have different worldviews and interpersonal styles that fit an individualistic culture more or less well.

A related challenge pertains to understanding how international students can promote the understanding of cultural differences and sensitivity in our training programs. A recent study found that 90% of counselor educators sampled agreed that the cross-cultural perspectives of international counseling students had positively enriched their program, and 83% agreed that working with international counseling students had positively affected them personally and professionally (Ng, 2006). We believe that we could learn much more from the international students currently enrolled on our campuses (see Heppner, 2006). Sometimes the learning in our training programs is perceived as primarily a unidirectional process (from instructor to student) as opposed to a bidirectional process where international students and U.S. students and faculty learn about cross-cultural issues from their interactions and discussions throughout the educational process. Moreover, having good relationships between domestic and international students today means networking with international leaders tomorrow. Promoting meaningful linkages between our domestic and international students may contribute to the internationalization of our profession. Thus, a related challenge for U.S. training programs is to identify ways to benefit maximally from the diverse cross-cultural awareness, knowledge, and skills that currently exist in many counselor training programs.

Finally, there is much to gain from U.S. graduate students studying abroad (e.g., see Alexander et al., 2005). There are many ways for students to learn from our international colleagues, such as workshops, brief 2-week immersions, semester- or year-long study abroad experiences, and dual-degree programs. Similar to the reports from Fulbright scholars, students report that their cross-cultural learning experiences are not only stimulating, but also sometimes transforming (e.g., Friedlander et al., 2002). But why are so few counseling psychology graduate students studying abroad? (J. Ponterotto, personal communication, February 22, 2007). Our challenge is to internationalize the training curriculum by developing effective cross-cultural learning opportunities for U.S. students in counseling psychology.

Challenge 9: Collaboration among Counseling Organizations

In analyzing the recent history of U.S. counseling psychology, Heppner et al. (2000) concluded, "the profession has now evolved beyond any one organization. Collaboration among Division 17, CCPTP [Council of Counseling Psychology Training Programs], ACCTA [Association of Counseling Center Training Agencies], and other groups has been and will continue to be critically important in the future" (p. 37). Yet collaboration only among U.S.-based counseling organizations will not be sufficient in the future. Rather, it will be increasingly important to collaborate across counseling organizations around the globe—"there are common elements in the development of counseling psychology across national boundaries, and the voices of counseling psychology leaders from one country can support and lend credence [in] another country" (Heppner, 2006, p. 168). We have much to share and learn from each other's experiences. The challenge is how to overcome cross-cultural obstacles to promote collaboration among counseling organizations around the world. It is incumbent on counseling leaders to understand the many benefits of such collaboration and to build the necessary organizational structures to promote global alliances.

CONCLUSION

In the process of writing this chapter, we originally thought about using 10 final recommendations for the future of the profession; 10 is a nice "round number," and a list of 10 recommendations is often seen as a good ending point in the United States. Although Chinese people do use phrases to describe the number 10 as perfect, they rarely use the number to end their work for several reasons. So we borrowed a Chinese belief that nine is the best and the luckiest number (e.g., there are often nine dragons in symbols on Chinese temples and walls) and used only nine challenges. Another Chinese belief is that nothing is perfect; there is always some space to improve the work. Thus, we end with nine challenges to indicate that there is much left to be done to internationalize U.S. counseling psychology.

Andre Gide, winner of the 1947 Nobel Prize in Literature, wrote. "Man [sic] cannot discover new oceans unless he has the courage to lose sight of the shore." Over 25 years ago, professional leaders proposed that multicultural counseling competencies were essential for future counseling psychologists (e.g., Sue, 1982). Recent history indicates those early visionaries were quite correct. The globalization of the twenty-first century demands that cross-cultural competencies will also be essential to the future of counseling psychology.

What our students learn today is mostly U.S.-based psychology and counseling psychology. Although this type of training has been successful in the past, it will not be sufficient in the future. Multiculturally and cross-culturally competent counseling psychologists are necessary to promote the cause of social justice (see Marsella, 2006). Although the next 25 years promise to be an exciting time for counseling psychology (Heppner, 2006), it will be necessary to take risks as we move into unchartered waters and "lose sight of the shore."

The internationalization of counseling psychology reflects global trends and societal needs, but does not signify a fusion of all cultures and knowledge. In the process of internationalizing U.S. counseling psychology, we can better recognize our own identities, boundaries, strengths, and limitations, as well as those of our international colleagues. We can learn from our international colleagues' indigenous perspectives, research, and counseling practice and work collaboratively to integrate the existing knowledge and create new global perspectives. Counseling psychologists in the future will collect knowledge from all corners of the world and put the puzzle together as an extraordinary picture of a worldwide psychology. Without a doubt, we cannot do this without each other's collective work. "This type of knowledge and psychological understanding of human behavior will be maximally useful to practitioners and researchers" (Leong & Blustein, 2000, p. 6). The whole will be greater than the sum of its parts (Sabourin, 2001).

REFERENCES

Ægisdóttir, S., Gerstein, L. H., & Canel, D. (in press). Methodological issues in cross-cultural counseling research: Equivalence, bias and translations. *Counseling Psychologist.*

Alexander, C. M., Kruczek, T., & Ponterotto, J. G. (2005). Building multicultural competencies in school counselor trainees: An immersion experience. *Counselor Education and Supervision, 44,* 255–266.

Altbach, P. G., & Lewis, L. S. (1998). *Internationalism and insularity: American faculty and the world.* Retrieved January, 25, 2007, from www.findarticles.com/p/articles/mi_m1254/is_n1_v30/ai_21162837.

American Psychological Association. (2003). Guidelines on multicultural education, training, research, practice, and organization change for psychologists. *American Psychologist, 58,* 377–402.

Ardila, R. (1993). Latin American psychology and world psychology. In U. Kim & J. Berry (Eds.), *Indigenous psychologies* (pp. 170–176). Newbury Park, CA: Sage.

Berry, J. W. (1989). Imposed etics-emics-derived etics: The operationalization of a compelling idea. *International Journal of Psychology, 24,* 721–735.

Blocher, D. H. (2000). *The evolution of counseling psychology.* New York: Springer.

Borgen, F. H. (1984). Counseling psychology. *Annual Review of Psychology, 35,* 579–604.

Chao, H. M., Wang, L. F., & Yang, K. U. (2006). Program evaluation of counseling psychology services in elementary schools. *Bulletin of Educational Psychology, 37,* 345–365.

Cheung, F. M. (1998). Cross-cultural psychopathology. In C. Belar (Ed.), *Comprehensive clinical psychology: Vol. 10. Sociocultural and individual differences* (pp. 35–51). Oxford: Pergamon.

Cheung, F. M. (2000). Deconstructing counseling in a cultural context. *Counseling Psychologist, 28,* 123–132.

Davis, J. (2000). Four international organizations in Psychology: An overview. *Eye on Psi Chi, 4,* 33–37.

Douce, L. A. (2004). Globalization of counseling psychology. *Counseling Psychologist, 32,* 142–152.

Faragher, J. M., Buhle, M. J., Czitrom, D., & Armitage, S. H. (1997). *Out of many: A history of American people.* Upper Saddle River, NJ: Prentice-Hall.

Fong, S. C. (2006). *Imagination, openness, courage* (Presidential address for the first hundred years of university education in Singapore). Retrieved January 25, 2007, from www.nus.edu.sg/vco/speeches/2006/pdf/IOC_Prof_Shih.pdf.

Fretz, B. R. (1985). New editor's introduction. *Counseling Psychologist, 13,* 3–10.

Friedlander, M. L., Carranza, V. E., & Guzman, M. (2002). International exchanges in family therapy: Training, research, and practice in Spain and United States. *Counseling Psychologist, 30,* 314–329.

Friedman, T. L. (2005). *The world is flat: A brief history of the twenty-first century.* New York: Farrar, Straus & Giroux.

Gelso, C. J. (1979). Research in counseling: Methodological and professional issues. *Counseling Psychologist, 8,* 7–35.

Gerstein, L. H. (2005). Counseling psychologists as international social architects. In R. L. Toporek, L. H. Gerstein, N. A. Fouad, G. Roysircar-Sodowsky, & T. Israel (Eds.), *Handbook for social justice in counseling psychology: Leadership, vision, and action* (pp. 377–387). Thousand Oaks, CA: Sage.

Gerstein, L.H., & Ægisdóttir, S. (2005a). Counseling around the world. *Journal of Mental Health Counseling, 27,* 95–184.

Gerstein, L. H., & Ægisdóttir, S. (2005b). Counseling outside of the United States: Looking in and reaching out! *Journal of Mental Health Counseling, 27,* 221–281.

Hedlund, D. E. (1988). Counseling psychology and the Zambian Fulbright program. *Counseling Psychologist, 16,* 288–292.

Heine, S. J., & Lehman, D. R. (2004). Move the Body, Change the Self: Acculturative Effects of the Self-Concept. In M., Schaller, & C. S. Crandall (Eds.), *The psychological foundations of culture* (pp. 305–331). Mahwah, NJ: Erlbaum.

Henderson, G., Spigner-Littles, D., & Milhouse, V. H. (2006). *A practitioner's guide to understanding indigenous and foreign cultures: An analysis of relationships between ethnicity, social class, and therapeutic intervention strategies.* Springfield, IL: Thomas.

Heppner, P. P. (1988). Cross-cultural outcomes of a research Fulbright in Sweden. *Counseling Psychologist, 16,* 297–302.

Heppner, P. P. (Ed.). (1990). *Pioneers in counseling and human development: Personal and professional perspectives.* Washington, DC: American Association of Counseling and Development.

Heppner, P. P. (1997). Building on strengths as we move into the next millennium. *Counseling Psychologist, 25,* 5–14.

Heppner, P. P. (2006). The benefits and challenges of becoming cross-culturally competent counseling psychologists. *Counseling Psychologist, 34,* 147–172.

Heppner, P. P., Casas, J. M., Carter, J., & Stone, G. L. (2000). The maturation of counseling psychology: Multifaceted perspectives from 1978–1998. In S. D. Brown & R. W. Lent (Eds.), *Handbook of counseling psychology* (3rd ed. pp. 3–49). New York: Wiley.

Heppner, P. P., Fouad, N. A., & Hansen, N. (Eds.). (2002). *First and second generation pioneers in the counseling profession: Personal and professional perspectives.* Columbia, MO: MU Custom Publishing.

Heppner, P. P., & Gerstein, L. H. (in press). International developments in counseling psychology. In F. T. L. Leong (Ed.), *Encyclopedia of counseling psychology*. Thousand Oaks, CA: Sage.

Heppner, P. P., Heppner, M. J., Lee, D.-G., Wang, Y.-W., Park, H.-J., & Wang, L.-F. (2006). Development and validation of a collectivistic coping styles inventory. *Journal of Counseling Psychology, 53*, 107–125.

Heppner, P. P., Wampold, B. E., & Kivlighan, D., Jr. (2008). *Research design in counseling* (3rd ed.) Pacific Grove, CA: Brooks/Cole.

Kim, U., & Berry, J.W. (Eds.). (1993). *Indigenous psychologies: Research and experiences in cultural contexts*. Newbury Park, CA: Sage.

Lent, R. W., Brown, S. D., Nota, L., & Soresi, S. (2003). Testing social cognitive interest and choice hypotheses across Holland types in Italian high school students. *Journal of Vocational Behavior, 62*, 101–118.

Lent, R. W., Tracey, T. J. G., Brown, S. D., Soresi, S., & Nota, L. (2006). Development of interests and competency beliefs in Italian adolescents: An exploration of circumplex structure and bidirectional relationships. *Journal of Counseling Psychology, 53*, 181–191.

Leong, F. T. L. (2002). Challenges for career counseling in Asia: Variations in cultural accommodation. *Career Development Quarterly, 50*, 277–284.

Leong, F. T. L., & Blustein, D. L. (2000). Toward a global vision of counseling psychology. *Counseling Psychologist, 28*, 5–9.

Leong, F. T. L., & Lee, S. H. (2006). A cultural accommodation model of psychotherapy: Illustrated with the case of Asian-Americans. *Psychotherapy: Theory, Research, Practice, and Training, 43*, 410–423.

Leong, F. T. L., & Ponterotto, J. G. (2003). A proposal for internationalizing counseling psychology in the United States: Rationale, recommendations, and challenges. *Counseling Psychologist, 31*, 381–395.

Leong, F. T. L., & Santago-Riveria, A. L. (1999) Climbing the multiculturalism summit: Challenges and pitfalls. In P. Pedersen (Ed.), *Multiculturalism as a fourth force* (pp. 61–74). Philadelphia: Brunner/Mazel.

Leong, F. T. L., & Savickas, M. L. (2007). Introduction to special issue on international perspectives on counseling psychology. *Applied Psychology: An International Review, 56*, 1–6.

Leong, F. T. L., & Serafica, F. (2001). Cross-cultural perspectives on Super's career development theory: Career maturity and cultural accommodation. In F. T. L. Leong & A. Barak (Eds.), *Contemporary models in vocational psychology: A volume in honor of Samuel H. Osipow* (pp. 167–205). Mahwah, NJ: Erlbaum.

Leong, F. T. L., & Tang, M. (2002). A cultural accommodation approach to career assessment with Asian Americans. In K. Kurasaki, S. Sue, & S. Okazaki (Eds.), *Asian American mental health: Assessment, theories and methods* (pp. 265–281). Dordrecht, The Netherlands: Kluwer Press.

Leung, S. A. (2003). A journey worth traveling: Globalization of counseling psychology. *Counseling Psychologist, 31*, 412–419.

Magrath, C. P. (1993). *Comments to the Board on Home Economics on November 12, 1993*. Washington, DC: National Association of State Universities and Land-Grant Colleges.

Marsella, A. J. (1998). Toward a "Global-Community Psychology": Meeting the needs of a changing world. *American Psychologist, 53*, 1282–1291.

Marsella, A. J. (2006). Justice in a global age: Becoming counselors to the world. *Counselling Psychology Quarterly, 19*, 121–132.

Marsella, A. J., & Pedersen, P. (2004). Internationalizing the counseling psychology curriculum: Toward new values, competencies, and directions. *Counseling Psychology Quarterly, 17*, 413–423.

McWhirter, J. J. (1988). The Fulbright program in counseling psychology. *Counseling Psychologist, 16*, 279–281.

McWhirter, J. J. (2000). And now, up go the walls: Constructing an international room for counseling psychology. *Counseling Psychologist, 28*, 117–122.

Morrow, S. L., Rakhsha, G., & Castaneda, C. L. (2001). Qualitative research methods for multicultural counseling. In J. G. Ponterotto, J. M. Casas, L. A. Suzuki, & C. M. Alexander (Eds.), *Handbook of multicultural counseling* (pp. 575–603). Thousand Oaks, CA: Sage.

Ng, K. (2006). Counselor educators' perceptions of and experiences with international students. *International Journal for the Advancement of Counselling, 28*, 1–19.

Norsworthy, K. L. (2005). Bringing social justice to international practices of counseling psychology. In R.L. Toporek, L.H. Gerstein, N.A. Fouad, G. Roysircar-Sodowsky, & T. Israel (Eds.), *Handbook for social justice in counseling psychology: Leadership, vision, and action* (pp. 421–441). Thousand Oaks, CA: Sage.

Nugent, F. A. (1988). Counseling psychology and the west German Fulbright program. *Counseling Psychologist, 16*, 293–296.

Nutt, R. L. (2006). Implications of globalization for training in counseling psychology. *Counseling Psychologist, 35*, 157–171.

Pawlik, K., & Rosenzweig, M. R. (Eds.). (2000). *International handbook of psychology.* Thousand Oaks, CA: Sage.

Pedersen, P. B. (1991). Multiculturalism as a generic approach to counseling. *Journal of Counseling and Development, 70*, 6–12.

Pedersen, P. B. (Ed.). (1999). *Multiculturalism as a fourth force.* Philadelphia: Taylor & Francis.

Pedersen, P. B. (2003). Culturally biased assumptions in counseling psychology. *Counseling Psychologist, 31*, 396–403.

Pedersen, P. B. (2005). Foreword. In R. Moodley & W. West (Eds.), *Integrating traditional healing practices into counseling and psychotherapy* (pp. xi–xii). Thousand Oaks, CA: Sage.

Pedersen, P. B., & Leong, F. (1997). Counseling in an international context. *Counseling Psychologist, 25*, 117–122.

Quintana, S. M., Troyano, N., & Taylor, G. (2001). Cultural validity and inherent challenges in quantitative methods for multicultural research. In J. G. Ponterotto, J. M. Casas, L. A. Suzuki, & C. M. Alexander (Eds.), *Handbook of multicultural counseling* (pp. 604–630). Thousand Oaks, CA: Sage.

Rogers, C. (1942). *Counseling and psychotherapy: Newer concepts in practice.* Boston: Houghton Mifflin.

Sabourin, M. (2001). International psychology: Is the whole greater than the sum of its parts? *Canadian Psychology/Psychologie Canadienne, 42*, 74–81.

Savickas, M. L. (in press). Helping people choose jobs: A history of the vocational guidance profession. In R. Van Esbroeck & J. Athanasou (Eds.), *International handbook of career guidance.* New York: Springer.

Scott, C. W. (1980). History of the division of counseling psychology: 1945–1963. In J. M. Whiteley (Ed.), *The history of counseling psychology* (pp. 25–40). Monterey, CA: Brooks/Cole.

Segall, M. H., Lonner, W. J., & Berry, J. W. (1998). Cross-cultural psychology as a scholarly discipline: On a flowering of culture in behavioral research. *American Psychologist, 53*, 1101–1110.

Sinha, D. (1993). Indigenization of psychology in India and its relevance. In U. Kim & J. W. Berry (Eds.), *Indigenous psychologies: Research and experiences in cultural contexts* (pp. 30–43). Newbury Park, CA: Sage.

Skovholt, T. M. (1988). Searching for reality. *Counseling Psychologist, 16*, 282–287.

Skovholt, T. M., Hansen, S., Goh, M., Romano, J., & Thomas, K. (2005). The Minnesota International Counseling Institute (MICI) 1989-present: History, joyful moments, and lessons learned. *International Journal for the Advancement of Counseling, 27*, 17–33.

Soresi, S., Nota, L., & Lent, R. W. (2004). Relation of type and amount of training to career counseling self-efficacy in Italy. *Career Development Quarterly, 52*, 194–201.

Sue, D. W. (1982). Position paper: Cross-cultural counseling competencies. *Counseling Psychologist, 10*, 45–52.

Sue, D. W., & Sue, D. (1990). *Counseling the culturally different: Theory and practice* (2nd ed.). New York: Wiley.

Tracey, T. J. G., Lent, R. W., Brown, S. D., Soresi, S., & Nota, L. (2006). Adherence to RIASEC structure in relation to career exploration and parenting style: Longitudinal and idiothetic considerations. *Journal of Vocational Behavior, 69*, 248–261.

Whiteley, J. M. (1980). *Counseling psychology: A historical perspective.* Schenectady, NY: Character Research Press.

Williamson, E. G. (1939). *How to counsel students: A manual of techniques for clinical counselors.* New York: McGraw-Hill.

Wrenn, C. G. (1962). *The counselor in a changing world.* Washington, DC: American Personnel and Guidance Association.

Wrenn, C. G. (1966). Birth and early childhood of a journal. *Journal of Counseling Psychology, 13*, 485–488.

CHAPTER 6

The Interface of Counseling Psychology and Positive Psychology: Assessing and Promoting Strengths

SHANE J. LOPEZ
LISA M. EDWARDS

Counseling psychology's tradition of studying and promoting the best in people was forged more than 50 years ago. As counseling psychology emerged from its vocational psychology roots, Donald Super (1955) called for a subdiscipline of psychology that would help all people make the most of their resources. The subscription to a strengths philosophy was evident at the second national conference on counseling psychology in 1964 when Division 17 members, reexamining the self-definition and standards of the profession, suggested that the "special emphases [of counseling psychologists] are on the appraisal and use of assets for furthering individual development" (Thompson & Super, 1964, pp. 3–4).

During the final half of the twentieth century, counseling psychology's "focus on people's assets and strengths, and on positive mental health, regardless of the degree of disturbance" (Gelso & Fretz, 2001, p. 6) was firmly established as one of the major unifying themes of the profession. In the past 10 years, counseling psychology has been recognized as a bona fide specialty with a "focus on healthy aspects and strengths of the client" (Commission for the Recognition of Specialties and Proficiencies in Professional Psychology [CRSPPP], n.d., ¶4; also see Gelso & Fretz, 2001). Indeed, the specialty has a record of scholarship examining human strengths and positive life outcomes (Lopez, Magyar-Moe, et al., 2006) and a philosophy of practice that capitalizes on clients' assets (Sox-Harris, Thoresen, & Lopez, in press; Uffelman, 2006).

The rigorous study of what is right and positive about people also has attracted the attention of other social scientists and of the general public during this early part of the twenty-first century. In this chapter, we first define positive psychology and describe its purview, citing counseling psychology-relevant topics that have been the focus of recent theory and research (e.g., positive emotions and traits). We then discuss promising tools for assessing, and methods for promoting, psychological strengths. The chapter concludes with a critique of strengths-based work and a discussion of future directions for counseling and positive psychology research and practice focused on strengths. Because it is not possible to survey all positive psychology scholarship in this chapter, we refer readers to other sources for more extensive coverage of particular topics (e.g., Lopez, in press; Lopez & Snyder, 2003; Peterson & Seligman, 2004; Snyder & Lopez, 2002, 2007).

POSITIVE PSYCHOLOGY

The term *positive psychology* first appeared in Abraham Maslow's (1954) final chapter of *Motivation and Personality*. He used the term in an aspirational manner, describing the makeup of a fully functioning person and of the field, humanistic psychology, poised to foster optimal human development. The term resurfaced in 1998 when Martin Seligman, then president-elect of the American Psychological Association (APA), described a positive psychology initiative, or the "scientific pursuit of optimal human functioning." Seligman argued that societal changes, the development of Veterans Administration hospitals, and the focus of federal research funding fueled a dramatic shift toward psychologists studying and treating mental illness (see Seligman & Csikszentmihalyi, 2000). In Seligman's view, mid-twentieth century psychologists transformed from professionals interested in helping people identify and improve meaningful and productive areas in their lives to professionals who almost entirely ignored individual strengths and virtues, in lieu of pathology, weakness, and damage. A positive psychology initiative, Seligman suggested, would serve to augment "negative" psychology as well as to help psychologists reclaim areas of scholarly inquiry and practice associated with optimal functioning.

Since the 1998 reintroduction of *positive psychology*, the term has been used with little precision and it now means many things to many people (as suggested by a cursory scan of the 855 references on PsycInfo and 10.3 million hits in a Google search); it describes a movement, a philosophy, a science, a practice, and a professional specialty. In our own writings, we have generally stayed true to the parsimonious 1998 definition (Lopez, in press; Lopez & Snyder, 2003; Snyder & Lopez, 2002, 2007): Positive psychology is the scientific and practical pursuit of optimal human functioning. A related definition appears on the Positive Psychology Center web site; "Positive Psychology is the scientific study of the strengths and virtues that enable individuals and communities to thrive" (www.ppc.sas.upenn.edu, retrieved November 14, 2006). Yet both definitions (a) fail to acknowledge the breadth of work focusing on what is right with people, (b) do not reference positive emotions, and (c) give only passing mention, at best, to the social aspects of optimal functioning and the positive functioning of institutions and communities.

Positive Traits and Emotions

When framing positive psychology, Seligman went beyond his definition and identified topics that mainstream psychological science had neglected—positive individual traits, positive emotions, and positive institutions. Based on our review of the articles in the *Journal of Positive Psychology* (since its inception in January 2005) and topics represented in positive psychology handbooks addressing assessment, research methods, practice, and current theories and models, scholarship related to two of these topics—positive traits and positive emotions—have yielded new programs of research and a wealth of findings. Indeed, a review of the contents in positive psychology textbooks (e.g., Peterson, 2006; Snyder & Lopez, 2007) reveals that positive personal traits such as hope, optimism, self-efficacy, emotional intelligence, wisdom, and courage, and more generally, humans strengths, have received the most attention from social scientists. Current positive emotions research, though quite fruitful and informative, is somewhat dominated by debates over the makeup of personal happiness and emerging theories about happiness (Lyubomirsky, Sheldon, & Schkade, 2005). Positive personal and interpersonal experiences, such as attachment, flow, spirituality, and mindfulness also have garnered attention. The third topic, positive institutions, has not yet attracted as much attention as the other two (Gable & Haidt, 2005).

In subsequent sections of this chapter, we discuss how the *sine qua non* of positive traits, human strengths, are measured and promoted. First, this section provides examples of important work focused on positive emotions. Our discussion of positive emotions is limited to the scholarship that examines how experiences of emotions such as joy, contentment, and interest stimulate coping, building of resources, and success across life domains.

Fredrickson's (2000, 2001, 2002) broaden and build model of positive emotions highlights the social and cognitive effects of positive emotional experiences. In testing her theoretical model over several studies, Fredrickson demonstrated that the experience of joy expands the realm of what a person feels like doing at a particular point in time—this is referred to as the *broadening* of an individual's thought-action repertoire. Following an emotion-eliciting film clip (the clips induced one of five emotions: joy, contentment, anger, fear, or a neutral condition eliciting neither positive or negative emotions), research participants were asked to list everything they would like to do at that moment. Those participants who experienced joy or contentment listed significantly more desired possibilities than did the people in the neutral or negative conditions.

It appears that through the effects of broadening processes, positive emotions also can help to *build* resources. Fredrickson and Joiner (2002) demonstrated this building phenomenon by assessing people's positive and negative emotions and broad-minded coping (solving problems with creative means) on two occasions, 5 weeks apart. The researchers found that initial levels of positive emotions predicted increases in creative problem solving that predicted further increases in positive emotion. This reciprocal cycle held true only for positive emotions, and *not* for negative emotions. Therefore, positive emotions such as joy may help to generate resources and maintain a sense of vital energy (i.e., more positive emotions). This theoretical model could inform new approaches to counseling individuals, couples, families, teams, and work groups.

Lyubomirsky, King, and Diener (2005) performed a meta-analysis examining the relationship between positive affect and success. These authors hypothesized that positive affect, the hallmark of happy people, actually engenders success (e.g., enjoyment of work, income, and social support) or behaviors paralleling success (e.g., physical well-being, coping, creativity). Lyubomirsky, King, et al. (2005) reviewed (a) cross-sectional studies to examine the correlation between positive affect and success or behaviors paralleling success, (b) longitudinal studies to test whether positive affect precedes success or behaviors paralleling success, and (c) experimental studies to assess whether positive affect leads to success or behaviors paralleling success. Consistent with their hypotheses, they concluded that positive affect is related to success across major life domains such as productive work ($r = .27$), satisfying relationships ($r = .27$), and good health ($r = .32$), as well as behaviors paralleling success such as prosocial behavior ($r = .32$), coping ($r = .34$), and immune functioning ($r = .26$). They also found from longitudinal studies that positive affect precedes many of these successful outcomes in particular domains, such as work ($r = .24$), relationships ($r = .21$), and mental and physical health ($r = .18$ for both). Finally, experimental studies suggest that positive affect can cause behaviors paralleling success such as sociability ($r = .51$), effective problem resolution skills ($r = .33$), and original thinking ($r = .25$). This work suggests that positive affect is linked to substantive outcomes in domains that counseling psychologists are most interested in, such as academic achievement and retention and occupational engagement and productivity.

Positive psychology is a robust area of inquiry that goes beyond Seligman's framework and that recently has spurred the development of new theories, measures, and change strategies. We next turn to research and practice on human strengths, the positive traits alluded to in Seligman's framework for positive psychology. We believe this work may resonate with most counseling psychologists. In the next two sections, we first describe the most comprehensive classifications and measures of strengths and then discuss strategies for promoting strengths.

ASSESSING HUMAN STRENGTHS

The past decade has seen much fruitful work on the assessment of human strengths. Two comprehensive measures of strengths are now available online at little or no cost. One measure, the Clifton Strengths-Finder (Buckingham & Clifton, 2000; Lopez, Hodges, & Harter, 2005), is based on a platform of 34 talent themes that are prevalent in society and predictive of educational and vocational success. The other, the Values in Action Inventory of Strengths (VIA-IS; Peterson & Seligman, 2004), is based on the belief that strengths are the lived manifestations of virtues and are associated with well-being; it measures 24 character strengths. We review each of them in this section.

Clifton StrengthsFinder

The development of the Clifton StrengthsFinder began with Donald Clifton. During his 50-year career, Clifton studied success across a wide variety of business and education domains (Buckingham &

Clifton, 2000; Clifton & Anderson, 2002; Clifton & Nelson, 1992). He believed that talents could be operationalized, studied, and accentuated in work and academic settings. He viewed *strengths* as extensions of talent. More precisely, the strength construct combines talent with associated knowledge and skills and is defined as the ability to provide consistent, near-perfect performance in a specific task. Clifton identified personal talents using empirically based, semi-structured interviews, which led to the creation of a structured measure of talent in the 1990s.

Based on earlier interview data, Clifton identified about three dozen talent themes. The resulting Clifton StrengthsFinder presents, in an online format (www.strengthsfinder.com), 180-item pairs designed to measure 34 talent themes (Buckingham & Clifton, 2000; Lopez et al., 2005). It is appropriate for administration with adolescents and adults with reading levels of 10th grade or higher and is available in 17 languages. Although it is used to identify personal talents, the supporting materials are intended to help individuals discover how to build on their talents in particular life roles (e.g., Buckingham & Clifton, 2000; Clifton & Anderson, 2002; Clifton & Nelson, 1992).

The Clifton StrengthsFinder provides information on an individual's Five Signature Themes—the five themes on which he or she scored highest. Remaining themes are not rank ordered or shared with respondents. These data are provided to foster intrapersonal development. However, this instrument is not designed or validated for use in employee selection or mental health screening, nor is it sensitive to change and, thus, it should not be used as a pre-post measure of growth.

Extensive psychometric research on the Clifton StrengthsFinder was conducted by Gallup researchers and summarized in a technical report by Lopez et al. (2005). Across samples, most scales (i.e., themes) have been found to yield acceptable internal consistency and test-retest reliability estimates over periods ranging from 3 weeks to 17 months. In a college student sample, the mean test-retest reliability estimate (with an 8- to 12-week interval) across the 34 themes was .70 (Schreiner, 2005). In terms of validity, intercorrelations among the themes suggest that they are relatively independent of one another. Preliminary construct validity evidence (Lopez et al., 2005; Schreiner, 2005) indicates that themes are related to expected Big Five personality constructs and scales on the Sixteen Personality Factors test (16PF; Cattell, 1993) and the California Personality Inventory-260 (Gough & Bradley, 1996).

Values in Action

The Values in Action (VIA; Peterson & Seligman, 2004) Classification of Strengths is intended to serve as the antithesis of the *DSM*. Peterson and Seligman noted that we currently have a shared language for speaking about the negative side of psychology, but we have no such equivalent terminology for describing human strengths. The VIA Classification of Strengths was intended to provide such a language. The VIA classification system, originally commissioned by the Mayerson Foundation, was generated in response to two basic questions: "(1) how can one define the concepts of 'strength' and 'highest potential' and (2) how can one tell that a positive youth development program has succeeded in meeting its goals?" (Peterson & Seligman, 2004, p. v).

After reviewing dozens of inventories of virtues and strengths, Peterson, Seligman, and colleagues arrived at a list of 24 strengths, organized under six overarching virtues (wisdom and knowledge, courage, humanity, justice, temperance, and transcendence) thought to "emerge consensually across cultures and throughout time" (Peterson & Seligman, 2004, p. 29). The measure of virtues and strengths, the VIA-IS, was designed to describe the individual differences of character strengths as continua rather than as distinct categories. The current iteration of the VIA-IS is available online (www.positivepsychology.org) and as a paper-and-pencil measure in English and several other languages. The 240 items (10 for each strength), answered along a 5-point Likert scale, can be completed in about 30 minutes.

Regarding reliability, all scales have produced satisfactory internal consistency and test-retest estimates over a 4-month period. In terms of validity, correlations among scales are higher than expected because the inventory was designed to measure 24 unique constructs. However, more favorable validity evidence includes findings that (a) self-ratings correlate appropriately with ratings of the target individual by friends and family members and (b) the majority of the scales correlate positively with measures of life satisfaction. Factor analytic findings suggest that the measure consists of five factors (strengths of restraint, intellectual strengths, interpersonal strengths, emotional strengths, theological strengths) instead of the six proposed virtues. Peterson and Seligman (2004) described studies comparing strengths across groups of people and argued that the VIA-IS can be used as an outcome measure for strengths-enhancing interventions. The researchers at the VIA Institute plan additional examinations of the psychometric properties of the measure.

DEVELOPING AND EVALUATING STRENGTHS-BASED PRACTICES

Most current strengths-based practices encourage clients and students to complete one or both of the previously described measures or to become familiar with a vocabulary of strengths closely associated with those talents or strengths identified by the Clifton StrengthsFinder and the VIA-IS. We next describe three approaches developed recently by counseling psychologists that have not yet undergone empirical scrutiny (Lopez, Tree, Bowers, & Burns, 2006; Smith, 2006; Wong, 2006) and two intervention packages that have received some degree of empirical support (Seligman, Rashid, & Parks, 2006; Seligman, Steen, Park, & Peterson, 2005). Table 6.1 summarizes the characteristics of each of these approaches.

Strengths-Centered Therapy

Strength-centered therapy (SCT; Wong, 2006) is a psychotherapeutic approach, grounded in social constructionism, designed to leverage character strengths and virtues (as defined by Peterson & Seligman, 2004) as facilitators of the change process. Over the course of SCT, the counselor and client use social constructionist metastrategies of creative language and polyvocality (i.e., use of clients' interpersonal resources to expand the number of voices bearing on the clients' experiences, including their strengths) to create a larger repertoire of personal strengths and their meaning in the client's life. With these

Table 6.1   Characteristics of Strengths-Based Practices

Strengths-Based Approach	Strengths Tool	Manualized Protocol	Undergirding Principles	Empirical Evidence
Strengths-centered therapy (Wong, 2006)	VIA-IS	No	Constructionism	No
Strengths-based counseling for adolescents (Smith, 2006)	None	No	Common factors	No
Strengths mentoring (Lopez, Tree, et al., 2006)	CSF	Yes	Common factors	No
Positive psychology interventions (Seligman et al., 2005)	VIA-IS	No	Positive emotion, engagement, meaning	Yes
Positive psychotherapy (Seligman et al., 2006)	VIA-IS	Yes	Positive emotion, engagement, meaning	Yes

meanings and a greater vocabulary of strengths, it is hypothesized that clients begin to attach their life experiences to that which is positive and adaptive. Strength-centered therapy employs weekly sessions, during which clients are assumed to cycle and recycle through four phases (explicitizing, envisioning, empowering, and evolving) over a few months.

In SCT, the process of naming the client's existing character strengths, which could be facilitated with the VIA-IS or interviews, is termed *explicitizing*. Next, clients use *envisioning* to identify the strengths they wish to develop through intentional use. During the *empowering* phase, clients are assumed to experience a boost in agency as they begin to believe that using their strengths can positively affect their lives. This agency may be derived from the development of habits (e.g., writing weekly thank-you notes to cultivate gratitude) that lead to the effective use of strengths. Finally, the *evolving* phase is most salient during the termination stage of psychotherapy and involves the process of making strengths development a never-ending process that transcends the formal psychotherapeutic process.

Strengths-Based Counseling for Adolescents

Strengths-based counseling (SBC) for adolescents (Smith, 2006) builds on the common factors of change and attempts to foster growth by helping clients use strengths to overcome some of life's problems. Strengths-based counseling guides the psychologist who "searches for what people have rather than what they do not have, what people can do rather than what they cannot do, and how they have been successful rather than how they have failed" (Smith, 2006, p. 38).

Strengths-based counseling involves 10 stages of counseling:

Stage 1: *Creating the therapeutic alliance* begins with discussion of the importance of personal strengths and honors personal struggles.

Stage 2: *Identifying strengths* relies on narrative techniques to help clients discover and internalize their strengths.

Stage 3: *Assessing presenting problems* serves to clarify the client's concerns.

Stage 4: *Encouraging and instilling hope* allows the strengths-based counselor to provide the client with feedback on individual effort and improvement.

Stage 5: *Framing solutions* relies heavily on solution-focused strategies.

Stage 6: *Building strength and competence* fosters the development of internal and external assets.

Stages 7 through 9: *Empowering, changing, and building resilience* are designed to promote agency and facilitate goal pursuit.

Stage 10: *Evaluating and terminating* allows the counselor and client to identify the strengths that were most valuable to the change process and to honor progress that has been made.

Though this approach lacks specific strengths-enhancing techniques, it provides the counselor with a general guide for strengths-based counseling.

Strengths Mentoring

Strengths mentoring (SM; Lopez, Tree, Bowers, & Burns, 2004; Lopez, Tree, et al., 2006) is a student development strategy designed to capitalize on the common factors of change and to boost academic self-efficacy (Bandura, 1977), hope (Snyder, 1994), and personal growth initiative (Robitschek, 1998). Strengths mentoring, a three-session manualized approach, promotes the intentional use of strengths, as measured by the Clifton StrengthsFinder, in students' daily lives. During SM, trained mentors and student mentees identify salient academic goals that could be attained over a semester. Using microcounseling skills and narrative and hope-enhancing techniques, the mentor helps mentees move through three stages of strengths development (naming, nurturing, and navigating).

In SM, students are assigned to mentors based on schedule availability. Before arriving for the *naming* session, mentees complete the Clifton StrengthsFinder and print out their feedback. During this structured first session, the mentor works to develop academic goals, to help the mentee understand the measure's feedback and how it relates to school-related goals, and to incorporate the five signature strengths into personal descriptions. The mentor walks the mentee through the Strengths Imagery (see Appendix: Part A) toward the end of the session. As homework given at the end of the first session, mentees are asked to share their feedback with people close to them and to craft stories about how their strengths are used. In the *nurturing* session, mentees are encouraged to complete narrative exercises designed to create a catalog of critical events that have been, or could be, resolved through intentional use of strengths or "doing what you do best." Nurturing homework involves completing additional storytelling exercises (that are emailed to the mentor after completion) about using strengths to attain goals. During the final session, focused on *navigating*, mentees are challenged to create pathways that could help resolve academic challenges or overcome real or perceived obstacles that might get in the way of academic success. Finally, the mentor and mentee discuss success experiences associated with using strengths and concerns about future strengths development and academic pursuits.

Positive Psychology Interventions: Promoting Strengths in the Pursuit of Happiness

The positive strategies described by Seligman et al. (2005) rest on the assumption that happiness can be increased via positive emotions, engagement, and meaning (Seligman, 2002). Central to three of the five exercises is the identification and understanding of a participant's *signature strengths*. Having this knowledge then allows participants to consider ways in which they might capitalize on their strengths to promote well-being. Accordingly, the first activity involves participants taking the VIA-IS to identify personal strengths (Peterson & Seligman, 2004). Then, participants are asked to try and use more of their signature strengths over the next week. A second exercise asks participants to use one of their top strengths in a new and different way during the upcoming week.

A third exercise, the gratitude visit, taps into positive emotion and engagement. This exercise asks participants to write and deliver a letter of gratitude to someone in their lives who had not been properly thanked before. In doing so, the participant engages in reflection about positive memories and enduring thankfulness. A fourth exercise involves documenting blessings in life. Participants are asked to write down three good things that went well each day for 1 week and to note the causes for each of these things. In this way, participants are encouraged to become oriented toward pleasurable events and engagement with life. A fifth exercise requires participants to write about a time when they were "at their best." In their retelling, participants are asked to note the personal strengths that they displayed in this situation, and how they used them to shine. Participants are then asked to review and reflect on this story once a day for a week.

To evaluate the effectiveness of these five exercises, Seligman et al. (2005) recruited 577 adult participants to participate in a randomized controlled trial via the Internet. Participants were asked to complete five exercises that were delivered via the Internet, one per week. The control group completed a placebo exercise that asked them to write about their early memories every night for 1 week. Participants' levels of happiness and depression were assessed via self-report before beginning the set of exercises and at the completion of each exercise. Findings indicated that participants in all conditions (exercise and placebo) tended to show initial increases in happiness and decreases in depressive symptoms, but the gratitude visit exhibited the most pronounced initial effects, while noting three good things and using signature strengths yielded better long-term gains.

Positive Psychotherapy: Treating Depression by Capitalizing on Strengths

Encouraged by the favorable findings regarding their Internet study (Seligman et al., 2005), Seligman et al. (2006) developed positive psychotherapy (PPT), a comprehensive, manualized set of positive psychology exercises specifically designed to relieve depression. As before, the therapy relies on knowledge and application of a client's signature strengths, identified with the VIA-Short Version (Peterson & Seligman, 2004). Specifically, the sessions begin with an orientation and introduction to the PPT framework, and then move to exercises that encourage identification and cultivation of signature strengths. Subsequent sessions involve the application of strengths and the enhancement of such skills as savoring, optimism, hope, love, and attachment. The five exercises used by Seligman et al. (2005) are included in these sessions, along with other exercises. A mid-therapy check and a final integration session serve to reinforce previous lessons.

Research on the effectiveness of PPT has included two studies with young adults, one with individuals with mild-to-moderate depression, and one with individuals with severe depression. In the first study, participants were randomly assigned to a treatment or no treatment condition, and the participants in the treatment condition received PPT in a group format for 6 weeks. Findings of this study suggested that the PPT was moderately effective at lowering depressive symptoms ($d = .48$ at posttest and .59 at 1-year follow-up) and increasing life satisfaction ($d = .30$ at posttest and .29 at 1-year follow-up).

In the second study, individuals with severe depression were randomly assigned either to individual PPT or a treatment as usual condition, which consisted of an integrative therapeutic approach (based on clinician's judgment of appropriate treatment for client) without following a particular manual or theoretical orientation. There also was a nonrandomized matched group of participants who received treatment as usual plus antidepressant medications. Individual PPT, which lasted up to 14 sessions, involved asking clients to tell a real-life story about themselves at their best, identifying their signature strengths, and then setting goals and receiving coaching to manage problems. Effectiveness was measured by decreases in depressive symptoms and improvements in overall outcome and self-reported levels of global functioning and well-being. In addition, the researchers developed criteria to determine if a client was in remission from their depression. Findings suggested that PPT substantially exceeded (a) treatment as usual plus medication on the measures of depressive symptoms and overall outcome ($d = 1.22$ and 1.13), and (b) treatment as usual on clinician-rated measures of depression and global functioning ($d = 1.41$ and 1.16). In addition, 64% of PPT clients met criteria for remission, as compared to 11% in treatment as usual and 8% in treatment as usual with medication (Seligman et al., 2006). These authors called for future research to replicate these findings and to elucidate further the processes behind the promotion of strengths.

FUTURE RESEARCH AND PRACTICE

Counseling psychology's philosophical commitment to studying and promoting strengths is well established (Brown & Lent, 2000; Lopez, Edwards, Magyar-Moe, Pedrotti, & Ryder, 2003; Super, 1955), though the extent to which that philosophy has been translated into research and practice has been critically examined in several recent articles (e.g., Gerstein, 2006; Lopez & Magyar-Moe, 2006; Sapp, 2006). Anecdotal evidence suggests that counseling psychologists are putting strengths measures to good use in counseling centers, career services, and classrooms. Our review reveals that counseling psychologists are developing formal strategies for promoting strengths—although these strategies require empirical scrutiny to determine their efficacy. We propose that strengths-based practices now become more culturally sensitive and that future research is needed to examine the role of positive emotions in strengths development.

Accounting for Cultural Nuances in Strength-Based Scholarship and Practice

Despite our specialty's long tradition of examining and promoting human strengths through research and practice, counseling psychology work is not immune to a common criticism of strengths-focused scholarship and practice: it often fails to address the nuances of cultural influences on strengths development and enhancement (Ahuvia, 2001; Bacigalupe, 2001; Leong & Wong, 2003; Sue & Constantine, 2003; Walsh, 2001). As U.S. society becomes increasingly diverse (APA, 2003), it is necessary to include a discussion of cultural context and cultural differences in the investigation of strengths practice and academic and vocational success.

In the broader field of psychology, the focus on issues of diversity has moved from models that viewed individuals of different backgrounds as psychologically inferior or pathological, to multicultural models that acknowledge and appreciate unique approaches to life demonstrated by individuals, cultures, and societies. In counseling psychology, the unifying theme of a focus on the environment and context (Gelso & Fretz, 2001) has naturally emphasized the importance of diverse approaches to theory, research, and practice. Counseling psychologists currently are leading the discussion about multiculturalism as a virtue (Fowers & Davidov, 2006). Thus counseling psychologists are already attuned to exploring strengths among people of diverse backgrounds and are cautious in applying theory and research that has only been studied in majority populations (Lopez, Magyar-Moe, et al., 2006).

Currently, counseling psychology researchers and practitioners contend with arguments about the universality of strengths that, if left unaddressed, could undermine efforts to foster strengths development. Some who espouse a culture-free approach argue that the objectivity inherently present in the field of social science can "transcend particular cultures and politics and approach universality" (Seligman & Csikszentmihalyi, 2000, p. 5). In contrast, researchers who propose a more culturally embedded approach suggest that cultural values can only be understood through a cultural context (Constantine & Sue, 2006; Snyder & Lopez, 2007). Thus, strengths can be found in all cultures, but may manifest themselves in different ways.

In counseling psychology, professionals support each of these approaches. A small survey (Pedrotti & Edwards, 2005) was conducted with prominent counseling psychologists who focus on multicultural work to explore perspectives on multiculturalism and positive psychology. Pedrotti and Edwards identified a list of 46 multicultural experts in the Society of Counseling Psychology and contacted each individually via email. Nine members (7 women and 2 men) responded, and each was asked to answer six open-ended questions on the interface between multiculturalism and positive psychology. The data provided by these qualitative responses were analyzed for specific themes and for points of divergence.

One question specifically addressed the universality of strengths: "It has been said that Positive Psychology is a descriptive science that can 'transcend particular cultures and politics, and approach universality.' Do you agree or disagree with this statement? Please explain." Results indicated that all participants agreed that cultural context shapes strengths and their manifestations. A quote that exemplifies that theme was: "What determines living 'optimally' is culturally dependent." However, half of the participants believed that there also may exist some universal strengths that transcend culture, as noted in the following response: "The fact that all humans have positive aspects of their behavior is universal certainly (all seek happiness, equilibrium, all work and try for healthy relationships). But, of course, the manifestations of that [are] culturally determined."

The findings from this small survey cannot be generalized to the field at large, but they provide a glimpse of the challenges we face as we strive to understand optimal human functioning while balancing the search for commonalities and unique experiences among individuals of all backgrounds. Given this sensitive issue, we must work more closely with scholars in other areas of psychology and other fields to facilitate the culturally sensitive study of human strengths. By bringing Eastern and Western philosophy and social and cognitive psychology to bear on our study of strengths development, for example, we may be able to construct culturally sensitive measures and programs.

Examining the Link between Strengths Discovery and Enhancement and Positive Emotions

Having assigned the completion of hundreds of VIA inventories and Clifton StrengthsFinders to students, clients, mentees, and research participants, we have observed that, typically, respondents view the process and the results positively, share the results with one or more people close to them, and are open to the idea of using their strengths in a novel way to improve functioning at work or school. Given these observations and the findings reviewed earlier regarding positive emotions and traits, we hypothesize that discovering and capitalizing on strengths may serve as a positive mood induction. This induction may promote the broadening phenomenon whereby a person who learns his or her strengths might build enduring social, physical, and intellectual resources, as suggested by Fredrickson's (2000, 2001, 2002) broaden and build model.

This proposed link between strengths and positive emotions could be examined with study of the emotional experience of people who have just completed a strengths measure and received their feedback; the immediate computer feedback associated with the VIA-IS and the Clifton StrengthsFinder could be used to facilitate such research. Similarly, the extent to which the counseling and mentoring protocols of Wong (2006), Smith (2006), and Lopez, Tree, et al. (2004) and the strengths-based strategies of Seligman et al. (2005, 2006) generate positive emotions could be researched. More complex designs could also be used to study the ways in which positive affect may relate to strengths discovery and promotion.

CLOSING REMARKS

Positive psychology discoveries regarding strengths are leading to new measures and approaches to helping people make bad lives good, and good lives better. Some of the strength-based practice strategies summarized in this chapter—though thoughtfully designed and well received in the practice community—lack a strong theoretical basis, need to be more culturally contextualized, and require empirical scrutiny. Preliminary results of the strategies from Seligman and colleagues (Seligman et al., 2005, 2006) are promising, and their manualized PPT will soon be made available to practitioners. Nevertheless, the extent to which the VIA-IS and related strategies are culturally relevant has not been examined.

The two strengths measures and the five practical approaches to strengths development would profit from further refinement and empirical scrutiny. Due to the specialty's long-standing philosophical commitment to emphasizing people's strengths, counseling psychologists readily embrace the idea that strengths strategies can help improve the lives of people regardless of their degree of normalcy or disturbance. Continued and intensified study of strengths development could help positive and counseling psychologists understand how and why a focus on strength facilitates well-being and success.

APPENDIX: STRENGTHS ENHANCEMENT: IMAGERY AND INTERACTION

SHANE J. LOPEZ
KELLY BOWERS

Part A: Strengths Imagery

I'd like you to relax in your chair, recline or lean back if you like, and close your eyes if you want to. First, I ask that you pay attention to the instructions that follow, as they are important. I invite you to think about a time when you wanted to achieve something important to you ... a time when you felt really motivated ... a time when you utilized your strengths for getting to your goal. Sometimes people find it helpful to close their eyes to see the images more clearly. Have you thought of a time like this? A time when you felt hopeful that you could achieve something important to you ... something that motivated you ... something that you had the strengths to achieve. (Long pause.) You might notice

---

Authors Shane J. Lopez and Kelly Bowers adapted the appendix from Berg (2006) and Snyder (1994).

how driven you felt . . . how empowered . . . you might remember times when you wanted to give up . . . but didn't . . . you kept going because of your commitment . . . your desire . . . instead, you might have worked harder . . . you may have tried a different strength for dealing with the hard times . . . you might have broken your goal down into steps . . . with each step you achieved making you feel more energized . . . more empowered . . . more confident . . . you may have noticed how you focused on the goal . . . adjusting the goal based on what was happening . . . so that you knew that your goal was challenging . . . difficult . . . but achievable . . . knowing that once you achieved your goal . . . you would feel confident . . . motivated . . . proud of yourself . . . knowing that you have everything that it takes . . . the motivation . . . the ability to utilize multiple strengths . . . the ability to set challenging goals . . . and achieve them . . . everything that it takes to be successful with future goals . . . Take a moment to absorb all of these thoughts and then open your eyes (if eyes are closed). (Speak very slowly and deliberately.)

Part B: Interactive Dialogue

What situation did you think of?

Why was this goal so important to you?

How did you maintain your motivation when things got difficult?

How did you decide how you were going to utilize your strengths to achieve your goal?

How did achieving this goal make you feel?

How did these experiences help you to prepare for the future?

What did you learn from this experience that will help you on the task?

Part C: Skills Enhancement

I'd like to share with you some things that we have found through extensive research that enhance a person's ability to reach goals. There are three main components necessary to reach your goals: (1) set goals, (2) utilize multiple strengths, and (3) increase motivation. Here are some strategies for the first component, *setting goals*:

- Set goals that will be difficult but achievable. Be sure to set goals that are in line with your expectations, not the expectations of others.
- Be specific about your goals; define them objectively.
- Take time in setting your goals, and allow yourself to adjust your goals once you have experiences to guide you.

The second component is your ability to *utilize multiple strengths* as strategies to reach your goals. Here are some ways to improve this skill:

- Think about the steps involved in reaching your goal.
- Think about the different strengths that you could utilize to reach the goal.
- In your mind, rehearse what you will need to do during the pursuit of your goal to be successful in reaching it. Also, anticipate the problems you might have in reaching your goal and the personal strengths you can use to overcome the problems.

The third component is the *motivation* to reach your goals. Here are some ways to increase motivation:

- Think about the process of reaching your goal as a journey. Anticipating roadblocks that you might face may be helpful in reminding you that, when you start to feel discouraged, it is a signal that you must increase your motivation and work harder.

- As you work toward your goal, remind yourself of how far you have come and think positively about your progress on the goal. Think about similar challenging situations where you were able to overcome the situation.

- Use positive self-talk like "I can do it," "Keep going," and "I am doing really well."

Which of these do you think you are particularly good at?
Which of these do you think you could stand improvement on?

REFERENCES

Ahuvia, A. (2001). Well-being in cultures of choice: A cross-cultural perspective. *American Psychologist, 56*, 77–78.

American Psychological Association. (2003). Guidelines on multicultural education, training, research, practice, and organizational change for psychologists. *American Psychologist, 58*, 377–402.

Bacigalupe, G. (2001). Is positive psychology only White psychology? *American Psychology, 56*, 82–83.

Bandura, A. (1977). Self-efficacy: Toward a unifying theory of behavioral change. *Psychological Review, 84*, 191–215.

Berg, C. (2006). *The effectiveness of a hope intervention for coping with cold pressor pain.* Unpublished dissertation, University of Kansas, Lawrence.

Brown, S. D., & Lent, R. W. (2000). *Handbook of counseling psychology*, Third Edition. New York: Wiley.

Buckingham, M., & Clifton, D. O. (2000). *Now, discover your strengths.* New York: Free Press.

Cattell, R. B. (1993). *The 16PF fifth edition*, Champagne, IL: Institute for Personality and Ability Testing.

Clifton, D. O., & Anderson, E. (2002). *Strengthsquest: Discover and develop your strengths in academics, career, on beyond.* New York: Gallup Press.

Clifton, D. O., & Nelson, P. (1992), *Soar with your strengths.* New York: Delacorte Press.

Commission for the Recognition of Specialties and Proficiencies in Professional Psychology. (n.d.). *Archival description of counseling psychology.* Retrieved June 12, 2002, from http://www.apa.org/crsppp/counseling.html.

Constantine, M., & Sue, D. W. (2006). Factors contributing to optimal human functioning of people of color in the United States. *Counseling Psychologist, 34*, 228–244.

Fowers, B. J., & Davidov, B. J. (2006). The virtue of multiculturalism: Personal transformation, character, and openness to the other. *American Psychologist, 61*, 581–594.

Fredrickson, B. L. (2000). Cultivating positive emotions to optimize health and well-being. *Prevention and Treatment, 3* Available at http://journals.apa.org/prevention.

Fredrickson, B. L. (2001). The role of positive emotions in positive psychology: The broaden-and-build theory of positive emotions. *American Psychologist, 56*, 218–226.

Fredrickson, B. L. (2002). Positive emotions. In C. R. Snyder & S. J. Lopez (Eds.), *The handbook of positive psychology* (pp. 120–134). New York: Oxford University Press.

Fredrickson, B. L., & Joiner, T. (2002). Positive emotions trigger upward spirals toward emotional well-being. *Psychological Science, 13*, 172–175.

Gable, S. L., & Haidt, J. (2005). What (and why) is positive psychology? *Review of General Psychology, 9*, 103–110.

Gelso, C., & Fretz, B. (2001). *Counseling psychology* (2nd ed.). Fort Worth, TX: Harcourt Brace Jovanovich.

Gerstein, L. H. (2006). Counseling psychology's commitment to strengths: Rhetoric or reality? *Counseling Psychologist, 34*, 276–292.

Gough, H., & Bradley, P. (1996). *CPI^{TM} manual* (3rd ed.) Palo Alto, CA: CPP Books.

Leong, F., & Wong, P. (2003). Optimal human functioning from cross-cultural perspectives: Cultural competence as an organizing framework. In W. B. Walsh (Ed.), *Counseling psychology and optimal human functioning* (pp. 123–150). Mahwah, NJ: Earlbaum.

Lopez, S. J. (Ed.). (in press). *The encyclopedia of positive psychology.* London: Blackwell.

Lopez, S. J., Edwards, L. M., Magyar-Moe, J. L., Pedrotti, J. T., & Ryder, J. (2003). Fulfilling its promise: Counseling psychology's efforts to understand and promote optimal human functioning. In B. Walsh (Ed.), *Counseling psychology and optimal functioning* (pp. 297–307). Mahwah, NJ: Earlbaum.

Lopez, S. J., Hodges, T., & Harter, J. (2005). *Technical report: Development and validation of the Clifton Strengths Finder*. Princeton, NJ: Gallup Organization.

Lopez, S. J., & Magyar-Moe, J. L. (2006). Positive psychology that matters. *Counseling Psychologist, 34*, 323–330.

Lopez, S. J., Magyar-Moe, J. L., Petersen, S. E., Ryder, J. A., Krieshok, T. S., Lichtenberg, J. W., et al. (2006). Counseling psychology's focus on positive aspects of human functioning: A major contribution. *Counseling Psychologist, 34*, 205–227.

Lopez, S. J., & Snyder, C. R. (Eds.). (2003). *Positive psychological assessment: A handbook of models and measures*. Washington, DC: American Psychological Association.

Lopez, S. J., Snyder, C. R., Magyar-Moe, J., Edwards, L. M., Pedrotti, J. T., Janowski, K., et al. (2004). Strategies for accentuating hope. In P. A. Linley, & S. Joseph (Eds.), *Positive psychology in practice* (pp. 388–404). Hoboken, NJ: Wiley.

Lopez, S. J., Tree, H., Bowers, K., & Burns, M. E. (2004). *KU Strengths Mentoring Protocol*. Unpublished mentoring protocol, University of Kansas, Lawrence.

Lopez, S. J., Tree, H., Bowers, K., & Burns, M. E. (2006, October). *Positive psychology on campus: Discovering students' strengths*. In S. J. Lopez's (Chair) Symposium: Positive psychology on campus. Presented at the 5th Gallup International Positive Psychology Summit Washington, D.C.

Lyubomirsky, S., King, L., & Diener, E. (2005). The benefits of frequent positive affect: Does happiness lead to success? *Psychological Bulletin, 131*, 803–855.

Lyubomirsky, S., Sheldon, K. M., & Schkade, D. (2005). Pursuing happiness: The architecture of sustainable change. *Review of General Psychology, 9*, 111–131.

Maslow, A. (1954). *Motivation and personality*. New York: Longman.

Pedrotti, J. T., & Edwards, L. M. (2005, August). *Positive psychology and multiculturalism: A counseling psychology perspective*. Roundtable facilitated at the annual meeting of the American Psychological Association, Washington, DC.

Peterson, C. (2006). *A primer in positive psychology*. New York: Oxford University Press.

Peterson, C., & Seligman, M. E. P. (2004). *Character strengths and virtues: A handbook and classification*. New York: Oxford University Press.

Robitschek, C. (1998). Personal growth initiative: The construct and its measure. *Measurement and Evaluation in Counseling and Development, 30*, 183–198.

Sapp, M. (2006). The strengths-based model for counseling at-risk youths. *Counseling Psychologist, 34*, 118–117.

Schreiner, L. (2005). *A technical report of the Clifton Strengths Finder with college students*. Princeton, NJ: The Gallup Organization.

Seligman, M. E. P. (2002). *Authentic happiness*. New York: Free Press.

Seligman, M. E. P., & Csikszentmihalyi, M. (2000). Positive psychology: An introduction. *American Psychologist, 55*, 5–14.

Seligman, M. E. P., Rashid, T., & Parks, A. C. (2006). Positive psychotherapy. *American Psychologist, 61*, 774–788.

Seligman, M. E. P., Steen, T. A., Park, N., & Peterson, C. (2005). Positive psychology progress. *American Psychologist, 60*, 410–421.

Smith, E. (2006). The strengths-based counseling model. *Counseling Psychologist, 34*, 13–79.

Snyder, C. R. (1994). *The psychology of hope: You can get there from here*. New York: Free Press.

Snyder, C. R., & Lopez, S. J. (2002). *Handbook of positive psychology*. New York: Oxford University Press.

Snyder, C. R., & Lopez, S. J. (2007). *Positive psychology: The scientific and practical explorations of human strengths*. Thousand Oaks, CA: Sage.

Sox-Harris, A., Thoresen, C., & Lopez, S. J. (in press). Examining the influence of positive psychology in healthcare settings. *Journal of Counseling and Development*.

Sue, D. W., & Constantine, M. G. (2003). Optimal human functioning in people of color in the United States. In W. B. Walsh (Ed.), *Counseling psychology and optimal human functioning* (pp. 151–169). Mahwah, NJ: Erlbaum.

Super, D. E. (1955). Transition: From vocational guidance to counseling psychology. *Journal of Counseling Psychology, 2*, 3–9.

Thompson, A. S., & Super, D. E. (Eds.). (1964). *The professional preparation of counseling psychologists* (Report of the 1964 Greystone Conference). New York: Columbia University, Teacher's College, Bureau of Publications.

Uffelman, R. (2006, Summer). Hope springs anew: Using hope theory in therapy with college students. *Naming and Nurturing: The E-Newsletter of the Positive Psychology Section of the Society of Counseling Psychology Division 17*, 6, 8.

Walsh, W. B. (2001). The changing nature of the science of vocational psychology. *Journal of Vocational Behavior, 59*, 262–274.

Wong, J. (2006). Strengths-centered therapy: A social constructionist, virtue-based psychotherapy. *Psychotherapy: Theory, Research, Practice, and Training, 43*, 133–146.

PART II
Diversity and Multicultural Psychology

CHAPTER 7

Conceptual and Measurement Issues in Multicultural Psychology Research

MATTHEW J. MILLER
HUNG-BIN SHEU

Multiculturalism has become a central force in psychology. What initially began as a social and political movement in the 1960s and 1970s has had a substantial impact on the field of psychology (Neville & Carter, 2005; Pope-Davis, Coleman, Liu, & Toporek, 2003; Sue & Sue, 2003). Although a review of the history of general psychology reveals a reluctance to address multicultural issues and, at times, an antipathy toward members of racial and ethnic groups (Neville & Carter, 2005), recent events (e.g., publication of the "Guidelines on Multicultural Education, Training, Research, Practice, and Organizational Change" by the American Psychological Association in 2003) suggest an increasing awareness and commitment to multiculturalism in psychology. The force and permanence of multicultural psychology is perhaps best evidenced by the plethora of handbooks, encyclopedias, books, and conceptual and empirical articles in the literature. Although multicultural psychology is not tied to a specific area in psychology, counseling psychology has been associated with the movement from its inception and continues to be at the forefront of multicultural theory, research, and practice (Ponterotto, Casas, Suzuki, & Alexander, 2001).

In this context, we review the multicultural psychology literature from a conceptual and measurement perspective. Instead of providing a comprehensive and exhaustive review of the literature and associated issues, our goal for the chapter is to identify issues that we feel are especially germane to research in multicultural psychology. We also intend to identify future directions that will perhaps facilitate the continued growth of this dynamic and evolving field. In the first section, we consider the multiple meanings of multiculturalism and present a discussion of universality versus specificity. The second section reviews the use of factor analysis in measurement development research, makes some recommendations for future use of this important data analytic strategy, and highlights the utility of measure equivalence strategies in multicultural research. Last, we suggest how traditional and novel meta-analytic strategies might be employed in theory development and testing research in multicultural psychology. Before proceeding, we wish to state our bias—that on both personal and professional levels we embrace diversity in all its forms and subscribe to the idea that an appropriate understanding of race, ethnicity, and culture (in the broadest sense) is essential for valid research and measurement. We also applaud the many pioneers who have provided the conceptual and empirical foundations on which the body of multicultural psychology knowledge is built.

CONCEPTUAL ISSUES IN MULTICULTURAL PSYCHOLOGY RESEARCH

A large number of important conceptual issues and considerations have received attention in the multicultural literature, including the implications of treating race as a categorical variable (see Delgado-Romero, Galván, Maschino, & Rowland, 2005), differing conceptual and operational definitions of key multicultural constructs (cf. Miller, in press), and efforts to differentiate between race, culture, and ethnicity (see Betancourt & López, 1993). In preparing this chapter, we chose to highlight two central issues in multicultural psychology research: the ways in which multiculturalism is conceptualized and the issue of universality versus specificity.

What (or Whom) Is Multicultural?

Although it is clear that multicultural psychology is an important force in psychology, less clear is what is actually meant by the term *multicultural*. To answer this question, it is necessary first to define what is meant by the term *culture*. Although numerous definitions of culture exist, we endorse the idea that culture is central to everyday life and is an evolving shared system of meaning that provides context and value through history, ideology, social norms, roles, beliefs, and values (Nagel, 1994; Noh, 2003; Triandis et al., 1980). There has been some discussion among scholars regarding what constitutes culture (e.g., culture tied to ethnicity versus culture tied to other social phenomena—college football or Craigslist members). According to Sue and Sue (2003), this discussion typically addresses whether culture should be used in the context of race and ethnicity (referred to as the *exclusive position*) or whether culture encompasses the myriad phenomenological experiences of groups (e.g., women; lesbian, bisexual, gay and transgender individuals; level of ability; age, religion) of people (referred to as the *inclusive position*). There is concern among some scholars that expanding the definition of multiculturalism beyond the scope of race and ethnicity will substantially dilute the meaningfulness of the term (Sue & Sue, 2003). In addition, Sue and Sue state that broad, inclusive definitions of multiculturalism enable those discomforted by issues related to race and racism to discount the importance of this domain of multicultural theory and practice. We realize that this is likely a complex discussion that cannot be adequately resolved in this chapter. We do, however, agree with Sue and Sue and follow their lead in embracing the inclusive definition of multiculturalism, while simultaneously focusing on multiculturalism as it pertains specifically to race and ethnicity. One reason we felt compelled to focus predominantly on race and ethnicity is that even though counseling psychology has been at the forefront of the multicultural movement, historically issues of race and ethnicity have been underrepresented in the empirical literature (Delgado-Romero et al., 2005). In addition, it has been suggested that historically, racial, ethnic, and cultural research has been based on European American standards and has tended to portray racial, ethnic, and cultural minorities in a negative manner (Sue, Ivey, & Pedersen, 1996). Thus, throughout the remainder of this chapter, we emphasize empirical examples that involve race, ethnicity, and culture. Broader discussions of multicultural issues may be found in other chapters in this *Handbook,* including Ponterotto (Chapter 8, this volume), Constantine, Miville, and Kindaichi (Chapter 9, this volume), Liu and Ali (Chapter 10, this volume), Nutt and Brooks (Chapter 11, this volume), Croteau, Bieschke, Fassinger, and Manning (Chapter 12, this volume), Peterson and Elliot (Chapter 13, this volume), Leong and Gupta (Chapter 19, this volume), and Fouad and Kantamneni (Chapter 24, this volume).

Universality versus Specificity

Some researchers (e.g., MacPhee, Kreutzer, & Fritz, 1994; Sue et al., 1996) have argued that most research conducted in North America is based on the assumption of universality, which is Eurocentric and treats White Americans as the reference group. For instance, Butcher, Cheung, and Lim's (2003) review of the cross-cultural utility of the Minnesota Multiphasic Personality Inventory (MMPI-2) revealed that the Philippines, Thailand, and South Korea do not have separate in-country norms and need to rely on U.S. norms as standards of comparison. They suggested that separate norms need to be established in these countries before meaningful cross-cultural comparisons involving the MMPI-2 can be made.

Moreover, although a construct may be universally meaningful, how the construct manifests itself can vary significantly in different cultures. A good example is Holland's (1997) hexagonal model of vocational interests. The concept of vocational interests has been found to be relevant in the career decision-making process across different cultures. However, empirical findings have shown that the structure of interests varies to some degree, especially in non-Western countries (e.g., Tang, 2001). These examples indicate that although most assessment tools and theories were originally developed with the U.S. population or, more specifically, White Americans, manifestations of underlying constructs may be different in other nations or ethnic minority groups. Simply assuming that a construct will hold up universally or applying norms derived from the majority group to different populations can lead to inaccurate conclusions or inappropriate diagnoses and treatment recommendations.

Because of different cultural experiences, theoretical perspectives developed for one group may not necessarily fit the life experiences of another group. Different models have been developed to conceptualize racial or ethnic identity development for African Americans, White Americans, Asian Americans, and Latino Americans (see Helms & Cook, 1999; Sue & Sue, 2003). Although these models share some common characteristics, such as the acknowledgment of sociopolitical influences in shaping a person's identity, they differ in accommodating each racial or ethnic group's history and interactions with the mainstream society. This example shows that even though a particular psychological construct has merit in explaining attitudes or behaviors of individuals with different backgrounds, assuming that the construct can be applied universally without modification may result in a failure to capture meaningful cultural nuances.

The negative consequences of the assumption of universality have been outlined by Burlew (2003), including (a) the temptation to accept and apply prematurely research conclusions derived from one group to another, (b) discouragement for revising existing theoretical models or developing new models to account for experiences of ethnic group members, and (c) failure to identify specific cultural variables that may serve as protective factors for surviving the challenges of minority status. These consequences deserve special attention in multicultural research. Given that developmental tasks, adjustment issues, and psychological disorders often present themselves in dissimilar ways across ethnic groups, multicultural counseling researchers need to determine whether the theoretical construct or concept under study is equivalent and relevant across the populations of interest. It seems somewhat unrealistic and perhaps impractical to aspire to develop counseling theories and models that are universally true. We suggest that future research continue to tease out which part of a theory has universal utility and which part is applicable only to a specific racial or ethnic group (e.g., Fischer, Jome, & Atkinson, 1998; Leong, 1993). We further propose that theoretically grounded studies of measurement equivalence— via factor analytic, measurement invariance, and meta-analytic methodologies—represent particularly powerful ways to elucidate the universal utility versus cultural specific nature of important psychological constructs. Thus, the main purpose of this chapter is to review critical issues involved in conducting factor analytic, measurement invariance, and meta-analytic research to address important questions in multicultural psychology.

USE OF FACTOR ANALYSIS IN MULTICULTURAL RESEARCH

Psychological measurement is an essential element in multicultural psychology research. Stevens (1946) defines psychological measurement as the assignment of numbers to aspects of individuals in a nonarbitrary fashion so that properties or aspects can be summarized and communicated. Simply put, it involves the translation of abstract constructs (e.g., racial identity) into (hopefully) concrete and meaningful operationalizations that can then be quantified, summarized, and communicated. Psychological measurement allows us to study empirically abstract constructs such as the counseling process, aptitude, and resilience. Multicultural psychology, like many areas in the broader field of psychology, deals with many critical yet abstract constructs such as acculturation, enculturation, bicultural competence, racial and ethnic identity, multicultural competence, race-related stress, and acculturative stress. These conceptually and practically meaningful constructs are often complex (involving numerous domains, dimensions, or factors) and nuanced (i.e., differences in level of magnitude are meaningful). It is therefore essential that researchers develop measures that adequately and appropriately capture the full meaning and breadth of the purported construct.

Numerous authors have heeded this call. Given the many and diverse constructs that have appeared in the multicultural literature, it is not surprising to see an ever-increasing number of measurement development studies. Since the publication of the third edition of the *Handbook of Counseling Psychology* in 2000, 19 newly developed measures of multicultural constructs have been published in the *Journal of Counseling Psychology* (*JCP*) and *Cultural Diversity and Ethnic Minority Psychology* (*CDEMP*)— two primary outlets for multicultural psychology research. These new measures (see Miller, 2006, for a complete list of references) represent important multicultural constructs such as (a) knowledge of and attitudes toward lesbian, gay, and bisexual individuals (Worthington, Dillon, & Becker-Schutte, 2005); (b) racism-related outcomes (Liang, Li, & Kim, 2004; Spanierman & Heppner, 2004); (c) multicultural environment (Pope-Davis, Liu, Nevitt, & Toporek, 2000); and (d) color-blind racial attitudes (Neville, Lilly, Duran, Lee, & Browne, 2000). More measures in this area are either in press or in development (e.g., Sheu & Lent, in press).

Given the conceptual and practical importance of multicultural constructs, the way in which the constructs are operationalized is of the *utmost* importance. General recommendations for measure development and construction are beyond the scope of this chapter and have been summarized by a number of authors (e.g., Anastasi & Urbina, 1997; Dawis, 2000; DeVellis, 2003). Instead, our intention is to highlight a few measurement specific issues we feel are most germane to multicultural psychology research. We focus on appropriate uses of factor analyses in this section and then turn our attention to measurement invariance methodologies in the next section.

In the multicultural literature, it seems rare to come across a construct that consists of a single domain or dimension. Some would argue that a truly unidimensional construct is a conceptual or empirical impossibility (Hattie, 1985; Hayduk, 1996). Given the nuanced and multifaceted nature of constructs of interest to multicultural scholars, it is not surprising that every newly developed multicultural measure published from 2000 to 2006 in *JCP* and *CDEMP* was multidimensional. A common data analytic approach to measurement development (used in each of the aforementioned 19 new measure development studies) is factor analysis. Factor analysis is typically used to "summarize the interrelationships among the variables [measured items] in a concise but accurate manner as an aid in conceptualization" (Gorsuch, 1983, p. 2). As researchers continue to produce measures of complex multifaceted constructs, factor analysis will continue to be the method of choice to summarize interrelationships among items representing multiple dimensions. Readers are referred to recent sets of recommendations for the appropriate implementation of both exploratory factor analysis (EFA; e.g., Fabrigar, Wegener, MacCallum, & Strahan, 1999; Kahn, 2006; Worthington & Whittaker, 2006) and confirmatory factor analysis (CFA; e.g., Martens, 2005; Quintana & Maxwell, 1999; Weston & Gore, 2006). In the following sections, we briefly review salient issues in EFA and CFA and then recommend best practices for implementing such data analytic strategies. In addition, we report how factor analysis has been used in the development and validation of recently published multicultural measures.

Exploratory Factor Analysis

Exploratory factor analysis is a widely used analytic strategy that was developed over 100 years ago (Spearman, 1904). There are a number of important components to consider when performing an EFA, such as (a) the appropriateness of the strategy given the researcher's purpose, (b) factor extraction method, (c) identifying the appropriate number of factors for retention, and (d) factor rotation (for a comprehensive discussion of these issues, see Fabrigar et al., 1999; Kahn, 2006; Worthington & Whittaker, 2006).

Appropriateness of Exploratory Factor Analysis Strategy

Exploratory factor analysis is most appropriate in the initial stages of measure development and when the researcher's goal is to derive a more parsimonious understanding of a broad set of measured items by identifying a set of underlying common factors. Principal components analysis (PCA) is often used inappropriately in place of EFA. This is problematic because there are fundamental differences between EFA and PCA (i.e., the way in which variance is represented) that make them suitable for different types of purposes. Principal components analysis is appropriate when the goal of analysis is simple data reduction (i.e., reduction of a large number of items or measures to fewer overarching categories), whereas EFA is more appropriate where the goal is to identify underlying latent factors (e.g., in measure development).

Extraction Method

After determining that the EFA approach is appropriate, the researcher must select an extraction method that will be used to fit a factor model to the observed data (Fabrigar et al., 1999). The most common extraction methods are principal axis factors and maximum likelihood (ML) estimation. The ML estimation is advantageous because it provides indices of goodness-of-fit. However, the ML approach requires the assumption of multivariate normality, the violation of which can produce distorted results (Curran, West, & Finch, 1996). When using the ML approach, it is essential to provide information on the distribution of the data to ensure that results are not attributable to measurement artifact. Although the Principal Axis Factors approach does not provide indices of fit, it also does not require multivariate normality and is therefore less likely to generate distorted results (Finch & West, 1997).

Factor Retention

Because of the exploratory nature of EFA, researchers are required to determine the appropriate number of factors (ranging from one to as high as the total number of measured items). Historically, the common approach for determining the appropriate number of factors for retention has been the use of eigenvalues and the scree plot (Fabrigar et al., 1999). However, parallel analysis, which compares observed eigenvalues to eigenvalues generated from numerous random sets of data (see Fabrigar et al., 1999), is the method of choice for determining the number of factors to retain because it is statistically based and more accurate than the aforementioned traditional approaches (O'Connor, 2000; Zwick & Velicer, 1986).

Factor Rotation

Any multifactor solution has a large number of plausible alternative configurations of the factors in multidimensional space (Fabrigar et al., 1999). Therefore, with the assistance of statistical software, factors are rotated in multidimensional space to identify the most interpretable solution. There exist two main rotation procedures—orthogonal and oblique. Orthogonal rotation assumes that the factors are unrelated and, therefore, does not estimate factor interrelations. Oblique rotation, however, allows for estimation of (expected) factor interrelations. Fabrigar et al. proposed several advantages of the oblique rotation method over the orthogonal approach. In particular, the oblique method better conforms to the reality that many psychological constructs are interrelated in practice; it is also more likely to produce interpretable solutions because it allows estimation of factor interrelations.

In sum, when conducting an EFA researchers should (a) avoid using PCA unless the goal is simply limited to data reduction; (b) be cognizant of the strengths and limitations of model-fitting procedures and, if using ML, be sure to assess for multivariate normality; (c) use parallel analysis to determine the appropriate number of factors for retention; and (d) ordinarily employ oblique rotation of multifactor solutions (unless there is good reason to assume that the factors are, according to theory, orthogonal).

Confirmatory Factor Analysis

Whereas EFA is most appropriate when attempting to identify the underlying factor structure of a measure or set of data, CFA is best suited for analyses in which the researcher has a substantiated a priori knowledge of the factor structure (Fabrigar et al., 1999). The prominence of CFA in counseling psychology research is reflected in the number of recent methodological reviews of this data-analytic procedure in the literature (e.g., Martens, 2005; Weston & Gore, 2006). Although a comprehensive review of the methodological issues specific to CFA is beyond the scope of this chapter, we wish to highlight what we and others (e.g., Martens, 2005; Quintana & Maxwell, 1999) think are especially important considerations in multicultural psychology research such as (a) identifying theoretically or empirically viable alternative models for comparison with the researcher's hypothesized model, (b) assessing for violations of the assumption of multivariate normality, (c) selecting a set of incremental and comparative fit indices a priori, (d) reporting all estimated model parameters, (e) eschewing model modification unless it is possible to validate the newly constructed model on a separate sample, and (f) avoiding the use of item parceling when the purpose of the study is measurement development (Bandalos & Finney, 2001; Martens, 2005).

Identification of Alternative Models

One of the strengths of the CFA approach is the ability of the researcher to assess the degree to which the data fit an a priori specified model. The degree to which the hypothesized model fits the observed data either confirms or disconfirms the researcher's assertion. However, when a researcher specifies and tests only one model, it is difficult to ascertain whether other plausible alternative models exist that explain the data equally well or even better than the hypothesized model. Historically, those employing CFA procedures in the published literature have often failed to account for alternate models (MacCallum, Wegener, Uchino, & Fabrigar, 1993). Analogous to ruling out rival hypotheses in establishing internal validity, it is imperative to identify and test plausible competing models (explanations) and to provide evidence that the researcher's hypothesized model best represents the data (MacCallum et al., 1993). It is also important to refrain from asserting that one has identified *the* best model in an absolute sense; rather, unless the researcher has tested all possible alternative models (which is unlikely), it is more appropriate to state that, compared to the other models tested, a particular model offers the best data-model fit in a particular study.

Multivariate Normality

Maximum likelihood is the foremost method of estimation in CFA studies (Curran et al., 1996; Kline, 1998). As previously indicated, ML requires that the data be normally distributed. This, however, poses a problem because nonnormal distributions are common in psychological research (Curran et al., 1996). All else being equal, when data are normally distributed, ML estimation produces reliable parameter estimates and standard errors (Bollen, 1989). However, when ML estimation is used in the presence of nonnormal data, there may be (a) an increase in Type I errors in goodness-of-fit chi-square tests resulting from an increase in the magnitude of chi-square values, and (b) a reduction in the estimation of standard errors of the parameter estimates, which may result in the false positive identification of significant factor loadings (Kline, 1998). The Satorra-Bentler scaled chi-square (SB χ^2; Satorra & Bentler, 1994) is a widely used approach for addressing violations of multivariate normality. The SB χ^2 adjusts for the inflation of the chi-square statistic due to distributional violations; that is, the greater the degree of nonnormality, the more the SB χ^2 reduces the inflated chi-square (Curran et al., 1996). When calculating the SB χ^2, most statistical packages such as EQS (pronounced like the letter "X"; Bentler, 1989) or LISREL (Jöreskog & Sörbom, 1996) also provide a more robust estimate of standard errors of parameter estimates. The increase in the size of standard errors of parameter estimates decreases the level of the statistical significance of the associated parameter estimate.

Assessment of Model Fit

Perhaps the primary goal of CFA is to assess whether the observed data confirm or disconfirm an author's postulated measurement model. Given the commonly stated difficulties with the chi-square statistic (e.g., Bryant & Baxter, 1997; Kline, 1998), the use of alternative fit indices is the typical approach in determining the degree to which the hypothesized model fits the observed data (typically a covariance matrix). There are a large number of available fit indices, each of which has different philosophical assumptions, advantages, and limitations. The myriad fit indices can be broadly categorized as either *comparative (incremental)* or *absolute fit indices*. Comparative fit indices assess whether the researcher's model provides a better fit to the data than a null model. Comparative fit indices typically estimate the goodness of model fit, where higher values indicate better fit (Hoyle, 1995). The Normed Fit Index (NFI), the Non-Normed Fit Index (NNFI), and the Comparative Fit Index (CFI) are examples of comparative fit indices.

Absolute indices of fit compare the researcher's model to a perfectly fitting model (a model that exactly reproduces the covariance matrix from the obtained data). Absolute fit indices assess how well the researcher's hypothesized model reproduces the covariance matrix obtained from the sample data (Hu & Bentler, 1998). These fit indices typically estimate "badness" of model fit in relation to a perfectly fitting model (Hoyle, 1995). Examples of absolute fit indices are the Goodness of Fit Index (GFI), the Standardized Root Mean Square Residual (SRMR), and the Root Mean Square Error of Approximation (RMSEA). As noted by Martens (2005), there is a lack of consensus regarding the best or most appropriate indices for determining model fit. Commonly used indices such as the GFI and the NFI have been found to be affected by such factors as sample size and model identification (Hu & Bentler, 1998; Marsh, Balla, & McDonald, 1998). Therefore, indices such as the NNFI, CFI, RMSEA, and SRMR are currently among the favored indices of model fit in confirmatory factor analysis (Martens, 2005; Quintana & Maxwell, 1999).

Reporting Model Parameters

Another important issue in CFA is the reporting of model parameters in the study results (MacCallum & Austin, 2000; McDonald & Ho, 2002). This often nonreported information may be important because even a perfectly fitting model may have nonsignificant model parameters (Quintana & Maxwell, 1999). By providing all of the estimated model parameters (e.g., factor loadings, unique error terms), the researcher allows the reader to gain a better understanding of the relationships among model components and leaves less room for ambiguity (Martens, 2005; McDonald & Ho, 2002).

Model Modification

As previously indicated, one of the strengths of the CFA approach is that it allows the researcher to confirm or disconfirm a priori hypothesized models. However, confirmatory approaches to factor analysis can be used in an exploratory manner. It is possible that after completion of data analysis via CFA, the researcher can identify both nonsignificant model parameters and essential parameters (via statistical software) that were not initially estimated and rerun the modified model with the ultimate aim of achieving a better model fit. The difficulty with this approach is that unless the newly modified model is validated in a separate sample, it is unclear whether the observed fit of the modified model is a function of "chance characteristics of the data" (MacCallum, Roznowski, & Necowitz, 1992, p. 490). Another potential limitation associated with model modifications is that it is an empirically (i.e., data) driven approach to model refinement (MacCallum et al., 1992). Therefore, it is imperative that the researcher first consider the theoretical appropriateness of any proposed model modifications before implementing any changes (Quintana & Maxwell, 1999). Given the limitations of a posteriori modification of models, such an approach is typically not recommended (e.g., MacCallum et al., 1992; McDonald & Ho, 2002).

Item Parceling

Item parceling is commonly used in structural equation modeling techniques, such as CFA (Little, Cunningham, Shahar, & Widaman, 2002). Item parcels are observed indicators made up of the sum or average of at least two measured items (Little et al., 2002). Although there are a number of advantages associated with the item parceling approach (e.g., smaller sample size requirements due to fewer estimated model parameters; decreased likelihood of distributional violations), its use is not without controversy (cf. Little et al., 2002; Miller, in press). And although there is no clear consensus on the appropriate use of item parceling, when the purpose of a CFA analysis is that of measure development or refinement, the use of item parceling is not recommended (Bandalos & Finney, 2001; Little et al., 2002).

Implementation of Exploratory and Confirmatory Factor Analysis in the Multicultural Measure Development Literature

Miller (2006) conducted a content analysis of the aforementioned population of 19 newly developed multicultural measures published in *JCP* and *CDEMP* from 2000 to 2006 to assess the degree to which authors were incorporating the recommendations for EFA and CFA in scale development. Specifically, Miller was interested in examining the way in which authors were conducting exploratory and confirmatory factor analyses in scale development studies. This aspect of measurement development was selected given the recent calls for appropriate use of factor analytic techniques in the literature. Of the 19 published studies, 5 conducted EFA only, 2 conducted CFA only, and the remaining 12 conducted both EFA and CFA.

In reviewing the fidelity with which studies adhered to recommendations for EFA, there emerged both strengths and limitations of the existing multicultural measure development literature: A majority (10 of 17) of studies used the appropriate EFA analysis, whereas 7 studies used PCA (though all studies reported that they had conducted an EFA). In addition, a majority (10 of 17) of studies used oblique rotation to identify an interpretable factor solution (6 used orthogonal, and 1 study did not provide information). However, perhaps the most disconcerting finding from the Miller (2006) analysis is that none of the identified EFA studies utilized parallel analysis in determining the number of factors to retain. Instead, all 17 studies used eigenvalues, scree plot, or a combination of the two to determine the number of factors to retain. Ten of these studies also used the criteria of interpretability for selecting the number of factors to retain.

The review of 14 studies that used CFA to develop measures of multicultural constructs revealed a number of strengths. Eight studies identified plausible alternative models for testing, 13 of the 14 studies used at least one of the recommended fit indices (see Martens, 2005), and 13 of the 14 studies did not conduct any model modification with the CFA analysis. Although there were a number of positive aspects of the reviewed CFA studies, three shortcomings were evident. First, none of the 14 studies reported any information on multivariate normality. This is problematic in that if any of the 14 data sets violated the assumption of normality, there is an increased likelihood that model parameters were incorrectly identified as significant. Second, only one of the studies actually reported all model parameter estimates. Third, one measurement development study used item parceling.

In sum, these findings suggest that although the multicultural measure development literature has incorporated a number of recommendations on the use of EFA and CFA, there is room for continued improvement. When using EFA, researchers are encouraged to employ parallel analysis to identify the underlying factor structure. When using CFA to test a measurement model, researchers should assess for violations of normality, and if present, use such statistics as the Satorra-Bentler scaled chi-square, along with robust estimation methods, to provide more accurate model parameter estimates. In addition, we suggest that multicultural psychology research could benefit from the inclusion of measure equivalence studies. This concept is discussed in the following section.

USE OF MEASUREMENT INVARIANCE APPROACHES IN MULTICULTURAL RESEARCH

Researchers and practitioners in multicultural psychology are often interested in examining group differences on a variable of interest (e.g., Do Asian American and African American women differ in their experience of barriers to career choice? Do differences in racial identity status affect the level of perceived prejudice? Is generational status related to levels of acculturation and enculturation?). Historically, the way in which group differences have been assessed is by comparing mean scores on specified measures and concluding that group differences exist in the population when a statistically significant difference emerges. However, a fundamental limitation in examining group differences via mean score comparisons is the assumption that the tool used to assess mean scores (e.g., the psychological measure) is being used in an equivalent fashion across groups (Byrne, Shavelson, & Muthén, 1989; Meredith, 1993; Widaman & Reise, 1997). Before we can assess whether mean score differences exist across different groups, it is imperative that we establish that the measurement of the construct of interest is operating in an equivalent fashion across the groups of interest (Widaman & Reise, 1997). It is necessary to establish measurement equivalence before assessing for mean score differences. The term *measurement equivalence* refers to the degree to which tests or inventories are measuring (operationalizing) a construct of interest in an equivalent fashion across different groups (Byrne et al., 1989).

Technically, one aspect of measurement equivalence or invariance pertains to the condition in which the relationship between test items and their respective latent factors are equivalent (or invariant) across groups (Widaman & Reise, 1997). The magnitude of the relationship between latent factor(s) and items must be statistically identical for measurement invariance to hold (Meredith, 1993). Without evidence of measurement equivalence, any interpretations of mean score differences (e.g., that differences in mean scores reflect *true* difference in the construct of interest) are at best tenuous and at worst erroneous (Horn & McArdle, 1992; Steenkamp & Baumgarnter, 1998). In addition, when instruments exhibit measurement nonequivalence, there are important issues (e.g., bias) to consider when using the instrument for selection and prediction (see Millsap, 1997; Millsap & Kwok, 2004).

There is a large body of between-group comparison research in the multicultural literature (e.g., studies comparing groups for differences in depression, identity, acculturation, and eating behaviors). Yet there is a dearth of measurement invariance evidence in this literature. Greater attention needs to be given to measurement equivalence research, and we summarize below the central issues involved in conducting such research.

Review of the Terminology

A review of the literature pertaining to measurement equivalence provides numerous (and at times confusing) terms describing this data analytic approach. The terms *measurement invariance, measurement equivalence/invariance,* and *factorial invariance* are often used interchangeably to refer to the degree to which instruments or models operate in a similar fashion across meaningfully distinct groups. Whereas the terms *measurement invariance* and *measurement equivalence* are not necessarily tied to a specific data analytic approach, factorial invariance is typically associated with factor analytic methods of assessing equivalence (i.e., the equivalence of measures is tested by examining factor analytically derived models across distinct groups).

Table 7.1   Synthesizing Differing Measurement Invariance Categories

Meredith (1993) Paradigm	Vandenberg and Lance (2000) Paradigm	Level of Invariance Assessed
—	Configural invariance	Same pattern of loadings
Weak factorial invariance	Metric invariance	Equivalent factor loadings
Strong factorial invariance	Metric and scalar invariance	Equivalence of factor loadings and item intercepts
Strict factorial invariance	Metric, scalar, and uniqueness invariance	Equivalence of factor loadings, items intercepts, and unique error terms
Structural invariance	Invariant factor variances Invariant factor covariances Invariant factor means	Equivalence of factor variances, covariances, and means

Source: "Assessing Factorial Invariance in Cross-Sectional and Longitudinal Studies" (pp. 153–175), by D. E. Bontempo and S. M. Hofer, in *Oxford Handbook of Methods in Positive Psychology,* A. D. Ong and M. H. M. van Dulmen (Eds.), 2007, New York: Oxford University Press.

In the factorial invariance literature, there is an increased opportunity for misunderstanding given the numerous, and often times overlapping, terms used to describe differing states of equivalence. Nuanced discussions of factorial invariance include a myriad number of terms such as *configural, weak, metric, strong, strict,* and *scalar* forms of factorial invariance. As Bontempo and Hofer (2007) noted, these numerous terms are derived from the different paradigms used to describe different tests and states of factorial invariance. Some researchers (e.g., Meredith, 1993) use the terms *weak factorial invariance, strong factorial invariance,* and *strict factorial invariance*, which refer to increasingly stringent degrees or categories of invariance. Others (e.g., Vandenberg & Lance, 2000) use the terms *configural, metric, scalar, uniqueness, factor variances, factor covariance,* and *factor means,* which refer to specific invariance tests. However, as seen in Table 7.1, these two paradigms are not mutually exclusive.

Factorial Invariance

One of the currently favored methods used to determine measurement equivalence is confirmatory factor analysis; therefore, for the rest of this section we use the term *factorial invariance* when discussing measurement equivalence. As noted earlier, in the factor analytic framework, the factorial invariance of instruments or models is tested by examining a measurement and/or structural model across distinct groups (Byrne et al., 1989; Millsap & Kwok, 2004; Steenkamp & Baumgartner, 1998). Factorial invariance assesses the degree to which parameters of a hypothesized model (e.g., factor loadings) have nonsignificantly different values across different groups or populations (Millsap & Kwok, 2004). Are there nonsubstantial differences across groups in the magnitude of model parameters (e.g., the influence of a latent factor on an observed indictor or item measure)? Establishing factorial invariance (i.e., measurement equivalence) requires two broad types of evidence: (1) measurement invariance and (2) structural invariance (Byrne et al., 1989; Vandenberg & Lance, 2000). *Measurement invariance* deals with whether the factor configurations, loadings, item intercepts, and unique error variances are similar or significantly different across groups. *Structural invariance* assesses whether factor variances, covariances, and latent means are equivalent across groups (Bontempo & Hofer, 2007; Byrne et al., 1989; Vandenberg & Lance, 2000).

In the next section, we review the specific tests of factorial invariance (i.e., configural, metric, scalar, uniqueness; each of increasing stringency) and structural invariance (i.e., factor variances, covariance, and means) based on the literature. See Vandenberg and Lance (2000), Meredith (1993), and Byrne et al. (1989) for comprehensive applied and mathematical discussions of factorial invariance.

Measurement Invariance

Equivalence of Covariance Matrices

Some suggest that a necessary first step in assessing factorial invariance is a test of the equivalence of covariance matrices (Jöreskog & Sörbom, 1996). This omnibus test of the equivalence of covariance matrices across groups assumes that if no difference in covariance matrices exists across different groups, then invariance has been established (Vandenberg & Lance, 2000)—that the covariance matrices of measured variables (e.g., items) are equivalent across groups. Others (e.g., Bontempo & Hofer, 2007) argue that this omnibus test of covariance matrices is not ideal because well-fitting components (i.e., model parameters) of the model may be confounded by poorly fitting ones.

Configural Invariance

Configural invariance assesses the degree to which the same *pattern* of estimated model parameters is appropriate for both samples independently (i.e., is the pattern of factor loadings the same across groups?). Establishing configural invariance is a prerequisite for conducting further tests of invariance (Vandenberg & Lance, 2000) and is typically tested via CFA by assessing the degree to which a posited measurement model produces an appropriate fit to the data for independent groups.

Metric Invariance

Metric invariance assesses the equivalence of the *magnitude* of factor loadings (i.e., assessing the degree to which test items relate to their respective factor in an equivalent fashion across groups; Horn & McArdle, 1992; Widaman & Reise, 1997). Testing for metric invariance requires the researcher to constrain factor loadings to be equivalent across independent samples rather than, as is the case of establishing configural invariance, simply testing model fit in different samples. It assesses the degree to which test items are being interpreted in the same way across different groups and is thus of particular importance to multicultural research (Byrne et al., 1989). We can infer that items are being interpreted in the same way when the equivalence of factor loadings is established.

Scalar Invariance

Scalar invariance assesses the equivalence of item *intercepts* across groups and is a requirement for comparisons of latent means (G. W. Cheung & Rensvold, 2002). Item intercepts provide an indication of the value of the measured item when the value of the common factor is zero (Bontempo & Hofer, 2007). Testing for scalar invariance involves constraining item intercepts of the measurement model to be equivalent across groups. A nonsignificant difference in intercept values suggests scalar invariance. The combination of configural, metric, and scalar invariance is sometimes referred to as strong factorial invariance. This test is rare in the literature because intercepts are often seen as sample-specific and arbitrary (Vandenberg & Lance, 2000). However, in the specific case of measure development, scalar variance across groups is "always undesirable" (Bontempo & Hofer, 2007, p. 164).

Uniqueness Invariance

In the measurement invariance literature, uniqueness refers to the unique variance in each measured indicator (e.g., item) that is not accounted for by the indicator's respective factor (i.e., is not common variance). Assessing the equivalence of uniqueness requires that unique error terms are constrained to be equal across groups. When configural, metric, scalar, and uniqueness invariance are established, strict factorial invariance is established.

In summary, establishing evidence of factorial invariance requires that the (a) hypothesized measurement model fits equally well across groups (configural invariance), (b) magnitude of factor loadings are equivalent across groups (metric invariance), (c) intercepts are the same across groups (scalar invariance), and (d) magnitude of errors are equal across groups (uniqueness invariance). Vandenberg and Lance (2000) recommended that these tests of measurement invariance (i.e., configural, metric, scalar, and uniqueness) be conducted *sequentially* (in the order presented earlier) and *prior* to tests of structural invariance.

Structural Invariance

Tests of measurement invariance focused primarily on the fit of the hypothesized measurement model across groups—whether the magnitude of factor loadings, intercepts, and errors are similar across groups. Tests of structural invariance, however, focus more on the equivalence of factor scores across groups by testing whether (a) the dispersion or variance of factor scores is equivalent across groups (equivalence of factor variances), (b) the factors intercorrelate similarly across groups (equivalence of factor covariance), and (c) the latent mean scores obtained on each factor are the same across groups. Establishing evidence of measurement invariance is a prerequisite for examining structural invariance (Widaman & Reise, 1997).

Equivalence of Factor Variances and Covariances

These tests of structural invariance assess whether the way in which the *breadth* (i.e., degree of variance) of the latent factor is being equivalently operationalized (equivalence of factor variances) and the degree to which the magnitude of factor intercorrelations are the same (equivalence of factor covariances) across meaningfully distinct groups (G. W. Cheung & Rensvold, 2002). Typical tests for this type of invariance involve constraining factor variances and covariances to be equal across groups.

Equivalence of Latent Factor Means

The test of equivalence of latent factor means is analogous to a *t* test or analysis of variance (ANOVA) comparison of observed mean scores; however, the test of latent factor means is advantageous because measurement error has been parceled out (Bontempo & Hofer, 2007; Vandenberg & Lance, 2000). Tests of equivalence of latent factor means are rare in the literature and, when conducted, are generally based on some theoretical consideration (G. W. Cheung & Rensvold, 2002).

Some researchers suggest that if metric measurement invariance is not established, then further tests of invariance (e.g., scalar invariance, equivalence of factor covariances) are not feasible; others, however, suggest that only partial measurement invariance is required for further invariance testing (Byrne et al., 1989; Reise, Widaman, & Pugh, 1993). Partial measurement invariance refers to the condition in which one or more model parameters, identified via metric, scalar, and uniqueness invariance tests, are found to be variant across identified groups. There is, however, a lack of consensus as to what is acceptable in terms of the number of variant parameters and which parameters (e.g., uniqueness, factor loadings, intercepts) can be variant before concluding that the entire model does not hold true across different groups (Bontempo & Hofer, 2007). Although there is a lack of consensus about the acceptable minimal levels of partial invariance, Byrne et al. (1989) proposed that a minimum of two invariant factor loadings per latent factor in metric invariance tests were required to establish partial measurement invariance. We, however, feel that a more conservative approach (e.g., invariance across the majority of loadings per latent factor in metric invariance tests) would produce results in which greater confidence can be placed regarding the common meaning of items or factor structure across groups.

Implementation of Measurement Equivalence in Multicultural Research

In light of the recent interest in the literature in measurement equivalence, we conducted a literature search to identify the degree to which measurement equivalence (i.e., factorial invariance) was being addressed in the multicultural psychology literature. Based on a title and keyword search using the term *factorial invariance* in the PsycInfo database (all years), we identified three published articles that included some test of measurement and/or structural invariance for a measure across different racial and/or ethnic groups (Mobley, Slaney, & Rice, 2005; Utsey, Brown, & Bolden, 2004; Wei, Russell, Mallinckrodt, & Zakalik, 2004). Two of these studies were published in *JCP* and one was published in *Educational and Psychological Measurement*. Of the three studies, each assessed for metric invariance, one addressed configural invariance, and two attended to equivalence of factor variances and covariances. In addition, one study assessed the equivalence of latent factor means. After rejecting the equivalence of factor variances and covariances, one study identified a model with partial structural invariance.

We would like to make five suggestions to encourage the further application of measurement invariance techniques to multicultural psychology research. First, we suggest that while providing evidence of each type of invariance would be ideal, at times this may not be necessary. For a number of research questions, a primary concern (in terms of invariance) might be whether measured items are being interpreted in an equivalent way across different groups, and issues related to factor structure may be of less concern. However, when the goal of a study is to test theory, we recommend obtaining evidence of structural invariance across different groups.

Second, consistent with the broader CFA and structural equation modeling literature, we encourage researchers to continue to address the issue of multivariate normality in factorial invariance studies. When using the SB χ^2, the traditional nested model testing approach (i.e., obtaining chi-square values for the two models being compared and assessing whether the difference between them is significant) tends to not be trustworthy (Satorra & Bentler, 2001). Therefore, when conducting nested model tests with nonnormally distributed data, it is necessary to use the scale difference chi-square test statistic (T_d; Satorra & Bentler, 2001), which provides a more accurate test for detecting meaningful differences between nested models when using the SB χ^2.

Third, we encourage the inclusion of scalar invariance tests when assessing latent factor means. Because intercept values are necessary in the identification of latent means, if intercepts are variant (or if no information is provided on their equivalence) across groups, it is not possible to determine if observed latent factor mean nonequivalence is due to actual differences or variance in intercept values (Vandenberg & Lance, 2000). It has been suggested that strict factorial invariance (see Table 7.1) should be established to make meaningful interpretations about the equivalence of latent factor means across different groups (Meredith, 1993).

Fourth, although the most relevant application of measurement equivalence in multicultural research is likely that of assessing the invariance of a measurement model of a multicultural measure (e.g., the CoBRAS), this analytic technique can also be used to test the equivalence of a structural model across different groups. Lent et al. (2005) assessed the equivalence of a structural model of academic interest and choice across male and female university students. Testing structural coefficients (i.e., the effect of one latent factor on another) aids theory validation (e.g., that the process by which interests and choices occur is equivalent across gender) or revision (in cases where structural nonequivalence is found). It could also be used to assess in-group variations (e.g., plausibility of a particular structural model for Asian Americans at different levels of acculturation).

Finally, we also wish to point out that tests of invariance can be conducted with both cross-sectional and longitudinal data (Bontempo & Hofer, 2007). The difference in application is that for cross-sectional data, analysis addresses the equivalence of model parameters across different (i.e., independent) groups, whereas longitudinal tests of invariance assess the equivalence of model parameters over time in the same group (see Meredith & Horn, 2001). The application of measurement invariance with longitudinal data may be especially useful in studying such issues as cultural adaptation or the experience of racism-related stress.

We believe that incorporating measurement equivalence in multicultural research is essential for the continued growth and development of the field. Attending to measurement equivalence could likely elucidate and refine our understanding of the nature and structure of multicultural constructs between groups (e.g., women and men, Asian Americans and Caucasians, Latinos and African Americans) and within groups (e.g., Puerto Ricans and Mexican Americans).

USE OF META-ANALYSES TO INTEGRATE FINDINGS AND TEST MULTIVARIATE MODELS

We began this chapter by referencing the impact of social forces external to counseling psychology that were responsible for the increasing attention paid to multicultural issues in the field. Counseling psychology has been well positioned to address salient social issues (e.g., racism, oppression, social justice) and has done so with vigor. Over the past few decades, numerous theoretical and empirical works pertinent to multicultural issues have been published (Neville & Carter, 2005). A recent review of the acculturation literature identified over 300 published articles since 2000 alone (Miller, Kasson, & Farrell, 2006). As the literature in multicultural psychology continues to grow, researchers will likely be in need of research methodologies that allow for the integration and synthesis of findings from a wide range of existing studies. We propose that traditional (i.e., bivariate) meta-analytic and structural equation modeling meta-analytic approaches have the potential to serve this purpose well.

Historically, meta-analysis has been used to shed light on validating and expanding old theories and developing new theories (e.g., Hunter & Schmidt, 2004). Although much progress has been made since the term *meta-analysis* was first coined in the 1970s, traditional meta-analytic approaches are limited in their ability to capture the complexity of modern data analysis techniques. Traditional meta-analyses have focused on bivariate effect sizes, such as correlations and *d* values. Using this technique, several meta-analyses have integrated findings across studies of the relationship between particular sets of theoretically related variables, such as the relation of cultural mistrust to attitudes and behaviors regarding mental health service use (e.g., Whaley, 2001). Although the traditional meta-analytic approach to research synthesis has provided invaluable information, this approach is limited in that it only assesses simultaneous associations between two variables. The traditional approach does not allow for the concurrent estimation of multiple associations (e.g., mediational models). Given the complexity of multicultural constructs and the nuanced conceptual frameworks (nomological networks) in which these constructs are placed, it would be valuable to take multiple variables (i.e., models of psychological processes germane to multicultural research) into account simultaneously to fully synthesize research findings and to test multicultural models and theories.

Recent developments in meta-analytic structural equation modeling (MASEM) provide a means to address such issues (M. W. L. Cheung & Chan, 2005; Shadish, 1996). Meta-analytic structural equation modeling is particularly suitable when researchers are interested in integrating data from multiple studies that are derived from a theoretical model or include the same set of constructs. This new approach can provide more accurate estimates of the effect sizes between any pair of variables included in the model because the joint effects of other variables are taken into account. By contrast, traditional approaches tend to overestimate bivariate effects. Although we were unable to identify any studies using the MASEM strategy in the multicultural literature, a recent meta-analysis (Sheu et al., 2006) tested the choice model of social cognitive career theory (Lent, Brown, & Hackett, 1994) with 39 independent correlation matrices that included the same set of four variables. In almost every instance, Sheu et al. found that the path coefficients obtained from MASEM were smaller, and presumably more accurate, than the correlations obtained from traditional bivariate approaches.

There are a number of areas in the field of multicultural psychology that we believe are ripe for synthesis and summary (e.g., acculturation literature, racial or ethnic identity literature). Because the MASEM approach requires multiple empirical studies that examine the same model (or components), traditional meta-analytic procedures would still be useful in synthesizing research from areas where only bivariate associations have been studied (e.g., acculturation and mental health outcomes, associations between racial and ethnic identity). Ultimately, we recommend the use of MASEM to obtain the most accurate estimates of effect sizes between variables in complex multicultural models (i.e., where multiple relations are being examined simultaneously). The use of meta-analytic procedures in such situations would not only serve to summarize current findings but would also identify issues for future research (e.g., possible mediator and moderator variables).

SUMMARY

Multicultural psychology began as a socially and politically inspired movement and, over the past few decades, has evolved into a relatively sophisticated, empirically based scholarly field due to the efforts of countless pioneers and their professional descendents. Our review of the multicultural psychology research literature revealed a number of positive trends in the implementation of sophisticated measurement development and data analytic methodologies. We summarized important factors to consider when using exploratory and confirmatory factor analytic strategies to develop and validate measures of important multicultural constructs. We also suggested that measurement invariance data analytic strategies are particularly powerful ways to enhance our understanding of both multicultural constructs and diverse cultural groups. Last, we highlighted traditional meta-analytic and structural equation modeling meta-analytic approaches and their utility for both theory validation and refinement. We hope this chapter assists researchers as they consider new ways to further understanding of multicultural phenomena in counseling psychology.

REFERENCES

American Psychological Association. (2003). Guidelines on multicultural education, training, research, practice, and organizational change for psychologists. *American Psychologist, 58*, 377–402.

Anastasi, A., & Urbina, S. (1997). *Psychological testing* (7th ed.). Upper Saddle River, NJ: Prentice Hall.

Bandalos, D. L., & Finney, S. J. (2001). Item parceling issues in structural equation modeling. In G. A. Marcoulides & R. E. Schumaker (Eds.), *Advanced structural equation modeling: New developments and techniques* (pp. 269–296). Mahwah, NJ: Erlbaum.

Bentler, P. M. (1989). *EQS: Structural equations program manual*. Los Angeles: BMDP Statistical Software.

Betancourt, H., & López, S. R. (1993). The study of culture, ethnicity, and race in American psychology. *American Psychologist, 48*, 629–637.

Bollen, K. A. (1989). *Structural equations with latent variables*. New York: Wiley.

Bontempo, D. E., & Hofer, S. M. (2007). Assessing factorial invariance in cross-sectional and longitudinal studies. In A. D. Ong & M. H. M. van Dulmen (Eds.), *Oxford handbook of methods in positive psychology* (pp. 153–175). New York: Oxford University Press.

Bryant, F. B., & Baxter, W. J. (1997). The structure of positive and negative automatic cognition. *Cognition and Emotion, 11*, 225–258.

Burlew, A. K. (2003). Research with ethnic minorities: Conceptual, methodological, and analytical issues. In G. Bernal, J. E. Trimble, A. K. Burlew, & F. T. L. Leong (Eds.), *Handbook of racial and ethnic minority psychology* (pp. 179–197). Thousand Oaks, CA: Sage.

Butcher, J. N., Cheung, F. M., & Lim, J. (2003). Use of the MMPI-2 with Asian populations. *Psychological Assessment, 15*, 248–256.

Byrne, B. M., Shavelson, R. J., & Muthén, B. (1989). Testing for the equivalence of factor covariance and mean structures: The issue of partial measurement invariance. *Psychological Bulletin, 105*, 456–466.

Cheung, G. W., & Rensvold, R.B. (2002). Evaluating goodness-of-fit indexes for testing measurement invariance. *Structural Equation Modeling, 9*, 233–255.

Cheung, M. W. L., & Chan, W. (2005). Classifying correlation matrices into relatively homogeneous subgroups: A cluster analytic approach. *Educational and Psychological Measurement, 65*, 954–979.

Curran, P. J., West, S. G., & Finch, J. F. (1996). The robustness of test statistics to nonnormality and specification error in confirmatory factor analysis. *Psychological Methods, 1*, 16–29.

Dawis, R. V. (2000). Scale construction and psychometric considerations. In H. E. A. Tinsley & S. B. Brown (Eds.), *Handbook of applied multivariate statistics and mathematical modeling* (pp. 65–94). New York: Academic Press.

Delgado-Romero, E. A., Galván, N., Maschino, P., & Rowland, M. (2005). Race and ethnicity in empirical counseling and counseling psychology research: A 10-year review. *Counseling Psychologist, 33*, 419–448.

DeVellis, R. F. (2003). *Scale development: Theory and applications* (2nd ed.). Thousand Oaks, CA: Sage.

Fabrigar, L. R., Wegener, D. T., MacCallum, R. C., & Strahan, E. J. (1999). Evaluating the use of exploratory factor analysis in psychological research. *Psychological Methods, 3*, 272–299.

Finch, J. F., & West, S. G. (1997). The investigation of personality structure: Statistical models. *Journal of Research in Personality, 31*, 439–485.

Fischer, A. R., Jome, L. M., & Atkinson, D. R. (1998). Reconceptualizing multicultural counseling: Universal healing condition in a culturally specific context. *Counseling Psychologist, 26*, 525–588.

Gorsuch, R. L. (1983). *Factor analysis* (2nd ed.). Hillsdale, NJ: Erlbaum.

Hattie, J. A. (1985). Methodology review: Assessing unidimensionality of tests and items. *Applied Psychological Measurement, 9*, 139–164.

Hayduk, L., (1996) *LISREL issues, debates, and strategies*. Baltimore, MD: Johns Hopkins University Press.

Helms, J. E., & Cook, D. A. (1999). *Using race and culture in counseling and psychotherapy: Theory and process*. Needham Heights, MA: Allyn & Bacon.

Holland, J. L. (1997), *Making vocational choice: A theory of vocational personalities and work environments* (3rd ed.). Odessa, FL: Psychological Assessment Resources.

Horn, J. L., & McArdle, J. J. (1992). A practical and theoretical guide to measurement invariance in aging research. *Experimental Aging Research, 18*, 117–144.

Hoyle, R. H. (1995). *Structural equation modeling: Concepts, issues, and applications*. Thousand Oaks, CA: Sage.

Hu, L., & Bentler, P. M. (1998). Fit indices in covariance structure modeling: Sensitivity to underparameterized model misspecification. *Psychological Methods, 3*, 424–453.

Hunter, J. E., & Schmidt, F. L. (2004). *Methods of meta-analysis: Correcting error and bias in research findings* (2nd ed.). Thousand Oaks, CA: Sage.

Jöreskog, K., & Sörbom, D. (1996). *LISREL 8: User's reference guide*. Lincolnwood, IL: Scientific Software International.

Kahn, J. H. (2006). Factor analysis in counseling psychology research, training, and practice: Principles, advances, and applications. *Counseling Psychologist, 34*, 684–718.

Kline, R. B. (1998). *Principles and practice of structural equation modeling*. New York: Guilford Press.

Lent, R. W., Brown, S. D., & Hackett, G. (1994). Toward a unifying social cognitive theory of career and academic interest, choice, and performance [Monograph]. *Journal of Vocational Behavior, 45*, 79–122.

Lent, R. W., Brown, S. D., Sheu, H., Schmidt, J., Brenner, B. R., Gloster, C. S., *et al.* (2005). Social cognitive predictors of academic interests and goals in engineering: Utility for women and students at historically Black universities. *Journal of Counseling Psychology, 52*, 84–92.

Leong, F. T. L. (1993). The career counseling process with racial-ethnic minorities: The case of Asian Americans. *Career Development Quarterly, 42*, 26–40.

Liang, C. T. H., Li, L. C., & Kim, B. S. K. (2004). The Asian American Racism-Related Stress Inventory: Development, factor analysis, reliability, and validity. *Journal of Counseling Psychology, 51*, 103–114.

Little, T. D., Cunningham, W. A., Shahar, G., & Widaman, K. F. (2002). To parcel or not to parcel: Exploring the question, weighing the merits. *Structural Equation Modeling, 9*, 151–173.

MacCallum, R. C., & Austin, J. T. (2000). Applications of structural equation modeling in psychological research. *Annual Review of Psychology, 51*, 201–226.

MacCallum, R. C., Roznowski, M., & Necowitz, L. B. (1992). Model modifications in covariance structure analysis: The problem of capitalization on chance. *Psychological Bulletin, 111*, 490–504.

MacCallum, R. C., Wegener, D. T., Uchino, B. N., & Fabrigar, L. R. (1993). The problem of equivalent models in applications of covariance structure analysis. *Psychological Bulletin, 114*, 185–199.

MacPhee, D., Kreutzer, J. C., & Fritz, J. J. (1994). Infusing a diversity perspective into human development courses. *Child Development, 65*, 699–715.

Marsh, H. W., Balla, J. R., & McDonald, R. P. (1998). Goodness-of-fit indices in confirmatory factor analysis: Effects of sample size. *Psychological Bulletin, 103*, 391–411.

Martens, M. P. (2005). The use of structural equation modeling in counseling psychology research. *Counseling Psychologist, 33*, 269–298.

McDonald, R. P., & Ho, M. R. (2002). Principles and practice in reporting structural equation analyses. *Psychological Methods, 7*, 64–82.

Meredith, W. (1993). Measurement invariance, factor analysis, and factorial invariance. *Psychometrika, 58*, 525–543.

Meredith, W., & Horn, J. L. (2001). The role of factorial invariance in modeling growth and change. In L. M. Collins (Ed.), *New methods for the analysis of change* (pp. 203–240). Washington, DC: American Psychological Association.

Miller, M. J. (2006). *A content analysis of the multicultural measurement development literature.* Unpublished manuscript.

Miller, M. J. (in press). A bilinear multidimensional measurement model of Asian American acculturation and enculturation: Implications for counseling interventions. *Journal of Counseling Psychology.*

Miller, M. J., Kasson, D., & Farrell, J. (2006). *An empirical review of the acculturation literature across disciplines.* Unpublished manuscript.

Millsap, R. E. (1997). Invariance in measurement and prediction: Their relationship in the single-factor case. *Psychological Methods, 2*, 248–260.

Millsap, R. E., & Kwok, O. (2004). Evaluating the impact of partial factorial invariance on selection in two populations. *Psychological Methods, 9*, 93–115.

Mobley, M., Slaney, R. B., & Rice, K. G. (2005). Cultural validity of the Almost Perfect Scale-Revised for African American college students. *Journal of Counseling Psychology, 52*, 629–639.

Nagel, J. (1994). Constructing ethnicity: Creating and recreating ethnicity and culture. *Social Problems, 41*, 152–176.

Neville, H. A., & Carter, R. T. (2005). Race and racism in counseling psychology research, training, and practice: A critical review, current trends, and future directions. *Counseling Psychologist, 33*, 413–418.

Neville, H. A., Lilly, R. L., Duran, G., Lee, R. M., & Browne, L. (2000). Construction and initial validation of the Color-Blind Racial Attitudes Scale (CoBRAS). *Journal of Counseling Psychology, 47*, 59–70.

Noh, E. R. (2003). *We are all bicultural: Different ways of integrating the cultures through the experience of Korean American college students.* Unpublished doctoral dissertation, Boston College.

O'Conner, B. P. (2000). SPSS and SAS programs for determining the number of components using parallel analysis and Velicer's MAP test. *Behavior Research Methods, Instruments, and Computers, 32*, 396–402.

Ponterotto, J. G., Casas, J. M., Suzuki, L. A., & Alexander, C. M. (Eds.). (2001). *Handbook of multicultural counseling* (2nd ed.). Thousand Oaks, CA: Sage.

Pope-Davis, D. B., Coleman, H. L. K., Liu, W. M., & Toporek, R. L. (Eds.). (2003). *Handbook of multicultural competencies in counseling and psychology.* Thousand Oaks, CA: Sage.

Pope-Davis, D. B., Liu, W. M., Nevitt, J., & Toporek, R. L. (2000). The development and initial validation of the Multicultural Environmental Inventory. *Cultural Diversity and Ethnic Minority Psychology, 6*, 57–64.

Quintana, S. M., & Maxwell, S. E. (1999). Implications of recent developments in structural equation modeling for counseling psychology. *Counseling Psychologist, 27*, 485–527.

Reise, S. P., Widaman, K. F., & Pugh, R. H. (1993). Confirmatory factor analysis and item response theory: Two approaches for exploring measurement invariance. *Psychological Bulletin, 114*, 552–566.

Satorra, A., & Bentler, P. M. (1994). Corrections to test statistics and standard errors on covariance structure analysis. In A. von Eye & C. C. Clogg (Eds.), *Latent variables analysis* (pp. 399–419). Thousand Oaks, CA: Sage.

Satorra, A., & Bentler, P. M. (2001). A scaled difference chi-square test statistic for moment structure analysis. *Psychometrika, 66*, 507–514.

Shadish, W. R. (1996). Meta-analysis and the exploration of causal mediating processes: A primer of examples, methods, and issues. *Psychological Methods, 1*, 47–65.

Sheu, H. B., & Lent, R. W.(in press). Development and initial validation of the Multicultural Counseling Self-Efficacy Scale—Racial Diversity Form. *Psychotherapy: Theory, Research, Practice, Training*.

Sheu, H. B., Miller, M. J., Lent, R. W., Brown, S. D., Hennessy, K., & Duffy, R. D. (2006, August). *The social cognitive choice model: Comparison of two meta-analytic approaches*. In R.W. Lent (Chair), Testing social cognitive career theory with diverse methodological tools. Paper presented at the 2006 annual Conference of the American Psychological Association, New Orleans, LA.

Spanierman, L. B., & Heppner, M. J. (2004). Psychosocial Costs of Racism to Whites Scale (PCRW): Construction and initial validation. *Journal of Counseling Psychology, 51*, 249–262.

Spearman, C. (1904). General intelligence, objectively determined and measured. *American Journal of Psychology, 15*, 201–293.

Steenkamp, J. E. M., & Baumgartner, H. (1998). Assessing measurement invariance in cross-national consumer research. *Journal of Consumer Research, 25*, 78–90.

Stevens, S. S. (1946). On the theory of scales of measurement. *Science, 103*, 677–680.

Sue, D. W., Ivey, A. E., & Pedersen, P. B. (1996). *A theory of multicultural counseling and therapy*. New York: Brooks/Cole.

Sue, D. W., & Sue, D. (2003). *Counseling the culturally diverse: Theory and practice* (4th ed.). Hoboken, NJ: Wiley.

Tang, M. (2001). Investigation of the structure of vocational interests of Chinese college students. *Journal of Career Assessment, 9*, 365–380.

Triandis, H., Lambert, W., Berry, J., Lonner, W., Heron, A., Brislin, R., et al. (Eds.), (1980) *Handbook of cross-cultural psychology* (Vols. 1–6). Boston: Allyn & Bacon.

Utsey, S. O., Brown, C., & Bolden, M. A. (2004). Testing the structural invariance of the Africultural Coping Systems Inventory across three samples of African descent populations. *Educational and Psychological Measurement, 64*, 185–195.

Vandenberg, R. J., & Lance, C. E. (2000). A review and synthesis of the measurement invariance literature: Suggestions, practices, and recommendations for organizational research. *Organizational Research Methods, 3*, 4–70.

Wei, M., Russell, D. W., Mallinckrodt, B., & Zakalik, R. A. (2004). Cultural equivalence of adult attachment across four ethnic groups: Factor structure, structured means, and associations with negative mood. *Journal of Counseling Psychology, 51*, 408–417.

Weston, R., & Gore, P. A. (2006). A brief guide to structural equation modeling. *Counseling Psychologist, 34*, 719–751.

Whaley, A. L. (2001). Cultural mistrust and mental health services for African Americans: A review and meta-analysis. *Counseling Psychologist, 29*, 213–531.

Widaman, K. F., & Reise, S. P. (1997). Exploring the measurement invariance of psychological instruments: Applications in the substance use domain. In K. J. Bryant & M. Windle (Eds.), *The science of prevention: Methodological advances from alcohol and substance abuse research* (pp. 281–324). Washington, DC: American Psychological Association.

Worthington, R. L., Dillon, F. R., & Becker-Schutte, A. M. (2005). Development, reliability, and validity of the Lesbian, Gay, and Bisexual Knowledge and Attitudes Scale for Heterosexuals (LGB-KASH). *Journal of Counseling Psychology, 52*, 104–118.

Worthington, R. L., & Whittaker, T. A. (2006). Scale development research: A content analysis and recommendations for best practice. *Counseling Psychologist, 34*, 806–838.

Zwick, W. R., & Velicer, W. F. (1986). Comparison of five rules for determining the number of components to retain. *Psychological Bulletin, 9*, 432–442.

CHAPTER 8

Theoretical and Empirical Advances in Multicultural Counseling and Psychology

JOSEPH G. PONTEROTTO

There is little debate that attention to multicultural issues in counseling psychology has increased substantially during the past 25 years. The rapid growth of the multicultural counseling field is not at all unexpected, especially in the past decade. At the turn of the twenty-first century, Neimeyer and Diamond (2001) conducted a Delphi poll surveying the anticipated future of counseling psychology in the United States. Training directors of counseling psychology programs were polled regarding their expectations for major developments in the field over the next decade. Respondents (51% response rate) rated 28 possible developments in three broad areas: (1) counseling psychology core identity, (2) research and training, and (3) professional training. Of 11 identified core areas, "Commitment to issues of diversity" received the highest ratings (Neimeyer & Diamond, 2001, p. 57). Developments over the past 5 years suggest that the Delphi poll predictions were on target (e.g., American Psychological Association, 2003).

Whereas multicultural inquiry in counseling psychology was still in its infancy at the time this *Handbook* was first published in 1984, it is now clearly in a state of rapid maturation. The literature on diversity is now so broad and expansive that it is hard to track or prioritize. This chapter synthesizes the growing literature in multicultural counseling and provides a summary of major developments in the field. I begin with a brief historical perspective on trends in the multicultural counseling literature. Second, I review theory and research in two emerging areas of multicultural psychology: (1) the universal-diverse orientation and (2) the multicultural personality. These constructs are directly relevant to counseling psychology, and both hold promise for advancing research and practice in our specialty.

HISTORICAL DEVELOPMENTS IN MULTICULTURAL COUNSELING

In briefly reviewing the history of theory and research in multicultural counseling, I borrow terminology introduced by sociologists Denzin and Lincoln (2005), who outlined the history of qualitative research along nine historical periods that they labeled *moments*. I next describe the development of multicultural counseling in a series of five moments beginning around the middle of the twentieth century.

First Moment: Benign Neglect (Pre-1960s)

The *first moment* in the specialty of multicultural counseling was characterized by a noticeable neglect of multicultural issues in counseling theory and research. A review of the counseling, clinical, and educational literatures during this time yields only a few articles focusing on cultural issues in counseling (Jackson, 1995; Westbrook, 1991). Jackson (1995) conducted a fairly comprehensive review of the journal literature during the 1950s and concluded that the majority of multicultural literature focused on African Americans, with little attention given to other American racial or ethnic minority groups.

With regard to topical foci, he noted an emphasis on educational achievement, testing issues across cultures (e.g., bias), and career development topics, with little attention to the counseling relationship or process.

Second Moment: Birth of a Movement (1960s and 1970s)

Spurred on by the civil rights movement and the passage of the Civil Rights Act of 1964, counseling psychology galvanized a commitment to attend to issues of mental health for non-White populations. The quantity of literature focusing on multicultural issues increased significantly during this period, and professional psychology organizations established numerous committees and commissions to address the field's former neglect of minority issues (Heppner, Casas, Carter, & Stone, 2000; Jackson, 1995). Research during this time tended to study race and ethnicity as categorical variables, and often focused on between-groups differences. During the early portion of this *second moment,* there was still a strong focus on African American issues; as the period progressed, increased attention was devoted to other racial/ethnic minority groups.

According to Atkinson and Thompson (1992), comprehensive reviews of the empirical literature during the 1970s revealed three major trends: (1) racial or ethnic minority clients tended to underutilize voluntary mental health services; (2) African Americans preferred to see an African American counselor over a White counselor; and (3) racial or ethnic minority professionals were underrepresented at all levels in counseling and clinical psychology.

Third Moment: Gaining Momentum and Establishing a Specialty (1980s)

There was unprecedented growth in attention to multicultural issues during the 1980s (see Jackson, 1995). During this *third moment,* major theoretical and empirical breakthroughs were made, accompanied by a major paradigm shift from between-group difference models to within-group difference models. The research zeitgeist shifted from comparing minority groups to Whites, to the identification of differences in cultural groups, absent the comparison to White "control" groups. Within-group difference models promoted strength-based perspectives in the study of mental health issues among racial or ethnic groups (Ponterotto & Casas, 1991).

Theories of Black and White racial identity development (e.g., Helms, 1984) took hold during the early 1980s and went on to have a profound impact on research generation over subsequent decades. Another within-group variable, acculturation, began to receive theoretical attention during this time and led to the development of popular acculturation measures for Hispanic Americans (Cuellar, Harris, & Jasso, 1980) and Asian Americans (Suinn, Rickard-Figueroa, Lew, & Vigil, 1987).

In their concise yet comprehensive review of the literature from 1981 through 1990, Atkinson and Thompson (1992) summarized studies on Black and White racial identity development, acculturation, counselor-client similarity matching (employing race or ethnicity, attitudes, and education as matching variables), and cultural mistrust. Ponterotto and Casas (1991) reviewed 91 empirical studies from 1983 through 1988 published in five leading counseling journals and noted that the most prevalent topics of study were counselor-client racial similarity and counseling process, career counseling, academic or educational counseling, assertiveness, client preferences for counselors' race, general attitudes toward counseling, client needs assessments, and multicultural instrument development and validation. Although coverage of non-African American groups continued to grow during this period, the *third moment* was still marked by a primary focus on African American issues in counseling.

Fourth Moment: Maturation and Expansion of a Specialty (1990s)

The *fourth moment* witnessed exponential growth in multiculturally focused journal articles and book chapters. Research trends in racial identity development and acculturation initiated in the *third moment* came to full fruition during this time period. By the mid 1990s, racial identity, acculturation, and worldview constructs constituted major foci in counseling research. New models of White racial identity, Black racial identity, and biracial or multiracial identity were presented, and increasing research appeared on non-White, non-African American racial or ethnic groups (e.g., see reviews in Ponterotto, Casas, Suzuki, & Alexander, 2001). This fourth moment also saw increasing theoretical and research attention devoted to nonracial or nonethnic minority groups, in particular, gay and lesbian populations, the elderly, and persons with disabilities (e.g., Atkinson & Hackett, 1998).

The 1990s also witnessed a move toward greater accountability in promoting counseling competency across cultures, leading to the development and testing of numerous multicultural counseling competency assessment instruments and tools (Ponterotto, Fuertes, & Chen, 2000). Complementing the increased attention to multicultural competency was a parallel growth in attention to multiculturalism in training. Surveys indicated that by 1995, 89% of counseling psychology programs required a multicultural course, and 57% of these programs reported success in integrating multicultural issues into all coursework (Ponterotto, 1997). During this *fourth moment*, multicultural counseling became an established specialty in the field.

Fifth Moment: Beyond Borders and Disciplines (2000-Present)

I characterize the present period as the *fifth moment* of multicultural counseling. Key markers of this moment include (a) the expansion of multicultural counseling issues beyond U.S and Canadian borders (Leong & Ponterotto, 2003); (b) the intersection of multicultural counseling with other psychological specialties, such as positive psychology (Constantine & Sue, 2006), personnel psychology (Van der Zee & Van Oudenhoven, 2000), and personality psychology (Van der Zee & Van Oudenhoven, 2001); and (c) the expansion of scientific methods to enhance the comprehensive study of multicultural counseling (Miller & Sheu, Chapter 7, this volume; Morrow, Rakhsha, & Castaneda, 2001). In addition to new directions, the fifth moment is characterized by a continuing focus on topics generated in previous moments; namely, the role of racial and ethnic identity (Cokley, 2007), acculturation (Sam & Berry, 2006), and worldview (Koltko-Rivera, 2004) in counseling process and outcome, and accountability in meeting the mental health needs of an increasingly diverse clientele through an emphasis on multicultural counseling competence (Constantine, Miville, & Kindaichi, Chapter 9, this volume).

One emphasis evident in this fifth moment is an expansion of theory and research from *emic* (culturally specific; e.g., models of Black and White racial identity development) to more *etic* (culturally transcendent) models. Although generating extensive research, emic models of racial identity development are limited in a number of ways. The majority of racial identity work is rooted only in counseling and developmental psychology, thus limiting the scope and application of the theory. Because emic models are culture-specific, they are limited in their ability to generalize and capture the experiences of a broad base of individuals. Ponterotto, Utsey, and Pedersen (2006) noted that having broader, "more universally inclusive (etic) models of cultural self-integration and multicultural interpersonal competence would be useful to researchers and teachers" (p. 128). Two particularly promising etic models in this regard are universal-diverse orientation (UDO) and the multicultural personality (MP). In the next sections, I review research in these two areas.

UNIVERSAL-DIVERSE ORIENTATION

Universal-diverse orientation was introduced into the counseling psychology literature by Miville et al. (1999), who defined the construct as follows:

> an attitude toward all other persons that is inclusive yet differentiating in that similarities and differences are both recognized and accepted; the shared experience of being human results in a sense of connectedness with people and is associated with a plurality of diversity of interactions with others. (p. 292)

In developing their construct, Miville et al. relied on existential counseling writings (Vontress, 1988), contending that therapeutic effectiveness requires counselors to ally themselves on some level with clients based on shared human similarities, and that they must also respect and accept the cultural differences that clients bring to the counseling process. In building conceptual support for UDO, Miville et al. linked it to Jung's (1968) constructs of universal images, archetypes, and the collective unconscious—all of which serve to connect individuals across culture and time. They also anchored UDO in Yalom's (1985) group counseling universality construct, and in the within-group differences literature on minority identity development (e.g., Helms, 1984). Although not cited by Miville et al., the UDO construct can also be linked to inquiry outside of the counseling and psychotherapy field—for example, to social psychologists Phillips and Ziller's (1997) theory of nonprejudice, which "is conceptualized, in part, as a universal orientation in interpersonal relations whereby perceivers selectively attend to, accentuate, and interpret similarities rather than differences between self and others" (p. 420).

Miville et al. (1999) perceived the UDO construct as including cognitive, behavioral, and emotional components. The cognitive component, which they termed Relativistic Appreciation of Oneself and Others, involved the "recognition and acceptance of the similarities and differences among people." The behavioral component tapped "previous and intended behaviors relevant to interpersonal contact with people of different backgrounds (e.g., race, gender, and religion)," and was titled Diversity of Contact. The emotional component, titled Sense of Connection, referred to "the emotional bond one feels toward others, reflected in the statement 'We are all in the same boat' " (p. 293).

From a nomological perspective, UDO should relate to a broad array of situations that involve close interpersonal interaction. Counselors need requisite levels of UDO to connect with clients and establish positive therapeutic relationships. Universal-diverse orientation would facilitate counselors' empathic responses to clients as well as their flexibility in understanding and working within clients' diverse worldviews. It would also be expected that UDO levels would influence significant others' ability to relate to each other, parents' ability to connect with their children, teachers' ability to relate to students, and friends' and students' ability to relate to one another. At present, the empirical research has only begun to tap this potentially extensive nomological network. The extant research in this regard is reviewed shortly, after a brief review of how UDO has been operationalized.

Measuring the Universal-Diverse Orientation Construct

In a series of four sequenced studies, Miville et al. (1999) developed the Miville-Guzman Universality-Diversity Scale (M-GUDS) and provided initial estimates of score reliability and validity. Initially, 75 Likert-type items, using both positive and negative (reverse-scored) wording, were written to represent the three UDO components. After a content validity assessment and an initial small sample ($N = 33$) item-analysis, the initial item pool was reduced to 45 items. Next, the 45-item UDO was distributed to a sample of 93 Caucasian undergraduate psychology students to establish score validity and reliability. An initial exploratory factor analysis yielded a broad general factor and two more minor factors (variance accounted for was not specified). The authors interpreted the pattern of factor loadings as consistent with a unidimensional structure, rather than the hypothesized three-factor structure, and proceeded to use only the M-GUDS total score in subsequent psychometric testing. The internal consistency reliability estimate for the single factor was high ($\alpha = .92$).

Additional tests of validity, using convergent and discriminant tests, generally supported score construct validity for the M-GUDS one-factor model. Miville et al. (1999) found that M-GUDS scores were positively correlated with the Pseudo-Independence ($r = .42$) and Autonomy statuses ($r = .48$; i.e., higher statuses) of Helms's (1984) White racial identity model, and negatively correlated with the Disintegration ($r = -.56$) and Reintegration ($r = -.60$) statuses. The latter two scales reflect less tolerant and more racist attitudes. Further, as would be expected, M-GUDS scores were negatively related to scores on homophobia ($r = -.33$) and dogmatism scales ($r = -.27$). Regarding discriminant validity, Miville et al. found M-GUDS total scores were not significantly correlated with Scholastic

Aptitude Test (SAT) verbal scores ($r = -.04$), but were significantly negatively correlated with SAT Quantitative scores ($r = -.21$). The pattern of correlations, to a large degree, supported the researchers' initial hypotheses, and provided initial validity and reliability evidence for M-GUDS total scores with their undergraduate student sample.

Subsequent studies reported in Miville et al. (1999) found that UDO scores correlated largely as expected with scores on measures of empathy ($rs = .04$ to $.54$), healthy narcissism ($rs = .46$ to $.49$), feminism ($r = .39$), femininity sex role ($r = .35$), and androgyny sex role ($r = .24$), but did not correlate highly with scores on measures of self-esteem ($rs = .04$ to $.17$). Additionally, among a subsample of African American students, UDO total scores correlated significantly with the Internalization stage of racial identity ($r = .29$).

The UDO construct has generated a good deal of research in the ensuing years. A summary of these studies is provided in Table 8.1, which first lists the UDO development studies and then presents the remainder, ordered alphabetically. The table also includes key study variables and effect size (ES) ranges, as well as select sample demographics (sample size, racial and gender composition) and coefficient alphas (when available). This latter set of data provides researchers with information necessary to begin conducting "reliability generalization" studies as the corpus of research on the M-GUDS (and M-GUDS-S) grows (see Henson & Thompson, 2002).

Important work on the construct validity of UDO was advanced by Fuertes, Miville, Mohr, Sedlacek, and Gretchen (2000) in a series of three studies designed to more closely examine the factor structure of the M-GUDS. Using a large undergraduate sample, the results of a principal components analysis found strong support for a three-component structure (accounting for 39% of the variance), consistent with the rationally and theoretically developed model initially hypothesized in Miville et al. (1999). Component 1 mostly included items assessing the Diversity of Contact (behavioral) component; Component 2 represented the cognitive component, labeled originally as Relativistic Appreciation; and Component 3 included items mostly tapping interpersonal comfort with diverse persons. This third component was aligned with the original emotional component (Sense of Connection), but was relabeled Comfort with Differences to reflect better the item content.

In their second study, Fuertes, Miville, et al. (2000) administered the original 45-item M-GUDS to a moderate size sample attending an orientation session for new undergraduates. In analyzing the M-GUDS scores, the authors extracted the highest loading 5 items from each of the three components to create a shortened 15-item scale (M-GUDS-S); they then subjected the data to confirmatory factor analysis (CFA) procedures. The CFA compared the single factor model recommended by Miville et al. (1999) with the originally hypothesized three-factor model supported in Fuertes, Miville, et al. (2000). The three-factor model fit the data better than the one-factor model (see Table 8.1 for specific fit indexes). The 15-item M-GUDS-S total score correlated .77 with the 45-item M-GUDS total score.

In Study 3, Fuertes, Miville, et al. (2000) administered the M-GUDS-S to a sample of graduate students in counseling and conducted a new CFA testing the 15-item, three-factor model identified in Study 2. The resultant goodness-of-fit was excellent (see Table 8.1). The M-GUDS-S appears to have significant research potential in that it conforms to the three-component theoretical model yet is much shorter than the original M-GUDS. The latter characteristic is likely to increase its appeal to researchers and to generate improved response rates from participants.

Factor Structure and Reliability Summary

Subsequent studies provided further evidence that the UDO construct as operationalized by the M-GUDS-S is best characterized multidimensionally. More specifically, four studies (two reported in Miville, Romans, Johnson, & Lone, 2004; Singley & Sedlacek, 2004; Strauss & Connerley, 2003) calculated the subscale intercorrelations. The Contact-Appreciation correlations ranged from .37 to .50 (mean and median = .44), the Contact-Comfort correlations ranged from $-.32$ to 46 (mean and median = .38), and the Appreciation-Comfort correlations ranged from $-.25$ to .40 (mean = .30 and median = .32).

Table 8.1 Summary of Studies on the Universal-Diverse Orientation (UDO) Construct Utilizing the M-GUDS or M-GUDS-S Scales

Authors	Scale Version	Coefficient Alpha				Sample			Criterion and Construct Validity	
		T	CT	AP	CM	N	White(%)	Female(%)	Variables Predicted	Effect Size (ES)
Miville et al. (1999) (1)	M-GUDS	.92				93	100	28	Autonomy, homophobia, dogmatism	Small to medium
Miville et al. (1999) (2)	M-GUDS	.94				110	70	30	Empathy, narcissism	Small to medium
Miville et al. (1999) (3)	M-GUDS	.89				153	53	35	Feminism, femininity, androgyny	Small to medium
Miville et al. (1999) (4)	M-GUDS	.89				135	0 (all Black)	71	Personal and collective self-esteem, internalized Black identity	Small
Fuertes, Miville, et al. (2000) (1)	M-GUDS					335	63	56	PCA yielded CT (=19%), AP (10%), CM (10%)	
Fuertes, Miville, et al. (2000) (2)	M-GUDS to M-GUDS-S		.82	.59	.92	206	63	59	15-item, 3-factor M-GUDS-S developed, CFA: CFI = .95	
Fuertes, Miville, et al. (2000) (3)	M-GUDS-S					186	61	82	New CFA on 3-factor model, CFI = .95	
Brummett et al. (2007)	M-GUDS-S	.75				124	56	75	Hierarchical regression (HR): hardiness, social functioning, esteem	Small to medium
Constantine & Arorash (2001)	M-GUDS	.91				186	86	72	HR: multicultural counseling competency expectations	Medium
Constantine et al. (2001)	M-GUDS-S		.80	.70	.79	100 school counselors	91	84	HR: CT, AP, CM with multicultural counseling knowledge and skills	Small to medium
Fuertes & Brobst (2002)	M-GUDS-S	.79				85 clients/past clients	58	80	UDO predicted satisfaction with current or prior counseling	Small
Fuertes & Gelso (1998)	M-GUDS					309	68	58	Asian Americans with lower UDO preferred a psychologist with similar personality	
Fuertes, Sedlacek, et al. (2000)	M-GUDS					206	63	55	Academic self-concept, attitudes toward help seeking and diversity	Medium to large

Study	Scale	RA	CM	CT	T	N	CFI	GFI	Findings	Effect size
Miville et al. (2004)	M-GUDS-S	.82	.74	.75		290	87	65	Efficacy, coping, optimism, connectedness, positive thoughts, esteem	Small to medium
Miville et al. (2006)	M-GUDS-S	.74				211	79	80	HR: various empathy subscales	Small to medium
Munley et al. (2004)	M-GUDS-S					165	81	81	HR: multicultural counseling knowledge and awareness	Small
Sawyerr et al. (2005)	M-GUDS-S	.76	.74	.59	.59	165	40	52	Openness to change, self-transcendence, self-enhancement, conservation	Small to medium
Singley & Sedlacek (2004)	M-GUDS-S	.83	.83	.76	.80	2,327	70	50	Top quartile ranked students scored higher on UDO	Medium to large
Strauss & Connerley (2003)	M-GUDS-S	.80	.77	.70	.71	252	62	53	Diverse environment exposure, race, gender, agreeableness, openness	Small to medium
Thompson et al. (2002)	M-GUDS	.73				106	63	86	Big Five plus openness to experience facet scores	Primarily in medium range
Yeh & Arora (2003)	M-GUDS	.93				159 school counselors			Multicultural workshops, interdependent self-construal	Large, Medium

Notes: M-GUDS = Relativistic Appreciation subscale; CFI = Comparative fit index; CM = Comfort with Differences subscale; CT = Diversity of Contact subscale; Miville-Guzman Universality-Diversity Scale; GFI = Goodness of fit index; HR = Hierarchical regression; PCA = Principal component analysis; T = Total score.

Theoretically, some overlap would be expected, but the moderate magnitude of the relations does suggest that the three factors are relatively distinct. These findings provide further support for the validity of Fuertes, Miville, et al.'s (2000) three-factor model.

With regard to the reliability of the M-GUDS total score, seven studies reported alphas ranging from .73 to .94, with the median alpha at .91 (see Table 8.1). Focusing on the total score for the M-GUDS-S, six studies reported alphas that ranged from .74 to .83 (Mdn = .78). For the separate M-GUDS-S subscales, alphas ranged from .74 to .83 (Mdn = .78) for Contact; .59 to .76 (Mdn = .70) for Appreciation; and .59 to .92 (Mdn = .77) for Comfort.

Although most of these internal consistency estimates would be considered marginally adequate, further work to achieve higher levels of internal consistency (e.g., by adding a few more good items to each subscale) could advance future research considerably. One particular outcome of such future scale development would be less biased estimates of the construct-level correlations of UDO components with important criterion constructs—the obtained correlations would be less attenuated (i.e., downwardly biased) by measurement error than those that have been summarized in Table 8.1.

Research Review

A review of the literature identified 22 studies across 16 peer-reviewed journal articles that focused on the UDO construct. Roughly half of these studies operationalized UDO as a unidimensional construct using either the M-GUDS or M-GUDS-S total score; the other half incorporated the three dimensional model of the M-GUDS-S: Contact, Appreciation, and Comfort subscales. The UDO construct has been examined primarily in young adult university samples, with some attention to counseling graduate students and business school students. Two studies have focused on practicing school counselors, while one study examined correlates of the construct among actual clients.

Studies with counseling graduate students (Miville, Carlozzi, Gushue, Schara, & Ueda, 2006; Munley, Lidderdale, Thiagarajan, & Null, 2004; Thompson, Brossart, Carlozzi, & Miville, 2002) and professional school counselors (Constantine et al., 2001; Yeh & Arora, 2003) have found UDO total scores to correlate significantly with scores on measures of empathy ($rs = -.11$ to .30), emotional intelligence ($r = .30$), openness to experience ($r = .56$), amount of multicultural training ($r = .57$), and interdependent self-construal ($r = .38$). Additionally, hierarchical regression studies with counseling students (Miville et al., 2006) and professionals (Munley et al., 2004) have reported that UDO total scores account for significant unique variance in empathy and multicultural knowledge and awareness over and above such other variables as gender, age, social desirability, race, and amount of multicultural training (R^2 change in these analyses have ranged from .02 to .21). Sampling university students who were at the time, or had previously been, in personal counseling, Fuertes and Brobst (2002) found UDO total scores to only minimally predict European American ($\Delta R^2 = .06$) and minority clients' ($\Delta R^2 = .07$) satisfaction with counseling.

Other hierarchical regression studies, with mostly undergraduate students (Brummett, Wade, Ponterotto, Thombs, & Lewis, 2007; Constantine & Arorash, 2001), have shown that M-GUD-S scores account for significant variance in psychological hardiness ($\Delta R^2 = .10$), psychosocial functioning ($\Delta R^2 = .05$), and multicultural counseling competence expectations ($\Delta R^2 = .16$) beyond the variance accounted for by participant age, race, and age- and gender-based political correctness. Still other studies (Fuertes, Sedlacek, Roger, & Mohr, 2000; Miville et al., 2004; Sawyerr, Strauss, & Yan, 2005; Strauss & Connerley, 2003) have reported that UDO total scores account for significant variance in attitudes toward diversity ($R^2_{adj.} = .35$), help seeking ($R^2_{adj.} = .12$), academic self-confidence ($R^2_{adj.} = .10$), social ($rs = .14$ to .31) and general self-efficacy ($rs = .15$ to .39), healthy coping skills ($rs = .05$ to .32), agreeableness ($rs = .27$ to .29), openness to experience ($rs = .13$ to .24), and self-transcendence ($rs = .15$ to .32). Finally, Singley and Sedlacek (2004) found that students graduating in the top 25% rank of their high school class scored higher on M-GUDS-S total scores than did the second quartile ranking

($\eta^2 = .15$), and furthermore, students graduating in the top 10% of their class scored higher than all other groups on the Contact ($\eta^2 = .08$) and Comfort ($\eta^2 = .10$) subscales.

Summary

The body of research reviewed in this section suggests that the UDO construct, whether measured by its total score or its separate dimensions (*Contact, Appreciation,* and *Comfort*), appears to relate to criterion variables of interest to psychologists generally, and to counseling psychologists specifically. Universal-diverse orientation appears to relate to counselors' perceived multicultural competence and their general ability to connect to others (e.g., interdependent self-construal). Additionally, UDO scores of general adolescent and young adult college student populations related to levels of empathy, maturity, acceptance of diverse others (particularly racial and sexual orientation minority groups), academic performance, and general psychological health.

The final column of Table 8.1 presents the range of effect sizes from the studies, expressed in most cases as Pearson's *r,* or as an R^2 for regression models. Using Cohen's (1988) general standards for inter-preting effect sizes—where for *r*'s, .10 is small, .30 is medium, and .50 is large; for *R2* or $R^2_{adj.}$ (or ΔR^2 for hierarchical regression models) .01 is small, .09 is medium, and .25 is large; and for η^2, .01 is small, .06 is medium, and .14 is large—most of the predicted relationships fell in the small to medium range. This range of effect sizes is consistent with the majority of medical and psychological research that has found most correlations to fall between *r* = .15 to .30 (2% to 9% of shared variance; Meyer et al., 2001). Given that counseling psychologists are increasingly working with culturally diverse clients (APA, 2003), it would appear that the UDO construct is one with great relevance to and promise for the field.

Recommendations for Research

Future research is needed to test the goodness-of-fit of Fuertes, Miville, et al.'s (2000) three-factor model across large and diverse samples. It would also be useful to test model fit across gender, racial or ethnic, and age groups. At present, there is limited research on nonstudent populations, and on later-stage adults and early adolescents. From a developmental perspective, it would be instructive to understand at approximately what age levels of UDO begin to crystallize.

Looking back to the potential nomological network for UDO, research needs to examine the con-struct as it relates to broader human interaction, such as parenting, intimate relationships, friendship formation and stability, and collegial interaction in the work environment. Furthermore, it would be useful to expand the scope of UDO research to examine its relationship to various career variables, academic/educational variables, and a broad base of both mental health and physical heath variables. Additionally, from a counseling process and outcome perspective, it would be of interest to know the impact of counselor-client matching on UDO levels. Finally, all of the UDO research reviewed in this chapter was conducted in the United States, and it would be of value to test the import of the construct across nations. I believe the *fifth moment* of multicultural counseling research will involve subjecting psychological constructs to the test of global relevance.

MULTICULTURAL PERSONALITY DEVELOPMENT

As the United States becomes increasingly culturally diverse (APA, 2003), what kind of person is more apt to adjust successfully and thrive in our increasingly diverse society? The construct of the multicultural personality (MP) addresses this question. The clinical psychologist Ramirez (1991) defined the multicultural personality as "a synthesis and amalgamation of the resources learned from different people and cultures to create multicultural coping styles, thinking styles, perceptions of the world (world views) and multicultural identities" (p. 26). More recently, Ponterotto and colleagues (Ponterotto et al., 2006, 2007) addressed the multicultural personality construct from a counseling and positive psychology base, linking multicultural personality dispositions to improved quality of life for individuals living in culturally heterogeneous environments.

Concurrent with work on MP in the United States, a team of researchers in the Netherlands, working in personnel and personality psychology, conceptualized an independent depiction of the construct. Van der Zee and Van Oudenhoven (2000) were interested in studying the characteristics of multicultural effectiveness in the global business environment. These authors defined multicultural effectiveness "as success in the fields of professional effectiveness, personal adjustment and intercultural interactions" (p. 293). They reasoned that MP traits would better predict international career success and personal adjustment than would broad, global traits of personality such as the Big Five (Costa & McCrae, 1992).

Nomologically speaking, MP should relate to any situation where individuals representing variant worldviews come together. In today's society, with the multiculturalization of the United States and other immigrant-accessible nations, and with a more globally inter-connected workforce, MP is potentially relevant to most individuals in most societies. As will be highlighted in the next section, MP research has primarily focused on career development and personal adjustment in international work situations, though the construct has clear applicability to a broad range of psychological issues salient across heterogeneous societies. At present, Van der Zee and Van Oudenhoven's (2000, 2001) conception of the multicultural personality is the only one that has undergone systematic empirical scrutiny, and thus their operationalization of MP is the focus of this section.

Measuring the Multicultural Personality Construct

After reviewing an extensive international literature on intercultural effectiveness, focusing on both adequate work performance and psychological well-being in new cultural environments, Van der Zee and Van Oudenhoven (2000) identified seven components of multicultural effectiveness: (1) cultural empathy, (2) open-mindedness, (3) emotional stability, (4) orientation to action, (5) adventurousness or curiosity, (6) flexibility, and (7) extraversion. These components were operationalized in the development of the Multicultural Personality Questionnaire (MPQ; Van der Zee & Van Oudenhoven, 2000). Initially, 12 to 15 items were written to represent each component; however, after a series of factor analyses and examination of subscale intercorrelations, the authors settled on a four-factor solution (accounting for 31% of the variance): Openness (combining items from Open-Mindedness and Cultural Empathy), Emotional Stability, Social Initiative (combining Extraversion and Orientation to Action), and Flexibility (combining Adventurousness and Flexibility).

In convergent tests of construct validity, Van der Zee and Van Oudenhoven (2000) found that MPQ subscale scores related to measures of the Big Five, need for change, and rigidity in theoretically predicted ways. The MPQ Openness correlated most highly with Big Five's Openness ($r = .57$), MPQ Emotional Stability correlated most highly with Big Five's Neuroticism ($r = -.77$), MPQ Social Initiative correlated most highly with Big Five's Extraversion ($r = .85$), whereas MPQ Flexibility correlated highest with a separate measure of need for change ($r = .67$). Furthermore, in hierarchical models, the four MPQ factors predicted variance in international career aspirations ($\Delta R^2 .10$) and international orientation (a measure of interest and perceived self-efficacy in succeeding at an international career) ($\Delta R^2 = .18$), beyond the variance predicted by the Big Five personality variables. For both models, MPQ Openness and Flexibility were the strongest predictors.

Van der Zee and Van Oudenhoven (2001) continued factor analytic work on the MPQ and settled on a five-factor structure as best representing the MPQ:

1. *Cultural Empathy:* The ability to empathize with the thoughts, behaviors, and feelings of culturally diverse individuals.

2. *Open-Mindedness:* An unprejudiced and open attitude toward cultural differences.

3. *Emotional Stability:* The ability to stay calm under stressful and novel situations.

4. *Social Initiative:* A tendency to actively approach social situations and exhibit initiative in these interactions.

5. *Flexibility:* The ability to conceptualize novel situations as a positive challenge and to adapt accordingly.

This study also found high levels of convergence between MPQ self-reports and MPQ assessments by significant others, with four of the five self-other correlations yielding medium or large effect sizes. Finally, in a criterion group comparison, students who had committed to studying abroad scored higher on all five subscales than a comparison student group not planning to study abroad (η^2 values ranged from .03 to .17).

Factor Structure and Reliability Summary

At present, the five-factor MPQ model developed by Van Der Zee and Van Oudenhoven (2001) appears to be the most robust and most widely incorporated. Two studies did find a higher order three-factor model (Ponterotto et al., 2007; Van der Zee, Van Oudenhoven, & de Grijs, 2004) wherein Cultural Empathy and Open-Mindedness items loaded together on a combined factor labeled Openness; Emotional Stability and Flexibility items loaded together on a new factor labeled Adaptation; and Social Initiative maintained its unique item structure. However, these factor analyses were exploratory in nature, not subjected to confirmatory factor analyses, and have not resulted in scale revision. The five-factor model, however, was replicated in a factor analysis of MPQ scores (30.3% variance accounted for) with adult job applicants in the Netherlands and Belgium (Van der Zee, Zaal, & Piekstra, 2003). Furthermore, confirmatory factor analyses conducted with samples of Italian and Dutch students (Leone, Lucidi, Ercolani, & Presaghi, 2003; Leone, Van der Zee, Van Oudenhoven, Perugini, & Ercolani, 2005) found satisfactory fit indexes for the five-factor model ($CFI = .90$ and $.91$).

To further assess the score construct validity of the five-factor model, it will be instructive to examine the factor intercorrelations. Based on 12 studies reporting subscale intercorrelations, the mean and median intercorrelations, respectively, were as follows: Cultural Empathy–Open-Mindedness, both mean and median intercorrelations = .54; Cultural Empathy–Social Initiative, .35, .31; Cultural Empathy–Emotional Stability, .12, .11; Cultural Empathy–Flexibility, both .16; Open-Mindedness–Social Initiative, .43, .45; Open-Mindedness–Emotional Stability, .25, .26; Open-Mindedness–Flexibility, both .41; Social Initiative-Emotional Stability, both .38; Social Initiative–Flexibility, .36, .35; and Emotional Stability–Flexibility, .35, .38. These intercorrelations are mostly in the small to moderate range, thus providing further support for the relative independence of the five subconstructs (some overlap is expected).

With regard to reliability, coefficient alphas across 14 studies for the five MPQ factors were very satisfactory (see Table 8.2): Cultural Empathy ranged from .76 to .93 (Mdn = .83); Open-Mindedness ranged from .75 to .93 (Mdn = .84); Emotional Stability ranged from .70 to .95 (Mdn = .86); Social Initiative ranged from .85 to .94 (Mdn = .89); and Flexibility ranged from .64 to .93 (Mdn = .74).

Research Review

Table 8.2 presents a summary of all MPQ studies found to date. Similar to Table 8.1, I first summarize the two development studies (Van der Zee & Van Oudenhoven, 2000, 2001), and then present the remainder alphabetically. Of the 15 studies listed in Table 8.2, 12 relied on the five-factor MPQ model. The majority of studies were conducted in Europe, with two conducted in the United States. European samples consisted primarily of university students or international workers and expatriates, whereas

Table 8.2 Summary of Studies on the Multicultural Personality (MP) Construct Utilizing the Multicultural Personality Questionnaire (MPQ)

Authors	Coefficient Alpha					Sample		Criterion and Construct Validity	
	CE	O	ES	SI	F	N	Female (%)	Variables Predicted	Effect Size (ES)
Van der Zee & Van Oudenhoven (2001)		.75	.70	.90	.85	257	71	HR: international self-efficacy	Medium
						98% Dutch		Multicultural aspirations	Small
Van der Zee & Van Oudenhoven (2001) Self	.81	.86	.91	.90	.80	211	76	Distinguished between those with and without international goals	Small to medium
Other	.88	.84	.91	.91	.74	92% Dutch			
Leone et al. (2003; Italian translation)	.85	.84	.85	.87	.72	533	56 (Italian students)	HR: multicultural activity, international orientation	Medium, Small
Leone et al. (2005) Italian	.76	.86	.85	.85	.65	421 Italians	62	HR: international orientation	Small
Dutch	.82	.83	.88	.89	.74	419 Dutch	75	5-factor model a good fit across samples	
Luijters et al. (2006)	.90	.88	.83	n/a	.78	108	54 (expatriates in Netherlands)	Dual identity preference, High CE related to cultural identity preference	High, Medium
Margavio et al. (2005)						244	30 (infomation science students)	Older, higher grades, socially involved, multicultural coursework/exp. higher on MPQ	
Mol, Van Oudenhoven, & Van der Zee (2001)	.77	.76	.76	.85	.67	205	52 (high school students in Taiwan)	Life satisfaction, physical health, psychological well-being, peer/mentor support	Primarily medium
Ponterotto et al. (2007; U.S. English adaptation)	.91		.87	.87	.86 (A)	270	77	Scales of psychological well-being	Small to medium

Study						N	Sample	Findings	Effect size
Stronkhorst (2005)						33 internship and 48 study abroad		MPQ scores rose marginally after living abroad	Primarily small
Van der Zee, Atsma, & Brodbeck (2004)	.93	.93	.95	.94	.93	228	49 U.K. graduate students (53% British)	MPQ F and ES positive impact on well-being under high diversity conditions	
Van der Zee, Van Oudenhoven, & de Grijs, (2004)	.86	.75	.86	.88	.84	160	72 (Dutch students)	MPQ A and O rated high stress conditions safer; O saw high stress as challenging	
Van der Zee & Brinkmann (2004)	.83	.84	.82	.90	.81	137	35 (employees from 21 countries)	MPQ predicts international career aspirations, Living abroad	Large, Medium
Van der Zee et al. (2003)	.87	.83	.83	.86	.72	264	26 (adult job applicants)	HR: behavioral competence, Various career interests	Medium, Small to Medium
Van Oudenhoven et al. (2003)	.83	.84	.84	.89	.64	102	20 (expats from 24 countries)	HR: life satisfaction, physical and psychological well-being, job satisfaction	Small to large
Van Oudenhoven and Van der Zee (2002)	.78	.78	.83	.87	.72	171	56 (international business students)	MPQ predicted foreign student adjustment more than domestic students	Medium

Notes: A = Adaptation subscale in three-factor MPQ model; CE = Cultural Empathy subscale; ES = Emotional Stability subscale; O = Open-mindedness subscale; SI = Social Initiative subscale: F = Flexibility subscale.

the U.S. samples were college students. At present, the current-use 91-item MPQ is available in Dutch (Van der Zee & Van Oudenhoven, 2001), Italian (Leone et al., 2003), U.K. English (Van Oudenhoven & Van der Zee, 2002), and U.S. English (Ponterotto et al., 2007).

Multicultural Personality in University and High School Student Samples

In addition to the Van der Zee and Van Oudenhoven (2000, 2001) MPQ development studies, six additional studies sampled undergraduate populations in Europe, primarily in the Netherlands, Italy, and the United Kingdom. Three of these studies incorporated regression models and found that the MPQ factors predicted variance in multicultural activity ($\Delta R^2 = .12$) and international orientation ($\Delta R^2 = .07$ and $\Delta R^2 = .09$) above and beyond the variance accounted for by the Big Five and other broad personality measures. MPQ *Open-Mindedness* and *Social Initiative* were the strongest individual predictors (Leone et al., 2003, 2005). Furthermore, Van Oudenhoven and Van der Zee (2002) found that that, as a set, MPQ scale scores predicted variance in participants' physical health ($R^2 = .13$), mental health ($R^2 = .17$), subjective well-being ($R^2 = .12$), academic achievement ($R^2 = .07$), and perceived peer support ($R^2 = .15$).

Using a creative experimental design, Van der Zee, Atsma, and Brodbeck (2004) organized graduate students completing an organizational behavior course into 43 work groups that varied in the group's overall level of diversity. Findings indicated that the MPQ factors of Flexibility and Emotional Stability had a positive impact on final course evaluations (exams and case study) under conditions of high group diversity; and Flexibility had a positive effect on evaluations under the conditions of high diversity, but a negative effect on evaluations under conditions of low diversity.

Van der Zee, Van Oudenhoven, et al. (2004) designed an innovative analog study where stress levels of various intercultural scenarios were manipulated. Incorporating the MPQ three-factor model, the findings indicated that under the high stress condition, respondents scoring higher on MPQ Adaptation ($\eta^2 = .03$) and Openness ($\eta^2 = .03$) were more inclined to appraise the intercultural scenario as safe. Furthermore, students higher in MPQ Openness tended to perceive the high stress vignette as challenging and adventurous ($\eta^2 = .03$). Finally, under the high stress scenario, respondents scoring higher in MPQ Openness ($\eta^2 = .05$) experienced more positive affect, while those students scoring lower on MPQ Adaptation ($\eta^2 = .03$) reported higher negative effect.

In the final European undergraduate study, Stronkhorst (2005) tracked students interning or studying abroad for 3 to 4 months to see if MPQ scores changed from the beginning to the end of the programs. The author found that for the internship abroad program, scores were higher in Cultural Empathy and Open-Mindedness at the program's conclusion; and in the exchange program, there was a score gain only for Flexibility. In interpreting these findings, Stronkhorst surmised that longer infusion periods may be necessary to more significantly alter MP profiles. However, this study was not a tightly controlled experiment, and score changes could have been due to factors independent of the *cultural immersion* experience; for example, to general participant maturation over time.

Two of the 15 studies highlighted in Table 8.2 took place in the United States and focused on university studies. Margavio, Hignite, Moses, and Margavio (2005) examined correlates of MPQ scores and found that students who were more involved in social activities scored higher on Emotional Stability and Social Initiative; those who expressed a desire to work internationally scored higher on Open-Mindedness and Flexibility; those who had completed international coursework scored higher on Cultural Empathy; and those reporting more multicultural experiences scored higher on Open-Mindedness, Social Initiative, and Flexibility. Using a slightly adapted U.S. English version of the MPQ, Ponterotto et al. (in press) found that MPQ factors tended to correlate in expected directions with various subscales of psychological well-being (rs from $-.04$ to $.36$).

In the only MPQ study to date focusing on young adolescents, Mol, Van Oudenhoven, and Van der Zee (2001) surveyed international high school students in Taipei (66% were from the United States) and found that select MPQ scale scores related to levels of well-being and social interaction. In a stepwise regression model, Open-Mindedness and Emotional Stability explained significant variance in life satisfaction ($R^2 = .12$), and Emotional Stability alone predicted variance in physical health ($R^2 = .04$) and psychological well-being ($R^2 = .17$). With regard to social interaction variables, Open-Mindedness plus Social Initiative predicted perceived social support from peers ($R^2 = .29$), and from mentors ($R^2 = .17$), whereas Open-Mindedness and Emotional Stability predicted participation in extracurricular activities ($R^2 = .06$).

Multicultural Personality in International Adult Worker Samples

A total of four studies were located that examined correlates of MPQ scores among adult worker populations in Europe (Luijters, Van der Zee, & Otten, 2006; Van der Zee & Brinkmann, 2004; Van der Zee et al., 2003; Van Oudenhoven, Mol, & Van der Zee, 2003). The collective findings of these studies indicated that MPQ scores correlated in predictable patterns with vocational interests and intercultural competence. Cultural Empathy was positively related to social interests ($r = .28$) and negatively related to scientific or technical interest ($r = -.18$), whereas Social Initiative was positively related to enterprising ($r = .31$) and managerial ($r = .20$) interests and negatively related to scientific or technical interest ($r = -.20$). Furthermore, MPQ factors correlated in predictable patterns with measures of intercultural sensitivity, intercultural communication, intercultural relationship building, conflict management, leadership, and tolerance for ambiguity (rs from .20 to .73; median $r = .46$).

These studies also found that after controlling for broad personality traits and biographical data (e.g., time in country, host country language mastery, and education level), MPQ scores predicted unique variance in competency assessments of job applicants ($\Delta R^2 = .14$; Cultural Empathy and Open-Mindedness alone yielded significant beta weights), satisfaction with life ($\Delta R^2 = .08$), physical well-being ($\Delta R^2 = .19$), psychological well-being ($\Delta R^2 = .39$), professional adjustment as measured by job satisfaction ($\Delta R^2 = .12$), and social adjustment as measured by perceived social support ($\Delta R^2 = .26$; MPQ Emotional Stability and Flexibility factors were generally the stronger predictors of the criterion variables).

Luijters et al. (2006) incorporated an experimental analog study to examine favorability ratings of 108 expatriates judging a hypothetical Turkish expatriate working in the Netherlands who exhibited one of four manipulated acculturation strategies: High commitment to both original cultural identity (Turkish) and the company identity, low commitment to both, a high cultural identity with a low company identity, or a low cultural identity with a high company identity. Findings indicated that respondents who were high in MPQ Cultural Empathy, rated the scenarios where there was high cultural commitment most favorably ($\eta^2 = .09$); and those high in Emotional Stability rated the dual high identity scenario most favorably ($\eta^2 = .14$). The authors interpreted this latter finding by noting that a person needs to be emotionally stable to negotiate integrating multiple identities simultaneously. The study's findings were generally consistent with theoretical predictions.

Summary

The pattern of correlations between the MPQ factors and a host of criterion variables provides strong support that the multicultural personality, as operationalized through the MPQ, is a salient and important construct for psychologists to consider. Though initially anchored in international research in personnel psychology, the multicultural personality construct is a fruitful avenue of research for counseling psychologists. Among the criterion variables sharing variance with one or more MPQ factors are international career orientation, job satisfaction, extent of multicultural activity, psychological well-being, coping with interculturally stressful situations, selected vocational interests, perceived peer and mentor support, and physical health. Furthermore, though somewhat related to broader personality constructs such as the Big Five, MPQ factors in a number of studies predicted variance in criterion variables beyond that accounted for by general personality. With regard to the magnitude of the validity coefficients, the majority of effect sizes across studies were in the small to medium range.

The quality of the MPQ studies reviewed in this chapter was, overall, quite strong. In addition to one-time sampling, some studies followed participants over time. The Van Oudenhoven and Van der Zee (2002) study found that although *Emotional Stability* was the best predictor of initial international adjustment, after 6 months living abroad, the groups' adjustment was best predicted by *Cultural Empathy*. Another interesting finding regarding the MPQ is that the pattern of scale score relationships with various criterion variables is stronger when participants are in novel multicultural situations. Finally, participants' MPQ self-ratings on the MPQ were highly correlated with significant others' ratings of the participants. This self-other comparison method is a common practice in personality research and represents a fruitful area for research on counseling constructs.

Recommendations for Research

Although the MPQ has been used in Europe since the early 1990s, it has only recently begun to see use in North America. The factor structure of the MPQ needs to be tested with large North American samples. The MPQ has also focused primarily on international students and workers, expatriates, or business students given the personnel psychology orientation of its developers (Van der Zee & Van Oudenhoven, 2000, 2001). Though Ponterotto et al. (2007) anchored their MPQ work in counseling and positive psychology, more research is needed to understand fully the place of multicultural personality development in counseling psychology. Does the MP construct need to be broadened to fit the paradigms of counseling and positive psychology? In a new, and as yet untested, model of the multicultural personality, Ponterotto et al. (2006) incorporated Van der Zee and Van Oudenhoven's (2000) model of the multicultural personality and Miville et al.'s (1999) UDO model as two of seven theoretical anchors of an expanded multicultural personality framework directed specifically to the work of counseling and positive psychologists. As such, it would be of value to understand the empirical relationship between UDO, MPQ, and other anchors underlying this expanded model. We would expect, for example, that MPQ scores and UDO scores would be moderately and positively correlated given that both constructs focus, to varying degrees, on understanding, accepting, and connecting with culturally diverse others.

Many of the criterion variables used in MPQ research have focused on variables salient to international students, workers, and expatriates. It is now important to test the predictive and incremental validity of the MPQ factors as they relate to criteria relevant to counseling psychologists, such as career development variables, academic and educational issues, development and prevention, social and family functioning, coping and problem solving, and expanded quality of life indicators. It would also be useful to examine multicultural personality development across the life span. At around what age can we detect the development of Cultural Empathy, Social Initiative, and other MPQ factors? Do MPQ scores vary by life-stage, extent of multicultural contact, and various life experiences in U.S. samples? How does MP develop over time and what factors influence that development? Can a person have too much MP?

IMPLICATIONS FOR PRACTICE

This chapter has selectively examined two constructs that are seen as representing the fifth moment in multicultural counseling history. Both UDO and MP are etic constructs in that they can transcend cultures and national boundaries, are anchored in multiple disciplines of psychology, and have the potential to advance the field of counseling psychology in meaningful ways. Although early research has largely been supportive of both constructs, the bodies of research are still somewhat limited, having only first appeared in 1999 (UDO) or 2000 (MPQ). Thus, the implications for practice highlighted in this section should be viewed as tentative.

Both constructs have salience for anyone living in a culturally heterogeneous environment, such as many areas of the United States, where individuals are increasingly coming into contact with people who are different on some cultural variable. Counseling psychology, which historically endorses a hygiological perspective (Lent, 2004), aims to improve the quality of life of individuals, and to help them with adjustment and adaptation issues across the life span. If the trends supporting UDO and MPQ as empirically meaningful constructs are maintained in future research across broadened U.S. samples, addressing these constructs through early intervention and prevention programs may prove fruitful in preparing individuals for living more effectively and comfortably among culturally diverse others. The impact of racism, sexism, and other "isms" in the United States is catastrophic from mental health, physical health, and quality of life perspectives (APA, 2003; Ponterotto et al., 2006), and higher levels of UDO and MP might serve to mitigate this impact.

Looking specifically at UDO, college students who have higher levels of this construct seem to do better academically, are more open to diverse others, are physically more healthy, and are better adjusted and happier psychologically. Thus student development programming throughout the college years could address student UDO development. Singley and Sedlacek (2004) noted that "UDO might be employed to give admissions committees a more holistic view of applicants" (p. 87). Though the state of research on UDO may be too limited at this time to warrant incorporating the M-GUDS-S in admissions' decisions, the point is an intriguing one. The same could be said for recruiting counseling trainees, as research has consistently linked UDO to higher levels of (at least) self-reported multicultural competence and empathy. Although UDO might be expected to be relevant outside of North American borders, the construct still has not been studied in terms of the test of global relevance.

With regard to the MP, research has consistently found that those who score higher on MPQ factors perform better professionally and are better adjusted psychologically in novel intercultural situations. The research, however, is heavily weighted toward the global business environment and life in more extreme cultural shifts, such as moving to and studying or working in a different country. Although initial findings with samples of U.S. college students are consistent with findings from European student and expatriate studies, more research is needed to fully understand the implications of high MP on U.S. residents migrating to or living in both urban and more rural areas.

I believe theory and research on both UDO and MP is well-aligned with counseling psychology's intersecting disciplines of positive psychology (Lopez & Edwards, Chapter 6, this volume) and international psychology (Heppner, Leong, & Chiao, Chapter 5, this volume) and will, over time, yield important implications for prevention and intervention. In closing, I hope this chapter stimulates expanded research on the etic constructs of UDO and MP.

REFERENCES

American Psychological Association. (2003). Guidelines on multicultural education, training, research, practice, and organizational change for psychologists. *American Psychologist, 58*, 377–402.

Atkinson, D. R., & Hackett, G. (Eds.). (1998). *Counseling diverse populations* (2nd ed.). Boston: McGraw-Hill.

Atkinson, D. R., & Thompson, C. E. (1992). Racial, ethnic, and cultural variables in counseling. In S. D. Brown & R. W. Lent (Eds.), *Handbook of counseling psychology* (2nd ed., pp. 349–382). New York: Wiley.

Brummett, B. R., Wade, J. C., Ponterotto, J. G., Thombs, B., & Lewis, C. (2007). Psychosocial well-being and a multicultural personality disposition. *Journal of Counseling and Development, 85*, 73–81.

Civil Rights Act of 1964, P. L. 88–353, 78 Stat. 241 (1964).

Cohen, J. (1988). *Statistical power analysis for the behavioral sciences.* New York: Wiley.

Cokley, K. (2007). Critical issues in the Measurement of Ethnic and Racial Identity: A referendum on the state of the field. *Journal of Counseling Psychology, 54*, 224–234.

Constantine, M. G., & Arorash, T. J. (2001). Universal-diverse orientation and general expectations about counseling: Their relation to college students' multicultural counseling expectations. *Journal of College Student Development, 42*, 535–544.

Constantine, M. G., Arorash, T. J., Barakett, M. D., Blackmon, S. M., Donnelly, P. C., & Edles, P. A. (2001). School counselors' universal-diverse orientation and aspects of their multicultural counseling competence. *Professional School Counseling, 5*, 1318.

Constantine, M. G., & Sue, D. W. (2006). Factors contributing to optimal human functioning in people of color in the United States. *Counseling Psychologist, 34*, 228–244.

Costa, P. T., Jr., & McCrae, R. R. (1992). *Revised NEO Personality Inventory (NEO-PI-R) and NEO Five Factor Inventory (NEO-FFI) professional manual.* Odessa, FL: Psychological Assessment Resources.

Cuellar, I., Harris, L. C., & Jasso, R. (1980). An acculturation scale for Mexican-American normal and clinical populations. *Hispanic Journal of Behavioral Sciences, 2*, 199–217.

Denzin, N. K., & Lincoln, Y. S. (2005). Introduction: The discipline and practice of qualitative research. In N. K. Denzin & Y. S. Lincoln (Eds.), *Sage handbook of qualitative research* (3rd ed., pp. 1–32). Thousand Oaks, CA: Sage.

Fuertes, J. N., & Brobst, K. (2002). Clients' ratings of counselor multicultural competency. *Cultural Diversity and Ethnic Minority Psychology, 8*, 214–223.

Fuertes, J. N., & Gelso, C. J. (1998). Asian-American, Euro-American, and African-American students' universal-diverse orientation and preferences for characteristics of psychologists. *Psychological Reports, 83*, 280–282.

Fuertes, J. N., Miville, M. L., Mohr, J. J., Sedlacek, W. E., & Gretchen, D. (2000). Factor structure and short form of the Miville-Guzman Universality-Diversity Scale. *Measurement and Evaluation in Counseling and Development, 33*, 157–169.

Fuertes, J. N., Sedlacek, W. E., Roger, P. R., & Mohr, J. J. (2000). Correlates of universal-diverse orientation among first-year university students. *Journal of the First-Year Experience, 12*, 45–59.

Helms, J. E. (1984). Toward a theoretical explanation of the effects of race on counseling: A Black and White model. *Counseling Psychologist, 12*, 153–165.

Henson, R. K., & Thompson, B. (2002). Characterizing measurement error in scores across studies: Some recommendations for conducting "Reliability Generalization" studies. *Measurement and Evaluation in Counseling and Development, 35*, 113–127.

Heppner, P. P., Casas, J. M., Carter, J., & Stone, G. L. (2000). The maturation of counseling psychology: Multifaceted perspectives, 1978–1998. In S. D. Brown & R. W. Lent (Eds.), *Handbook of counseling psychology* (3rd ed., pp. 3–49). New York: Wiley.

Jackson, M. L. (1995). Multicultural counseling: Historical perspectives. In J. G. Ponterotto, J. M. Casas, L. A. Suzuki, & C. M. Alexander (Eds.), *Handbook of multicultural counseling* (pp. 3–16). Thousand Oaks, CA: Sage.

Jung, C. G. (1968). *The archetypes and the collective unconscious* (2nd ed., R. F. C. Hull, Trans.). Princeton, NJ: Princeton University.

Koltko-Rivera, M. (2004). The psychology of worldviews. *Review of General Psychology, 8*, 3–58.

Lent, R. W. (2004). Toward a unifying theoretical and practical perspective on well-being and psychosocial adjustment. *Journal of Counseling Psychology, 51*, 482–509.

Leone, L., Lucidi, F., Ercolani, A. P., & Presaghi, F. (2003). Versione Italiana del Multicultural Personality Questionnaire (MPQ). *Bollettino di Psicologia Applicata, 240*, 27–35.

Leone, L., Van der Zee, K. I., Van Oudenhoven, J. P., Perugini, M., & Ercolani, A. P. (2005). The cross-cultural generalizability and validity of the Multicultural Personality Questionnaire. *Personality and Individual Differences, 38*, 1449–1462.

Leong, F. T. L., & Ponterotto, J. G. (2003). A proposal for internationalizing counseling psychology in the United States: Rationale, recommendations, and challenges. *Counseling Psychologist, 31*, 381–395.

Luijters, K., Van der Zee, K. I., & Otten, S. (2006). Acculturation strategies among ethnic minority workers and the role of intercultural personality traits. *Group Processes and Intergroup Relations, 9*, 561–575.

Margavio, T., Hignite, M., Moses, D., & Margavio, G. W. (2005). Multicultural effectiveness assessment of students in IS courses. *Journal of Information Systems Education, 16*, 421–427.

Meyer, G. J., Finn, S. E., Eyde, L. D., Kay, G. G., Moreland, K. L., Dies, R. R., et al. (2001). Psychological testing and psychological assessment: A review of evidence and issues. *American Psychologist, 56*, 128–165.

Miville, M. L., Carlozzi, A. F., Gushue, G. V., Schara, S. L., & Ueda, M. (2006). Mental health counselor qualities for a diverse clientele: Linking empathy, universal-diverse orientation, and emotional intelligence. *Journal of Mental Health Counseling, 28*, 151–165.

Miville, M. L., Gelso, C. J., Pannu, R., Liu, W, Touradji, P., Holloway, P., et al. (1999). Appreciating similarities and valuing differences: The Miville-Guzman Universality-Diversity Scale. *Journal of Counseling Psychology, 46*, 291–307.

Miville, M. L., Romans, J. S. C., Johnson, D., & Lone, R. (2004). Universal-diverse orientation: Linking social attitudes with wellness. *Journal of College Student Psychotherapy, 19*, 61–79.

Mol, S. T., Van Oudenhoven, J. P., & Van der Zee, K. I. (2001). Validation of the Multicultural Personality Questionnaire among an internationally oriented student population in Taiwan. In F. Salili & R. Hoosain (Eds.), *Multicultural education: Issues, policies and practices* (pp. 167–186). Greenwich, CT: Information Age Publishing.

Morrow, S. L., Rakhsha, G., & Castaneda, C. L. (2001). Qualitative research methods for multicultural counseling. In J. G. Ponterotto, J. M. Casas, L. A. Suzuki, & C. M. Alexander (Eds.), *Handbook of multicultural counseling* (2nd ed., pp. 575–603). Thousand Oaks, CA: Sage.

Munley, P. H., Lidderdale, M. A., Thiagarajan, M., & Null, U. (2004). Identity development and multicultural competency. *Journal of Multicultural Counseling and Development, 32*(Extra), 283–295.

Neimeyer, G. J., & Diamond, A. K. (2001). The anticipated future of counseling psychology in the United States: A Delphi poll. *Counselling Psychology Quarterly, 14*, 49–65.

Phillips, S. T., & Ziller, R. C. (1997). Toward a theory and measure of the nature of nonprejudice. *Journal of Personality and Social Psychology, 72*, 420–434.

Ponterotto, J. G. (1997). Multicultural counseling training: A competency model and national survey. In D. B. Pope-Davis & H. L. K. Coleman (Eds.), *Multicultural counseling competencies: Assessment, education and training, and supervision* (pp. 111–130). Thousand Oaks, CA: Sage.

Ponterotto, J. G., & Casas, J. M. (1991). *Handbook of racial/ethnic minority counseling research*. Springfield, IL: Thomas.

Ponterotto, J. G., Casas, J. M., Suzuki, L. A., & Alexander, C. M. (Eds.). (2001). *Handbook of multicultural counseling* (2nd ed.). Thousand Oaks, CA: Sage.

Ponterotto, J. G., Costa-Wooford, C. I., Brobst, K., Spelliscy, D., Mendelsohn-Kacanski, J., Scheinholtz, J., et al. (2007). Multicultural personality dispositions and psychological well-being. *Journal of Social Psychology, 147*, 119–135.

Ponterotto, J. G., Fuertes, J. N., & Chen, E. C. (2000). Models of multicultural counseling. In S. D. Brown & R. W. Lent (Eds.), *Handbook of counseling psychology* (3rd ed., pp. 639–669). New York: Wiley.

Ponterotto, J. G., Utsey, S. O., & Pedersen, P. B. (2006). *Preventing prejudice: A guide for counselors, educators, and parents* (2nd ed.). Thousand Oaks, CA: Sage.

Ramirez, M., III (1991). *Psychotherapy and counseling with minorities: A cognitive approach to individual and cultural differences*. New York: Pergamon Press.

Sam, D. L., & Berry, J. W. (Eds.). (2006). *The Cambridge handbook of acculturation psychology*. Cambridge: Cambridge University Press.

Sawyerr, O. O., Strauss, J., & Yan, J. (2005). Individual value structures and diversity attitudes: The moderating effects of age, gender, race, and religiosity. *Journal of Managerial Psychology, 20*, 498–521.

Singley, D. B., & Sedlacek, W. (2004). Universal-diverse orientation and precollege academic achievement. *Journal of College Student Development, 45*, 84–89.

Strauss, J. P., & Connerley, M. L. (2003). Demographics, personality, contact, and universal-diverse orientation: An exploratory examination. *Human Resource Management, 42*, 159–174.

Stronkhorst, R. (2005). Learning outcomes of international mobility at two Dutch institutions of higher education. *Journal of Studies in International Education, 9*, 292–315.

Suinn, R. M., Rickard-Figueroa, K., Lew, S., & Vigil, P. (1987). The Suinn-Lew Asian Self-Identification Acculturation Scale: An initial report. *Educational and Psychological Measurement, 47*, 401–407.

Thompson, R. L., Brossart, D. F., Carlozzi, A. F., & Miville, M. L. (2002). Five-factor model (big five) personality traits and universal-diverse orientation in counselor trainees. *Journal of Psychology, 136*, 561–572.

Van der Zee, K., Atsma, N., & Brodbeck, F. (2004). The influence of social identity and personality on outcomes of cultural diversity in teams. *Journal of Cross-Cultural Psychology, 35*, 283–303.

Van der Zee, K., & Brinkmann, U. (2004). Construct validity evidence for the Intercultural Readiness Check against the Multicultural Personality Questionnaire. *International Journal of Selection and Assessment, 12*, 285–290.

Van der Zee, K., & Van Oudenhoven, J. P. (2000). The Multicultural Personality Questionnaire: A multidimensional instrument of multicultural effectiveness. *European Journal of Personality, 14*, 291–309.

Van der Zee, K., & Van Oudenhoven, J. P. (2001). The Multicultural Personality Questionnaire: Reliability and validity of self- and other ratings of multicultural effectiveness. *Journal of Research in Personality, 35*, 278–288.

Van der Zee, K., Van Oudenhoven, J. P., & de Grijs, E. (2004). Personality, threat, and cognitive and emotional reactions to stressful intercultural situations. *Journal of Personality, 72*, 1069–1096.

Van der Zee, K., Zaal, J. N., & Piekstra, J. (2003). Validation of the Multicultural Personality Questionnaire in the context of personnel selection. *European Journal of Personality, 17*, 77–100.

Van Oudenhoven, J. P., Mol, S., & Van der Zee, K. (2003). Short note: Study of the adjustment of western expatriates in Taiwan ROC with the Multicultural Personality Questionnaire. *Asian Journal of Social Psychology, 6*, 159–170.

Van Oudenhoven, J. P., & Van der Zee, K. I. (2002). Predicting multicultural effectiveness of international students: The Multicultural Personality Questionnaire. *International Journal of Intercultural Relations, 26*, 679–694.

Vontress, C. E. (1988). An existential approach to cross-cultural counseling. *Journal of Multicultural Counseling and Development, 16*, 78–83.

Westbrook, F. D. (1991). Forty years of using labels to communicate about nontraditional students: Does it help or hurt? *Journal of Counseling and Development, 70*, 20–28.

Yalom, I. D. (1985). *The theory and practice of group psychotherapy* (2nd ed.). New York: Basic Books.

Yeh, C. J., & Arora, A. K. (2003). Multicultural training and interdependent and independent self-construal as predictors of universal-diverse orientation among school counselors. *Journal of Counseling and Development, 81*, 78–83.

CHAPTER 9

Multicultural Competence in Counseling Psychology Practice and Training

MADONNA G. CONSTANTINE
MARIE L. MIVILLE
MAI M. KINDAICHI

Increased attention to multicultural issues in the field of counseling psychology has paralleled the rapidly growing population of people of color in the United States and the emerging awareness of the mental health needs of these populations (Constantine, 2002). According to recent estimates, people of color, including those of multiracial heritages, comprise over 30% of the U.S. population (U.S. Census Bureau, 2004). Over the next 50 years, the racial and ethnic landscape of the United States is projected to be more diverse, such that the percentage of individuals who identify as White alone is expected to decrease by 10%, and the percentages of those who identify as Latino(a), Black, and Asian are expected to increase to nearly 25%, 15%, and 8%, respectively, of the total population (U.S. Census Bureau, 2004). In addition, the cumulative percentage of people who identify as Native American, Pacific Islander, Native Hawaiian, or as having two or more races, is projected to double by 2050. Hence, in the coming years, the probability of mental health providers interacting with a broad range of culturally diverse clients is high.

As the U.S. population continues to diversify, counseling psychologists and other mental health service providers have an obligation to examine cultural sensitivity issues in practice and training and to facilitate multicultural counseling competence in a pluralistic society (Constantine & Sue, 2005). In addition, psychologists are charged with understanding the roles that race and other dimensions of culture play in individuals' development and experiences (American Psychological Association [APA], 2003), including factors that contribute to quality mental health care to people of color. Because complex racial and cultural disparities continue to characterize current mental health practices (U.S. Department of Health and Human Services [USDHHS], 2001), promoting counseling psychologists' multicultural competence can be considered an act of social justice promotion (e.g., Constantine, Hage, Kindaichi, & Bryant, 2007).

Over the past 25 years, counseling psychologists have taken leadership in promoting the need for multicultural competence among psychologists who function as helpers, educators, researchers, consultants, and advocates for social change (e.g., APA, 2003; Arredondo et al., 1996; Constantine & Sue, 2005). There has been steady growth in research that investigates the complex intrapersonal and interpersonal processes through which counselors engage in culturally responsive care. The primary conceptualization that has guided this research has been the tripartite model of multicultural counseling competence (D. W. Sue, Arredondo, & McDavis, 1992; D. W. Sue et al., 1982). Multicultural counseling competence has been viewed as the integration of helping professionals' (a) *awareness* of themselves and of others' cultural attitudes and beliefs, (b) *knowledge* of the rich histories and present-day experiences of diverse groups of people, and (c) *skills* needed to work with clients of diverse cultural backgrounds. The tripartite model also has been influential in the development of training and practice guidelines for counselors and counseling psychologists (APA, 2003; Constantine & Sue, 2005).

This chapter summarizes conceptual writings and empirical research relevant to multicultural competence in clinical assessment, counseling, and training. We begin by discussing vital considerations for multiculturally competent assessment. Next, we present recent models of multicultural counseling and then move to discussing issues regarding the measurement of multicultural counseling competence. Issues related to training in multicultural counseling also are presented, followed by implications and future research directions for multicultural counseling and training.

MULTICULTURAL ASSESSMENT CONSIDERATIONS

Culture contextualizes how individuals make meaning of their various experiences. In the language of counseling and psychotherapy, culture frames definitions of normality and adjustment, constructions of illness and wellness, and what are considered appropriate sources of support (Ridley, Li, & Hill, 1998). Although writers have underscored the importance of considering cultural variables in assessment (e.g., Dana, 2005; Suzuki, Ponterotto, & Meller, 2001), few comprehensive models have been offered in the literature. Moreover, although studies have identified the damage that culturally insensitive and neglectful assessment processes might inflict (e.g., Garb, 1997; Nguyen, Huang, Arganza, & Liao, 2007), models and guidelines for multiculturally competent clinical assessment generally have not been tested empirically.

Multiculturally Competent Assessment

Multiculturally competent assessment has profound implications for client care and the integrity of the profession of counseling psychology (Roysircar, 2005). In a sample of professional counseling, clinical, and school psychologists, Hansen et al. (2006) found nearly half of the respondents reported rarely or never using cultural formulations and culture-specific diagnoses of the *DSM-IV-TR* (American Psychiatric Association, 2000). Further, many multicultural competence behaviors were endorsed infrequently, including (a) using culturally congruent resources (e.g., cultural literature and indigenous healers) to supplement treatment, (b) referring clients to more qualified colleagues, (c) developing plans to improve cultural competence, and (d) using multiculturally sensitive data-gathering techniques. Finally, statistically significant differences between respondents' beliefs about their work and their actual reported practices implied that clinicians, despite holding beliefs to the contrary, may not always exhibit helping behaviors that are important for sound practice. In accordance with the "Guidelines on Multicultural Education, Training, Research, Practice, and Organizational Change for Psychologists" (APA, 2003), it is a priority for the field of professional psychology to attend to issues of multicultural competence, especially in clinical assessment (Roysircar, 2005).

Clinician Bias

It has been suggested that clinician bias detracts from culturally competent assessment. Garb (1997) found that African American and Latino(a) clients were more likely than White clients to be diagnosed with schizophrenia, even when diagnostic criteria had not been met. Garb also found that higher socioeconomic status (SES) predicted better clinical prognoses, and that clinicians were less likely to diagnose clients when they were of higher SES. Nguyen et al. (2007) found that Black and Native Hawaiian children were more likely than White children to be diagnosed with conduct-related concerns and disruptive behavioral disorders, whereas depression and dysthymia were more likely to be diagnosed among White children than Latino(a) or Native Hawaiian children. In addition, Rainey and Nowak (2005) discussed biases that clinicians may have toward African American youth wherein clinicians' ethnocentrism, stereotype-based fears, individualistic perspectives, and assumptions of superiority may compromise assessment as well as relationship building.

Cultural considerations may be misappropriated in clinical assessment processes as a function of clinicians' oversight or overemphasis. Practitioners may surmise that the client has a diagnosable mental health condition without considering the cultural framework surrounding the client's situation; this is the equivalent of a Type I error (Ridley et al., 1998). The equivalent of a Type II error occurs when practitioners overemphasize the role of culture or adjust their subjective thresholds of wellness and pathology such that they fail to identify the severity of a mental health condition that does exist (Ridley et al., 1998). Judgment mistakes in how cultural information is considered in assessment may have far-reaching implications for interventions, clients' experiences in therapy, and outcomes. It is imperative that counseling psychologists purposefully and systematically consider the cultural contexts of clients, the therapeutic dyad, assessment procedures themselves, and their roles as helping professionals in conducting culturally appropriate assessment (APA, 2003).

Conceptualizations of Multicultural Assessment

Several models of multicultural assessment have appeared in the literature, although none have yet to receive rigorous empirical testing. The multicultural assessment procedure (MAP; Ridley et al., 1998) is a four-phase guided process through which clinicians make critical decisions relevant to information gathering and ongoing hypothesis testing to derive sound assessments of their clients.

In Phase 1 (*identify cultural data*), clinicians use data from the clinical interview and other sources to arrive at a consideration of the severity of clients' conditions across cultural contexts. Identifying and categorizing the information gleaned in Phase 1 allows clinicians to *interpret cultural data* (Phase 2) with respect to base-rate information about mental health conditions that may be dependent on clients' race, class, gender, age, and other determinants. Gathering such base-rate information allows the clinician to use this information to formulate working hypotheses that address the ego-syntonic and ego-dystonic consequences of a set of client behaviors, the extent to which clients' behaviors may be extreme, even within their cultural contexts, and clients' interpretations of their psychological presentations.

In Phase 3, clinicians *engage in hypotheses testing* to rule out alternate explanations for clients' circumstances (e.g., medical conditions). Through the process of hypotheses testing, clinicians are thought to *arrive at clear assessment decisions* (Phase 4) that ultimately will inform intervention and treatment plans. Ridley et al. underscored the cyclic and reciprocal nature of MAP, amending previous conceptualizations of clients' psychological concerns in light of new treatment information or events.

Ponterotto, Gretchen, and Chauhan (2001) noted that multicultural assessment necessitates clinicians' systematic appraisal of their own cultural identities. They summarized various cultural identity development assessment models and several semi-structured interview protocols regarding cultural identity, using the outline of the *DSM-IV-TR* cultural formulation as a framework. Areas of inquiry in their model included language fluency, endorsement of individualistic or collectivistic worldview values, acculturation level and related distresses, incidences of subtle and overt racism, and concerns related to sexual orientation, in addition to psychosocial concerns relevant to education, work, and family. Ponterotto et al. suggested that their framework can be used to facilitate understanding of clients' worldviews and perception of their concerns, culture-based explanations for their distress and concerns, experiences of their families' cultures, and cultural and power dynamics in the counseling relationship. Roysircar (2005) developed an intake form that clinicians might use to guide their initial interactions with their clients based on Ponterotto et al.'s suggestions.

Roysircar-Sodowsky and Kuo (2001) offered suggestions for multicultural assessment that emphasize practitioners' role in establishing therapeutic working alliances, explaining assessment processes clearly to clients, and consulting with professionals who are knowledgeable and experienced with clients' backgrounds in interpreting assessment results. They recommended that clinicians encourage clients to give feedback about their assessment results. Roysircar-Sodowsky and Kuo stressed practitioners' responsibility to be critical about which psychological tests are to be administered, the cultural relevance of given tests, and any concerns regarding psychometric and cultural validity. Clinicians are responsible for determining whether there is a need for non-English instruments or for a language trans- lator. Further, similar to Ridley et al. (1998), Roysircar-Sodowsky and Kuo recommended that clinicians draw from multiple sources of information, including interviews with family members, self-ratings, and behavioral observation.

Liu and Clay (2002) and Rainey and Nowak (2005) offered suggestions and cautions related to clinical assessment with youth. These authors recommended that clinicians attend to their own cultural self-awareness, identify the culturally salient concerns of young clients, and draw on multiple sources of data (e.g., interviews with important others, collaborations with teachers and coaches, behavioral checklists). In particular, Liu and Clay specified five steps that may inform clinical assessment with culturally diverse youth:

1. Identify relevant cultural aspects (e.g., reference groups and identity attitudes related to reference groups, gender role socialization processes and beliefs).

2. Determine the level of information and skill needed to provide treatment or to suggest a referral (e.g., knowledge of clients' cultural norms and the shared experiences of specific racial and ethnic groups).

3. Incorporate cultural issues (e.g., consider how clients' culture-based values may inform their attitudes toward treatment or goals).

4. Understand the cultural assumptions inherent in interventions (e.g., the extent to which interven- tions emphasize separation/autonomy or individualism versus collectivism).

5. Implement interventions from a strengths-based perspective.

Rainey and Nowak (2005) encouraged clinicians to be knowledgeable about diagnoses given more commonly to children of color (e.g., Oppositional Defiant Disorder and Conduct Disorder) and to as- sess for abuse or maltreatment, learning difficulties, communication disorders, major depression, or sub- stance use. Additionally, they underscored the importance of clinicians operating from a strengths-based perspective that considers protective factors that youth have in their cultural contexts and implementing interventions that engage these protective factors.

In sum, multiculturally competent assessment necessitates psychologists' attention to clients' holistic experiences as cultural beings and careful consideration of how the assessment process itself may be culture bound. The models and guidelines described earlier stress psychologists' commitment to their own cultural self-exploration and awareness, particularly because the clinician is the primary instrument and interpreter of clinical information. Moreover, multicultural assessment rests on the input from multiple sources of information to augment clients' disclosures, counselors' responses and observations, and information from potential referral sources. Further, in the spirit of ethical practice, counseling psychologists are encouraged to be mindful about the limits of their multicultural competence, as they risk harming clients through inappropriate clinical assessment, determination of treatment goals and interventions, and overall care.

MULTICULTURAL COUNSELING CONSIDERATIONS

Models of Multicultural Counseling

Neville and Mobley (2001) presented a nonlinear ecological model of multicultural counseling processes (EMMCCP) wherein sociocultural factors and cultural identities are incorporated systemically across multiple areas of influence. Their model rests on the assumptions that personal characteristics shape how individuals interact with and respond to their environments; that culture necessarily influences human behavior; and that society is stratified across various social locations and identities, including race, gender, class, and sexual orientation.

In the EMMCCP, the interaction between macrosystems and the individual is explicated from a multicultural perspective. Neville and Mobley (2001) included five concentric systems in their ecological model to organize the sociocultural influences:

1. The *individual/personal system* includes the interaction of reference group identities, sex role beliefs, acculturation, and counselors' multicultural counseling competencies with personality style, age, and interpersonal competence.

2. The *microsystem* includes culture-related experiences in proximal systems such as family, school, work, and peer groups, and the level of cultural competence of local structures in which counselors and clients interact, such as the counseling center.

3. The *mesosystem* includes the interaction between the mental health profession, systems of education, and work with sociocultural group organization.

4. The *exosystem* includes the context of social policies and professional organizations that promote parity in care across health care, law, education, and employment.

5. The *macrosystem* structures experiences and functions in the subordinate systems and includes social identity structures, sociocultural values, and group-level cultural responses to oppressive hierarchies, such as institutional racism. Individual and reference group responses to ubiquitous and repeated experiences of oppression and dominance may serve as a background to understanding multicultural counseling interactions across the outlined strata (Neville & Mobley, 2001).

Constantine and Ladany (2001) presented an expanded model of multicultural counseling competence in response to Fischer, Jome, and Atkinson's (1998) call for attention to helping processes thought to be common across cultures. Constantine and Ladany proposed that multicultural counseling competence consists of six dimensions:

1. *Counselor self-awareness* involves recognition of how multiple cultural identities and racial-cultural socialization experiences influence counselors' attitudes, beliefs, and values.

2. *General knowledge about multicultural issues* includes continually learning about psychosocial issues regarding living in a pluralistic society through conceptual, empirical, and popular readings as well as professional and personal experiences.

3. *Multicultural counseling self-efficacy* is counselors' belief that they can enact skills and behaviors reflective of multicultural competence.

4. *An understanding of unique client variables* refers to counselors' recognition of the interplay between personal and situational factors to affect specific clients in their unique contexts.

5. *An effective counseling working alliance* refers to clients' and counselors' agreement about the goals, tasks, and emotional bond, allowing exploration of racial and cultural issues.

6. *Multicultural counseling skills* are counselors' abilities to address multicultural issues effectively, including their sensitively in identifying cultural-related content and dynamics.

Although there is limited empirical evidence to support these models of culturally responsive care, we next turn to recent explorations into aspects of multicultural competent counseling practices that indirectly support aspects of the above models.

Counseling Processes and Attention to Racial and Cultural Issues in Treatment

Some research has explored multicultural counseling competence in relation to therapeutic process and outcome variables. Constructs that have drawn attention have included empathy, working alliance, and satisfaction with counseling. Although empathy is considered a core competency across different forms of counseling, research has suggested that cultural empathy, in particular, is essential to aspects of multicultural counseling competence (Constantine, 2001a). Constantine (2000) found that, after controlling for social desirability attitudes and gender, affective empathy was significantly and positively predictive of self-reported multicultural counseling knowledge ($\beta = .31$, $p < .01$) and awareness ($\beta = .19$, $p < .05$) among 124 counseling professionals. Furthermore, Fuertes and Brobst (2002) reported that, after accounting for client multicultural awareness, White and ethnic minority clients' perceptions of their therapists' empathy explained significant variance in client-rated satisfaction with counseling ($\beta = .44$, $p < .001$). Among 51 therapy dyads consisting of client and therapist pairings of same- and cross-race or gender, Fuertes et al. (2006) found a positive relationship between clients' ratings of therapists' multicultural competence and empathy ($r = .81$, $p < .001$).

Over the past 10 years, research in counseling psychology also has paid attention to the complex and intersecting influences of racial-cultural attitudes and beliefs in counseling. Rollock and Gordon (2000) asserted that, "there is a special urgency in rooting out racism in mental health contexts because of the personal distress and social cost that mental health issues inevitably entail" (p. 5). Research has suggested that expressions of racism occurring in the context of therapy can have profound implications for therapists' perceived multicultural counseling competence and for therapeutic processes and outcomes (e.g., Abreu, 1999; Burkard & Knox, 2004; Constantine, 2007; D'Andrea & Daniels, 2001; Neville, Worthington, & Spanierman, 2001; Thompson & Neville, 1999). Over and above prior training in multicultural issues, greater endorsement of racism attitudes has been associated negatively with aspects of counselors' multicultural counseling competence; namely, their ability to conceptualize cases by integrating salient cultural information ($\beta = -.21$, $p < .05$; Constantine & Gushue, 2003).

It has been found that more advanced racial identity attitudes generally have been related to higher levels of self-perceived multicultural counseling competence among counseling trainees (Vinson & Neimeyer, 2000). Although more sophisticated racial identity attitudes may imply greater awareness of race-related contexts, the practice implications of such awareness may be complex. Abreu (1999) reported that studies relying on clinical data revealed a tendency to assess clients of color more severely than White clients; however, when race was an obvious variable of interest, respondents assessed clients of color equally or less severely than White clients.

Counseling psychologists' perspectives about race and unconscious racial biases may be manifested in therapy behaviors (Ridley, 2005). The term *racial microaggressions* has been used to describe subtle, daily, and often overlooked manifestations of racial oppression and hostility that occur regularly in the lives of people of color (e.g., Constantine, 2007; Pierce, Carew, Pierce-Gonzalez, & Willis, 1978; Solórzano, Ceja, & Yosso, 2000). Examples of racial microaggressions that may appear in the counseling context include counselors' locating the responsibility for a client's hardship (either race-related hardship or otherwise) primarily or exclusively on the client (Burkard & Knox, 2004), minimizing the role of race and racism in individuals' experiences (e.g., colorblind racial ideology: Neville et al., 2001), and shifting standards of therapeutic judgments to accommodate negative stereotypes of people of color (e.g., Gushue, 2004).

The endorsement of colorblind racial attitudes has been positively related to modern racism (Neville, Lilly, Duran, Lee, & Browne, 2000) and negatively related to empathy for clients (Burkard & Knox, 2004). Additionally, Neville, Spanierman, and Doan (2006) reported that endorsing colorblind racial attitudes contributed negatively to the prediction of therapists' self-reported multicultural counseling awareness ($\beta = -46$, $p \leq .01$) and knowledge ($\beta = -21$, $p \leq .05$) beyond their multicultural training experiences, racial-cultural self-identification, and social desirability attitudes; colorblind racial attitudes also were found to be related negatively to the frequency with which therapists considered race in case conceptualization activities ($r = -.35$, $p < .05$). Gushue (2004) found that, after controlling for motivation to respond without prejudice and client race, lower colorblind racial identity attitude scores were associated with lower ratings of a fictional Black client's distress ($\beta = .36$, $p < .01$). In this latter study, it was suggested that helping professionals might alter evaluative standards of psychological wellness based on the client's race and contextual information.

The manner in which race-related concerns are shared in therapeutic contexts may have implications for clients' experiences in therapy and therapeutic outcomes. Thompson and Jenal (1994) qualitatively examined one-time interactions between Black female clients and Black or White race-avoidant female counselors and characterized them based on the quality of their interactions. Findings suggested that the degree to which race-related content (e.g., clients' experiences, racial identity experiences, degree of affiliation with the counselor by race) is addressed in counseling might affect counseling interactions. Thompson, Worthington, and Atkinson (1994) reported that African American clients disclosed more freely with, and were more likely to self-refer to, counselors who demonstrated attention to cultural content and overall cultural responsiveness versus counselors who used more universalistic counseling approaches.

Recently, Constantine (2007) used structural equation modeling and found that perceived racial microaggressions by African American clients were negatively predictive of clients' ratings of (a) the therapeutic working alliance with White therapists, (b) their therapists' general and multicultural counseling competence, and (c) their overall satisfaction with counseling. Moreover, African American clients' dissatisfaction with counseling due to the experience of subtle racial indignations in therapy was not significantly mediated by their perceptions of therapists' general counseling competence or the therapeutic working alliance. Thus, in the language of the tripartite model of multicultural counseling competence, research regarding the potential effects of therapists' racial microaggressions suggests that multicultural awareness and knowledge is essential to providing meaningful and ethically conscionable care to diverse clients (Constantine, 2007).

Evidence-Based Practice

Evidence-based practices in psychology (EBPP) have been defined as "the integration of the best available research with clinical expertise in the context of patient characteristics, culture, and preferences" (APA Presidential Task Force on Evidence-Based Practice, 2006). Professional dialogues concerning EBPP and related constructs (e.g., empirically validated treatment, empirically supported treatment) have been provocative and continue to spark debate among researchers and practitioners across professional psychology generally and in counseling psychology specifically (e.g., Coleman & Wampold, 2003; Wampold, Lichtenberg, & Waehler, 2002). Wampold et al. (2002) provided a comprehensive history of the movement in psychology toward evidence-based practices and offered seven principles by which counseling psychologists could review evidence that purports to support given interventions.

At present, it appears that there has been limited study of EBPP in relation to multicultural populations (see Coleman & Wampold, 2003). Evidence-based practice research among adult and pediatric samples appears to suggest some potential differences or treatment nuances attributable to race or culture (Clay, Mordhorst, & Lehn, 2002). It has been argued that research in support of EBPPs fails to use samples with adequate representation of people of color, assume rather than test generalizability of psychological theories across cultures, and neglect to consider mediating or moderating effects of race or cultural values (S. Sue, 1998). The simple inclusion of people of color in efficacy research is not a sufficient means to address the questionable validity EBPPs may have on diverse people, as race, ethnicity, language, worldview, social class, and other markers of social location are confounded and may have complex implications for individuals' responses to treatment and intervention approaches (Coleman & Wampold, 2003; Miranda, Nakamura, & Bernal, 2003).

Coleman and Wampold (2003) drew from Neville and Mobley's (2001) ecological model to describe contextual frameworks that inform counseling interventions and provided a guide to developing culture-specific treatment. Counseling psychologists invested in issues of multicultural counseling competence could participate in practice and research dialogues through systemically and mindfully developing culture-specific interventions and examining the efficacy of these interventions with given populations. However, as has been the circumstance with much of the multicultural counseling process research (e.g.,

Constantine, 2007; Fuertes et al., 2006), there may be challenges regarding data collection, particularly in attempts to collect data from "real" clients in counseling settings. Nonetheless, such data seem vital if counseling psychologists are to meet effectively the mental health needs of diverse cultural populations.

MEASUREMENT OF MULTICULTURAL COUNSELING COMPETENCE

Several quantitative instruments based conceptually on the tripartite model of multicultural counseling competence have contributed to the increase in multicultural counseling competence research over the past 2 decades (Dunn, Smith, & Montoya, 2006; Kitaoka, 2005). These instruments have included the Cross-Cultural Counseling Inventory—Revised (CCCI-R; LaFromboise, Coleman, & Hernandez, 1991); the Multicultural Awareness-Knowledge-Skills Survey (MAKSS; D'Andrea, Daniels, & Heck, 1991); the Multicultural Counseling Inventory (MCI; Sodowsky, Taffe, Gutkin, & Wise, 1994); and the Multicultural Counseling Knowledge and Awareness Scale (MCKAS; Ponterotto, Gretchen, Utsey, Rieger, & Austin, 2002), which is a revision of the Multicultural Counseling Awareness Scale-Form B (MCAS-B; Ponterotto et al., 1996).

The CCCI-R (LaFromboise et al., 1991), originally developed as a measure in which supervisors evaluated their supervisees' abilities to counsel culturally diverse clients, is a 20-item scale that has been modified to be a self-report instrument in several studies (e.g., Constantine & Ladany, 2000; Ladany, Constantine, Inman, & Hofheinz, 1997). Although the supervisor rating form has yielded a three-factor solution (cross-cultural counseling skills, sociopolitical awareness, and cultural sensitivity; LaFromboise et al., 1991), only a single factor has been consistently derived from the self-report version of this instrument. Alpha coefficients have ranged from .88 (Ladany et al., 1997) for the scores on the single self-report scale to .95 (LaFromboise et al., 1991) for scores on the full scale of the supervisor-rating form.

The MAKSS (D'Andrea et al., 1991) is a 60-item self-report scale consisting of three subscales that measure multicultural counseling knowledge, skills, and awareness. Reliability coefficients of .75, .90, and .96 for the awareness, knowledge, and skills subscales, respectively, were reported for graduate students who participated in initial psychometric testing of the MAKSS (D'Andrea et al., 1991). A revision of the MAKSS, the MAKSS-CE-R (Kim, Cartwright, Asay, & D'Andrea, 2003), consists of 33 items from the original MAKSS. Among samples of graduate students in counseling psychology, reliability coefficients for the three MAKSS-CE-R subscales ranged from .71 (awareness) to .87 (knowledge and skills). Additionally, subscale scores on the MAKSS-CE-R were found to converge with subscales of other self-report measures of multicultural counseling competence (e.g., the knowledge and awareness subscales of the MCKAS).

The MCI (Sodowsky et al., 1994) was developed to assess counselors' considerations of differences related to acculturation, nationality, worldview, and language, in addition to race. The MCI is a 40-item scale that consists of four subscales measuring multicultural awareness (i.e., counselors' cultural responsiveness and sensitivity as related to personal life experiences and interactions), knowledge (i.e., counselors' case conceptualization, treatment strategies, and research knowledge), and skills (i.e., counselors' ability to retain culturally diverse clients, recognize and recover from cultural impasses, and provide effective interventions), along with the multicultural counseling relationship (i.e., counselors' interactional qualities with culturally diverse clients). Among counseling center practitioners in Sodowsky et al.'s (1994) validation sample, reliability coefficients of .80, .80, .81, and .67, respectively, were reported for the awareness, knowledge, skills, and relationship subscales. The MCI also has been positively correlated with other self-report measures of multicultural counseling competence (e.g., Constantine & Ladany, 2000).

The MCKAS (Ponterotto et al., 2002) is a 32-item scale that consists of two subscales: (1) multicultural knowledge and (2) awareness. Among a sample of graduate students, coefficient alphas for the knowledge and awareness subscales of the MCKAS were both .85 (Ponterotto et al., 2002). The MCKAS

Knowledge subscale was found to be significantly and positively correlated with the MCI Knowledge, Skills, and Awareness subscales; in addition, the MCKAS Awareness subscale was positively correlated with the MCI Relationship subscale.

Although the use of self-report multicultural counseling competence instruments has been widespread in the literature (Worthington, Soth, & Moreno, 2006), some researchers have identified several limitations with regard to their use. Despite the common tripartite theoretical framework on which the self-report multicultural counseling competence scales were based (D. W. Sue et al., 1982), some researchers (e.g., Constantine, Gloria, & Ladany, 2002; Constantine & Ladany, 2000; Pope-Davis & Dings, 1995) have noted inconsistencies in the number and types of factors across these quantitative measures. Whereas the MAKSS consists of three subscales reflecting dimensions of multicultural attitudes/beliefs, knowledge, and skills, the MCKAS has a two-factor structure (i.e., multicultural counseling knowledge and awareness) and the MCI has a four-factor structure (i.e., awareness, knowledge, skills, and relationship). Furthermore, even the factors that claim to measure the same construct by name may not do so psychometrically (Constantine et al., 2002; Kitaoka, 2005).

Other limitations associated with using self-report multicultural counseling competence scales pertain to issues of social desirability by test takers. Constantine and Ladany (2000) found social desirability attitudes to correlate significantly and positively with most self-report multicultural counseling competence instruments (r's $= .18$ to $.30$, p's $< .05$). Moreover, they found that the relationship between self-reported multicultural counseling competence and multicultural case conceptualization ability (an aspect of *demonstrated* multicultural counseling competence) was nonsignificant after controlling for social desirability. Similarly, Worthington, Mobley, Franks, and Tan (2000) indicated that self-reported multicultural counseling competence, as measured by the MCI, was positively correlated with social desirability ($r = .31$, $p < .05$).

In an attempt to rely less on self-report ratings of multicultural counseling competence, some investigators have turned to using observer or third-party (e.g., multicultural counseling "experts," supervisors, and clients) ratings of multicultural counseling competence to obtain more accurate depictions of therapists' ability to work effectively with culturally diverse populations. In a sample of 38 university counseling center practitioners, Worthington et al. (2000) found that, after controlling for social desirability attitudes, self-reported multicultural counseling knowledge was the only unique significant predictor of multicultural counseling competence as observed by independent raters ($\beta = .46$, $p < .01$). Furthermore, Constantine (2001b) explored predictors of observer ratings of multicultural counseling competence in a racially diverse group of 52 counselor trainees. Her findings indicated that African American ($\beta = .66$, $p < .001$) and Latino(a) American ($\beta = .66$, $p < .001$) trainees were rated as more multiculturally competent than their White American peers. In addition, Fuertes et al. (2006) reported a nonsignificant relationship between clients' ratings of therapists' multicultural counseling competence and the therapists' self-reported multicultural competence ($r = -.03$, $p > .05$). They also reported that clients' ratings of their therapists' multicultural competence ($\beta = .40$, $p = .001$), general counseling competence (conceptualized as counselors' expertness, attractiveness, trustworthiness; $\beta = .17$, $p = .03$), and empathy ($\beta = .44$, $p = .003$) each accounted for unique significant variance in clients' satisfaction with counseling. Moreover, Constantine (2007) found that African American clients' perceptions of their therapists' multicultural counseling competence was positively related to these clients' satisfaction with the counseling services they received ($r = .59$, $p < .001$). It is clear that research exploring multicultural counseling competence using methods other than self-report represents a promising and critical area of further investigation.

TRAINING IN MULTICULTURAL COUNSELING COMPETENCE

In light of the primary importance now being given to training in multicultural counseling in psychology, one important empirical question is: What is currently being done in counseling psychology training programs to facilitate multicultural counseling competence? Several early studies explored the extent to which such training exists in both academic and internship programs. One of the first studies was undertaken by Hills and Strozier (1992), who found that all but one program offered a multicultural counseling course or unit and that 59% of programs required students to take at least one multicultural course. Their findings also indicated that "much of the burden for multicultural activities" was carried out by assistant or adjunct professors (p. 48). However, they also found that it was senior faculty, particularly full professors, who had the greatest influence in enacting the integration of multicultural issues in the training programs.

Quintana and Bernal (1995) explored multicultural training differences between counseling and clinical psychology programs. Surveys were sent to all APA-accredited programs in counseling ($n = 61$) and clinical ($n = 148$) psychology, with response rates of 67% ($n = 41$) and 70% ($n = 104$), respectively. They found:

> a majority of counseling and clinical programs [a] offered instruction on minority issues within specific courses [73% and 62% for counseling and clinical programs, respectively] . . . [b] integrated these topics into preexisting courses [approximately 88% for both program types] . . . [c] provided practicum sites that served minority populations [66% and 59%, respectively] . . . and [d] had faculty continuing their own education on minority issues [76% and 66%, respectively]. (p. 107)

Quintana and Bernal also found that counseling psychology programs typically had proportionally larger numbers of faculty of color as well as had higher faculty of color to students of color ratios. In sum, counseling psychology programs demonstrated a higher level of commitment on all dimensions of multicultural training. However, the authors were careful to note that average effect size differences between the two program types were small.

Ponterotto, Alexander, and Grieger (1995) developed the Multicultural Competency Checklist (MCCL) as a practical means of assessing attention to issues of multicultural competence in academic training programs. The MCCL contains 22 items based on six themes: (1) minority representation (e.g., percentage of minority faculty and students of color), (2) curriculum issues (e.g., required multicultural counseling course), (3) counseling practice and supervision (e.g., work with clients of color), (4) research considerations (e.g., faculty research productivity in multicultural research), (5) evaluation (e.g., annual student evaluations assess multicultural competence), and (6) physical environment (e.g., visible displays of multicultural art). Constantine, Ladany, Inman, and Ponterotto (1996) administered the MCCL to doctoral students at 67 APA-accredited counseling psychology training programs. Of 536 possible surveys, 178 were returned (33% response rate). Results indicated that an average of 10.81 of the possible 22 competencies were present in respondents' programs. Most frequently endorsed items included a required multicultural course (although 20% reported no such required course), use of diverse teaching styles, use of varied assessment methods, and presence of faculty members whose primary research interests were on multicultural issues. Least frequently endorsed items included presence of bilingual faculty, a multicultural committee, and physical space devoted to multicultural issues. Despite the existence of multicultural competence measures, over 75% of respondents stated their programs did not incorporate such methods in student evaluations. Ponterotto (1997) conducted a similar study utilizing the MCCL with counseling psychology program faculty. His findings generally were consistent with those of Constantine et al. (1996), except that faculty tended to rate the presence of some multicultural issues more than did students. The somewhat discrepant findings between students and faculty with regard to attention to multicultural issues in training programs is curious and warrants further empirical attention.

Rogers, Hoffman, and Wade (1998) explored salient components of training in five APA-accredited counseling psychology and five APA-accredited school psychology programs considered to be notable in their approach to multicultural counseling competence training. Programs were selected through nominations by prominent multicultural scholars. Selected programs received the highest numbers of nominations as well as the highest rankings relative to other nominated programs. Data included descriptive information about the programs (e.g., review of student application materials) as well as semi-structured interviews with two faculty members from each program. Results indicated that at least two faculty members (usually associate and full professors) taught multicultural issues in each program, and a third of the doctoral students were students of color. Notable aspects of these programs centered on (a) curricular requirements (e.g., required multicultural course, practicum experience with diverse clients), (b) recruitment techniques to attract students of color (e.g., including networking with other institutions and professionals in the field and personal contacts from faculty), (c) retention techniques (e.g., student mentors and exposure to diverse others), (d) institutional climate (e.g., department and university multicultural committees), and (e) common definitions of multicultural counseling competence among the faculty.

Two recent studies (Maton, Kohout, Wicherski, Leary, & Vinokurov, 2006; Rogers & Molina, 2006) reviewed a key aspect of multicultural counseling competence training identified by Ponterotto et al. (1995)—minority representation among students in doctoral psychology programs. Maton et al. noted both "disquieting and encouraging trends" between 1989 and 2003 regarding students of color in the psychology graduate pipeline. They found increasing numbers of students of color had received their bachelor's (25%) and master's (20%) degrees in psychology. However, growth rates for the receipt of the PhD in psychology had stalled since 1999, particularly the percentages of African Americans and Latinos matriculating into doctoral programs. Rogers and Molina identified exemplary efforts of 11 departments and programs in psychology in their recruitment and retention of students of color. Common strategies included involving current faculty and students of color in recruitment, offering excellent financial aid, personal contacts by faculty, and having a critical mass of students and faculty of color.

Another important empirical question is whether multicultural training leads to increases in multicultural counseling competence. Smith, Constantine, Dunn, Dinehart, and Montoya (2006) conducted a meta-analytic review of studies conducted over a 30-year period regarding the effectiveness of multicultural education in applied psychology programs, including counseling psychology, clinical psychology, and community psychology. Many, though not all of the studies, utilized multicultural counseling competence measures as criterion variables; other variables included racial identity, racial prejudice, and client-counselor relationship. The authors identified two types of empirical studies in this area: (a) 45 retrospective studies "that surveyed individuals regarding their level of education in multicultural issues" (p. 134), totaling nearly 6,000 participants, and (b) 37 outcome studies, involving over 2,000 individuals, which evaluated multicultural competence after the completion of a specific education intervention, such as a course or workshop. Results from the first set of studies indicated that participants who had received some form of multicultural education scored moderately higher on various multicultural competence measures than those who had not received this education (random effects weighted average effects size: $d = .49$). However, the authors cautioned that this finding does not provide information as to how increased competence specifically might lead to more effective practice with culturally different clients.

The second set of studies similarly found that participants consistently benefited from specific multicultural education activities, and Smith et al. noted "large increases in multicultural competence" (random weighted average effects size: $d = .98$) after the completion of such activities (p. 140). Indeed, only 2 of the 37 studies had effect sizes smaller than .30, and none had negative effect sizes. The authors summarized the findings as indicating that "rather than attempting to select applicants on the basis of previous multicultural education [Meta analysis 1], [employers] would be better off to provide multicultural education to all new hires [Meta analysis 2]" (p. 140). In other words, providing specific educational activities directed toward particular outcomes (e.g., populations) might be a more effective means for conducting multicultural counseling competence training.

Training level also may be important to consider in evaluating the effectiveness of multicultural counseling training. In an exploratory study of interns at a counseling center over a 10-year period, Manese, Wu, and Nepomuceno (2001) found that only the knowledge and skills component of multicultural counseling competence (using the MCAS-B; Ponterotto et al., 1996) increased over the course of the internship year. The authors attributed this finding to the general training emphases of the internship as being skill-focused, which includes multicultural counseling skills. Issues of multicultural awareness might more likely be addressed during participants' academic programs.

Other important questions regarding multicultural counseling competence is how training is provided and what are best practices? Several scholars (e.g., Alvarez & Miville, 2003; Ridley, Mendoza, & Kanitz, 1994; Vazquez & Garcia-Vazquez, 2003) have suggested a number of important considerations. Alvarez and Miville identified three major sets of considerations in planning training activities: (1) pedagogical assumptions (e.g., role of students and instructors, nature of learning, identity development, and sociopolitical framework), (2) structural considerations (e.g., depth versus breadth of multiculturalism, content, format, and assignments), and (3) process (e.g., group norms, dealing with conflict and resistance, and instructor process). Fouad and Arredondo (2007) further suggested that issues of multicultural counseling competence should be infused in the entire curriculum and that students be annually evaluated regarding their multicultural counseling competence.

A number of scholars have commented that in addition to traditional didactic activities, of greatest importance are more experiential activities that allow participants to grapple openly and honestly with the complex emotional aspects of becoming multiculturally competent (e.g., Kim & Lyons, 2003; Roysircar, 2004). Mio and Barker-Hackett (2003) noted that using self-reflective essays or journals might be particularly useful for topics that are emotionally charged (e.g., owning racist beliefs or privilege). Sanchez-Hucles and Jones (2005) also called for multicultural competence training that "better prepares individuals to have difficult dialogues about race and other taboo topics" (p. 549). Activities involving such dialogues, while potentially fraught with tension and conflict, can be a primary means of developing consciousness and confidence. Experiential training activities make a great deal of intuitive sense, and there is much anecdotal evidence to suggest their effectiveness. Unfortunately, there are currently little empirical data to support these types of educational interventions.

A final consideration regarding multicultural counseling training is the assessment of multicultural counseling competence among students. Indeed, in light of problems associated with self-report measures, programs should not rely solely on such measures to assess student competence; instead "multitrait, multimethod [and] multiinformant" (Kaslow, 2004, p. 778) assessment strategies are more effective. Multiple measures of students' attitudes may be gathered through the use of self-reports, supervisor evaluations, peer reviews, and client feedback. A more recent approach is the use of 360-degree evaluations "in which systematic input is gleaned by means of a comprehensive survey (often computerized) from one's supervisors, a diverse cadre of both peers and subordinates, and oneself . . . can provide input" about multicultural counseling competence (Kaslow, 2004, p. 778). Coleman and Hau (2003) suggested the use of portfolios as a way to collect a range of multicultural counseling competence information about students across their matriculation in training programs.

Current research indicates that multicultural counseling training has positive outcomes, more so than if trainees do not receive such training. Smith et al. (2006) summarized several excellent critiques on the status of multicultural counseling training: (a) a continuing lack of sound theoretical basis and training philosophy as well as institutional support to guide the development of a coherent program; (b) a focus more on competencies linked with awareness and knowledge, leaving very little emphases on skill development necessary for competent practice; and (c) the need for "multicultural education initiatives and the construct of multicultural competence [to] undergo ongoing and rigorous scrutiny if they are to continue receiving widespread support from mental health professionals" (p. 142).

IMPLICATIONS AND FUTURE RESEARCH DIRECTIONS IN PRACTICE AND TRAINING

As discussed earlier, there have been notable advances in conceptual and empirical work relevant to multicultural competence in both the assessment and treatment of people of color. Regarding assessment, current evidence points to continuing problems with mis- or overdiagnoses of certain disorders for many clients of color. Researchers also have explored the impact of biases in counselor attitudes and therapy skills (e.g., racial microaggressions). Further, recent models of assessment and treatment offer exciting prospects for future research. In sum, the available conceptual and empirical work points to a number of directions for future research and practice in multicultural counseling competence.

There is continued need for programmatic research exploring the theory-derived competencies of skills, knowledge, and awareness (e.g., Arredondo et al., 1996), as well as other culture-relevant variables that may affect counseling processes or outcomes (e.g., identity, acculturation, and language). A common problem in the extant literature has been the heavy reliance on self-perceptions of multicultural counseling competence. A number of researchers have found significant relationships between self-reported multicultural counseling competence and social desirability attitudes (e.g., Constantine & Ladany, 2000; Worthington et al., 2000), raising questions about the validity of self-rated multicultural competence measures. Likewise, much of the research on multicultural competence has utilized either analogue or convenience samples, leading to external validity concerns (Worthington et al., 2006). Thus, research that incorporates instrumentation beyond self-reported ratings (e.g., knowledge) and that explores actual skill use and effectiveness with actual client samples is much in demand.

The multicultural counseling models proposed in the past decade provide an incredibly rich conceptual base from which to design programmatic research (e.g., Constantine & Ladany, 2001; Neville & Mobley, 2001; Ponterotto, Fuertes, & Chen, 2000). The EMMCCP model (Neville & Mobley, 2001) identifies several concentric systems in which clients are nested, only one level of which (the individual or personal system) has received serious attention in the literature. Research on interactions across these levels (e.g., individual or personal systems and mesosystems) may provide important information about the various feedback loops that affect therapy outcomes. The six competence dimensions proposed by Constantine and Ladany (2001) also represent an innovative way of exploring the "common factors" approach to therapy (Wampold, 2000). Researchers might explore the individual and collective impact of each of these dimensions on client retention, satisfaction, and change. Study of traditional counseling variables with clients of color, focusing on both counselor (e.g., attractiveness, credibility, and expertise) and client factors (e.g., level of functioning, readiness to change) also is warranted (Fuertes & Gretchen, 2001).

In addition, studies of multicultural counseling competence for specific cultural populations are greatly needed. Although there are now book-length works focusing on the treatment of Latinos and Latinas (e.g., Santiago-Rivera, Arredondo, & Gallardo-Cooper, 2002), much more empirical work must be done examining potential outcome moderators (e.g., age, generation, language abilities, and relational and process variables). Moreover, more research must be conducted exploring the impact on therapy of racial or ethnic group-specific concerns based, for instance, on sociohistorical backgrounds, prejudice and discrimination, immigration status, poverty, and specific cultural values and beliefs.

The impact of therapists from varying racial or cultural backgrounds on clients from other racial-cultural backgrounds also deserves further study. Much of the available literature presumes that either the counselor or client is White. Thus, the potential impact of biased attitudes of therapists from one racial-ethnic group toward another racial or ethnic group is largely unexplored. Other issues of bias based on age, gender, class, sexual orientation, or disability status also remain largely unexplored in relation to multicultural counseling competence. In short, much more research needs to be conducted to provide sufficient information for counseling psychologists and other mental health professionals to conduct evidenced-based practice for clients of color (Coleman & Wampold, 2003).

Another prime area for future research involves training for multicultural counseling competence and its specific subcompetencies. The original position paper developed by D. W. Sue et al. (1982), which ultimately served as a framework for the *Multicultural Guidelines* approved much later by the APA (2003), described 11 specific multicultural counseling competencies. Other scholars, such as D. W. Sue et al. (1998), Ridley et al. (1994), Arredondo et al. (1996), Constantine and Ladany (2001), and Fouad and Arredondo (2007), have presented multicultural counseling competencies in depth. However, as Ponterotto et al. (2000) noted, a "basic question remains unanswered: Do counselors who possess these competencies evidence improved counseling outcome with clients across cultures?" (p. 641).

Counseling psychologists have been leaders in advancing the state of research, theory, practice, and training in multicultural competence. Great strides have been made regarding the advocacy and inclusion of multicultural competence for all professional psychologists, such that competence in cultural diversity has been identified as a foundational (Kaslow, 2004) and cross-cutting (Lichtenberg, 2006) set of professional competencies, meaning that knowledge, attitudes, and skills necessary to work effectively with diverse clients are seen as necessary for all aspects of science and practice. However, empirical demonstrations that link training in multicultural counseling to actual counseling outcomes are critical areas for further programmatic research.

REFERENCES

Abreu, J. M. (1999). Conscious and nonconscious African American stereotypes: Impact on first impression and diagnostic ratings by therapists. *Journal of Consulting and Clinical Psychology, 67*, 387–393.

Alvarez, A. N., & Miville, M. L., (2003). Walking a tightrope: Strategies for teaching undergraduate multicultural counseling courses. In D. B. Pope-Davis, H. L. K. Coleman, W. M. Liu, & R. L. Toporek (Eds.), *Handbook of multicultural competencies in counseling and psychology* (pp. 528–547). Thousand Oaks, CA: Sage.

American Psychiatric Association. (2000). *Diagnostic and statistical manual of mental disorders* (4th ed., text rev.). Washington, DC: Author.

American Psychological Association. (2003). Guidelines on multicultural education, training, research, practice, and organizational change for psychologists. *American Psychologist, 58*, 377–402.

American Psychological Association Presidential Task Force on Evidence-Based Practice. (2006). Evidence-based practice in psychology. *American Psychologist, 61*, 271–298.

Arredondo, P., Toporek, R., Brown, S. P., Jones, J., Locke, D. C., Sanchez, J., et al. (1996). Operationalization of the multicultural counseling competencies. *Journal of Multicultural Counseling and Development, 24*, 42–78.

Burkard, A. W., & Knox, S. (2004). Effect of therapist color-blindness on empathy and attributions in cross-cultural counseling. *Journal of Counseling Psychology, 51*, 387–397.

Clay, D. L., Mordhorst, M. J., & Lehn, L. (2002). Empirical supported treatments in pediatric psychology: Where is the diversity? *Journal of Pediatric Psychology, 27*, 325–337.

Coleman, H. L. K., & Hau, J. M. (2003). Multicultural counseling competency and portfolios. In D. B. Pope-Davis, H. L. K. Coleman, W. M. Liu, & R. L. Toporek (Eds.), *Handbook of multicultural competencies in counseling and psychology* (pp. 168–182). Thousand Oaks, CA: Sage.

Coleman, H. L. K., & Wampold, B. E. (2003). Challenges to the development of culturally relevant, empirically supported treatment. In D. B. Pope-Davis, H. L. K. Coleman, W. M. Liu, & R. L. Toporek (Eds.), *Handbook of multicultural competencies in counseling and psychology* (pp. 227–246). Thousand Oaks, CA: Sage.

Constantine, M. G. (2000). Social desirability attitudes, sex, and affective and cognitive empathy as predictors of self-reported multicultural counseling competence. *Counseling Psychologist, 28*, 857–872.

Constantine, M. G. (2001a). Multicultural training, theoretical orientation, empathy, and multicultural case conceptualization ability in counselors. *Journal of Mental Health Counseling, 23*, 357–372.

Constantine, M. G. (2001b). Predictors of observer ratings of multicultural counseling competence in Black, Latino, and White American trainees. *Journal of Counseling Psychology, 48*, 456–462.

Constantine, M. G. (2002). Predictors of satisfaction with counseling: Racial and ethnic minority clients' attitudes toward counseling and ratings of their counselors' general and multicultural counseling competence. *Journal of Counseling Psychology, 49*, 255–263.

Constantine, M. G. (2007). Racial microaggressions against African American clients in cross-racial counseling relationships. *Journal of Counseling Psychology, 54*, 1–16.

Constantine, M. G., Gloria, A. M., & Ladany, N. (2002). The factor structure underlying three self-report multicultural counseling competence scales. *Cultural Diversity and Ethnic Minority Psychology, 8*, 334–345.

Constantine, M. G., & Gushue, G. V. (2003). School counselors' ethnic tolerance attitudes and racism attitudes as predictors of their multicultural case conceptualization of an immigrant student. *Journal of Counseling and Development, 81*, 185–190.

Constantine, M. G., Hage, S. M., Kindaichi, M. M., & Bryant, R. M. (2007). Social justice and multicultural issues: Implications for the practice and training of counselors and counseling psychologists. *Journal of Counseling and Development, 85,* 24–29.

Constantine, M. G., & Ladany, N. (2000). Self-report multicultural counseling competence scales: Their relation to social desirability attitudes and multicultural case conceptualization ability. *Journal of Counseling Psychology, 47,* 155–164.

Constantine, M. G., & Ladany, N. (2001). New visions for defining and assessing multicultural counseling competence. In J. G. Ponterotto, J. M. Casas, L. A. Suzuki, & C. M. Alexander (Eds.), *Handbook of multicultural counseling* (2nd ed. pp. 482–498). Thousand Oaks, CA: Sage.

Constantine, M. G., Ladany, N., Inman, A. G., & Ponterotto, J. G. (1996). Students' perceptions of multicultural training in counseling psychology programs. *Journal of Multicultural Counseling and Development, 24,* 241–253.

Constantine, M. G., & Sue, D. W. (Eds.). (2005). *Strategies for building multicultural competence in mental health and educational settings.* Hoboken, NJ: Wiley.

Dana, R. H. (2005). *Multicultural assessment: Principles, applications, and examples.* Mahwah, NJ: Erlbaum.

D'Andrea, M., & Daniels, J. (2001). Expanding our thinking about White racism: Facing the challenge of multicultural counseling in the 21st century. In J. G. Ponterotto, J. M. Casas, L. A. Suzuki, & C. M. Alexander (Eds.), *Handbook of multicultural counseling* (2nd ed., pp. 289–310). Thousand Oaks, CA: Sage.

D'Andrea, M., Daniels, J., & Heck, R. (1991). Evaluating the impact of multicultural counseling training. *Journal of Counseling and Development, 70,* 143–170.

Dunn, T. W., Smith, T. B., & Montoya, J. A. (2006). Multicultural competency instrumentation: A review and analysis of reliability generalization. *Journal of Counseling and Development, 84,* 471–482.

Fischer, A. R., Jome, L. M., & Atkinson, D. R. (1998). Reconceptualizing multicultural counseling: Universal healing conditions in a culturally specific context. *Counseling Psychologist, 26,* 525–588.

Fouad, N. A., & Arredondo, P. (2007). *Becoming culturally oriented: Practical advice for psychologists and educators.* Washington, DC: American Psychological Association.

Fuertes, J. N., & Brobst, K. (2002). Clients' ratings of counselor multicultural competency. *Cultural Diversity and Ethnic Minority Psychology, 8,* 214–223.

Fuertes, J. N., & Gretchen, D. (2001). Emerging theories of multicultural counseling. In L. A. Suzuki, J. G. Ponterotto, & P. J. Meller (Eds.), *Handbook of multicultural assessment: Clinical, psychological, and educational applications* (2nd ed., pp. 509–541). San Francisco: Jossey-Bass.

Fuertes, J. N., Stracizzi, T. I., Bennett, J., Schienholtz, J., Mislowack, A., Hersh, M., et al. (2006). Therapist multicultural competency: A study of therapy dyads. *Psychotherapy: Theory, Research, Practice, Training, 43,* 480–490.

Garb, H. N. (1997). Race bias, social class bias, and gender bias in clinical judgment. *Clinical Psychology: Science and Practice, 4,* 99–120.

Gushue, G. V. (2004). Race, color-blind racial attitudes, and judgments about mental health: A shifting standards perspective. *Journal of Counseling Psychology, 51,* 398–407.

Hansen, N. D., Randazzo, K. V., Schwartz, A., Marshall, M., Kalis, D., Frazier, R., et al. (2006). Do we practice what we preach? An exploratory survey of multicultural psychotherapy competencies. *Professional Psychology: Research and Practice, 37,* 66–74.

Hills, H. I., & Strozier, A. L. (1992). Multicultural training in APA-approved counseling psychology programs: A survey. *Professional Psychology: Research and Practice, 23,* 43–51.

Kaslow, N. J. (2004). Competencies in professional psychology. *American Psychologist, 59,* 774–781.

Kim, B. S. K., Cartwright, B. Y., Asay, P. A., & D'Andrea, M. J. (2003). A revision of the Multicultural Awareness, Knowledge, and Skills Survey—Counselor Edition. *Measurement and Evaluation in Counseling and Development, 36,* 161–180.

Kim, B. S. K., & Lyons, H. Z. (2003). Experiential activities and multicultural counseling competence training. *Journal of Counseling and Development, 81,* 400–408.

Kitaoka, S. K. (2005). Multicultural counseling competencies: Lessons from assessment. *Journal of Multicultural Counseling and Development, 33,* 37–47.

Ladany, N., Constantine, M. G., Inman, A. G., & Hofheinz, E. W. (1997). Supervisee multicultural case conceptualization ability and self-reported multicultural competence as functions of supervisee racial identity and supervisor focus. *Journal of Counseling Psychology, 44,* 284–293.

LaFromboise, T. C., Coleman, H. L. K., & Hernandez, A. (1991). Development and factor structure of the Cross-Cultural Counseling Inventory—Revised. *Professional Psychology: Research and Practice, 22*, 380–388.

Lichtenberg, J. (2006, February). *Competencies in counseling psychology: An overview of the issues.* Invited presentation at the annual CCPTP midwinter meeting, Tampa, FL.

Liu, W. M., & Clay, D. L. (2002). Multicultural counseling competencies: Guidelines in working with children and adolescents. *Journal of Mental Health Counseling, 24*, 177–187.

Manese, J. E., Wu, J. T., & Nepomuceno, C. A. (2001.) The effect of training on multicultural counseling competencies: An exploratory study over a 10-year period. *Journal of Multicultural Counseling and Development, 29*, 31–40.

Maton, K. I., Kohout, J. L., Wicherski, M., Leary, G. E., & Vinokurov, A. (2006). Minority students of color and the psychology graduate pipeline. *American Psychologist, 61*, 117–131.

Mio, J. S., & Barker-Hackett, L. (2003). Reaction papers and journal writing as techniques for assessing resistance in multicultural courses. *Journal of Multicultural Counseling and Development, 31*, 12–19.

Miranda, J., Nakamura, R., & Bernal, G. (2003). Including ethnic minorities in mental health intervention research: A practical approach to a long-standing problem. *Culture, Medicine, and Psychiatry, 27*, 467–486.

Neville, H. A., Lilly, R. L., Duran, G., Lee, R., & Browne, L. (2000). Construction and initial validation of the Color-Blind Racial Attitudes Scale (CoBRAS). *Journal of Counseling Psychology, 47*, 59–70.

Neville, H. A., & Mobley, M. (2001). Social identities in contexts: An ecological model of multicultural counseling psychology processes. *Counseling Psychologist, 29*, 471–486.

Neville, H. A., Spanierman, L., & Doan, B.-T. (2006). Exploring the association between color-blind racial ideology and multicultural counseling competencies. *Cultural Diversity and Ethnic Minority Psychology, 12*, 275–290.

Neville, H. A., Worthington, R. L., & Spanierman, L. B. (2001). Race, power, and multicultural counseling psychology: Understanding White privilege and color-blind racial attitudes. In J. G. Ponterotto, J. M. Casas, L. A. Suzuki, & C. M. Alexander (Eds.), *Handbook of multicultural counseling* (2nd ed., pp. 257–288). Thousand Oaks, CA: Sage.

Nguyen, L., Huang, L. N., Arganza, G. F., & Liao, Q. (2007). The influence of race and ethnicity on psychiatric diagnoses and clinical characteristics of children and adolescents in children's services. *Cultural Diversity and Ethnic Minority Psychology, 13*, 18–25.

Pierce, C., Carew, J., Pierce-Gonzalez, D., & Willis, D. (1978). An experiment in racism: TV commercials. In C. Pierce (Ed.), *Television and education* (pp 62–88). Beverly Hills, CA: Sage.

Ponterotto, J. G. (1997). Multicultural counseling training: A competency model and national survey. In D. B. Pope-Davis & H. L. K. Coleman (Eds.), *Multicultural counseling competencies: Assessment, education and training, and supervision* (pp. 111–130). Thousand Oaks, CA: Sage.

Ponterotto, J. G., Alexander, C. M., & Grieger, I. (1995). A multicultural competency checklist for counseling training programs. *Journal of Multicultural Counseling and Development, 23*, 11–23.

Ponterotto, J. G., Fuertes, J. N., & Chen, E. C. (2000). Models of multicultural counseling. In S. D. Brown & R. W. Lent (Eds.), *Handbook of counseling psychology* (3rd ed., pp. 639–669). New York: Wiley.

Ponterotto, J. G., Gretchen, D., & Chauhan, R. V. (2001). Cultural identity and multicultural assessment: Quantitative and qualitative tools for the clinician. In L. A. Suzuki, J. G. Ponterotto, & P. J. Meller (Eds.), *Handbook of multicultural assessment: Clinical, psychological, and educational applications* (2nd ed., pp. 67–99). San Francisco: Jossey-Bass.

Ponterotto, J. G., Gretchen, D., Utsey, S. O., Rieger, B. P., & Austin, R. (2002). A revision of the Multicultural Counseling Awareness Scale. *Journal of Multicultural Counseling and Development, 30*, 153–180.

Ponterotto, J. G., Rieger, B. T., Barrett, A., Harris, G., Sparks, R., Sanchez, C. M., et al. (1996). Development and initial validation of the Multicultural Counseling Awareness Scale. In G. R. Sodowsky & J. C. Impara (Eds.), *Multicultural assessment in counseling and clinical psychology* (pp. 247–282). Lincoln, NE: Buros Institute of Mental Measurements.

Pope-Davis, D. B., & Dings, J. G. (1995). The assessment of multicultural counseling competencies. In J. G. Ponterotto, J. M. Casas, L. A. Suzuki, & G. Alexander (Eds.), *Handbook of multicultural counseling* (pp. 287–311). Thousand Oaks, CA: Sage.

Quintana, S. M., & Bernal, M. E. (1995). Ethnic minority training in counseling in counseling psychology: Comparisons with clinical psychology and proposed standards. *Counseling Psychologist, 23*, 102–121.

Rainey, J. A., & Nowak, T. M. (2005). Mental health assessment with African American children and adolescents. In D. A. Harley & J. M. Dillard (Eds.), *Contemporary mental health issues among African Americans* (pp. 255–277). Alexandria, VA: American Counseling Association.

Ridley, C. R. (2005). *Overcoming unintentional racism in counseling and therapy* (2nd ed.). Thousand Oaks, CA: Sage.

Ridley, C. R., Li, L. C., & Hill, C. L. (1998). Multicultural assessment: Reexamination, reconceptualization, and practical application. *Counseling Psychologist, 26*, 827–910.

Ridley, C. R., Mendoza, D. W., & Kanitz, B. E. (1994). Multicultural training: Reexamination, operationalization, and integration. *Counseling Psychologist, 22*, 277–289.

Rogers, M. R., Hoffman, M. A., & Wade, J. (1998). Notable multicultural training in APA-approved counseling psychology and school psychology programs. *Cultural Diversity and Mental Health, 4*, 212–226.

Rogers, M. R., & Molina, L. E. (2006). Exemplary efforts in psychology to recruit and retain graduate students of color. *American Psychologist, 61*, 143–156.

Rollock, D., & Gordon, E. W. (2000). Racism and mental health into the 21st century: Perspectives and parameters. *American Journal of Orthopsychiatry, 70*, 5–13.

Roysircar, G. (2004). Cultural self-awareness assessment: Practice examples from psychology training. *Professional Psychology: Research and Practice, 35*, 658–666.

Roysircar, G. (2005). Culturally sensitive assessment, diagnosis, and guidelines. In M. G. Constantine & D. W. Sue (Eds.), *Strategies for building multicultural competence in mental health and educational settings* (pp. 19–38). Hoboken, NJ: Wiley.

Roysircar-Sodowsky, G., & Kuo, P. Y. (2001). Determining cultural validity of personality assessment: Some guidelines. In D. B. Pope-Davis & H. L. K. Coleman (Eds.), *The intersection of race, class, and gender: Implications for multicultural counseling* (pp. 213–239). Thousand Oaks, CA: Sage.

Sanchez-Hucles, J., & Jones, N. (2005). Breaking the silence around race in training, practice, and research. *Counseling Psychologist, 33*, 547–558.

Santiago-Rivera, A., Arredondo, P., & Gallardo-Cooper, M. (2002). *Counseling Latinos and la familia: A practical guide*. Thousand Oaks, CA: Sage.

Smith, T. B., Constantine, M. G., Dunn, T. W., Dinehart, J. M., & Montoya, J. A. (2006). Multicultural education in the mental health professions: A meta-analytic review. *Journal of Counseling Psychology, 53*, 132–145.

Sodowsky, G. R., Taffe, R. C., Gutkin, T. B., & Wise, S. L. (1994). Development of the Multicultural Counseling Inventory: A self-report measure of multicultural competencies. *Journal of Counseling Psychology, 41*, 137–148.

Solórzano, D., Ceja, M., & Yosso, T. (2000). Critical race theory, racial microaggressions, and campus racial climate: The experiences of African American college students. *Journal of Negro Education, 69*, 60–73.

Sue, D. W., Arredondo, P., & McDavis, R. J. (1992). Multicultural counseling competencies and standards: A call to the profession. *Journal of Multicultural Counseling and Development, 20*, 64–88.

Sue, D. W., Bernier, J. B., Duran, M., Feinberg, L., Pedersen, P., Smith, E., et al. (1982). Position paper: Cross-cultural counseling competencies. *Counseling Psychologist, 10*, 45–52.

Sue, D. W., Carter, R. T., Casas, J. M., Fouad, N. A., Ivey, A. E., Jensen, M., et al. (1998). *Multicultural counseling competencies: Individual and organizational development*. Thousand Oaks, CA: Sage.

Sue, S. (1998). In search of cultural competence in psychotherapy and counseling. *American Psychologist, 53*, 440–448.

Suzuki, L. A., Ponterotto, J. G., & Meller, P. J. (Eds.). (2001). *Handbook of multicultural assessment: Clinical, psychological, and educational applications* (2nd ed.). New York: Jossey-Bass.

Thompson, C. E., & Jenal, S. T. (1994). Interracial and intraracial quasi-counseling interactions when counselors avoid discussing race. *Journal of Counseling Psychology, 41*, 484–491.

Thompson, C. E., & Neville, H. A. (1999). Racism, mental health, and mental health practice. *Counseling Psychologist, 27*, 155–223.

Thompson, C. E., Worthington, R., & Atkinson, D. R. (1994). Counselor content orientation, counselor race, and Black women's cultural mistrust and self-disclosures. *Journal of Counseling Psychology, 41*, 155–161.

U.S. Census Bureau. (2004). *U.S. interim projections by age, sex, race, and Hispanic origin*. Retrieved on February 1, 2007, from www.census.gov/ipc/www/usinterimproj/.

U.S. Department of Health and Human Services. (2001). *Mental health: Culture, race and ethnicity—A supplement to mental health: A report of the surgeon general*. Rockville, MD: U.S. Department of Health and Human Services, Public Health Office, Office of the Surgeon General.

Vazquez, L. A., & Garcia-Vazquez, E. (2003). Teaching multicultural competence in the counseling curriculum. In D. B. Pope-Davis, H. L. K. Coleman, W. M. Liu, & R. L. Toporek (Eds.), *Handbook of multicultural competencies in counseling and psychology* (pp. 546–561). Thousand Oaks, CA: Sage.

Vinson, T. S., & Neimeyer, G. J. (2000). The relationship between racial identity development and multicultural counseling competency. *Journal of Multicultural Counseling and Development, 28*, 177–192.

Wampold. B. E. (2000). Outcomes of individual counseling and psychotherapy: Empirical evidence addressing two fundamental questions. In S. D. Brown & R. W. Lent (Eds.), *Handbook of counseling psychology* (3rd ed., pp. 711–739). New York: Wiley.

Wampold, B. E., Lichtenberg, J. W., & Waehler, C. A. (2002). Principles of empirically supported interventions in counseling psychology. *Counseling Psychologist, 30*, 197–217.

Worthington, R. L., Mobley, M., Franks, R. P., & Tan, J. A. (2000). Multicultural counseling competencies: Verbal content, counselor attributions, and social desirability. *Journal of Counseling Psychology, 47*, 460–468.

Worthington, R.L., Soth, A.M., & Moreno, M.V. (2006, August). *Multicultural counseling competencies research: A 20-year content analysis*. Paper presented at the annual meeting of the American Psychological Association, New Orleans, LA.

CHAPTER 10

Social Class and Classism: Understanding the Psychological Impact of Poverty and Inequality

WILLIAM MING LIU
SABA RASHEED ALI

Psychologists need to integrate social class and classism into research, training, and practice (American Psychological Association [APA], 2007; M. T. Brown, Fukunaga, Umemoto, & Wicker, 1996; Fouad & Brown, 2001; Liu, 2001, 2006; Liu, Ali, et al., 2004; Liu, Soleck, Hopps, Dunston, & Pickett, 2004; Lott, 2002; Smith, 2005). But confusion exists about what social class is and how it may function in a person's life (Frable, 1997; Liu, 2002; Liu, Ali, et al., 2004). Social class affects a person's life through poverty, classism, and other forms of economic inequality. But for counseling psychologists, what are these affects? How do we conceptualize and understand the impact of poverty and inequality in an individual's life? How might we change our research and practice to better meet the experiences and needs of these impoverished communities? This chapter first provides some conceptual clarification of the terms *social class, socioeconomic status (SES), poverty,* and *inequality*. Second, we use Bronfenbrenner's (1986) ecological theory to understand the macro and micro affects of poverty and inequality on the individual. Finally, we discuss clinical implications for working with clients who live in impoverished circumstances.

DEFINING SOCIAL CLASS AND CLASSISM

For psychologists, understanding the terms *social class, classism,* and *SES* is often problematic because they are generally used atheoretically and operationalized poorly in research and theory (M. T. Brown et al., 1996; Liberatos, Link, & Kelsey, 1988; Oakes & Rossi, 2003). Additionally, much of the psychological research has imported sociological approaches to investigating social class by using indices of income, education, and occupation to represent a social class position (e.g., middle-class; M. T. Brown et al., 1996). Several researchers have found that these "objective" indices do not account for much variance after a subjective social class question has been asked such as "What is your social class?" (Ostrove, Adler, Kuppermann, & Washington, 2000). Researchers have also found that each index may be related to separate types of outcomes. Education may be a good predictor of occupational type among men but not women (Gottfried, 1985; Hoffman, 2003). And income is notoriously difficult to measure because it is subject to inaccurate reporting, short-term fluctuations, and high reactivity (Duncan, 1988). Croizet and Claire (1998) found evidence that asking about income may elicit negative self-thoughts (stereotype threat) from participants and change (i.e., depress) their performance.

Even though research has not supported this aggregate approach to measuring social class, psychologists continue to use income, education, and occupation, or some combination of these three, to categorize people into social class groups (Liu, Ali, et al., 2004). Liu (2002) frames this method as a stratification paradigm wherein individuals are situated in fabricated social class groups or pseudosocial class groupings. Of the many limitations to this approach, one is the potentially unlimited number of social class groups (striations) that any given researcher can create (e.g., middle working-class). For psychologists, the most significant limitation is the assumption that everyone in a specific social class category has the same worldview and reacts to this worldview in the same way. Other limitations include the assumptions that social class and classism are only adult experiences and that everyone is motivated to ascend the social class hierarchy (i.e., upward mobility bias; Liu, 2002).

Social Class, Socioeconomic Status, and Classism

A main source of confusion is terminology: Should we use *social class* or *SES*? Several authors have shown that there is no agreed-on definition of social class or SES in the psychological literature (Oakes & Rossi, 2003), and that researchers have used both terms interchangeably (Liu, Ali, et al., 2004). Both terms have been used to allude to status gradients, mobility, status, positions, access to resources, power, and privilege. But SES seems to be used often to refer to gradients and mobility, whereas social class is used to refer to positions and relationships to resources (APA, 2007). In either case, both terms have not been sufficiently differentiated. Alternatively, Liu, Ali, et al. (2004) suggest that psychologists should use social class to describe a psychological experience that includes such concepts as identity, acculturation, stress, or worldview. These authors draw a parallel to the study of race and racism, where psychologists tend to study racial identity, the effects of racism, and acculturation, rather than the physical aspects of race per se.

In the social class worldview model (SCWM; Liu, 2002), the term *worldview* refers to the beliefs and attitudes that help people comprehend the demands of their social class's economic culture, develop behaviors to meet the social class economic culture demands, and recognize how classism functions in their lives. The use of the term *social class* is also intentional. Social class is nominally easier to link with classism. But social class reflects the authors' beliefs that people regard each other in categories and not as mobile individuals on a gradient (i.e., class versus status). Finally, the use of the term *social class* is also a reminder that inequalities exist between social class groups.

Classism is also a broad term that functions at the macro and micro level of interpersonal relationships. Certainly, the terms *economic exploitation, inequality,* and *poverty* are forms of classism but using these constructs without clearly specifying their psychological meaning and intent leads to confusion. Liu (2002) uses the term *classism* to identify an interpersonal form of prejudice and discrimination that functions in relation to the SCWM at several levels. Different forms of classism may elicit diverse feelings (anxiety, frustration, depression) and also can have different consequences for individuals. Based on the assumption that people will conceptually categorize others in social classes and then treat others accordingly, Liu (2002) explicates various types of potential classism: *Downward classism* is conceptualized as prejudice and discrimination against those perceived in a lower social class group; *upward classism* is prejudice and discrimination against those perceived in a higher social class group; and *lateral classism* is prejudice experienced in maintaining your perceived social class position (i.e., "keeping up with the Joneses"). Liu (2002) also speculates that individuals may experience *internalized classism* that is apprehension and depression when a person is unable to maintain a perceived social class position.

Smith (2006) critiqued Liu's (2006) conceptualization of classism as not recognizing differences in power across powerful and disempowered groups and as having the power to do disservice to people who are economically poor by attributing a level of agency to the poor that they really do not have. However, Liu (2006) proposed that power and interpersonal relationships need to move beyond a binary of "haves" and "have-nots" and instead, power should be redefined as exercised in relationship networks wherein people are constantly negotiating between privilege, empowerment, and marginalization (Liu & Pope-Davis, 2003a, 2003b). Liu (2006) is also interested in the microaggressions (Sue, 2003) of classism that help to perpetuate inequality, exploitation, and poverty. It is these inter- and intragroup classisms that fuel discrimination and prejudice and contribute to structural inequalities. Therefore, individuals are constantly targets as well as perpetrators of classism.

Poverty and Inequality

Poverty, as defined by the Census Bureau (2003), focuses only on the material conditions of an individual and family. Originally developed in 1963/1964 (Fisher, 1992), the definition of poverty was based on the amount needed to purchase basic food stuffs multiplied by three. There are a number of problems related to the current definition of poverty, and Liu (in press) identified three: First, the basic definition of poverty is national in scope and does not take into account variability related to geography and locale. Second, although the poverty threshold is adjusted annually for inflation (Census Bureau, 2005), it does not account for changes in consumption. In other words, the poverty threshold reflects today's dollar needs but the consumption behavior of 1963 (Short & Garner, 2002). The poverty threshold does not account for the cost of fuel, health care, or child care. Third, the poverty threshold is an absolute value. Anyone living above the dollar amount for poverty is considered "not in poverty." Even though some may live in poor or near-poor conditions or live a life of deprivation, they are not counted as living "in poverty" (Liu, in press).

For psychologists, poverty is difficult to research and conceptualize because it represents a constellation of causes and consequences. Thus, it is inaccurate to study "poverty" as a singular psychological construct. Similarly, counseling psychologists who find themselves in clinical practice with people in poverty situations may find it difficult to conceptualize what poverty looks like from the client's perspective. Conceptual challenges also arise with the notion of economic inequality. Inequality, especially economic or social class inequality, is related to disparities in resources in a population or community (Wilkinson & Pickett, 2006). Inequality refers to a situation in which the poor not only have exponentially fewer resources than the rich, but also have restricted access and limited social class mobility in a society. Moreover, in those countries where a substantial difference exists between rich and poor, the overall mental health of the population is poorer than in countries with less inequality (Wilkinson & Pickett, 2006). Therefore, a substantial gap exists in resources, their allocation and access, and the chronic absence of these resources has led to conditions of inequality wherein increasing income alone is insufficient to close the gap.

An example of inequality and the effects of closing the income gap come from a quasi-experiment by Costello, Compton, Keeler, and Angold (2003). They found that after the income on a reservation had been increased by a new casino, American Indian children living on the reservation showed a 40% decrease in incidences of deviant behaviors, but no change in rates of affective disorders. By all accounts, the American Indian children prior to the casino's opening were persistently poor. As a result, their odds of having psychiatric problems were 59% higher than never-poor children. After the increase in income, diagnosed conduct and oppositional disorders decreased, whereas anxiety and depression persisted. Although many factors may be related to the psychiatric symptoms that declined and persisted, Costello et al. (2003) suggested that this difference at least supports a social causation hypothesis for conduct and oppositional disorders. Thus, the lack of power among those who are poor and in poverty is a central defining characteristic of inequality. In this chapter, we discuss poverty and inequality as interdependent constructs because poverty is a form of inequality. Although poverty and being poor address the material condition of the individual, inequality addresses the issue of lack of power.

Poverty and inequality are important to understand as social justice and multicultural issues (Vera & Speight, 2003), but are somewhat more difficult to conceptualize as psychological constructs for research and clinical practice. How do these societal level issues manifest in the psychotherapy relationship? To expand our understanding of these specific social class issues, we discuss the development of mental health problems using Bronfenbrenner's (1986) ecological theory. We chose ecological theory because it best reflects current research that suggests that some mental health problems and other forms of psychological distress are a result of a person's social class (social causation) rather than a cause of his or her social class (social selection). Before doing so, however, we need also to understand the links between social class and various mental health outcomes.

Social Class Gradients and Mental Health

The social class gradient for mental health suggests that individuals at higher social classes are more likely to have better mental and physical health than those at lower social classes (Adler, Boyce, Chesney, Folkman, & Syme, 1993). The gradient posits a monotonic relationship between social class and health, such that, with increasing social class, the health of the individual increases (Gallo & Matthews, 2003). The gradient should also predict that the higher a person is in social class, the higher a person's self-esteem. However, Twenge and Campbell (2002) conducted a meta-analysis of 446 samples ($N = 312,940$), and found that the relation between social class and self-esteem, although statistically significant, was small ($d = .15$, $r = .08$). Other findings from the Twenge and Campbell meta-analysis suggested that the relationship between social class and self-esteem starts out to be quite small in children, increases with age, and then returns to a smaller relationship at around 60 years of age. Some sex differences were also reported—the relationship seemed to increase in women, but decrease in men over time. Thus, in this one indicator of psychological health, social class is a small contributor, varies by gender, and appears to be curvilinear with age.

Research also suggests that the social class and mental health gradient may vary depending on a number of factors such as age, exposure to environmental toxins, higher stress levels, and limited access to health care (Hopps & Liu, 2006). Other disparities and inequalities are also negatively and heavily weighted toward the lower social class spectrums; that is, for all diseases and all cause-mortality, the gradient is steepest in the lowest social classes (Gallo & Matthews, 2003), but then levels off significantly at higher social class levels.

There are two major explanations for this gradient: (1) Social causation theory suggests that people become vulnerable to psychological stress arising from conditions of poverty (Beiser, Johnson, & Turner, 1993). (2) By contrast, social selection theory suggests that individuals with mental health problems come from poor conditions and are likely to experience downward mobility as a result of their life problems. Some research suggests that the interaction of the two theories best explains mental health issues of people in poverty (Tiffin, Pearce, & Parker, 2005), but other researchers have found significant and substantial evidence to support the social causation theory (Bosma, van de Mheen, & Mackenbach, 1999; Costello et al., 2003; Gallo, Bogart, Vranceanu, & Matthews, 2005).

Gallo et al. (2005) researched a type of social causation theory called the reserve capacity theory in which people in lower social classes have less, and are less able to generate financial and social support. The reserve capacity model suggests that environmental demands create psychological costs that have a cascade affect across other dimensions of the person's life. The threat of physical harm—a constant threat for many living in poor neighborhoods—may create constant conditions of arousal and anxiety that are difficult to sustain psychologically and physically. Moreover, when faced with environmental stresses, interpersonal conflicts and stressors, and other demands, the poor have fewer resources to draw on, are likely to deplete their resources more quickly, and benefit less from resource mobilization than those in higher social classes. Thus, resource allocation is not equally distributed but must be weighted toward the steepest part of the gradient. Contributing to the depletion of personal resources is the constant exposure to daily stressors, a feeling of being out of control, and high levels of social conflicts (Gallo et al., 2005). Gallo et al. (2005) found that those in lower social classes had fewer material, personal, and interpersonal resources, which made them more susceptible to negative emotions and cognitions (depression, hopelessness, hostility, and anxiety) than those from higher social class backgrounds (Gallo & Matthews, 1999, 2003). Conversely, individuals in low social class situations who had good social support and believed they had personal control "did not display elevated emotional distress relative to those with high social status" (Gallo & Matthews, 2003, p. 35). Therefore, it may be that individuals in low social classes who feel they have no control over their environments are the most susceptible to the deleterious affects of poverty, whereas those with greater levels of perceived control may be somewhat protected.

Gallo and Matthews (1999) also posited that social drift versus social selection is a more likely explanation for individuals with mental illness falling into lower social class groups. In their reserve capacity model, a chronic state of negative emotions may increase the possibility of psychiatric disorders and make the individual less competitive for certain types of employment or other forms of economic security. Therefore, a form of social selection may appear, but primarily as a result of the impact of social causation in creating the preconditions for mental health problems.

In this elaboration of poverty, inequality, and social class, poverty is most likely to affect certain populations more and more extremely than others. In particular, poverty is more likely to affect new immigrants, people of color (African, Asian, Latino, and Native American communities), and women (Edelman & Jones, 2004; Geronimus, Bound, Waidmann, Hillemeier, & Burns, 1996). If there is any intersection in which race, social class, and inequality is most prominent, it is in the context of poverty (Liu, Hernandez, Mahmood, & Stinson, 2006).

Even for those ethnic racial group members who have been able to make some social class gains and upward mobility, their social class status may constantly be threatened. Heflin and Pattillo (2006) found that, during times of duress, middle-class African Americans are less likely to have other middle-class family members and siblings to turn to for assistance. African American middle-class members may, therefore, be more socially isolated than middle-class and poor Whites. They may also feel that their social class position is constantly under threat and may be vigilant to signs of status loss. Thus, in the research on social class, poverty, and race, researchers need also to focus on the social class groups that appear to be successful, but also face salient threats to their stability.

Although the research covered in this section is predicated on the ill effects of poverty and low social class status on physical and psychological health, the reserve capacity model could also provide a basis for the design of psychological interventions. As Gallo and Matthews (2003) have discovered, social support and access to material resources are both equally important in preventing and treating psychological distress. Because this is a form of social causation, psychologists need to assess for the variety of stressors, across multiple environments, which could fill or deplete these resources and affect individual's access to, or feelings about, important sources of social support.

ECOLOGICAL THEORY AND THE IMPACT OF POVERTY

Bronfenbrenner's ecological model (1986) is clear about the need to further understand the impact of social class, poverty, and inequality on human development. His model was designed as a heuristic to frame the multiple effects that various environments can have on a child's growth and development. The model posits that the physical and psychological maturation and development of a child into adulthood is affected by a number of systems and factors. Although the family is the main source of socialization and has the most impact on the child's development, occupational experiences, schooling, governmental action, societal norms and beliefs, and the passage of time are all variables needing consideration (Bronfenbrenner, 1986, 1989).

According to this theory, children live in a series of co-centric rings or levels of influence, with each level representing a different type of impact on the child's development. First, the child lives in a microsystem consisting mainly of family and peers. In the microsystem, the child has the most contact with his or her immediate surroundings. There is a bidirectional influence in the microsystem such that the environment affects the child but the child also potentially changes the life of the caretakers. The next ring is the mesosystem, which includes relationships between the family and other microsystems, such as school and church. The next level is the exosystem. Although the child does not encounter this level directly, he or she can be affected indirectly by it. For instance, the parents' workplace demands and stresses may affect the child. The final level is the macrosystem, including society's laws, norms, customs, and values. If the society favors families led by heterosexual, married parents, anyone not meeting this expectation may experience stress and strain that may impact how a parent interacts with a child.

Although Bronfenbrenner alludes to the direct impact of poverty and inequality on children, he does not specify how they affect the developmental life span or the worldview of the individual.

Current research on poverty and inequality provide some evidence to suggest that early experiences with poverty and inequality have consequences throughout the life span (McLoyd, 1998), and counseling psychologists might wish to be aware of these issues in practice and research.

DEVELOPMENT OF MENTAL HEALTH PROBLEMS

Using Bronfenbrenner's ecological theory (1986, 1989), we discuss the possible effects of each system on the individual, using specific examples in each system, and move from distal (i.e., macrosystem) to proximal (i.e., microsystem) influences.

Macrosystems

One prominent value and expectation in the United States is materialism. A materialistic value orientation (MVO) may be defined as "the belief that it is important to pursue the culturally sanctioned goals of attaining financial success, having nice possessions, the right image (produced in large part, through consumer goods), and a high social status (defined mostly by the size of a person's pocketbook and the scope of a person's possessions)" (Kasser, Ryan, Couchman, & Sheldon, 2004, p. 13). An MVO may also be related to upward mobility bias and endorsement of the protestant work ethic (PWE). The PWE values work over leisure (Mudrack, 1997), and internal psychological strengths (e.g., delay of gratification) over social strengths (e.g., relying on others). Similarly, the upward mobility bias assumes that all individuals are motivated to ascend the social class hierarchy, and deviance is attributed to those who do not subscribe to this belief. Consequently, work is primarily valued as a means to acquire material wealth, and material objects are used to reflect a person's social class mobility.

Even though research suggests that materialism and upward mobility are not robustly related to subjective evaluations of happiness (Boven, 2005; Burroughs & Rindfleisch, 2002), the dominant cultural (i.e., macrosystem) belief in the United States is that money (or at least possessions) can buy happiness. Materialism seems to be valued across the social class continuum, and neither the poor or rich are immune. M. Wood (1998) found that levels of impulsive buying were more strongly related to levels of education than to income level (and age and gender). Some research also suggests that teens at high levels of social class disadvantage and who live in poor neighborhoods tend to have high MVO (Cohen & Cohen, 1996; Kasser, Ryan, Zax, & Sameroff, 1995).

Materialism is also socialized early for many children and material objects may be used to cue a child's awareness of social class differences (Tulkin & Kagan, 1972). Achenreiner and John (2003) found that children learn to relate to brand names and start to develop preferences as early as 8 years old. As early as 12 years old, brand names become an important cue in many children's consumer habits. Liu (2002) speculated that the awareness of social class differences and the use of material objects as markers of social class may contribute to discriminatory and marginalizing behaviors (classism) toward children who do not meet expectations of normality.

Psychological distress may contribute to materialism (Solberg, Diener, & Robinson, 2004). Yet, the paradox of salving psychological stress through material possessions is the increased stress resulting from borrowing to finance materialistic needs. Watson (2003) found that people who had high MVO perceived themselves as "spenders" and as having positive attitudes toward borrowing and debt. Those with a high MVO also tend to value shopping over saving, are interested in new products, and are responsive to advertising about these new products (Goldberg, Gorn, Peracchio, & Bamossy, 2003). Yet as people spend and consume, high, nonmortgage debt is also negatively related to subjective well-being (S. Brown, Taylor, & Price, 2005).

Other research shows that people with a high MVO, or valuing of money, tend to have poorer subjective well-being (Solberg et al., 2004) and a sense of insecurity and self-doubt (Chang & Arkin, 2002; Christopher, Morgan, Marek, Keller, & Drummond, 2005). To compensate for these feelings of insecurity and self-doubt, these individuals may invest in material objects (Chang & Arkin, 2002). Advertisers understand the relationship between negative emotions and consumption and will use negative affect in advertisements to trigger an emotional response toward purchasing (Cotte & Ritchie, 2005).

Interpersonally, people with a high MVO may try to avoid presenting themselves as helpless and weak, vulnerable, and approachable, and attempt to impress others (Christopher et al., 2005). But ironically, these same individuals may doubt their ability to impress others (Christopher et al., 2005). Additionally, a high MVO is related to having fewer friends, poorer social skills (Solberg et al., 2004), and a higher sense of social anxiety in comparison to those with a low MVO (Christopher et al., 2005; Vohs, Mead, & Goode, 2006). In a series of experimental studies, Vohs et al. (2006) showed that participants primed to think about money tended to work on projects longer than participants not primed for money ($d = .86$), but were less helpful to others ($d = .66$), tended to prefer more interpersonal distance with potential new acquaintances ($d = .85$), and preferred individually focused leisure activities over more socially oriented experiences ($d = 1.06$). Vohs et al. (2006) concluded that reminding people of money increases self-reliance, but also decreases interpersonal dependence and the quality of relationships. Thus, the macrosystem value of materialism may be contradictory to the individual's physical and mental health. An overemphasis on materialism may isolate an individual and may involve him or her in a cycle of consumption, self-doubt, and distress.

Exosystems

One example of an exosystem effect on the individual, especially in child development, is parental workplace demands and stress. Research suggests that social class may be related to work-role salience (M. T. Brown et al., 1996; Diemer & Blustein, 2006), occupational expectations (Diemer & Hsieh, in press), vocational or educational aspirations (Ali & McWhirter, 2006), views of the world of work (Chaves et al., 2004), occupational self-concept implementation (Blustein et al., 2002), and career decision making self-efficacy (Thompson & Subich, 2006). Although research has explored various aspects of career development and decisions making, it is also important to understand the psychological impact of certain types of work.

The types of work most open to people who are poor or in poverty tend to be characterized as blue-collar and service occupations (e.g., maid, waiter, mechanic) that are often monotonous and repetitious and frequently provide little personal autonomy and control to the individual (Sapolsky, 2005). Karasek and Theorell (1990) described these types of jobs as lacking in decision authority (an inability to make decisions) and skill discretion. As a consequence, individuals in these work settings are often exposed to acute and chronic environmental and interpersonal stressors. The results of constant exposure to work stress may include cognitive deterioration, depressed mood, compromised immune functioning, and higher rates of cardiovascular disease (Boma et al., 1997; Griffin, Fuhrer, Stansfeld, & Marmot, 2002). Individuals working in these job settings who also lack significant personal resources may start to doubt their own self-worth (Gurin & Brim, 1984).

It is possible that the affects of unemployment, underemployment, and workplace stress can be transferred to a person's home relationships, which may result in marital conflict and strain and parent-child conflicts (Conger, Ge, Elder, Lorenz, & Simons, 1994; Gilbert & Rader, this volume). McLoyd, Jayaratne, Ceballo, and Borquez (1994) found that current unemployment and past work disruptions were related to increases in depressive symptoms among African American mothers. Depressive symptoms were, in turn, related to more frequent punishment of their children and adolescents, and to increased cognitive distress and depressive symptoms for adolescents (McLoyd et al., 1994). But even in blue-collar and service occupations, research has also shown that, regardless of the social class of the individual, increased sense of mastery and lower perceived job constraints were related to better subjective health, life satisfaction, and lower depressive symptoms (Lachman & Weaver, 1998). Similarly, increasing work demands and varying the type of work may also increase positive affect about work because the individual feels challenged and may use a diverse set of skills to meet the changing demands (Gallo & Matthews, 2003).

Furthermore, economic and work-related stressors, tended to increase parent dysphoria and marital and parent-child conflict (Conger et al., 1994). There may also be increases in aggressive and hostile communications between parents, especially over money matters and a general increase in family hostility (Conger et al., 1994). Increases in family hostility and conflict can increase the chances of child and adolescent behavioral and emotional problems (Conger et al., 1994).

In sum, individuals who have experienced poverty may also have been affected by job-related stressors of parents. Counselors may wish to consider the career perceptions and aspirations of these individuals and the occupational socialization they received from parents. They might also consider that living in poverty can increase family conflict and hostility and be careful about attributing negative intent to parents without considering the possibility of sociostructural and work-related stressors.

Mesosystems

The mesosystem connects the individual to his or her community. In a discussion of poverty and inequality, the environmental and material conditions related to poverty must be understood. The material conditions of impoverished communities may be easily identified as poor and dilapidated neighborhoods (Inagami, Cohen, Finch, & Asch, 2006) and lack of consumer, municipal, and health resources.

Poverty represents the convergence of multiple forms of inequality and classism. It is not a single event or condition, and its effects are not limited to the time in poverty. For many individuals who have experienced poverty, its consequences may last throughout their lives (D. Wood, 2003). Sapolsky (2005) reported a study of American nuns who, in their adult lives, had similar health and dietary habits. Yet their rates of disease and dementia were correlated with their social class status 50 years before they became nuns. Some reasons for why these effects may last a lifetime may be related to the aggregate affects of impoverished environments. The impact of poverty does not start when the child is born. Even in prenatal stages, the poor health care a mother receives begins the consequences of poverty. Before birth, mothers living in poverty are less likely to have prenatal care, and are likely to have premature or low birth weight infants (Case, Fertig, & Paxson, 2005). Problem births are also related to high infant mortality, cognitive impairment, psychosocial retardation, and other health problems, such as respiratory and cardiac difficulties, and obesity (Case et al., 2005; Chen, Matthews, & Boyce, 2002; Farah et al., 2006).

Additionally, people living in poor neighborhoods often experience increased incidences of violence (Rasmussen, Aber, & Bhana, 2004), lack of supermarkets, and poor school environments (Liu, Fridman, & Hall, in press; Liu & Hernandez, in press). Unsafe neighborhoods, inability to play outside, and lack of healthy food alternatives contribute to unhealthy lifestyles (e.g., tobacco use), obesity, and depression (Abernathy, Webster, & Vermeulen, 2002; Burdette & Whitaker, 2005; Finkelstein, Kubzansky, & Goodman, 2006).

Finally, in communities with low social capital or mutual trust, people are more likely to have poorer health (Kawachi, Kennedy, & Glass, 1999). When individuals are not likely to help each other, people are more likely to have poorer health. The additive affect of all these conditions (i.e., early prenatal influences, exposure to violence, lack of neighborhood resources, interpersonal mistrust) is an increasingly steep grade of poverty such that it becomes even more impossible to overcome for many.

Microsystems

The setting in which individuals live, the microsystem, has the most direct impact on them. The microsystem is also the environment in which people are socialized about social class and construct their social class worldview. Research suggests that people in lower social class groups tend to describe their world as more hostile, dominating, and unfriendly in comparison to their higher social class counterparts

(Gallo, Smith, & Cox, 2006). Additionally, those in lower social class groups tend to perceive themselves as the recipient of dominating and controlling behaviors from others and are likely to anticipate less than friendly interactions (Gallo et al., 2006). Gallo et al. (2006) posited that people in lower social class occupations tend to be repeatedly reminded of their subordinate status, which reinforces their perception of a hostile world.

Children in these environments may mirror their parents' perceptions of the world. Chen and Matthews (2001) found that children who are poor tend to interpret ambiguous situations as potentially threatening and to become angrier in those situations when compared to higher social class children. It may be that, in contexts of poverty, children learn to become hyper-vigilant to possible threats in their environments, and over time, these coping styles become dispositional worldviews wherein people are not to be trusted and ambiguous situations are likely to be viewed negatively (Chen & Matthews, 2001). Furthermore, Bosma et al. (1999) showed that fathers who did unskilled manual work tended to have poor coping skills or an absence of active problem-focused coping, an external locus of control, and a negative personality pattern, and their children had poor subjective health and tended to reflect negative aspects of the father's personality.

Interactions with parents and peers are also important in socializing materialistic attitudes. Parents who value materialistism tend to have children who are materialistic (Goldberg et al., 2003). Moreover, adolescents who associate happiness with material possessions are likely to report high levels of family stress and disruption (especially due to divorce) in comparison to those not linking happiness with materialism (Roberts, Tanner, & Manolis, 2005). Family disruptions often increase the level of materialism, perhaps as compensation for distress and family upheaval (Roberts et al., 2005). In one study of 2,218 secondary school children, Flouri (2004) found that parental conflict was positively associated with increased materialistic attitudes in the child, and mother's negative relationship with the child was also positively associated with materialistic attitudes. Unfortunately, high materialistic values also are slightly negatively related to school satisfaction and performance (Goldberg et al., 2003).

Clients may reflect their parents' worldviews and experiences growing up (or living in) impoverished neighborhoods. Materialistic values, negative perceptions about others, and hyper-vigilance toward threats are potential results of living in poverty (Gallo et al., 2006). Moreover, clients from such backgrounds may prefer direct guidance, advice, and less-ambiguous psychotherapy formats that come closer to the interpersonal interactions in their families of origin. But this is speculation based on other research about communication styles and interpersonal beliefs (e.g., Gallo et al., 2006). Currently, no research has examined the process and outcomes of counseling and psychotherapy with individuals living in poverty.

In sum, the ecological model suggests that social class, especially poverty and inequality, has an impact across the different levels in an individual's life. Starting from before birth and continuing into adulthood, the development of certain perceptions about the world, about the self, and about others may be affected by poverty and inequality. Even when an individual is able to move out of poverty its ill affects can leave an imprint. Ecological theory can provide a framework for understanding the connections between societal values, beliefs, and the micro-affects of poverty and inequality. It can also be used to inform research and practice.

PRACTICING THE SOCIAL CLASS WORLDVIEW MODEL

The SCWM (Liu, 2001, 2002) was developed as a subjective approach to understanding the individual's social class worldview and experiences with classism that does not equate a person's objective life circumstances (i.e., income level) with a particular social class. Rather, Liu assumes that people form self-perceptions that may be congruent or incongruent with their life situation, and that these self-perceptions do more to define their social class than the objective conditions in which they live. Some research supports this hypothesis by suggesting that a subjective assessment of a person's social class is a better predictor, for instance, of subjective well-being and health than the person's actual social class. Individuals from lower SES backgrounds who rate themselves as living in a higher social class position, often also report better health than do those who more accurately judge their positions in society (Ostrove et al., 2000). Additionally, Liu suggested that a theory of social class should incorporate an understanding of classism because both are interdependent constructs. In clinical practice, the SCWM may be used to explicate the various levels of social class perceptions in a person's life and connect cognitions and affect related to social class experiences (Liu & Arguello, in press).

Defining Social Class Worldview Model

The SCWM assumes that individuals live in economic cultures (ECs) that exert demands and expectations on them. Similar to Bronfenbrenner's (1986) theory, ECs are represented by the exosystems in which individuals live. The EC of any single individual represents any group, neighborhood, or community the individual values and in which he or she seeks a social class position or status (e.g., a work environment). The demands and expectations the individual experiences in his or her EC may come in the form of cultural capital (aesthetics important in the EC), social capital (important relationships), and human capital (important physical or intellectual skills). Not all capitals are equally valued in an EC, and the capitals are types of resources to be used by the individual to maintain his or her social class. Counseling psychology graduate students exist in academic EC's that value the development of human capital (e.g., intellectual and counseling skills) but also social capital (social networks) and graduate students must develop both types of capital to prosper in a graduate school environment.

The worldview is a type of lens through which the individual conceptualizes the EC demands. The worldview is developed in meso- and microsystem interactions with individuals, peers, and family members. An individual's SCWM contains aspects of social class that comprise the whole worldview. Aspects contributing to the whole worldview are socialization messages the individual receives from friends and peers, family, and other groups to which the individual aspires. Additional aspects are the individual's materialistic attitudes, social class congruent behaviors (e.g., etiquette, accent), and lifestyle considerations, such as the way a person spends time (e.g., leisure, work, vacations).

Finally, the individual perceives (and uses strategically) different types of classism in his or her life. These forms of classism were elaborated earlier as upward, downward, lateral, and internalized. In using these forms of classism, the individual is able to maintain his or her social class and thus maintain homeostasis. Classism is, however, viewed as a negative coping response and often focuses on negative attributions about people in other social class groups. Thus, individuals may constantly shift through all forms of classism in an effort to maintain their social class homeostasis. Some individuals may be constantly vigilant to threats, demands, and expectations that may weaken their social class position. Threats or the inability to maintain homeostasis is related to feelings of internalized classism or anxiety, depression, and frustration. Internalized classism motivates the individual to increase efforts to reach homeostasis, shift social class EC, or do nothing and experience increasing levels of noxious affect.

Using the Social Class Worldview

The SCWM is a theoretical framework that may guide clinicians when addressing issues of social class. At this time of writing, no empirical research has tested this model or the various clinical implications that can be drawn from it. However, we think that clinicians may use the SCWM as a framework that can assist them to help clients to (a) understand their social class and classism experiences, (b) connect affect and cognitions, and (c) develop potentially effective ways to change their situations. Although it is unlikely that clients come to psychotherapy with a presenting issue of social class or classism, the SCWM suggests that clinicians need to be sensitive to social class and classism concerns. In counseling a first-generation college student who is seeking help for severe feelings of psychological distress, a clinician working from an SCWM perspective, might consider newly experienced materialistic expectations engendered via interactions with wealthier peers as a potential source of distress. These considerations may not be as evident to a counselor unfamiliar with the SCWM. We, therefore, suggest that clinicians might find the SCWM a helpful heuristic tool that will allow them to (a) gain a fuller understanding of potential sources for clients' presenting concerns, (b) develop questions to direct counseling sessions, and (c) help clients frame and reframe their experiences.

Table 10.1 illustrates a sample set of queries and possible social class and classism factors that can guide SCWM-based counseling efforts.

Table 10.1   Social Class Interventions

The social class interventions are targeted toward the client's experiences of classism. Upward, downward, lateral, and internalized classisms are the focus of the therapist. Through collaboration, the client is helped to gain:

Insight about their experiences of classism, their worldview, and the pressures they experience as a part of an economic culture.

Empathy by the therapist toward the client's classism experiences is important.

The therapist challenges the client's irrational cognitions about their social status and what they need to do to maintain or achieve a social status.

The therapist helps the client integrate their history with their current situation.

The client is encouraged to develop self-efficacy in coping and managing their situation.

The client is helped to identify situations in which certain feelings are tied to classism experiences.

Step 1— Help the client identify and understand his or her economic culture.

Sample query: Tell me what kind of pressure you feel/experience as you try to keep up with your friends.

Identify answers that touch on cultural, social, and human capital pressures/expectations.

Step 2—Help the client identify the social class messages he or she receive(d).

Sample query: What would your parent(s)/peers say about your current situation?

How would your parent(s)/peers help you resolve your current situation?

List the ways you are acting to live out messages given to you by your parent(s)/peers.

Tell me about your peer group. Your support network.

Identify answers that focus on strong/salient cultural socialization messages still running in the client's mind, which drive the client's behavior and attitudes.

Step 2a—Help the client identify social class behaviors, lifestyles, and material possessions that are salient to the client in his or her current situation.

Sample query: Tell me how you imagine your life.

How would you ideally be spending your time?

What do others have that you want?

What do you notice about how other people act/behave that you like?

Identify answers that pinpoint the client's materialism values; how he has changed his lifestyle to fit into a new group, and how he has changed his behavior to belong in a new group.

Step 3—Identify the client's experiences with classism and move toward developing an adaptive, realistic, and healthy expectation about him- or herself.

Sample query: Do people look down on you?

Do you look down on others who are not like you?

What do your peers expect from you to maintain your status with them?

What does it feel like for you when you can't keep up with your peers? What do you do?

Identify answers that express high social class expectations and the negative consequences related to not meeting specific demands. Additionally, in what ways is the client participating in classism to maintain her social class standing?

(Continued)

Table 10.1 (Continued)

Step 4—Help the client integrate his or her experiences of classism.

Sample query: Now that we've started talking about all these aspects of your social class experience, tell me what it means to you?

What are you aware of about yourself that you didn't know before we started?

Identify an ability to understand and integrate the social class discussions into other aspects of the client's life.

Step 4a—Help the client take action and make changes in his or her life.

Sample query: What is the one thing you could do to change your awareness, situation, or perception?

Identify an ability to make personal changes in the client's life.

As shown in Table 10.1, at the first step, clinicians work with clients to understand the broader community in which they live and how this EC communicates social class expectations. In the second step, the clinician tries to better understand the ways in which the individual acts to meet these expectations, either successfully or unsuccessfully. In the third step, the clinician and client explore experiences with classism. In this step, the clinician might be sensitive to the possibility that the client is not only the recipient but might also be a perpetrator of classism. Thus, someone in a low social class position may experience downward classism, but could act in upwardly or laterally classist ways.

Using this SCWM framework, clients who live in poverty may be helped to explore their perceptions of their economic culture. In this case, being in poverty may bring with it certain EC demands and expectations. Even though the client may not be aware of these expectations, there may be material, cultural, and social types of capital that the individual may be expected to develop. Additionally, it may be useful for the clients to articulate their perception of power relationships and any feelings of marginalization or disempowerment. Clients might also explore how they negotiate privilege and power in their own EC.

In the final step, the client is encouraged to summarize and integrate his or her understanding of the social class discussions. The intent of this discussion is to (a) help the client integrate and synthesize the new awareness of him- or herself regarding social class, and (b) move toward possible action. The move toward action may be personal in terms of changing a person's own perception, awareness, and behaviors, such as decreasing a type of classism. Another type of action may be motivating the client toward larger social action and social justice. In discussing social class expectations, power, and inequality, clients may be sufficiently motivated not only to make personal changes but also to become social change agents. Again, using Bronfenbrenner's model, clients may be made aware that social justice and change may take place across different levels, from the personal to the institutional and the societal level (Sue & Sue, 2003).

CONCLUSION

This chapter provided a perspective on social class and classism by considering the effects of poverty and economic inequality in the context of Bronfenbrenner's (1986) ecological model. The intent was to show how poverty and inequality are contexts that set in motion a number of psychological consequences. The intent was also to enable counselors interested in working with people from impoverished settings to understand how poverty and inequality manifest in clinical practice and research. The mental health gradient is not a gentle slope where upward mobility is easy and without barriers. The gradient is steep, especially for those in poverty, and the inequality they experience can be quite deleterious.

In practice and research, people living in poverty may sometimes be perceived as resistant to change. But psychological interventions developed on middle-class participants in research may not address the wide range of barriers and lack of material and personal resources weighing down those in poverty.

Research has not fully explored the contextual issues needing to be addressed in therapy for those living in poverty. However, some research suggests that treating low-income individuals for psychological distress necessitates a context-driven approach to meeting multiple levels of physical (e.g., daycare, transportation, education) as well as psychological needs (i.e., depression; Miranda et al., 2003). Thus, in counseling-related research and applications, it seems important to develop theories to understand the lives of those in poverty and experiencing inequality. It is also important that social class-related research focus on the worldview, experiences, and identity of those individuals not in poverty. Much of the current social class research explores the deleterious effects of poverty. Yet, living in the middle-class may also bring psychological problems such as duress related to debt (Brooks, 2000), substance use (Schwartz & Hayden, 1986), and suicide (Rotheram-Borus, Walker, & Ferns, 1996). By adding the dimension of social class, it may be possible to tease apart the sources of problems and provide effective psychotherapy. Additionally, as the counseling psychology profession continues to expand into new spheres and populations, it is well to consider that current theories may be insufficient as a framework for working with clients who are not middle-class or upwardly mobile.

REFERENCES

Abernathy, T. J., Webster, G, & Vermeulen, M. (2002). Relationship between poverty and health among adolescents. *Adolescence, 37*, 55–67.

Achenreiner, GB., & John, D. R. (2003). The meaning of brand names to children: A developmental investigation. *Journal of Consumer Psychology, 13*, 205–219.

Adler, N. E., Boyce, W. T., Chesney, M., Folkman, S., & Syme, L. (1993). Socioeconomic inequalities in health: No easy solution. *Journal of the American Medical Association, 269*, 3140–3145.

Ali, S. R., & McWhirter, E. H. (2006). Rural Appalachian youth's vocational/educational post-secondary aspirations: Applying social cognitive career theory. *Journal of Career Development, 33*, 87–111.

American Psychological Association. (2007). *Taskforce report on socioeconomic status*. Retrieved January 31, 2007, from ww2.apa.org/pi/SES_task_force_report.pdf.

Beiser, M., Johnson, P. J., & Turner, R. J. (1993). Unemployment, underemployment, and depressive effect among Southeast Asian refugees. *Psychological Medicine, 23*, 731–743.

Blustein, D. L., Chaves, A. P., Diemer, M. A., Gallagher, L. A., Marshall, K. G, Sirin, S., et al. (2002). Voices of the forgotten half: The role of social class in the school-to-work transition. *Journal of Counseling Psychology, 49*, 311–323.

Boma, H., Marmot, M. G, Hemingway, H., Nicholson, A. C., Brunner, E., & Stansfeld, S. A. (1997). Low job control and risk of coronary heart disease in Whitehall II (prospective cohort) study. *British Medical Journal, 314*, 558–565.

Bosma, H., van de Mheen, H. D., & Mackenbach, J. P. (1999). Social class in childhood and general health in adulthood: Questionnaire study of contribution of psychological attributes. *British Medical Journal, 318*, 18–22.

Boven, L. V. (2005). Experientialism, materialism, and the pursuit of happiness. *Review of General Psychology, 9*, 132–142.

Bronfenbrenner, U. (1986). Ecology of the family as a context for human development: Research perspectives. *Developmental Psychology, 22*, 723–742.

Bronfenbrenner, U. (1989). Ecological systems theory. In R. Vasta (Ed.), *Annals of child development* (Vol. 6, pp. 185–246). Greenwich, CT: JAI Press.

Brooks, D. (2000). *Bobos in paradise: The new upper-class and how they got there*. New York: Simon & Schuster.

Brown, M. T., Fukunaga, C., Umemoto, D., & Wicker, L. (1996). Annual review, 1990–1996: Social class, work, and retirement behavior. *Journal of Vocational Behavior, 49*, 159–189.

Brown, S., Taylor, K., & Price, S. W. (2005). Debt and distress: Evaluating the psychological cost of credit. *Journal of Economic Psychology, 26*, 642–663.

Burdette, H. L., & Whitaker, R. C. (2005). A national study of neighborhood safety, outdoor play, television viewing, and obesity in preschool children. *Pediatrics, 116*, 657–662.

Burroughs, J. E., & Rindfleisch, A. (2002). Materialism and well-being: A conflicting values perspective. *Journal of Consumer Research, 29,* 348–370.

Case, A., Fertig, A., & Paxson, C. (2005). The lasting impact of childhood health and circumstance. *Journal of Health Economics, 24,* 365–389.

Census Bureau. (2003). Poverty in the United States: 2002. *Current Population Reports, P60–222.* Washington, DC: U.S. Department of Commerce.

Census Bureau. (2005). Alternative poverty estimates in the United States: 2003. *Current Population Reports, P60–227.* Washington, DC: U.S. Department of Commerce.

Chang, L., & Arkin, R. M. (2002). Materialism as an attempt to cope with uncertainty. *Psychology and Marketing, 19,* 389–406.

Chaves, A. P., Diemer, M. A., Blustein, D. L., Gallagher, L. A., DeVoy, J. E., Casares, M. T., et al. (2004). Conceptions of work: The view from urban youth. *Journal of Counseling Psychology, 51,* 275–286.

Chen, E., & Matthews, K. A. (2001). Cognitive appraisal biases: An approach to understanding the relationship between socioeconomic status and cardiovascular reactivity in children. *Annals of Behavioral Medicine, 23,* 101–111.

Chen, E., Matthews, K. A., & Boyce, T. (2002). Socioeconomic differences in children's health: How and why do these relationships change with age? *Psychological Bulletin, 128,* 295–329.

Christopher, A. N., Morgan, R. D., Marek, P., Keller, M., & Drummond, K. (2005). Materialism and self-presentation styles. *Personality and Individual Differences, 38,* 137–149.

Cohen, P., & Cohen, J. (1996). *Life values and adolescent mental health.* Mahwah, NJ: Erlbaum.

Conger, R. D., Ge, X., Elder, GH., Jr., Lorenz, F. O., & Simons, R. L. (1994). Economic stress, coercive family process, and developmental problems of adolescents. *Child Development, 65,* 541–561.

Costello, E. J., Compton, S. N., Keeler, G, & Angold, A. (2003). Relationships between poverty and psychopathology: A natural experiment. *Journal of the American Medical Association, 290,* 2023–2029.

Cotte, J., & Ritchie, R. (2005). Advertisers' theories of consumers: Why use negative emotions to sell? *Advances in Consumer Research, 32,* 24–31.

Croizet, J. C., & Claire, T. (1998). Extending the concept of stereotype threat to social class: The intellectual underperformance of students from low socioeconomic backgrounds. *Personality and Social Psychology Bulletin, 24,* 588–594.

Diemer, M. A., & Blustein, D. L. (2006). Critical consciousness and career development among urban youth. *Journal of Vocational Behavior, 68*(2), 220–232.

Diemer, M. A., & Hsieh, C. (in press). Sociopolitical development and vocational expectations among lower-SES adolescents of color. *Career Development Quarterly.*

Duncan, GJ. (1988). The volatility of family income over the life course. In P. Baltes & R. M. Lerner (Eds.), *Life span development and behavior* (Vol. 9, pp. 317–358). Hillsdale, NJ: Erlbaum.

Edelman, M. W., & Jones, J. M. (2004). Separate and unequal: America's children, race, and poverty. *Future of Children, 14*(2), 134–137.

Farah, M. J., Shera, D. M., Savage, J. H., Betancourt, L., Giannetta, J. M., Brodsky, N. L., et al. (2006). Childhood poverty: Specific associations with neurocognitive development. *Brain Research, 1110,* 166–174.

Finkelstein, D. M., Kubzansky, L. D., & Goodman, E. (2006). Social status, stress, and adolescent smoking. *Journal of Adolescent Health, 39,* 678–685.

Fisher, GM. (1992). The development and history of the poverty thresholds. *Social Security Bulletin, 55*(4), 3–14.

Flouri, E. (2004). Exploring the relationship between mothers' and fathers' parenting practices and children's materialist values. *Journal of Economic Psychology, 25,* 743–752.

Fouad, N. A., & Brown, M. T. (2001). Role of race and social class in development: Implications for counseling psychology. In S. D. Brown & R. W. Lent (Eds.), *Handbook of counseling psychology* (pp. 379–408). New York: Wiley.

Frable, D. E. S. (1997). Gender, racial, ethnic, sexual, and class identities. *Annual Review Psychology, 48,* 139–162.

Gallo, L. C., Bogart, L. M., Vranceanu, A. M., & Matthews, K. A. (2005). Socioeconomic status, resources, psychological experiences, and emotional responses: A test of the reserve capacity model. *Journal of Personality and Social Psychology, 88,* 386–399.

Gallo, L. C., & Matthews, K. A. (1999). Do negative emotions mediate the association between socioeconomic status and health? *Annals of the New York Academy of Sciences, 896,* 226–245.

Gallo, L. C., & Matthews, K. A. (2003). Understanding the association between socioeconomic status and physical health: Do negative emotions play a role? *Psychological Bulletin, 129*, 10–51.

Gallo, L. C., Smith, T. W., & Cox, C. M. (2006). Socioeconomic status, psychosocial processes, and perceived health: An interpersonal perspective. *Annals of Behavioral Medicine, 31*, 109–119.

Geronimus, A. T., Bound, J., Waidmann, T. A., Hillemeier, M. M., & Burns, P. B. (1996). Excess mortality among blacks and whites in the United States. *New England Journal of Medicine, 355*, 1552–1558.

Goldberg, M. E., Gorn, GJ., Peracchio, L. A., & Bamossy, G(2003). Understanding materialism among youth. *Journal of Consumer Psychology, 13*, 278–288.

Gottfried, A. W. (1985). Measures of socioeconomic status in child development research: Data and recommendations. *Merrill-Palmer Quarterly, 31*, 85–92.

Griffin, J. M., Fuhrer, R., Stansfeld, S. A., & Marmot, M. (2002). The importance of low control at work and home on depression and anxiety: Do these effects vary by gender and social class? *Social Science and Medicine, 54*, 783–798.

Gurin, P., & Brim, O. G, Jr. (1984). Change in self in adulthood: The example of sense of control. In P. B. Baltes & O. G. Brim Jr. (Eds.), *Life-span development and behavior* (Vol. 6, pp. 218–334). New York: Academic Press.

Heflin, C. M., & Pattillo, M. (2006). Poverty in the family: Race, siblings, and socioeconomic heterogeneity. *Social Science Research, 35*, 804–822.

Hoffman, L. W. (2003). Methodological issues in studies of SES, parenting, and child development. In M. H. Bornstein & R. H. Bradley (Eds.), *Socioeconomic status, parenting, and child development* (pp. 125–143). Hillsdale, NJ: Erlbaum.

Hopps, J., & Liu, W. M. (2006). Working for social justice from within the health care system: The role of social class in psychology. In R. L. Toporek, L. H. Gerstein, N. A. Fouad, GRoysircar, & T. Israel (Eds.), *Handbook for social justice in counseling psychology: Leadership, vision, and action* (pp. 318–337). Thousand Oaks, CA: Sage.

Inagami, S., Cohen, D. A., Finch, B. K., & Asch, S. M. (2006). You are where you shop: Grocery store locations, weight, and neighborhoods. *American Journal of Preventive Medicine, 31*, 10–17.

Karasek, R., & Theorell, T. (1990). *Healthy work: Stress productivity and the reconstruction of working life.* New York: Basic Books.

Kasser, T., Ryan, R. M., Couchman, C. E., & Sheldon, K. M. (2004). Materialistic values: Their causes and consequences. In T. Kasser & A. D. Kanner (Eds.), *Psychology and consumer culture: The struggle for a good life in a materialistic world* (pp. 11–28). Washington, DC: American Psychological Association.

Kasser, T., Ryan, R. M., Zax, M., & Sameroff, A. J. (1995). The relations of maternal and social environments to late adolescents' materialist and prosocial values. *Developmental Psychology, 31*, 907–914.

Kawachi, I., Kennedy, B. P., & Glass, R. (1999). Social capital and self-rated health: A contextual analysis. *American Journal of Public Health, 89*, 1187–1193.

Lachman, M. E., & Weaver, S. L. (1998). The sense of control as a moderator of social class differences in health and well-being. *Journal of Personality and Social Psychology, 74*, 763–773.

Liberatos, P., Link, B. G, & Kelsey, J. L. (1988). The measurement of social class in epidemiology. *Epidemiologic Reviews, 10*, 87–121.

Liu, W. M. (2001). Expanding our understanding of multiculturalism: Developing a social class worldview model. In D. B. Pope-Davis & H. L. K. Coleman (Eds.), *The intersection of race, class, and gender in counseling psychology* (pp. 127–170). Thousand Oaks, CA: Sage.

Liu, W. M. (2002). The social class-related experiences of men: Integrating theory and practice. *Professional Psychology: Research and Practice, 33*, 355–360.

Liu, W. M. (2006). Classism is much more complex. *American Psychologist, 61*, 337–338.

Liu, W. M. (in press). Poverty. In F. T. L. Leong (Ed.), *Encyclopedia of counseling.* Thousand Oaks, CA: Sage.

Liu, W. M., Ali, S. R., Soleck, G, Hopps, J., Dunston, K., & Pickett, T., Jr. (2004). Using social class in counseling psychology research. *Journal of Counseling Psychology, 51*, 3–18.

Liu, W. M., & Arguello, J. (in press). Social class and classism in counseling. *Counseling and Human Development.*

Liu, W. M., Fridman, A., & Hall, T. (in press). Social class and school counseling. In H. L. K. Coleman & C. Yeh (Eds.), *Handbook of school counseling.* New York: Earlbaum.

Liu, W. M., & Hernandez, J. (in press). Social class and educational psychology. In N. J. Salkind (Ed.), *Encyclopedia of educational psychology.* Thousand Oaks, CA: Sage.

Liu, W. M., Hernandez, J., Mahmood, A., & Stinson, R. (2006). The link between poverty, classism, and racism in mental health. In D. W. Sue & M. GConstantine (Eds.), *Racism as a barrier to cultural competence in mental health and educational settings* (pp. 65–86). Hoboken, NJ: Wiley.

Liu, W. M., & Pope-Davis, D. B. (2003a). Moving from diversity to multiculturalism: Exploring power and the implications for psychology. In D. B. Pope-Davis, H. L. K. Coleman, W. M. Liu, & R. L. Toporek (Eds.), *Handbook of multicultural competencies in counseling and psychology* (pp. 90–102). Thousand Oaks, CA: Sage.

Liu, W. M., & Pope-Davis, D. B. (2003b). Understanding classism to effect personal change. In T. B. Smith (Ed.), *Practicing multiculturalism: Internalizing and affirming diversity in counseling and psychology* (pp. 294–310). New York: Allyn & Bacon.

Liu, W. M., Soleck, G, Hopps, J., Dunston, K., & Pickett, T. (2004). A new framework to understand social class in counseling: The social class worldview and modern classism theory. *Journal of Multicultural Counseling and Development, 32*, 95–122.

Lott, B. (2002). Cognitive and behavioral distancing from the poor. *American Psychologist, 57*, 100–110.

McLoyd, V. C. (1998). Socioeconomic disadvantage and child development. *American Psychologist, 53*, 185–204.

McLoyd, V. C., Jayaratne, T. E., Ceballo, R., & Borquez, J. (1994). Unemployment and work interruption among African American single mothers: Effects on parenting and adolescent socioemotional functioning. *Child Development, 65*, 562–589.

Miranda, J., Chung, J. Y., Green, B. L., Krupnick, J., Siddique, J., Revicki, D. A., et al. (2003). Treating depression in predominantly low-income young minority women: A randomized controlled trial. *Journal of the American Medical Association, 290*, 57–65.

Mudrack, P. E. (1997). Protestant work-ethic dimensions and work orientations. *Personality and Individual Differences, 23*, 217–225.

Oakes, J. M., & Rossi, P. H. (2003). The measurement of SES in health research: Current practice and steps toward a new approach. *Social Science and Medicine, 56*, 769–784.

Ostrove, J. M., Adler, N. E., Kuppermann, M., & Washington, A. E. (2000). Objective and subjective assessments of socioeconomic status and their relationship to self-rated health in an ethnically diverse sample of pregnant women. *Health Psychology, 19*, 613–618.

Rasmussen, A., Aber, M. S., & Bhana, A. (2004). Adolescent coping and neighborhood violence: Perceptions, exposure, and urban youths' efforts to deal with danger. *American Journal of Community Psychology, 33*, 61–75.

Roberts, J. A., Tanner, J. F., Jr., & Manolis, C. (2005). Materialism and the family structure-stress relation. *Journal of Consumer Psychology, 15*, 183–190.

Rotheram-Borus, M. J., Walker, J. U., & Ferns, W. (1996). Suicidal behavior among middle-class adolescents who seek crisis services. *Journal of Clinical Psychology, 52*, 143–197.

Sapolsky, R. (2005, December). Sick of poverty. *Scientific American, 293*(6), 92–99.

Schwartz, R. H., & Hayden, GF. (1986). Marijuana use among middle-class adolescents. *Southern Medical Journal, 79*, 927–930.

Short, K. S., & Garner, T. I. (2002, July). *A decade of experimental poverty thresholds: 1990–2000.* Paper presented at the annual meeting of the Western Economic Association, Seattle, WA.

Smith, L. (2005). Psychotherapy, classism, and the poor: Conspicuous by their absence. *American Psychologist, 60*, 687–696.

Smith, L. (2006). Addressing classism, extending multicultural competence, and serving the poor. *American Psychologist, 61*, 338–339.

Solberg, E. G, Diener, E., & Robinson, M. D. (2004). Why are materialists less satisfied? In T. Kasser & A. D. Kanner (Eds.), *Psychology and consumer culture: The struggle for a good life in a materialistic world* (pp. 29–48). Washington, DC: American Psychological Association.

Sue, D. W. (2003). *Overcoming our racism: The journey to liberation.* San Francisco: Jossey-Bass.

Sue, D. W., & Sue, D. (2003). *Counseling the culturally diverse: Theory and practice* (4th ed.) Hoboken, NJ: Wiley.

Thompson, M. N., & Subich, L. M. (2006). The relation of social status to the career decision process. *Journal of Vocational Behavior, 69*, 289–301.

Tiffin, P. A., Pearce, M. S., & Parker, L. (2005). Social mobility over the lifecourse and self-reported mental health at age 50: Prospective cohort study. *Journal of Epidemiology and Community Health, 59*, 870–872.

Tulkin, S. R., & Kagan, J. (1972). Mother-child interaction in the first year of life. *Child Development, 43*, 31–41.

Twenge, J. M., & Campbell, W. K. (2002). Self-esteem and socioeconomic status: A meta-analytic review. *Personality and Social Psychology Review, 6*, 59–71.

Vera, E. M., & Speight, S. L. (2003). Multicultural competence, social justice, and counseling psychology: Expanding our roles. *Counseling Psychologist, 31*, 253–272.

Vohs, K. D., Mead, N. L., & Goode, M. R. (2006). The psychological consequences of money. *Science, 314*, 1154–1156.

Watson, J. J. (2003). The relationship of materialism to spending tendencies, saving, and debt. *Journal of Economic Psychology, 24*, 723–739.

Wilkinson, R. G, & Pickett, K. E. (2006). Income inequality and population health: A review and explanation of the evidence. *Social Science and Medicine, 62*, 1768–1784.

Wood, D. (2003). Effect of child and family poverty on child health in the United States. *Pediatrics, 112*, 707–711.

Wood, M. (1998). Socio-economic status, delay of gratification, and impulse buying. *Journal of Economic Psychology, 19*, 295–320.

CHAPTER 11

Psychology of Gender

ROBERTA L. NUTT
GARY R. BROOKS

Although it may once have seemed acceptable to assume that the theories and practice of psychotherapy could remain isolated from their social and cultural contexts, it has more recently become clear that competent practitioners must attend to the rich diversity of their clients' lives. Gender is a significant variable that shapes how clients identify, experience, and attribute responsibility for their problems, choose to address them, and behave in the psychotherapy office. In addition, gender affects the behavior of practitioners themselves. Thus, competent and ethical therapeutic practice requires that practitioners become as knowledgeable as they can be about the emerging literature on gender and its implications for practice.

Girls and boys, and women and men, are socialized into different gender-defined cultures in the United States and most other countries (Philpot, Brooks, Lusterman, & Nutt, 1997). Socialized expectations are continually replicated throughout the life span, an active process that has been described as "doing gender" (Deaux & Major, 1987). Although some may assume that men and women are therefore too different to understand one another (Gray, 1992), the reality is that women and men are more similar than different (Hyde, 2005). Exaggerating gender differences may actually cause harm to individuals, families, relationships, education, the workplace, and society (Barnett & Rivers, 2004). However, ignoring differences may diminish important elements of a person's identity. Just as ethnic background may be a source of pride and crucial to understanding an individual's development and personality, understanding a person's sense of gender role may also be critical. Theories of therapy and research on evidence-based practices often do not adequately address gender as an aspect of diversity (Levant & Silverstein, 2005). Hence, this chapter examines gender role socialization issues that are important for effective counseling practice with individuals, couples, and families.

GENDER SOCIALIZATION ACROSS THE LIFE SPAN

The socialization of boys and girls is a ubiquitous process that is carried out by a variety of cultural agents. Of these, parents, schools, and the media are especially important.

Agents of Gender Socialization for Infants, Children, and Adolescents

Parents

The differential treatment of girls and boys may begin in utero when parents choose to employ amniocentesis to learn the sex of their child. Although few gender differences are apparent in newborns (Maccoby, 1998), most adults treat girl and boy babies differently. Adults tend to handle girls more gently and play with boys more roughly, give children sex-typed toys and books, and reinforce gender-appropriate behaviors and appearance (Evans & Davies, 2000; Lindsey & Mize, 2001). Boys and girls are dressed differently, with girls' clothing more likely being pastel and frilly representing delicacy

176

and boys' clothing being sturdier for rougher play. Similarly, boys' rooms are more often decorated in primary colors and girls' rooms in pastels and lace (Pomerleau, Bolduc, Malcuit, & Cossette, 1990). These experiences begin the process of telling girls to be ladylike, pretty (i.e., they are valued most for their appearance), and cautious, and boys to be strong and take risks.

Parents tend to talk differently to girls and boys. Mothers talk more to their daughters and use more supportive speech, which may encourage girls to develop better empathic and relational skills (Bosacki & Moore, 2004). Boys are more likely to be encouraged to be independent, which Pollack (1998) has suggested happens so early that it negatively affects the ability of boys and men to perceive others with empathy and form relationships (cf. Jordan, Kaplan, Miller, Stiver, & Surrey, 1991). Early on, girls are typically taught better relationship skills, whereas boys gain better skills at navigating the world alone, with both genders losing balance between the two needed life skills.

Gender role socialization research in the United States has been done mostly with White, middle-class families, so it is likely that these messages and behaviors vary across ethnic groups in the United States and abroad. Gender roles are less differentiated among African American children who see many assertive and independent Black women (Reid, Haritos, Kelly, & Holland, 1995). There is also evidence that the birth of boys is more welcome than that of girls, especially as a family's firstborn, in many cultures (Gonzalez & Koestner, 2005). In the extreme, there are cultures in which girl babies are killed or sold (Neft & Levine, 1997). Such examples reflect ways in which girls and women are taught to feel lesser and unimportant.

School Systems

A long history of research demonstrates that boys and girls are treated differently in schools. In general, teachers pay more attention to boys and give them clearer feedback (Jones & Dindia, 2004). Black girls are given even less attention than White girls (AAUW, 1996). Boys are called on more often, given more time to answer questions, and often asked to elaborate on their answers, which leads them to think more deeply. Girls are more often praised for their good behavior (Golombok & Fivush, 1994). Girls are taught to look good (Wolf, 1991) and depend on others, particularly men, to take care of and rescue them. This theme is further carried out in children's books in which girls are underrepresented and generally shown in caretaker roles (Doyle & Paludi, 1998). Boys and men tend to be shown in active or occupational roles and as aggressive and competitive (Evans & Davies, 2000) but seldom as fathers (D. A. Anderson & Hamilton, 2005). These messages may result in girls feeling that they should be passive or that they are not as important, bright, competent, or able to take care of themselves (Tepper & Cassidy, 1999)—feelings which may follow them into adulthood. These messages may also influence the broader culture to view girls and women as less competent or important, and more dependent, than boys and men (Vandell & Dempsey, 1991).

Media

Television, films, newspapers, magazines, video games, cartoons, advertising, and other media sources have been shown to have a strong impact on shaping gender roles at all ages, and particularly for adolescents. As in children's books, girls and women are underrepresented (Glascock & Preston-Schreck, 2004). Although some change has occurred in the past 30 years, boys and girls are still portrayed in primarily traditional roles (Furnham & Mak, 1999), which reinforces messages children receive about what is appropriate.

Television viewing has been shown to relate to increased aggressiveness in boys and overconcern with appearance in girls. Television often presents idealized images of women that stereotypically emphasize youth, extreme thinness, and sexuality (Fouts & Burggraf, 2000). Research suggests that media attention on female appearance has led to an increased preoccupation with weight, body image, and overall appearance, which has had a direct impact on eating disorders in Western societies (see

Mintz, Hamilton, Bledman, and Franko, Chapter 33, this volume). This impact is greater on White and Asian American girls and women and less on African Americans (Demarest & Allen, 2000). On the average, American children watch 8 to 14 hours of television each week (Wright, Huston, Vandewater, et al., 2001). Meta-analyses have established a positive correlation (rs ranging from .10 to .21) between the amount of television viewing and the acceptance of gender role stereotypes (Herrett-Skjellum & Allen, 1996), suggesting that television viewing has a small but consistent relationship to the acceptance of gender role stereotypes.

Impact of Gender Socialization on Girls and Women

All the influences described in the previous list and many more carry gender role messages relevant to self-esteem and mental health during the gender socialization of girls.

Biological Issues

From the beginning of menstruation, adolescent girls are faced with the complex issues of reproduction. The beginning of menarche may have profound effects on body image, self-esteem, peer relationships, and social power, with White girls more likely to suffer symptoms of depression than Hispanic or African American girls (Hayward, Hotlib, Schraedley, & Litt, 1999). In addition, as girls mature and menses begins, their bodies gain more body fat, which violates the cultural thin ideal and may lead to further body dissatisfaction, negative body image, and eating disorders. Girls growing up in cultures or subcultures that view menarche as either a natural event or a positive affirmation of womanhood report more positive experiences (Bishop, 1999). Some findings indicate that college-age women view menstruating women as stronger and more trustworthy (Forbes, Adams-Curtis, White, & Holmgren, 2003).

Appearance

The impact of gender role messages from childhood and adolescence generally continues into adulthood for women. The emphasis on valuing women for their appearance illustrates objectification theory, which postulates that women are viewed and treated as objects (Fredrickson & Roberts, 1997) both by themselves and others. Women's over-attention to body and appearance and resulting self-objectification may lead to shame, anxiety, and lessened productivity, self-esteem, and self-confidence (Quinn, Kallen, Twenge, & Fredrickson, 2006). Half or more of all women of all ages reportedly suffer from some form of body dissatisfaction (McLaren & Kuh, 2004). One way this objectification is reinforced is by the sexualized, thin images of women in the media (Bessenoff, 2006; Fouts & Burggraf, 2000).

Women and the Workplace

In the workplace, women in general continue to earn less than men; be disproportionately represented in jobs that underutilize their talents and capabilities; hold jobs that have little status or opportunity for advancement; confront a lack of external support structures such as child care, flexible work schedules, and paid maternity leave; face discrimination in hiring and promotion; suffer sexual harassment and other forms of devaluation; and carry the majority of home responsibilities (APA, 2007; Fassinger, 2002; Gilbert & Rader, Chapter 25, this volume). These problems may be exacerbated for women of color, women with disabilities, or women of lower socioeconomic status.

Early theories of career development were based on White, middle-class male models that ignored or minimized the career development of women and people of color (Fassinger, 2002). Very early researchers believed that women did not even have a need for achievement and therefore did not need to be included in theory and research (McClelland, 1961). Although psychology no longer believes that women lack aspirations or drive, there is still evidence that some women are brought up to under-aspire and may face discrimination and harassment in the workplace, particularly in male-dominated professions. Sexual harassment and the hostile work environment it creates can lead women to leave educational programs and other training, change jobs and careers, suffer decreased job satisfaction and lowered morale, and become less productive and more self-critical (Levy & Paludi, 1997). Figures for 2003 indicated that 47% of the workforce in the United States was comprised of women (Statistical Abstracts, 2004–2005) and in families with two wage earners, they contributed about 40% of the family's income (Gilbert & Rader, Chapter 25, this volume). Thus, their job stress and productivity impact not only the lives of women and their families but the entire economy.

In 2005, women earned 81% of the salary earned by men (Gilbert & Rader, Chapter 25, this volume). These ratios decrease for women of color, women with disabilities, and women heading single-parent households (Costello, Wight, & Stone, 2003). In addition to generalized discrimination, roadblocks that impede women's career advancement include the glass ceiling, or the concept that women are allowed to advance only so far (Federal Glass Ceiling Commission, 1995) and lack of effective mentoring and role models, effective leadership training, and experience (Lockwood, 2006). Work-family conflict is also expected to impact women's work and achievements, and there is ample evidence that working women still take responsibility for the major portion of household work, including child care (Gilbert & Rader, Chapter 25, this volume).

Violence and Abuse

Women and girls are at substantial risk for experiences of violence and trauma (Wolfe & Kimerling, 1997). Partner abuse occurs in all types of couples (married, unmarried, gay, lesbian; Renzetti, 1997), but most frequently the woman is likely to be injured in heterosexual couples of all SES levels, ethnic groups, and in most countries (Krahé, Bieneck, & Möller, 2005). Recent data estimate 47 assaults per 1,000 American women, although under-reporting of assaults is suspected (National Center for Injury Prevention and Control [NCIPC], 2005) and an actual prevalence rate of 29% has been estimated (Coker & Davies, 2002). Battering can result in a full range of injuries from bruises and cuts to concussions, broken bones, brain injury, and even death (Ackerman & Banks, 2003). A suggested contributor to women's remaining in battering situations is female gender role socialization that leads women to feel devalued, lacking in self-confidence, undeserving of respect, self-sacrificing, unassertive, helpless, and overvaluing of love relationships (Nutt, 1999). Hendy, Eggen, Gustitus, McLeod, and Ng (2003) also described such reasons as concern for children and their need for a father, hoping for husband's reform, financial concerns, fear of her attacker and potential reprisals, lack of support from others, and having no place to go or live.

Rape and sexual assault are additional sources of traumatic stress for girls and women, with recent estimates that 15% of women are raped or sexually assaulted at some time in their lives (Rozee & Koss, 2001). Rape survivors suffer acute distress for generally a month or two after the rape, but fear and anxiety plus problems with sexuality and trust may persist for much longer (McMullin & White, 2006). Many turn to prescription drugs and alcohol to cope (Sturza & Campbell, 2005). Some survivors endure additional stress if they blame themselves (Littleton & Breitkopf, 2006), which may be more marked for Black women (Neville, Heppner, Oh, Spanierman, & Clark, 2004).

Reproduction and Childbirth

Issues associated with reproduction and childbirth can evoke a wide range of emotions in women from joy to fear. Many women experience pregnancy and motherhood as very positive despite the accompanying physical and hormonal changes, but these feelings are neither consistent nor universal (Rice & Else-Quest, 2006). Some of the joyful feelings are associated with planning for the child's future and envisioning happy family scenes (Bondas & Eriksson, 2001), whereas stressors can include increased violence toward women during pregnancy (Leigh & Huff, 2006) and postpartum depression (Seguin, Potvin, St-Denis, & Loiselle, 1999), which may be exacerbated for women who lack social or financial support.

For some women, voluntary childlessness and abortion may be chosen options (Russo, 2000). Response to abortion has been related to personal control perceptions, high self-esteem, and preabortion levels of optimism (Major, Richards, Cooper, Cozzarelli, & Zubek, 1998). Those women who choose not to have children may feel criticized by those who consider them selfish or abnormal, particularly extended family members, which has led to the coining of a new term to reflect their status: *childfree* (Park, 2002). Many women and couples who wish to conceive children and are unable to do so confront fertility issues and feelings of loss, grief, and mourning (K. M. Anderson, Sharpe, Rattay, & Irvine, 2003). For some, adoption has been a positive solution (Zamostny, O'Brien, Baden, & Wiley, 2003).

Women and Aging

Cultural stereotypes of women as they age are increasingly negative in a culture that values youth and beauty. Older women are seldom seen on television or in films, and when they are, the characters are often negatively portrayed as poor and dependent (Kjaersgaard, 2005). As they age, women are subject to many negative stereotypes as well as financial problems and discrimination against any disabilities or change in physical status associated with aging (APA, 2004). The most frequent victims of elder abuse are women over 75 years of age (Bergeron, 2005). Married women tend to outlive their spouses and are less likely to remarry than widowers, which leaves many elderly women with years of single life to fill with friends and extended family (Garner & Mercer, 2001).

There are particularly negative stereotypes of menopause and postmenopausal women. Medical models have treated menopause as a deficiency disease characterized by depression, irritability, and mood swings rather than a natural biological phenomenon (Avis, 2003). In actuality, menopausal women have reported positive attitudes toward menopause and increased independence and self-confidence with age (Etaugh, 1993). As many women age, they have been found to be healthier than younger women, less concerned about loneliness, more autonomous, engaged in lively and satisfying friendships, actively engaged in social issues, assertive, creative, welcoming of new experiences, and displaying high levels of life satisfaction (Rose, 2007). Life expectancy for women has increased, nutrition is better, people exercise more, and quality of life is better. With the greater number of role choices and no more fears of accidental pregnancy, concern for the opinions and possible criticisms of others tends to lessen (Arnold, 2005), whereas joy in living and autonomy increase (Muhlbauer & Chrisler, 2007).

Impact of Gender Socialization on Boys and Men

Although many writers have described the advantages of being male in patriarchal cultures, there is emerging evidence that gender role expectations for boys and men also have their limitations. According to the gender role strain paradigm (Pleck, 1995), gender roles constrict the lives of both males and females across the life cycle. Furthermore, there is evidence that boys are expected to conform to a narrower range of behaviors, are sanctioned more severely when they violate acceptable gender role norms, and actively avoid any behaviors deemed feminine (Hughes & Seta, 2003).

Emotion Socialization

The role restrictiveness of boyhood is dramatically illustrated in the area of emotion socialization, whereby young men are indoctrinated into normative male alexithymia (Levant & Kopecky, 1995). Through this process of emotion socialization, boys are discouraged from expressing emotions in general, with special prohibitions against softer or tender emotions, such as compassion, vulnerability, or fear. Group interactions in childhood reinforce this process, as girl playgroups tend to be intimate and relationship-focused, whereas boy playgroups tend to emphasize structured games, competition, and toughness (Maccoby, 1990).

Relationships

Closely related to this conceptualization of normative alexithymia is the self-in-relation perspective that posits widely differing relational emphases for young girls and boys (Jordan et al., 1991). Bergman (1995) has contended that early male development emphasizes the need for detachment and places minimal importance on the development of relational skills. Real (1997) proposed that this loss of the relational aspect of young men's lives generates unresolved grief that lays the groundwork for depression in middle adulthood.

Violence and Abuse

In the very early stages of boyhood, young men are forced to confront issues of violence and aggression that profoundly affect their self-esteem, emotional well-being, and status with other males. Despite the pretension that violence and physical aggression are unacceptable, many young men come to learn that violence is actually the crucible of manhood. David and Brannon's (1976) classic framework of masculinity norms identified "Give'em Hell" as a central part of traditional manhood. Lisak (2001) noted that young boys are so regularly exposed to coercion and physical aggression from fathers, peers, and the media that they commonly repress traumatic experiences of childhood physical abuse or dismiss them as trivial. Boys who do not repress their emotional reactions and do not adopt the required toughness are subject to further abuse and bullying as they become identified as weak. Survival in this environment may require a cauterizing of interpersonal sensitivity and compassion, which may lead to a pronounced deficit in empathy or empathic disconnection (Miller & Eisenberg, 1988).

Socialization into Sexuality

In their later adolescent development, males encounter an eruption of hormonal activity and burgeoning sexual interest for which they are minimally prepared. At one time, female sexuality was considered complex and issue-laden, whereas male sexuality was considered relatively straightforward and free of any issues other than acquiring willing partners and maintaining high standards of performance. Of late, however, many have questioned the basic underpinnings of men's entire approach to sexuality. Brooks (1995, 1998) has decried the dysfunctional manner by which many young men are introduced to sexual activity, including the objectification of women and the lack of intimacy in nonrelational sexuality.

Work and Career

Consistent with the "Big Wheel" component of David and Brannon's (1976) model of masculinity, men generally equate their degree of masculinity with their success in the workplace or their capacity to function as the good provider. Men learn to experience masculinity as hierarchical, demanding that they continually measure themselves against other men and always meet the expectations of the male chorus (Brooks, 1998). Status as a worker may be particularly important to blue-collar or working-class manhood. Men's career choices are commonly affected by their view of the manliness of potential occupations, with loss of the worker role identified as a critical precipitant to men's depression and suicidal ideation (Cochran & Rabinowitz, 2000). Loss of work identity can create difficulties for men who become disabled, and many men struggle in accommodating to retirement (Sternbach, 2001).

Marriage

In adulthood, men are expected to demonstrate emotional maturity by settling down through heterosexual marriage (at the time of this writing, marriage remains generally unavailable to gay men). Despite the historically popular images of marriage as distasteful to men, men actually benefit considerably from traditional marriages. In the sexual division of labor in conventional marriages, men receive benefits in terms of marital services, household labor, child care, caretaking, and emotion facilitation. In return, traditional men expect that the proper execution of their marital responsibilities requires that they unfailingly function as family leaders, providers, and protectors (Gilbert & Rader, Chapter 25, this volume). Even those men who wish to take advantage of recent cultural shifts such as shared child care and housework or allowances for parental leave find that peers, family, and corporate culture may frown on men who do so.

Fatherhood

Fatherhood has always been a central component in virtually all cultural prescriptions of masculinity (Cabrera, Tamis-LeMonda, Bradley, Hofferth, & Lamb, 2000), yet the role of the father has undergone substantial transformation over the past several decades. The traditional father was expected to be a "responsible provider, a disciplinarian who instills a sense of morality in his children, and a role model who is physically strong and remains calm in the face of danger" (Silverstein, Auerbach, & Levant, 2002, p. 362). Part of that formula was the assumption that the father would be emotionally less connected to his children and free from domestic labor and child-rearing responsibilities, as well as frequently absent from the home and important events in family life.

Over the past several decades, a new image of the father has appeared, a model that expected more of men as fathers and also celebrated the multiple benefits that fathering provides (Levant & Kopecky, 1995). New fathering roles have become possible (and necessary) with dramatic shifts in the structure and composition of contemporary families. Modern fathering roles call for men to participate more actively with their children, to be more emotionally accessible and less authoritarian, and to be intimate and egalitarian with their wives (Silverstein et al., 2002). Some men have responded well to these shifts in fathering expectations, but other men have encountered significant gender role strain. The neoconservative men's movement is a call for a return to more traditional fathering roles, whereas the Promise Keepers push actively for reestablishment of male leadership in families (Brickner, 1999).

Dark Side of Masculinity

Adult men are far more likely than women to engage in a range of behaviors that are markedly harmful to others and to themselves. More men than women abuse alcohol and illicit substances (see Martens et al., Chapter 32, this volume), perpetrate domestic violence (Harway & Hansen, 2004), commit rape and sexual assault (Rozee & Koss, 2001), sexually harass (Levy & Paludi, 1997), demonstrate road rage and instigate automobile fatalities (Galovski, Malta, & Blanchard, 2006), and abandon financial responsibilities to their children (Boumil & Friedman, 1996). An argument can be made that even though most men never engage in most of these behaviors, all are exposed to masculinity norms that subtly or overtly encourage aggression, sexual preoccupation, risk taking, and resolving differences with power tactics and interpersonal domination (David & Brannon, 1976). This perspective posits that when these destructive behaviors are recognized as partially an exaggerated outgrowth of normative male socialization, the behaviors may be more fully understood, with opportunities for the design of more creative and effective interventions.

Men's Health

Perhaps nothing better illustrates the penalties of male gender role strain than the statistics showing that men live shorter lives than women (Courtenay, 2000). The differential life expectancies for women and men have been estimated to be approximately 7 years (and African American men tend to die 8 years sooner than Caucasian men). Although these differences in life expectancies may be attributed to many causes, one relevant explanation ties men's mortality to their masculinity socialization and its harmful health-related behaviors and nonbehaviors. Most obviously, the male warrior role subjects men to military duty and warfare fatalities. Additionally, the previously noted proclivity for men to perpetrate violence, abuse alcohol and illicit substances, speed in vehicles, and engage in high-risk behaviors contributes to earlier death. Further, although workplaces are changing, men remain more likely to occupy the most physically dangerous occupations (U.S. Department of Labor, 1999).

More subtle, yet equally important, are the contributions to men's health problems that are directly connected to their attitudes toward their bodies, their physical health needs, and their overall recognition of vulnerability and self-care. Courtenay (2000) has noted that men often avoid regular visits with their physicians, ask fewer questions, have lower levels of necessary knowledge about their health status, and engage in far fewer preventative behaviors (seat belts, teeth brushing, and healthy diets). In sum, there continues to be much empirical validation for the early observation of Goldberg (1976) that masculinity is hazardous to men's health.

Homophobia, Male Friendships, and Social Isolation

Among the poorly recognized issues for men are the issues of social isolation and limited social networks. Social psychologists have identified important gender differences in friendships and have noted the shortcomings of men's relationship patterns, particularly in terms of male-male friendships. Caldwell and Peplau (1982) noted that although women and men claim similar numbers of same-sex friendships, male-male friendships were characterized by far less actual contact, minimal sharing of emotional material, and a general focus on action and doing versus intimacy and sharing innermost thoughts. The potential to counter men's emotional isolation has been considered to be a primary factor in the advantages of male therapy groups (Brooks, 1998), a central appeal of Robert Bly's mythopoetic men's movement, and a significant aspect of the Promise Keepers movement (Brickner, 1999).

Many factors have been proposed as contributing to men's avoidance of intimate relationships with other men and their emotional dependence on women, including structural factors such as the simple reality that men have historically had less time to nurture relationships. Nevertheless, much of this pattern is likely related to male socialization about competition, alexithymia, confusion of intimacy and sexuality, and homophobia (Plummer, 1999).

Late-Life Issues for Men

The aforementioned negative stereotypes and ageism that are so problematic for women in later life seem to have a differential impact on the lives of older men. Many observers have reported on vastly different images of the older man and the older woman, with many more positive attributes ascribed to the former. Developmental researchers have long posited that aging has many psychological benefits for men, as it may free them from the anxieties and role restrictions of earlier years. Although there appears to be limited empirical support for this generally accepted concept, it has been commonly thought that older men tend to incorporate their feminine side and expand their gender role behaviors (Thompson, 1994). There is abundant evidence, however, that this life stage also presents difficulties for men in general and ethnic minority men, working class men, and gay men, in particular. At this point in their lives, men face numerous physical, psychological, and spiritual challenges, including issues of failing health, postretirement adjustment, altered sexual functioning, limited social support systems, and meaning of life issues (Thompson & Whearty, 2004).

IMPLICATIONS FOR PRACTICE WITH GIRLS AND WOMEN

Just as in all the practice guidelines approved by the American Psychological Association (APA; 2000, 2003, 2004, in press), working with any group requires, among other things, knowledge of that groups' development, identity formation, biological issues, socialization patterns, needs, issues of oppression and discrimination, and intergenerational history. The earlier sections of this chapter touched briefly on a number of important gender issues.

Counselor Awareness of Stereotypes

Psychologists and counselors need to be aware of the socialization processes for girls and women (and boys and men), recognize the stereotypes that result, and understand how these may affect their life experiences and well-being. Research has demonstrated that when women are aware of the potential impact of stereotypes they are less vulnerable to their negative effects (Martens, Johns, Greenberg, & Schimel, 2006). Professionals must recognize that girls and women, as well as boys and men, are socialized into multiple group memberships that create complex, multifaceted identities. Tied to these identities are issues regarding the extent to which the individual accepts or denies each identity and the oppression or privilege associated with that identity. This recognition includes the professional being cognizant of his or her own multiple identities and stereotypes of others to avoid bias in service provision (APA, 2000, 2003, 2004; O'Neil & Egan, 1992).

It is critical that practitioners base their interventions on gender-fair research, have the ability to critique research findings using a gender lens, and employ language that is inclusive and conveys respect for all persons. Psychologists and counselors need particular skills in understanding and explaining the impact of gender role socialization and expectations on their clients. Pittman (1985) coined the term *gender broker* to describe this needed skill in gender role analysis that allows clients to examine old messages and make conscious re-decisions to accept some socialization messages and reject others (Philpot et al., 1997). Helping a woman understand how her family and educational system reinforced her for silence could allow her to find her voice. This process also includes awareness of what types of client issues and problems may be internal to the client and what issues may be externally based on discrimination, societal limits, or other external obstacles. Knowledge of and appreciation for power issues and their impact are essential to understanding client circumstances (Worell & Remer, 2003). This knowledge could be particularly useful in understanding the impact of sexual harassment in the workplace, violence in the home, or distribution of household chores.

Bias in Assessment, Theory, and Diagnosis

Practitioners must evaluate and use only those assessment instruments that have demonstrated themselves to be gender-fair. Biased instruments have been used to misdiagnose and misclassify women in general, persons of color, and women with disabilities (e.g., see Constantine, Miville, & Kindaichi, Chapter 9, this volume). Biases present in theories of therapy also require scrutiny. Theories that overvalue individualism and autonomy, undervalue connections and relational variables, overvalue rationality, undervalue emotional responses, pay inadequate attention to the context of the client's life, portray mothers in negative and critical ways, overemphasize achievement drive and workplace objectivity, and tie definitions of mental health to characteristics typically considered masculine may lead to interventions that are biased and do harm. There is need for more theories that view mental health in the context of balancing family, work, recreation, creativity, spirituality, friendships, and other interests.

There is continuing evidence of bias in diagnosis by gender, ethnicity, race, age, disability, sexual orientation, and social class (Caplan & Cosgrove, 2004). The gender role socialization of girls and women plus their economic status, ethnicity, sexual orientation, and disability status create perceptions that may lead to inappropriate use and overuse of certain diagnoses, such as histrionic, borderline, and dependent personality disorders, somatization, premenstrual dysphoric syndrome, eating disorders, agoraphobia, and depression (Cosgrove, 2004). These diagnostic categories and their symptoms may be viewed as exaggerations of the stereotyped female gender role expectations and behaviors, such as being overly emotional or passive or overdoing caretaking behaviors. Hence, psychologists need to be particularly careful when diagnosing girls and women to recognize the context of their clients' behavior and symptoms and to avoid stereotype bias. Counselors should also be aware that sexual abuse and rape are likely to be found in the history of women diagnosed as borderline, histrionic, or dependent, with one study finding that sexual and physical abuse had occurred for 81% of women diagnosed with personality disorders (Herman, Perry, & van der Kolk, 1989). Additionally, symptoms in girls may be overlooked because girls are more likely to internalize problems, blame themselves, or show less overt symptoms (Seiffge-Krenke & Stemmler, 2002).

Context and Interventions

Practitioners who work with girls and women have an obligation to know about the challenges, strengths, identities, and social contexts of these clients. Knowledge of specific interventions that are associated with positive outcomes for girls and women in particular problem areas is necessary. When working with girls and women concerned with body size and suffering from body dissatisfaction, objectification, and eating disorders, therapies that teach the client to modify negative internalized self-attitudes and expectations have been found to be effective (see Mintz, Hamilton, Bledman, and Franko, Chapter 33, this volume). Treatments for depression, as well as some eating disorders, that challenge distorted and ruminative thinking and focus on interpersonal issues have demonstrated success.

Approaches that aid women to restore a sense of self-control and self-efficacy have been shown to be helpful for women diagnosed with Postraumatic Stress Disorder (PTSD; Blake & Sonnenberg, 1998). Research has demonstrated that psychologists, counselors, physicians, and other health professionals often fail to assess for domestic violence and sexual abuse (Harway & Hansen, 2004). In treating these survivors, interventions that help them cope with intrusive memories and that challenge and change any mistaken sense of responsibility and shame have led to better coping and positive change (Kubany, Hill, & Owens, 2003). If couples' counseling is to be employed in cases of domestic violence, it may be crucial to treat the individuals separately until the batterer has made sufficient progress to make seeing them together safe (Philpot et al., 1997).

Tapping into women's and girls' strength and resilience is another important element of successful treatment (Worell & Remer, 2003). Strong relationships, positive self-image, assertiveness, problem-solving skills, internal locus of control, and self-efficacy have been shown to promote healthy functioning (Enns, 2000). Active participation of the client as a partner in therapy seems also to increase empowerment, self-direction, and positive outcome (Riger, 2000). Finally, awareness and understanding of clients' multiple interacting identities, including the fluidity of their salience over time, are essential to positive outcome (APA, 2000, 2003, 2004, 2007). These diversities include gender, culture, ethnicity, race, sexual orientation, disability, and religion.

IMPLICATIONS FOR PRACTICE WITH BOYS AND MEN

As noted earlier, there has been concern that mental health practices may fail to comprehend how traditional socialization may contribute to overdiagnosing, overmedicating, and overtreating girls and women (Caplan & Cosgrove, 2004). In contrast, a case can be made that the mental health community has contributed to underdiagnosing and undertreating boys and men. Evidence has accumulated indicating that men are far less likely than women to seek professional help, and particularly psychotherapy (Addis & Mahalik, 2003). Even when men appear in counselors' offices, they frequently have not chosen freely to come and are not enthusiastic about being there (Scher, 1990). Much of this gender discrepancy in utilization of mental health services may be attributed to male socialization, with its emphasis on emotional stoicism and self-reliance (David & Brannon, 1976). Also, mental health providers may not recognize the special needs of men and their difficulties in functioning as ideal therapy clients. Sensitive and ethical gender-fair work requires the practitioner to possess the necessary awareness, attitudes, knowledge, and skills.

Counselor Attitudes and Beliefs (Awareness)

Because all mental health practitioners are themselves raised in a gendered culture, they have also internalized values and beliefs about expected gender role behavior. The attitudes and values of therapists regarding gender roles will likely influence their assessment, diagnosis, and treatment of clients. Wisch and Mahalik (1999) found that male therapists holding traditional gender role attitudes viewed nontraditional male clients as less likeable, were less empathic toward them, and held a poorer prognosis for them. A special challenge for practitioners may be the potential for reactivity based in distaste for men who exhibit behaviors associated with the dark side of masculinity (e.g., substance abuse, violence, inappropriate sexual behavior, flight from responsibilities). As a result, special efforts may be needed to develop an empathic connection and working alliance with them.

Viewing Men's Presenting Problems in Gender Context (Knowledge)

When men's most common presenting problems are viewed in isolation, they can be a source of embarrassment or shame for a new male client. To counter this problem, it is frequently beneficial to help the male client understand how his problematic behavior might (to some extent) be grounded in male socialization. Philpot et al. (1997) referred to this process as *gender inquiry*, whereas Addis and Mahalik (2003) described it as *gender role analysis*, and Pittman (1985) described it as *serving as a gender broker*. At their core, these processes share the identical objectives of lessening self-blame and developing greater insight into the many forces shaping a man's behavior (without absolving men from individual responsibility for their actions).

Therapist Skills

Many observers have noted that traditional psychotherapy's emphasis on emotional expression, disclosing vulnerability, ceding control, acknowledging mistakes and failures, recognizing feelings of shame, and admitting dependency needs can create difficulties for males socialized to adhere to traditional stoic masculine roles (Brooks, 1998; Cochran & Rabinowitz, 2000). As a result, the early stages of a counseling relationship might be productively spent in finding ways to "change the services to fit the 'average' man" (Addis & Mahalik, 2003, p. 14). Such activities might include discussing a man's expectations and correcting erroneous ones, particularly those related to pressures to reveal vulnerabilities prematurely, explore painful emotions, or cede control in therapy sessions (Mahalik, Good, & Englar-Carlson, 2003).

Kiselica (2001) recommended a number of male-friendly therapy practices, including use of shorter sessions, informal settings outside the office (e.g., playgrounds for young men), instrumental activities, humor, self-disclosure, and psychoeducational groups. Additionally, a more comfortable counseling environment can be created by providing greater opportunities for reciprocity (e.g., men's groups), increasing awareness of the normativeness of a male client's problems (e.g., depression or insecurities), or recognizing the positive or constructive aspects of male clients' behaviors or intentions (Addis & Mahalik, 2003; Brooks, 1998).

With appropriate accommodations, most established therapeutic approaches can be useful in working with men. For psychoanalytic treatment, Pollack (2005) suggested modifications to support "the patient's need to believe, for long periods of time and without interpretation or challenge to his denial, that both the therapist and the therapy are unimportant to him" (p. 535). He further recommended that analysts be especially aware of issues with men's shame. Cognitive psychotherapy approaches can be helpful to men because of their reliance on thinking versus feeling (Levant & Kopecky, 1995). Group therapy has been advocated as a rich format for countering men's emotional isolation (Brooks, 1998). Mahalik (2005) proposed that interpersonal psychotherapy has the potential to counter many men's overreliance on the detached and dominant interpersonal style and "add flexibility to a man's behavioral repertoire"

(p. 245). Behavioral therapies can be attractive to traditional men because of their emphasis on discrete practical problems and appeal to men's concerns with performance.

Many men who would resist formal therapy, might be more willing to participate in any of several therapylike interventions. Executive coaching (Sperry, 2003) is one of the more recent models for intervening with men, and it may be well suited to men who find seeking formal psychotherapeutic help aversive. Embedded in this model is the recognition that autocratic and dispassionate leadership models and effective leaders (more frequently men) must augment their interpersonal styles. This approach is quite similar to many well-established psychoeducational interventions such as assertiveness training, emotional skills training, anger management training, and many aspects of popular marital communications paradigms. Another example of the application of psychoeducational programs to specific male problems is Levant's (1998) intervention model for male alexithymia that adopts a skills-based model and incorporates a consciousness-raising component regarding men's fear of emotional expression.

Recognizing the long-standing problems in persuading men to enter the offices of mental health professionals, there can be great advantage in considering ways to bring mental health services to places where men are already present. The aforementioned success of the executive coaching model, whereby basic psychological concepts are re-packaged in common business (male-friendly) language, represents a prime example of this concept. These approaches share the common philosophy that considerable emotional and relationship benefit can be provided to men, even when these men never enter traditional therapy.

Customizing Interventions to Diverse Masculinities (Awareness, Knowledge, and Skills)

Although it is important to appreciate the impact of the dominant masculinity template (White, heterosexual, able-bodied, and middle-class), ethical practice also requires recognition of diversities in the male experience. The concepts of male privilege and advantage have far different meaning when viewed in the context of racial oppression, gay bashing, and marginalization of men who fail to meet the desired masculine stereotype. The concept of multiple oppressions, most often applied to minority group women, may also have applicability to men who are not privileged in terms of race or ethnicity, sexual orientation, physical status, or social class. In addition to developing awareness of general issues in counseling men, practitioners are urged to recognize the special situations and needs of African American men, Hispanic men, Asian men, gay or bisexual men, physically challenged men, and working-class men.

IMPLICATIONS FOR PRACTICE WITH COUPLES AND FAMILIES

As suggested earlier, women and girls and men and boys are all socialized into different cultures. Hence, when a man and a woman come together in a heterosexual marriage or partnership, there is the potential for a clash between cultures that may create misunderstandings and conflicting expectations. Moreover, the gender socialization process not only teaches each partner appropriate gender roles, it also teaches them what to expect as stereotypic characteristics and behavior of the other gender (Philpot et al., 1997). Partners may, therefore, not only misunderstand each other, they may have a set of expectations that do not fit their partner. In gay and lesbian couples, the possibility of a partnership between two individuals with similar socialization experiences may create a different set of clashes and role negotiation issues based on faulty assumptions of sameness.

A critical part of therapy with a heterosexual couple may be helping them understand the gender socialization of the other to break through their miscommunications and misunderstandings. This process may include helping the partners recognize their own gender role journey (O'Neil & Egan, 1992; Pittman, 1985) and the gender role journey of their partner. One strategy to aid in this mutual understanding is gender inquiry, in which the partners are taught to interview each other regarding family-of-origin messages and expectations, peer group influences, educational system rewards and challenges, work experiences, and relationship history (Philpot et al., 1997). In addition to serving as conduits for deeper understanding, using these strategies early in counseling before focusing on particularly emotional current issues may lay a foundation for supporting work on the current difficulties (Nutt, 2005).

In Western cultures, a common misunderstanding may occur in a couple in which the man has been brought up to believe that his most important role as breadwinner also confers the right to make key decisions in his family. In contrast, his wife may have been reared in a family that taught that all gender voices are equal, women are expected to develop careers in addition to families, and housework should be shared. The couple could be expected to clash on financial issues, childrearing, household maintenance, and a myriad of other issues. Without careful examination of the origins of their gendered messages, there is danger that they will each become entrenched in their points of view and perceive their partner as wrong. Hence, a stalemate could result in which the couple is stuck. An additional part of this gender examination may also include knowledge of how men and women are taught to use language differently (Dindia & Canary, 2006; Gray, 1992).

In gay and lesbian relationships, there may be a different set of gendered roles and expectations. Lesbian relationships tend to be stable and committed over long periods of time (Hill, 1999), which fits with partners who were likely both brought up to make and value emotional connections. They are also more likely to seek egalitarian solutions to problems, whereas gay couples might struggle more with issues of control that often characterize male socialization (Patterson, 2000). Practitioners must also be sensitive to issues of discrimination, hate crimes, homophobia, and other stressors that may affect lesbian and gay relationships.

Interventions that are effective with couples may also be useful in working with families. All family members have received gender socialization messages that may be creating conflicts and misunderstandings in the household. Many Euro-centered family therapy theories have assumed that the appropriate role of fathers is as breadwinner and mothers as nurturer. Mothers have been blamed for family problems by assuming they were overinvolved or enmeshed with their children. Boundaries have been overemphasized at the expense of connection and family intimacy, and therapist neutrality has supported the status quo of gender power differentials.

A possible intervention is to examine the gender role stereotype expectations in any given culture and their impact on family functioning. These stereotypes will be affected by the individualistic versus collectivistic orientation of the culture. The goal is empowerment of all family members in the context of their appropriate subsystem (e.g., parental, sibling) and the cultural expectations of family structure. The status and voice of each family member deserves attention and respect. Power issues may be directly addressed, including issues of respect and family loyalty in collectivistic cultures. This can be particularly important in couples' and family therapy in a culture in transition between collectivism and individualism in which expectations may be mixed and confusing. The parental subsystem is encouraged to take its appropriate place at the head of the family, and children are supported and encouraged to take increasing self-responsibility as they mature. Family chores are examined to determine the extent of their gender typing (e.g., in the United States, do men and boys mow the lawn and girls and women do the dusting and cooking?). Children need to learn all household skills for their adult futures in most cultures. The work activities outside and inside the home of men and women are equally respected as are child-care responsibilities. Western men may welcome equality when they see its benefits for balancing their lives, a realization often accompanied by relief. Again, for lesbian and gay families, and families of varying ethnic backgrounds, the influences of these diversities and their cultural underpinnings must be addressed.

SUMMARY AND CONCLUSION

Much as there has been recognition of the central importance of race, ethnicity, sexual preference, social class, age, and ability status in shaping how a client views the world, there is also clear recognition of the fundamental role of gender-based beliefs and values. Feminist critics first identified the damage produced by ignorance of women's experiences and failure to appreciate issues of differential access to power and opportunities. Men's studies scholars have joined this critique and highlighted the need to understand male socialization and its limiting effects on men's lives. This chapter has reviewed the growing literature on gender studies, highlighting the need for awareness and skill development among practitioners to expand their intervention options with female and male clients. There remains a need for greater study and understanding of the intersections between gender and other areas of diversity.

REFERENCES

Ackerman, R. J., & Banks, M. E. (2003). Assessment, treatment, and rehabilitation for interpersonal violence victims: Women sustaining head injuries. In M. E. Banks & E. Kaschak (Eds.), *Women with visible and invisible disabilities: Multiple intersections, multiple issues, multiple therapies* (pp. 343–363). New York: Haworth Press.

Addis, M. E., & Mahalik, J. R. (2003). Men, masculinity, and the contexts of help seeking. *American Psychologist, 58*, 5–14.

American Association of University Women (AAUW). (1996). *Girls in the middle: Working to succeed in school.* Washington, DC: AAUW's Educational Foundation.

American Psychological Association. (2000). Guidelines for psychotherapy with lesbian, gay, and bisexual clients. *American Psychologist, 55*, 1440–1451.

American Psychological Association. (2003). Guidelines on multicultural education, training, research, practice, and organizational change for psychologists. *American Psychologist, 58*, 377–402.

American Psychological Association. (2004). Guidelines for psychological practice with older adults. *American Psychologist, 59*, 236–260.

American Psychological Association. (in press). Guidelines for psychological practice with girls and women. *American Psychologist, 62*.

Anderson, D. A., & Hamilton, M. (2005). Gender role stereotyping of parents in children's picture books: The invisible father. *Sex Roles, 52*, 145–151.

Anderson, K. M., Sharpe, M., Rattay, A., & Irvine, D. S. (2003). Distress and concerns in couples referred to a specialist infertility clinic. *Journal of Psychosomatic Research, 54*, 353–355.

Arnold, E. (2005). A voice of their own: Women moving into their fifties. *Health Care for International, 26*, 630–651.

Avis, N. E. (2003). Depression during the menopausal transition. *Psychology of Women Quarterly, 27*, 91–100.

Barnett, R., & Rivers, C. (2004). *Same difference: How gender myths are hurting our relationships, our children, and our jobs.* New York: Basic Books.

Bergeron, L. R. (2005). Abuse of elderly women in family relationships: Another form of violence against women. In. K. Kendall-Tarkett (Ed.), *The handbook of women, stress, and trauma* (pp. 141–157). New York: Brunner-Routledge.

Bergman, S. J. (1995). Men's psychological development: A relational perspective. In W. S. Pollack & R. F. Levant (Eds.), *New psychotherapy for men* (pp. 68–90). New York: Wiley.

Bessenoff, G. R. (2006). Can the media affect us? Social comparison, self-discrepancy, and the thin ideal. *Psychology of Women Quarterly, 30*, 239–251.

Bishop, T. A. (1999). *A qualitative study of young adult women's recollections of menarche.* Unpublished dissertation, California School of Professional Psychology, Berkeley/Alameda.

Blake, D. D., & Sonnenberg, R. T. (1998). Outcome research on behavioral and cognitive behavior treatments for trauma survivors. In V. M. Follette, J. Ruzek, & F. Abueg (Eds.), *Trauma in context* (pp. 15–47). New York: Guilford Press.

Bondas, T., & Eriksson, K. (2001). Women's lived experiences of pregnancy: A tapestry of joy and suffering. *Qualitative Health Research, 11*, 824–840.

Bosacki, S. L., & Moore, C. (2004). Preschoolers' understanding of simple and complex emotions: Links with gender and language. *Sex Roles, 50*, 659–675.

Boumil, M. M., & Friedman, J. (1996). *Deadbeat dads: A national child support scandal.* New York: Praeger.

Brickner, B. W. (1999). *The Promise Keepers: Politics and promises.* Lanham, MD: Lexington Books.

Brooks, G. R. (1995). *The Centerfold Syndrome: How men can overcome objectification and achieve intimacy with women.* San Francisco: Jossey-Bass.

Brooks, G. R. (1998). *A new psychotherapy for traditional men*. San Francisco: Jossey-Bass.

Cabrera, N. J., Tamis-LeMonda, C. S., Bradley, R. H., Hofferth, S., & Lamb, M. E. (2000). Fatherhood in the twenty-first century. *Child Development, 71*, 127–136.

Caldwell, M., & Peplau, L. (1982). Sex differences in same-sex friendships. *Sex Roles, 8*, 721–732.

Caplan, P. J., & Cosgrove, L. (Eds.). (2004). *Bias in psychiatric diagnosis*. Northvale, NJ: Aronson.

Cochran, S., & Rabinowitz, F. (2000). *Men and depression: Clinical and empirical perspectives*. New York: Academic Press.

Coker, A. L., & Davies, K. E. (2002). Physical and mental health effects of intimate partner violence for men and women. *American Journal of Preventive Medicine, 23*, 260–268.

Cosgrove, L. (2004). Gender bias and sex distribution of mental disorders in the DSM-IV-TR. In P. J. Caplan & L. Cosgrove (Eds.), *Bias in psychiatric diagnosis* (pp. 127–140). Northvale, NJ: Aronson.

Costello, C. B., Wight, V. R., & Stone, A. J. (2003). *The American woman 2003–2004*. New York: Palgrave Macmillan.

Courtenay, W. H. (2000). Constructions of masculinity and their influence on men's well-being: A theory of gender and health. *Social Science and Medicine, 50*, 1385–1401.

David, D., & Brannon, R. (Eds.). (1976). *The forty-nine percent majority*. Reading, MA: Addison-Wesley.

Deaux, K., & Major, B. (1987). Putting gender into context: An interactional model of gender-related behaviors. *Psychological Bulletin, 94*, 369–389.

Demarest, J., & Allen, R. (2000). Body image: Gender, ethnic, and age differences. *Journal of Social Psychology, 140*, 465–472.

Dindia, K., & Canary, D. (Eds.). (2006). *Sex differences and similarities in communication*. Mahwah, NJ: Erlbaum.

Doyle, J., & Paludi, M. A. (1998). *Sex and gender: The human experience* (4th ed.). New York: McGraw-Hill.

Enns, C. Z. (2000). Gender issues in counseling. In S. D. Brown & R. W. Lent (Eds.), *Handbook of counseling psychology* (3rd ed., pp. 601–638). New York: Wiley.

Etaugh, C. (1993). Women in the middle and later years. In F. L. Denmark & M. A. Paludi (Eds.), *Psychology of women: A handbook of issues and theories* (pp. 213–246). Westport, CT: Greenwood.

Evans, L., & Davies, K. (2000). No sissy boys here: A content analysis of the representation of masculinity in elementary school reading textbooks. *Sex Roles, 42*, 255–270.

Fassinger, R. E. (2002). Hitting the ceiling: Gendered barriers to occupational entry, advancement and achievement. In L. Diamant & J. Lee (Eds.), *The psychology of sex, gender, and jobs: Issues and solutions* (pp. 21–46). Westport, CT: Greenwood.

Federal Glass Ceiling Commission. (1995, March). *Good for business: Making full use of the nation's human capital*. Washington, DC: U.S. Department of Labor.

Forbes, G. B., Adams-Curtis, L. E., White, K. B., & Holmgren, K. M. (2003). The role of hostile and benevolent sexism in women's and men's perceptions of the menstruating woman. *Psychology of Women Quarterly, 27*, 58–63.

Fouts, G., & Burggraf, K. (2000). Television situation categories: Female weight, male negative comments, and audience reactions. *Sex Roles, 42*, 925–932.

Fredrickson, B. L., & Roberts, T. (1997). Objectification theory: Toward understanding women's lived experiences and mental health risks. *Psychology of Women Quarterly, 21*, 173–206.

Furnham, A., & Mak, T. (1999). Sex-role stereotyping in television commercials: A review and comparison of fourteen studies done on five continents over 25 years. *Sex Roles, 41*, 413–437.

Galovski, T. E., Malta, L. S., & Blanchard, E. B. (2006). *Road rage: Assessment and treatment of the angry, aggressive driver*. Washington, DC: American Psychological Association.

Garner, J. D., & Mercer, S. O. (Eds.). (2001). *Women as they age* (2nd ed.) New York: Haworth Press.

Glascock, J., & Preston-Schreck, C. (2004). Gender and racial stereotypes in daily newspaper comics: A time-honored tradition? *Sex Roles, 51*, 423–431.

Goldberg, H. (1976). *The hazards of being male*. New York: New American Library.

Golombok, S., & Fivush, R. (1994). *Gender development*. New York: Cambridge University Press.

Gonzalez, A. Q., & Koestner, R. (2005). Parental preference for sex of newborn as reflected in positive affect in birth announcements. *Sex Roles, 52*, 407–411.

Gray, J. (1992). *Men are from Mars, women are from Venus: A practical guide for improving communication and getting what you want in your relationships*. New York: HarperCollins.

Harway, M., & Hansen, M. (2004). *Spouse abuse: Treating battered women, batterers and their children* (2nd ed.). Sarasota, FL: Professional Resource Press.

Hayward, C., Hotlib, I., Schraedley, P. D., & Litt, I. F. (1999). Ethnic differences in association between pubertal status and symptoms of depression in adolescent girls. *Journal of Adolescent Health, 25*, 143–149.

Hendy, H. M., Eggen, D., Gustitus, C., McLeod, K. C., & Ng, P. (2003). Decision to leave scale: Perceived reasons to stay or leave violent relationships. *Psychology of Women Quarterly, 27*, 162–173.

Herman, J. L., Perry, J. C., & van der Kolk, B. A. (1989). Childhood trauma in borderline personality disorders. *American Journal of Psychiatry, 146*, 490–495.

Herrett-Skjellum, J., & Allen, M. (1996). Television programming and sex stereotyping: A meta-analysis. In. B. Burleson (Ed.), *Communication yearbook 19* (pp. 157–185). Thousand Oaks, CA: Sage.

Hill, C. A. (1999). Fusion and conflict in lesbian relationships? *Feminism and Psychology, 9*, 179–185.

Hughes, F. M., & Seta, C. E. (2003). Gender stereotypes: Children's perceptions of future compensatory behavior following gender roles. *Sex Roles, 49* (11–12), 685–691.

Hyde, J. S. (2005). The gender similarities hypothesis. *American Psychologist, 60*, 581–592.

Jones, S. M., & Dindia, K. (2004). A meta-analytic perspective on sex equity in the classroom. *Review of Educational Research, 76*, 443–471.

Jordan, J. V., Kaplan, A. G., Miller, J. B., Stiver, I. P., & Surrey, J. L. (1991). *Women's growth in connection*. New York: Guilford Press.

Kiselica, M. S. (2001). A male-friendly therapeutic process with school-age boys. In G. R. Brooks & G. E. Good (Eds.), *The handbook of counseling and psychotherapy with men: A guide to settings and approaches* (Vol. I, pp. 43–58). San Francisco: Jossey-Bass.

Kjaersgaard, K. S. (2005). Aging to perfection or perfectly aged? The image of women growing older on television. In E. Cole & J. H. Daniel (Eds.), *Featuring females: Feminist analyses of media* (pp. 199–210). Washington, DC: American Psychological Association.

Krahé, B., Bieneck, S., & Möller, I. (2005). Understanding gender and intimate partner violence from an international perspective. *Sex Roles, 52*, 807–828.

Kubany, E. S., Hill, E. E., & Owens, J. A. (2003). Cognitive trauma therapy for battered women with PTSD: Preliminary findings. *Journal of Traumatic Stress, 16*, 81–91.

Leigh, W. A., & Huff, D. (2006). *Women of color health data book: Adolescents to seniors* (3rd ed., NIH Publication No. 06-4247). Bethesda, MD: National Institutes of Health, Office of Research on Women's Health.

Levant, R. F. (1995). Toward the reconstruction of masculinity. In R. F. Levant & W. S. Pollack (Eds.), *A new psychology of men* (pp. 229–251). New York: Basic Books.

Levant, R. F. (1998). Desperately seeking language: Understanding, assessing, and treating normative male alexithymia. In W. S. Pollack & R. F. Levant (Eds.), *New psychotherapy for men* (pp. 35–56). New York: Wiley.

Levant, R. F., & Kopecky, G. (1995). *Masculinity reconstructed: Changing the rules of manhood, in relationships, and in family life*. New York: Dutton.

Levant, R. F., & Silverstein, L. B. (2005). Gender is neglected by both evidence based practices and "treatment as usual. In J. C. Norcross, L. Beutler, & R. F. Levant (Eds.), *Evidence based practice in mental health: Debate and dialogue on the fundamental questions* (pp. 338–345). Washington, DC: American Psychological Association.

Levy, A., & Paludi, M. A. (1997). *Workplace sexual harassment*. Englewood Cliffs, NJ: Prentice-Hall.

Lindsey, E. W., & Mize, J. (2001). Contextual differences in parent-child play: Implications for children's gender role development. *Sex Roles, 44*, 155–176.

Lisak, D. (2001). Male survivors of trauma. In G. R. Brooks & G. E. Good (Eds.), *The new handbook of psychotherapy and counseling with men* (pp. 278–292). San Francisco: Jossey-Bass.

Littleton, H., & Breitkopf, C. R. (2006). Coping with the experience of rape. *Psychology of Women Quarterly, 30*, 106–116.

Lockwood, P. (2006). "Someone like me can be successful": Do college students need same-gender role models? *Psychology of Women Quarterly, 30*, 36–46.

Maccoby, E. E. (1990). Gender and relationships: A developmental account. *American Psychologist, 45*, 513–520.

Maccoby, E. E. (1998). *The two sexes: Growing up apart, coming together*. Cambridge, MA: Harvard University Press.

Mahalik, J. R. (2005). Interpersonal psychotherapy for men. In G. E. Good & G. R. Brooks (Eds.), *The new handbook of psychotherapy and counseling with men: A comprehensive guide to settings, problems, and treatment* (pp. 234–247). San Francisco: Jossey-Bass.

Mahalik, J. R., Good, G. E., & Englar-Carlson, M. (2003). Masculinity scripts, presenting concerns, and help seeking: Implications for practice and training. *Professional Psychology: Research and Practice, 34*, 123–131.

Major, B., Richards, C., Cooper, M. L., Cozzarelli, C., & Zubek, J. (1998). Personal resilience, cognitive appraisals, and coping: An integrative model of adjustment to abortion. *Journal of Personality and Social Psychology, 74*, 735–752.

Martens, A., Johns, M., Greenberg, J., & Schimel, J. (2006). Combating stereotype threat: The effect of self-affirmation on women's intellectual performance. *Journal of Experimental Social Psychology, 42*, 236–243.

McClelland, D. (1961). *The achieving society*. New York: Van Nostrand.

McLaren, L., & Kuh, D. (2004). Body dissatisfaction in midlife women. *Journal of Women and Aging, 16*, 35–54.

McMullin, D., & White, J. W. (2006). Long-term effects of labeling a rape experience. *Psychology of Women Quarterly, 30*, 96–105.

Miller, P. A., & Eisenberg, N. (1988). The relation of empathy to aggressive and externalizing/antisocial behavior. *Psychological Bulletin, 103*, 324–344.

Muhlbauer, V., & Chrisler, J. C. (2007). Introduction. In V. Muhlbauer & J. C. Chrisler (Eds.), *Women over 50: Psychological perspectives* (pp. 1–8). New York: Springer.

National Center for Injury Prevention and Control. (2005). *Intimate partner violence: Fact sheet*. Washington, DC: Centers for Disease Control and Prevention.

Neft, N., & Levine, A. (1997). *Where women stand: An international report on the status of women in 140 countries, 1997–1998*. New York: Random House.

Neville, H. A., Heppner, M. J., Oh, E., Spanierman, L. B., & Clark, M. (2004). General and culturally specific factors influencing Black and White rape survivors' self-esteem. *Psychology of Women Quarterly, 28*, 83–94.

Nutt, R. L. (1999). Women's gender-role socialization, gender-role conflict, and abuse. In M. Harway & J. M. O'Neil (Eds.), *What causes men's violence against women?* (pp. 117–134). Thousand Oaks, CA: Sage.

Nutt, R. L. (2005). Feminist and contextual work. In M. Harway (Ed.), *Handbook of couples therapy* (pp. 228–249). Hoboken, NJ: Wiley.

O'Neil, J. M., & Egan, J. (1992). Men's and women's gender role journeys: A metaphor for healing, transition, and transformation. In B. R. Wainrib (Ed.), *Gender issues across the life cycle* (pp. 107–123). New York: Springer.

Park, K. (2002). Stigma management among the voluntarily childless. *Sociological Perspectives, 45*, 21–45.

Patterson, C. J. (2000). Family relationships of lesbians and gay men. *Journal of Marriage and the Family, 62*, 1052–1069.

Philpot, C. L., Brooks, G. R., Lusterman, D.-D., & Nutt, R. L. (1997). *Why men and women clash and how therapists can bring them together*. Washington, DC: American Psychological Association.

Pittman, F. (1985). Gender myths: When does gender become pathology? *Family Therapy Networker, 9*, 25–33.

Pleck, J. H. (1995). The gender role strain paradigm: An update. In R. F. Levant & W. S. Pollack (Eds.), *A new psychology of men* (pp. 11–32). New York: Basic Books.

Plummer, D. (1999). *One of the boys: Masculinity, homophobia, and modern manhood*. New York: Haworth Press.

Pollack, W. S. (1998). *Real boys: Rescuing our sons from the myths of boyhood*. New York: Random House.

Pollack, W. S. (2005). "Masked men": New psychoanalytically oriented treatment models for adult and young adult men. In G. E. Good & G. R. Brooks (Eds.), *The new handbook of psychotherapy and counseling with men* (Rev. ed., pp. 203–216). San Francisco: Jossey-Bass.

Pomerleau, A., Bolduc, D., Malcuit, G., & Cossette, L. (1990). Pink or blue: Environmental gender stereotypes in the first two years of life. *Sex Roles, 22*, 359–367.

Quinn, D. M., Kallen, R. W., Twenge, J. M., & Fredrickson, B. L. (2006). The disruptive effect of self-objectification on performance. *Psychology of Women Quarterly, 30*, 59–64.

Real, T. (1997). *I don't want to talk about it: Overcoming the secret legacy of male depression*. New York: Simon & Schuster.

Reid, P. T., Haritos, C., Kelly, E., & Holland, N. E. (1995). Socialization of girls: Issues of ethnicity in gender development. In H. Landrine (Ed.), *Bringing cultural diversity to feminist psychology: Theory, research, and practice* (pp. 93–112). Washington, DC: American Psychological Association.

Renzetti, C. M. (1997). Violence in lesbian and gay relationships. In L. O'Toole & J. R. Schiffman (Eds.), *Gender violence: Interdisciplinary perspectives* (pp. 285–293). New York: New York University Press.

Rice, J. K., & Else-Quest, N. (2006). The mixed messages of motherhood. In J. Worell & C. D. Goodheart (Eds.), *Handbook of girls' and women's psychological health: Gender and well-being across the lifespan* (pp. 339–349). New York: Oxford University Press.

Riger, S. (2000). What's wrong with empowerment. In S. Riger (Ed.), *Transforming psychology: Gender in theory and practice* (pp. 97–106). New York: Oxford University Press.

Rose, S. M. (2007). Enjoying the returns: Women's friendships after 50. In V. Muhlbauer & J. C. Chrisler (Eds.), *Women over 50: Psychological perspectives* (pp. xx). New York: Springer.

Rozee, P. D., & Koss, M. P. (2001). Rape: A century of resistance. *Psychology of Women Quarterly, 25*, 295–311.

Russo, N. F. (2000). Understanding emotional responses after abortion. In J. C. Chrisler, C. Golden, & P. D. Rozee (Eds.), *Lectures on the psychology of women* (pp. 113–128). Boston: McGraw-Hill.

Scher, M. (1990). The effect of gender role incongruities on men's experience as clients in psychotherapy. *Psychotherapy, 27*, 322–326.

Seguin, L., Potvin, L., St.-Denis, M., & Loiselle, J. (1999). Depressive symptoms in the late postpartum among low socioeconomic status women. *Birth, 26*, 157–163.

Seiffge-Krenke, I., & Stemmler, M. (2002). Factors contributing to gender differences in depressive symptoms: A test of three developmental models. *Journal of Youth and Adolescence, 31*, 405–417.

Silverstein, L. B., Auerbach, C. F., & Levant, R. F. (2002). Contemporary fathers reconstructing masculinity: Clinical implications of gender role strain. *Professional Psychology: Research and Practice, 33*, 361–369.

Sperry, L. (2003). *Executive coaching: The essential guide for mental health professionals.* New York: Brunner-Routledge.

Statistical Abstracts of the United States. (2004–2005). *Section 12: Labor force, employment, and earnings.* Washington, DC: U.S. Census Bureau.

Sternbach, J. (2001). Psychotherapy with the Young OlderMan. In G. R. Brooks & Glenn E. Goods (Eds.). *The New handbook of psychotherapy and counseling: A comprehensive guide to settings, problems, and treatment approaches.* San Francisco, CA: Jossey-Bass (pp. 464–480).

Sturza, M. L., & Campbell, R. (2005). An exploratory study of rape survivors' prescription drug use as a means of coping with sexual assault. *Psychology of Women Quarterly, 29*, 353–363.

Tepper, C. A., & Cassidy, K. W. (1999). Gender differences in emotional language in children's picture books. *Sex Roles, 40*, 265–280.

Thompson, E. H. (1994). Older men as invisible men in contemporary society. In E. H. Thompson (Ed.), *Older men's lives* (pp. 1–21). Newbury Park, CA: Sage.

Thompson, E. H., & Whearty, P. M. (2004). Older men's social participation: The importance of masculinity ideology. *Journal of Men's Studies, 13*, 5–24.

U. S. Department of Labor. (1999). *Most dangerous occupation of 1997? Timber cutting.* Washington, DC: Bureau of Labor Statistics.

Vandell, K., & Dempsey, S. B. (1991). *Stalled agenda: Gender equity and the training of educators.* Washington, DC: American Association of University Women.

Wisch, A. F., & Mahalik, J. R. (1999). Male therapists' clinical bias: Influence of client gender roles and therapist gender role conflict. *Journal of Counseling Psychology, 46*, 51–60.

Wolfe, J., & Kimerling, R. (1997). Gender issues in the assessment of posttraumatic stress disorder. In J. P. Wilson & T. M. Keane (Eds.), *Assessing psychological trauma and PTSD* (pp. 192–238). New York: Guilford Press.

Wolfe, N. (1991). *The Beauty of Myth.* New York: William Morrow.

Worell, J., & Remer, P. (2003). *Feminist perspectives in therapy: Empowering diverse women.* (2nd ed.). Hoboken, NJ: Wiley.

Wright, J. C., Huston, A. C., Vandewater, E. A., Bickham, D. S., Scantlin, R, Kotler, J., et al. (2001). American children's use of electronic media in 1997: A national survey. *Journal of Applied Developmental Psychology, 22*, 31–47.

Zamostny, K. P., O'Brien, K. M., Baden, A. L., & Wiley, M. O. (2003). The practice of adoption: History, trends and social context. *Counseling Psychologist, 31*, 651–678.

CHAPTER 12

Counseling Psychology and Sexual Orientation:

History, Selective Trends, and Future Directions

JAMES M. CROTEAU
KATHLEEN J. BIESCHKE
RUTH E. FASSINGER
JESSICA L. MANNING

The past 3 decades witnessed a revolution in psychology's approach to science and practice on lesbian, gay, bisexual, and transgender (LGBT) issues. Prior to the mid-1970s, the predominant approach was one of pathology with a focus on curing or treating homosexuality (e.g., Rothblum, 2000). Two forces joined to change this approach radically. First, the open organizing of lesbian and gay communities combined with the burgeoning lesbian and gay rights movement began to change prevailing anti-LGBT social norms (Rothblum, 2000). Second, as a more affirmative perspective on LGBT people became visible in wider society, pioneering psychologists such as Evelyn Hooker were conducting scientific studies with improved methodological rigor (Rothblum, 2000). This research began to establish that same-sex sexual orientation per se was not associated with deficiencies in mental health.

These changes provided the impetus for professional activism in psychology (Fassinger, 1991; Morgan & Nerison, 1993; Rothblum, 2000). The American Psychiatric Association's 1973 removal of homosexuality from their list of mental disorders was a monumental historical event (Rothblum, 2000). The American Psychological Association (APA) followed suit in 1975 and further charged psychology with removing the stigma associated with homosexuality (Conger, 1975). The Committee on Lesbian, Gay, and Bisexual Concerns was established in the APA, as was the Association of Lesbian and Gay Psychologists, which became APA Division 44 (Society for the Psychological Study of Lesbian, Gay, and Bisexual Issues) in 1984 (Morgan & Nerison, 1993; Rothblum, 2000). Further, the APA governing council, challenged to follow through on its resolution to remove the stigma associated with homosexuality, has passed a number of resolutions in the past 2 decades, including those focusing on hate crimes, therapeutic responses to sexual orientation, LGB youth, parenting, teachers, the military, and marriage rights (see www.apa.org/pi/lgbc/policy/pshome.html). Psychology has undergone a radical transformation, and the prevailing model has shifted from pathology to affirmation and from locating homosexuality as the problem to identifying anti-LGBT social and institutional prejudices and practices as the problem.

In the past 15 years, the LGBT literature has grown so dramatically in quantity and breadth that a complete review is well beyond the scope of this chapter. For such overviews, readers can turn to two editions of a handbook on LGBT affirmative psychotherapy (Bieschke, Perez, & DeBord, 2007; Perez, DeBord, & Bieschke, 2000). Our aim here is to urge more counseling psychologists to become active contributors to LGBT affirmative psychology by focusing on scholarly contributions situated in our discipline and highlighting important ways that counseling psychologists can advance such work. Accordingly, in the first section, we discuss the history and current status of LGBT affirmative perspectives in counseling psychology. The second section discusses three areas of LGBT scholarship and research that are particularly suited to the perspectives of counseling psychology and in which counseling psychologists have made significant contributions: (1) sexual identity development, (2) vocational psychology, and (3) professional training and education. In the third section, we turn to counseling practice, review key findings in counseling research, and discuss the implications of these findings. Our critical review of the literature is selective, focusing on publications from within the past decade and emphasizing, but not limited to, contributions in counseling psychology.

We also note here our choices regarding LGBT terminology. Lesbian women, gay men, bisexual men and women, and transgender people often are considered together as sexual minorities due to shared oppression related to sexual and gender expression (Fassinger & Arseneau, 2007). Although a full discussion of the complexities of definition, identification, and labeling related to these groups is beyond the scope of this chapter (see Fassinger & Arseneau, 2007), we believe it is important to consider all four groups and we use the terms *LGBT* and *sexual and gender minorities* when doing so. When referring to a particular study or scholarly literature, we use terms indicative of the group(s) actually considered in that work.

HISTORY AND CURRENT STATUS OF LESBIAN, GAY, BISEXUAL, AND TRANSGENDER AFFIRMATIVE PERSPECTIVES

Counseling psychology was slow to embrace the study of sexual orientation issues and the affirmative perspective on LGBT people that emerged in the mid-1970s and 1980s. The *Counseling Psychologist* (*TCP*) and the *Journal of Counseling Psychology* (*JCP*) published only four articles on sexual orientation prior to the 1990s. In 1991, there was a landmark issue of *TCP* containing four articles that introduced counseling psychologists to lesbian and gay affirmative practice and served as a primer on sexual orientation issues for counseling psychologists (see Fassinger, 1991). Around this same time, the Society of Counseling Psychology (SCP, Division 17 of APA) began to attend to LGBT issues in its organization. An ad-hoc committee on LGB issues was formed, eventually becoming one of the first sections in the newly re-organized SCP in 1996. That group, now known as the Section on Lesbian/Gay/Bisexual Awareness, is very active in the Society (see www.div17.org/lgba/default.htm).

The 1990s saw a great expansion of LGBT affirmative perspectives in the counseling psychology literature. Indeed, we found that the numbers of articles in *TCP* and *JCP* have increased 10-fold in the past 15 years, including four multi-article major contributions in *TCP* and 13 research studies in *JCP*. Phillips, Ingram, Smith, and Mindes (2003) provided a content analysis of the LGBT literature in eight counseling psychology-related journals from 1990 to 1999, including *TCP* and *JCP*. The authors found a total of 119 articles in the eight journals, an average of almost 12 articles per year; this was a significant increase over an earlier period (1978–1989) in which a review of six of the eight journals yielded only 43 articles, an average of only 3.5 per year. Our own search of all eight journals over the years 2000 through 2005 revealed that the level of production has continued, with an average of 14 articles per year. Just 15 years ago, publications related to sexual orientation were few in number and almost any empirical study represented a contribution by filling a void in the knowledge base. Those circumstances have changed dramatically as an existing scholarly foundation has been built. Practice-oriented scholarship that provides very basic information about working with sexual minority clients in isolation from research and theory is no longer needed. Theory and research now must be built on prior findings, and issues of rigor, relevance, and complexity must be addressed more fully. Although the quality and rate of scholarship production clearly has increased significantly, Phillips and her colleagues found that only 2% of all articles reviewed focused on sexual orientation. This rate is much lower than might be expected given the percentage of the population affected by sexual and gender orientation issues; thus, increased attention to sexual orientation is a continuing concern.

Bieschke, Croteau, Lark, and Vandiver (2005) provided an additional perspective on the status of LGBT issues in counseling psychology in their examination of the narratives of diverse counseling professionals of all sexual orientations (cf. Croteau, Lark, Lidderdale, & Chung, 2005). They found that heterosexism is still strong in counseling and counseling psychology at both overt and covert levels and that this heterosexist discourse is supported by silence regarding sexual orientation issues. At the same time, an LGBT affirmative discourse is definitely present in the profession, but it needs strengthening in several important ways. Bieschke and colleagues asserted that the LGBT affirmative discourse in the profession is often shallow, affirming that "gay is okay" but failing to promote advocacy that would change systemic inequalities and heterosexist norms. They also challenged counseling professionals to move the LGBT affirmative discourse toward a recognition that sexual orientation exists in a web of interrelated social and cultural identities and contexts, and toward an incorporation of more complex and socially constructed notions of sexual orientation and identity. Further, the authors asserted that the profession must embrace the emerging concept of "difficult dialogues" and engage in exploration of the conflicts and tensions that exist around LGBT affirmation, especially regarding anti-LGBT religious beliefs and the inclusion of sexual orientation in definitions of multiculturalism.

This call for a deepening of the LGBT affirmative professional discourse in counseling psychology echoes some contemporary literature on the movement of LGBT psychology toward a new paradigm based on multiplicity of experience and contexts; on racial, ethnic, and cultural sensitivity and inclusion; and on embracing bisexual and transgender issues (see Garnets, 2002). This emerging paradigm no longer employs overly simplistic and dichotomous gay-straight notions of sexual orientation, single pathway models for developing a positive identity related to having a same- or both-gender sexual orientation, or decontextualized views that consider sexual orientation as separate from other social and cultural group statuses and contexts. In the following sections of this chapter, we note the extent to which this new paradigm has (or has not) been incorporated into the scholarly literature on the topics under consideration.

LESBIAN, GAY, BISEXUAL, AND TRANSGENDER AFFIRMATIVE SCHOLARSHIP AND RESEARCH IN COUNSELING PSYCHOLOGY

We selected sexual identity theory, vocational psychology, and professional training as areas for review because they fit well with counseling psychology's unique emphases and values and because they are areas in which counseling psychologists have made major contributions.

Sexual Identity Theory

Counseling psychologists have played a significant role in helping to shape what may be the most studied concept in LGBT affirmative psychology: sexual identity development, the process by which individuals develop a psychological sense of themselves that embraces their sexual orientation amidst pervasive societal heterosexism and sexual prejudice. The first lesbian and gay sexual identity models were developed in the late 1970s and 1980s (e.g., Cass, 1979, 1984; Coleman, 1978). Although there is widespread agreement among contemporary scholars that these models are often overly simplistic, exclusive, and decontextual (Fassinger & Arseneau, 2007; McCarn & Fassinger, 1996), they provided a much-needed theoretical cornerstone for the then-newly emerging LGB affirmative psychology.

Contemporary conceptions of sexual identity are slowly becoming consistent with the new paradigm for LGBT psychology that is more inclusive, culturally sensitive, and contextual. Newer theories of sexual identity give increasing attention to the experiences of women, bisexual men and women, and transgender people (e.g., Lev, 2007; Potoczniak, 2007; Sophie, 1985–1986) and address the ways in which racial, ethnic, and cultural differences profoundly influence the construction of sexual identity (e.g., Fukuyama & Ferguson, 2000; Greene, 2000). Moreover, scholars have turned toward perspectives that recognize the socially constructed nature of sexual identity, the necessity of anchoring conceptions of identity in particular social and cultural contexts, and the identification of differing pathways to identity based on those contexts. Counseling psychologists have played key roles in this evolution toward more complex conceptualizations of sexual identity, particularly in reference to the three areas of theory development discussed in the following subsections.

Dual Trajectory Lesbian and Gay Identity Model

Early sexual identity models involved a single developmental trajectory that included an (implicit or explicit) assumption that LGB individuals come to a sense of identity about their own internal experience of sexuality simultaneously with open identification as a member of a LGB reference group. Fassinger and her colleagues (Fassinger & Miller, 1996; McCarn & Fassinger, 1996) proposed the first sexual identity development model with two independent trajectories—one involving increased positive identification with a person's own internal sense of same-sex attraction and the other involving increased identification with an LGB reference group. Sexual minority individuals were hypothesized to move through phases of *awareness* (of difference), *exploration* (of a person's nascent feelings and attractions as well as the existence of LGBT people), *deepening* or *commitment* (to same-sex choices and group identification), and *internalization* or *synthesis* (of sexual minority identity and community into overall life) along each of these trajectories, with circular progressions, re-cycling, and location in multiple phases simultaneously possible. An individual also could be at different phases along each trajectory, and the trajectories might (or might not) influence one another. Further, individuals could develop a positive sense of self in relation to a same-sex orientation without strong identification with, involvement in, or political consciousness about the oppression of a particular reference group or community (i.e., could be in latter phases of individual and early phases of group trajectories).

This model is inclusive in that it allows possibilities for healthy negotiation of a same-sex orientation in contexts where living as an openly lesbian woman or gay man, connecting to lesbian and gay communities, or having a political consciousness about sexual orientation is not permissible or is culturally foreign. Moreover, it accounts for the successful integration of an individual sexual or romantic sense of self among a wide range of people with same-sex attractions (e.g., women in long-term relationships living in rural areas without connections to lesbian communities; racial or ethnic minority men who are sexually or romantically involved with men but identify primarily with their ethnic communities and do not identify as gay men). Although exhibiting the influences of earlier linear stage models and not explicitly framed from a social constructionist point of view, this model represents a significant departure from the notion that a single linear pathway can capture adequately the diverse experiences associated with sexual minority identities. The model has been recognized for its inclusiveness and for its rich applicability to counseling practice (e.g., Bieschke, Paul, & Blasko, 2007; Potoczniak, 2007). Empirical support for the model initially was provided by two Q-sort studies of small, diverse samples of lesbian women (McCarn, 1991) and gay men (Fassinger & Miller, 1996). These studies found that participants were able to sort items reliably that corresponded to the different phases of identity development as postulated in the model.

Subsequent research (see Fassinger, 2007) yielded two separate measures (Lesbian Identity Questionnaire [LIQ], Gay Identity Questionnaire [GIQ]) with subscales to assess each of the eight possible phases. Internal consistency reliability estimates for the eight phase subscales have ranged from poor (.29) to excellent (.94) across nine known studies; reliabilities for individual phase subscales (range = .57 to .94) generally have been found to be higher than those of the group phases (range = .29 to .82), and middle phase subscales somewhat lower than earlier and later phase subscales. These results are consistent with other kinds of identity development research (e.g., racial, feminist identity). These studies also have demonstrated that the identity phases and dual trajectories of the model are related in predictable ways to other relevant psychological variables such as self-esteem, identity disclosure, and community identification (which are related positively to later phases of development), as well as internalized homophobia and propensity to seek conversion therapy (which are related positively to earlier phases of development). Fassinger and colleagues currently are working on a large-scale validation of the model and measures with LGBT people of color (Risco & Fassinger, 2007). Some scholarship on the applicability of this model to practice also has appeared (e.g., Ritter & Terndrup, 2002), suggesting that there are many possibilities for counseling psychologists to use this model to explore the effects of dual identity trajectories in LGBT development.

Heterosexual Identity Models

Few scholars and researchers had addressed the development of heterosexual identity prior to a 2002 major contribution in *TCP* devoted to heterosexual identity that included two different models of heterosexual development (Mohr, 2002; Worthington, Savoy, Dillon, & Vernaglia, 2002). Worthington et al. (2002) created a developmental model that in some ways parallels the lesbian and gay dual trajectory model reviewed previously. Here we focus on the model developed by Mohr because it is particularly concerned with applying heterosexual identity concepts to counselors' work with LGBT clients. According to the model, counselors' experiences with personal sexuality and exposure to social information about sexual orientation influence the development of *working models of sexual orientation* (democratic, compulsory, politicized, and integrative). *Core motivations* of the individual (social acceptance and psychological consistency) reciprocally influence and inform the working models to form an adult heterosexual identity. There are fluctuations even when heterosexual identity is relatively stable. Thus, individuals enact a particular *identity state* for each specific *sexual orientation stimulus* and *immediate context* encountered. A heterosexual man whose working model of sexual orientation involves affirming LGB people (either from a politicized or integrative model), for example, may respond with polite laughter to a homophobic slur in a locker room context that values heterosexist masculinity. Thus, counselors must be vigilant about their own biases that might surface as stimuli and contexts change.

Little research and application concerning Worthington and colleagues' model (2002) has been published to date, and none concerning the Mohr (2002) model. Nevertheless, these foundational models offer many possibilities for counseling psychologists to explore ways in which heterosexuals understand their own sexual orientation and the oppression of LGBT people. The models can be applied and studied in relation to clinical work, anti-heterosexism education, and the training and supervision of heterosexual psychologists in LGBT affirmative practice.

Gender-Transgressive Identity Enactment

Fassinger and Arseneau's (2007) model of gender-transgressive sexual minority identity enactment takes a social constructionist and critical theory perspective that centralizes the contexts in which identity is enacted. Although the models reviewed earlier provide multiple pathways and possibilities for identity development, this latest model represents the most radical departure from prior work by abandoning logical positivist perspectives that seek to identify linear developmental sequences or common psychological experiences. This model is also unique in its umbrella focus on identities that transgress gender expectations both in terms of the gender of an individual's sexual or romantic partners (i.e., sexual orientation) and in terms of an individual's gender related expression (i.e., gender orientation or roles). Thus, the model is inclusive of consideration of both common and varying experiences across such identities as *lesbian, gay, bisexual,* and *transgender.*

Four contexts must be considered in understanding an individual's gender-transgressive sexual minority identity: (a) *gender orientation* or a sense of self in reference to male/female or masculine/feminine; (b) *sexual orientation* or a sense of sexuality and relational intimacy; (c) *cultural orientation* or sense of self along multicultural dimensions such as race, ethnicity, religion, disability status, and social class; and (d) *temporal influences* that include both the historical cohort of LGBT people to which an individual belongs and the individual's actual chronological age. Gender-transgressive sexual minorities enact their contextualized identity in four developmental arenas that include mental and physical health, relationships and families, education and work, and legal and political rights. Rather than providing a developmental categorization applied decontextually to sexual minority individuals, this model allows infinite variation in how gender-transgressive sexual identity is formed and expressed across many life arenas. Essentially the model is a broad mapping of contexts that may influence identity enactment for gender-transgressive people of all gender, racial, ethnic, cultural, and other social groups.

The model can be seen as a "bold" attempt to attend to the "complexities that separate lesbian, gay, bisexual and transgender communities" while still asserting the commonality of gender transgression (Bieschke, Perez, et al., 2007, p. 15). Perez (2007) points out that prior linear stage models have failed to take into account historical and community contexts and complexities, whereas this theoretical perspective "challenges therapists to question existing notions of identity construction and to begin considering the multiple constructions, layers, and methods through which LGBT identities (and even non-LGBT identities) are enacted" (p. 404). Given its recency, there is no empirical work yet to support (or challenge) its assumptions. This leaves many avenues for counseling psychologists to pursue, such as creating measures to tap the model's main constructs; exploring the complexities of gender orientation in a particular arena, such as education or work; or conceptualizing the integration of cultural and sexual orientation.

Lesbian, Gay, Bisexual, and Transgender Vocational Psychology

Only a few isolated efforts to address lesbian and gay vocational issues existed before two landmark publications of special issues and sections of the *Journal of Vocational Behavior* (Croteau & Bieschke, 1996) and the *Career Development Quarterly* (Pope, 1995). A subsequent review of the literature recognized these publications as major initial steps in building an LGBT vocational psychology (Croteau, Anderson, Distefano, & Kampa-Kokesch, 2000). This review also identified five primary areas of study in LGB vocational psychology: (1) LGB identity development; (2) discrimination and workplace climate; (3) managing sexual identity at work; (4) the influences of societal messages on occupational interests, choices, and perceptions; and (5) career interventions. Of these five areas, only two have received sustained scholarly attention: (1) discrimination and workplace climate and (2) disclosing or managing sexual identity (Lidderdale, Croteau, Anderson, Tovar-Murray, & Davis, 2007). We first discuss these two areas and then turn briefly to the "traditional" arenas that have been so central to the broader vocational psychology—career development, choice, and assessment. In the discussion that follows, it is important to note that the research and scholarship on LGBT career issues has devoted little attention to racial, ethnic, bisexual, and transgender diversity (Croteau et al., 2000). The general lack of inclusion in this literature is a strong cautionary note to any conclusions regarding LGBT career behavior that might be drawn based on existing theory or research. The new paradigm focused on multiplicity of experiences and cultural contexts very much remains an important front for future work in this area.

Early empirical work suggested that experiences of discrimination and hostility in the workplace are pervasive and that sexual identity negotiation in the workplace may be critical (Croteau, 1996; Croteau et al., 2000). Early quantitative studies lacked clear conceptual definitions and adequate measurement of these constructs, a problem that plagues more recent studies as well (see Croteau, Anderson, & VanderWal, in press). Further, inconsistency in definition and measurement across studies often makes it difficult to draw clear integrative conclusions. One example of this inconsistency is the research that finds negative workplace climates are related to limited identity disclosure by lesbian and gay workers. All of these studies have problems in defining one or both variables as well as inconsistency in measurement across studies, thus, preventing any firm conclusions about the relationship between climate and identity disclosure. Led largely by counseling psychologists, there have been promising advances recently in defining and measuring workplace climate and sexual identity management. As conceptual definition and measurement are critical to advancing research in this area, we focus here on these issues.

Workplace Climate

We identified three trends in the way in which workplace climate has been considered in the research literature: as the (1) presence or absence of nondiscrimination policies (e.g., Ragins & Cornwell, 2001), (2) level of LGBT supportiveness in the workplace (e.g., Griffith & Hebl, 2002), or (3) degree of heterosexism, homophobia, or discrimination in the workplace (e.g., Lyons, Brenner, & Fassinger, 2005). The presence or absence of LGBT-related organizational policies might be measured adequately by a few straightforward questions due to the relatively concrete and objective nature of this construct. The presence of support or heterosexism in a work climate, however, cannot be measured as simply. The abstract nature of such concepts can be understood differently across participants and, thus, clear conceptual definitions and careful operational measurement are needed.

Waldo (1999) and Liddle, Luzzo, Hauenstein, and Schuck (2004) have developed promising approaches to defining and measuring workplace climate that account for more than the simple presence of policies. Modeled on measures of the sexual harassment of women, Waldo developed the Workplace Heterosexism Experiences Questionnaire (WHEQ) to measure LGB workers' perceptions of harassment and discrimination based on their sexual orientation, ranging from subtle slights to overt hostility. Original psychometric evaluation yielded an internal consistency reliability estimate for the full scale of .93 and a two-factor structure involving indirect and direct experiences of heterosexism. Two other studies have shown similar reliability estimates and expected relationships to constructs such as unsupportive social interactions, depression, and distress (Lyons et al., 2005; Smith & Ingram, 2004).

More recently, Liddle and colleagues (2004) developed the Lesbian, Gay, Bisexual, and Transgendered Climate Inventory (LGBTCI), and it appears to be the most rigorously developed measure to date. The LGBTCI is intended to measure both positive and negative aspects of LGBT-related workplace climates, and item development occurred both qualitatively and quantitatively. In the final measure, internal consistency, split-half, and test-retest reliability estimates for total scores were excellent (.96, .97, and .87, respectively). Further, the measure correlated in expected ways with other measures of discrimination and with work satisfaction.

There also have been calls for theoretical contributions aimed at organizing and interpreting research, as well as guiding practice, related to LGBT workplace climate (Croteau et al., 2000; Lonborg & Phillips, 1996). Chung (2001) proposed the only theoretical model to date that attempts to explain dynamics relevant to workplace climate and provide a guide for career counseling practice. Chung identified three dimensions of workplace discrimination: (1) *formal* (institutional policies and decisions) versus *informal* (interpersonal dynamics and atmosphere); (2) *potential* (what might happen if sexual orientation is known) versus *encountered* (experienced discrimination); and (3) *real* (objective assessment of discrimination) versus *perceived* (subjective assessment of discrimination). Chung further explicated how workers cope with discrimination. Vocational choice coping involves three possible strategies: (1) self-employment, (2) entering jobs or careers known to be LGB affirmative, or (3) choosing to enter potentially hostile workplaces due to the impossibility of enacting the first two strategies, or because of the compelling nature of some careers or jobs. Those who work in less than fully affirmative environments have to cope with discrimination through work adjustment processes (e.g., silence, confrontation, or seeking support) or through managing the disclosure of their identity (see next section).

Counseling psychologists wishing to advance understanding of the impact of workplace climate on LGBT workers would do well to make use of these psychometric and theoretical advances in the literature. It is time for workplace climate to be approached with more theoretical and empirical rigor, and counseling psychologists can continue to take the lead in doing so.

Sexual Identity Management

Early quantitative research most often focused on the degree of self-disclosure of lesbian and gay workers, usually measured by asking for estimates of the number of people at work who knew of the worker's minority sexual orientation. At the same time, qualitative studies demonstrated that dealing with a lesbian or gay identity at work involves a complex series of decisions about disclosure that are motivated by multiple factors, indicating a need for an expanded focus on the process of identity management rather than quantity of disclosure (Anderson, Croteau, Chung, & DiStephano, 2001; Croteau et al., in press; Lidderdale et al., 2007). From a study of lesbian and gay teachers, Griffin (1992) developed a model involving four identity management strategies (*passing, covering, implicitly out*, and *explicitly out*) that fall along a continuum from safety-seeking nondisclosure at one end to integrity-seeking disclosure at the other end. In a study of gay men in the corporate world, Woods (1993) developed a framework involving the strategies of *counterfeiting, avoiding, acknowledging*, and *advocating*. Both of these models offer promise in capturing the multifaceted and ongoing nature of managing sexual identity at work as described in qualitative studies (Anderson et al., 2001; Croteau, 1996; Croteau et al., 2000), and both models have been advanced through measurement development.

Button's (2004) scale of identity management strategies was designed to measure Woods' (1993) framework. Button found internal consistency reliability values for the four subscales ranging from .80 to .88, but a factor analysis determined that a three-factor model best fit the data, containing subscales of counterfeiting, avoiding, and integrating. Similar internal consistency reliability estimates on these factor-derived three subscales have been found in other studies (e.g., Chrobot-Mason, Button, & DiClementi, 2001).

Anderson et al. (2001) developed a measure of workers' use of Griffin's (1992) four identity management strategies. An initial administration of the inventory revealed a range of internal consistency reliability estimates: (a) explicitly out (.87), (b) implicitly out (.53), (c) covering (.73), and (d) passing (.37). Factor analysis suggested that passing and covering combined into one factor. The measure also was shown to correlate generally in expected directions with measures of workplace disclosure and endorsement of descriptions of the identity management strategies. Both scales are promising self-report measures of sexual identity management (Anderson et al., 2001; Button, 2004); however, there needs to be more research attention, particularly in relation to factor structures. A study examining both instruments together could be especially enlightening.

Although specific strategies for sexual identity management have been proposed and studied, efforts to understand theoretically how different strategies become preferred and implemented have been much more limited. Croteau et al. (in press) identified only three such theoretical efforts—two from the organizational psychology literature and one from counseling psychology. The two organizational psychology models are somewhat similar and use stigma theory to explain how LGB workers might anticipate the consequences and weigh the costs and benefits of disclosing an invisible and stigmatized identity (Clair, Beatty, & MacLean, 2005; Ragins, in press). Ragins proposes that disclosure decisions are related to four types of antecedents: (1) the anticipated consequences of disclosure, including both costs and benefits; (2) the socially constructed characteristics of the anti-LGBT stigma (e.g., the degree that being LGB is perceived by others as disruptive); (3) psychological factors of LGB workers (e.g., the centrality of sexual identity to a worker's sense of self); and (4) environmental factors related to support for LGB people in the work environment. Ragins also conceptualizes the "disconnects" that can occur when disclosure varies across work and nonwork settings.

In counseling psychology, Lidderdale et al. (2007) proposed a social cognitive model of how LGB workers learn about, make sense of, and choose identity management strategies. The Workplace Sexual Identity Model (WSIM) focuses on how socially learned self-efficacy beliefs and outcome expectations about a range of sexual identity management strategies interact with contextual influences to determine strategy preferences, intentions, and behaviors. Person inputs and distal contextual influences combine with sexual and other social and cultural identity statuses to shape initial learning experiences that workers have in relation to sexual identity management strategies. Continual learning occurs as the worker experiences and makes cognitive sense of outcomes of actual or vicariously observed sexual identity management behaviors. These evolving learning experiences shape each LGBT worker's self-efficacy beliefs and outcome expectations about the various strategies for identity management, creating cognitions that determine both the range of, and preferences for, identity management strategies. Workers then develop intentions about which strategies to use and what behaviors to employ to implement intended strategies. Many proximal work-related and nonwork-related contextual factors moderate how preferences are translated into intentions as well as how intentions are translated into identity management behaviors. These proximal contextual influences include the immediate work situation, the workplace climate, the nature of the work role, interpersonal aspects of the worker's personal life, and the context of the larger community. Although this model holds promise for guiding both research and practice, it has not been empirically explored or tested.

We encourage future researchers to focus on sexual identity management processes rather than a simplistic quantification of disclosure. The measures described herein are promising and deserve more attention. Further, to test and employ WSIM, the central tenets of the model need verification. Measurement work must be done, particularly on self-efficacy beliefs and outcome expectations regarding various identity management strategies (Croteau et al., in press; Lidderdale et al., 2007). Moreover, attention should be given to the ways in which additional marginalized identity locations (e.g., due to race, ethnicity, gender, class, disability) increase the complexity of the identity management process. Counseling psychologists are particularly well prepared for this important work based on their training in psychometrics, vocational issues, and diversity.

Career Development, Choice, and Assessment

Career development and choice long have been a primary focus of vocational counseling psychologists, but attention to LGBT populations in this regard only recently has begun. Early efforts included several articles applying widely used vocational theories to the career issues of lesbians and gay men (Dunkle, 1996; Mobley & Slaney, 1996; Morrow, Gore, & Campbell, 1996). Although these articles offered useful practice applications and identified directions for research, empirical work has been limited. Chung and Harmon (1994) found that the Holland code classifications of gay men's career aspirations were less gender traditional than those of heterosexual men. Empirical data relative to Super's theory were reported by House (2004), Boatwright, Gilbert, Forrest, and Ketzenberger (1996), and Schmidt and Nilsson (2006), who found that the career development trajectories of their participants were compromised by sexual minority identity (e.g., facing discrimination, losing vocational energy due to coming out processes). One study investigated Latino lesbian and gay career development using a Social Cognitive Career Theory lens and found a complex interplay of contextual influences on vocational choice and planning (Adams, Cahill, & Ackerling, 2004). Nauta, Saucier, and Woodard (2001) used the role modeling aspect of social learning theory to investigate LGB students' experiences with vocational role models and found that, although LGB students reported having role models, they perceived less guidance and support from others in their academic and career decision making than did heterosexual students. Lyons et al. (2005) used the Theory of Work Adjustment to examine the extent to which person-environment fit mediated the impact of workplace heterosexism on job satisfaction, finding that almost half of LGB employees' job satisfaction was accounted for by perceptions of fit in their work environment, and that fit mediated the effects of workplace climate on job satisfaction. Finally, Tomlinson and Fassinger (2003) used Chickering's developmental theory to explore the effects of climate and identity variables on the vocational development of lesbian college students, finding that identity and campus climate interacted in their effects on both interpersonal relationship and vocational variables.

Another line of research in the traditional purview of vocational psychology includes work regarding career assessment and counseling. What little work that exists regarding sexual minority career clients is primarily conceptual. Chung (2003a, 2003b) offered thorough analyses of the state of the literature on career assessment and counseling with sexual minorities, highlighting the focus of existing work on gay men and urging more attention to lesbians as well as bisexual and transgender people. In one of the very few data-based efforts on career counseling with sexual minorities, Bieschke and Matthews

(1996) investigated career counselors' attitudes toward LGB clients, and found that counselors' own sexual orientation and a nonheterosexist organizational climate were the strongest predictors of gay affirmative career counseling.

Overall, as pointed out in several comprehensive reviews, very little research has explored career development, choice, counseling, or assessment with these populations (Croteau et al., 2000; Lidderdale et al., 2007). At this point, virtually nothing is known about what career counselors actually do with LGBT clients, including the extent to which they use formal assessment and how they deal with the potential inapplicability of existing concepts and measures to these populations. This area is ripe for future research, and the theoretical and limited empirical base in the area provides a useful foundation on which to build, using both qualitative and quantitative research approaches.

Professional Training and Education

Counseling psychologists long have been leaders in studying clinical supervision and graduate training. LGBT-affirmative training includes a wide range of professional training activities, such as clinical supervision, mentoring, changing trainee attitudes, counseling skills training, and attending to LGBT issues across the curriculum (Phillips, 2000). We first review recent research on the status of LGB affirmative training and then focus on studies that inform training indirectly by exploring graduate trainees' attitudes about LGB issues and clinical judgment. Finally, we discuss disparate scholarship focused on specific aspects of training.

State of Lesbian, Gay, and Bisexual Affirmative Training

Phillips and Fischer (1998) randomly selected programs in clinical and counseling psychology and asked training directors to administer a survey to six students in their final year of training prior to internship. Results from 108 usable surveys (a response rate of 36%) indicated that 94% of respondents scored toward the positive or accepting end of a homophobia scale. Additionally, students reported integration of mainly lesbian and gay, rather than bisexual, issues into a few of their courses (transgender issues were not studied). About half of the students reported being challenged to examine heterosexist bias, and students in counseling programs reported more attention to LGB issues than students in clinical programs. Results indicated inadequate training in LGB concerns overall, as respondents reported being unprepared to work with lesbian or gay clients, and particularly unprepared to work with bisexual clients. Formal coursework, exploration of personal biases, and contact with gay men accounted for a significant amount of variance in feelings of preparedness. Overall, the Phillips and Fischer study documents the importance of a wide range of training elements in the development of trainees' feelings of preparedness.

In 2005, Sherry, Whilde, and Patton surveyed training directors of accredited counseling and clinical programs about the incorporation of sexual minority issues into their programs. Fifty-one percent of those sampled responded to the survey. The majority reported that their programs meaningfully incorporated sexual minority issues into the curricula, but only a few reported that they assessed LGB competencies in yearly evaluations of students. Training directors of counseling programs reported more attention to LGB issues than did directors of clinical programs. Although the results of this study suggest more attention to sexual minority issues than was reported 7 years earlier in the Phillips and Fischer study, direct comparisons are ill-advised because Sherry et al. examined the perceptions of training directors, whereas Phillips and Fischer examined the perceptions of trainees.

These studies document important, but insufficient, inclusion of LGBT affirmative perspectives in graduate education in counseling psychology. Additional research that assesses the current state of training in LGBT issues on an ongoing basis is necessary, particularly concerning the extent to which programs are providing training in LGBT affirmative psychology that is inclusive and culturally sensitive. There seems to be a lack of inclusion of bisexual issues, and a completely unexplored issue is the extent to which training about transgender populations is provided. Further, little is known about how students learn to deal with the unique concerns of LGBT people further marginalized by oppression based on race, ethnicity, social class, disability, and other social statuses.

Trainee Attitudes and Clinical Judgments

Studies of trainee attitudes have found relatively high levels of self-reported affirmation of LGB individuals (Bieschke, McClanahan, Tozer, Grzegorek, & Park, 2000; Bieschke, Paul, et al., 2007). An analogue study of the relationship between client sexual orientation and counselor trainee homophobia revealed that homophobic trainees assigned significantly fewer positive adjectives to gay and lesbian than to heterosexual clients (Barrett & McWhirter, 2002). For male participants in particular, there was a positive relation between homophobia scores and the tendency to assign unfavorable adjectives to gay or lesbian clients, accounting for 16% of the variance.

In a rare effort addressing bisexual issues, Mohr, Israel, and Sedlacek (2001) investigated the degree to which attitudes about bisexuality influenced clinical practice. A sample of 97 counselor trainees participated in an analogue study using an intake vignette of a bisexual woman. Results indicated that attitudes toward bisexuality accounted for 25% of the variance in clinical judgment and reaction variables. Trainees who felt positively about bisexuality were more likely to view work with these clients positively and to perceive them to have high levels of psychosocial functioning. Additionally, trainees who viewed bisexuality as a stable and legitimate sexual orientation were less likely than others to rate the bisexual client in stereotypic ways, particularly in regard to problems with intimacy.

Kerr, Walker, Warner, and McNeill (2003) also used an analogue approach to investigate whether the lesbian sexual orientation of a client with dysthymic disorder influenced the clinical judgment of 157 trainees in clinical and counseling psychology programs. Participants who read a lesbian client vignette tended to attribute the client's dysthymic disorder to sexual orientation significantly more often than did participants who read the heterosexual client vignette. Students were not quick, however, to attribute dysthymia to sexual orientation—in all conditions, attributions for dysthymia were first attributed to two or three other presenting concerns.

Findings from these studies suggest that trainee attitudes about sexual minorities do influence their client appraisals. The mechanisms and nuances of such biases need further study. Future research also should move beyond analogue studies to include naturalistic studies of how trainees interact with actual sexual minority clients. Again, studies of reactions to transgender clients and to clients who face dual oppression (e.g., LGBT people of color) would facilitate a more inclusive understanding of sexual orientation attitudes and clinical judgments.

Specific Aspects of Professional Training

Seeking to investigate the process of developing LGB affirmative attitudes among counselors-in-training, Dillon et al. (2004) used consensual qualitative research to examine changes among members of a research team that was studying attitudes of heterosexuals toward sexual minorities. Results suggested that "team members' growth was evident, moving from maintaining socialized heterosexist and homophobic beliefs, assumptions, and behaviors toward becoming professional and personal heterosexual allies of the LGB community" (p. 174). Participants emphasized that an atmosphere characterized by safety and trust was necessary to explore their own biases and sexual identities. It is likely that the voluntary nature of the research team also contributed to meaningful exploration of attitudes toward LGB individuals; indeed, the authors identified "motivation" as one of the themes.

Lark and Croteau (1998) provided a rare focus on the experiences of LGB trainees. Utilizing a grounded theory approach to describe the mentoring experiences of 14 LGB doctoral students in counseling psychology, these authors found two themes that appeared to shape the mentoring relationship. One theme was the students' ongoing concern for their safety as LGB individuals in the training environment. The other theme was about how "out" to be, which involved the fear that disclosure might negatively influence their professional careers. Based on their data, the authors made several recommendations regarding mentoring. First, it seems important for mentors to convey clearly their affirmation of LGB individuals. Further, mentors must be perceived as safe, particularly in training environments characterized by silence or hostility. In addition, students with varying levels of outness will have different mentoring needs, and those with multiple identities may face additional complexities. Both LGB and heterosexual mentors need to consider carefully how their own sexual orientation influences the mentoring relationship, and mentors also must attend to unique boundary issues due to the relatively small size of many LGB communities.

Israel and Hackett (2004) are the only known researchers to employ experimental methods to investigate the effects of training on therapist attitudes toward LGB individuals. Their four conditions included (1) information only, (2) attitude exploration only, (3) information and attitude exploration, and (4) placebo. Participants who were assigned to one of the information conditions were significantly more knowledgeable at postintervention testing than those who did not receive information. Surprisingly, however, those assigned to one of the attitude exploration conditions reported significantly more negative attitudes after attitude training on LGB issues than trainees who had not explored their own attitudes. The authors explained the latter finding as possibly involving a reassessment of attitudes after becoming more conscious of personal biases (i.e., recognizing that previously held attitudes were not as positive as originally assumed). Bieschke, Paul, et al. (2007) speculated that another possible reason for this finding is that participants felt more comfortable being honest about their attitudes after prolonged exposure to the trainers' honesty.

Finally, in a unique application of theory to training, Bieschke, Eberz, Bard, and Croteau (1998) applied social cognitive career theory to trainees' experiences of LGBT affirmative research training. The authors discussed the influence of individual and contextual variables on the development of self-efficacy beliefs and outcome expectations specific to conducting LGBT-related research, and made specific recommendations for effective LGB affirmative scholarly training. Although focused on research training, this theoretical contribution may help counseling psychologists to be more deliberate in the design and implementation of training experiences across all professional roles and activities (e.g., clinical practice, supervision, teaching, advocacy). This theory lends itself to understanding key trainee cognitions related to developing or pursuing LGBT-related professional interests and also allows an understanding of contextual factors in the training environment that catalyze students' development or pursuit of such interests.

Overall, the literature on training in LGBT issues indicates definite attempts to provide affirmative training in graduate programs, but notable deficits in this literature need to be addressed. First, actual training interventions need to be designed, implemented, and evaluated more formally. Second, although a theoretical model of LGB affirmative supervision recently has been generated (see Halpert, Reinhardt, & Toohey, 2007), there have been no published empirical studies of affirmative supervision. Finally, almost no inquiry has been based in the emerging more inclusive and culturally sensitive paradigm in LGBT psychology (e.g., no research on training about transgender issues or LGBT people of color).

COUNSELING PRACTICE WITH SEXUAL MINORITY CLIENTS

In two reviews of research on the provision of counseling to LGB individuals, Bieschke and her colleagues concluded that the evidence suggests that lesbian and gay people are likely to seek therapy at higher rates than heterosexuals (Bieschke et al., 2000; Bieschke, Paul, et al., 2007). Reasons for this high utilization pattern have not been ascertained, although it has been speculated that distress created by the social stigma of sexual minority status may play a role (Cochran, Sullivan, & Mays, 2003). It also is reasonable to speculate that these high utilization rates indicate that clients find treatment useful, and the existing empirical data largely support such a conclusion (Bieschke et al., 2000; Bieschke, Paul, et al., 2007). High utilization rates and positive perceptions of helpfulness seem to indicate that professional psychologists are generally responsive to the needs of sexual minority clients (Bieschke et al., 2000; Bieschke, Paul, et al., 2007). We first review one of the most important recent trends in LGBT affirmative counseling research: establishing competencies for the provision of LGB-affirmative counseling and therapy. We then discuss a disturbing and controversial trend in recent research: the increased attention to providing conversion therapy.

Recent Developments Regarding LGBT Affirmative Counseling Competencies

Fassinger and Sperber Richie (1997) were among the first to suggest that models of multicultural counseling competency might be applied meaningfully to sexual orientation. Others have elaborated on this conceptualization and provided suggestions to enhance counseling competence in the three domains of attitudes, skills, and knowledge. Here we review several research efforts to elaborate or develop measures related to such competencies.

Israel, Ketz, Detrie, Burke, and Shulman (2003) used a Delphi technique to generate and rate counselor competencies. Ultimately, 33 knowledge, 23 attitude, and 32 skills competencies for working with LGB clients were identified as either "helpful" or "very important" by experts. These compose a taxonomy of competencies that could be used in both research and practice.

Bidell (2005) developed the Sexual Orientation Counselor Competency Scale (SOCCS) using multicultural counselor competency models. Results of an exploratory factor analysis supported a three-factor (attitudes, knowledge, and skills) solution that accounted for 40% of the total scale variance. Internal consistency reliability estimates on the three factor-analytically derived subscales ranged from .76 to .91, and 1-week test-retest reliability estimates ranged from .83 to .85. Preliminary validity data indicated that the SOCCS correlated as expected with measures of multicultural awareness and counselor self-efficacy. The SOCCS appears to be a promising instrument for research on counselor competencies, although it shares similar limitations with other multicultural competency self-report instruments concerning social desirability effects and an as yet undocumented relationship to treatment outcome.

Dillon and Worthington (2003) developed the Lesbian, Gay, and Bisexual Affirmative Counseling Self-Efficacy Inventory (LGB-CSI). Using exploratory and confirmatory factor analytic techniques, a five-factor measure was established, including Application of Knowledge, Advocacy Skills, Awareness, Relationship, and Assessment. Internal consistency estimates for each of the five factors were adequate (.83 to .96). Two-week test-retest reliability estimates ranged from .37 to .51. Evidence for discriminant validity suggested that the LGB-CSI was not strongly associated with socially desirable responding. As Dillon and Worthington noted, although their findings regarding the LGB-CSI are in need of replication and extension, the measure holds promise for use in understanding potentially important cognitive factors in training students to be competent with LGBT populations.

Conversion Therapy

Some clients experience considerable conflict about their minority sexual orientation and these clients may seek to change their sexual orientation via conversion therapy. Conversion therapy is defined as an attempt to change a same-sex sexual orientation, not merely an attempt to alter an individual's engagement in sexual behaviors with members of the same sex. Conversion therapy is often referred to as "reparative" or "reorientation" therapy, labels we eschew because they imply a faulty client sexual orientation.

Empirical research on conversion therapy suggests that clients who seek this kind of help tend to be religious and to experience their religious identity as incompatible with a sexual minority identity (Bieschke, Paul, et al., 2007). Tozer and Hayes (2004) found that participants who held homonegative beliefs, had an intrinsic religious identity, or were in the early phases of lesbian or gay identity development were more likely to view conversion therapy as an option. They also found that internalized homonegativity may serve to mediate the relationship between an intrinsic religious orientation and propensity to seek conversion therapy.

In their review of the recent research on conversion therapy, Bieschke, Paul, et al. (2007) concluded that it is ineffective in changing sexual orientation. Across studies, evidence pointed to a small number of highly motivated individuals reporting some type of change, usually a shift in their behavior toward same-sex others rather than a change in their orientation, feelings, or attractions. Some participants in qualitative studies reported that, even when sexual orientation change was unsuccessful, the process of exploring the conflict between their religious and sexual identity was beneficial. A very small minority of participants also reported a belief that they had made a sexual orientation shift, but it is difficult to interpret these results in the absence of accurate measurement of sexual orientation prior to intervention as well as long-term follow-up studies.

More important, there is substantial evidence to suggest that conversion therapy has the potential to cause harm (Beckstead & Morrow, 2004; Schroeder & Shidlo, 2001; Shidlo & Schroeder, 2002), and the APA has issued a resolution strongly criticizing its use with clients. We agree with Morrow and Beckstead (2004) that a dichotomous conceptualization of a person's status in regard to sexual orientation (e.g., out-gay versus ex-gay) precludes the exploration of a wide variety of options for identity expression. We recommend that readers consult Beckstead and Israel (2007) and other sources cited there for help in working with clients involving identity conflict and religious issues.

CONCLUSION

We were highly selective about the topics reviewed here; there are many other areas of study in LGBT affirmative psychology in which counseling psychologists have made significant contributions as well as important areas for counseling psychologists to consider for future study. Some of these areas include couples and relationships; parenting; adolescents and school safety; aging and gerontology; and prevention and psychoeducation (see Bieschke, Perez, et al., 2007; Perez et al., 2000). Our intention here is to encourage more scholarly contributions to LGBT affirmative psychology, and we have suggested a number of viable research directions for counseling psychologists to pursue.

We particularly encourage scholarship that fosters the movement of LGBT psychology toward the new paradigm that we have outlined here. This paradigm would produce research that incorporates a multiplicity of experiences and contexts; racial, ethnic, and cultural sensitivity; and the embracing of bisexual and transgender issues. As multiculturalism increasingly becomes central to the way that counseling psychologists conceptualize their work—both in science and practice—it becomes more and more critical to ensure that sexual orientation is understood as fully integrated with gender, race, ethnicity, culture, class, disability, and other aspects of social location. Counseling psychologists are uniquely positioned by their history, values, and training to take the lead in creating a truly inclusive LGBT affirmative psychology, and it is our hope that this chapter provides direction for our colleagues in undertaking this timely and essential work.

REFERENCES

Adams, E. M., Cahill, B. J., & Ackerling, S. J. (2004). A qualitative study of Latino lesbian and gay youths' experiences with discrimination and the career development process. *Journal of Vocational Behavior, 66*, 199–218.

Anderson, M. Z., Croteau, J. M., Chung, Y. B., & DiStephano, T. M. (2001). Developing an assessment of sexual identity management for lesbian and gay workers. *Journal of Career Assessment, 9*, 243–260.

Barrett, K. A., & McWhirter, B. T. (2002). Counselor trainees' perceptions of clients based on client sexual orientation. *Counselor Education and Supervision, 41*, 219–232.

Beckstead, A. L., & Israel, T. (2007). Affirmative counseling and psychotherapy focused on issues related to sexual orientation conflicts. In K. J. Bieschke, R. M. Perez, & K. A. DeBord (Eds.), *Handbook of counseling and psychotherapy with lesbian, gay, bisexual, and transgender clients* (2nd ed., pp. 221–244). Washington, DC: American Psychological Association.

Beckstead, A. L., & Morrow, S. L. (2004). Mormon clients' experiences of conversion therapy: The need for a new treatment approach. *Counseling Psychologist, 32*, 651–691.

Bidell, M. P. (2005). The Sexual Orientation Counselor Competency Scale: Assessing attitudes, skills, and knowledge of counselors working with lesbian, gay, and bisexual clients. *Counselor Education and Supervision, 44*, 267–279.

Bieschke, K. J., Croteau, J. M., Lark, J. S., & Vandiver, B. J. (2005). Toward a discourse of sexual orientation equity in the counseling professions. In J. M. Croteau, J. S. Lark, M. A. Lidderdale, & Y. B. Chung (Eds.), *Deconstructing heterosexism in the counseling professions: A narrative approach* (pp. 189–210). Thousand Oaks, CA: Sage.

Bieschke, K. J., Eberz, A. B., Bard, C. C., & Croteau, J. M. (1998). Applying social cognitive theory to the creation of GLB-affirmative research training environments. *Counseling Psychologist, 26*, 735–753.

Bieschke, K. J., & Matthews, C. (1996). Career counselor attitudes and behaviors toward gay, lesbian, and bisexual clients. *Journal of Vocational Behavior, 48*, 243–255.

Bieschke, K. J., McClanahan, M., Tozer, E., Grzegorek, J. L., & Park, J. (2000). Programmatic research on the treatment of lesbian, gay, and bisexual clients: The past, the present, and the course for the future. In R. M. Perez, K. A. DeBord, & K. J. Bieschke (Eds.), *Handbook of counseling and psychotherapy with lesbian, gay, and bisexual clients* (pp. 309–336). Washington, DC: American Psychological Association.

Bieschke, K. J., Paul, P. L., & Blasko, K. A. (2007). Review of empirical research focused on the experience of lesbian, gay, and bisexual clients in counseling and psychotherapy. In K. J. Bieschke, R. M. Perez, & K. A. DeBord (Eds.), *Handbook of counseling and psychotherapy with lesbian, gay, bisexual, and transgender clients* (2nd ed., 293–316) Washington, DC: American Psychological Association.

Bieschke, K. J., Perez, R. M., & DeBord, K. A. (Eds.). (2007). *Handbook of counseling and psychotherapy with lesbian, gay, bisexual, and transgender clients* (2nd ed.). Washington, DC: American Psychological Association.

Boatwright, K. J., Gilbert, M. S., Forrest, L., & Ketzenberger, K. (1996). Impact of identity development upon career trajectory: Listening to the voices of lesbian women. *Journal of Vocational Behavior, 48*, 210–228.

Button, S. B. (2004). Identity management strategies utilized by lesbian and gay employees: A quantitative investigation. *Group and Organization Management, 29*, 470–494.

Cass, V. C. (1979). Homosexual identity formation: A theoretical model. *Journal of Homosexuality, 4*, 219–236.

Cass, V. C. (1984). Homosexual identity formation: Testing a theoretical model. *Journal of Sex Research, 20*, 143–167.

Chrobot-Mason, D., Button, S. B., & DiClementi, J. D. (2001). Sexual identity management strategies: An exploration of antecedents and consequences. *Sex Roles, 45*, 321–336.

Chung, Y. B. (2001). Work discrimination and coping strategies: Conceptual frameworks for counseling lesbian, gay, and bisexual clients. *Career Development Quarterly, 50*, 33–44.

Chung, Y. B., (2003a). Career counseling with lesbian, gay, bisexual, and transgendered persons: The next decade. *Career Development Quarterly, 52*, 78–86.

Chung, Y. B. (2003b). Ethical and professional issues in career assessment with lesbian, gay, and bisexual persons. *Journal of Career Assessment, 11*, 96–112.

Chung, Y. B., & Harmon, L. W. (1994). The career interests and aspirations of gay men: How sex-role orientation is related. *Journal of Vocational Behavior, 45*, 223–239.

Clair, J. A., Beatty, J. E., & MacLean, T. L. (2005). Out of sight but not out of mind: Managing invisible social identities in the workplace. *Academy of Management Review, 30*, 78–95.

Cochran, S. D., Sullivan, J. G., & Mays, V. M. (2003). Prevalence of mental disorders, psychological distress, and mental health services use among lesbian, gay and bisexual adults in the United States. *Journal of Consulting and Clinical Psychology, 71*, 53–61.

Coleman, E. (1978). Toward a new model of homosexuality: A review. *Journal of Homosexuality, 3*, 345–359.

Conger, J. (1975). Proceedings of the American Psychological Association, Incorporated, for the year 1974: Minutes of the annual meeting of Council of Representatives. *American Psychologist, 30*, 620–651.

Croteau, J. M. (1996). Research on the work experiences of lesbian, gay, and bisexual people: An integrative review of methodology and findings [Special issue]. *Journal of Vocational Behavior, 48*, 195–209.

Croteau, J. M., Anderson, M. Z., Distefano, T. M., & Kampa-Kokesch, S. (2000). Lesbian, gay, and bisexual vocational psychology: Reviewing and planning construction. In R. M. Perez, K. A. DeBord, & K. J. Bieschke (Eds.), *Handbook of counseling and psychotherapy with lesbian, gay, and bisexual clients* (pp. 383–408). Washington, DC: American Psychological Association.

Croteau, J. M., Anderson, M. Z., & VanderWal, B. L. (in press). Models of workplace sexual identity disclosure and management: Reviewing and extending concepts. *Group and Organizational Management.*

Croteau, J. M., & Bieschke, K. J. (1996). Beyond pioneering: An introduction to the special issue on the vocational issues of lesbian women and gay men [Special issue]. *Journal of Vocational Behavior, 48,* 119–124.

Croteau, J. M., Lark, J. S., Lidderdale, M. A., & Chung, Y. B. (Eds.). (2005). *Deconstructing heterosexism in the counseling professions: A narrative approach.* Thousand Oaks, CA: Sage.

Dillon, F. R., & Worthington, R. L. (2003). The Lesbian, Gay, and Bisexual Affirmative Counseling Self-Efficacy Inventory (LGB-CSI): Development, validation, and training implications. *Journal of Counseling Psychology, 50,* 235–251.

Dillon, F. R., Worthington, R. L., Savoy, H. B., Rooney, S. C., Becker-Schutte, A., & Guerra, R. M. (2004). On becoming allies: A qualitative study of lesbian-, gay-, and bisexual-affirmative counselor training. *Counselor Education and Supervision, 43,* 162–178.

Dunkle, J. H. (1996). Toward an integration of gay and lesbian identity development and Super's life-span approach. *Journal of Vocational Behavior, 48,* 149–159.

Fassinger, R. E. (1991). The hidden minority: Issues and challenges in working with lesbian women and gay men. *Counseling Psychologist, 19,* 151–176.

Fassinger, R. E. (2007). *Measuring lesbian and gay identity development processes: Testing a dual-trajectory model.* Unpublished manuscript, University of Maryland.

Fassinger, R. E., & Arseneau, J. R. (2007). "I'd rather get wet than be under that umbrella": Differentiating the experiences and identities of lesbian, gay, bisexual, and transgender people. In K. J. Bieschke, R. M. Perez, & K. A. DeBord (Eds.), *Handbook of counseling and psychotherapy with lesbian, gay, bisexual, and transgender clients* (2nd ed., pp. 19–50). Washington, DC: American Psychological Association.

Fassinger, R. E., & Miller, B. A. (1996). Validation of an inclusive model of sexual minority identity formation on a sample of gay men. *Journal of Homosexuality, 32,* 53–78.

Fassinger, R. E., & Sperber Richie, B. (1997). Sex matters: Gender and sexual orientation training for multicultural counseling competency. In D. B. Pope-Davis & H. L. K. Coleman (Eds.), *Multicultural counseling competencies: Assessment, education and training, and supervision* (pp. 83–110). Thousand Oaks, CA: Sage.

Fukuyama, M. A., & Ferguson, A. D. (2000). Lesbian, gay, and bisexual people of color: Understanding cultural complexity and managing multiple oppressions. In R. M. Perez, K. A. DeBord, & K. J. Bieschke (Eds.), *Handbook of counseling and psychotherapy with lesbian, gay, and bisexual clients* (pp. 81–106). Washington, DC: American Psychological Association.

Garnets, L. D. (2002). Sexual orientations in perspective. *Cultural Diversity and Ethnic Minority Psychology, 8,* 115–129.

Greene, B. (2000). Beyond heterosexism and across the cultural divide: Developing an inclusive lesbian, gay, and bisexual psychology: A look to the future. In B. Greene (Ed.), *Education, research, and practice in lesbian, gay, bisexual, and transgendered psychology* (pp. 1–45). Thousand Oaks, CA: Sage.

Griffin, P. (1992). From hiding out to coming out: Empowering lesbian and gay educators. In K. M. Harbeck (Ed.), *Coming out of the classroom closet* (pp. 167–196). Binghamton, NY: Harrington Park Press.

Griffith, K. H., & Hebl, M. R. (2002). The disclosure dilemma for gay men and lesbians: "Coming out" at work. *Journal of Applied Psychology, 87,* 111–119.

Halpert, S. C., Reinhardt, B., & Toohey, M. J. (2007). Affirmative clinical supervision. In K. J. Bieschke, R. M. Perez, & K. A. DeBord, (Eds.), *Handbook of counseling and psychotherapy with lesbian, gay, bisexual, and transgender clients* (2nd ed., pp. 341–358). Washington, DC: American Psychological Association.

House, C. J. C. (2004). Integrating barriers to Caucasian lesbians' career development and Super's life-span, life-space approach. *Career Development Quarterly, 52,* 246–255.

Israel, T., & Hackett, G. (2004). Counselor education on lesbian, gay, and bisexual issues: Comparing information and attitude exploration. *Counselor Education and Supervision, 43,* 179–191.

Israel, T., Ketz, K., Detrie, P. M., Burke, M. C., & Shulman, J. L. (2003). Identifying counselor competencies for working with lesbian, gay, and bisexual clients. *Journal of Gay and Lesbian Psychotherapy, 7,* 3–21.

Kerr, S. K., Walker, W. R., Warner, D. A., & McNeill, B. W. (2003). Counselor trainees' assessment and diagnosis of lesbian clients with dysthymic disorder. *Journal of Psychology and Human Sexuality, 15,* 11–26.

Lark, J. S., & Croteau, J. M. (1998). Lesbian, gay, and bisexual doctoral students' mentoring relationships with faculty in counseling psychology: A qualitative study. *Counseling Psychologist, 26,* 754–776.

Lev, A. I. (2007). Transgender communities: Developing identity through connection. In K. J. Bieschke, R. M. Perez, & K. A. DeBord (Eds.), *Handbook of counseling and psychotherapy with lesbian, gay, bisexual, and transgender clients* (2nd ed., pp. 147–176). Washington, DC: American Psychological Association.

Lidderdale, M. A., Croteau, J. M., Anderson, M. Z., Tovar-Murray, D., & Davis, J. M. (2007). Building lesbian, gay, and bisexual vocational psychology: A theoretical model of workplace sexual identity management. In K. J. Bieschke, R. M. Perez, & K. A. DeBord (Eds.), *Handbook of counseling and psychotherapy with lesbian, gay, bisexual, and transgender clients* (2nd ed., pp. 245–270). Washington, DC: American Psychological Association.

Liddle, B. J., Luzzo, D. A., Hauenstein, A. L., & Schuck, K. (2004). Construction and validation of the lesbian, gay, bisexual, and transgendered climate inventory. *Journal of Career Assessment, 12,* 33–50.

Lonborg, S. D., & Phillips, J. M. (1996). Investigating the career development of gay, lesbian, and bisexual people: Methodological considerations and recommendations [Special issue]. *Journal of Vocational Behavior, 48,* 176–194.

Lyons, H. Z., Brenner, B. R., & Fassinger, R. E. (2005). A multicultural test of the theory of work adjustment: Investigating the role of heterosexism and fit perceptions in the job satisfaction of lesbian, gay, and bisexual employees. *Journal of Counseling Psychology, 52,* 537–548.

McCarn, S. R. (1991). *Validation of a model of sexual minority (lesbian) identity development.* Unpublished master's thesis, University of Maryland at College Park.

McCarn, S. R., & Fassinger, R. E. (1996). Revisioning sexual minority identity formation: A new model of lesbian identity and its implications for counseling and research. *Counseling Psychologist, 24,* 508–534.

Mobley, M., & Slaney, R. B. (1996). Holland's theory: Its relevance for lesbians and gay men. *Journal of Vocational Behavior, 48,* 125–135.

Mohr, J. J. (2002). Heterosexual identity and the heterosexual therapist: An identity perspective on sexual orientation dynamics in psychotherapy. *Counseling Psychologist, 30,* 532–566.

Mohr, J. J., Israel, T., & Sedlacek, W. E. (2001). Counselors' attitudes regarding bisexuality as predictors of counselors' clinical responses: An analogue study of a female bisexual client. *Journal of Counseling Psychology, 48,* 212–222.

Morgan, K. S., & Nerison, R. M. (1993). Homosexuality and psychopolitics: An historical overview. *Psychotherapy: Theory, Research, Practice, Training, 30,* 133–140.

Morrow, S. L., & Beckstead, A. (2004). Conversion therapies for same-sex attracted clients in religious conflict: Context, predisposing factors, experiences, and implications for therapy. *Counseling Psychologist, 32,* 641–650.

Morrow, S. L., Gore, P. A., & Campbell, B. W. (1996). The application of a sociocognitive framework to the career development of lesbian women and gay men. *Journal of Vocational Behavior, 48,* 136–148.

Nauta, M. M., Saucier, A. M., & Woodard, L. E. (2001). Interpersonal influences on students' academic and career decisions: The impact of sexual orientation. *Career Development Quarterly, 49,* 352–362.

Perez, R. M. (2007). The "boring" state of research and psychotherapy with lesbian, gay, bisexual, and transgender clients: Revisiting Barón (1991). In K. J. Bieschke, R. M. Perez, & K. A. DeBord (Eds.), *Handbook of counseling and psychotherapy with lesbian, gay, bisexual, and transgender clients* (2nd ed., pp. 399–418). Washington, DC: American Psychological Association.

Perez, R. M., DeBord, K. A., & Bieschke, K. J. (Eds.). (2000). *Handbook of counseling and psychotherapy with lesbian, gay, and bisexual clients.* Washington, DC: American Psychological Association.

Phillips, J. C. (2000). Training issues and considerations. In R. M. Perez, K. A. DeBord, & K. J. Bieschke (Eds.), *Handbook of counseling and psychotherapy with lesbian, gay, and bisexual clients* (pp. 337–358). Washington, DC: American Psychological Association.

Phillips, J. C., & Fischer, A. R. (1998). Graduate students' training experiences with lesbian, gay, and bisexual issues. *Counseling Psychologist, 26,* 712–734.

Phillips, J. C., Ingram, K. M., Smith, N. G., & Mindes, E. J. (2003). Methodological and content review of lesbian-, gay-, and bisexual-related articles in counseling journals: 1990–1999. *Counseling Psychologist, 31,* 25–62.

Pope, M. (1995). Gay and lesbian career development: Introduction to the special section. *Career Development Quarterly, 44,* 146–147.

Potoczniak, D. J. (2007). Development of bisexual men's identities and relationships. In K. J. Bieschke, R. M. Perez, & K. A. DeBord (Eds.), *Handbook of counseling and psychotherapy with lesbian, gay, bisexual, and transgender clients* (2nd ed., 119–146) Washington, DC: American Psychological Association.

Ragins, B. R. (in press). Disclosure disconnects: Antecedents and consequences of disclosing invisible stigmas across life domains. *Academy of Management Review.*

Ragins, B. R., & Cornwell, J. M. (2001). Pink triangles: Antecedents and consequences of perceived workplace discrimination against gay and lesbian employees. *Journal of Applied Psychology, 86*, 1244–1261.

Risco, C., & Fassinger, R. E. (2007). *Exploring identity processes for LGB people of color: Validation of a dual-trajectory model of sexual minority development.* Unpublished manuscript, University of Maryland.

Ritter, K. Y., & Terndrup, A. I. (Eds.). (2002). *Handbook of affirmative psychotherapy with lesbians and gay men.* New York: Guilford Press.

Rothblum, E. D. (2000). "Somewhere in Des Moines or San Antonio": Historical perspectives on lesbian, gay, and bisexual health. In R. M. Perez, K. A. DeBord, & K. J. Bieschke (Eds.), *Handbook of counseling and psychotherapy with lesbian, gay, and bisexual clients* (pp. 57–80). Washington, DC: American Psychological Association.

Schmidt, C. K., & Nilsson, J. E. (2006). The effects of simultaneous developmental processes: Factors relating to the career development of lesbian, gay, and bisexual youth. *Career Development Quarterly, 55*, 22–37.

Schroeder, M., & Shidlo, A. (2001). Ethical issues in sexual orientation conversion therapies: An empirical study of consumers. *Journal of Gay and Lesbian Psychotherapy, 5*, 131–166.

Sherry, A., Whilde, M. R., & Patton, J. (2005). Gay, lesbian, and bisexual training competencies in American Psychological Association accredited graduate programs. *Psychotherapy: Theory, Research, Practice, Training, 42*, 116–120.

Shidlo, A., & Schroeder, M. (2002). Changing sexual orientation: A consumers' report. *Professional Psychology: Research and Practice, 33*, 249–259.

Smith, N. G., & Ingram, K. M. (2004). Workplace heterosexism and adjustment among lesbian, gay, and bisexual individuals: The role of unsupportive social interactions. *Journal of Counseling Psychology, 51*, 57–67.

Sophie, J. (1985–1986). A critical examination of stage theories of lesbian identity development. *Journal of Homosexuality, 12*, 39–51.

Tomlinson, M., & Fassinger, R. E. (2003). Career development, lesbian identity development, and campus climate among lesbian college students. *Journal of College Student Development, 44*, 845–860.

Tozer, E. E., & Hayes, J. A. (2004). Why do individuals seek conversion therapy? *Counseling Psychologist, 32*, 716–741.

Waldo, C. R. (1999). Working in a majority context: A structural model of heterosexism as minority stress in the workplace. *Journal of Counseling Psychology, 46*, 218–232.

Woods, J. D. (1993). *The corporate closet: The professional lives of gay men in America.* New York: Free Press.

Worthington, R. L., Savoy, H. B., Dillon, F. R., & Vernaglia, E. R. (2002). Heterosexual identity development: A multidimensional model of individual and social identity. *Counseling Psychologist, 30*, 496–531.

CHAPTER 13

Advances in Conceptualizing and Studying Disability

DAVID B. PETERSON
TIMOTHY R. ELLIOTT

Counseling psychology has maintained an historic interest in the well-being of people who live with chronic and disabling health conditions. Indeed, the term *counseling psychologist* was coined by the Veterans Administration as it formalized psychological services for veterans returning from World War II. Many of these veterans had incurred disabling conditions in service to their country (Whitely, 1984). However, it may be argued that, over subsequent decades, counseling psychology has strayed from its initial concern with research, service, and policy issues associated with disability. This evolution has been partly influenced by federal and state funding agencies that assumed leadership for resolving the health, vocational, and social inequities faced by persons with disabilities. During the golden age of this federal sponsorship (Rusalem, 1976), federal legislation mandated funds to expand health, vocational, and educational services to persons with disabilities; train professionals to provide these services; and increase architectural accessibility (see Elliott & Leung, 2005).

Many counseling psychology training programs benefited from this support. Counseling psychology faculty at the University of Minnesota obtained funds that sponsored the development and refinement of the Minnesota Theory of Work Adjustment (Dawis & Lofquist, 1984). Federal funds obtained by the counseling psychology faculty at the University of Missouri-Columbia resulted in the publication of one of the most influential documents in vocational rehabilitation (McGowan & Porter, 1967). Federal funds also supported graduate students who would eventually assume leadership positions in the Division of Counseling Psychology. Many counseling psychologists (e.g., John McGowan, Cecil Patterson) were also elected to leadership positions of associations representing rehabilitation counseling.

Federal initiatives were responsible for initiating the systematic study of psychological and social issues related to disabilities, helping to spur the growth of counseling psychology. Studies of attitudinal and social factors that impede access to services formed some of the early pioneering work that defined the social-clinical-counseling psychology interface. Federal initiatives also mandated the study of racial and ethnic factors in disability and adjustment, long before multicultural issues were realized as the "fourth force" in psychology (Pedersen, 2000). However, much of this work was atheoretical in nature as a clear premium was placed on the refinement of existing medical and vocational services to persons with disability.

Over the past 40 years, studies of disability have become synonymous with the field of vocational rehabilitation. During this time, psychologists in medical settings and comfortable with medical model conceptions of disability have been increasingly likely to study psychological aspects of the disability experience and to provide psychological services to persons with disabilities. Counseling psychology's involvement in the study of disability has waned during this same period. This decline is reflected in the decreased appearance of disability-related articles in the *Journal of Counseling Psychology*. Disability-related topics (physical, intellectual, and sensory disabilities and associated services) appeared in the titles of 18 articles published in the 10 volumes of the journal published from 1970 through 1979. But it took another 27 volumes of the journal for the next set of 18 articles on disability to accumulate over the years 1980 through 2006 (volumes 27 through 53).

Many factors now compel us to regard disability from a new perspective as counseling psychology enters the twenty-first century. Persons with disabilities constitute one of the largest minority groups in the United States. In addition, an estimated 45% of persons in the United States live with a chronic health condition that has some disabling features (World Health Organization [WHO], 2002). Health care policy and service delivery systems have been overwhelmed by the costs incurred in responding to the acute and long-term needs of these individuals. These changes have ushered in new challenges and unanticipated opportunities for counseling psychologists. This chapter is based on the assumption that it is important to prepare the current and next generation of counseling psychologists for these challenges and opportunities. To aid this process, we review historical conceptions of disability, and in particular, how these conceptions have been altered by a new classification system developed by the World Health Organization—the *International Classification of Functioning, Disability, and Health* (*ICF*; WHO, 2001). The *ICF* is reviewed next and its implications for counseling psychology theory, research, practice, and training is discussed.

PREVALENCE OF DISABILITY

Approximately 49.7 million people in the United States live with some type of long-lasting health condition or disability (U.S. Census Bureau, 2003). Of this number, 9.3 million (almost 4%) have a sensory disability involving sight or hearing; 2.2 million (over 8%) have a condition limiting basic physical activities, such as walking, climbing stairs, reaching, lifting, or carrying; 12.4 million (almost 5%) live with a physical, mental, or emotional condition causing difficulty in learning, remembering, or concentrating; 6.8 million (2.6%) live with a physical, mental, or emotional condition causing difficulty in dressing, bathing, or getting around inside the home; 18.2 million people aged 16 and older live with conditions that make it difficult to go outside the home to shop or visit a doctor; and 21.3 million of those age 16 to 64 live with a condition that affects their ability to work at a job or business. Disability rates escalate with age for both men and women, and over 46% of people with a disability report having more than one disabling condition. Persons between the ages of 16 and 64 are less likely to be employed if they are disabled and 8.7 million people with disabilities experience low socioeconomic status (U.S. Census Bureau, 2003). These data are based on reports from only those persons who responded to the Census 2000 form and, thus, may significantly under-represent persons living with chronic disabilities in the United States.

Increases in Disability Rates

Chronic health and disabling conditions are increasing throughout the world (WHO, 2002). In the next 15 years, it is estimated that chronic, disabling conditions and mental disorders will account for 78% of the global disease burden in developing countries (WHO, 2002, p. 13). The disability experience can be influenced by access to rehabilitative services, cultural stereotypes among service providers, national differences in approaches to treating disabilities, service utilization and health care costs in different countries and cultures, disparities in the epidemiology of various disabilities at the international level, differences in governmental policies, collaborative efforts between health care providers and grassroots leaders, and differences in values and views of disability in various societies (WHO, 2002). Differences may also exist in cultural meanings attached to disability and quality of life, in attitudes and perceptions of disability, and in the role of the family and society relative to disability management (Murdick, Shore, Chittooran, & Gartin, 2004).

Causes and Costs

Advancements in medical technology have resulted in improved treatment of acute medical conditions and longer life expectancy for people with disabilities (Peterson & Aguiar, 2004; Tarvydas, Peterson, & Michaelson, 2005). Many disabilities result from lifestyle factors that include unhealthy behaviors and consumption patterns, inadequate prevention of disease and injuries, or from improper management of other chronic health conditions (WHO, 2002). Well-known health problems associated with disability include diabetes (American Diabetes Association, 2003), obesity (National Task Force on the Prevention and Treatment of Obesity, 2000), cardiovascular disease (Keil et al., 1989), and multiple visual impairments (Rudberg, Furner, Dunn, & Cassel, 1993).

Disability imposes serious economic consequences (WHO, 2002). Direct and indirect costs associated with disability are expected to escalate with the increasing number of persons who will live with a disability over the next several decades (U.S. Department of Health & Human Services, 2000). On average, persons with disabilities spend more than four times as much on medical care, services, and equipment as their nondisabled counterparts (Max, Rice, & Trupin, 1995). In general, higher health care costs are associated with chronic physical disability and its secondary complications. These costs include loss in employment productivity, impaired quality of life, problems with psychosocial functioning, and management of chronic disease and disability, along with the acute episodes of care associated with such conditions (Hansen, Fink, Frydenberg, & Oxhoj, 2002; Kessler, Greenberg, Mickelson, Meneades, & Wang, 2001).

Challenge of Defining Disability

Disability has usually been defined by the prevailing medical and legal systems in particular cultures. Less attention has been given to contextual factors (e.g., social and technological contributions) and subjective attributes that substantially affect a person's experience of disability. Although consensus as to what is or is not disability has not been easy to achieve, it is critically important to agree how disability is identified. In doing so, those who are disadvantaged by their experience of disability can be identified, their life experiences compared with those who are not disabled, and disparities in life experiences can be noted so that inequalities can be observed, measured, and ultimately remedied (Leonardi, Bickenbach, Üstün, Kostanjsek, & Chatterji, 2006).

The various and multidisciplinary definitions of disability in clinical, legal, and academic circles have complicated efforts to develop, sponsor, and enact effective policy and service for persons who live with disabling conditions (Walkup, 2000). We next discuss several models of disability, including the impact of the WHO's (2001) latest health classification system (the *ICF*) on how disability is defined and classified today.

FOUNDATIONAL MODELS OF DISABILITY

Several different models of disability have dominated professional thinking over the years, including the medical model, the social model, and the biopsychosocial model. Although it continues to be influential, the medical model's shortcomings, the ascendance of the civil rights movement in the United States, and related disability activism gave rise to an opposing social model of disability. Given a growing population of people with disabilities and a related increase in stakeholders, more recent models of disability acknowledge the central role of social factors in understanding the causes and consequences of disability, supporting a more integrative biopsychosocial model of disability. In this section, we describe and critique three major models of disability, and compare their development to the evolution of the *ICF*.

Medical Model

Early efforts to describe population health originally focused on the prevalence of medical diagnoses and causes of death (see Peterson, 2005). The *medical model* of disability grew out of this focus, which emphasized the diagnosis and treatment of disease, disorder, or injury (WHO, 2001); health problems are diagnosed and specialized services are prescribed to cure the problem (Kaplan, 2002). This perspective has been relatively effective in the detection and treatment of acute health problems.

Over time, advances in science, directed largely by the medical model, have allowed researchers to describe disease processes and their related etiologies more accurately. Thus, the medical model is responsible for the rapid and effective response to the acute needs of persons with physical disabilities and other chronic health conditions, and the first initiatives to address issues of improved care, survival, and quality of life can be attributed to professions that embraced the medical model. In the United States, medical definitions of disability provide the cornerstone for determining disability for legal and occupational purposes, and for determining eligibility for financial assistance (Chan & Leahy, 1999; Tarvydas et al., 2005). The *International Statistical Classification of Diseases and Related Health Problems,* tenth revision (*ICD-10;* WHO, 1992) was first formalized in 1893 as the Bertillon Classification or the *International List of Causes of Death* (the *ICD* acronym persists to this day). The *ICD* provides an etiological classification of health conditions (e.g., diseases, disorders, injuries) related to mortality (death) and morbidity (illness). The *ICD* is a good example of the medical model's influence on the classification of health and disability.

The value of the medical model is clearly apparent in several areas, such as in the design of triage services that preserve life and allay acute problems following the onset of physical disability, and in serving the acute care needs of those living with disability. However, the model has difficulty accommodating the types of permanent and chronic long-term care needs that would promote optimal health and life quality in persons living with a disability. The needs of increasing numbers of persons with chronic health conditions are also not adequately addressed by institutions that are committed to the delivery of services for acute, short-term conditions.

The medical model relies heavily on measures and tests of the disease process. Consequently, the model places a limited value on subjective reports of quality of life and well-being. Adherence to the medical model can also lead health providers to undervalue patient input concerning treatment options and recommendations for prescribed regimens. From the medical model perspective, the successful diagnosis and treatment of acute conditions does not hinge substantially on the accuracy or quality of patient input.

A growing body of research suggests that diagnostic information alone, without functional data, may not adequately reflect an individual's health condition. Disease or impairment may manifest differently across individuals; similar functioning does not imply similar health conditions. Diagnoses alone do not sufficiently predict length (McCrone & Phelan, 1994) or outcome (Rabinowitz, Modai, & Inbar-Saban, 1994) of hospitalization, level of necessary care (Burns, 1991), service needs (National Advisory Mental Health Council, 1993), work performance (Gatchel, Polatin, Mayer, & Garcy, 1994), receipt of disability benefits (Bassett, Chase, Folstein, & Regier, 1998; Massel, Liberman, Mintz, & Jacobs, 1990; Segal & Choi, 1991), or social integration (Ormel, Oldehinkel, Brilman, & vanden Brink, 1993). Leonardi et al. (2006) note that it is important to distinguish between objective descriptions of the "disability experience" and an individual's satisfaction with that experience: "...data about quality of life, well-being, and personal satisfaction with life are useful for health and policy planning; but these data are not necessarily predicted by the presence or extent of disability" (p. 1220).

The course of chronic disease and disability over the life span is substantially influenced by behavioral and social mechanisms. The medical model and related diagnostic information have been shown to have limited capacity for assessing and making changes in these important domains. Further, health care services provided in the medical model paradigm are contingent on third-party reimbursement and the ability of specific programs and administrative systems to absorb financial losses not covered by third-party payers. Financial costs associated with chronic and disabling conditions have strained health care delivery systems grounded in the medical model; cost-containment efforts have often involved cuts in disability services and insurance coverage.

Social Model

In contrast to the medical model, the social model of disability considers the role of environmental facilitators and barriers in health and functioning (Hurst, 2003; Smart, 2005). In this paradigm, disability is not just a personal attribute, but a complex social construct reflecting the interaction between the individual and environment (WHO, 2001). The social model focuses on the barriers and facilitators to daily activities, life skills, social relations, life satisfaction, and participation in society. This model suggests that any problem related to disability is not just due to the person with the disability, but rather is also influenced by societal attitudes and barriers in the environment.

The social model, favored by advocates for the civil rights of persons with disability, highlights the need for increased access and opportunities for people with disabilities; it disapproves of the medical model as a template for policy decisions concerning disability. Variations of the social model have appeared in the "new paradigm" of disability and as a social-constructionist model in the disability studies literature (see Olkin, 1999). In this paradigm, the individual is seen as the organizing core, but impairments are defined by the environment. The environment is typically construed as the "major determinant of individual functioning" (Pledger, 2003, p. 281).

Despite underscoring the social conditions that affect the quality of life of persons living with a disability, the social model does not clearly distinguish who qualifies as a person with a disability (or how disability is measured or determined). Researchers in this tradition have yet to establish a distinct body of scholarship that systematically posits empirically testable and potentially falsifiable hypotheses. Moreover, some proponents appear to regard psychological theory and scholarship as a continuation of a medical model that equates disability with person-based pathology that is largely independent of environmental and social factors (see Olkin & Pledger, 2003).

Biopsychosocial Model

The *biopsychosocial model* integrates useful aspects of both the medical and social models (Peterson & Rosenthal, 2005; Simeonsson et al., 2003; Ueda & Okawa, 2003). This perspective permeates the psychological literature and is consistent with contemporary rehabilitation processes and practice (Frank & Elliott, 2000; Parker, Szymanski, & Patterson, 2005). The biospsychosocial model of disability considers the interactive effects of disease (disability parameters), psychosocial stressors, and personal and environmental factors that account for varying degrees of adaptation. Rehabilitation professionals have long acknowledged the role of environmental and attitudinal barriers in society, and advocated for their mitigation to improve life conditions for persons with disabilities (Scherer et al., 2004).

Biopsychosocial models—usually developed to study adjustment associated with specific disability diagnoses (e.g., spinal cord injury, traumatic brain injury, multiple sclerosis)—have proliferated in the rehabilitation psychology literature (e.g., see Frank & Elliott, 2000). These models typically attempt to integrate medical aspects of a given diagnostic condition with important psychological (e.g., personality traits, coping abilities) and social (e.g., stress, social support) variables and their various interactions in the prediction of optimal adjustment. More recent variants of this model emphasize the primacy of subjective, phenomenological appraisals of resources, stressors, and contextual issues across diagnostic conditions (Elliott, Kurylo, & Rivera, 2002). This shift is based partly on evidence that (a) individual differences and other psychological characteristics usually account for greater variance in the prediction of adjustment among persons with disability than does any condition-specific variable, and that (b) stressors appear to vary as a function of psychological and social characteristics rather than being due to specific diagnostic conditions (with a few exceptions occurring among conditions that impose severe disruptions in brain-behavior relations).

Emanating from the biopsychosocial approach, the *ICF* is based on an integration of the medical and social models of disability and addresses biological, individual, and societal perspectives on health (Peterson, 2005). The *ICF*'s interactive conceptual framework illustrates how facilitators and barriers in the environment are key factors in understanding disability and how advocacy occurs through social change (Hurst, 2003). Most important, the individual's appraisals of environmental assets and liabilities, personal body functions, and his or her ability to participate in desired personal and social activities, are important considerations in classifying functioning, disability, and health with the *ICF* (see Peterson & Threats, 2005, for a discussion of the 11 provisions for ethical use of the *ICF*). We next turn to a discussion of the *ICF*.

DISABILITY AND THE INTERNATIONAL CLASSIFICATION OF FUNCTIONING, DISABILITY AND HEALTH

The paradigm shift from the medical to social and biopsychosocial models of disability is reflected in the evolution of the *ICF* (WHO, 2001). The *ICF* has enjoyed support from professions and consumer advocacy groups throughout the international community. The promise of the *ICF* is that it can be a stimulus for significant developments in theory, research, policy, and practice applications (Bruyère & Peterson, 2005), the results of which can be used to help identify, mitigate, or remove societal hindrances to the full participation of people with disabilities in mainstream society (Peterson & Rosenthal, 2005).

A variety of literature reviews have discussed and critiqued the *ICF* (see volume 50 of *Rehabilitation Psychology*, 2005; volume 19 of *Rehabilitation Education*, 2005; and volume 25 of *Disability & Rehabilitation*, 2003). Although the *ICF* is described briefly in the next section, such an overview is not an adequate substitute for reviewing the *ICF* itself in its entirety, the related literature, or for attending training provided by those who are expert in its use.

The *ICF* is "a classification of human functioning and disability" (WHO, 2001, p. 21). Initially drafted as the *International Classification of Impairments, Disabilities, and Handicaps (ICIDH)* by the World Health Organization (WHO, 1980), the *ICF* was intended to complement its sister classification system, the *ICD* (WHO, 1992), currently in its tenth revision. The *ICD* classifies mortality and morbidity, whereas the *ICF* classifies functioning, disability, and health, and they are designed to be used together.

The *ICF* was endorsed for international use by the 54th World Health Assembly in 2001, and was subsequently accepted by 191 countries as the international standard to classify health and health-related states (Bruyère & Peterson, 2005). The *ICF* provides a new way to talk about health that avoids the use of diagnostic labels exclusively and promotes a complementary use of universal classifications of function. The *ICF* uses a culturally sensitive, integrative, and interactive model of health and functioning that is sensitive to social and environmental aspects of health and disability (Üstün, Chaterji, Bickenbach, Kostanjsek, & Schneider, 2003).

The *ICF* definitions have a noticeably positive, health-oriented focus. *Impairments* are no longer defined as *problems,* but as:

> a loss or abnormality in body structure or physiological function (including mental functions). Abnormality here is used strictly to refer to a significant variation from established statistical norms (i.e., as a deviation form a population mean within measured standard norms) and should be used only in this sense. (WHO, 2001, p. 213)

The *ICF* codes classify a variety of functional data that enhance our ability to target appropriate interventions and effectively measure their outcomes (Leonardi et al., 2006; Peterson, 2005).

Disability Defined by the International Classification of Functioning, Disability and Health

The *ICF* conceptualizes *disability* as an overarching term that refers to any impairments, activity limitations, or participation restrictions, or "the outcome or result of a complex relationship between an individual's health condition and personal factors, and of the external factors that represent the circumstances in which the individual lives" (WHO, 2001, p. 17). The term *disability* emphasizes the interaction between individual, societal, and body-related aspects of impairments, activity limitations, and participation restrictions in the environment that can be used to describe both how environmental factors are key to understanding disability, and how disability advocacy occurs through social change (Hurst, 2003). Although disability is defined in the *ICF* proper, it is operationalized by "activity limitations" (p. 213). The antiquated term *handicap* is replaced by *participation restriction*: "Impairments are interactions affecting the body; activity limitations are interactions affecting [an] individual's actions or behavior; participation restrictions are interactions affecting [a] person's experience of life" (Leonardi et al., 2006, p. 1220).

International Classification of Functioning, Disability and Health Conceptual Framework

The *ICF* conceptual framework is depicted in Figure 13.1 (WHO, 2001, p. 18). The *ICF* uses labels complementary to the biopsychosocial model of disability, and permits separate ratings along dimensions of body structure and function or impairment at the organ level, activity (versus activity limitation) and participation (versus participation restriction) at the person level, and environmental facilitators or barriers at the societal level. It allows for an analysis of functioning across several dimensions and does not regard a specific medical diagnosis as a concept that determines functioning, health, or disability.

Universe of Well-Being

The *ICF* focuses on *health and well-being* by referring to components of health that are typically a focus of health care professionals (e.g., seeing, hearing, speaking, remembering, learning, walking), and to components (*health-related components of well-being*) that are not typically a focus of health care systems (e.g., labor, education, employment, social interactions, and transportation). Thus, the *ICF*

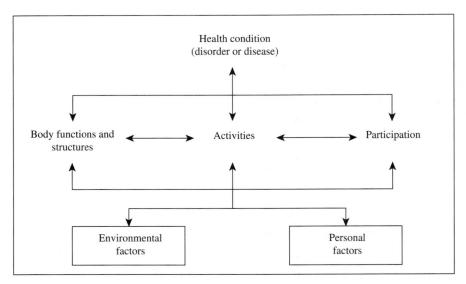

Figure 13.1   Interactions between the Components of the *ICF*.
Source: The International Classification of Functioning, Disability and Health (p. 18), by the World Health Organization, 2001, Geneva, Switzerland: Author. Copyright 2001 by the World Health Organization. Reprinted with permission.

was not designed to classify disability exclusively; it also classifies *health* and *health-related* states that make up a *universe of well-being.*

Functioning in the *ICF* includes all body functions, activities, and participation in society. As Figure 13.1 suggests, the *ICF*'s conceptual framework provides a model of functioning and disability that is dynamic, with reciprocal relationships between the various health-related conditions in the context of environmental and personal factors. The *ICF* does not currently classify personal circumstances such as socioeconomic status, race, gender, religion, or culture that may restrict full participation in society for reasons not related to health. The Personal Factors component in the conceptual framework of the *ICF* is important because it highlights the need to consider complex ipsative and social factors that inform classifications of health and functioning.

Impairment

Impairments are the manifestations of dysfunction in the body structures or functions. The etiology of a particular dysfunction is not the focus of the *ICF*, but rather is the focus of its sister classification, the *ICD-10* (WHO, 1992). Impairments do not necessarily imply the presence of a disorder or disease but "represent a deviation from certain generally accepted population standards" of functioning (WHO, 2001, p. 12). Determination of impairment is made by "those qualified to judge physical and mental functioning according to these standards" (p. 12).

Structure of the International Classification of Functioning, Disability and Health

The *ICF* is made up of two parts, each with two components: The first part of the *ICF* describes the individual via *Functioning and Disability;* the second part addresses *Contextual Factors.* All components are further divided into chapters that contain categories of function in a given domain of health and health-related states. The units of classification are qualified with numeric codes that specify the magnitude or extent of disability or function in a given category or, within the case of environment, the extent to which a factor in the environment is a facilitator or a barrier.

There are two versions of the *ICF*: the full version that provides four levels of classification detail, and the short version that provides two levels of classification. In addition to an alphabetical index that organizes the hardcopy version of the *ICF*, the WHO created an electronic version of the *ICF* that is searchable through the *ICF* Browser (www.who.int/classifications/ICF/en/) or CD-ROM (WHO, 2001).

Part One: The Individual

In the first part, Functioning and Disability, there are two components: The first component, Body, consists of two parallel classifications, Body Functions and Body Structures. The second component, Activities and Participation, covers domains of functioning from both an individual and societal perspective. The two components of functioning in the first part of the *ICF* can be expressed either as nonproblematic functioning or as disabilities (i.e., impairment, activity limitation, or participation restriction), and are operationalized through four separate but related constructs. Body Functions and Structures are interpreted through *changes in physiological systems* or *anatomical structures,* and Activities and Participation are interpreted though *capacity* and *performance* (WHO, 2001).

Part Two: The Context

The second part of the *ICF* classification describes Contextual Factors through two components, Environmental Factors and Personal Factors. Environmental Factors are factors in the physical, social, or attitudinal world ranging from the immediate to more general environment. Environmental Factors are qualified as either facilitating or hindering functioning. The second component of Contextual Factors is

Personal Factors, which is comprised of personal attributes such as race, age, fitness, religion, lifestyle, habits, upbringing, coping styles, social background, education, profession, past and current experience, overall behavior pattern and character style, and individual psychological assets (WHO, 2001). A summary of the *ICF* chapters is listed in Table 13.1.

Levels of Classification

Domains in the *ICF* are practical and meaningful sets of related physiological functions, psychological functions, and anatomical structures. These functions also include actions, tasks, and areas of life described from bodily, individual, and societal perspectives (WHO, 2001).

The one-level classification of the *ICF* includes the following components:

- The *Body Functions* component contains 8 chapters that address "physiological functions of body systems (including psychological functions)" (WHO, 2001, p. 12).

- The *Body Structures* component contains 8 chapters that parallel the *Body Functions* component and deal with "anatomical parts of the body such as organs, limbs, and their components" (p. 12).

- The *Activities and Participation* component contains 9 chapters, with *Activities* addressing "the execution of a task or action by an individual" and *Participation* addressing "involvement in a life situation" (p. 14).

- The *Environmental Factors* component contains 5 chapters focusing on "the physical, social, and attitudinal environment in which people live and conduct their lives" (p. 171), organized from the immediate to more general environment.

The two-level classification is comprised of specific chapter headings. For each chapter, alphanumeric codes are used to indicate chapters (e.g., *b* for Body Functions, *s* for Body Structures, *d* for Activities and Participation, and *e* for Environmental Factors) and specific categories in each chapter. For example, the classification associated with the psychological function of emotion is found in the first chapter of Body Functions (code "b") under the specific mental function section, called *Emotional Functions,* or alphanumeric code b152 (WHO, 2001).

The *Detailed Classification with Definitions* lists all categories in the *ICF* along with their definitions, inclusions, and exclusions, providing the greatest level of detail using four- and five-digit numeric codes. Examples of the detail level in Emotional Functions could include appropriateness of emotion (b1520), regulation of emotion (b1521), and range of emotion (b1522).

Body Functions and Structures

The criteria for impairment are the same for Body Functions and Structures and are classified according to (a) loss or lack, (b) reduction, (c) addition or excess, and (d) deviation. Codes have qualifiers to indicate a magnitude or level of health for a given code. The Body Function component qualifies impairment with a Likert-type scale (ranging from "mild" to "complete" impairment; WHO, 2001, p. 47). The Body Structure component also uses a Likert-type scale to qualify severity of impairment and the nature of change in a specific body structure. A different qualifier is used to indicate the location of the impairment.

Activities and Participation, and Capacity and Performance

This second component under Functioning and Disability classifies nine domains of functioning from both individual and societal perspectives (see Table 13.1). In all instances, the Body Functions and Structures component is intended to be used with the Activities and Participation component. The

Table 13.1 Summary of *ICF* Chapters

Components	Body Functions	Body Structures	Activities and Participation	Environmental Factors
Code letter	*b*	*s*	*d*	*e*
	8 PARALLEL CHAPTERS		*9 CHAPTERS*	*5 CHAPTERS*
Chapter 1	Mental functions	Structures of the nervous system	Learning and applying knowledge	Products and technology
Chapter 2	Sensory functions and pain	The eye, ear, and related structures	General tasks and demands	Natural environment and human-made changes to environment
Chapter 3	Voice and speech functions	Structures involved in voice and speech	Communication	Support and relationships
Chapter 4	Functions of the cardiovascular, hematological, immunological, and respiratory systems	Structures of the cardiovascular, immunological, and respiratory systems	Mobility	Attitudes
Chapter 5	Functions of the digestive, metabolic, and endocrine systems	Structures related to the digestive, metabolic, and endocrine systems	Self-care	Services, systems, and policies
Chapter 6	Genitourinary and reproductive functions	Structures related to the genitourinary and reproductive systems	Domestic life	
Chapter 7	Neuromusculoskeletal and movement-related functions	Structures related to movement	Interpersonal interactions and relationships	
Chapter 8	Functions of the skin and related structures	Skin and related structures	Major life areas	
Chapter 9			Community, social, and civic life	

Source: ICF: International Classification of Functioning, Disability and Health, by the World Health Organization, 2001, Geneva: Author. Reprinted with permission.

term *activity* is defined as the execution of a task or action by an individual such as sitting, copying, calculating, or driving. The term *participation* is defined as involvement in a life situation. As with the term *impairment, activity limitations* and *participation restrictions* "are assessed against a generally accepted population standard" (WHO, 2001, p. 15) for someone without a similar health condition.

The domains of the Activities and Participation component are operationalized through the use of the qualifiers capacity and performance. *Capacity* "describes an individual's ability to execute a task or an action," or more specifically, "the highest probable level of functioning that a person may reach in a given domain at a given moment" (WHO, 2001, p. 15). One must apply the capacity qualifier in the context of a "uniform" or "standard" environment; a heuristic for capacity could be *what a person can do*. The *performance* qualifier describes "what a person does in his or her current environment" (p. 15); a heuristic for performance could be *what a person does do*.

The performance and capacity qualifiers are rated on the same 0 to 4 scale as the first qualifier of Body Functions and Structures, substituting the term *difficulty* for *impairment*. Performance and capacity can be considered both with and without assistive devices or personal assistance, forming four possible qualifiers (performance with and without assistance, and capacity with and without assistance).

Contextual Factors

Environmental Factors (the physical, social, and attitudinal worlds) are classified in the *ICF* by whether they facilitate or hinder functioning. Environmental Factors are organized into three levels: (1) individual level (e.g., support network), (2) services level (e.g., vocational rehabilitation), and (3) cultural or legal systems level (e.g., worldviews, laws). Table 13.1 lists the five chapters that comprise Environmental Factors.

Although it is not currently classified, the Personal Factors component of the *ICF* is comprised of personal characteristics such as gender, race, age, fitness, religion, lifestyle, habits, upbringing, coping styles, social background, education, profession, past and current experience, overall behavior pattern and character, individual psychological assets, and other health conditions. It is believed that all of these descriptors can impact health and functioning, and users are encouraged to consider these issues qualitatively while classifying other areas of health and functioning. Great interest has been expressed by a variety of stakeholders to further develop this component of the *ICF* (e.g., Hurst, 2003). In its current iteration, these issues must be considered as they may affect the outcome of a given health care intervention when classifying health and functioning using the *ICF*. An integrative overview of the *ICF* is illustrated in Table 13.2.

Contrasting the International Classification of Functioning, Disability, and Health with the Medical Model

An example may help to contrast the utility of the *ICF* with that of the traditional medical model. When an individual incurs a spinal cord injury (SCI), he or she will likely be assessed for an inpatient rehabilitation program. This determination will be made by a physician. The prevailing model for categorizing SCI relies on medical technology and expertise to determine the level of the injury (in the spinal column) and the degree to which the spinal cord may be impaired (complete versus incomplete; Elliott & Rivera, 2003). Various disciplines on an multidisciplinary team will conduct assessments that represent their particular expertise (e.g., nursing, physical therapy, psychology, social work), and this information ideally is used to develop a clinical treatment plan. However, the medical condition—an SCI (e.g., paraplegia, tetraplegia) and the completeness of lesion—serves as the overriding diagnosis that determines the clinical treatment plan and corresponding decisions concerning length of stay, reimbursement for services, and qualification for possible services postdischarge. The SCI *is* the "disability."

Table 13.2   Overview of the *ICF*

Two Parts (A dynamic interaction)	Part 1: Functioning and Disability		Part 2: Contextual Factors	
Components	Body Functions and Structures	Activities and Participation	Environmental Factors	Personal Factors
Domains (Contain the categories or units of classification of the *ICF*)	Body Functions (including Psychological Functioning) Body Structures	Life areas (tasks, actions)	External influences on functioning and disability	Internal influences on functioning and disability
Constructs (Defined through use of qualifiers that modify the extent or magnitude of function or disability)	Change in body function (physiological) Change in body structure (anatomical)	Capacity: Executing tasks in a standard environment ("can do") Performance: Executing tasks in the current environment ("does do")	Facilitating or hindering impact of features of the physical, social, and attitudinal world	Impact of attributes of the person
Positive aspect	Functioning Functional and structural integrity Activities Participation		Facilitators	Not classified in the *ICF*
Negative aspect	Disability Impairment Activity limitation Participation restriction		Barriers/hindrances	

Source: ICF: International Classification of Functioning, Disability, and Health, by the World Health Organization, 2001, Geneva: Author. Reprinted with permission.

The *ICF* dictates a more thorough appreciation of the condition, the individual, and environmental factors, and it considers psychological and social factors that might impose impairment above and beyond the medical diagnosis (see Table 13.1). A person diagnosed with "incomplete paraplegia" may have nerve damage that results in a loss of motor movement of the lower limbs, but it may also spare sensations at or below the site of the lesion. This person would retain chest, hand, arm, shoulder, and neck functions. Under the Body Functions component, the *ICF* emphasizes factors like *mental functions* (including personality traits, coping behaviors, mental status) and *sensory functions* (e.g., persistent pain often associated with incomplete lesions) just as much as it rates damage to the spinal cord and where this damage is located (under Body Structures). This coding scheme—and the corresponding evaluations of impairment—may then have greater explanatory power in appreciating impairment imposed by persistent pain, ineffective coping skills in regulating emotions, and subsequent depression, beyond the initial medical diagnosis alone.

IMPLICATIONS FOR COUNSELING PSYCHOLOGY

The *ICF* has numerous implications for professional psychology, generally, and for counseling psychology, specifically. First, disability should no longer be equated with a medical diagnostic condition, and disability issues need no longer be considered as synonymous with vocational rehabilitation or restricted to the services of any single health profession or medical specialty. From the perspective of the *ICF*, any health condition (including such varied conditions as depression, asthma, diabetes mellitus, schizophrenia, or HIV) can have disabling features that can be understood (and rated) along the components in the *ICF* framework.

Second, the *ICF* functions as a working model, and it does not purport to stand alone as a comprehensive theory of any particular condition (or associated component). It simply provides an organizing scheme for appreciating factors related to an individual that can impose limitations and complicate or facilitate function and adjustment. Third, the *ICF* does not serve any specific health profession and does not constrain the disability experience to any particular agency or outcome. Although vocational rehabilitation remains an important aspect of adjustment, this feature does not limit the wide array of possible services, opportunities, and options for persons with disabling conditions.

One by-product of the *ICF* is that it highlights the ways in which professional psychology has implicitly adopted a medical model in defining psychological specialties and respective areas of expertise and practice. It implies a compartmental approach in which health and rehabilitation psychologists work with people with physical disabilities, and nonspecialists (e.g., counseling psychologists) do not. Olkin and colleagues have argued that this implicit stance limits the available psychological services and opportunities for people who live with some disabling condition (Olkin, 1999; Olkin & Pledger, 2003).

Although counseling psychology research has documented that persons with disabilities lack access to mental health services and encounter barriers that impede their participation in psychological services (e.g., poor transportation; Pelletier, Rogers, & Dellario, 1985), it is unfortunate that most doctoral programs in clinical and counseling psychology do not address disability in coursework or practica (Leung, Sakata, & Ostby, 1990; Spear & Schoepke, 1981). The *ICF* presents considerable research and practice opportunities for counseling psychologists. We briefly describe several of them below.

Measurement and Assessment

To facilitate implementation of the *ICF* in the United States, the American Psychological Association (APA) and WHO formed a series of interdisciplinary teams to develop *The Procedural Manual and Guide for the Standardized Application of the ICF: A Manual for Health Professionals* (Reed et al., 2005). Given the size of the volume to date (over 800 pages), it may be useful to develop computerized matching systems in using the *ICF* (Peterson & Rosenthal, 2005). Once the *Procedural Manual* is published, the guide can be used for training to promote consistent coding. Studies will be needed to evaluate the clarity and utility of the manual to clinical practice, and to validate the application of the *ICF* given the new implementation guidelines (Peterson & Rosenthal, 2005).

The *ICF* is designed as a system that requires the active participation of a consumer in a collaborative and informational process, and is not something that is done *to* a consumer (Peterson, 2005; Peterson & Threats, 2005; Threats & Worrall, 2004). Eleven ethical provisions were established in the sixth Annex of the *ICF* (WHO, 2001, pp. 244–245) to reduce the risk of disrespectful or harmful use of the newly revised classification system. Coordinators of the WHO revision efforts for the *ICIDH* (WHO, 1980) included people with disabilities and disability advocates in the revision process, which led to important changes in the content and structure of the *ICF* (WHO, 2001). The 11 ethical provisions address three critical areas: (1) respect and confidentiality, (2) clinical use of the *ICF*, and (3) social use of *ICF* information (WHO, 2001).

There are several potential pitfalls in the *ICF* classification process that may affect ratings. These pitfalls reflect more general problems in clinical judgment and assessment biases, and in the interactional dynamics between raters and participants. Counseling psychologists who are interested in these issues will need to receive training in the use of the *ICF* and become involved in its use to study these biases. Several health professions are now using item response theory to convert the *ICF* into measurement systems that individualize the assessment process, reduce respondent burden, and increase measurement precision (Velozo, 2005). In one recent conference, professionals from rehabilitation psychology (DiCowden, 2005), nursing (Coenen, 2005), occupational therapy (Velozo, 2005), and physical therapy (Mayo & McGill, 2005) discussed efforts to develop instruments and protocols based on the *ICF* model.

Other psychologists have participated in the development and refinement of measures to (a) evaluate and quantify the extent of physical disability and capacity for self-care, (b) identify limitations for discharge and rehabilitation, (c) identify outcomes associated with rehabilitation interventions, and (d) inform the identification of goals for rehabilitation (Heinemann, 2005; Mermis, 2005). The increased emphasis on activities, access, and capacities (particularly in the pursuit of personal goals for optimal well-being) will likely require greater use of quantitative methods in individual assessment, program evaluation, and longitudinal models to identify personal and social variables predictive of optimal and complicated adjustment over time. This will permit counseling psychologists to examine theoretical perspectives that are related to adjustment (e.g., career development of women with disabilities; Noonan, Gallor, Hensler-McGinnis, Fassinger, & Goodman, 2004).

Counseling psychologists can also contribute by studying and refining concepts that may eventually be subsumed in the Personal Factors components (which is not yet classified), including characteristics such as gender, race, age, fitness, religion, lifestyle, habits, coping styles, and individual psychological assets. Ideally, future versions of the *ICF* will include psychometrically sound items for rating characteristics that prove important in understanding present and subsequent functioning. Creating such measures will be a formidable task, requiring identification of relatively few measurable constructs that could be efficiently included in the *ICF* from among the vast array of potential person-psychological variables. Counseling psychologists are well suited to participate in this process given the field's interest in the roles of gender, culture, age, and religion in health and well-being across the life span. Counseling psychology's concerns with psychometrics and studying and promoting "positive assets" also fit well with the explicit valence the *ICF* places on access and well-being and on developing sound ways to measure important person and environmental inputs.

Certain specific, measurable constructs studied in counseling psychology research may hold promise in distinguishing "behavioral patterns" that predict both self-reported adjustment and objective health outcomes. Ineffective social problem-solving abilities are associated with greater distress and self-reported psychosocial impairment beyond variance attributable to the physical limitations imposed by a physical disability (Elliott, Godshall, Herrick, Witty, & Spruell, 1991). Ineffective problem-solving abilities are also predictive of expensive, preventable, and potentially life-threatening secondary complications over a 3-year period among persons with severe physical disability (Elliott, Bush, & Chen, 2006). Such constructs are particularly attractive because they have implications for interventions that can be delivered by nondoctoral level service providers in a variety of ways (e.g., via long-distance technologies, such as telephone counseling; Grant, Elliott, Weaver, Bartolucci, & Giger, 2002).

Developing Services and Policy

The implications of the *ICF* for developing, providing, and evaluating services for persons with disabling conditions are immense. The WHO model of disability champions advocacy and consumer perspectives. The use of the *ICF* will encourage services that attempt to promote independent living via improved access to institutions, improved role functioning and mobility, and reduced disability. This will hopefully create service delivery systems and associated policies that promote better collaborative partnerships with persons who live with a disabling condition and increased community and home-based services (Institute of Medicine, 2001; WHO, 2002). Consequently, a greater premium will be placed on the provision and use of assistive devices and enhanced computer technologies, and the removal of existing environmental barriers (Scherer, 2002). Psychological interventions have demonstrated considerable impact in the treatment of specific disability adjustment issues and in enhancing role function (Elliott & Jackson, 2005; Elliott & Leung, 2005). Consumers will likely want a greater emphasis on health promotion, exercise, and leisure activities than previously observed (Rimmer & Braddock, 2002).

Agencies may experience some difficulty in developing *collaborative partnerships* that recognize consumers as active stakeholders in their own health and well-being. Psychologists who use qualitative methods and conduct participatory action research (Kidd & Kral, 2005) may assume influential roles in developing, implementing, and evaluating such services. Social-constructionist views of disability (Olkin, 1999) may also be used to help design interventions consonant with the aspirations of the *ICF*. Counseling psychologists may also realize more influential roles in developing and providing assistive services as an extension of public and health care policy.

The managed care industry has caused health professionals to be more outcome-focused in their reports to third-party payers, rather than reporting only traditional diagnostic information (Tarvydas et al., 2005). The *ICF* provides a system to document functional outcomes that complement the diagnostic information in other health classification efforts.

The use of the *ICF* in service delivery will eventually impact both academic and research discourse on disability. Bodenreider (2005) has recently mapped the *ICF* onto the National Library of Medicine's Unified Medical Language System (UMLS). *ICF* concepts were associated with a related term in the UMLS, so that in the future the *ICF* could be cross-referenced with other information systems that are already linked to the UMLS. Previous UMLS initiatives were primarily influenced by the medical model. The *ICF*'s taxonomy has challenged the UMLS to develop new categories that better reflect functional information rather than diagnostic information alone.

The *ICF* may also assist in managing the ever-increasing amount of medical information. Chute (2005) suggested that, although measures and classifications of functioning are the overall metric of organic well-being, the evolving knowledge base of medical information has outgrown our ability to consume it effectively. He suggested that systems like the *ICF* can help us to develop shared semantics, vocabularies, and terminologies, in a way that helps us to use medical knowledge effectively in treating people in health care settings.

CONCLUSION

The *ICF* has influenced many health care entities internationally and is now in use in several countries including the United States, Australia, Canada, and the Netherlands (Bickenbach, 2003; Holloway, 2004; Madden, Choi, & Sykes, 2003). Work on the World Health Survey, built on the *ICF* conceptual framework, has been implemented in 74 countries (Üstün et al., 2003). Future research and implementation efforts with the *ICF* promise to (a) revolutionize the way stakeholders in health care delivery systems think about and classify health, (b) improve the quality of health care for individuals across the world, (c) generate innovative outcome-based research, and (d) influence culturally sensitive global health policy (Peterson & Rosenthal, 2005; Stucki, Ewert, & Cieza, 2003).

REFERENCES

American Diabetes Association. (2003). Economic costs of diabetes in the U.S. in 2002. *Diabetes Care, 26*, 917–932.

Bassett, S. S., Chase, G. A., Folstein, M. F., & Regier, D. A. (1998). Disability and psychiatric disorders in an urban community: Measurement, prevalence and outcomes. *Psychological Medicine, 28*, 509–517.

Bickenbach, J. E. (2003). Functional status and health information in Canada: Proposals and prospects. *Health Care Financing Review, 24* (3), 89–102.

Bodenreider, O. (2005, June). *Mapping new vocabularies to the UMLS: Experience with ICF*. Symposium conducted at the meeting of the World Health Organization's North American Collaborating Center, Mayo Clinic, Rochester, MN.

Bruyère, S. M. & Peterson, D. B. (2005). Introduction to the special section on the International Classification of Functioning, Disability and Health (*ICF*): Implications for rehabilitation psychology. *Rehabilitation Psychology, 50,* 103–104.

Burns, C. (1991). Parallels between research and diagnosis: The reliability and validity issues of clinical practice. *Nurse Practitioner, 16,* (42), 45, 49–50.

Chan, F., & Leahy, M. (Eds.). (1999). *Health care and disability case management.* Lake Zurich, IL: Vocational Consultants Press.

Chute, C. G. (2005, June). *The spectrum of clinical data representation: A context for functional status*. Symposium conducted at the meeting of the World Health Organization's North American Collaborating Center, Mayo Clinic, Rochester, MN.

Coenen, A. (2005, June). *Mapping ICF to the International Classification for Nursing Practice (ICNP)*. Symposium conducted at the meeting of the World Health Organization's North American Collaborating Center, Mayo Clinic, Rochester, MN.

Dawis, R., & Lofquist, L. H. (1984). *A psychological theory of work adjustment.* Minneapolis: University of Minnesota Press.

DiCowden, M. A. (2005, June). *The impact of ICF coding in practice*. Symposium conducted at the meeting of the World Health Organization's North American Collaborating Center, Mayo Clinic, Rochester, MN.

Elliott, T., Bush, B., & Chen, Y. (2006). Social problem solving abilities predict pressure sore occurrence in the first three years of spinal cord injury. *Rehabilitation Psychology, 51,* 69–77.

Elliott, T., Godshall, F., Herrick, S., Witty, T., & Spruell, M. (1991). Problem-solving appraisal and psychological adjustment following spinal cord injury. *Cognitive Therapy and Research, 15,* 387–398.

Elliott, T., & Jackson, W. T. (2005). Cognitive-behavioral therapy in rehabilitation psychology. In A. Freeman (Editor-in-Chief), *Encyclopedia of cognitive behavior therapy* (pp. 324–327). New York: Springer Science + Business Media.

Elliott, T., Kurylo, M., & Rivera, P. (2002). Positive growth following an acquired physical disability. In C. R. Snyder & S. Lopez (Eds.), *Handbook of positive psychology* (pp. 687–699). New York: Oxford University Press.

Elliott, T., & Leung, P. (2005). Vocational rehabilitation: History and practice. In W. B. Walsh & M. Savickas (Eds.), *Handbook of vocational psychology* (3rd ed., pp. 319–343). New York: Erlbaum.

Elliott, T., & Rivera, P. (2003). Spinal cord injury. In A. Nezu, C. Nezu, & P. Geller (Eds.), *Handbook of psychology: Vol. 9. Health psychology* (pp. 415–435). Hoboken, NJ: Wiley.

Frank, R. G., & Elliott, T. (2000). *Handbook of rehabilitation psychology.* Washington, DC: American Psychological Association Press.

Gatchel, R. J., Polatin, P. B., Mayer, T. G., & Garcy, P. D. (1994). Psychopathology and the rehabilitation of patients with chronic low back pain disability. *Archives of Physical Medicine and Rehabilitation, 75,* 666–670.

Grant, J., Elliott, T., Weaver, M., Bartolucci, A., & Giger, J. (2002). A telephone intervention with family caregivers of stroke survivors after hospital discharge. *Stroke, 33,* 2060–2065.

Hansen, M. S., Fink, P., Frydenberg, M., & Oxhoj, M. L. (2002). Use of health services, mental illness, and self-rated disability and health in medical inpatients. *Psychosomatic Medicine, 64,* 668–675.

Heinemann, A. (2005). Putting outcome measurement in context: A rehabilitation psychology perspective. *Rehabilitation Psychology, 50,* 6–14.

Holloway, J. D. (2004, January). A new way of looking at health status. *Monitor on Psychology, 35,* 32.

Hurst, R. (2003). The international disability rights movement and the *ICF. Disability and Rehabilitation, 25,* 572–576.

Institute of Medicine. (2001). *Crossing the quality chasm: A new health system for the 21st century.* Washington, DC: National Academy Press.

Kaplan, R. M. (2002). Quality of life: An outcomes perspective. *Archives of Physical Medicine and Rehabilitation, 83* (Suppl. 2), S44–S50.

Keil, J. E., Gazes, P. C., Sutherland, S. E., Rust, P. F., Branch, L. G., & Tyroler, H. A. (1989). Predictors of physical disability in elderly blacks and whites of the Charleston Heart Study. *Journal of Clinical Epidemiology, 42,* 521–529.

Kessler, R. C., Greenberg, P. E., Mickelson, K. D., Meneades, L. M., & Wang, P. S. (2001). The effects of chronic medical conditions on work loss and work cutback. *Journal of Occupational and Environmental Medicine, 43,* 218–225.

Kidd, S. A., & Kral, M. J. (2005). Practicing participatory action research. *Journal of Counseling Psychology, 52,* 187–195.

Leonardi, M., Bickenbach, J., Üstün, T. B., Kostanjsek, N., & Chatterji, S. (2006). Comment: The definition of disability: What is in a name? *Lancet, 368* (9543), 1219–1221.

Leung, P., Sakata, R., & Ostby, S. (1990). Rehabilitation psychology professional training: A survey of APA accredited programs. *Rehabilitation Education, 4,* 177–183.

Madden, R., Choi, C., & Sykes, C. (2003). The *ICF* as a framework for national data: The introduction of the *ICF* into Australian data dictionaries. *Disability and Rehabilitation, 25,* 676–682.

Massel, H. K., Liberman, R. P., Mintz, J., & Jacobs, H. E. (1990). Evaluating the capacity to work of the mentally ill. *Psychiatry: Journal for the Study of Interpersonal Processes, 53,* 31–43.

Max, W., Rice, D. P., & Trupin, L. (1995). *Medical expenditures for people with disabilities* (Disability Statistics Abstract, Number 12). Washington, DC: U.S. Department of Education, National Institute on Disability and Rehabilitation Research.

Mayo, N. E., & McGill, J. (2005, June). *Standardizing clinical assessments to the ICF*. Symposium conducted at the meeting of the World Health Organization's North American Collaborating Center, Mayo Clinic, Rochester, MN.

McCrone, P., & Phelan, M. (1994). Diagnosis and length of psychiatric in-patient stay. *Psychological Medicine, 24,* 1025–1030.

McGowan, J., & Porter, T. (1967). *An introduction to the vocational rehabilitation process: A training manual.* Washington, DC: U.S. Department of Health, Education, and Welfare, Vocational Rehabilitation Administration.

Mermis, B. J. (2005). Developing a taxonomy for rehabilitation outcome measurement. *Rehabilitation Psychology, 50,* 15–23.

Murdick, N., Shore, P., Chittooran, M. M., & Gartin, B. (2004). Cross-cultural comparison of the concept of "otherness" and its impact on persons with disabilities. *Education and Training in Developmental Disabilities, 39,* 310–316.

National Advisory Mental Health Council. (1993). Health care reform for Americans with severe mental illness: Report of the National Advisory Mental Health Council. *American Journal of Psychiatry, 150,* 1447–1465.

National Task Force on the Prevention and Treatment of Obesity. (2000). Overweight, obesity, and health risk. *Archives of Internal Medicine, 160,* 898–904.

Noonan, B. M., Gallor, S., Hensler-McGinnis, N., Fassinger, R. E., & Goodman, J. (2004). Challenge and success: A qualitative study of the career development of highly achieving women with physical and sensory disabilities. *Journal of Counseling Psychology, 51,* 68–80.

Olkin, R. (1999). *What psychotherapists should know about disability.* New York: Guilford Press.

Olkin, R., & Pledger, C. (2003). Can disability studies and psychology join hands? *American Psychologist, 58,* 296–304.

Ormel, J., Oldehinkel, T., Brilman, E., & vanden Brink, W. (1993). Outcome of depression and anxiety in primary care: A three wave 3~HF year study of psychopathology and disability. *Archives of General Psychiatry, 50,* 759–766.

Parker, R. M., Szymanski, E. M., & Patterson, J. B. (Eds.). (2005). *Rehabilitation counseling: Basics and Beyond* (4th ed.) Austin, TX: ProEd.

Pedersen, P. (2000). *A handbook for developing multicultural awareness* (3rd ed.) Alexandria, VA: American Counseling Association.

Pelletier, J. R., Rogers, S. E., & Dellario, D. (1985). Barriers to the provision of mental health services to individuals with severe physical disability. *Journal of Counseling Psychology, 32,* 422–430.

Peterson, D. B. (2005). International Classification of Functioning, Disability and Health (*ICF*): An introduction for rehabilitation psychologists. *Rehabilitation Psychology, 50,* 105–112.

Peterson, D. B. & Aguiar, L. (2004). History & systems: United States. In T. F. Riggar & D. R. Maki (Eds.), *The handbook of rehabilitation counseling* (pp. 50–75). New York: Springer.

Peterson, D. B. & Rosenthal, D. R. (2005). The International Classification of Functioning, Disability and Health (*ICF*) as an allegory for history and systems in rehabilitation education. *Rehabilitation Education, 19*, 75–80.

Peterson, D. B. & Threats, T. T. (2005). Ethical and clinical implications of the International Classification of Functioning, Disability and Health (*ICF*) in rehabilitation education. *Rehabilitation Education, 19*, 129–138.

Pledger, C. (2003). Discourse on disability and rehabilitation issues: Opportunities for psychology. *American Psychologist, 58*, 279–284.

Rabinowitz, J., Modai, I., & Inbar-Saban, N. (1994). Understanding who improves after psychiatric hospitalization. *Acta Psychiatrica Scandidavica, 89*, 152–158.

Reed, G. M., Lux, J. B., Bufka, L. F., Trask, C., Peterson, D. B., Stark, S., et al. (2005). Operationalizing the International Classification of Functioning, Disability and Health (*ICF*) in clinical settings. *Rehabilitation Psychology, 50*, 122–131.

Rimmer, J. H., & Braddock, D. (2002). Health promotion for people with physical, cognitive, and sensory disabilities: An emerging national priority. *American Journal of Health Promotion, 16*, 220–224.

Rudberg, M. A., Furner, S. E., Dunn, J. E., & Cassel, C. K. (1993). The relationship of visual and hearing impairments to disability: An analysis using the longitudinal study of aging. *Journal of Gerontology, 48*, M261–M265.

Rusalem, H. (1976). A personalized recent history of vocational rehabilitation in America. In H. Rusalem & D. Malikin (Eds.), *Contemporary vocational rehabilitation* (pp. 29–45). New York: New York University Press.

Scherer, M. (Ed.). (2002). *Assistive technology: Matching device and consumer for successful rehabilitation.* Washington, DC: American Psychological Association.

Scherer, M., Blair, K. L., Banks, M. E., Brucker, B., Corrigan, J., & Wegener, J. H. (2004). Rehabilitation psychology. In W. E. Craighead & C. B. Nemeroff (Eds.), *The concise Corsini encyclopedia of psychology and behavioral science* (3rd ed., pp. 801–802). Hoboken, NJ: Wiley.

Segal, S. P., & Choi, N. G. (1991). Factors affecting SSI support for sheltered care residents with serious mental illness. *Hospital and Community Psychiatry, 42*, 1132–1137.

Simeonsson, R. J., Leonardi, M., Lollar, D., Bjorck-Akesson, E., Hollenweger, J., & Martinuzzi, A. (2003). Applying the International Classification of Functioning, Disability and Health (*ICF*) to measure childhood disability. *Disability and Rehabilitation, 25*, 602–610.

Smart, J. (2005). The promise of the International Classification of Functioning, Disability and Health (*ICF*). *Rehabilitation Education, 19*, 191–199.

Spear, J., & Schoepke, J. (1981). Psychologists and rehabilitation: Mandates and current training practices. *Professional Psychology, 12*, 606–612.

Stucki, G., Ewert, T., & Cieza, A. (2003). Value and application of the *ICF* in rehabilitation medicine. *Disability and Rehabilitation, 25*, 628–634.

Tarvydas, V. M., Peterson, D. B., & Michaelson, S. D. (2005). Ethical issues in case management. In F. Chan, M. Leahy, & J. Saunders (Eds.), *Case management for rehabilitation health professionals* (2nd ed., pp. 144–175). Osage Beach, MO: Aspen Professional Services.

Threats, T. T. & Worrall, L. (2004). Classifying communication disability using the ICF. *Advances in Speech Language Pathology, 6*, 53–62.

Ueda, S. & Okawa, Y. (2003). The subjective dimension of functioning and disability: What is it and what is it for? *Disability and Rehabilitation, 25*, 596–601.

U. S. Census Bureau. (2003, March). *Disability status: 2000*. Washington, DC: U.S. Department of Commerce, Economics and Statistics Administration.

U. S. Department of Health and Human Services. (2000). *Healthy people 2010*. Washington, DC: U.S. Department of Health and Human Services.

Üstün, T. B., Chaterji, S., Bickenbach, J., Kostanjsek, N., & Schneider, M. (2003). The international classification of functioning, disability and health: A new tool for understanding disability and health. *Disability and Rehabilitation, 25*, 565–571.

Velozo, C. A. (2005, June). *Tutorial: Developing measures based on the ICF*. Symposium conducted at the meeting of the World Health Organization's North American Collaborating Center, Mayo Clinic, Rochester, MN.

Walkup, J. (2000). Disability, health care, and public policy. *Rehabilitation Psychology, 45*, 409–422.

Whitely, J. M. (1984). *Counseling psychology: A historical perspective*. Schenectady, NY: Character Research Press.

World Health Organization. (1980). *ICIDH: International classification of impairments, disabilities, and handicaps. A manual of classification relating to the consequences of disease.* Geneva, Switzerland: Author.

World Health Organization. (1992). *International statistical classification of diseases and related health problems, tenth revision (ICD-10).* Geneva, Switzerland: Author.

World Health Organization. (2001). *ICF: International Classification of Functioning, Disability and Health.* Geneva, Switzerland: Author.

World Health Organization. (2002). *Innovative care for chronic conditions: Building blocks for action.* Geneva, Switzerland: Author.

PART III
Counseling and Supervision

CHAPTER 14

Measuring and Improving Psychotherapy Outcome in Routine Practice

MICHAEL J. LAMBERT
DAVID A. VERMEERSCH

The measurement of client outcome is central to evaluating the effects of counseling and psychotherapy and to improving therapeutic services (Kendall, Holmbeck, & Verduin, 2004). For decades, many researchers have argued that the central issue in all social science research is measurement (Nunnaly, 1978). In psychotherapy outcome research, the ability to accurately assess client response to treatment throughout the course of therapy, at termination, and/or at follow-up is directly related to the quality and appropriateness of the measure(s) being used for this purpose (Ogles, Lambert, & Fields, 2002). When client changes are not detected on an outcome measure, either treatment did not work or the instrument was inadequate in detecting changes that occurred (Guyatt, 1988). Therefore, it is imperative that appropriate measures of outcome are used, or else treatment gains may go undetected, a mistake that clinicians and researchers can ill afford to make in an age of increased accountability.

Of the thousands of psychological tests that have been published to date, most have been specifically designed to serve one or more of the following purposes: discrimination, prediction, and evaluation (Kirshner & Guyatt, 1985). A *discriminative* measure distinguishes between individuals or groups based on an underlying dimension when no external criterion or gold standard is available. Intelligence tests such as the Wechsler Adult Intelligence Scale (WAIS) and personality inventories such as the Minnesota Multiphasic Personality Inventory (MMPI) are examples of discriminative measures. Discriminative measures are often used as diagnostic instruments because they are specifically designed to discriminate between different individuals (based on their scores on a measure) at a single point in time.

A *predictive* measure classifies individuals into categories when a gold standard is available, either concurrently or prospectively to determine whether individuals have been classified correctly. This type of measure is generally used as a screening instrument to identify which specific individuals have or will develop a target condition. When a measure is used to assist in assessing whether a client is appropriate for a specific type of treatment (e.g., using a measure to assess a client's ego strength for the purpose of predicting whether he or she will be able to meaningfully participate in brief dynamic therapy), it is being used for predictive purposes. The Child Abuse Potential Inventory (Milner, Gold, Ayoub, & Jacewitz, 1984) is an example of a predictive measure in that it is designed to detect individuals who are at an increased risk of committing abusive acts.

An *evaluative* measure measures change over time (e.g., pre- and posttreatment, weekly change over the course of treatment) in an individual or group on the dimension(s) of interest. Tests designed to assess treatment benefits or outcomes are examples of evaluative measures. Outcome measures are quite different from discriminative and predictive measures because they are designed to measure intraindividual change over time via repeated administrations, rather than to discriminate between different individuals at a single point in time (Kirshner & Guyatt, 1985).

Psychological measures are often used, either appropriately or inappropriately, for some combination of the aforementioned purposes. A measure may be used to assist in determining a client's appropriateness for a specific type of treatment (i.e., predictive purpose), and then subsequently used to track that client's progress throughout the course of treatment and status at termination (i.e., evaluative purpose). Although this is justified in cases in which a measure has demonstrated utility in serving multiple purposes—such a practice often represents an application of a measure for a purpose for which that measure was not designed—and may lead to the inaccurate assessment of a client. Froyd, Lambert, and Froyd (1996) reported the MMPI to be among the 10 most frequently used self-report measures of outcome (i.e., evaluative purpose) although the MMPI was specifically designed for diagnostic purposes (i.e., discriminative purpose). The MMPI is not an appropriate instrument for measuring outcome because it contains many items that are not sensitive to changes in clients receiving treatment, is excessively long, and is relatively expensive. As this example suggests, it is extremely important that care is taken when selecting instruments to measure client response to treatment.

Given the importance of outcome measurement, clinicians would benefit from being aware of the qualities associated with sound outcome measures. The development of selection criteria (i.e., characteristics of instruments that will lead to the most accurate measurement of client change) for outcome measures to be implemented in practice has received increased attention in recent years (Trabin, 1995). Because professional practices may come to rely heavily on the demonstration of measured effects of treatments, it is imperative that outcome measures possess characteristics that will lead to the most accurate reflection of client improvement. Some authors (Horowitz, Milbrath, & Stinson, 1997; Pilkonis, 1997; Shea, 1997) have proposed selection criteria for instruments aimed at measuring changes in symptomatology associated with a specific disorder (e.g., Major Depressive Disorder) or a major diagnostic category (e.g., Personality Disorders). Others have focused on the development of universally accepted selection criteria that can be applied to the evaluation of any outcome measure (Lambert, Horowitz, & Strupp, 1997; Newman & Ciarlo, 1994). Although there are some differences between the selection criteria proposed by various authors, there appears to be considerable overlap as well.

Synthesizing and building on the available literature, Lambert et al. (1997) suggested that the following 13 criteria consistently emerge as an appropriate means of selecting methods and measures of outcome:

1. Relevance to target group;
2. Simple, teachable methods;
3. Use of measures with objective referents;
4. Use of multiple respondents;
5. Psychometric strengths and the availability of norms;
6. Low measure costs relative to its use;
7. Understanding by nonprofessional audiences, easy feedback, uncomplicated interpretation;
8. Useful in-clinical services;
9. Compatibility with a variety of clinical theories and practices;
10. The possibility of multiple administrations;
11. Comprehensiveness;
12. Ties to a diagnostic classification system (e.g., *DSM*); and
13. Sensitivity to change (i.e., the ability of an outcome measure to detect change following an intervention).

Attention to the aforementioned criteria will increase the likelihood of selecting a measure that provides the most accurate reflection of client outcome. Accurate assessment of client outcome will allow clinicians to demonstrate treatment effectiveness more convincingly and alter treatment strategies in response to client change if needed.

FROM OUTCOME MEASUREMENT AND MONITORING TO MANAGEMENT

A major emerging trend in psychotherapy outcome research is the shift from merely *measuring* or *monitoring* outcome to *managing* outcome. For many decades, and even to the present day, psychotherapy outcome research, with the notable exception of the behavior therapies, has relied heavily on study designs that measure client outcome at pretreatment and posttreatment. Although such designs have proven beneficial in establishing the general efficacy (through studies conducted under highly controlled experimental conditions; e.g., randomized clinical trials) and effectiveness (through studies conducted under less controlled conditions that are more representative of routine clinical practice) of the treatments under investigation, they are limited in that outcome data from these studies (because they are collected following termination from treatment) cannot be used to positively influence the treatment process of the individual clients under investigation. Pre- and posttreatment assessments are essentially a postmortem analysis of outcome because clients have already terminated treatment and nothing can be done to improve their outcomes, even if they experienced no change or even deteriorated in treatment.

A more recent trend in outcome research is the increased emphasis on regularly monitoring or tracking outcome throughout the treatment process. Regular monitoring of client progress has—in addition to answering questions related to the general efficacy and effectiveness of treatments—allowed researchers to explore more sophisticated questions related to psychotherapy outcome. Through regularly monitoring client change throughout treatment, researchers have been able to better understand patterns of change in psychotherapy, as evidenced in the growing and evolving body of literature related to the dose-response relationship in psychotherapy. However, similar to what has historically occurred in studies involving the pre- and posttreatment assessment of outcome, researchers have not typically used data from studies involving the regular monitoring of client progress in real time to positively influence treatment process and outcome. Although this is not a significant concern for the large number of clients who respond well to treatment and attain a positive outcome, it is particularly problematic for the large minority of clients who proceed completely through a course of treatment and experience no change (approximately 30% to 40%) or actually deteriorate (5% to 15%) in therapy (Hansen, Lambert, & Forman, 2002; Lambert & Ogles, 2004).

Outcome management extends the practice of measuring and monitoring client progress throughout the course of treatment by using these data to influence positively the treatment process and outcome of the clients under investigation. The major advantage of psychotherapy outcome management is that outcome data can be regularly gathered and used by administrators and clinicians for the purpose of making needed alterations in intervention strategy if clients are either unresponsive to or deteriorating in treatment, which is a primary concern of virtually all stakeholders in the treatment process.

Several psychotherapy outcome management systems has been developed and implemented in clinical service delivery settings worldwide. Though the specific procedures employed in each of these quality management systems vary, a common feature across all of them is the monitoring of client outcome throughout treatment and the use of these data to improve outcomes. The first system to arrive on the scene was developed by Howard and colleagues, using the COMPASS (Lueger et al., 2001). Kordy, Hannöver, and Richard (2001) developed a computer-assisted, feedback-driven psychotherapy quality management system in Germany; Barkham and colleagues (2001) created the Clinical Outcomes in Routine Evaluation (CORE) system widely used in the United Kingdom; and Kraus and Horan (1999) developed the Treatment Outcome Package (TOPS) system. In general, these later two systems have emphasized the administrative use of data rather than feedback to therapists during the course of psychotherapy. Administrative use allows managers of mental health services to examine the periodic and final outcome of interventions and compare outcomes to appropriate benchmarks. The Partners for Change Outcome Management System (PCOMS; Miller, Duncan, Sorrell, & Brown, 2005) is an ultra-brief measure that employs two, 4- item scales, one focusing one outcome and the other aimed at assessing the therapeutic alliance. Because of its brevity, this system is very clinician friendly and insures discussion of assessment results by client and therapist at each session. Each of these systems has advantages and disadvantages and each has achieved various levels of acceptance and use. However, because none of the preceding systems has evaluated the effects of feedback on client outcome using randomized controlled trials, conclusions about the relative value of each of these systems for enhancing client outcome will have to wait for the accumulation of evidence.

The remainder of this chapter describes one specific psychotherapy quality management system that has been developed, implemented, and empirically evaluated through multiple, randomized controlled trials (Harmon et al., 2007; Hawkins et al., 2004; Lambert, Whipple et al., 2001; Whipple et al., 2003). The major components of this system are detailed, as well as how the provision of regular feedback to clinicians on their clients' progress has been used to improve outcomes, particularly for those clients who are not having a favorable response to therapy.

THE OUTCOME QUESTIONNAIRE PSYCHOTHERAPY QUALITY MANAGEMENT SYSTEM

Given the demand for regular and efficient outcome assessment in psychotherapy outcome management, a suitable but brief measure was selected for implementation in the outcome questionnaire psychotherapy quality management system. The Outcome Questionnaire-45 (OQ-45; Lambert, Morton et al., 2004) is a 45-item, self-report measure designed for repeated administration throughout the course of treatment and at termination. In accordance with several reviews of the literature (e.g., Lambert, 1983), the OQ was conceptualized and designed to assess three domains of client functioning: (1) symptoms of psychological disturbance (particularly anxiety and depression), (2) interpersonal problems, and (3) social role functioning. Consistent with this conceptualization of outcome, the OQ-45 provides a total score, based on all 45 items, as well as Symptom Distress, Interpersonal Relations, and Social Role subscale scores. Each of these subscales contains some items related to the quality of life of the individual. Higher scores on the OQ-45 are indicative of greater levels of psychological disturbance.

Research has indicated that the OQ-45 is a psychometrically sound instrument, with excellent internal consistency (Cronbach's alpha = .93), adequate 3-week test-retest reliability (r = .84), and strong concurrent validity estimates ranging from .55 to .88 (all significant at p < .01) when the total score and the subscale scores were correlated with scores from the MMPI-2, Symptom Checklist 90—Revised (SCL-90R), Beck Depression Inventory (BDI), Zung Depression Scale, Taylor Manifest Anxiety Scale, State-Trait Anxiety Inventory, Inventory of Interpersonal Problems, and Social Adjustment Scale (Lambert, Morton et al., 2004). Furthermore, the OQ-45 has been shown to be sensitive to changes in multiple client populations over short periods of time while remaining relatively stable in untreated individuals (Vermeersch, Lambert, & Burlingame, 2002; Vermeersch et al., 2004). In short, the OQ-45 is a brief measure of psychological disturbance that is reliable, valid, and sensitive to changes clients make during psychotherapy. It is well suited for tracking client status during and following treatment.

Defining a Positive and Negative Outcome

A key element in psychotherapy quality management research is defining and operationalizing the concepts of positive and negative outcome. Jacobson and Truax (1991) offered a methodology by which client changes on an outcome measure can be classified in the following categories: recovered, reliably improved, no change, deteriorated. There are two pieces of information necessary to make these client outcome classifications: (1) a Reliable Change Index (RCI) and (2) a normal functioning cutoff score. Clinical and normative data were analyzed by Lambert, Morton, and colleagues (2004) to establish a Reliable Change Index (RCI) and a cutoff score for the OQ-45. The RCI obtained on the OQ-45 was 14 points, indicating that client changes of 14 or more points on the OQ-45 can be considered reliable (i.e., not due to measurement error). The cutoff score for normal functioning on the

OQ-45 was calculated to be 63, indicating that scores of 64 or higher are more likely to come from a dysfunctional population than a functional population, and scores of 63 or lower are more likely to come from a functional population than a dysfunctional population. Using this information, clients can be placed in the following categories based on the change observed in their OQ scores:

- *Recovered* (i.e., clinically significant change): Clients whose score decreases by 14 or more points and passes below the cutoff score of 64
- *Improved* (i.e., reliably changed): Clients whose score decreases by 14 or more points but does not pass below the cutoff score of 64
- *No change:* Clients whose score changes by less than 14 points in either direction
- *Deteriorated:* Clients whose score increases by 14 or more points

Support for the validity of the OQ-45's reliable change and cutoff score has been reported by Lunnen and Ogles (1998) and Beckstead et al. (2003). Having a method to classify each client's treatment response is an essential component of client-focused research because the primary purpose of psychotherapy outcome management is to understand and improve the gains each individual is making during the course of treatment. Furthermore, the ability to classify individual client change bridges the gap between traditional efficacy and effectiveness studies (that focus on changes made by groups of clients) and clinical practice (Kendall, Marrs-Garcia, Nath, & Sheldrick, 1999).

Prediction of Treatment Failure

A core element of outcome management systems is the prediction of treatment failure. To improve outcomes of clients who are responding poorly to treatment, such clients must be identified before termination from treatment and, ideally, as early as possible in the course of treatment. Although many studies have investigated the value of several client, therapist, client-therapist interaction, and extra-therapeutic variables in predicting outcome, very few of the variables explored are consistently highly predictive of outcome. Research utilizing the OQ-45 has indicated that the best predictors of outcome are initial severity of distress (i.e., pretreatment OQ-45 total score) and change score following separate sessions early in the course of treatment. Brown and Lambert (1998) found that pretreatment OQ-45 total score and change scores from Sessions 1 through 3 accounted for approximately 40% of the variance in final outcome, and that after taking these variables into account, all other variables combined (e.g., diagnosis, client demographics, therapist demographics, therapist theoretical orientation) accounted for less than 1% of the variance in final outcome. In prior studies using the OQ-45, the best way to predict outcome was to know how distressed clients were prior to treatment and whether the changes they made early in the treatment process were positive or negative.

One limitation in the aforementioned research relates to the extent to which these findings may be a function of mono-source bias (because the client was the source of both ratings) and common method variance (because the OQ-45 was both the predictor and the outcome criterion). However, change scores on the OQ have been found to correlate highly with change scores noted on other measures that are frequently used to assess outcome (Beckstead et al., 2003).

Given research on the variables most predictive of outcome, an empirically derived signal-alarm system was developed to alert clinicians to potential treatment failures (Finch, Lambert, Schaalje, 2001). This system plots a statistically generated expected recovery curve for differing levels of pretreatment distress on the OQ-45 and uses this as a basis for identifying clients who are not making expected treatment gains and are at risk of having a poor outcome. The accuracy of this signal-alarm system has been evaluated in a number of empirical investigations (Ellsworth, Lambert, & Johnson, 2006; Lambert, Whipple, Bishop, et al., 2002; Lutz et al., 2006; Percevic, Lambert, & Kordy, 2006; Spielmans, Masters, & Lambert, 2006), and, although an extensive discussion of the results of these studies is beyond the scope of this chapter, the signal-alarm system is highly sensitive in that it is able to accurately predict a poor outcome in about 88% of cases that actually end with a negative outcome (as measured by the OQ), and it is also far superior to clinical judgment in its ability to identify clients who are at risk of having a negative treatment outcome (Hannan et al., 2005).

Provision of Feedback and Clinical Support Tools

The signal-alarm system has been used as an intervention for preventing deterioration and enhancing positive outcomes in clients because it alerts clinicians to potential treatment failures and allows them to modify their treatment approach in an attempt to improve the outcomes of clients who are having a poor response to treatment and are predicted to have a poor outcome. Once a client takes the OQ-45, commences treatment, and completes a session of treatment, the signal-alarm system can be used to generate feedback regarding the client's progress. The feedback to therapists consists of several components, among which are a progress graph that includes all the client's OQ-45 total scores from pretreatment to the current session and a color-coded message (white, green, yellow, or red) that indicates the status of client progress. The specific language of the feedback messages varies not only as a function of client progress, but also as a function of the session at which the feedback is provided (e.g., the same amount of negative change may prompt a red message at session 2, but a red message at session 20 will be stated with more urgency). A summary of each feedback message follows:

- *White message:* The client is functioning in the normal range. Consider termination.
- *Green message:* The rate of change the client is making is in the adequate range. No change in the treatment plan is recommended.
- *Yellow message:* The rate of change the client is making is less than adequate. Consider altering the treatment plan by intensifying treatment, shifting intervention strategies, and monitoring progress especially carefully. This client may end up with no significant benefit from therapy.
- *Red message:* The client is not making the expected level of progress. Chances are he or she may drop out of treatment prematurely or have a negative treatment outcome. Steps should be taken to carefully review this case and decide on a new course of action such as referral for medication or intensification of treatment. The treatment plan should be reconsidered. Consideration should also be given to presenting this client at a case conference. The client's readiness for change may need to be reassessed.

Over the past 25 years, methodologies have been used in medical research and practice to manage clinical interventions in areas such as drug dosage, diagnosis, and preventive care. These interventions are often used in a stepwise approach that assists physicians in clinical decision making and provides recommendations to improve the quality of patient health care. Similarly, a set of clinical support tools (CST) was developed and integrated into the existing psychotherapy quality management system in an attempt to augment the feedback provided to therapists and further improve outcomes of nonresponding and deteriorating clients (Lambert et al., 2004; Whipple et al., 2003). As such, the CSTs are intended to be utilized by therapists when one of their clients is predicted to have a poor outcome (i.e., when a therapist receives a red or yellow warning message, indicating that the client is not responding or is deteriorating in treatment).

The CSTs are composed of a problem-solving decision tree designed to systematically direct therapists' attention to certain factors that have been shown to be consistently related to client outcome in the empirical literature, such as the therapeutic alliance, social support, readiness to change, diagnostic formulation, and need for psychiatric referral. Specific measures aimed at assisting therapists to assess the quality of the therapeutic alliance, client readiness for change, and client perceptions of social support are also included. These measures have included the Revised Helping Alliance Questionnaire

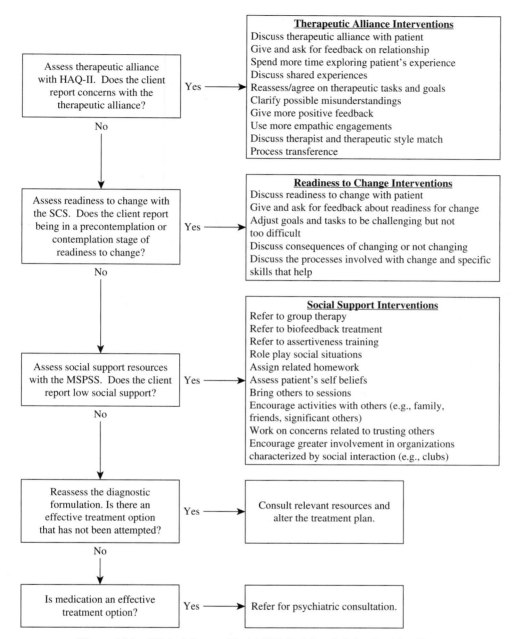

Figure 14.1   Clinical Support Tool (CST) Problem-Solving Decision Tree.

(HAQ-II; Luborsky, 1994), Multidimensional Scale of Perceived Social Support (MSPSS; Zimet, Dahlem, Zimet, & Farley, 1988), and Stages of Change Scale (SCS). Furthermore, the CSTs provide specific intervention strategies that could be used by therapists if problems were detected in the afore-mentioned domains. Figure 14.1 depicts the CST problem-solving decision tree provided to therapists in cases in which their clients were predicted to have a poor outcome.

In addition to providing feedback regarding client progress and CSTs to therapists, feedback can also be provided directly to clients. Client feedback messages (i.e., white, green, yellow, or red) that correspond to the aforementioned therapist feedback messages have been developed in an effort to directly inform clients of their progress in treatment and enhance client-therapist collaboration in treatment (Harmon et al., 2007; Hawkins et al., 2004). A summary of each of the client feedback messages (that can be provided between sessions 2 through 4) follows (each message is prefaced by the following statement, "The information presented below is based on your responses to the questionnaire that you complete prior to each therapy session."):

White message: It appears that you are experiencing low levels of distress as measured by your responses. If your level of progress is maintained, you will likely have a positive therapy outcome. Your responses to the questionnaire suggest that you feel more like those persons who are not overly burdened by their distress, and who do not believe they have a need for treatment. We *encourage* you to continue working as hard as you have to obtain the most you can from therapy.

Green message: It appears that your level of improvement is similar to the majority of patients who are receiving treatment. Although your current level of progress suggests that you are on course for a positive outcome, we *encourage* you to continue working hard so that you may receive maximum benefit from treatment. You may also want to consider discussing with your therapist the aspects of treatment that have been most and least helpful to experience the greatest benefit from your treatment.

Yellow/red message: It appears that you have not experienced a reduced level of distress. Because you may not be experiencing the expected rate of progress, it is possible that you have even considered terminating treatment, believing that therapy may not be helpful for you. Although you have yet to experience much relief from therapy, it is still early in treatment and there is the potential for future improvement. However, we *urge* you to discuss openly any concerns that you may be having about therapy with your therapist because there are strategies that can be used to help you receive the most out of your therapy. It may also require your willingness to complete additional questionnaires that may shed light about why you are not experiencing the expected rate of progress.

The administration of the OQ-45 (whether via paper and pencil or computerized), scoring, application of the signal-alarm system, and generation of feedback reports (for therapists and/or clients) can all be integratively and almost instantaneously processed through software called OQ-Analyst (administration of the measure and generation of the feedback report takes a total time of approximately 5 to 7 minutes). Figure 14.2 depicts a screen shot of a therapist feedback report generated by the OQ-Analyst software. This feedback report illustrates the progress of a client from intake to Session 9. At session 9, the client's degree of deterioration (i.e., an increase of 21 points, from a 58 at pretreatment to a 79 at session 9) prompted a red feedback message to be given to the therapist. The feedback report also allows the therapist to view all prior OQ-45 scores and associated feedback messages (e.g., this therapist first received a red feedback message at Session 3, then again at Sessions 5 and 9). At every session, the therapist is able to look below the graph and read the message that is provided. Feedback messages vary depending on the size of the deviation from expected treatment response (the dark sloping line) and amount of therapy. Client scores are also displayed in the graph in relation to the horizontal line at a score of 63, which as previously mentioned, represents the cutoff score between client and nonclient populations on the OQ-45. The feedback report also provides information about the client's answer to five critical items, as well as other information (e.g., whether the client's change at the current session meets clinical significance criteria for recovery, improvement, no change, or deterioration) that may potentially be helpful to a therapist working with such a client.

Impact of Feedback on Client Outcome

Five controlled studies have been published that examine the effects of providing client progress feedback to therapists and clients (Harmon et al., 2007; Hawkins et al., 2004; Lambert, Whipple, et al., 2001; Lambert, Whipple, Vermeersch, et al., 2002; Whipple et al., 2003). Each of the studies required about 1 year of daily data collection and evaluated the effects of providing feedback about a client's improvement through the use of progress graphs and warnings about clients who were not demonstrating expected treatment responses (signal-alarm cases). Each of these studies asked the primary question: Does formal feedback to therapists (and in two studies, clients) on client progress improve

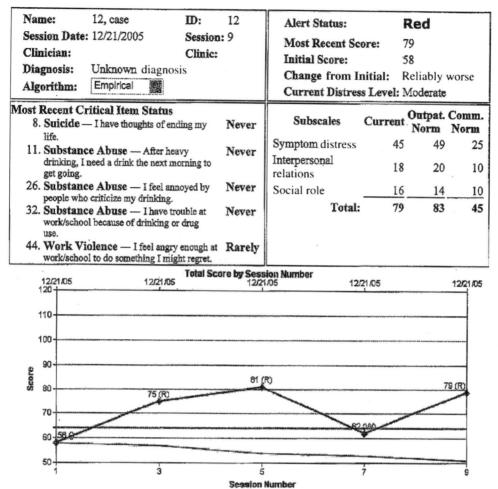

Name:	12, case	ID:	12
Session Date: 12/21/2005		Session: 9	
Clinician:		Clinic:	
Diagnosis:	Unknown diagnosis		
Algorithm:	Empirical		

Alert Status:	**Red**
Most Recent Score:	79
Initial Score:	58
Change from Initial:	Reliably worse
Current Distress Level:	Moderate

Most Recent Critical Item Status

8. **Suicide** — I have thoughts of ending my life. **Never**
11. **Substance Abuse** — After heavy drinking, I need a drink the next morning to get going. **Never**
26. **Substance Abuse** — I feel annoyed by people who criticize my drinking. **Never**
32. **Substance Abuse** — I have trouble at work/school because of drinking or drug use. **Never**
44. **Work Violence** — I feel angry enough at work/school to do something I might regret. **Rarely**

Subscales	Current	Outpat. Norm	Comm. Norm
Symptom distress	45	49	25
Interpersonal relations	18	20	10
Social role	16	14	10
Total:	79	83	45

Total Score by Session Number

Graph Label Legend:
(R) = Red: High chance of negative outcome   (Y) = Yellow: Some chance of negative outcome
(G) = Green: Making expected progress   (W) = White: Functioning in normal range

Feedback Message:
The patient is deviating from the expected response to treatment. They are not on track to realize substantial benefit from treatment. Chances are they may drop out of treatment prematurely or have a negative treatment outcome. Steps should be taken to carefully review this case and identify reasons for poor progress. It is recommended that you be alert to the possible need to improve the therapeutic alliance, reconsider the client's readiness for change and the need to renegotiate the therapeutic contract, intervene to strengthen social supports, or possibly alter your treatment plan by intensifying treatment, shifting intervention strategies, or decide on a new course of action, such as referral for medication. Continuous monitoring of future progress is highly recommended.

Figure 14.2   OQ-Analyst Screen Shot Illustrating Feedback Report of Client Progress Provided to Therapist.

psychotherapy outcomes? The hypothesis in each of these studies predicted: Clients identified as signal-alarm cases (those predicted to have a poor final treatment response) whose therapist received feedback will show better outcomes than similar clients whose therapists did not receive feedback.

The five studies shared many things in common:

- Consecutive cases seen in routine care regardless of client diagnosis or comorbid conditions (rather than being disorder specific).

- Random assignment of client to experimental (feedback) and treatment-as-usual conditions (no feedback) was made in all but one of the studies.

- Psychotherapists provided a variety of theoretically guided treatments, with most adhering to cognitive behavioral and eclectic orientations and fewer representing psychodynamic and experiential orientations.
- Different types of clinicians were involved—postgraduate therapists and graduate students each accounted for about 50% of clients seen.
- Therapists saw both experimental (feedback) and no feedback cases, thus limiting the likelihood that outcome differences between conditions could be due to therapist effects.
- The outcome measure as well as the methodology rules or standards for identifying signal-alarm clients (failing cases) remained constant.
- The length of therapy (dosage) was determined by client and therapist rather than by research design or arbitrary insurance limits.

Client characteristics such as gender, age, and ethnicity were generally similar across four of the studies and came from the same university counseling center, whereas the fifth sample (Hawkins et al., 2004) was older, more disturbed, and treated in a hospital-based outpatient clinic.

Another notable difference in the studies was that two of the studies (Harmon et al., 2007; Whipple et al., 2003) included a second experimental condition that was intended to strengthen the feedback intervention by encouraging therapists to use the CSTs (i.e., problem-solving decision tree, additional measures and cutoffs, and suggestions for alternative clinical interventions) with signal-alarm cases. The Harmon et al. and Hawkins et al. studies also included two experimental conditions aimed at comparing treatment-as-usual with feedback to therapists, and feedback to both therapists and clients. Design features of the five studies are detailed in Table 14.1.

Results from the combined studies are presented graphically in Figure 3. As can be seen, the clients identified as Not-on-Track (NOT) had a different outcome course depending on assignment to the no-feedback or feedback treatment conditions. Up to the point that these signal-alarm cases were first signaled (or in the case of the no-feedback treatment, could have been signaled), the graph illustrates an average worsening of around 10 points (about one-half a standard deviation on the OQ-45). From the point of the signal-alarm, all the experimental (feedback) groups improved, whereas the no feedback control (treatment as usual; TAU) cases improved to an average score near 80 but were, as a group, slightly worse off than when they entered treatment. Also displayed is the outcome for On-Track (OT) cases where therapists did get feedback (OT- FB) and did not get feedback (OT-NFb). As can be seen,

Table 14.1 Summary of Design Characteristics of Controlled Outcome Studies Aimed at Reducing Deterioration and Enhancing Positive Outcome

Study	Clients/ Therapists N	TAU	Therapist Feedback	Therapist/Client Feedback	Clinical Support Tools
Lambert, Whipple, et al. (2001)	609/31	X	X		
Lambert, Whipple, Vermeersch, et al. (2002)	1020/49	X	X		
Whipple et al. (2003)	981/48	X	X		X
Hawkins et al. (2004)	201/5	X	X	X	
Harmon et al. (2007)	1374/47		X	X	X

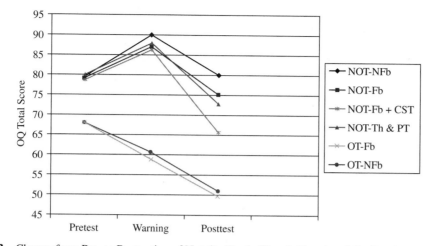

Figure 14.3   Change from Pre- to Posttesting of Not-On-Track (Signal-Alarm) and On-Track Patients.
Note: NOT-NFb = Signal-alarm cases whose therapist got no signal or message, treatment as usual; NOT-Fb = Signal-alarm cases whose therapist got a red or yellow signal, indicating client was at risk for treatment failure, treatment as usual; NOT-Fb + CST = Signal-alarm cases whose therapist got feedback and used the Clinical Support Tools; NOT-Th & P = Signal-alarm cases in which both therapists and clients received direct feedback; OT-Fb = Clients whose therapist got a green or white signal and message and who were predicted to have a positive outcome; OT-NFb = Clients who were making satisfactory progress and whose therapist never received any information about their progress, that is treatment as usual. Pretest OQ = Average client scores on the OQ-45 at intake; Warning OQ = Average client score on the OQ-45 at the point at which a patient qualified for a yellow or red message(the time of warning varied across patients); Posttest OQ = Average client OQ-45 score at the session they terminated treatment (number of sessions until termination occurred varied).

these clients made steady progress and left treatment, as a group, well in the ranks of normal functioning. It appeared to make little difference in outcome for feedback (Green or White messages) to have been given.

In the individual studies themselves, the effect sizes (Cohen's *d*) for the difference between various feedback conditions for the NOT clients and TAU controls ranged from a low of .34 (when NOT clients whose therapists received feedback regarding their clients' progress were compared with TAU controls whose therapists received no feedback) to .92 (when NOT clients whose therapists received feedback regarding their clients' progress and used the CSTs to improve outcomes in these clients were compared with TAU controls whose therapists received no feedback). Such effect sizes are surprisingly large when we consider an average effect for comparative studies (active treatments) typically falls between .00 and .20 (Lambert & Ogles, 2004) and is widely considered important enough to lead to a recommendation of a "best practice." Across the five studies, some inconsistent results have been found. Usually the provision of NOT feedback increases the number of sessions that clients attend by about 2 to 3 sessions (as compared to NOT no-feedback) and decreases sessions for OT cases by two thirds of a session (as compared to OT no-feedback), but this was not found in the Hawkins et al. (2004) study where number of sessions attended by both NOT groups was equal and number of sessions attended by both OT groups was also equal. In about half the studies, feedback to OT cases improved outcomes despite reducing treatment length. Direct feedback to clients in the form of a written message improved outcomes dramatically in the Hawkins et al. (2004) study, but had no impact in the Harmon et al. (2007) replication.

Table 14.2 presents a classification of signal-alarm clients based on their final treatment status at termination. As shown, 20% of the signal-alarm cases seen by therapists who received no feedback showed a negative treatment outcome at termination. In contrast, when therapists received feedback that identified their client as not-on-track, only 15%, 12%, and 8% depending on treatment condition deteriorated. The rates for signal-alarm cases (NOT) showing clinically significant or reliable change were also markedly different, with the highest rates of improvement in the therapist-feedback plus CSTS

Table 14.2   Percent of Not-On-Track (Signal-Alarm) Cases Meeting Criteria for Clinically Significant Change at Termination

	TAU	T-Fb	T-Fb + CST	T/C-Fb
Outcome classification	N (%)	N (%)	N (%)	N (%)
Deteriorated[a]	64 (20)	90 (15)	12 (8)	19 (12)
No change	184 (58)	316 (53)	73 (47)	71 (46)
Reliable/or clinically significant change[b]	70 (22)	196 (33)	169 (45)	57 (37)

Notes: TAU = Patients who were not on track and whose therapist was not given feedback; T-Fb = Patients who were not on track and whose therapist received feedback; T-Fb + CST = Patients who were not on track and whose therapist received feedback and used clinical support tools; T/C-Fb = Therapist feedback plus written direct feedback to clients.
[a]Worsened by at least 14 points on the OQ from pretreatment to posttreatment.
[b]Improved by at least 14 points on the OQ or improved and passed the cutoff between dysfunctional and functional populations.

condition (45%), compared to 22% in the TAU condition. These data suggest the improved outcomes for clients in the experimental conditions are not only statistically significant but possess considerable clinical meaning for the individual client.

Therapist Effects and Improving Outcomes: Another Form of Outcome Management

Using the rather large data base that has accumulated over the years, the outcome of clients as it relates to specific therapists has been examined in two overlapping studies (Okiishi et al., 2003, 2006). After testing for the effects of different therapeutic orientations, therapist experience, gender, and age and finding that these variables did not make a significant difference with regard to client outcome, comparisons of outcome were made across 71 therapists who treated clients with equivalent levels of initial severity. Each therapist saw a minimum of 30 clients (range 30 to 350+). As might be expected, which therapist the client saw for therapy had a larger impact on outcome than any of the other variables. Most therapists could not be distinguished from one another based on their clients' outcome. However, there was enough variability in client outcome by therapist to provide an opportunity to enhance client treatment response through the use of this information. Although the results of these studies will not be elaborated on here, the upper and lower 10% showed enough difference to warrant exploration of differences in the way these individuals practice. This issue is being explored in an ongoing investigation.

To give an example of the differences in outcomes for these extreme groups, therapists whose clients had the best outcomes had an improved/recovery rate of 44% and a deterioration rate of 5%. In contrast, therapists whose clients demonstrated the poorest outcomes improved/recovered at a rate of 28% and 11% deteriorated. One therapist saw over 160 clients who had a 19% deterioration rate, whereas another saw over 300 clients with less than 1% deteriorating. Because therapists were given anonymity in return for participation in the data analysis, this information could not be directly and immediately used to enhance client outcome, but a further understanding and use of this information for scientific and humanitarian purposes is highly desirable.

SUMMARY AND CONCLUSION

The program of research described in this chapter has taken over a decade to complete. It began with the simple aim of applying research to practice with the goal of enhancing client outcomes. Outcome was defined conceptually as including symptoms of psychopathology, interpersonal difficulties, social role functioning, and well-being. The elements of these constructs were operationally defined through a 45-item self-report scale that could be administered on a session-by-session basis throughout psychotherapy. The scale was constructed and validated with particular attention to including items that remained constant over time if a person went untreated, but demonstrated positive change with increasing doses of psychotherapy.

Following the progress of thousands of clients during treatment allowed for the study of longitudinal trends of change over time. These longitudinal data led to the generation of expected recovery curves and the determination of the amount of deviation from expected recovery that is predictive of a poor outcome. From this information, an empirically derived signal-alarm system for providing ongoing feedback to therapists (with particular emphasis placed on providing feedback about potential treatment failure) was developed and its predictive accuracy was tested and supported. This signal-alarm system ultimately led to the creation of software that made providing this information to therapists and clients nearly instantaneous.

Perhaps most important, the signal-alarm system has been successfully implemented in five clinical trials that clearly demonstrate that feedback provided to therapists about impending treatment failure improves the outcome for clients at risk for having no response to treatment or a poor outcome. These studies have led to the development and use of CSTs and feedback to clients to further improve outcomes of these potential treatment failures. Evidence that these strategies are feasible and improve client outcome is mounting, but further investigations of the impact of CSTs and feedback to clients are needed. Given the large sample sizes of the five clinical trials, and a combined overall sample size of over 4,000 clients, the current findings seem compelling and suggest that the provision of feedback to therapists in cases that are at-risk for treatment failure should be considered an evidence-based practice in psychology (American Psychological Association, 2006). Given the relatively large effect sizes obtained in these and other studies of feedback (Berking, Orth, & Lutz, 2006), particularly in comparison to the effect sizes obtained in controlled comparative studies of "different" therapies, it is conceivable that future psychotherapy outcome management efforts may yield as much, if not more, benefit to client outcome as any search for new and specific treatments for specific disorders.

This research has also made it very apparent that there is considerable variability in client outcomes as a function of the person providing treatment. In contrast to the fact that most practitioners see themselves as *above average* therapists—a phenomenon not restricted to mental health professionals and psychotherapy (Kruger, 1999)—client outcome is normally distributed and there are a few therapists who produce unusually good and poor outcomes. Studies aimed at understanding what these therapists do and how this may enhance training and practice are underway.

Despite the compelling nature of these findings, several limitations to this research program should be noted: First, most of the results summarized on feedback were based on data collected in a university counseling center. Studies in other settings are needed. A recent study of a 30-day inpatient treatment program in Switzerland (Berking et al., 2006) using similar methods has replicated the effects of progress feedback, and we found similar positive effects in a hospital-based outpatient clinic, but many more studies will be needed before the limitations and generalizability of such interventions are known.

Second, no attempts were made in any of the five controlled studies to dictate how feedback was used by therapists (e.g., therapists were free to share the information with clients or not, depending on therapist preferences). Although this methodology increases the likelihood that the results reflect what will happen in other clinical settings, clinicians' actions with regard to looking at feedback, sharing it with clients, and modifying treatment, remain largely unknown (with the exception of the two studies in which feedback was directly delivered to clients).

Third, this research utilizes a single self-report measure of improvement and therefore provides only one view of the impact of therapy on clients. Decisions regarding the continued provision of treatment, modification of ongoing treatment, and the like, cannot be made based on a single questionnaire or independent from clinical judgment. Nevertheless, the results of these studies do seem to suggest that the feedback system should be viewed as supplementing clinical decision making—a "lab test" result to be used by clinicians, rather than a replacement for the clinician's judgment.

Observations regarding the practicality of implementing a feedback system in routine care are also warranted. Generally speaking, clinicians do not see the value of frequent assessments based on standardized scales (Hatfield & Ogles, 2004), possibly because they are confident in their ability to accurately observe client worsening and provide an appropriate response. Despite evidence that suggests psychotherapists are not alert to treatment failure (Hannan et al., 2005; Yalom & Lieberman, 1971), and strong evidence that clinical judgments are usually found to be inferior to actuarial methods across a wide variety of predictive tasks (Meehl, 1954), therapists' confidence in their clinical judgment stands as a barrier to implementation of monitoring and feedback systems. In addition, clinicians are used to practicing in private and with considerable autonomy. Monitoring and managing client treatment response makes the effects of practice somewhat public and transparent. Such transparency inevitably raises evaluation anxiety and fears of losing control. Implementation requires the cooperation of therapists and takes time before it is apparent to clinicians that the feedback is helpful.

The practical difficulties of adding monitoring and managing activities to busy practices can also be an important barrier to implementation. Fortunately, recent developments in software programs make the possibility of instantaneous feedback to clinicians easy to implement. If the client takes the OQ-45 immediately prior to the scheduled psychotherapy session, feedback through the OQ-Analyst is available to the therapist prior to beginning that session. Despite the aforementioned limitations and challenges, it is hoped that the study of these research results convinces practitioners that systematically monitoring their clients with the methods described in this chapter is in the best interest of clients and that researchers will consider replication, improvement, and expansion of these findings.

REFERENCES

American Psychological Association. (2006). Evidence-based practice in psychology. *American Psychologist, 61* (4), 271–285.

Barkham, M., Margison, F., Leach, C., Lucock, M., Mellor-Clark, J., Evans, C., et al. (2001). Service profiling and outcomes benchmarking using the CORE-OM: Toward practice-based evidence in the psychological therapies. *Journal of Consulting and Clinical Psychology, 69*, 184–196.

Beckstead, D. J., Hatch, A. L., Lambert, M. J., Eggett, D. L., Goates, M. K., & Vermeersch, D. A. (2003). Clinical significance of the Outcome Questionnaire (OQ-45.2). *Behavior Analyst Today, 4*, 79–90.

Berking, M., Orth, U., & Lutz, W. (2006). Wie effekiv sind systematische Ruckmeldungen des therapieverlaufs an den therapeuten? Eine empirishe studie in einem stationar-verhaltenstherapeutischen setting, *Zeitchrift fur Klinishe Psychologie und Psychotherapie, 35*, 21–29.

Brown, G. S., & Lambert, M. J. (1998, June). *Tracking patient progress: Decision making for cases who are not benefiting from psychotherapy*. Paper presented at the annual meeting of the Society for Psychotherapy Research, Snowbird, UT.

Ellsworth, J. R., Lambert, M. J., & Johnson, J. (2006). A comparison of the Outcome Questionnaire-45 and Outcome Questionnaire-30 in classification and prediction of treatment outcome. *Clinical Psychology and Psychotherapy, 13*, 379–392.

Finch, A. E., Lambert, M. J., & Schaalje, B. G. (2001). Psychotherapy quality control: The statistical generation of expected recovery curves for integration into an early warning system. *Clinical Psychology and Psychotherapy, 8*, 231–242.

Froyd, J. E., Lambert, M. J., & Froyd, J. D. (1996). A survey and critique of psychotherapy outcome measurement. *Journal of Mental Health, 5*, 11–15.

Guyatt, G. (1988). Measuring health status in chronic airflow limitation. *European Respiratory Journal, 1*, 560–564.

Hannan, C., Lambert, M. J., Harmon, C., Nielsen, S. L., Smart, D. W., Shimokawa, K. et al. (2005). A lab test and algorithms for identifying clients at risk for treatment failure. *Journal of Clinical Psychology: In Session, 61*, 155–163.

Hansen, N. B., Lambert, M. J., & Forman, E. V. (2002). The psychotherapy dose-response effect and its implications for treatment delivery services. *Clinical Psychology: Science and Practice, 9*, 329–343.

Harmon, S. C., Lambert, M. J., Smart, D. W., Hawkins, E. J., Nielsen, S. L., Slade, K., et al. (2007). Enhancing outcome for potential treatment failures: Therapist/client feedback and clinical support tools. *Psychotherapy Research, 17*, 380–391.

Hatfield, D. R., & Ogles, B. M. (2004). The current climate of outcome measures use in clinical practice. *Professional* Psychology: *Research and Practice, 35*, 325–337.

Hawkins, E. J., Lambert, M. J., Vermeersch, D. A., Slade, K., & Tuttle, K. (2004). The effects of providing patient progress information to therapists and patients. *Psychotherapy Research, 14*, 308–327.

Horowitz, M. J., Milbrath, C., & Stinson, C. H. (1997). Assessing personality disorders. In H. H. Strupp, L. M. Horowitz, & M. J. Lambert (Eds.), *Measuring patient changes in mood, anxiety, and personality disorders: Toward a core battery* (pp. 401–432). Washington, DC: American Psychological Association.

Jacobson, N. S., & Truax, P. (1991). Clinical significance: A statistical approach to defining meaningful change in psychotherapy research. *Journal of Consulting and Clinical Psychology, 59*, 12–19.

Kendall, P. C., Holmbeck, G., & Verduin, T. (2004). Methodology, design, and evaluation in psychotherapy research. In M. J. Lambert (Ed.), *Bergin and Garfield's handbook of psychotherapy and behavior change* (5th ed., pp. 16–43). Hoboken, NJ: Wiley.

Kendall, P. C., Marrs-Garcia, A., Nath, S. R., & Sheldrick, R. C. (1999). Normative comparisons for the evaluation of clinical significance. *Journal of Consulting and Clinical Psychology, 67*, 285–299.

Kirshner, B., & Guyatt, G. (1985). A methodological framework for assessing health indices. *Journal of Chronic Diseases, 38*, 27–36.

Kordy, H., Hannöver, W., & Richard, M. (2001). Computer-assisted feedback-driven quality management for psychotherapy: The Stuttgart-Heidelberg model. *Journal of Consulting and Clinical Psychology, 69*, 173–183.

Kraus, D. R., & Horan, F. P. (1999). Outcomes roadblocks: Problems and solutions. *Behavioral Health Management, 17*(5), 22–26.

Kruger, J. (1999). Lake Wobegon be gone! The 'below-average effect' and the egocentric nature of comparative ability judgments. *Journal of Personality and Social Psychology, 77*(2), 221–232.

Lambert, M. J. (1983). Introduction to assessment of psychotherapy outcome: Historical perspective and current issues. In M. J. Lambert, E. R. Christensen, & S. S. DeJulio (Eds.), *The assessment of psychotherapy outcome* (pp. 3–32). New York: Wiley.

Lambert, M. J., Horowitz, L. M., & Strupp, H. H. (1997). Conclusions and recommendations. In H. H. Strupp, L. M. Horowitz, & M. J. Lambert (Eds.), *Measuring patient changes in mood, anxiety, and personality disorders: Toward a core battery* (pp. 491–502). Washington, DC: American Psychological Association.

Lambert, M. J., Morton, J. J., Hatfield, D., Harmon, C., Hamilton, S., Reid, R. C., et al. (2004). *Administration and Scoring Manual for the Outcome Questionnaire-45.* Salt Lake City, UT: OQ Measures.

Lambert, M. J., & Ogles, B. M. (2004). The efficacy and effectiveness of psychotherapy. In M. J. Lambert (Ed.), *Bergin and Garfield's handbook of psychotherapy and behavior change* (5th ed., pp. 139–193). Hoboken, NJ: Wiley.

Lambert, M. J., Whipple, J. L., Bishop, M. J., Vermeersch, D. A., Gray, G. V., & Finch, A. E. (2002). Comparison of empirically derived and rationally derived methods for identifying clients at risk for treatment failure. *Clinical Psychology and Psychotherapy, 9*, 149–164.

Lambert, M.J., Whipple, J. L., Harmon, C., Shimokawa, K., Slade, K., & Christofferson, C. (2004). *Clinical Support Tools Manual.* Provo, UT: Department of Psychology, Brigham Young University.

Lambert, M. J., Whipple, J. L., Hawkins, E. J., Vermeersch, D. A., Nielsen, S. L., & Smart, D. W. (2003). Is it time for clinicians to routinely track patient outcome?: A meta-analysis. *Clinical Psychology: Science and Practice, 10*, 288–301.

Lambert, M. J., Whipple, J. L., Smart, D. W., Vermeersch, D. A., Nielsen, S. L., & Hawkins, E. J. (2001). The effects of providing therapists with feedback on client progress during psychotherapy: Are outcomes enhanced? *Psychotherapy Research, 11*, 49–68.

Lambert, M. J., Whipple, J. L., Vermeersch, D. A., Smart, D. W., Hawkins, E. J., Nielsen, S. L., et al. (2002). Enhancing psychotherapy outcomes via providing feedback on client progress: A replication. *Clinical Psychology and Psychotherapy, 9*, 91–103.

Luborsky, L. B. (1994). Therapeutic alliances as predictors of psychotherapy outcomes: Factors explaining the predictive success. In A. O. Horvath & L. S. Greenberg (Eds.), *The working alliance: Theory, research, and practice* (pp. 38–50). New York: Wiley.

Lueger, R. J., Howard, K. I., Martinovich, Z., Lutz, W., Anderson, E. E., & Grissom, G. (2001). Assessing treatment progress of individual clients using expected treatment response models. *Journal of Consulting and Clinical Psychology*, *69*, 150–158.

Lunnen, K. M., & Ogles, B. M. (1998). A multiperspective, multivariable evaluation of reliable change. *Journal of Consulting and Clinical Psychology, 66*, 400–410.

Lutz, W., Lambert, M. J., Harmon, S. C., Stulz, N., Tschitsaz, A., & Schürch, E. (2006). The probability of treatment success, failure and duration: What can be learned from empirical data to support decision making in clinical practice? *Clinical Psychology and Psychotherapy, 13*, 223–232.

Meehl, P. E. (1954). *Clinical versus statistical prediction*. Minneapolis: University of Minnesota Press.

Miller, S. D., Duncan, B. L., Sorrell, R., & Brown, G. S. (2005). The partners for change outcome system. *Journal of Clinical Psychology: In Session, 61*, 199–208.

Milner, J. S., Gold, R. G., Ayoub, C., & Jacewitz, M. M. (1984). Predictive validity of the Child Abuse Potential Inventory. *Journal of Consulting and Clinical Psychology, 52*(5), 879–884.

Newman, F. L. & Ciarlo, J. A., (1994). Criteria for selecting psychological instruments for treatment outcome assessments. In M. E. Maruish (Ed.), *The use of psychological testing for treatment planning and outcome assessment* (pp. 98–110). Hillside, NJ: Erlbaum.

Nunnaly, J. C. (1978). *Psychometric theory*. New York: McGraw-Hill.

Ogles, B. M., Lambert, M. J., & Fields, S. A. (2002). *Essentials of outcome assessment*. Hoboken, NJ: Wiley.

Okiishi, J. C., Lambert, M. J., Eggett, D., Nielsen, S. L., Dayton, D. D., & Vermeersch, D. A. (2006). An analysis of therapist treatment effects: Toward providing feedback to individual therapists on their patients' psychotherapy outcome. *Journal of Clinical Psychology, 62*(9), 1157–1172.

Okiishi, J. C., Lambert, M. J., Nielsen, S. L., & Ogles, B. M. (2003). In search of supershink: Using patient outcome to identify effective and ineffective therapists. *Clinical Psychology and Psychotherapy, 10*, 361–373.

Pilkonis, P. A. (1997). Measurement issues relevant to personality disorders. In H. H. Strupp, L. M. Horowitz, & M. J. Lambert (Eds.), *Measuring patient changes in mood, anxiety, and personality disorders: Toward a core battery* (pp. 371–388). Washington, DC: American Psychological Association.

Percevic, R., Lambert, M. J., & Kordy, H. (2006). What is the predictive value of responses to psychotherapy for its future course? Empirical explorations and consequences for outcome monitoring. *Psychotherapy Research, 16*, 364–373.

Shea, M. T. (1997). Core battery conference: Assessment of change in personality disorders. In H. H. Strupp, L. M. Horowitz, & M. J. Lambert (Eds.), *Measuring patient changes in mood, anxiety, and personality disorders: Toward a core battery* (pp. 389–400). Washington, DC: American Psychological Association.

Spielmans, G. I., Masters, K. S., & Lambert, M. J. (2006). A comparison of rational versus empirical methods in prediction of negative psychotherapy outcome. *Clinical Psychology and Psychotherapy, 13*, 202–214.

Trabin, T. (1995). Making quality and accountability happen in behavioral healthcare. *Behavioral Healthcare Tomorrow, 4*(3), 5–6.

Vermeersch, D. A., Lambert, M. J., & Burlingame, G. M. (2002). Outcome questionnaire: Item sensitivity to change. *Journal of Personality Assessment, 74*, 242–261.

Vermeersch, D. A., Whipple, J. L., Lambert, M. J., Hawkins, E. J., Burchfield, C. M., & Okiishi, J. C. (2004). Outcome questionnaire: Is it sensitive to changes in counseling center clients? *Journal of Counseling Psychology, 51*, 38–49.

Whipple, J. L., Lambert, M. J., Vermeersch, D. A., Smart, D. W., Nielsen, S. L., & Hawkins, E. J. (2003). Improving the effects of psychotherapy: The use of early identification of treatment failure and problem solving strategies in routine practice. *Journal of Counseling Psychology, 58*, 59–68.

Yalom, I. D., & Lieberman, M. A. (1971). A study of encounter group casualties. *Archives of General Psychiatry, 25*, 16–30.

Zimet, G. D., Dahlem, N. W., Zimet, S. G., & Farley, G. K. (1988). The multidimensional scale of perceived social support. *Journal of Personality Assessment, 52*, 30–41.

CHAPTER 15

The Importance of Treatment and the Science of Common Factors in Psychotherapy

ZAC E. IMEL
BRUCE E. WAMPOLD

In any scientific experiment, having a sophisticated understanding of the phenomenon that is to be manipulated (i.e., the independent variable) is important. Unlike other psychological experiments in which the independent variable can be tightly controlled, psychotherapy is notoriously difficult to study. Furthermore, the proliferation of treatment models and techniques (Bergin & Garfield, 1994) results in a tremendously diverse set of healing practices that, at first glance, have little in common. One common strategy for dealing with this complexity is to treat each psychotherapy or technique as a distinct phenomenon, developing explicit criteria for the implementation of treatment-specific interventions so that mechanisms unique to each procedure can be examined. Consequently, distinctive and detailed theories of change are needed for each therapy. Alternatively, a *common factors* approach to understanding the effects of psychotherapy holds that the unique theoretical content of an intervention is not an important guide to the mechanisms responsible for client change. Instead, this approach is concerned with determining the core ingredients inherent in all successful psychotherapies so that a more parsimonious understanding of therapy can be developed (Norcross, 2005). Cognitive-behavioral therapies (CBT), psychodynamic therapy, experiential and existential therapies, as well as other psychological treatments, although apparently quite diverse, share much in common.

This chapter reviews evidence that suggests the common factors perspective is scientifically valid and has the potential to increase the benefits of psychotherapy to clients. First, we discuss the alternative to common factors, the medical model. Second, we review evidence suggesting that the medical model is less valid than the common factors model in the domain of psychotherapy. Third, we provide a broad overview of the common factors literature, citing predominant common factor schemes and noting their critiques. Finally, to address these critiques, we highlight processes and mechanisms that are central to one common factors perspective, *the contextual model*.

MEDICAL MODEL

The medical model suggests psychotherapy is best understood as an analogue to Western medical procedures. *Specificity,* the essence of the medical model, holds that healing and symptom relief occur through discovery of an underlying disease state and treatments designed to directly address the underlying biological dysfunction (Wampold, 2001a, 2001b). This is similar to an antibiotic for a bacterial infection—the antibiotic agent kills the bacteria that are the cause of the illness and the patient improves. Whatever improvement is accomplished through hope, expectation, or the therapeutic relationship is considered unimportant (or perhaps less important). The antibiotic is the critical ingredient and the context in which the pill is administered is relatively unimportant.

249

In psychotherapy, the equivalent of the medical model and the corresponding notion of specificity is the assumption that a treatment is effective because it alters a particular psychological dysfunction; namely, those outlined in the treatment's theoretical rationale. Accordingly, the therapeutic techniques (e.g., interpretation of maladaptive relational patterns or changing core cognitive schema), which are derived from the treatment theory, are responsible for the benefits of psychotherapy—and not other factors such as the creation of adaptive expectations, hope, or remoralization. A modern psychodynamically oriented therapist may hold that depression is the result of a maladaptive relational pattern learned in childhood interactions with important adult figures. Improvement occurs as the therapist develops an understanding of this relational pattern in the therapeutic relationship; by making this pattern more explicit, the therapist helps the client develop alternative methods of relating to others (Strupp & Binder, 1984). Without an accurate interpretation of the relational pattern and a corresponding change in relating to others, it is assumed that the depression would persist.

Having now outlined the assumptions of the medical model, we briefly review the evidence derived from psychotherapy outcome research that suggests that in psychotherapy that this underlying explanatory model may be flawed.

FINDINGS FROM OUTCOME RESEARCH

There are several predictions that follow from a medical model of psychotherapy. If the predictions of the medical model in psychotherapy hold, it is unlikely that the common factors model is valid or important. We briefly examine two areas: (1) treatment differences, and (2) theory-specific predictors of outcome.

Treatment Differences

If specific ingredients are responsible for the efficacy of psychotherapy, research should reveal some differences among treatments. Thus, treatments whose specific ingredients more adequately address the underlying dysfunction (e.g., are more "potent") should be superior to others, presumably those with flawed theoretical rationales. Over the past 50 years, researchers have conducted hundreds of clinical trials, comparing the effects of one psychotherapy to others.

Meta-analyses of psychotherapy studies have consistently demonstrated that there are no substantial differences in outcomes among treatments (D. A. Shapiro & Shapiro, 1982; Smith & Glass, 1977; Wampold et al., 1997). This suggests two possibilities: (1) psychotherapies may contain different but equally potent ingredients and thus are similarly effective treatments or (2) therapies that look different on the surface could be quite similar in their actual therapeutic ingredients (similar to two aspirins with different colored coatings; Frank & Frank, 1991; Wampold, 2001b).

Despite substantiated findings that there are no differences in effectiveness between differing therapeutic approaches in general, it is possible that in specific problems or disorders, certain treatments are more effective than others (cf. Crits-Christoph, 1997). Indeed, the medical model predicts that certain specific techniques will be uniquely curative for specific underlying dysfunctions. For mild disorders (e.g., minor depression or adjustment disorders), common factors (e.g., a relationship with an empathic healer) may be sufficiently curative, whereas for more severe, chronic, and intransigent disorders (e.g., alcohol dependence and abuse, major depression, posttraumatic stress disorder), some specific treatments may be more effective than others (Crits-Christoph, 1997). As yet, however, little evidence suggests that any one treatment consistently outperforms any other for any specific psychological disorders (Wampold, 2006; Westen, Novotny, & Thompson-Brenner, 2004). Consider the following examples.

Alcohol Use Disorders

In the psychological treatment of alcohol dependence and abuse there are a number of treatment options that rely on very different and often incompatible rationales. Not surprisingly, the acrimony between treatment advocates has been quite palpable. Interestingly, more than 20 years ago, Mark and Linda Sobell (Sobell & Sobell, 1973) demonstrated that a regimen of controlled drinking was at least as effective as an abstinence based program, which was counter to the dominant abstinence-based models of treatment (see also Marlatt, 1983). The Sobells' conclusion that training in moderation was as effective as abstinence was subjected to an unprecedented level of criticism (e.g., congressional hearings) by advocates of the disease model of alcoholism (see Pendery, Maltzman, & West, 1982). Although the Sobells were eventually vindicated from any wrong-doing, controlled drinking has never gained wide acceptance in the United States. Most recently, a large clinical trial ($n = 1,726$) comparing CBT (Kadden et al., 1992), motivational interviewing (W. R. Miller & Rollnick, 2002), and 12-Step facilitation (Nowinski, Baker, & Carroll, 1992) revealed no evidence of differences among treatments (Project Match Research Group, 1997). Despite the staunch promotion of various treatments for alcoholism, little hard evidence remains to suggest that any one treatment is superior (Berglund et al., 2003).

Severe Depression

There is mixed evidence regarding the differential effectiveness of psychotherapies for severe depression. Although no one convenient definition of severe depression exists, the most agreed-on definition is an extreme elevation on some depression severity index, usually the Beck Depression Inventory or Hamilton Rating Scale for Depression (Nemeroff, 2007). Findings from the National Institute of Mental Health (NIMH) Treatment of Depression Collaborative Research Protocol (TDCRP) initially indicated individuals with more severe depression were more successfully treated with interpersonal therapy (IPT) than with cognitive therapy (CT; Elkin et al., 1989). More recently, researchers demonstrated that an expanded version of behavioral activation (BA) was superior to CT in the treatment of severe depressions (Dimidjian et al., 2006).

Researchers have offered both methodological and substantive explanations for the poor performance of CT in these trials (cf. Dimidjian et al., 2006; Jacobson & Hollon, 1996; Kim, Wampold, & Bolt, 2006). A recent reanalysis of the TDCRP data indicated that the superiority of IPT over CT in severe depression may have been an artifact of the failure to consider differences between therapists (Kim, Wampold, & Bolt, 2006). More important, the lack of a priori hypotheses regarding the relative efficacy of BA, IPT, and CT in severe depression makes the findings difficult to interpret. Thus, there remains little consistent evidence to suggest that a particular therapeutic ingredient included in BA or IPT and not in CT is critical to the treatment of severe depression, as would be needed to support a medical model of treatment.

Anxiety Disorders

An area for which it is often claimed that particular treatments are necessary is anxiety disorders. A number of researchers (even common factors researchers, e.g., Frank & Frank, 1991) have suggested that for anxiety disorders, treatments that contain exposure as an explicit therapeutic procedure are required (DeRubeis, Brotman, & Gibbons, 2005; Ogles, Anderson, & Lunnen, 1999). There are certainly a number of highly effective exposure-based treatments for anxiety disorders (Emmelkamp, 2004), but interestingly there are few studies that have compared exposure-based treatments to nonexposure-based treatments, perhaps because the inclusion of exposure is thought to be ubiquitous in all viable treatments of anxiety disorders with avoidant behavior; indeed it is difficult to design a treatment that does not contain any form of (in-vivo or imaginal) exposure (Wampold, 2005). However, consider recent findings indicating that present-centered therapy (PCT) was as effective as CBT with exposure. Present-centered therapy is a common factor control treatment for PTSD, with the explicit goal of avoiding any exposure-type interventions, including imaginal exposure; consequently, patients are not allowed to talk about their trauma in the session and are redirected to discuss contemporaneous issues. Interestingly, when PCT was manualized and therapists received rigorous training from PCT experts, it was found comparable to CBT with exposure-based components (McDonagh et al., 2005; Schnurr et al., 2003). Another example of the efficacy of nonexposure treatment is a study conducted by the developer of applied relaxation (AR). In this study, AR, which is not based on exposure principles, was comparable to CBT in the treatment of panic (Öst & Westling, 1995). Moreover, Wampold (2006) reviewed the literature on anxiety disorders and concluded that there was no evidence that any particular anxiety treatment was superior to any other treatment that was intended to be therapeutic and that was delivered adequately.

Theory-Specific Mediators of Outcome

The finding that treatments are equivalent does not necessarily imply that common factors are those primarily responsible for change. It could be that each treatment is effective through distinct and theory-specific mechanisms. There are three primary methods that researchers have used to test this notion: (1) placebo or common factor controls, (2) component designs, and (3) rating adherence.

Common Factor Controls

If the specific ingredients designed to address an underlying disorder are essential in producing client change, then the absence of the ingredient should attenuate the effectiveness of the treatment. In medicine, this possibility is established by comparing a drug to a placebo. In the pharmacological context, a placebo is a treatment with no specific active chemical ingredient. As there is nothing chemically potent about the drug, pharmacologists consider any beneficial effects of a placebo to be the result of "nonspecific" psychological mechanisms and, therefore, unimportant. To determine the potency of the chemical agents contained in a drug, researchers conduct a double-blind clinical trial in which the efficacy of the drug is compared to a placebo, usually a sugar pill with no known chemical effects. Ideally, patients, administrators of the drug, and evaluators are blind to the conditions (known as a *triple-blind* study). Because neither the researcher, patient, nor evaluator knows which treatment the patient is receiving, blinding controls for any potential bias. Consequently, the only difference between the two treatment conditions is the purported active chemical agents in the pill. Thus, any observed differences in patient symptoms posttreatment can be attributed to the chemical makeup of the drug (A. K. Shapiro & Shapiro, 1997).

In psychotherapy research, the analogue to the randomized double-blinded placebo control group, which involves the use of a psychological placebo (often called *nonspecific, supportive counseling,* or *common factor* control), dates back to 1956 (Rosenthal & Frank, 1956). These *common factors control groups* (the term to be used hereafter) involve a treatment that is designed not to contain ingredients related to the psychological mechanisms of the treatment to which it is being compared. Common factor controls are often devoid of a bona fide or credible treatment rationale, are not intended to be therapeutic, may prohibit specific therapist interventions, or may involve less patient contact than the treatment condition. Research indicates that bona fide psychotherapies that are intended to be therapeutic for a particular disorder (as defined by Wampold et al., 1997) regularly surpass the effects of common factor control groups (Stevens, Hynan, & Allen, 2000). Many researchers interpret this as evidence for the specific effects of treatment techniques included in bona fide therapies (cf. DeRubeis et al., 2005; Stevens et al., 2000). However, there are numerous problems with this conclusion (Kirsch, 2005; Wampold, Minami, Tierney, Baskin, & Bhati, 2005).

The first critical issue is that therapists are necessarily aware of the treatment they are providing and, consequently, they are not blind to the treatment being offered. Thus, a therapist's belief in the effectiveness of the control is compromised. Such studies are, at best, single blind and often not blinded at all. This problem renders the findings derived from comparisons of psychotherapies to common factor controls difficult to interpret. Differences between treatments could be due to a therapist's lack of belief in the treatment or a client's knowledge that he or she is receiving the control treatment, rather than to the specific techniques included in the experimental treatment.

A second problem confounding the blinding procedure is that common factors controls and bona fide psychotherapies are often not *structurally equivalent*. Structural equivalence refers to the similarity of two compared treatments in terms of therapist training, number and length of sessions, format (group versus individual), and whether the clients were allowed to discuss topics that were logically germane to the treatment (Baskin, Tierney, Minami, & Wampold, 2003). The differences between a common factors control and a bona fide psychotherapy may be attributed to structural differences and not the specific therapeutic techniques. Baskin et al. (2003) evaluated the effect of structural equivalence in a recent meta-analysis and found that as the structural equivalence of a control condition approached that of the bona fide therapy, differences between conditions became quite small—reduced from an effect size (*d*) of .47 to .15 (Baskin et al., 2003). Thus, the differential effectiveness of common factor controls and bona fide psychotherapies is not likely due to the effects of specific techniques.

Component Designs

Another method for directly assessing the impact of specific techniques is the component design, in which a critical component of treatment is subtracted (dismantling design) or added to an existing treatment. An exemplary component study was conducted by Jacobson et al. (1996), who dismantled CBT for depression by comparing CBT to behavioral treatment (BT). Cognitive-behavioral therapy and BT were structurally equivalent except that BT lacked the cognitive component. Results revealed no differences between treatments, and theory-specific moderators (e.g., measures of irrational thoughts) did not differentially predict treatment efficacy (Jacobson et al., 1996). The similarity of BT and CBT indicated that the cognitive component of cognitive therapy may not be an essential ingredient of treatment. In addition, Ahn and Wampold (2001) completed a meta-analysis of component studies and found no evidence to support the claim that adding a specific ingredient to a treatment augmented psychotherapy outcome.

The findings reviewed earlier suggest that theory-specific interventions are not the entities responsible for the effects of psychotherapy. Adding or subtracting supposedly critical aspects of interventions has little effect on outcome, and common factors controls, although logically flawed in the context of psychotherapy, nevertheless demonstrate effects that are similar to established treatments when structurally equivalent.

Adherence

If a specific ingredient offered in a treatment is critical to the success of the treatment, the degree to which the therapist adheres to the treatment protocol should be related to the outcome. Yet the relationship between therapist adherence and outcome is mixed. Although some evidence suggests that some degree of adherence is important, other findings indicate that there is either no relationship between adherence and outcome, or that high and possibly rigid levels of adherence may even be *detrimental*.

There are studies that indicate that therapist adherence is related to outcome. Luborsky (1985) reported a significant correlation (*r* = .38) of *treatment purity,* defined as the ratio of adherence to the administered treatment to adherence to the alternative treatment, and outcome. In a comparative study of CBT and mutual support groups, Bright, Baker, and Neimeyer (1999) found a moderate (*r* = .38) association between treatment purity and outcome on one of the four outcome measures used in the study, but no significant association on the other three.

Despite studies that indicate a positive relationship, there are several large and well-designed studies that indicate either a null or a negative relationship between adherence and treatment outcome. In the NIMH TDCRP that compared IPT to CT, researchers investigated the relationship of adherence to outcome. After controlling for pretreatment symptoms and the provision of support by the therapist, adherence measures were unrelated to outcome. More interesting, however, is that TDCRP researchers also investigated the relationship between therapist competence and outcome. Although the initial zero order correlation revealed no statistically significant association between competence and outcome, including adherence and competence in the model simultaneously revealed a significant correlation between competence and outcome. Thus, when adherence to treatment protocol was controlled or suppressed, the effect of therapist competence on outcome increased. This suggests that the aspects of competence related to adherence are not related to outcome (Shaw et al., 1999).

Two additional studies offer evidence that the effect of adherence on outcome is negative. Castonguay, Goldfried, Wiser, and Raue (1996) found that the degree to which the therapist focused on the client's distorted cognitions (a treatment-specific factor in cognitive therapy) was *negatively* correlated with posttreatment outcome. Specifically, those clients whose therapists spent more time focused on the impact of distorted cognitions actually faired worse. Earlier studies of time-limited dynamic psychotherapy (TLDP), revealed that an attempt to dictate therapist behaviors in therapy, with a primary focus on helping therapists manage negative interpersonal interactions, had an unexpected and negative influence on therapeutic process (Henry, Strupp, Butler, Schacht, & Binder, 1993; Henry, Schacht, Strupp, Butler, & Binder, 1993). The researchers concluded, "although 'the *treatment* was delivered'.... the *therapy* did not always occur" (Henry, Strupp et al., 1993, p. 438, italics added).

A limitation of any statistical relationship between adherence and outcome (positive or negative) is that findings may be the result of client characteristics. Specifically, it may be easier for therapists to adhere to a prescribed treatment protocol when clients are motivated to engage in the treatment and have better prognoses, which might explain the positive outcomes. The adherence literature does not provide strong support for specificity and also suggests that absolute adherence to a protocol may be detrimental.

Conclusion

The predictions of specificity and the medical model in psychotherapy are predominantly inconsistent with research evidence. Hundreds of clinical trials have failed to document that any psychotherapy is consistently superior to any other psychotherapy, both generally and for specific disorders. What evidence does exist is problematic and has not been consistently replicated. As a result, little treatment-specific understanding of client improvement has emerged from empirical research. The addition or subtraction of theory-specific interventions does not seem to affect outcomes, and structurally equivalent common factor controls often approach the effectiveness of bona fide psychotherapies. Finally, the degree to which a therapist adheres to a treatment protocol has, at best, a mixed relationship with treatment outcome.

EMERGENCE OF COMMON FACTOR MODELS

Given the limitations of the medical model in psychotherapy, researchers have developed alternative explanations for the benefits of psychotherapy. One alternative explanation is that the mechanisms of change are the therapeutic actions common across all effective treatments. Next, we describe the genesis of the common factors perspective, outlining several current summaries of common factors research, a number of critiques, and then perspectives that are responsive to these critiques.

Overview of Common Factors Perspective

The idea that some set of common factors is responsible for the effects of psychotherapy was first advanced by Saul Rosenzweig in 1936. In his classic paper, Rosenzweig noticed that the majority of psychotherapy schools boasted claims of therapeutic success and parlayed that evidence as support for the validity of their therapeutic ideology and (illogically) the inferiority of competing models. The success of numerous conflicting therapeutic ideologies led Rosenzweig to the conclusion that treatment effectiveness provides little information about the validity of a change theory. Rosenzweig then described a number of *implicit common factors* that may better explain treatment successes, including: (a) the inspiring or stimulating aspects of the therapist's personality, (b) the reintegration of personality through the systematic application of some therapeutic ideology, (c) implicit psychological processes such as catharsis or social reconditioning, and (d) the reformulation of psychological events (Rosenzweig, 1936).

The typical strategy of common factors proponents has been to highlight one or a list of factors that are believed to be critical in psychotherapy. One of the most widely noted and well-articulated attempts to develop such a list is found in the work of Sol Garfield. In his book, *Psychotherapy: An Eclectic-Integrative Approach* (1995), he described the following change mechanisms as common to all therapies: (a) the therapeutic alliance; (b) interpretation, insight, and understanding; (c) cognitive modifications; (d) catharsis, emotional expression, and release; (e) reinforcement; (f) desensitization; (g) relaxation; (h) information; (i) reassurance and support; (j) expectancies; (k) exposure to and confronting of a problem situation; (l) time; and (m) the placebo response.

As the number of treatment variables offered as potential common factors has increased, reviewers have begun to distill the common factors literature into more manageable frameworks—to look for commonalities among the common factors. Lambert and Ogles (2004) categorized common factors in terms of their temporal occurrence in therapy: (a) support factors, (b) learning factors, and (c) action factors. More specifically, support precedes learning, which is then followed by action. These categories are composed of over 30 specific agents per category. In another review, Grencavage and Norcross (1990) found over 89 common factors and organized them into four broad categories: (1) therapist qualities, (2) change processes, (3) treatment structures, and (4) relationship. Forty-one percent of the common factors cited referred to some change process that may be common across psychotherapies. The most commonly cited factors were the therapeutic alliance, catharsis, practice and acquisition of new behaviors, and positive client expectations.

Tracey, Lichtenberg, Goodyear, Claiborn, and Wampold (2003) conducted a multidimensional scaling and cluster analysis of the factors listed by Grencavage and Norcross. Experienced psychologists were asked to compare the similarity of common factors culled from 14 larger categories. Analyses indicated two dimensions of commonalities: (1) thinking (cool) and (2) feeling (hot) therapeutic activities. They also found three clusters: (1) bond, (2) information, and (3) role. Unlike previous reviews, this analysis provided an empirically derived structure of the therapeutic commonalities. Moreover, these findings were less determined by the conscious models of the researchers and therefore more likely to provide insight into how common factors are present in actual practice.

However defined, common factors seem to be important to the success of psychotherapy. Lambert and Barley (2002) summarized their impression of the psychotherapy literature, concluding that the common factors account for 30% of the variance in treatment outcomes, expectation or placebo effects for 15%, extra-therapeutic factors for 40%, and specific techniques for 15%. In a large quantitative review, Wampold (2001b) found that 70% of the benefits of psychotherapy were due to common factors and only 8%, at most, were due to specific ingredients, whereas the remainder was undetermined.

Although these summaries present only a broad overview of the common factors literature, they provide a useful introduction. Research suggests that common factors account for a sizable portion of the variance (from 30% to 70%) in therapeutic outcomes and thus are likely important variables in the process of psychotherapy. Further, this summary suggests that there is an array of theoretically viable common factors. There is general consensus on several factors (e.g., therapeutic relationship), but there is by no means unanimity. Some researchers consider expectation to be a result of the placebo effect and not a true common factor (cf. Lambert & Barley, 2002), whereas others do not make such a distinction (Garfield, 1995; Grencavage & Norcross, 1990).

Criticism

There are several criticisms of the proposed common factors listed earlier. Critiques are primarily concerned with the notion that the common factors are *necessary* ingredients, but not *sufficient* to produce change. What is assumed to be sufficient is the provision of common factors plus some specific technique that addresses some specific disorder or problem. Specific ingredients are thus considered critical to the therapeutic process and are needed to provide "an extra boost" for change (Asay & Lambert, 1999). In the following sections, we highlight the comments of concerned psychotherapy researchers, including the beliefs that (a) accepting common factors as sufficient obviates the need for specific treatments, (b) common factors can be reduced to a warm relationship, and (c) the common factors are vague and not scientific.

Common Factors Dismiss the Need for Techniques

The first critique of the common factors position is that a focus on common factors necessarily conflicts with the competent implementation of a particular treatment. Sexton, Ridley, and Kleiner (2004) have argued that the provision of independent common factors disconnected from the provision of actual treatment has deleterious consequences. As noted by London (1964), "it is techniques, not theories, that are actually used on people" (London, 1964, as cited in Lazarus, 1989, p. 33). As an illustration of a common factors approach *sans* a specific treatment, consider the following tongue-in-cheek first session by a well-meaning but misguided common factors therapist:

> The counseling I offer is based on extensive empirical research. About 40% of your cure will come directly from you. If you're motivated, your problems aren't too big, and you've cultivated some helpful friends and family, then we're in good shape. Another 30% of your cure comes from us developing a positive therapeutic relationship . . . so let's work together to try and like each other. Then, the other 30% of your cure is based on how well I can get you to have hope that this procedure will help you and on the particular counseling techniques I'll be using . . . So I think the best place for us to start is by getting right to work on establishing a positive therapeutic alliance. (Sommers-Flanagan & Sommers-Flanagan, 2004, p. 16)

This quote illustrates how an understanding of common factors becomes problematic when isolated from the specific treatments in which they are usually embedded. Although the therapist's actual statement is consistent with one summary of the empirical literature on psychotherapy outcomes (Lambert & Barley, 2002), this disembodied therapy is similar to eating ketchup or chutney for dinner. Although these condiments can be quite tasty, they tend to be more fulfilling with something to put them on (Sommers-Flanagan & Sommers-Flanagan, 2004). Our misguided therapist provides an illustration of how the common factors lose their meaning and, ironically, may be difficult to provide when decontextualized from a specific treatment.

Common Factors Equals a Warm Relationship

A discussion of decontextualized therapies leads to another criticism of the common factors position; namely, that the common factors can be reduced to a warm and empathic therapeutic relationship. Practically stated, therapists should just go build a warm relationship with a client, and the client will magically improve. Reviewers of the common factors literature, both pro and con, typically include a critical analysis of the literature concerned with the therapeutic relationship (cf. DeRubeis et al., 2005; Elkin, 1995; Wampold, 2005; Weinberger, 1995). Here, the therapeutic relationship may be a victim of its own success. The logic appears to be: If the therapeutic relationship is the exemplar common factor and the literature concerned with this relationship is flawed, then the common factors perspective must be equally flawed.

Although the therapeutic relationship has received more attention and is the most consistent predictor of psychotherapy available (Horvath & Bedi, 2002; see also Gelso & Samstag, this volume), there are limitations worthy of consideration. The correlation between the therapeutic relationship and outcome is, at most, moderate (approximately $r = .24$), allowing for the operation of other process variables (Crits-Christoph, Gibbons, & Hearon, 2006). In addition, any correlational finding is limited in that researchers cannot make causal inferences about the direction of the predictor-outcome relation. The quality of the relationship may lead to change or it may be that previous symptom change leads to a quality relationship. It is also possible that some unmeasured third variable (e.g., client characteristics, therapist behaviors) may be responsible for the correlation. Researchers have addressed several of these limitations by controlling for prior symptom change (cf. Constantino, Arnow, Blasey, & Agras, 2005), but it is clear that the therapeutic relationship cannot be construed as a source of unequivocal support for common factors (DeRubeis et al., 2005).

Common Factors Are Not Scientific

In addition to critiques of the therapeutic alliance, there is a belief that the common factors-specificity debate necessitates a polemic between, on the one hand, advocates of specific treatments who value the role of clinical trials and scientific knowledge and, on the other, advocates of common factors who eschew the findings of science in favor of a more humanistic, "touchy-feely" view of therapeutic change (cf. Carey, 2004). This perception has a number of possible sources.

The first source is the relative lack of integrated theories of change in the common factors literature. The gradual accumulation of purported common factors, the lack of differences between treatments, and the variety of summaries of the common factors literature have resulted in the perception that psychotherapists and researchers alike can pick from a grab bag of common factors and forgo the more arduous application of a specific theory. Many descriptions of the factors are quite broad or offered in list form, with relatively little attention to the mechanisms through which change might occur (Sexton et al., 2004; Weinberger, 1995).

The second possible source may be the separation of common factors research from more basic psychological science. Common factors models, contrarian in their very nature, are offered as alternatives when specific psychological treatments, often based on psychological theories, fail to hold up to empirical scrutiny. As common factors models are developed with the primary intent of accounting for the effects of conflicting theories that advocate sometimes diametrically opposed treatment rationales (e.g., cognitive versus behavioral), it is not surprising that common factors theories are often avowedly atheoretical (Orlinsky & Howard, 1986).

Although many common factors models emerged in an attempt to explain the findings of process outcome research (which would seem to imply that common factors models are quite scientific), the models are often not couched in terms of experimental or social psychology. Positive therapist characteristics are often cited as an important common factor, but it is unclear why certain characteristics lead to change (Beutler et al., 2004). Reviews of the therapeutic relationship's impact on psychotherapy outcome are often not accompanied by in depth discussions of social or developmental psychology (e.g., attachment theory). Positive client expectations are also often cited as a common factor that is related to outcome; however, theories of how expectation leads to change rarely drive this discussion (R. P. Greenberg, Constantino, & Bruce, 2006).

A third source of the anti-science perception is the overwhelming success of the medical model in modern medicine. The medical model arose from the successful application of scientific principles to the treatment of physical illness (e.g., germ theory, antibiotics), which effectively transported medicine from the dark ages (A. K. Shapiro & Shapiro, 1997; Wampold, 2001a). In Western medicine, science and specificity have become aligned. As a result, to be legitimate and scientific, psychotherapy must emulate the medical model. Acceptance of a common factors model of psychotherapy, in which treatment theories are not viewed as important guides to change mechanisms, distinguishes psychotherapy from the medical model and harms its prestige (Wampold, 2001a). Essentially, to reject the medical model is to reject science.

Criticisms Revisited: Clarifications and Elaboration

Although the earlier critiques orient theorists to key issues, they are based on a limited view of the common factors literature. We believe that a more comprehensive understanding of common factors and attention to recent findings from both basic and clinical science reveals this to be the case. The common factors need not be perceived as disembodied, mechanistically vague placeholders for failed specific treatments. A thorough consideration of one common factors perspective, the contextual model, reveals (a) a coherent treatment is a crucial vehicle for the common factors, (b) a number of integrated models stipulate relationships between common factors, and (c) common factors can be outlined with a relatively high degree of mechanistic specificity.

Centrality of a Coherent Treatment

Although common factors models have been critiqued as leading to the abdication of a coherent treatment and as being dependent on the therapeutic alliance, a contextual model of psychotherapy demonstrates how this critique is flawed. The contextual model is an extension of the perspective offered in Jerome Frank's seminal work, *Persuasion and Healing: A Comparative Study of Psychotherapy* (e.g., see Frank & Frank, 1991). Frank positioned psychotherapy in the tradition of other cultural healing practices and emphasized the importance of theory-driven treatment. Frank (1985) argued:

> All psychotherapeutic methods are elaborations and variations of age-old procedures of psychological healing. These include confession, atonement and absolutions, encouragement, positive and negative reinforcements, modeling, and promulgation of a particular set of values. These methods become embedded in theories as to the causes and cures of various conditions which often become highly elaborate. (p. 49–50)

Of particular relevance is that the theory of change is *embedded* in the process of therapy. Consequently, the theory of any treatment is an organizing construct through which other common factors are delivered.

The finding that psychotherapies often outperform common factor controls (Stevens et al., 2000), rather than providing evidence for specific ingredients, serves to reiterate how providing a treatment that is intended to be therapeutic is a common factor. Although common factors controls are created to facilitate the provision of common factors without an accompanying specific treatment, this logic, as noted earlier, is flawed. An important distinction between the study of chemically based and psychologically based treatments exists. The specific ingredients of a chemical treatment (e.g., fluoxetine) can be removed without influencing the psychological processes involved in the provision of treatment. However, this is not the case in psychologically based treatments (Kirsch, 2005).

Rogerian therapy, as it focuses on the facilitation of an empathic therapeutic relationship, is often utilized as a common factors control. However, when offered as control treatment, therapists providing Rogerian treatment are often (a) aware that they are providing the control treatment, which may inhibit belief in the treatment, and (b) not allowed to provide a cogent, believable therapeutic rationale and related therapeutic interventions. Therapists are not guided by modern experiential treatment rationales (e.g., L. S. Greenberg & Watson, 2005), but rather by a trimmed version of early person-centered therapy. Further, therapists are not allowed to perform interventions an experiential therapist would normally provide. When used as a control treatment, Rogerian therapy is often more defined by what the therapist should not do, then what the therapist should do. As a result, Rogerian therapy controls do not contain a variety of common factors (e.g., expectation, coherent therapeutic rationale) and thus any observed inferiority to intact treatments ironically provides support for the importance of common factors. Regardless, there is evidence to suggest that Rogerian therapy, even as a control treatment, when offered with enthusiasm and an intention to be therapeutic, is as effective as other empirically supported treatments (see Markowitz, Kocsis, Bleiberg, Christos, & Sacks, 2005).

In contrast to the medical model, the contextual model holds that it is not the specific ingredients of a particular treatment, but the healing context created by a treatment that is clinically potent. The provision of an *acceptable* explanation or *naming* is an active ingredient, but a scientifically correct explanation is not essential (Frank & Frank, 1991; Garfield, 1995; Marmor, 1962; Wampold, Imel, Bhati, & Johnson-Jennings, 2006). According to Torrey (1972), "The identification of the offending agent may activate a series of associated ideas in the patient's mind producing confession, abreaction, and general catharsis. It also conveys to the patient that someone understands" (p. 71). Although there is no compelling evidence that the veridicality of a treatment's rationale is clinically potent (cf. Wampold et al., 2006), it remains important that the therapist knows the *right* name for the client's distress (Torrey, 1972).

To know the right name, the therapist must share some aspect of the client's worldview, especially that aspect related to the problem at hand. A client immersed in a culture of scientific positivism may quickly reject an explanation that his or her phobia is related to possession by an ancestral spirit. Alternatively, a therapist's explanation that a phobia is related to the failure of the prefrontal cortex to inhibit messages from a hyperactive amygdala may be met with a blank stare by a client with mystic religious beliefs and no exposure to modern science (Torrey, 1972). The multicultural implications of the contextual approach, and its shift in perspective from *what* treatment is provided to *how* treatment is provided, are noteworthy. The key issue is not whether a treatment's rationale provides accurate diagnostic picture of a client's problems, but the extent to which the rationale is experienced as a compelling framework for understanding the problem (see Wampold et al., 2006). The context, both interpersonal and cultural, in which the treatment occurs, is critical to its utility and legitimacy (Frank & Frank, 1991; Torrey, 1972). A contextual model holds that, to be effective, the explanation must be (a) offered in the expected cultural frame of the healing practice (e.g., an explanation of a chi imbalance would be incongruent in a Western medical doctor's office), (b) proximal to the client's currently held explanation of distress, and (c) consistent with the client's belief system (Coleman & Wampold, 2003; Wampold et al., 2006). These assertions are consistent with a body of research that suggests the importance of therapeutic rationales that are consistent with an individual's worldview or cultural belief system (cf. Addis & Jacobson, 1996; Atkinson, Worthington, Dana, & Good, 1991).

Integrated Theoretical Models

An additional criticism of common factors models is that their structure is often poorly explicated, primarily offered in lists or summaries of the psychotherapy literature. However, a close inspection of the common factors literature reveals the potential for an integrated model of common factors. Both Jerome Frank and E. Fuller Torrey have offered similar transcultural models of psychotherapy (Frank & Frank, 1991; Torrey, 1972; see also Kleinman & Sung, 1979). An additional example of a highly integrated theoretical model is the *generic model of psychotherapy* articulated by Orlinsky and Howard (1986). Taken together, these models form the theoretical basis of the contextual model and suggest that several aspects of the treatment process interact to activate clinical improvement, including (a) an emotionally charged, confiding relationship, (b) an acceptable explanation of psychological distress, and (c) a treatment that is consistent with the explanation.

Researchers have proposed a variety of relationships between these three factors. Briefly, the provision of a therapeutic rationale inspires hope or positive expectation (a change mechanism that is discussed later) and provides a framework for unpleasant emotions, suggesting it is possible to cope and enhance the client's sense of self-efficacy. Achieving insight also inspires a feeling of success ("I understand!") and may be considered rewarding in itself (Frank & Frank, 1991; Wampold et al., 2006). Providing a treatment may also be considered a vehicle that maintains the therapeutic relationship. The therapist's use of theory-derived techniques may serve to increase the status of the therapist and arouse emotion, augmenting the affective bond between the therapist and client (Frank & Frank, 1991; Wampold et al., 2006). Adherence to a shared myth also creates a powerful affective bond (Frank & Frank, 1991). The bond, which is the quality of the real human relationship between the therapist and client, has both direct and indirect effects on therapeutic outcome. The direct effect occurs through the remoralizing effects of the bond. The indirect effect is mediated through the implicit affective messages (e.g., "I am worthy") that a strong therapeutic bond communicates to the client (Orlinsky & Howard, 1986).

Common Mechanisms of Change: Expectation as a Case in Point

The final critique involves the contention that common factors models are mechanistically vague. One mechanism through which the processes described in the contextual model may operate is through a change in expectations. Indeed, most studies indicate a positive relationship between expectations and outcome (Arnkoff, Glass, & Shapiro, 2002; R. P. Greenberg et al., 2006). Unfortunately, the expectation literature in psychotherapy is limited by a preponderance of correlational findings (similar to other process or outcome findings), flawed attempts at expectancy manipulation, measurement problems, and a lack of theory-driven research. When considered in isolation, psychotherapy research does not allow firm conclusions regarding how or if it is a change in expectancies that leads to change in psychotherapy outcome (R. P. Greenberg et al., 2006).

Despite a lack of clarity in the psychotherapy literature, an examination of the placebo concept offers utility for elucidating the complex role of expectation in psychotherapy (Wampold et al., 2005). That is, one explanation for the beneficial effect of placebos is that of expectation. Response expectancy theory holds that the effects of expectancy on subjective experience (e.g., emotion) are unmediated and have a direct effect on experience (Kirsch, 1985). "The perception is not just of the experience, it is the experience" (Kirsch, 1999, p. 7).

Basic science that is concerned with revealing the mechanisms that drive the placebo effect compellingly demonstrates that the expectation of an experience affects the experience (Benedetti, Mayberg, Wager, Stohler, & Zubieta, 2005). Consider the classic study by Thomas (1987) who demonstrated that the expectation a general practitioner creates is responsible for the reduction of certain symptoms. Thomas assigned patients suffering from minor problems such as pain, cough, or tiredness to a placebo treatment versus a no treatment condition (e.g., some inert treatment or no treatment at all) and a positive versus negative consultation context (e.g., "*You will soon be well*" or "*I am not sure this treatment will help*"). Results indicated no differences in outcome between the placebo treatment and no treatment, but a significant difference between the positive and negative consultation contexts. This finding suggests that the expectation created by the provider was critical to symptomatic improvement (Thomas, 1987).

Biological studies of the placebo suggest that positive expectancy for analgesia results in the release of endogenous opioids, a substance with known analgesic effects. Essentially, the expectation of analgesia creates analgesia (Amanzio, Pollo, Maggi, & Benedetti, 2001; Levine, Gordon, & Fields, 1978). A recent study indicated that the expectation that a person will receive a less noxious taste (then previously expected) influenced activation in the primary taste cortex (even though the actual taste stimulus remained the same). Expectation of taste influenced the actual experience of the taste (Nitschke et al., 2006). In sum, a review of the available evidence contradicts the critique that the common factors are not scientific. This assertion of scientific rigor is especially clear concerning expectation.

SUMMARY: IMPLICATIONS FOR RESEARCH AND PRACTICE

The important distinction between the medical model and common factors models is an emphasis on specific techniques that supposedly effect change differently across therapies as opposed to an emphasis on common therapeutic mechanisms that are similar across therapies. Whereas the medical model is popular and has been quite successful in medicine, its prediction are often inconsistent with psychotherapy outcome research. Alternatively, a contextual model of psychotherapy is consistent with current findings in basic and clinical science and is simultaneously responsive to a number of critiques of the common factors.

Implications for Research

Although extant research is inconsistent with the medical model, our review highlights a number of gaps in the psychotherapy literature that, if addressed, could further illuminate the debate between medical or common factors models.

First, the findings from comparative trials of psychotherapies for specific disorders have not yet been meta-analyzed in a manner that allows an omnibus test of treatment differences (see Wampold et al., 1997). Future meta-analyses of treatment differences should focus on analyzing the similarity of effects garnered from studies that compare two psychotherapies in the treatment of a specific disorder, addressing the question: "Are there any differences between psychotherapies for a specific disorder when they are directly compared." Because the medical model predicts differences between treatments will emerge in the treatment of a specific disorder (i.e., some treatments will contain the appropriate ingredients for a particular disorder, some will not), this strategy would provide a fairer test of the medical model than previous analyses of treatment differences in which researchers collapsed across disorders (cf. Smith & Glass, 1977). If these meta-analyses provide no evidence of treatment differences, this would further indicate that the differences in theoretical content that drive scientific interest in comparative trials are relatively minor sources of variability in treatment outcomes.

Second, future research could address the diverging explanations for process-outcome correlations offered by the medical and common factors models. Consider the example of adherence: A medical model suggests that differences in adherence to treatment protocols are due to the therapist—whether the therapist follows the treatment manual. Thus, the medical model predicts that there will be a positive correlation between outcome and adherence and that the correlation is due to the therapist (i.e., a between-therapist correlation). However, an alternate view predicts that any positive correlation between adherence and outcome would be attributable to client variables—clients with good prognoses (i.e., motivated clients with sufficient psychological resources) will comply with treatment and improve, regardless of the therapist (a within-therapist correlation; see Bohart and Tallman, 1999). However, an examination of a simple correlation obscures any possible complex combination of therapist and client factors and makes it impossible to examine how adherence is related to outcome. One potential strategy for dealing with this issue is the use of multilevel modeling strategies (cf. Raudenbush & Bryk, 2002), which model the fact that clients are nested within therapists (i.e., each therapist treats many clients and therapists have an effect on outcome). Multilevel models provide estimates of between- and within-therapist correlations so that the therapist and patient contributions to the process-outcome correlation can be determined. In this way, it could be determined whether patient or therapist contributions to adherence predict outcome.

Finally, if the study of common factors is to advance, the focus of research must change from examining *if* common factors are important to *how*. Although clinical research will continue to be important, this strategy is limited by an inability to draw strong causal inferences.

Accordingly, researchers interested in the psychological mechanisms through which common factors are effective should compliment traditional process outcome research with an attention to basic psychological science. As illustrated earlier, research on the placebo effect, although not directly concerned with psychotherapy, offers strong evidence that alterations in expectation are one mechanism through which psychological change can occur. As a further example, we might consider the surge of scientific interest in mirror neurons and empathy (e.g., Iacaboni et al., 2004; Preston & de Waal, 2002). Recently, a group of psychotherapy researchers found that moment-to-moment concordance of patient and therapist skin conductance ratings (SCR—a physiological measure of the sympathetic nervous system and emotional arousal) was associated with positive client and therapist socioemotional responses. In addition, the degree of SCR concordance was significantly correlated with client ratings of therapist empathy ($r = .47$; Marci, Ham, Moran, & Orr, 2007). Coan, Schaefer, and Davidson (2006) demonstrated that neural response to the threat of electric shock was reduced when individuals' spouses or partners held their hands. Moreover, the magnitude of neural response was related to a self-report measure of relationship quality. Similar studies that examine the process of empathic connection in human relationships and psychotherapy have the potential to inform greatly how it is that the therapeutic relationship heals.

Implications for Practice

At first glance, the debate between advocates of specific treatments and common factors seems to require a choice between the two positions: Either the techniques offered by a particular therapy address some key underlying dysfunction, or some list of common factors are all that is necessary for change. On the contrary, a contextual model illustrates that a coherent treatment that includes an explanation, therapeutic actions, and a therapeutic relationship are necessary common factors of therapeutic change. Consequently, the clinical implications of a common factors model of practice are surprisingly mundane. The most pragmatic way for clinicians to ensure they are providing the common factors of therapeutic change is to provide a coherent treatment.

What remains controversial, however, is what the clinician considers to be the source of change. From the common factors perspective, it is how treatment is administered, not the particular type of therapy or the empirical veracity of the therapeutic rationale that determines outcome. The choice of a particular treatment likely depends on a variety of complex factors including personality variables and the cultural background of the client and therapist, not predictions offered in the medical model. Rather than undercutting the scientific credibility of psychotherapy, the diversity of treatment models, techniques, and rationales that are currently available provides therapists who work with diverse populations a number of avenues through which the common factors may be provided.

The unquestioning use of one treatment protocol with a parsimonious scientific explanation may be unhelpful for some clients. Even if the rationale of cognitive therapy provides an accurate portrayal of the etiology of depression, certain clients may experience the rationale as objectionable. This assertion is consistent with the finding that adherence to a treatment protocol can suppress the effect of therapist competency (Shaw et al., 1999). Indeed, a common factors model suggests that the competent therapist might stray from a treatment protocol if it is ineffective. Consequently, practicing clinicians and administrators should ensure that therapeutic work is guided by the wisdom found in the variety of treatments available, but be mindful that the mandating of specific treatments is not supported by current scientific evidence. Alternatively, clinical attention to the patient's acceptance of the therapeutic rationale, the therapeutic relationship, and the patient's expectations for change are recommended.

Although polemics regarding the most appropriate treatments for certain clients will likely continue in the foreseeable future, a more pragmatic approach likely to directly benefit clients is increased clinical attention to the degree to which clients improve. As stated by Irvin Yalom (1995):

> Controversies arise when we discuss not the process or the purpose or the effects of explanation but the content of explanation. . . . When we focus on change rather than on self-understanding as our ultimate goal, we cannot but conclude that an explanation is correct if it leads to change. (p. 85)

Indeed, there is evidence to suggest that if therapists receive feedback regarding their client's change trajectory vis-à-vis the trajectory of clients with similar levels of pretreatment severity, the likelihood of positive outcome is enhanced (Lambert, Hansen, & Finch, 2001; S. D. Miller, Duncan, & Hubble, 2005).

REFERENCES

Addis, M. E., & Jacobson, N. S. (1996). Reasons for depression and the process and outcome of cognitive-behavioral psychotherapies. *Journal of Consulting and Clinical Psychology, 64*, 1417–1424.

Ahn, H., & Wampold, B. E. (2001). Where oh where are the specific ingredients? A meta-analysis of component studies in counseling and psychotherapy. *Journal of Counseling Psychology, 48*, 251–257.

Amanzio, M., Pollo, A., Maggi, G., & Benedetti, F. (2001). Response variability to analgesics: A role for non-specific activation of endogenous opioids. *Pain, 90*, 205–215.

Arnkoff, D. B., Glass, C. R., & Shapiro, S. J. (2002). Expectations and preferences. In J. C. Norcross (Ed.), *Psychotherapy relationships that work: Therapist contributions and responsiveness to patients* (pp. 335–356). New York: Oxford University Press.

Asay, T. P., & Lambert, M. J. (1999). The empirical case for the common factors in therapy: Quantitative findings. In M. A. Hubble, B. L. Duncan, & S. D. Miller (Eds.), *The heart and soul of change: What works in therapy* (pp. 23–55). Washington, DC: American Psychological Association.

Atkinson, D. R., Worthington, R. L., Dana, D. M., & Good, G. E. (1991). Etiology beliefs, preferences for counseling orientations, and counseling effectiveness. *Journal of Counseling Psychology, 38*, 258–264.

Baskin, T. W., Tierney, S. C., Minami, T., & Wampold, B. E. (2003). Establishing specificity in psychotherapy: A meta-analysis of structural equivalence of placebo controls. *Journal of Consulting and Clinical Psychology, 71*, 973–979.

Benedetti, F., Mayberg, H. S., Wager, T. D., Stohler, C. S., & Zubieta, J. (2005). Neurobiological mechanisms of the placebo effect. *Journal of Neuroscience, 25*, 10390–10402.

Bergin, A. E., Garfield, S. L. (Eds.). (1994). *Handbook of psychotherapy and behavior change* (4th ed.) New York: Wiley.

Berglund, M., Thelander, S., Salaspuro, M., Franck, J., Andréasson, S., & Öjehagen, A. (2003). Treatment of alcohol abuse: An evidence-based review. *Alcoholism: Clinical and Experimental Research, 27*, 1645–1656.

Beutler, L. E., Malik, M., Alimohamed, S., Harwood, T. M., Talebi, H., Noble, S., et al. (2004). Therapist variables. In M. J. Lambert (Ed.), *Bergin and Garfield's handbook of psychotherapy and behavior change* (5th ed. pp. 227–306). Hoboken, NJ: Wiley.

Bohart, A. C., & Tallman, K. (1999). *How clients make therapy work: The process of active self-healing.* Washington, DC: American Psychological Association.

Bright, J. I., Baker, K. D., & Neimeyer, R. A. (1999). Professional and paraprofessional group treatments for depression: A comparison of two treatments. *Journal of Consulting and Clinical Psychology, 67*, 491.

Carey, B. (2004, August 10). For psychotherapy's claims, skeptics demand proof. *New York Times*, F1–F4.

Castonguay, L. G., Goldfried, M. R., Wiser, S., & Raue, P. J. (1996). Predicting the effect of cognitive therapy for depression: A study of unique and common factors. *Journal of Consulting and Clinical Psychology, 64*, 497–504.

Coan, J. A., Schaefer, H. S., & Davidson, R. J. (2006). Lending a hand: Social regulation of neural response to threat. *Psychological Science, 17*, 1032–1039.

Coleman, H. L. K., & Wampold, B. E., (2003). Challenges to the development of culturally relevant, empirically supported treatment. In D. B. Pope-Davis, H. L. K. Coleman, W. M. Liu, & R. L. Toporek (Eds.), *Handbook of multicultural competencies in counseling and psychology* (pp. 227–246). Thousand Oaks, CA: Sage.

Constantino, M. J., Arnow, B. A., Blasey, C., & Agras, W. S. (2005). The association between patient characteristics and the therapeutic alliance in cognitive-behavioral and interpersonal therapy for bulimia nervosa. *Journal of Consulting and Clinical Psychology, 73*, 203–211.

Crits-Christoph, P., (1997). Limitations of the dodo bird verdict and the role of clinical trials in psychotherapy research: Comment on Wampold et al. (1997). *Psychological Bulletin, 122*, 216–220.

Crits-Christoph, P., Gibbons, M. B. C., & Hearon, B. (2006). Does the alliance cause good outcome? Recommendations for future research on the alliance. *Psychotherapy: Theory, Research, Practice, Training, 43*, 280–285.

DeRubeis, R. J., Brotman, M. A., & Gibbons, C. J. (2005). A conceptual and methodological analysis of the non-specifics argument. *Clinical Psychology: Science and Practice, 12*, 174–183.

Dimidjian, S., Hollon, S. D., Dobson, K. S., Schmaling, K. B., Kohlenberg, R. J., Addis, M. E., et al. (2006). Randomized trial of behavioral activation, cognitive therapy, and antidepressant medication in the acute treatment of adults with major depression. *Journal of Consulting and Clinical Psychology, 74*, 658–670.

Elkin, I. (1995). Further differentiation of common factors. *Clinical Psychology: Science and Practice, 2*, 75–78.

Elkin, I., Shea, M., Watkins, J., Imber, S., Sotsky, S., Collins, J., et al. (1989). NIMH treatment of depression collaborative research program: General effectiveness of treatments. *Archives of General Psychiatry, 46*, 971–982.

Emmelkamp, P. M. G. (2004). Behavior therapy with adults. In M. Lambert (Ed.), *Bergin and Garfield's handbook of psychotherapy and behavior change* (5th ed., pp. 393–446). Oxford: Wiley.

Frank, J. D. (1985). Therapeutic components shared by all psychotherapies. In M. Mahoney & A. Freeman (Eds.), *Cognition and psychotherapy* (pp. 39–80). New York: Plenum Press.

Frank, J. D., & Frank, J. B. (1991). *Persuasion and healing: A comparative study of psychotherapy* (3rd ed.). Baltimore: Johns Hopkins University Press.

Garfield, S. L. (1995). *Psychotherapy: An eclectic-integrative approach* (2nd ed.). Oxford: Wiley.

Greenberg, L. S., & Watson, J. C. (2005). *Emotion-focused therapy for depression*. Washington, DC: American Psychological Association.

Greenberg, R. P., Constantino, M. J., & Bruce, N. (2006). Are patient expectations still relevant for psychotherapy process and outcome? *Clinical Psychology Review, 26*, 657–678.

Grencavage, L. M., & Norcross, J. C. (1990). Where are the commonalities among the therapeutic common factors? *Professional Psychology: Research and Practice, 21*, 372–378.

Henry, W. P., Butler, S. F., Strupp, H. H., Schacht, T. E. (1993). Effects of training in time-limited dynamic psychotherapy: Changes in therapist behavior. *Journal of Consulting and Clinical Psychology, 61*, 434–440.

Henry, W. P., Schacht, T. E., Strupp, H. H., & Butler, S. F., (1993). Effects of training in time-limited dynamic psychotherapy: Mediators of therapists' responses to training. *Journal of Consulting and Clinical Psychology, 61*, 441–447.

Horvath, A. O., & Bedi, R. P. (2002). The alliance. In J. C. Norcross (Ed.), *Psychotherapy relationships that work: Therapist contributions and responsiveness to patients* (pp. 37–69). New York: Oxford University Press.

Iacaboni, M., Lieberman, M. D., Knowlton, B. J., Molnar-Szakacs, I., Mornitz, M., Throop, C. J., et al. (2004). Watching social interactions produces dorsomedial prefrontal and medial parietal bold fMRI signal increases compared to resting baseline. *Neuroimage, 21*, 1167–1173.

Jacobson, N. S., Dobson, K. S., Truax, P. A., Addis, M. E., Koerner, K., Gollan, J. K., et al. (1996). A component analysis of cognitive-behavioral treatment for depression. *Journal of Consulting and Clinical Psychology, 64*, 295–304.

Jacobson, N. S., & Hollon, S. D. (1996). Prospects for future comparisons between drugs and psychotherapy: Lessons from the CBT-versus-pharmacotherapy exchange. *Journal of Consulting and Clinical Psychology, 64*, 104–108.

Kadden, R., Carroll, K., Donovan, D., Cooney, N., Monti, P., Abrams, D., et al. (1992). *Cognitive-behavioral coping skills therapy manual: A clinical research guide for therapists treating individuals with alcohol abuse and dependence*. Rockville, MD: NIAA.

Kim, D., Wampold, B. E., & Bolt, D. M. (2006). Therapist effects in psychotherapy: A random-effects modeling of the national institute of mental health treatment of depression collaborative research program data. *Psychotherapy Research, 16*, 161–172.

Kirsch, I. (1985). Response expectancy as a determinant of experience and behavior. *American Psychologist, 40*, 1189–1202.

Kirsch, I. (1999). *How expectancies shape experience*. Washington, DC: American Psychological Association.

Kirsch, I. (2005). Placebo psychotherapy: Synonym or oxymoron? *Journal of Clinical Psychology, 61*, 791–803.

Kleinman, A., & Sung, L. H. (1979). Why do indigenous practitioners successfully heal? *Social Science and Medicine, 13*, 7–26.

Lambert, M. J., & Barley, D. E. (2002). Research summary on the therapeutic relationship and psychotherapy outcome. In J. C. Norcross (Ed.), *Psychotherapy relationships that work: Therapist contributions and responsiveness to patients*. (pp. 17–32). New York: Oxford University Press.

Lambert, M. J., Hansen, N. B., & Finch, A. E. (2001). Patient-focused research: Using patient outcome data to enhance treatment effects. *Journal of Consulting and Clinical Psychology, 69,* 159–172.

Lambert, M. J., & Ogles, B. M. (2004). The efficacy and effectiveness of psychotherapy. In M. J. Lambert (Ed.), *Bergin and Garfield's handbook of psychotherapy and behavior change* (5th ed., pp. 139–193). Oxford: Wiley.

Lazarus, A. A. (1989). Why I am an eclectic (not an integrationist). *British Journal of Guidance and Counselling, 17,* 248–258.

Levine, J. D., Gordon, N. C., & Fields, H. L. (1978). The mechanism of placebo analgesia. *Lancet, 2,* 654–657.

London, P. (1964). *The modes and morals of psychotherapy* (2nd ed.). New York: Harper.

Luborsky, L. (1985). Therapist success and its determinants. *Archives of General Psychiatry, 42,* 602–611.

Marci, C. D., Ham, J., Moran, E., & Orr, S. P. (2007). Physiologic correlates of perceived therapist empathy and social-emotional process during psychotherapy. *Journal of Nervous and Mental Disease, 195,* 103–111.

Markowitz, J. C., Kocsis, J. H., Bleiberg, K. L., Christos, P. J., & Sacks, M. (2005). A comparative trial of psychotherapy and pharmacotherapy for 'pure' dysthymic patients. *Journal of Affective Disorders, 89,* 167–175.

Marlatt, G. A. (1983). The controlled-drinking controversy: A commentary. *American Psychologist, 38,* 1097–1110.

Marmor, J. (1962). Psychoanalytic therapy as an educational process. In J. H. Massernan (Ed.), *Science and psychoanalysis* (pp. 286–299). New York: Grune & Stratton.

McDonagh, A., Friedman, M., McHugo, G., Ford, J., Sengupta, A., Mueser, K., et al. (2005). Randomized trial of cognitive-behavioral therapy for chronic posttraumatic stress disorder in adult female survivors of childhood sexual abuse. *Journal of Consulting and Clinical Psychology, 73,* 515–524.

Miller, S. D., Duncan, B. L., & Hubble, M. A. (2005). Outcome-informed clinical work. In J. C. Norcross & M. R. Goldfried (Eds.), *Handbook of psychotherapy integration* (2nd ed., pp. 84–102). New York: Oxford University Press.

Miller, W. R., & Rollnick, S. (2002). *Motivational interviewing* (2nd ed.). New York: Guilford Press.

Nemeroff, C. B. (2007). The burden of severe depression: A review of diagnostic challenges and treatment alternatives. *Journal of Psychiatric Research, 41,* 189–206.

Nitschke, J. B., Dixon, G. E., Sarinopoulos, I., Short, S. J., Cohen, J. D., Smith, E. E., et al. (2006). Altering expectancy dampens neural response to aversive taste in primary taste cortex. *Nature Neuroscience, 9,* 435–442.

Norcross, J. C. (2005). A primer on psychotherapy integration. In J. C. Norcross & M. R. Goldfried (Eds.), *Handbook of psychotherapy integration* (2nd ed., pp. 3–23). New York: Oxford University Press.

Nowinski, J., Baker, S., & Carroll, K. (1992). *Twelve step facilitation therapy manual: A clinical research guide for therapists treating individuals with alcohol abuse and dependence.* Rockville, MD: NIAA.

Ogles, B. M., Anderson, T., & Lunnen, K. M. (1999). The contribution of models and techniques to therapeutic efficacy: Contradictions between professional trends and clinical research. In M. A. Hubble, B. L. Duncan, & S. D. Miller (Eds.), *The heart and soul of change: What works in therapy* (pp. 201–225). Washington, DC: American Psychological Association.

Orlinsky, D. E., & Howard, G. S. (1986). Process and outcome in psychotherapy. In A. E. Bergin & S. L. Garfield (Eds.), *Handbook of psychotherapy and behavior change* (3rd ed., pp. 311–384). Oxford: Wiley.

Öst, L., & Westling, B. E. (1995). Applied relaxation vs. cognitive behavior therapy in the treatment of panic disorder. *Behaviour Research and Therapy, 33,* 145–158.

Pendery, M. L., Maltzman, I. M., & West, L. J. (1982). Controlled drinking by alcoholics? New findings and a reevaluation of a major affirmative study. *Science, 217,* 169–175.

Preston, S. D., & de Waal, F.B. M. (2002). Empathy: Its ultimate and proximate bases. *Behavior and Brain Sciences, 25,* 1–72.

Project Match Research Group. (1997). Matching alcoholism treatments to client heterogeneity: Project MATCH post-treatment drinking outcomes (1997). *Journal of Studies on Alcohol, 58,* 7–29.

Raudenbush, S. W., & Bryk, A. S. (2002). *Hierarchical linear models: Applications and data analysis methods.* New York: Sage.

Rosenthal, D., & Frank, J. D. (1956). Psychotherapy and the placebo effect. *Psychological Bulletin, 53,* 294–302.

Rosenzweig, S. (1936). Some implicit common factors in diverse methods of psychotherapy. *American Journal of Orthopsychiatry, 6,* 412–415.

Schnurr, P. P., Friedman, M. J., Foy, D. W., Shea, M. T., Hsieh, F. Y., Lavori, P. W., et al. (2003). Randomized trial of trauma-focused group therapy for posttraumatic stress disorder: Results from a department of veterans affairs cooperative study. *Archives of General Psychiatry, 60,* 481–489.

Sexton, T. L., Ridley, C. R., & Kleiner, A. J. (2004). Beyond common factors: Multilevel-process models of therapeutic change in marriage and family therapy. *Journal of Marital and Family Therapy, 30*, 131–149.

Shapiro, A. K., & Shapiro, E. (1997). *The powerful placebo: From ancient priest to modern physician*. Baltimore: Johns Hopkins University Press.

Shapiro, D. A., & Shapiro, D. (1982). Meta-analysis of comparative therapy outcome studies: A replication and refinement. *Psychological Bulletin, 92*, 581–604.

Shaw, B. F., Elkin, I., Yamaguchi, J., Olmsted, M., Vallis, T. M., Dobson, K. S., et al. (1999). Therapist competence ratings in relation to clinical outcome in cognitive therapy of depression. *Journal of Consulting and Clinical Psychology, 67*, 837–846.

Smith, M. A., & Glass, G. V. (1977). Meta-analysis of psychotherapy outcome studies. *American Psychologist, 32*, 752–760.

Sobell, M. B., & Sobell, L. C. (1973). Individualized behavior therapy for alcoholics. *Behavior Therapy, 4*, 49–72.

Sommers-Flanagan, J., & Sommers-Flanagan, R. (2004). *Counseling and psychotherapy theories in context and practice: Skills, strategies, and techniques*. Hoboken, NJ: Wiley.

Stevens, S. E., Hynan, M. T., & Allen, M. (2000). A meta-analysis of common factor and specific treatment effects across the outcome domains of the phase model of psychotherapy. *Clinical Psychology: Science and Practice, 7*, 273–290.

Strupp, H. H., & Binder, J. L. (1984). *Psychotherapy in a new key: A guide to time-limited dynamic psychotherapy*. New York: Basic Books.

Thomas, K. B. (1987). General practice consultations: Is there any point in being positive? *British Medical Journal, 294*, 1200–1202.

Torrey, E. F. (1972). What western psychotherapists can learn from witchdoctors. *American Journal of Orthopsychiatry, 42*, 69–76.

Tracey, T. J. G., Lichtenberg, J. W., Goodyear, R. K., Claiborn, C. D., & Wampold, B. E. (2003). Concept mapping of therapeutic common factors. *Psychotherapy Research, 13*, 401–413.

Wampold, B. E. (2001a). Contextualizing psychotherapy as a healing practice: Culture, history, and methods. *Applied and Preventive Psychology, 10*, 69–86.

Wampold, B. E. (2001b). *The great psychotherapy debate: Models, methods, and findings*. Hillsdale, NJ: Erlbaum.

Wampold, B. E. (2005). Establishing specificity in psychotherapy scientifically: Design and evidence issues. *Clinical Psychology: Science and Practice, 12*, 194–197.

Wampold, B. E. (2006). Do therapies designated as empirically supported treatments for specific disorders produce outcomes superior to non-empirically supported treatment therapies? In J. C. Norcross, L. E. Beutler, & R. F. Levant (Eds.), *Evidence-based practices in mental health: Debate and dialogue on the fundamental questions* (pp. 299–328). Washington, DC: American Psychological Association.

Wampold, B. E., Imel, Z. E., Bhati, K. S., & Johnson-Jennings, M. D. (2006). Insight as a common factor. In L. Castonguay & C. E. Hill (Eds.), *Insight in psychotherapy* (pp. 119–139). Washington, DC: American Psychological Association.

Wampold, B. E., Minami, T., Tierney, S. C., Baskin, T. W., & Bhati, K. S. (2005). The placebo is powerful: Estimating placebo effects in medicine and psychotherapy from randomized clinical trials. *Journal of Clinical Psychology, 61*, 835–854.

Wampold, B. E., Mondin, G. W., Moody, M., Stich, F., Benson, K., & Ahn, H. (1997). A meta-analysis of outcome studies comparing bona fide psychotherapies: Empirically, 'all must have prizes.' *Psychological Bulletin, 122*, 203–215.

Weinberger, J. (1995). Common factors aren't so common: The common factors dilemma. *Clinical Psychology: Science and Practice, 2*, 45–69.

Westen, D., Novotny, C. M., & Thompson-Brenner, H. (2004). The empirical status of empirically supported psychotherapies: Assumptions, findings, and reporting in controlled clinical studies. *Psychological Bulletin, 130*, 631–663.

Yalom, I. D. (1995). *The theory and practice of group psychotherapy*. (4th ed.) New York: Basic Books.

CHAPTER 16

A Tripartite Model of the Therapeutic Relationship

CHARLES J. GELSO
LISA WALLNER SAMSTAG

It is an understatement to say that there are many ways of framing the relationship that exists between a client and therapist in counseling and psychotherapy. The frame that we have selected for this chapter divides the relationship into three interrelated components: a working alliance, a transference-countertransference configuration, and what may be termed a real relationship. This view of the therapeutic relationship was first proposed by the great psychoanalyst, Ralph Greenson, in his treatise on classical psychoanalysis and psychoanalytic psychotherapy (Greenson, 1967). Thus, the tripartite conception of the therapeutic relationship examined here originated from psychoanalysis. However, the model and its components have been extrapolated to psychotherapy in general, and in the present review, we focus on theoretical and empirical findings that stem from nonanalytic as well as psychoanalytic treatments.

The tripartite model, as it is formulated here, rests on the assumption that each and every psychotherapy relationship consists, to one degree or another, of a working alliance, a transference-countertransference configuration, and a real relationship. In the reality of the psychotherapy hour, however, the components are intertwined and often not sharply distinguishable elements of the gestalt, or whole relationship. We say more about this interrelated aspect of the components later in this chapter.

The degree to which each of these components emerges, and the importance of each, varies according to the individual relationship and the therapist's theory of treatment. For example, transference may tend to be manifested more in psychoanalytic than cognitive-behavioral therapies, but transference also does occur in cognitive-behavioral treatment and is likely an important element in that treatment (e.g., Ryan & Gizinski, 1971). At the same time, the emergence and interpretation of transference are unlikely to be as important in the cognitive-behavioral treatments as in therapies that place an emphasis on it.

This chapter focuses on the tripartite model. First we present definitional issues and offer our preferred definition of each major component. We then summarize theoretical controversies and key empirical findings related to each component. We conclude by briefly discussing the operation of the relationship components in practice and pointing to useful future directions for work on the tripartite model. Throughout the chapter, our emphasis is on how the key components of the therapeutic relationship operate transtheoretically, despite their psychoanalytic roots.

THE THERAPEUTIC RELATIONSHIP DEFINED

Given the voluminous literature over the past half century on the therapeutic relationship (see Norcross, 2002), it is rather amazing how little effort has been devoted to defining it. Often the relationship has been confused with therapist-offered conditions (e.g., empathy, positive regard, genuineness), whereas these conditions only represent one side of the relationship, the therapist side. Our conception is bipersonal and centrally includes the client. At times, the relationship has also been equated with the therapeutic or working alliance. Such a conception is much too limited, in our view, because the alliance is better seen as one part of the overall relationship, albeit an important one.

For the purposes of this chapter, we adopt the definition first proposed by Gelso and Carter (1985, 1994). The relationship may be seen as *the feelings and attitudes the therapy participants have toward one another and the manner in which these are expressed*. There have been some disagreements about this very general definition. For example, Hill (1994) argued that the inclusion of "the manner in which they are expressed" makes the definition so inclusive that it includes everything that happens in treatment. Gelso and Hayes (1998) countered that a definition must include how the feelings and attitudes are expressed because it is their very expression that demonstrates or enacts the relationship. It is important to underscore, however, that relational feelings and attitudes may be expressed in a wide range of ways, many of which are not explicitly verbal and some of which are quite subtle (e.g., eye movements, posture) and some not so subtle. Moreover, we believe that the manner of expressing what is felt and thought by the participants is a necessary part of any definition of relationship.

In addition to defining what a phenomenon is, it is important to specify what the phenomenon is not. In particular, the therapeutic relationship is not the techniques used by the therapist that are usually tied to one or another theory. For example, the analytic therapist tends to prefer certain kinds of interpretation; the cognitive-behavioral therapist uses persuasive and conditioning techniques; and the person-centered therapist tends to use reflections of feeling. These techniques may be influenced by the quality of the relationship. For example, the timing, tone, frequency, and quality of a technique are likely affected by how the participants feel about one another. In turn, the nature and timing of techniques will themselves affect the relationship. But techniques are not the relationship.

THE WORKING ALLIANCE—ITS RUPTURE AND REPAIR

Of the three parts of the therapeutic relationship, the working alliance is the one that is most clearly operationalized and, consequently, has been studied most extensively. Gelso and Carter viewed the working alliance as "probably the most fundamental if therapy is to proceed effectively at all" (1994, p. 297). They also defined this alliance as,

> the alignment that occurs between counselor and client or, more precisely, between the reasonable side of the client (the observing or reasonable ego, in analytic terms) and the counselor's working or therapizing side .... This permits the client to experience negative feelings toward the counselor without disruption of the work .... It is the working alliance also ... that creates the sense that the participants ... are joined together in a shared enterprise, each making his or her contribution to the work. (Gelso & Carter, 1985, pp. 162–163)

In our view, this definition is advantageous in that it is not exclusive to any one particular theoretical model of change and, as such, has transtheoretical applicability. Although the concept of the alliance emerged from psychoanalysis, the "working" and "therapizing" features can accommodate any type of clinical intervention.

Working Alliance Theory

Freud first identified the importance of engaging the patient as a collaborator (Breuer & Freud (1893–1895) and the requirement that patients experience positive transference for the analyst in successful treatment (S. Freud, 1912/1958). Positive transference is defined as a basic respect and trust the patient feels for the analyst, based on past experiences with authority figures (transference is the topic of the next section in this chapter). Although the working alliance shares some features of positive transference, Greenson (1965) unfortunately did not completely distinguish the two constructs. This lack of theoretical precision in defining the alliance as distinct from transference reflects the confusion about the construct that exists to this day.

We believe it is important to highlight the *working* aspect of the working alliance in Gelso and Carter's (1985) definition. Many different terms, such as working alliance (Greenson, 1965), helping alliance (Luborsky, 1976), and therapeutic alliance (Zetzel, 1956) have been used in the literature, further contributing to conceptual confusion about this part of the therapeutic relationship. We prefer the label *working alliance* because it captures the importance of purposive and collaborative effort on the part of the client and the therapist—as distinct from the concept of the therapeutic alliance, which has been identified more specifically as the affective bond the client develops for the therapist (Gaston, 1990). The term therapeutic alliance is problematic because it is too easily equated with the overall therapeutic relationship or general affective tone of the interactions, and the concept then loses its unique theoretical value.

Bordin (1979, 1994) extended Greenson's work by articulating differentiated features of the working alliance. Bordin's conceptualization focused on (a) the client's presenting complaints and treatment *goals*, (b) the agreement between the client and therapist regarding the techniques or therapeutic *tasks* that will achieve those goals, and (c) the establishment of a basic trust and confidence (called the *bond*) that the tasks will be effective. He also discussed how the alliance develops and may change during treatment, and the potential for "strains" or "ruptures" in the alliance to occur at any time.

Relevant to these strains or ruptures, Gelso and Carter's (1985) definition of the working alliance also addressed the importance of a client's negative feelings having room to emerge in the treatment, if necessary. Negative feelings can be expressed toward the therapist as implicit or explicit hostility and, if ill-managed, may lead to the development of a negative therapeutic process, poor overall outcome, and premature termination. Despite the theorized importance of the working alliance, relatively little has been written on how a therapist is to develop and sustain this alliance, especially in the context of negative therapeutic process. Difficulties in managing expressions of client hostility and improving a poor alliance can occur at all levels of expertise, even for the most seasoned clinicians (e.g., Hill et al., 2003).

One important exception to this gap in knowledge is the inquiry on alliance ruptures. Ruptures are defined as a negative shift in the alliance over time or as difficulty in establishing an alliance. Ruptures are considered to be inevitable over the course of therapy, and their repair often involves a specific focus on aspects of the alliance (e.g., renegotiating the client's treatment goals, communicating about the quality of interaction between the client and therapist; Safran & Muran, 2000). Hostility expressed between client and therapist has been operationalized as two general types of alliance ruptures—client withdrawal and confrontation (Safran, Crocker, McMain, & Murray, 1990; Samstag, Muran, & Safran, 2004)—with distinct interventions and repair processes outlined for each type (Safran, Muran, Samstag, & Stevens, 2002).

Research on the Working Alliance

The enormous body of empirical work on the working alliance can be divided into two general domains. In one domain, researchers have asked the question, "Is an early working alliance necessary for a good overall outcome?" Results have demonstrated an affirmative response. Two meta-analyses of alliance-outcome studies, including a range of clinical orientations, found client's self-report ratings of the alliance to be the strongest predictors of overall outcome, with estimates ranging from $r = .22$ to .26 (Horvath & Symonds, 1991; Martin, Garske, & Davis, 2000). In the studies included in these meta-analyses, alliance and outcome ratings were generally obtained within the first third of time-limited therapy (e.g., sessions 3 to 5). While the magnitude of these correlations is relatively small, they are reliable and robust findings that are especially important given the vast number of variables that make up the totality of a psychotherapy experience. The alliance has also been found to predict overall outcome separately from early symptom alleviation (e.g., Connolly Gibbons et al., 2003; Constantino, Arnow, Blasey, & Agras, 2005).

One of the most commonly used measures of the alliance is the Working Alliance Inventory (WAI: Horvath & Greenberg, 1989), which is a transtheoretical tool based on Bordin's conceptualization of the alliance. The instrument has client and therapist self-report and observer-rated versions. Examples of items from the client scale are: "I like and respect my therapist" (bond component), and "I believe the way that we are working with my problems is correct" (task component). An important issue for further study and debate in the assessment of the working alliance is the extent to which the alliance construct is considered to be a transtheoretical or common factor versus one rooted in a particular theory of change (Wampold, 2001). Hatcher and Barends (2006) recommended modifications to the WAI that emphasize the connection to the work of therapy more explicitly (e.g., "I like and respect my therapist enough to do the work I need to do in therapy"). Ultimately, a more thorough and meaningful assessment of the working alliance may require focus on both its common and theory-specific factors, perhaps tapped by separate instruments (Samstag, 2006).

Some studies have focused on identifying predictors of the alliance itself early in therapy. The predictors have included client variables (e.g., attachment, psychological mindedness, personality features; Constantino et al., 2005; Mallinckrodt, 1991; Muran, Segal, Samstag, & Crawford, 1994) and therapist variables (e.g., flexibility, lack of criticalness; Ackerman & Hilsenroth, 2001, 2003). However, this cross-sectional research is limited in the sense that it risks isolating the working alliance as a static entity that manifests only in the early phase of treatment.

A second general domain of alliance research has examined the trajectory of alliance development over the entire course of therapy. For instance, some researchers have demonstrated links between V-shaped shifts in alliance over time in good outcome cases (e.g., Stiles et al., 2004). A V-shaped shift refers to a distinctive high-low-high pattern of alliance ratings across sessions. This pattern is consistent with Safran and Muran's (1996) model of rupture-repair sequences observed within sessions and with earlier theoretical writings (Bordin, 1979, 1994; Gelso & Carter, 1994). An emerging area is the study of training techniques focused on monitoring and improving working alliances continuously over the course of treatment (e.g., Crits-Christoph, Connolly Gibbons, Narducci, Schamberger, & Gallop, 2006; Muran, Safran, Samstag, & Winston, 2005; Safran, Muran, Samstag, & Winston, 2005). This type of research is a critical next step in furthering understanding of the role of working alliance in effecting change. More study is also needed on the working alliance in longer-term therapy. (Interested readers are referred to Castonguay & Beutler, 2005, and Castonguay, Constantino, & Holtforth, 2006, for recent reviews of working alliance research.)

TRANSFERENCE: THEORETICAL AND EMPIRICAL PERSPECTIVES

The definition of transference and its role in the change process have gone through considerable transformation since its inception. Changes in thinking about transference, and a dynamic theory of mind more broadly, have been significantly influenced by the interpersonal, relational, intersubjective, and feminist movements. Psychodynamic theories may now be distinguished by different conceptualizations of what is inside the client in the form of mental representations of past relationships, or "objects," and what is outside the client in the form of a "real" person (see Aron, 1996). While transference emerged as a central component of psychoanalytic theories, it is a phenomenon found within all adult human relationships and is beginning to be addressed more consistently as a transtheoretical construct (Gelso & Hays, 1998).

Transference is generally agreed to be a phenomenon whereby internalized objects that exist within a patient—a kind of distillation of past important relationships—are displaced onto the therapist, influencing the nature of the therapeutic relationship in ways that are consistent with the client's relationship history (Greenberg & Mitchell, 1983). However, it is the conception of transference as a displacement or distortion, resulting in an illusory relationship between client and therapist, whereby theoretical diversions are found. For instance, Gill (1982) offered a view of transference as contextual, emphasizing that the patient's distortions of the therapist could be seen as plausible when the therapist's actual responses are taken into account. Thus, from a relational perspective, a client's transference, independent of a therapist's reactions, is a clinically meaningless concept. The radical change in understanding transference as being exclusively within the client, to being part of an interactional phenomenon that must also include the therapist, consequently turns other classical analytic concepts such as the "neutral" clinician and "free association" on their heads (see Hoffman, 1998).

S. Freud (1912/1958) identified three types of transferences: the unobjectionable positive transference, negative transference, and erotic transference. The adaptive, unobjectionable positive transference is defined as the patient's conscious attitude of basic trust and respect for the analyst and is based on gratifying experiences the patient has had with authority figures in the past. While aspects of positive transference were considered by Freud to be a requirement for effective treatment to occur, this motivating transference was not fully distinguished theoretically from the concept of the working alliance or the real relationship, leading to conceptual confusion about the different components of the therapeutic relationship and how they function in treatment. We emphasize here how the transference functions more fluidly, sometimes in a facilitating capacity as part of the working alliance, and sometimes in an obstructing capacity as part of negative transference or resistance to change.

Developmental perspectives on transference have been elaborated, addressing how internalized schemas of self-other relationships form. Bowlby (1973) used the term "working models" and Stern (1985) used "representations of interactions that have been generalized" to describe the structure and function of an individual's mental representations of relationships with oneself and others. Schemas provide expectations for future relationships based on what happened with significant others in the past. Individuals' response to their expectations of others, rather than to actual behavior, provides one explanation for why schemas of even destructive patterns of interactions with others become self-fulfilling prophecies. Wachtel (1981) applied the Piagetian notions of assimilation and accommodation to explain how transference can be understood from a cognitive developmental perspective, underscoring how reality is both perceived and constructed: New information that is perceived is *assimilated* into a preexisting mental schema; a preexisting schema can also be shifted to *accommodate* perceived information that does not fit it. Accordingly, transference can be defined as the predominance of assimilation over accommodation.

In sum, a classical definition of transference that emphasizes the experience of distortion and displacement is useful because it theoretically distinguishes transference from the working alliance and real relationship. In their comparative analysis of different theories of transference, Gelso and Hayes (1998) identify distortion as a particularly complex and controversial component of transference. They concluded that:

> although transference involves distortion, it is not distortion alone that makes the phenomena transferential. In fact, it can easily be argued that all perceptions of present figures in our lives are distortions to one degree or another—carryovers from both our immediate and our distant past. The quality that makes an experience transferential is that the client clings to the perception or experience of the therapist, failing to let go of it in the face of contrary evidence. (pp. 53–54)

We emphasize that transference is not simply synonymous with distortion and cannot be meaningfully considered in isolation of other components of the therapeutic relationship.

Empirical Perspectives on Transference

Efforts to study transference empirically have been impeded by difficulties in defining and measuring this highly complex phenomenon. At this stage in the research, studies may be broadly categorized in terms of three different rating perspectives—observer, client, and therapist—and the corresponding definitions of transference consistent with each perspective (Gelso & Hayes, 1998; Kivlighan, 2002).

Each perspective and surrounding set of empirical methodologies comes with strengths and limitations, which are discussed briefly next.

Early research on transference defined it from the perspective of the trained outside observer. A number of systems were developed into psychotherapy process measures in which characteristic patterns of relationships were identified from clients' descriptions of their interactions with others and rated by reliable observers on a variety of dimensions. Two of the most frequently used psychotherapy process measures are the Core Conflictual Relationship Theme method (CCRT; Luborsky & Crits-Christoph, 1998) and the Plan Formulation Method (PFM; Silberschatz, 2005; Weiss, Sampson, and the Mount Zion Psychotherapy Research Group, 1986). An advantage of these kinds of observer ratings is that they reflect sophisticated theories of personality and therapeutic action and thus capture a degree of the complexity of ongoing therapy, including shifts in the way a client experiences his or her relationship with the therapist. As a result, clinicians may find results from studies using the CCRT and PFM to be consistent with their observations of their own clients and with their own guiding theories of change. For example, over the course of treatment, clients have shown an overall reduction in the pervasiveness of transference reactions on the CCRT (i.e., elements of conflictual relationships, such as negative expected responses of others), corresponding with an expected decrease in symptoms (Crits-Christoph & Luborsky, 1990). Similarly, results using the PFM to evaluate the extent to which a therapist disconfirmed a client's "pathogenic belief" or negative expectation of what occurs in relationships with others, were statistically related to improvement in the client's presenting problems (Silberschatz & Curtis, 1993).

Results from studies using observer measures identify internalized relationship patterns that can provide clues as to the types of transferences that will be experienced in treatment and offer promising leads in terms of identifying potential predictors of transference. At the same time, the complexity of the observer measures renders them time consuming and challenging to learn. Clinical raters typically require many hours of training on the measures, followed by intensive inter-rater reliability testing. Sample sizes of studies using process measures are usually small, limiting generalizability.

From the client's perspective, transference is defined as self-reported experiences of relationships with others, components of which may impede therapy. Barber, Foltz, and Weintraub (1998) developed a standardized instrument of self-reported characteristic interactions with significant others, based on the CCRT, called the Central Relationship Questionnaire (CRQ). The CRQ, with similar components to the CCRT, such as the client's expected responses of others, responses of self, and intention or underlying wish in relationships, has demonstrated reliability and concurrent validity with scales assessing symptomotology and interpersonal functioning. For instance, students with a history of mental illness were found to score higher on items tapping an expected negative response of others compared to students with no history of mental illness (Barber et al., 1998), and a sample of offspring having mothers who were Holocaust survivors reported unique relationship patterns (e.g., a wish to be in conflict with parents) and greater interpersonal distress compared to a group whose mothers were not Holocaust survivors (Weisman et al., 2002).

Compared to observer measures, a client-rated instrument such as the CRQ is a much less labor-intensive tool for measuring transference. However, self-report information cannot capture important elements of transference, such as distortion of the therapist's behaviors, reactions, and intentions—elements that, by definition, remain outside of the client's awareness.

From the clinician's perspective, therapists have provided descriptions and ratings of a client's transference, such as using an adjective checklist of positive and negative distorted client reactions after sessions or completed treatments (e.g., the Missouri Identifying Transference Scale [MITS], Multon, Patton, & Kivlighan, 1996). The MITS demonstrates strong internal reliability for positive and negative transference subscores derived by factor analysis. Preliminary evidence suggests that scores on the MITS are consistent with client-ratings of their relationships with their parents (Multon et al., 1996). The Psychotherapy Relationship Questionnaire (Westen, 2000) is a clinician-rated instrument that, compared to the MITS, assesses more elaborated patterns of transference. Initial findings suggest a five-factor structure (angry/entitled, anxious/preoccupied, secure/engaged, avoidant/counterdependent, sexualized transference dimensions), with certain factors correlating in expected directions with *DSM-IV* Axis-II disorders (Bradley, Heim, & Westen, 2005).

While there is also some evidence to suggest that therapist ratings of the amount of transference differentiate successful from less successful treatments (e.g., Graff & Luborsky, 1977) and that transference can be identified by therapists from a range of theoretical orientations (e.g., Gelso, Kivlighan, Wine, Jones, & Friedman, 1997), it may be noted that therapists, like clients, have perceptual biases and selectively attend to each others' features based on their unique interpersonal histories. As a result, transference cannot be assessed fully by therapist ratings alone. Hilliard, Henry, and Strupp (2000) found that overall outcome in short-term dynamic psychotherapy was affected by the early relationship histories of both clients and their therapists, and that this link was mediated by the quality of the alliance. Thus, an advantage of using observer rated measures is reduced rater bias (although the possible impact of observers' relational histories on the results is, as yet, undetermined).

In conclusion, research on transference from each of these three perspectives has produced some important first steps in assessing this construct reliably and validly. However, no one rating perspective or definition of transference by itself adequately captures the complexity of the construct. While it may be appealing to see client- and therapist-rated instruments as quick methods for evaluating transference, we believe the field would suffer in the long run if it lost sight of the nuance, complexity, and ambiguity that is an inherent part of the transference.

THE DOUBLE HELIX OF COUNTERTRANSFERENCE

Countertransference has had a long and complicated history in psychotherapy and psychoanalysis. For many years, countertransference was viewed as a destructive force, something to be eliminated if therapy was to succeed. By contrast, it has also been seen as an indispensable tool of the therapist. Epstein and Feiner (1988) captured this ambivalence when they observed that these two themes—countertransference as a hindrance and an aid to treatment—"have been intertwined, like a double helix, throughout the historical development of psychoanalytic conceptions of countertransference" (p. 282) and of analytic treatment.

S. Freud's early comments on countertransference (1910/1957, 1912/1959) may have set the stage for this ambivalence (see Gelso & Hayes' [2007] review of the history of countertransference). S. Freud suggested that therapists need to understand their unconscious as deeply as possible, while at the same time eliminating countertransference and, in fact, putting aside all their feelings toward the patient. In any event, the pejorative view of countertransference held sway for many decades. As a consequence, the clinical and, especially, empirical literatures suffered (see Gelso & Hayes, 2007, Chapter , this volume). If countertransference is a bad thing, then the experience of it may be seen as shameful, something hard to admit to yourself and certainly to colleagues. Such an attitude makes it difficult to study a phenomenon. However, a shift in how countertransference was defined that took place around the mid-twentieth century brought about greater theoretical and clinical attention to the topic, followed by an increase in empirical research.

Definitions of Countertransference

At least four different definitions of countertransference exist (Epstein & Feiner, 1988; Gelso & Hayes, 2007), ranging from the rather narrow classical definition to the all-encompassing totalistic one. In the *classical* conception (S. Freud, 1912/1959), countertransference is seen as the therapist's mostly unconscious, conflictual (i.e., largely neurotic) reactions to the client's transference. The *totalistic* conception, which emerged during the 1950s, viewed virtually all of the therapist's emotional reactions as countertransference. With this broadened definition, countertransference was seen as something that could be invaluable to the therapist. By studying their own internal reactions, therapists could best understand how clients affected significant others in their lives, how others reacted to clients, and how clients reacted to others.

Other conceptions of countertransference focus on the inherently interactive nature of the phenomenon (Kiesler, 1996; Mitchell, 1997; Racker, 1957; Teyber, 2005). In an attempt to draw upon the strengths of these different perspectives, while avoiding their limitations, Gelso and Hayes (2007) provided what they termed an integrative conception. They defined countertransference as "the therapist's internal and external reactions that are shaped by the therapist's past and present emotional conflicts and vulnerabilities" (p. 25). This conception acknowledges the influence of the client and the nontransference basis of some of the client's reactions to which countertransference responds. The definition also incorporates the nontransference basis for some therapist countertransference. Unlike the totalistic conception, the integrative conception also allows for a delineation of what countertransference is not. Finally, the integrative conception is consistent with most countertransference research conducted over the past three decades.

Empirical Findings on Countertransference, Therapy Process, and Therapy Outcome

With a few notable exceptions, research on countertransference did not begin in earnest until the 1980s. As is the case with any young area of research, there are many scattered and unreplicated findings. Next we summarize key findings, focusing mostly on those that have at least some replication.

Occurrence, Origins, and Manifestation of Countertransference

How often does countertransference occur? Little base rate data exist. However, even using a more conservative definition of countertransference similar to the classical view, the limited available data suggest that it occurs a great deal. For example, Hayes et al. (1998) studied eight experienced, highly reputed, and theoretically diverse therapists, who each worked with one client for 12 to 20 sessions. These therapists reported countertransference in 80% of their sessions, which for a variety of reasons may be a conservative estimate. The origins of countertransference appear to be manifold and multilayered. Therapist characteristics, blind spots, and self-reports of sources of countertransference have been studied. In their review, Gelso and Hayes (2007) concluded that countertransference may stem from therapists' unresolved issues with their family of origin, roles as parents and partners, narcissism, unmet needs, grandiosity, and professional self-concept. Typically, the origins that are exhibited in the therapy hour have their roots in earlier unresolved issues in the therapist.

Countertransference is manifested through a therapist's behavior, affect, and cognitions. It most likely begins internally, as thoughts and feelings that, if not understood and managed in one way or another, may be acted out behaviorally. At the affective level, a consistent finding has been that when therapists' unresolved issues are stimulated, therapists experience increased anxiety (Gelso & Hayes, 2007). This finding supports long-standing clinical theory. However, other emotional reactions may also occur. Thus, Hayes et al. (1998) found that countertransference reactions may take the form of anger, sadness, nurturing feelings, pity, disappointment, boredom, inadequacy, guilt, and envy.

At the cognitive level, a classic study by Cutler (1958) revealed that countertransference may be manifested through memory distortions. Cutler found that when the client's material touched on an area that is conflictual for the therapist, the likelihood that the therapist would accurately recall what was discussed was decreased. Other studies (Fiedler, 1951; Gelso, Fassinger, Gomez, & Latts, 1995; McClure & Hodge, 1987) support the idea that therapists are more likely to incorrectly recall particular verbal expressions or misperceive the client's personality when the therapist's conflicts are invoked.

At the behavioral level, several studies suggest that when therapists' unresolved issues are stimulated, they tend to pull away from clients. Indeed, therapist avoidance is the most commonly found overt manifestation of countertransference (Gelso & Hayes, 2007; Hayes & Gelso, 2001). Such avoidance can take the form of ignoring the clients' feelings, disapproving, changing the topic, or making less personally involving statements. Although avoidance is the most commonly found behavioral manifestation, as theoretically expected, the other extreme (i.e., over-involvement) has also been found. For example, in a qualitative study of seven novice therapist-trainees, Williams, Judge, Hill, and Hoffman (1997) found that clinical supervisors of two of these trainees noticed over-involvement in the client's problems (e.g., taking the client's side against parents).

Countertransference Interaction Hypothesis

A number of studies have sought to determine what client factors serve as triggers of countertransference. Studies have examined presenting problems (e.g., same-sex relationship problems, rape, HIV infection) and styles (e.g., hostility, seductiveness, dependency). The search for such triggers generally has not been fruitful. Instead, what has been commonly found is that whether the client's problems or style creates countertransference will depend on the therapist's conflicts and vulnerabilities. For example, a study by Mohr, Gelso, and Hill (2005) used attachment theory to make predictions about countertransference behavior. It was found that counselor-trainees with dismissing styles of attachment were more likely to exhibit hostile and rejecting countertransference behavior with clients who had preoccupied attachment styles; meanwhile preoccupied-attached counselors displayed this kind of countertransference with dismissing clients. Thus, client triggers appear to interact with therapist vulnerabilities in the experience of countertransference.

Countertransference, Countertransference Management, and Outcome

There is a paucity of research on the relation of countertransference to outcome. We are aware of only one such study (Hayes, Riker, & Ingram, 1997), which found countertransference to be associated with poorer outcomes among the less successful cases of brief therapy. This partial support is buffered by findings that countertransference is associated with variables themselves known to relate to outcome. For example, a negative association has been found between countertransference behavior and the working alliance that develops between therapists and clients (Ligiero & Gelso, 2002; Rosenberger & Hayes, 2002). These quantitative studies are supported by qualitative data on brief and long-term therapy that underscore how countertransference hinders treatment (Gelso, Hill, Mohr, Rochlen, & Zack, 1999; Hill, Nutt-Williams, Heaton, Thompson, & Rhodes, 1996; Williams et al., 1997). What is missing in this literature is the link of countertransference, other important variables (e.g., working alliance, resistance) and outcome. Studies examining the extent to which the relation of countertransference to outcome may be mediated by other variables would be very useful.

It will be recalled that there are two elements to the double helix of countertransference. What of the positive side? Clinical theory suggests that if therapists can understand and work with their countertransference-based feelings and cognitions, they are less likely to act them out and, instead, can use them to better understand the client. In keeping with this view, over the past several years a litera-ture has developed on the topic of countertransference management. For example, VanWagoner, Gelso, Hayes, and Diemer (1991) developed a theory of countertransference management (CM). They asserted that CM is composed of five therapist factors: anxiety management, self-insight, self-integration, em-pathy, and conceptualizing ability. It was proposed that therapists possessing CM ability would be more likely to provide effective treatment. Research has largely supported this theory. CM has been associated with reduced countertransference behavior in counseling (Friedman & Gelso, 2000; Hayes et al., 1997), general excellence as a therapist (VanWagoner et al., 1991), strength of working alliance (Rosenberger & Hayes, 2002), and treatment outcome (Gelso, Latts, Gomez, & Fassinger, 2002). Despite this support, we still know little about how the five factors work separately and together to affect treatment. Some findings point to complex interactions (Latts & Gelso, 1995; Robbins & Jolkovski, 1987). Little is also known about just what therapists do to manage countertransference-based feelings and thoughts so as to not act them out. Beginning efforts in this area are highly promising (e.g., Williams, Hurley, O'Brien, & DeGregorio, 2003), suggesting a range of in-session and extra-session behavior that is used to manage countertransference.

PSYCHOTHERAPY'S HIDDEN DIMENSION: THE REAL RELATIONSHIP

The idea of a real relationship in psychotherapy has been around for a long time (See A. Freud, 1954; Menaker, 1942). The early literature on this construct came from psychoanalysis, and the real relationship was often contrasted with transference. The most theoretically influential early work was probably that of Greenson (1967) who, as indicated earlier, divided the overall therapeutic relationship into the working alliance, the transference (including countertransference), and the real relationship. His separation of real relationship from working alliance was particularly notable. For Greenson, the working alliance was an artifact of treatment, and the only reason for its existence was to foster successful therapy. The working alliance *emerged from* the real relationship, which was seen as a fundamental aspect of all human relationships.

Real Relationship Defined

Despite its long existence, the concept of real relationship seemed to reside in the background of clinical theory and had never been investigated empirically until recently. In part, this status was due to the lack of a clear definition and to the resulting absence of measurement tools. Over the past two decades, Gelso and his collaborators have sought to refine theoretically the concept of real relationship (e.g., Gelso, 2002; Gelso & Carter, 1985, 1994; Gelso & Hayes, 1998) and to develop measures of this construct (Gelso et al., 2005; Kelley, Gelso, Fuertes, Marmarosh, & Holmes, in press).

Following Greenson (1967), Gelso and colleagues suggested that the real relationship consisted of two fundamental elements, genuineness and realism. Genuineness is "the ability to be who one truly is, to be nonphoney, to be authentic in the here and now" (Gelso, 2002, p. 37). Realism is "the experiencing or perceiving the other in ways that befit him or her, rather than as projections of wished for or feared others (i.e., transference)" (p. 37). In combining the elements of genuineness and realism, Gelso (2004) defined the real relationship as "the personal relationship existing between two or more people as reflected in the degree to which each is genuine with the other and perceives the other in ways that befit the other" (p. 6).

In elaborating this definition, Gelso and colleagues argued that two additional concepts are necessary if real relationship is to make sense theoretically and clinically: magnitude and valence. Magnitude pertains to how much of a real relationship (genuineness and realism) exists, and rests on the idea that genuineness and realism vary in terms of how much of them are present at any moment. The notion of valence is predicated on the idea that within the context of a real relationship, clients' and therapists' feelings toward one another may range from very positive to very negative. For example, a client may genuinely not like certain qualities in his or her therapist, qualities that are realistically perceived.

While varying in strength, the real relationship has been theorized as existing from the first moment of contact between all therapists and clients and as having a significant impact on the process and outcome of all treatments. The stronger the real relationship, the more effective will be the treatment (Gelso & Hayes, 1998). In contrast to these theoretical claims, the concept of a real relationship in therapy has been quite controversial. Three fundamental arguments have been posed against the value of the construct. First, since everything in the therapeutic relationship is real, the concept of a real relationship is redundant and unnecessary. Second, who can know what is real and thus be the arbiter of reality? This criticism focuses on the fact that early psychoanalysts often wrote as if they had the market on what was real. Finally, the concept of real relationship has been challenged because even if there is a reality, it can never be fully known.

Each of these arguments has been addressed by Gelso (2002). He suggested that, despite the fact that everything is real in the therapeutic relationship, a concept of real relationship adds something significant to other relational constructs, and thus has incremental value. Also, consistent with postmodern thought, neither member of a therapeutic dyad need be seen as the total arbiter of what is real. Instead, what is real is perceptual and is co-constructed by the dyad. Finally, Gelso pointed out that the concept of real relationship is in no way negated by the fact that we can never fully know what is real. In the human sciences, no theoretical construct is or probably can be fully known.

Empirical Efforts to Study the Real Relationship

Eugster and Wampold (1996) conducted the first study examining the role of the real relationship in psychotherapy. These researchers found that clients' perceptions of the real relationship offered by their highly expert therapists were the most powerful of nine predictors of treatment satisfaction. However, therapists' perceptions of the real relationship that they offered to clients were negatively associated with their ratings of satisfaction. This implied that for clients, the therapist-offered real relationship was extremely important, whereas for therapists it was not helpful. Instead, for the therapists, other therapist variables (e.g., expertness) were far more significant in relation to satisfaction. The finding that the real relationship was so much more helpful in the clients' eyes raises questions about just what is helpful and what is not helpful, and why this would vary according to the participants' roles.

Two qualitative studies shed further light on clients' and therapists' experiences associated with the real relationship. Based on interviews, Knox, Hess, Peterson, and Hill (1997) found that for 13 clients, their therapists' self-disclosures fostered a sense of these therapists' realness and humanness, thus strengthening the real relationship. Gelso et al. (1999) found that for 11 psychodynamic therapists, each reporting on one long-term successful case, the real relationship helpfully facilitated clients' expression of difficult transference feelings.

Measuring the Real Relationship

A key impediment to the empirical study of the real relationship has been the lack of sound and economical measures. Recently, both therapist and client forms have been developed and have demonstrated promising reliability and validity. Both the therapist (Gelso et al., 2005) and client (Kelley et al., 2007) measures contain 24 items, with 12-item subscales assessing genuineness and realism. The scales also contain items tapping the magnitude and valence of the real relationship. As theoretically expected, the therapist form (Gelso et al., 2005) has been found to relate positively to therapists' ratings of their working alliance with clients, session outcome, clients' level of insight, and negative transference (negatively). The client form (Kelley et al., 2007) was found to relate to other measures of the real relationship, therapist congruence, clients' observing ego, and clients' tendency to hide true feelings in order to meet others' expectations (negative correlation).

To date, two studies have been completed using these new measures. Fuertes et al. (2007) found that clients' ratings of real relationship were related to their progress in treatment, above and beyond the variance in progress accounted for by their ratings of working alliance, therapist empathy, and attachment to their therapist. Therapists' scores on the real relationship measure were also related to progress, although marginally so. Marmarosh, Gelso, Markin, and Majors (2007) also found that both clients' and therapists' ratings of the strength of their real relationships were associated with treatment outcome, above and beyond the variance accounted for by working alliance. However, for clients, the aspect of real relationship that predicted outcome was the Genuineness subscale, whereas for therapists the aspect-predicting outcome was the Realism subscale. Given the theoretical similarity of real relationship and working alliance, these two studies are significant in suggesting that the strength of the real relationship may relate to treatment progress and outcome independent of the variance accounted for by working alliance.

CURRENT STATUS AND FUTURE DIRECTIONS

In this chapter, we described, in broad brushstrokes, theoretical developments and empirical findings related to the tripartite model of the psychotherapy relationship. Although the components of the relationship have been reviewed separately, as we have noted early on, they are far from separate in the lived experience of the psychotherapy hour. During the hour, within the confines of most theoretical orientations, the therapist's role is to listen empathically and take in what the client is expressing, verbally and nonverbally, and then to respond in a way that is in keeping with the therapist's implicit or explicit theory of treatment. Thus, for example, the person-centered therapist may respond with empathic reflections, the cognitive-behavioral therapist with suggestions, and the psychoanalytic therapist with interpretations.

The components all work at the same time, each influencing and at times merging into the other as the hour unfolds. The simultaneous and overlapping manifestation of the components is always at play, albeit mostly silently. Still, at times, one or the other of the components becomes salient. When stressed or ruptured, or when most needed, the working alliance becomes salient. At other times, the transference or countertransference takes center stage, and in some instances their emergence is so strong that even therapists who do not focus on them will notice and respond to their press. The real relationship, too, may stand out most at certain points, for example, early and late in the treatment.

There is another way in which the components operate interactively. That is, within the tripartite model, each may be theorized to influence the other. Thus, as we have suggested, the working alliance has been theorized as emerging from the real relationship. In turn, the working alliance and real relationship influence the extent to which the client is able to express and gain insight into difficult and painful transference feelings. These transferences influence the working alliance and real relationship.

Furthermore, just as transference is affected by the real relationship and the working alliance, so too is countertransference influenced by them, and by transference, as well. Regarding the latter, consistent with most psychoanalytic theories, the client may be seen as unconsciously aiming to influence the therapist through the transference. That is, the client wishes to create certain feelings and thoughts in the therapist, some aimed at maintaining the client's defenses, and some aimed at establishing conditions for growth. Countertransference, at least as inwardly experienced by the therapist, may be seen as partly a reflection of this client press or influence. How the countertransference is then dealt with by the therapist will have a major impact on the therapeutic process.

Empirical Beginnings in the Study of Interacting Components

Over a decade ago, Gelso and Carter (1994) theorized about how the components of the relationship unfold and interact during treatments of all theoretical persuasions. A series of theoretical propositions were offered that cut across theories of therapy. Some of the theorized relations have subsequently been studied. We paraphrase propositions that have been studied and summarize the key findings next.

Transference and the Working Alliance Mutually Influence One Another

Using time-series analysis to examine time-dependent relationships, Patton, Kivlighan, and Multon (1997) found that the working alliance appeared to influence transference. That is, when working alliance was high in a session, the following two sessions exhibited high levels of transference. However, alliance was not similarly influenced by transference.

Countertransference and the Working Alliance Mutually Influence One Another

In two studies, therapists' countertransference with clients was negatively related to working alliance (Ligiero & Gelso, 2002; Rosenberger & Hayes, 2002). Rosenberger and Hayes also found that countertransference management ability was positively associated with alliance. Myers and Hayes (2006) found in a laboratory analogue that when alliances are poor, therapists' disclosure of their countertransference issues resulted in participants' perceptions that sessions were shallower and the therapists less expert.

Real Relationship and the Working Alliance Mutually Influence One Another

The recent series of studies on real relationship described earlier find this component to be strongly related to working alliance, although causal direction remains unclear.

As Transference or Real Relationship Comes to the Foreground, the Other Recedes to the Background

This complex proposition would predict, among other things, a negative relationship between transference and real relationship. One study to date did find that transference was related negatively to real relationship (Gelso et al., 2005).

Although the study of the interaction among the four components is in its early stages, the initial findings have been promising. In addition to theorizing about the ways in which the components interact, Gelso and Carter (1994) offered propositions about how each component unfolds during brief and long-term treatment. Little research has been done on this topic. However, two studies (Kivlighan & Shaughnessy, 2000; Stiles et al., 2004) examined the working alliance across the course of brief therapy. Each found different kinds of alliance patterns. In both studies, some clients demonstrated a stable and strong alliance throughout, whereas another cluster evidenced a linearly improving alliance. In both studies, a cluster of clients who experienced a declining alliance followed by a strengthened alliance improved the most. This supports one of Gelso and Carter's propositions, and suggests that ruptures followed by repairs in the working alliance at some point in brief therapy tend to be associated with the best outcomes. In the area of transference, Gelso et al. (1997) demonstrated that in brief therapy the curves of negative transference for the more successful cases showed an increase and then decline, a pattern that appears to be opposite the V-shaped curves related to successful outcome in the two working alliance studies. Like the study of interactions among components, the investigation of how the components unfold, individually and jointly, is in its infancy and represents a growing edge of research on the tripartite model.

We would like to conclude by pointing to one of the major tensions in the study of relationship components: The requirements of clinical practice and theory construction, on the one hand, and traditional science on the other. The tension is especially strong when the focal point is made up of highly complicated constructs that implicate unconscious processes and is nowhere more evident than in the study of transference. The psychodynamically based theoretician develops highly complex theories based on anxiety and defense, and the practitioner attends to this great complexity within the context of an amazingly complex and nuanced human relationship. The traditional scientist, on the other hand, must simplify and reduce in order to study, and scientific findings invariably pertain to only tiny pieces of a complex puzzle. The practitioner/theoretician often believes that such simplifications miss the point, whereas the scientist feels they are the point, and will eventually allow us to paint a reasonably comprehensive portrait of the process or construct. Practitioners and theoreticians often do not take research findings seriously because of the limitations just noted. This tension has existed from the beginning of clinical thought on topics such as transference, countertransference, and real relationship; and it may be part of the slow progress of research on these topics. There is no simple way to resolve this tension, in our view, although the development of scientific methods that are not fundamentally reductionistic, such as qualitative approaches, may be helpful in the years ahead. At the same time, the study of components of the tripartite model from a variety of vantage points and using a range of methodologies to address questions of how the components affect the process and outcome of brief and long-term therapy, how they interact with one another, and how they develop over the course of more and less successful therapy will be of great benefit. Such studies will help us understand and eventually enhance the efficacy of psychotherapy.

REFERENCES

Ackerman, S. J., & Hilsenroth, M. J. (2001). A review of therapist characteristics and techniques negatively impacting the therapeutic alliance. *Psychotherapy, 38*, 171–185.

Ackerman, S. J., & Hilsenroth, M. J. (2003). A review of therapist characteristics and techniques positively impacting the therapeutic alliance. *Clinical Psychology Review, 23*, 1–33.

Aron, L. (1996). *A meeting of minds: Mutuality in psychoanalysis.* Hillsdale, NJ: Analytic Press.

Barber, J. P., Foltz, C., & Weintraub, R. M. (1998). The Central Relationship Questionnaire: Initial report. *Journal of Counseling Psychology, 45*, 131–142.

Bordin, E. S. (1979). The generalizability of the psychoanalytic concept of the working alliance. *Psychotherapy, 16*, 252–260.

Bordin, E. S. (1994). Theory and research on the therapeutic working alliance: New direction. In A. O. Horvath & L. S. Greenberg (Eds.), *The working alliance: Theory, research, and practice* (pp. 13–37). New York: Wiley.

Bowlby, J. (1973). *Attachment and loss: Vol. II. Separation.* London: Hogarth Press and the Institute of Psychoanalysis.

Bradley, R., Heim, A., & Westen, D. (2005). Transference phenomena in the psychotherapy of personality disorders: An empirical investigation. *British Journal of Psychiatry, 186*, 342–349.

Breuer, J., & Freud, S. (1893–1895). Studies on hysteria. In J. Strachey (Eds.), *The standard edition of the complete psychological works of Sigmund Freud* (Vol. 2, pp. 3–335). London: Hogarth Press.

Castonguay, L. G., & Beutler, L. E. (Eds.). (2005). *Principles of therapeutic change that work.* New York: Oxford University Press.

Castonguay, L. G., Constantino, M. J., & Holtforth, M. G. (2006). The working alliance: Where are we and were should we go? *Psychotherapy, 43*, 271–279.

Connolly Gibbons, M. B., Crits-Christoph, P., de la Cruz, C., Barber, J. P., Siqueland, L., & Gladis, M. (2003). Pretreatment expectations, interpersonal functioning, and symptoms in the prediction of the therapeutic alliance across supportive-expressive psychotherapy and cognitive therapy. *Psychotherapy Research, 13*, 59–76.

Constantino, M. J., Arnow, B. A., Blasey, C., & Agras, W. S. (2005). The association between patient characteristics and the therapeutic alliance in cognitive-behavioral and interpersonal therapy for bulimia nervosa. *Journal of Consulting and Clinical Psychology, 73*, 203–211.

Crits-Christoph, P., Connolly-Gibbons, M. B., Narducci, J., Schamberger, M., & Gallop, R. (2006). Can therapists be trained to improve their alliances? A pilot study of Alliance-Fostering therapy. *Psychotherapy Research, 16*, 268–281.

Crits-Christoph, P., & Luborsky, L. (1990). The changes in CCRT pervasiveness during psychotherapy. In L. Luborsky & P. Crits-Christoph (Eds.), *Understanding transference: The Core Conflictual Relationship Theme Method* (pp. 133–146). New York: Basic Books.

Cutler, R. L. (1958). Countertransference effects in psychotherapy. *Journal of Consulting Psychology, 22*, 349–356.

Epstein, L., & Feiner, A. H. (1988). Countertransference: The therapist's contribution to treatment. In B. Wolstein (Ed.), *Essential papers on countertransference* (pp. 292–303). New York: New York University Press.

Eugser, S. L., & Wampold, B. E. (1996). Systematic effects of participant role on evaluation of the psychotherapy session. *Journal of Consulting and Clinical Psychology, 64*, 1020–1028.

Fiedler, F. E. (1951). On different types of countertransference. *Journal of Clinical Psychology, 7*, 101–107.

Freud, A. (1954). The widening scope of indications for psychoanalysis. *Journal of the American Psychoanalytic Association, 2*, 607–620.

Freud, S. (1957). Future prospects of psychoanalytic psychotherapy. In J. Strachey (Ed. & Trans.), *The standard edition of the complete psychological works of Sigmund Freud* (Vol. 11, pp. 139–151). London: Hogarth Press. (Original work published 1910)

Freud, S. (1958). The dynamics of transference. In J. Strachey (Ed.), *The standard edition of the complete psychological works of Sigmund Freud* (Vol. 12, pp. 99–108). London: Hogarth Press. (Original work published 1912)

Freud, S. (1959). Recommendations for physicians on the psycho-analytic method of treatment. In J. Riviere (Ed. & Trans.), *Collected papers of Sigmund Freud* (Vol. 2, pp. 323–341). (Original work published 1912)

Friedman, S. M., & Gelso, C. J. (2000). The development of the inventory of countertransference behavior. *Journal of Clinical Psychology, 56,* 1221–1235.

Fuertes, J., Mislowack, C., Brown, S., Shovel, G-A., Wilkinson, S., & Gelso, C. (2007). Correlates of the real relationship in psychotherapy: A study of dyads. *Psychotherapy Research. 17,* 423–430.

Gaston, L. (1990). The concept of the alliance and its role in psychotherapy: Theoretical and empirical considerations. *Psychotherapy, 27,* 143–153.

Gelso, C. J. (2002). Real relationship: The "something more" of psychotherapy. *Journal of Contemporary Psychotherapy, 32,* 35–41.

Gelso, C. J. (2004). *A theory of the real relationship in psychotherapy.* Paper presented at the International Conference of the Society for Psychotherapy Research, Rome, Italy.

Gelso, C. J., & Carter, J. (1985). The relationship in counseling and psychotherapy: Components, consequences, and theoretical antecedents. *Counseling Psychologist, 13,* 155–243.

Gelso, C. J., & Carter, J. (1994). Components of the psychotherapy relationship: Their interaction and unfolding during treatment. *Journal of Counseling Psychology, 41,* 296–306.

Gelso, C. J., Fassinger, R., Gomez, M., & Latts, M. (1995). Countertransference reactions to lesbian clients: The role of homophobia, counselor gender, and countertransference management. *Journal of Counseling Psychology, 42,* 356–364.

Gelso, C. J., & Hayes, J. (1998). *The psychotherapy relationship: Theory, research, and practice.* New York: Wiley.

Gelso, C. J., & Hayes, J. (2007). *Countertransference and the therapist's inner experience: Perils and possibilities.* Hillsdale, NJ: Erlbaum.

Gelso, C. J., Hill, C., Mohr, J., Rochlen, A., & Zack, J. (1999). Describing the face of transference: Psychodynamic therapists' recollections about transference in cases of successful long-term therapy. *Journal of Counseling Psychology, 46,* 257–267.

Gelso, C. J., Kelley, F., Fuertes, J., Marmarosh, C., Holmes, S., Costa, C., et al. (2005). Measuring the real relationship in psychotherapy: Initial validation of the therapist form. *Journal of Counseling Psychology, 52,* 640–649.

Gelso, C. J., Kivlighan, D., Wine, B., Jones, A., & Friedman, S. (1997). Transference, insight, and the course of time-limited therapy. *Journal of Counseling Psychology, 44,* 209–217.

Gelso, C. J., Latts, M., Gomez, M., & Fassinger, R. (2002). Countertransference management and therapy outcome: An initial evaluation. *Journal of Clinical Psychology, 58,* 861–867.

Gill, M. M. (1982). *The analysis of transference.* (Vol. 1). New York: International Universities Press.

Graff, H., & Luborsky, L. (1977). Long-term trends in transference and resistance: A report on a quantitative-analytic method applied to four psychoanalyses. *Journal of the American Psychoanalytic Association, 25,* 471–490.

Greenberg, J. R., & Mitchell, S. A. (1983). *Object relations in psychoanalytic theory.* Cambridge, MA: Harvard University Press.

Greenson, R. R. (1965). The working alliance and the transference neurosis. *Psychoanalytic Quarterly, 34,* 155–181.

Greenson, R. R. (1967). *The technique and practice of psychoanalysis* (Vol. 1). New York: International Universities Press.

Hatcher, R. L., & Barends, A. W. (2006). How a return to alliance theory could help alliance research. *Psychotherapy, 43,* 292–299.

Hayes, J. A., & Gelso, C. J. (2001). Clinical implications of research on countertransference: Science informing practice. *Journal of Clinical Psychology/In Session, 57,* 1041–1052.

Hayes, J. A., McCracken, J. E., McClanahan, M. K., Hill, C. E., Harp, J. S. & Carozzoni, P. (1998). Therapist perspectives on countertransference: Qualitative data in search of a theory. *Journal of Counseling Psychology, 45,* 468–482.

Hayes, J. A., Riker, J. R., & Ingram, K. M. (1997). Countertransference behavior and management in brief counseling: A field study. *Psychotherapy Research, 7*, 145–153.

Hill, C. E. (1994). What is the therapeutic relationship? A reaction to Sexton and Whiston. *Counseling Psychologist, 22*, 90–97.

Hill, C. E., Kellems, I. S., Kolchakian, M. R., Wonell, T. L., Davis, T. L., & Nakayama, E. Y. (2003). The therapist experience of being the target of hostile versus suspected-unasserted client anger: Factors associated with resolution. *Psychotherapy Research, 13*, 475–491.

Hill, C. E., Nutt-Williams, E., Heaton, K., Thompson, B., & Rhodes, R. (1996). Therapist retrospective recall of impasses in long-term psychotherapy: A qualitative analysis. *Journal of Counseling Psychology, 43*, 207–217.

Hilliard, R. B., Henry, W. P., & Strupp, H. H. (2000). An interpersonal model of psychotherapy: Linking patient and therapist development history, therapeutic process, and types of outcome. *Journal of Consulting and Clinical Psychology, 68*, 125–133.

Hoffman, I. Z. (1998). *Ritual and spontaneity in the psychoanalytic process: A dialectical-constructivist view.* Hillsdale, NJ: Analytic Press.

Horvath, A. O., & Greenberg, L. S. (1989). Development and validation of the Working Alliance Inventory. *Journal of Counseling Psychology, 36*, 223–233.

Horvath, A. O., & Symonds, B. (1991). Relation between working alliance and outcome in psychotherapy: A meta-analysis. *Journal of Counseling Psychology, 38*, 139–149.

Kelley, F., Gelso, C., Fuertes, J., Marmarosh, C., & Holmes, S. (2007). *The Real Relationship Inventory: Development and psychometric investigation of the Client Form.* Manuscript submitted for publication.

Kiesler, D. (1996). *Contemporary interpersonal theory and research.* New York: Wiley.

Kivlighan, D. M., Jr. (2002). Transference, interpretation, and insight: A research-practice model. In G. S. Tryon (Ed.), *Counseling based on process research: Applying what we know* (pp. 166–196). Boston: Allyn & Bacon.

Kivlighan, D. M., & Shaughnessy, P. (2000). Patterns of working alliance development: A typology of clients' working alliance ratings. *Journal of Counseling Psychology, 47*, 362–371.

Knox, S., Hess, S., Peterson, D., & Hill, C. (1997). A qualitative analysis of client perceptions of the effects of helpful therapist self-disclosure in long-term therapy. *Journal of Counseling Psychology, 44*, 273–283.

Latts, M., & Gelso, C. J. (1995). Countertransference behavior and management with survivors of sexual assault. *Psychotherapy, 32*, 405–415.

Ligiero, D., & Gelso, C. J. (2002). Countertransference, attachment, and the working alliance: The therapist's contributions. *Psychotherapy, 39*, 3–11.

Luborsky, L. (1976). Helping alliances in psychotherapy: The groundwork for a study of their relationship to its outcome. In J. L. Claghorn (Ed.), *Successful psychotherapy* (pp. 92–116). New York: Brunner/Mazel.

Luborsky, L., & Crits-Christoph, P. (1998). *Understanding transference: The core conflictual relationship theme method* (2nd ed.). New York: Basic Books.

Mallinckrodt, B. (1991). Clients' representations of childhood emotional bonds with parents, social support, and formation of the working alliance. *Journal of Counseling Psychology, 38*, 401–409.

Marmarosh, C., Gelso, C., Markin, R., & Majors, R. (2007). *The real relationship in psychotherapy: Relations to adult attachment, working alliance, and therapy outcome.* Manuscript submitted for publication.

Martin, D. J., Garske, J. P., & Davis, K. M. (2000). Relation of the therapeutic alliance with outcome and other variables: A meta-analytic review. *Journal of Consulting and Clinical Psychology, 68*, 438–450.

McClure, B. A., & Hodge, R. W. (1987). Measuring countertransference and attitude in therapeutic relationships. *Psychotherapy, 24*, 325–335.

Menaker, E. (1942). The masochistic factor in the psychoanalytic situation. *Psychoanalytic Quarterly, 11*, 171–186.

Mitchell, S. (1997). *Influence and autonomy in psychoanalysis.* Hillsdale, NJ: Analytic Press.

Mohr, J. J., Gelso, C. J., & Hill, C. E. (2005). Client and counselor-trainee attachment as predictors of session evaluation and countertransference behavior in first counseling sessions. *Journal of Counseling Psychology, 52*, 298–309.

Multon, K. D., Patton, M. J., & Kivlighan, D. M., Jr. (1996). Development of the Missouri identifying transference scale. *Journal of Counseling Psychology, 43*, 259–260.

Muran, J. C., Segal, Z. V., Samstag, L. W., & Crawford, C. E. (1994). Patient interpersonal problems and therapeutic alliance in short-term cognitive therapy. *Journal of Consulting and Clinical Psychology, 62*, 185–190.

Muran, J. C., Safran, J. D., Samstag, L. W., & Winston, A. (2005). Evaluating an alliance-focused treatment for personality disorders. *Psychotherapy, 42*, 532–545.

Myers, D. & Hayes, J. A. (2006). Effects of therapist general self-disclosure and countertransference disclosure on ratings of the therapist and session. *Psychotherapy: Theory, Research, Practice, Training, 43*, 173–185.

Norcross, J. (2002). *Psychotherapy relationships that work.* New York: Oxford University Press.

Patton, M. J., Kivlighan, D. M., & Multon, K. D. (1997). The Missouri psychoanalytic counseling research project: Relation of changes in counseling process and outcome. *Journal of Counseling Psychology, 44*, 189–208.

Racker, H. (1957). The meanings and uses of countertransference. *Psychoanalytic Quarterly, 26*, 303–357.

Robbins, S. B., & Jolkovski, M. P. (1987). Managing countertransference feelings: An interactional model using awareness of feeling and theoretical framework. *Journal of Counseling Psychology, 34*, 276–282.

Rosenberger, E. W., & Hayes, J. A. (2002). Origins, consequences, and management of countertransference: A case study. *Journal of Counseling Psychology, 49*, 221–232.

Ryan, V. L., & Gizinski, M. N. (1971). Behavior therapy in retrospect: Patients' feelings about their behavior therapy. *Journal of Consulting and Clinical Psychology, 37*, 1–9.

Safran, J. D., Crocker, P., McMain, S., & Murray, P. (1990). The therapeutic alliance rupture as a therapy event for empirical investigation. *Psychotherapy, 27*, 154–165.

Safran, J. D., & Muran, J. C. (1996). The resolution of ruptures in the therapeutic alliance. *Journal of Consulting and Clinical Psychology, 64*, 447–458.

Safran, J. D., & Muran, J. C. (2000). *Negotiating the therapeutic alliance.* New York: Guilford Press.

Safran, J. D., Muran, J. C., Samstag, L. W., & Stevens, C. (2002). Repairing alliance ruptures. In J. C. Norcross (Ed.), *Psychotherapy relationships that work* (pp. 235–254). New York: Oxford University Press.

Safran, J. D., Muran, J. C., Samstag, L. W., & Winston, A. (2005). Evaluating alliance-focused intervention for potential treatment failures: A feasibility study. *Psychotherapy, 42*, 512–531.

Samstag, L. W. (2006). The working alliance in psychotherapy: An overview of the invited papers in the special section. *Psychotherapy, 43*, 300–307.

Samstag, L. W., Muran, J. C., & Safran, J. D. (2004). Defining and identifying alliance ruptures. In D. Charman (Ed.), *Core processes in brief psychodynamic psychotherapy* (pp. 187–214). Hillsdale, NJ: Erlbaum.

Silberschatz, G. (2005). *Transformative relationships: The control-mastery theory of psychotherapy.* New York: Routledge.

Silberschatz, G., & Curtis, J. (1993). Measuring the therapist's impact on the patient's therapeutic progress. *Journal of Consulting and Clinical Psychology, 61*, 401–411.

Stern, D. (1985). *The interpersonal world of the infant.* New York: Basic Books.

Stiles, W. B., Glick, M. J., Osatuke, K., Hardy, G. E., Shapiro, D. A., Agnew-Davies, R., et al. (2004). Patterns of alliance development and the rupture-repair hypothesis: Are productive relationships U-shaped or V-shaped? *Journal of Counseling Psychology, 51*, 81–92.

Teyber, E. (2005). *Interpersonal process in psychotherapy* (5th ed.) Belmont, CA: Brooks/Cole.

VanWagoner, S., Gelso, C., Hayes, J., & Diemer, R. (1991). Countertransference and the reputedly excellent therapist. *Psychotherapy, 28*, 411–421.

Wachtel, P. L. (1981). Transference, schema, and assimilation: The relevance of Piaget to the psychoanalytic theory of transference. *Annual Review of Psychoanalysis, 8*, 59–76.

Wampold, B. E. (2001). *The great psychotherapy debate.* Mahwah, NJ: Erlbaum.

Weisman, H., Barber, J. P., Raz, A., Yam, I., Foltz, C., & Livne-Snir, S. (2002). Parental communication of Holocaust experiences and interpersonal patterns in offspring of Holocaust survivors. *International Journal of Behavioral Development, 26*, 371–381.

Weiss, J., Sampson, H., & the Mount Zion Psychotherapy Research Group. (1986). *The psychoanalytic process: Theory, clinical observation and empirical research.* New York: Guilford Press.

Westen, D. (2000). *Psychotherapy Relationship Questionnaire (PRQ)* [Manual]. Available from www.psychsystems.Net/lab.

Williams, E., Hurley, K., O'Brien, K., & DeGregorio, A. (2003). Development and validation of the Self-awareness and Management Strategies Scales for therapists. *Psychotherapy, 40*, 278–288.

Williams, E., Judge, A., Hill, C., & Hoffman, M. A. (1997). Experiences of novice therapists in prepracticum: Perceptions of therapists' personal reactions and management strategies. *Journal of Counseling Psychology, 44*, 390–399.

Zetzel, E. R. (1956). Current concepts of transference. *International Journal of Psychoanalysis, 37*, 369–375.

CHAPTER 17

Facilitating Insight in Counseling and Psychotherapy

CLARA E. HILL
SARAH KNOX

Having an explanation for our thoughts, feelings, and behaviors provides us with a sense of control over our world (Frank & Frank, 1991; Hanna & Richie, 1995). If we know why things happen, we feel better able to change them or to accept them as they are. In addition, attaining such self-understanding and insight has often been considered a noble goal in and of itself. In this light, Socrates claimed that "The unexamined life is not worth living," and the motto written over a Delphic temple translates as "Know yourself." Many of us, then, highly value self-examination. We want to understand our motivations for doing things, and we want to know how and why we affect others as well as how and why they affect us.

Although people can certainly attain insight on their own, counseling and psychotherapy have become the socially sanctioned forums in modern society for pursuing healing through self-understanding (Frank & Frank, 1991). Relatedly, Castonguay and Hill (2007) have suggested that insight is fundamental to the therapy process. Hence, it seems appropriate to examine what we know about insight within counseling and psychotherapy. In this chapter, we provide a definition of insight, describe how insight has been conceptualized within the three major theoretical orientations, review the empirical literature about insight in counseling and psychotherapy, and conclude with some recommendations for practice and research.

DEFINITION OF INSIGHT

A panel of experts (Hill, Castonguay, et al., 2007) agreed that insight: (a) is conscious (as opposed to implicit or unconscious), (b) involves a sense of newness (i.e., seeing or understanding something in a new way), (c) involves making connections between things that previously seemed disparate (e.g., between past and present events, therapist and significant others, emotion and cognition, behaviors and emotions), and (d) involves causality (e.g., finding a reason or explanation for events, behaviors, emotions, or thoughts). In addition, we consider insight to be both an event (something one attains, a discrete discovery that happens) as well as more of an overall amount or level of self-understanding. Thus, insight can be both a small "o" outcome (a single event that occurs within therapy) and a big "O" Outcome (major changes in self-understanding or self-schema that arise as a result of therapy).

Although we agree that insight must involve a sense of newness or be an "aha" experience, we also acknowledge that it is often difficult to assess the newness of insight. For example, a rater listening to a therapy session may have a hard time determining whether an insight was new, although he or she could certainly sense the arousal or excitement over the discovery in the client's voice. In addition, it can even be difficult for clients to assess whether an insight is truly new or whether it just hits them in a new way at the moment. Clients may, for instance, feel a sense of newness even when the insight itself is not entirely new.

One controversy related to the definition of insight involves cognitive versus emotional insight (Holtforth et al., 2007; Messer & McWilliams, 2007; Reid & Finesinger, 1952; Singer, 1970). Some argue that for insight to be effective in therapy, it must have an emotional component (i.e., the person must experience the new understanding at an affective or gut level, not just acknowledge an intellectual explanation). In our view, however, invoking such a requirement confounds insight with emotional arousal. Therefore, we suggest that insight be defined as a cognitive event that may, or may not, be accompanied by emotional arousal.

Synonyms for insight are new meaning and new explanation. A related (but not entirely synonymous) term is *self-understanding,* which differs from insight primarily in terms of newness (i.e., self-understanding need not be new; see above). Another related term is self-knowledge, which is also not necessarily new and could be implicit or unconscious (a person might generally understand that he or she is shy and have some ideas about why that is, but might not be able to articulate these ideas). A third related term is *self-awareness,* which involves neither a sense of newness nor causality (e.g., we can be aware of feeling sad but not know the reasons for the sadness). Finally, we distinguish insight, which is a state, from insightfulness or psychological-mindedness, which are traits.

Given all of these considerations, the definition that comes closest to capturing the complexity of this construct and that fits our conceptualization of insight is one that has been used in a number of studies: Insight occurs when a "client expresses an understanding of something about him/herself and can articulate patterns or reasons for behaviors, thoughts, or feelings. Insight usually involves an 'aha' experience, in which the client perceives self or world in a new way" (Hill et al., 1992, pp. 548–549). Note that we omitted the last part of Hill et al.'s definition ("The client takes appropriate responsibility rather than blaming others, using 'shoulds' imposed from the outside world, or rationalizing") because responsibility may be associated with insight but is not necessarily part of it.

THEORETICAL PERSPECTIVES ON INSIGHT

Most of the major theoretical approaches to psychotherapy have discussed insight, although they have defined it in different ways and also differ with regard to beliefs about its value in therapy. In this section, we briefly describe psychoanalytic/psychodynamic, humanistic/experiential, and cognitive/behavioral perspectives on insight. We note, however, that a theoretically driven explanation (i.e., insight) for clients' difficulties is a factor common to all therapeutic approaches (Wampold, Imel, Bhati, & Johnson-Jennings, 2007). Furthermore, client acceptance of the explanation (i.e., the explanation/insight makes sense to the client and fits the client's worldview) may be more important than the specific explanatory system itself (e.g., psychoanalytic/psychodynamic, humanistic/experiential, cognitive/behavioral) or even the truth of the explanation (Wampold et al., 2007).

Psychoanalytic/Psychodynamic Therapy

Psychodynamic approaches are built on the pursuit of insight, which is considered the "pure gold" of therapy. The centrality of insight in this orientation likely arose from the assumption among early psychoanalysts that achieving insight into psychic processes was linked with mental health (Messer & McWilliams, 2007). Freud (1923/1963) believed, for example, that insight into areas of difficulty could facilitate problem resolution. Later, advocates of ego psychology asserted that the most valuable and healing insights emerged within an affectively laden transference relationship. The term insight was used in this orientation variously to mean "awareness of one's feelings" or "self-understanding," and suggested both the process of self-examination as well as its content. With the emergence of relational theorists came greater attention to insight as an outcome of therapy, one founded more on an authentic therapeutic collaboration between patient and therapist than on therapists' dispensing insight via interpretation. Thus, insight began with Freud as a means to an end (i.e., reducing symptoms), but later came to occupy a broader position in the therapy endeavor as an end in itself.

Humanistic/Experiential Therapy

In his early work, Carl Rogers (1942) defined insight as "an experience which the client achieves" (p. 177) or as a form of connecting and acceptance that was felt rather than intellectual. In addition, Rogers asserted that insight occurs through experiential awareness and gaining a new perspective *in vivo* (Pascual-Leone & Greenberg, 2007). In his later work, Rogers referred less to insight and more to awareness and felt experience, suggesting that when clients experience something in the moment in the therapy relationship, consciously feel as deeply and intensely as they can, experience this completely for the first time, and welcome and accept the experience (Rogers, 1959, pp. 52–53), therapy moves forward and insight has occurred. Thus, insight is viewed as the product of explicating and creating new meanings via a continuous process of awareness (Gendlin, 1981), as an experience-near, in-the-moment meta-awareness of oneself as both living and observing oneself in the process of living (Pascual-Leone & Greenberg, 2007). In this view, the actual content of the insight is relatively unimportant in comparison to the effect that the insight has on clients in fostering empowerment, agency, and a sense of the potential for change (Yalom, 1981). In experiential approaches, insight is achieved through clients deeply and fully exploring their experiences, and through the resulting uncovering of new aspects of themselves (Greenberg & van Balen, 1998). Clients are the creators of their insights, with therapists helping clients discover something to which the therapist (and until the insight occurs, the client) is not yet privy (Bohart, 2007).

Cognitive/Behavioral Therapy

In cognitive-behavioral therapy (CBT), insight is defined as the acquisition of a new understanding of yourself or others, and is often based on clients recognizing the irrationality of their automatic thoughts and becoming aware of alternative cognitions, a process that may lead directly to therapeutic change (Holtforth et al., 2007). The concept of insight was initially dismissed by the early behaviorists (from which CBT arose) because insight suggested the existence of unconscious processes (Cautela, 1993), was deemed a process of "social conversion" in which clients learned and adopted therapists' points of view (Bandura, 1969), and was considered an epiphenomenal by-product rather than a cause of symptom change (Holtforth et al., 2007). However, cognitive elements were later integrated into a newer CBT view of insight. Indeed, contemporary CBT theorists use terms similar to insight (e.g., cognitive change, cognitive restructuring, rational restructuring, cognitive realignment, rational reevaluation, discovery of irrationality, and schema change; Holtforth et al., 2007). In this view, insight involves a change in schemas about self and others (i.e., a change in our "cognitive representation of individuals, past experiences with other people, situations, and [our]selves, which helps [us] to construe events within that particular aspect of life"; Goldfried, 2003, p. 56). Although some CBT theorists agree that insight (or change in self-schemas) involving emotional arousal may lead to stronger and more durable therapeutic benefit, some have also argued that emotional processes are not necessary for insight (Holtforth et al., 2007). Thus, although insight may be more powerful and have greater therapeutic impact when coupled with emotion, insight without emotion may also be helpful (Holtforth et al., 2007).

Summary

Clearly, insight has a role in each of the three major theoretical perspectives. With regard to the *focus* of the insight, psychoanalytic/psychodynamic and humanistic/experiential theorists focus on the self (of the client), whereas cognitive/behaviorists focus on the self and others. *Emotion* seems central to insight for humanistic/experiential theorists but has a lesser role for the other two orientations.

Psychoanalytic/psychodynamic and cognitive/behavioral adherents consider the *content* of the insight important, whereas the fostering of empowerment and self-agency is given more weight in the humanistic/experiential view. Finally, the *purpose* of insight is increased self-understanding for humanistic/experiential adherents, whereas it is to enhance mental health in psychoanalytic/ psychodynamic and cognitive/behavioral perspectives (with the latter also seeking adaptive changes in thoughts and behaviors).

EMPIRICAL STUDIES OF INSIGHT

We located studies through a PsycINFO search using the terms *insight* and *self-understanding*. We included *self-understanding* because this term is quite similar to our definition of insight (see earlier discussion). We limited our search to studies that (a) were published in English, (b) appeared in peer-reviewed journals, (c) were conducted with human participants, and (d) were related to psychotherapeutic counseling or psychotherapy. We also located studies through references in previously identified research and through references in a recent chapter reviewing the empirical literature on insight in psychotherapy (Gibbons, Crits-Christoph, Barber, & Schamberger, 2007). We then selected only those studies that met our working definition of insight; hence, we eliminated some early research (e.g., Mann & Mann, 1959; Vargas, 1954) that defined insight as self-awareness or as congruence between one's own and another's description of self. To be included in this review, studies also had to directly assess insight. Thus, for example, research that assessed the relationship between therapist interpretations and treatment outcome was only included if client insight was directly assessed rather than assumed.

We divided studies into three categories: (1) evidence for insight in therapy, (2) facilitators of insight, and (3) the relationship of insight to other outcomes. Hence, we first establish that insight does occur in therapy, then discuss how such insight might arise, and finally investigate the effects of insight. Because of space limitations, we did not review studies examining the relationship of insight to other process variables, such as client experiencing.

Evidence for Insight in Therapy

Several different methods have been used to assess client insight, ranging from microlevel assessment (small "o") of the expression of insight within sessions (e.g., client verbal behavior), to postsession reports of insight as a helpful event and of gains in insight (medium-level "o"), to assessments of macrolevel changes in overall insight (big "O") as a result of therapy. We review studies within each of these areas.

Coding Insight as a Client Verbal Behavior in Therapy Sessions (Small "o")

Several researchers have developed category systems for trained judges to code client verbal behavior (i.e., what the client says) in therapy sessions, with insight as one category in such systems. For example, Snyder (1947) included an insight-understanding category, and Hill et al. (1992) included a category of insight defined as seeing themes, patterns, or causal relationships. In comparison with other client behaviors (e.g., description, exploration), client insight occurred infrequently. For example, the amount of judged insight ranged from 1% of all client statements in a case of brief therapy (Hill, Carter, & O'Farrell, 1983), to 3% for eight clients in middle sessions of brief therapy (Hill et al., 1992), to 8% to 29% for five cases of nondirective therapy (Snyder, 1947). In addition, Seeman (1949) found that a single category of client behavior involving understanding, insight, and outcomes increased across quintiles for 10 cases of client-centered therapy (4%, 6%, 9%, 17%, 19%).

Mahrer and Nadler (1986) developed a system for judges to code good moments in therapy (i.e., when clients exhibit good process, therapeutic change, or progress). One such good moment is "client expressing insight-understanding." In middle sessions of experiential therapy, Mahrer, Dessaulles, Nadler, Gervaize, and Sterner (1987) found that 2% of good moments and 0% of very good moments involved insight-understanding. Similar figures for good moments were reported by Mahrer, Nadler, Sterner, and White (1989) for client statements in sessions conducted by Albert Ellis (6%), Carl Rogers (4%), and Alvin Mahrer (2%). In contrast, 15% of good moments in short-term dynamic psychotherapy were classified as insight-understanding (Stalikas, de Stefano, & Bernadelli, 1997), which makes sense because insight is more central to psychodynamic psychotherapy than to other therapies.

In the Insight Rating Scale, judges rate each segment of client speech on the following nine items:

> (a) patient recognizes specific phenomena (ideation, affect, behavior) relevant to the behavior being discussed; (b) patient recognizes habitual patterns of behavior; (c) patient recognizes that he or she plays an active rather than a passive role in producing his or her symptoms and experiences; (d) patient recognizes particular behaviors as indications of defensiveness or resistance; (e) patient connects two problems that were previously unconnected, or sees their immediate relevance; (f) patient becomes increasingly aware of previously unconscious (repressed) thoughts, feelings, or impulses; (g) patient is able to relate present events to past events; (h) patient is able to relate present experiences to childhood experiences; and (i) patient's awareness of psychological experiences appears to be cumulative. (Crits-Christoph, Barber, & Beebe, 1993, p. 415)

Using this scale, Kivlighan, Multon, and Patton (2000) regressed session number on client insight (summed across the 9 items). They found that client insight increased linearly over the course of 20 sessions for 12 cases of psychoanalytic therapy (adjusted $R^2 = .21, p < .05$).

In a study of five cases of brief, time-limited, psychodynamic therapy, O'Connor, Edelstein, Berry, and Weiss (1994) coded client speech for how much it involved pro-plan insight (which they defined as clients coming to understand the unconscious ways that they test therapists). In all five cases, which ranged in outcome, clients started at a moderate level of insight, had less insight at the end of therapy, and then showed increased insight in the posttherapy and six-month follow-up interviews.

Using the Client Verbal Response Mode System (Hill et al., 1992), Shechtman and Ben-David (1999) found no differences in insight between individual and group treatment in a sample of aggressive boys and girls. In a later study involving boys only, Shechtman (2003) found that emotional awareness-insight was more present in group than in individual treatment.

Client insight as represented in verbal behavior has also been coded as one step within the Assimilation of Problematic Experiences Scale (APES; Stiles, 2002). Once a specific client problem has been identified, the client's level of functioning on that problem is rated on the APES (0 = warded off/dissociated, 4 = understanding/insight, 7 = integration/mastery) across the course of therapy. Two examples illustrate findings representative of the many studies that have used this model: Brinegar, Salvi, Stiles, and Greenberg (2006) found that one client (Margaret) showed verbal behavior reflective of insight in 9 of her 17 sessions; Honos-Webb, Surko, Stiles, and Greenberg (1999) found that another client (Jan) demonstrated insight by understanding and ultimately integrating two conflicting parts of herself.

In sum, based on a number of studies using a variety of measures and methodologies, there is clear evidence that clients express insight within therapy sessions. In terms of frequency, it appears that insight occurs less frequently than other client behaviors (e.g., description or exploration). Furthermore, it may be that psychodynamic therapists as compared to other therapists elicit more client insight, although these results need to be replicated. The evidence was conflicting about whether insight changed systematically across the course of individual therapy, and whether there were differences in client insight between individual and group therapy. Although we cannot tell for sure without seeing examples of coded transcripts, the definitions of insight used across these studies appeared to be relatively similar. If so, differences between studies may be due to different samples and therapeutic approaches rather than to differences in conceptualizing or assessing insight.

Insight as a Helpful Event in Therapy (Medium-Level "o")

In their review of client experiences in therapy, Elliott and James (1989) found that the most often cited helpful event in therapy was self-understanding/insight (cited in 12 out of 21 studies). Because a number of different methods have been used to assess helpful events, and because other studies have been conducted since the Elliott and James review, we present studies according to their particular methodology.

In several studies, clients and therapists reported the most and least helpful events in sessions using the Helpful Aspects of Therapy. These events were then coded into categories (one of which was insight) using the Therapeutic Impact Content Analysis System. For example, Elliott, James, Reimschuessel, Cislo, and Sack (1985) found that the categories of insight (defined as client "realizing something new about self," p. 622) and understanding (defined as being accurately or deeply understood by the therapist) were the two most common helpful impacts. In Llewelyn (1988), therapists most frequently cited clients' gaining cognitive and affective insight as the most helpful event, whereas clients most frequently cited reassurance/relief and problem solution as the most helpful events. In Booth, Cushway, and Newnes (1997), insight was one of the most frequently cited helpful events for clients. In addition, Llewelyn, Elliott, Shapiro, Hardy, and Firth-Cozens (1988) found that clients reported personal insight more often in exploratory (i.e., psychodynamic) than in prescriptive (i.e., cognitive/behavioral) therapy.

Using a similar methodology where participants' responses to probes about important events in sessions were coded using Mahrer and Nadler's (1986) list of good moments, Martin and Stelmaczonek (1988) found that the expression of insight or understanding was the most frequently coded category for both clients and therapists (31% and 28%, respectively). In addition, they found no changes over time (early, middle, and late sessions of brief therapy) in the frequency of insight as a helpful event. Using a similar method, Cummings, Slemon, and Hallberg (1993) found that experienced counselors recalled insight as an important client event more often than did novice counselors (42% versus 23%), although clients who were paired with experienced versus novice therapists did not differ in how often they recalled insight as an important event. Cummings et al. also found that clients identified more insight events in the middle of brief therapy than in the beginning or end, although therapists did not differ in their report of insight across the course of therapy.

Helpful events have also been assessed in group therapy. Block and Reibstein (1980) reported that both therapists and clients cited self-understanding (defined as "the patient learns something important about his behavior or assumptions or motivations or unconscious thoughts," p. 275) as the most important event in group therapy (38% and 37%, respectively, of all reported important events). Similarly, in Kivlighan, Multon, and Brossart (1996), emotional awareness-insight was one of the most helpful client-rated impacts of group counseling.

Finally, in several studies asking clients about the most helpful events in dream work using the Hill model, the most often cited helpful event in every study was insight (Cogar & Hill, 1992; Hill, Diemer, & Heaton, 1997; Hill et al., 2000; Hill, Rochlen, Zack, McCready, & Dematatis, 2003). Given that insight is a major goal of the Hill dream model, it is not surprising that clients report gaining insight as one of the most helpful events.

Thus, across different research teams and methods of assessment, insight consistently emerged as the most or as one of the most frequently cited helpful events in therapy. Combining this conclusion with the findings of studies on the expression of insight reviewed earlier, it seems that clients often recall insight as the most helpful event in therapy, although insight does not occur very frequently in therapy. These results suggest that insight may be more salient or memorable than other events (e.g., description, exploration) that occur in therapy.

Post session Self-Report Measures of Insight Attainment (Medium-Level "o")

Elliott and Wexler (1994) developed the Session Impact Scale to assess what clients report attaining from experiential therapy sessions. Of the 10 positive items on this scale, insight into self was rated by clients as occurring moderately frequently ($M = 3.03$, $SD = 1.40$ on a 5-point scale where $1 =$ not at all, and $5 =$ very much). In contrast, other positive impacts, such as feeling understood and definition of problem, were rated as occurring more often, and insight into others and progress on problems were rated as occurring less often.

In a set of eight studies of dream sessions (see review in Hill & Goates, 2004), clients in seven of the eight studies indicated on self-report postsession measures (Mastery-Insight Scale, Session Impacts Scale—Understanding Subscale) that they had gained insight as a result of participating in dream sessions. In fact, the level of these insight gains was consistently more than a standard deviation higher than that reported by clients in regular therapy (i.e., not working with dreams).

Another set of studies focused on intellectual versus emotional insight. Using 5-point scales ($1 =$ no insight, $5 =$ high insight), Gelso, Hill, and Kivlighan (1991) found that therapists rated their clients at an average of 3.32 ($SD = .75$) for intellectual insight (defined as "an understanding of the cause-effect relationships but lacks depth because it does not connect to affects underlying client's thoughts," p. 430) and 2.78 ($SD = .95$) for emotional insight (defined as "connected emotionally to his or her understanding," p. 430) after middle sessions of ongoing psychotherapy. Using the same scales, Gelso, Kivlighan, Wine, Jones, and Friedman (1997) found that therapists rated client insight an average of 3.22 ($SD = .72$) for intellectual insight and 2.52 ($SD = .76$) for emotional insight after sessions of brief therapy. However, no changes in either type of insight were found across the course of therapy.

In summary, both clients and therapists reported on standardized measures that clients gained insight in both regular therapy sessions and in dream sessions. In addition, focusing on dreams led to more client insight than did regular therapy, and intellectual insight occurred more often than emotional insight.

Changes in Insight as an Outcome of Therapy (Big "O")

In this section, we calculated effect sizes ($d =$ the difference between means divided by the pooled standard deviations) for changes in insight over time in therapy. According to Cohen (1988), .20 is a small effect size, .50 is a medium effect size, and .80+ is a large effect size (note, however, that these cutoffs apply to between-subjects data and may provide liberal estimates for within-subjects data).

Connolly and colleagues (1999) randomly assigned clients with generalized anxiety disorder to either supportive-expressive therapy or medication. They found a large effect size ($d = 1.14$) on the Self-Understanding of Interpersonal Patterns Scale (SUIP) after 16 weeks of supportive-expressive therapy, but only a medium effect size ($d = .43$) for medication, suggesting that a treatment aimed at insight resulted in more insight gains than one not oriented toward insight. In addition, clients in two different case studies of therapists using immediacy (talking about the here-and-now relationship) in brief therapy showed considerable improvement on the SUIP ($d = .44$ in Kasper, Hill, & Kivlighan, 2006; $d = 1.50$ in Hill, Crook-Lyon, et al., 2006).

In addition, gains in insight have been studied via changes in judge-rated insight in client interpretations of their dreams before and after single sessions of dream work (Hill, Crook-Lyon, et al., 2006; Hill et al., 2001); two sessions of dream work (Davis & Hill, 2005); 12 sessions of therapy involving working on both troubling dreams and troubling events (Diemer, Lobell, Vivino, & Hill, 1996); eight sessions of group dream work (Falk & Hill, 1995); and two sessions of couples dream work (Kolchakian & Hill, 2002). Using a 9-point rating scale ($1 =$ low insight, $9 =$ high insight), the average level of insight before sessions across studies was 4.12, whereas the average level after dream work was 5.00, yielding a medium effect size ($d = .53$) across eight samples in the six studies. The average d for single sessions was .72, for two sessions was .48, and over extended sessions was .44. In the only one of these 7 studies to include random assignment to a wait list control, Falk and Hill (1995) found no change in insight for the wait list control ($d = .02$). Thus, clients gained a moderate amount of insight into their dreams as a result of working with their dreams, whereas clients randomly assigned to a wait list control did not change in insight related to their dreams.

In sum, clients have shown increases in overall insight after therapy, using both a client self-report measure of insight and judges' ratings of insight in dream interpretations. Thus, it appears that supportive-expressive therapy and therapy focused on working with dreams, both of which aim to foster insight, do effect changes in client insight. It may be that other treatment approaches also foster insight, but these have not yet been tested.

Summary of Evidence for Insight in Therapy

Using a variety of different methods, researchers have found that insight occurs in psychotherapy. First, judges have coded client verbal behavior as insight in up to one-third of client speech (though more typically it is less than 10%). Second, clients and therapists have indicated that insight is either the most helpful or one of the most helpful or important events in therapy. Third, using psychometrically sound postsession measures, both clients and therapists have reported that clients gain insight in sessions. And finally, clients changed in overall level of insight over the course of therapy as assessed by a psychometrically sound self-report measure of insight and by judges' ratings of insight in clients' dream interpretations. Unfortunately, evidence is either lacking or conflicting about insight for different kinds of clients, different theoretical orientations, and for patterns of changes in insight over the course of therapy. Given this strong empirical evidence that clients do indeed gain insight in therapy, we next review the literature about how insight develops in therapy.

Facilitators of Insight

The literature related to how insight develops in therapy includes: therapist interventions associated with insight gains, client characteristics associated with insight gains, and patterns of interactions between therapists and clients associated with insight gains.

Therapist Interventions Associated with Insight Attainment

In this section, we review studies that focused on specific therapist interventions directly associated with client insight. In the first study, Morgan, Luborsky, Crits-Christoph, Curtis, and Solomon (1982) found that client in-session insight was positively related to judge-rated therapist facilitative behaviors ($r =$ .43 with therapist being helpful, $r = .67$ with therapist being involved). Unfortunately, these researchers did not specify which therapists' interventions were associated with being helpful or involved.

In a sequential analysis of therapist and client behavior in a case study of 12 sessions of brief therapy, Hill et al. (1983) found evidence that client insight immediately followed therapist interpretation, silence, open question, and confrontation more often than would be expected by chance, but followed therapist minimal encouragers less often than would be expected by chance. In similar analyses of another case study of 20 sessions of brief therapy with the same therapist but a different client, O'Farrell, Hill, and Patton (1986) found that client insight followed therapist interpretation, direct guidance, and confrontation more often than would be expected by chance, but followed therapist minimal encouragers and restatements less often than would be expected by chance.

Elliott and his colleagues also found inconsistent results when examining the relationship between specific therapist interventions and insight. In an analogue study of volunteer clients seen by graduate students for single 20-minute sessions, Elliott (1985) found that client insight correlated positively ($r =$ .32) with therapist open questions and negatively with therapist reassurance ($r = -.25$). In an ongoing treatment sample, client insight correlated positively ($r = .35$) with therapist interpretation (Elliott et al., 1985). In a later study using qualitative methods, Elliott et al. (1994) suggested that therapist interpretation facilitated client insight in both psychodynamic-interpersonal and cognitive-behavioral therapy.

Fretter, Bucci, Broitman, Silberschatz, and Curtis (1994) found that clients had more insight immediately after nontransference than transference interpretations in two cases, but they found no difference in client insight between the two types of interpretation in a third case. When they added an assessment, based on control mastery theory, of the compatibility (suitability or accuracy) of the interpretations, they found no differences in insight for the three cases for transference versus nontransference interpretations. (No data were provided for these results, precluding the calculation of effect sizes.) Furthermore, compatibility of the therapist interpretation was correlated significantly ($r = .45, .32, .35$) with client insight in all three cases. Fretter et al. suggested that the accuracy of the interpretation for the specific client was more important than whether or not the interpretation reflected transference material.

Kivlighan et al. (1996) found that client ratings of emotional awareness-insight as a helpful impact of group counseling were positively correlated ($r = .30$) with group leaders being technical (being dominant, conditional, and offering conceptual input). Unfortunately, the specific therapist interventions that were associated with being technical were not specified.

Using Consensual Qualitative Research (CQR), Knox, Hess, Petersen, and Hill (1997) examined client perceptions of the effects of helpful therapist self-disclosure in long-term therapy. Among the positive effects reported, clients stated that therapist self-disclosure gave them insight or a new perspective from which they could make important changes.

Raingruber (2000), in an interpretive phenomenological investigation of eight matched therapist-client pairs who were asked, via videotape review, to describe significant interactions and responses in their sessions, found that focusing on feelings during sessions helped clients develop self-understanding. More specifically, "self understanding was linked to feeling heard, being recognized by the therapist, and to 'finding' themselves in the therapist's response. Being with feelings . . . enabled clients to experience and feel what had been unclear, pay attention to another's response, and understand something new about themselves in the process" (p. 49).

Hill et al. (2003) compared a low input condition (i.e., therapists offered empathy and probes for insight) with a high input condition (i.e., therapists offered empathy and probes for insight along with at least one interpretation and at least one idea for action) in a single dream session. They found no differences in judge-rated client insight between the two conditions ($d = .15$), suggesting that therapist use of interpretation did not yield additional insight beyond what is gained through probing for insight.

Hill, Crook-Lyon, et al. (2006) found that clients who gained the most insight in single dream sessions had therapists who were judged to adhere to and be competent using the dream model. The researchers further examined insight attainment in these data by closely examining three cases (two that gained insight, one that declined in insight) from the Hill, Crook-Lyon, et al. (2006) data set. In these three case studies (Hill, Knox, et al., 2007; Knox, Hill, Hess, & Crook-Lyon, in press), a consistent finding was that therapist probes for insight (e.g., "What do you think it means that you dreamt of your mother?") were each associated with client insight; therapist interpretation and reflection of feelings were associated with insight in two of the three cases. In another analysis from the larger data set, examining only the insight stage of the dream model for a subset of 40 clients, Baumann and Hill (2006) found that clients had higher immediate levels of insight after therapists used probes for insight and interpretation. Hence, from this set of studies, it appears that therapist probes for insight were consistently associated with client insight, whereas therapist interpretation and reflections were associated with insight only for some clients.

Finally, Levitt, Butler, and Hill (2006) conducted a grounded theory study of adults who, between two months and one year earlier, had completed at least eight sessions of individual therapy. They found that clients identified several therapist interventions (homework, cathartic techniques, role-playing, questioning, challenging, suggesting new perspectives, paraphrasing, reflecting, pointing out patterns in client behavior) as helpful in leading them to new insights.

In sum, therapist probes for insight have been consistently associated with client insight gains. The evidence for therapist interpretation is more mixed, with some studies finding support but others not finding support. Evidence suggested that transference interpretations did not lead to more client insight than did nontransference interpretations. One study suggested that the accuracy of the therapist interpretation is crucial for client insight. Other therapist interventions found in more than one study to be associated with insight gains were confrontation, paraphrases/reflection of feelings, and open question. A number of other therapist interventions (e.g., silence, direct guidance, self-disclosure, focusing on feelings, homework, cathartic techniques, role-plays) were associated with insight in single studies.

Client Contributions to Insight Attainment

In a qualitative study of client-identified insight events in both psychodynamic-interpersonal and cognitive-behavioral therapies, Elliott et al. (1994) found that client discussions of recent painful or puzzling life events served as a stimulus for the occurrence of insight. Thus, expression of painful or puzzling events may be a marker indicating that clients are ready for insight.

Diemer et al. (1996) conducted a study of brief therapy (12 sessions) involving two sessions focused on interpretation of dreams and two sessions focused on interpretation of troubling events. In correlating five measures of client insightfulness and insight before treatment with six measures of client insight posttreatment, four (out of a possible 30) significant correlations were found. Client pretreatment self-reported insightfulness was negatively correlated ($r = -.42$) with therapist postsession ratings of insight; judge-rated pretreatment client insight in dream interpretations was positively correlated with posttreatment therapist-rated client insight ($r = .43$) and negatively correlated with change in judge-rated insight across treatment ($r = -.63$); judge-rated pretreatment insight into recent troubling events was negatively correlated with change in judge-rated insight in such events across treatment ($r = -.60$). Thus, mixed results were found (three findings suggested that low levels of pretreatment levels of insightfulness and insight were associated with insight during therapy, one suggested that high levels of these variables were associated, and 26 found no association).

Kolden and Klein (1996) found that clients with marked personality pathology and severe symptomatic distress reported more insight and learning (which they called realizations) than did clients with less pathology and symptomatic distress. In a follow-up study with the same data, Kolden et al. (2005) found that clients with Cluster B personality disorders (i.e., antisocial, borderline, histrionic, narcissistic) reported more insight than did clients with Cluster C pathology (i.e., avoidant, dependent, obsessive-compulsive), although clients with Cluster C pathology experienced more insight if they had interpersonal distress. Kolden et al. proposed that without some interpersonal distress, those with Cluster C pathology experience less insight.

In their search for predictors of insight with 157 volunteer clients who participated in single dream sessions, Hill, Crook-Lyon, et al. (2006) found that those clients who gained the most insight started at low levels of initial insight and were very involved in the process of the session. In addition, in their qualitative analyses of single dream sessions for two cases that attained insight and one that declined in insight, Hill, Knox, et al. (2007) and Knox et al. (2006) found that the clients who gained the most insight had dreams that were at least moderately salient, had positive attitudes toward dreams, seemed ready for gaining insight, and did not have overwhelming affect. Interestingly, client psychological mindedness did not seem to be a prerequisite for insight.

In sum, conflicting findings emerged with regard to levels of client insightfulness and insight pretherapy as predictors of insight. In addition, talking about difficult events, client involvement in sessions, client readiness for insight, salience of dreams and attitudes toward dreams in the case of dream work, a lack of overwhelming affect, and personality pathology and interpersonal distress were all found in single studies to be associated with client insight but need to be replicated. Clearly, then, we cannot draw any conclusions about possible client contributors to insight until more research is completed.

Patterns of Interactions between Therapists and Clients Associated with Insight Gains

Two investigators have examined more complex therapist-client sequences that might facilitate client insight gains. Sexton (1993) interpreted the results of his time-series analysis linking therapy process to inter-session and posttreatment outcomes as suggesting that there was a three-stage process of insight acquisition: (1) an emotionally warm bond between therapist and client existed in sessions prior to (2) therapists' reporting client improvement, and (3) clients then reported acquiring insight in subsequent sessions. Insight, however, did not lead to symptom reduction, and was likewise unrelated to intermediate or overall outcome. Based on another time-series analysis, Sexton (1996) posited that there was a slightly different three-step process. First, clients were engaged in their therapy. Second, they described an emotionally positive experience in a session, one that included "good contact" with their therapist. Finally, in the next session, within which it was likely that therapists focused on developing insight, clients achieved insight.

Angus and Hardtke (2007) used a narrative process model to examine the relationship between change in a client's (i.e., Margaret's) narratives and the emergence of insight. As Margaret more fully experienced her painful emotions arising from an earlier difficult experience with her mother, and in the presence of her therapist's consistent empathic responses, she began to realize the extent to which her continuing distress over this event had affected her relationship with her husband. She began to understand that what she had perceived as her husband's emotional abandonment of her and his lack of interest in her past was, in fact, his attempt to protect her from having to relive difficult memories and painful emotions. Thus, "Margaret's disclosure of an emotionally salient autobiographical memory . . . set the stage for the emergence of a new insight . . . [within] a strong therapeutic alliance in which Margaret felt safe and secure to tell her stories" (p. 201).

In sum, not enough studies exist about the interaction between clients and therapists in the process of insight attainment to make even any conjectural conclusions. These preliminary results do suggest, however, that insight attainment involves a more complicated process than just a single therapist intervention leading to client insight.

Summary of Facilitators of Insight

Some evidence suggests that therapist probes for insight are consistently associated with insight, whereas evidence for the association between therapist interpretations and client insight is more mixed. Less consistent evidence has been found for other therapist interventions. Furthermore, although it makes sense that client characteristics might be predictive of insight attainment, no consensus has been found in this area, perhaps because the studies investigated different client characteristics. Finally, some studies suggest that a complex sequence of events consisting of therapist interventions, client characteristics, and the therapeutic relationship produce client insight, but these findings need to be replicated. It is important to note, as well, that all of the studies in this area have been correlational rather than experimental, and thus the causal direction of the observed effects cannot be determined.

The Association between Insight and Other Therapeutic Outcomes

In this section, we review research on the relationship of insight to other therapy outcomes. In effect, we change lenses here. Earlier in the chapter, we talked about *insight* as a small "o," medium "o," or big "O" outcome. Now we're talking about insight (whether small "o," medium "o," or big "O" outcome) as it relates to other types of outcomes in therapy (and these outcomes could be assessed as small "o," medium "o," or big "O," depending on when the outcome is measured). Stated another way, how do insight gains relate to other consequences of therapy (e.g., reductions in symptomatology, behavior change). For instance, insight might mediate other outcomes (e.g., is insight necessary for action?). Note that all of the studies here are also correlational. Thus, we cannot posit that insight causes other outcomes, just that it is associated with these outcomes. Insight, then, could be related to these outcomes, but be neither necessary nor sufficient to attain the outcomes.

Some studies found a positive relationship between insight and other therapy outcomes. In a hierarchical regression analysis, Gelso et al. (1991) found that therapist-rated client transference did not predict therapist-rated session quality. The increment when client intellectual and emotional insight was added to transference, however, was significant (R^2 change $= .24, p < .01$), suggesting that insight was related to session quality. Furthermore, the addition of the interaction between transference and insight was significant (R^2 change $= .16, p < .05$), such that clients with the best therapist-rated session quality were judged by therapists as having both high transference and high insight in the session. In a subsequent study, Gelso et al. (1997) found no significant correlations between therapist-rated client intellectual or emotional insight and outcome (either client-judged or therapist-judged). In a hierarchical regression analysis, however, the addition of the transference by emotional insight interaction was significant in relation to combined client and therapist-rated outcome for the first session (R^2 change $= .12, p < .05$) and the first quarter of treatment (R^2 change $= .58, p < .001$). Clients with the best outcomes from therapy (as judged by both therapists and clients) had both high transference (either positive or negative) and high emotional insight.

In addition, O'Connor et al. (1994) found that the rank order of the average judge-rated suitability or accuracy of client insight within sessions was exactly the same as the rank order of client-rated outcome (averaged across symptom change, change in target complaints, overall change) for five cases. Using the Insight Rating Scale applied to clients' postsession reports of the most helpful events in sessions, Kivlighan et al. (2000) found a significant negative relationship ($r = -.53$) between judge-rated client insight and target complaints, such that increases in client insight preceded sessions with lower target complaints. Additional analyses found that symptom reduction did not precede insight. These results suggest that insight leads to reductions in target complains, whereas reductions in target complaints do not lead to insight. Hoffart, Versland, and Sexton's (2002) examination of dispositional variables among patients diagnosed with panic disorder and/or agoraphobia and Cluster C personality traits revealed that client-rated self-understanding (i.e., insight) in the first session was significantly associated with decreases in negative/maladaptive schema belief ($r = -.40$) and emotional distress ($r = -.26$) throughout therapy. In Detert, Llewelyn, Hardy, Barkham, and Stiles (2006), all of the cases experiencing good outcomes in terms of reductions in depression and general symptomatology reached APES assimilation level 4 (understanding/insight), whereas none of the poor outcome cases did. The difference in the assimilation ratings between the good and bad outcome cases was quite substantial ($d = 2.5$).

In contrast, other studies found no relationship between insight and therapy outcome. Morgan et al. (1982) found that judge-rated insight in client speech did not differ for the 10 most and 10 least improved cases from a large data set. In Sexton's (1996) time-series analysis of brief eclectic psychotherapy, client-rated insight (as measured by the single item, "The session gave me important new thoughts and understandings") did not precede changes in symptom levels. Booth et al. (1997) found that the frequency of insight cited by clients as a helpful event did not correlate with changes in outcome (quality of life, goal attainment) as a result of brief therapy. Hill, Crook-Lyon, et al. (2006) found that gain in judge-rated insight from single dream sessions was not correlated with other outcome measures such as changes in judge-rated action ideas, client-rated session evaluation, or changes in the target problem.

In sum, six studies found that insight was positively related to session and treatment outcome, but four studies found no significant relationships. There was no pattern of results in terms of who rated insight and outcome, suggesting that the differing results could not be accounted for by the source of the rating. In addition, evidence suggests that the relationship between insight and outcome may be quite complicated. For example, it may be the interaction between transference and emotional insight that is important for outcome, rather than just the amount of insight. Given the variety of ways in which insight was assessed, the different measures of therapy outcome, and the different types of therapy involved, we cannot draw any definitive conclusions about the association between insight and other therapy outcomes.

CONCLUSIONS AND NEW DIRECTIONS

Based on this literature, we feel very comfortable concluding that clients do achieve insight, both during and as a result of therapy, and that clients value insight gains in therapy. We feel less comfortable, however, drawing any conclusions about how clients gain insight, what therapist interventions facilitate insight, which clients are most likely to gain insight, or the relationship of insight to other therapy outcomes. Given the range of findings in the literature, it seems crucial for researchers to pay more attention to client insight so that we may better understand how it develops, what role it may have in therapy outcome, and thus how to foster it more effectively in clients. Hence, we next propose several ideas for future research.

Measurement of Insight

We propose that insight is situation-specific, such that a person can have insight into one situation but could be unaware of the reasons for her or his behavior in other situations. For example, a person could understand that she acts in self-defeating ways in situations with men, but she might not understand why she cannot motivate herself to finish her college degree. If insight is situation-specific, then we need to measure it using methods that allow us to capture such complexity. Similar to the way in which insight has been assessed in the dream area (see Hill & Goates, 2004), researchers could have clients identify their target problems and write their understanding of the cause of each problem before, during, and after therapy. Judges could then rate the level of insight into each target problem at each point in time. Alternatively, as Stiles (2002) has done with his research on assimilation, researchers could identify the target problems by listening to tapes of the entire therapy and then going back and rating the client's level of insight in any discussions about that target problem.

In addition, insight needs to be measured in a dimensional format rather than as a dichotomous event, because there seem to be different levels of insight rather than it being all-or-nothing. Some insights could also reflect major new realizations, whereas others could be insignificant. The former insights would probably have a much different impact on clients than the latter. Or it may be that insight evolves through a gradual accretion (similar to gold dust) rather than in a sudden burst (similar to a gold nugget), a process that could only be tested with a continuous type of rating scale.

Insight Attainment

It is clearly too simplistic to examine single therapist interventions in relation to client insight, for doing so fails to capture the complex sequence of events between therapists and clients in insight acquisition. Rather, we need to examine what is likely to be a quite complicated process of attaining insight, as some researchers are beginning to do (e.g., Angus & Hardtke, 2007; Hill, Knox, et al., 2007; Knox et al., 2006; Sexton, 1993, 1996).

Recently, a panel of experts proposed a conceptual model that might prove useful for investigating the process of insight attainment. Hill, Castonguay, et al. (2007) suggested that therapists: (a) set the foundation for insight by establishing a strong therapeutic alliance; (b) prepare clients for insight by reducing client defenses, educating clients about insight, and encouraging client exploration of memories, painful or puzzling stories, or narratives; (c) look for markers (e.g., puzzlement, desire for understanding) indicating that the client is ready for insight; (d) actively promote insight through interventions that may directly facilitate client insight (e.g., probes for insight, empathic reflections, challenges, interpretations, reframes) or interventions intended to help clients change specific behaviors, which in turn might facilitate insight (e.g., behavioral assignments, paradoxical directives); and finally (e) help clients consolidate their insight gains by using interventions such as reinforcement, help clients symbolize or articulate the insight in a clear or memorable form, and help clients repeat the insight in different ways to enable them to generalize their learning.

Researchers could investigate this model through innovative methods such as task analysis (e.g., Greenberg, 2007) or qualitative methods such as those used by Angus and Hardtke (2007), or Hill, Knox, et al. (2007) and Knox et al. (2006), and then modify the model based on the empirical evidence. In addition, it would be valuable to investigate the effects of emotional arousal on the attainment of cognitive insight. In particular, researchers could examine whether cognitive insights that are accompanied by emotional arousal are more related to other therapy outcomes (e.g., symptom improvement, better adaptive functioning, improved interpersonal relationships) than cognitive insights not accompanied by emotional arousal.

Therapist versus Client Generation of Insight

Some (particularly early) researchers presumed that therapists "bequeath" insight to clients through interpretations, implying that clients cannot develop insight on their own or that therapist interpretation could speed up the process of clients developing insight. Thus, for example, therapists sought to give interpretations at a level that clients could tolerate (e.g., Speisman, 1959), and therapist interpretation was linked with treatment outcome without even assessing client insight (see Gibbons et al., 2007). Other theorists (e.g., Bohart, 2007), however, have suggested a more egalitarian role in the development of insight, in that clients are viewed as self-healers whose therapists coach them in the healing process or help them remove blocks (and return) to the self-healing process. Relatedly, some recent research has also placed the generation of insight at least equally in the client's hands (e.g., Hill, Knox, et al., 2007; Knox et al., in press). Such an evolution in the potential source of client insight leads us to wonder whether there is any difference between therapist-provided insights and client-generated insights. For example, do clients value their own versus therapist-generated insights differently? Do insights from these varying sources have different effects—do some insights "stick" better and lead to greater symptom reduction and improvement in client functioning? Are some clients better served by therapist- versus client-generated insights? Do therapist- and client-generated insights differentially affect the therapy process and relationship?

Role of Therapist Interpretation in Client Insight Acquisition

We are also curious about why therapist interpretations do not consistently lead to client insight. Although early theorists asserted that therapist interpretations were the primary means for clients to achieve insight, and practiced accordingly, the extant research affirms neither the necessity nor the consistent effectiveness of interpretation for insight (see also Spiegel & Hill, 1989). How might we explain the impact, or lack thereof, of therapist interpretations on client insight? Some research (Crits-Christoph, Cooper, & Luborsky, 1988; Fretter et al., 1994) suggests that therapists' interpretations need to be accurate or fit clients' concerns to be effective. More research along this line is needed.

Another possibility is that interpretations are ineffective if they require a level of understanding for which the client is not yet ready, either cognitively or emotionally (see also Speisman, 1959). In contrast, an interpretation may offer so marginal a new understanding (provide little beyond what the client already knows) that minimal growth in self-understanding (i.e., insight) occurs. Or perhaps the interpretation is offered at an inappropriate time: If clients are heavily into affect, for example, a more cognitively based interpretation may derail her/him from affective engagement. Similarly, maybe the therapist's delivery of the interpretation is off-putting to the client (e.g., offered haughtily or in a manner that disempowers the client).

Or perhaps the impact of interpretation takes a longer period of time to develop, and thus requires a different empirical approach to examine. For instance, clients may have one type of response to an interpretation immediately after it is given, but a different type of response after some time has elapsed. Perhaps clients need time to "chew on" the interpretation, to wrestle with it intellectually and emotionally, before its final impact emerges and thus can be assessed. For interpretations that do lead to insight, how are they experienced differently from those that do not yield insight? Asking clients to discuss both effective and ineffective interpretations would be one way to examine these differential effects (Spiegel & Hill, 1989).

Cognitive processing may be yet another angle to consider. That is, for an interpretation to "work," the client needs, at minimum, to perceive, remember, reflect upon, and, ultimately, accept it. Therapists may presume, however, that the "brilliance" of the interpretation alone is what matters, and that such brilliant interpretations will somehow work their way into clients' understandings. But if the client is too preoccupied with other concerns to hear or encode the interpretation, it might as well never have been delivered. Furthermore, clients may hear, but simply disagree with, the therapist's interpretation; if so, such "resistance" will likely affect the interpretation's impact. Given the potential roles of cognitive processing and social influence in insight acquisition, advances may arise from applying knowledge derived from cognitive psychology (Caspar & Berger, 2007) and social psychology (Haverkamp & Tashiro, 2007) to the assessment and understanding of interpretation and insight.

Value of Insight

Adherents of the psychodynamic tradition assert that insight is the "pure gold" of therapy, valuable in and of itself, whether or not it leads to change. In contrast, many therapists adhering to a CBT orientation value insight only if it leads to symptom reduction or behavioral change. Our position is that insight is valuable in its own right as an outcome of therapy, and that it also may lead to other desirable outcomes (see argument by Gelso & Hayes, 2007, about the interaction between insight and action). In support of this position, we note the findings in the literature suggesting that clients experience the attainment of insight as one of the most helpful aspects of therapy. Based on our view that insight attainment is just as valuable an outcome as changes in symptomatology or interpersonal functioning, we argue that insight/self-understanding should be included in outcome batteries assessing the effects of therapy and should be investigated for its role in therapy. We acknowledge that this position on the inherent value of insight reflects our theoretical orientation and may be controversial (e.g., managed care organizations may not wish to pay for attainment of insight, unless it is found to lead consistently to symptom reduction or unless the values within society change).

Insight may also be a precondition for, or a mediator of, other changes (i.e., a person must attain insight before he or she can make robust behavioral changes). Does insight enable clients to make such changes, for instance, or does insight yield benefits apart from behavioral changes? Insight is sometimes related to other therapy outcomes and sometimes not—what might account for such differences? What contributes to some clients being more versus less able to translate insight into action/changes in their lives? If clients were to be asked years after therapy, what would they say about the effects of insight that occurred in therapy on their lives now? These questions are worthy of examination.

CONCLUSION

The recent theorizing and research on insight (see Castonguay & Hill, 2007) has led to a new level in the understanding of insight. We are hopeful that we, and others, can continue to both deepen and broaden this research and thus add to the growing knowledge of this construct. Despite its inherent "messiness," insight merits further attention given its central role as both an outcome of therapy in and of itself, and also as a potential mediator of other outcomes in therapy.

REFERENCES

Angus, L., & Hardtke, K. (2007). Margaret's story: An intensive case analysis of insight and narrative process change in client-centered psychotherapy. In L. G. Castonguay & C. E. Hill (Eds.), Insight in psychotherapy (pp. 187–205). Washington, DC: American Psychological Association.

Bandura, A. (1969). *Principles of behavior modification.* New York: Holt, Rinehart and Winston.

Baumann, E., & Hill, C. E. (2006). *Insight gains in the insight stage of the Hill dream model: The influence of client reactance and therapist response modes.* Manuscript in preparation.

Block, S., & Reibstein, J. (1980). Perceptions by patients and therapists of therapeutic factors in group psychotherapy. *British Journal of Psychiatry, 137*, 274–278.

Bohart, A. (2007). Insight and the active client. In L. G. Castonguay & C. E. Hill (Eds.), *Insight in psychotherapy* (pp. 257–277). Washington, DC: American Psychological Association.

Booth, H., Cushway, D., & Newnes, C. (1997). Counselling in general practice: Clients' perceptions of significant events and outcome. *Counselling Psychology Quarterly, 10*, 175–187.

Brinegar, M. G., Salvi, L. M., Stiles, W. B., & Greenberg, L. S. (2006). Building a meaning bridge: Therapeutic progress form problem formulation to understanding. *Journal of Counseling Psychology, 53*, 165–180.

Caspar, F., & Berger, T. (2007). Insight and cognitive psychology. In L. G. Castonguay & C. E. Hill (Eds.), *Insight in psychotherapy* (pp. 375–399). Washington, DC: American Psychological Association.

Castonguay, L. G., & Hill, C. E. (2007). Introduction: Examining insight in psychotherapy. In L. G. Castonguay & C. E. Hill (Eds.), *Insight in psychotherapy* (pp. 3–5). Washington, DC: American Psychological Association.

Cautela, J. R. (1993). Insight in behavior therapy. *Journal of Behavior Therapy and Experimental Psychiatry, 24*, 155–159.

Cogar, M. M., & Hill, C. E. (1992). Examining the effects of brief individual dream interpretation. *Dreaming, 2*, 239–248.

Cohen, J. (1988). *Statistical power analysis for the behavioral sciences* (2nd ed.). Hillsdale, NJ: Erlbaum.

Crits-Christoph, P., Barber, J. P., & Beebe, K. (1993). Evaluating insight. In N. E. Miller, L. Luborsky, J. P. Barber, & J. P. Docherty (Eds.), *Psychodynamic treatment research: A handbook for clinical practice* (pp. 407–422). New York: Basic Books.

Crits-Christoph, P., Cooper, A., & Luborsky, L. (1988). The accuracy of therapists' interpretations and the outcome of dynamic psychotherapy. *Journal of Consulting and Clinical Psychology, 56*, 490–495.

Cummings, A. L., Slemon, A. G., & Hallberg, E. T. (1993). Session evaluation and recall of important events as a function of counselor experience. *Journal of Counseling Psychology, 40*, 156–165.

Davis, T. L., & Hill, C. E. (2005). Including spirituality in the Hill model of dream interpretation. *Journal of Counseling and Development, 83*, 492–503.

Detert, N. E., Llewelyn, S. P., Hardy, G. E., Barkham, M., & Stiles, W. B. (2006). Assimilation in good- and poor-outcome cases of very brief psychotherapy for mild depression. *Psychotherapy Research, 16*, 393–407.

Diemer, R. A., Lobell, L. K., Vivino, B. L., & Hill, C. E. (1996). Comparison of dream interpretation, event interpretation, and unstructured sessions in brief therapy. *Journal of Counseling Psychology, 43*, 99–112.

Elliott, R. (1985). Helpful and nonhelpful events in brief counseling interviews: An empirical taxonomy. *Journal of Counseling Psychology, 32*, 307–322.

Elliott, R., & James, E. (1989). Varieties of client experience in psychotherapy: An analysis of the literature. *Clinical Psychology Review, 9*, 443–467.

Elliott, R., James, E., Reimschuessel, C., Cislo, D., & Sack, N. (1985). Significant events and the analysis of immediate therapeutic impact in psychotherapy. *Psychotherapy, 22*, 620–630.

Elliott, R., Shapiro, D. A., Firth-Cozens, J., Stiles, W. B., Hardy, G. E., Llewelyn, S. P., et al. (1994). Comprehensive process analysis of insight events in cognitive-behavioral and psychodynamic-interpersonal psychotherapies. *Journal of Counseling Psychology, 41*, 449–463.

Elliott, R., & Wexler, M. M. (1994). Measuring the impact of sessions in process-experiential therapy of depression: The Session Impacts Scale. *Journal of Counseling Psychology, 41*, 166–174.

Falk, D. R., & Hill, C. E. (1995). The process and outcome of dream interpretation groups for divorcing women. *Dreaming, 5*, 29–42.

Frank, J. D., & Frank, J. B. (1991). *Persuasion and healing: A comparative study of psychotherapy* (3rd ed.) Baltimore: Johns Hopkins University Press.

Fretter, P. B., Bucci, W., Broitman, J., Silberschatz, G., & Curtis, J. T. (1994). How the patient's plan relates to the concept of transference. *Psychotherapy Research, 4*, 58–72.

Freud, S. (1963). *Character and culture*. Oxford: Crowell-Collier. (Original work published 1923)

Gelso, C. J., & Hayes, J. (2007). Insight, action, and the therapeutic relationship. In L. G. Castonguay & C. E. Hill (Eds.), *Insight in psychotherapy* (pp. 293–311). Washington, DC: American Psychological Association.

Gelso, C. J., Hill, C. E., & Kivlighan, D. M. (1991). Transference, insight, and the counselors' intentions during a counseling hour. *Journal of Counseling and Development, 69*, 428–433.

Gelso, C. J., Kivlighan, D. M., Wine, B., Jones, A., & Friedman, S. C. (1997). Transference, insight, and the course of time-limited therapy. *Journal of Counseling Psychology, 44*, 209–217.

Gendlin, E. T. (1981). *Focusing* (2nd ed.). New York: Bantam Books.

Gibbons, M. B. C., Crits-Christoph, P., Barber, J. P., & Schamberger, M. (2007). Insight in psychotherapy: A review of empirical literature. In L. G. Castonguay & C. E. Hill (Eds.), *Insight in psychotherapy* (pp. 143–165). Washington, DC: American Psychological Association.

Goldfried, M. R. (2003). Cognitive-behavioral therapy: Reflections on the evolution of a therapeutic orientation. *Cognitive Therapy and Research, 27*, 53–69.

Greenberg, L. S. (2007). A guide to conducting a task analysis of psychotherapeutic change. *Psychotherapy Research, 17*, 15–30.

Greenberg, L. S., & van Balen, R. (1998). The theory of experience-centered therapies. In L. S. Greenberg, J. C. Watson, & G. Lietaer (Eds.), *Handbook of experiential psychotherapy* (pp. 28–57). New York: Guilford Press.

Hanna, F. J., & Richie, M. H. (1995). Seeking the active ingredients of psychotherapeutic change: Within and outside the context of therapy. *Professional Psychology: Research and Practice, 26*, 176–183.

Haverkamp, B. E., & Tashiro, T. (2007). Cognitive structures and motives as barriers to insight: Contributions from social cognition research. In L. G. Castonguay & C. E. Hill (Eds.), *Insight in psychotherapy* (pp. 355–374). Washington, DC: American Psychological Association.

Hill, C. E., Carter, J. A., & O'Farrell, M. K. (1983). A case study of the process and outcome of time-limited counseling. *Journal of Counseling Psychology, 30*, 3–18.

Hill, C. E., Castonguay, L. G., Elliott, R., Gelso, C. J., Goldfried, M. R., Stiles, W. B., et al. (2007). Insight in psychotherapy: Definitions, processes, consequences, and research directions. In L. G. Castonguay & C. E. Hill (Eds.), *Insight in psychotherapy* (pp. 441–454). Washington, DC: American Psychological Association.

Hill, C. E., Corbett, M. M., Kanitz, B., Rios, P., Lightsey, R., & Gomez, M. (1992). Client behavior in counseling and therapy sessions: Development of a pantheoretical measure. *Journal of Counseling Psychology, 39*, 539–549.

Hill, C. E., Crook-Lyon, R. E., Hess, S., Goates, M. K., Roffman, M., Stahl, J., et al. (2006). Prediction of process and outcome in the Hill dream model: Contributions of client dream-related characteristics and the process of the three stages. *Dreaming, 16*, 159–185.

Hill, C. E., Diemer, R., & Heaton, K. J. (1997). Dream interpretation sessions: Who volunteers, who benefits, and what volunteer clients view as most and least helpful. *Journal of Counseling Psychology, 44*, 53–62.

Hill, C. E., & Goates, M. K. (2004). Research on the Hill cognitive-experiential dream model. In C. E. Hill (Ed.), *Dream work in therapy: Facilitating exploration, insight, and action* (pp. 245–288). Washington, DC: American Psychological Association.

Hill, C. E., Kelley, F. A., Davis, T. L., Crook, R. E., Maldonado, L. E., Turkson, M. A., et al. (2001). Predictors of outcome of dream interpretation sessions: Volunteer client characteristics, dream characteristics, and type of interpretation. *Dreaming, 11*, 53–72.

Hill, C. E., Knox, S., Hess, S., Crook-Lyon, R., Goates-Jones, M., & Sim, W. (2007). The attainment of insight in the Hill dream model: A single case study. In L. Castonguay & C. E. Hill (Ed.), *Insight in psychotherapy* (pp. 207–230). Washington, DC: American Psychological Association.

Hill, C. E., Rochlen, A. B., Zack, J. S., McCready, T., & Dematatis, A. (2003). Working with dreams using the Hill Cognitive-Experiential Model: A comparison of computer-assisted, therapist empathy, and therapist empathy + input conditions. *Journal of Counseling Psychology, 50*, 211–220.

Hill, C. E., Sim, W., Spangler, P., Stahl, J., Sullivan, C., & Teyber, E. (2006). *Immediacy in therapy: A second case study*. Manuscript in preparation.

Hill, C. E., Zack, J., Wonnell, T., Hoffman, M. A., Rochlen, A., Goldberg, J., et al. (2000). Structured brief therapy with a focus on dreams or loss for clients with troubling dreams and recent losses. *Journal of Counseling Psychology, 47*, 90–101.

Hoffart, A., Versland, S., & Sexton, H. (2002). Self-understanding, empathy, guided discovery, and schema belief in schema-focused cognitive therapy of personality problems: A process-outcome study. *Cognitive Therapy and Research, 26*, 199–219.

Holtforth, M. G., Castonguay, L. G., Boswell, J. F., Wilson, L. A., Kakouros, A., & Borkovec, T. D. (2007). Insight in cognitive-behavioral therapy. In L. G. Castonguay & C. E. Hill (Eds.), *Insight in psychotherapy* (pp. 57–80). Washington, DC: American Psychological Association.

Honos-Webb, L., Surko, M., Stiles, W. B., & Greenberg, L. S. (1999). Assimilation of voices in psychotherapy: The case of Jan. *Journal of Counseling Psychology, 46*, 448–460.

Kasper, L., Hill, C. E., & Kivlighan, D. (2006). *A case study of immediacy in therapy*. Manuscript in preparation.

Kivlighan, D. M., Multon, K. D., & Brossart, D. F. (1996). Helpful impacts in group counseling: Development of a multidimensional rating system. *Journal of Counseling Psychology, 43*, 347–355.

Kivlighan, D. M., Multon, K. D., & Patton, M. J. (2000). Insight and symptom reduction in time-limited psychoanalytic counseling. *Journal of Counseling Psychology, 47*, 50–58.

Knox, S., Hess, S. A., Petersen, D. A., & Hill, C. E. (1997). A qualitative analysis of client perceptions of the effects of helpful therapist self-disclosure in long-term therapy. *Journal of Counseling Psychology, 44*, 274–283.

Knox, S., Hill, C. E., Hess, S., & Crook-Lyon, R. (in press). *The attainment of insight in the Hill dream model: Replication and extension. Psychotherapy Research.*

Kolchakian, M. R., & Hill, C. E. (2002). Working with unmarried couples with dreams. *Dreaming, 12*, 1–16.

Kolden, G. C., & Klein, M. H. (1996). Therapeutic process in dynamic therapy for personality disorders: The joint influence of acute distress and dysfunction and severity of personality pathology. *Journal of Personality Disorders, 10*, 107–121.

Kolden, G. C., Klein, M. H., Strauman, T. J., Chisholm-Stockard, S., Heerey, E., Schneider, K. L., et al. (2005). Early psychotherapy process and cluster B and C personality pathology: Similarities and differences in interactions with symptomatic and interpersonal distress. *Psychotherapy Research, 15*, 165–177.

Levitt, H., Butler, M., & Hill, T. (2006). What clients find helpful in psychotherapy: Developing principles for facilitating moment-to-moment change. *Journal of Counseling Psychology, 53*, 314–324.

Llewelyn, S. P. (1988). Psychological therapy as viewed by clients and therapists. *British Journal of Clinical Psychology, 27*, 223–237.

Llewelyn, S. P., Elliott, R., Shapiro, D. A., Hardy, G., & Firth-Cozens, J. (1988). Client perceptions of significant events in prescriptive and exploratory periods of individual therapy. *British Journal of Clinical Psychology, 27*, 105–114.

Mahrer, A., Dessaulles, A., Nadler, W. P., Gervaize, P. A., & Sterner, I. (1987). Good and very good moments in psychotherapy: Content, distribution, and facilitation. *Psychotherapy: Theory, Research, Practice, Training, 24*, 7–14.

Mahrer, A., & Nadler, W. P. (1986). Good moments in psychotherapy: A preliminary review, a list, and some promising research avenues. *Journal of Consulting and Clinical Psychology, 54*, 10–15.

Mahrer, A., Nadler, W. P., Sterner, I., & White, M. V. (1989). Patterns of organization and sequencing of "good moments" in psychotherapy sessions. *Journal of Integrative and Eclectic Psychotherapy, 8*, 125–139.

Mann, J. H., & Mann, C. H. (1959). Insight as a measure of adjustment in three kinds of group experience. *Journal of Consulting Psychology, 23*, 91.

Martin, J., & Stelmaczonek, K. (1988). Participants' identification and recall of important events in counseling. *Journal of Counseling Psychology, 35*, 385–390.

Messer, S. B., & McWilliams, N. (2007). Insight in psychodynamic therapy: Theory and assessment. In L. G. Castonguay & C. E. Hill (Eds.), *Insight in psychotherapy* (pp. 9–29). Washington, DC: American Psychological Association.

Morgan, R. W., Luborsky, L., Crits-Christoph, P., Curtis, H., & Solomon, J. (1982). Predicting the outcomes of psychotherapy using the Penn Helping Alliance rating method. *Archives of General Psychiatry, 39*, 397–402.

O'Connor, L. E., Edelstein, S., Berry, J. W., & Weiss, J. (1994). Changes in the patient's level of insight in brief psychotherapy: Two pilot studies. *Psychotherapy, 31*, 533–544.

O'Farrell, M. K., Hill, C. E., & Patton, S. (1986). Comparison of two cases of counseling with the same counselor. *Journal of Counseling and Development, 65*, 141–145.

Pascual-Leone, A., & Greenberg, L. S. (2007). Insight and awareness in experiential therapy. In L. G. Castonguay & C. E. Hill (Eds.), *Insight in psychotherapy* (pp. 31–56). Washington, DC: American Psychological Association.

Raingruber, B. (2000). Being with feelings as a recognition practice: Developing clients' self-understanding. *Perspectives in Psychiatric Care, 36*, 41–50.

Reid, J. R., & Finesinger, J. E. (1952). The role of insight in psychotherapy. *American Journal of Psychiatry, 108*, 726–734.

Rogers, C. R. (1942). *Counseling and psychotherapy: Newer concepts in practice.* Boston: Houghton Mifflin.

Rogers, C. R. (1959). The essence of psychotherapy: A client-centered view. *Annals of Psychotherapy, 1*, 51–57.

Seeman, J. (1949). A study of the process of non-directive therapy, *Journal of Consulting Psychology, 13*, 157–168.

Sexton, H. (1993). Exploring a psychotherapeutic change sequence: Relating process to intersessional and post-treatment outcome. *Journal of Consulting and Clinical Psychology, 61*, 128–136.

Sexton, H. (1996). Process, life events, and symptomatic change in brief eclectic psychotherapy. *Journal of Consulting and Clinical Psychology, 64*, 1358–1365.

Shechtman, Z. (2003). Therapeutic factors and outcomes in group and individual therapy of aggressive boys. *Group Dynamics: Theory, Research, and Practice, 7*, 225–237.

Shechtman, Z., & Ben-David, M. (1999). Individual and group psychotherapy of childhood aggression: A comparison of processes and outcomes. *Group Dynamics: Theory, Research, and Practice, 3*, 263–274.

Singer, E. (1970). *New concepts on psychotherapy*. New York: Basic Books.

Snyder, W. U. (1947). A comparison of one unsuccessful with four successful nondirectively counseled cases. *Journal of Consulting Psychology, 11*, 38–42.

Speisman, J. C. (1959). Depth of interpretation and verbal resistance in psychotherapy. *Journal of Consulting Psychology, 23*, 93–99.

Spiegel, S. B., & Hill, C. E. (1989). Guidelines for research on therapist interpretation: Toward greater methodological rigor and relevance to practice. *Journal of Counseling Psychology, 36*, 121–129.

Stalikas, A., de Stefano, J., & Bernadelli, A. (1997). Client process in short term dynamic psychotherapy. *Counselling Psychology Quarterly, 10*, 29–38.

Stiles, W. B. (2002). Assimilation of problematic experiences. In J. C. Norcross (Ed.), *Psychotherapy relationships that work: Therapist contributions and responsiveness to patients* (pp. 357–365). New York: Oxford University Press.

Vargas, M. J. (1954). Changes in self-awareness during client-centered therapy. In C. R. Rogers & R. F. Dymond (Eds.), *Psychotherapy and personality change*. Chicago: University of Chicago Press.

Wampold, B. E., Imel, Z. E., Bhati, K. S., & Johnson-Jennings, M. D. (2007). Insight as a common factor. In L. G. Castonguay & C. E. Hill (Eds.), *Insight in psychotherapy* (pp. 119–139). Washington, DC: American Psychological Association.

Yalom, I. D. (1981). *Existential psychotherapy*. New York: Basic Books.

CHAPTER 18

Therapist Self-Awareness: Interdisciplinary Connections and Future Directions

ELIZABETH NUTT WILLIAMS
JEFFREY A. HAYES
JAMES FAUTH

Therapist self-awareness has been long identified as a critical component of psychotherapy (Mattison, 2000; Strong, 1970; Uhlemann & Jordan, 1981). Particularly in the psychoanalytic literature, therapist self-awareness has been seen as a vital aspect of successful therapeutic process (Ehrlich, 2001; Jacobs, 1991). Indeed, psychotherapy scholars of all therapeutic orientations continue to argue for the importance of therapist self-awareness (Hagedorn, 2005; Jennings & Skovholt, 1999; Norcross, 2000), with particular emphasis on the importance of self-awareness in multicultural counseling competence (Baker, 1999; Roysircar, 2004).

Though therapist self-awareness has been hailed as inherently positive (Coster & Schwebel, 1997), necessary for ethical practice (Rubin, 2000), and critical for skillful psychotherapeutic work (Edwards & Bess, 1998), the use of the term "*self-awareness*" in these contexts generally refers to "self-knowledge" or "self-insight"—the importance of knowing your own issues, biases, strengths, and weaknesses. However, an alternate definition of self-awareness (as a momentary state of heightened self-focus, e.g., Williams & Fauth, 2005) has also been suggested—a definition that allows for the possibility for self-awareness to be negative or hindering. Because researchers tend to use the same term (self-awareness) to refer to both self-insight and moment-to-moment states of self-focus, there exists some definitional confusion in the psychotherapy literature.

In this chapter, we review the various definitions of self-awareness, as well as examine major theories of self-awareness and empirical findings outside of counseling psychology and psychotherapy research. We then discuss the specific findings within the counseling literature in relation to therapist self-talk, self-awareness, and countertransference, including a review of the strategies therapists use to manage countertransference and distracting self-awareness. Finally, we will explore the concept of mindfulness as a potentially useful construct for understanding and developing therapist self-awareness and offer specific suggestions for future research.

DEFINITIONS, THEORIES, AND EMPIRICAL FINDINGS FROM OUTSIDE OF COUNSELING PSYCHOLOGY

The confusion over the meaning of the term "self-awareness" found within the psychotherapy literature can also be seen in the broader psychology literature, where the vast majority of studies on self-awareness have been conducted. For example, in the social and cognitive psychology literatures, self-awareness has often been associated with self-consciousness and self-focused attention. However, there are important

---

Special thanks to Jessica Hoehn and Jessica Wood for their assistance with the literature search for this chapter.

303

definitional distinctions. For example, whereas *self-awareness* was defined by Fenigstein, Scheier, and Buss (1975) as a state of self-directed attention, *self-consciousness* has usually been defined as a trait (e.g., "the enduring tendency of persons to direct attention toward themselves," Fenigstein, 1979, p. 76). *Self-focused* attention has been defined by Ingram (1990) as "an awareness of self-referent, internally generated information" (p. 156). It has been referred to as more of "an umbrella term" (Mor & Winquist, 2002), which can incorporate varying dimensions of self-awareness (e.g., rumination, self-absorption, self-reflection).

Several theories have also been developed to explain the cognitive, emotional, and behavioral consequences of self-awareness. In 1972, S. Duval and Wicklund introduced *objective self-awareness theory,* which postulated that a state of self-focused attention could cause one to engage in self-evaluation and increased dispositional attributions (e.g., blaming the self). They also posited that existing affect (both positive and negative) could be intensified by self-awareness. In 1981, Carver and Scheier extended objective self-awareness theory by suggesting that the self-evaluation provoked by internally directed attention is part of a self-regulatory cycle in which one compares one's current state with an ideal or standard. According to this model, if there is a perceived discrepancy between the current state and the ideal, then self-evaluation can occur, along with concurrent increases in negative affect. Pyszczynski and Greenberg (1987) proposed that some individuals cannot disengage from this self-regulatory cycle. As a result of this perseveration, an individual may develop a style that consistently presents with intense negative affect, poor task performance, and reductions in self-esteem. More recently, researchers have been reexamining some of these original theories and suggesting alternative or updated approaches (e.g., T. S. Duval & Silvia, 2001; Trapnell & Campbell, 1999), with a greater focus on the interaction of self-awareness and a variety of personality variables, such as attachment security (e.g., Alden, Teschuk, & Tee, 1992).

These theories have received varying levels of empirical support. One popular area of research has been the relation of self-awareness (and, more broadly, self-focused attention) to affective states and experiences. It has been widely documented that self-focused attention can be related to negative affect (Fejfar & Hoyle, 2000; Gibbons et al., 1985; Palfai & Salovey, 1992) and to various forms of psychopathology (Ingram, 1990), such as depression (Sloan, 2005), suicidality (Baumeister, 1991), alcoholism (Hull, 1981), and obsessive-compulsive disorder (Cohen & Calamari, 2004). Several theorists have hypothesized that self-focused attention contributes to the maintenance of negative mood and thus depression (Lewinsohn, Hoberman, Teri, & Hautzinger, 1985; Pyszczynski & Greenberg, 1987), and several studies have supported this idea (Ingram, Lumry, Cruet, & Sieber, 1987; T. W. Smith & Greenberg, 1981).

Others, however, suggest that there is a more complex (and possibly more positive) relationship between self-awareness and emotion (e.g., Silvia & O'Brien, 2004). For example, Silvia (2002b) found that persons who thought emotions should be inhibited were significantly less happy when they were highly self-focused; in contrast, persons who did not feel the need to inhibit their emotions were unaffected by self-focus. Thus, Silvia has argued that rather than intensifying affect, self-awareness merely reinforces standards we already hold about emotionality. In fact, Silvia (2002a) found that high levels of self-awareness were associated with a decrease in or dampening of emotional intensity. Silvia concluded that people experiencing high levels of self-focused attention may be "more likely to notice their affective experiences, *not* to experience emotions more strongly" (p. 210).

The research on anxiety and self-focused attention has also been mixed. Although Woody and Rodriguez (2000) found, under conditions of self-focused attention, that participants reported higher levels of anxiety and appeared more anxious to others, Bögels, Rijsemus, and De Jong (2002) found no relation between heightened self-awareness and indicators of social anxiety (e.g., blushing, physiological arousal, negative thoughts). They suggested that self-awareness may only increase negative emotions in those people who are already predisposed to experience those emotions (e.g., phobic individuals: Woody, 1996).

Thus, the relationship between self-focus and affect has been extensively studied but with many contradictory results. In fact, Campbell et al. (1996) referred to these contradictions as the "self-absorption paradox" (p. 142)—that much of the research suggests a strong relationship between self-focused awareness and negative affect and various forms of psychopathology (see Ingram, 1990, for a review) but others have found positive effects of self-awareness, such as providing a buffer against stress (e.g., Mullen & Suls, 1982; Suls & Fletcher, 1985) and generating more clear and consistent views of self (e.g., Nasby, 1985, 1989). Thus, "despite their higher levels of psychological distress and pathology, self-focused individuals possess a clearer, better articulated self-structure than do less focused individuals" (Campbell et al., 1996, p. 142). Based on their own research, these authors suggested that this paradox may be explained by the ways in which self-awareness has been operationalized and that the *frequency* of self-focused awareness may be less important than the *motive* for attending to the self (e.g., for purposes of self-reflection or rumination).

In addition to studies on the relationship between self-focused attention and affect, a second area of research has focused on the impact of self-awareness on self-evaluation. S. Duval and Wicklund (1972) originally postulated that attributions of personal responsibility would follow heightened states of self-awareness. In other words, a person who is self-focused should, according to objective self-awareness theory, be more likely to make internal causal attributions. For example, S. Duval and Wicklund (1973) found that participants who became self-focused (in the presence of a mirror) attributed more causal responsibility to themselves for hypothetical outcomes (e.g., winning the lottery). While this finding has been replicated in some studies (e.g., Fenigstein & Levine, 1984; Silvia & Duval, 2001), Gibbons (1990), in his review of the literature, concluded that self-focused attention does not always increase personal attributions of responsibility. Much like the relationship of self-focused attention to negative affect, the relationship between self-focused attention and personal attributions appears to be quite complex. For example, Chen, Yates, and McGinnies (1988) found that, when self-aware, people may make greater internal attributions of success but greater external attributions of failure.

A third area of research has focused on the relationship between self-awareness and task performance. Carver and Scheier (1981) theorized that self-focus should intensify or exacerbate a person's task performance, such that those who perceive themselves as performing below standard will do even worse and those who perceive themselves as performing at or above standard will do even better. Burgio, Merluzzi, and Pryor (1986), in support of Carver and Scheier's (1981) theory, found just such an interaction between expectations of performance ability and self-focus. Specifically, they found that those with negative expectancies performed more poorly than those with positive expectancies (according to observers), but only in the presence of a camera (i.e., when their attention was self-focused). Thus, the impact of self-focus in and of itself was limited; however, the interaction between self-focus and expectancy level produced observable changes in task performance. Similarly, Matthews, Davies, and Lees (1990) found that arousal was consistently associated with better performance under conditions requiring sustained attention. Although there has been some evidence that heightened arousal leads to self-awareness (e.g., Fenigstein & Carver, 1978), others have not found such a relationship (e.g., Panayiotou & Vrana, 1998; Rapee & Lim, 1992). Thus, the extent to which self-awareness has any direct relationship to performance remains unclear.

In sum, the cognitive and social psychological literatures on self-awareness remain contradictory and full of paradox (Campbell et al., 1996). Although there is a large body of evidence that self-focused attention has a direct relationship with negative affect and psychopathology (e.g., Ingram, 1990), other research suggests a potentially more complex relationship between self-awareness and mood. Silvia (2002a), for example, suggested that increases or decreases in affect as facilitated by self-awareness may be moderated by the importance we place on our personal feelings and their display. Similarly, though there is some support for the idea that self-focused awareness increases anxiety (e.g., Woody & Rodriguez, 2000), others suggest that only those predisposed to anxiety will show heightened anxiety under conditions of self-focus (Bögels et al., 2002). There is also still much to be learned about the relationship of self-awareness to both self-evaluation and performance. The literature suggests a complex relationship between self-awareness and its cognitive, behavioral, and emotional consequences.

THERAPIST SELF-AWARENESS IN THE PSYCHOTHERAPY LITERATURE

The potential importance of cognitive processes in psychotherapists has been a subject of research interest for the past 20 years (cf. Hill & O'Grady, 1985; Martin, Martin, Meyer, & Slemon, 1986). In fact, several models for training novice therapists and supervisors have focused on the importance of cognitive factors (e.g., Borders, Rainey, Crutchfield, & Martin, 1996; Fong, Borders, Ethington, & Pitts, 1997; Morran, Kurpius, Brack, & Brack, 2001). For example, based on the idea that therapist self-talk would be evaluative in nature and thus associated with greater anxiety, Kline (1983) devised a method of training (aimed at therapist self-talk) designed to reduce anxiety and increase ability to concentrate. In addition to reducing anxiety, Richardson and Stone (1981) found that novice therapists who received cognitive instructional training demonstrated better communication skills. Similarly, Kurpius, Benjamin, and Morran (1985) found that teaching cognitive self-instruction strategies to novice counselors positively affected the quality of counselors' clinical hypothesis formulation. R. C. Smith, Dorsey, Lyles, and Frankel (1999) found that teaching self-awareness recognition strategies resulted in additional mastery of patient interviewing skills of medical residents. These training models all rely on the potential impact of therapist self-talk and self-awareness and seek to help trainees minimize the interference effects of distracting self-talk.

Despite the clinical significance of therapist self-awareness, in contrast to the volumes of research that have been conducted on self-awareness in the cognitive and social psychology literatures, there has been relatively little empirical focus on therapist self-awareness in the psychotherapy literature (with the exception of studies of countertransference as one form of self-awareness). This section includes a review of empirical findings related to three relevant constructs in the counseling literature: therapist self-talk, therapist self-awareness and its management, and countertransference and its management.

Therapist Self-Talk

Interest in the concept of therapist self-talk gained popularity in the 1980s, based in part on the literature in the 1970s that suggested the power of internal dialogue to affect individuals' perceptions and emotions (e.g., Beck, 1976; A. Ellis, 1975; Meichenbaum, 1977). Early studies on therapist self-talk focused almost entirely on ways to categorize the types of self-talk that therapists experience. For example, Fuqua, Newman, Anderson, and Johnson (1986) developed a classification system for self-talk along six dimensions (social comparison, anxiety, task management, stimulus discrimination, personal adequacy, and anticipation of outcome), which they further classified into two global subscales (task-facilitative and task-distractive self-talk). They found that task-distractive self-talk was strongly correlated with counselors' negative self-ratings of performance and was moderately correlated with anxiety. Morran (1986) used Fuqua et al.'s measure and found that counselors (ranging from novice to experienced) displayed a moderate level of task-facilitative self-talk and a relatively low level of task-distractive self-talk, and that neither related to measures of counselor performance. Morran did note, however, that having fewer task-distractive thoughts was associated with the generation of higher-quality clinical hypotheses, thus suggesting an indirect connection between task-distractive self-talk and therapeutic skill.

Similarly, Uhlemann, Lee, and Hiebert (1988) designed the Counsellor Self-Talk Inventory to assess both the positive and negative self-talk of novice therapists. They found that most trainees reported positive thoughts about their work. However, much like Morran (1986), they found no relationship between the novice therapists' self-talk (before a session) and their effectiveness during a session. In contrast, Hiebert, Uhlemann, Marshall, and Lee (1998) found that counselor anxiety was associated with negative self-talk and poor performance. It is important to note, however, that the measurement of self-talk they used (which asks for counselors' *pre-session* self-talk statements) differs from other self-talk category systems, which code specific *in-session* therapist self-talk.

In another attempt to code therapist self-talk, Borders, Fong-Beyette, and Cron (1988) used Dole et al.'s (1982) Counselor Retrospective Coding System in a case study of a novice counselor's in-session cognitions. Dole et al.'s system involves six categorical dimensions: time (past, present, or future), place (in-session or out-of-session events and feelings), focus (client, counselor, client-counselor interaction-relationship, or supervisor), locus (external or internal), orientation (professional or personal), and mode (cognitive [neutral or planning] or affective [positive or negative]). Borders et al. found that the counselor revealed an intense self-scrutiny as well as little conscious awareness of intentionality. For example, the counselor's thoughts were coded primarily as self-focused, and over half of these self-focused retrospections were coded as negative, reflecting the counselors' self-doubts and negative feelings. Interestingly, Borders (1989) found that novice counselors with higher ego development reported fewer negative thoughts about their clients and themselves.

Morran, Kurpius, and Brack (1989) also developed a categorization system of counselor self-statements, including 14 different categories (behavioral observations, client-focused questions, summarizations, associations, inferences or hypotheses, relationship assessment, self-instruction, anxiety or self-doubt, corrective self-feedback, positive self-feedback, reaction to client, self-questions, external, and self-monitoring). The four most common categories were inferences or hypotheses followed by client-focused questions, self-instructions, and summarizations. The categories related to self-focus represented 38% of the counselors' reported thoughts. However, negative self-focused thoughts (e.g., anxiety or self-doubt) made up only 5% of the counselors' thoughts.

Finally, Nutt-Williams and Hill (1996) examined therapist self-talk using a rating system based on focus (self or other) and valence (negative to positive). They studied the self-talk of 31 therapists-in-training, using Cacioppo and Petty's (1981) thought listing procedure. They found that, although only 13% of trainees' thoughts were both negative and self-focused, negative therapist self-talk was associated with lower client ratings of the therapist's helpfulness and a greater proportion of negative client reactions (from the therapist's perspective).

Overall, the research on therapist self-talk has found a fairly consistent relationship between negative or task-distractive self-talk and trainee anxiety and diminished self-assessments of performance. Though some of the measures have focused on global approaches to self-talk (e.g., Fuqua et al., 1986) and others have focused on rating specific instances of therapist self-talk within counseling sessions (e.g., Nutt-Williams & Hill, 1996), all studies of self-talk have emphasized cognitions to the exclusion of other types of therapist personal reactions (e.g., awareness of emotional, behavioral, or visceral reactions).

Therapist Self-Awareness

More recently, research has shifted from self-talk to the broader concept of therapist self-awareness. One point of connection remains the interest in how self-awareness and therapist anxiety might be related. For example, Hale and Stoltenberg (1988) manipulated self-awareness in undergraduate students participating as counselors in a role play counseling session. They told the participants they would be videotaped (and pointed out the equipment) in order to foster self-focus. They found that those in the self-focused conditions reported greater anxiety. In contrast, M. V. Ellis, Krengel, and Beck (2002) found no impact of self-focus on counselor anxiety or performance. They, too, manipulated therapists' self-awareness using a videotape (cf. Carver & Scheier, 1978) and also a mirror combined with an audiotape of the session (cf. Buss, 1980). Though they confirmed that the manipulations did in fact increase self-focus as in previous research, they found no decrease in task performance or increase in reported anxiety. M. V. Ellis et al. suggested that perhaps the construct of self-awareness has been "overly pathologized" and that "the complexity inherent in the counseling session may outstretch the original formulation of self-awareness theory" (p. 113). However, both Hale and Stoltenberg (1988) and M. V. Ellis et al. (2002) used experimental designs in which self-awareness was purposefully manipulated, leaving open the question of the impact of naturally occurring states of self-awareness.

In assessing such naturally occurring states of self-awareness, Williams, Judge, Hill, and Hoffman (1997) examined novice therapists' reports of their own personal reactions using a combined qualitative and quantitative approach. They wanted to examine "the types of reactions with which beginning therapists struggle during counseling sessions as well as their awareness of these reactions" (p. 390). Over the course of a semester of clinical training, novice therapists completed forms after each session that assessed therapists' in-session reactions and the ways in which they managed those reactions. In addition, therapists completed pre-semester and post-semester measures of state anxiety and counseling self-efficacy, and supervisors completed post-semester measures of supervisees' countertransference management and therapeutic skill.

Williams et al. (1997) found that, over time, trainees became less anxious, developed greater therapeutic skill and self-efficacy, and became better able to manage countertransferential reactions. However, they also typically reported feeling distracted and anxious about their skills and performance. Difficulties managing their reactions were manifested via negative or incongruent behaviors in session. Although the sample size was small and the majority of results were qualitative (therefore limited in generalizability), the results provided a new avenue for research into therapist self-awareness, its consequences, and potential management strategies.

Williams, Polster, Grizzard, Rockenbaugh, and Judge (2003) extended this line of research by interviewing both novice and experienced therapists about their experiences of self-awareness. Using Consensual Qualitative Research (CQR; Hill, Thompson, & Williams, 1997), they analyzed interview data for six novice therapists and six experienced therapists. They found that novice therapists were typically aware of anxiety, critical self-talk, confusion, their bodies, and nonverbal behaviors. In contrast, experienced therapists were more often aware of feeling bored and distracted by extra-therapy issues (e.g., needing to return a phone call, worrying about financial matters). All therapists were typically cued to their self-awareness by internal and physiological reactions (e.g., heart palpitations, sweat), but only novice therapists reported being cued to self-awareness by their clients' behavior or expectant looks. Over time, both novice and experienced therapists reported feeling less nervous about their role as therapists; experienced therapists also reported feeling more comfortable, flexible, competent, and confident. They also, however, reported feeling less "vigilant" than when they were novices. Thus, some self-awareness changes over time, and in positive ways; however, the gains in feeling less anxious might be contrasted with the loss of focus reported by more experienced therapists.

Because the previous studies had used primarily qualitative designs to study therapist self-awareness, Williams, Hurley, O'Brien, and de Gregorio (2003) developed a scale for measuring therapist self-awareness—the Self-Awareness and Management Strategies (SAMS) Scales for Therapists. The SAMS was administered to a national sample of 301 practicing psychologists. The items rated as occurring most frequently included awareness of physical self and changes in intensity of self-awareness. Also common were thoughts unrelated to the client or session and thoughts about performance. Factor analyses of the items yielded two subscales related to hindering self-awareness (Anxious and Distracting) as well as five subscales pertaining to management strategies (Self-Care/Self-Reflection, Cognitive/Relaxation Techniques, Actively Returning the Focus to the Client, Attempting to Suppress or Ignore Self-Awareness, and Returning to Basic Therapeutic Techniques).

Because of the potential for therapist self-awareness to be hindering (anxiety-producing or distracting), Williams engaged in a series of studies to examine the relationship of therapist self-awareness (e.g., moment-to-moment states of self-focus during sessions) to other aspects of the therapy process. For example, Williams (2003) assessed the perspectives of novice therapists and their clients, using video-assisted recall after therapy sessions. Williams found evidence that therapists' self-awareness may indeed be hindering at times. Specifically, when therapists rated themselves as more self-aware, clients rated them as *less* helpful. In contrast, Fauth and Williams (2005) and Williams and Fauth (2005) found that therapists' in-session self-awareness was generally helpful rather than hindering. This finding applied to both novice helpers (Fauth & Williams, 2005) and more advanced therapists (Williams & Fauth, 2005). In fact, Fauth and Williams found that clients reported feeling closer to and more supported by therapists who reported being more self-aware.

The role of self-awareness in psychotherapy is both intriguing and seemingly complex. For example, it could be that, much like Csikszentmihalyi's (1990) psychology of "flow," momentary states of heightened self-awareness (which counters the flow experience) can be disruptive and related to negative affective states during therapy sessions. Yet others have found that self-awareness can reduce egocentrism and thus increase one's ability to take another's perspective (Stephenson & Wicklund, 1983)—suggesting that self-awareness could increase a counselor's empathic attunement. The few empirical studies of therapist self-awareness confirm this complexity. In fact, to date, it remains unclear whether momentary states of self-awareness are hindering, helpful, or more likely, both. When therapists ought to be focused primarily on the client, as would be expected most of the time in session, therapists' self-directed attention can be interfering. However, the reality of clinical work is that therapists must maintain a bifurcated attention, aware of what is happening with the client as well as within themselves. In this way, self-awareness is not only useful, but necessary. Thus, the extent to which therapist self-awareness is helpful is probably a matter of degree—when it becomes excessive and takes the form of self-preoccupation, it is likely to have deleterious effects.

In instances where therapist self-awareness is indeed hindering, it may become necessary for the therapist to manage his or her awareness to reduce the potentially negative impact on the client or the session. The literature on therapists' management of distracting self-awareness has been fairly consistent. Several studies have suggested that therapists often attempt to (a) focus on intervention planning; (b) refocus their attention on the client; (c) use their self-awareness to gain greater understanding of the client, themselves, or the process; or (d) merely suppress their awareness (Williams, 2003; Williams, Hurley, et al., 2003; Williams et al., 1997; Williams, Polster, et al., 2003). Additionally, novice therapists report employing self-disclosure as a strategy to manage feelings of anxiety or of being lost (Williams, Polster, et al., 2003). Williams, Hurley, et al. identified two additional management strategies, which they labeled Self-Care/Self-Reflection and Cognitive/Relaxation Techniques. Among the kinds of management strategies in the Self-Care/Self-Reflection cluster are seeking supervision or consultation, seeking personal therapy, and taking a vacation. Cognitive/Relaxation Techniques included deep breathing, self-coaching, and thought stopping.

In an attempt to investigate whether particular management strategies were more effective than others, Fauth and Williams (2005) recruited novice helpers to participate in a one-time counseling session. Surprisingly, Fauth and Williams found that, although increases in self-awareness predictably resulted in increased use of management strategies, increased use of management strategies was linked with decreased personal involvement (i.e., engagement and presence in the session) on the part of the therapist and less positive client ratings of the therapeutic relationship. They suggested that "perhaps some low-to-moderate baseline level of self-awareness may be facilitative, but fluctuations above that baseline may be distracting . . . because of the increasing amount of energy required to manage it" (p. 446). In a follow-up study with more advanced therapists, Williams and Fauth (2005) found that although use of basic techniques (e.g., asking a question, using a paraphrase) was the most common management strategy, no one management strategy was more effective than others.

Williams and Fauth (2005) acknowledged the limitations in the research on therapist self-awareness and management strategies, such as the use of brief counseling analogues rather than ongoing therapeutic encounters and the need for greater diversity of participants. However, they also suggested that inconsistencies in findings across studies may be related to the relative infancy of this line of research. In particular, they suggested that future research on therapist self-awareness focus more on the valence of the self-awareness rather than on its perceived usefulness (e.g., whether it is perceived as helpful or hindering), arguing that even negative self-awareness may be helpful to the therapist's understanding of the therapy process. In addition, though much of the self-awareness research has taken a categorization approach in both qualitative (e.g., Williams et al., 1997; Williams, Polster, et al., 2003) and quantitative studies (e.g., Williams, Hurley, et al., 2003), more research is needed on the specific and unique content of in-session self-awareness. For example, perhaps worries about your personal life are distracting whereas worries about feeling useful to the client are helpful. In addition, the research connecting therapist self-awareness to anxiety merits further scrutiny, as some studies have found a strong relationship (e.g., Hale & Stoltenberg, 1988; Williams, 2003) and others have found little or even an inverse relationship (e.g., M. V. Ellis et al., 2002; Williams & Fauth, 2005).

One area of research that may help shed light on the complexities of the self-awareness literature might be the study of therapist countertransference management. Specifically, the countertransference literature may illuminate the connections between distracting self-focus and the types of management strategies that may prove useful. In particular, we explore the construct of self-insight and the relatively new application of mindfulness to both the management of countertransference and more broadly to the management of distracting self-awareness.

Self-Insight and Mindfulness in the Management of Countertransference

Many definitions of countertransference exist (Gelso & Hayes, 2007), although they all have in common the notion that countertransference involves a reaction on the part of the therapist that is atypical in some regard (Kiesler, 2001). That is, countertransference reactions differ from reactions the therapist usually has to clients in general or to a particular client, or they differ from reactions other therapists would tend to have to a client. These reactions may be in response to a variety of stimuli, and they may be covert, in the form of thoughts, feelings, and visceral sensations, or overt, in the form of behavior (Gelso & Hayes, 2007). Assuming that what the therapist typically thinks, feels, and does is beneficial to the client, the atypical nature of countertransference reactions makes them potentially problematic. In fact, countertransference has long been thought to affect psychotherapy negatively (Freud, 1910/1959; Gelso & Hayes, 2007), and research evidence to this effect is beginning to accumulate (Hayes, 2004). We suggest that all therapists, no matter how experienced, credentialed, or otherwise reputable, experience countertransference with some frequency. In fact, in a qualitative study of eight seasoned therapists, these expert therapists reported experiencing countertransference, defined as reactions stemming from areas of unresolved personal conflict, in 80% of their sessions (Hayes et al., 1998). To avoid countertransference reactions altogether, a therapist would either need to stop seeing clients or overcome the basic human condition. In other words, countertransference reactions seem to be an inevitable part of the work of therapy. Therefore, much like the construct of hindering self-awareness, the question arises as to how countertransference reactions can be managed to minimize their negative impact on the process and outcome of therapy.

Several therapist qualities have been suggested to be central to managing countertransference reactions: empathy, conceptual skills, self-integration, anxiety management, and self-insight (e.g., Hayes, Gelso, Van Wagoner, & Diemer, 1991; Hayes, Riker, & Ingram, 1997; Van Wagoner, Gelso, Hayes, & Diemer, 1991). For the purposes of this chapter, we focus on self-insight—a form of self-knowledge from which one might differentially experience moment-by-moment levels of self-focused attention. From an empirical perspective, psychotherapy experts consider self-insight to be an important component of countertransference management (Hayes et al., 1991), and therapists judge self-insight to be one factor that distinguishes excellent from ordinary clinicians (Van Wagoner et al., 1991). However, several studies have failed to detect a relationship between therapists' self-insight and both countertransference behavior, operationalized as therapist avoidance behavior (Gelso, Fassinger, Gomez, & Latts, 1995), and therapy outcome (Hayes et al., 1997).

Additional research provides clues as to why therapists' self-insight may be insufficient in preventing countertransference behavior. Two different studies found that therapists exhibited less countertransference behavior only when they had an awareness of their countertransference feelings *and* were able to use theory to understand their reactions to clients (Latts & Gelso, 1995; Robbins & Jolkovski, 1987).

In other words, to prevent negative countertransference behavior, therapists may need to have enough self-insight to know that they are experiencing countertransference feelings and also to have sufficient conceptualizing skills to know what to do with their reactions. Reich (1951, p. 25) described this process as locating an "outside position in order to be capable of an objective evaluation of what [was] just now felt within."

On the whole, research to date has not provided extensive support for the idea that therapist self-insight, in and of itself, is critical to countertransference management. This seems both puzzling and ironic given the importance attached in the theoretical and clinical literature to therapists' understanding of what is going on inside themselves, affectively, cognitively, and viscerally. One possible explanation is that countertransference researchers have yet to adequately measure therapist self-insight. In one study, for example, therapists' ratings of their self-insight were not correlated with supervisors' ratings, calling into question the accuracy with which self-insight was measured (Hayes et al., 1997).

Self-insight does present enormously challenging, and almost inherently paradoxical, measurement issues. On the one hand, self-report may be the most dependable way to assess self-insight, and on the other hand, dating back to early experiments in psychology, introspection is known to be fraught with problems. For instance, the paradox of self-insight is that therapists who are more knowledgeable about themselves recognize how relatively little they actually know, while less self-insightful therapists think that the small amount they comprehend about themselves is all there is to know. Another reason why self-insight has not been found to be critical to managing countertransference could be that self-insight as a trait may be less important than a therapist's moment-to-moment awareness of her or his experience in a given session, and most research on countertransference and its management has measured self-insight as a trait rather than as a state.

Assuming that research has yet to catch up to clinical reality and that self-insight is, in fact, important in managing countertransference, a practically significant question arises as to whether there are particular practices that therapists can engage in to further their self-insight. In seeking to answer this question, Baehr (2004) interviewed 12 psychologists about activities that facilitated their self-insight. Much like the self-awareness literature (e.g., Williams, Hurley, et al., 2003), he discovered that a good number of therapists found it useful to spend time engaging in both self-care and self-reflection. Baehr also found that meditation was identified as facilitating therapist self-insight. The practice of meditation, in any number of forms, has been found to enhance mindfulness, or a moment-to-moment awareness and acceptance of what one is experiencing (Ryan & Brown, 2003; Walsh & Shapiro, 2006). Thus, the concept of mindfulness has arisen as a potential approach to managing countertransference reactions (e.g., Morgan, 2005) and, we argue, to managing distracting forms of self-awareness more broadly defined.

Mindfulness involves the cognitive processes of both awareness and attention in the present moment (Germer, 2005). According to Brown and Ryan (2003), "awareness and attention are intertwined, such that attention continually pulls 'figures' out of the 'ground' of awareness" (p. 822). One of the challenges of conducting psychotherapy is to be aware of and attend to numerous phenomena simultaneously—what the client is saying, how the client is saying it, what the client is not saying, how the client is feeling, and how much time is left in the session, not to mention the therapist's own emotions, thoughts, visceral sensations, self-talk, countertransference reactions, behaviors, fantasies, and other associations to what is and is not transpiring in the moment. Of course, therapists cannot attend concurrently to all of these things, nor should they. Clinical experience, we hope, brings refined judgment about the relative importance of these and many other happenings on a moment-to-moment basis. However, novice therapists can become preoccupied with themselves in ways that diminish their presence to clients (e.g., Williams, 2003). Furthermore, research has demonstrated that countertransference can cause even seasoned clinicians to pull back from and lose emotional contact with clients or to over-identify with clients and become less aware of their own experience (Fauth & Hayes, 2006; Hayes & Gelso, 1993; Rosenberger & Hayes, 2002).

In contrast, when therapists are mindful, they are aware of and accepting of their experience in the present. According to Bishop et al. (2004):

> In a state of mindfulness, thoughts and feelings are observed as events in the mind, without overidentifying with them and without reacting to them in an automatic, habitual pattern of reactivity. This dispassionate state of self-observation is thought to introduce a "space" between one's perception and response. Thus mindfulness is thought to enable one to respond to situations more reflectively (as opposed to reflexively). (p. 235)

Mindfulness includes not just awareness but also acceptance of your experiences (Safran & Muran, 2000; Shapiro, Schwartz, & Bonner, 1998), and acceptance may be a pivotal component in managing countertransference. When therapists are able to recognize, without judgment, their reactions to clients, no matter how unpleasant or painful, several benefits may ensue. Therapists are less likely to act out on countertransference thoughts and feelings. They can attend to their internal reactions, learn from them, and make use of them without the complications of secondary emotions such as shame and remorse.

Mindfulness, according to Germer (2005, p. 4) "is a skill that allows us to be less reactive," not only to clients but to ourselves as well. In addition, by practicing self-acceptance, therapists provide positive modeling for clients. Consider, by way of contrast, a therapist who is aware of his countertransference-based thoughts, sensations, or feelings and yet is so troubled by them that he denies them, projects them onto the client, or punishes himself—or the client—for having them. None of these scenarios will facilitate the management of countertransference. Thus, it is not simply awareness or insight that is important, but rather it is what therapists do with their self-awareness that matters. Again, it is our contention that therapists need to acknowledge and accept their internal reactions, rather than blame or judge themselves for having them, and that this acceptance is a critically important component of managing these reactions.

FUTURE RESEARCH ON THERAPIST SELF-AWARENESS

This chapter has highlighted the numerous paradoxes, inconsistencies, and complexities that characterize the current state of research on self-awareness within and outside of the counseling and psychotherapy literatures. The meanings and assumptions associated with the term seem to vary quite a bit, and the results of research have been inconsistent and equivocal. What accounts for this state of affairs in research on self-awareness? We believe that a primary obstacle to productive research on self-awareness is the definitional confusion about the construct. For instance, the term *self-awareness* is sometimes used to refer to a state-like experience but other times as more of a trait-like characteristic. Consistent research findings are hard to come by in such state of definitional flux.

For self-awareness research to become more productive and cumulative, we need to achieve consensus on an appropriate definition of the term. Our position is that the term self-awareness should be reserved for momentary, state-like experiences, thereby conforming more closely to common usage of the term. Other terms, such as self-knowledge or self-insight, should be used to refer to the trait-like characteristic of being "self-aware." Applied to the therapeutic situation, then, our definition of self-awareness would be "therapists' momentary recognition of and attention to their immediate thoughts, emotions, physiological responses, and behaviors during a therapy session" (Williams & Fauth, 2005, p. 374). Researchers investigating self-awareness should ensure that the methods they use to measure and manipulate the construct are congruent with this definition, thereby making research more directly comparable and potentially cumulative in nature.

Beyond basic definitional clarity, it would also be helpful to classify different "types" of self-awareness and to develop a more nuanced description and understanding of the multiple dimensions along which experiences of self-awareness vary. In line with previous research by Williams and colleagues (Nutt-Williams & Hill, 1996; Williams et al., 1997; Williams, Polster, et al., 2003), continued intensive qualitative inquiry into the nature of self-awareness experiences in therapy situations would be helpful in this regard. For example, thought-listing techniques and process-recall methodologies could be used to tap more directly into therapists' experiences of self-awareness in their work with clients. In analogue situations, where we have a bit more methodological freedom, we could interrupt "sessions" in progress at various points and ask therapists to share their experience of self-awareness in relation to various client stimuli or therapeutic situations.

Based on our clinical experience, as well as the foregoing research review, we have some educated guesses about dimensions of self-awareness that might emerge from such research. First, it seems that self-awareness can vary in terms of its scope. While self-awareness can be, at times, very narrowly focused on some particular aspect of the therapist's experience, at other times it can be much more expansive, including a holistic sense of the self-in-context. The content associated with self-awareness also ranges considerably. For example, we might be aware of thoughts, feelings, or sensations about ourselves, our clients, the therapeutic situation, or outside events that are positive, neutral, or negative in valence. Finally, our reaction to our self-awareness can be quite different, ranging from rejecting to accepting reactions.

With a more sophisticated description and understanding of the construct in hand, researchers might then be able to measure and manipulate self-awareness in a more precise manner. For example, the social and cognitive psychology literatures abound with examples of how self-awareness can be manipulated, such as through the placement of a mirror (Bögels et al., 2002; Silvia, 2002a), the writing of personally focused essays (Fenigstein & Levine, 1984; Pyszcynski, Holt, & Greenberg, 1987), and instructing participants to focus on some aspect of themselves (e.g., R. J. Ellis & Holmes, 1982; Lyubomirsky & Nolen-Hoeksema, 1995). Unfortunately, we do not know what type, or dimension(s), of self-awareness such manipulations affect. Likewise, in the therapy literature, self-awareness has been manipulated primarily by videotaping therapists, resulting in widely varying results (M. V. Ellis et al., 2002; Hale & Stoltenberg, 1988). If we understood and measured self-awareness in a more nuanced manner, however, we might bring more order to the seemingly chaotic current state of self-awareness research. We could also make comparisons between induced (manipulated) states of self-awareness and reports of naturally occurring self-focus.

Several areas of therapeutic self-awareness research await further investigation. First, we believe that it is important to extend existing research (Fauth & Williams, 2005; Williams & Fauth, 2005) about the links among therapists' self-awareness, emotions, and interpersonal behaviors in therapy sessions. Second, the frequent assumption that self-awareness plays a critical role in the successful management of countertransference reactions also needs to be more thoroughly studied. Third, researchers should explore the relationships between therapists' personal characteristics, self-awareness, and emotions; for example, some evidence suggests that the relationship between self-awareness and negative affect may be stronger for women than men (Mor & Winquist, 2002). Fourth, the nature and experience of self-awareness during "critical" therapy events, such as alliance rupture events (Safran & Muran, 2000), might be profitably explored. Ultimately, the direct or indirect links between therapist self-awareness and therapy outcomes should also be explored.

Two constructs that deserve special attention in future research on therapist self-awareness are mindfulness and attentional flexibility. Empirically, mindfulness training has been associated with reductions in stress and chronic pain (Chang et al., 2004; Kabat-Zinn, 1982; Shapiro et al., 1998) as well as with gains in quality of life and overall well-being (e.g., Galantino, Baime, Maguire, Szapary, & Farrar, 2005; Reibel, Greeson, Brainard, & Rosenzweig, 2001). Yet, despite these established benefits of mindfulness, very little research has been done to study the effects of mindfulness on psychotherapy, and in particular, on psychotherapists. In one of the few studies related to the effects of mindfulness on psychotherapists, Lesh (1970) found that, compared to a nonrandomized control group, counselors who practiced meditation for four weeks demonstrated greater gains in empathy. Similarly, Shapiro et al. (1998) found that an eight-week mindfulness-based training program increased empathy among medical students. Thus, we suggest, and encourage, more research on the use of mindfulness in psychotherapy.

In particular, we are interested in mindfulness as a potential strategy for increasing a therapist's ability to stay present and self-aware while at the same time reducing reactivity that could become distracting or hindering.

In addition, current research strongly suggests that therapists' negative emotions and reactions, in particular, are linked with various countertherapeutic processes (Fauth & Hayes, 2006; Ligiéro & Gelso, 2002). The mindfulness literature suggests that mindful self-awareness might help therapists attend to and manage their emotional experience more reflectively and effectively (Fulton, 2005; Safran & Muran, 2000). Therefore, research is needed on how mindfulness affects therapists' experience of their negative emotions. Perhaps when they are mindful, therapists experience their emotions as less intense? Or maybe mindfulness alters the nature of the relationship between therapists' negative reactions and the therapy process. We also encourage research on the effects mindfulness meditation training or other mindfulness practices on therapists' self-awareness with clients.

Another potentially productive line of research to pursue relates to the concept of *attentional flexibility*. Friedman and Förster (2005) have defined attentional flexibility as the ability to purposefully "shift focus among cognitive operations using executive control" (p. 70). Though much research in this area has focused primarily on older adults (e.g., Hahn & Kramer, 1995; Stankov, 1988), the concept can be easily applied to a wide variety of populations and to the therapeutic setting. For example, Hymer (2004) suggested that clients who exhibit the most attentional flexibility may also benefit the most from treatment.

Based on Muraven's (2005) suggestion that "poor self-regulation of attention may help to account for individual differences in cognitive performance" (p. 396), we suggest that differences in therapeutic performance (e.g., therapist helpfulness) may be related to attentional flexibility. In fact, the broader concept of attentional control might be a useful framework for future empirical studies. For example, what happens when therapists experience a nonpurposeful attentional lapse (see Smallwood et al., 2004)? Some research has suggested that attention can "slip" when individuals are worried or bored (Reason & Lucas, 1984). Thus, attentional flexibility or control may offer an additional focus for research on the connection between therapist anxiety and therapist attention.

CONCLUSION

We have attempted to present a new perspective on therapist self-awareness by reviewing the literature outside the psychotherapy field as well as by reviewing empirical studies of therapist self-talk, self-awareness, and countertransference management. Collectively, these bodies of research offer fertile directions for future inquiry on the psychotherapy process. Though the existing research continues to be ripe with paradox, such a state of complexity should not be surprising, given that the endeavor of psychotherapy is complex in its essence.

Because of the conflicts and complexities of the research at this state, we are hesitant to provide any concrete suggestions for practice. However, we suggest that practicing therapists explore the mindfulness literature as well as the literature on management of hindering self-awareness and countertransference for more specific and practical guidance for clinical practice. For psychotherapy researchers, we hope that the previous section has provided ample ideas for new empirical studies, inspiring them to jump into these new arenas. We look forward to the next, "adolescence" phase of research on therapist self-awareness and its potentially helpful impact on the practice of psychotherapy.

REFERENCES

Alden, L. E., Teschuk, M., & Tee, K. (1992). Public self-awareness and withdrawal from social interactions. *Cognitive Therapy and Research, 16*, 249–267.

Baehr, A. P. (2004). *Wounded healers and relational experts: A grounded theory of experienced psychotherapists' management and use of countertransference.* Unpublished doctoral thesis, Pennsylvania State University.

Baker, K. A. (1999). The importance of cultural sensitivity and therapist self-awareness when working with mandatory clients. *Family Process, 38*, 55–67.

Baumeister, R. F. (1991). *Escaping the self*. New York: Basic Books.

Beck, A. T. (1976). *Cognitive therapy and the emotional disorders*. New York: International Universities Press.

Bishop, S. R., Lau, M., Shapiro, S., Carlson, L., Anderson, N. D., Carmody, J., et al. (2004). Mindfulness: A proposed operational definition. *Clinical Psychology: Science and Practice, 11*, 230–241.

Bögels, S. M., Rijsemus, W., & De Jong, P. J. (2002). Self-focused attention and social anxiety: The effects of experimentally heightened self-awareness on fear, blushing, cognitions, and social skills. *Cognitive Therapy and Research, 26*, 461–472.

Borders, L. D. (1989). Developmental cognitions of first practicum supervisees. *Journal of Counseling Psychology, 36*, 163–169.

Borders, L. D., Fong-Beyette, M. L., & Cron, E. A. (1988). In-session cognitions of a counseling student: A case study. *Counselor Education and Supervision, 28*, 59–70.

Borders, L. D., Rainey, L. M., Crutchfield, L. B., & Martin, D. W. (1996). Impact of a counseling supervision course on doctoral students' cognitions. *Counselor Education and Supervision, 35*, 204–217.

Brown, K., & Ryan, R. (2003). The benefits of being present: Mindfulness and its role in psychological well-being. *Journal of Personality and Social Psychology, 84*, 822–848.

Burgio, K. L., Merluzzi, T. V., & Pryor, J. B. (1986). Effects of performance expectancy and self-focused attention on social interaction. *Journal of Personality and Social Psychology, 50*, 1216–1221.

Buss, A. H. (1980). *Self-consciousness and social anxiety*. San Francisco: Freeman.

Cacioppo, J. T., & Petty, R. E. (1981). Social psychological procedures for cognitive response assessment: The thought-listing technique. In T. V. Merluzzi, C. R. Glass, & M. Genest (Eds.), *Cognitive assessment* (pp. 309–342). New York: Guilford Press.

Campbell, J. D., Trapnell, P. D., Heine, S. J., Katz, I. M., Lavallee, L. F., & Lehman, D. R. (1996). Self-concept clarity: Measurement, personality correlates, and cultural boundaries. *Journal of Personality and Social Psychology, 70*, 141–156.

Carver, C. S., & Scheier, M. F. (1978). Self-focusing effects of dispositional self-consciousness, mirror presence, and audience presence. *Journal of Personality and Social Psychology, 37*, 324–332.

Carver, C. S., & Scheier, M. F. (1981). *Attention and self-regulation*. New York: Springer-Verlag.

Chang, V. Y., Palesh, O., Caldwell, R., Glasgow, N., Abramson, M., Burke, A., et al. (2004). The effects of a mindfulness-based stress reduction program on stress, mindfulness self-efficacy, and positive states of mind. *Stress and Health: Journal of the International Society for the Investigation of Stress, 20*, 141–147.

Chen, H., Yates, B. T., & McGinnies, E. (1988). Effects of involvement on observers' estimations of consensus, distinctiveness, and consistency. *Personality and Social Psychology Bulletin, 14*, 468–478.

Cohen, R. J., & Calamari, J. E. (2004). Thought-focused attention and obsessive-compulsive symptoms: An evaluation of cognitive self-consciousness in a nonclinical sample. *Cognitive Therapy and Research, 28*, 457–471.

Coster, J. S., & Schwebel, M. (1997). Well-functioning in professional psychologists. *Professional Psychology: Research and Practice, 28*, 5–13.

Csikszentmihalyi, M. (1990). *Flow: The psychology of optimal experience*. New York: Harper & Row.

Dole, A. A., Burton, L., Gold, J., Lerner, J., Nissenfeld, M., & Weis, D. (1982). Six dimensions of retrospections by therapists and counselors—A manual for research. *JSAS: Catalog of Selected Documents in Psychology, 12*, 23 (MS2454).

Duval, S., & Wicklund, R. A. (1972). *A theory of objective self-awareness*. New York: Academic Press.

Duval, S., & Wicklund, R. A. (1973). Effects of objective self-awareness on attributions of causality. *Journal of Experimental Social Psychology, 9*, 17–31.

Duval, T. S., & Silvia, P. J. (2001). *Self-awareness and causal attribution: A dual systems theory*. Boston: Kluwer Academic Press.

Edwards, J. K., & Bess, J. M. (1998). Developing effectiveness in the therapeutic use of self. *Clinical Social Work Journal, 26*, 89–106.

Ehrlich, F. M. (2001). Levels of self-awareness: Countertransference in psychoanalysis, couple, and family therapy. *Contemporary Psychoanalysis, 37*, 283–296.

Ellis, A. (1975). *A new guide to rational living*. Oxford: Prentice-Hall.

Ellis, M. V., Krengel, M., & Beck, M. (2002). Testing self-focused attention theory in clinical supervision: Effects on supervisee anxiety and performance. *Journal of Counseling Psychology, 49*, 101–116.

Ellis, R. J., & Holmes, J. G. (1982). Focus of attention and self-evaluation in social interaction. *Journal of Personality and Social Psychology, 43,* 67–77.

Fauth, J., & Hayes, J. A. (2006). Counselors' stress appraisals as predictors of countertransference behavior with male clients. *Journal of Counseling and Development, 84,* 430–439.

Fauth, J., & Williams, E. N. (2005). The in-session self-awareness of therapist-trainees: Hindering or helpful? *Journal of Counseling Psychology, 52,* 443–447.

Fejfar, M. C., & Hoyle, R. H. (2000). Effect of private self-awareness on negative affect and self-referent attribution: A quantitative review. *Personality and Social Psychology Review, 4,* 132–142.

Fenigstein, A. (1979). Self-consciousness, self-attention, and social interaction. *Journal of Personality and Social Psychology, 37,* 75–86.

Fenigstein, A., & Carver, C. S. (1978). Self-focusing effects of heartbeat feedback. *Journal of Personality and Social Psychology, 36,* 1242–1250.

Fenigstein, A., & Levine, M. P. (1984). Self-attention, concept activation, and the causal self. *Journal of Experimental Social Psychology, 20,* 213–245.

Fenigstein, A., Scheier, M. F., & Buss, A. H. (1975). Public and private self-consciousness: Assessment and theory. *Journal of Consulting and Clinical Psychology, 43,* 522–527.

Fong, M. L., Borders, L. D., Ethington, C. A., & Pitts, J. H. (1997). Becoming a counselor: A longitudinal study of student cognitive development. *Counselor Education and Supervision, 37,* 100–114.

Freud, S. (1959). Future prospects of psychoanalytic psychotherapy. In J. Strachey (Ed. & Trans.), *The standard edition of the complete psychological works of Sigmund Freud* (Vol. 11, pp. 139–151). London: Hogarth Press. (Original work published 1910)

Friedman, R. S., & Förster, J. (2005). The influence of approach and avoidance cues on attentional flexibility. *Motivation and Emotion, 29,* 69–81.

Fulton, P. R. (2005). Mindfulness as clinical training. In C. K. Germer, R. D. Siegel, & P. R. Fulton (Eds.), *Mindfulness and psychotherapy* (pp. 55–72). New York: Guilford Press.

Fuqua, D. R., Newman, J. L., Anderson, M. W., & Johnson, A. W. (1986). Preliminary study of internal dialogue in a training setting. *Psychological Reports, 58,* 163–172.

Galantino, M. L., Baime, M., Maguire, M., Szapary, P., & Farrar, J. T. (2005). Association of psychological and physiological measures of stress in health-care professionals during an 8-week mindfulness meditation program: Mindfulness in practice. *Stress and Health: Journal of the International Society for the Investigation of Stress, 21,* 255–261.

Gelso, C. J., Fassinger, R. E., Gomez, M. J., & Latts, M. G. (1995). Countertransference reactions to lesbian clients: The role of homophobia, counselor gender, and countertransference management. *Journal of Counseling Psychology, 42,* 356–364.

Gelso, C. J., & Hayes, J. A. (2007). *Countertransference and the therapist's inner experience: Perils and possibilities.* Mahwah, NJ: Erlbaum.

Germer, C. K. (2005). Mindfulness: What is it? What does it matter? In C. K. Germer, R. D. Siegel, & P. R. Fulton, (Eds.), *Mindfulness and psychotherapy* (pp. 3–27). New York: Guilford Press.

Gibbons, F. X. (1990). Self-attention and behavior: A review and theoretical update. In M. P. Zanna (Ed.), *Advances in experimental social psychology* (Vol. 23, pp. 249–303). New York: Academic Press.

Gibbons, F. X., Smith, T. W., Ingram, R. E., Pearce, K., Brehm, S. S., & Schroeder, D. J. (1985). Self-awareness and self-confrontation: Effects of self-focused attention on members of a clinical population. *Journal of Personality and Social Psychology, 48,* 662–675.

Hagedorn, W. B. (2005). Counselor self-awareness and self-exploration of religious and spiritual beliefs: Know thyself. In C. S. Cashwell & J. S. Young (Eds.), *Integrating spirituality and religion into counseling: A guide to competent practice* (pp. 63–84). Alexandria, VA: American Counseling Association.

Hahn, S., & Kramer, A. F. (1995). Attentional flexibility and aging: You don't need to be 20 years of age to split the beam. *Psychology and Aging, 10,* 597–609.

Hale, K. K., & Stoltenberg, C. D. (1988). The effects of self-awareness and evaluation apprehension on counselor trainee anxiety. *Clinical Supervisor, 6,* 49–69.

Hayes, J. A. (2004). The inner world of the psychotherapist: A program of research on countertransference. *Psychotherapy Research, 14,* 21–36.

Hayes, J. A., & Gelso, C. J. (1993). Male counselors' discomfort with gay and HIV-infected clients. *Journal of Counseling Psychology, 40,* 86–93.

Hayes, J. A., Gelso, C. J., Van Wagoner, S. L., & Diemer, R. A. (1991). Managing countertransference: What the experts think. *Psychological Reports, 69*, 139–148.

Hayes, J. A., McCracken, J. E., McClanahan, M. K., Hill, C. E., Harp, J. S., & Carozzoni, P. (1998). Therapist perspectives on countertransference: Qualitative data in search of a theory. *Journal of Counseling Psychology, 45*, 468–482.

Hayes, J. A., Riker, J. R., & Ingram, K. M. (1997). Countertransference behavior and management in brief counseling: A field study. *Psychotherapy Research, 7*, 145–153.

Hiebert, B., Uhlemann, M. R., Marshall, A., & Lee, D. Y. (1998). The relationship between self-talk, anxiety, and counseling skill. *Canadian Journal of Counselling, 32*, 163–171.

Hill, C. E., & O'Grady, K. E. (1985). List of therapist intentions illustrated in a case study and with therapists of varying theoretical orientations. *Journal of Counseling Psychology, 32*, 3–22.

Hill, C. E., Thompson, B. J., & Williams, E. N. (1997). A guide to conducting consensual qualitative research. *Counseling Psychologist, 25*, 517–572.

Hull, J. G. (1981). A self-awareness model of the causes and consequences of alcohol consumption. *Journal of Abnormal Psychology, 90*, 586–600.

Hymer, S. (2004). Being in the moment and shifting self-perspectives. *American Journal of Psychoanalysis, 64*, 27–38.

Ingram, R. E. (1990). Self-focused attention in clinical disorders: Review and a conceptual model. *Psychological Bulletin, 107*, 156–176.

Ingram, R. E., Lumry, A., Cruet, D., & Sieber, W. (1987). Attentional processes in depression disorders. *Cognitive Therapy and Research, 11*, 351–360.

Jacobs, T. (1991). *The use of the self: Countertransference and communication in the analytic setting.* Madison, CT: International Universities Press.

Jennings, L., & Skovholt, T. M. (1999). The cognitive, emotional, and relational characteristics of master therapists. *Journal of Counseling Psychology, 46*, 3–11.

Kabat-Zinn, J. (1982). An outpatient program in behavioral medicine for chronic pain and empirical referents. *Journal of Clinical Psychology/In Session, 57*, 1053–1063.

Kiesler, D. J. (2001). Therapist countertransference: In search of common themes and empirical referents. *Journal of Clinical Psychology/In Session, 57*, 1053–1063.

Kline, W. B. (1983). Training counselor trainees to talk to themselves: A method of focusing attention. *Counselor Education and Supervision, 22*, 296–302.

Kurpius, D. J., Benjamin, D., & Morran, D. K. (1985). Effects of teaching a cognitive strategy on counselor trainee internal dialogue and clinical hypothesis formulation. *Journal of Counseling Psychology, 32*, 263–271.

Latts, M. G., & Gelso, C. J. (1995). Countertransference behavior and management with survivors of sexual assault. *Psychotherapy: Theory, Research, and Practice, 32*, 405–415.

Lesh, T. (1970). Zen meditation and the development of empathy in counselors. *Journal of Humanistic Psychology, 10*, 39–74.

Lewinsohn, P. M., Hoberman, H., Teri, L., & Hautzinger, M. (1985). An integrative theory of depression. In S. Reiss & R. Bootzin (Eds.), *Theoretical issues in behavior therapy* (pp. 331–359). New York: Academic Press.

Ligiéro, D., & Gelso, C. (2002). Countertransference, attachment, and the working alliance: The therapist's contributions. *Psychotherapy: Theory, Research, Practice, Training, 39*, 3–11.

Lyubomirsky, S., & Nolen-Hoeksema, S. (1995). Effects of self-focused rumination on negative thinking and interpersonal problem solving. *Journal of Personality and Social Psychology, 69*, 176–190.

Martin, J., Martin, W., Meyer, M., & Slemon, A. (1986). Empirical investigation of the cognitive mediational paradigm for research on counseling. *Journal of Counseling Psychology, 34*, 251–260.

Matthews, G., Davies, D. R., & Lees, J. L. (1990). Arousal, extraversion, and individual differences in resource availability. *Journal of Personality and Social Psychology, 59*, 150–168.

Mattison, M. (2000). Ethical decision-making: The person in the process. *Social Work, 45*, 201–213.

Meichenbaum, D. H. (1977). *Cognitive behavioral modification: An integrative approach.* New York: Plenum Press.

Mor, N., & Winquist, J. (2002). Self-focused attention and negative affect: A meta-analysis. *Psychological Bulletin, 128*, 638–662.

Morgan, S. P. (2005). Depression: Turning toward life. In C. K. Germer, R. D. Siegel, & P. R. Fulton (Eds.), *Mindfulness and psychotherapy* (pp. 130–151). New York: Guilford Press.

Morran, D. K. (1986). Relationship of counselor self-talk and hypothesis formulation to performance level. *Journal of Counseling Psychology, 33*, 395–400.

Morran, D. K., Kurpius, D. J., Brack, C. J., & Brack, G. (2001). A cognitive-skills model for counselor training and supervision. *Journal of Counseling and Development, 73*, 384–389.

Morran, D. K., Kurpius, D. J., & Brack, G. (1989). Empirical investigation of counselor self-talk categories. *Journal of Counseling Psychology, 36*, 505–510.

Mullen, B., & Suls, J. (1982). "Know thyself": Stressful life changes and the ameliorative effect of private self-consciousness. *Journal of Experimental Social Psychology, 18*, 43–55.

Muraven, M. (2005). Self-focused attention and the self-regulation of attention: Implications for personality and pathology. *Journal of Social and Clinical Psychology, 24*, 382–400.

Nasby, W. (1985). Private self-consciousness, articulation of the self-schema, and recognition memory of trait adjectives. *Journal of Personality and Social Psychology, 49*, 704–709.

Nasby, W. (1989). Private and public self-consciousness and articulation of the self-schema. *Journal of Personality and Social Psychology, 56*, 117–123.

Norcross, J. C. (2000). Psychotherapist self-care: Practitioner-tested, research-informed strategies. *Professional Psychology: Research and Practice, 31*, 710–713.

Nutt-Williams, E., & Hill, C. E. (1996). The relationship between self-talk and therapy process variables for novice therapists. *Journal of Counseling Psychology, 43*, 170–177.

Palfai, T. P., & Salovey, P. (1992). The influence of affect on self-focused attention: Conceptual and methodological issues. *Consciousness and Cognition, 1*, 306–339.

Panayiotou, G., & Vrana, R. S. (1998). Effect of self-focused attention on the startle reflex, heart rate, and memory performance among anxious and non-anxious individuals. *Psychophysiology, 35*, 1–9.

Pyszczynski, T., & Greenberg, J. (1987). Self-regulatory perseveration and the depressive self-focusing style: A self-awareness theory of reactive depression. *Psychological Bulletin, 102*, 122–138.

Pyszczynski, T., Holt, K., & Greenberg, J. (1987). Depression, self-focused attention, and expectancies for positive and negative future life events for self and others. *Journal of Personality and Social Psychology, 52*, 994–1001.

Rapee, R. M., & Lim, L. (1992). Discrepancy between self- and observer ratings of performance in social phobics. *Journal of Abnormal Psychology, 101*, 728–731.

Reason, J., & Lucas, D. (1984). Absent-mindedness in shops: Its incidence, correlates and consequences. *British Journal of Clinical Psychology, 23*, 121–131.

Reibel, D., Greeson, J., Brainard, G., & Rosenzweig, S. (2001). Mindfulness-based stress reduction and health-related quality of life in a heterogeneous patient population. *General Hospital Psychiatry, 23*, 183–192.

Reich, A. (1951). On countertransference. *International Journal of Psychoanalysis, 32*, 25–31.

Richardson, B., & Stone, G. L. (1981). Effects of a cognitive adjunct procedure within a microcounseling situation. *Journal of Counseling Psychology, 28*, 168–175.

Robbins, S. B., & Jolkovski, M. P. (1987). Managing countertransference feelings: An interactional model using awareness of feeling and theoretical framework. *Journal of Counseling Psychology, 34*, 276–282.

Rosenberger, E. W., & Hayes, J. A. (2002). Origins, consequences, and management of countertransference: A case study. *Journal of Counseling Psychology, 49*, 221–232.

Roysircar, G. (2004). Cultural self-awareness assessment: Practice examples from psychology training. *Professional Psychology: Research and Practice, 35*, 658–666.

Rubin, S. (2000). Differentiating multiple relationships from multiple dimensions of involvement: Therapeutic space at the interface of client, therapist, and society. *Psychotherapy: Theory, Research, Practice, and Training, 37*, 315–324.

Ryan, R. M., & Brown, K. W. (2003). Why we don't need self-esteem: On fundamental needs, contingent love, and mindfulness. *Psychological Inquiry, 14*, 71–76.

Safran, J. D., & Muran, J. C. (2000). *Negotiating the therapeutic alliance: A relational treatment guide.* New York: Guilford Press.

Shapiro, S., Schwartz, G., & Bonner, G. (1998). Effects of mindfulness-based stress reduction on medical and premedical students. *Journal of Behavioral Medicine, 21*, 581–599.

Silvia, P. J., (2002a). Self-awareness and emotional intensity. *Cognition and Emotion, 16*, 195–216.

Silvia, P. J., (2002b). Self-awareness and the regulation of emotional intensity. *Self and Identity, 1*, 3–10.

Silvia, P. J., & Duval, T. S. (2001). Objective self-awareness theory: Recent progress and enduring problems. *Personality and Social Psychology Review, 5,* 230–241.

Silvia, P. J., & O'Brien, M. E. (2004). Self-awareness and constructive functioning: Revisiting "the human dilemma." *Journal of Social and Clinical Psychology, 23,* 475–489.

Sloan, D. M. (2005). It's all about me: Self-focused attention and depressed mood. *Cognitive Therapy and Research, 29,* 279–288.

Smallwood, J., Davies, J. B., Heim, D., Ginnigan, F., Sudberry, M., O'Connor, R., et al. (2004). Subjective experience and the attentional lapse: Task engagement and disengagement during sustained attention. *Consciousness and Cognition: An International Journal, 13,* 657–690.

Smith, R. C., Dorsey, A. M., Lyles, J. S., & Frankel, R. M. (1999). Teaching self-awareness enhances learning about patient-centered interviewing. *Academic Medicine, 74,* 1242–1248.

Smith, T. W., & Greenberg, J. (1981). Depression and self-focused attention. *Motivation and Emotion, 5,* 323–331.

Stankov, L. (1988). Aging, attention, and intelligence. *Psychology and Aging, 3,* 59–74.

Stephenson, B. O., & Wicklund, R. A. (1983). Self-directed attention and taking the other's perspective. *Journal of Experimental Social Psychology, 19,* 58–77.

Strong, S. R. (1970). Causal attribution in counseling and psychotherapy. *Journal of Counseling Psychology, 17,* 388–399.

Suls, J., & Fletcher, B. (1985). Self-attention, life stress, and illness: A prospective study. *Psychosomatic Medicine, 47,* 469–481.

Trapnell, P. D., & Campbell, J. D. (1999). Private self-consciousness and the five-factor model of personality: Distinguishing rumination from reflection. *Journal of Personality and Social Psychology, 76,* 284–304.

Uhlemann, M. R., & Jordan, D. (1981). Self awareness and the effective counsellor: A framework for assessment. *Canadian Counsellor, 15,* 70–73.

Uhlemann, M. R., Lee, D. Y., & Hiebert, B. (1988). Self-talk of counsellor trainees: A preliminary report. *Canadian Journal of Counselling, 22,* 73–79.

Van Wagoner, S. L., Gelso, C. J., Hayes, J. A., & Diemer, R. A. (1991). Countertransference and the reputedly excellent therapist. *Psychotherapy, 28,* 411–421.

Walsh, R., & Shapiro, S. L. (2006). The meeting of meditative disciplines and western psychology: A mutually enriching dialogue. *American Psychologist, 61,* 227–239.

Williams, E. N. (2003). The relationship between momentary states of therapist self-awareness and perceptions of the counseling process. *Journal of Contemporary Psychotherapy, 33,* 177–186.

Williams, E. N., & Fauth, J. (2005). A psychotherapy process study of therapist in session self-awareness. *Psychotherapy Research, 15,* 374–381.

Williams, E. N., Hurley, K., O'Brien, K., & de Gregorio, A. (2003). Development and validation of the Self-Awareness and Management Strategies (SAMS) scales for therapists. *Psychotherapy: Theory, Research, Practice and Training, 40,* 278–288.

Williams, E. N., Judge, A. B., Hill, C. E., & Hoffman, M. (1997). Experiences of novice therapists in prepracticum: Trainees', clients', and supervisors' perceptions of therapists' personal reactions and management strategies. *Journal of Counseling Psychology, 44,* 390–399.

Williams, E. N., Polster, D., Grizzard, M. B., Rockenbaugh, J., & Judge, A. B. (2003). What happens when therapists feel bored or anxious? A qualitative study of distracting self-awareness and therapists' management strategies. *Journal of Contemporary Psychotherapy, 33,* 5–18.

Woody, S. R. (1996). Effects of focus of attention on social phobics' anxiety and social performance. *Journal of Abnormal Psychology, 105,* 61–69.

Woody, S. R., & Rodriguez, B. F. (2000). Self-focused attention and social anxiety in social phobics and normal controls. *Cognitive Therapy and Research, 24,* 473–488.

CHAPTER 19

Culture and Race in Counseling and Psychotherapy: A Critical Review of the Literature

FREDERICK T. L. LEONG
ARPANA GUPTA

With the influx of immigrants into the United States, there has been a continual increase in diversity, both racially and ethnically (U.S. Department of Health & Human Services, 2001). In 2000, 30% of the population was composed of ethnic minorities (U.S. Census Bureau, 2001). These changing demographics mean that mental health care professionals will be increasingly encountering clients from diverse backgrounds, cultures, languages, religions, customs, and traditions. These clients will be presenting with issues that are different and unique from what most counselors have previously seen. Consequently, it is imperative that health care providers be able to meet the needs of this new diverse population. To be multiculturally competent, service providers will have to be able to increase their cultural awareness and their cultural abilities. This process of cross-cultural competence development is complex, multidimensional, and continuous.

A central issue has been whether ethnic minority clients need different psychological interventions, assessments, or treatments or whether similar approaches to the mainstream society can be used (Leong, Chang, & Lee, 2006). Most research addressing this question has focused on (a) ethnic minority clients' preferences for therapists of similar ethnicity and (b) the effects on counseling outcome of seeing ethnically similar versus ethnically different (usually White) therapists. In this chapter, we review the research on these two important questions as well as research on the effectiveness of psychotherapy with ethnic minority clients in order to promote greater multicultural awareness and competence among counselors and therapists seeing an ethnically diverse clientele. Due to space limitations, we consider only issues related to the provision of therapy with three of the larger ethnic minority groups: African Americans, Hispanic/Latino Americans, and Asian Americans. Our intention is not to ignore or undervalue other ethnic groups, however, other ethnic groups have not received sufficient research attention in the counseling and psychotherapy literature to draw even tentative conclusions about their preferences or about the effectiveness of counseling with them. When possible, information relevant to these other groups is introduced.

First we present an overview of client characteristics that might be associated with preferences for ethnically similar therapists and that, if ignored, might affect counseling outcome. In subsequent sections, we review research on client preferences and client-therapist matching, counseling process and outcome with ethnic minority clients, and cultural sensitivity and training. In the final two sections of the chapter, we consider two recent theories and models for cross-cultural counseling and discuss future research needs and recommendations.

CLIENT VARIABLES

A central tenet of most theories of multicultural counseling is that it is important to consider the cultural lens from which ethnic and racial groups view themselves and the world. This is because, according to most theories, an understanding of the personality characteristics and worldviews of these diverse groups is critical to providing the best and most appropriate therapy for them. It is this tenet that has directed most research on client preferences and therapeutic outcome. It is first important to understand the personalities and worldviews that clients bring with them to counseling because they might form the bases of their preferences for therapists and affect the outcomes that they attain from counseling.

According to Leong (1986), a comprehensive understanding of ethnically related client factors requires that information be collected from empirical studies of (a) the personalities and worldviews of members of ethnic minority groups, (b) their conceptions of mental health and expectations for counseling services, and (c) relevant theories. In this chapter, all three of these sources will be used to help identify client characteristics that have the potential to influence counseling perceptions and outcome. It is noted that all ethnic minority groups display a considerable amount of within-group heterogeneity. Therefore, the client variables that are discussed here may not "universally" describe all members of a particular ethnic group, but they seem to be descriptive of a significantly large number of persons within each ethnic group. They represent cultural factors of which all counselors and therapists must be aware.

African Americans

According to Helms and Carter (1991), most of the research focused on culturally sensitive therapy with African Americans has tried to address three main issues: (a) whether this racial/ethnic group prefers same race/ethnicity therapists, (b) whether African Americans possess similar within-group characteristics that determine these therapist preferences, and (c) whether the desire to seek therapists from the same race/ethnicity reflects a more encompassing need for finding those who share similar backgrounds and characteristics. Theory and research with African Americans has suggested that African Americans may prefer ethnically similar therapists (e.g., Fuertes & Gelso, 1998). For example, Helms (1984) developed a model of racial identity for African Americans and proposed that African American clients who exhibit a preference for therapists of the same race/ethnicity are in a stage where they accept their Africanness and are skeptical of the White culture, values, and norms (Parham & Helms, 1981). Later in the chapter, research that has tested such hypotheses will be discussed, but it is clear that client racial identity is only one among an array of variables that could affect clients' preferences for therapists. For instance, other variables that may influence therapist preference include similarity in attitudes and social class, and therapist attractiveness.

Personalities and Values

African Americans may have distinct characteristics and preferences that set them apart from other ethnic and racial groups. Some differences in values exist between African Americans and Whites; for instance, a preference for collective values versus individualism has been found (Nobles, 1980). This value preference could affect client and counselor attitudes, expectations, and behavioral patterns. Western-based psychotherapies tend to focus on solutions to problems at the individual level, and this may not be adequate for addressing the problems that many African Americans experience. African Americans have historically been subject to prejudice, discrimination, and other disadvantages that minorities experience. This, in turn, could affect the therapeutic relationship and thus re-create a minority status in therapy sessions.

Gibbs and Huang (1989) highlighted the various intricacies associated with establishing therapeutic relationships with ethnic and racial minority clients. They described what may happen when African

American clients encounter therapists from different backgrounds and orientations. For instance, African American clients who value interpersonal versus more individual process may encounter, approach, and evaluate therapy from this interpersonal perspective and will value attempts made by therapists to enhance the interpersonal process. It has also been found (Gibbs & Huang, 1989) that African American clients may portray an outward demeanor of "coolness" in therapy which serves, in part, to assess their therapist. As in therapy with all clients, if the therapist is able to establish a trusting and strong therapeutic relationship with the client, the client may respond favorably by increasing involvement, commitment, and engagement in the therapy process. In this case, the development of such a relationship with many African American clients may require the therapist to understand the interpersonal preferences of their African American clients and the rationale for the attitude of "coolness" that they might display during early sessions.

Psychotherapy theories have proposed that many African American therapists have a different orientation toward therapy than their White counterparts because they are more likely to approach therapy in an interpersonal manner, whereas the latter tend to focus more on the goal- or task-related aspects of the client-therapist relationship (Zane, Hall, Sue, Young, & Nunez, 2004). These two therapy orientations are very different and may be incompatible. Misunderstandings and problems in communication and goal setting could result during psychotherapy if the client and therapist hold differing orientations. This theory has yet to be empirically tested.

Attitudes and Preferences

African Americans are a heterogeneous ethnic/racial group in their attitudes and preferences. The few empirical investigations that have appeared in the literature are limited in their scope and application because they were conducted only on students and so cannot easily be generalized to the rest of the African American population. These studies also involved analogue procedures rather than actual psychological treatment (Hall, 2001). Recently, there have been increased efforts to conduct appropriate and realistic studies with African Americans. Hall (2001) highlights some of the current empirically supported therapies (EST) and culturally sensitive therapies (CST) involving African Americans. For instance, a study conducted by Clark, Anderson, Clark, and Williams (1999) discussed how ethnic identity could affect coping responses toward racism and discrimination.

Hispanic/Latino Americans

Despite significant heterogeneity among Hispanic and Latino Americans, one experience that many share is a history of Spanish colonization that affected cultural and religious views and practices, language, and worldviews. There is also a shared history of uprooting, separation, immigration, and exposure to oppression, prejudice, and discrimination.

Acculturation and Immigration

The history of Latin American immigration to the United States is different from that of European Americans for several reasons. First, many Latinos—including Mexicans, Puerto Ricans, and Panamanians—came to the United States to fill the labor demands of U.S. industries. However, many Cubans, Dominicans, Salvadorans, and Nicaraguans came to the United States as refugees for political and foreign policy reasons. Second, the literature suggests that Latin Americans are often not viewed as immigrants at all, but as a racial/ethnic/linguistic caste. This means that as a result of historic linguistic and racial conflicts, Latin Americans are considered separate from mainstream White Americans. Initially, this caste system was reflected through the discrimination of dark- versus light-skinned Latinos (Rodriguez, 1998). However, many Latinos today are viewed as visible racial/ethnic minorities and, therefore, are often discriminated against as much as other visible racial/ethnic minorities. Most Latino immigrants also entered the United States during the postindustrial era when the United States was already recognized as a world power and when the gap between the wealthy and poor grew enormously. Thus, many Latinos who immigrated during this time had little hope of benefiting from the unskilled factory jobs that had helped many European immigrants move into the middle class during the industrial era. This same pattern of exclusion has been true of other racial and ethnic groups, but Latinos are the most recent immigrant group to suffer from this difficult integration.

Two out of five Latinos are immigrants despite the fact that many Latinos are considered native Americans (Rios-Ellis et al., 2005). One in 10 children resides in mixed-status families where only some family members are legal U.S. citizens (Rios-Ellis et al., 2005). Acculturation is an issue with which many Latino immigrants contend, as is also true of Asian Americans. Many Latino immigrants undergo an adjustment process in which they cross a cultural *puente* (bridge) from South America to North America. This opportunity to cross from the South to the North offers Latino immigrants an opportunity for U.S. citizenship and its associated benefits. Therefore, Latinos traveling along this cultural bridge may feel that they are in limbo, living in the "hyphen" between the opportunities available in the United States versus the comforts of being home. In these instances, they are considered as both outsiders and insiders (Stavans, 1996).

Family Ties

Many Latinos maintain strong ties with their countries of origin and their families there. They make frequent trips to visit family, and they continue to support their families financially. A growing number of Latinos form businesses in the United States and this number continues to increase (Suro, 1999) in efforts to increase the financial statuses for themselves and their families. This reciprocity in infusion of cultures needs to be considered when trying to meet Latino client therapy needs because this can affect the client's therapy preferences and outcomes.

Worldview

Many Latinos also display what is known as self-orientation, which is defined as the tendency to see themselves and the social world in a particular manner (Triandis, 1989). Self-orientation consists of two orthogonal parts: *allocentrism* and *idiocentrism*. Allocentrism involves the definition of self in relation to others, and centers on concepts such as group values and social support. Idiocentrism involves the definition of self in isolation from others and centers on attaining personal goals and reliance on self for support and soothing. Both these concepts of self are independent from each other and remain stable over time and contexts. La Roche (2002) stressed that most Latino subgroups define themselves in allocentric terms but underscore individualistic assumptions. This balance of individual goal attainment and social connectedness may be common across races/ethnicities, but La Roche (2002) maintained that Latino participants who are more allocentric in nature tend to show greater adherence to treatment than do idiocentric Latinos, and thus, this has implications for counseling processes and outcomes.

Asian Americans

Asian Americans are a very diverse group of individuals, comprised of about 43 varying groups having about 100 languages and dialects (U.S. Department of Health and Human Services, 2001). The biggest challenge with Asian Americans is the great degree of within-group heterogeneity that is present. Various factors need to be considered when working with Asian Americans, such as cultural differences, native country of origin, circumstances under which they came to the United States, generational status, and native language spoken.

Personality Characteristics

Asian Americans, as a group, often exhibit personality traits that are influenced by their cultural heritage, which places an emphasis on factors such as humility, modesty, strict self-monitoring, leniency toward others, family obligations and loyalty, conformity, obedience, subordination to authority, interpersonal harmony, role hierarchy, and self-restraint (Chien & Banerjee, 2002). Given these worldviews and personality traits, Asian Americans tend to exhibit respect for counselors. In counseling, many Asian Americans may, therefore, be less verbally and emotionally expressive than whites, which could erroneously be interpreted as repression, inhibition, or shyness (D. Sue, 1998).

Certain cultural values are important to Asian Americans. Often racial identity and gender can influence the cultural value held by Asian Americans (C. Yeh, Carter, & Pieterse, 2004). Asian American personality characteristics differ by gender, and they can be influenced by gender, roles, societal pressures, and acculturation processes (D. Sue, 2001). Techniques such as reframing and discussing cultural conflicts can help traditional Asian men deal with living up to societal and cultural expectations. More acculturated Asian men may be helped by didactic presentations of men's roles in the United States versus using introspective techniques. Counselors sometimes fail to appreciate that these personality characteristics are consistent with the cultural norms and values of Asian Americans. Cognitive behavioral techniques may be more effective with Asian men than with Asian women or men from other ethnic groups. It is important to select interventions that are consistent with the worldview and personality characteristics of Asian Americans clients.

Language

Language is another client characteristic that often needs attention when counseling Asian Americans because it can be a barrier to effective communication. Those who speak little or no English or who are bilingual could be misunderstood by counselors who cannot converse with them in their native language. This interference in communication could result in Asians trying to use nonverbal methods or interpreters, which can also be misinterpreted or distorted (Marcos, 1979).

Family

Family plays a central role in the lives of most Asian Americans. Counselors need to move toward a process of integration of family into the therapeutic process rather than differentiation of the individual from the family's values and customs. This is especially important for families who face difficulties associated with social isolation, adjustment, and cultural and language barriers. Issues like cultural and language barriers could lead to parent-child conflicts (Hong & Ham, 1992). Other family factors that need to be noted include parenting styles (Lim & Lim, 2004), adaptation experience of Asian Americans (B. S. K. Kim, Brenner, Liang, & Asay, 2003), and differences stemming from intergenerational gaps and acculturation (J. M. Kim, 2003). Differing parenting styles are also indicative of the personality development and life experiences of Asian Americans (H. Kim & Chung, 2003). Counselors may need to consider the family as both a potential pillar of support and resource as well as a potential stressor for their Asian American clients. This applies specifically to Asian Americans due to the importance placed on family connectedness and values within this ethnic/racial group.

Acculturation

Acculturation is a complex, multidimensional process that represents the degree to which Asian Americans identify and integrate with the host culture versus their culture of origin (Chun, Organista, & Marin, 2003). Acculturation overlaps with racial identity, involves aspects of behavioral, cultural, and social adaptations (Leong, 2001) and can result in cultural conflicts. These conflicts can consist of intergenerational, interpersonal, or gender role conflicts. Acculturation can also affect an Asian American's willingness to seek psychological help, response to the therapy process, and therapeutic outcome (Gim, Atkinson, & Whiteley, 1990). Research has indicated that acculturation is significantly predictive of mental health symptoms (C. J. Yeh, 2003), and is also linked to career development, such as job satisfaction and occupational stress and strain (Leong, 2001).

Counseling Expectations

Asian Americans can have certain expectations for the counseling process. Many Asian American students, especially the less acculturated, view counseling as a directive, paternalistic, and authoritarian process. Consequently, they are likely to expect advice, information, direction, empathy, and nurturance from their therapists (Yuen & Tinsley, 1981). The therapist is often expected to be an expert, while clients expect to take on low levels of responsibility, openness, and self-motivation (Yuen & Tinsley, 1981).

Help-Seeking Attitudes

A review of the literature suggests that Asian Americans underutilize, and have high rates of premature termination from, mental health services (Bui & Takeuchi, 1992). Help-seeking attitudes are affected by factors such as acculturation (Zhang & Dixon, 2003), gender (Gim, Atkinson, & Whiteley, 1990), and social-network orientation (Tata & Leong, 1994). Certain barriers are associated with these low utilization rates: cognitive (e.g., stigmas), affective (e.g., shame), values (e.g., collectivist orientation), and physical barriers (e.g., access to resources; Leong & Lau, 2001). Since a cultural analogy of therapy is not present in the Asian American culture, therapy may not be considered as an option and instead symptoms may be expressed somatically. Yep (2000) suggests culturally acceptable ways in which mental illness can be broached with Asian Americans (e.g., somatic complaints may be viewed as acceptable and normal expressions of mental illness within this cultural context).

Experiences of Psychological Distress

Asians, like all other ethnic and racial groups, experience mental health problems (Takeuchi, Mokuau, & Chun, 1992) despite being considered the "model minority" group. As mentioned, Asian Americans tend to attribute symptoms of psychological distress to somatic rather than environmental factors. Ethnic identity is also important to understanding the cultural experience of Asian Americans, especially within the context of racism and discrimination. Acculturation, adaptation, and bicultural stress have been shown to have important mental health consequences for Asian American immigrants (C. J. Yeh, 2003). Therefore, within-group differences attributed to immigration status (e.g., international, permanent residents, naturalized citizens) need to be taken into account when trying to understand and contextualize the life experiences of Asians.

Coping Mechanisms

Many Asian Americans use social withdrawal and avoidance strategies as coping mechanisms when their problems involve outsiders. Their usual support and coping systems usually include family and religious practices rather than professionals such as physicians or therapists (C. Yeh & Wang, 2000). Indigenous coping resources, such as traditional folk healers, spiritual identifications, and religious practices (e.g., Buddhism) may be useful resources for Asian Americans. Social support systems such as family, friends, and even international student offices can offer Asian international students a buffering system against cultural adjustment difficulties. A few studies suggest that Asian Americans show a lesser need for social support than do European Americans (e.g., Wellisch et al., 1999). Some studies have also concluded that Asian Americans exhibit higher levels of depressive symptoms, withdrawal behaviors, and social problems.

RESEARCH ON CLIENT PREFERENCES AND CLIENT-THERAPIST MATCHING

To provide appropriate and effective treatments to diverse racial and ethnic groups, it is important to identify therapist variables that have been suggested, even tentatively, by research. A way to do this is by looking at client preferences and client-therapist matching factors. There are also a number of therapist variables that could pose barriers to effective and appropriate psychotherapy, such as the therapist's prejudice or cultural bias, and lack of intercultural skills and culture-specific knowledge of diverse ethnic and racial groups. It is likely that most counselors' bias toward other ethnic and racial groups comes from two main sources: their own cultural and personal backgrounds, and their professional training. Many of the client variables mentioned can be linked to therapist variables. For instance, some Asian American clients prefer therapists of their own race and ethnicity. One common factor associated with therapeutic outcome, regardless of client race and ethnicity, is the client-therapist relationship (see Gelso & Samstag, Chapter 16, this volume; Imel & Wampold, Chapter 15, this volume).

Client Preferences

Helms and Carter (1991) investigated the effect of clients' gender and race on their preferences for African American or White therapists. It was found that, for Whites, a preference for White therapists was influenced by racial identity and gender, but not social class. The preferences of African American clients generally did not differ as a function of therapist race, but at times African American clients' racial identity attitudes reflected a preference for White male counselors. This study indicates that the prediction of therapist preference is a complex and interactive phenomenon, one that can depend on the gender and ethnicity of the participants; or that the ethnicity of the therapist can be one of many characteristics important to African American clients. This finding has yielded mixed results, suggesting that at times ethnic matching produces enhanced outcomes; and at other times did not. A review of the literature suggests that the effect sizes of these outcomes are usually small (Zane et al., 2004). There were also differences between cultural match and ethnic match. It could be possible that cultural match has more of an effect than ethnic match, as culture encompasses a broader range of factors than does ethnicity. These relationships need to be investigated further, but these findings are indicative of the fact that African Americans are a heterogeneous group that exhibits much within-group variability.

According to Atkinson (1986), Latino/as do not appear to have a preference for ethnically or racially similar therapists. The literature does not reveal any ethnicity effects on therapy process variables such as perceived therapist credibility, perceived therapist effectiveness, and client verbal behaviors. In a study investigating Mexican attitudes toward therapists, Ruelas, Atkinson, and Ramos-Sanchez (1998) reported that satisfaction with their therapists was positively related to the degree to which Mexican American community college students perceived their therapists to have behaved consistently with Mexican cultural values. In the same study, levels of client acculturation were not correlated with perceived counselor credibility. There is some research on the effects of therapist style on therapy process and outcomes with Latino/a clients. Ponce and Atkinson (1989) found that a sample of Mexican American clients preferred a more directive counseling style. Pomales and Williams (1989) also reported that Puerto Rican and Mexican American students generally tended to prefer directive counseling styles. This preference for direction and guidance during counseling superseded the need for attention to level of acculturation.

Since many Asian Americans have a lower tolerance for ambiguity than members of most other ethnic groups, it has been suggested that their preferences for therapy are more likely to be for structured, solution-focused, directive, and crisis-orientated counseling (Berg & Jaya, 1993). This suggests that many Asian American clients prefer a therapist who is an authority but is not authoritative (Leong et al., 2006). Asian American clients often described their counselors as more credible and competent if they came from an Asian background (Atkinson, Wampold, Lowe, Matthews, & Ahn, 1998).

Client-Therapist Match

One of the most pressing issues investigated here is whether ethnic minority groups should see therapists of the same ethnicity. Thompson, Worthington, and Atkinson (1994) examined multicultural awareness toward African American clients in a sample of two African American therapists and two White therapists. Results indicated that therapists, regardless of race, who addressed issues associated with being African American were perceived as being more trustworthy than therapists who did not attend to the African American experiences of their clients. Clients of the former therapists were also more likely to disclose intimate information and to return for further sessions.

S. Sue, Fujino, Hu, Takeuchi, and Zane (1991) conducted a large-scale study at the Los Angeles County Mental Health system on the effects of ethnic client-therapist matches on the treatment durations and outcomes of African Americans. They demonstrated that, when an ethnic match was present, a larger number of sessions were needed, but ethnic match did not make a difference on Global Assessment Scale (GAS) ratings. However, this study did not investigate the effects on treatment outcome that client "preference" had for therapist ethnicity. Based on this study, it is unclear if African American clients prefer African American therapists, but the findings do seem to indicate that match may only be weakly, if at all, related to outcome. Using the same data, M. Yeh, Eastman, and Cheung (1994) found evidence that client-therapist match may be related to (a) early termination, (b) number of sessions attended, and (c) therapist-rated psychological functioning at discharge. The relation of therapist-client match to premature termination and attendance has been replicated in a national study of Veterans Administration outpatient clients. African American clients who were not matched (i.e., were treated by White therapists) versus those who were matched with African American therapists displayed greater early termination (29% versus 14% dropout after 1st session) and attended fewer therapy sessions (17 sessions when not ethnically matched versus 25 when matched; Rosenheck, Fontana, & Cottrol, 1995).

Studies conducted in an outpatient substance abuse setting found that ethnic matching of African American clients with therapists did not result in greater numbers of sessions attended (Fiorentine & Hillhouse, 1999). These authors did find a positive relation between ethnic matching and client-perceived counselor credibility. The results of this study suggest that there could be other factors at work here, such as therapist competence and training in dealing with drug abuse issues. It appears that there is some evidence to suggest that ethnic matching may reduce the probability of African American clients terminating prematurely from therapy and increase their attendance, but it does not appear to be associated to any discernable extent to other outcomes (e.g., symptom reduction, global functioning).

S. Sue et al. (1991) studied a sample of Mexican Americans who had English as their primary language and those who did not. Among clients for whom English was not the primary language, ethnic matching predicted a decrease in premature termination, an increase in the number of sessions, and positive treatment outcomes in the form of favorable therapist ratings. This suggests that for non-English-speaking clients, ethnic and language matching mattered, especially with regard to the psychological process and outcome. These findings were replicated (Russell et al., 1996; M. Yeh et al., 1994), indicating that language match, ethnic-racial match, and community location may help to determine client dropout and other treatment outcomes.

Acosta and Cristo (1981) highlighted the importance of language match when treating monolingual Spanish-speaking Latino/a clients. These researchers investigated the effects of using English-speaking therapists along with language interpreters. Results indicated that this practice improved communication with therapists because it helped these clients feel understood and helped, in comparison with bilingual Mexican clients who spoke to their therapists in English (Kline, Acosta, Austin, & Johnson, 1980). These studies highlight the importance of language match in determining therapy process and outcomes.

Other variables in addition to ethnic and language match have been investigated. Similar to the study summarized for African Americans earlier, Latino/a Americans who were matched on gender and ethnicity with their substance abuse counselors displayed better outcomes and higher rates of utilization of services (Fiorentine & Hillhouse, 1999). Dansereau, Joe, Dees, and Simpson (1996) demonstrated that individually tailored counseling methods were optimal in enhancing communication with the therapist, in enhancing treatment attendance, and in increasing effectiveness in reducing positive drug urine tests. Tailoring counseling processes helps to increase the match between the client and the therapist (S. Sue & Zane, 1987).

In a study exploring the relation of ethnicity in Asian American clients to therapist bias, it was found that the Asian clients produced more favorable GAS ratings and attended more sessions when assigned to ethnically matched therapists (Gamst, Dana, Der-Karabetian, & Kramer, 2001). Similarly, in another study where age and gender were controlled, ethnically matched clients were evaluated as having higher mental health functioning. Ito and Maramba (2002) suggest broadening cultural match theories to extend beyond ethnicity or language variables in order to deliver effective, culturally appropriate services and to increase retention.

S. Sue and Zane (1987) suggested that client-therapist ethnic-match studies show significant results, but the effect sizes of these studies are small and may be a function of the large sample sizes or weak outcome measures used in these studies. Ethnic match would indicate matching along the lines of racial demarcations. Cultural matching would include broader concepts such as language and cultural background. The S. Sue et al. (1991) study demonstrated large effect sizes for the relationship between ethnic-matching and drop-out rates, especially for those clients who are less acculturated to the mainstream culture and who may also have less proficiency in the English language. However, the drop-out base rates in this study for ethnically matched and ethnically mismatched therapist-client pairs were low to begin with.

COUNSELING PROCESS AND OUTCOME WITH ETHNIC MINORITY CLIENTS

Much of the current research on counseling processes and outcomes with ethnically and racially diverse populations is based on comparisons of particular ethnic minority groups with Whites. This section examines the counseling process and outcome among all the ethnic groups in unison versus individually. It seems reasonable that despite the considerable amount of overlap present between groups, there are certain issues that are salient for specific ethnic/racial groups.

Treatment processes and outcomes can be measured using empirical studies that use techniques such as parallel services (e.g., health care, psycho-education) or ethnic/language matching between client and therapist. These variables can also be investigated using indices such as treatment utilization rates, treatment length, and premature termination. Treatment process and outcome measures for ethnic minorities are important because they provide some indication of the effectiveness of treatment by and to ethnic minority groups. Treatment process and outcomes can also be measured using more direct, but biased measures such as client and therapist ratings. This can be a difficult method to use in evaluating the effectiveness of therapy because there are often problems associated with the delivery of culturally sensitive and appropriate mental health services to culturally/ethnically/racially diverse populations (U.S. Department of Health & Human Services, 2001). These problems associated with service delivery can involve the unavailability of sufficient ethnic-related data, either due to small sample sizes or noncompliance issues. There are also sociocultural and structural barriers associated with the under-representation of ethnic minority groups in mainstream mental health practices. This under-representation could influence compliance or cause under-utilization rates among ethnic groups. These issues can also create problems in getting client and therapist ratings as they influence individuals' attitudes and behaviors toward help seeking (Leong & Lau, 2001).

Treatment processes and outcomes among ethnic and racial groups can best be understood if we make a research shift from more static and unidimensional models to more dynamic and interactional ones. This multidimensional counseling approach is best represented by Bryan Kim and colleagues (B. S. K. Kim et al., 2003), who simultaneously examined the effects of acculturation, cultural values, and counseling style preferences. This type of research is consistent with that advocated by Helms (1990), whereby racial identity is investigated via regressive, progressive, and parallel therapist-client relationships. Not only are these new methods more appropriate, but they also are more ecologically valid and better reflect the realities of cross-cultural counseling (Leong et al., 2006). Some evidence for the advantages of multidimensional models (i.e., those that consider the interactions between universal and cultural dimensions in understanding human behavior) versus unidimensional models (i.e., those that consider only the universal *or* the cultural dimensions and not their interactions) come from ethnic match studies. For example, Fujino, Okazaki, and Young (1994), in studying over 1,000 Asian American women who used mental health services in Los Angeles, found that "ethnic and/or gender match conditions were significantly associated with reduced premature termination, increased treatment duration, and the assignment of higher functioning at admission in comparison to the no-match condition" (p. 164). In other words, adding the ethnic dimension improved various clinical outcomes for Asian American clients.

Reviews of the literature on the effectiveness of psychotherapy among African Americans have been evaluated in various ways and reveal divergent findings depending on the methodology and focus of the study. For example, Brown, Schulberg, Sacco, Perel, and Houck (1999) found that interpersonal therapy and nortriptyline are effective ways of treating depression in African Americans. Similarly, cognitive-behavioral therapy was found to reduce Beck Depression Inventory scores for severe depression in African American adults (Organista, Munoz, & Gonzalez, 1994). Cognitive behavior therapy was also found to reduce anxiety symptoms in African Americans. Since many studies investigating treatment outcomes among African Americans (like the studies mentioned above) use different outcome measures, it is difficult to draw general conclusions. The findings are mixed. Some research suggests that mainstream treatments are effective for African Americans and that there are no ethnic differences in treatment outcomes. Other studies suggest that the treatments were less beneficial for African Americans than for Whites.

There is evidence suggesting that mainstream therapeutic methods are less effective for Hispanic/Latino populations, as evidenced by indicators such as utilization rate and treatment length. These are useful process or intermediate outcome variables to investigate as it might be expected that utilizing therapy or increased treatment length will lead to positive outcomes, like symptom relief and increased levels of functioning. There has also been a move toward developing more culturally sensitive and appropriate treatment methods for Latinos. S. Sue et al. (1991) showed that posttreatment GAS scores increased for Mexican Americans, and some research suggests that cognitive-behavioral and interpersonal therapeutic methods are effective in treating depression among Latino/a Americans (Rosello & Bernal, 1999). However, in general, Mexican Americans underutilize mental health services.

Leong (1986) has demonstrated that in the past there was a significant lack of empirical evidence demonstrating the effectiveness and current status of treatment process and outcome for Asian Americans, but this has changed more recently. Asian Americans continue to underutilize mental health services (U.S. Department of Health and Human Services, 2001). Leong and Lau (2001) suggest that there are internal (individual and cultural group) and external (social, systems, and institutional) barriers that account for these low treatment utilization rates among Asian Americans. Further research is needed to examine Ethnic Specific Services (ESS), which help reduce underutilization rates and ultimately help improve treatment processes and outcomes. For example, Zane, Hatanaka, Park, and Akutsu (1994) in their study of ESS, evaluated the patterns of utilization and treatment outcomes in an ethnic specific clinic in Los Angeles and found no significant differences between Whites and Asian American groups. In areas where ESS services cannot be provided, it has been suggested that, at the very least, culturally responsive services should be made available (Leong et al., 2006).

CULTURAL SENSITIVITY AND TRAINING

Counselors' Bias

Professional therapists often have different cultural backgrounds and personal characteristics than their ethnic minority clients. At times, the amount of stereotyping found in therapists can be as much as that found in the general public, and unfortunately this stereotyping can lead to cases of misdiagnosis. Lack of culture-specific knowledge is a barrier to effective and appropriate therapy. Therapists need to address client issues at both the macro- and microlevels in culturally appropriate ways. Stereotyping ethnic minority clients hinders the therapeutic process and outcome (Berg & Jaya, 1993).

Training Bias

Lack of cultural skills and knowledge can mean that clients will not get much needed and appropriate care. The professional training received by counselors can be a source of bias as most training programs involve traditional methods. Evaluating if procedures are culturally appropriate for a specific client in a specific situation is essential. It is important that social and cultural variables be emphasized as they can affect the client's help-seeking behaviors, experiences of distress, manifestation of symptoms, and therapeutic process and outcome (Lu, Du, Gaw, & Lin, 2002).

Cultural Competency and Appropriateness of Treatment

Cross-cultural training has been recognized as an important and vital part of educating and training professionals. An example of such a training program is the Cross-Cultural Training Institute for Mental Health Professionals, developed by Lefley (1985). Wade and Bernstein (1991) investigated the effects of this four-hour program on African American clients' perceptions of therapist-participants. They found that trained therapists were viewed as being more trustworthy and attractive, and as having greater experience, empathy, and unconditional positive regard than those who did not receive cross-cultural training. Clients also attended more sessions with trained versus untrained therapists. These results were impressive, especially for such a brief training program.

D'Andrea, Daniels, and Heck (1991) conducted a study to assess the efficacy of three different types of graduate multicultural training programs. The three programs were similar in content but varied in intensity: 3 hours/week for 15 weeks, 6 hours/week for 6 weeks, and intense weekend workshops for 3 weeks. These researchers found that all three training programs were associated with significant improvements in therapist multicultural awareness, knowledge, and skill acquisition. There were no significant differences on these variables as a function of training intensity. These results indicate that the content of training programs may be more important than their length. By contrast, Pope-Davis and Dings (1995) found that these same multicultural workshops helped improve multicultural awareness, but had no effects on improving cross-cultural knowledge or skills. Unfortunately, none of these studies investigated the effects of multicultural training on therapeutic outcome.

Cultural sensitivity is a process that requires a person to be willing to address issues of race and ethnicity. The development of cultural sensitivity training and awareness is imperative in order for therapists to be able to provide effective and appropriate services to ethnic and racial minority populations (Acosta, Yamamoto, & Evans, 1982; Lefley, 1985). Acosta (1984) reviewed psychotherapy studies dealing with Mexican Americans. In one study reviewed by Acosta, counselors received an orientation program for working with low-income and minority clients. The orientation program consisted of a series of seminars with topics drawn from the book, *Effective Psychotherapy for Low-Income and Minority Patients* (Acosta et al., 1982). Post-program evaluations demonstrated that the program did increase the therapists' knowledge and sensitivity in dealing with low-income and minority patients. Patient follow-up data suggested that the orientation program helped the therapists become more effective, as indexed by both self and patient reports (Yamamoto, Acosta, Evans, & Skilbeck, 1984). Lefley's (1985) program, described here, has also been shown to be effective in training Latino/a therapists. Preliminary research supports the efficacy of cultural sensitivity training, but further research needs to be conducted to replicate these findings. The effects of cultural sensitivity training on therapy outcome also need to be assessed.

There is growing awareness in the literature of the need to examine the appropriateness of Western psychotherapies for racial/ethnic groups. For example, it is important to consider the appropriateness of psychotherapy approaches in terms of their congruence with such Asian values as familial relations, interpersonal harmony, role hierarchy, self-restraint, and collectivism (Chien & Banerjee, 2002). Some work is being done to modify Western practices to better meet the cultural needs of diverse populations (Tseng, 2004).

Since many Asians place a strong emphasis on family connectivity and involvement, it is important that Western family approaches be modified in order to be more congruent with Asian values and norms (Chao, 2002). Confucian-based values, such as emphasis on collectivism, saving face, family structure, family hierarchy, and family priorities, need to be highlighted (E. Y. K. Kim, Bean, & Harper, 2004). Bae and Kung (2000) proposed a five-stage model for working with Asian American families, including *preparation* (preparing providers for effective service delivery), *engagement* (aggressive outreach to prevent early drop-out), *psycho-education* (broad-based family psycho-education about treatment), *family sessions* (individualized intervention coupled with facilitating family social support network), and *ending* stage (evaluating treatment). The authors provide details about the content and focus of these stages.

RECENT THEORIES AND MODELS OF CROSS-CULTURAL COUNSELING

Finally, in addition to the need for more process and outcome research, there is also a need for more theory development. While there have been some promising developments in terms of new theories and models of cross-cultural counseling, most of them have not yet been empirically validated. However, it is worthwhile to highlight a couple of these theories with the hope that it will stimulate systematic empirical research on their validity and utility. The theory of multicultural counseling and therapy proposed by D. W. Sue, Ivey, and Pedersen (1996) was an excellent start, but what is needed now are systematic and empirical investigations of the propositions of that theory.

Whereas D. W. Sue et al.'s (1996) theory is comprehensive (6 major propositions and 49 corollaries), more mid-range models of cross-cultural psychotherapy have also been developed. In contrast to comprehensive models, mid-range models focus only on several key aspects of the cross-cultural counseling dyad as opposed to attempts to specify all elements. For example, Leong and his colleagues (Leong & Lee, 2006; Leong & Serafica, 2001; Leong & Tang, 2002) developed the cultural accommodation model (CAM) of cross-cultural psychotherapy. CAM is aimed at providing more culturally relevant and effective psychotherapy for racial and ethnic minority groups. This model involves three steps: (1) identifying the cultural gaps or cultural blind spots in an existing theory that restricts the cultural validity of the theory, (2) selecting current culturally specific concepts and models from cross-cultural and ethnic minority psychology to fill in the cultural gaps and accommodate the theory to racial and ethnic minorities, and (3) testing the culturally accommodated theory to determine if it has incremental validity above and beyond the culturally unaccommodated theory.

As Leong and Lee (2006) have pointed out, a review of the cultural-general aspects of Western models of psychotherapy should provide an estimate of the degree of confidence with which we can apply these models to racial and ethnic minority clients. Their assumption is that the cultural-general aspects of a model or its degree of cultural loading is an important index. The higher the cultural loading, the more likely that the model may not readily transfer to other racial and ethnic minority groups. An index of the amount of cultural loading in a particular model of psychotherapy may, therefore, inform therapists about the amount of cultural accommodation that may be necessary (Leong & Lee, 2006).

For example, it has been pointed out that Freud's conceptualization of repressed sexuality as the root cause of neurosis has a high cultural loading because it is highly related to the sexual mores for women in the Victorian era.

According to Leong and Lee (2006), once Western models of psychotherapy have been reviewed with regard to their cross-cultural validity and degree of cultural loading, culture-specific constructs need to be identified in order to fill the gaps. This constitutes the second step in CAM. It is essentially an incremental validity model whereby the universal or culture-general aspects of these Western models need to be supplemented with culture-specific information. It is proposed that adding the culture-specific elements to Western models in order to accommodate the cultural dynamics of racial and ethnic minority clients will produce a more effective and relevant approach to psychotherapy with these clients.

FUTURE RESEARCH NEEDS AND RECOMMENDATIONS

The research on counseling and psychotherapy we have reviewed for African Americans has mainly focused on specific issues such as depression and anxiety. However, none of these studies were conducted within the context of a control group design and, therefore, this makes their conclusions tentative and inconclusive. Similarly, psychotherapy research done with Latino groups has shown that there is not sufficient data to draw definitive conclusions. Research on client and therapist variables, and treatment processes and outcomes for Asian Americans have also produced inconsistent findings, largely due to differences in level of analysis and sample characteristics. With Asian Americans, samples are usually drawn from smaller-scale analogue studies that consist of either international students or more acculturated college student samples. These restricted samples raise questions about the generalizability of these studies to clinical settings and populations (Leong et al., 2006). Therefore, the overall conclusion is that more psychotherapy research is needed. Much of the literature on psychotherapy with ethnic minorities is conceptual in nature but is limited in terms of empirical hypothesis-testing.

In their excellent review of the literature, Zane et al. (2004) identified some of the major research needs within this area. Since their review covers the same literature as that of the current chapter, some of their observations bear repeating here. Zane et al. (2004) noted that studies have varied greatly in the ways in which they have operationalized cultural variables. They proposed that ethnic affiliation may not be an adequate representation of cultural variation since ethnic differences and cultural differences are not equivalent. Because observing ethnic differences only implies differences in culture, they went on to recommend that cultural differences be studied directly in terms of variations in actual attitudes, values, and perceptual constructs.

They also noted the frequent use of analogue studies, over-reliance on volunteer students rather than real clients, assessment of change over one treatment session rather than over the entire course of therapy, and examination of client preferences for therapists' characteristics. Zane et al. (2004) questioned whether the brevity and simulated nature of the treatment sessions in most of these analogue studies really help advance knowledge of psychotherapy with racial and ethnic minority groups. They also noted limitations in the samples selected in these studies. Researchers have frequently noted the heterogeneity within each ethnic minority group (e.g., Leong, 1986). Indeed, significant variations in psychosocial characteristics such as social class, educational level, acculturation level, and immigration experiences are often not accounted for in these studies. The impact of these moderator variables need to be systematically examined in future studies, and their interaction with other cultural variables needs to be teased apart.

Zane et al. (2004) also questioned whether the most appropriate measures have been used in these studies. They noted that ethnic and cultural differences can be obscured by the use of unreliable, invalid, or insensitive measures. They point to the numerous investigators who have already lamented that clinical assessments of racial and ethnic minority groups often over- or underpathologize the symptoms of these clients when evaluations are based on norms developed on White populations and when little or no attention is paid to the issue of measurement equivalence (see Miller & Sheu, Chapter 7 this volume).

In addition to the observations of Zane et al. (2004), the review of the literature in this chapter has highlighted some other research needs. It is understandable that much of the research on counseling and psychotherapy with culturally diverse populations has tended to focus on outcomes. After all, if psychotherapy does not produce positive effects, then our entire enterprise will be called into question. However, the over-reliance on studies of outcomes has neglected the need for studies of the psychotherapy process. As Leong (1986) has pointed out, much of what we know about the therapy process with Asian Americans came from clinical formulations. That observation from 20 years ago remains true to this day and appears to apply equally to other racial and ethnic minority groups. Only when we begin to examine the process of psychotherapy with culturally diverse populations will we begin to understand how to provide effective therapy to these groups. In recognition of the need to "get at the heart of psychotherapy with culturally diverse clients" and stimulate more process research, Leong and Lopez (2006) guest edited a special issue of *Psychotherapy: Theory, Research, Practice and Training.*

Another major problem in our knowledge base on psychotherapy with culturally diverse populations lies in the research gaps within the cross-cultural competence research movement. In a review of the instruments designed to assess cross-cultural competence, Leong (1998) noted that many of the instruments are more concerned with the relationship-building elements in cross-cultural counseling than the actual treatment process. To date, there have been very few cross-cultural counseling process studies to help delineate what actually happens in cross-cultural counseling relationships beyond the initial few sessions. Instead, most studies have been based on analogue designs rather than clinical field studies with real clients being treated by practicing counselors. Further, there is little demonstrated linkage between these cross-cultural counseling measures and actual counseling outcomes. There are even fewer studies of counseling outcomes in cross-cultural counseling relationships than studies of the counseling process.

Leong (1998) also commented on the problem of distinguishing between knowledge and skills in cross-cultural counseling competencies as delineated in the conceptual model outlined in Division 17's position paper on cross-cultural counseling competencies (D. W. Sue et al., 1982). Conceptually, the knowledge-skills distinction makes sense since it is quite possible that a newly trained counselor in a good training program would possess the knowledge about cross-cultural counseling, but not necessarily the skills. It is only with extended application of this knowledge with real-life clients that such skills develop. Yet, at least one of the instruments find that these two dimensions are combined for their respondents (i.e., knowledge and skills are not qualitatively different; Leong, 37). For the other measures, we suspect that the skills dimension is being measured at a global and generic level and does not represent a well-sampled domain. We have only to review some of the items representative of the skills domain to see how global and nonspecific they are. This problem is probably due to the fact that we have not conducted many empirical studies into the actual counseling process in cross-cultural counseling dyads to identify the relevant elements to be measured. As such, our current measurement of cross-cultural counseling skills are quite crude and of unknown predictive validity in relation to actual counseling outcomes.

As noted by Leong and Lee (2006), the key question becomes what cultural variables should be used for this accommodation process. There are a myriad of cultural variables that may be implicated in the cross-cultural dyad. They propose that the selection of these culture-specific variables be guided by the evidence-based practice approach. As suggested by Cochrane (1979), we need to be guided by a critical summary of the best available scientific evidence for how we approach our practice. It should be no different in how we select cultural variables for accommodation in the CAM. In particular, we need to go to the scientific literature to identify those culture-specific variables that have been systematically studied to use in modifying our approach to psychotherapy with racial and ethnic minority clients. Ultimately, the CAM approach predicts that cultural accommodation will be superior to ignoring cultural variables when conducting cross-cultural psychotherapy.

CONCLUSION

It is becoming increasingly important to address issues of culture and race in therapy, especially with regard to the recent increase in diversity. Professionals need to provide culturally sensitive and effective therapies and interventions. This means that there is a need to address issues related to specific client variables, client preferences, therapist variables, and client-therapist matching. Increased research efforts will need to be directed toward evaluating the process and outcome of counseling with ethnic minority clients, and, where deficiencies exist, new theories will need to be developed and tested. Gaps in our knowledge and training will need to be filled. Our review suggests that some steps have already been taken, but more needs to be done to meet the needs of an increasingly diverse clientele.

REFERENCES

Acosta, F. X. (1984). Psychotherapy with Mexican Americans: Clinical and empirical gains. In J. L. Martinez Jr. & R. H. Mendoza (Eds.), *Chicano psychology* (pp. 163–189). Orlando, FL: Academic Press.

Acosta, F. X., & Cristo, M. H. (1981). Development of a bilingual interpreter program: An alternative model for Spanish-speaking services. *Professional Psychology, 12,* 474–482.

Acosta, F. X., Yamamoto, J., & Evans, L. A. (1982). *Effective psychotherapy for low-income and minority patients.* New York: Plenum Press.

Atkinson, D. R. (1986). Similarity in counseling. *Counseling Psychologist, 14,* 319–354.

Atkinson, D. R., Wampold, B. E., Lowe, S. M., Matthews, L., & Ahn, H. (1998). Asian American preferences for counselor characteristics: Application of the Bradley Terry-Luce model to paired comparison data. *Counseling Psychologist 26*(1), 101–123.

Bae, S. W., & Kung, W. W. M. (2000). Family intervention for Asian Americans with a schizophrenic patient in the family. *American Journal of Orthopsychiatry, 70*(4), 532–541.

Berg, I. K., & Jaya, A. (1993). Different and same: Family therapy with Asian-American families. *Journal of Marital and Family Therapy, 19*(1), 31–38.

Brown, C., Schulberg, H. C., Sacco, D., Perel, J. M., & Houck, P. R. (1999). Effectiveness of treatments for major depression in primary medical care practice: A post hoc analysis of outcomes for African American and white patients. *Journal of Affective Disorders, 53,* 185–192.

Bui, K. T., & Takeuchi, D. T. (1992). Ethnic minority adolescents and the use of community mental health care services. *American Journal of Community Psychology, 20*(4), 403–417.

Chao, C. M. (2002). The central role of culture: Working with Asian children and families. In F. W. Kaslow (Ed.), *Comprehensive handbook of psychotherapy: Interpersonal/humanistic/existential* (Vol. 3, pp. 35–58). Hoboken, NJ: Wiley.

Chien, W. W., & Banerjee L. (2002). Caught between cultures: The young Asian American in therapy. In E. D. Russell (Ed.), *The California School of Professional Psychology handbook of multicultural education, research, intervention, and training* (pp. 210–220). San Francisco: Jossey-Bass.

Chun, K. M., Organista, P. B., & Marin, G. (2003). *Acculturation: Advances in theory, measurement, and applied research.* Washington, DC: American Psychological Association.

Clark, R., Anderson, N. B., Clark, V. R., & Williams, D. R. (1999). Racism as a stressor for African Americans: A biopsychosocial model. *American Psychologist, 54,* 805–816.

Cochrane, A. L. (1979). 1931–1971: A critical review, with particular reference to the medical profession. In *Medicines for the year 2000* (pp. 1–11). London: Office of Health Economics.

D'Andrea, M., Daniels, J., & Heck, R. (1991). Evaluating the impact of multicultural counseling training. *Journal of Counseling and Development, 70,* 143–148.

Dansereau, D. F., Joe, G. W., Dees, S. M., & Simpson, D. D. (1996). Ethnicity and the effects of mapping-enhanced drug abuse counseling. *Addictive Behaviors, 21,* 363–376.

Fiorentine, R., & Hillhouse, M. P. (1999). Drug treatment effectiveness and client-counselor empathy. *Journal of Drug Issues, 29,* 59–74.

Fuertes, J. N., & Gelso, C. J. (1998). Asian-American, Euro-American, and African-American students' universal-diverse orientation and preferences for characteristics of psychologists. *Psychological Reports, 83,* 280–282.

Fujino, D. C., Okazaki, S., & Young, K. (1994). Asian American women in mental health system: An examination of ethnic and gender match between therapist and client. *Journal of Community of Psychology, 22,* 164–176.

Gamst, G., Dana, R. H., Der-Karabetian, A., & Kramer, T. (2001). Asian American mental health clients: Effects of ethnic match and age on global assessment and visitation. *Journal of Mental Health Counseling, 23*(1), 57–71.

Gibbs, J. T., & Huang, L. N. (1989). *Children of color: Psychological interventions with minority youths.* San Francisco: Jossey-Bass.

Gim, R. H., Atkinson, D. R., & Whiteley, S. (1990). Asian-American acculturation, severity of concerns, and willingness to see a counselor. *Journal of Counseling Psychology, 37*(3), 281–285.

Hall, G. C. N. (2001). Psychotherapy research with ethnic minorities: Empirical, ethical, and conceptual issues. *Journal of Consulting and Clinical Psychology, 69*(3), 502–510.

Helms, J. E. (1984). Toward a theoretical explanation of the effects of race on counseling: A Black and White model. *Counseling Psychologist, 12,* 153–164.

Helms, J. E. (1990). *Black and white racial identity: Theory, research, and practice.* New York: Greenwood Press.

Helms, J. E., & Carter, R. T. (1991). Relationships of White and Black racial identity attitudes and demographic similarity to counselor preferences. *Journal of Counseling Psychology, 38,* 446–457.

Hong, G. K. & Ham, M. D. (1992). Impact of immigration of the family life cycle: Clinical implications for Chinese Americans. *Journal of Family Psychotherapy, 3*(3), 27–40.

Ito, K. L., & Maramba, G. G. (2002). Therapeutic beliefs of Asian American counselors: Views from an ethnic-specific clinic. *Transcultural Psychiatry, 39*(1), 33–73.

Kim, B. S. K., Brenner, B. R., Liang, C. T. H., & Asay, P. A. (2003). A qualitative study of adaptation experiences of 1.5-generation Asian Americans. *Cultural Diversity and Ethnic Minority Psychology, 9*(2), 156–170.

Kim, E. Y. K., Bean, R. A., & Harper, J. M. (2004). Do general treatment guidelines for Asian American families have applications to specific ethnic groups? The case of culturally-competent therapy with Korean Americans. *Journal of Marital and Family Therapy, 30*(3), 359–372.

Kim, H., & Chung, R. H. (2003). Relationship of recalled parenting style to self-perception in Korean American college students. *Journal of Genetic Psychology, 164*(4), 481–492.

Kim, J. M. (2003). Structural family therapy and its implications for the Asian American family. *Family Journal Counseling and Therapy for Couples and Families, 11*(4), 388–392.

Kline, F., Acosta, F. X., Austin, W., & Johnson, R. G. (1980). The misunderstood Spanish-speaking patient. *American Journal of Psychiatry, 137,* 1530–1533.

La Roche, M. J. (2002). Psychotherapeutic considerations in treating Latinos. *Cross-cultural Psychiatry, 10,* 115–122.

Lefley, H. P. (1985). Mental health training across cultures. In P. Pedersen (Ed.), *Handbook of cross-cultural counseling and therapy* (pp. 259–266). Westport, CT: Greenwood Press.

Leong, F. T. L. (1986). Counseling and psychotherapy with Asian Americans: Review of the literature. *Journal of Counseling Psychology, 33*(2), 196–206.

Leong, F. T. L., (1998, December). *Definitions and measurement of cross-cultural counseling competencies.* Paper presented at the Roundtable on Conceptualizing and Measuring Cultural Competence convened by the Western Interstate Commission on Higher Education (WICHE) and the Evaluation Center at HSRI, Denver, CO.

Leong, F. T. L. (2001). The role of acculturation in the career adjustment of Asian American workers: A test of Leong and Chou's (1994) formulations. *Cultural Diversity and Ethnic Minority Psychology, 7*(3), 262–273.

Leong, F. T. L., Chang, D., & Lee, S. H. (2006). Counseling and psychotherapy with Asian Americans: Process and outcomes. In F. T. L. Leong et al. (Eds.), *Handbook of Asian American psychology* (2nd ed., pp. 429–447). Thousand Oaks, CA: Sage.

Leong, F. T. L., & Lau, A. S. L. (2001). Barriers to providing effective mental health services to Asian Americans. *Mental Health Services Research, 3*(4), 201–214.

Leong, F. T. L., & Lee, S. H. (2006). A cultural accommodation model for cross-cultural psychotherapy: Illustrated with the case of Asian Americans. *Psychotherapy: Theory, Research, Practice, and Training, 43,* 410–423.

Leong, F. T. L., & Lopez, S. (2006). Guest editor's introduction. *Psychotherapy: Theory, Research, Practice, and Training, 43*(4), 378–379.

Leong, F. T. L., & Serafica, F. C. (2001). Cross-cultural perspective on Super's career development theory: Career maturity and cultural accommodation. In F. T. L. Leong & A. Barak (Eds.), *Contemporary models in vocational psychology: A volume in honor of Samuel H. Osipow* (pp. 167–205). Mahwah, NJ: Erlbaum.

Leong, F. T. L., & Tang, M. (2002). A cultural accommodation approach to career assessment with Asian Americans. In K. S. Kurasaki, S. Okazaki, & S. Sue (Eds.), *Asian American mental health: Assessment theories and methods* (pp. 265–279). New York: Kluwer Academic/Plenum Press.

Lim, S. L., & Lim, B. K. (2004). Parenting style and child outcomes in Chinese and immigrant Chinese families—current findings and cross-cultural considerations in conceptualization and research. *Marriage and Family Review, 35*(3/4), 21–43.

Lu, F. G., Du, N., Gaw, A., & Lin, K. M. (2002). A psychiatric residency curriculum about Asian-American issues. *Academic Psychiatry, 26*(4), 225–236.

Marcos, L. R. (1979). Effects of interpreters on the evaluation of psychopathology in non-English-speaking patients. *American Journal of Psychiatry, 136*(2), 171–174.

Nobles, W. W. (1980). African philosophy: Foundations for Black psychology. In R. Jones (Ed.), *Black psychology* (pp. 99–105). New York: Harper & Row.

Organista, K. C., Munoz, R. F., & Gonzalez, G. (1994). Cognitive-behavioral therapy for depression in low-income and minority medical outpatients: Description of a program and exploratory analyses. *Cognitive Therapy and Research, 18*, 241–259.

Parham, T. A., & Helms, J. E. (1981). The influence of Black students' racial identity attitudes on preferences for counselor's race. *Journal of Counseling Psychology, 28*, 250–257.

Pomales, J., & Williams, V. (1989). Effects of level of acculturation and counseling style on Hispanic students' perceptions of counselor. *Journal of Counseling Psychology, 36*, 79–83.

Ponce, F. Q., & Atkinson, D. R. (1989). Mexican-American acculturation, counselor ethnicity, counseling style, and perceived counselor credibility. *Journal of Counseling Psychology, 36*, 203–208.

Pope-Davis, D. B., & Dings, J. G. (1995). The assessment of multicultural counseling competencies. In J. G. Ponterotto, J. M. Casas, L. A. Suzuki, & C. M. Alexander (Eds.), *Handbook of multicultural counseling* (pp. 287–311). Thousand Oaks, CA: Sage.

Rios-Ellis, B., Aguilar-Gaxiola, S., Cabassa, L., Caetano, R., Comas-Diaz, L., Flores, Y., et al. (2005). *Critical disparities in Latino Mental Health: Transforming research into action*. Washington, DC: Institute for Hispanic Health, National Council of La Raza. Available from www.nclr.org/content/publications/download/34795/.

Rodriguez, C. (1998). *Latino manifesto*. Columbia, MD: Cimarron.

Rosenheck, R., Fontana, A., & Cottrol, C. (1995). Effect of clinician-veteran racial pairing in the treatment of posttraumatic stress disorder. *American Journal of Psychiatry, 152*, 555–563.

Rossello, J., & Bernal, G. (1999). The efficacy of cognitive-behavioral and interpersonal treatments for depression in Puerto Rican adolescents. *Journal of Consulting and Clinical Psychology, 67*, 734–745.

Ruelas, S. R., Atkinson, D. R., & Ramos-Sanchez, L. (1998). Counselor helping model, participant ethnicity and acculturation level, and perceived counselor credibility. *Journal of Counseling Psychology, 45*, 98–103.

Russell, G. L., Fujino, D. C., Sue, S., Cheung, M., & Snowden, L. R. (1996). The effects of therapist-client ethnic match in the assessment of mental health functioning. *Journal of Cross-Cultural Psychology, 27*, 598–615.

Stavans, L. (1996). *The Hispanic condition: Reflections on culture and identity in America*. New York: Harper Perennial.

Sue, D. W. (1998). The interplay of sociocultural factors on the psychological development of Asians in America. In G. Morten & D. R. Atkinson (Eds.), *Counseling American minorities* (5th ed., pp. 205–213). New York: McGraw-Hill.

Sue, D. W. (2001). Asian American masculinity and therapy: The concept of masculinity in Asian American males. In G. E. Good & G. R. Brooks (Eds.), *The new handbook of psychotherapy and counseling with men: A comprehensive guide to settings, problems, and treatment approaches* (Vols. 1 & 2, pp. 780–795). San Francisco: Jossey-Bass.

Sue, D. W., Bernier, J. E., Durran, A., Feinberg, L., Pedersen, P., Smith, E., et al. (1982). Position paper: Cross-cultural counseling competencies. *Counseling Psychologist, 10*, 45–52.

Sue, D. W., Ivey, A. E., & Pedersen, P. B. (1996). *A theory of multicultural counseling and therapy*. Pacific Grove, CA: Brooks/Cole.

Sue, S., Fujino, D. C., Hu, L. T., Takeuchi, D. T., & Zane, N. W. S. (1991). Community mental health services for ethnic minority groups: A test of the cultural responsiveness hypothesis. *Journal of Counseling Psychology, 59*, 533–540.

Sue S., & Zane, N. (1987). The role of culture and cultural techniques in psychotherapy: A critique and reformulation. *American Psychologist, 42*, 37–45.

Suro, R. (1999). *Strangers among us: Latinos' lives in a changing America*. New York: Vintage Books.

Takeuchi, D. T., Mokuau, N., & Chun, C. A. (1992). Mental health services for Asian Americans and Pacific Islanders. *Journal of Mental Health Administration, 19*(3), 237–245.

Tata, S. P., & Leong, F. T. L. (1994). Individualism-collectivism, social-network orientation, and acculturation as predictors of attitudes toward seeking professional psychological help among Chinese Americans. *Journal of Counseling Psychology, 41*(3), 280–287.

Thompson, C. E., Worthington, R., & Atkinson, D. R. (1994). Counselor content orientation, counselor race, and Black women's cultural mistrust and self-disclosures. *Journal of Counseling Psychology, 41*, 155–161.

Triandis, H. C. (1989). The self and social behavior in differing cultural contexts. *Psychological Review, 96*, 506–520.

Tseng, W. S. (2004). Culture and psychotherapy: Asian perspectives. *Journal of Mental Health, 13*(2), 151–161.

U. S. Census Bureau. (2001). *Resident population estimates of the United States by sex, race, and Hispanic origin: April 1, 1990 to July 1, 1999, with Short-Term Projection to November 1, 2000*. Available from www.census.gov/Press-Release/www/2003/cb03-16.html.

U. S. Department of Health and Human Services. (2001). *Mental health: Culture, race and ethnicity—A supplement to mental health: A report of the surgeon general*. Rockville, MD: U.S. Department of Health and Human Services, Public Health Service, Office of the Surgeon General.

Wade, P., & Bernstein, B. (1991). Culture sensitivity training and counselor's race: Effects on Black female clients' perceptions and attrition. *Journal of Counseling Psychology, 38*, 9–15.

Wellisch, D., Kagawa-Singer, M., Reid, S. L., Lin, Y. J., Nishikawa-Lee, S., & Wellisch, M. (1999). An exploratory study of social support: A cross-cultural comparison of Chinese-, Japanese-, and Anglo-American breast cancer patients. *Psycho Oncology, 8*(3), 207–219.

Yamamoto, J., Acosta, F. X., Evans, L. A., & Skilbeck, W. M. (1984). Orienting therapists about patients' needs to increase patient satisfaction. *American Journal of Psychiatry, 141*, 274–277.

Yeh, C. J. (2003). Age, acculturation, cultural adjustment, and mental health symptoms of Chinese, Korean, and Japanese immigrant youths. *Cultural Diversity and Ethnic Minority Psychology, 9*(1), 34–48.

Yeh, C. J., Carter, R. T., & Pieterse, A. L. (2004). Cultural values and racial identity attitudes among Asian American students: An exploratory investigation. *Counseling and Values, 48*(2), 82–95.

Yeh, C. J., & Wang, Y. W. (2000). Asian American coping attitudes, sources, and practices: Implications for indigenous counseling strategies. *Journal of College Student Development, 41*(1), 94–103.

Yeh, M., Eastman, K., & Cheung, M. K. (1994). Children and adolescents in community health centers: Does the ethnicity or the language of the therapist matter? *Journal of Community Psychology, 22*, 153–163.

Yep, G. A. (2000). Explaining illness to Asian and Pacific Islander Americans: Culture, communication, and boundary regulation. In B. B. Whaley (Ed.), *Explaining illness: Research, theory, and strategies* (pp. 283–297). Mahwah, NJ: Erlbaum.

Yuen, R. K., & Tinsley, H. E. (1981). International and American students' expectancies about counseling. *Journal of Counseling Psychology, 28*(1), 66–69.

Zane, N., Hall, G. C. N., Sue, S., Young, K., & Nunez, J. (2004). Research on psychotherapy with culturally diverse populations. In M. J. Lambert, A. E. Bergin, & S. L. Garfield (Eds.), *Handbook of psychotherapy and behavior change* (5th ed., pp. 767–804). Hoboken, NJ: Wiley.

Zane, N., Hatanaka, H., Park, S., & Akutsu, P. (1994). Ethnic-specific mental health services: Evaluation of parallel approach for Asian American clients. *Journal of Community of Psychology, 22*, 68–81.

Zhang, N., & Dixon, D. N. (2003). Acculturation and attitudes of Asian international students toward seeking psychological help. *Journal of Multicultural Counseling and Development, 31*(3), 205–222.

CHAPTER 20

Developments in Counseling Skills Training and Supervision

NICHOLAS LADANY
ARPANA G. INMAN

Beutler (1995) proposed the "germ theory myth" of psychotherapy training, which essentially highlights the erroneous myth that simple exposure to counseling and psychotherapy principles via coursework will result in trainee counseling competence. In many other professions such as medical training, practicing a skill (e.g., surgery) prior to engaging in that skill with a live person is a hallmark of the training. At best, professional psychology programs offer a course or two on counseling skills, (in the midst of many more courses on theory and research), followed by on-the-job supervision of counseling. The argument from educators is that content-based theory and research courses prepare students to embark on counseling activities. The extent to which this assumption is supported empirically has yet to be tested. Even if it were tested, researchers would likely have a difficult time finding a clear and significant link between content-based courses and demonstrated counseling skills, given how distant and varied the predictors are from the criterion. What has been attended to is the adequacy with which, and the parameters under which, training programs provide counseling skills training to students prior to seeing actual clients, as well as the supervision of counselor trainees. This chapter reviews the two primary and most directly related aspects of counselor training that pertain to the work of counseling: *counseling skills training* and *supervision*.

COUNSELING SKILLS TRAINING

The need to attend to counseling skills first received attention in the late 1960s with the influence of Carl Rogers' work on facilitative conditions in the therapeutic process. Since then, a major focus of counseling skills training has been based on a didactic-experiential training model in which students receive coursework on counseling theories and basic helping skills, and training protocols are used to assist them in developing basic relationship and discrete counseling skills (e.g., open-ended questions, reflections). While helping skills training continues to be viewed as an important initiation into the counselor role (with several new training models developed), it has received little attention in recent years. In fact, as we enter a new era for the 4th edition of the *Handbook of Counseling Psychology,* it is interesting to note that apart from a chapter in the first edition (Russell, Crimmings, & Lent, 1984), chapters in subsequent editions made limited or no mention of the role of counseling skills training within training programs. Our intention in this chapter is to bring back the focus on the counseling skills literature by reviewing two important areas: helping skills training models and counseling skills research. We further highlight critical gaps pertinent to counseling skills training and research.

The authors would like to thank Amanda Busby for her superb literature review assistance.

Helping Skills Training Models

The late 1960s and early 1970s saw the initial development of systematic and structured training models that focused on teaching counselor trainees discrete helping skills. Varied in their views of learning (Nerdrum & Rønnestad, 2002), approaches to training (e.g., rating scales, video/audiotaped feedback), and their empirical support, four stand out as most useful to counselor educators: human resource training (HRT) or integrated didactic experiential training (IDET; Carkhuff, 1971), microcounseling (MC; Ivey, 1971), interpersonal process recall (IPR; Kagan, 1984), and Hill's helping skills model (Hill, 2004; Hill & O'Brien, 1999).

Human Relations Training or Integrated Didactic Experiential Training

Based on Rogers' (1957) relational focus of empathy, warmth, and genuineness, Carkhuff (1971) developed a didactic cognitive-experiential (self-awareness) training model. Trained within a three-stage model of self-exploration, understanding, and action, trainees use helping skills that focus on empathy (e.g., nonverbal attending, reflection of feelings), advanced empathy (e.g., interpretation, self-disclosure, immediacy), and direct guidance skills (e.g., problem solving, decision making), respectively.

Microcounseling Skills Training

While having a similar focus as HRT, Ivey's MC model proposes a metatheory of counseling. Using both theoretical (dream interpretation) and practical training skills (attending behaviors), trainees are systematically taught to be intentional in their work with their clients. Ivey proposes a hierarchy of skills ranging from easier (attending behaviors) to more difficult skills (reflection of feelings), which then get integrated into a personal theory. There are four training components (instruction, modeling, practice, and feedback) used to teach basic interviewing skills.

Interpersonal Process Recall

A third major model, IPR focuses on teaching trainees about interpersonal dynamics in the counseling process via a unique recall process whereby an "inquirer" has trainees review and reflect on their in-session thoughts, feelings, and bodily sensations that may have interfered with the therapeutic process. Based on a discovery approach to learning, reflection is then used to foster growth in the therapist and the client. An important assumption that IPR makes is that even beginning trainees have the requisite skills when working with their clients, although these skills may be hampered by performance anxiety and a desire for impression management (Hill & Lent, 2006a). IPR is used in both counseling skills training and supervision.

Hill's Helping Skills Model

Hill's three-stage theoretically integrated approach to helping skills focuses on exploration, insight, and action. In addition to integrating aspects of the previous three models (HRT, MC, and IPR), and focusing on building a good working alliance, this model provides a theoretical basis for each stage. Specifically, client-centered therapy lays the foundation for exploration, psychodynamic-interpersonal theories inform the insight stage, and cognitive-behavioral theories influence the action stage.

Counseling Skills Research

Although several variables (training model, trainer, trainee, and context) can influence the development of counseling skills, only training models have received significant attention in the literature. Three major meta-analyses of the counseling skills training research (Baker & Daniels, 1989; Baker, Daniels, & Greeley, 1990; Hill & Lent, 2006b) have collectively yielded important insights about the effectiveness of three counseling skills training models (HTR, MC, and IPR) and specific components related to skill improvement among counselor trainees. The first part of this section summarizes the findings of these meta-analyses; the second part highlights areas in need of further investigation.

Meta-Analytic Findings

Meta-analytic reviews of helping skills training models have shown that HRT ($d = 1.07$) seems to outperform MC ($d = .63$) and IPR ($d = .20$) for graduate students in promoting skill acquisition (Baker et al., 1990). Further, an earlier meta-analysis of MC revealed larger effect sizes for undergraduates ($d = 1.18$) but a moderate effect size for graduate students ($d = .66$; Baker & Daniels, 1989). (The d statistic in these analyses refers to the difference in standard deviation units between training and control groups, with d's of .2, .5. and .8 reflecting small, medium, and large effect sizes, respectively; Cohen, 1988.) The relatively small effect size for IPR compared to HRT and MC suggests that guided and structured training (e.g., instruction with a curricular focus) may be more effective at imparting counseling skills than a discovery-oriented learning approach (Mayers, 2004).

In attempting to understand what makes training programs effective, Hill and Lent (2006b) conducted meta-analyses to evaluate specific components (e.g., instruction, modeling) of these three programs. Particular training components, including modeling ($d = .90$), instruction ($d = .63$), and feedback ($d = .89$), yielded medium to large effects compared to no training, and a combination of the components (e.g., modeling plus instruction) was more effective than the provision of a single component (e.g., either modeling or instruction alone; $d = .51$). Further, the type of skill measure used (ratings of trainees' skills in interviews versus analogue situations) did not produce substantially different effect sizes. Despite these positive findings, the few studies that have been done and their methodological and conceptual problems limit the weight of these conclusions.

Areas for Future Investigation

Although a focus on training models and their components provides us with some information on skills training, there are several variables (e.g., trainer, trainee, context) that can moderate the development of counseling skills. Further, counseling skills training is often accompanied by other skills such as self-awareness, multicultural competencies, developing a theoretical framework, and case conceptualization abilities (Hill & Lent, 2006a). An exclusive focus on helping skills training, without also exploring the moderating variables and other aspects of counseling training, can produce a very limited understanding of the effects of training on counselor development and the complexity of the clinical process. To date, no attention has been given to trainer effects, and empirical research that has examined variables such as gender, level of training, cognitive complexity, and self-efficacy (e.g., Lent, Hill, & Hoffman, 2003) has been too fragmented to make clear conclusions (Hill & Lent, 2006a).

A major criticism of skills training programs has been their lack of attention to higher-order skills (e.g., self-awareness of therapist; Albert & Edelstein, 1990) and limited focus on trainee experiences (Nerdrum & Rønnestad, 2002). While rare, a few qualitative explorations in this area have yielded some important findings. For instance, Williams, Judge, Hill, and Hoffman's (1997) study on prepracticum trainee experiences during counseling sessions revealed that trainees acknowledge a struggle with reactions to their clients' presenting issues, concerns about their therapeutic role (e.g., taking sides), and potential conflicts with their clients. Similarly, Howard, Inman, and Altman's (2006) examination of trainee journals in their first practicum experience (preceded by a helping skills course, based on Hill's work) highlighted trainees' discussions about countertransferential issues, sense of self-efficacy, and specific client dynamics. In a similar vein, Nerdrum and Rønnestad's findings revealed that trainees not only reflected on the cognitive challenges of incorporating a new style (empathic) into their preexisting theoretical orientations, but also realized the need for a greater personal and emotional involvement in the therapeutic process since entering graduate school. These findings highlight the importance of engaging in qualitative methodologies to obtain a more in-depth analysis and complex assessment of trainees' experiences.

Research has focused on helping skills in analogue or highly controlled situations, but limited attention has been paid to how to handle particular situations or challenges in counseling. Thus, another area of inquiry would be to train and assess the transferability of helping skills to feelings of sexual attraction (Ladany, O'Brien, et al., 1997), handling anger (Hess, Knox, & Hill, 2006), cultural issues (Ladany, Inman, Constantine, & Hofheinz, 1997), and other such scenarios.

Despite the importance of culture in counselor training, helping skills training has not traditionally considered the role of culture in trainees' use of specific helping skills (Hill & Lent, 2006b). Although not directly a part of the helping skills literature, studies have examined the influence of didactic training (e.g., coursework, workshops) on self-reported multicultural competencies, obtaining inconsistent results (e.g., Inman, Meza, Brown, & Hargrove, 2004). Other studies have examined the influence of experiential (e.g., exposure, contact, cultural immersion) approaches on multicultural competence and revealed a moderate to strong relationship with self-reported multicultural competencies (e.g., Díaz-Lázaro & Cohen, 2001). Proponents suggest that a lack of cultural awareness can result in miscommunications and imposition of incongruent cultural interventions on culturally different clients (Ancis & Ali, 2005).

In a related fashion, little attention has been given to trainees' understanding of the "larger picture" and how theory might influence case conceptualization or case formulation abilities in counseling settings. While there is some initial support for Hill's three-stage theoretical model (Hill & Kellem, 2002; Hill & Lent, 2006a) in that it provides a conceptual framework for trainees to work from, trainees need to understand client dynamics in order to develop appropriate interventions. Case formulations help organize the complicated and at times contradictory nature of the counseling experience. Thus, in formulating a case, multiple client (e.g., biological, psychological, social, cultural) and therapist factors (e.g., theoretical orientation, worldview) that influence the therapeutic process (e.g., hindering and facilitating factors; Elles, 2002) and guide the types of goals and interventions (e.g., microskills, higher order skills) one might use in the counseling process must be considered. In essence, case formulations provide a link between theory and practice (Elles, 2002).

There is some evidence to suggest that case formulation approaches can be used to reliably assess client problems and to predict counseling process and outcome (Elles, 2002). However, the utility of theoretically based conceptualizations that integrate multicultural issues requires further study (see Constantine et al., Chapter 9, this volume). Successful multicultural counseling requires not only an accurate assessment of client issues but an in-depth understanding of critical cultural factors that influence the client's experience (Grieger & Ponterotto, 1994). Thus, further exploration in this area is clearly needed. Finally, it would also be beneficial to develop or refine measures (e.g., Helping Skills Measure, case conceptualization abilities; Hill & Kellem, 2002) that help integrate the different skills needed and provide a holistic picture of counselor skills development.

SUPERVISION

Unlike the long tradition of inquiry on counseling and psychotherapy, theory and research related to supervision has primarily received attention over the past two decades. Moreover, there has been limited interplay between theory and research in the realm of supervision. Specifically, there have been a few "large" theoretical models of supervision, and of these models, few have been empirically based or tested. This section is divided into two minimally related parts, one examining supervision theory and the other reviewing the empirical supervision literature. We also focus our review on individual supervision of individual counseling, which is where the bulk of the supervision literature has concentrated.

Supervision Theories

Theoretical models of supervision can be broadly divided into two classes: psychotherapy-based models and supervision-based models. Psychotherapy-based models generally approach supervision in a manner similar to the provision of psychotherapy. Although this approach may seem reasonable on the surface, we believe it has limitations because the goals of supervision (e.g., helping the counselor to conceptualize and work effectively with the client) differ from those of psychotherapy. We argue that there is a fundamental assumptive flaw with this approach, namely, that processes relevant to a psychotherapeutic approach would be relevant and applicable to supervision. We therefore focus our attention on supervision-based theoretical models, giving most attention to those models that are relatively comprehensive in nature.

Supervision-based models begin with the assumption that supervision is a unique enterprise in and of itself, containing processes, outcomes, and phenomena that are distinctive and not likely to be experienced in the same manner in other contexts. To be sure, there are elements of supervision that mimic counseling, such as when the supervisor reflects what the supervisee is feeling. However, even in these moments the supervision experience may contain elements that differ from counseling (e.g., involuntary nature, evaluation), influencing the experience of both offering and receiving reflections. In some respects, supervision can be thought of as a blending of two interrelated activities: counseling and teaching and, as a result, is a unique phenomenon.

Theoretical models of supervision can be further divided into models that are relatively comprehensive, typically found in book format, and those that are relatively circumscribed in scope (e.g., attending to an aspect or particular process of supervision), typically originating in journal article form. The more circumscribed models have considered supervision elements such as supervision competencies (Falender & Shafranske, 2004), interpersonal process recall (Kagan, 1984), reflective learning (Ward & House, 1998), schema-focused supervision (Greenwald & Young, 1998), Socratic supervision (Overholser, 2004), supervisor self-disclosure (Ladany & Walker, 2003), and constructivist-based training (Zuber-Skerritt & Roche, 2004).

Three of the (earlier) circumscribed models can be seen as setting the stage for each of the three comprehensive models we review. Hogan's (1964) developmental framework can be found in aspects of Stoltenberg, McNeill, and Delworth's (1998) integrated developmental model (IDM). Bernard's (1979) discrimination model, which attends to the roles and functions of the members of the dyad, can be seen in Holloway's systems approach to supervision (SAS; 1995). Bordin's (1983) model of the supervisory working alliance can be seen as a foundation of Ladany, Friedlander, and Nelson's (2005) critical events supervision (CES) model.

We chose three theoretical models (Holloway, 1995; Ladany et al., 2005; Stoltenberg et al., 1998) for the crux of our review because they (a) are comprehensive in scope, (b) have an empirical foundation on which they were based, (c) present areas for research via testable hypotheses, (d) have aspects that are both prescriptive and descriptive, and (e) are derived specifically for the supervision context. For each of these models, we identify and summarize the framework of the model, its primary constructs, and strengths and weaknesses.

Integrated Developmental Model

The basis for IDM is that supervisees developmentally change over time and that three structures can reflect the supervisee's level of development: motivation (e.g., interest, anxiety), autonomy (e.g., dependence to independence), and self and other awareness (e.g., cognition, affect). These structures, in turn, inform eight domains of clinical activity: (1) intervention skills competence, (2) assessment techniques, (3) interpersonal assessment, (4) client conceptualization, (5) individual differences, (6) theoretical orientation, (7) treatment plans and goals, and (8) professional ethics. With knowledge of the structures and domains, supervisors can intervene according to the supervisees' level of development (Stoltenberg et al., 1998).

Similar to the developmental work in supervision, the supervisory relationship is seen as differing across three trainee developmental levels. For a Level 1 supervisee, the supervisor should focus on empathy, understanding, and validation to take into account the supervisee's anxiety. For a Level 2 supervisee, the relationship is believed to undergo significant conflict and stress, in part, based on previous supervisory experiences. As such, supervisors are encouraged to attend to the here-and-now. Level 3 supervisees are expected to have the capacity to quickly develop a relationship that allows for the exploration of personal dynamics.

A strength of the IDM is that it addresses many of the shortcomings of earlier developmental models that were seen as overly simplistic. Also, a hallmark of a good theory is that it evolves over time based on clinical and empirical evidence, something that IDM has done. One critique of the model is that although it indicates that the supervisory relationship is critical, the relationship itself and the supervisor tasks that could be used to change it are ill-defined. In addition, the extent to which supervisees, in general, can be characterized based on a sequence of developmental issues with limited within-group variation (e.g., most supervisees enter Level 1 as highly anxious, motivated, and dependent, with little self-awareness) needs more clear empirical support.

Systems Approach to Supervision

The SAS conceptualizes supervision as consisting of seven factors that include (1) the supervision relationship, (2) the client (i.e., client characteristics, identified problems and diagnosis, counseling relationship), (3) the trainee (i.e., experience in counseling, theoretical orientation to counseling, learning needs and style, cultural characteristics, self-presentation), (4) the institution (agency clientele, organizational structure and climate, professional ethics and standards), (5) the supervisor (professional experience, role in supervision, theoretical orientation to counseling, cultural characteristics, self-presentation), (6) the functions of supervision (monitoring/evaluating, advising/instructing, modeling, consulting, and supporting/sharing), and (7) supervision tasks (counseling skill, case conceptualization, professional role, emotional awareness, and self-evaluation). Process is defined as a combination of the tasks and the functions (Holloway, 1995).

The supervision relationship is the core factor and consists of three elements. First, there is the interpersonal structure that includes the power inherent in the supervisor role, and involvement, or level of intimacy and attachment between the supervisor and trainee. Second, the relationship progresses through phases, from beginning to mature to termination. Third, it involves the contract where the supervisor and supervisee negotiate the expectations for their learning goals.

A clear strength of the SAS model is that it takes into account just about anything that can occur in supervision. For instance, it highlights the influence of institutional factors on supervision. Institutional factors have garnered almost no attention in the supervision literature. Although the SAS identifies the relationship as the core factor, and notes that it changes over time, the model does not specify how the relationship is formed, maintained, or repaired, when necessary. This specificity would assist practitioners in implementing the model. A second critique of the model is that it has stimulated little research since its creation.

Critical Events in Supervision

The fundamental premise of the CES is that the most meaningful aspects of supervision involve critical events of learning. The most frequent and challenging events were identified and were believed to occur either within a session or across multiple sessions. These events included (a) remediating skill difficulties and deficits, (b) heightening multicultural awareness, (c) negotiating role conflicts, (d) working through countertransference, (e) managing sexual attraction, (f) repairing gender-related misunderstandings, and (g) addressing problematic supervisee emotions and behaviors. The supervision work on these events occurred in three phases: the marker, the task environment, and the resolution—all of which were embedded in the supervisory working alliance (Ladany et al., 2005).

The supervisory working alliance, considered the foundation of the model, was derived from Bordin's (1983) model and viewed as consisting of a mutual agreement between the supervisor and supervisee about the goals and tasks of supervision, in addition to an emotional bond. The alliance serves as the figure and ground for the work related to the critical events, emerging when the supervisory relationship is in need of attention or when the tasks become challenging, and receding when the relationship is solid.

With the alliance in place, the first phase of a critical event is the *marker,* or a supervisee statement or behavior (e.g., feeling stuck with a client, chronically arriving late to supervision) that signals a need for the supervisor to intervene. Following the marker, and depending on the event, supervision enters the task environment where the supervisor engages in a subset of interaction sequences that may include a focus on the supervisory alliance, the therapeutic process, exploration of feelings, countertransference, parallel processes, self-efficacy, skill, normalizing experience, evaluation, or multicultural awareness or knowledge. The final phase involves a resolution that involves changes in levels of self-awareness, knowledge, skills, or the supervisory alliance.

A strength of the model is that it is empirically informed and designed to promote future empirical work. Empirical tests of the model would essentially involve finding an event in supervision and examining the types of markers, interaction sequences, and resolutions that occur. Similar to the other models, it has heuristic value for the supervisor-practitioner. However, this model does not address "noncritical" or normative events (e.g., case review) in supervision. In addition, the hypothesized sequences are still to be supported empirically.

Supervision Research

Since the last edition of the *Handbook,* the empirical articles in supervision have continued at a slow but steady rate of typically less than 10 published articles per year. The reasons for the low output likely reflect a few challenging conditions. First, conducting quality supervision research is a difficult and arduous endeavor, and available samples are relatively small compared to counseling research. Second, a comprehensive look at supervision would involve collecting data on supervisees, their clients, and their supervisors—an enormous undertaking (e.g., Ladany, Walker, Pate-Carolan, & Gray, in press). Finally, only a handful of supervision researchers are conducting programmatic research.

For our review, we included research conducted across disciplines (e.g., social work, counselor education, counseling psychology), focusing on research conducted primarily since the last edition of the *Handbook* and on variables that have a history of investigation and that continue to be salient and relevant to practice. In addition, two issues that are addressed to varying degrees in the aforementioned theoretical models, yet seem central to understanding supervision, are the importance of the supervisory relationship and the evaluation process. Both of these have also received moderate research attention. Research on the supervisory relationship has also been driven by a circumscribed theoretical model of the supervisory working alliance (Bordin, 1983). We, therefore, start by discussing Bordin's model and summarizing research that has been derived from it and other models of the supervisory working alliance. We then turn to a review of research on the evaluation process in supervision and other research areas that have garnered some recent empirical attention, especially emerging research on multicultural issues and conflict in supervision. We also present a series of supervision variables that have received limited empirical work but would be good avenues for future research.

The Supervisory Relationship

A challenge in the supervision literature has been how to define the supervisory relationship. In some cases, the relationship has been defined as everything that happens in supervision. However, we believe that such a definition of the relationship is ambiguous and ill-defined. Alternatively, the supervisory relationship has been approached from a more circumscribed perspective, with more beneficial results.

Bordin's (1983) model of the supervisory working alliance offers the most cogent definition of the supervisory relationship and has also been the most investigated. Extrapolated from his conceptualization of the therapeutic working alliance (Bordin, 1979), Bordin identified three components of the supervisory working alliance: mutual agreement between the supervisee and supervisor on the goals of supervision, mutual agreement between the supervisee and supervisor on the tasks of supervision, and an emotional bond between the supervisee and supervisor.

The model identified and described eight goals for supervision. These include: (1) mastery of specific skills (e.g., empathy, assertiveness training), (2) enlarging one's understanding of clients (i.e., expanding the overall conceptualization of the client), (3) enlarging one's awareness of process issues (i.e., seeing therapeutic process as incremental and as evolving over time), (4) increasing awareness of self and its impact on process (i.e., using one's own reactions in therapy to facilitate understanding of the therapy work), (5) overcoming personal and intellectual obstacles toward learning and mastery (i.e., countertransference), (6) deepening one's understanding of concepts and theory (i.e., therapeutic approaches), (7) providing a stimulus to research (i.e., supervision as a place to identify research questions), and (8) maintenance of standards of service (e.g., professional ethics).

Bordin identified a series of mutually agreed upon tasks and indicated that the tasks may change slightly depending on the goal of the supervisor. Examples of tasks include feedback on reports, focusing on the therapist's feelings, providing alternative conceptualizations, observing the therapeutic work through supervisee self-report, audiotape, or videotape, and having the supervisee select the topics of discussion in supervision. In terms of the emotional bond, Bordin posited that the strength of the bond component is based on mutual trust, likeability, and care between the supervisee and supervisor. As with the other components, the concept of mutuality is critical. In addition to the three components, Bordin referred to other key processes that help to establish the alliance. These include empathizing with the supervisee as a means of establishing the alliance, actively diffusing the hierarchical relationship inherent in supervision, and balancing critical feedback with an acknowledgment of the supervisee's strengths.

Bordin's model has been tested empirically in relation to a variety of supervision variables. The findings from these studies indicate that a stronger supervisory working alliance is related to greater supervisor attractiveness and interpersonal sensitivity (Ladany, Walker, & Melincoff, 2001); goal-setting and feedback (Lehrman-Waterman & Ladany, 2001); trainee satisfaction (Ellis & Ladany, 1997; Inman, 2006); supervisor self-disclosure (Ladany & Lerhman-Waterman, 1999); and supervisors and supervisees who were at advanced stages of racial identity (Ladany, Brittan-Powell, & Pannu, 1997). A weaker supervisory alliance is related to greater trainee role conflict and ambiguity (Ladany & Friedlander, 1995); lower supervisor multicultural competence (Inman, 2006); and poorer supervisor adherence to ethical behaviors (Ladany, Lehrman-Waterman, Molinaro, & Wolgast, 1999). One tentative conclusion based on this series of investigations is that the supervisory working alliance is a foundation upon which effective supervision is based (Ladany et al., 2005).

Evaluation

Beyond its nonvoluntary nature, the one clear process that distinguishes supervision from counseling is evaluation. Lehrman-Waterman and Ladany (2001) developed an instrument to assess the process of supervisor evaluation. This measure, along with the theoretical model on which it is based, provides a structure for understanding the process of evaluation. In essence, evaluation was described as consisting of two functions: goal-setting and feedback. The effectiveness of goal-setting was based on how well the supervisor could facilitate the development of goals that were specific, clear, feasible in relation to capacity, opportunity, and resources, related to tasks, modifiable over time, measurable, prioritized, mutually agreed upon, and that would require supervisees to "stretch" themselves. Two types of feedback were identified: formative, which is ongoing throughout supervision, and summative, which involves a more formal review, typically at the middle and end of an academic semester. This study found that more effective perceptions of evaluation were related to the supervisory working alliance, supervisee self-efficacy, and satisfaction.

To be sure, this lone study needs replication and extension to both further validate the measure of perceived evaluation as well as to test the theoretical propositions in relation to evaluation. There are, however, two qualitative investigations that may shed additional light on the role of formative and summative evaluation in supervision. In one study, there was preliminary evidence that formative feedback was seen as important for good supervision among psychiatry trainees and their supervisors (Chur-Hansen & McLean, 2006). In a second study, Hoffman, Hill, Holmes, and Freitas (2005) examined reasons supervisors gave for easy, difficult, or no feedback. Their results indicated that easy feedback was typically about clinical problems, was provided directly, was positively received, and involved supervisees who were open. Difficult feedback pertained to clinical, personal, and professional issues, was likely to be provided indirectly, and involved supervisees who were not very open. Finally, no feedback was typically given when the issues pertained to supervisee personal concerns (e.g., aloofness) and involved observations of the supervisee by other people (e.g., staff) that were shared with the supervisor.

Knowing the process of effective evaluation and some of the considerations governing decisions about giving feedback, supervisors are left with what is arguably the most daunting task, namely, *what* should be evaluated. To date, many evaluation instruments have been developed. Lambert and Ogles (1997) concluded that evaluation instruments are most useful when they attend to specific trainee behaviors and when several rating sources are used. However, they found numerous (e.g., psychometric) problems with published measures. In addition, it has been found that trainees are most likely to be evaluated qualitatively (Norcross & Stevenson, 1984; Norcross, Stevenson, & Nash, 1986); most supervisors rely on supervisee self-report to assess the counseling work, with less than 60% relying on audiotapes and less than 40% relying on videotapes (Ladany & Lehrman-Waterman, 1999); trainee likeability influences evaluation (Carey, Williams, & Wells, 1988; Dodenhoff, 1981); and supervisors do not always evaluate their supervisees ethically (Ladany, Lehrman-Waterman, et al., 1999). Another aspect to consider in relation to supervisee evaluation instruments is how well the instrument does what it is supposed to do—that is, the validity of the obtained scores in predicting important supervision-related criteria. Ladany and Muse-Burke (2001) identified a series of components that could be used to determine the utility of a given measure (although no single evaluation instrument is expected to attend to all of the components). These components include: (a) mode of counseling (e.g., individual, group), (b) domain of supervisee behavior (e.g., counseling, supervision), (c) competence area (e.g., helping skills, conceptualization skills, multicultural competence, supervision behaviors), (d) method (e.g., supervisee self-report, case notes, audiotape), (e) proportion of case load (e.g., number of clients, one client), (f) segment of experience (e.g., one session, segment of session), (g) time period (e.g., late in client treatment, early in training experience), (h) evaluator (e.g., supervisor, supervisee, client), (i) level of proficiency (e.g., relative to cohort group), (j) reliability, (k) validity, and (l) format (e.g., quantitative, qualitative).

Multicultural Issues

As indicated earlier, the work related to multicultural training has increased since Goodyear and Guzzardo's (2000) chapter in the last edition of the *Handbook*. However, only five relevant studies have been published specifically on multicultural aspects of supervision since 2000. We refer readers to Constantine et al. (Chapter 9, this volume) for a summary of the literature pertaining to multicultural competencies.

In a rich qualitative investigation, Burkard et al. (2006) explored the differences between culturally responsive and unresponsive supervision. In culturally responsive supervision, supervisees experienced support when exploring cultural issues. In culturally unresponsive supervision, supervisees felt that cultural issues were ignored, actively discounted, or dismissed by their supervisors. Supervisees of color reported experiencing culturally unresponsive supervision more often than their White counterparts. Using a blend of qualitative and analogue methodology, Utsey, Hammar, and Gernat (2005) found their sample of White supervisees in a focus group to be uncomfortable discussing racial issues, particularly their own. Both of these studies shed light on complex perspectives regarding racial issues in supervision.

In the realm of gender and supervision, Szymanski (2005) examined the relationship between feminist identity and supervision practices. The results indicated that feminist identity, including a critical examination of traditional gender roles, anger over sexism, connection with women's communities, and activism, were related to feminist supervision practices. This study is an excellent example of how the field can move beyond sex as a categorical variable to study the psychological aspects of gender. Walker, Ladany, and Pate-Carolan (in press) studied gender-related events in supervision from the perspectives of women supervisees. Roughly half of the identified events were supportive in nature (e.g., helping supervisees use gender in case conceptualizations, processing feelings about gender in supervision, professional development discussions that integrate gender), while the other half were nonsupportive (e.g., the supervisor making stereotypical comments about the trainee or a client, dismissing gender, or inappropriate behavior toward the supervisee). In all, these studies point to the reality that gender issues continue to be prevalent and influential in supervision.

There has been very limited study of sexual orientation and supervision. Sherry, Whilde, and Patton (2005) found that most training directors of counseling psychology and clinical psychology programs believed that sexual orientation issues were discussed in practicum and supervision experiences, although the survey did not identify the specifics regarding how this was done. Clearly, more empirical work is needed in this neglected area.

Ancis and Ladany (2001) offered a theoretical framework for conceptualizing multicultural identity issues as well as multicultural supervision competencies. As part of their Heuristic Model of Nonoppressive Interpersonal Development, they recommended ways for supervisors and supervisees to conceptualize multicultural identities (e.g., gender, race, sexual orientation, ethnicity, disability, and socioeconomic status) in the client-counselor-supervisor triad. Their model incorporates other identity models (e.g., Helms, 1990), defines phases of identity development (i.e., adaptation, incongruence, exploration, and integration) for those who are from socially oppressed and socially privileged groups, and describes types of supervisory relationships based on these phases (progressive, parallel-advanced, parallel-delayed, and regressive). In addition, multicultural supervision competencies are identified and defined across six domains (i.e., supervisor-focused personal development, supervisee-focused development, conceptualization, skills/interventions, process, and outcome/evaluation). Inman (2006) adapted this model and developed a measure to assess supervisor multicultural competence.

Conflicts in Supervision

Research has demonstrated that supervision is not always a safe place for learning and, in fact, can cause psychological harm to the supervisee. In particular, two studies each examined supervisee perspectives on conflictual supervision experiences using a qualitative methodology (Gray, Ladany, Walker, & Ancis, 2001; Nelson & Friedlander, 2001). Many similarities were found across these investigations. One commonality is that the supervisor's style in conflictual supervision involved a lack of support, disrespect, and blame (e.g., supervisor exhibited unstable moods). The supervisee also felt unclear about expectations and roles, and the conflict led to negative feelings (e.g., fear) and reduced self-efficacy. Typically, the supervisee sought support and additional supervision from others, including peers. Supervisees were typically able to see positive aspects of the experience as well, such as becoming more knowledgeable about the difference between effective and poor supervision.

Veach (2001) offered a model for classifying conflictual events in supervision that is organized along seven dimensions: (1) type of event (e.g., abuse, neglect), (2) content focused, (3) intentionality, (4) overt versus covert, (5) intensity, (6) frequency, (7) timing in relationship, and (8) recency of event.

It appears that there is no one type of poor supervision and there are many ways in which a supervisor can harm a supervisee (Veach, 2001). Ellis (2001) added five recommendations for future work in the area of harmful supervision: (1) More in-depth analysis needs to be made of supervision that causes harm; (2) an examination of the supervisee's contribution to the supervisory conflict, without victim-blaming, should occur; (3) a prevalence study is in order to determine how widespread the phenomenon is; (4) assessment of due process procedures should be in place at training sites that include a "supervisee bill of rights"; and (5) more attention should be devoted to the training of supervisors.

Research to Practice and Practice to Research Linkages: Future Directions

Research and practice in relation to supervision need an infusion of energetic investigators willing to take on a host of fruitful areas of scholarship, using practical experience to guide these endeavors and, in turn, presenting the research in a clinically meaningful manner. The stalled nature of supervision research leads us to point toward supervision variables that are ripe for inquiry, in addition to the aforementioned supervision variables. Although a single study into a phenomenon, as is the case in some of these areas, limits the critical mass from which theory can be built or results can be generalized, it can point to meaningful areas of future programmatic research. To that end, we mention the following research-practice directions, as well as tentative conclusions based on early studies.

Covert Processes

Sometimes, what is *not* said in supervision is as critical or more critical than what *is* said in supervision (Farber, Berano, & Capobianco, 2006). Research into covert processes has found that supervisees and supervisors keep many things from one another that could influence client care (e.g., Ladany, Hill, Corbett, & Nutt, 1996). Investigations into covert processes could be expanded to include such variables as supervisee and supervisor self-talk, intentions, and reactions.

Supervisee Development

Historically, supervisee development, defined broadly, has garnered considerable attention in the supervision literature, although support for developmental hypotheses remains suspect (Ellis & Ladany, 1997). Overall, it seems that supervisees see themselves differently as they gain experience and that supervisors perceive trainees differently depending on the trainee's experience level. Since the previous *Handbook* chapter, there have been no empirical studies that specifically attended to developmental hypotheses. Clearly more work is needed to test specific developmental hypotheses in a theoretically consistent manner to determine if developmental changes are reliable and predictable.

Parallel Process

Parallel process can be thought of as ways in which the counseling work, as well as interactions between the client and counselor, are mimicked in supervision with the interactions between the supervisee and supervisor (Doehrman, 1976). Limited primarily to case study research (e.g., Friedlander, Siegel, & Brenock, 1989), it appears that parallel processes may occur at times, however, the specific manner in which they occur and can be used for beneficial purposes is less clear. Approaching an understanding of parallel process from both qualitative and experimental perspectives is a critical next step.

Supervisee Sexual Attraction toward Clients and Use of Supervision

One of the more difficult areas of discussion in supervision happens when supervisees are sexually attracted to their clients (Ladany, O'Brien, et al., 1997). Preliminary evidence suggests that supervisees believe that their sexual attraction toward clients influences counseling process and outcome, and that supervisors are reluctant to talk about it in supervision. The processes involved in discussing and managing sexual attraction, both for counselors and supervisors, is an important avenue of future investigation.

Self-Supervision

A skill infrequently discussed in the literature is the process of supervisee self-supervision, where supervisees reflect, monitor, critique, and manage their behaviors in counseling. Dennin and Ellis' (2003) findings indicate that self-regulation training, an aspect of self-supervision, increased supervisees' ability to use metaphors but did not influence their use of empathy. Given the unquestionable reliance on self-supervision, the adequacy and appropriateness of self-supervision during and after training warrants additional attention.

Supervisor Self-Disclosure

Preliminary evidence suggests that supervisor self-disclosure, particularly about counseling struggles, is related to the supervisory working alliance (Ladany & Lehrman-Waterman, 1999). Ladany and Walker (2003) developed a model of supervisor self-disclosure in which it was proposed that the content (i.e., personal material, therapy experiences, professional experiences, reactions to the trainee's clients, and supervision experiences) and the personalization (i.e., discordant to congruent, nonintimate to intimate, and in the service of the supervisor or trainee) of the self-disclosure would to varying degrees lead to changes in the supervisory working alliance, supervisee disclosure, and supervisee learning. Testing this model would offer supervisors a theoretical basis on which to determine the efficacy of their self-disclosures.

Taping Supervisees

The importance of taping counselors for use in feedback has a long history in counselor supervision. To date, the one study that examined taping found that using one-way mirrors, audiotaping, and videotaping had negligible effects on supervisees (Ellis, Krengel, & Beck, 2002). Given the critical role that taping plays in counselor supervision, it would behoove researchers to examine the multifaceted implications of taping, both the potential positive and negative consequences.

Supervision Ethics

Although ethical guidelines for supervision have been created for all of the mental health professions, limited empirical work has examined ethical behaviors in supervision. Ladany, Lehrman-Waterman, et al. (1999) found that more than half of their sample of trainees reported that their supervisor departed from professional ethics in their supervision. The most frequently violated guidelines pertained to inadequate performance evaluation and to confidentiality issues. With the potential of so many ethical violations, it appears critical to examine the influence of ethics on supervision process and outcome.

Supervisor Countertransference

Supervisor countertransference has been defined pantheoretically and empirically as follows:

> an exaggerated, unrealistic, irrational, or distorted reaction related to a supervisor's work with a trainee. This reaction may include feelings, thoughts, and behaviors that are likely to be in response to both the trainee's interpersonal style and the supervisor's unresolved personal issues and may also be in response to trainee-supervision environmental interactions, problematic client-trainee interactions, trainee-supervisor interactions, or supervisor-supervision environment interactions. (Ladany, Constantine, Miller, Erickson, & Muse-Burke, 2000, p. 111)

Supervisor countertransference seems to occur and may influence supervision process and outcome. However, the extent of its influence is yet to be determined.

Supervisor Training

The bulk of the research has attended to the training of supervisees, and only recently has supervisor training received some attention. This is the case even though models of supervisor training have been present in the literature for some time (Holloway, 1992). In addition, states are beginning to design and require supervisor training for psychologists in order for them to engage in supervision practice. Scott, Ingram, Vitanza, and Smith (2000) examined the state of supervisor training among professional psychology programs as well as internship sites. Their results indicated that counseling psychology programs were more likely to offer supervision training than their clinical psychology counterparts, and counseling center internships were more likely to include supervision training than other internship sites. In addition to these results, it is important to consider if supervisor training indeed influences the work in supervision.

Specialization Areas of Supervision

Most supervision work has attended to supervisees who are engaged in general mental health counseling with individual clients. However, specialized forms of supervision for specialized populations, clinical problems, and counseling deserve theoretical and empirical attention. These areas include supervision of career counseling (Bronson, 2001) and assessment (Prieto & Stoltenberg, 1997); group supervision of individual counseling (Carroll, 1996); peer group supervision (Bernard & Goodyear, 2004); supervision of family counseling (Liddle, Becker, & Diamond, 1997); supervision of counselors working with children and adolescents (Neill, 2006) and older adults (McDonald & Haney, 1988); supervision of school counseling (Magnuson, Norem, & Bradley, 2001); postdegreed supervision (King & Wheeler, 1999); supervision of couples counseling (Stratton & Smith, 2006); and supervision with international trainees (Nilsson & Anderson, 2004). As can be seen, the empirical work in supervision can take many directions.

Supervision and Client Outcome

It can be reasonably argued that the ultimate goal of supervision is to influence client outcome (Holloway, 1992). Because client outcome is at least one step removed from supervision work, it would not be surprising if the influence that supervision has on client outcome is limited. Moreover, given the methodological complexities involved in obtaining triadic samples, it is not surprising that research in this area is sparse (Ladany et al., in press). However, two investigations offer a sense of how supervision can be used to influence client outcome. Specifically, it is possible that counselors receiving information about poor client progress can use supervision to alter the course of treatment (Lambert, Hansen, & Finch, 2001) and that focusing supervision on a particular skill may alter use of that skill in counseling (Bambling, King, Raue, Schweitzer, & Lambert, 2006). In the end, the influence of supervision on client outcome may be the ultimate challenge for supervision researchers to demonstrate the efficacy of supervision.

CONCLUSION

The clearest statement we can make about counselor training and supervision is that we need to learn a great deal more. The question must continue to be asked: How much and what type of training is enough to prepare students to see clients; and once they begin to see clients, how does supervision help them become more effective?

REFERENCES

Alberts, G., & Edelstein, B. (1990). Therapist training: A critical review of skill training studies. *Clinical Psychology Review, 10*(5), 497–511.

Ancis, J. R., & Ali, S. R. (2005). Multicultural counseling training approaches: Implications for pedagogy. In C. Z. Enns & A. L. Sinacore (Eds.), *Teaching and social justice: Integrating multicultural and feminist theories in the classroom* (pp. 85–97). Washington, DC: American Psychological Association.

Ancis, J. R., & Ladany, N. (2001). Multicultural supervision. In L. J. Bradley & N. Ladany (Eds.), *Counselor supervision: Principles, process, and practice* (3rd ed., pp. 63–90). Philadelphia: Brunner-Routledge.

Baker, S. B., & Daniels, T. G. (1989). Integrating research on the microcounseling program: A meta-analysis. *Journal of Counseling Psychology, 36*, 213–222.

Baker, S. B., Daniels, T. G., & Greeley, A. T. (1990). Systematic training of graduate-level counselors: Narrative and meta-analytic reviews of three major programs, *Counseling Psychologist, 18*, 355–421.

Bambling, M., King, R., Raue, P., Schweitzer, R., & Lambert, W. (2006). Clinical supervision: Its influence on client-rated working alliance and client symptom reduction in the brief treatment of major depression. *Psychotherapy Research, 16*, 317–331.

Bernard, J. M. (1979). Supervisor training: A discrimination model. *Counselor Education and Supervision, 19*, 60–68.

Bernard, J. M., & Goodyear, R. K. (2004). *Fundamentals of clinical supervision* (3rd ed.). Needham Heights, MA: Allyn & Bacon.

Beutler, L. E. (1995). The germ theory myth and the myth of outcome homogeneity. *Psychotherapy: Theory, Research, Practice, Training, 32*, 489–494.

Bordin, E. S. (1979). The generalizability of the psychoanalytic concept of the working alliance. *Psychotherapy: Theory, Research and Practice, 16*, 252–260.

Bordin, E. S. (1983). Supervision in counseling: Vol. II. Contemporary models of supervision: A working alliance based model of supervision. *Counseling Psychologist, 11*, 35–42.

Bronson, M. K. (2001). Supervision of career counseling. In L. J. Bradley & N. Ladany (Eds.), *Counselor supervision: Principles, process, and practice* (3rd ed., pp. 222–244). New York: Brunner-Routledge.

Burkard, A. W., Johnson, A. J., Madson, M. B., Pruitt, N. T., Contreras-Tadych, D. A., Kozlowski, J. M., et al. (2006). Supervisor cultural responsiveness and unresponsiveness in cross-cultural supervision. *Journal of Counseling Psychology, 53*, 288–301.

Carey, J. C., Williams, K. S., & Wells, M. (1988). Relationship between dimensions of supervisor influence and counselor trainees' performance. *Counselor Education and Supervision, 28*, 130–139.

Carkhuff, R. R. (1971). *The development of human resources*. New York: Holt, Rinehart and Winston.

Carroll, M. (1996). *Counseling supervision: Theory, skills, and practice*. London: Cassell.

Chur-Hansen, A., & McLean, S. (2006). On being a supervisor: The importance of feedback and how to give it. *Australian Psychiatry, 14*, 67–71.

Cohen, J. (1988). *Statistical power analysis for the behavioral sciences* (2nd ed.). New York: Wiley.

Dennin, M. K., & Ellis, M. V. (2003). Effects of a method of self-supervision for counselor trainees. *Journal of Counseling Psychology, 50*, 69–83.

Díaz-Lázaro, C., & Cohen, B. B. (2001). Cross-cultural contact in counseling training. *Journal of Multicultural Counseling and Development, 29*, 41–56.

Dodenhoff, J. T. (1981). Interpersonal attraction and direct-indirect supervisor influence as predictors of counselor trainee effectiveness. *Journal of Counseling Psychology, 28*, 47–52.

Doehrman, M. J. (1976). Parallel processes in supervision and psychotherapy. *Bulletin of the Menninger Clinic, 40*, 3–104.

Eells, T. D. (2002). Formulation. *Encyclopedia of Psychotherapy 1*, 815–822.

Ellis, M. V. (2001). Harmful supervision, a cause for alarm: Comment on Gray et al. and Nelson and Friedlander (2001). *Journal of Counseling Psychology, 48*, 401–406.

Ellis, M. V., Krengel, M., & Beck, M. (2002). Testing self-focused attention theory in clinical supervision: Effects on supervisee anxiety and performance. *Journal of Counseling Psychology, 49*, 101–116.

Ellis, M. V., & Ladany, N. (1997). Inferences concerning supervisees and clients in clinical supervision: An integrative review. In C. E. Watkins (Ed.), *Handbook of psychotherapy supervision* (pp. 447–507). New York: Wiley.

Falender, C. A., & Shafranske, E. P. (2004). *Clinical supervision: A competency-based approach*. Washington, DC: American Psychological Association.

Farber, B. A., Berano, K. C., & Capobianco, J. A. (2006). A temporal model of patient disclosure in psychotherapy. *Psychotherapy Research, 16*, 463–469.

Friedlander, M. L., Siegel, S. M., & Brenock, K. (1989). Parallel process in counseling and supervision: A case study. *Journal of Counseling Psychology, 36*, 149–157.

Goodyear, R. K., & Guzzardo, C. R. (2000). Psychotherapy supervision and training. In S. Brown & R. W. Lent (Eds.), *Handbook of counseling psychology* (3rd ed., pp. 83–108). New York: Wiley.

Gray, L. A., Ladany, N., Walker, J. A., & Ancis, J. R. (2001). Psychotherapy trainees' experience of counterproductive events in supervision. *Journal of Counseling Psychology, 48*, 371–383.

Greenwald, M., & Young, J. (1998). Scheme-focused therapy: An integrative approach to psychotherapy [Special issue]. *Journal of Cognitive Psychotherapy, 12*, 109–126.

Grieger, I., & Ponterotto, J. G. (1994). A framework for assessment in multicultural counseling. In J. G. Ponterotto, J. M. Casas, L. A. Suzuki, & C. H. Alexander (Eds.), *Handbook of multicultural counseling* (pp. 357–374). Thousand Oaks, CA: Sage.

Helms, J. E. (1990). *Black and White racial identity: Theories, research, and practice*. Westport, CT: Greenwood Press.

Hess, S., Knox, S., & Hill, C. E. (2006). Teaching graduate students trainees how to manage client anger: A comparison of three types of training. *Psychotherapy Research, 16*, 282–292.

Hill, C. E. (2004). *Helping skills: Facilitating explorations, insight, and action* (2nd ed.). Washington, DC: American Psychological Association.

Hill, C. E., & Kellem, I. S. (2002). Development and use of the Helping Skills Measure to assess client perceptions of the effects of training and of helping skills in sessions. *Journal of Counseling Psychology, 49*, 264–272.

Hill, C. E., & Lent, R. W. (2006a). A narrative and meta-analytic review of helping skills training: Time to review a dormant area of inquiry. *Psychotherapy: Theory, Research, Practice, Training, 43*, 154–172.

Hill, C. E. & Lent, R. W. (2006b). Training for novice therapists: Skills plus. *Psychotherapy Bulletin, 41*, 11–16.

Hill, C. E., & O'Brien, K. (1999). *Helping skills: Facilitating explorations, insight, and action*. Washington, DC: American Psychological Association.

Hoffman, M. A., Hill, C. E., Holmes, S. E., & Freitas, G. F. (2005). Supervisor perspective on the process and outcome of giving easy, difficult, or no feedback to supervisees. *Journal of Counseling Psychology, 52*, 3–13.

Hogan, R. A. (1964). Issues and approaches in supervision psychotherapy. *Psychotherapy: Theory, Research, and Practice, 1*, 139–141.

Holloway, E. L. (1992). Supervision: A way of teaching and learning. In S. D. Brown & R. D. Lent (Eds.), *Handbook of counseling psychology* (2nd ed., pp. 177–214). New York: Wiley.

Holloway, E. L. (1995). *Clinical supervision: A systems approach*. Thousand Oaks, CA: Sage.

Howard, E., Inman, A. G., & Altman, A. (2006). Critical incidents among novice trainees. *Counselor Education and Supervision, 46*, 88–102.

Inman, A. G. (2006). Supervisor multicultural competence and its relation to supervisory process and outcome. *Journal of Marital and Family Therapy, 32*, 73–85.

Inman, A. G., Meza, M., Brown, A., & Hargrove, B. K. (2004). Students and program faculty's perceptions of multicultural training in marriage and family therapy programs and its relation to students' perception of multicultural competence. *Journal of Marital and Family Therapy, 30*, 113–129.

Ivey, A. E. (1971). *Microcounseling: Innovations in interviewing training*. Oxford: Charles C. Thomas.

Kagan, N. (1984). Interpersonal process recall: Basic methods and recent research. In D. Larson (Ed.), *Teaching psychological skills: Models for giving psychology away* (pp. 229–244). Monterey, CA: Brooks/Cole.

King, D., & Wheeler, S. (1999). The responsibilities of counsellor supervisors: A qualitative study. *British Journal of Guidance and Counselling, 27*, 215–229.

Ladany, N., Brittan-Powell, C. S., & Pannu, R. K. (1997). The influence of supervisory racial identity interaction and racial matching on the supervisory working alliance and supervisee multicultural competence. *Counselor Education and Supervision, 36*, 284–304.

Ladany, N., Constantine, M. G., Miller, K., Erickson, C. D., & Muse-Burke, J. L. (2000). Supervisor countertransference: A qualitative investigation into its identification and description. *Journal of Counseling Psychology, 47*, 102–115.

Ladany, N., & Friedlander, M. L. (1995). The relationship between the supervisory working alliance and trainees' experience of role conflict and role ambiguity. *Counselor Education and supervision, 34*, 356–368.

Ladany, N., Friedlander, M. L., & Nelson, M. L. (2005). *Critical events in psychotherapy supervision: An interpersonal approach*. Washington, DC: American Psychological Association.

Ladany, N., Hill, C. E., Corbett, M., & Nutt, L. (1996). Nature, extent, and importance of what therapy trainees do not disclose to their supervisors. *Journal of Counseling Psychology, 43*, 10–24.

Ladany, N., Inman, A. G., Constantine, M. G., & Hofheinz, E. (1997). Supervisee multicultural case conceptualization ability and self-reported multicultural competence as functions of supervisee racial identity and supervisor focus. *Journal of Counseling Psychology, 44*, 284–293.

Ladany, N., & Lehrman-Waterman, D. E. (1999). The content and frequency of supervisor self-disclosures and their relationship to supervisor style and the supervisory working alliance. *Counselor Education and Supervision, 38*, 143–160.

Ladany, N., Lehrman-Waterman, D. E., Molinaro, M., & Wolgast, B. (1999). Psychotherapy supervisor ethical practices: Adherence to guidelines, the supervisory working alliance, and supervisee satisfaction. *Counseling Psychologist, 27*, 443–475.

Ladany, N., & Muse-Burke, J. L. (2001). Understanding and conducting supervision research. In L. J. Bradley & N. Ladany (Eds.), *Counselor supervision: Principles, process, and practice* (3rd ed., pp. 304–329). Philadelphia: Brunner-Routledge.

Ladany, N., O'Brien, K. M., Hill, C. E., Melincoff, D., Knox, S., & Petersen, D. A. (1997). Sexual attraction towards clients, use of supervision, and prior training: A qualitative study of predoctoral psychology interns. *Journal of Counseling Psychology, 44*, 413–424.

Ladany, N., & Walker, J. A. (2003). Supervisor self-disclosure: Balancing the uncontrollable narcissist with the indomitable altruist. *Journal of Clinical Psychology/In Session, 59*, 611–621.

Ladany, N., Walker, J., & Melincoff, D. S. (2001). Supervisee integrative complexity, experience, and preference for supervisor style. *Counselor Education and Supervision, 40*, 203–219.

Ladany, N., Walker, J., Pate-Carolan, L., & Gray, L. (in press). *Experiencing counseling and psychotherapy: Insights from psychotherapy trainees, their clients, and their supervisors*. New York: Taylor & Francis.

Lambert, M. J., Hansen, N. B., & Finch, A. E. (2001). Patient-focused research: Using patient outcome data to enhance treatment effects. *Journal of Consulting and Clinical Psychology, 69*, 159–172.

Lambert, M. J., & Ogles, B. M. (1997). The effectiveness of psychotherapy supervision. In C. E. Watkins (Ed.), *Handbook of psychotherapy supervision* (pp. 421–446). New York: Wiley.

Lehrman-Waterman, D., & Ladany, N. (2001). Development and validation of the evaluation process within supervision inventory. *Journal of Counseling Psychology, 48*, 168–177.

Lent, R. W., Hill, C. E., & Hoffman, M. A. (2003). Development and validation of the Counselor Activity Self-Efficacy Scales. *Journal of Counseling Psychology, 50*, 97–108.

Liddle, H. A., Becker, D., & Diamond, G. M. (1997). Family therapy supervision. In C. E. Watkins (Ed.), *Handbook of psychotherapy supervision* (pp. 400–418). New York: Wiley.

Magnuson, S., Norem, K., & Bradley, L. J. (2001). Supervising school counselors. In L. J. Bradley & N. Ladany (Eds.), *Counselor supervision: Principles, process, and practice* (3rd ed., pp. 207–221). New York: Brunner-Routledge.

Mayers, R. E. (2004). Should there be a three-strike rule against discovery learning? The case for guided methods of instruction. *American Psychologistital, 59*, 14–19.

McDonald, P. A., & Haney, H. (1988). *Counseling the older adult: A training manual in clinical gerontology* (2nd ed.). Lexington, MA: Lexington Books.

Neill, T. K. (2006). *Helping others help children: Clinical supervision of child psychotherapy*. Washington, DC: American Psychological Association.

Nelson, M. L., & Friedlander, M. L. (2001). A close look at conflictual supervisory relationships: The trainee's perspective. *Journal of Counseling Psychology, 48*, 384–395.

Nerdrum, P., & Rønnestad, M. H. (2002). The trainees' perspective: A qualitative study of learning empathic communication in Norway. *Counseling Psychologist, 30*, 609–629.

Nilsson, J. E., & Anderson, M. Z. (2004). Supervising international students: The role of acculturation, role ambiguity, and multicultural discussions. *Professional Psychology: Research and Practice, 35*, 306–312.

Norcross, J. C., & Stevenson, J. F. (1984). How shall we judge ourselves? Training evaluation in clinical psychology programs. *Professional Psychology: Research and Practice, 15*(4), 497–508.

Norcross, J. C., Stevenson, J. F., & Nash, J. M. (1986). Evaluation of internship training: Practices, problems and prospects. *Professional Psychology: Research and Practice, 17*, 280–282.

Overholser, J. C. (2004). The four pillars of psychotherapy supervision. *Clinical Supervisor, 23*, 1–13.

Prieto, L. R., & Stoltenberg, C. D. (1997). The supervision of psychological assessment: Toward parsimony and empirical evidence for developmental supervision theory. *Professional Psychology: Research and Practice, 28*, 593–594.

Rogers, C. R. (1957). The necessary and sufficient conditions of therapeutic personality change. *Journal of Consulting Psychology, 21*, 95–103.

Russell, R. K., Crimmings, A. M., & Lent, R. W. (1984). Therapist training and supervision: Theory and research. In S. Brown & R. W. Lent (Eds.), *Handbook of counseling psychology* (pp. 281–625). New York: Wiley.

Scott, K. J., Ingram, K. M., Vitanza, S. A., & Smith, N. G. (2000). Training in supervision: A survey of current practices. *Counseling Psychologist, 28*, 403–422.

Sherry, A., Whilde, M. R., & Patton, J. (2005). Gay, lesbian, and bisexual training competencies in American Psychological Association accredited graduate programs. *Psychotherapy: Theory, Research, Practice, Training, 42*, 116–120.

Stoltenberg, C. D., McNeill, B., & Delworth, U. (1998). *IDM supervision: An integrated developmental model for supervising counselors and therapists.* San Francisco: Jossey-Bass.

Stratton, J. S., & Smith, R. D. (2006). Supervision of couples cases. *Psychotherapy: Theory, Research, Practice, Training, 43*, 337–348.

Szymanski, D. M. (2005). Feminist identity and theories as correlates of feminist supervision practices. *Counseling Psychologist, 33*, 739–747.

Utsey, S. O., Hammar, L., & Gernat, C. A. (2005). Examining the reactions of white, black, and Latino/a counseling psychologists to a study of racial issues in counseling and supervision dyads. *Counseling Psychologist, 33*, 565–573.

Veach, P. (2001). Conflict and counterproductivity in supervision: When relationships are less than ideal—Comment on Nelson and Friedlander (2001) and Gray et al. (2001). *Journal of Counseling Psychology, 48*, 396–400.

Walker, J., Ladany, N., & Pate-Carolan, L. (in press). Gender-related events in psychotherapy supervision: Female trainee perspectives. *Counselling and Psychotherapy Research.*

Ward, C. C., & House, R. M. (1998). Counseling supervision: A reflective model. *Counselor Education and Supervision, 38*, 23–33.

Williams, E. N., Judge, A. B., Hill, C. E., & Hoffman, M. A. (1997). Experiences of novice therapists in prepracticum: Trainees', clients', and supervisors' perceptions of therapists' personal reactions and management strategies. *Journal of Counseling Psychology, 44*, 390–399.

Zuber-Skerritt, O., & Roche, V. (2004). A constructivist model for evaluating postgraduate supervision: A case study. *Quality Assurance in Education, 12*, 82–93.

PART IV

Career Development and Vocational Psychology

CHAPTER 21

Advances in Vocational Theories

NANCY E. BETZ

In this chapter, I review theoretical and empirical advances in the major theories of career development and vocational behavior. I take as my reference point the excellent review done by Swanson and Gore (2000) in the third edition of this *Handbook*. Because it is not possible to offer a comprehensive literature review in the available space, I focus on those theories that have received the most empirical attention over roughly the past 10 years: Holland's theory, social cognitive career theory, and developmental-contextual theories. I also briefly discuss the theory of work adjustment and Gottfredson's theory of circumscription and compromise.

More comprehensive coverage of career theories is contained in Brown and Lent's (2005) *Career Development and Counseling: Putting Theory and Research to Work* and the third edition of the *Handbook of Vocational Psychology* (Walsh & Savickas, 2005). Fouad (2007) also provides an excellent review and analysis of the field of vocational behavior. Those interested in the use of theories in career counseling may want to consult Luzzo (2000), Swanson and Fouad (1999), and Walsh and Heppner (2006).

A good theory should have the following hallmarks. For testability and heuristic value, a theory must propose clear, measurable constructs and testable interrelationships among constructs; it must generate research and consequent theory explication and extension based on research findings. For utility, a theory must have practical applications to career assessment and counseling and have relevance for the career development of an increasingly diverse clientele in a global social environment (Spokane, Fouad, & Swanson, 2003). More recent criteria for the utility and relevance of a theory derive from changes in the nature of the workplace—the increasing intertwining of work and personal lives as women's involvement in the workforce approaches both the prevalence and salience of that of men, the reduced predictability of the world of work (Fouad, 2007), the fact that many people do not have much choice in what work they will do (Blustein, 2006), and the increasing ubiquity of career transitions throughout life (Fouad, 2007).

TRAIT-FACTOR THEORIES

Parson's (1909) "matching model" of career choice, which provided a foundation for the study of vocational behavior and career development, postulated that optimal career choices involved three steps: knowledge of self, knowledge of work environments, and some means of matching the two to provide a good fit. This simple but profound statement was followed by nearly 100 years of research and development on methods of measuring individual differences in work-related characteristics—interests, abilities, values, and personality (Armstrong & Rounds, Chapter 22, this volume; Hansen, 2005; Tyler, 1995). Other researchers have focused on the measurement and classification of occupational characteristics and work environments (Gore & Hitch, 2005) and on means of matching person and environment. Two of the best-known operationalizations of the matching model are Holland's theory and the theory of work adjustment.

Holland's Theory

Interest in Holland's theory continues at a high level. The theory identifies six basic vocational personality or interest types—Realistic, Investigative, Artistic, Social, Enterprising, and Conventional—and six corresponding work environments. Holland (1997) summarized 30 years of research on the correlates—personality, abilities and competencies, values, and other self-descriptive characteristics—of the six types. The theory assumes that choices are optimal when they constitute a match between person and environment (congruence), and that congruent choices are most likely to lead to good outcomes: "vocational satisfaction, stability and achievement depend on the congruence between one's personality and the environment in which one works" (Holland, 1997, p. 10). Holland postulated that the types can be arranged in a hexagonal configuration. In addition to congruence and the hexagonal structure, Holland's theory contains the concepts of consistency, differentiation, and identity (see Holland, 1997). Because these concepts have not been extensively studied since 2000, they are not covered here.

Tests of Congruence Hypotheses

Considerable research has addressed two postulates—that people tend to make congruent choices, and that congruence leads to desirable work outcomes. In general, there is strong evidence for the usefulness of the congruence postulate in predicting choices of college major and occupation (Holland, 1997; Spokane & Cruza-Guet, 2005). People tend to choose and remain in congruent environments. At least two major means of studying congruence have been used in this research. The most common one involves some means of operationalizing or measuring the degree of similarity between the individual's Holland code type (from one to three letters) and the Holland code of his or her college major or occupation. Tracey and Robbins (2005) examined the congruence hypothesis in middle and high school students, finding that congruence increased from 8th to 10th grade but then decreased by 12th grade, suggesting a reexamination as the end of high school draws near. Gupta and Tracey (2005) found, among other findings, that Asian Indian college students in the United States were more likely than White students to emphasize duty to family over congruence in making career decisions.

One of the difficulties in this method of studying congruence is the existence of many alternative congruence indices that do not necessarily yield the same results (Brown & Gore, 1994; Eggerth, Bowles, Tunick, & Andrew, 2005). Different measures of the Holland interest types or environments may also yield different results (e.g., Armstrong, Hubert, & Rounds, 2003; Eggerth et al., 2005).

The second major method of examining level of congruence is to use discriminant analysis and MANOVA procedures to examine the extent to which Holland theme scores predict membership (hit rates and percentage of group membership variance accounted for) in college major or occupational groups. In these studies, both Holland interest and confidence theme (broad measures of self-efficacy that correspond to the six Holland types) scores have been found to substantially predict occupational or academic major group membership, and each variable set (interests and confidence) contributes incremental variance to that prediction. Betz, Borgen, and Harmon (2006) found that the Holland interest themes accounted for 77% to 79% of occupational differences, and the Holland confidence themes accounted for 80% to 82% of occupational differences. Tracey and Hopkins (2001) and Rottinghaus, Betz, and Borgen (2003) also reported that both RIASEC interest and confidence scores (ability self-estimates in the Tracey and Hopkins study) accounted for significant amounts of variance in college major and career clusters and in occupational choice, respectively. Such findings support the focus on congruence as an important basis for identifying potentially satisfying choice options.

Outcomes of Congruence

A large body of research has examined the extent to which congruent choices actually predict desirable work outcomes. Spokane, Meir, and Catalano (2000) reviewed 66 studies done between 1985 and 1999.

They concluded that the relationships of congruence to job satisfaction, well-being, and supervisor's evaluation of job performance had each been supported by two or more studies, and that the average correlation was about .25, accounting for 5% of the variance in the dependent (outcome) variables.

More recently, Tsabari, Tziner, and Meir (2005) analyzed correlations from 26 studies done between 1988 and 2003, including 53 samples and over 6,500 participants. They reported a mean congruence-satisfaction correlation of .17, lower than that reported by Spokane et al. They also found evidence for culture and age as moderator variables—the mean congruence correlation was higher in Israel (.23 over 9 studies) than the United States (.13 over 29 studies). Congruence was higher in younger (aged 20 to 30) individuals than individuals over 30, and it was higher with more years of job tenure ($r = .64$). Although these findings appear contradictory, the authors note that there was far more within variable heterogeneity in tenure than there was for age, so the results for age may be difficult to generalize due to restriction in range.

Finally, Gore and Brown (2006) note that many of the studies cited in the meta-analyses are characterized by serious restrictions in range on one or both of the two major variables—either Holland code types, satisfaction, or both. If one assumes that the people remaining in an occupation are those who have some degree of initial fit and who are mostly satisfied, there is an inevitable restriction in range on the variables of interest that attenuates the magnitude of any correlations obtained from such samples.

Like research on the congruence of choices, research on the outcomes of congruence often yields different results depending on which congruence index is used. Tinsley (2000) presented a number of arguments in support of three of the available indices (the C, K-P, and HC methods) and recommended that studies use at least two of them. Brown and Gore's (1994) C-Index received further elaboration by Eggerth and Andrew (2006) and Gore and Brown (2006), although Tinsley (2006) offers an alternative view of the utility of these elaborations.

Interest Structures and Individual Differences

The dimensionality and structure of interests, as indexed by Holland themes, has been an active area of research. In general, findings have shown that the Holland interest themes approximate a circular (rather than strictly hexagonal) pattern across gender, ethnicity, and nationality (e.g., Armstrong et al., 2003; Darcy & Tracey, 2007; Rounds & Tracey, 1993). However, some findings suggest that fit of the RIASEC structure is better in more versus less Westernized countries (Yang, Stokes, & Hui, 2005).

Although most research has examined the circular order model, some researchers have examined a more stringent circulant model that specifies equal distances between the six sides of the hexagon. Results have more strongly supported the less restrictive circular order model than the circulant model (e.g., Armstrong et al., 2003; Yang et al., 2005), and this support for the less restrictive model has been fairly consistent across gender and racial-ethnic groups and across college student and adult samples.

In addition to gender, race, and ethnicity differences in interest structure, research has continued to address gender and race/ethnicity differences in response patterns (level) of Holland theme scores, because score level has practical implications for choice of college majors and careers. Gender differences in the themes continue to prevail, with men scoring higher on Realistic and women on Social across types of measures (e.g., Fouad, 2002; Tracey & Robbins, 2005). Race and ethnicity differences in score levels are less apparent. Fouad (2002) found large effect sizes for gender, small to moderate for age, and small effect sizes for race, with the exception that Asian Americans scored higher on the Investigative scale than did other groups. Betz and Gwilliam's (2002) findings led them to conclude that gender trumps race in influencing RIASEC score differences on interest and confidence inventories. Fouad (2002) urged the continuing use of same-gender norms in interest inventories to minimize the effects of these continuing gender differences. In a study designed to probe the factors underlying possible bases of RIASEC interest item endorsement, Fouad and Walker (2005) found that differential item endorsement could be traced to differential availability of same-race role models and differential perceived occupational opportunities.

Integrating Measures of Personality

Research on Holland's theory has included studies of the personality correlates of the six Holland themes (see Holland, 1997). The past few years have witnessed an explosion of research on the relationships of personality to vocational constructs in general, and Holland's theory in particular (e.g., Barrick, Mount, & Gupta, 2003; Sullivan & Hansen, 2004; Thoresen, Kaplan, Barsky, Warren, & de Chermont, 2003). One of the most frequently studied topics has been the relationships of the Big Five personality traits (McCrae & Costa, 1997) with the Holland RIASEC dimensions for both interests and confidence perceptions. Meta-analyses of the relationships of RIASEC interests to the Big Five (Barrick et al., 2003; Larson, Rottinghaus, & Borgen, 2002) have strongly supported the relationships of Extraversion to both Social and Enterprising interests, Openness to Artistic and Investigative interests, Agreeableness to Social Interests, and Conscientiousness to Conventional interests.

The relationships of Big Five Factors and RIASEC confidence measures have also been examined (Nauta, 2004; Schaub & Tokar, 2005). This research has indicated some parallels with the relations found between RIASEC interests and the Big Five: Extraversion is related to Enterprising and Social confidence as well as interests (Larson et al., 2002). In addition, some research has found more generalized relations of a personality dimension with self-efficacy dimensions. Nauta (2004) found that Openness showed statistically significant correlations with all six Holland confidence themes (.18 [R] to .48 [A]). Nauta also found small, negative relationships between Neuroticism and all six Holland confidence themes (five were statistically significant). Conscientiousness showed significant positive associations with three of six efficacy themes (.18 [C] to .28 [S]), as did Extraversion (.16 [A] to .39 [E]). Thus, some of the common variance between Big Five factors and Holland confidence themes may be due to specific content overlap (e.g., Extraversion and Social Confidence both involve self-ratings of interpersonal behavior), while some of it may reflect more global personality-confidence relations (e.g., those with high neuroticism scores may generally doubt their vocational capabilities; cf. Lent, Brown, & Hackett, 1994).

Summary

Holland's theory continues to generate a large body of research, and there is continuing growth in our understanding of its dimensionality, correlates, and cross-cultural validity and utility. The RIASEC constructs and measures are often integrated within research on other major theories of career choice and adjustment, as discussed in subsequent sections. Although the six Holland themes are by no means the only way of conceptualizing or assessing the educational and occupational world, they have a widespread appeal and staying power for both applied and scientific objectives. Holland's theory continues as the most popular basis for career assessment, used in countless career interest and confidence inventories, career guidance programs, and computerized and online career assessment and guidance systems. Holland's typology has been incorporated into the major government sponsored occupational information system (O*NET; see Eggerth et al., 2005) and is used in career assessment programs all over the world.

Theory of Work Adjustment

The other major trait-factor, or P-E fit, theory is the theory of work adjustment (TWA; Dawis & Lofquist, 1984). As recently reviewed by Dawis (2005), TWA is both a fit theory and an interaction theory, describing the relationships between people and work environments. The theory focuses on two major individual variables: needs and skills. Work environments have two parallel or commensurate features, reinforcer systems and skill requirements. The predictive model has two major propositions: (1) the correspondence between the individual's needs and the reinforcer systems of the work environment should predict level of job satisfaction; and (2) the correspondence between the individual's skills and the skill requirements of the work environment should predict level of satisfactoriness. Satisfaction and satisfactoriness together predict tenure in the work environment. Other factors such as interests and personality traits are also suggested to influence satisfaction, satisfactoriness, and tenure, although no specific postulates are stated about them. The theory also proposes that when individuals are in a state of discorrespondence, some change needs to occur, such as changing self, changing the environment, or seeking a more correspondent environment.

Like Holland's theory, a strength of TWA is that the central concepts have been well operationalized (see Dawis, 2005). Earlier research supported the postulates concerning the importance of correspondence to both satisfaction and satisfactoriness and the relationship of the latter two (especially satisfaction) to tenure. Dawis (2005) noted that the two most important inferences that can be drawn from research are that "correspondence makes for satisfaction and dissatisfactoriness drives adjustment behavior" (p. 17). Although the theory has not generated a great deal of research recently, Lyons and O'Brien (2006) found that correspondence was substantially related to work satisfaction among a large sample of African American workers, and that these workers' perceptions of the racial climates of their work environments did not add significant unique variance to the prediction of satisfaction. Similarly, Lyons, Brenner, and Fassinger (2005) found that correspondence was a significant predictor of work satisfaction in a sample of lesbian and gay workers.

Summary

TWA's propositions and the supportive research have important implications for helping people make correspondent choices and for helping them understand or address problems in satisfaction or satisfactoriness after occupational entry. The ideas can also be useful in interventions to increase the retention of college students. Because TWA is a dynamic model of adjustment, it may also be productively used with developmental models that examine the transitions that occur throughout the career life span. Hesketh and Griffin (2005) noted the increasing emphasis in the work adjustment literature on the concept of adaptability and the ways in which TWA can be used to organize conceptions of adaptability as proactive behavior, reactive behavior, and tolerant behavior (p. 261). Recent research on the applicability of the "correspondence makes for satisfaction" hypothesis for African American (Lyons & O'Brien, 2006) and lesbian and gay workers (Lyons et al., 2005) suggests that the cross-cultural study of TWA's major hypotheses would be a fruitful direction for future research.

SOCIAL COGNITIVE CAREER THEORY

Social cognitive career theory (SCCT; Lent, Brown, & Hackett, 1994, 2000) has generated a great deal of research in recent years. Bandura's (1977) theory of self-efficacy expectations was introduced to the career literature by Hackett and Betz (1981) and subsequently generated much empirical research. In 1994, Lent et al. integrated the concept of self-efficacy into an expanded and comprehensive social cognitive model of interest development, choice making, and performance. The theory includes several building blocks, beginning with three "person variables"—self-efficacy beliefs, outcome expectations, and personal goals—that were derived from Bandura's (1986) theory.

Self-efficacy expectations are "people's judgments of their capabilities to organize and execute courses of action required to attain designated types of performances" (Bandura, 1986, p. 391). Outcome expectations refer to beliefs about the outcomes or consequences of certain behaviors, and personal goals are intentions to engage in particular activities or to work for certain goals. Personal goals include "choice content goals, that is, the type of activity or career that the individual wishes to pursue, and performance goals, the level or quality of performance the individual plans to achieve" (Lent 2005, p. 105). The model also includes demographic variables such as gender and ethnicity, traditional traitlike variables such as measured ability and values, and "background contextual affordances" (qualities of the environment, broadly defined) for determining the quality of learning experiences that shape self-efficacy and outcome expectations.

Efficacy and outcome expectations are postulated to be related to each other and to influence interest development. Interests, along with efficacy and outcome expectations, influence choice goals, and all four of the former influence choice actions. Proximal contextual factors (environmental supports and barriers near the point of choice-making) also influence choice goals and actions. Finally, choice actions are postulated to affect performance domains and attainments, including choice stability over time.

Measurement Issues

Research continues to be directed at the development of measures of the constructs, especially self-efficacy expectations. This process is complicated in SCCT by the behavior domain-specificity of both the model and the constructs (Betz & Hackett, 2006; Lent & Brown, 2006b). An SCCT model might be used to predict choice of a science major, so what must be measured are science-related self-efficacy beliefs, outcome expectations, and interests as well as barriers and supports to a choice in science. Research on self-efficacy per se is so popular that 11% of all articles published between 2001 and 2006 in the *Journal of Counseling Psychology, Journal of Career Assessment,* and *Journal of Vocational Behavior* included a reference to self-efficacy in their titles or abstracts (Gore, 2006). There has been much less research on outcome expectations (see Fouad & Guillen, 2006), detracting from efforts to test the model comprehensively.

Some major areas on which recent measurement efforts have focused can be organized according to Lent and Brown's (2006b) four-category system. Examples of the first category, *content or task-specific self-efficacy*, include measures of science and engineering majors and careers (Lent, Brown, Schmidt, et al., 2003), other academic disciplines such as social studies, art, and English (Fouad, Smith, & Zao, 2002), the six themes of Holland's theory (Lindley & Borgen, 2002), basic dimensions of vocational activity such as leadership and public speaking (Betz et al., 2006; Rottinghaus, Betz, & Borgen, 2003), research competencies (Bieschke, 2006), and general academic self-efficacy (Gore, 2006).

Coping self-efficacy, Lent and Brown's second category, has been measured by Byars (2006) and by Lent, Brown, Schmidt, et al. (2003). *Process self-efficacy* includes skills necessary for any area of career pursuit such as career decision self-efficacy (see Betz, Hammond, & Multon, 2005). *Self-regulatory self-efficacy* could refer to a person's beliefs in his or her abilities to organize and manage time and workload to facilitate success or career adaptability (see Hesketh & Griffin, 2005; Rottinghaus, Day, & Borgen, 2005).

Hypothesis Testing

Recent research has examined the validity of the theory's major hypotheses. Most research supports the relationships of self-efficacy and outcome expectations, with correlations between .45 and .55 (Ali, McWhirter, & Chronister, 2005; Nauta & Epperson, 2003). Lent, Brown, Nota, and Soresi (2003) found correlations ranging from .68 to .79 between self-efficacy and outcome expectations across the Holland themes in Italian high school students. The hypothesis that low self-efficacy expectations for male-dominated careers limited women's consideration of those options (Hackett & Betz, 1981) continues to receive empirical support (see Lindley, 2006).

Other studies have shown incremental predictive validity of self-efficacy and outcome expectations relative to interests, goals, and performance (Flores, Navarro, Smith, & Ploszaj, 2006; Fouad et al., 2002; Gore & Leuwerke, 2000; Lent et al., 2001; Lent et al., 2005; Nauta & Epperson, 2003). Lent, Brown, Nota, et al. (2003) found that the combination of self-efficacy and outcome expectations explained large amounts of variance in interests in the Holland themes, and that interests were in turn a good predictor of occupational consideration. Gore and Leuwerke (2000) found that self-efficacy and outcome expectations were more powerful predictors of occupational considerations than was person-environment congruence.

Support has also been found for the hypothesized paths between self-efficacy and outcome expectations, interests, and choice goals and outcome behaviors (Lent et al. 2001 2005), and a path between choice goals and goal stability (persistence) in students in engineering (Lent, Brown, Schmidt, et al., 2003). Nauta and Epperson (2003) found that self-efficacy predicted interests which, in turn, predicted choice of major in 204 college women who had participated in a science- and math-related career exploration conference while in high school. Gore (2006) and Kahn and Nauta (2001) reported that academic self-efficacy is significantly related to first-year academic performance (GPA) when self-efficacy is measured at the end of the first semester or during the second semester. Bieschke (2006) reported that research self-efficacy was strongly related to research productivity, and research outcome expectations were strongly related to research interests. Gore (2006) reported that course self-efficacy was related to persistence, whereas Kahn and Nauta (2001) found that outcome expectations and performance goals were related to persistence.

Environmental and Contextual Influences

Interest in the environmental influences in SCCT has expanded, partially as a result of Lent et al.'s (2000) emphasis on the conceptualization and role of environmental barriers and supports. They distinguished distal from proximal influences and suggested that the latter, being closer to the goal action, may influence goals or actions directly or moderate the relations of interests to goals and goals to actions.

Research on contextual supports and barriers has included studies by Flores and O'Brien (2002) on the roles of acculturation, parental support, and occupational barriers relative to the career choice goals of Mexican American high school girls; Flores et al. (2006) on acculturation and parental support in Mexican American high school boys; and Ali et al. (2005) on the role of peer, sibling, and parental support in lower socioeconomic status students. Lent et al. (2002) reported qualitative research leading to the development of structured measures of domain-specific (math and science) barriers and supports. They found four classes of barriers (financial, instructional, social and familial, and gender or race discrimination) and four classes of supports (social support and encouragement, instrumental assistance, access to role models and mentors, and financial resources).

In testing the relations of supports and barriers to choice goals, Lent et al. (2001) found that, contrary to predictions, the barriers and supports measures were only minimally related to the choice measures. Rather, the data supported a partial mediation model wherein barriers and supports affect self-efficacy which, in turn, affects outcome expectations and interests and, through them, choice intentions. Such partial mediation was also found by Lent, Brown, Schmidt, et al. (2003) and Lent, Brown, Nota, et al. (2003), suggesting that barriers and supports, even when proximally perceived, exert their influence largely through their effects on self-efficacy rather than directly by hindering (in the case of barriers) or facilitating (in the case of supports) the choices that people make.

Relationships of Self-Efficacy and Interests

One topic that has long been of interest to researchers has been the relationship between self-efficacy and interests. Interest-confidence correlations are typically in the .40s to .50s; for example, .53 in the Lent et al. (1994) meta-analysis and .46 in the Lent et al. (2005) sample of engineering students. Rottinghaus, Larson, and Borgen's (2003) meta-analysis of 53 independent samples, which examined parallel measures of interests and self-efficacy, found average RIASEC self-efficacy–interest correlations to range from .50 (Enterprising) to .68 (Investigative).

In terms of causality, although acknowledging the reciprocal relations between self-efficacy and interests, SCCT posits an a priori location of self-efficacy in the model, as one of the causes of interests, and Bandura (1977) has agreed with this ordering. Recent research has tested causal relations between self-efficacy beliefs and interests. Tracey (2002) examined RIASEC confidence and interest scores obtained over a 1-year interval in fifth- and seventh-grade students and found support for a reciprocal influence model in which interests led to competence development and vice versa. Nauta, Kahn, Angell, and Cantarelli (2002), using a cross-lagged panel design, also found evidence for reciprocal causation among college students. At the longest time period, however, which was 7 months, the data more strongly supported the role of self-efficacy as an antecedent of interests. Lent, Tracey, Brown, Soresi, and Nota (2006) also found evidence for a bidirectional model for all six Holland themes.

Silvia (2003) examined a hypothesis that too much self-efficacy can lead to reduced interest, creating boredom. In two experimental studies, he found the predicted quadratic relationship—interests increased as self-efficacy increased, but then decreased as self-efficacy became very high. He pointed out that unless the possibility of a nonlinear relationship is examined, traditional correlational procedures will not reveal the existence of one. Schaub and Tokar (2005) examined the extent to which learning experiences and self-efficacy expectations mediated the relationship of personality to Holland interests. They found that self-efficacy mediated some of these relationships, and these mediating effects sometimes supported a content-correspondence hypothesis; for example, artistic self-efficacy mediated the relationship between openness and artistic interests.

Diverse Groups

One of the most active and important areas of SCCT research involves its applicability to diverse groups. Considerable research has examined social cognitive variables as a function of gender, ethnicity, or both. Flores and her colleagues have found somewhat different patterns in support factors for Mexican American boys (Flores et al., 2006) versus girls (Flores & O'Brien, 2002). Ali and Saunders (2006) found that both self-efficacy beliefs and parental support predicted Appalachian youths' expectations of attending college. Ali et al. (2005) found that sibling and peer support predicted self-efficacy beliefs. Lent et al. (2005) compared engineering students at two types of university, finding that those at historically Black universities reported significantly higher self-efficacy, outcome expectations, technical interests, social support, and educational goals than did students at a predominantly White university. Gushue and Whitson (2006) found that career decision self-efficacy fully mediated the relation of two background contextual factors, gender role attitudes and ethnic identity, to career choice goals in Black and Latina girls. Byars (2006) found that nationalist and assimilationist racial ideologies were related to career self-efficacy, outcome expectations, interests, and perceived barriers.

Williams and Subich (2006) examined the hypothesis, originally proposed by Hackett and Betz (1981), that differential access to learning experiences leads to women's lower self-efficacy in Realistic and Investigative domains and men's lower self-efficacy in Social domains. They found, as hypothesized, differential reporting of access to efficacy information as a function of gender. Men reported greater access to information in the Realistic and Investigative areas, whereas women reported more experience with learning experiences in the Social area. Consistent with social cognitive theory (Bandura, 1997; Lent et al., 1994), these learning experiences, in turn, predicted both self-efficacy and outcome expectations.

Lindley (2006) provides an excellent review of research on self-efficacy in diverse populations. Among other observations, she noted that more research is needed on those with intersecting identities, such as African Americans with disabilities or gay Asian Americans. She also noted the paucity of research on outcome expectations or on interventions with diverse groups.

Interventions

A major application of social cognitive constructs to career intervention has been the development of parallel measures of interests and self-efficacy for use in career counseling. The optimal conditions for choice are moderate to high levels of both interests and confidence, but where there is interest without high levels of confidence, Bandura's (1977) sources of efficacy information can be used to increase self-efficacy and thus, possibly, expand career options. There are now many options for parallel assessment of interests and self-efficacy (confidence), and these are reviewed by Betz and Rottinghaus (2006).

More generally, SCCT is a theory with rich implications for career interventions through efforts designed to strengthen self-efficacy and outcome expectations, and also through methods of strengthening support systems and reducing or buffering barriers. In her review of intervention research, Gainor (2006) noted that research designs have included a few analogue studies, program evaluations, and about 16 quasi-experimental and experimental studies since 1981. Most studies have focused on increasing either career decision self-efficacy (Uffelman, Subich, Diegelman, Wagner, & Bardash, 2004) or on increasing women's self-efficacy for male-dominated career fields (Turner & Lapan, 2004). Although this research suggests optimism concerning the effectiveness of efficacy-focused interventions, Gainor noted that more research should focus on increasing contextual support and on eliminating social and economic barriers in educational and vocational arenas as well as on strengthening individuals' self-efficacy beliefs. Research reviewed earlier, finding that contextual supports and barriers operate in the choice-making process primarily through their influences on evolving self-efficacy beliefs and outcome expectations, would suggest that support-enhancing and barrier-reducing efforts may also be a way to influence persons' self-efficacy beliefs in various occupational domains.

Satisfaction

Finally, Lent and Brown (2006a) recently proposed an extension of SCCT to the area of job and work satisfaction (including satisfaction with educational pursuits). This extension represents an integration of trait with social cognitive perspectives, and includes a strong emphasis on personality as well as environmental factors in satisfaction. The model builds on the recent research suggesting the importance of personality variables, especially positive and negative affect and extraversion, in predicting job satisfaction (Thoresen et al., 2003).

Summary

Social cognitive career theory has received considerable interest from vocational researchers. Advances in both measuring the constructs and studying their hypothesized interrelations have been extensive. Explicit focus on conceptualizing and measuring environmental and contextual influences, especially barriers and supports, is an important direction, as is work on the relationships, reciprocal or causal, of interests and self-efficacy expectations. Studies of learning experiences relevant to the development of self-efficacy expectations have much promise. The importance of SCCT to the understanding of the career development of women and members of racial and ethnic groups has only begun to be understood; much more remains to be done in designing and evaluating interventions based on the theory. The theory has relevance for understanding a wide range of vocational behaviors relevant to both career choice and adjustment. It is likely that it will continue to receive extensive research attention.

DEVELOPMENTAL THEORIES

Over 50 years ago, Donald Super revolutionized the field of vocational psychology with his developmental career theory (Super, 1953). Among his many groundbreaking ideas was that we must consider vocation not as a one-point-in-time decision, but as a developmental process that occurs over the course of a lifetime—hence the term *career development*. His well-known developmental stages included growth, exploration, establishment, maintenance, and disengagement. Inventories assessing career development and maturity during the exploration stage were widely used in research (e.g., Crites & Savickas, 1996; Savickas & Hartung, 1996), and continue to be used internationally as well as in the

United States (Hardin, Leong, & Osipow, 2001; Leong & Serafica, 2001). Other key ideas included the postulates that career development involves an implementation of the self-concept and that individuals have many life roles differing in their salience.

Several other scholars have extended and expanded themes begun by Super's work. Examples include a developmental-contextual model of career development (Vondracek & Hartung, 2002; see also Richardson, Constantine, & Washburn, 2005) and a recent emphasis on postmodern philosophy and social constructionism in vocational theory (Richardson et al., 2005). Postmodernism in general and social constructionism in particular (see Blustein, 2006; Blustein, Schultheiss, & Flum, 2004; Savickas, 2002) challenge the view of science as an objective, unbiased endeavor and emphasize that knowledge is socially and culturally based and embedded. The contextual view also contains a strong emphasis on the connections between relational functioning and vocational functioning (Blustein et al., 2004; Richardson et al., 2005; Schultheiss, 2003). Collin and Young (2000) suggest that it is impossible to consider working without also attending to the relational context in which working occurs and the life roles with which it intersects. Blustein et al. (2004) note that relational life affects all life domains, including the domain of work and career. (A relational focus is not unique to developmental-contextual theories, but is prominent in SCCT and has been central as well in the study of women's career development and of the home-career interface; see, e.g., Gilbert & Rader, Chapter 25, this volume.)

Career constructionists agree that the term *career* has many meanings that are subjective, unique, and embedded within a social context (Blustein et al., 2004; Collin & Young, 2000). For Savickas (2002), "career denotes a reflection on the course of one's vocational behavior, rather then vocational behavior itself. This reflection can focus on actual events such as one's occupations (objective career) or on their meaning (subjective career)" (p. 152). Because the meaning of career is unique to the individual, such therapeutic techniques as autobiography, storytelling, and finding themes in one's life and behavior provide essential material in counseling (Savickas, 2002).

Super's Career Stages

There continues to be substantial research related to Super's career stages, although the amount of attention varies for the stages. Hartung, Porfeli, and Vondracek (2005) provide an excellent review of the research done on childhood vocational development, from ages 3 to 14. They conclude that vocational development begins in childhood and that much progress in vocational tasks—exploration, awareness, aspirations, interests, and adaptability (maturity)—occurs during that time. Their review communicates a rich view of early development, but this richness has not captured much empirical attention in recent years (Tracey, 2002, is one exception). Hartung et al. stress the need for longitudinal research.

Most career developmental research has addressed Super's exploration stage of career development, a major focus of which is the roles of familial and other support systems in the career exploration behaviors of young people (Kenny & Bledsoe, 2005; Kenny, Blustein, Chaves, Grossman, & Gallagher, 2003). Kenny et al. (2003) reported that support was a much stronger predictor of adaptive educational and career attitudes and behaviors than were perceived barriers in urban, largely minority ninth graders. Kenny and Bledsoe (2005) reported that family, teacher, and friend support and peer belief systems about the value of education were significantly related to four indices of career adaptability—school identification, perceptions of educational barriers, outcome expectations, and progress in career planning.

There also continues to be research on the third phase of the exploration stage, actualizing a choice, and on disruptions to the process such as career indecision, drifting, or floundering. Wiesner, Vondracek, Capaldi, and Porfeli (2003) examined predictors of four career pathways in at-risk males—they found that the most significant predictors of long-term unemployment (versus short-term unemployment, employment, and college education) included academic attainment during adolescence. This latter was in turn predicted in part by parental variables, including involvement and expectations for the child.

There is also now an increasing emphasis within the developmental/constructionist tradition on the process of career transitions for those traditionally left out of vocational research (see Blustein, Kenna,

Murphy, DeVoy, & DeWine, 2005). Exemplary studies include those of poor and working-class youth (Kenny & Bledsoe, 2005), the noncollege-bound for whom the school-to-work transition is immediate rather than delayed (Blustein, Juntunen, & Worthington, 2000; see also Hartung & Blustein, 2002); those who flounder after leaving high school, pursuing neither employment nor further education or training (e.g., Wiesner et al., 2003); and those transitioning from welfare to work (Juntunen et al., 2006).

With respect to stages following the exploration stage, Savickas (2001) has argued convincingly that the concept of career maturity makes little sense because it implies a linear, unidimensional, and hierarchical process. The establishment, maintenance, and disengagement stages do not necessarily involve linear processes (Savickas, 2001). Savickas (2001 2002) and others have suggested that the notion of "career adaptability" makes more sense as the necessary ingredient for successful negotiation of the adult career developmental process. "Career adaptability is a psychological construct that denotes an individual's readiness and resources for coping with current and anticipated tasks of vocational development" (Savickas, 2002, p. 156). (Note the overlap here with the SCCT construct of coping self-efficacy. The concept of career adaptability is also increasingly used as an indicator of work adjustment, from a trait-factor perspective; see Hesketh & Griffin, 2005.)

Savickas's (2002) reconceptualization of Super's maintenance stage as the "management" stage conveys a proactive, positively oriented set of coping mechanisms. The reduced predictability of work lives (Fouad, 2007) resulting from more frequent changes in organizations toward downsizing or even closure can include sudden unemployment and reduction or loss of anticipated retirement income. Such unpredictability requires adaptation, coping, and resiliency. In a longitudinal study, Zikic and Klehe (2006) examined predictors of reemployment status in individuals experiencing involuntary job loss. Career planning and career exploratory behaviors were significant predictors of more positive outcomes 6 months after the unemployment had occurred.

Vondracek and Hartung (2002) noted that the final stage in Super's theory, the disengagement stage, must be reconceptualized because not all careers have predetermined end points any longer. Little is known about extended careers, serial careers, and multiple retirements. Disengagement simply does not describe many career patterns today.

From Stages to Communities

Blustein's (2006) psychology of working calls for a change of focus from people who have the freedom to make career choices based on such concepts as person-environment fit and implementation of the self-concept to those who must work to eat and provide shelter for themselves and their children. He also urges much more attention to addressing societal inequalities and unequal opportunity in our research. He urges a community focus in determining the work-related needs and goals of community members and the design of interventions, which should be oriented toward social change and changes in public policy. Blustein has described this as the "emancipatory communitarian" approach to the psychology of working (Blustein, McWhirter, & Perry, 2005), which is closely related to broader social justice approaches within counseling psychology (Juntunen et al., 2006; Speight & Vera, Chapter 4, this volume).

Summary

This tradition is rich with new ideas and emphases, with scholars involved in the discussion, but it is at the same time probably the most elusive in terms of concrete research hypotheses, and its scope is so broad that there are many points of empirical entry—too many for a review of this type. The theory covers the whole life span and includes reference to all major social roles. It covers developmental tasks and vocational self-concepts and career and life themes. It includes references as well to matching concepts of trait-factor theories and self-referent ideas of SCCT, although these linkages are rarely acknowledged. No single model can summarize the theory or any statement of hypotheses to be tested.

An added complexity is that many of the concepts are intentionally subjective—this subjectivity may be relevant to career counseling, as narratives, stories, and themes provide richness and uniqueness. However, subjectivity makes communication among scientists more difficult. Methodologically, the contextual-constructionist theories lend themselves well to qualitative research, which is increasingly frequent within this tradition (see Blustein et al., 2005). Longitudinal research is also required to examine developmental processes, and more emphasis is needed in this area.

Gottfredson's Theory

Gottfredson's (2002) theory describes the cognitive career decision-making process as a developmental process involving the principles of circumscription and compromise. She postulates that a first stage of career development in childhood is the development of a social self-image, a view of one's role in the social world. This view can be influenced by gender and social class, among other things (see Gottfredson & Lapan, 1997). Also part of this view is a sense of the occupational world and its contents.

Next, children begin to narrow the range by a successive series of narrowing criteria—these begin with sex-type (where presumably occupations associated with the other sex are rejected, occurring during ages 6 to 8) and then move to social class or prestige, whereby occupations outside one's range of acceptable class level are rejected (ages 9 to 13). This latter rejection can include occupations that are perceived as more difficult as well as those perceived as below the boundaries of social level acceptability. Finally, during ages 14 and older, individuals integrate more abstract concepts like interests into their growing self-knowledge

Following this narrowing of occupational possibilities or circumscription process, compromise occurs. In this process, the individual seeks to find a balance between desirability and accessibility, to give up highly preferred but less accessible alternatives for less preferred but more realistic options. Although Gottfredson originally theorized that in making choices individuals will compromise interests first, followed by prestige, and then sex type, she revised her theory in 1996 to state that whether sex type, prestige, or interests receive priority in the compromise process depends on the discrepancy between the ideal and realistic choice. In the case of small discrepancies, interests can receive top priority; with moderate discrepancies, prestige will receive priority; and with large discrepancies, people will sacrifice interests before compromising on sex type or prestige level. Gottfredson suggests that most individuals will settle for a good, as opposed to an "optimal," choice.

Hartung et al. (2005) provide an excellent review of the roles of gender stereotypes, prestige, socioeconomic status, and interests in children's perceived vocational options, development, and aspirations. They concluded that all four have an influence. Although these conclusions suggest that gender stereotypes, prestige, and SES play an influential role in the vocational development of children, they do not provide a direct test of Gottfredson's hypotheses about the primacy of these factors at different stages of the process. One study done since 2000 (Blanchard & Lichtenberg, 2003) examined the order of prioritization under conditions of low, moderate, and high compromise. It was found that, under conditions of low compromise, Gottfredson's theory is supported in that interests receive priority, followed by prestige, and then sex type. Under conditions of moderate and high compromise, however, prestige and sex type were equally important, and both were more important than interests.

Summary

Overall, there has not been extensive research on this theory in recent years. It is difficult to study the internal processes of children, and retrospective studies have many methodological problems. Given the specificity in the ages at which the processes are to occur, and the order in which sex type, prestige, and interests are to take precedence, sophisticated research designs are needed to examine the postulates of the theory.

CONCLUSION

Most research and writing done since 2000 has focused on three vocational theories—Holland's theory, SCCT, and developmental/contextual/constructionist theories. In examining this literature, I am struck by the increasing frequency with which theorists and researchers are using concepts from more than one theory and the extent to which certain concepts are studied across theoretical orientations. As a few examples of theoretical commingling, SCCT integrates social cognitive constructs with traditional individual differences constructs, such as vocational interests, and, in the Lent and Brown (2006a) model of job satisfaction, personality and SCCT perspectives are explicitly integrated. There is great interest in the interrelationships of interests (especially the Holland interest themes) and self-efficacy (again especially the Holland confidence themes), thus further mingling trait-factor and SCCT orientations. The research of Kenny and colleagues (Kenny et al., 2003; Kenny & Bledsoe, 2005) integrates concepts and measures of supports, barriers, career development, and outcome expectations, though without noting the linkages of these concepts to other theoretical positions.

Other concepts are now used across theories. The importance of context and culture are endorsed throughout vocational research. The study of the effects of early family relationships on career development could have its basis in relational theories in the developmental tradition and in SCCT (background contextual affordances). Early family relationships are also included among the background learning experiences in studies of the development of confidence in the Holland themes (e.g., Schaub & Tokar, 2005) and of the relationships of parenting style to RIASEC circumplex structure (Tracey et al., 2006). A study of career barriers could just as easily emerge from SCCT, from constructionist perspectives, or from trait-factor approaches to studying women's career development. The major theories are being studied for relevance and utility across ethnic groups, cultures, and social classes.

Thus, although we are not at a point of full theoretical integration or convergence (see Savickas & Lent, 1994), we definitely have theoretical commingling. Researchers have realized that there are useful concepts in vocational psychology, not all associated originally with a single theoretical model. This is a positive trend—each theory can offer us some useful ideas, but our ability to increase our understanding of vocational behavior and career development across groups and across the life span may be enhanced by multiple concepts and postulates. At the same time, I would reemphasize the importance of theory-driven research—much of the richness of our vocational literature can be traced to the existence of several theories offering measurable concepts and testable hypotheses. All things considered, vocational theory and research are vibrant and growing and present a positive picture for the field of counseling psychology.

REFERENCES

Ali, S. R., McWhirter, E., & Chronister, K. (2005). Self-efficacy and vocational outcome expectations for adolescents of lower SES: A pilot study. *Journal of Career Assessment, 13*, 40–58.

Ali, S. R., & Saunders, J. L. (2006). College expectations of rural Appalachian youth: An exploration of social cognitive career theory factors. *Career Development Quarterly, 55*, 38–51.

Armstrong, P., Hubert, L., & Rounds, J. B. (2003). Circular unidimensional scaling: A new look at group differences in interest structure. *Journal of Counseling Psychology, 50*, 297–308.

Bandura, A. (1977). Self-efficacy: Toward a unifying theory of behavioral change. *Psychological Review, 84*, 191–215.

Bandura, A. (1986). *Social foundations of thought and action*. Englewood Cliffs, NJ: Prentice Hall.

Bandura, A. (1997). *Self-efficacy: The exercise of control*. New York: Freeman.

Barrick, M. R., Mount, M. K., & Gupta, R. (2003). Meta-analysis of the relationship between the Five-Factor Model and Holland's occupational types. *Personnel Psychology, 56*, 45–74.

Betz, N., Borgen, F., & Harmon, L. (2006). Vocational confidence and personality in the prediction of occupational group membership. *Journal of Career Assessment, 14*, 36–55.

Betz, N., & Gwilliam, L. (2002). The utility of measures of the Holland themes for African American and European American college students. *Journal of Career Assessment, 10*, 283–300.

Betz, N., & Hackett, G. (2006). Career self-efficacy: Back to the future. *Journal of Career Assessment, 14*, 3–11.

Betz, N., Hammond, M., & Multon, K. (2005). Reliability and validity of five-level response continua for the Career Decision Self-efficacy Scale. *Journal of Career Assessment, 13*, 131–149.

Betz, N., & Rottinghaus, P. (2006). Current research on parallel measures of interests and confidence for basic dimensions of vocational activity. *Journal of Career Assessment, 14*, 56–76.

Bieschke, K. (2006). Research self-efficacy beliefs and research outcome expectations: Implications for developing scientifically minded psychologists. *Journal of Career Assessment, 14*, 77–91.

Blanchard, C. A., & Lichtenberg, J. W. (2003). Compromise in career decision-making: A test of Gottfredson's theory. *Journal of Vocational Behavior, 62*, 250–271.

Blustein, D. (2006). *The psychology of working*. Mahwah, NJ: Erlbaum.

Blustein, D., Juntunen, C., & Worthington, R. (2000). The school-to-work transition: Adjustment challenges of the forgotten half. In S. D. Brown & R. W. Lent (Eds.), *Handbook of counseling psychology* (3rd ed., pp. 435–470). New York: Wiley.

Blustein, D., Kenna, A., Murphy, K., DeVoy, J., & DeWine, D. (2005). Qualitative research in career development. *Journal of Career Assessment, 13*, 351–370.

Blustein, D., McWhirter, E., & Perry, J. (2005). An emancipatory commutarian approach to vocational development theory, research, and practice. *Counseling Psychologist, 33*, 141–179.

Blustein, D., Schultheiss, D., & Flum, H. (2004). Toward a relationship perspective of the psychology of careers and working: A social constructionist analysis. *Journal of Vocational Behavior, 64*, 423–440.

Brown, S. D., & Gore, P. A. (1994). An evaluation of interest congruence indices: Distribution characteristics and measurement properties. *Journal of Vocational Behavior, 45*, 310–327.

Brown, S. D., & Lent, R. W. (Eds.). (2005). *Career development and counseling*. Hoboken, NJ: Wiley.

Byars, A. (2006). Racial ideology in predicting social cognitive career variables for Black undergraduates. *Journal of Vocational Behavior, 69*, 134–148.

Collin, A., & Young, R. (2000). The future of career. In A. Collin & R. Young (Eds.), *The future of career* (pp. 276–300). Cambridge: Cambridge University Press.

Crites, J. O., & Savickas, M. (1996). Revision of the Career Maturity Inventory. *Journal of Career Assessment, 4*, 131–138.

Darcy, M., & Tracey, T. (2007). Circumplex structure of Holland's RIASEC interests across gender and time. *Journal of Counseling Psychology, 54*, 17–31.

Dawis, R. V. (2005). The Minnesota Theory of Work Adjustment. In S. D. Brown & R. W. Lent (Eds.), *Career development and counseling* (pp. 3–24). Hoboken, NJ: Wiley.

Dawis, R. V., & Lofquist, L. (1984). *A psychological theory of work adjustment*. Minneapolis: University of Minnesota Press.

Eggerth, D. E., & Andrew, M. E. (2006). Modifying the C index for use with Holland codes of different length. *Journal of Career Assessment, 14*, 267–275.

Eggerth, D. E., Bowles, S. M., Tunick, R. H., & Andrew, M. E. (2005). Convergent validity of ONET Holland code classifications. *Journal of Career Assessment, 13*, 150–168.

Flores, L., Navarro, R., Smith, J., & Ploszaj, A. (2006). Testing a model of non-traditional career choice goals with Mexican American high school men. *Journal of Career Assessment, 14*, 214–234.

Flores, L., & O'Brien, K. M. (2002). The career development of Mexican American adolescent women. *Journal of Counseling Psychology, 49*, 14–27.

Fouad, N. A. (2002). Cross cultural differences in vocational interests: Between group differences on the Strong Interest Inventory. *Journal of Counseling Psychology, 49*, 283–289.

Fouad, N. A. (2007). Work and vocational psychology: Theory, research, and applications. *Annual Review of Psychology, 58*, 1–22.

Fouad, N. A., & Guillen, A. (2006). Outcome expectations: Looking to the past and potential future. *Journal of Career Assessment, 14*, 130–142.

Fouad, N. A., Smith, P., & Zao, K. E. (2002). Across academic domains: Extensions of the social cognitive career model. *Journal of Counseling Psychology, 49*, 164–171.

Fouad, N. A., & Walker, C. M. (2005). Cultural influences on responses to items on the Strong Interest Inventory. *Journal of Vocational Behavior, 66*, 104–123.

Gainor, K. A. (2006). Twenty five years of self-efficacy in career assessment and practice. *Journal of Career Assessment, 14*, 143–160.

Gore, P. A. (2006). Academic self-efficacy as a predictor of college outcomes. *Journal of Career Assessment, 14*, 92–115.

Gore, P. A., & Brown, S. (2006). Simpler may be better: A reply to Eggerth and Andrew. *Journal of Career Assessment, 14*, 276–282.

Gore, P. A., & Hitch, J. (2005). Occupational classification and sources of occupational information. In S. D. Brown & R. W. Lent (Eds.), *Career development and counseling* (pp. 382–416). Hoboken, NJ: Wiley.

Gore, P. A., & Leuwerke, W. C. (2000). Predicting occupational considerations: A comparison of self-efficacy beliefs, outcome expectations, and person-environment congruence. *Journal of Career Assessment, 8*(2), 37–250.

Gottfredson, L. (2002). Gottfredson's theory of circumscription, compromise, and self-creation. In D. Brown & Associates (Eds.), *Career choice and development* (4th ed., pp. 85–148). San Francisco: Jossey-Bass.

Gottfredson, L., & Lapan, R. (1997). Assessing gender based circumscription of occupational aspirations. *Journal of Career Assessment, 5*, 355–474.

Gupta, S., & Tracey, T. (2005). Dharma and interest-occupation congruence in Asian Indian college students. *Journal of Career Assessment, 13*, 320–336.

Gushue, G. V., & Whitson, M. L. (2006). The relationship of ethnic identity and gender role attitudes to career choice goals among Black and Latina girls. *Journal of Counseling Psychology, 53*, 379–385.

Hackett, G., & Betz, N. E. (1981). A self-efficacy approach to the career development of women. *Journal of Vocational Behavior, 18*, 326–339.

Hansen, J. C. (2005). Assessment of interests. In S. D. Brown & R. W. Lent (Eds.), *Career development and counseling* (pp. 281–304). Hoboken, NJ: Wiley.

Hardin, E., Leong, F., & Osipow, S. (2001). Cultural relativity in the conceptualization of career maturity. *Journal of Vocational Behavior, 58*, 36–52.

Hartung, P., & Blustein, D. (2002). Reason, intuition, and social justice: Elaborating on Parson's career decision making model. *Journal of Counseling and Development, 80*, 41–47.

Hartung, P., Porfeli, E., & Vondracek, F. (2005). Child vocational development: A review and reconsideration. *Journal of Vocational Behavior, 66*, 385–419.

Hesketh, B., & Griffin, B. (2005). Work adjustment. In W. B. Walsh & M. Savickas (Eds.), *Handbook of vocational psychology* (3rd ed., pp. 245–266). Mahwah, NJ: Erlbaum.

Holland, J. L. (1997). *Making vocational choices: A theory of vocational personalities and work environments* (3rd ed.). Odessa, FL: PAR.

Juntunen, C., Cavett, A., Clow, R. B., Rempel, V., Darrow, R., & Guilmino, A. (2006). Social justice through self-sufficiency. In R. Toporek, L. Gerstein, N. Fouad, G. Roysicar, & T. Israel (Eds.), *Handbook of social justice in counseling psychology* (pp. 294–312). Thousand Oaks, CA: Sage.

Kahn, J., & Nauta, M. (2001). Social cognitive predictors of first year college persistence. *Research in Higher Education, 42*, 633–652.

Kenny, M. E., & Bledsoe, M. (2005). Contributions of the relational context to career adaptability among urban adolescents. *Journal of Vocational Behavior, 66*, 257–272.

Kenny, M. E., Blustein, D., Chaves, A., Grossman, A., & Gallagher, L. (2003). The role of perceived barriers and relational support in the educational and vocational lives of urban high school students. *Journal of Counseling Psychology, 50*, 142–155.

Larson, L. M., Rottinghaus, P. J., & Borgen, F. H. (2002). Meta-analyses of big six interests and big five personality variables. *Journal of Vocational Behavior, 61*, 217–239.

Lent, R. W. (2005). A social cognitive view of career development and counseling. In S. D. Brown & R. W. Lent (Eds.), *Career development and counseling: Putting theory and research to work* (pp. 101–130). Hoboken, NJ: Wiley.

Lent, R. W., & Brown, S. D. (2006a). Integrating person- and situation perspectives on work satisfaction: A social cognitive view. *Journal of Vocational Behavior, 69*, 236–247.

Lent, R. W., & Brown, S. D. (2006b). On conceptualizing and assessing social cognitive constructs in career research: A measurement guide. *Journal of Career Assessment, 14*, 12–35.

Lent, R. W., Brown, S. D., Brenner, B., Chopra, S. B., Davis, T., Talleyrand, R., et al. (2001). The role of contextual supports and barriers in the choice of math/science educational options. *Journal of Counseling Psychology, 48*, 474–483.

Lent, R. W., Brown, S. D., & Hackett, G. (1994). Toward a unifying social cognitive theory of career and academic interest, choice, and performance. *Journal of Vocational Behavior, 45*, 79–122.

Lent, R. W., Brown, S. D., & Hackett, G. (2000). Contextual supports and barriers to career choice: A social cognitive analysis. *Journal of Counseling Psychology, 31*, 356–362.

Lent, R. W., Brown, S. D., Nota, L., & Soresi, S. (2003). Testing social cognitive interest and choice hypotheses across Holland types in Italian high school students. *Journal of Vocational Behavior, 62*, 101–118.

Lent, R. W., Brown, S. D., Schmidt, J., Brenner, B., Lyons, H., & Treistman, D. (2003). Relation of contextual supports and barriers to choice behavior in engineering majors. *Journal of Counseling Psychology, 50*, 458–465.

Lent, R. W., Brown, S. D., Sheu, H.-B., Schmidt, J., Brenner, B., Gloster, C. S., et al. (2005). Social cognitive predictors of academic interests and goals in engineering: Utility for women and students at historically black universities. *Journal of Counseling Psychology, 52*, 84–92.

Lent, R. W., Brown, S. D., Talleyrand, R., McPartland, E. B., Davis, T., Chopra, S. B., et al. (2002). Career choice barriers, supports, and coping strategies. *Journal of Vocational Behavior, 60*, 61–72.

Lent, R. W., Tracey, T. J. G., Brown, S. D., Soresi, S., & Nota, L. (2006). Development of interests and competency beliefs in Italian adolescents: An exploration of circumplex structure and bidirectional relationships. *Journal of Counseling Psychology, 53*, 181–191.

Leong, F., & Serafica, F. (2001). Cross-cultural perspective on Super's career development theory. In F. Leong & A. Barak (Eds.), *Contemporary models in vocational psychology* (pp. 167–206). New York: Erlbaum.

Lindley, L. D. (2006). The paradox of self-efficacy: Research with diverse populations. *Journal of Career Assessment, 14*, 143–160.

Lindley, L. D., & Borgen, F. H. (2002). Generalized self-efficacy, Holland theme self-efficacy, and academic performance. *Journal of Career Assessment, 10*, 301–314.

Lyons, H., Brenner, B., & Fassinger, R. (2005). A multicultural test of the theory of work adjustment: Investigating the role of heterosexism and fit perceptions in the job satisfaction of lesbian, gay, and bisexual employees. *Journal of Counseling Psychology, 52*, 537–548.

Lyons, H., & O'Brien, K. (2006). The role of person-environment fit in the job satisfaction and tenure intentions of African American employees. *Journal of Counseling Psychology, 53*, 387–396.

Luzzo, D. (2000). *Career counseling of college students.* Washington, DC: American Psychological Association.

McCrae, R. R., & Costa, P. T. (1997). Personality trait structure as a human universal. *American Psychologist, 52*, 509–516.

Nauta, M. (2004). Self-efficacy as a mediator of the relationships between personality factors and career interests. *Journal of Career Assessment, 12*, 381–394.

Nauta, M., & Epperson, D. (2003). A longitudinal examination of the social-cognitive model applied to high school girls' choices of nontraditional college majors and aspirations. *Journal of Counseling Psychology, 50*, 448–457.

Nauta, M., Kahn, J. H., Angell, J. W., & Cantarelli, E. A. (2002). Identifying the antecedent in the relation between career interests and self-efficacy. *Journal of Counseling Psychology, 49*, 290–301.

Parsons, F. (1909). *Choosing a vocation.* Boston: Houghton Mifflin.

Richardson, M. S., Constantine, K., & Washburn, M. (2005). New directions for theory development in vocational psychology. In W. B. Walsh & M. Savickas (Eds.), *Handbook of vocational psychology* (3rd ed., pp. 51–84). Mahwah, NJ: Erlbaum.

Rottinghaus, P. J., Betz, N., & Borgen, F. (2003). Validity of parallel measures of vocational interests and confidence. *Journal of Career Assessment, 11*, 355–378.

Rottinghaus, P. J., Day, S. X., & Borgen, F. H. (2005). The Career Futures Inventory: A measure of career related adaptability and optimism. *Journal of Career Assessment, 13*, 3–24.

Rottinghaus, P. J., Larson, L. M., & Borgen, F. H. (2003). The relation of self-efficacy and interests: A meta-analysis of 60 samples. *Journal of Vocational Behavior, 62*, 221–236.

Rounds, J., & Tracey, T. (1993). Prediger's dimensional representation of Holland's RIASEC circumplex. *Journal of Applied Psychology, 78*, 875–890.

Savickas, M. (2001). Toward a comprehensive theory of career development. In F. Leong & A. Barak (Eds.), *Contemporary models in vocational psychology* (pp. 295–320). Mahwah, NJ: Erlbaum.

Savickas, M. (2002). Career construction: Developmental theory of vocational behavior. In D. Brown & Associates (Eds.), *Career choice and development* (4th ed., pp. 149–205). San Francisco: Jossey-Bass.

Savickas, M., & Hartung, P. J. (1996). The Career Development Inventory in review: Psychometric and research findings. *Journal of Career Assessment, 4,* 171–188.

Savickas, M. L., & Lent, R.W. (Eds.). (1994). *Convergence in career development theories.* Palo Alto: CPP Books.

Schaub, M., & Tokar, D. (2005). The role of personality and learning experiences in social cognitive career theory. *Journal of Vocational Behavior, 66,* 304–325.

Schultheiss, D. E. P. (2003). A relational approach to career counseling. *Journal of Counseling and Development, 81,* 301–310.

Silvia, P. J. (2003). Self-efficacy and interest: Experimental studies of optimal incompetence. *Journal of Vocational Behavior, 62,* 237–249.

Spokane, A. R., & Cruza-Guet, M. C. (2005). Holland's theory of vocational personalities in work environments. In S. D. Brown & R. W. Lent (Eds.), *Career development and counseling* (pp. 24–41). Hoboken, NJ: Wiley.

Spokane, A. R., Fouad, N., & Swanson, J. (2003). Culture-centered career intervention. *Journal of Vocational Behavior, 62,* 453–458.

Spokane, A. R., Meir, E. I., & Catalano, M. (2000). Person-environment congruence and Holland's theory: A review and reconsideration. *Journal of Vocational Behavior, 57,* 137–187.

Sullivan, B. A., & Hansen, J. C. (2004). Mapping associations between interests and personality: Toward a conceptual understanding of individual differences in vocational behavior. *Journal of Counseling Psychology, 51,* 287–298.

Super, D. (1953). A theory of vocational development. *American Psychologist, 8,* 185–190.

Swanson, J. L., & Fouad, N. (1999). *Career theory and practice.* Thousand Oaks, CA: Sage.

Swanson, J. L., & Gore, P. A. (2000). Advances in vocational psychology theory and research. In S. D. Brown & R. W. Lent (Eds.), *Handbook of counseling psychology* (3rd ed., pp. 233–269). New York: Wiley.

Thoresen, C. J., Kaplan, S. A., Barsky, A. P., Warren, C. R., & de Chermont, K. (2003). The affective underpinnings of job perceptions and attitudes. *Psychological Bulletin, 129,* 914–945.

Tinsley, H. E. A. (2000). The congruence myth: An examination of the efficacy of the person-environment fit model. *Journal of Vocational Behavior, 56,* 147–179.

Tinsley, H. E. A. (2006). A pig in a suit is still a pig: A comment on "Modifying the C index for use with Holland codes of unequal length." *Journal of Career Assessment, 14,* 283–288.

Tracey, T. J. G. (2002). Development of interests and competency beliefs. *Journal of Counseling Psychology, 49,* 148–163.

Tracey, T. J. G., & Hopkins, N. (2001). Correspondence of interests and abilities with occupational choice. *Journal of Counseling Psychology, 48,* 113–172.

Tracey, T. J. G., Lent, R. W., Brown, S. D., Soresi, S., & Nota, L. (2006). Adherence to RIASEC structure in relation to career exploration and parenting style: Longitudinal and idiothetic considerations. *Journal of Vocational Behavior, 69,* 248–261.

Tracey, T. J. G., & Robbins, S. B. (2005). Stability of interests across ethnicity and gender: A longitudinal examination of grades 8 through 12. *Journal of Vocational Behavior, 67,* 335–364.

Tsabari, O., Tziner, A., & Meir, E. I. (2005). Updated meta-analysis on the relationship between congruence and satisfaction. *Journal of Career Assessment, 13,* 216–232.

Turner, S. L., & Lapan, R. T. (2004). Evaluation of an intervention to increase non-traditional career interests and career-related self-efficacy among middle school adolescents. *Journal of Vocational Behavior, 66,* 516–531.

Tyler, L. E. (1995). The challenge of diversity. In D. Lubinsky & R. Dawis (Eds.), *Assessing individual differences in human behavior* (pp. 1–13). Palo Alto, CA: Davies Black.

Uffelman, R. A., Subich, L. M., Diegelman, N. M., Wagner, K. S., & Bardash, R. J. (2004). Effect of mode of interest assessment on clients' career decision self-efficacy. *Journal of Career Assessment, 12,* 366–380.

Vondracek, F. W., & Hartung, P. (2002). Innovating career development using advances in life course and life span planning. *Journal of Vocational Behavior, 61,* 375–380.

Walsh, W. B., & Heppner, M. (2006). *Handbook of career counseling of women.* Mahwah, NJ: Erlbaum.

Walsh, W. B., & Savickas, M. (2005). *Handbook of vocational psychology* (3rd ed.). Mahwah, NJ: Erlbaum.

Wiesner, M., Vondracek, F., Capaldi, D., & Porfeli, E. (2003). Childhood and adolescent predictors of early adult career pathways. *Journal of Vocational Behavior, 63,* 305–328.

Williams, C. M., & Subich, L. (2006). The gendered nature of career-related learning experiences: A social cognitive career theory perspective. *Journal of Vocational Behavior, 69*, 262–275.

Yang, W., Stokes, G. S., & Hui, C. H. (2005). Cross cultural validation of Holland's interest structure in Chinese population. *Journal of Vocational Behavior, 67*, 379–396.

Zikic, J., & Klehe, U.-C. (2006). Job loss as a blessing in disguise. *Journal of Vocational Behavior, 69*, 391–409.

CHAPTER 22

Vocational Psychology and Individual Differences

PATRICK IAN ARMSTRONG
JAMES B. ROUNDS

According to estimates from the U.S. Department of Labor's Bureau of Labor Statistics, there are more than 140 million employed adults in the United States, and this number is projected to increase to more than 160 million by 2014 (Hecker, 2005). The wide range of options available to individuals entering the labor market can make educational and career choices difficult and stressful. A critical role for vocational psychology is to facilitate the linking of individuals to educational and career opportunities in which they can become successful and satisfied. This chapter focuses on how measures of individual differences help counseling psychologists in their work with clients struggling to resolve issues related to career decisions and work adjustment. We also examine how individual differences measures are used in the field of vocational psychology to predict work performance and satisfaction.

This chapter begins with a brief overview of applications of individual differences in vocational psychology and conceptualizations of career success. The discussion of individual differences measures is divided into sections on the validity evidence for cognitive and noncognitive predictors of career-related outcomes such as job performance and career choices. Traditionally, cognitive and noncognitive measures have been viewed as distinct, separate areas of study. However, there have been attempts to combine information obtained using both types of measures to predict career-related outcomes. We review issues related to the development of integrated models of individual differences, including methodological issues related to using multiple indicators in predicting career-related outcomes. We also examine models put forward to integrate cognitive and noncognitive individual differences measures, and provide a critical look at how sex differences in these measures may play an important role in the ongoing debate over the poor representation of women in the "hard" sciences, mathematics, and engineering.

APPLICATIONS OF INDIVIDUAL DIFFERENCES

Individual Differences and Counseling Psychology

Working with individuals to promote successful career development using individual differences measures is not a new role for counseling psychologists (Dawis, 1992). Although the mandate of counseling psychology has expanded beyond its vocational roots, as evidenced by the wide range of issues and research findings in this volume, issues related to career development remain a cornerstone of our profession. Individual difference measures used in vocational psychology can predict what Ozer and Benet-Martinez (2006) refer to as consequential outcomes: "Certain life outcomes and events are widely recognized as important—important for individuals and important for the society in which they live" (p. 402). From this perspective, measures of individual differences are important to the extent that they can be used to predict meaningful, or consequential, career-related outcomes.

The authors thank David Lubinski for his feedback on this chapter.

In the field of counseling psychology we are often interested in more than simply predicting outcomes, no matter how consequential they may be. The prediction of career choices and job performance is important, and provides validity evidence for individual differences measures. As noted by Prediger and Johnson (1979), however, counseling often involves expanding the range of options being considered by clients. Therefore, the notion of consequential outcomes in the field of counseling psychology can be viewed more broadly to include goals such as expanding the range of options considered by career counseling clients. The ultimate goal of this expanded view is to help clients make choices that have the best chance of maximizing their occupational success and satisfaction.

Defining Career Success

Career success can be viewed as arising primarily from two sources: intrinsic and extrinsic rewards (Judge, Higgins, Thoresen, & Barrick, 1999; Ozer & Benet-Martinez, 2006). *Intrinsic* career success reflects the level of job satisfaction obtained by an individual. *Extrinsic* career success reflects concepts such as work performance, income level, and occupational status. There may be some overlap between these conceptualizations because an individual may be satisfied with a career choice because of its financial rewards. However, the key distinction between intrinsic and extrinsic career success lies in the difference between an internalized, subjective sense of success experienced by the individual versus an externalized measure of the rewards associated with an occupation.

In addition to satisfaction produced by intrinsic and extrinsic rewards, the fit between individuals and career choices can be measured by comparing abilities with job performance requirements, and needs with job reinforcers. *Satisfactoriness* is the term often used to describe the extent to which cognitive abilities possessed by individuals are compatible with the cognitive demands of occupations (Dawis & Lofquist, 1984). From an employer's perspective, workers are sought who possess the abilities, skills, and training (or the capacity to become trained) to fulfill job requirements. From the individual's perspective, potential employment opportunities are evaluated based primarily on their intrinsic and extrinsic rewards. Individuals are satisfactory for a job to the extent that they have the intellectual capacities and associated skills and training to perform job tasks, but individuals will be satisfied with a job to the extent that their needs are met by the job, and they perceive the job as being consistent with their interests, personality traits, and abilities. The challenge when studying career decisions, therefore, is to develop methods to balance both cognitive abilities with cognitive demands, and noncognitive traits with intrinsic and extrinsic rewards.

The gravitational hypothesis, first proposed by McCormick, Jeanneret, and Mecham (1972), has been put forward as a model of how cognitive and noncognitive individual differences impact career development over time. McCormick, DeNisi, and Shaw (1979) proposed: "People tend to gravitate toward and remain in jobs that they are able to perform and that are reasonably compatible with their personal characteristics" (p. 52). Individual differences in the capacity to perform job requirements will lead to gravitation toward occupations with higher or lower levels of cognitive demands in accordance with the individual's intellectual capacities. Simultaneously, individual differences in noncognitive traits, combined with variability in the rewards offered by occupations, will lead to gravitation toward those occupations that provide the most desirable intrinsic and extrinsic rewards (Reeve & Heggestad, 2004; Wilk, Desmarais, & Sackett, 1995). Career adjustment is impacted by experiences in the environment, as individuals strive to match both cognitive and noncognitive characteristics to the demands and rewards of the workplace (Hogan & Roberts, 2004; Roberts, Caspi, & Moffitt, 2003).

COGNITIVE AND NONCOGNITIVE MEASURES

Our review of individual differences measures in vocational psychology is divided into two sections: cognitive and noncognitive measures. Measures of cognitive abilities, especially General Mental Ability (GMA), are frequently used to predict job performance, and noncognitive measures of interests and personality are frequently used to predict job satisfaction and career choices, as well as job performance. Research on job performance criteria can be used to develop selection criteria for employment decisions, and selection criteria are most effective when the number of applicants is large relative to the number of positions (Taylor & Russell, 1939). Counseling psychologists do not have the luxury of choosing the best clients from a large pool of applicants. They are ethically bound to provide services to individuals from diverse backgrounds and will often focus on noncognitive measures such as interests, personality, and self-efficacy beliefs. Both types of individual differences measures provide useful information for linking people to career options (Dawis, 1996).

Cognitive Predictors of Career-Related Outcomes

Cognitive measures of General Mental Ability (GMA) are effective predictors of job performance and level of occupational attainment (Schmidt & Hunter, 1998, 2004). In a review of 85 years of research on selection criteria that are used in personnel decision making, Schmidt and Hunter (1998) found that GMA measures had a mean validity coefficient (r) of .51 for overall job performance. A recent meta-analysis performed in the United Kingdom found similar results (Beruta, Anderson, & Salgado, 2005). GMA is also an important predictor of performance in academic settings (Kuncel, Hezlett, & Ones, 2001, 2004). Kuncel and Hezlett (2007) have subsequently synthesized nine meta-analyses and demonstrated that standardized admission tests (e.g., Graduate Record Examination, Law School Admissions Test, Medical College Admissions Test) predict many measures of student success better than academic grades. Nevertheless, a combination of standardized test scores and grades are the best predictors of success.

Schmidt and Hunter (2004) reported that the effects of GMA on job performance and training success are contingent on the level of cognitive complexity for an occupation, with the highest validity coefficients observed in occupations at the highest levels of cognitive complexity. They also cited the findings of Judge et al. (1999), who reported that general mental ability level measured in early adolescence can predict adult levels of occupational attainment ($r = .51$) and income ($r = .53$). There is an important caveat to the conclusions drawn by Schmidt and Hunter: "GMA predicts one's ultimate attained job level, but it does not predict which occupation at that level one will enter. That role falls to interests" (Schmidt & Hunter, 2004, p. 163).

The meta-analytic work by Schmidt and Hunter (1998 2004) demonstrates the importance of GMA in predicting job performance, training success, and level of occupational attainment. Longitudinal research by Austin and Hanisch (1990) also supports the central role of GMA in job performance in an analysis of the predictors of occupational attainment from the Project Talent dataset (more than 13,000 high school students with an 11-year follow-up after graduation). The discriminant function analyses they conducted included variables measuring abilities, interest, gender, and socioeconomic status. Overall, Austin and Hanisch found that the best predictor of attainment was a composite score interpreted as representing general mental ability, with the second best predictor being a composite score of gender and mathematics. These first two factors primarily representing cognitive abilities and gender accounted for 81.9% of the variance in occupational attainment. Three additional composite scores that included interest variables increased the variance accounted for to 96.8%, which supports the incremental validity of noncognitive predictors of occupational attainment.

Austin and Hanisch (1990) showed that individual differences measures are effective predictors of career-related outcomes over an extended 13-year period, despite being measured at a young age. These results highlight the central importance of cognitive ability in the career development process. Austin and Hanisch questioned the relative utility of interests in the counseling process: "Given the proportions of between-groups variance accounted for by the first two functions, counseling psychologists may have been using interest to a greater extent than warranted by their influence on occupational attainment" (pp. 84–85). If the goal of career counseling is to predict occupational attainment, then Austin and Hanisch are right to suggest a move toward an increased emphasis on cognitive measures. The field of counseling psychology does not have a narrow focus on using measures of individual differences to predict levels of occupational attainment (see Dawis, 1992; Prediger & Johnston, 1979). Issues related to predicting occupational attainment are important to career-related outcomes, but career practitioners are also interested in predicting occupational satisfaction as well as attainment. Furthermore, as discussed in the following subsection, personality and interest measures add incremental validity to measures of GMA when predicting occupational attainment and do a better job than GMA in predicting occupational satisfaction. Thus, both cognitive and noncognitive variables are useful in vocational research.

Longitudinal analyses on the relationships among personality, GMA, and career success were also conducted by Judge et al. (1999). This research is notable because it included separate analyses of intrinsic and extrinsic concepts of career success. Data were obtained from three longitudinal studies obtained from the intergenerational studies program at the University of California at Berkeley; participants were recruited from 1928 to 1931 and followed through retirement. For measures of intrinsic career success, the key predictors were personality, with a multivariate R of .42; in comparison, the R value for GMA was .09 which showed no incremental validity over personality in predicting intrinsic career success. For extrinsic success, the Rs for personality traits and GMA were .54 and .53, respectively, with a combined R for the two sets of constructs of .64. From a usefulness standpoint, these results suggest that personality traits play a role in determining both intrinsic and extrinsic career success, whereas GMA is primarily involved in extrinsic success.

Gottfredson (2003) has claimed that cognitive assessments in career counseling have been limited because of potential difficulties in presenting results to clients. With an interest measure, the finding that one person prefers working with things and another person prefers working with ideas does not necessarily imply the superiority of one person over the other. Although some individuals may attach greater prestige, status, and desirability to some types of occupations than to others, a career counselor can explore the notion of interests without implying that some choices are inherently superior. The challenge with using cognitive measures in counseling, therefore, is to find ways to include this information in the career counseling process to constructively expand the range of options considered by individuals, and not simply to predict their level of success. For example, measures of specific abilities may help clients fine-tune their occupational choices by identifying occupations that make the most effective use of their particular constellations of abilities (see Dawis, 2005; Dawis & Lofquist, 1984; Humphreys, Lubinski, & Yao, 1993; Lubinski & Benbow, 2006).

Noncognitive Predictors of Career-Related Outcomes

Literature by vocational psychologists has explored a wide range of noncognitive constructs when compared with the cognitive predictor literature, where debate focuses primarily on interpretations of GMA. Research on the utility of noncognitive measures such as interests and personality typically focuses on two issues: (1) the incremental validity of noncognitive measures in predicting job performance over and above GMA, and (2) the use of interests, personality, and self-efficacy beliefs to predict work satisfaction and career choices. There is a long tradition in vocational psychology of using interest measures to predict career choices (see, e.g., Fryer, 1931). Interests reflect preferences for activities and work environments, and as such can be effective for predicting future aspirations of students and the occupations they choose up to 23 years later (Campbell, 1971; Hansen & Campbell, 1985; Hansen & Dik, 2005). Additional validity evidence is found in research examining the extent to which interest measures can predict the current occupations of employed individuals (Dik & Hansen, 2004; Donnay & Borgen, 1996).

Interests are stable over time (Low, Yoon, Roberts, & Rounds, 2005), which may contribute to their strong predictive validity. Low et al. (2005) estimated the stability of vocational interests at different life stages in a meta-analytic review of 66 longitudinal studies. Interests were observed to be relatively stable, even in early adolescence. Stability estimates for different age periods from adolescence to middle adulthood suggest that, contrary to popular notions about interest development, rank order and profile stabilities of vocational interests changed very little during the greater part of adolescence (Low & Rounds, in press). Also, contrary to common wisdom (e.g., Campbell, 1971), stability rose markedly only during the beginning of emerging adulthood (ages 18 to 22) and reached a plateau for the remainder of the next 2 decades.

There are several explanations for this observed developmental trend. The marked increase in stability during the age period of 18 to 22 years coincides with emerging adulthood in which adolescents leave their families and high schools for novel settings such as college or the workforce. With fewer environmental constraints, individuals are more likely to choose the contexts (e.g., educational courses, work, leisure activities, and social relationships) that best fit their interests. These experiences can reinforce the characteristics that led people to those experiences in the first place, resulting in an elaboration, refinement, and stability of interests. After the period of 18 to 22 years when interests plateau, the individual enters adulthood. This involves increased commitment to other life roles, such as being a worker, spouse, or parent (Levinson, 1986). These commitments restrict the latitude an individual has in changing environments. A person's talents, expectations, irreversible choices, and credentials further diminish the range of movement after entry into the workforce. Interests, therefore, increase in stability within a small window of time (18 to 22 years), after which the constancy of workplace environments limits the frequency of new experiences, as well as curtails further elaboration of fit between the individual and new environments.

Interest-based research typically focuses on Holland's (1959, 1997) RIASEC model of vocational personality types and work environments. Holland's model includes six categories of interests and types of work environments: Realistic (R), Investigative (I), Artistic (A), Social (S), Enterprising (E), and Conventional (C). This model has been used to classify individuals' interests and occupations and has influenced the development of interest measures (Campbell & Borgen, 1999). By matching an individual's interests to occupational characteristics by Holland category, it is possible to identify potential career choices for career counseling clients (McDaniel & Snell, 1999). A spatial model of the types was proposed by Holland, Whitney, Cole, and Richards (1969), using a hexagon to represent the interrelations between the types ordered clockwise, resulting in what is frequently termed the R-I-A-S-E-C model. As illustrated in Figure 22.1, the degree of similarity between any two of the types is inversely proportional to the distances between them on the hexagon. Areas of the spatial model where

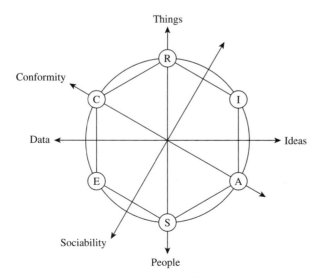

Figure 22.1   Prediger's (1982) Data-Ideas and People-Things Dimensions and Hogan's (1983) Sociability and Conformity Dimensions Embedded in Holland's RIASEC Model. Gender differences in the People-Things dimension may be implicated in the different career trajectories of mathematically talented men and women (Lubinski & Benbow, 2006).

the individual's interests are strongest can be identified using the results of an interest inventory, and the level of congruence for an occupational choice can be assessed by the distance between the location of strongest interests and an occupational choice (Rounds & Day, 1999).

Meta-analyses of studies reporting correlations between RIASEC interest types have generally supported the structure of Holland's theory (Rounds & Tracey, 1993; Tracey & Rounds, 1993). Day, Rounds, and Swaney (1998), for example, examined the fit of Holland's model with large representative samples of students who completed the ACT Interest Inventory (ACT, 1995), and found a good fit for the Holland model with both male and female samples representing different U.S. racial-ethnic groups. Fouad, Harmon, and Borgen (1997) reported similar results to those of Day and colleagues with large representative samples of successfully employed adults from U.S. racial-ethnic groups who completed the Strong Interest Inventory (SII; Harmon, Hansen, Borgen, & Hammer, 1994). Anderson, Tracey, and Rounds (1997) found the fit of the RIASEC data to be similar for both males and females who completed the SII. This research provides evidence for the construct validity of Holland's RIASEC types and structural hypothesis.

There continues to be some debate about the fit of the Holland model in U.S. minority group and international samples. In a comprehensive meta-analysis, Rounds and Tracey (1996) compared the fit of RIASEC correlation matrices from 20 U.S. ethnic group samples and 76 international samples with a U.S. benchmark group of 74 matrices. Rounds and Tracey reported that Holland's model was a better fit for the benchmark samples than for the U.S. ethnic groups and international samples, and found that an alternative model proposed by Gati (1979, 1991) was a better fit than the Holland model.

Armstrong, Hubert, and Rounds (2003) reanalyzed the Day et al. (1998) and Fouad et al. (1997) data using recent statistical methods developed to fit circular structures (Hubert, Arabie, & Meulman, 1997), and found the fit of the Holland model to be lower for African American and Hispanic samples than for Caucasian and Asian American samples. As illustrated in Figure 22.2, by examining the pattern of unequal distances between types for racial-ethnic groups, it may be possible to identify areas of improvement for RIASEC-based measures. Armstrong and colleagues identified two patterns of structural inconsistency across racial-ethnic groups, *type isolation* and *type compression*. Both patterns suggest that additional work is needed to improve the construct validity of the measures for use with diverse groups. Type isolation occurs when the distances between a type and its two adjacent types account for more than 50% of the circumference of the circular structure, effectively isolating that type on one half of the circumplex. This structural pattern can be seen with the Artistic scale for the Hispanic American men and women who completed the Strong Interest Inventory, which suggests that additional work is needed to increase the integration of the isolated types into the work continuum being represented by the six RIASEC scales.

In comparison, type compression occurs when the distance between two scales is very small. This occurs for Realistic-Investigative and for Enterprising-Conventional with African American men and women and also for Hispanic American women who completed the SII. Realistic-Investigative type compression was also observed for female students in a longitudinal study by Darcy and Tracey (2007) and is an issue in samples drawn from China (Long & Tracey, 2006). Overall, these results suggest that distinctions between types made in Holland's model may not be as salient for members of diverse racial-ethnic groups.

Interests can also be assessed more narrowly by focusing on basic interests rather than RIASEC types (Day & Rounds, 1997). The first set of widely used basic interest measures were developed by Campbell, Borgen, Eastes, Johansson, and Peterson (1968) for the Strong Vocational Interest Blank (Campbell, 1971; Strong, 1943). Basic interest scales were created to provide interpretive information to enhance Strong's empirically developed Occupational Scales by providing insight into the "organization of an individual's choices" (Campbell et al., 1968, p. 54). Campbell et al. noted that the Occupational Scales were effective for identifying potential interest in specific occupational titles, but the heterogeneous content of these scales made it difficult to expand the interpretation of results to other occupations. By grouping items into homogeneous content areas, Basic Interests provided a structured, standardized way to begin a discussion of how interests can be expanded beyond the scope of a specific occupation.

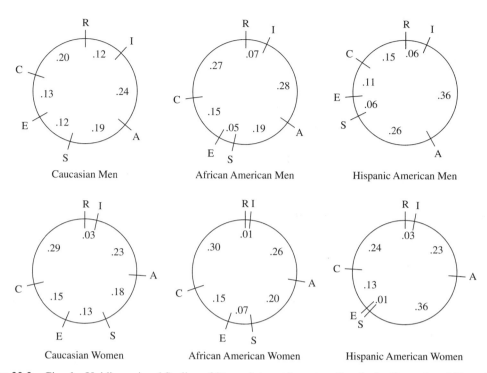

Figure 22.2   Circular Unidimensional Scaling of Strong Interest Inventory Results for Caucasian, African American, and Hispanic American Men and Women. Group differences in the structure of RIASEC types suggest that additional work is needed to improve the construct validity of Holland-based measures for diverse racial-ethnic groups.
   Source: "Circular Unidimensional Scaling: A New Look at Group Differences in Interest Structure," by P. I. Armstrong, L. Hubert, and J. Rounds, 2003, *Journal of Counseling Psychology, 50,* pp. 303–306. Copyright 2003 by the American Psychological Association. Adapted with permission.

When comparing the validity of the Basic Interest Scales of the 1994 edition of the Strong Interest Inventory with the Holland-based General Occupational Themes, Donnay and Borgen (1996) found the basic interest scales to be the most valid predictors of occupational group membership and concluded: "Basic interest scales more effectively deal with the reality of a complex multivariate space" (p. 288).

To augment information obtained from interest assessments, measures of other noncognitive constructs, such as personality and self-efficacy, can provide useful information for predicting work performance, job satisfaction, and career choices. Gasser, Larson, and Borgen (2004) found that after controlling for gender, the California Personality Inventory scales of Achievement via Independence, Conceptual Fluency, and Insightfulness as well as the Strong Interest Inventory Investigative and Learning Environment scales all provided unique information for predicting future educational aspirations. Betz and Rottinghaus (2006) reported that basic interest measures had higher validity in predicting occupational membership than a set of corresponding self-efficacy measures, but the combined use of both sets of measures was more effective than using either set independently (see also Donnay & Borgen, 1999). Ralston, Borgen, Rottinghaus, and Donnay (2004) reported similar incremental validity results for combining interests and self-efficacy measures when predicting a major program of study in a sample of college students. A recent meta-analysis by Judge, Jackson, Shaw, Scott, and Rich (2007) demonstrated that self-efficacy measures provide little incremental validity for predicting job performance after controlling for GMA and the big five personality factors. Thus, self-efficacy beliefs may add incremental validity to interests in predicting occupational and college major choices, but may not add above GMA and various personality characteristics (e.g., conscientiousness) in predicting work performance, especially for complex work tasks.

Meta-analytic research on the correlations between interest and self-efficacy support the unique contributions of each measure (Rottinghaus, Larson, & Borgen, 2003). This research also suggests that there is a strong association between individuals' liking of an area of work and having confidence in their ability to do the work. In short, people tend to like doing things they are good at, and dislike things they are not good at, but unique information is provided by measures of both interests and self-efficacy (Betz & Rottinghaus, 2006). Addressing discrepancies between interests and efficacy beliefs can be effective in counseling for career choices because a focus on discrepancies can provide an opening for expanding the range of careers considered by individuals and also for developing interventions to increase self-efficacy beliefs in areas of higher interest than confidence. Interest and self-efficacy data can also help clients consider the accuracy of their occupational knowledge in areas where self-efficacy is higher than interests. The latter is suggested by Social Cognitive Career Theory's (SCCT; Lent, Brown, & Hackett, 1994) interest model whereby interests are seen as a joint function of self-efficacy beliefs and outcome expectations (expected outcomes of occupational pursuit). Thus, in areas where self-efficacy is higher than interests, SCCT would suggest that outcome expectations for that occupational area may be somewhat low and that clients should search out more information on the occupation to ensure that their outcome expectations for that occupation are accurate (see Brown & Lent, 1996).

Linkages between personality, as measured by the five-factor model of personality (Goldberg, 1993), and interests as measured by Holland's (1997) RIASEC types, have been explored in meta-analyses by Mount, Barrick, Scullen, and Rounds (2005), and Larson, Rottinghaus, and Borgen (2002). Mount et al. reported a clear distinction between personality and interest measures in their analyses. Their results support the distinctiveness of the two sets of constructs, providing a mandate for the continued use of both personality and interests in vocational research and practice. Mount et al. proposed and identified from a motivational perspective, two higher-order dimensions among the Big Five personality traits and Holland's RIASEC interests. One dimension represented a contrast between *striving for accomplishment* (desire and motivation for getting things done) and *striving for personal growth* (seeking new experiences, venturesome encounters with life, creative expression, and new ideas). When compared with Prediger's (1982) interest-based Data-Ideas dimension, the accomplishment–personal growth dimension reflects more general individual differences in the relative importance of intrinsic (for personal growth–oriented individuals) versus extrinsic (for accomplishment-oriented individuals) rewards and may have important implications for job satisfaction and performance. The second dimension, similar to Hogan's (1983) sociability dimension or Prediger's (1982) People-Things dimension, tapped social interaction versus working alone. Mount et al. suggest that combining traits and interests (e.g., Openness and Artistic interests) and developing multifaceted measures may predict motivational and performance outcomes better than either attribute measured separately.

Both interests and personality measures provide incremental validity over measures of GMA in the prediction of job performance (Austin & Hanisch, 1990; Judge et al., 1999). There is also evidence linking personality development with work experiences (Roberts et al., 2003). The results of the Mount et al. (2005) meta-analysis identifying dimensions linking personality traits and interests supports the use of both measures in counseling and other applied settings. Their findings suggest that using a combination of RIASEC interest measures and five-factor model personality measures may help clients connect personal goals, such as a need for accomplishment or personal growth, with their activity interests and career choices, including preferences for working with either people or things. Clients with a pattern of personality and interest scores suggesting an orientation to growth and working with people would likely find different occupations satisfying than those found by persons with a people and accomplishments or a things and accomplishment orientation.

INTEGRATIVE MODELS AND OTHER FUTURE DIRECTIONS

Multiple Indicators and Prediction of Career-Related Outcomes

Ahadi and Diener (1989) suggested that there is often an implicit assumption underlying discussions of effect sizes that behaviors are caused by single versus multiple determinants. Mischel (1968) questioned the practical utility of conscientiousness as a predictor of work performance because the correlation between this personality trait and various measures of work performance rarely exceeds values of $r = .30$. There are two difficulties with Mischel's argument. First, the criticism of conscientiousness as having only a .30 correlation with work behavior assumes a one-to-one relationship with the trait, and second, it ignores the role of other traits and factors that influence work behavior. If work behavior has a single determinant, then the personality trait of conscientiousness, with a correlation of .30, appears to be a poor predictor of that behavior. However, if one acknowledges that multiple factors influence behaviors, then the finding that a single measure of conscientiousness has a correlation of .30 with a specific behavior is impressive.

Ahadi and Diener (1989) evaluated different theoretical models of the relationship between traits and behaviors using Monte Carlo simulations to generate upper-bound estimates for the possible correlations between traits and behaviors. When a behavior was modeled as being determined entirely by three traits, the upper-bound correlation between single behavior and trait measures was found to be approximately .50; and when the behavior was determined by four traits, the upper-bound correlation between a single behavior and trait measures was .45. There are two key implications of these results for vocational psychology research and practice. First, most behaviors of interest to vocational psychologists and career counselors (e.g., work performance and job satisfaction) are multiply determined. Thus, it is unrealistic to expect any single predictor to explain a large amount of variance in these multiply determined outcomes. A variable that explains some variance in such outcomes represents a potentially important target for assessment and exploration in career counseling although the correlation may seem small in an absolute sense. Second, these findings suggest that additive and integrative models of the effects of multiple traits should increasingly become the focus of research and practice.

Integrative Models of Individual Differences

Integrative models that combine cognitive and noncognitive measures to predict important career outcomes have appeared in the literature in recent years. Ackerman and Heggestad (1997) have put forward the notion of "trait complexes" as a model to describe the linkages among cognitive abilities, interests, and personality. As presented in Figure 22.3, based on meta-analytic reviews of research studying interrelations among these individual differences domains, four trait complexes were identified: (1) the *Social* trait complex, which includes the people-oriented Enterprising and Social interest types, the personality traits of extraversion and social potency, and subjective well-being; (2) the *Clerical/Conventional* trait complex, which includes the Conventional interest types, personality traits of control, conscientiousness, and traditionalism, and perceptual speed ability; (3) the *Science/Math* trait complex, which includes Realistic and Investigative interests, visual perception, and math reasoning ability; and (4) the *Intellectual/Cultural* trait complex, which includes Investigative and Artistic interests, openness to experience, typical intellectual engagement, idea fluency, and general cognitive ability.

The work of Ackerman and Heggestad (1997) suggests that abilities, interests, and personality may develop in tandem, resulting in the emergence of important trait complexes. The socioanalytic model of personality development, proposed by Hogan (1983; Hogan & Roberts, 2004; Hogan & Sheldon, 1998), also supports the notion that cognitive and noncognitive individual differences are interdependent in their development. Development occurs as part of an iterative process of feedback between abilities, interests, personality, and other traits. As illustrated in Figure 22.3, the trait complexes proposed by Ackerman and Heggestad (1997) emerge in the context of Holland's RIASEC circumplex model of interests. In particular, the Social and Science/Math complexes appear aligned with the People/Things dimension proposed by Prediger (1982). The Clerical/Conventional and Intellectual/Cultural complexes appear to be aligned with the second interest dimension, and may be consistent with what Armstrong, Smith, Donnay, and Rounds (2004) refer to as the Structured/Dynamic interest dimension and what Hogan (1983) refers to as the Conformity dimension.

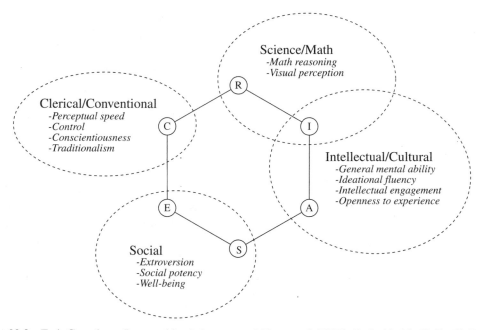

Figure 22.3   Trait Complexes Proposed by Ackerman and Heggestad (1997), Embedded in Holland's RIASEC Model.

When considering the role of individual differences in vocational psychology, integrative models (e.g., Ackerman & Heggestad, 1997) may provide effective frameworks for developing research questions and counseling applications. Ackerman and Heggestad's data suggest that counselors can obtain a more complete picture of clients' likely occupational preferences by combining cognitive, interest, and personality information to assess where they might fall in each of the trait complexes. The information provided by such integrative assessments might end up being more predictive of individuals' preferences and choices than data provided by ability, interest, or personality alone. Also generating occupational possibilities for clients on the bases of these trait complexes may yield better choices than simply generating possibilities separately on the basis of ability, interests, and personality and subsequently combining them. Such possibilities are ripe avenues for future research.

Another example of an integrative model of individual differences that uses interests as an organizational framework is the Strong Ring (Armstrong et al., 2004), which combines an occupational interest structure with occupational data from the U.S. Department of Labor's O*NET database. Compared with Ackerman and Heggestad's (1997) model, which used RIASEC dimensions to operationalize interests, the Strong Ring's interest structure was developed from the SII Basic Interest scales. A hierarchical model of 9 general interest areas and 19 more specific occupational clusters was fit into a three-dimensional ringlike structure. Data on 62 occupational characteristics, including values, knowledge areas, skills, work activities, and work contexts were obtained from the O*NET database and embedded in the three-dimensional structure using property vector fitting (Kruskal & Wish, 1978). Figure 22.4 displays the first two dimensions of the Strong Ring, with O*NET characteristics embedded in the structure, thereby facilitating the linkage of interests with other work requirements. The results of Armstrong et al.'s study also demonstrate that adding a third dimension to their model increased the occupational characteristics that could be integrated into an interest structure beyond the results that are possible using a two-dimensional model like Holland's (1959, 1997) theory.

Lubinski (2000) offered an additional viewpoint on the integration of individual differences domains, focusing primarily on the areas of cognitive abilities, interests, and personality. Lubinski suggests that individuals who have similar levels of extraversion may display different behavioral patterns if they vary in their level of conscientiousness and also argues that individual differences in behavior will

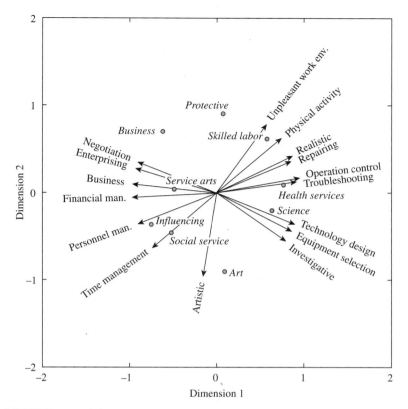

Figure 22.4   O*NET Characteristics Embedded in Dimensions 1 and 2 of the Strong Ring, Integrating Data from the U.S. Department of Labor into an Interest-Based Model of Occupations. The integration of occupational data into interest structures facilitates its use in counseling and other applied settings.

Source: "The Strong Ring: A Basic Interests Model of Occupational Structure," by P. I. Armstrong, T. J. Smith, D. A. C. Donnay, and J. Rounds, 2004, *Journal of Counseling Psychology, 51,* p. 309. Copyright 2004 by the American Psychological Association. Reprinted with permission.

be determined by multiple factors that span across the traditionally discrete individual differences domains. Therefore, two students with strong spatial ability skills may be pulled in different directions academically depending on their scores on the people/things dimension of interests. The motivational dimensions identified by Mount et al. (2005) also reflect the integrative potential of trait complexes. Individuals who are oriented toward striving either for accomplishment or for personal growth will seek out different career opportunities and respond to different rewards offered in the workplace. Lubinski argues that the emergence of trait complexes may be important to understanding individual differences in occupational attainment when comparing individuals with similar levels of GMA: "Increments for personality measures typically range between 0.05 and 0.15, which may seem small when contrasted with what ability constructs offer, but their economic and social gains are huge" (Lubinski, 2000, p. 428).

Gender Differences and Career Development

The challenge of integrating information across multiple sets of individual differences measures can also be seen in the recurrent debate over gender differences in the career development process. In particular, there are ongoing concerns about potential gender differences in both cognitive and noncognitive individual differences measures, and the potential impact of these measures on the career development of women. Recent reviews of the research on gender differences have provided strong evidence that male-female difference effect sizes across a wide range of psychological constructs are small. Hyde (2005) reviewed 124 effect sizes from 46 meta-analyses of gender differences, including measures of cognitive abilities, communication, social and personality variables, psychological well-being, motor behaviors, and a miscellaneous category that includes moral behavior and job performance. Hyde reported that 78% of the observed gender differences effect sizes were small or close to zero. Exceptions to this trend of small differences between males and females included motor performance, incidences of masturbation, and levels of aggression.

Spelke (2005) identified three common hypotheses used to explain how gender differences in cognitive abilities lead to the differential representation of men and women in math, science, and engineering careers. These hypotheses include the suggestion that, beginning in childhood, males are more focused on interacting with objects and because of this are predisposed to learn more about mechanical systems. It has also been proposed that males are more likely to have strong spatial and numerical abilities that result in higher levels of math proficiency, and that the larger variability in male cognitive ability scores, when compared with scores of females, increases the probability of males having very high levels of mathematical talent. To challenge these three hypotheses, Spelke noted that systematic research on object perception in children finds no gender differences in performance, and that male and female students display equal capacities to learn advanced college-level mathematics despite gender differences on standardized tests.

Vocational interests are an area of gender differences research that is conspicuously absent from the reviews by Hyde (2005) and Spelke (2005). Research by Lippa (1998, 2005) on gender differences in the People-Things dimension of interests (Prediger, 1982; see Figure 22.1) has consistently demonstrated large effect sizes of at least 1.20 standard deviations, suggesting that women tend to have substantially stronger interests in people-oriented activities and occupations than do men, while the opposite is true for interest in things-oriented occupations and activities. In a 35-year longitudinal study of individuals with high levels of math proficiency, Lubinski and Benbow (2006) reported that women with high levels of math ability were less likely than their male counterparts to pursue careers in fields such as math, science, and engineering. However, these women often chose other careers that require math ability, such as medicine and the social sciences, as well as prestigious careers in law and business administration. Lubinski and Benbow (2006) suggested that these patterns of sex differences in highly prestigious and complex fields may be largely the results of gender differences in interests and values— that men and women with equally high math abilities gravitate toward different, but equally prestigious, professional fields on the basis of gender-typed interests and values. Gender differences in interests, therefore, may have important implications for understanding the different career trajectories of men and women. However, the same may not be true for race and ethnicity differences in interests and occupational choices. Fouad (2002; Fouad & Mohler, 2004) found that racial-ethnic group differences in interests were quite small compared with the differences usually found between men and women on the same interest scales.

Vocational interests are effective in predicting the current occupation of employed individuals (Borgen & Lindley, 2003; Donnay & Borgen, 1996; Larson & Borgen, 2002) and also in predicting future aspirations of students and the occupations they choose up to 23 years later (Campbell, 1971; Hansen & Campbell, 1985). In addition to the predictive validity of these measures, there is also evidence that feedback received from interest inventory results impacts the career development of students (Luzzo & Day, 1999; Uffelman, Subich, Diegelman, Wagner, & Bardash, 2004). Prediger and Johnson's (1979) classic paper on the gender bias in interest measurement raises the issue of the importance of prediction in career counseling, and the implications this has for the development of less sex-restrictive interest measures. They made an interesting point about the role of predictive validity in the context of career counseling: The primary goal of career counseling, according to Prediger and Johnson, is not to predict occupational choice, but rather to generate a range of occupational possibilities for clients. Although it would be difficult to justify using measures in the career counseling process that are not related to, or cannot predict career choices in some way (Rounds & Armstrong, 2005), the key issue is a trade-off between predictive validity and development of a measure that helps clients consider a range of viable occupational options that is as wide as possible (Prediger, 1977). Interest measures producing the highest levels of predictive validity may, therefore, provide a good snapshot of current gender imbalances. A more gender-neutral measure may sacrifice some predictive validity relative to more traditional interest measures, but this loss may be more than offset by improved utility of gender-neutral measures to promote a wider range of career options for both men and women.

Returning to the notion of consequential outcomes, gender differences can affect the career choices people make as well as the personnel selections made by employers. Reardon, Vernick, and Reed (2004) examined changes in the distribution of Holland's (1997) RIASEC interest categories in the labor market from 1960 to 1990 using census data. Their findings demonstrate that complexity of work is clearly related to the Holland type assigned to an occupation: Investigative and Artistic occupations typically have the highest level of complexity, and Conventional and Realistic occupations tend to have the lowest levels of complexity. Gender is also related to Holland type because the distribution of the labor market by gender is unequal across the six RIASEC categories. Realistic and Investigative occupations tend to be male dominated, whereas Social and Conventional occupations are female dominated. Therefore, when Holland-based measures are used to recommend careers, implicit messages are being communicated about the complexity of work that is appropriate for individuals based on their gender, which may have implications for the levels of intrinsic and extrinsic career success experienced by men and women.

SUMMARY AND CONCLUSION

Individual differences measures are central to the field of vocational psychology, and can be used to predict job performance, career choice, and intrinsic and extrinsic career success. The research reviewed in this chapter demonstrates that there are positive correlations between general mental abilities and virtually all the variables that are used to measure desirable work outcomes. From a personnel selection standpoint, measures of cognitive abilities can be used to select those applicants who are most likely to be successful by selecting those applicants with the highest scores. However, cognitive ability is a potentially loaded question for counseling psychologists because differences between high and low scores are often interpreted in terms of strengths and weaknesses. Unlike interests, where learning that one is interested in a particular area of work does not necessarily imply a limited future, results from cognitive assessments have the potential to imply limits for future success. Nevertheless, cognitive assessments in vocational psychology can identify strengths and also facilitate the gravitational process of matching individuals to levels of employment where they are most likely to experience both intrinsic and extrinsic career success.

Noncognitive measures are also implicated in job performance, and provide incremental validity over measures of cognitive ability. Individuals who, relatively speaking, are more interested in performing the work activities associated with a job, are motivated to succeed, and have personalities and values that match the work are more likely to be productive workers. In comparison, from a counseling perspective the issue of how to work with individual differences measures is more complicated because, unlike employers, counselors do not have the luxury of selecting a small number of clients from a large pool of applicants. The challenge facing vocational psychologists who work in the field of counseling psychology is to develop integrative models that combine information from cognitive and noncognitive measures. The continued development of, and research on, integrative models of individual differences will offer opportunities to expand the utility of individual differences in vocational psychology.

REFERENCES

Ackerman, P. L., & Heggestad, E. D. (1997). Intelligence, personality, and interests: Evidence for overlapping traits. *Psychological Bulletin, 121,* 219–245.

ACT. (1995). *Revised unisex edition of the ACT Interest Inventory (UNIACT)* [Technical manual]. Iowa City, IA: Author.

Ahadi, S., & Diener, E. (1989). Multiple determinants and effect size. *Journal of Personality and Social Psychology, 56*, 398–406.

Anderson, M. Z., Tracey, T. J. G., & Rounds, J. (1997). Examining the invariance of Holland's vocational interest model across gender. *Journal of Vocational Behavior, 50*, 349–364.

Armstrong, P. I., Hubert, L., & Rounds, J. (2003). Circular unidimensional scaling: A new look at group differences in interest structure. *Journal of Counseling Psychology, 50*, 297–308.

Armstrong, P. I., Smith, T. J., Donnay, D. A. C., & Rounds, J. (2004). The strong ring: A basic interests model of occupational structure. *Journal of Counseling Psychology, 51*, 299–313.

Austin, J. A., & Hanisch, K. A. (1990). Occupational attainment as a function of abilities and interests: A longitudinal analysis using project TALENT data. *Journal of Applied Psychology, 75*, 77–86.

Beruta, C., Anderson, N., & Salgado, J. F. (2005). The predictive validity of cognitive ability tests: A UK meta-analysis. *Journal of Occupational and Organizational Psychology, 78*, 387–409.

Betz, N. E., & Rottinghaus, P. J. (2006). Current research on parallel measures of interests and confidence for basic dimensions of vocational activity. *Journal of Career Assessment, 14*, 56–76.

Borgen, F. H., & Lindley, L. D. (2003). Individuality and optional human functioning: Interest, self-efficacy, and personality. In W. B. Walsh (Ed.), *Counseling psychology and optimal human functioning* (pp. 55–91). Mahwah, NJ: Erlbaum.

Brown, S. D., & Lent, R. W. (1996). A social cognitive framework for career choice counseling. *Career Development Quarterly, 44*, 354–366.

Campbell, D. P. (1971). *Handbook for the strong vocational interest blank.* Stanford, CA: Stanford University Press.

Campbell, D. P., & Borgen, F. H. (1999). Holland's theory and the development of interest inventories. *Journal of Vocational Behavior, 55*, 86–101.

Campbell, D. P., Borgen, F. H., Eastes, S. H., Johansson, C. B., & Peterson, R. A. (1968). A set of basic interest scales for the Strong Vocational Interest Blank for Men. *Journal of Applied Psychology Monograph, 52*, (6, Whole No. 2).

Darcy, M. U. A., & Tracey, T. J. G. (2007). Circumplex structure of Holland's RIASEC interests across gender and time. *Journal of Counseling Psychology, 54*, 17–31.

Dawis, R. V. (1992). The individual differences tradition in counseling psychology. *Journal of Counseling Psychology, 39*, 7–19.

Dawis, R. V. (1996). Vocational psychology, vocational adjustment, and the work force: Some familiar and unanticipated consequences. *Psychology, Public Policy, and Law, 2*, 229–248.

Dawis, R. V. (2005). The Minnesota Theory of Work Adjustment. In S. D. Brown & R. W. Lent (Eds.), *Career development and counseling: Putting theory and research to work* (pp. 3–23). Hoboken, NJ: Wiley.

Dawis, R. V., & Lofquist, L. (1984). *A psychological theory of work adjustment: An individual differences model and its applications.* Minneapolis: University of Minnesota Press.

Day, S. X., & Rounds, J. (1997). "A little more than kin, and less than kind": Basic interests in vocational research and career counseling. *Career Development Quarterly, 45*, 207–220.

Day, S. X., Rounds, J., & Swaney, K. (1998). The structure of vocational interests for diverse racial-ethnic groups. *Psychological Science, 9*, 40–44.

Dik, B. J., & Hansen, J. C. (2004). Development and validation of discriminant functions for the Strong Interest Inventory. *Journal of Vocational Behavior, 64*, 182–197.

Donnay, D. A. C., & Borgen, F. H. (1996). Validity, structure, and content of the 1994 Strong Interest Inventory. *Journal of Counseling Psychology, 43*, 275–291.

Donnay, D. A. C., & Borgen, F. H. (1999). The incremental validity of vocational self-efficacy: An examination of interest, self-efficacy, and occupation. *Journal of Counseling Psychology, 46*, 432–447.

Fouad, N. A. (2002). Cross-cultural differences in vocational interests: Between-groups differences on the Strong Interest Inventory. *Journal of Counseling Psychology, 49*, 283–289.

Fouad, N. A., Harmon, L. W., & Borgen, F. H. (1997). Structure of interests in employed male and female members of U.S. racial-ethnic minority and nonminority groups. *Journal of Counseling Psychology, 44*, 339–345.

Fouad, N. A., & Mohler, C. J. (2004). Cultural validity of Holland's theory and the Strong Interest Inventory for five racial/ethnic groups. *Journal of Career Assessment, 12*, 423–439.

Fryer, D. (1931). *The measurement of interests.* New York: Henry Holt.

Gasser, C. E., Larson, L. M., & Borgen, F. H. (2004). Contributions of personality and interests to explaining the educational aspirations of college students. *Journal of Career Assessment, 12*, 347–365.

Gati, I. (1979). A hierarchical model for the structure of interests. *Journal of Vocational Behavior, 15*, 90–106.

Gati, I. (1991). The structure of vocational interests. *Psychological Bulletin, 109*, 309–324.

Goldberg, L. R. (1993). The structure of phenotypic personality traits. *American Psychologist, 48*, 26–34.

Gottfredson, L. S. (2003). The challenge and promise of cognitive career assessment. *Journal of Career Assessment, 11*, 115–135.

Harmon, L. W., Hansen, J. C., Borgen, F. H., & Hammer, A. L. (1994). *Strong Interest Inventory applications and technical guide*. Stanford, CA: Stanford University Press.

Hansen, J. C., & Campbell, D. P. (1985). *Manual for the SVIB-SCII*. Palo Alto, CA: Consulting Psychologists Press.

Hansen, J. C., & Dik, B. J. (2005). Evidence of 12-year predictive and concurrent validity for SII occupational scale scores. *Journal of Vocational Behavior, 67*, 365–378.

Hecker, D. E. (2005). Occupational employment projections to 2014. *Monthly Labor Review, 128*(11), 70–101.

Hogan, R. (1983). A socioanalytic theory of personality. In M. M. Page (Ed.), *Nebraska Symposium on Motivation 1982—Personality: Current theory and research* (pp. 55–89). Lincoln: University of Nebraska Press.

Hogan, R., & Roberts, B. (2004). A socioanalytic model of maturity. *Journal of Career Assessment, 12*, 207–217.

Hogan, R., & Sheldon, D. (1998). A socioanalytic perspective on job performance. *Human Performance, 11*, 129–144.

Holland, J. L. (1959). A theory of occupational choice. *Journal of Counseling Psychology, 6*, 35–45.

Holland, J. L. (1997). *Making vocational choices: A theory of vocational personalities and work environments* (3rd ed.). Odessa, FL: Psychological Assessment Resources.

Holland, J. L., Whitney, D. R., Cole, N. S., & Richards, J. M., Jr. (1969). *An empirical occupational classification derived from a theory of personality and intended for practice and research* (ACT Research Report No. 29). Iowa City, IA: American College Testing.

Hubert, L., Arabie, P., & Meulman, J. (1997). Linear and circular unidimensional scaling for symmetric proximity matrices. *British Journal of Mathematical and Statistical Psychology, 50*, 253–284.

Humphreys, L. G., Lubinski, D., & Yao, G. (1993). Utility of predicting group membership and the role of spatial visualization in becoming an engineer, physical scientist, or artist. *Journal of Applied Psychology, 78*, 250–261.

Hyde, J. S. (2005). The gender similarities hypothesis. *American Psychologist, 60*, 581–592.

Judge, T. A., Higgins, C. A., Thoresen, C. J., & Barrick, M. R. (1999). The big five personality traits, general mental ability, and career success across the lifespan. *Personnel Psychology, 52*, 621–652.

Judge, T. A., Jackson, C. L., Shaw, J. C., Scott, B. A., & Rich, B. L. (2007). Self-efficacy and work related performance: The integral role of individual differences. *Journal of Applied Psychology, 92*, 107–127.

Kruskal, J. B., & Wish, M. (1978). *Multidimensional scaling*. Newbury Park, CA: Sage.

Kuncel, N. R., & Hezlett, S. A. (2007). Standardized tests predict graduate student success. *Science, 315*, 1080–1081.

Kuncel, N. R., Hezlett, S. A., & Ones, D. S. (2001). A comprehensive meta-analysis of the predictive validity of the graduate record examinations: Implications for graduate student selection and performance. *Psychological Bulletin, 127*, 162–181.

Kuncel, N. R., Hezlett, S. A., & Ones, D. S. (2004). Academic performance, career potential, creativity, and job performance: Can one construct predict them all? *Journal of Personality and Social Psychology, 86*, 148–161.

Larson, L. M., & Borgen, F. H. (2002). Convergence of vocational interests and personality: Examples in an adolescent gifted sample. *Journal of Vocational Behavior, 60*, 91–112.

Larson, L. M., Rottinghaus, P. J., & Borgen, F. H. (2002). Meta-analyses of big six interests and big five personality factors. *Journal of Vocational Behavior, 61*, 217–239.

Lent, R. W., Brown, S. D., & Hackett, G. (1994). Toward a unifying social cognitive theory of career and academic interest, choice, and performance [Monograph]. *Journal of Vocational Behavior, 45*, 79–122.

Levinson, D. J. (1986). A conception of adult development. *American Psychologist, 41*, 3–13.

Lippa, R. (1998). Gender-related individual differences and the structure of vocational interests: The importance of the people-things dimension. *Journal of Personality and Social Psychology, 74*, 996–1009.

Lippa, R. (2005). Subdomains of gender-related occupational interests: Do they form a cohesive bipolar M-F dimension? *Journal of Personality, 73*, 693–729.

Long, L., & Tracey, T. J. G. (2006). Structure of RAISEC scores in China: A structural meta-analysis. *Journal of Vocational Behavior, 68*, 39–51.

Low, K. S. D., & Rounds, J. (in press). Interest change and continuity from early adolescence to middle adulthood. *International Journal of Educational and Vocational Guidance*.

Low, K. S. D., Yoon, M., Roberts, B. W., & Rounds, J. (2005). The stability of vocational interests from early adolescence to middle adulthood: A quantitative review of longitudinal studies. *Psychological Bulletin, 131*, 713–737.

Lubinski, D. (2000). Scientific and social significance of assessing individual differences: "Sinking shafts at a few critical points." *Annual Review of Psychology, 51*, 405–444.

Lubinski, D., & Benbow, C. P. (2006). Study of mathematically precocious youth after 35 years: Uncovering antecedents for the development of math-science expertise. *Perspectives on Psychological Science, 1*, 316–345.

Luzzo, D. A., & Day, M. A. (1999). Effects of Strong Interest Inventory feedback on career decision-making self-efficacy and social cognitive career beliefs. *Journal of Career Assessment, 7*, 1–17.

McCormick, E. J., DeNisi, A. S., & Shaw, J. B. (1979). Use of the Position Analysis Questionnaire for establishing the job component validity of tests. *Journal of Applied Psychology, 64*, 51–56.

McCormick, E. J., Jeanneret, P. R., & Mecham, R. C. (1972). A study of job characteristics and job dimension as based on the Position Analysis Questionnaire (PAQ). *Journal of Applied Psychology, 56*, 347–368.

McDaniel, M. A., & Snell, A. F. (1999). Holland's theory and occupational information. *Journal of Vocational Behavior, 55*, 74–85.

Mischel, W. (1968). *Personality and assessment*. New York: Wiley.

Mount, M. K., Barrick, M. R., Scullen, S. M., & Rounds, J. (2005). Higher-order dimensions of the big five personality traits and the big six vocational interest types. *Personnel Psychology, 58*, 447–478.

Ozer, D. J., & Benet-Martinez, V. (2006). Personality and the prediction of consequential outcomes. *Annual Review of Psychology, 57*, 401–421.

Prediger, D. J. (1977). Alternatives for validating interest inventories against group membership criteria. *Applied Psychological Measurement, 1*, 275–280.

Prediger, D. J. (1982). Dimensions underlying Holland's hexagon: Missing link between interests and occupations? *Journal of Vocational Behavior, 21*, 259–287.

Prediger, D. J., & Johnson, R. W. (1979). *Alternatives to sex-restrictive vocational interest assessment* (ACT Research Report No. 79). Iowa City, IA: ACT.

Ralston, C. A., Borgen, F. H., Rottinghaus, P. J., & Donnay, D. A. C. (2004). Specificity in interest measurement: Basic interest scales and major field of study. *Journal of Vocational Behavior, 65*, 203–216.

Reardon, R. C., Vernick, S. H., & Reed, C. A. (2004). The distribution of the U.S. workforce from 1960 to 1990: A RIASEC perspective. *Journal of Career Assessment, 12*, 99–112.

Reeve, C. L., & Heggestad, E. D. (2004). Differential relations between general cognitive ability and interest-vocation fit. *Journal of Occupational and Organizational Psychology, 77*, 385–402.

Roberts, B. W., Caspi, A., & Moffitt, T. E. (2003). Work experiences and personality development in young adulthood. *Journal of Personality and Social Psychology, 84*, 582–593.

Rottinghaus, P. J., Larson, L. M., & Borgen, F. H. (2003). The relation of self-efficacy and interests: A meta-analysis of 60 samples. *Journal of Vocational Behavior, 62*, 221–236.

Rounds, J., & Armstrong, P. I. (2005). Assessment of needs and values. In S. D. Brown & R. W. Lent (Eds.), *Career development and counseling: Putting theory and research to work* (pp. 305–329). Hoboken, NJ: Wiley.

Rounds, J., & Day, S. X. (1999). Describing, evaluating and creating vocational interest structures. In M. L. Savickas & A. R. Spokane (Eds.), *Vocational interests: Meaning, measurement, and counseling use* (pp. 103–133). Palo Alto, CA: Davies-Black.

Rounds, J., & Tracey, T. J. (1993). Prediger's dimensional representation of Holland's RIASEC circumplex. *Journal of Applied Psychology, 78*, 875–890.

Rounds, J., & Tracey, T. J. (1996). Cross-cultural structural equivalence of RIASEC models and measures. *Journal of Counseling Psychology, 43*, 310–329.

Schmidt, F. L., & Hunter, J. E. (1998). The validity and utility of selection methods in personnel psychology: Practical and theoretical implications of 85 years of research findings. *Psychological Bulletin, 124*, 262–274.

Schmidt, F. L., & Hunter, J. E. (2004). General mental ability in the world of work: Occupational attainment and job performance. *Journal of Personality and Social Psychology, 86*, 162–173.

Spelke, E. S. (2005). Sex differences in intrinsic aptitude for mathematics and science? A critical review. *American Psychologist, 60*, 950–958.

Strong, E. K. (1943). *Vocational interests of men and women*. Stanford, CA: Stanford University Press.

Taylor, H. C., & Russell, J. T. (1939). The relationship of validity coefficients to the practical effectiveness of tests in selection: Discussion and tables. *Journal of Applied Psychology, 23,* 565–578.

Tracey, T. J., & Rounds, J. (1993). Evaluating Holland's and Gati's vocational-interest models: A structural meta-analysis. *Psychological Bulletin, 113,* 229–246.

Uffelman, R. A., Subich, L. M., Diegelman, N. M., Wagner, K. S., & Bardash, R. J. (2004). Effect of mode of interest assessment on clients' career decision-making self-efficacy. *Journal of Career Assessment, 12,* 366–380.

Wilk, S. L., Desmarais, L. B., & Sackett, P. R. (1995). Gravitation to jobs commensurate with ability: Longitudinal and cross-sectional tests. *Journal of Applied Psychology, 80,* 79–85.

CHAPTER 23

Conceptualizing and Diagnosing Problems in Vocational Decision Making

STEVEN D. BROWN
CHRISTOPHER C. RECTOR

Career interventions for choice-making difficulties are demonstrably, but modestly, effective. Two meta-analyses of the career intervention outcome literature (Brown & Ryan Krane, 2000; Whiston, Brecheisen, & Stephens, 2003) have converged to suggest that the average client participating in career interventions achieves about a third of a standard deviation better outcome than the average control client ($ds = .30$ to $.34$). Although these effects can be viewed as clinically important (Brown & McPartland, 2005), they are still considered small by contemporary standards (Cohen, 1988). Several reasons for these somewhat disappointing, albeit clinically important, effect sizes have been offered in the literature, and several suggestions have been made to improve the effectiveness of career interventions for choice-making difficulties.

A major reason that has been offered to explain the modest effects of career interventions is that most interventions in the outcome literature are theoretically truncated (Achter & Lubinski, 2005; Brown & McPartland, 2005; Miller & Brown, 2005). They are based primarily on a single theory (Holland, 1997) and fail to incorporate other empirically supported theories; as a result, they focus primarily on interests as the primary source of self-understanding and occupational consideration. Thus, some writers (e.g., Brown & McPartland, 2005) have suggested that career interventions can be improved by incorporating more fully other empirically supported theories and other personal (e.g., needs, values, and abilities) and contextual (e.g., external barriers and supports) variables that have been shown to relate to occupational choice, satisfaction, and success.

Several writers (e.g., Brown & McPartland, 2005; Miller & Brown, 2005) have also suggested that the most theoretically complete intervention may still yield modest (albeit larger) effects if clients are treated, as they seem to be in the outcome literature, uniformly—as if their reasons for seeking counseling and the sources of their choice-making difficulties are identical. Brown and McPartland (2005) pointed out that most interventions seem to be developed under the assumption that all clients are seeking more options even though clients' goals are typically more diverse. Alternative reasons for seeking counseling may include confusion because of an overwhelming number of options, a need to make a choice among a few good options, or a desire to confirm an already made choice. Thus, Brown and McPartland (2005) suggested that outcome effects might be improved simply by asking clients about their goals at the outset of counseling and tailoring intervention efforts to these goals rather than assuming that everyone who seeks career counseling is without options.

Relatedly, most interventions that have appeared in the outcome literature seem to ignore (or at least fail to assess for) the underlying reasons that might be responsible for clients' choice-making difficulties and consequently fail to target intervention efforts to the sources of clients' indecision. Brown and

The authors thank Xiaoan Fan, Denada Hoxha, Kristen Lamp, Justin Li, Jodi Roth, Kyle Telander, Selena Traymane, and Ryan Williams for their contributions to the research presented herein.

and McPartland (2005) noted that interventions in the research literature tended to treat all clients not only as if they have no options, but also as if their main source of difficulty revolves around a lack of self-knowledge (usually) and occupational information (occasionally) despite abundant evidence that self-knowledge and information deficits are not the sole sources of indecision problems. In fact, a variety of personal (e.g., anxiety, fear of commitment, goal instability) and contextual (e.g., interpersonal conflicts, external barriers) factors have been found to relate to vocational indecision and may, individually or collectively, contribute to individuals' vocational choice-making difficulties.

As consumers of the career decision-making literature, we have been disappointed that it seems to have had such little impact on practice and to have moved to the periphery of career inquiry in the past 10 to 15 years (Kelly & Lee, 2002). We suggest that a closer look at this body of research will reveal why it seems to have had such little appeal for those who develop career interventions and why investigators might have lost interest in the topic. Our goals in writing this chapter are to reinvigorate research on sources of vocational indecision and to suggest how research can better inform practice. We first provide a brief review of past research on factors related to vocational indecision. We conclude the first section by speculating about why this research has had such little influence on practice and by suggesting how future research might be approached to increase its clinical impact. We then present new data that may bring conceptual and empirical clarity to the literature; we also suggest how these data may be used by clinicians to tailor treatments and by researchers to design aptitude-treatment interactions studies. We hope this chapter improves the services that diverse clients receive for choice-making difficulties and moves outcome research beyond the "one size fits all" approach that has dominated it for many decades.

PAST RESEARCH

Although understanding the differences between vocationally decided and undecided persons has had a long history in vocational psychology (e.g., Crites, 1969; Williamson, 1965), much of the empirical research on career indecision seems to have been stimulated by a few seminal writings. First, Holland and Holland (1977) observed that vocational indecision is a multidimensional construct and suggested that several subtypes seek help from career counselors: (a) persons with information and skill deficits, (b) those with significant environmental and personal barriers, and (c) individuals with diffuse and unclear identities and significant levels of anxiety and immaturity. Second, Salomone (1982), in one of a series of important articles based on his clinical experiences, suggested that many of his clients seemed to be chronically indecisive—although they entered counseling seeking help for career choice-making difficulties, they had a long history of difficulty in making important life decisions and often presented with a constellation of characteristics that included chronic feelings of helplessness, dependency, immaturity, anxiety, and frustration, and low levels of self-confidence and self-esteem. They often also had a tendency to ruminate extensively about their situation, chronically felt that they did not have enough information, and wanted others to provide answers for them.

Together these two papers suggest that problems in vocational decision making can be caused by a host of psychological, cognitive, emotional, and contextual factors, and that different subtypes of clients can be identified based on informational and identity deficits and other psychological characteristics and contextual experiences they bring with them to counseling. Much of the subsequent research on problems of vocational indecision seemed to have been driven by these two important insights. Scales began, and continue, to be developed to measure multiple causes of indecision. Correlational and factor analytic studies have been undertaken to identify psychological, emotional, motivational, cognitive, and (more recently) contextual correlates of indecision. Cluster analytic investigations have sought to identify subtypes of vocationally undecided clients. We next briefly review measurement development, correlational, and factor analytic research. We then introduce cluster analytic research, but subsequently revisit this research in light of newer data on the structure of vocational indecision.

Measurement of Vocational Indecision

Several multiscale measures of vocational indecision have been developed over the years; most notably, the *Career Decision Profile* (CDP; Jones, 1989), *Career Factors Inventory* (CFI; Chartrand, Robbins, Morrill, & Boggs, 1990), *Career Decision Difficulties Questionnaire* (CDDQ; Gati, Krausz, & Osipow, 1996), and the *Career Decision Scale* (CDS; Osipow, 1986). The purpose of each scale is to provide measures of multiple factors that were hypothesized by the scale developers to be related to vocational indecision.

The CDP, developed from a three-dimensional model of vocational decision status, includes scales to measure levels of decidedness and comfort and four reasons for indecision: lack of occupational information, lack of self-clarity, generalized indecisiveness, and low choice/work importance. Research has largely supported the factor structure of the instrument and has yielded internal consistency estimates from .68 for scores on the Lack of Occupational Information scale to .77 for Lack of Self-Clarity scores (e.g., Jones, 1989).

The CFI was based on the assumption that the primary antecedents of vocational indecision are both informational and affective. The measure, therefore, contains two informational subscales (Need for Occupational Information and Need for Self-Information) and two affective subscales (Generalized Indecisiveness and Career Choice Anxiety). Although research has largely supported the four factor structure of the instrument (Chartrand & Nutter, 1996), the correlations between the two affective and two informational subscales are sufficiently large to suggest a two-factor (Information and Affective) structure (see interscale correlation matrices in Chartrand & Nutter, 1996). Internal consistency estimates have ranged from .79 (Indecisiveness) to .91 (Career Choice Anxiety).

The CDDQ, the most conceptually complex of the three measures, was developed from a cognitive-information processing model of career indecision. This model posits three broad factors (lack of readiness, lack of information, and inconsistent information) that underlie vocational decision-making problems, with lack of readiness most influential prior to engaging in decision making and lack of information and inconsistent information most influential during the act of decision making. Each of the three major cognitive/informational factors is further broken down hierarchically into subfactors. Thus, an individual who is not ready to make a decision may be stymied because of generalized indecisiveness, beliefs in dysfunctional career myths, or simply because of being unmotivated to make a decision. Similarly, persons who are stuck in the process of making a decision because of a lack of information may lack self- or occupational information, may need information on the decision-making process, or may not know how to gather additional information. Finally, persons who are dealing with inconsistent information may be getting unreliable information from others or experiencing internal or external conflicts.

In all, 13 scores are obtainable from the CDDQ—3 scores on the higher-order Lack of Readiness, Lack of Information, and Inconsistent Information scales, and 10 scores on the subscales that are assumed to define each of the higher-order factors. Reliability estimates have suggested that the Lack of Readiness scale may be somewhat less homogeneous (Cronbach's alphas = .63 to .70) than the other two higher-order scales (Cronbach's alphas of .91 to .95 on the Inconsistent Information and Lack of Information scales, respectively). The subscale scores tend to yield somewhat lower reliability estimates, with scores on several of the subscales being substantially influenced by measurement error (e.g., internal consistency estimates on lack of motivation and career myths scores have been as low as .29 and .53, respectively). Factor analytic results, although generally supportive of the hierarchical structure of the instrument, have sometimes found the subscales to load on different factors in different analyses (Gati et al., 1999; Kelly & Lee, 2002; Tien, 2005).

The CDS was the first measure of indecision that sought concurrently to assess respondents' levels of indecision and reasons for their indecision. It contains 2 items measuring certainty of educational and career choices and 16 items measuring antecedents of decidedness and certainty. Initial factor analyses (Osipow, Carney, & Barak, 1976) of the latter 16 items yielded a four factor structure (lack of structure and confidence, perceived external barriers, positive choice conflict, and personal conflict).

This structure was rarely replicated in subsequent research, leading Osipow (1986) to recommend use of a total score as an overall measure of indecision. More recent factor analyses, using more appropriate factor analytic strategies (principal axis versus principal components analyses) and rotation methods (oblique rather than orthogonal), suggested a replicable four factor structure that included (1) identity diffusion, (2) lack of support for decisions, (3) approach-approach conflict, and (4) internal and external barriers (Shimizu, Vondracek, & Schulenberg, 1994; Shimizu, Vondracek, Schulenberg, & Hostetler, 1988). Nonetheless, total scores for certainty and overall indecision are typically the only scores reported in research using the CDS.

In summary, there are similarities and differences in the scores that can be obtained from the multi-factor indecision inventories. All three instruments from which subscales scores are obtained (i.e., CDP, CFI, and CDDQ) provide measures of generalized indecisiveness and occupational information needs. Also, the questions in the generalized indecision scales from all three instruments seem to have been faithfully derived from Salomone's (1982) clinical definition of indecisiveness as involving a long-standing, chronic difficulty in making decisions in different contexts.

Each of these instruments also provides scores on unique sets of factors (owing largely to the conceptions of indecision that drove their development). The CFI provides a measure of state anxiety (career choice-making anxiety) that the others do not. The CDP uniquely includes scales that allow for the assessment of respondents' feelings of self-clarity and whether making a vocational choice is important to the client at the present moment. The CDDQ also includes a similar Lack of Motivation scale as well as measures of career myths, unreliable information, and internal and external barriers. Finally, an approach-approach conflict factor has emerged from factor analyses of CDS items along with a barriers factor that is similar to the CDDQ internal and external barriers subscales.

Correlational and Factor Analytic Research

A second body of literature on vocational indecision has sought to explore correlates of indecision and to identify higher-order factors that account for substantial variance in scores on the many manifest variables that have been included in correlational investigations. The overall goal of the latter studies has been to identify latent variables that might underlie vocational decision-making difficulties. The general strategy in both types of investigation has been to employ one or more of the multifactor measures of indecision along with measures of other variables that were hypothesized to relate to indecision. The latter variables were of two types. The first type included variables derived from specific vocational theories (e.g., career decision-making self-efficacy beliefs, career maturity attitudes, fear of commitment, self-concept crystallization, decision-making styles, and vocational identity). The second type involved variables that had not been derived from the vocational literature, but were hypothesized as contributing to decision-making problems. Examples include anxiety (trait and state), self-esteem, depression, goal instability, personality, locus of control, problem-solving control and confidence, identity achievement status, attachment styles, psychological independence from parents, and coping strategies and styles. Indeed, we counted over 50 variables that have been included in research on correlates of indecision.

With this volume of correlates, it is not surprising that several investigators have used factor analytic methodology to try to bring some conceptual order to the literature (Fuqua & Newman, 1989; Kelly & Lee, 2002; Stead & Watson, 1993; Tinsley, Bowman, & York, 1989). Unfortunately, three of the studies (Fuqua & Newman, 1989; Stead & Watson, 1993; Tinsley et al., 1989) used inappropriate principal component analyses to extract factors (see Fabrigar, Wegener, MacCallum, & Strahan, 1999; Miller & Sheu, Chapter 7, this volume), and all used orthogonal rotation procedures to arrive at the final solution, although the latent reasons for indecision are probably, to some extent, related. There was some overlap in the measures employed in the studies (the CDS was employed in all four studies, whereas the CDP and CFI were used in two), but most of them used measures that were unique to the study. Finally, two of the studies (Fuqua & Newman, 1989; Tinsley et al., 1989) factored scale and subscale scores, while two others (Kelly & Lee, 2002; Stead & Watson, 1993) used interitem correlation matrices as their input.

A total of 20 factors emerged from these analyses, ranging in individual studies from 3 (Fuqua & Newman, 1989; Tinsley et al., 1989) to 8 (Kelly & Lee, 2002). Nonetheless, there appears to be some consistency across the different solutions. The authors of all four studies labeled one factor as measuring trait or chronic indecisiveness. This factor was marked in three studies primarily by CDP and CFI indecisiveness scale scores and by CDS items asking about general problems in decision making and reliance on others (Tinsley et al.'s, 1989, indecisiveness factor was marked only by total scores on the 16-item CDS indecision scale, although the data we later present suggest that this factor is mislabeled). Another point of consistency is that all four studies yielded an information deficit factor, although Kelly and Lee's (2002) eight-factor solution yielded two information factors, one reflecting a need for information and the other representing a lack of information. Other factors that emerged from these analyses, albeit less consistently, included those labeled by the authors as career choice anxiety (Kelly & Lee, 2002; Stead & Watson, 1993), self-concept clarity, crystallization, or diffusion (Kelly & Lee, 2002; Tinsley et al., 1989), and decision-making obstacles or conflicts with others (Kelly & Lee, 2002; Tinsley et al., 1989).

Thus, despite the substantial differences among studies, several consistent higher-order potential sources of decision-making difficulty emerged from these analyses—trait indecisiveness, information deficits, self-concept clarity or diffusion, and obstacles and conflicts. Two studies (Kelly & Lee, 2002; Stead & Watson, 1993) also identified a unique state anxiety (i.e., career choice anxiety) factor. One question that remains, however, is whether these four (or maybe five) factors will consistently emerge when more appropriate factor extraction (principal factor analysis) and rotation (oblique) methods are employed. We address this question in the second part of the chapter.

Cluster Analytic Studies

Another area of investigation has used a variety of different measures (including a few of those used in the factor analytic studies) to perform cluster analyses to identify unique subtypes of undecided persons. As with the factor analytic studies, the participants in the cluster analytic studies have been quite variable, including high school students (Multon, Heppner, & Lapan, 1995; Rojewski, 1994), samples from the general college population (Larson, Heppner, Ham, & Dugan, 1988; Lucas & Epperson, 1990; Wanberg & Muchinsky, 1992), college students taking a career planning course (Chartand et al., 1994; Kelly & Lee, 2002), and college counseling center clients (Lucas, 1993).

Two of the studies employing general samples of college students clustered undecided students separately from the more decided students, but used different criteria to identify the vocationally undecided sample. Larson et al. (1988) defined vocational undecidedness as having not declared a college major in a timely manner, while Lucas and Epperson (1990) selected their undecided sample on the basis of low scores on My Vocational Situation's Vocational Identity Scale (Holland, Daiger, & Power, 1980). Wanberg and Muchinsky (1992) clustered all college students in their sample together. Finally, a stunningly large number of variables were included across the studies, with very few measures used in more than one study. The CDP and CFI were employed in one study, while the CDS was used in two studies. Other variables that were measured in at least one study included vocational identity (3 studies), state and trait anxiety (2 studies), self-esteem (2 studies), locus of control (2 studies), career salience and commitment (2 studies), goal instability, feelings of inadequacy, social anxiety, public and private self-consciousness, decision-making styles, problem-solving confidence, career myths, support systems, pressure to make a decision, knowledge of the world of work, career-planning behaviors, and self-efficacy for self-assessment, information search, and academic skills.

Needless to say, results of studies that were based on such a large and nonoverlapping set of variables and that used such disparate samples are very difficult to integrate. It is also probably one reason why these and the factor analytic studies have had such little influence on research and practice. We suggest, however, that these findings might be made clearer and more clinically useful by approaching them from a different methodological perspective. We reasoned that cluster analytic studies might yield more consistent and interpretable sets of client types if the disparate manifest variables used in these studies could be shown, via appropriate factor analytic methodology, to be markers of a smaller number of latent variables (prior factor analytic studies have suggested four or five good possibilities). Although a single factor analytic study employing measures of some 50 manifest variables would stretch the patience of the most dedicated research participant and the resources of the most resource-rich investigator, we thought that the task might be easier if we approached it from a meta-analytic perspective—collecting and factoring correlation matrices used in investigations of correlates of vocational indecision, and combining the resulting factor pattern matrices in a meta-analytic manner. In the following section, we describe this methodology, and the findings we obtained from it.

A FOUR FACTOR MODEL OF VOCATIONAL INDECISION

As we noted above, we believe one reason why research on vocational indecision has had such little impact on practice and on career counseling outcome and process research revolves around the plethora of variables that have been studied in the literature. It was also our contention that many of the variables that have been studied in the indecision literature intercorrelate to such an extent that they actually represent the same underlying construct and serve to define a few (maybe four or five) overarching sources of decision-making difficulties. If true, then these overarching, latent sources of difficulty might make cluster analytic results more clearly interpretable and form the foundations for the types of vocational problem diagnostic systems that have been called for in the literature for many years (e.g., Brown & Ryan Krane, 2000; Rounds & Tinsley, 1984; Savickas, 1989). In this section, we present the methodology and results of our initial meta-analytic attempt to identify sources of vocational decision-making difficulties (see Rector, 2006, for a more complete description of the methodology).

Methods and Results

We started by identifying, through comprehensive literature search strategies, 28 published correlation matrices that seemed amenable to factor analysis (e.g., adequate sample sizes and variable to potential factor ratios as recommended by Fabrigar et al., 1999) and included at least two manifest variables that on conceptual grounds might serve as markers for previously suggested (e.g., Brown & Ryan Krane, 2000) or identified latent variables (e.g., indecisiveness, choice anxiety, information needs, identity diffusion, choice barriers and conflicts). Four of these matrices were subsequently eliminated based on Bartlett chi square test results, unacceptably low communality estimates, and convergence failure in factor analytic runs. References to the studies from which the 28 matrices were drawn are available in Rector (2006).

Each of the final 24 matrices was subjected individually to principal axis factoring with oblique rotations, using Kaiser and scree criteria to determine the number of factors to extract prior to rotation. The 24 correlation matrices yielded from one to four factor solutions, with minimal salient cross-loadings, accounting for substantial amounts of total variance in their input correlation matrices (medians were 71%, 69%, 66%, and 86% for the one, two, three, and four factor solutions, respectively). The final rotated factor pattern matrices were then inspected to identify common factors. Analyses began with two matrices that yielded single factor solutions. Serling and Betz (1990) administered measures of trait anxiety, state anxiety, self-esteem, and fear of commitment in a validation study of a scale developed to measure fear of commitment, and they presented separate correlation matrices for male and female samples. Both matrices, in our analyses, yielded a single factor solution with loadings ranging in absolute value from .70 to .96 for the female sample and from .64 to .95 for the male sample. Self-esteem loaded negatively on this factor, while the other measures loaded positively.

The remaining 23 factor pattern matrices were then inspected to identify whether a similar factor appeared that included measures of trait anxiety, state anxiety, self-esteem, or fear of commitment as marker variables. We used an iterative process by identifying factors that included one of the Serling and Betz (1990) marker variables, recording other variables that loaded on this factor, and then using this expanded set of marker variables to inspect subsequent matrices. This procedure resulted in 11 matrices that appeared to have yielded a highly similar factor. Manifest variables with significant positive loadings on this factor included measures of trait, state, career choice, and social anxiety; depression; fear of commitment; trait neuroticism; external locus of control; chronic indecisiveness; dependent decision-making style; and self-criticism. Measures of self-esteem, psychological hardiness, problem-solving confidence and control, and problem-focused coping styles had salient negative loadings on this factor.

We then sequentially inspected the matrices that yielded two-, three-, and four-factor solutions using the same iterative procedure to identify other factors that were common across the remaining 22 matrices and variables that showed salient loadings on them. These procedures yielded an additional three common factors and suggested that four latent sources may underlie career decision-making difficulties. We finally calculated summary loadings (median loadings when possible) of each manifest variable on every factor on which it loaded in the 24 matrices to estimate the strength with which each defined its primary latent variable and to inspect for possible salient cross-loadings. The results appear in Table 23.1.

Factor Interpretation

The first factor (as described previously) is defined primarily by (a) anxiety (both trait and state), depressive affect, and trait neuroticism; (b) low levels of self-esteem, psychological hardiness, and general problem-solving confidence; (c) a tendency to focus on and fear what will go wrong with decisions (fear of commitment), engagement in avoidant rather than approach coping efforts, and reliance on others when making important decisions (dependent decision-making style); and (d) beliefs that life is under the control of chance, powerful others, or other external factors. It is also marked by high scores on the CDP and CFI indecisiveness scales.

The presence of this factor, we think, confirms that chronic indecisiveness may represent a significant source of vocational decision-making difficulties; it also allows us to understand the constellation of characteristics that chronically indecisive clients might bring with them to counseling. They are likely to be self-critical and anxiety prone, to see themselves as having little control over their lives and little confidence in their abilities to solve problems generally. As a result, they prefer to avoid rather than approach problematic situations and may seek out and rely heavily on the opinions, views, and dictates of others in such situations. A final characteristic that may contribute substantially to these clients' long-standing difficulties in decision making and may have important implications for counseling is their tendency to focus on the negative rather than positive consequences of decisions—to become stymied by fears of what will go wrong if they follow a specific course of action (fear of commitment).

These characteristics bear remarkable similarity to the characteristics of chronically indecisive clients described by Salomone (1982). They also collectively come close to representing the core characteristics of trait negative affectivity (Watson & Clark, 1984)—a construct that consistently relates negatively to work and life satisfaction and to decision-making difficulties in a variety of life spheres (see Lent, Chapter 27, this volume). We have tentatively labeled this as an *Indecisiveness/Trait Negative Affect* factor to capture fully its major characteristics, although measures of trait negative affectivity need to be included in subsequent research to confirm the accuracy of this label.

The second factor reflects a *Lack of Information* latent dimension. All CDDP lack of information subscales loaded saliently on this factor along with the CFI lack of self and occupational information subscales and the CDP lack of occupational information subscale. Scales developed by Callanan and Greenhaus (1990) to measure lack of self-information and internal and external work information also loaded strongly on this factor. The only other manifest variable that loaded on this factor came from the

Table 23.1   Summary Factor Pattern Matrix

Manifest Variables	Factors			
	I	**II**	**III**	**IV**
Trait anxiety[a] (k = 12)	**.90**	.09	.08	.06
Hardiness (k = 2)	**−.88**	—	—	−.04
Depression (k = 4)	**.85**	—	—	.14
State anxiety[b] (k = 12)	**.76**	.10	.11	.11
Fear of commitment (k = 6)	**.69**	—	—	**.30**
Self-esteem (k = 7)	**−.67**	—	−.03	−.07
Indecisiveness[c] (k = 3)	**.63**	.05	.06	.26
Trait neuroticism (k = 1)	**.61**	—	—	.13
Self-criticism (k = 2)	**.60**	—	—	—
Dependent decision-making style (k = 1)	**.52**	—	—	.02
External locus of control[d] (k = 7)	**.48**	—	.15	.06
Problem-solving confidence (k = 2)	**−.48**	—	—	−.12
Positive (behavioral) coping style (k = 4)	**−.48**	—	—	—
Finding additional information (k = 4)	.01	**.91**	.07	.09
Lack of occupational information (k = 9)	.07	**.75**	.05	.12
Lack of self information (k = 7)	.15	**.66**	.22	**.33**
Lack of information on the process (k = 4)	—	**.64**	.06	.23
Approach-approach conflict (k = 2)	.05	**.53**	**.31**	—
External barriers (k = 3)	.17	.20	**.68**	—
Situational constraints (k = 1)	.08	.13	**.62**	.28
Interpersonal conflict (k = 6)	.10	.05	**.52**	.04
Unreliable information (k = 4)	.01	**.41**	**.50**	.09
CDS indecision (k = 8)	.05	.17	.18	**.88**
Vocational exploration and commitment (k = 2)	—	—	.09	**−.88**
Career decision-making self-efficacy (k = 5)	—	—	−.09	**−.85**
Vocational identity (k = 4)	−.12	−.21	−.03	**−.84**
Rational decision-making style (k = 1)	−.02	—	—	**−.76**
Lack of motivation (k = 4)	—	.12	.14	**.71**
Lack of self-clarity (k = 8)	.10	.14	.11	**.70**
Goal instability (k = 3)	—	—	.08	**.67**
Intuitive decision-making style (k = 1)	.07	—	—	**.67**
Career maturity attitudes (k = 2)	−.05	−.29	—	**−.66**
Dysfunctional thinking/career myths (k = 5)	.09	.01	.06	**.62**
Achieved ego identity status (k = 2)	—	—	—	**−.54**
Trait conscientiousness (k = 1)	−.11	—	—	**−.46**
Choice/work importance (k = 4)	—	.16	—	**−.44**
Approach-avoidance style (k = 1)	.13	—	—	**.35**

Notes: Empty cells indicate that the row variable was never included with other markers of the column factor. Salient loadings of .30 or higher are in bold. k = Number of matrices that included a measure of this manifest variable. Factor I = Indecisiveness/ Trait Negative Affect; Factor II = Information Deficits; Factor III = Interpersonal Conflicts and Barriers; Factor IV = Lack of Readiness.

[a]Includes measures of trait and manifest anxiety.
[b]Includes measures of state, career choice, and social anxiety.
[c]Includes CFI and CDP Indecisiveness scales.
[d]Includes measures of external, powerful others, and chance locus of control.

CDS approach-approach conflict subscale (indecision caused by conflict between or among appealing occupational options). Although the loading of this variable on a lack of information factor may, at first blush, be hard to understand, it might reflect that persons seeking counseling for a lack of information may be doing so to resolve this conflict. Stated another way, it may be that many clients who indicate that they lack information are really not seeking out more options (as is assumed in the outcome literature), but are rather needing further information to help them choose between or among an already crystallized set of options.

The third factor seems to reflect vocational decision-making problems involving *Interpersonal Conflicts and Barriers*. Manifest variables that loaded highly on this factor included indices of conflict involving disagreements with significant others (e.g., the CDDQ external conflict subscale), perceptions of external barriers (e.g., CDS barriers subscales), and situational constraints (e.g., Callanan & Greenhaus's 1990 situational constraints subscale). Also, experiences of approach-approach conflict had a salient (.31) secondary loading on this factor, suggesting, perhaps, that persons experiencing conflicts with significant others and other forms of external barriers may be stuck between two occupational options—one preferred by the client and the other preferred by significant others. Another possibility is a conflict between a preferred option that seems to be closed off to the person via external barriers and a less preferred, but more available option. In either case, our results suggest that information deficits (Factor II) and barriers or interpersonal conflicts (Factor III) may bring many people to counseling for help in deciding among attractive options and not to generate even more options.

The fourth factor resembles the identity diffusion factor suggested by others (e.g., Brown & Ryan Krane, 2000; Kelly & Lee, 2002) but is, we think, more than that. Although this factor is defined by identity diffusion (e.g., low MVS-Identity scores) and a lack of self-clarity (e.g., high scores on the CDP Lack of Self-Clarity scale), it is also marked by variables reflecting a lack of confidence in career decision-making skills, immature career attitudes (including adherence to career myths and other dysfunctional attitudes), unstable career goals, a reduced likelihood of being in an ego-identity-achieved status, and a concurrent lack of motivation to make and commit to a vocational decision. This pattern of loadings is consistent with developmental conceptions of a *Lack of Readiness* to make a career decision (e.g., Peterson, Sampson, Lenz, & Reardon, 2002; Phillips, 1992). Thus, high scorers on this factor may simply not yet have developed the attitudes, self-knowledge, and decision-making and goal-setting skills to make and commit to a vocational decision. Such a pattern of deficits is developmentally expected and may not become problematic until persons reach an age where vocational choice making is required or expected.

Several other interesting patterns of loadings on this factor might provide some insights into a person's lack of readiness, along with implications for counseling. First, measures of trait conscientiousness showed negative loadings on this factor. In the personality literature, conscientious persons are described as achievement-oriented, dependable, goal-directed, rational (versus intuitive), orderly, and deliberate (see Costa & McRae, 1985). These findings, along with the positive loadings of measures of intuitive (versus rational) decision-making styles on this factor, suggest that (a) low trait conscientiousness might be a risk factor for later problems of readiness, and (b) counseling persons with readiness difficulties may be made more difficult where low trait conscientiousness is present.

Second, several investigators (e.g., Chartrand et al., 1994; Tinsley et al., 1989) have used CDS total indecision scores to define chronic indecisiveness. Our data, however, suggest that these scores are the strongest markers of lack of readiness and might be used to identify vocationally unready clients. Identifying indecisive clients, on the other hand, requires measures that ask directly about the pervasiveness of a client's decision-making difficulties (e.g., CDP and CFI indecisiveness scales). Third, the full pattern of loadings also highlights the differences between our indecisiveness and lack of readiness factors. All variables that load on the indecisiveness factor represent cross-situational (e.g., trait anxiety, neuroticism, self-esteem, problem-solving confidence) contributors to vocational decision-making problems, whereas manifest variables that define the readiness factors are largely domain (vocational) specific (e.g., career decision-making self-efficacy beliefs, vocational identity, self-clarity, career choice salience). Thus, the readiness factor seems to represent difficulties in making a specific type of decision (a vocational decision), whereas the indecisiveness factor represents more pervasive problems.

Low readiness and the variables that define it, therefore, do not indicate more pervasive problems that need counselors' attention unless diagnostic data suggest that the lack of readiness is accompanied by indicators suggesting more pervasive problems. Similarly, chronic indecisiveness is not the same as a lack of readiness. Persons may enter counseling displaying chronic problems in decision making, but this does not mean that they lack goals or are unclear about their identities (or even have information deficits). In fact, our reanalyses of the cluster analytic studies will suggest that some chronically indecisive clients may be quite vocationally ready to make a decision, but are stymied by the dispositional tendencies that they bring with them to counseling.

A Reconceptualization of Cluster Analytic Data

As indicated earlier, several studies have sought to identify homogeneous subtypes of vocationally undecided people using a variety of (often non-overlapping) samples and measures. Despite this methodological disparity, our four factor model of indecision, when applied to these studies, may suggest some patterns of cross-study consistency that have potentially important implications for counseling and future research.

Chronic Indecisiveness

Four of the studies seemed to yield a cluster of potentially chronically indecisive persons who were marked *only* by the manifest variables included on our chronic indecisiveness/trait negative affect factor—high trait and state anxiety (Chartrand et al., 1994; Lucas, 1993; Wanberg & Muchinsky, 1992), indecisiveness (Wanberg & Muchinsky, 1992), and external locus of control (Lucas, 1993; Wanberg & Muchinsky, 1992); low self-esteem (Chartrand et al., 1994; Lucas, 1993; Wanberg & Muchinsky, 1992) and problem solving self-confidence (Larson et al., 1988); and a dependent decision-making style (Lucas, 1993).

Further inspection of these chronically indecisive clusters yielded important insights that, if confirmed, have important implications for counseling. Wanberg and Muchinsky (1992) clustered students drawn from the general college student population and identified two clusters of decided and two clusters of undecided students on the basis of the two-item CDP decidedness scale scores. One of the decided clusters (labeled by Wanberg & Muchinsky as "concerned decided individuals") displayed a pattern of scores on other measures that would clearly define them, in our model, as chronically indecisive—high state and trait anxiety and indecisiveness, and low self-esteem. These findings suggest that at least some chronically indecisive students may seek counseling because they cannot commit to a tentatively made decision and not because they are either without options or undecided.

Thus, cluster analytic and counseling outcome studies that use only "undecided" samples will miss a potentially large number of persons with profound decision-making difficulties. For example, indecisive students made up 40% of Wanberg and Muchinsky's (1992) sample, but only 4% of Larson et al.'s (1988) sample of college students who had not declared their major. Thus, Larson et al.'s (1988) failure to include students who had declared a major, but who were uncomfortable or less than committed to it, may have caused them to miss a potentially large number of chronically indecisive students. Finally, Chartrand et al.'s (1994) and Lucas's (1993) "indecisive" clusters made up 24% of career course students and 32% of counseling center clients, respectively.

Collectively, these results have at least two important implications: indecisive clients may seek out career services in somewhat large numbers, but may not present as being as undecided as we might otherwise expect. They, therefore, may not be searching for options, but seeking help in committing to, and feeling more comfortable with, some already made decisions. However, helping indecisive clients achieve comfort with their choices will probably not be a straightforward and easy task and will, we hypothesize, require helping them manage their dispositions toward negative affectivity (see Brown, Ryan, & McPartland, 1996).

Unreadiness

Three studies identified a cluster of persons who, by our model, seemed to be developmentally unready to make a decision—Rojewski's (1994) transitionally undecided ninth graders (38% of the sample), Wanberg and Muchinsky's (1992) indifferent undecided college students (25%), and perhaps Larson et al.'s (1988) uninformed group of students who had not declared a college major (48%). All three groups scored relatively high on the CDS indecision scale which was the primary marker of lack of readiness in our analyses. Rojewski's transitionally undecided ninth graders also displayed low levels of choice certainty and commitment, while the two college student samples also displayed a lack of self-clarity, diffuse vocational identities, low levels of choice importance (Wanberg & Muchinsky, 1992), and adherence to career myths (Larson et al., 1988).

Clear clusters of developmentally unready students failed to emerge from the studies of college students enrolled in career courses (Chartrand et al., 1994) or counseling center clients (Lucas, 1993). These findings may suggest that developmentally unready college-age students may be somewhat indifferent about choosing an occupation or college major and may not use career services extensively until the need to make a choice becomes more imminent or unless other sources of difficulty co-occur with their lack of readiness—a possibility we discuss next.

Unready Indecisives

Several cluster analytic studies found that problems of indecisiveness and a lack of readiness may co-occur. (Also, the median correlation between these factors in our factor analyses was .45.) Lucas and Epperson (1990) identified a cluster of students (Cluster 1), comprising 21% of their total sample, who reported diffuse vocational identities and low choice importance (lack of readiness) along with high anxiety and low self-esteem, a dependent decision-making style, and an external locus of control (chronic indecisiveness). Chartrand et al. (1994) labeled as "indecisive" a cluster of students who may be more accurately characterized as unready and indecisive—low goal stability and identity diffusion (unreadiness) and high choice anxiety, indecisiveness, and low self-esteem (indecisiveness). This cluster made up 38% of career course takers in the sample. Wanberg and Muchinsky's (1992) "anxious undecided" group (15% of total sample) obtained relatively low scores on measures of decidedness, choice importance, self-clarity, and vocational identity (lack of readiness) along with high scores on measures of state, trait, and social anxiety and external locus of control. Finally, Larson et al.'s (1988) "planless avoiders" reported low career decision-making self-efficacy beliefs and self-clarity and high career myths (lack of readiness) along with lack of confidence in general problem-solving abilities and an avoidant problem-solving style, comprising 21% of their undeclared majors sample. These findings suggest that (a) problems of indecisiveness and lack of readiness may co-occur in college student samples, (b) such students will report themselves as being vocationally undecided or unable to declare a college major in a timely manner, and (c) unready indecisives avail themselves of career services much more frequently than those who are simply developmentally unready.

The two studies of high school students likewise revealed a cluster of developmentally unready students who might also be developing characteristics associated with chronic indecisiveness. This cluster was most clearly identified in Multon et al.'s (1995) study of 10th through 12th graders: 24% of their sample reported themselves as being undecided about a career decision and displayed mostly developmentally appropriate levels of goal instability and lack of self-clarity, but also obtained high scores on a measure of trait negative affectivity. Rojewski (1994), in his study of ninth graders, uncovered a cluster of students who scored high on the CDS indecision scale (the primary marker of lack of readiness in our analyses) and displayed immature career attitudes and competencies along with the type of avoidant coping style that loaded on our indecisiveness/negative affectivity factor. These students made up 24% of Rojewski's sample.

The two high school student studies have potentially far-reaching implications. They suggest that as early as ninth grade, a sizable number of adolescents (24% of both samples) may be at risk for later problems associated with chronic indecisiveness and trait negative affectivity; in particular, pervasive decision-making difficulties and less than optimal vocational satisfaction and success. Thus, identifying and intervening with high school students who are at risk for becoming chronically indecisive in later years may have implications for their later abilities to make and commit to vocational decisions and achieve work satisfaction and success.

The manifest variables that defined our indecisiveness factor may provide some potential targets for early intervention efforts. These include (to name a few possibilities) anxiety management, problem-solving skills, and coping skills training. Central to all of these efforts may be helping these at-risk students to understand and manage their dispositional tendencies to focus on, and ruminate about, the potential negative versus positive consequence of decisional alternatives (see also Brown et al., 1996). These are precisely the intervention strategies that we think will also be necessary in working with adults who enter counseling because of problems of indecisiveness, whether or not they are associated with readiness or other (e.g., information deficit or interpersonal conflict) problems.

Information Deficits

All studies uncovered a cluster of participants who showed primarily information deficits, ranging from 10% of career counseling clients (Lucas, 1993) to 25% of students without a college major (Larson et al., 1998) to 32% of students enrolled in a career planning course (Chartrand et al., 1994). An interesting implication of these data is that students with information deficits may be much less likely to seek help from a career counseling center than those with more pervasive problems associated with indecisiveness alone or indecisiveness in combination with readiness deficits. In contrast, students with primarily or solely information deficits might be more likely to enroll in career courses than to seek career counseling. Our data also collectively suggest that career courses may attract a diverse set of students: our reanalysis of Chartrand et al.'s (1994) data suggest that career courses may be sought by chronically indecisive (24%) and unready indecisive (38%) as well as by information-seeking (32%) persons. Thus, future research on career courses should explore whether these courses are equally beneficial for information seeking, indecisive, and unready indecisive students. Although purely unready students will probably not choose to enroll in such courses, their effectiveness with unready students should be explored when enrollment is mandated for undecided students (see Kelly & Lee, 2002).

Finally, our exploration of cluster analytic results suggested that information deficits may also co-occur with problems of readiness (Lucas & Epperson, 1990; Multon et al., 1995; Rojewski, 1994). The factor intercorrelations obtained from our factor analyses confirm this (Mdn $r = .48$) and suggest that information deficits also share some variance with indecisiveness (Mdn $r = .46$) and interpersonal conflicts and barriers (Mdn $r = .49$).

Interpersonal Conflicts and Barriers

Only one study (Kelly & Lee, 2002) clustered students on the bases of their interpersonal conflicts and barriers and found a unique cluster of students enrolled in a career course whose choice-making difficulties might be due to interpersonal conflicts (primarily) and barriers. Although Kelly and Lee (2002) did not report on the number or percentage of their career course clients who experienced such conflicts, it is clear from these and our meta-analytic results that barriers and interpersonal conflicts can represent a significant source of decision-making difficulties for some clients. Thus, future research should study more fully the roles of barriers and interpersonal conflicts in the choice-making process, especially among women, the poor, and people of color. Several theories (e.g., Cook, Heppner, & O'Brien, 2002; Lent et al., 1994) have highlighted the potential career-inhibiting influence of such factors, especially external barriers. These theories may provide a fertile source of ideas about how barriers and interpersonal conflicts may underlie problems in choice-making as well as useful intervention suggestions, including how support building might counteract the inhibiting influences of external barriers (e.g., Brown & McPartland, 2005; Brown & Ryan Krane, 2000; Miller & Brown, 2005).

RECOMMENDATIONS AND CONCLUSION

In writing this chapter, we wanted to renew interest in research on causes of vocational indecision. We hope that our review of past research and the model that we presented stimulates new investigations on this important topic. Such investigations might take several forms. One would be to test the validity of our model. Although there are many ways to approach this task, a fruitful approach would be to conduct a series of confirmatory factor analytic studies testing our four factor model against plausible alternatives. In using this approach, investigators would initially select a subset of measures of marker variables for each of our four factors, administer these measures to appropriately large samples of participants, and then conduct confirmatory factor analyses on this data set. Subsequent studies could then include at least one marker variable for each factor from the earlier studies, add another new subset of marker measures, administer these measures to a new (but comparable) sample of participants, and repeat the confirmatory factor analytic tests of our four factor model versus other reasonable models that might have emerged from the earlier investigations.

A related important area of investigation would be to use our model to explore other potential sources of vocational indecision. For example, we suspect that our data set included a trait positive affectivity counterpart to our Indecisiveness/Trait Negative Affect factor that we could not adequately verify. To explain, several of the 24 matrices included measures of such positive characteristics as hope, agency, trait extraversion and agreeableness, and various positive cognitions that typically loaded together onto a single factor with surprisingly weak to nonexistent cross-loadings on any of our four identified factors. Unfortunately, each study relied on unique sets of these positive characteristics and thus provided no markers that we could use to verify whether these factors were study specific or collectively represented a common latent positive affectivity factor.

The existence of this factor could have important implications for refining our understanding of vocational indecision. The literature on trait positive and negative affectivity (see Watson & Tellegen, 1985) is clear that these are relatively independent dimensions of human affectivity and that the experience of negative emotion is not the bipolar opposite of the experience of positive emotion. Rather, the "negative pole" of positive affectivity is characterized by tiredness, apathy, boredom, and lethargy and not by negative emotional states. Thus, we wonder whether low positive affectivity might be an additional independent contributor to vocational indecision; that is, some people may be vocationally undecided simply because of their dispositional tendencies to be bored with choices and to have little energy to engage in exploration activities.

Another important research question is whether low positive affectivity is just another dispositional contributor to lack of readiness or whether it represents an independent cause of vocational indecision. If it emerges as a fifth major factor in subsequent tests of our model, we wonder whether knowledge of clients' dispositional tendencies toward boredom and lethargy might allow us to fine-tune our understanding of a client's apparent lack of readiness. Low positive affectivity and unreadiness may signal a dispositional cause for the client's lack of readiness versus a situational cause if positive affectivity is in the average or above-average range. Thus, future research should explore other potential sources, including trait positive affectivity, of vocational indecision.

Measurement development is an additional important area for investigation. Currently, no instrument provides a direct measure of each of the factors in our four factor model. Although counselors and researchers who want to begin to apply our model can piece together an assessment battery from extant instruments, aptitude-treatment interaction research and counseling practice would be greatly aided by a single instrument that would validly measure clients' indecisiveness, information deficits, interpersonal conflicts, and readiness. In the meantime, our results suggest some candidates for an assessment battery. The short CFI, CDP, or CDDQ indecisiveness scales may provide adequate ways to screen for potential chronic indecisiveness/trait negative affect. Follow-ups, with other questionnaires or interviews, could then be conducted to explore other constellations of characteristics (e.g., trait anxiety, fear of commitment, external locus of control, dependent decision-making styles, general lack of problem-solving confidence) that might become important targets for intervention.

Total CDS scores served as the primary marker of *lack of readiness* in our analyses and, therefore, might be used to screen for this important cause for indecision. Although the double- and triple-barreled nature of the items on this questionnaire causes us some concern, it still might provide an adequate initial screen for lack of readiness that can be further refined by adequate follow-ups. We would not recommend the CDDQ Lack of Readiness scale for this purpose because total scores on this scale are obtained from scores on subscales measuring indecisiveness, lack of motivation, and dysfunctional myths. The former subscale is misplaced according to our analysis and the reliability estimates obtained on the scores of the latter two subscales are sometimes inadequate.

The CDDQ External Conflicts subscale might be a useful screening measure for *interpersonal conflicts and barriers* and its Lack of Information scale might identify clients with *information deficits*. However, the CFI information subscales and the CDP Lack of Occupational Information scale yield the same information with fewer items and nearly equally adequate internal consistency estimates. Combining Choice Anxiety and Indecisiveness scores on the CFI will also yield data on overall indecisiveness. Thus, two instruments (CFI and CDS) and a measure of interpersonal conflicts and barriers (e.g., the CDDQ subscale) may provide a short, but useful screening battery for future research and practice.

We have reviewed research on factors related to vocational indecision and presented new data confirming that vocational indecision is multiply determined. We hope that this chapter renews interest in, and provides an important building block for, research on this important topic. We also hope counselors can use our data and speculations to improve the services that they provide to their vocationally undecided clients and that we can begin to move intervention research in a direction that will provide counselors with information that is useful to the diverse undecided clients they see in their practices.

REFERENCES

Achter, J. A., & Lubinski, D. (2005). Blending promise with passion: Best practices for counseling intellectually talented youth. In S. D. Brown & R. W. Lent (Eds.), *Career development and counseling: Putting theory and research to work* (pp. 600–624). Hoboken, NJ: Wiley.

Brown, S. D., & McPartland, E. B. (2005). Career interventions: Current status and future directions. In W. B. Walsh & M. L. Savickas (Eds.), *Handbook of vocational psychology* (3rd ed., 195–226). Mahwah, NJ: Erlbaum.

Brown, S. D., & Ryan Krane, N. E. (2000). Four (or five) sessions and a cloud of dust: Old assumptions and new observations about career counseling. In S. D. Brown & R. W. Lent (Eds.), *Handbook of counseling psychology* (3rd ed., pp. 740–766). New York: Wiley.

Brown, S. D., Ryan, N. E., & McPartland, E. B. (1996). Why are so many people happy and what do we do for those who aren't? *A reaction to Lightsey. Counseling Psychologist, 24*, 751–757.

Callanan, G. A., & Greenhaus, J. H. (1990). The career indecision of managers and Professionals: Development of a scale and a test of a model. *Journal of Vocational Behavior, 37*, 79–103.

Chartrand, J. M., Martin, W. F., Robbins, S. B., McAuliffe, G. J., Pickering, J. W., & Calliotte, J. A. (1994). Testing a level versus interactional view of career indecision. *Journal of Career Assessment, 2*, 40–54.

Chartrand, J. M., & Nutter, K. J. (1996). The Career Factors Inventory: Theory and applications. *Journal of Career Assessment, 4*, 205–218.

Chartrand, J. M., Robbins, S. B., Morrill, W. H., & Boggs, K. (1990). Development and evaluation of the Career Factors Inventory. *Journal of Counseling Psychology, 37,* 491–501.

Cohen, J. (1988). *Statistical power analysis for the behavioral sciences* (2nd ed.). Hillsdale, NJ: Erlbaum.

Cook, E. P., Heppner, M. J., & O'Brien, K. M. (2002). Career development of women: Color and White women—Assumptions, conceptualizations, and interventions from an ecological perspective. *Career Development Quarterly, 50,* 291–305.

Costa, P. T., & McRae, R. R. (1985). *The NEO Personality Inventory manual.* Odessa, FL: Psychological Assessment Resources.

Crites, J. O. (1969). *Vocational psychology: The study of vocational behavior and its development.* New York: McGraw-Hill.

Fabrigar, L. R., Wegener, D. T., MacCallum, R. C., & Strahan, E. J. (1999). Evaluating the use of exploratory factor analysis in psychological research. *Psychological Methods, 4,* 272–299.

Fuqua, D. R., & Newman, J. L. (1989). An examination of the relations among career subscales. *Journal of Counseling Psychology, 36,* 487–491.

Gati, I., Krausz, M., & Osipow, S. H. (1996). A taxonomy of difficulties in career decision making. *Journal of Counseling Psychology, 43,* 510–526.

Holland, J. L. (1997). *Making vocational choices: A theory of vocational personalities and work environments* (3rd. ed.). Odessa, FL: Psychological Assessment Resources.

Holland, J. L., Daiger, D. C., & Power, P. G. (1980). *My vocational situation.* Palo Alto, CA: Consulting Psychologists Press.

Holland, J. L., & Holland, J. E. (1977). Vocational indecision: More evidence and speculation. *Journal of Counseling Psychology, 24,* 404–414.

Jones, L. K. (1989). Measuring a three-dimensional construct of career indecision among college students: A revision of the Vocational Decision Scale—The career decision profile. *Journal of Counseling Psychology, 36,* 477–486.

Kelly, K. R., & Lee, W. C. (2002). Mapping the domain of career decision problems. *Journal of Vocational Behavior, 61,* 302–326.

Larson, L. M., Heppner, P. P., Ham, T., & Dugan, K. (1988). Investigating multiple subtypes of career indecision through cluster analysis. *Journal of Counseling Psychology, 35,* 439–446.

Lent, R. W., Brown, S. D., & Hackett, G. (1994). Toward a unifying social cognitive theory of career and academic interest, choice, and performance [Monograph]. *Journal of Vocational Behavior, 45,* 79–122.

Lucas, M. S. (1993). A validation of types of career indecision at a counseling center. *Journal of Counseling Psychology, 40,* 440–446.

Lucas, M. S., & Epperson, D. L. (1990). Types of vocational undecidedness: A replication and refinement. *Journal of Counseling Psychology, 37,* 382–388.

Miller, M. J., & Brown, S. D. (2005). Counseling for career choice: Implications for improving interventions and working with diverse populations. In S. D. Brown & R. W. Lent (Eds.), *Career development and counseling: Putting theory and research to work* (pp. 441–465). Hoboken, NJ: Wiley.

Multon, K. D., Heppner, M. J., & Lapan, R. T. (1995). An empirical derivation of career decision subtypes in high school students. *Journal of Vocational Behavior, 47,* 76–92.

Osipow, S. H. (1986). *Career Decision Scale manual.* Odessa, FL: Psychological Assessment Resources.

Osipow, S. H., Carney, C. G., & Barak, A. (1976). A scale of educational-vocational undecidedness: A typological approach. *Journal of Vocational Behavior, 9,* 233–243.

Peterson, G. W., Sampson, J. P., Jr., Lenz, J. G., & Reardon, R. C. (2002). A cognitive information approach to career problem solving and decision making. In D. Brown & Associates (Eds.), *Career choice and development* (4th ed., pp. 312–369). San Francisco: Jossey-Bass.

Phillips, S. D. (1992). *Career counseling: Choice and implementation.* In S. D. Brown & R. W. Lent (Eds.), *Handbook of counseling psychology* (2nd ed., 513–547). New York: Wiley.

Rector, C. C. (2006). *Toward a career indecision diagnostic typology: An exploratory factor analysis.* Unpublished doctoral dissertation, Loyola University, Chicago

Rojewski, J. W. (1994). Career indecision subtypes for rural adolescents from disadvantaged and nondisadvantaged backgrounds. *Journal of Counseling Psychology, 41,* 356–363.

Rounds, J. B., & Tinsley, H. E. A. (1984). Diagnosis and treatment of vocational problems. In S. D. Brown & R. W. Lent (Eds.), *Handbook of counseling psychology* (pp. 137–177). New York: Wiley.

Salomone, P. R. (1982). Difficult cases in career counseling: Pt. II. The indecisive client. *Personnel and Guidance Journal, 60*, 496–499.

Savickas, M. L. (1989). Annual review: Practice and research in career counseling and development, 1988. *Career Development Quarterly, 38*, 100–134.

Serling, D. A., & Betz, N. E. (1990). Development and evaluation of a measure of fear of commitment. *Journal of Counseling Psychology, 37*, 91–97.

Shimizu, K., Vondracek, F. W., & Schulenberg, J. (1994). Unidimensionality versus multidimensionality of the Career Decision Scale: A critique of Martin, Sabourin, Lapante, and Coallier. *Journal of Career Assessment, 2*, 1–14.

Shimizu, K., Vondracek, F. W., Schulenberg, J. E., & Hostetler, M. (1988). The factor structure of the Career Decision Scale: Similarities across selected studies. *Journal of Vocational Behavior, 32*, 213–225.

Stead, G. B., & Watson, M. B. (1993). How similar are the factor structures of the Career Decision Scale, the Career Decision Profile, and the Career Factors Inventory? *Educational and Psychological Measurement, 53*, 281–290.

Tien, H. S. (2005). The validation of the Career Decision-Making Difficulties Scale in a Chinese culture. *Journal of Career Assessment, 13*, 114–127.

Tinsley, H. E. A., Bowman, S., & York, D. C. (1989). Career Decision Scale, My Vocational Situation, Vocational Rating Scale, and Decisional Rating Scale: Do they measure the same constructs. *Journal of Counseling Psychology, 36*, 115–120.

Wanberg, C. R., & Muchinsky, P. M. (1992). A typology of career decision status: Validity of the vocational decision status model. *Journal of Counseling Psychology, 39*, 71–80.

Watson, D., & Clark, L. A. (1984). Negative affectivity: The disposition to experience aversive emotional states. *Psychological Bulletin, 96*, 465–490.

Watson, D., & Tellegen, A. (1985). Toward a consensual structure of mood. *Psychological Bulletin, 98*, 219–235.

Whiston, S. C., Brecheisen, B. K., & Stephens, J. (2003). Does treatment modality affect career counseling effectiveness? *Journal of Vocational Behavior, 62*, 390–410.

Williamson, E. G. (1965). *Vocational counseling: Some historical, philosophical, and theoretical perspectives.* New York: McGraw-Hill.

CHAPTER 24

Contextual Factors in Vocational Psychology: Intersections of Individual, Group, and Societal Dimensions

NADYA A. FOUAD
NEETA KANTAMNENI

It is a time of exciting change for vocational psychology. On the one hand, the real world issues that vocational psychologists address are growing more complex, as the world of work changes. On the other hand, the field itself is changing, influenced by concerns that research has neglected a large percentage of the population for whom work and choice are an oxymoron, and by a strong push to understand how the context of people's lives influences their career and work development. These changes are occurring at a time when research in vocational psychology has powerful policy implications, such as ameliorating gender and racial/ethnic inequities in work, identifying mechanisms to support employment of the unemployed, predicting successful reforms to welfare programs, empowering individuals to create satisfying work lives, and developing model programs to support men and women's work-life balance.

Traditional notions of career and work are dramatically changing. Globalization, technological advances in nearly every occupational area, and social contracts between corporations and individuals have shifted the emphasis from careers and jobs as a single choice made early in life to a series of choices that individuals make over a life span. And choices are increasingly made involuntarily as individuals are fired or laid off from jobs that they thought were stable. As Fouad (2007) noted, vocational psychologists try to help individuals make choices in a world of work that is, in many ways, a moving target. And yet work is a crucial aspect of life in the United States.

The context in which career and vocational decisions are made is critical in understanding both the process and content of those decisions. Similar to Merriam Webster's definition, we define context as the interrelated, reciprocal, and dynamic environment in which career decisions are made. The circumstances surrounding the individual and his or her environment at the time decisions are made strongly shape those decisions. The career and work choices made by a White, middle-class, midwestern, Christian, heterosexual male in his early 20s may be quite different from choices made by an African American Christian young woman, who is lesbian and living in the South. Their decisions are shaped by the environment in which they live, including their families, their socioeconomic status, the opportunity structure of the labor market around them, and their exposure to racism and discrimination. It is impossible to understand the choices of either of these individuals, predict the outcome, or intervene to help them make better choices without understanding the context of their decision making.

Vocational psychologists have, in fact, argued for over 2 decades that we need to broaden our understanding of context. Scholars first challenged the field to examine the role of gender (Betz & Hackett, 1981; Farmer, 1985) and race and ethnicity (Fouad, Cudeck, & Hansen, 1984; Smith, 1980) in influencing career decisions. These scholars criticized vocational psychology research as too focused on the career experiences of relatively privileged men, for whom career development appeared to follow a linear trajectory. As Fitzgerald and Betz (1994) noted, "Career development theories have always had the most to say about the smallest segment of the population, that is, white middle class heterosexual men" (p. 105). Career development research has begun to provide more information on the work experiences of women, and to some extent, people of color. In the past decade, factors such as social class (Blustein, 2006; M. T. Brown, Fukunaga, Umemoto, & Wicker, 1996), family (Schultheiss, Palma, Predragovich, & Glasscock, 2002; Whiston, 1996), relationships (Flum, 2001; Schultheiss, 2003), and geographic location (C. Brown, Darden, Shelton, & Dipoto, 1999; Chaves et al., 2004) also have been identified as important areas for vocational psychologists to incorporate in their research and practice. More recently, some have argued (Blustein, 2006; Fouad, 2007) that we need to examine multiple dimensions (e.g., race *and* gender *and* social class) of context.

Despite the calls for understanding context in career decision making, most research focuses on single snapshots of contextual influences, typically at one point in time. Capturing the multiple dimensions of context that can influence career decisions is a difficult feat. Consider an adolescent girl who is struggling with whether to go to college. The most important influences on her decision may be her interest in math, her gender, her race, the opportunity to take additional math courses, her mother's support, and her hometown's proximity to a college. However, when that same girl becomes an employed adult, the influences on her career choices may differ. Her math interests, her education, her mother's support, and her gender and race may influence her career path, but so might her sexual orientation, her cultural values, and the opportunity structure for work. All these contextual factors interrelate and may be reciprocal. A contextual framework that captures these multiple levels of influence is needed in vocational psychology, and we propose such a model in this chapter.

We are not the first to suggest the need for such a model. Vondracek, Lerner, and Schulenberg (1986) called for a contextual lens on vocational choices in their developmental-contextualism model. They postulated that the person-environment interaction is dynamic and changes over the life span. Thus, the model has both an interdisciplinary and developmental focus, incorporating concepts from developmental psychology. It is also a dynamic model, in that change in one context produces change in other levels of context, and people have some effect on their own environment. Individuals are both shaped by and shape their environment. Savickas (2002) noted that the contribution of the developmental contextualism model was recognizing the individual's potential for change and encouraging psychologists to empower individuals to effect that change. The model has not been further developed since 1986, and there has been little direct empirical evidence for the approach (Osipow & Fitzgerald, 1996). However, Vondracek et al. were the first to argue that career choices are the result of "interlocking factors" situated in the individual's social and family context (Young, Valach, & Collin, 2002); this perspective has shaped the field of vocational psychology in the past 20 years.

Bronfenbrenner's ecological developmental model (Bronfenbrenner, 1977) has also begun to influence vocational psychology, most notably in an application to career counseling with women (Cook, Heppner, & O'Brien, 2002). Cook et al. noted that the ecological model is particularly helpful for career counseling with women because their "behavior is . . . a representation of the complex interaction[s] among the myriad factors" that affect their lives (p. 296). Cook et al. believe that an ecological approach aids career counselors not only to empower women, but to understand the influences from the microlevel (e.g., home, school), exolevel (e.g., external environments such as parental workplace), macrolevel (e.g., society), and mesolevel (e.g., interactions among the different levels) that may circumscribe the real options that women have. Betz (2002) cautioned that the ecological model "increases the complexity of assessment and makes research difficult" (p. 338), and encouraged future research to focus on how to assess the various levels influencing individual vocational behavior.

We agree with Betz (2002) that an ecological model makes research more difficult, but we also believe that it is critical to develop a framework to better understand the reciprocal influences of context on individuals' career decisions. Bronfenbrenner's model is complex, consisting of several interacting systems. In this chapter, we propose a modified model that builds on previous models (Bronfenbrenner, 1977) by examining contextual influences, yet is specifically related to vocational psychology, and is rooted in a multicultural framework. Our model is somewhat less complex than Bronfenbrenner's;

we postulate two layers of contextual influences that operate on individual vocational variables rather than four. Similar to Vondracek et al. (1986) and Cook et al. (2002), we suggest that the environment consists of both group-level factors (e.g., gender, race and ethnicity, social class, family) and societal factors (e.g., acculturation, influences from majority culture). These factors intersect with each other and with individual factors (e.g., interests, abilities, values) to help shape decisions. Thus, interests may be shaped by the expectations from an individual's family and the opportunity structure in his or her environment. To fully capture the conceptual framework, then, we have proposed a three-dimensional model. The model highlights the reciprocal and dynamic ways contextual factors influence career development and provides a conceptual framework to guide future research and interventions in this area. In particular, we hope that this model will guide research in understanding factors that increase resilience and empower individuals in making strong vocational decisions. Our chapter is organized around this model, described more fully in the following section. We briefly review selected studies in each of the model's three dimensions, with an emphasis on group and societal factors. The last part of the chapter is a brief discussion of the implications for research and interventions in the ways that individual, family, and cultural factors interact.

PROPOSED MODEL

Our proposed model integrates the multiple dimensions of contextual factors on vocational development. This model captures the dynamic, complex, and interactive nature of how contextual factors influence the meaning made in career and work decisions. The first dimension includes the individual factors on which contextual factors operate. This dimension encompasses the traditional areas that vocational psychologists have believed shape career choices, including interests, values, and abilities. The second dimension comprises group level variables. This dimension includes gender, race and ethnicity, SES, family variables, religion, sexual orientation, and relationships. The third dimension is the society in which individuals reside, including their culture of origin (e.g., cultural values), their culture's difference from the majority culture (e.g., discrimination and cultural barriers), and influences directly from the societal mainstream culture (e.g., schooling, the labor market, and opportunity structure).

Our proposed model is depicted in Figure 24.1. Because of space limitations, we can only discuss the research related to some aspects of the model. Other areas (e.g., disability, sexual orientation, religion) have not received much empirical examination in vocational psychology and, though important, are not discussed in the chapter. We refer readers to Croteau, Bieschke, Fassinger, and Manning (Chapter 12, this volume) on sexual orientation and Peterson and Elliott (Chapter 13, this volume) on disability for in-depth discussions in these areas.

A key component of our model is the interaction among the various dimensions, highlighting the multifaceted nature of the role context plays in vocational development. Individuals may differ among the variables within each dimension at different points in their lives. Similarly, the variables within each dimension can, and often do, interact with one another as well as with variables in other dimensions to create a context unique for each individual. Furthermore, we suggest that the salience of each of these contextual factors varies greatly depending on the individual and his or her developmental stage.

DIMENSION 1: INDIVIDUAL INFLUENCES

We briefly discuss individual influences here, but refer readers to Amstrong and Rounds (Chapter 22, this volume) for an in-depth discussion. The first dimension includes the individual differences that shape career decisions and choices. These are the variables that have historically been a focus of vocational psychology research; we propose that contextual influences act on individual differences. Individuals differ on various psychological attributes, often portrayed as mean differences on an assessment of those

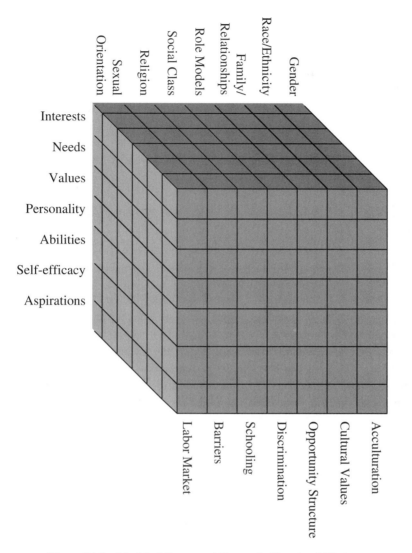

Figure 24.1   Model of Contextual Factors in Vocational Choice

attributes. Dawis (1996) noted that the psychology of individual differences provided a scientific basis for the development of vocational psychology. Indeed, he argued that the study of individual differences is one of the five roots of counseling psychology in general (Dawis, 1992).

Dawis (1992 1996) traced the history of vocational psychology's emphasis on the assessment of individual differences in aptitude, skills, intelligence, interests, and values. Fundamentally, vocational psychologists were influenced strongly by Parsons' (1909) person-environment matching model. Efforts to understand individual differences focused on explaining differences among individuals, which eventually led to efforts in predicting person-environment fit. Contemporary reviews of research indicate that vocational psychologists are still focusing on how individuals differ on the dimensions of interests, abilities, and needs/values (Hansen, 2005; Krane & Tirre, 2005; Rounds & Armstrong, 2005). This is not to suggest that vocational psychologists have not asked additional questions in the past century of research. Indeed, they have argued that individual differences in other constructs, such as career beliefs, barriers, and personality, need to be assessed, as do the factors that contribute to those differences (Swanson & D'Achiardi, 2005). One of the prevailing concerns among vocational psychologists is that an overemphasis on assessment of individual differences may lead to the misuse of tests for assessing those differences (Hartung, 2005).

DIMENSION 2: GROUP-LEVEL INFLUENCES

The second dimension includes group-level influences—the immediate context of our social environment. These differences include influences often categorized by an orientation to specific demographic groups defined by gender, race/ethnicity, relational influences, and social class. Group-level differences may also include sexual orientation or the influence of religion on vocational choice. Researchers have long argued that group-level factors influence vocational development as well as the meaning a person makes of the world of work (Blustein, 2006).

Gender

We briefly review here the empirical research on the role of gender in career decision making, but readers are referred to Betz (2005) and Cook, Heppner, and O'Brien (2002) for in-depth discussions of gender and career choices. As these authors point out, gender plays an important role throughout individuals' careers; however, most of the research on the effect of gender on career decisions has focused on predictors of initial choice.

Studies of occupational aspirations have found that both girls and boys aspire to careers that are gender-stereotypic. In longitudinal studies of high school students, the perception that some occupations are only appropriate for women decreases over time, but girls continue to say they aspire to female-dominated careers (Miller & Budd, 1999). Farmer and her students (Farmer, Wardrop, Anderson, & Risinger, 1995) found that girls were less likely than boys to want to pursue a science career 10 years after high school, and the higher the girls' career commitment, the more likely they were to choose a different, more gender-stereotypic, career. The effect size was moderate for the relationship between career commitment and a shift to traditional careers for girls, but the pattern was not found for boys.

The difference between what youth want to do versus what they expect to do when they grow up has been the subject of research to understand why there are often differences between aspirations and expectations. Armstrong and Crombie (2000) focused on this discrepancy, finding that eighth graders who had the most differences between their aspirations and expectations changed their initial career choice in the direction of their expectations by 10th grade, often to a more gender-traditional occupation.

Research over 25 years has also shown differences in the perception of what girls think they can do, particularly in the math and science areas. As Betz (2005) noted, these differences tend to follow traditional gender role socialization patterns. This is reflected in gender differences in vocational interests. Studies have consistently shown a moderate effect size for women scoring higher on Artistic and Social interests and lower on Realistic interests than men (Aros, Henly, & Curtis, 1998; Fouad, 2002; Fouad & Walker, 2005). Recent research shows that these gender differences are also found in the learning opportunities and experiences in different fields that women and men seek out (Williams & Subich, 2006).

Gender differences in interests and learning experiences are predicted by Social Cognitive Career Theory (Lent, Brown, & Hackett, 1994). Betz and Hackett (1981), in their seminal 1981 study, found that college women had higher self-efficacy (confidence in abilities to do the tasks) for gender-traditional occupations (e.g., nurse and teacher) and lower self-efficacy for nontraditional occupations such as math, science, or technical occupations (e.g., engineer, physician). Betz (2005) reviewed other studies on gender and self-efficacy expectations, concluding "low self-efficacy, especially in relationship to male-dominated careers . . . may reduce the self-perceived career options of women" (p. 259).

Gender also influences the rationale that individuals give for making career decisions. Davey (2001) asked high school seniors why they chose an occupational goal, and found a moderate effect ($r =$ .31) for differences between girls and boys in pattern of reasons for choice. Males were more likely to choose an occupation on the basis of interests, while girls were more likely to cite altruistic reasons. Men and women differ in the role that prestige plays in choosing a career (Farmer, Rotella, Anderson, & Wandrop, 1998). Echoing Davey's study, Farmer et al. also found for engineering occupations that men and women had similar scientific (Investigative) interests, but the second Holland code was Social for women and Realistic for men.

While women's career choices have been examined for over 3 decades, researchers have just begun to examine the role of gender role traditionality in men's career choices. Jome and Tokar (1998) found that one discriminant function accounted for 15% of the difference between men in gender traditional and nontraditional majors, with the highest loading variables including antifeminist attitudes, restrictive emotionality, attitudes toward toughness, and two indicators of homophobic attitudes. In a second study, Tokar and Jome (1998) found that social interests were the only interest area that mediated the relationship between masculinity and gender-traditional career choices (men with stronger versus weaker social interests are more likely to chose gender atypical fields). Lease (2003) investigated factors that led to boys' persistence in their nontraditional aspirations, finding that liberal social attitudes predicted nontraditional choice, but socioeconomic status and higher educational aspirations were predictive of more male-traditional occupations.

Gender influences career and work choices throughout the life span. It influences individuals' perception of what careers might be appropriate, their self-efficacy beliefs for traditional and nontraditional careers, and their interests for gender-traditional and nontraditional occupations. Gender plays an influential role in career decision making, but few studies have investigated how other contextual factors influence gender and gender role socialization throughout the career development process.

Race and Ethnicity

Race and ethnicity play an influential role in career development, career decision making, and how individuals find meaning through work. These background variables are such strong social stratification variables (Helms, Jernigan, & Mascher, 2005) that they help create an unequal occupational landscape for racial/ethnic minority group members. Data indicate that African Americans and Hispanics are underrepresented in professional, management, and related occupations (35%, 26%, and 17%, respectively) (U.S. Bureau of Labor Statistics [BLS], 2006). Conversely, Blacks and Hispanics are overrepresented in lower-paying positions, such as service (23% and 24%, respectively), production, transportation, and material moving occupations (16% and 19%, respectively) when compared with their White counterparts (15% and 12%, respectively). Unemployment status also differs across racial/ethnic categories, with unemployment rates for African Americans and Hispanics higher than for Whites. These statistics from the Bureau of Labor indicate that race and ethnicity are related to opportunities to work.

Researchers have also shown that the reality of racism and discrimination encountered in the workforce negatively influences the hiring of African Americans and Hispanics (Pager & Quillian, 2005). Once racial/ethnic minority individuals are hired, racism adversely affects their perceptions of the workplace and their mental health (Parker et al., 2003; Roberts, Swanson, & Murphy, 2004). Whereas the occupational landscape and the impact of discrimination differ for individuals from minority backgrounds, many individual factors also affect how career decisions are made. There are many differences in the resilience of individuals to the influences of discrimination on career development. An example of this can be seen in Richie et al's (1997) qualitative analysis of high-achieving African American women, which indicates that we also need to understand factors that empower individuals to achieve despite barriers.

Although there are racial/ethnic differences in work choices, it is not known how these differences in career and work choices occur, or whether these reflect choices or compromises, because few empirical studies have systematically examined this complex variable. We briefly review here the empirical research on the role of race and ethnicity in career decision making, but refer readers to Worthington, Flores, Navarro, Brown, and Lent (2005) and M. T. Brown, Yamini-Diouf, and Ruiz de Esparza (2005) for more in-depth discussions.

A recent meta-analysis examined the role of race and ethnicity on factors related to adolescents' initial career decisions: career aspirations, career expectations, interests, and decision making (Fouad

& Byars-Winston, 2005). The authors examined 16 studies, and found no significant differences among racial/ethnic groups in career aspirations or decision-making attitudes, but race and ethnicity appeared to relate to perceptions of career opportunities and barriers. The effect sizes associated with perceptions of career-related opportunities and barriers ($g = 0.38$) were moderate and revealed ethnic minority group members perceived more barriers and fewer opportunities than did the average White American. The authors concluded that while career dreams and aspirations appeared to be similar for all individuals ($g = 0.01$), perceptions of opportunities to recognize and achieve these dreams differed across racial/ethnic groups.

While current research has focused on mean differences between racial/ethnic groups on various career variables such as future career expectations and aspirations, barriers and supports, and factors influencing career goals (Chung & Harmon, 1999; Luzzo & McWhirter, 2001), little is known about how members of racial/ethnic minority groups construct their careers. It is not known if differences in employment choices reflect variations in cultural values about work, access to role models, discrimination and racism, perceptions of opportunities, or some combination of all these factors. In exploring these questions, several qualitative studies have focused on the construction of meaning through work for individuals from varying ethnic groups. Juntunen and her colleagues (2001), examining the construction of meaning of career among 18 American Indian adults, found several general themes. Participants viewed career as a lifelong endeavor with a strong emphasis on planning, goal setting, and looking to the future. Participants also viewed career as being strongly related to personal and family goals, and an important part of a person's identity.

Researchers have qualitatively examined variables related to career development of high-achieving minority women (Gomez et al., 2001; Richie et al., 1997). Gomez et al. investigated the career development of 20 notable Latinas and found that the career paths of these participants tended to be unplanned and nonlinear. Contextual background variables such as educational experiences and social status influenced the participants' career decisions as did family and cultural variables (cultural value of *familismo*, collectivism, messages about gender roles, and familial career aspirations). Participants also indicated they had developed a bicultural identity to navigate two cultures, balancing Latina cultural values without appearing as if selling out to mainstream culture.

Richie et al. (1997) interviewed 9 high-achieving African American women and found that being a woman in a sexist context impacted the participants, both in their personal and professional lives. The combination of sexism and racism was prevalent, presenting barriers for these participants in the workforce. However, all the participants were high achievers and attributed their success in overcoming these barriers to feelings of passion about their work and the support that they received from others, particularly from their families. In a separate qualitative study, Pearson and Bieschke (2001) also interviewed 14 high-achieving African American women and found that a strong value on education within their families influenced the participants' vocational development; families also provided lessons about how to pursue, enter, and maintain careers. Furthermore, gender role socialization within the family, either flexible or androgynous, influenced participants' career development, although most participants reported that they did not feel limited by their gender in their career choices.

Racial/ethnic background appears to affect vocational development in multiple ways. Individuals from racial/ethnic minority backgrounds are not represented in all types and levels of employment as are White Americans (BLS, 2006), yet their career dreams and aspirations are similar to those of their White counterparts. This may be due to racism and discrimination within the workforce, precluding opportunities, rather than as a direct result of their aspirations. Qualitative studies investigating the process of constructing meaning in career development have indicated that various contextual factors such as cultural values and familial values may be related to career choice. These studies provide the groundwork for understanding how members of racial/ethnic minority groups construct meaning from their careers. These studies also revealed several factors that may be related to resilience in the participants, particularly familial support. Race and ethnicity appear to play an important role in career development and will be covered in other sections of this chapter as well.

Relational and Familial Influences

It has been proposed that psychology is undergoing a relational revolution (Blustein, 2001). The past decade has seen an emphasis in researchers' focus and attention on the central role that interpersonal relationships play in human development (Blustein, Schultheiss, & Flum, 2004). Strong positive relationships can act as a motivating force behind career exploration by providing a foundation from which individuals make career decisions (Blustein et al., 2004; Richie et al., 1997). The opposite is also true; negative relationships can impede career exploration by restricting exploratory behavior. Several studies have highlighted the influences that family can have on vocational development, finding, for example, that sibling and parental support are positively related to career exploration, commitment, (Leal-Muniz & Constantine, 2005), self-efficacy (Ali, McWhirter, & Chronister, 2005), school engagement, aspirations (Kenny, Blustein, Chaves, Grossman, & Gallagher, 2003), and overcoming barriers (Richie et al., 1997).

A comprehensive review of 77 studies by Whiston and Keller (2004) found that family-of-origin influences were related to career development in specific, and largely predictable, ways (e.g., supportive family environments were related to increased career exploration). Family process variables such as family interactions, parental expectations, and relational factors were both positively (e.g., strong parental expectations) and negatively (e.g., unrealistic parental expectations) associated with career-related factors. The authors noted that parents often interact with children and adolescents on career-related issues, and family members had more influence on career decision making than peers. Whiston and Keller also found that some familial influences, such as parental attachment, appeared to be related to such career choice outcomes as vocational exploration, career decidedness, and commitment to a career. An important conclusion of this review was that while much research has investigated the role of familial influences on career development, family factors cannot be examined in isolation. Instead, family needs to be considered with other contextual factors such as gender, socioeconomic status, and race.

Finally, role models play an influential role in vocational development. It has been hypothesized that identification with role models can be critical in career decision making (Gibson, 2004). Role models can act as mentors by providing information about outcomes associated with specific careers as well as influence career decision making. Empirical research has found that role models have a small positive relationship to career maturity ($r = .06$) (Flouri & Buchanan, 2002), vocational identity ($r = .22$), and career certainty ($r = .28$) (Nauta & Kokaly, 2001). Role models also are an important source of self-efficacy and outcome expectation information (Lent et al., 1994).

Relationships can influence vocational development in multiple ways. Whereas relational influences can both hinder and promote career exploration, much of the recent research has highlighted the positive association between strong relationships, particularly within one's family, and vocational development. Both qualitative and quantitative research projects have found that strong relationships can empower individuals to create satisfying work lives.

Social Class

We briefly review the empirical research on the role of social class in vocational development, but refer readers to Chapter 10, this volume, by Liu and Rasheed for an in-depth discussion of social class. Few scholars have focused on exploring social class as a contextual influence. In fact, a major criticism of vocational psychology is that research has neglected the concerns of poor or working-class individuals compared with middle-class or wealthy individuals (Blustein, 2006). Yet, social class has been hypothesized to act as an influential structural factor in vocational development, shaping access to resources and influencing occupational attainment, aspirations, and career development (Blustein et al., 2002). Researchers have suggested that social class affects occupational attainment, access to work, and values placed on work (M. T. Brown et al., 1996; Fouad & Brown, 2000).

A recent qualitative study of 20 young adults by Blustein et al. (2002) found that individuals from more affluent backgrounds had greater access to resources as well as more support from families and schools. Poorer youth reported more barriers to career choices. In addition, social class appeared to affect the meaning that working-class youth made of their vocational development. Perhaps the most poignant finding of this study was that youth from poorer backgrounds appeared to travel on a "one-way journey to a world of unskilled and dead-end jobs," such as fast-food worker, whereas middle-class youth appeared to be simply taking these jobs on their way to a "more personally and financially satisfying work life" (Blustein et al., 2002, p. 321). An additional qualitative study by Chaves et al. (2004) examined urban adolescents' conceptions of work and found that students from low-income backgrounds viewed work as a means to an end. Moreover, these students from different backgrounds received similar messages about the role of work from their families.

Gender, race and ethnicity, relational and familial influences, and social class appear to be related to vocational development. However, little research has focused on how these constructs directly influence vocational development and the meaning people make of the role of work in their lives. More research is needed to examine the interrelationships among group-level variables, as well as between individual and group-level variables.

DIMENSION 3: SOCIETAL-LEVEL INFLUENCES

The third dimension in our model represents the societies in which individuals reside that create a larger context for work and career decisions. This includes the morals, values, traditions, and customs that help create institutions in that society, including educational systems and labor markets. Societal influences shape policies on schooling, higher education, transitions in and out of work (such as family leave and unemployment policies), and age and the process of retirement. These policies and societal decisions stem from values and attitudes inherent in that society. Although there are within-group differences, the United States, as a society, places an emphasis on individual achievement and gain, whereas Asian countries place a higher value on collective achievement; these differences become evident in the pay structure in each society, in the value placed on emotional relationships, and in the role of teams for achieving individual success (Gelfand, Erez, & Aycan, 2007).

For many immigrants and racial/ethnic minorities, the societal dimension also includes their culture of origin, and the context that results from differences between the culture of origin and mainstream culture. A woman who immigrated to the United States from Saudi Arabia would be influenced by the societal expectations and prescriptions for women in her native Saudi Arabia, by the opportunities available to her in the United States, and by her ability to negotiate the differences between the two societies.

Culture of Origin

The role and nature of work in an individual's life are influenced by societal beliefs and values. An individual's culture of origin shapes how that individual constructs meaning in his or her work, his or her career development trajectories, and the extent to which he or she engages in career exploration. Aspects of an individual's culture of origin include factors such as family influences and cultural values. Familial factors were discussed in Dimension 2; in this section, we focus on cultural values.

Although work values have traditionally been thought to be an individual variable, the values and messages people receive from their cultures of origin affect their views on work and the meaning they give to their careers. And cultures differ on the variables that influence work decisions (Gelfand et al., 2007). In addition to differences due to individualism and collectivism, societies differ in their emphasis on doing versus being: the former is a value placed on work as a worthy end in itself, whereas being focuses on work as a means to other aspects of life, such as family and friend relationships. Another area in which cultures differ is whether individuals are judged by what they have achieved or by the family and class into which they were born. Finally, cultures vary in their comfort with uncertainty and the typical perceived differences between those in power and their employees (power distance). In some cases, cultural values may expand the role that work plays in people's lives, whereas in other cases, values may limit occupational choices and career exploration. Values are often culturally situated variables, and it may be necessary to explore these values to gain a full understanding of the meaning of work in people's lives (Kim, Yang, & Hwang, 2006).

Although cultural values have been hypothesized to play an influential role in career development, little research has investigated this relationship empirically. A qualitative analysis found cultural values to be influential in Latina career development with participants reporting a strong collectivistic value and identity that they espoused throughout adulthood (Gomez et al., 2001). The cultural value of familismo was central to many of the participants. In addition, the cultural values of *dharma*, an Indian value of tradition and duty, were investigated in relation to interest-occupation congruence (Gupta & Tracey, 2005). Gupta and Tracey found that Indians displayed a higher adherence to dharma ($r = .43$) and interests were less congruent with their occupational choices when compared with Caucasians ($r = -.25$), although dharma was not found to significantly predict congruence. Although research on the role of cultural values in career decision making is sparse, these values may have a long-standing impact on vocational development.

Differences from Mainstream Culture

In addition to culture of origin, differences between culture of origin and the mainstream culture may also help to shape vocational development. Individuals from diverse backgrounds may encounter conflicting experiences and messages related to the world of work. Qualitative studies found that racial/ethnic minority individuals often felt they were living in two worlds and had to navigate between two cultures to balance values and norms (Gomez et al., 2001; Juntunen et al., 2001). Participants reported that they developed a bicultural identity to incorporate values from both cultures in their career decision making.

A factor that may influence this navigation is acculturation. Acculturation describes the way individuals change, accommodate, or adopt cultural patterns of mainstream society (Kohatsu, 2005). The role of acculturation can be influential in creating vocational identity. On the one hand, Flores and O'Brien (2002) found that acculturation level had a small relationship ($r = .23$) with the selection of nontraditional careers in a sample of Mexican American adolescent women; those who had higher Anglo orientation chose less prestigious and more gender-traditional careers. On the other hand, Flores, Ojeda, Huang, Gee, and Lee (2006) found that Mexican American students who were acculturated to Anglo culture were more likely to have higher educational goals than students who were less acculturated to Anglo culture, with a moderate effect found ($r = .34$). In addition, these researchers found that educational goals were unrelated to Mexican-oriented acculturation. Similarly, Leong (2001) found that Asian Americans' acculturation to mainstream culture was positively and moderately related to job satisfaction ($r = .34$ to $.44$) and supervisors' performance ratings ($r = .37$), and was negatively related to occupational stress and strain ($r = -.25$ to $.31$). Although these studies found mixed results for the role that acculturation plays in career development, the research investigating acculturation is limited and further research is needed.

Discrimination also influences how individuals navigate between two cultures. Data from the Bureau of Labor Statistics (2006), as earlier described, highlights the potential impact of this discrimination, with individuals from racially diverse backgrounds being employed in different types of positions and having higher rates of unemployment when compared with their White counterparts. This may, in part, be due to restriction of choices because of anticipated discrimination or the perceptions of occupational opportunities. Chung and Harmon (1999) supported this in a larger quantitative study, finding a moderate effect size for differences in perceptions of discrimination in the workplace: racial/ethnic minority individuals perceived more discrimination from Whites than Whites believed there was discrimination against racial/ethnic minorities.

Often, discrimination influences the perceived and actual barriers an individual experiences, shaping the context of his or her vocational development. Social cognitive career theory describes supports and barriers as contextual variables that influence progress toward a career choice (Lent, Brown, & Hackett, 2000). Much of the empirical research available on supports has focused primarily on relational supports, such as family and peer supports. This research has been previously discussed under the second domain. Yet, a substantial amount of literature has focused on the role of barriers in career and vocational development. Fouad and Byars-Winston's (2005) meta-analysis, described earlier, documented the differences between racial/ethnic minorities and Whites on perceptions of barriers, with racial/ethnic minorities perceiving more barriers than European Americans. Furthermore, several studies have found that perceptions of barriers are related to outcome expectations ($r = -.44$) (Chronister & McWhirter, 2004), career indecision ($r = .28$) (Constantine, Wallace, & Kindaichi, 2005), premature foreclosure of career options ($r = .25$) (Leal-Muniz & Constantine, 2005), school engagement ($r = -.23$ to $-.25$), and career aspirations ($r = -.15$ to $-.27$) (Kenny et al., 2003). Although effect sizes ranged from low to moderate, perceived barriers are correlated with individuals' vocational development and how career choices are made.

Barriers affect vocational development, but despite this hindrance, many individuals achieve successful careers. Much more research is needed to understand factors that empower individuals to overcome and succeed in the face of barriers. The qualitative studies described earlier (e.g., Gomez et al., 2001; Richie et al., 1997) that focused on high-achieving women from racial/ethnic minority groups have provided the foundation for these investigations. These participants reported that strong support from their families, a strong sense of identity, and feelings of passion about their work increased their resilience in overcoming barriers.

Influences from Mainstream Culture

Individuals in the United States interact with the larger U.S. societal culture on a daily basis, and their vocational development is influenced in multiple ways by the larger mainstream culture. Research has shown that the United States is highly individualistically oriented. The U.S. culture emphasizes doing, rather than being; places a high value on achievement; and is somewhat low on tolerance for uncertainty and somewhat low on power distance (the distance between those in authority and subordinates) (Gefland et al., 2007). These values shape policies, such as welfare reform that places a high value on women seeking work, and educational systems that are designed to provide opportunities for high-achieving students, regardless of their background. The types of school that individuals attend and the opportunity structures available also affect how careers are chosen and how views on work are formed. In addition, the changing labor market and globalization also have an effect on how individuals view careers, make sense of the world of work, and construct their vocational identity. Individuals who feel insecure about their jobs, who worry about the safety of their pensions, and who are encouraged to develop new communication and technological skills are less likely to make career transitions voluntarily (Burke, 2002).

Mainstream culture can influence the opportunity structures available to people. Opportunity structures are defined as "one's access to the resources and supports that frame the process of planning, training, locating, and adjusting to work" (Blustein, 2006, p. 143). These include financial support for education and training, supportive family, strong and effective education, and safe and adequate housing and residential areas (Blustein, 2006). Depending on their backgrounds, the opportunity structures to which individuals have access affect their vocational development and their views on the world of work.

Researchers have argued that it is necessary and vital to investigate opportunity structures and poverty when understanding the context surrounding vocational development (American Psychological Association [APA], 2; Blustein, 2006). The American Psychological Association (2000) adopted a

Resolution on Poverty and Socioeconomic Status guiding psychologists in addressing the issues and concerns related to poverty in research, assessment and evaluation, graduate training, public policy, and intervention programs. Furthermore, poverty and access to opportunities affect career-decision making. Individuals who have greater access to structures such as a stronger secondary education or financial support for postsecondary education may be more likely to find jobs as well as choose careers related to individual reasons (e.g., interests, values) rather than external reasons (e.g., pay bills). Social class strongly influences access to opportunity structures (M. T. Brown et al., 1996; Fouad & Brown, 2000), with individuals from higher socioeconomic status often having much more access to opportunity structures than those who come from lower SES groups.

Within the United States, the context around education differs dramatically across varying types of schools. The education provided in an inner-city school experiencing a shortage in funding, overcrowding of students, and a poor teacher retention rate differs greatly from that of a school with ample funding, effective learning environments, and motivated, passionate teachers (Kozol, 2005). Many schools serving minority children, specifically Blacks and Hispanics, lack the basics necessary for a strong education—clean classrooms, hallways, restrooms, up-to-date books, and appropriate supplies (Kozol, 2005). Furthermore, faced with accountability mandates, school administrators and teachers use commanding and controlling teaching strategies rather than creative learning opportunities (Kozol, 2005). There are variations in educational quality, and these variations often create differences in the vocational development for students.

In addition, the changing labor market also affects vocational development. Traditional views of work and career are dramatically shifting as the labor market changes within the United States and an increasingly global market is changing the labor force in critical ways. Occupational insecurity is resulting from changes in retirement packages and layoffs due to mergers, company adjustments, and changes to pension plans. These changes have influenced expectations in secondary and postsecondary education as well as the skills required for future jobs.

Changing working environments are forcing employees to adapt to a new world of work. From globalization to a changing labor market to different sets of required skills, individuals are now viewing work in a different manner. Gone are the days when career decisions were implemented straight out of school, when an individual worked for one company for years, and retired with secure pensions and benefits. Instead, the labor force is now being asked to engage in lifelong learning, to continuously modify and adjust, and to acclimate to changing work environments. These changes are influencing vocational development.

INTERSECTIONS: IMPLICATIONS FOR RESEARCH AND PRACTICE

We have reviewed the empirical studies on selected factors in each of the dimensions that are part of Figure 24.1. However, individuals' career development and decision making also are shaped by the intersections of individual, group, and societal dimensions. In this section, we discuss the intersections between Individual and Group Dimensions, between Individual and Societal Dimensions, Group and Societal Dimensions, and finally, the implications for understanding context in the intersections among all three dimensions. Where literature is available, we briefly review relevant research in the intersecting area (e.g., race differences in interests), but because so few studies exist, our discussion focuses primarily on our suggestions for further research and the implications for practice.

Individual and Group Intersections

Some scholars have examined the intersections between the individual and group dimensions. Research in the past 20 years has examined various aspects of the influence of race and ethnicity on interests (e.g., Armstrong, Hubert, & Rounds, 2003; Fouad, 2002; Fouad & Walker, 2005). Much of this research has evaluated whether the current tools designed to assess interests may be applied across cultural groups. Research has found, for the most part, that there are few differences in measured interests across racial/ ethnic groups. However, Fouad and Walker found differences in endorsement pattern of items across groups, suggesting that items of interest inventories may have additional meanings across groups due, in part, to cultural expectations and role modeling. Most of the items on interest instruments are individualistically oriented, and it is possible that these assessments are tapping into a narrow domain of preferences for activities and are not accurately capturing the interests across racial/ethnic groups. Future research on the intersection between individual and group-level dimensions needs to focus on continuing to systematically examine the applicability of assessment tools across populations (Subich, 2005). Future research also needs to examine the domain of interests for more collectivistically oriented individuals in the United States to better understand their interests from an emic perspective, instead of in comparison to those who are individualistically oriented.

Although most of the research on individual variables in vocational psychology has been quantitative, newer studies on the role of socioeconomic status and family influence in career development have been qualitative. Blustein and Kenny and their colleagues (Blustein et al., 2004; Chaves et al., 2004; Kenny et al., 2003) have argued that poor urban youth view the world of work qualitatively differently than do individuals from more affluent backgrounds. These studies have given vocational psychologists an important perspective, but much more research is needed to determine the factors involved in this influence. Does social class influence the opportunities to express interests? Do individuals who are from affluent backgrounds develop interests and values in different ways, and if so, how does that process differ? Is it important to intervene to alter the process so that everyone develops interests and values in the same way, or is it important to merely understand that process, rather than alter it?

Just as it is important to study the process that influences the impact of social class on career development, it is important to examine the intersections for individual variables and family factors. Most of the research on the role of family has shown that families do, indeed, influence their children, often in empowering ways. In positive family interactions, that influence is evident in support and guidance, and in relationships through which children can explore the world from a safe vantage point. In negative interactions, families hinder an individual's overall development. Researchers and practitioners need to understand the varying dimensions of family influence, from family support to family expectations and obligations. What is the role of family in the development of interests, if children's occupational choice is based on family obligations, rather than individual choice? How do we understand the supportive mechanisms of families in career choice?

Finally, it is critical to further examine the intersection between race and ethnicity and individual variables. The census data we discussed under Dimension 2 shows that members of racial/ethnic minority groups in the United States are distributed disproportionately across occupational areas. This uneven distribution suggests that different factors may be operating in the choices of racial/ethnic minority and majority culture individuals. Research has shown that these differences do not stem from differences in the initial career aspirations, but more research is needed to understand the salience of individual factors for different racial/ethnic groups. Do interests play less of a role in career choices or do values play more of a role across racial/ethnic groups? Practitioners also need to assess a broad array of interests and assess the weight of factors related to interests, social class, and family influence in their clients' career decisions.

Individual and Societal Intersections

The few studies that have examined the intersection between individual and societal dimensions have focused on the differences in interests (Farh, Leong, & Law, 1998) and values across cultures (Leong, Austin, Sekaran, & Komarraju, 1998; Leung & Hou, 2001), as well as the role of acculturation in interests (Tang, 2002; Tang, Fouad, & Smith, 1999). Overall, studies have found that values are influenced by the culture of origin, and Subich (2005) recommends using caution when applying U.S.-normed values instruments across populations. Most studies have also shown that Holland's (Spokane, Meir, & Catalano, 2000) circular theory of interests is supported across cultures. Tang's work has found that acculturation affects the relative influence of interests on career choice; those who are less acculturated are more influenced by family expectations than by their interests.

There is much that remains to be determined in the intersection between individual and societal dimensions. Gelfand et al. (2007) noted that there are cross-cultural differences in the ways that individuals are motivated to achieve; they hypothesized that these differences stem from differences in cultural values, including collectivism. These have clear implications for the development of interests, and the role that values play in choices. Much more information is needed on the role of cultural values, and the ways that individuals negotiate the differences between the values from their culture of origin and the culture of the larger U.S. society.

Group and Societal Intersections

Most counseling and vocational psychologists focus at the individual level, and few researchers have examined the interaction between group and societal factors. Chaves et al. (2004) focused on the intersection between race and ethnicity and societal context for urban youth. This research indicated that poor urban youth who had greater critical consciousness had greater career adaptability skills. Though no other research has focused on the intersection between group and societal intersections, the implications from these studies appear to be important for community and school-level interventions. Research and practice could focus on interventions that provide parental education and information on overcoming barriers to education and achievement. Other programs could examine school-based programs designed to help people cope with discrimination. Community-based programs in low-income areas could also be designed to promote career development. An example of the latter might be inner-city programs for teen mothers to help them set feasible career goals and develop plans to achieve them.

Individual, Group, and Societal Intersections

No research to date has focused on the intersections among all three levels, and this is the area in which the most research is needed. Future research could focus, for example, on understanding the cultural transmission of values to parents, who in turn influence their child's development of interests. Other questions might include the role of schooling in interaction with social class to shape opportunities to develop interests, how self-efficacy interacts with gender and race in school to affect vocational development, or how work values intersect with peer and family relationships and acculturation. Another area for investigation is potential moderators of the relationships among the dimensions, such as gender, disability, or developmental stage. Further investigation of the intersection of all three dimensions would provide ways to conceptualize the context of an individual's career.

SUMMARY

We have argued that a conceptual framework is needed to provide direction to researchers and practitioners in understanding the context of vocational choices. The model we proposed includes three dimensions that begin to capture the context for individuals. The dimensions include individual difference variables (such as interests, values, self-efficacy), group-level differences (gender, race and ethnicity, family, social class), and societal differences (culture, mainstream society, and difference between the two). We echo Cook et al.'s (2002) argument that understanding the context in which individuals make decisions is critical in effectively empowering individuals to make the best decisions they can. Vocational psychologists need to understand the influences of group and societal factors that help to shape not only the development of vocational interests and values, but individuals' ability to implement those choices. Researchers have just begun to examine contextual factors, and we are sure that future researchers will continue to refine and add to our proposed model.

REFERENCES

Ali, S. R., McWhirter, E. H., & Chronister, K. M. (2005). Self-efficacy and vocational outcome expectations for adolescents of lower socioeconomic status: A pilot study. *Journal of Career Assessment, 13*, 40–58.

American Psychological Association. (May, 2000). *Resolution on poverty and socioeconomic status.* Retrieved September 13, 2007, from www.apa.org/pi/urban/povres.html.

Armstrong, P. I., & Crombie, G. (2000). Compromises in adolescents' occupational aspirations and expectations from grades 8 to 10. *Journal of Vocational Behavior, 56*, 82–98.

Armstrong, P. I., Hubert, L., & Rounds, J. (2003). Circular unidimensional scaling: A new look at group differences in interest structure. *Journal of Counseling Psychology, 50*, 297–308.

Aros, J. R., Henly, G. A., & Curtis, N. T. (1998). Occupational sextype and sex differences in vocational preference-measured interest relationships. *Journal of Vocational Behavior, 53*, 227–242.

Betz, N. E. (2002). Explicating an ecological approach to the career development of women. *Career Development Quarterly, 50*, 335–338.

Betz, N. E. (2005). Women's career development. In S. D. Brown & R. W. Lent (Eds.), *Career development and counseling: Putting theory and research to work* (pp. 253–277). Hoboken, NJ: Wiley.

Betz, N. E., & Hackett, G. (1981). The relationship of career-related self-efficacy expectations to perceived career options in college women and men. *Journal of Counseling Psychology, 28*, 399–410.

Blustein, D. L. (2001). Extending the reach of vocational psychology: Toward an inclusive and integrated psychology of working. *Journal of Vocational Behavior, 59*, 171–182.

Blustein, D. L. (2006). *Psychology of working: A new perspective on career development, counseling, and public policy.* Mahweh, NJ: Erlbaum.

Blustein, D. L., Chaves, A. P., Diemer, M. A., Gallagher, L. A., Marshall, K. G., Sirin, S., et al. (2002). Voices of the forgotten half: The role of social class in the school-to-work transition. *Journal of Counseling Psychology, 49*, 311–323.

Blustein, D. L., Schultheiss, D. E. P., & Flum, H. (2004). Toward a relational perspective of the psychology of careers and working: A social constructionist analysis. *Journal of Vocational Behavior, 64*, 423–440.

Bronfenbrenner, U. (1977). Toward an experimental ecology of human development. *American Psychologist, 32*, 513–531.

Brown, C., Darden, E. E., Shelton, M. C., & Dipoto, M. C. (1999). Career exploration and self-efficacy of high school students: Are there urban/suburban differences? *Journal of Career Assessment, 7*, 227–237.

Brown, M. T., Fukunaga, C., Umemoto, D., & Wicker, L. (1996). Annual review, 1990–1996: Social class, work, and retirement behavior. *Journal of Vocational Behavior, 49*, 159–189.

Brown, M. T., Yamini-Diouf, Y., & Ruiz de Esparza, C. (2005). Career interventions for racial/ethnic minority persons: A research agenda. In W. B. Walsh & M. L. Savickas (Eds.), *Handbook of vocational psychology* (3rd ed., pp. 227–244). Mahweh, NJ: Erlbaum.

Burke, R. J. (2002). Organizational transitions. In C. L. Cooper & R. J. Burke (Eds.), *The new world of work* (pp. 3–28). Oxford: Blackwell.

Chaves, A. P., Diemer, M. A., Blustein, D. L., Gallagher, L. A., DeVoy, J. E., Casares, M. T., et al. (2004). Conceptions of work: The view from urban youth. *Journal of Counseling Psychology, 51*, 275–286.

Chronister, K. M., & McWhirter, E. H. (2004). Ethnic differences in career supports and barriers for battered women: A pilot study. *Journal of Career Assessment, 12*, 169–187.

Chung, Y. B., & Harmon, L. W. (1999). Assessment of perceived occupational opportunity for Black Americans. *Journal of Career Assessment, 7*, 45–62.

Constantine, M. G., Wallace, B. C., & Kindaichi, M. M. (2005). Examining contextual factors in the career decision status of African American adolescents. *Journal of Career Assessment, 13*, 307–319.

Cook, E. P., Heppner, M. J., & O'Brien, K. M. (2002). Career development of women of color and White women: Assumptions, conceptualization, and interventions from an ecological perspective. *Career Development Quarterly, 50*, 291–305.

Davey, F. H. (2001). The relationship between engineering and young women's occupational priorities. *Canadian Journal of Counselling, 35*, 221–228.

Dawis, R. V. (1992). The individual differences tradition in counseling psychology. *Journal of Counseling Psychology, 39*, 7–19.

Dawis, R. V. (1996). Vocational psychology, vocational adjustment, and the workforce: Some familiar and unanticipated consequences. *Psychology, Public Policy, and Law, 2*, 229–248.

Farh, J.-l., Leong, F. T. L., & Law, K. S. (1998). Cross-cultural validity of Holland's model in Hong Kong. *Journal of Vocational Behavior, 52*(3), 425–440.

Farmer, H. S. (1985). Model of career and achievement motivation for women and men. *Journal of Counseling Psychology, 32*, 363–390.

Farmer, H. S., Rotella, S., Anderson, C., & Wandrop, J. (1998). Gender differences in science, math, and technology careers: Prestige level and Holland interest type. *Journal of Vocational Behavior, 53*, 73–96.

Farmer, H. S., Wardrop, J. L., Anderson, M. Z., & Risinger, R. (1995). Women's career choices: Focus on science, math, and technology careers. *Journal of Counseling Psychology, 42*, 155–170.

Fitzgerald, L. F., & Betz, N. E. (1994). Career development in cultural context: The role of gender, race, class, and sexual orientation. In M. L. Savikas & R. W. Lent (Eds.), *Convergence in career development theories: Implications for science and practice* (pp. 103–117). Palo Alto, CA: CPP Books.

Flores, L. Y., & O'Brien, K. M. (2002). The career development of Mexican American adolescent women: A test of social cognitive career theory. *Journal of Counseling Psychology, 49*, 14–27.

Flores, L. Y., Ojeda, L., Huang, Y.-P., Gee, D., & Lee, S. (2006). The relation of acculturation, problem-solving appraisal, and career decision-making self-efficacy to Mexican American high school students' educational goals. *Journal of Counseling Psychology, 53*, 260–266.

Flouri, E., & Buchanan, A. (2002). The role of work-related skills and career role models in adolescent career maturity. *Career Development Quarterly, 51*, 36–43.

Flum, H. (2001). Relational dimensions in career development. *Journal of Vocational Behavior, 59*, 1–16.

Fouad, N. A. (2002). Cross-cultural differences in vocational interests: Between-group differences on the Strong Interest Inventory. *Journal of Counseling Psychology, 49*, 283–289.

Fouad, N. A. (2007). Work and vocational psychology: Theory, research and applications. *Annual Review of Psychology, 57*, 543–564.

Fouad, N. A., & Brown, M. T. (2000). Role of race and social class in development: Implications for counseling psychology. In S. D. Brown & R. W. Lent (Eds.), *Handbook of counseling psychology* (3rd ed., pp. 379–408). New York: Wiley.

Fouad, N. A., & Byars-Winston, A. M. (2005). Cultural context of career choice: Meta-analysis of race/ethnicity differences. *Career Development Quarterly, 53*, 223–233.

Fouad, N. A., Cudeck, R., & Hansen, J.-I. C. (1984). Convergent validity of the Spanish and English forms of the Strong-Campbell Interest Inventory for bilingual Hispanic high school students. *Journal of Counseling Psychology, 31*, 339–348.

Fouad, N. A., & Walker, C. M. (2005). Cultural influences on responses to items on the Strong Interest Inventory. *Journal of Vocational Behavior, 66*, 104–123.

Gelfand, M. J., Erez, M., & Aycan, Z. (2007). Cross-cultural organizational behavior. *Annual Review of Psychology, 58*, 479–514.

Gibson, D. E. (2004). Role models in career development: New directions for theory and research. *Journal of Vocational Behavior, 65*, 134–156.

Gomez, M. J., Fassinger, R. E., Prosser, J., Cooke, K., Mejia, B., & Luna, J. (2001). Voces abriendo caminos [voices foraging paths]: A qualitative study of the career development of notable Latinas. *Journal of Counseling Psychology, 48*, 286–300.

Gupta, S., & Tracey, T. J. G. (2005). Dharma and interest-occupation congruence in Asian Indian college students. *Journal of Career Assessment, 13*, 320–336.

Hansen, J.-I. C. (2005). Assessment of interests. In S. D. Brown & R. W. Lent (Eds.), *Career development and counseling: Putting theory and research to work* (pp. 281–304). Hoboken, NJ: Wiley.

Hartung, P. J. (2005). Integrated career assessment and counseling: Mindsets, models and methods. In W. B. Walsh & M. L. Savickas (Eds.), *Handbook of vocational psychology* (pp. 371–395). Mahwah, NJ: Erlbaum.

Helms, J. E., Jernigan, M., & Mascher, J. (2005). The meaning of race in psychology and how to change it: A methodological perspective. *American Psychologist, 60*, 27–36.

Jome, L. M., & Tokar, D. M. (1998). Dimensions of masculinity and major choice traditionality. *Journal of Vocational Behavior, 52,* 120–134.

Juntunen, C. L., Barraclough, D. J., Broneck, C. L., Seibel, G. A., Winrow, S. A., & Morin, P. M. (2001). American Indian perspectives on the career journey. *Journal of Counseling Psychology, 48,* 274–285.

Kenny, M. E., Blustein, D. L., Chaves, A., Grossman, J. M., & Gallagher, L. A. (2003). The role of perceived barriers and relational support in the educational and vocational lives of urban high school students. *Journal of Counseling Psychology, 50,* 142–155.

Kim, U., Yang, K.-S., & Hwang, K.-K. (2006). Contributions to indigenous and cultural psychology: Understanding people in context. In U. Kim, K.-S., Yang & K.-K. Hwang (Eds.), *Indigenous and cultural psychology: Understanding people in context* (pp. 3–25). New York: Springer Science + Business Media.

Kohatsu, E. L. (Ed.). (2005). *Acculturation: Current and future directions* (Vol. 1). Hoboken, NJ: Wiley.

Kozol, J. (2005). *The shame of the nation: The restoration of apartheid schooling in America.* New York: Crown.

Krane, N. E. R., & Tirre, W. C. (2005). Ability assessment in career counseling. In S. D. Brown & R. W. Lent (Eds.), *Career development and counseling: Putting theory and research to work* (pp. 330–352). Hoboken, NJ: Wiley.

Leal-Muniz, V., & Constantine, M. G. (2005). Predictors of the Career Commitment Process in Mexican American College Students. *Journal of Career Assessment, 13,* 204–215.

Lease, S. H. (2003). Testing a model of men's nontraditional occupational choices. *Career Development Quarterly, 51,* 244–258.

Lent, R. W., Brown, S. D., & Hackett, G. (1994). Toward a unifying social cognitive theory of career and academic interest, choice, and performance. *Journal of Vocational Behavior, 45,* 79–122.

Lent, R. W., Brown, S. D., & Hackett, G. (2000). Contextual supports and barriers to career choice: A social cognitive analysis. *Journal of Counseling Psychology, 47,* 36–49.

Leong, F. T. L. (2001). The role of acculturation in the career adjustment of Asian American workers: A test of Leong and Chou's (1994) formulations. *Cultural Diversity and Ethnic Minority Psychology, 7,* 262–273.

Leong, F. T. L., Austin, J. T., Sekaran, U., & Komarraju, M. (1998). An evaluation of the cross-cultural validity of Holland's theory: Career choices by workers in India. *Journal of Vocational Behavior, 52,* 441–455.

Leung, S. A., & Hou, Z.-J. (2001). Concurrent validity of the 1994 Self-Directed Search for Chinese high school students in Hong Kong. *Journal of Career Assessment, 9*(3), 283–296.

Luzzo, D. A., & McWhirter, E. H. (2001). Sex and ethnic differences in the perception of educational and career-related barriers and levels of coping efficacy. *Journal of Counseling and Development, 79,* 61–67.

Miller, L., & Budd, J. (1999). The development of occupational sex-role stereotypes, occupational preferences and academic subject preferences in children at ages 8, 12, and 16. *Educational Psychology, 19,* 17–35.

Nauta, M. M., & Kokaly, M. L. (2001). Assessing role model influences on students' academic and vocational decisions. *Journal of Career Assessment, 9,* 81–99.

Osipow, S. H., & Fitzgerald, L. F. (1996). *Theories of career development* (4th ed.). Boston: Allyn & Bacon.

Pager, D., & Quillian, L. (2005). Walking the talk? What employers say versus what they do. *American Sociological Review, 70,* 355–380.

Parker, C. P., Baltes, B. B., Young, S. A., Huff, J. W., Altmann, R. A., Lacost, H. A., et al. (2003). Relationships between psychological climate perceptions and work outcomes: A meta-analytic review. *Journal of Organizational Behavior, 24,* 389–416.

Parsons, F. (1909). *Choosing a vocation.* Boston: Houghton Mifflin.

Pearson, S. M., & Bieschke, K. J. (2001). Succeeding against the odds: An examination of familial influences on the career development of professional African American women. *Journal of Counseling Psychology, 48,* 301–309.

Richie, B. S., Fassinger, R. E., Linn, S. G., Johnson, J., Prosser, J., & Robinson, S. (1997). Persistence, connection, and passion: A qualitative study of the career development of highly achieving African American-Black and White women. *Journal of Counseling Psychology, 44,* 133–148.

Roberts, R. K., Swanson, N. G., & Murphy, L. R. (2004). Discrimination and occupational mental health. *Journal of Mental Health, 13,* 129–142.

Rounds, J. B., & Armstrong, P. I. (2005). Assessment of needs and values In S. D. Brown & R. W. Lent (Eds.), *Career development and counseling: Putting theory and research to work* (pp. 305–329). Hoboken, NJ: Wiley.

Savickas, M. L. (2002). A developmental theory of vocational psychology. In D. Brown (Ed.), *Career choice and development* (4th ed., pp. 149–205). San Francisco: Jossey-Bass.

Schultheiss, D. E. P. (2003). A relational approach to career counseling: Theoretical integration and practical application. *Journal of Counseling and Development, 81*, 301–310.

Schultheiss, D. E. P., Palma, T. V., Predragovich, K. S., & Glasscock, J. M. J. (2002). Relational influences on career paths: Siblings in context. *Journal of Counseling Psychology, 49*(3), 302–310.

Smith, E. J. (1980). Career development of minorities in nontraditional fields. *Journal of Non-White Concerns in Personnel and Guidance, 8*, 141–156.

Spokane, A. R., Meir, E. I., & Catalano, M. (2000). Person-environment congruence and Holland's theory: A review and reconsideration. *Journal of Vocational Behavior, 57*, 137–187.

Subich, L. M. (2005). Career assessment with culturally diverse individuals. In W. B. Walsh & M. L. Savickas (Eds.), *Handbook of vocational psychology* (3rd ed., pp. 397–421). Mahwah, NJ: Erlbaum.

Swanson, J. L., & D'Achiardi, C. (2005). Beyond interests, needs/values, and abilities: Assessing other important career constructs across the life span. In S. D. Brown & R. W. Lent (Eds.), *Career development and counseling: Putting theory and research to work* (pp. 353–381). Hoboken, NJ: Wiley.

Tang, M. (2002). A comparison of Asian American, Caucasian American, and Chinese college students: An initial report. *Journal of Multicultural Counseling and Development, 30*(2), 124–134.

Tang, M., Fouad, N. A., & Smith, P. L. (1999). Asian Americans' career choices: A path model to examine factors influencing their career choices. *Journal of Vocational Behavior, 54*, 142–157.

Tokar, D. M., & Jome, L. M. (1998). Masculinity, vocational interests, and career choice traditionality: Evidence for a fully mediated model. *Journal of Counseling Psychology, 45*, 424–435.

U.S. Bureau of Labor Statistics. (2006). *Labor force statistics from the current population survey*. Retrieved December 12, 2006, from www.bls.gov/cps/home.htm#data.

Vondracek, F., Lerner, R., & Schulenberg, J. (1986). *Career development: A life-span developmental approach.* Hillsdale, NJ: Erlbaum.

Whiston, S. C. (1996). The relationship among family interaction patterns and career indecision and career decision-making self-efficacy. *Journal of Career Development, 23*(2), 137–149.

Whiston, S. C., & Keller, B. K. (2004). The influences of the family of origin on career development: A review and analysis. *Counseling Psychologist, 32*, 493–568.

Williams, C. M., & Subich, L. M. (2006). The gendered nature of career related learning experiences: A social cognitive career theory perspective. *Journal of Vocational Behavior, 69*, 262–275.

Worthington, R. L., Flores, L. Y., Navarro, R. L., S. D., Brown, & Lent, R. W. (2005). Career development in context: Research with people of color. In S. D. Brown & R. W. Lent (Eds.), *Career development and counseling: Putting theory and research to work* (pp. 225–252). Hoboken, NJ: Wiley.

Young, R. A., Valach, L., & Collin, A. (2002). A contextualist explanation of career. In D. Brown (Ed.), *Career choice and development* (4th ed., pp. 206–254). San Francisco: Jossey-Bass.

CHAPTER 25

Work, Family, and Dual-Earner Couples: Implications for Research and Practice

LUCIA ALBINO GILBERT
JILL RADER

> In years gone by, the problem of balancing work and family was thought to be a women's issue. We now know better. Men live in families, too. And the welfare of families is not simply a matter of concern for individuals. Balancing paid and domestic work is a social issue. (Crosby & Sabattini, 2005, p. 350)

Contemporary theorists and researchers focus on modern solutions instead of the traditional assumptions that women and men always must make agonizing choices between their work and personal lives (Barnett & Hyde, 2001; Greenhaus & Powell, 2006). Such scholars have challenged problem-focused theories that frame work and family as inherently at odds and have cited strong evidence that work and family roles are compatible and mutually enhancing, with experiences in one role capable of producing positive experiences and outcomes in the other. Whether families experience conflict between occupational and personal lives depends largely on the availability of progressive workplace policies as well as new thinking about how men and women conceptualize their roles within the family. Counseling psychologists play a role in helping those in dual-earner families achieve greater balance; they further act to affect government and workplace policies so that employers can be more family-friendly.

The focus of this chapter is on family and work relations in dual-earner households in the United States. The majority of studies on work and family are largely based on middle-class samples (Barnett & Hyde, 2001). In addition, although the material included in the chapter may pertain to the work and family relations of single-earner families, this group is not a primary focus. The chapter is organized to orient the reader to recent thinking about family and work convergence and to offer directions for future research and practice.

We begin by describing the context in which women and men are raising families in the current economic system. We provide current Department of Labor statistics for workplace participation and income, and illustrate how these numbers interact with individual factors such as biological sex, race, and educational attainment. We also attend to the modern realities of workplace policies and societal beliefs about roles for women and men in the workplace and at home. We then examine more closely this interface between work and family life and what the research shows in terms of how employers and families influence each other (and how they might continue to influence each other, given the never-ending challenge of balancing economic realities with the equally compelling needs for love and relationships).

In light of the research on work-family convergence, we examine important implications for research and practice for counseling psychologists, implications that affect each member of a dual-earner household in a real and personal way (e.g., one's feelings about fairness, or how one communicates with a partner). We provide case examples to illustrate the real-world implications of the aforementioned research. Finally, we explore directions for future research and practice, directions that capture the richness

426

and diversity of the field. These new paths range from examining counselors' roles as social justice agents, to critically evaluating the gendered practices of the home and workplace, to better illuminating the sometimes invisible role of the working father.

THE SOCIETAL CONTEXT OF FAMILY AND WORK RELATIONS

We begin with the larger societal context of dual-earner families and provide current statistics on workforce participation, education, and earnings. We then turn briefly to sociocultural factors such as belief systems and work-family policies that further shape the societal context for dual-earner families.

Demographics

Contemporary dual-earner families emerged in the second half of the twentieth century in the context of women's changing status and educational and employment opportunities. The single most important change influencing work and family relations today is not women's increased involvement in paid work per se; rather, it is this paid work involvement coupled with changes in the status and nature of women's work, which in turn have brought about changes in men's roles, in family responsive workplace practices, and in the law.

Employment

According to a 2006 report by the Bureau of Labor Statistics examining 2005 data, 82% of families had at least one employed member, and this percentage was unchanged from 2004 to 2005. In addition, there was little or no change over the year in the proportions of employed members in European American (83%), African American (78%), Asian American (90%), and Hispanic families (87%; U.S. Bureau of Labor Statistics, 2006a). Among married-couple families, 84% had an employed parent in 2005. The proportion of all married-couple families in which only the husband worked (20%) edged down in 2005, as did the proportion of married-couple families in which only the wife worked (7%). Less than 10% of families with children in the home were single-earner families with a stay-at-home mother. In contrast, the proportion of dual-worker couples rose to 51% (U.S. Bureau of Labor Statistics, 2006a), a proportion that has been steadily increasing over the past 2 decades. Since the early 1990s, the dual-earner family has represented the modal family form in the United States. Thus, across various ethnic groups and educational levels, both spouses are employed full-time in the majority of U.S. married families (Bond, Galinsky, & Swanberg, 1998; Crosby & Sabattini, 2005).

Education

Women's educational achievement is now on par with men's. The past 30 to 40 years have witnessed increased access to education for women, improved job opportunities, laws to protect them from discriminatory practices, and a status and meaning separate from their affiliations with men (Gilbert, 2006). Women and men now graduate from high school and college in about the same proportions. Approximately 84% of both women and men are high school graduates and 28% are college graduates (Rhodes, 2006). This compares with the 10% overall (13% men and 7% women) who were college graduates 40 years ago (Rhodes, 2006).

Women are entering and graduating with advanced degrees from fields such as law, medicine, the life sciences, and business administration at comparable rates to men. However, this is less true in the physical sciences, computer sciences, and engineering, where significantly fewer women receive advanced degrees (Smallwood, 2003). Graduate student enrollment in American colleges and universities continued to increase in 2005, and this growth was attributed to a growing number of female and African

American students (Porter, 2006). Women now account for 58% of all graduate students (Porter, 2006). The increasing enrollment of women, including minority women, is a positive development. However, as we will see in the next section, income disparity remains, regardless of education level.

Income

The wage gap is also narrowing. In 2005, women earned 81 cents for every dollar earned by men, up from 76.1 cents in 2001 and 66.6 cents in 1983 (U.S. Census Bureau, 2006). Research from the American Association of University Women (AAUW, 2003), however, indicates that women with 4-year college degrees continue to earn, on average, $17,600 per year less than men with the same level of education. Statistics by type of industry indicate the gendered processes of career selection, advancement, and salary. In each of the 20 industry sectors examined by the Census Bureau, men earned more than women. Men earned the most in the fields of management and enterprise, followed by the professional, scientific, and technical services sectors. Best incomes for women were in the utilities, management, and enterprise groups, although women's earnings in none of these sectors equaled those of men (U.S. Census Bureau, 2006). In addition, women more than men continue to be pigeonholed in traditional occupations that do not offer significant room for advancement and provide less financial security (Michaels, 2006). The highest proportions of women with a college education are elementary school teachers and nurses (AAUW, 2003).

As a general rule, women are still underrepresented in the highest paying occupations and over-represented in the lowest (U.S. Bureau of Labor Statistics, 2006b). Race and ethnicity can widen the income gap for some minority women; for example, Latina women remain the most poorly compensated of workers in the United States (U.S. Census Bureau, 2006). There is considerable variability within women's and men's salaries, however, particularly at higher educational levels. Across various ethnic groups, 40% of college-educated women earn as much or more than their spouses (Stebbins, 2001), and married women on average provide 40% of their families' income (AAUW, 2003).

Sociocultural Factors Framing Family and Work Relations

Culture refers broadly to the pattern of arrangements, material or behavioral, characterizing a particular society. It includes social institutions and knowledge, belief systems about gender, ethnic identity and minority status, and morals and customs. Work and family relations develop and change as social institutions, opportunities, and belief systems change. In this section, we briefly note two sociocultural factors particularly important to understanding today's dual-earner families: belief systems and workplace practices and polices.

Belief Systems

Work and family issues differ along dimensions of race, ethnicity, sexual orientation, and gender (the meanings societies and individuals ascribe to male and female categories). As Tatum (1997) commented, we live in a smog of racism, homophobia, and sexism. Access to education and occupational opportunity and supportive institutional and workplace practices and policies, which can vary on these dimensions, are key aspects of the context of dual-earner family life. Despite some positive trends in salary and educational trends previously noted, workplace practices still significantly limit opportunities for women, ethnic minorities, and gays and lesbians (see Carli & Eagly, 2001, whole issue; Meyerson, 2003). For example, partners in same-sex families, or the biological children of same-sex partners, often are not entitled to the same health benefits as are heterosexual partners.

Beliefs about gender are particularly pervasive in considerations of family and work relations. The personal lives of individuals are always played out within the constraints of societal norms and values and social institutions. In the United States and globally, these constraints are permeated with conventional notions of sex and gender. Researchers today have a much better understanding of how biological sex forms the basis of a social classification system—namely, gender—and how views of what it means to be a woman or man in a culture are conveyed through cultural discourses that preserve and perpetuate existing practices, beliefs, and power relationships (Marecek, 1995). The fact that women across all ethnic groups earn less than men with comparable levels of education has less to do with women's and men's abilities and more to do with societal views of who is entitled to be paid more.

Workplace Practices and Polices

A global economy, encroaching corporatization, and the changing nature of large segments of the workplace have brought about a shift from expectations of lifetime employment to the growing recognition that vocational life is one of constant adaptation. Today's workers enter an ever-changing marketplace requiring career flexibility, continuing education and skills training, and geographic moves. Many employees are entering into a different contract with their employers today than in the past (Stone, 2005). Under the traditional employment contract, good performers were ensured job stability and often advancement. Loyalty and low turnover were important organizational goals. In the modern contract, firms plan for regular employee turnover and encourage employees to view their employment as a short-time arrangement in which they are to take responsibility for developing their own career paths. The modern contract promises employability security, general training, networking opportunities, and market-based pay as opposed to job security, firm-specific training, promotion opportunities, and longevity-linked pay and benefits (Stone, 2005).

It is too soon to know what effects these changes will have on partners in dual-earner families. There is the promise of positive aspects related to flexibility, autonomy, and balance, but there also appear to be significant negative aspects related to new forms of employment discrimination and the further blurring of how "business as usual" determines private lives (Fineman & Dougherty, 2005; Okin, 1989). This crucial area of study has received little research attention from the perspective of the individuals in dual-earner families.

In contrast to aspects of the emerging modern employment contract, family-responsive workplace practices are designed to help employees manage their work and family roles as well as help organizations attract and retain employees by enhancing their job satisfaction and performance. Current practices include programs such as dependent care support (child care and elder care), workplace child care, paid maternity and paternity leave, flexible work schedules, and telecommuting. Most employers offer family-friendly benefits, but there is considerable variability among employers in the type and quality of benefits offered (Foley, 2006). More versus less supportive family-friendly workplaces are associated with higher levels of job satisfaction and more commitment to company success (Jacobs & Gerson, 2001), lower work-family conflict, and lower levels of turnover and absenteeism (Glass & Finley, 2002; Lobel, 1999).

In addition, under the Family and Medical Leave Act of 1993, companies with 50 or more employees are required to provide 12 weeks of unpaid leave for childbirth, adoption, and other family-related situations. Because leaves mandated by FMLA are unpaid, this policy provides a minimal level of benefit for many employees (Armenia & Gerstel, 2006). In heterosexual families, in which men often earn more than woman, there is less incentive for men to take leave, perpetuating the dynamic that women give care and men provide salary.

Although less so than in the past, fathering and mothering are still linked to prevailing ideologies that legitimize fathers' lesser availability to their children and view mothers as the primary caretaker for a developing child (Thompson & Walker, 1995). Fewer men than women use family benefits and FMLA (Levine & Pittinsky, 1997; Wayne & Cordeiro, 2003). Either implicitly or explicitly, men are often discouraged from making use of these benefits, leaving greater family responsibilities on women and lowering the benefits of work-family balance. This is another insufficiently studied topic. Existing studies typically focus on who uses benefits (women), rather than on who does not and why (men).

INTERFACE BETWEEN PAID WORK AND THE SPOUSE/PARTNER RELATIONSHIP

How occupational work interfaces with the spouse/partner relationship is of central importance to vocational psychology. This interface influences career paths, relationship stability and satisfaction, and the socialization of children within families and society at large. Much can be said based on a large body of empirical research emanating from a number of disciplinary perspectives (e.g., economics, law, psychology, and sociology) and using a broad range of methods (e.g., personal diaries, interviews, time survey approaches, and case and historical studies). We identify two main areas of consensus in this research. The first has to do with the convergence of partners' self-concepts and behaviors about work and family roles and theories of work-family enrichment. The second has to do with more recent areas of study that have emerged in attempts to further understand the lives of dual-earner families.

Work-Family Convergence

The past 30 years have witnessed profound changes in views of work and family lives and the assumptions embedded in theories that guide research in these areas. These changes include a rethinking of traditional conceptions of motherhood and fatherhood, understanding of internal and external barriers to women's and men's work-family development, and awareness of restrictions that conventional views of gender place on women's public authority and on men's emotional and relational lives. In contemporary society, work and family engagement are important components of both women's and men's identities and well-being (Schneider & Waite, 2005). Leading scholars have identified a work-family convergence in which employment and involvement with family are recognized as an appropriate, normative, healthy, and intrinsically rewarding aspect of women's and men's adult lives (Barnett & Hyde, 2001; Bianchi, Robinson, & Milkie, 2006; Greenhaus & Powell, 2006).

The similarity in work-family issues for women and men is part of the convergence theme that has emerged. Fathers and mothers both experience conflict between their work and family roles, and both desire more flexibility in their work schedules and more time with their families (Bond et al., 1998; Brownson & Gilbert, 2002; Thoits, 1992). Although household work and parenting remain unevenly divided in many marriages, the distribution of income and participation in family roles is more equitable than in past decades (Stebbins, 2001). Husbands' participation in housework increases when wives earn more of the family income (Stebbins, 2001) and when husbands participate more in the care and nurturing of their children (Coltrane & Adams, 2001). Approximately 20% of spouses in dual-earner families work different shifts in order to share child rearing (Smith, 2000).

In addition, contemporary theorists and researchers have challenged traditional theories that frame work and family as inherently in conflict and stress-producing, citing evidence that work and family roles are instead compatible and mutually enhancing, with experiences in one role producing positive experiences and outcomes in the other role (Barnett, 1998; Barnett & Hyde, 2001; Greenhaus, Collins, & Shaw, 2003; Greenhaus & Powell, 2006). Findings indicate that multiple-role engagement is linked to such indices as physical and psychological well-being, relational health, and life satisfaction in men and women (Barnett, Brennan, Raudenbush, & Marshall, 1994; Barnett & Hyde, 2001; Rice, Frone, & McFarlin, 1992). Participation in both work and family roles has also been found to positively moderate distress when one of these roles is less satisfactory (Barnett, Marshall, & Pleck, 1992; Barnett, Marshall, & Sayer, 1992).

Partners can integrate and balance their employment and home roles in many ways. These variations depend to a large degree on partners' attitudes and values, personal needs, educational and career preparation, incomes, and employment situation (Barnett & Rivers, 1996; Coltrane, 2000; Gilbert, 1993; Goodnow & Bowes, 1994; Stebbins, 2001; Steil, 1997). Studies indicate that at least one-third of heterosexual two-career families have established egalitarian role-sharing arrangements, although many families who are not role-sharing describe their situation as equitable in the context of their work and family situation (Bianchi et al., 2006; Gerson, 1993; Steil, 2001). Same-sex dual-earner families, although less studied than heterosexual partners, are reported to be quite egalitarian in their role patterns (Eldridge & Gilbert, 1990; Kurdek, 2007).

Generally speaking, the predictors of marital satisfaction include active, problem-focused coping strategies (Bouchard, Sabourin, Lussier, Wright, & Richer, 1998), partners holding similar attitudes about women's and men's roles, and partners maintaining good communication (e.g., Greenstein, 1996; Huston & Geis, 1993; Nielsen, 2005). For partners holding egalitarian views, more sharing of the responsibilities of the household and parenting is associated with greater marital happiness (e.g., Nielsen, 2005; Sanchez & Kane, 1996; Thompson & Walker, 1989).

There is evidence of men's increased participation in parenting and household work (Barnett & Rivers, 1996; Lee, 2005); however, women on average still do more household work and child-care activities, and men on average devote more hours to occupational work (Bianchi et al., 2006). A large-scale study of dual-earner families using time diaries found that mothers today spend at least as much time with their children as mothers did 40 years ago. However, time diaries from male partners indicated that the amount of child care and housework performed by fathers has sharply increased (Bianchi et al., 2006). These findings are consistent with those reported by Barnett and others (Barnett & Hyde, 2001).

Although there is an underlying theme of work-family convergence, it is important to recognize that dual-earner families, as a group, vary considerably. Partners' choices and negotiations are framed by the occupational and societal factors described in the first section of the chapter, and also are influenced by partners' own personal values, personalities, and skills. Patterns of work-family relations range from traditional to role-sharing, regardless of the family's economic status (Gilbert, 2006).

To summarize, relationship satisfaction and stability in dual-earner families are generally associated with the following conditions (obtained effect sizes are typically in the small to medium range): (a) partners holding less traditional views of gender; (b) partners discussing during courtship their plans for integrating careers and family life; (c) partners affirming each other's occupational pursuits and aspirations; (d) partners being happy with their occupational work; (e) partners viewing each other's involvement in home roles as fair; (f) partners feeling supported for their lifestyle choices; (g) partners experiencing little discrimination based on gender, race, ethnicity, or sexual orientation in their workplace; (h) employers of both partners having benefit policies that are family responsive; and (i) both partners actively participating in parenting, feeling comfortable sharing parenting with child-care personnel, and being satisfied with the child care they are using.

Current Areas of Study

A number of personal, family, sociopsychological, and societal factors influence the family and work relations of partners as well as the socialization of their children. Because several of these have been addressed in earlier sections of the chapter, we focus here on two more recent research areas central to partners' day-to-day lives and to their marital happiness and stability: relational work within the family and parenting of adolescent children.

Relational Work and the Mutuality of Partner Support

Relational work not only involves valuing and affirming a partner's abilities and goals, it also involves emotional support, empathic listening, and the ability to nurture. Jessie Bernard (1974) noted some time ago that spousal support and emotional sensitivity and responsivity play a key role in dual-earner families. Men have typically depended on women for support and affirmation, and society has long assumed that women are the societal carriers of relational responsibility (Fletcher, 2001). Wilcox and Nock (2006) write, "Women are particularly vested in the emotional quality of their marriages because they have long borne the primary emotional burdens of family life. Their stake in the emotional character of their marriages is also rooted in gendered patterns of childhood socialization that encourage female proficiency in and sensitivity toward emotional dynamics in relationships" (p. 1321).

In dual-earner marriages, men's ability to give women the emotional support and encouragement women traditionally give to men is especially crucial to spouses' marital happiness. Poor emotional quality is an important predictor of women's decisions to seek divorce (Sayer & Bianchi, 2000; Wilcox & Nock, 2006). Women's assessments of the equitable division of household chores, along with men's ability to provide emotional support, are critical components of relationship satisfaction (Wilcox & Nock, 2006).

Inextricably tied to the ability to be sensitive and offer support is how each partner conceptualizes that need for support. Partners in successful dual-earner relationships reframe social support as an interpersonal process involving both giving and receiving and mutual empowerment and strength. By reconceptualizing the relation between gender and emotion, heterosexual partners can move beyond viewing emotion as a characteristic on which wives and husbands differ and can instead view it as an interpersonal process that serves as a vehicle for the development of mutuality between partners (Gilbert, 1994; Shields, 2002).

Marital quality is further enhanced by love, sexual satisfaction, communication, and satisfaction with the dual-earner lifestyle (Perrone & Worthington, 2001). Contrary to popular belief, men and women seem to value intimacy, sexual exclusivity, and commitment to one's partner to the same degree (Dion & Dion, 2001). However, although intimacy is important to both men and women, women still tend to contribute more to creating this sense of closeness in relationships (Dion & Dion, 2001). Research in this area is in its early stages, and much still needs to be learned.

Parenting of Adolescents

Although research on dual-earner families has typically focused on the parenting of young children, greater interest and concern have recently shifted to the adolescent years. This shift appears to be related to the lessened concern about parenting in the earlier years and the possible effects of caregivers other than the mother. In fact, findings indicate that exposure to child care per se does not harm children or jeopardize their emotional and cognitive development (Perry-Jenkins, Repetti, & Crouter, 2000; Scarr & Eisenberg, 1993). The shift in focus may also stem from concerns about peer group influences on adolescents. A comprehensive review reaffirmed the significance of parents and parent-child interactions in influencing which peers children select and in moderating susceptibility to peer influence (Collins, Maccoby, Steinberg, Hetherington, & Bornstein, 2000).

Erikson (1968) described adolescents and young adults as striving to achieve a self-definition that not only gives them a sense of knowing where they are going, but that also receives support and approval from the significant others in their lives, particularly parents and other influential adults. According to Erikson, attaining a sense of inner identity represents the ability of individuals to adapt their special skills, capacities, and strengths synthesized during childhood to the prevailing role structure and social system in which they are socially embedded. Children reared in dual-earner families live within a changing social and family system in which the traditional framework of conceptual dichotomies—occupational work versus parenthood, his work versus her work—no longer predicts how individuals will live their adult lives. The literature indicates that adolescents reared in dual-earner families, girls more so than boys, are likely to actively consider and plan for integrating and combining work and family roles in their own lives (Galinsky, 1999). They also seek partners who share these views (Gilbert, 1993).

How do parents in dual-earner families influence their adolescents' identities? Studies on factors such as role management, occupational identity, gender role ideology, and education-related beliefs and values indicate that adolescents' identities are shaped through a dynamic engagement with their parents (Hammack, 2005). Parents provide the most immediate role models for their children's social learning, and the ways parents manage and feel about their occupational and family roles likely influence adolescents' work and family values and expectations. How parents balance work and relationships also provides a paradigm for how children live out their own adult lives.

Adolescents experience their parents' work within the context of the family. Father's work-related stress has been reported to be particularly pervasive, with fathers' negative emotions more likely than mothers to spill over to other family members (Hammack, 2005). On average, mothers more than fathers know more about their adolescents' daily experiences, but this varies according to partners' hours of employment (Coltrane, 1996). Marchena (2005) investigated adolescent assessments of parental role management and found their assessments to be quite positive. Many adolescents in their study accepted their parents' work roles as a normative part of family life, and a vast majority of the study's participants expected to be part of a dual-earner family when they themselves had adolescent children. These findings are consistent with an earlier large-scale survey (Galinsky, 1999).

The role of family relationships and parent-child dynamics in shaping children's future gendered family patterns is not well understood, however. Several studies have found that mothers' gender role attitudes are consistently associated with their children's attitudes (e.g., Cunningham, 2001). More recent studies include both mothers and fathers and investigate both attitudes and behaviors. Findings indicate that parents' actual division of household tasks in the home is a much stronger predictor of adolescents' role expectations than parents' attitudes per se (Weinshenker, 2005). Because family work occurs in the home, parents' behavior can be directly observed by their children, and thus takes the form of both social learning and modeling. Weinshenker (2005) reported that children who observed fathers who did very little housework constructed different notions about appropriate gender roles than did children in families where the parents shared roles equitably. Parents who shared housework roles also showed more warmth and support toward their children. The role of parental attitudes and behaviors relative to children's gender role attitudes and behavior is an important area for continuing research.

ACHIEVING WORK-LIFE BALANCE: IMPLICATIONS FOR PRACTICE

Examples from clients are provided to illustrate work-family dynamics that emerge in practice. These examples involve two issues that often emerge with clients seeking assistance: achieving fairness in the relationship and deepening emotional connection and reciprocity.

Views of Fairness

Spouses' perceptions of what constitutes fairness directly relate to marital quality and personal well-being (Steil, 1997). Equality of power is not the issue; rather, it is the perception of equity within the relationship. Wives who define themselves as co-providers, rather than as persons who generate a second income, are more likely to expect their husbands to participate in family work and feel relatively unsatisfied if they perceive their husbands as not doing their fair share of that work. Similarly, husbands typically involve themselves more in family work when wives make greater financial contributions to the family and when both partners attribute greater meaning and importance to the wife's employment (Gilbert & Kearney, in press).

Women who perceive themselves as coproviders but who are hesitant to ask their husbands to do more at home may inadvertently act in ways that keep husbands in the dominant position—at the cost of their own marital happiness. Studies indicate that wives who perceive husbands as doing too little, and husbands who disagree that they are doing too little, report lower marital satisfaction than wives and husbands who either equitably share roles or who agree in their perceptions that the wife is doing more (Gottman & Notarius, 2000; Nielsen, 2005; Stanley, Markham, & Whitton, 2003). These findings underscore the value of partners creating norms of fairness for self and other. This becomes complicated when what is viewed as fair is decided through a lens that may reproduce gendered patterns (Magnusson, 2005), a topic to be discussed later.

Counseling psychologists employed in clinical settings are advised to stay informed of evolving research in the field and to build these findings into their interventions with clients. The following is an example of how a counseling psychologist might respond to a fairness issue in a clinical setting.

Case Example

Imagine working with a married, Mexican American, heterosexual woman who has sought counseling to deal with conflict in her relationship with her spouse. Central to the couple's conflicts are disagreements about who does, and should, maintain order and cleanliness in the household. Your client admits to performing the bulk of housecleaning and grocery shopping, and feels she should be doing more of that work because she is working fewer hours per week and paying a smaller proportion of the family's bills. She is also performing most of the child care for the couple's 3-year-old son, but indicates that this has not been a source of conflict within the marriage. She explains that she accepted a 30-hour position at work so that she could spend more time with her son and reports that she is happy with this arrangement.

However, the client, who was raised in a traditional, Catholic, two-parent household with a stay-at-home mother, admits that she has fears of reproducing the same relationship dynamic as that modeled by her parents. She reports having an internal conflict between craving the stability of the relationship model she observed as a child and wanting a more egalitarian, emotionally intimate relationship with her husband. She says that her arguments with her husband often arise out of feeling that she is "taken for granted" by him relative to housework and shopping duties, and that she feels closer to him when he offers to share some of those tasks with her.

Therapist Intervention

How can a therapist best respond to this client? A therapist who is uninformed about evolving views of work and family life, as well as gender socialization and its impact on heterosexual relationships, may be more likely to validate the client's perceptions that stability in a marriage comes at a cost to a woman's sense of emotional well-being and intimacy with her husband. An alternative, based on more recent scholarship, is to consider a new paradigm for viewing and creating mutually satisfying relationships. A therapist might assist the client to challenge preconceived notions of a woman's role in the family and to examine what aspects of that role are most satisfying for her. A more conscious, deliberate analysis of the family system and how she fits into that system could further help the client to renegotiate previously unspoken rules about who does what in the household, as well as who nurtures the marital relationship. Such renegotiation could yield a greater sense of egalitarianism that the client has stated she longs for. Attention to the client's culture would be an important component of counseling, as the client might further need to examine how her role as a woman and mother interacts with feelings about her ethnicity and religious background.

Communication, Mutuality, and Spousal Support

As noted, the quality of the communication, support, and affirmation between partners is central to the success of dual-earner families. Partners must create time together as a couple to increase communication (Barnett & Rivers, 1996; Zimmerman, Haddock, Current, & Ziemba, 2003). Dual-earner partners often struggle to make this time amid the daily tasks of running a household (e.g., cooking meals, mowing the lawn, performing child care), with very little time available to focus exclusively on their relationship with one another. Relationships benefit when partners communicate care and interest in each other's occupational activities, in addition to praising family involvement and support (Nielsen, 2005; Stevens, Kiger, & Riley, 2001; Zimmerman et al., 2003). The following is an example of how a counseling psychologist might respond to a communication issue in a clinical setting.

Case Example

Imagine working with a married, African American, heterosexual male. He has sought counseling at the behest of his spouse of 7 years, who would like him to "get help with listening" to her. The couple has two daughters, ages 5 and 2. Both the client and his spouse work full time in professional jobs. However, the client earns a significantly higher income and works longer hours. Child care is available through his partner's workplace.

The client reports general satisfaction with his family life. However, he expresses frustration with regard to how he and his partner communicate. He admits that when his partner expresses dissatisfaction with some aspect of their home life, he either switches immediately into "problem-solving mode" or feels defensive, as if he is being attacked. He says that these responses irritate his partner, who indicates a desire to be heard or to "vent."

The client was raised by his mother in a single-parent household and was the oldest child. He expresses pride in the fact that he can support not only his aging mother but also his family, and he cannot understand why his efforts are not "good enough" for his partner. He also expresses some sadness about being unable to spend more time with his young daughters, as they are often already in bed by the time he arrives home from work.

Therapist Intervention

A therapist with a traditional worldview of relationships between men and women might validate (and perpetuate) the client's beliefs that men and women communicate differently and need different things, and that this is an inevitable state of affairs. In the interest of affirming his masculinity and self-esteem related to performing the traditional male role, such a therapist might also affirm his viewpoint that monetary support is his most important contribution to family life.

Operating from the perspective of current research on dual-earner families, as well as evolving thinking about gender roles, however, one may assume the challenging task of validating the client's values while challenging him in those areas in which a new way of thinking might be beneficial. For example, a therapist might want to help him to explore his own definitions of partner, father, and son, and to clarify which aspects of those roles best serve his emotional and relational needs. One could also engage in psychoeducation about gender socialization and its possible impact on communication patterns between women and men, and discuss strategies for equalizing the ways in which each partner seeks emotional support or expresses vulnerability. Further, it may be valuable to address the client's sadness about lost time with his children. Desire for closeness and connection with children is an important aspect of fatherhood, and helping this client to develop strategies for creating those connections would likely be beneficial. Counseling psychologists can offer their clients a unique opportunity to redefine their goals in a space where traditional notions of male or female success can be gently challenged and broadened.

WHERE TO FROM HERE?

In this final section, we discuss additional areas for future research, theory, and practice, building on recommendations offered in earlier sections. A theme of the chapter is that partners' family and work relations occur within a larger social context over which they have little direct control, which remains inequitable in many areas, and which resists enactment of policies that would foster and support the growing work-family convergence. Where we go from here must engage these areas of inequity.

Helping Counseling Psychologists Be Social Justice Agents

The relevant issue is not whether one is racist or sexist or homophobic, but whether one is actively working against traditional systems of advantage (Tatum, 1997). Goodman et al. (2004) urged counseling psychologists to engage in social justice work, and this is precisely what is needed to further the goals and well-being of dual-earner families, especially those of more modest means. For many dual-earner families, family incomes are not keeping up with the amount of time spent at work, and that disparity is greatest among those with the lowest incomes (Dau-Schmidt & Brun, 2006). Women and men in lower-income dual-earner families can thus find themselves in a no-win situation as they struggle to protect their economic futures while holding together what has become one of the few sources of stability in changing times—the family, or one's relationships with partners, children, and parents.

Many areas need attention, ranging from studying the diverse population of dual-earner families to bringing about more flexible work arrangements, higher rates for minimum wage, increased benefits, and greater job security (Fineman & Dougherty, 2005). The practice of social justice offers many tools, such as ongoing self-evaluation, giving voice, consciousness-raising, and building on strengths. How counseling psychologists can be successful social justice agents and apply these tools to larger social issues needs much more attention. Counseling psychology is known for considering the context of individuals' lived experiences. However, historically, and still today, the main focus of research and practice is on the individual client. Even in some feminist approaches, the goal is to empower individual clients.

As Goodman et al. (2004) noted, "The opportunities to break new ground are vast" (p. 830). But how do we get there from here? Shifting our perspectives to intervene in structures and systems that shape individual lives requires transformations in the theories that guide our work as well as changes in how we construct an understanding of the forces influencing individuals. Getting there will likely involve working across disciplinarly boundaries with economists, sociologists, and legal scholars to elucidate and change practices that maintain the status quo. It will also require rethinking what we mean by social problems.

Redefining Social Problems

The definition of a social problem is time, place, and context bound (Seidman & Rappaport, 1986). What becomes defined as a social problem is often filtered through the implicit assumptions of one's culture, which in turn can predetermine who or what is seen as a problem and its possible solutions. For example, views of women as primarily caregivers have limited the development of national social policies in the areas of child care and parental leave.

Counseling psychologists have a role in redefining today's social problems and illuminating the pathways leading to possible solutions. We hold a responsibility for establishing valid research strategies that facilitate social change. We need to identify and understand the structural, relational, and psychological components of injustice. A case in point is minimum wage. The level set for minimum wage salaries occurs within a societal context of fairness, yet the reality of minimum wage on families may not be fair. At the time this chapter was written, the U.S. Senate was in a 2-week stalemate about whether to increase the minimum wage from $5.15 an hour, where it had been set for the past 10 years, to $7.25 an hour. (Editor's note: The final decision was to raise the wage to $7.25, but this will not go into effect until July of 2009.)

According to Seidman and Rappaport (1986), the unexamined and implicit premises and processes that undergird our culture's construction of a social problem create simple, stereotyped problem definitions. These, in turn, lead to similarly narrow and constrained solutions. We turn next to what we see as a particular social problem that needs redefining and that holds important implications for research and social action.

Changing Paradigms for Comparing Women and Men

In her summary of themes from 3 decades of research on gender, Kay Deaux (1999) maintained:

> Whatever the forces, there is little doubt that a sex difference tradition will continue within gender research. Assumptions of difference are embedded in the culture and transmitted regularly through media and conversation. Nor is there doubt that women and men do differ, on some dimensions, in some circumstances,

and at least some of the time. I only hope that psychologists can continue to document the complexities and variations of gender, as it is constructed and interpreted, eventually forcing an increasing sophistication in the discourse and representations that convey gender in the larger world. (p. 18)

Sex—being a women or a man biologically—distinguishes human individuals. Gender, in contrast, refers to the meanings society and individuals ascribe to someone who is born biologically female or male. Gender as difference is the assumption that one set of characteristics, abilities, and interests belongs to one sex, and that another set belongs to the other or "opposite sex." Researchers have always compared women and men, often with the assumption that any differences had inherent meaning tied to biology and that no other theoretical framework was necessary. In addition, the nonconscious ideology of opposite sexes often results in differences in degree on gender-related traits and abilities being misreported as differences in kind between women and men and then framed as intrinsic sex differences. Variability in responses within women and within men and the overlap of distributions of female and male responses is often not considered, even when statistical analyses show zero to small effect sizes in the many meta-analyses for most psychological variables and workplace behaviors (Hyde, 2005). These include cognitive variables, such as abilities; social or personality variables, such as leadership and helping behavior; psychological well-being, such as self-esteem; and motor behaviors, such as throwing distance. Indeed, sex differences and their inevitability have become central to our public discourse, despite the lack of scientific evidence to support these differences (Barnett & Rivers, 2004). Popular books such as *Men Are from Mars, Women Are from Venus* (Gray, 1992) provide a clear example of how the nonconscious ideology of opposite sexes is perpetuated (Barnett & Rivers, 2004). This book, as suggested by the title, asserts the notion that men and women are as different as beings from other planets but provides no empirical research to supports its claims.

How is this a social problem? Current theorists seek to move beyond difference as a model for studying gender (Hyde, 2005) but, as Seidman and Rappaport (1986) indicated, people prefer simplified models that fit their personal observations and confirm their social prejudices. Women, in particular, "have been trapped for generations by people's willingness to accept their own intuitions about the truth of gender stereotypes" (Mednick, 1989, p. 1122). As our understanding of dual-earner families moves toward work-family convergence and theories of work-family enrichment, it is important to frame our research questions within paradigms that contextualize gender and allow for sameness between women and men. A case in point is emotional expression and satisfaction, which are increasingly recognized as central criteria for marital happiness (Glenn, 1998). Wethington (2005) argued that researchers are only now documenting that gender differences are very small within samples of married couples, and that situation and context are more likely to be associated with variations in emotions than is gender at the daily level of observation. Traditional paradigms on the relationship between work and family directed researchers' attention toward differences in emotion, and studies were designed and interpreted from that perspective (Shields, 2002). Future research need not be similarly constrained.

Continuing the debate about whether there are truly sex differences in personality and abilities is no longer a useful enterprise (Barnett & Hyde, 2001; Mednick, 1989; Riger, 1997). The fact that one is male or female is not his or her most important characteristic. James (1997) recommended steps toward providing a more contextualized understanding of gender as a social construct by considering (a) within-group diversity, (b) the transfer of group characteristics from one situation to another and from public to private contexts, and (c) the ways in which group characteristics have changed and continue to change over time. A case in point with regard to the ways in which group characteristics have changed over time is work-family convergence. The evidence is clear that as women's and men's lives become more similar, there are fewer and fewer psychological differences between them (Barnett & Hyde, 2001).

Making Working Fathers More Visible

The way that scholars think about fatherhood has changed over the past 40 years, but current research efforts continue to focus more on mothers than fathers. Although the word "parenting" may be used in reported findings, participants more often than not are mostly mothers. In addition, the term "working fathers" rarely appears in the research literature in contrast to the normative use of the term "working mothers." Language and naming provide social phenomena with visibility. Making visible that men and women both parent their children brings men more firmly into the social discourses about parenting and work-family convergence.

Fathering appears to be uniquely sensitive to interpersonal and contextual variables, such as the mother's expectations and behaviors and the availability of family-supportive workplace policies. Current research indicates that being a partner in a caring, committed, and collaborative marriage promotes responsible fathering and active participation (Doherty, Kouneski, & Erickson, 1998). As mentioned earlier, fathers' involvement in household work and with their children likely influences children's gender-related cognitions and behaviors as well as men's own self-definitions and interpersonal qualities. The process of men's involvement in home roles may also result in ongoing revisions of conventional views of manliness. Family roles, traditionally included in the study of women's well-being, are increasingly being considered in understanding men's well-being, but are still at an early stage of study. Research is needed to assist in further recognizing the legitimate status of working fathers as a group and highlighting the dramatic role changes taking place among men.

Studying Power and Equity

Power and access form an important dynamic in the public sector, yet the tradition of considering romance as private often obscures how relationships develop within a cultural and societal context (Cancian, 1987; Frisco & Williams, 2003; Okin, 1989). Who does what in the home and the workplace often is determined by societal views of gender roles, although partners assume these are their personal decisions (Steil, 1997).

Equity between couples is typically framed according to two paradigms: exchange theory and the bargaining model (Bittman, England, Folbre, Sayer, & Matheson, 2003). According to exchange theory, the partner who is more economically dependent on the other's income will give more and receive less in the marital exchange. The spouse with the smaller income might shoulder more of the housekeeping and child-rearing work in exchange for the higher income provided by her or his partner. According to the bargaining model, negotiation within a marriage is conducted according to level of perceived threat (e.g., divorce threat, or the threat of the higher-earning spouse withholding support). Whether divorce is considered to be an option, money affects the balance of power within the relationship.

Bittman et al. (2003) reported that the division of housework reported in various studies is consistent with exchange and bargaining theories. Women consistently do much more housework than men, and men earn higher salaries (Bianchi, Milkie, Sayer, & Robinson, 2000). However, this comes with a cost. Perceived inequity in the division of household labor is negatively associated with both husbands' and wives' reported marital happiness and is positively associated with the odds of divorce among wives but not husbands (Frisco & Williams, 2003; Saginak & Saginak, 2005).

What is missing from the exchange and bargaining paradigms is an analysis of the actual dialogue engaged in by partners in reaching decisions. Theorizing needs to go beyond conventional assumptions that the partner who earns more does less in the home, or that equity between couples rests on a foundation of one's fear of abandonment. Recent theorists are using a different paradigm based on gender discourse. According to this paradigm, societal discourses, such as "housework is women's work," are unconsciously reproduced in partners' negotiations and serve to maintain inequities (Blain, 1994; Magnusson, 2005; Saginak & Saginak, 2005).

Dominant discourses, such as housework is women's work, are the mechanisms through which traditional views of various groups, and members of groups, are presented and preserved in the majority culture. Dominant discourses are linguistic (including verbal and nonverbal communication) and nonlinguistic (including everyday practices and institutional structures) and typically preserve the status quo by perpetuating the values of the most powerful groups in society. Blain (1994) and Magnusson

(2005) used the concept of dominant discourse to investigate the systematic structuring of social relations surrounding the family responsibilities and practices of spouses in dual-earner families. Both researchers' analyses identified themes characteristic of spouses' talk in the area of family work. For couples not sharing household and parenting responsibilities, nearly all the themes that emerged to explain one's own behavior and the behavior of one's spouse either relied on supposedly essential characteristics on which women and men differ (e.g., women need to take care of children) or ignored the larger social context of power relations in marriage. Couples who agreed that they did not share tasks portrayed the woman's expertise as naturally giving them more responsibility for the household. By contrast, couples who viewed tasks as equally shared talked about negotiations and strategies to move away from traditional assumptions that placed the woman in the expert position.

As these examples make clear, the gender-as-difference discourse interferes with the real conversation that is needed to make relationships work and allow partners to honestly engage each other on issues of power and assumed difference; as a result, this gender-as-difference discourse may have negative consequences for relationship commitment and stability. Strategies are needed to change such gendered discourses. We know from clinical settings that communication is particularly important in negotiating egalitarian roles, particularly in asking for and receiving support. The language of interactions, especially language that disrupts conventional assumptions about gender, can help partners communicate concern, support, and caring in their efforts to maintain a loving relationship. Although there are few studies to guide us here, clinical observations would indicate that this is a fruitful direction for research.

CONCLUSION

Although it is not a new family form, the dual-earner family is evolving as work becomes more similar for women and men and as women's and men's traditional sex-specialized roles converge. This chapter documents the importance, viability, and vitality of the dual-earner family and the work-family convergence that is taking place. A great deal of research has already been done and some areas are more in need of further understanding and attention than others. Counseling psychologists have an important role in all aspects of work and family relations—from working with individual clients to advocating for needed social change.

REFERENCES

American Association of University Women. (2003). *Women at work*. Washington, DC: AAUW Educational Foundation.

Armenia, A., & Gerstel, N. (2006). Family leaves, the FMLA, and gender neutrality: The intersection of race and gender. *Social Science Research, 35*(4), 871–891.

Barnett, R. C. (1998). Toward a review and reconceptualization of the work/family literature. *Genetic, Social, and General Psychology Monographs, 124*, 125–182.

Barnett, R. C., Brennan, R. T., Raudenbush, S. W., & Marshall, N. L. (1994). Gender and the relationship between marital-role quality and psychological distress: A study of women and men in dual-earner couples. *Psychology of Women Quarterly, 18*, 105–127.

Barnett, R. C., & Hyde, J. S. (2001). Women, men, work, and family. *American Psychologist, 56*, 781–796.

Barnett, R. C., Marshall, N. L., & Pleck, J. H. (1992). Men's multiple roles and their relationship to men's psychological distress. *Journal of Marriage and the Family, 54*, 358–367.

Barnett, R. C., Marshall, N. L., & Sayer, A. (1992). Positive-spillover effects from job to home: A closer look. *Women and Health, 19*(2/3), 13–41.

Barnett, R. C., & Rivers, C. (1996). *She works, he works: How two income families are happier, healthier, and better off*. San Francisco: Harper.

Barnett, R. C., & Rivers, C. (2004, September 3). Men are from earth and so are women: It's faulty research that sets them apart. *Chronicle of Higher Education*, B11–B13.

Bernard, J. (1974). *The future of motherhood*. New York: Dial Press.

Bianchi, S. M., Milkie, M. A., Sayer, L. C., & Robinson, J. P. (2000). Is anyone doing the housework? Trends in the gender division of household labor. *Social Forces, 79*, 191–234.

Bianchi, S. M., Robinson, J. P., & Milkie, M. A. (2006). *Changing rhythms of American family life*. New York: Russell Sage Foundation.

Bittman, M., England, P., Folbre, N., Sayer, L., & Matheson, G. (2003). When does gender trump money? Bargaining and time in household work. *American Journal of Sociology, 109*, 186–214.

Blain, J. (1994). Discourses of agency and domestic labor: Family discourse and gendered practice in dual-career families. *Journal of Family Issues, 15*, 515–549.

Bond, J. T., Galinsky, E., & Swanberg, J. E. (1998). *The 1997 national study of the changing workforce*. New York: Families and Work Institute.

Bouchard, G., Sabourin, S., Lussier, Y., Wright, J., & Richer, C. (1998). Predictive validity of coping strategies on marital satisfaction: Cross-sectional and longitudinal evidence. *Journal of Family Psychology, 12*, 112–131.

Brownson, C., & Gilbert, L. A. (2002). The development of the Discourses about Fathers Inventory: Measuring fathers' perceptions of their exposure to discourses. *Psychology of Men and Masculinity, 3*(2), 97–106.

Cancian, F. M. (1987). *Love in America: Gender and self-development*. New York: Cambridge University Press.

Carli, L. L., & Eagly, A. H. (Eds.). (2001). Gender, hierarchy, and leadership [Special issue]. *Journal of Social Issues, 57*(4).

Collins, W. A., Maccoby, E. E., Steinberg, L., Hetherington, E. M., & Bornstein, M. H. (2000). Contemporary research on parenting: The case for nature and nurture. *American Psychologist, 55*, 218–232.

Coltrane, S. (1996). *Family man, fatherhood, housework, and gender equity*. New York: Oxford University Press.

Coltrane, S. (2000). Research on household labor: Modeling and measuring the social embeddedness of routine family work. *Journal of Marriage and the Family, 62*, 363–389.

Coltrane, S., & Adams, M. (2001). Men's family work: Child-centered fathering and the sharing of domestic labor. In R. Hertz & N. L. Marshall (Eds.), *Working families: The transformation of the American home* (pp. 72–102). Berkeley: University of California Press.

Crosby, F. J., & Sabattini, L. (2005). Family and work balance. In J. Worell & C. Goodheart (Eds.), *Handbook of girls' and women's psychological health* (pp. 350–358). New York: Oxford University Press.

Cunningham, M. (2001). The influence of parental attitudes and behaviors on children's attitudes toward gender and household work in early adulthood. *Journal of Marriage and the Family, 63*, 111–122.

Dau-Schmidt, K. G., & Brun, C. (2006). Protecting families in a global environment. *Indiana Journal of Global Legal Studies, 13*(1), 165–205.

Deaux, K. (1999). An overview of research on gender: Four themes from three decades. In W. B. Swann Jr., J. Langlois, & L. A. Gilbert (Eds.), *Sexism and stereotypes in modern society: The gender science of Janet Taylor Spence* (pp. 11–33). Washington, DC: American Psychological Association.

Dion, K. K., & Dion, K. L. (2001). Gender and relationships. In R. Unger (Ed.), *Handbook of the psychology of women and gender* (pp. 256–271). New York: Wiley.

Doherty, W. J., Kouneski, E. F., & Erickson, M. F. (1998). Responsible fathering: An overview and conceptual framework. *Journal of Marriage and the Family, 60*, 277–292.

Eldridge, N. S., & Gilbert, L. A. (1990). Correlates of relationship satisfaction in lesbian couples. *Psychology of Women Quarterly, 14*, 43–62.

Erikson, E. (1968). *Identity and the life cycle*. New York: Norton.

Fineman, A. A., & Dougherty, T. (Eds.). (2005). *Feminism confronts homo economicus: Gender, law, and society*. Ithaca, NY: Cornell University Press.

Fletcher, J. K. (2001). *Disappearing acts: Gender, power, and relational practice at work*. Cambridge, MA: MIT Press.

Foley, S. (2006). Family-responsive workplace policies. In J. H. Greenhaus (Ed.), *Encyclopedia of career development* (pp. 317–319). Thousand Oaks, CA: Sage.

Frisco, M. L., & Williams, K. (2003). Perceived housework equity, marital happiness, and divorce in dual-earner households. *Journal of Family Issues, 24*, 51–73.

Galinsky, E. (1999). *Ask the children: What America's children really think about working parents*. New York: William Morrow.

Gerson, K. (1993). *No man's land: Men's changing commitments to family and work*. New York: Basic Books.

Gilbert, L. A. (1993). *Two careers/one family*. Newbury Park, CA: Sage.

Gilbert, L. A. (1994). Reclaiming and returning gender to context: Examples from studies of dual-career families. *Psychology of Women Quarterly, 18*, 539–558.

Gilbert, L. A. (2006). Two-career relationships. In J. H. Greenhaus (Ed.), *Encyclopedia of career development* (pp. 822–828). Thousand Oaks, CA: Sage.

Gilbert, L. A., & Kearney, L. (in press). Sex, gender, and dual-earner families: Implications and applications for career counseling for women. In B. Walsh & M. Heppner (Eds.), *Handbook of career counseling for women*. Mahwah, NJ: Erlbaum.

Glass, J., & Finley, A. (2002). Coverage and effectiveness of family-responsive workplace policies. *Human Resources Management Review, 12*, 313–337.

Glenn, N. (1998). The course of marital success and failure in five American 10-year marriage cohorts. *Journal of Marriage and the Family, 60*, 569–576.

Goodman, L. A., Liang, B., Helms, J. E., Latta, R. E., Sparks, E., & Weintraub, S. R. (2004). Training counseling psychologists as social justice agents. *Counseling Psychologist, 32*, 793–837.

Goodnow, J. J., & Bowes, J. M. (1994). *Men, women, and household work*. New York: Oxford University Press.

Gottman, J., & Notarius, C. (2000). Decade review: Observing marital interaction. *Journal of Marriage and the Family, 62*, 927–947.

Greenhaus, J. H., Collins, K. M., & Shaw, J. D. (2003). The relation between work-family balance and quality of life. *Journal of Vocational Behavior, 63*, 510–531.

Greenhaus, J. H., & Powell, G. N. (2006). When work and family are allies: A theory of work-family enrichment. *Academy of Management Review, 31*, 72–92.

Greenstein, T. N. (1996). Husbands' participation in domestic labor: Interactive effects of wives' and husbands' gender ideologies. *Journal of Marriage and the Family, 58*, 585–595.

Gray, J. (1992). *Men are from Mars, women are from Venus: A practical guide for improving communication and getting what you want in your relationships*. New York: HarperCollins.

Hammack, P. L. (2005). Parenting and adolescent development: Overview. In B. Schneider & L. J. Waite (Eds.), *Being together, working apart: Dual-career families and the work-life balance* (pp. 331–332). Cambridge: Cambridge University Press.

Huston, T. L., & Geis, G. (1993). In what ways do gender-related attitudes and beliefs affect marriage? *Journal of Social Issues, 49*(3), 87–106.

Hyde, J. S. (2005). The gender similarities hypothesis. *American Psychologist, 60*, 581–592.

Jacobs, J. A., & Gerson, K. (2001). Overworked individuals or overworked families? Explaining trends in work, leisure, and family time. *Work and Occupations, 28*, 40–63.

James, J. B. (1997). What are the social issues involved in focusing on difference in the study of gender? *Journal of Social Issues, 53*(2), 213–232.

Kurdek, L. (2007). The allocation of household labor by partners in gay and lesbian couples. *Journal of Family Issues, 28*(1), 132–148.

Lee, Y. (2005). Measuring the gender gap in household labor: Accurately estimating wives' and husbands' contributions. In B. Schneider & L. J. Waite (Eds.), *Being together, working apart: Dual-career families and the work-life balance* (pp. 229–247). Cambridge: Cambridge University Press.

Levine, J. A., & Pittinsky, T. L. (1997). *Working fathers: New strategies for balancing work and family*. Reading, MA: Addison-Wesley.

Lobel, S. A. (1999). Impacts of diversity and work-life initiatives in organizations. In G. N. Powell (Ed.), *Handbook of gender and work* (pp. 453–476). Thousand Oaks, CA: Sage.

Magnusson, E. (2005). Gendering or equality in the lives of Nordic heterosexual couples with children: No well-paved avenues. *Nordic Journal of Women's Studies, 13*(3), 153–163.

Marchena, E. (2005). Adolescents' assessment of parental role management in dual-earner families. In B. Schneider & L. J. Waite (Eds.), *Being together, working apart: Dual-career families and the work-life balance* (pp. 333–360). Cambridge: Cambridge University Press.

Marecek, J. (1995). Gender, politics, and psychology's way of knowing. *American Psychologist, 50*, 162–163.

Mednick, M. T. (1989). On the politics of psychological constructs: Stop the bandwagon—I want to get off. *American Psychologist, 44*, 1118–1123.

Meyerson, D. E. (2003). *Tempered radicals*. Cambridge, MA: Harvard Business School Press.

Michaels, W. B. (2006, November 2). Celebrating 125 years of university women. *Diverse: Issues in Higher Education, 23*(19), 11.

Nielsen, M. R. (2005). Marriage and family overview. In B. Schneider & L. J. Waite (Eds.), *Being together, working apart: Dual-career families and the work-life balance* (pp. 167–168). Cambridge: Cambridge University Press.

Okin, S. M. (1989). *Justice, gender, and the family*. New York: Basic Books.

Perrone, K. M., & Worthington, E. L. (2001). Factors influencing ratings of marital quality for individuals within dual-career marriages: A conceptual model. *Journal of Counseling Psychology, 48*, 3–9.

Perry-Jenkins, M., Repetti, R., & Crouter, A. (2000). Work and family in the 1990s. *Journal of Marriage and the Family, 62*, 981–998.

Porter, J. R. (2006, September 22). With more women and African-Americans, enrollments rise at graduate schools. *Chronicle of Higher Education, 53*(5), A10.

Rhodes, F. H. T. (2006, November 24). After 40 years of growth and change, higher education faces new challenges. *Chronicle of Higher Education*, A18–A20.

Rice, R. W., Frone, M. R., & McFarlin, D. B. (1992). Work-nonwork conflict and the perceived quality of life. *Journal of Organizational Behavior, 13*, 155–168.

Riger, S. (1997). From snapshots to videotape: New directions in research on gender differences. *Journal of Social Issues, 53*(2), 395–408.

Saginak, K. A., & Saginak, M. A. (2005). Balancing work and family: Equity, gender, and marital satisfaction. *Family Journal, 13*(2), 162–166.

Sanchez, L., & Kane, E. W. (1996). Women's and men's constructions of perceptions of housework fairness. *Journal of Family Issues, 17*, 385–387.

Sayer, L. C., & Bianchi, S. M. (2000). Women's economic independence and the probability of divorce. *Journal of Family Issues, 21*(7), 906–943.

Scarr, S., & Eisenberg, M. (1993). Child care research: Issues, perspectives, and results. *Annual Review of Psychology, 44*, 613–644.

Schneider, B., & Waite, L. J. (Eds.). (2005). *Being together, working apart: Dual-career families and the work-life balance*. Cambridge: Cambridge University Press.

Seidman, E., & Rappaport, J. (1986). *Redefining social problems*. New York: Plenum Press.

Shields, S. A. (2002). *Speaking from the heart: Gender and the social meaning of emotion*. Cambridge: Cambridge University Press.

Smallwood, S. (2003, December 12). American women surpass men in earning doctorates. *Chronicle of Higher Education*, A10.

Smith, K. (2000). *Who's minding the kids? Child care arrangements: Fall 1995* (Current populations reports, P70–70). Washington, DC: U.S. Census Bureau.

Stanley, S., Markham, H., & Whitton, S. (2003). Communication, conflict, and commitment: Insights on the foundations of relationship success from a national survey. *Family Process, 41*, 659–675.

Stebbins, L. F. (2001). *Work and family in America: A reference handbook*. Santa Barbara, CA: ABC-CLIO.

Steil, J. M. (1997). *Marital equality: Its relationship to the well-being of husbands and wives*. Thousand Oaks, CA: Sage.

Steil, J. M. (2001). Family forms and member well-being: A research agenda for the decade of behavior. *Psychology of Women Quarterly, 25*, 344–363.

Stevens, D., Kiger, G., & Riley, P. J. (2001). Working hard and hardly working: Domestic labor and marital satisfaction among dual-earner couples. *Journal of Marriage and Family, 63*, 514–526.

Stone, K. V. W. (2005). The new faces of employment discrimination. In M. A. Fineman & T. Dougherty (Eds.), *Feminism confronts home economics: Gender, law, and society* (pp. 297–323). Ithaca, NY: Cornell University Press.

Tatum, B. (1997). *Why are all the Black kids sitting together in the cafeteria?* New York: Basic Books.

Thoits, P. A. (1992). Identity structures and psychological well-being: Gender and marital status comparisons. *Social Psychological Quarterly, 55*, 236–256.

Thompson, L., & Walker, A. J. (1989). Women and men in marriage, work, and parenthood. *Journal of Marriage and the Family, 51*, 845–872.

Thompson, L., & Walker, A. J. (1995). The place of feminism in family studies. *Journal of Marriage and the Family, 57*, 847–865.

U.S. Bureau of Labor Statistics. (2006a, April). *Employment characteristics of families in 2005*. Washington, DC: U.S. Government Printing Office.

U.S. Bureau of Labor Statistics. (2006b, March). *Women still underrepresented among highest earners*. Washington, DC: U.S. Government Printing Office.

U.S. Census Bureau. (2006). *Income, earnings, and poverty data from the 2005 American Community Survey* (ACS-02). Washington, DC: U.S. Government Printing Office.

Wayne, J. H., & Cordeiro, B. L. (2003). Who is a good organizational citizen? Social perception of male and female employees who use family leave. *Sex Roles, 49*(5/6), 233–246.

Weinshenker, M. N. (2005). Imagining family roles: Parental influences on the expectations of adolescents in dual-earner families. In B. Schneider & L. J. Waite (Eds.), *Being together, working apart: Dual-career families and the work-life balance* (pp. 365–388). Cambridge: Cambridge University Press.

Wethington, E. (2005). Marriage and family overview. In B. Schneider & L. J. Waite (Eds.), *Being together, working apart: Dual-career families and the work-life balance* (pp. 190–195). Cambridge: Cambridge University Press.

Wilcox, W. B., & Nock, S. L. (2006). What's love got to do with it? Equality, equity, commitment, and women's marital quality. *Social Forces, 84*(3), 1321–1345.

Zimmerman, T. S., Haddock, S. A., Current, L. R., & Ziemba, S. (2003). Intimate partnership: Foundation to the successful balance of family and work. *American Journal of Family Therapy, 31*, 107–124.

CHAPTER 26

Vocational Counseling Process and Outcome

SUSAN C. WHISTON
DARYN RAHARDJA

Juntunen (2006) contended that work is a pervasive aspect of most individuals' lives, yet many applied psychologists have little interest, training, or competence related to assisting individuals with increasingly complex work issues. As many have argued (e.g., DeBell, 2002; Swanson, 1995), one of the major distinctions between counseling psychology and other psychological specialties is the focus on work and career issues, including expertise in vocational counseling. Whether the centrality of vocational or work interests will remain in counseling psychology is uncertain. Heppner, O'Brien, Hinkelman, and Flores (1996) found that counseling psychology students were significantly less interested in career-vocational counseling than in social-emotional counseling.

We argue that counseling psychologists should embrace and enhance their expertise in vocational (or career) counseling, not only to retain the field's unique and traditional identity, but also to address the pressing and significant clinical needs in this area. As Juntunen (2006) documented, work is a major force in psychological health; a growing body of evidence links job satisfaction and work-related issues to psychological well-being (Akerboom & Maes, 2006; Carr, Schmidt, Ford, & DeShon, 2003; Parker et al., 2003). Moreover, negative spillover from work to other aspects of life and relationships is exceedingly common and is associated with increased probabilities of developing mood, anxiety, or substance abuse disorders (Frone, 2000). Furthermore, if counseling psychologists are interested in issues of social justice, then ignoring issues related to work and the psychology of working is analogous to ignoring the proverbial elephant in the room. For many individuals, lacking work or working at minimum wage jobs can lead to other disparities, such as inadequate health care or poor educational access.

If counseling psychologists continue their tradition of recognizing the importance of work in people's lives, then it follows that every counseling psychologist must develop expertise at providing vocationally related interventions and acquire knowledge about the interventions that are most effective with their clients. Some writers have made definitional distinctions between career counseling and career intervention. Swanson (1995), for example, defined career counseling as "an ongoing, face to face interaction between counselor and client, with career- or work-related issues as the primary focus" (p. 219). Career interventions, on the other hand, have been defined as "any treatment or effort intended to enhance an individual's career development or to enable the person to make better career-related decisions" (Spokane & Oliver, 1983, p. 100).

This chapter focuses on process and outcome research related to both career counseling and the broader spectrum of work-related interventions. In discussing psychotherapy research, Hill and Lambert (2004) defined process as what happens in psychotherapy sessions (e.g., therapist interpretation of a client's comment), and outcome as immediate and long-term changes that occur as a result of the therapeutic process. Despite these definitions, the distinction between process and outcome is sometimes difficult to differentiate because process and outcome are inextricably linked. There are constructs, such as the working alliance, that are used as both process and outcome variables. Consistent with Swanson (1995), career counseling process and outcome are discussed as separate entities, yet the somewhat artificial separation between the two is acknowledged. This chapter is organized around four central themes or questions: (1) Are vocational counseling and interventions effective? (2) Do input variables, such as client factors, counselor variables, or modality of delivery, influence outcome? (3) What processes produce the best results? (4) What works for whom under what circumstance?

ARE VOCATIONAL COUNSELING AND INTERVENTIONS EFFECTIVE?

The seemingly simple question of whether vocational counseling and interventions are effective implies some thorny and complex issues related to what constitutes effectiveness. As Wampold, Lichtenberg, and Wahler (2002) underscored, no single study can validate any intervention, and conclusions related to empirical support should be based on an appropriate synthesis of studies bearing on the efficacy of the intervention. We first, therefore, review the meta-analytic evidence on the overall effectiveness of career interventions and then explore whether intervention effectiveness may vary depending on the type of outcome that is used.

How Effective Are Career Interventions?

Four primary meta-analyses have been conducted that compared vocational interventions to no treatment (Brown & Ryan Krane, 2000; Oliver & Spokane, 1988; Spokane & Oliver, 1983; Whiston, Sexton, & Lasoff, 1998). These studies involved a wide range of career interventions (e.g., classes, computer systems), not just vocational counseling.

Oliver and Spokane (1988) added more recently published studies to their earlier meta-analysis (Spokane & Oliver, 1983), finding that those receiving career interventions scored almost a standard deviation higher (delta = .82) on various outcome measures than those who did not receive an intervention or received a placebo intervention. Delta, the effect size estimate used by Smith, Glass, and Miller (1980) in their classic meta-analysis of psychotherapy outcomes, is calculated by subtracting the mean of the control group from the mean of the treatment group and dividing by the standard deviation of the control group. Subsequent to Oliver and Spokane's studies, meta-analytic techniques became more sophisticated, finding that dividing by a pooled within group standard deviation rather than the control group standard deviation and weighting individual effect sizes, before averaging, by the inverse of their variances yields a more unbiased overall effect size estimate (d_+) than simple unweighted averaging (Hedges & Olkin, 1985). Using the Hedges and Olkin weighting procedure to examine mean differences between treatment and control groups, Brown and Ryan Krane (2000) and Whiston et al. (1998) found similar average effect sizes for career interventions that were substantially smaller than those found by Oliver and Spokane (1988). Using these more sophisticated procedures, Brown and Ryan Krane (2000) focused on the impact of interventions on career choice outcomes (e.g., decidedness, certainty, choice satisfaction) and constructs related to career choice (e.g., self-efficacy, career maturity); they found an average effect size of .34.

In their meta-analysis of a wider variety of vocational outcomes, Whiston et al. (1998) determined effect sizes using different weighting procedures. They found when effect sizes were weighted simply by sample size, the overall average effect size was .44, which was similar to Oliver and Spokane's sample size weighted effect size of .48. However, when Whiston et al. used the procedures suggested by Hedges and Olkin in which weighting also included the inverse variance, their findings ($d_+ = .30$) were similar to Brown and Ryan Krane's findings.

In combining the findings from meta-analytic studies, the average overall effect sizes for career interventions tend to fall in the range of .30 to .50, particularly when the appropriate statistical adjustments are made. Although these weighted effect sizes are smaller than Oliver and Spokane's original unweighted effect size of .82, even the more conservative effect size estimates are all statistically and practically significant. Using Cohen's (1988) rules of thumb for interpreting the magnitude of effect sizes, career interventions would be considered as having small to moderate effects. To clarify further the practical significance of these effect sizes, Brown and McPartland (2005) converted Brown and Ryan Krane's (2000) effect size of $d_+ = .34$ to a correlation in order to provide a Binomial Effect Size (BES; Rosenthal & Rubin, 1982) interpretation of career intervention effectiveness. This conversion suggested that, all else being equal, 17% more persons would show improvement on important career choice outcomes if they receive career interventions than if they do not. In addition, even when using the most conservative effect size of $d_+ = .30$, the average career client is likely to exceed 62% of the control group clients on a wide range of vocational outcomes (Whiston, 2002).

Does Career Intervention Effectiveness Vary by Outcome?

Without a clear understanding of the status and quality of the outcome measures used, there is little practical utility in the conclusion that those who received vocational interventions consistently exceeded those who did not. Brown and McPartland (2005) argued that, in their experience, most individuals seek assistance related to work or career issues to (a) make or remake a career or occupational choice, (b) implement an already made (or remade) choice, or (c) achieve adjustment. They also concluded that the majority of studies have involved career choice interventions and, therefore, the interpretation of vocational outcome research should primarily focus on choice-related outcomes.

Brown and Ryan Krane's (2000) meta-analysis focused on choice-related outcomes (e.g., choice satisfaction, certainty, or level of decidedness) and other outcomes that have been found to be related to choice-making success (congruence, vocational identity, career maturity, and career decision-making self-efficacy beliefs). Whiston et al. (1998) found that 40% of all outcome measures used in studies published between 1983 and 1995 involved either measures of certainty and decidedness or career maturity. Whiston et al. found a small average weighted effect size ($d_+ = .19$) for career interventions that were evaluated with certainty/decidedness measures and a somewhat larger one ($d_+ = .53$) when measures of career maturity were used. Brown and Ryan Krane (2000) found that the largest effect sizes were associated with measures of vocational identity ($d_+ = .63$), and Whiston et al. found a larger average effect size ($d_+ = .81$) for outcome measures that evaluated participants' performance of career-related skills (e.g., interviewing, writing, problem solving).

Folsom and Reardon (2003) documented the evolution of outcome measures used to evaluate career courses in higher education between 1976 and 2001. They reported that measures of career maturity had declined, and recent studies were more likely to use instruments that assessed decidedness, vocational identity, and career thoughts. In examining the effectiveness of career counseling courses, they found that in 34 out of the 38 studies that they identified, career counseling courses resulted in positive outcomes related to career maturity, career decision making, vocational identity and thoughts, and locus of control. Furthermore when the outcomes were course satisfaction and retention (both to the next semester and until graduation), 13 out of the 15 studies had positive findings. Thus, both qualitative reviews (e.g., Folsom & Reardon, 2003) and quantitative reviews (e.g., Brown & Ryan Krane, 2000) have indicated that vocational outcome researchers have predominately relied on client self-report measures rather than on behavioral or long-term outcomes.

In summarizing the findings related to the general effectiveness of vocational counseling and interventions, outcome researchers tended to find positive outcomes. The general mean effect sizes seemed to be in the small to moderate range; however, there was significant variation in effect sizes depending on the type of outcome. The majority of research has focused on choice-related outcomes (e.g., decidedness) and other outcomes that are related to choice-making success (e.g., career maturity). Larger effect sizes tended to be associated with measures of career maturity, vocational identity, and performance of career-related skills than with measures of certainty or decidedness. Thus, it may be that career interventions are quite effective at promoting more intermediate outcomes that should make the choice-making process easier (i.e., career maturity, vocational identity), but their immediate postintervention effects on distal decision-making outcomes (e.g., decidedness and certainty) seem to be more modest.

DO INPUT VARIABLES INFLUENCE OUTCOME?

Whiston et al. (1998) found that career interventions were not a homogeneous group and that there was significant variation in effectiveness across different interventions, which directs attention to the possible influences of input factors and process variables on career intervention outcome. As indicated earlier, typical input factors are related to client demographics and counselor and site characteristics (e.g., degree of structure or intervention modalities).

Client Factors

The pertinent issue here is whether career counseling is more effective for some clients than others. In a seminal paper published more than 20 years ago, Fretz (1981) made an eloquent plea for more research related to which clients benefit from what type of career counseling. Fretz's call for research on client aptitude-by-treatment interactions is relevant today as we still know very little about the interaction between client factors and intervention outcomes. Whiston (2002) found that 49% of the career treatment-control group comparison studies since 1950 were conducted with college students. Related to client factors, Mau and Fernandes (2001) found that younger college students (less than 26 years old) were more likely to use career counseling services compared with older students, but there were no differences between the two age groups related to their satisfaction with career counseling. Shivy and Koehly (2002) found that, in general, college students preferred to receive career services off-campus and for those vocational services to be time limited. Nevertheless, this heavy reliance on research with college students and the lack of data related to the effectiveness of career counseling with different age groups poses problems in determining the types of client that benefit most from career counseling or how vocational counseling should be adapted to correspond to client demographic and contextual factors.

Gender

Most of the research related to clients' gender and vocational counseling have focused on clients' perceptions, expectations, and attitudes toward the vocational counseling process. In their meta-analysis, Brown and Ryan Krane (2000) identified 18 studies that examined gender differences in outcome; however, only 3 out of the 18 studies reported significant outcome differences between men and women. In each of these three studies, women had higher levels of career maturity at posttreatment than men. Mau and Fernandes (2001) found no significant gender difference in usage of career counseling services; however, they found that women reported somewhat higher levels of satisfaction with career counseling than men ($d = .05$). Conversely, Healy (2001) did not find gender differences in terms of satisfaction with either a brief career program or a more in-depth individual career counseling approach.

Rochlen and colleagues conducted a series of studies related to men's attitudes toward career counseling. Rochlen, Mohr, and Hargrove (1999) found that men were more likely to report a higher stigma attached to career counseling than women ($r = .35$). Rochlen and O'Brien (2002) found that men who tended to be restrictive in expressing emotions and uncomfortable with closeness with other men were more inclined to view career counseling as having more of a stigma. In contrast, they did not find differences between more and less traditional men concerning their views on the value of career counseling;

both groups viewed career counseling in positive terms. Although the authors predicted that more traditional men would prefer a person-environment-fit approach compared with a psychodynamic-integrated approach, both groups of men preferred a person-environment approach to career counseling. In another study, Rochlen, Blazina, and Raghunathan (2002) examined the impact of a gender-specific (targeted toward men) or a gender-neutral brochure on men's willingness to engage in career counseling. They found that both brochures produced equivalent gains in attitudes toward career counseling.

Race and Ethnicity

Brown and Ryan Krane (2000) contended that, although much has been written about the unique career development needs of racial and ethnic minorities, as of 2000 there had been very little exploration of the effects of varying career interventions with these different groups. Our reading of the career intervention outcome literature suggests that, 8 years later, there is still little research on racial/ethnic differences in career intervention outcome or on the relative effectiveness of interventions designed specifically for racial/ethnic minority groups versus more traditional interventions.

Shivy and Koehly (2002) found no difference in terms of preferences for career services among students from different racial and ethnic backgrounds. Nevertheless, Shivy and Koehly found that minority and international students' perceptions of career services typically available on a college campus were different from those of White students, which indicated a need for career services personnel to clarify with students of color the vocational services available. Carter, Scales, Juby, Collins, and Wan (2003) found that race was related to the number of sessions at a university-based career development center. Black students were most likely to attend only one session, Asian and Hispanic students were most likely to attend 2 to 9 sessions, and White students were most likely to attend 10 or more sessions. Moreover, although counselors perceived most clients as having made at least minimal progress, they saw Black clients as significantly more likely than other clients to achieve no change.

Diagnosis and Distress

Rounds and Tinsley (1984) called for the development of a vocational problem diagnostic scheme that could be used by both researchers and practitioners. As Brown and Rector (Chapter 23, this volume) indicate, researchers have only recently begun to agree on some commonalities in a diagnostic scheme for vocational problems. Furthermore, there is very little research related to the effectiveness of vocational counseling with clients diagnosed with differing vocational needs or problems. A rudimentary attempt to conduct this type of research found no differences in outcome between uncertain/minimally distressed and undecided/distressed clients after one session of career counseling (Rochlen, Milburn, & Hill, 2004).

Although some psychologists may have the impression that clients entering counseling with vocational concerns are less distressed than other clients, some studies suggest otherwise. Lucas (1992) found that college students seeking career counseling did not differ from students seeking personal counseling in terms of the problems they were experiencing. Other research has indicated that career and noncareer clients do not differ in levels of emotional discomfort (Gold & Scanlon, 1993) or on precounseling measures of personal adjustment (Lewis, 2001). Fouad et al. (2006) found that college students simultaneously reported high levels of career decision difficulties and psychological distress. Multon, Heppner, Gysbers, Zook, and Ellis-Kalton (2001) found that 60% of adults seeking counseling related to work issues could be classified as psychologically distressed, and the "undecided/distressed" clients in the Rochlen et al. (2004) study scored a full standard deviation higher than the normative mean for outpatient mental health clients on a standardized measure of psychological distress completed at intake.

Counselor Factors

In a meta-analysis that compared different modalities and approaches to career interventions, Whiston, Brecheisen, and Stephens (2003) found that counselor-free interventions were significantly *less* effective than any other type of intervention (e.g., individual counseling, group counseling, classes) that involved counselors. Hence, counselor involvement in the career intervention process appears to be critical. Whiston et al.'s meta-analysis further supported the importance of counselor involvement in that computer-assisted career guidance systems supplemented by counseling were found to have significantly better outcomes than interventions that relied solely on the computerized system.

Although Whiston et al. (2003) found that counselor-free interventions were less effective than those involving some sort of counseling, there appears to be very little research related to what factors contribute to being an effective vocational counselor. Similar to psychotherapy research, where neither training nor experience appear to consistently affect outcome (Beutler et al., 2004), meta-analytic reviews of vocational interventions (Oliver & Spokane, 1988; Whiston et al., 1998) have not found that master's- or doctoral-level clinicians are any more effective than counseling students or other service providers (e.g., teachers). Consistent with other findings regarding experience, Gati and Ram (2000) found that more experienced psychologists did not differ from students in terms of their abilities to accurately assess career-related interests of clients. In one of the rare studies to examine counselor attributes in vocational process and outcome research, Heppner, Multon, Gysbers, Ellis, and Zook (1998) found that counselor trainees' self-efficacy did increase with additional career counseling experience, but trainees' self-efficacy did not appear to be related to any of the process (e.g., counseling relationship) or outcome measures (e.g., decidedness, vocational identity) employed in the study.

Modalities

The definitional distinctions between input variables and process variables are often difficult to delineate, particularly when discussing different modalities (individual, small group, or large class interventions). We have somewhat arbitrarily labeled our discussion of differences in approaches or modalities as an input variable because that decision is often made before the vocational intervention process begins. In combining the effect sizes from Oliver and Spokane (1988) and Whiston et al. (1998) related to modality differences, Whiston (2002) found that individual counseling and career classes were the most effective treatment modalities. Brown and Ryan Krane (2000), however, concluded that providing career interventions in small groups that involve specific critical ingredients (discussed later in this chapter) could be effective.

If the intent of providing career interventions is to assist clients in the most efficient and timely manner, then individual counseling has been found consistently to be the most efficacious modality. Whiston et al. (1998) found individual career counseling to have the largest effect size compared with other modalities (e.g., group, classes) and the gains associated with individual counseling were accomplished on average in less than an hour. This is not to suggest, however, that career counseling should only be conducted in less than an hour, as compelling research indicates that optimum dose effect or number of sessions is 4 to 5 sessions (Brown & Ryan Krane, 2000).

Further support for the efficacy of individual career counseling comes from other recent studies. For adult clients who had attended between 3 and 12 sessions, Heppner et al. (1998) found that both levels of decidedness and target goal scores increased significantly after each individual career counseling session. Mau and Fernandes (2001) found that most clients who participated in career counseling were satisfied with the counseling they had received. In fact, Anderson and Niles (2000) found that clients evaluated their career counseling significantly more positively than did their counselors. Also, client gains achieved in career counseling appear to last. In following up with clients 1 to 12 months after receiving career counseling, Healy (2001) found that 85% of the clients reported continued progress (e.g., pursuing degrees, gathering information, and changing occupations); only 15% indicated they had done nothing since their last career counseling session.

Both qualitative (Folsom & Reardon, 2003) and quantitative (Whiston, 2002) reviews have also indicated that career classes are one of the more effective types of career intervention. In Folsom and Reardon's review, 34 out of the 38 studies of career courses for college students reported positive results, whereas Whiston found an unweighted effect size of 1.17 when career class participants are compared with nonparticipants. In one of the few vocational intervention studies that involved man-ualized treatments, Vernick, Reardon, and Sampson (2004) found that students over a 5-year period consistently rated this career course higher than other academic courses in terms of class demands and student-instructor involvement.

Small groups that typically involve 8 to 12 individuals are another popular modality for providing career interventions. In comparing career interventions, Whiston et al. (2003) found that structured vocational counseling groups were significantly more effective than unstructured groups. In conducting vocational group interventions, however, practitioners should consider Brown and Ryan Krane's (2000) critical ingredients, particularly individualized feedback and interpretation. Hence, when the goal is effective career choice counseling, a hybrid of group and individual vocational counseling may be the most effective and cost-efficient approach.

Conclusions about Input Factors

The finding that counselor-free interventions are significantly less effective than any other treatment modalities suggests that vocational interventions require the involvement of clinicians. These results indicate that vocational decision making and planning should not be relegated to only having a client use a computer or access the Internet; these issues are more effectively addressed by infusing counseling with Internet or computer-based programs. For researchers, this finding, coupled with the dearth of information concerning counselor attributes, should generate many questions about the characteristics of effective career counselors. Further, the limited research on sex differences suggests that women tend to report being somewhat more satisfied with their experiences than men and that some men may avoid seeking career services because of the stigma that they attach to such services. In closing this overview of input factors, we note that input factors in isolation account for only a small percentage of the variance in outcome measures. To adequately explain variations in vocational outcome, it is imperative to examine the interaction of input factors and process variables.

WHAT PROCESSES PRODUCE THE BEST RESULTS?

In psychotherapy, a wealth of process research can inform the clinician; however, there is less research in career counseling on the relationship between process and outcome (Blustein & Spengler, 1995). Heppner and Heppner (2003) referred to career counseling process variables as the overt and covert thoughts, feelings, and behaviors of both clients and counselors while engaged in counseling. Process variables should be distinguished from input variables, which describe the characteristics of the client and counselor as well as the setting in which career counseling is provided. Heppner and Heppner also differentiated process from outcome, stating that outcome encompasses the changes that resulted from career counseling, both directly and indirectly.

Critical Ingredients

Brown and Ryan Krane (2000) expanded on a meta-analysis conducted originally by Ryan (1999) and found that five critical ingredients positively influenced outcome regardless of modality or format. These five critical ingredients are written exercises, individualized interpretations, occupational information, modeling, and attention to building support. Healy (2001) found somewhat similar results; clients reported that the most helpful elements of career counseling were clarifying assets and values, receiving feedback from testing, and getting information. According to Brown and Ryan Krane, not only were the five critical ingredients important individually, but combinations of them resulted in larger effect sizes than any one individually. Although their analyses did not include any study that employed all five critical ingredients, adding one, two, or three critical ingredients yielded average standardized mean differences effect sizes (d_+'s) of .45, .61, and .99, respectively. Brown et al. (2003) also found that this increase in effect sizes was not based on the number of sessions or simply on longer career counseling being better. When they examined the simple addition of noncritical ingredients, there were no similar incremental increases in effect sizes as they found with the critical ingredients.

Written Exercises

Written exercises consist of activities or interventions that either encourage or require clients to record reflections, thoughts, or feelings concerning their career development (Brown & Ryan Krane, 2000; Ryan, 1999). In a further analysis of these data, Brown et al. (2003) found that the content of the written materials varied among more versus less effective career interventions that used written exercises. The more effective interventions tended to provide written exercises that required comparing occupations, which were followed by written materials that engaged clients in future planning. Thus, counseling psychologists who are considering activities that could be researched and implemented should develop written exercises that (a) provide clients with written analyses and comparisons of occupations, and (b) assist clients to articulate plans and activities related to achieving those goals.

Individualized Interpretation and Feedback

Brown and Ryan Krane (2000) also identified individualized feedback as a critical ingredient in career counseling. Their results did not indicate that the entire process needed to be conducted one-on-one. However, they found that, at some point, counselors need to work individually with clients on their future goals and plans. In comparing group interventions that included some individualized attention, Brown et al. (2003) found particularly large effect size differences between these and group interventions that lacked this critical one-on-one interaction (d_+'s of 1.47 versus .53, respectively).

Brown et al. (2003) suggested individual attention may be most critical for persons with difficult-to-interpret assessment results and in reviewing written client goals. In analyzing research related to interpretation of tests, Goodyear (1990) concluded that when given a preference, clients preferred to receive results individually and reported more satisfaction, clarity, and helpfulness when the interpretation was performed individually compared with other formats, such as groups.

Occupational Information

Occupational information is a traditional aspect of career counseling. Its importance was acknowledged by Frank Parsons (1909), whose tripartite model of career counseling included knowledge of the requirements and conditions of success, advantages and disadvantages, compensation, opportunities, and prospects in different lines of work. Galassi, Crace, Martin, James, and Wallace (1992) found that clients want to discuss information on specific careers in counseling and are willing to read, research information, and interview individuals outside sessions. This corresponds with Brown and Ryan Krane's (2000) findings that clients report better outcome when occupational information is processed within a vocational counseling session, and with Brown et al.'s (2003) finding of a strong positive correlation ($r = .82$) between outcome and career information-seeking effect sizes. Leso and Neimeyer (1991) and Neimeyer and Leso (1992) found that individuals were better at processing occupational information when they were provided with structured constructs (e.g., salary, occupational status) than when they attempted to develop their own set of constructs in which to process the information.

Modeling

Ryan (1999) defined modeling as exposing clients to individuals who have attained success in career exploration, decision making, or the implementation of goals. Although the conclusions of Brown and his colleagues about modeling (Brown & Ryan Krane, 2000; Brown et al., 2003) were based on substantially fewer studies than were some of the other critical ingredients, modeling interventions still appeared to significantly influence outcome. The efficacy of these interventions seems logical when viewed from a social cognitive theoretical perspective (e.g., Bandura, 1986; Lent, Brown, & Hackett, 1994), as vicarious learning is hypothesized to be the second most potent method for influencing self-efficacy perceptions. Hence, if the intent of the interventions is to help people become more efficacious in career decision making or in implementing career goals, then it seems quite logical to purposefully structure interventions where clients have opportunities to observe models who have successfully used decision making or career implementation strategies.

Attention to Building Support

The final ingredient has received the least attention, but Brown and Ryan Krane (2000) found some substantial effect sizes when career counselors devoted attention to helping clients build support for their career choices and plans. This support may be particularly important when clients are coping with existing or perceived barriers. This critical ingredient is also consistent with recent research on the roles of supports versus barriers on the career development of women and members of racial/ethnic minority groups (e.g., Kenny & Bledsoe, 2005; Richie et al., 1997).

In addition to the five critical ingredients in vocational counseling, there is research related to the efficacy of other process factors. In investigating important events in career counseling, Anderson and Niles (2000) found that both clients and counselors identified events related to client self-exploration and emotional support as being most helpful. In a qualitative study that analyzed the career counseling cases of 12 well-respected vocational psychologists, Whiston, Lindeman, Rahardja, and Reed (2005) found that experts were likely to use exploration interventions in the vocational counseling process. In a study of process factors in career counseling, Kirschner, Hoffman, and Hill (1994) found insight and challenge to be the most helpful counselor intentions. Other counselor intentions that also were found to be helpful included providing information, focusing on feelings, focusing on change, and focusing on the relationship. Nagel, Hoffman, and Hill (1995) found support for an active approach, where information giving, direct guidance, paraphrasing, and closed questions were involved in career counseling.

Niles, Anderson, and Cover (2000) reported that, while clients entered career counseling to obtain assistance with career-related concerns, the process of career counseling often entailed both personal and other factors that are not necessarily directly associated with the initial presenting career issue. Clients, counselors and expert witnesses all agreed that career guidance interviews were more effective if the counselor helped the client to feel comfortable in discussing personal information (Bimrose, Barnes, Hughes, & Orton, 2004).

In their qualitative study, Whiston et al. (2005) found that 12 vocational counseling experts often incorporated aspects of Hill and O'Brien's (1999) three-stage model for helping (exploration, insight, action) in their case studies. These experts frequently emphasized the importance of establishing therapeutic relationships and providing clients with support and encouragement during the exploration stage. After establishing a therapeutic relationship, many of these experts reported they also used challenging interventions as well as those designed to identify and clarify clients' presenting concerns, which are interventions typically used in Hill and O'Brien's insight stage. In discussing their approaches to career counseling, many experts reported using cognitive behavioral techniques, such as identifying self-imposed obstacles and irrational thoughts, and helping clients address cognitions that may constrict their exploration of viable options.

Career Assessments and Technology-Based Interventions

Despite having been a popular practice throughout the history of vocational psychology, surprisingly little research is related to the effectiveness of interpreting the results of career assessments to clients (Whiston & Oliver, 2005). In analyzing research published between 1983 and 1995, Whiston et al. (1998) found no studies related to individual test interpretation that employed a control group. Oliver and Spokane (1988) found an unweighted effect size of .62 for individual test interpretation based on only two studies. After reviewing 65 studies on test interpretation outcome, Tinsley and Chu (1999) failed to find a credible body of evidence to document the helpfulness of interpretation of interest inventories by trained clinicians. Yet Tinsley and Chu's conclusions related to interest inventories must be considered in light of Brown et al.'s (2003) findings that individualized feedback and interpretation are critical components of vocational counseling, especially when the clients present with problematic or otherwise difficult to interpret test profiles (e.g., inconsistent interest profiles or flat ability profiles).

Although findings related to traditional test interpretation are not definitive, the world of career assessment is changing, and evolving technologies are having a substantial impact on how career assessments are delivered and interpreted (Chartrand & Walsh, 2001). Osborn, Peterson, Sampson, and Reardon (2003) found that before using a computer-assisted career guidance system, clients anticipated that the system would increase their career options, enhance self-knowledge, and expand occupational knowledge. In a 6-year follow-up of individuals who used a computer-assisted career decision-making system, Gati, Gadassi, and Shemesh (2005) found significant differences in job satisfaction between those who were employed in one of the occupations that was recommended by the computerized program (*Making Better Decisions*) versus individuals who were employed in an occupation that was not recommended by the program. For those employed in an occupation that was congruent with the program, 100% were at least moderately satisfied with this choice (84% were highly satisfied with the occupation, and 16% were moderately satisfied). In comparison, of those who were employed in occupations not recommended by the program, 82% expressed at least moderate satisfaction with their choice (38% were highly satisfied and 44% were moderately satisfied), while 18% reported being dissatisfied with their occupation.

Although Internet-based vocational assessments resemble paper-and-pencil and traditional computer-assisted systems, a number of researchers (e.g., Gati & Saka, 2001; Oliver & Zack, 1999) have noted that professionals do not normally monitor a client taking an Internet-based assessment, whereas there is typically at least some oversight of the other types of assessment. In examining Israeli users' evaluation of an Internet-based career planning site, Gati, Kleiman, Saka, and Zakai (2003) found that 84% of the users were willing to recommend that site to their friends. Conversely, the use of this site was rarely associated with increases in the levels of vocational decidedness of the users.

There are substantial issues with consumers being unable to differentiate between psychometrically sound Internet assessments and those that are visually attractive but not scientifically based (see Gore & Leuwerke, Chapter 3, this volume). Furthermore, in considering Internet assessments, it is important to note Whiston et al.'s (2003) findings that counselor-free interventions were less effective than other modalities. Thus, when clinicians simply refer clients to the Internet for vocational decision making or planning, they are not providing clients with empirically supported assistance.

Working Alliance

The importance of the counseling relationship or working alliance in psychotherapy has been well documented, with research indicating that the quality of the relationship has a significant influence on counseling outcome (Gelso & Samstag, Chapter 16, this volume; Gelso & Hayes, 1998). In the psychotherapy literature, the working alliance is frequently conceptualized as (a) agreement between the counselor and client on the goals of therapy, (b) client and counselor agreement on the tasks to achieve those goals, and (c) the quality of the personal bond between the client and counselor.

Although Meara and Patton (1994) contended that a working alliance is essential to effective career counseling, the research on this issue has produced somewhat mixed findings. Two studies (Lewis, 2001; Vargo-Moncier & Jessell, 1995) that compared the counseling relationship in career and personal counseling found that the quality of the relationship was as important in career counseling as it was in personal counseling. Kirschner et al. (1994) found that the counselor intention of focusing on relationships was one of the most helpful interventions in career counseling process. However, research exploring the relationship of the working alliance and career counseling outcome has found that, despite significant increases in the strength of the alliance over the course of counseling, working alliance is either weakly (Multon et al., 2001) or not at all (Heppner et al., 1998) related to outcome. Multon et al. (2001) found that the working alliance accounted for a maximum of 12% of variance in career counseling outcome compared with the more than 26% outcome variance typically explained by the working alliance in psychotherapy (Horvath & Symonds, 1991).

Many factors probably contribute to findings that the relationship between the working alliance in career counseling and outcome is small, at best. A possible explanation is that practitioners may place less importance on the development of a working alliance with clients who present with career versus personal-social issues (Heppner et al., 1996). Another may be that the relationship is indeed less important in career counseling than other aspects of the process (e.g., helping clients understand their work personalities, establish goals, and seek out and use relevant sources of occupational information).

Dose Effect

In psychotherapy research, there have been several studies of the effect of the number of sessions on outcome (Lambert & Cattani-Thompson, 1996; Lambert & Ogles, 2004). Analogous to medical or pharmaceutical research, where the interest is on how much of the prescribed treatment is necessary, this area of psychotherapy research is often labeled the "dose effect." Research has also been conducted on the dose effect of career counseling. Oliver and Spokane (1988) stated that the only significant predictor of effect size was treatment intensity (number of hours and number of sessions entered as a block). Whiston et al. (1998), however, were unable to replicate the significance of treatment intensity. Healy (2001) did not find a difference in level of satisfaction with career counseling between clients who chose to complete the entire counseling process compared with those who terminated prematurely. Brown and Ryan Krane (2000) found a nonlinear, yet interesting, correlation between career outcomes and the number of counseling sessions. In plotting the number of sessions by outcome, they found an increase in effect size between one session to four or five sessions; however, the effect sizes dramatically decreased after five sessions.

Negative Effects

A somewhat limited body of research on process variables is associated with poor outcomes in vocational counseling. Participants in a study conducted by Healy (2001) indicated that the following factors hindered the effectiveness of their vocational counseling: (a) tests that failed to produce new leads, (b) processes that did not yield sufficient career direction, (c) counselors who were perceived as being inadequate (e.g., inattentive, mechanical test interpretation), and (d) disappointment in the availability of career information. Similarly, Anderson and Niles (2000) found that both clients and counselors cited ineffective counselor-structure activities (interventions that were either poorly selected or implemented in a haphazard manner) as being the least helpful interventions.

Conclusions about Process Factors

Research on the process of vocational counseling has identified five critical ingredients for assisting clients with vocational choices. Two of the five critical ingredients—building support and modeling effective career choice strategies—are not automatically integrated into many of the common approaches to vocational counseling; thus, we hope practitioners will be particularly attentive to incorporating these ingredients into their counseling. In addition, written exercises, including writing about goals, seem to be particularly efficacious. Individualized interpretation of written exercises is another critical component in the vocational counseling process as is attending individually to difficult-to-interpret assessment information. Counselors should also focus on using sound occupational information and finding innovative strategies for motivating clients to access and utilize this information.

Findings also indicate that counselors need to be actively involved in the career counseling process and should emphasize activities that facilitate exploration and the development of client insight. There are also some indications that optimum results in vocational counseling can occur in around four to five sessions. The skillfulness of the clinician may also play a role in successful vocational counseling as clients cite poorly implemented interventions as being least helpful to them. Despite the increasing exploration of process factors, additional research is needed to explicate process factors that positively influence vocational counseling outcome.

WHAT WORKS FOR WHOM UNDER WHAT CIRCUMSTANCE?

Brown and McPartland (2005) argued persuasively for moving research beyond the "one size fits all" approach to vocational counseling and instead exploring differential treatment approaches for clients from various backgrounds and with differing vocational needs. There have been a few exemplary studies in the quest to determine what works best for which clients under what circumstances. Chronister and McWhirter (2006) evaluated two group approaches designed to assist battered women with vocational issues. In this study, participants were assigned to a vocational counseling group that included Brown and Ryan Krane's (2000) critical ingredients, a group that offered the same vocational strategies plus interventions for enhancing participants' understanding of the effects of domestic violence, or a wait-list control group. At posttest, both the standard ($d = .98$) and the standard plus enhanced ($d = .52$) groups scored significantly higher than the control group on measures of career search self-efficacy. Interestingly, both the standard career ($d = .24$) and enhanced ($d = .55$) groups scored significantly higher than the control group on a measure of critical consciousness of domestic violence, which measured awareness of domestic violence and level of empowerment to exert control over one's life. At 5-week follow-up, the enhanced group had a significantly higher effect size on this measure of critical consciousness than the standard career group ($d = .57$).

Kim and colleagues (Kim & Atkinson, 2002; Kim, Li, & Liang, 2002; Li & Kim, 2004) have initiated an interesting line of research that responds to the calls for investigating issues of culture and whether differing approaches are more effective with clients from diverse backgrounds. They have studied Asian American college students, with a focus on the interaction of process factors and clients' adherence to Asian cultural values. Kim and Atkinson (2002) examined the relationships among Asian American adherence to cultural values, counselor ethnicity, counselor expression of cultural values, and client evaluation of the career counseling process. Although they hypothesized that Asian American clients would evaluate vocational counseling more positively with an Asian American counselor, the findings suggested just the opposite—clients tended to evaluate European counselors more positively. However, counselors' endorsement of, and attention to, Asian values seemed to be more important than race or ethnicity in that client ratings of empathy and credibility were positively related to counselor endorsement of Asian values, regardless of whether the counselor was White or Asian American.

Kim et al. (2002) extended this research on cross-cultural career counseling by having a European American counselor focus either on immediate problem resolution or the attainment of insight through the exploration of emotions and cognitions with Asian American clients. Once again, the results were somewhat contradictory as the Asian clients exposed to the immediate resolution condition reported a stronger working alliance than those in the expression of emotion condition; yet, those in the expression of emotion condition perceived greater counselor cross-cultural competence than those in the immediate resolution condition. Kim et al. found some differences in how effective Asian American clients perceived the career counseling session depending on clients' levels of Asian cultural values. In Li and Kim (2004), the European American career counselors employed either a directive or nondirective style. Asian American clients rated the directive style more positively on four of the five outcome measures regardless of their level of Asian cultural values. Kim's research is noteworthy in its consistent use of actual clients and counselors rather than analog conditions; this series of studies serves as a model of programmatic research aimed at understanding the relation of cultural variables to career counseling outcomes.

FUTURE RESEARCH

As noted throughout this chapter, there are numerous areas where additional research is needed to inform effective vocational counseling. Whiston et al. (1998) documented a declining interest in vocational intervention research, and we hope that trend has abated. This possible dwindling of interest among counseling psychologists in vocational interventions seems counterintuitive given the rapidly changing and evolving world of work and the pressures associated with those changes (see DeBell, 2006). Many individuals are facing increased uncertainty about work because of the economy's volatility, the globalization of the labor force, rapid advances in technology, and the ambiguity related to preparing for an ever-changing occupational landscape. Hence, additional research is needed to inform counseling psychologists on ways to assist a growing population of individuals with work-related issues.

Consistent with Brown and McPartland (2005), little can be gained from additional studies that employ vague, one-size-fits-all treatments; such research perpetuates the uniformity myth that career interventions are fairly standard across clients, regardless of their background characteristics, goals, and underlying reasons for experiencing vocational difficulties. Career counseling is known to be effective, but according to Brown and Ryan Krane (2000), it is still questionable how these interventions work and with which client populations they are more versus less effective. Endemic in the career counseling process and outcome literature are problems related to treatment integrity and the lack of multiple clinical trials of specific types of vocational counseling interventions. Even for career courses for college students, Folsom and Reardon (2003) found wide variation in terms of design, scope, and function. Therefore, to know if a type of career counseling is effective, researchers need to replicate studies where that defined type of counseling is verified and evaluated.

Moreover, many of the career interventions that have been studied lack a clear theoretical base. Many vocational interventions used in practice also lack a sound empirical base. Swanson and Gore (2000) argued that historically there has been an interdependence between theory and practice in vocational psychology, yet this alliance is rarely evident in intervention-based studies. We found some studies that attempted to incorporate social cognitive career theory (Lent et al., 1994), but these were often one-shot studies that did not include a theoretically based manual that could facilitate appropriate replication. Whiston (2003) called for a theoretical renaissance, a period where there would be significant theoretical advancement and synergy among theoreticians, researchers, and practitioners.

Given that the primary goal of process/outcomes research is to determine what works for whom under what conditions (Savickas, 1989), it is important to consider client characteristics. Even related to demographic variables such as gender, race or ethnicity, sexual orientation, or socioeconomic status, many researchers have previously failed to adequately describe the sample, which hinders application and replication of the study. Brown and Ryan Krane (2000) contended that much has been written about the unique career development needs of racial and ethnic minorities; yet, there has been very little exploration of the effects of varying career interventions with these different groups. Another pertinent issue related to determining what types of vocational interventions are effective with which types of clients concerns assessing clients' needs, goals, and problems. In the first edition of this *Handbook*, Rounds and Tinsley (1984) asserted that an adequate understanding of the process and outcome of vocational interventions could only be accomplished with the development of a diagnostic system of vocational issues and problems (see Brown & Rector, Chapter 23, this volume). Without a systematic diagnostic classification system, it is difficult to determine what interventions work with which specific types of client. Although much can be gained by developing and testing the effectiveness of interventions designed for specific groups, Brown and McPartland (2005) recommended performing comparative outcome studies where a specified set of interventions would be offered uniformly to clients from different groups. With this approach, researchers could examine if the same treatment results in differing outcomes for differing groups. Hence by combining research that closely examines the same and differing approaches to vocational counseling with various client groups, we can extend our body of knowledge and facilitate more empirically based decisions about tailoring career interventions to match clients' needs and background.

In psychotherapy research, there is a history of using dismantling and constructive design strategies in which interventions or components are added, subtracted, or varied and outcome is then assessed (Hoglend, 1999). These strategies generally have not been used in vocational process and outcome research, although they may be particularly useful in future examinations of the critical ingredients of vocational counseling and the most effective length or dose effect with certain client groups. It would also be useful to do cost/benefit analyses to assess whether the addition of individual interpretation, specific formal assessments, and commercial computer-assisted career guidance programs are worth the monetary investment.

Research is also needed to focus on sound assessments of the short- and long-term benefits of career interventions and the quality of the outcome measures. Consideration of the quality of vocational outcome assessments is not a recent phenomenon (see Fretz, 1981; Spokane & Oliver, 1983), but attention to outcome measures has become particularly crucial in this age of accountability. As Whiston (2001) contended, there needs to be congruence between the outcome measures and the intent or goals of the vocational counseling. Hence, for vocational counseling designed to assist clients in making career decisions, many of the commonly used measures (e.g., Career Decision Scale, Career Decision-Making Self-Efficacy Scale) are logical choices. However, if counseling is designed to lessen work-to-family conflict, measures of decidedness are most likely inappropriate. In many of the previous studies, immediate outcomes were assessed and there is a need for longitudinal studies in which long-term effects may be demonstrated.

Oliver and Spokane (1988) called for increased examination of the cost-effectiveness of vocational counseling; yet, little research has been reported regarding cost-benefit analyses. It might be helpful for counseling psychologists to demonstrate that interventions designed to facilitate career decision making increase levels of certainty, but also reduce the number of times college students change their majors and the tuition dollars spent in obtaining a degree. Financial factors are not the only outcomes to be considered in cost-benefit analyses and, although not prevalent in vocational counseling research, there are indications that occupational stress and work satisfaction are related to mental and physical health outcomes (Barling, Kelloway, & Frone, 2005). Hence, we encourage researchers to include measures of psychological distress and life satisfaction in outcome studies. Although our experiences tend to support the view that vocational counseling can affect the psychological, physical, and financial well-being of individuals, additional systematic research is needed to verify our perspective.

CONCLUSION

Swanson (1995) claimed that more is known about the outcome of vocational counseling than about its process and about what factors contribute to positive outcomes. Research has demonstrated that counselor-free career interventions tend to be ineffective and that vocational counseling becomes increasingly effective with addition of critical ingredients. Although the critical ingredients identified by Brown and Ryan Krane (2000) need additional empirical verification, these findings provide counseling psychologists with a foundation in which to design effective vocational counseling. Our endorsement of the five critical ingredients, however, should not be construed as supporting a "cookbook" approach to vocational counseling, where everyone receives these ingredients in a fixed and measured manner. Also, there is an ongoing need to study how different forms of career counseling interact with such individual differences as age, gender, race or ethnicity, socioeconomic status, and sexual orientation. Given the importance of work in most individuals' lives and its direct impact on factors related to both physical and mental health, counseling psychologists must be skilled clinicians in issues related to work and stay abreast of literature related to vocational counseling.

REFERENCES

Akerboom, S., & Maes, S. (2006). Beyond demand and control: The contributions of organizational risk factors in assessing the psychological well-being of health care employees. *Work and Stress, 20*, 21–36.

Anderson, W. P., Jr., & Niles, S. G. (2000). Important events in career counseling: Client and counselor perceptions. *Career Development Quarterly, 48*, 251–264.

Bandura, A. (1986). *Social foundations of thought and actions: A social cognitive theory*. Englewood Cliffs, NJ: Prentice-Hall.

Barling, J., Kelloway, E. K., & Frone, M. R. (2005). *Handbook of work stress*. Thousand Oaks, CA: Sage.

Beutler, L. E., Malik, M., Alimohamed, S., Harwood, T. M., Noble, S., & Wong, E. (2004). Therapist variables. In M. J. Lambert (Ed.), *Bergin and Garfield's handbook of psychotherapy and behavior* (5th ed., pp. 227–306). Hoboken, NJ: Wiley.

Bimrose, J., Barnes, S. A., Hughes, D., & Orton, M. (2004). *What is effective guidance? Evidence from longitudinal case studies in England*. Retrieved June 6, 2006, from Warwick Institute for Employment Research Web site: www2.warwick.ac.uk/fac/soc/ier/publications/bydate/2004.

Blustein, D. L., & Spengler, P. M. (1995). Personal adjustment: Career counseling and psychotherapy. In W. B. Walsh & S. H. Osipow (Eds.), *Handbook of vocational psychology* (2nd ed., pp. 295–329). Hillsdale, NJ: Erlbaum.

Brown, S. D., & McPartland, E. B. (2005). Career interventions: Current status and future directions. In W. B. Walsh & M. L. Savickas (Eds.), *Handbook of vocational psychology: Theory, research, and practice* (3rd ed., pp. 195–226). Mahwah, NJ: Erlbaum.

Brown, S. D., & Ryan Krane, N. E. (2000). Four (or five) sessions and a cloud of dust: Old assumptions and new observations about career counseling. In S. D. Brown & R. W. Lent (Eds.), *Handbook of counseling psychology* (3rd ed., pp. 740–766). New York: Wiley.

Brown, S. D., Ryan Krane, N. E., Brecheisen, J., Castelino, P., Budisin, I., Miller, M., & Edens, L. (2003). Critical ingredients of career choice interventions: More analyses and new hypotheses. *Journal of Vocational Behavior, 62*, 411–428.

Carr, J. Z., Schmidt, A. M., Ford, J. K., & DeShon, R. P. (2003). Climate perceptions matter: A meta-analytic path analysis relating molar climate cognitive and affective states, and individual level work outcomes. *Journal of Applied Psychology, 88*, 605–619.

Carter, R. T., Scales, J. E., Juby, H. L., Collins, N. M., & Wan, C. M. (2003). Seeking career services on campus: Racial differences in referral, process, and outcome. *Journal of Career Assessment, 11*, 393–404.

Chartrand, J. M., & Walsh, W. B. (2001). Career assessment: Changes and trends. In F. T. L. Leong & A. Barak (Eds.), *Contemporary models of vocational psychology* (pp. 231–255). Mahwah, NJ: Erlbaum.

Chronister, K. M., & McWhirter, E. H. (2006). An experimental examination of two career interventions for battered women. *Journal of Counseling Psychology, 53*, 151–164.

Cohen, J. (1988). *Statistical power analysis for the behavioral sciences* (2nd ed.). New York: McGraw-Hill.

DeBell, C. (2002). Practice for a paradigm shift: A complete model for an integrative course. *Counseling Psychologist, 30*, 858–877.

DeBell, C. (2006). What all applied psychologists should know about work. *Professional Psychology: Research and Practice, 37*, 342–350.

Folsom, B., & Reardon, R. (2003). College career courses: Design and accountability. *Journal of Career Assessment, 11*, 421–450.

Fouad, N. A., Guillen, A., Harris-Hodge, E., Henry, C., Novakovic, A., Terry, S., et al. (2006). Need, awareness, and use of career services for college students. *Journal of Career Assessment, 14*, 407–420.

Fretz, B. R. (1981). Evaluating the effectiveness of career interventions [Monograph]. *Journal of Counseling Psychology, 28*, 77–90.

Frone, M. R. (2000). Work-family conflict and employee psychiatric disorders: The national comorbidity survey. *Journal of Applied Psychology, 85*, 888–895.

Galassi, J. P., Crace, R. K., Martin, G. A., James, R. M., & Wallace, R. L. (1992). Client preferences and anticipations in career counseling: A preliminary investigation. *Journal of Counseling Psychology, 39*, 46–55.

Gati, I., Gadassi, R., & Shemesh, N. (2005). The predictive validity of computer-assisted career decision-making system: A 6-year follow-up. *Journal of Vocational Behavior, 68*, 205–219.

Gati, I., Kleiman, T., Saka, N., & Zakai, A. (2003). Perceived benefits of using an internet-based interactive career planning system. *Journal of Vocational Behavior, 62*, 272–286.

Gati, I., & Ram, G. (2000). Counselors' judgments of the quality of the prescreening stage of the career decision-making process. *Journal of Counseling Psychology, 47*, 414–428.

Gati, I., & Saka, N. (2001). Internet-based versus paper-and-pencil assessment: Measuring career decision-making difficulties. *Journal of Career Assessment, 9*, 301–321.

Gelso, C. J., & Hayes, J. A. (1998). *The psychotherapy relationship: Theory, research, and practice*. New York: Wiley.

Gold, J. M., & Scanlon, C. R. (1993). Psychological distress and counseling duration of career and noncareer clients. *Career Development Quarterly, 42*, 186–191.

Goodyear, R. K. (1990). Research on the effects of test interpretation: A review. *Counseling Psychologist, 18*, 240–257.

Healy, C. C. (2001). A follow-up of adult career counseling clients of a university extension center. *Career Development Quarterly, 49*, 363–373.

Hedges, L. V., & Olkin, I. (1985). *Statistical methods for meta-analysis*. New York: Academic Press.

Heppner, M. J., & Heppner, P. P. (2003). Identifying process variables in career counseling: A research agenda. *Journal of Vocational Behavior, 62*, 429–452.

Heppner, M. J., Multon, K. D., Gysbers, N. C., Ellis, C. A., & Zook, C. E. (1998). The relationship of trainee self-efficacy to the process and outcome of career counseling. *Journal of Counseling Psychology, 45*, 393–402.

Heppner, M. J., O'Brien, K. M., Hinkelman, J. M., & Flores, L. Y. (1996). Training counseling psychologists in career development: Are we our own worst enemies? *Counseling Psychologist, 24*, 105–125.

Hill, C. A., & Lambert, M. J. (2004). Methodological issues in studying psychotherapy process and outcome. In M. J. Lambert (Ed.), *Bergin and Garfield's handbook of psychotherapy and behavior change* (5th ed., pp. 84–135). Hoboken, NJ: Wiley.

Hill, C. A., & O'Brien, K. M. (1999). *Helping skills: Facilitating exploration, insight, and action*. Washington, DC: American Psychological Association.

Hoglend, P. (1999). Psychotherapy research: New findings and implications for training and practice. *Journal of Psychotherapy Practice and Research, 8*, 257–263.

Horvath, A. O., & Symonds, B. D. (1991). Relation between working alliance and outcome in psychotherapy: A meta-analysis. *Journal of Counseling Psychology, 38*, 139–149.

Juntunen, C. L. (2006). The psychology of working: The clinical context. *Professional Psychology: Research and Practice, 37*, 342–350.

Kenny, M. E., & Bledsoe, M. (2005). Contributions of the relational context of career adaptability among urban adolescents. *Journal of Vocational Behavior, 66*, 257–272.

Kim, B. S. K., & Atkinson, D. R. (2002). Effects of Asian American client adherence to Asian cultural values, counselor expression of cultural values, and counselor ethnicity on career counseling process. *Journal of Counseling Psychology, 49*, 3–13.

Kim, B. S. K., Li, L., & Liang, C. T. H. (2002). Effects of Asian American client adherence to Asian cultural values, session goal, and counselor emphasis of client expression on career counseling process. *Journal of Counseling Psychology, 49*, 342–354.

Kirschner, T., Hoffman, M. A., & Hill, C. E. (1994). Case study of the process and outcome of career counseling. *Journal of Counseling Psychology, 41*, 216–226.

Lambert, M. J., & Cattani-Thompson, K. (1996). Current findings regarding the effectiveness of counseling: Implications for practice. *Journal of Counseling and Development, 74*, 601–608.

Lambert, M. J., & Ogles, B. M. (2004). The efficacy and effectiveness of psychotherapy. In M. J. Lambert (Ed.), *Bergin and Garfield's handbook of psychotherapy and behavior* (5th ed., pp. 139–193). Hoboken, NJ: Wiley.

Lent, R. W., Brown, S. D., & Hackett, G. (1994). Toward a unifying social cognitive theory of career and academic interests, choice, and performance [Monograph]. *Journal of Vocational Behavior, 45*, 79–122.

Leso, J. F., & Neimeyer, G. J. (1991). Role of gender and construct type vocational complexity and choice of academic major. *Journal of Counseling Psychology, 38*, 182–188.

Lewis, J. (2001). Career and personal counseling: Comparing process and outcome. *Journal of Employment Counseling, 38*, 82–90.

Li, L. C., & Kim, B. S. K. (2004). Effects of counseling style and client adherence to Asian cultural values on counseling process with Asian American college students. *Journal of Counseling Psychology, 51*, 156–167.

Lucas, M. S. (1992). Problems expressed by career and non-career help seekers: A comparison. *Journal of Counseling and Development, 70*, 417–420.

Mau, W., & Fernandes, A. (2001). Characteristics and satisfaction of students who used career counseling services. *Journal of College Student Development, 42*, 581–588.

Meara, N. M., & Patton, M. J. (1994). Contribution of the working alliance in the practice of counseling. *Career Development Quarterly, 43*, 161–177.

Multon, K. D., Heppner, M. J., Gysbers, N. C., Zook, C., & Ellis-Kalton, C. A. (2001). Client psychological distress: An important factor in career counseling. *Career Development Quarterly, 49*, 324–335.

Nagel, D. P., Hoffman, M. A., & Hill. C. E. (1995). A comparison of verbal response modes used my master's-level career counselors and other helpers. *Journal of Counseling and Development, 74*, 101–104.

Neimeyer, G. J., & Leso, J. F. (1992). Effects of occupational information on personal versus provided constructs: A second look. *Journal of Counseling Psychology, 39*, 331–334.

Niles, S. G., Anderson, W. P., & Cover, S. (2000). Comparing intake concerns and goals with career counseling concerns. *Career Development Quarterly, 49*, 135–145.

Oliver, L. W., & Spokane, A. R. (1988). Career-intervention outcome: What contributes to client gain? *Journal of Counseling Psychology, 35*, 447–462.

Oliver, L. W., & Zack, J. S. (1999). Career assessment on the internet: An exploratory study. *Journal of Career Assessment, 8*, 323–356.

Osborn, D. S., Peterson, G. W., Sampson, J. P., Jr., & Reardon, R. C. (2003). Client anticipations about computer-assisted career guidance system outcomes. *Career Development Quarterly, 51*, 356–367.

Parker, C. P., Baltes, B. B., Young, S. A., Huff, J. W., Altmann, R. A., LaCost, H. A., et al. (2003). Relationships between psychological climate perceptions and work outcomes: A meta-analytic review. *Journal of Organizational Behavior, 24*, 389–416.

Parsons, F. (1909). *Choosing a vocation*. Boston: Houghton Mifflin.

Richie, B. S., Fassinger, R. E., Linn, S. G., Johnson, J., Prosser, J., & Robinson, S. (1997). Persistence, connection, and passion: A qualitative study of the career development of highly achieving African American-Black and white women. *Journal of Counseling Psychology, 44*, 133–148.

Rochlen, A. B., Blazina, C., & Raghunathan, R. (2002). Gender role conflict, attitudes toward career counseling, career decision-making, and perceptions of career counseling advertising brochures. *Psychology of Men and Masculinity, 3*, 127–137.

Rochlen, A. B., Milburn, L., & Hill, C. E. (2004). Examining the process and outcome of career counseling for different types of career counseling clients. *Journal of Career Development, 30*, 263–275.

Rochlen, A. B., Mohr, J. J., & Hargrove, B. K. (1999). Development of the Attitudes toward Career Counseling Scale. *Journal of Counseling Psychology, 46*, 196–206.

Rochlen, A. B., & O'Brien, K. M. (2002). The relation of male gender role conflict and attitudes toward career counseling to interest in and preferences for different career counseling styles. *Psychology of Men and Masculinity, 3*, 9–21.

Rosenthal, R. & Rubin, D. B. (1982). A simple general purpose display of magnitude of experimental effect. *Journal of Educational Psychology, 74*, 166–169.

Rounds, J. B., & Tinsley, T. J. (1984). Diagnosis and treatment of vocational problems. In S. D. Brown & R. W. Lent (Eds.), *Handbook of counseling psychology* (pp. 137–177). New York: Wiley.

Ryan, N. E. (1999). *Career counseling and career choice goal attainment: A meta-analytically derived model for career counseling practice.* Unpublished doctoral dissertation, Loyola University, Chicago.

Savickas, M. L. (1989). Annual review: Practice and research in career counseling and development, 1988. *Career Development Quarterly, 38,* 100–134.

Shivy, V. A., & Koehly, L. M. (2002). Client perceptions of and preferences for university-based career services. *Journal of Vocational Behavior, 60,* 40–60.

Smith, M. L., Glass, G. V., & Miller, T. I. (1980). *The benefits of psychotherapy.* Baltimore: Johns Hopkins University Press.

Spokane, A. R., & Oliver, L. W. (1983). Outcomes of vocational intervention. In S. H. Osipow & W. B. Walsh (Eds.), *Handbook of vocational psychology* (pp. 99–136). Hillsdale, NJ: Erlbaum.

Swanson, J. L. (1995). The process and outcome of career counseling. In W. B. Walsh & S. H. Osipow (Eds.), *The handbook of vocational psychology* (pp. 217–259). Mahwah, NJ: Erlbaum.

Swanson, J. L., & Gore, P. A. (2000). Advances in vocational psychology theory and research. In S. D. Brown & R. W. Lent (Eds.), *Handbook of counseling psychology* (3rd ed., pp. 740–766). New York: Wiley.

Tinsley, H. E. A., & Chu, S. (1999). Research on test and interest inventory interpretation outcomes. In M. L. Savickas & A. R. Spokane (Eds.), *Vocational interests: Meaning, measurement, and counseling use* (pp. 257–276). Palo Alto, CA: Davies-Black.

Vargo-Moncier, C. L., & Jessell, J. C. (1995). Quality of counselors' intake evaluations as a function of client presenting concern. *Journal of Counseling Psychology, 42,* 100–104.

Vernick, S. H., Reardon, R. C., & Sampson, J. P., Jr., (2004). Process evaluation of a career course: A replication and extension. *Journal of Career Development, 30,* 201–213.

Wampold, B. E., Lichtenberg, J. W., & Wahler, C. A. (2002). Principles of empirically supported interventions in counseling psychology. *Counseling Psychologist, 30,* 197–217.

Whiston, S. C. (2001). Selecting career outcome assessments: An organizational scheme. *Journal of Career Assessment, 9,* 215–228.

Whiston, S. C., (2002). Application of the principles: Career counseling and interventions. *Counseling Psychologist, 30,* 218–228.

Whiston, S. C. (2003). Career counseling: 90 years old yet still healthy and vital. *Career Development Quarterly, 52,* 35–42.

Whiston, S. C., Brecheisen, B. K., & Stephens, J. (2003). Does treatment modality affect career counseling effectiveness. *Journal of Vocational Behavior, 62,* 390–410.

Whiston, S. C., Lindeman, D. L., Rahardja, D., & Reed, J. H. (2005). Career counseling process: A qualitative analysis of experts' cases. *Journal of Career Assessment, 13,* 169–187.

Whiston, S. C., & Oliver, L. W. (2005). Career counseling process and outcome. In W. B. Walsh & M. Savickas (Eds.), *Handbook of vocational psychology* (3rd ed., pp. 155–194). Hillsdale, NJ: Erlbaum.

Whiston, S. C., Sexton, T. L., & Lasoff, D. L. (1998). Career intervention outcome: A replication and extension. *Journal of Counseling Psychology, 45,* 150–165.

CHAPTER 27

Understanding and Promoting Work Satisfaction: An Integrative View

ROBERT W. LENT

The topic of affect in the workplace—how people feel at and about their work—has long fascinated industrial-organizational and vocational scholars. This broad topic includes such affect-oriented constructs as job satisfaction and work stress. Tracing this line of inquiry to the early 1930s, Brief and Weiss (2002) argued that the innovation and diversity of early research on work affect eventually gave way to studies of narrower methodological and conceptual focus. However, they cited the past 20 years as a time when organizational researchers "rediscovered affect" (p. 282), bringing fresh approaches to the study of job satisfaction and related emotional constructs. Over the years, there have been a number of important reviews of the job satisfaction literature in particular (e.g., Brief, 1998; Locke, 1976; Spector, 1997), the enormous size of which has become a formidable challenge for any contemporary reviewer.

It is not difficult to fathom the reasons for psychology's continuing fascination with job satisfaction. Most people spend a good deal of their lives engaged in work, and it is typically assumed that how they feel about their work is of considerable consequence to themselves, their organizations, and their significant others. Even though the findings have often been less dramatic and more complex than might have initially been envisioned, the notion that "happy workers are more productive" (and also more responsible in their attendance, helpful to their coworkers, and likely to remain in their jobs) has sparked a great deal of inquiry (e.g., see Brief, 1998; Fritzsche & Parrish, 2005). Job satisfaction is also assumed to have the potential to spill over into people's nonwork lives (e.g., Judge & Ilies, 2004; Rain, Lane, & Steiner, 1991). In addition, job satisfaction may be viewed as an integral part of work adjustment and overall mental health, and has been linked to indices of physical health and even longevity (Lofquist & Dawis, 1984; Spector, 1997).

Although both counseling-vocational and industrial-organizational psychologists have long studied job satisfaction, they have tended to focus on somewhat different aspects of this construct. Vocational psychology, historically concerned with person-focused outcomes, has tended to conceptualize and study job satisfaction as one aspect of individuals' adaptation to work. For instance, the theory of work adjustment (TWA) highlights factors that promote individuals' job satisfaction, as well as the linkage of satisfaction to work tenure (Lofquist & Dawis, 1984). By contrast, organizational research has tended to emphasize employer-focused aspects of job satisfaction that are of particular relevance to staffing and unit productivity, such as the relation of job satisfaction to work performance, role engagement, and employee turnover (Fritzsche & Parrish, 2005). Of course, these foci can be viewed as complementary more than as competing since workers and employers share mutual interests, for example, in job retention.

Perhaps a more consequential area of divergence is that the two psychological specialties differ in the intensity of inquiry they have devoted to job satisfaction, particularly in recent years. As judged by prior editions of this *Handbook* as well as the *Handbook of Vocational Psychology* (Walsh & Savickas, 2005), job satisfaction and other aspects of adult career development have received far less coverage than have the prework or work entry concerns of adolescence and early adulthood (e.g., vocational interests, major choice, career decision making). Vocational psychology research has generally been more focused on what fields people wind up in and how they get there and less focused on how they feel and fare after they arrive. Nevertheless, important inquiry on, and reviews of, job satisfaction have appeared in the vocational literature over the years (e.g., Dawis, 2005; Holland, 1997; Lofquist & Dawis, 1984; Walsh & Eggerth, 2005). A goal of this chapter is to encourage a revival of interest in this topic among vocational psychologists. Because most people spend much more of their lives actually working than they do in preparing to work, a rebalanced agenda that devotes at least as much attention to the study of work adjustment (including job satisfaction) as to earlier developmental tasks will, no doubt, lend added vigor and relevance to vocational psychology.

This chapter first considers the typical ways that job, or work, satisfaction has been defined and measured. The second section of the chapter examines the major sources, or origins, of job satisfaction. Vocational and organizational researchers have converged on an overlapping set of person, environment, and person-environment fit predictors or determinants of job satisfaction. My coverage of sources and predictors of job satisfaction incorporates inquiry from both specialties. It also draws on the relevant literature on subjective well-being (SWB) emanating from personality and other basic areas of psychological research. The third section focuses on emerging integrative theoretical perspectives that consider how multiple sources of job satisfaction interrelate. Finally, I suggest implications of the review for future research and practice.

Given the enormity of the literature on job satisfaction, the review that follows is necessarily selective. A few decision rules were adopted for this purpose. In particular, since major theoretical positions and research reviews have appeared elsewhere (e.g., Brief, 1998; Fritzsche & Parrish, 2005), and mostly in the organizational literature, this chapter samples topics that are deemed relatively new (or of continuing import) and of particular relevance to counseling psychology, including adult career development practitioners. In addition, I relied on my earlier review of the general well-being literature (Lent, 2004) to construct an organizing scheme for selecting and presenting inquiry on the sources of job satisfaction and for considering the relation of job satisfaction to other aspects of adjustment.

JOB SATISFACTION: DEFINITIONS AND MEASURES

Although specific definitions abound, job satisfaction is commonly conceived as an attitudinal construct containing both affective and cognitive components (Brief, 1998). Locke's (1976) classic definition referred to "a pleasurable or positive *emotional state* resulting from the *appraisal* of one's job or job experiences" (p. 1300; italics added to emphasize the affective and cognitive aspects). Somewhat more simply, job satisfaction can be defined as the extent to which people like their jobs (Spector, 1997). The degree to which popular measures of job satisfaction adequately sample both affective and cognitive elements is a matter of some controversy (Brief & Weiss, 2002). But it would seem difficult to eliminate either element in asking people to *report* (a cognitive distillation) on how they *feel* about their jobs; thus, job satisfaction may be seen as an admixture of cognition and affect.

The working definition of job satisfaction in this chapter, then, emphasizes people's cognitive constructions of their work enjoyment. Job satisfaction is typically assessed by self-report. Such a focus enables respondents to weigh whatever specific factors they deem relevant to their work enjoyment. In other words, satisfaction is an idiographic appraisal. Although it is possible to obtain satisfaction ratings through alternative means (e.g., judgments of a target person's job satisfaction made by his or her supervisor, spouse, or coworkers), individuals are typically assumed to provide the best source of information about their own job satisfaction. As one article title in the SWB literature asserts, "If you want to know how happy I am, you'll have to ask me" (Irwin, Kammann, & Dixon, 1979).

Job Satisfaction Vis-à-Vis Subjective Well-Being

Job satisfaction may be viewed as a central element of SWB. Although the latter is often defined as consisting of global life satisfaction, the presence of positive affect, and the absence of negative affect, the focus on life satisfaction may be broadened to include satisfaction within more specific life domains, such as work and family (Diener, Suh, Lucas, & Smith, 1999). In a sense, then, job satisfaction represents an important aspect of *workplace well-being* (i.e., SWB as experienced within the context of work). It has been argued that domain-specific forms of satisfaction provide more accessible targets for counseling interventions than do overall life satisfaction (Lent, 2004). It may also be argued that satisfaction ratings, whether domain-specific or global, are necessary but not sufficient indicators of positive adaptation—that how well people are functioning is not only a matter of how they are feeling (a phenomenological judgment) but also how they are doing (a behavioral one). I return to this more inclusive view of work adjustment later in the chapter.

Global versus Facet Job Satisfaction

A key distinction in the measurement of job satisfaction involves *global* versus *facet* satisfaction. Global measures tap general or overall feelings about one's job. Examples include the Index of Job Satisfaction (Brayfield & Rothe, 1951) and the Job in General Scale (Ironson, Smith, Brannick, Gibson, & Paul, 1989). The latter asks respondents to rate their job in terms of a set of affectively (e.g., "enjoyable") and evaluatively oriented (e.g., "good") adjectives. Facet measures assess satisfaction with specific aspects of one's job or working conditions, which tend to fall into four main categories: the work itself, rewards, context, and people (Locke, 1976). Examples of facet measures include the Job Descriptive Index (Smith, Kendall, & Hulin, 1969) and the Minnesota Satisfaction Questionnaire (D. J. Weiss, Dawis, England, & Lofquist, 1967).

Temporal Considerations

Another key matter is the temporal frame of the assessment. Job satisfaction can be measured in terms of how people feel about their jobs either over nonspecific (e.g., "most of the time"; Ironson et al., 1989) or defined time periods (e.g., the past week, today, this moment). Job satisfaction ratings have been found to be somewhat stable over time. Staw and Ross (1985) reported stability coefficients over 3- and 5-year intervals, respectively, of .32 and .29. However, stability coefficients tended to be higher when workers remained in the same positions than when they changed employers or occupations. Such findings suggest that job satisfaction is responsive both to dispositional and situational factors (i.e., it is not an immutable quality of the person alone).

Because job satisfaction can fluctuate over time and conditions (e.g., Judge & Ilies, 2004), the temporal frame of reference is an important consideration. Nonspecific or longer time frames pose challenges for remembering, weighting, and combining information involved in rating satisfaction (Kahneman, 1999). More proximal and online ratings avoid some of this heuristic load and may yield a more precise and dynamic picture of the factors that promote satisfaction on a short-term basis. Some studies have used experience-sampling methods to examine the interplay between job satisfaction, situational mood, and affective traits (Ilies & Judge, 2002; Judge & Ilies, 2004).

Summary

Job satisfaction may be defined as a person's perceived enjoyment or liking of his or her work, either in a global, overall sense or in terms of particular work facets (e.g., pay, coworkers). Such ratings involve a combination of cognitive and affective elements in that they require respondents to appraise, weigh, and report their work-related feelings. Although job satisfaction is typically assessed through self-report and in relation to a general past or indefinite time frame, researchers are increasingly interested in more immediate and time-bound satisfaction ratings (e.g., moods or online affect). Past-oriented and indefinite temporal renderings may be seen as synonymous with a *trait* conception of job satisfaction wherein how one feels about work is a relatively stable aspect of the person. More proximal and situation-specific assessment may be equated with a *state* view that assumes job satisfaction can fluctuate over time and in response to specific events or conditions. (Global and facet measures may be either of the trait or state variety, depending on their temporal referent; e.g., most of the time versus right now.) This is not to imply that trait and state (or global and facet) measures of job satisfaction are unrelated, but it is useful to distinguish between them for conceptual and practical purposes. For example, knowing that a client has generally been satisfied at work most of the time (global, trait) but is currently unhappy with a particular work aspect, such as interactions with a supervisor (facet, state), may have important implications for intervention.

Parenthetically, in the remainder of this chapter, I use the terms *job* and *work* satisfaction synonymously to refer to work domain enjoyment. However, work satisfaction may be considered the more inclusive term because it can include satisfaction with one's job globally, the specific facets or conditions of one's work, or the larger work environment in which one's job is embedded. Most of the research discussed herein involves job satisfaction over a general or nonspecific time frame, although examples of research on situation-specific job affect will also be cited.

MULTIPLE SOURCES OF JOB SATISFACTION

This section presents major categories of variables that have been linked to work satisfaction: personality dispositions and affective traits; overall life satisfaction; work conditions (e.g., social support, role stressors) and person-environment (P-E) fit variables (e.g., needs-supplies fit, interest congruence); and social cognitive variables (e.g., goals, self-efficacy, outcome expectations). Although they are presented as putative sources, or precursors, of job satisfaction, at least some of the variables in this section have also been conceptualized as having a reciprocal, or bidirectional, relation to job satisfaction.

Personality and Affective Traits

Several meta-analyses have examined the relations of affective (positive and negative affect) and personality traits (the Big Five factors—neuroticism, extraversion, openness to experience, agreeableness, and conscientiousness) to work and life satisfaction. Judge, Heller, and Mount (2002) reported "true score correlations" (which adjust for psychometric limitations in the predictor and criterion variables) of extraversion, neuroticism, and conscientiousness to job satisfaction, respectively, of .25, −.29, and .26. Together, these three traits explained 17% of the variance in job satisfaction. Connolly and Viswesvaran (2000) observed somewhat higher true score correlations of negative affect (−.33) and positive affect (.49) to job satisfaction, though a more modest positive affect-job satisfaction meta-analytic correlation (.34) has been reported by others (Thoresen, Kaplan, Barsky, Warren, & de Chermont, 2003). The two traits together have been found to explain 30% of the variance in job satisfaction (Ilies & Judge, 2003).

Ilies and Judge (2003) also reported that 29% of the variance in job satisfaction may be due to genetic factors and that positive-negative affect accounts for nearly half of this genetic influence, whereas the Big Five factors explain only about one-quarter of the variance. They concluded that "genetic influences on job satisfaction are mediated primarily by affective traits and not by the broad personality factors" (p. 755). Such findings are impressive, especially with respect to the potential contribution of the affective traits to job satisfaction, and have led to the conclusion that "job satisfaction is, in part, dispositionally based" (Judge et al., 2002, p. 530). This heritability estimate, however, does not preclude the operation of nongenetic sources of job satisfaction. Situational and cognitive variables have, in fact, been found to predict job satisfaction independently of traits (e.g., Watson & Slack, 1993; H. M. Weiss, Nicholas, & Daus, 1999). Moreover, the specific paths by which traits may affect job satisfaction need to be explored. Trait-satisfaction relationships likely operate through "multiple channels" (Brief & Weiss, 2002, p. 286) or pathways. Much work remains to examine variables and processes that mediate these relationships (e.g., Brief, 1998; Heller, Watson, & Ilies, 2004; H. M. Weiss & Cropanzano, 1996)—in addition to exploring nontrait contributors to job satisfaction.

Life Satisfaction

Job satisfaction has often been studied in relation to overall life satisfaction (e.g., Brief, 1998; Heller, Judge, & Watson, 2002; Heller et al., 2004). Interest in the relation between the two constructs follows naturally from the observation that work is an important part of life for most persons—and that the boundaries between work and other life domains are often permeable. For example, social ties (Rain et al., 1991) and moods at work (Judge & Ilies, 2004) may carry over into one's nonwork hours, just as family and other nonwork factors can affect work. Consistent with such expectations, job and life satisfaction tend to covary substantially; Tait, Padgett, and Baldwin (1989) reported a meta-analytic correlation of .44 between them.

Life satisfaction is typically indexed by measures that ask people how happy they are with their lives on the whole. Some writers consider life satisfaction to be a dispositional variable, much like personality and affective traits (McCrae & Costa, 1991). As with job satisfaction, findings suggest that life satisfaction, or general happiness, has a heritable component (Lykken & Tellegen, 1996) and other traitlike features. However, other findings indicate that life satisfaction is responsive to environmental conditions and life changes and that it becomes less stable over longer time intervals (Veenhoven, 1994). Because life satisfaction is often considered as distinct from (but related to) positive and negative affect (Diener et al., 1999), it will here be considered separately from personality and affective trait influences.

An enduring question has been whether job satisfaction leads to life satisfaction or vice versa—that is, whether being happy in one's work carries over to the rest of life or whether people who are generally happy are simply likely to find happiness at work (because they are predisposed to be happy anywhere). In the "top-down" or dispositional view, job satisfaction is a manifestation of more general affective or personality tendencies; the causal arrow is, therefore, drawn from life satisfaction (qua trait) and other traits (e.g., positive and negative affect) to job satisfaction. In the "bottom-up" or situational view, work satisfaction (along with other domain satisfactions and, depending on the specific model, other situational, cognitive, and social variables) is accorded the potential to affect life satisfaction.

Cross-sectional findings offer support for both directional paths (e.g., Heller et al., 2004), though some longitudinal research suggests that life-to-job satisfaction may be the more potent of the two paths (Judge & Watanabe, 1993). At present, the "spillover hypothesis" (i.e., job and life satisfaction spill over into and mutually influence one other) remains a popular theoretical notion (Rain et al., 1991). A corollary is that the strength and primary direction of the causal path may depend on moderator variables, such as the importance of one's job relative to other life roles. For instance, for an individual whose work is the key feature of his or her identity, work satisfaction may have a predominant influence on overall life satisfaction.

Work Conditions and Person-Environment Fit

The job satisfaction literature was dominated for many years by a focus on aspects of the work environment that may have affective implications for individuals (Spector, 1997). A wide variety of work characteristics, conditions, and outcomes (or reinforcers) have been linked to job satisfaction. The variables in this section may be divided into three somewhat overlapping categories: (1) general job characteristics, conditions, and outcomes; (2) person-environment fit; and (3) perceived organizational support and role stressors.

General Job Characteristics, Conditions, and Outcomes/Values

A prevalent theoretical view has been that job satisfaction depends on the degree to which people perceive that their work environment provides a general set of favorable conditions, characteristics, or value fulfillment opportunities. Examples include Hackman and Oldham's (1976) job characteristics model, which focuses on the effects of five core job dimensions (e.g., skill variety, autonomy), and expectancy-value models (Mitchell, 1974, 1982), which highlight individuals' expectations about the sorts of outcomes that are contingent on their work efforts and the value that they place on these outcomes.

Warr (1999) organized commonly studied work characteristics and values into a set of 10 job features (e.g., opportunity for personal control, supportive supervision, valued social position, availability of money) that have been associated with job-specific well-being indices. Several of Warr's categories involve social aspects of work environments. Among other things, work offers opportunities for companionship, emotional support, belongingness, and practical assistance (Turner, Barling, & Zacharatos, 2002)—and such social-relational benefits have often been linked to satisfaction outcomes in the larger well-being literature (Ryan & Deci, 2001). The perceived social climate of work has been found to relate substantially to job satisfaction ($r = .46$) in a recent meta-analysis (Carr, Schmidt, Ford, & DeShon, 2003).

Forms of Person-Environment Fit

A second broad perspective assumes that it is not the presence, absence, or anticipation of generally favorable job characteristics or conditions that leads to work satisfaction. Instead, it is the capacity of the work environment to provide specific resources that individuals desire (or that complement their work personality, e.g., by providing a good outlet for one's interests). For instance,. the theory of work adjustment holds that individuals will be satisfied with their work to the extent that the environment offers a set of reinforcers that correspond well with their personal work needs (e.g., Dawis, 2005). Thus, a person who most highly values autonomy, altruism, and variety in his or her work would likely report job satisfaction to the extent that the work environment contains these features. Likewise, Holland's (1997) theory assumes that satisfaction will depend on the degree of congruence between an individual's vocational interests and those of persons in his or her occupational environment.

Although Dawis's and Holland's theories have been quite fertile, research on P-E fit has also been done outside the aegis of these theories. In much of this work, fit has been assessed subjectively by asking individuals how well they believe their job fulfills their needs or how well they fit their organization, work group, or supervisor along various dimensions, such as value compatibility (e.g., Kristof-Brown, Zimmerman, & Johnson, 2005). (By contrast, research on TWA and Holland's theory typically assesses fit by comparing individuals' measured values or interests, respectively, to separately obtained indexes of the reinforcement patterns or interest profiles of their work environment or occupational category.) A popular example of inquiry on subjective fit has involved perceived needs-supplies fit, that is, degree of fit between what the person wants from work and what the environment is seen as providing (Cable & DeRue, 2002).

Recent meta-analytic findings indicate that perceived fit between individuals and their specific jobs or work tasks (i.e., person-job fit as distinct from broader person-occupation fit) is strongly correlated (.56) with job satisfaction. Other types of perceived fit, including fit between the person and the larger work organization, specific work group, and supervisor have shown moderate correlations with job satisfaction (range = .31 to .44; Kristof-Brown et al., 2005). By contrast, P-E fit as assessed by Holland's (1997) and Dawis's (2005) theories have typically yielded lower relations with job satisfaction. Tranberg, Slane, and Ekeberg (1993) reported a mean correlation of .17 between interest congruence and job satisfaction.

Despite its apparent predictive utility, perceived fit may be subject to conceptual and methodological flaws. For example, on the basis of their findings, Edwards, Cable, Williamson, Lambert, and Shipp (2006) suggested that perceived fit and satisfaction each reflect common underlying affective content, such that "when people indicate that they fit the environment, they are not reporting the result of a [P-E] comparison process but instead are effectively saying they are satisfied with the environment" (p. 822). Moreover, assessing fit and job satisfaction subjectively and from the same perspective (that of the individual) capitalizes on monomethod and monosource bias and is, therefore, likely to inflate predictor-satisfaction relations. Indeed, such perceived fit methods produce meta-analytic correlations of person-job fit to satisfaction near .60, whereas calculation of fit based on separate measures of P and E yields a more modest effect size (.28; Kristof-Brown et al., 2005).

In defending the perceived fit approach, Kristof-Brown et al. (2005) noted that reliance on individuals' perception of fit is not unreasonable because satisfaction is likely to be affected more by fit to the environment as one experiences it subjectively than by objective features of the environment. As in the assessment of satisfaction itself, the individual may be the best arbiter of how well the job meets his or her needs. Despite the reasonableness of this argument, the "phenomenology of fit" remains a lively topic of debate at the moment and further research is needed to clarify the meaning of, and relations among, the various methods of assessing P-E fit (Edwards et al., 2006).

Perceived Organizational Support and Role Stressors

Several specific supportive or distressing work conditions—such as affectively relevant work events (H. M. Weiss & Cropanzano, 1996), role stressors (stress-producing environmental conditions such as role ambiguity, conflict, and overload; Beehr & Glazer, 2005), and invidious interpersonal conditions (e.g., workplace incivility, harassment; Lim & Cortina, 2005)—have also been reliably linked to job satisfaction (or dissatisfaction). Further, several of these work conditions have been shown to account for significant unique variance in job satisfaction or dissatisfaction independently of affective dispositions (e.g., Schaubroeck, Ganster, & Fox, 1992).

Organizational support theory and its research base (Rhoades & Eisenberger, 2002; Shore & Shore, 1995) suggest that the effect of the preceding conditions on job satisfaction and related outcomes (e.g., affective organizational commitment) may be mediated, at least in part, by employees' perceptions of organizational support or nonsupport—that is, the degree to which individuals feel that the organization is concerned about their welfare, values their contributions, and is committed to them. Experiences of workplace unfairness or harassment, nonresponsive supervision, stressful and ambiguous working conditions, and unfair reward systems may lead persons to perceive their workplaces as unsupportive which, in turn, increases feelings of work dissatisfaction. Perceived organizational support may, therefore, be a central mechanism that helps explain how diverse work conditions affect satisfaction.

Social Cognitive Variables

This category includes a variety of cognitive, behavioral, and environmental variables that have been studied in relation to job satisfaction (or the closely linked topic of life satisfaction) and that may be brought together under the conceptual umbrella of social cognitive theory (Bandura, 1986). Relative to research on temperament, work conditions, and P-E fit predictors, social cognitive predictors represent a somewhat recent thrust of research on work satisfaction.

Goals and Goal-Directed Behavior

In social cognitive (Bandura, 1986) and related theories, goals are usually defined as one's determination to effect a particular outcome (e.g., to pursue a given career path) or to attain a certain level of performance or productivity. People differ in the nature and salience of their personal goals. Various goal properties (e.g., simply having goals, having valued goals, being committed to one's goals, progressing toward one's goals) have been linked to well-being (Ryan & Deci, 2001). Perceived goal progress has been found to be a particularly useful predictor of educational satisfaction in cross-sectional research (Lent et al., 2005) and of job satisfaction (Maier & Brunstein, 2001) and SWB (Brunstein, 1993) in longitudinal studies. Such findings validate long-held assumptions that satisfaction is linked to successful efforts at attaining personally valued goals (e.g., Strong, 1955).

In contrast to dispositional determinants of job and life satisfaction, which are often viewed as highly resistant to change (e.g., Lykken & Tellegen, 1996), goal pursuit and progress represent more dynamic processes through which people contribute to their own well-being (Cantor & Sanderson, 1999). Thus, goal-directed behavior, and the variables that influence it, may be particularly relevant from a counseling perspective on job satisfaction. By setting and pursuing personal goals, people are seen as partly able to promote their own work satisfaction. This does not imply that goals function entirely independently of traits. It has been suggested that traits place limits on one's characteristic satisfaction "reaction range," but that "within this broad range, changes in people's environments, perceptions, feelings, and behaviors can increase or decrease their level of satisfaction" (Heller et al., 2004, p. 593).

Self-Efficacy

From the perspective of social cognitive theory, goal-directed behavior and domain-specific affect are each partly determined by self-efficacy, outcome expectations, and environmental supports and resources (Bandura, 1986, 1997). It is assumed that people will be more likely to set and pursue goals that are consistent with their beliefs about their personal capabilities, the expected consequences of goal pursuit, and available or accessible contextual resources. For present purposes, self-efficacy may be defined as personal beliefs about one's capability to perform particular behaviors necessary to achieve valued work-related goals or, more generally, to perform tasks requisite to success in one's work context.

Although career researchers have primarily explored the role of self-efficacy beliefs relative to educational-vocational interest, choice, and performance (Lent, Brown, & Hackett, 1994), these beliefs are also assumed to have important implications for the experience of affect and the management of affective states. For example, perceiving oneself as efficacious at key work behaviors may itself be satisfying (as a source of pride) and also partly influence how one interprets and copes with potentially stressful work events and conditions. Feeling competent may enable one to construe setbacks as less threatening, and may encourage use of more active coping strategies when one is beset by adverse conditions. Self-efficacy has been found to be moderately to strongly predictive of job satisfaction in employed workers (e.g., Caprara, Barbaranelli, Borgogni, & Steca, 2003; Chen, Goddard, & Casper, 2004). Other relevant findings suggest that self-efficacy may be related to domain satisfaction directly as well as indirectly through its relation to perceived goal progress (e.g., Lent et al., 2005).

Outcome Expectations

As noted, work values play a key role in TWA and in other conceptualizations of work satisfaction. In addition to the work conditions or rewards that the environment supplies or that people feel they have received, work values can be conceptualized in terms of the conditions or rewards that people prospectively anticipate their work environment to provide. This view entails expectancy-value beliefs (e.g., ratings of work-relevant outcomes and their importance to the individual; Mitchell, 1982) that can also be indexed as outcome expectations, or beliefs about the likelihood of receiving particular future outcomes contingent on one's work behavior (Bandura, 1986; Lent et al., 1994). Expected outcomes have been found to explain unique variance in job satisfaction apart from self-efficacy (e.g., Singer & Coffin, 1996) and situational and dispositional affect (H. M. Weiss et al., 1999).

Goal and Efficacy-Relevant Environmental Supports and Barriers

A special class of environmental variables are those that are specifically relevant to pursuit of one's personal goals or to fostering self-efficacy percepts. Goal-specific environmental supports and resources (e.g., social and material support for one's personal goals) are likely to promote satisfaction (Cantor & Sanderson, 1999; Diener & Fujita, 1995), while the absence of goal supports, or the presence of environmental obstacles that impede goal progress, may diminish it. Particular environmental features, such as encouragement, provision of modeling, and performance feedback, may also be construed as determinants of self-efficacy and outcome expectations (Bandura, 1986; Lent et al., 1994) which, in turn, facilitate goal pursuit and satisfaction. Goal-specific or more general environmental supports have been found to relate to both job (Maier & Brunstein, 2001) and educational (Lent et al., 2005) satisfaction.

Summary

This selective review indicates that many variables have been studied as predictors of job satisfaction. Even though they can be reduced to a relatively small number of larger variable classes (e.g., trait, environmental, social-cognitive), one is still left with the impression that there are multiple routes to job satisfaction. To create a unified understanding of work satisfaction, and a more systematic basis for intervention, it is valuable to consider how these various types of predictors function together and what may be the nature of the relations among them. Fortunately, there have been several attempts in recent years to begin construction of integrative models of job satisfaction. This is the focus of the next section.

INTEGRATIVE VIEWS OF WORK SATISFACTION

Earlier models of job satisfaction generally focused on single classes of predictors (e.g., job characteristics or dispositions). These single-source models tended to be either of the top-down (e.g., satisfaction is preordained by inheritance of a favorable temperament) or bottom-up (e.g., satisfaction is constructed by exposure to favorable situations) variety. The key limitation of such models is that each source alone tells only part of the story. An abundance of findings indicates that satisfaction is not merely a reflection of personality *or* a function of situation but rather a combination of the two (e.g., Heller et al., 2004). Their joint operation may account for more variance in satisfaction than either source alone, though maximizing amount of variance may be "less important than building a theoretical framework with both dispositions and situations existing harmoniously in the service of explanation" (H. M. Weiss & Cropanzano, 1996, p. 9).

Older P-E fit models, like TWA, transcended the single-source limitation in that they focused on aspects of persons (e.g., values) in relation to characteristics of the work setting (e.g., availability of resources to satisfy personal values). However, they may be limited in their assumption that better "objectively" defined matches between P and E invariably lead to greater satisfaction on the part of the person. Such models may not adequately take into account the variables and processes that likely mediate and moderate the pathway from fit to satisfaction. As suggested earlier, because of the phenomenological nature of satisfaction judgments, externally derived indicators of fit may affect satisfaction only to the extent that individuals *perceive* that the environment is meeting their needs. The combination of separate measures of P and E may yield a prediction that an individual's work environment contains the things he or she needs to be happy at work, but unless that individual experiences the fit as optimal (based on his or her own idiosyncratic mental calculations), this external perspective may not accurately forecast his or her felt level of satisfaction. This is one compelling reason why objective fit tends to predict job satisfaction less well than indicators of subjective or perceived fit (i.e., fit as defined by the researcher versus by the research participant; Kristof-Brown et al., 2005).

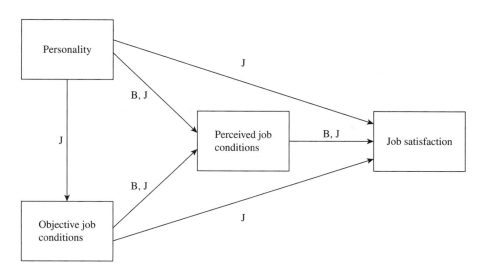

Figure 27.1 Perceived Job Characteristics as a Mediator of Personality and Objective Conditions. *Note:* This figure combines the models of Brief (1998) and Judge, Bono, and Locke (2000). B = Paths posited by Brief; J = Paths posited by Judge et al. (2000). Adapted with permission.

A new generation of job and life satisfaction models has been emerging in recent years. Although they differ in their specifics and their degree of comprehensiveness—and none has yet had the opportunity to be the object of sustained empirical attention—they share a common focus on bringing personality and situational variables together within an integrative perspective on satisfaction. Several examples are briefly described here.

Perceived Job Characteristics as a Mediator of Personality and Objective Conditions

The most parsimonious of the integrative models is Brief's (1998) conception, included in Figure 27.1. Brief held that global personality dimensions (e.g., negative affect) and objective job conditions (e.g., actual pay received) jointly affect individuals' interpretations of their job circumstances (e.g., perceived adequacy of work outcomes or conditions). It is these subjective interpretations that lead directly to satisfaction. In other words, the effects of personality and objective conditions on satisfaction operate through (are fully mediated by) the perceived work context. Thus, two individuals might have quite divergent views of the same work environment.

Judge, Bono, and Locke's (2000) model (also represented in Figure 1) is conceptually related to that of Brief (1998). In particular, Judge et al. (2000) similarly posited that personality and objective job conditions both affect perceived job conditions which, in turn, shape job satisfaction. However, unlike Brief, Judge, et al. specified direct (as well as indirect) paths from personality and objective conditions to satisfaction. In other words, they saw perceived job conditions as a partial, rather than a full, mediator of personality and objective work conditions. In addition, Judge et al. took a somewhat unusual approach to the definition of objective job conditions and personality. The former was conceptualized in terms of job complexity (the complexity of the work tasks required by one's job); the latter was represented by core self-evaluations, a novel personality construct represented by self-esteem, generalized self-efficacy, locus of control, and neuroticism. A test of their model with self-report data suggested that perceived job conditions fully mediated the relation of objective conditions, and partially mediated the relation of personality, to job satisfaction (Judge et al., 2000, Study 1).

Simultaneous Consideration of Job and Life Satisfaction

Heller et al. (2004) proposed and tested an integrative model of domain and life satisfaction using meta-analytic data (see the paths labeled "H" in Figure 27.2). It may be a bit of a stretch to classify their

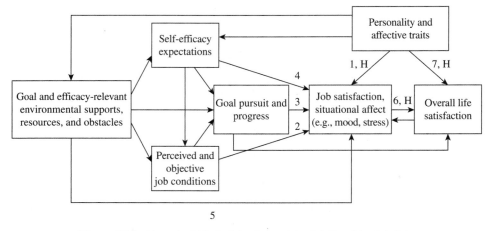

Figure 27.2   Domain-Life Satisfaction and Social Cognitive Models.
Note: This figure combines the models of Heller et al. (2004) and Lent and Brown (2006). H = Paths posited by Heller et al. (2004). Numbered paths refer to the Brown-Lent Model. Adapted with permission.

approach as an integrative model of job satisfaction because its focus was actually on life satisfaction as the ultimate criterion variable. I include this model here because it represents an important effort to consider how job and life satisfaction interrelate and how both are linked to personality. As in the model by Judge et al. (2000), Heller et al. envisioned a direct path from personality to job satisfaction. However, this scheme differs in that (a) personality is represented by four of the Big Five factors rather than by core self-evaluations, (b) life satisfaction and another form of domain satisfaction (marital satisfaction) are added to the model, and (c) job conditions are not included because Heller et al. were primarily concerned with the nature of the relations between domain and life satisfaction.

In addition to the direct path of personality to life satisfaction, Heller et al. posited that personality would affect life satisfaction indirectly through job and marital satisfaction (e.g., more favorable personality factors would promote job satisfaction which, in turn, would increase life satisfaction). Although they found support for this model in their meta-analysis, they also found support for an alternative model in which life satisfaction is portrayed as leading to job and marital satisfaction (see the return path from life to job satisfaction in Figure 27.2). These two plausible alternative constructions reflect the view that satisfaction in central life domains may be reciprocally related to life satisfaction. Because job conditions were not included in their models, Heller et al. could not test the joint operation of personality and job conditions relative to job satisfaction, as posited by the Brief (1998) and Judge et al. (2000) models.

Affective Events Theory

H. M. Weiss and Cropanzano's (1996) affective events theory (AET) takes a more unusual approach, focusing on relatively dynamic versus stable features of work environments and affect. As shown in Figure 27.3, the work environment gives rise to proximal work events (e.g., getting a raise, having an argument with a coworker) that can provoke changes in situational affect or mood and, in turn, ratings of overall job satisfaction. In addition to being influenced by situational affective reactions, job satisfaction is seen as directly affected by work conditions (as in the Judge et al., 2000 model). In a departure from the other models, personality is posited to influence job satisfaction indirectly by making certain types of situational affective reactions more or less likely (e.g., high trait negative affect may incline people to react to certain work events with greater levels of negative mood). Support has been found for some of the model's hypothesized links, such as the relation of mood to job satisfaction (Ilies & Judge, 2002; Judge & Ilies, 2004; H. M. Weiss et al., 1999). By highlighting the flux, rather than stability, of factors

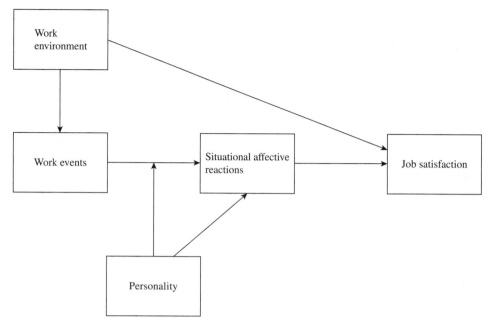

Figure 27.3   Affective Events Theory.

Note: This is a simplified version of H. M. Weiss and Cropanzano's (1996) model, omitting additional (nonsatisfaction) criterion variables. Adapted with permission.

that lead to job satisfaction, AET may be more compatible than the previous models with counseling psychology's focus on interventions that can promote job satisfaction.

Social Cognitive Model of Work Satisfaction

Lent and Brown (2006) offered a social cognitive model of work satisfaction linked to a larger model of domain and life satisfaction (Lent, 2004). Their model appears in Figure 27.2. Like some of the prior integrative models, the social cognitive model posits that satisfaction is affected directly by personality (path 1) and work conditions (path 2). Within their conception of work conditions, Lent and Brown included a wide array of variables that capture objective and perceived features of the environment, such as outcome expectations, needs-supplies fit, and perceived organizational support. Likewise, personality includes a variety of factors that have been empirically linked to job satisfaction (e.g., positive and negative affect). This model complements the others by highlighting additional, agentic paths to work satisfaction (e.g., self-efficacy, goal pursuit) that, like AET, may shed light on relatively dynamic processes that lead to job satisfaction—and that, theoretically, could be harnessed for therapeutic ends.

Of special relevance for counseling and developmental interventions, this model posits that work satisfaction is affected by setting and making progress at personally relevant work goals (path 3), self-efficacy at performing work tasks and at achieving one's work goals (path 4), and access to environmental resources for promoting self-efficacy and goal pursuit (path 5). The implication of these paths is that work satisfaction can be promoted by focusing on those aspects of the individual (e.g., self-efficacy, outcome expectations, goal selection, commitment, and progress) and environment (job enrichment and redesign) over which workers and supervisors have some control.

The model also acknowledges several specific indirect paths through which personality and environmental factors may affect work satisfaction (e.g., certain personality factors may promote or deflate perceptions of self-efficacy and environmental support that, in turn, influence satisfaction). Although such paths add complexity to the model, they represent an effort to capture the means by which person and situation factors operate jointly relative to job satisfaction. Consistent with Heller et al.'s (2004) models, the social cognitive model also posits that work satisfaction and life satisfaction affect one another bidirectionally (path 6) and that personality influences life satisfaction (path 7) as well as job satisfaction. Initial tests of full and partial versions of the social cognitive model have yielded supportive findings with college students (e.g., Lent et al., 2005; Lent, Singley, Sheu, Schmidt, & Schmidt, 2007), but studies of the model with employed adults have yet to be conducted.

Summary

This section briefly described five recent models that attempt to integrate person and situation perspectives on job satisfaction. The models focus to varying degrees on the role of personality in satisfaction, both as a direct effect (e.g., characteristic positive affect is likely to prompt ratings of overall job satisfaction) and as a mediated pathway (e.g., positive affect promotes favorable views of work conditions that, in turn, prompt satisfaction). Such theorizing can nurture a sophisticated understanding of the causal routes though which traits relate to satisfaction. Some of the models also contend with the nature of the relation between job and life satisfaction; the role of situational affect or mood as a dynamic link in the causal chain between the environment, the person, and satisfaction ratings; and the impact of social cognitive variables, like self-efficacy and goals, on satisfaction. Collectively, the integrative models have the potential to stimulate renewed research on work satisfaction and to inform therapeutic efforts aimed at its promotion.

DIRECTIONS FOR FUTURE INQUIRY AND PRACTICE

In this final section, I suggest a few broad directions for future inquiry on work satisfaction and also consider some implications of the existing literature for intervention efforts.

Directions for Research and Theory

Based on the preceding review, one of the most fruitful directions for inquiry on job satisfaction at this time would be to devote more effort to testing the new integrative models, both individually and comparatively. In comparative tests, the goal need not be to conduct an empirical horserace to identify which models (or individual variables) explain the most variance in job satisfaction. Rather, as suggested by H. M. Weiss and Cropanzano (1996), it would be valuable at this point to examine how specific person and environmental variables function together in the service of job satisfaction. For instance, we now know that certain affective traits are good predictors of job satisfaction (e.g., Heller et al., 2004; Judge et al., 2002), but we need to know more about the pathways through which they are linked to job satisfaction. Such work will require examining emotional, cognitive, behavioral, and environmental variables that may mediate or moderate trait-satisfaction relations.

It would be useful to employ longitudinal and experimental designs to a greater degree in doing model testing. Existing research on the integrative models has been largely cross-sectional in nature. Although such research can suggest predictor-criterion paths that are consistent with causal assumptions, it cannot conclusively demonstrate cause-effect relations. Longitudinal designs can at least test assumptions about the temporal predominance of putative causes and effects—a necessary if not sufficient condition for causal inference. Experimental designs do an even better job of testing what leads to what. Of course, it may not be viable to manipulate certain independent variables, like relatively stable personality factors, to examine their impact on satisfaction. In such cases, longitudinal designs offer a reasonable alternative.

Independent variables that are more dynamic and changeable are good candidates for experimental or quasi-experimental designs, and such variables are especially relevant from an intervention perspective because they represent aspects of job satisfaction over which some control may be exercised. Although some people may well be born with predispositions toward general happiness (Lykken & Tellegen, 1996), it still seems quite reasonable to identify person (e.g., goal setting) and environmental (e.g., social support) factors that may promote satisfaction or allay dissatisfaction. If experimental methods can be shown to modify these factors and, in turn, raise satisfaction levels, this would bode very well for therapeutic applications. A related research need is to derive and test systematic interventions for preventing or ameliorating job dissatisfaction. Such research could serve the dual purposes of testing theoretical assumptions about causal relations and exploring the practical utility of the integrative models.

Given that the preponderance of research has examined job satisfaction from a global, cross-situational perspective (both predictors and dependent variables have usually been conceptualized and measured as relatively static, traitlike properties), it would be useful to devote more study to state, temporally specific, and dynamic aspects of job satisfaction. Affective events theory highlights the potential of transient work events to influence situational affect that, in turn, may affect overall perceptions of job satisfaction (H. M. Weiss & Cropanzano, 1996), and recent experience-sampling research has begun to study the spillover of work events and moods to other areas of life (e.g., Judge & Illies, 2004). More such research would be valuable, particularly because of its potential to illuminate variables and processes that are relatively fluid, open to agentic control and, hence, relevant to intervention.

Finally, it is important to expand the purview of research on job satisfaction to encompass other aspects of work adjustment. As long suggested by TWA, it is useful to view satisfaction as a central marker of work adjustment, but not as the only criterion of successful work functioning (Dawis, 2005). Other criteria might include work role effectiveness (satisfactoriness, in TWA's terms), organizational citizenship behavior, tolerable levels of work stress, and absence of withdrawal and counterproductive work behaviors. While such variables are sometimes discussed as correlates or consequences of job satisfaction, and their bivariate relations to job satisfaction have been explored (Fritzsche & Parrish, 2005), it would be useful to better understand the nature of their interrelations with job satisfaction. For instance, satisfied workers may be more likely to perform prosocial behavior, but the goodwill that such behavior creates for them may also yield social rewards such as support and praise from coworkers and supervisors that, in turn, promote further satisfaction within a positive feedback loop. Research on such complex, reciprocal pathways and microprocesses could inform understanding of the ways that people adjust to their work environments as well as how they manage less than optimal fit or adverse work conditions. Such research could also lead to larger, multicomponent models of positive work adaptation.

Implications for Intervention

Perhaps the most obvious practical implication of the review is that job satisfaction is a multiply determined phenomenon. At a nomothetic level, many variables have been linked to the experience of job satisfaction and dissatisfaction. Despite occasional claims to the contrary (e.g., Lykken & Tellegen, 1996), research has thus far not unearthed a single source that trumps all the others in determining domain or overall life satisfaction. Nevertheless, at an idiographic level, there are likely to be particular environmental conditions, personality factors, and behaviors that spark or inhibit job satisfaction in individual workers, some of whom may seek remedial or developmental counseling or coaching services. Part of the challenge, then, is to identify those specific sources that are most relevant to a particular individual or, in the case of organizational interventions, to a group of individuals who share a common work environment.

As suggested, particularly with the emergence of integrative person-situation models of work satisfaction, there is a need to design and test theory-derived interventions aimed at the promotion of work satisfaction or the alleviation of dissatisfaction. In the current absence of such interventions, a few general guidelines might be distilled. Because of space limitations, I will focus on remedial more so than developmental or preventive objectives.

First, either informal or structured assessment methods could be employed to detect the most salient causes of work dissatisfaction. A perceived P-E fit orientation might provide a useful overarching structure for informal assessment. Two orienting questions could be (1) What are you not getting that you want in (or from) your work? and (2) What are you getting that you don't want? The first question aims to clarify needs-supplies fit issues (e.g., lack of variety, poor pay, absence of interpersonal support); the second seeks to identify invidious work conditions or role strain issues (e.g., harassment, undue stress, role ambiguity, and conflict). The perspective of affective events theory would also suggest a focus on specific, recent, affectively relevant work events (e.g., conflict with a supervisor). Alternatively, a facet measure of job satisfaction could be used to survey a range of conditions that represent potential sources of dissatisfaction.

The preceding suggestions largely focus on the perceived work environment. But another, complementary approach would be to explore other person, behavior, and contextual factors that can contribute to job satisfaction. For example, the social cognitive model would encourage exploration of such considerations as personal goal setting and progress (e.g., does the worker have central, personal goals? What sort of progress is the worker making on them? What goal barriers or supports might need to be addressed?); self-efficacy regarding goal pursuit and work task competence; coping skills; and involvement with valued work tasks. The work-family interface literature would suggest examining the potential spillover between work and other life domains that has the potential either to stir up (e.g., interrole conflicts) or lessen (e.g., family support) work dissatisfaction (see Gilbert & Rader, Chapter 25, this volume).

A trait or dispositional perspective on work satisfaction could also be entertained. Although a focus on potentially malleable features of the self (e.g., perceptions, behaviors) and environment is clearly conducive to counseling and self-initiated change efforts, it is valuable to consider the degree to which job dissatisfaction is a trait versus a state matter for a particular individual. Measures of trait or overall job and life satisfaction, positive affect (or extraversion), and negative affect (or neuroticism) could be used to explore the individual's general affective balance and level of satisfaction.

Depending on the sources of job dissatisfaction suggested by a thorough assessment phase, interventions might well be structured to address one or more of these sources, framed as the primary targets of counseling. Possible interventions could include (but not be limited to) developing strategies to access desired work conditions or reinforcers (e.g., via job redesign or skill updating) or to cope with negative aspects of one's job (e.g., managing stress); refining interpersonal, self-regulation, or technical job skills to maximize work success and the benefits it can bring; fostering goal progress (e.g., by helping individuals set and monitor progress toward clear, proximal, intrinsic, attainable yet challenging, valued goals); marshaling needed supports and resources for goal pursuit; enhancing task and goal-related self-efficacy; environmental advocacy to deal with harsh work conditions; and counseling for job or career change when P-E *mis*fit appears too great to be managed within the current job context.

Although situation and person-focused intervention approaches may be useful for many individuals, it is also important to consider that, for some, job dissatisfaction may well reflect, or be exacerbated by, personality traits or affective dispositions (e.g., characteristically high levels of negative affect). In such cases, it is well to consider that dispositions may place an upper bound on intervention effects (e.g., Heller et al., 2004). For example, counseling may help reduce job dissatisfaction but may not reset a chronically low affective baseline. Yet it is also useful to consider that traits may be more malleable than is sometimes assumed (Staw & Ross, 1985) and that work experiences or environments may affect personality as well as the other way around, at least at certain life stages (Roberts, Caspi, & Moffitt, 2003). Although full-fledged personality restructuring may not be a realistic goal, counseling may profitably help chronically unhappy clients to understand and manage the cognitive and behavioral aspects of their affective tendencies (e.g., how negative affectivity can shape perceptions of job events and how negative interpretations can be challenged; Brown, Ryan, & McPartland, 1996). Thus, it seems possible to assert some degree of affective self-regulation even under less than optimal personal or environmental conditions.

Summary

Despite the volumes of existing research on job satisfaction, recent advances—especially the emergence of newer, integrative models of job satisfaction and of domain-life satisfaction—offer exciting directions for new research as well as renewed potential to craft methods for promoting job satisfaction and reducing job dissatisfaction. Promising research directions include opportunities for model testing, exploring person-situation linkages via longitudinal and experimental methods, and developing and validating theory-derived interventions. Although more intervention research is needed, current knowledge of the multiply determined nature of job satisfaction does suggest a host of application possibilities, both for working with clients whose job dissatisfaction is linked to relatively situational and facet features of their work and for those who experience job dissatisfaction more chronically.

CONCLUSION

This is an exciting period in the study of job satisfaction. Advances have been made over the past few decades in identifying particular situational and person factors that predict job satisfaction and other aspects of work-related affect. Given the sizable number of individual variables that have been linked to job satisfaction, the present review organized them into a few larger classes of predictors and also described five promising integrative models, each of which considers how multiple sources of job satisfaction may interrelate. The potential of this literature to stimulate new inquiry and practical applications was also discussed.

Finally, a goal of this chapter was to encourage vocational psychologists to rediscover the value of studying work satisfaction and adjustment, as a complement to their focus on prework entry issues. By reengaging with organizational psychology in the study of job satisfaction, vocational psychology can help promote an integrative perspective that is relevant to the interests of both workers and employers. Such a perspective can offer a more comprehensive understanding of what individuals can do to promote their own work satisfaction as well as what organizations can do to facilitate this mutually beneficial outcome.

REFERENCES

Bandura, A. (1986). *Social foundations of thought and action: A social cognitive theory*. Englewood Cliffs, NJ: Prentice-Hall.

Bandura, A. (1997). *Self-efficacy: The exercise of control*. New York: Freeman.

Beehr, T. A., & Glazer, S. (2005). Organizational role stress. In J. Barling, E. K. Kelloway, & M. R. Frone (Eds.), *Handbook of work stress* (pp. 7–33). Thousand Oaks, CA: Sage.

Brayfield, A. H., & Rothe, H. F. (1951). An index of job satisfaction. *Journal of Applied Psychology, 35*, 307–311.

Brief, A. P. (1998). *Attitudes in and around organizations*. Thousand Oaks, CA: Sage.

Brief, A. P., & Weiss, H. M. (2002). Organizational behavior: Affect in the workplace. *Annual Review of Psychology, 53*, 279–307.

Brown, S. D., Ryan, N. E., & McPartland, E. B. (1996). Why are so many people happy and what do we do for those who aren't? A reaction to Lightsey (1996). *Counseling Psychologist, 24*, 751–757.

Brunstein, J. C. (1993). Personal goals and subjective well-being: A longitudinal study. *Journal of Personality and Social Psychology, 65*, 1061–1070.

Cable, D. M., & DeRue, D. S. (2002). The convergent and discriminant validity of subjective fit perceptions. *Journal of Applied Psychology, 87*, 875–884.

Cantor, N., & Sanderson, C. A. (1999). Life task participation and well-being: The importance of taking part in daily life. In D. Kahneman, E. Diener, & N. Schwarz (Eds.), *Well-being: The foundations of hedonic psychology* (pp. 230–243). New York: Russell Sage Foundation.

Caprara, G. V., Barbaranelli, C., Borgogni, L., & Steca, P. (2003). Efficacy beliefs as determinants of teachers' job satisfaction. *Journal of Educational Psychology, 95*, 821–832.

Carr, J. Z., Schmidt, A. M., Ford, J. K., & DeShon, R. P. (2003). Climate perceptions matter: A meta-analytic path analysis relating molar climate, cognitive and affective states, and individual level work outcomes. *Journal of Applied Psychology, 88*, 605–619.

Chen, G., Goddard, T. G., & Casper, W. J. (2004). Examination of the relationships among general and work-specific self-evaluations, work-related control beliefs, and job attitudes. *Applied Psychology: An International Review, 53*, 349–370.

Connolly, J. J., & Viswesvaran, C. (2000). The role of affectivity in job satisfaction: A meta-analysis. *Personality and Individual Differences, 29*, 265–281.

Dawis, R. V. (2005). The Minnesota Theory of Work Adjustment. In S. D. Brown & R. W. Lent (Eds.), *Career development and counseling: Putting theory and research to work* (pp. 3–23). Hoboken, NJ: Wiley.

Diener, E., & Fujita, F. (1995). Resources, personal strivings, and subjective well-being: A nomothetic and idiographic approach. *Journal of Personality and Social Psychology, 68*, 926–935.

Diener, E., Suh, E. M., Lucas, R. E., & Smith, H. L. (1999). Subjective well-being: Three decades of progress. *Psychological Bulletin, 125*, 276–302.

Edwards, J. R., Cable, D. M., Williamson, I. O., Lambert, L. S., & Shipp, A. J. (2006). The phenomenology of fit: Linking the person and environment to the subjective experience of person-environment fit. *Journal of Applied Psychology, 91*, 802–827.

Fritzsche, B. A., & Parrish, T. J. (2005). Theories and research on job satisfaction. In S. D. Brown & R. W. Lent (Eds.), *Career development and counseling: Putting theory and research to work* (pp. 180–202). Hoboken, NJ: Wiley.

Hackman, J. R., & Oldham, G. R. (1976). Motivation through the design of work: Test of a theory. *Organizational Behavior and Human Performance, 16*, 250–279.

Heller, D., Judge, T. A., & Watson, D. (2002). The confounding role of personality and trait affectivity in the relationship between job and life satisfaction. *Journal of Organizational Behavior, 23*, 815–835.

Heller, D., Watson, D., & Ilies, R. (2004). The role of person versus situation in life satisfaction: A critical examination. *Psychological Bulletin, 130*, 574–600.

Holland, J. L. (1997). *Making vocational choices: A theory of vocational personalities and work environments* (3rd ed.). Odessa, FL: Psychological Assessment Resources.

Ilies, R., & Judge, T. A. (2002). Understanding the dynamic relationships among personality, mood, and job satisfaction: A field experience sampling study. *Organizational Behavior and Human Decision Processes, 89*, 1119–1139.

Ilies, R., & Judge, T. A. (2003). On the heritability of job satisfaction: The mediating role of personality. *Journal of Applied Psychology, 88*, 750–759.

Ironson, G. H., Smith, P. C., Brannick, M. T., Gibson, W. M., & Paul, K. B. (1989). Construction of a job in general scale: A comparison of global, composite, and specific measures. *Journal of Applied Psychology, 74*, 193–200.

Irwin, R., Kammann, R., & Dixon, G. (1979). If you want to know how happy I am, you'll have to ask me. *New Zealand Psychologist, 8*, 10–12.

Judge, T. A., Bono, J. E., & Locke, E. A. (2000). Personality and job satisfaction: The mediating role of job characteristics. *Journal of Applied Psychology, 85*, 237–249.

Judge, T. A., Heller, D., & Mount, M. K. (2002). Five-factor model of personality and job satisfaction: A meta-analysis. *Journal of Applied Psychology, 87*, 530–541.

Judge, T. A., & Ilies, R. (2004). Affect and job satisfaction: A study of their relationship at work and at home. *Journal of Applied Psychology, 89*, 661–673.

Judge, T. A., & Watanabe, S. (1993). Another look at the job satisfaction-life satisfaction relationship. *Journal of Applied Psychology, 78*, 939–948.

Kahneman, D. (1999). Objective happiness. In D. Kahneman, E. Diener, & N. Schwarz (Eds.), *Well-being: The foundations of hedonic psychology* (pp. 3–25). New York: Russell Sage Foundation.

Kristof-Brown, A. L., Zimmerman, R. D., & Johnson, E. C. (2005). Consequences of individuals' fit at work: A meta-analysis of person-job, person-organization, person-group, and person-supervisor fit. *Personnel Psychology, 58*, 281–342.

Lent, R. W. (2004). Toward a unifying theoretical and practical perspective on well-being and psychosocial adjustment. *Journal of Counseling Psychology, 51*, 482–509.

Lent, R. W., & Brown, S. D. (2006). Integrating person and situation perspectives on work satisfaction: A social-cognitive view. *Journal of Vocational Behavior, 69,* 236–247.

Lent, R. W., Brown, S. D., & Hackett, G. (1994). Toward a unifying social cognitive theory of career and academic interest, choice, and performance [Monograph]. *Journal of Vocational Behavior, 45,* 79–122.

Lent, R. W., Singley, D., Sheu, H., Gainor, K.A., Brenner, B.R., Treistman, D., et al. (2005). Social cognitive predictors of domain and life satisfaction: Exploring the theoretical precursors of subjective well-being. *Journal of Counseling Psychology, 52,* 429–442.

Lent, R. W., Singley, D., Sheu, H., Schmidt, J. A., & Schmidt, L. C. (2007). Relation of social-cognitive factors to academic satisfaction in engineering students. *Journal of Career Assessment, 15,* 87–97.

Lim, S., & Cortina, L. M. (2005). Interpersonal mistreatment in the workplace: The interface and impact of general incivility and sexual harassment. *Journal of Applied Psychology, 90,* 483–496.

Locke, E. A. (1976). The nature and causes of job satisfaction. In M. D. Dunnette (Ed.), *Handbook of industrial and organizational psychology* (pp. 1297–1349). Chicago: Rand McNally.

Lofquist, L. H., & Dawis, R. V. (1984). Research on work adjustment and satisfaction: Implications for career counseling. In S. D. Brown & R. W. Lent (Eds.), *Handbook of counseling psychology* (pp. 216–237). New York: Wiley.

Lykken, D., & Tellegen, A. (1996). Happiness is a stochastic phenomenon. *Psychological Science, 7,* 186–189.

Maier, G. W., & Brunstein, J. C. (2001). The role of personal work goals in newcomers' job satisfaction and organizational commitment: A longitudinal analysis. *Journal of Applied Psychology, 86,* 1034–1042.

McCrae, R. R., & Costa, P. T. (1991). Adding liebe und arbeit: The full five-factor model and well-being. *Personality and Social Psychology Bulletin, 17,* 227–232.

Mitchell, T. R. (1974). Expectancy models of job satisfaction, occupational preferences and effort: A theoretical, methodological, and empirical appraisal. *Psychological Bulletin, 81,* 1053–1077.

Mitchell, T. R. (1982). Expectancy-value models in organizational psychology. In N. R. Feather (Ed.), *Expectancies and actions: Expectancy-value models in psychology* (pp. 293–312). Hillsdale, NJ: Erlbaum.

Rain, J. S., Lane, I. M., & Steiner, D. D. (1991). A current look at the job satisfaction/life satisfaction relationship: Review and future considerations. *Human Resources, 44,* 287–307.

Rhoades, L., & Eisenberger, R. (2002). Perceived organizational support: A review of the literature. *Journal of Applied Psychology, 87,* 698–714.

Roberts, B. W., Caspi, A., & Moffitt, T. E. (2003). Work experiences and personality development in young adulthood. *Journal of Personality and Social Psychology, 84,* 582–593.

Ryan, R. M., & Deci, E. L. (2001). On happiness and human potentials: A review of research on hedonic and eudaimonic well-being. *Annual Review of Psychology, 52,* 141–166.

Schaubroeck, J., Ganster, D. C., & Fox, M. L. (1992). Dispositional affect and work-related stress. *Journal of Applied Psychology, 77,* 322–335.

Shore, L. M., & Shore, T. H. (1995). Perceived organizational support and organizational justice. In R.S. Cropanzano & K. M. Kacmar (Eds.), *Organization politics, justice, and support: Managing the social climate of the workplace* (pp. 149–164). Westport, CT: Quorum.

Singer, M. S., & Coffin, T. K. (1996). Cognitive and volitional determinants of job attitudes in a voluntary organization. *Journal of Social Behavior and Personality, 11,* 313–328.

Smith, P. C., Kendall, L. M., & Hulin, C. L. (1969). *The measurement of satisfaction in work and retirement: A strategy for the study of attitudes.* Chicago: Rand McNally.

Spector, P. E. (1997). *Job satisfaction: Application, assessment, causes, and consequences.* Thousand Oaks, CA: Sage.

Staw, B. M., & Ross, J. (1985). Stability in the midst of change: A dispositional approach to job attitudes. *Journal of Applied Psychology, 70,* 469–480.

Strong, E. K. (1955). *Vocational interests 18 years after college.* Minneapolis: University of Minnesota Press.

Tait, M., Padgett, M. Y., & Baldwin, T. T. (1989). Job and life satisfaction: A reevaluation of the strength of the relationship and gender effects as a function of the date of the study. *Journal of Applied Psychology, 74,* 502–507.

Thoresen, C. J., Kaplan, S. A., Barsky, A. P., Warren, C. R., & de Chermont, K. (2003). The affective underpinnings of job perceptions and attitudes: A meta-analytic review and integration. *Psychological Bulletin, 129,* 914–945.

Tranberg, M., Slane, S., & Ekeberg, E. (1993). The relation between interest congruence and satisfaction: A metaanalysis. *Journal of Vocational Behavior, 42,* 253–264.

Turner, N., Barling, J., & Zacharatos, A. (2002). Positive psychology at work. In C. R. Snyder & S. J. Lopez (Eds.), *Handbook of positive psychology* (pp. 715–728). New York: Oxford University Press.

Veenhoven, R. (1994). Is happiness a trait? Tests of the theory that a better society does not make people any happier. *Social Indicators Research, 32*, 101–160.

Walsh, W. B., & Eggerth, D. E. (2005). Vocational psychology and personality: The relationship of the five-factor model to job performance and job satisfaction. In W. B. Walsh & M. L. Savickas (Eds.), *Handbook of vocational psychology* (3rd ed., pp. 267–295). Mahwah, NJ: Erlbaum.

Walsh, W. B., & Savickas, M. L. (Eds.). (2005). *Handbook of vocational psychology* (3rd ed.). Mahwah, NJ: Erlbaum.

Warr, P. (1999). Well-being and the workplace. In D. Kahneman, E. Diener, & N. Schwarz (Eds.), *Well-being: The foundations of hedonic psychology* (pp. 392–412). New York: Russell Sage Foundation.

Watson, D., & Slack, A. K. (1993). General factors of affective temperament and their relation to job satisfaction over time. *Organizational Behavior and Human Decision Processes, 54*, 181–202.

Weiss, D. J., Dawis, R. V., England, G. W., & Lofquist, L. H. (1967). *Manual for the Minnesota Satisfaction Questionnaire*. Minneapolis: University of Minnesota Press.

Weiss, H. M., & Cropanzano, R. (1996). Affective events theory: A theoretical discussion of the structure, causes, and consequences of affective experiences at work. In B. M. Staw & L. L. Cummings (Eds.), *Research in organizational behavior* (Vol. 18, pp. 1–74). Greenwich, CT: JAI.

Weiss, H. M., Nicholas, J. P., & Daus, C. S. (1999). An examination of the joint effects of affective experiences and job beliefs on job satisfaction and variations in affective experiences over time. *Organizational Behavior and Human Decision Processes, 78*, 1–24.

PART V

Development and Prevention

CHAPTER 28

Risk and Resilience

CONSUELO ARBONA
NICOLE COLEMAN

In the 1980s, developmental psychopathologists coined the term *resilience* to refer to the dynamic process observed in children and adolescents who achieve successful adaptation in the context of adversity. The emergence of the concept of resilience is associated with Norman Garmezy's studies of schizophrenia and Emmy Werner's pioneering longitudinal study of the children of Kauai, Hawaii (Masten & Powell, 2003). Garmezy's interest in understanding the etiology of schizophrenia led him and his team to focus on the children of mentally ill parents, who were at high risk for psychopathology. Motivated by the observation that many children developed well despite being raised by schizophrenic mothers, Garmezy's team changed their focus from studying risk to examining competence among children who experienced adversity because of parental mental illness, poverty, and other stressful life events (Garmezy & Tellegen, 1984). Werner and Smith's (2001) naturalistic study of the long-term developmental trajectory of a cohort of children born in 1955 on the island of Kauai is considered the first systematic investigation of risk and resilience (Masten & Powell, 2003).

The groundbreaking work of these and other resilience researchers (e.g., Anthony, 1974; Rutter, 1987) brought attention to the strengths of children and adolescents in at-risk groups who, up to that point, were primarily thought of in terms of their deficits and problems in development. These researchers reasoned that an understanding of the process of adaptation that allows some individuals to overcome adversity or traumatic experiences could help guide prevention and intervention efforts with others facing similar circumstances (Masten, 1994). Because it emphasizes strengths rather than deficits, the resilience model is consistent with counseling psychology's traditional philosophical stance and professional emphasis.

Since its inception as a specialty, counseling psychology has emphasized the study of normative processes of development and the facilitative personal and environmental conditions that lead to adaptive outcomes (Gelso & Fretz, 2001). In recent years, the field of psychology has recognized the importance of paradigms that focus on positive aspects of human functioning (Seligman & Csikszentmihalyi, 2000). Counseling psychologists have actively participated in the rediscovery of positive psychology, proposing theoretical, empirical, and clinical perspectives that emphasize well-being, optimal development, and strength-based approaches to counseling (e.g., Lent, 2004; Smith, 2006). The resilience paradigm provides an integrative framework for understanding the role of risk and protective factors in development that is consistent with counseling psychology's commitment to positive development, multicultural psychology, and the understanding of human functioning in the context of person-environment transactions. Therefore, this chapter provides an overview of the risk and resilience model, as developed and implemented by developmental psychologists, with a focus on how this model may be applied to research in counseling psychology.

In its relatively short history, the resilience paradigm has yielded valuable findings for furthering developmental theory and suggesting interventions to help those at risk. However, this approach has been criticized primarily because of variability in the definition and measurement of key constructs such as resilience, risk, protective and vulnerability factors, competence, and positive adaptation (e.g., Kaplan, 1999; Tolan, 1996). In the first section of the chapter, we provide an overview of the guidelines offered by leading resilience researchers regarding the definition and measurement of these key constructs and describe the most salient strategies in resilience research (Luthar, Cicchetti, & Becker, 2000; Luthar & Cushing, 1999; Masten & Powell, 2003; Rutter, 2000).

Several authors have published comprehensive reviews of empirical studies about resilient adaptation in the context of major threats to development (e.g., Luthar, 2006; Masten & Powell, 2003). We have not attempted to replicate this work; instead, in the second section of the chapter, we provide a brief overview of major themes in resilience research gleaned from these reviews. In the third section, we discuss the emerging empirical literature about the psychological implications of racial discrimination of African American youth from the perspective of the risk-resilience framework. This topic has not been widely covered in other reviews (Carter, 2007; Szalacha et al., 2003). The chapter concludes with a discussion of research and practice implications of the race-related resilience literature.

DEFINITION AND MEASUREMENT OF RESILIENCE-RELATED CONSTRUCTS

Resilience

Researchers have debated the meaning of resilience as a developmental construct (Luthar et al., 2000). A question frequently asked is, "Does resilience refer to a trait, a process, or an outcome?" In everyday language, resilience typically is located within the person; people who in adverse circumstances beat the odds and do better than expected are often described as resilient. Initially, developmental psychologists also conceptualized resilience in terms of protective personality traits; at-risk children who demonstrated positive outcomes were described as "stress-resistant" or "invulnerable" (Anthony, 1974; Garmezy & Tellegen, 1984). The conceptualization of resilience as a psychological attribute has been criticized as a quintessentially U.S. concept reminiscent of the Horatio Alger myth that exalts the individual's sense of agency and determination in overcoming difficult odds to achieve success (Rigsby, 1994). Empirical studies have demonstrated that contextual factors, including the family and the wider environment, contribute greatly to adaptive developmental outcomes among children and youth exposed to adversity (Kumpfer, 1999; Luthar, 2006; Luthar & Zelazo, 2003; Masten, 1994). Therefore, denoting resilience as a strictly personal characteristic is not only inaccurate, but may have the deleterious implication that less successful at-risk children and youth are to blame for their problems.

Developmental psychologists emphasize that resilience does not denote a personal attribute but refers to profiles or developmental trajectories of individuals who achieve successful adaptation in the context of risk and adversity (Luthar, 2006; Luthar & Zelazo, 2003; Masten & Powell, 2003). It is important to distinguish resilience from the construct of ego resiliency developed by Block and Block (1980). Ego resiliency refers to a personal disposition characterized by general resourcefulness and flexibility that does not presuppose the experience of risk and adversity. In contrast, resilience describes a dynamic developmental process of adaptation in the context of adversity that is associated with both personal attributes and contextual influences (Luthar et al., 2000; Masten, 2001). To distinguish between the constructs of resilience and resiliency, proponents of the resilience paradigm recommend that researchers use the word *resiliency* to connote a personality trait and avoid using the word *resilient* to describe children and youth. Instead, the term *resilient adaptation* is preferred because it conveys the transactional, process-oriented meaning of the resilience construct (Luthar & Zelazo, 2003; Masten, 1994).

Another topic of frequent debate among researchers is how to measure resilience. Luthar and Cushing (1999) state that conceptualized as a process, resilience is never directly observed, it is inferred. The inference of resilience in a person's developmental trajectory requires the assessment of the dimensions that anchor the process: (a) risks or threats to development, (b) competence or positive adaptation, and (c) protective and vulnerability factors associated with the outcomes observed (Luthar & Cushing, 1999). Next, we present an overview of the definitions and measurements of these key constructs in resilience research.

Risk

The assessment of resilience in a person's developmental trajectory presupposes the presence of risks—stressful, disruptive, or challenging circumstances that threaten positive adaptation. Risk factors include both individual (e.g., perinatal stress, cognitive functioning) and family and environmental (e.g., violence, poverty, parental psychopathology) variables that are linked to subsequent negative outcomes (Kaplan, 1999; Masten, 1994). A life condition qualifies as an indicator of risk only if the incidence of problems is measurably higher in the identified at-risk group compared with the normative group (Luthar & Zelazo, 2003). Poverty and parental depression are examples of at-risk conditions. Compared with their more affluent peers, children raised in poverty are twice as likely to repeat a grade and 1.3 times as likely to exhibit parent-reported social, emotional, or behavioral problems (Brooks-Gunn & Duncan, 1997). Among children and adolescents of depressed parents, 20% to 26% are diagnosed with major depressive disorder compared with 10% among the offspring of nondepressed parents (Hammen, 2003). Risk is a statistical concept that is appropriately used to describe groups but not individuals; belonging to an at-risk group is associated with the probability, not the certainty, of negative outcomes (Masten, 1994).

The three strategies typically used to assess risk in resilience research include multiple-item measures of adverse negative life experiences, assessment of the presence or absence of specific stressors, and consideration of constellations of multiple risk factors. These approaches are briefly described here and interested readers are referred to Luthar and Cushing (1999) for detailed information and examples of specific assessment strategies within each approach.

The most frequently used multiple-item measures of risk are scales that list negative life events and ask respondents to select the events they have experienced within a specified amount of time (e.g., past year, in their lives). Items in these scales refer to both uncontrollable events (e.g., death of parent, community violence) and events that to some extent are under the control of the respondent (e.g., failing grades, divorce). The life events sampled in these scales may differ in the potential negative impact of each stressor and the extent to which the stressor is chronic or acute. Life event scales allow researchers to compare groups that differ in level of exposure to stressful experiences without having to recruit different high- versus low-risk groups.

The second strategy for assessing risk in resilience research is to identify individuals who have experienced an adverse or stressful life circumstance, which may include chronic or acute single stressors such as child abuse or neglect, parental psychopathology, divorce, chronic illnesses, or poverty. The third strategy involves summative scales that yield a global index of adversity. Summative scales may be calculated by adding the number of specific stressful conditions experienced by each individual. In the case of continuous measures of risk conditions, standardized scores on the various scales are added to yield a measure of overall risk. Like life event scales, summative scales include adverse conditions that vary in the degree of threat or risk they pose.

Researchers must consider several issues in the selection of type of risk assessment to use in resilience research. Multiple psychosocial stressors coexist in life (e.g., poverty, community violence); therefore, summated scales that assess constellations of risk factors have high face validity. Furthermore, because maladjustment is positively related to both the number and the intensity of risks experienced, composite risk scales generally explain more variance in relation to adaptive outcomes than measures of single risk factors. However, composite scales do not allow researchers to determine which risk conditions are more influential or to identify factors that may ameliorate the impact of specific risk conditions—information that is crucial in devising intervention efforts (Luthar & Cushing, 1999; Sameroff, Gutman, & Peck, 2003).

A conceptual dilemma in the assessment of risk in relation to resilience is that negative life events and global adverse conditions like poverty or parental mental illness often present distal risks that do not affect children and youth directly (Luthar et al., 2000). The effects of these global risks in children's development often are moderated by multiple proximal variables. Research findings suggest that parental supervision and warmth (proximal variable) moderate the relation of poverty and environmental stressors (more distal risks) to children's developmental outcomes (Masten & Coatsworth, 1998). The question then is, to what extent are all children exposed to distal adverse circumstances (e.g., poverty, parental mental illness) equally at risk? Do children who experience distal risks and exhibit positive outcomes really demonstrate resilient adaptation if, in fact, elements in their environment shielded them from exposure to the same level of proximal risks as their less successful counterparts? Some researchers contend that because of this dilemma the construct of resilience lacks validity. In response to this criticism, Luthar and Cushing (1999) note that because resilience is defined as an interaction of the person with the environment, identifying those protective factors among people facing life adversity is exactly what resilience research is about.

Competence

In addition to risk, the inference of resilience requires the observation of competence or positive developmental outcomes. Competence is defined both broadly, in terms of success with major developmental tasks across behavioral domains such as completing high school, and more narrowly, in terms of specific behaviors and psychological conditions such as absence of depression or prosocial conduct (Masten & Coatsworth, 1998; Werner & Smith, 2001). Because resilience is a multidimensional construct, to avoid a narrow or misleading view of success in the midst of adversity, competence should be assessed across different domains. However, Luthar and Zelazo (2003) caution that it is reasonable to expect that outcomes in unrelated domains will not always be consistent. Among inner-city adolescents, resilience as indicated by conventionally conforming behaviors, such as academic achievement and school attendance, may not be related (or may be negatively related) to resilience as indicated by peer acceptance, a task in the social domain.

There is debate in the literature about the selection of relevant competence domains, the relative importance of the identified domains, and the level of competence a person must reach to demonstrate resilient adaptation (Windle, 1999). Resilience researchers have recognized that the criteria used to identify relevant competence domains and to determine what is considered a desirable or undesirable outcome is influenced by the researcher's social class, racial, and cultural vantage points. Masten notes that competence should be defined "on the basis of an observable track record of meeting the major expectations of a given society or culture in historical context for the behavior of children of that age and situation" (Masten & Coatsworth, 1998, p. 206). Therefore, researchers should carefully consider social, cultural, and contextual issues in defining expected developmental tasks.

In addition, Luthar and colleagues recommend that competence dimensions should be theoretically linked to the specific type of risk examined (Luthar, 1991; Luthar et al., 2000; Luthar & Zelazo, 2003). Socially responsible behaviors may be a more appropriate marker of competence in studies that examine resilience among children at risk for conduct disorder (Seidman & Pedersen, 2003), whereas lack of internalizing symptoms may be a more appropriate outcome in studies that examine adaptation among children of clinically depressed parents (Hammen, 2003). Similarly, the level of competence expected to determine resilience should be linked to the severity of risks experienced. For individuals experiencing serious trauma, lack of psychopathology or average-level functioning should be enough to demonstrate resilience. However, when risks faced are moderate, superior competence may be required to demonstrate resilient adaptation (Luthar & Cushing, 1999; Luthar & Zelazo, 2003).

The most common approaches used by resilience researchers to assess competence include multiple-item scales of specific adjustment dimensions, summative measures of several adjustment dimensions, and diagnosis of the presence or absence of psychopathology. A brief description of these approaches to assess competence follows; interested readers may consult Luthar and Cushing (1999) for more extensive information and examples of specific assessment strategies within each approach.

As with measures of risk, multiple-item scales are frequently used to measure competence. These scales assess the continuum between adjustment and maladjustment in terms of specific behavioral indicators of emotional health (e.g., depressive symptoms, anxiety) and developmental tasks (e.g., conduct, peer socialization skills). The target individuals as well as persons in their environment (e.g., parents, teachers, peers, spouse) typically respond to items these in scales. Among children and adolescents, measures of academic success (e.g., grades, scores on standardized achievement tests, school attendance) also are used as indicators of competence. The second strategy used to assess competence involves aggregating scores from multiple-item scales that reflect adjustment in several spheres of life (e.g., education, family, peers, employment). Thus, these summative scales provide a comprehensive measure of competence. Sometimes researchers apply data reduction procedures to adjustment scores across informants and measures to identify composite competence dimensions (e.g., Luthar, 1991). The third assessment strategy, determining the absence or presence of psychopathology, is most often used as a measure of competence in studies that examine resilience among people at risk because of exposure to traumatic experiences (e.g., war, sexual abuse) or to parental mental illness. The information needed to arrive at a psychological diagnosis is typically collected via structured or semistructured interviews from the target individuals and from persons in their lives (Luthar & Cushing, 1999).

To determine positive adaptation with multiple-item or summative scales, researchers often compare at-risk individuals with each other, and those who show the highest levels of adjustment are deemed to demonstrate resilient adaptation. In a study with inner-city adolescents, positive adaptation was defined as scoring in the top 16% of the distribution within the study's sample in scales assessing either social competence or school grades (Luthar, 1991). A problem with this practice is that, without an outside reference group, it is difficult to determine to what extent at-risk individuals with the highest scores are truly competent or just the best performers among a poorly functioning group. Luthar and Cushing (1999) suggest that to compensate for the absence of comparison reference groups, researchers should provide descriptive profiles of competence levels among individuals demonstrating resilient and nonresilient adaptation.

Protective and Vulnerability Factors

As stated, the goal of resilience research is to identify the personal and environmental factors that facilitate adaptive outcomes among individuals who have experienced adversity. Therefore, the third critical component embedded in the construct of resilience includes protective and vulnerability factors (Kaplan, 1999; Luthar & Zelazo, 2003). Protective factors are assets or resources that ameliorate the effects of adversity in a person's development, whereas vulnerability factors refer to conditions that exacerbate those effects. Most protective and vulnerability factors reflect continuous bipolar dimensions that at one end of the continuum are associated with resilient adaptation and at the other end are associated with maladjustment. Intelligence is a case in point; high cognitive abilities typically predict academic achievement, whereas a low level of cognitive abilities is associated with academic difficulties (Masten, 2001). Factors that are only associated with either maladjustment or competence are rare. Child maltreatment is considered only a vulnerability index because its presence is associated with dysfunction, but its absence does not necessarily lead to excellence. Conversely, artistic talent may be considered a protective factor, but lack of it is not associated with dysfunction (Luthar, 2006).

A review of the resilience literature shows that similar factors (e.g., self-esteem, peer relations, conduct) are used as measures of competence in some studies and as protective factors in others (Fergus & Zimmerman, 2005; Luthar & Zelazo, 2003; Masten, 1994). Therefore, to assess vulnerability and protective factors researchers have used strategies like the ones described in the previous two sections to assess risk and competence, respectively. Luthar and Zelazo (2003) argue that the interchangeable use of constructs as outcomes or predictors does not reflect confusion in the resilience literature, but stems from what Masten has called "cascading" effects in development. Because of the reciprocal nature of human development, competences in behavioral domains are related to each other within and across developmental stages (Masten & Coatsworth, 1998). The use of a particular construct as a predictor or as an outcome of resilient adaptation will depend on the researchers' conceptual framework and the timing of the assessment. For example, in research with African American youth, an achieved racial identity may be construed as both a desirable outcome in adolescent development and as a predictor or as a moderator of later adjustment (e.g., racial identity may moderate the relation of racial discrimination to psychological distress; e.g., Caldwell, Zimmerman, Bernat, Sellers, & Notaro, 2002).

STRATEGIES IN RESILIENCE RESEARCH

Researchers have primarily used two strategies to examine resilience among children and youth. The first approach, labeled variable-focused, examines the associations between discrete risk, vulnerability, protective, and adjustment variables. The second strategy takes a holistic, person-focused approach that emphasizes the identification of assets and resources that differentiate groups of individuals who vary in risk and adjustment levels (Luthar & Cushing, 1999; Masten, 2001). Even though both approaches have been implemented in cross-sectional studies, longitudinal studies that examine the relation of risk and protective variables to changes in developmental outcomes over time have been of most interest to resilience researchers.

Variable-focused studies of resilience typically use multiple regression analyses or structural equation modeling to examine to what extent measures of adversity and of assets and resources predict a desirable outcome. These analyses have revealed both main and moderated effects of protective factors in relation to measures of adjustment (Fergus & Zimmerman, 2005; Luthar & Cushing, 1999; Luthar & Zelazo, 2003; Masten, 2001). Main effects refer to assets or resources that show independent, direct associations with a positive outcome in the presence of the risk factor. Moderated effects, on the other hand, refer to assets or resources that show statistically significant interaction effects with specific risk conditions in predicting positive adaptation.

In his seminal work, Rutter (1987) defined protective factors only as those that showed interactive effects with risk conditions. Partly because interaction effects tend to have small effect sizes and are difficult to detect in multivariate analyses, some researchers advocate the use of the term *protective* to refer to all variables that distinguish at-risk individuals who show resilient adaptation from their peers who show maladjustment (Luthar & Cushing, 1999; Masten, 2001). Other researchers refer to assets and resources that have a general positive association with desired outcomes in the presence of risk as *promotive or compensatory*; and consistent with Rutter's initial formulation, they limit the use of the term *protective* for variables that moderate the relation of adversity to developmental outcomes (e.g., Sameroff et al., 2003).

Findings from a longitudinal study with African American adolescents in a suburban setting that examined academic outcomes in the presence of multiple risks illustrate the difference between promotive and protective factors (Gutman, Sameroff, & Eccles, 2002; Sameroff et al., 2003). Parental school involvement emerged as a promotive factor because it was positively associated with school grades among all adolescents regardless of risk level; parents' presence seemed to promote achievement among low-risk children and compensate for the problems experienced by those facing more adversity. In contrast, peer support seemed to operate as a protective factor. Higher level of risk was associated with low math achievement only among adolescents experiencing low levels of peer support (but not among students showing high levels of peer support), which suggests that peer support in some way protected the most vulnerable students from the effects of the risk factors, facilitating their math achievement. Finally, consistent parental discipline had both promotive and protective qualities because it was positively associated with school attendance among all youth, but the association of risk level with problems in school attendance was weaker among adolescents who reported higher levels of consistent parental discipline (parental discipline showed both direct and moderated effects).

In the person-focused approach, rather than examining the association among discrete risk and protective variables, researchers compare groups of individuals who vary in constellations of risk and adjustment factors to identify the personal assets and environmental resources that differentiate members of well-adjusted groups from their less well-adjusted counterparts. This approach considers risk and protective factors as they naturally occur; both exposure to risks and positive adaptation are judged on multiple criteria simultaneously. Most of the person-focused studies of resilience have compared individuals from the same at-risk samples who have shown adaptive and maladaptive outcomes (e.g., Werner & Smith, 2001).

Werner and Smith (2001) utilized the person-focused strategy in their now classic study of children born in the island of Kauai. These researchers identified as at-risk children those who by 2 years of age had experienced at least four negative factors, including perinatal stress, poverty, and uneducated, alcoholic, or mentally ill parents. About one-third of the cohort met those criteria for being at risk. When these at-risk children were 10 and 18 years old, researchers identified those who showed successful adaptation in both academic and peer socialization tasks, and compared them with their less successful peers. Results indicated that children and adolescents who demonstrated resilient outcomes had received better parenting, had a more easygoing temperament, better cognitive test scores, and more positive self-perceptions than their at-risk peers with less successful outcomes. Collectively, these factors appeared to protect children from the negative consequences of the combined risk conditions to which they were exposed.

As might be expected, these two research strategies have advantages and disadvantages. Because in variable-focused studies protective and risk factors are measured quantitatively on an a priori basis, these studies maximize statistical power and allow for the identification of specific and differential effects of personal assets and environmental resources in mitigating the impact of risk conditions on developmental outcomes. In variable-focused studies, however, it is not always possible to know to what extent at-risk participants with the best outcomes truly show high enough levels of competence compared with their normative peers or to what extent the identified protective factors confer benefits to those showing the highest levels of risk (Luthar, 2006). In contrast, person-focused approaches allow for rich, textured descriptions of the characteristics and circumstances that distinguish at-risk individuals who show adaptive and maladaptive outcomes. However, person-focused studies do not allow for the examination of the effects of specific protective factors in relation to specific at-risk conditions because participants are classified as at-risk or not based on constellations of risk and protective factors (Luthar & Cushing, 1999; Masten, 2001).

Results of variable- and person-focused studies have converged on three sets of protective factors associated with resilient adaptation throughout the life span: individual characteristics of the child such as intelligence and temperament; material and emotional resources provided by the family; and support received from persons or institutions in the wider community (Luthar et al., 2000; Masten & Powell, 2003). In the next section, we discuss briefly major themes related to these protective factors that have emerged from the accumulated evidence of about 5 decades of resilience research with children and youth. We have extracted these themes from several comprehensive reviews of the resilience literature that have been published in the recent past (Fergus & Zimmerman, 2005; Glantz & Johnson, 1999; Luthar, 2006; Luthar & Cushing, 1999; Luthar & Zelazo, 2003; Masten, 2001, Masten & Powell, 2003; Rutter, 2000; Szalacha et al., 2003; Wang & Gordon, 1999; Werner & Smith, 2001).

THEMES IN RESILIENCE RESEARCH

Resilience researchers have examined vulnerability and protective processes among children and adolescents in the context of major threats to development, including parental psychopathology, poverty, divorce, child maltreatment, and community violence. Findings from these studies have shown that resilient adaptation is not a permanent outcome, but changes across developmental periods as new vulnerabilities and strengths emerge with changing circumstances. Similarly, adaptation is not always consistent across domains. Children may show positive adaptation in some behavioral domains, but not in others (e.g., social versus academic), and behaviorally stellar youth may experience high levels of psychological distress (Luthar & Zelazo, 2003). In view of such findings, researchers prefer to conceptualize resilience in relation to specific risks, such as poverty, parental mental illness, or racial discrimination (Cauce, Stewart, Rodriguez, Cochran, & Ginzler, 2003; Hammen, 2003; Szalacha et al., 2003), and specific adaptive outcomes, such as educational or emotional resilience (Wang & Gordon, 1999).

In her extensive review of the empirical literature published during the past 5 decades, Luthar (2006) concluded that "strong supportive relationships are critical for achieving and sustaining resilient adaptation" (p. 780). The evidence suggests that to overcome adversity, children and youth must experience positive relationships in at least one of the contexts in which they live: the immediate and extended family, the school, or the larger community. In the face of many adverse circumstances, adequate parenting (by parental figures or caretakers) that provides children and youth with warmth, support, limit-setting, and monitoring is one of the most robust processes associated with resilient adaptation across the life span. At the same time, maltreatment, in the form of physical, sexual, or emotional abuse, is one of the most deleterious risks faced by children and adolescents.

Good parenting is often compromised by adverse circumstances such as poverty and parental psychopathology (Luthar & Zelazo, 2003). However, in situations where parental systems are not optimal, community resources also seem to contribute to resilient adaptation. These resources include quality child-care programs, comprehensive family services, supportive relationships with peers and adults outside the family (including teachers among K-12 students), high levels of community cohesion, and participation in structured community activities (Luthar, 2006). In adulthood, intimate relationships like marriage also are associated with positive outcomes in the face of ongoing life challenges (Luthar, 2006; Werner & Smith, 2001).

In addition to quality relationships in the family and wider community, personal attributes contribute to resilient adaptation among at-risk children and youth (Luthar, 2006; Masten & Coatsworth, 1998; Werner & Smith, 2001). Even though good intellectual functioning, a sociable, easygoing temperament, and high levels of self-efficacy and self-esteem seem to make a difference in the lives of at-risk children, Luthar (2006) has argued that research and resilience-related interventions should emphasize family and community factors rather than the personal characteristics of children and adolescents, as is typically the case. She notes that from an applied perspective, it seems more reasonable to strengthen family and community resources and reduce environmental risks, than attempt to change young children's personal characteristics. Furthermore, studies have indicated that children's attributes such as intelligence and self-efficacy that are commonly identified in research studies as protective, are themselves shaped by environmental influences.

Studies with adoptees from Romanian orphanages (Rutter & Romanian Adoptees Study Team, 1998; as cited in Luthar, 2006) and with twins exposed to domestic violence (Koenen, Moffit, Caspi, Taylor, & Purcell, cited in Luthar, 2006) have shown that environmental risk factors negatively influence children's IQ levels. Similar evidence exists for the influence of proximal interpersonal relations in the development of other protective personal attributes including self-regulation, self-efficacy, and internal locus of control. Therefore, it is important not to overemphasize the exclusive effects of children's attributes on positive adaptation when such attributes are subject to influence by family and community factors (Luthar, 2006).

Longitudinal studies have indicated that even though childhood experiences are crucial for resilient adaptation across the life span, there are turning points that allow some adults to "bounce back" from the effects of early adverse circumstances (Laub & Sampson, 2003; Masten, 1994). Werner and Smith (2001) found that most of the problematic adolescents in their cohort of at-risk children (e.g., teen mothers, delinquent boys, and mentally ill adolescents) showed adaptive outcomes in relation to family, work, and society by the time they were in their 30s and 40s. Turning points for these adolescents included vocational skills acquired in the armed forces, marriage to a stable partner, and attainment of postsecondary education. Similarly, Laub and Sampson (2003) reported that marriage accounted for as much as 40% reduction in criminal activity involvement among delinquent adolescents who were followed through the adult years.

In variable-focused studies with children and adolescents, good intellectual functioning and relationships with caring, prosocial adults are the factors most widely and consistently associated with positive adaptation in both favorable and unfavorable circumstances (Masten & Coatsworth, 1998). Results from person-focused studies that have included low-risk participants indicate that at-risk children and youth who do well typically possess similar levels of psychosocial resources (e.g., IQ, parenting quality, and self-concept) as their competent low-risk counterparts. These findings have led Masten (2001) to conclude that the promotive factors identified in resilience studies are general correlates of competence and that resilience is the product "of ordinary adaptive resources and systems" (p. 234) located in the individual and in the family context. Therefore, she argues, intervention efforts to ameliorate the impact of adversity in children and youth should be geared to strengthen and develop these basic adaptive systems.

In contrast to Masten's (2001) optimistic view of resilience as "ordinary magic," several authors have pointed out the limits of the resilience model among youth facing very high levels of environmental risks (Cauce et al., 2003; Sameroff et al., 2003). In a review of findings from two longitudinal research projects, Sameroff et al. (2003) concluded that personal resources (including self-efficacy, IQ, academic achievement, and mental health) were not enough to help children and adolescents facing a high number of family and environmental risk conditions to beat the odds. Similarly, in other studies, personal, family, and community factors that were beneficial at moderate levels of risk exposure seemed to offer little protection to children and youth living in communities characterized by very high levels of poverty (more than 40% of residents are poor) or of violence (Cauce et al., 2003; Luthar & Goldstein, 2004).

These findings are sobering because they suggest that resilient adaptation is rare in environments that present exceedingly high levels of risk. As Cauce et al. (2003) cautioned, an exclusive focus on personal and family attributes may shift away needed attention from addressing the larger social issues that make it possible for children to grow up in toxic environments. Policy and community-level changes that reduce poverty and enhance community safety may be the only effective interventions to facilitate resilient adaptation among those facing the most severe levels of these at-risk conditions.

The literature shows that resilient adaptation is the product of a complex, interactive process that includes multiple environmental, psychological, and biological variables. Research related to risk and resilience for the most part has studied naturally occurring events. The knowledge gained from these studies needs to be tested in experimental studies that examine the effectiveness of interventions designed to reduce known risk factors and promote environmental conditions and personal skills that have shown protective effects among those at risk. Luthar (2006) recommends that in selecting variables for research and intervention purposes, researchers prioritize factors that show "high promotive potential" (p. 782). Such factors are salient in a particular risk setting and proximal to the person, are malleable to environmental interventions, exert their influence for long periods of time, and are likely to lead to the development of other assets. Parental skills is an example of a factor with high promotive potential. Adequate parenting is a proximal factor that tempers the negative association of economic stress to childhood problems (Werner & Smith, 2001), it can be fostered by environmental interventions, and it impacts children's development for several years and in more than one dimension (emotional, social, and cognitive).

In research and intervention efforts, it is important to consider the context because vulnerability and protective processes often are specific to certain groups and circumstances. For example, studies have shown that optimal levels of parental monitoring and autonomy-granting depend on the level of risk faced by youth. Stricter parental control is associated with better academic and prosocial outcomes among youth living in high-risk urban environments, whereas youth in lower-risk environments fare better with higher levels of autonomy (Luthar, 2006; Sameroff et al., 2003).

In the resilience literature, it is widely acknowledged that ethnicity and race are contextual factors that present unique challenges to members of ethnic and racial minority groups (Luthar, 2006). One of these challenges is racial discrimination. Researchers have begun to examine the risks associated with perceived racial discrimination and the extent to which racial identity mitigates the negative impact of perceived discrimination on the lives of racial minority youth (Szalacha et al., 2003). In the next section we provide a review of this emerging literature with African Americans, the group that has been studied most frequently.

RACIAL DISCRIMINATION AND RACIAL IDENTITY: RISK AND RESILIENCE

The social climate of the United States historically has been and continues to be plagued by racism. For the purposes of this chapter, we define racism as a system whose function is aimed at maintaining a racial hierarchy in which Whites represent the dominant group and members of racial/ethnic minorities represent subordinate groups. This institutional racism manifests itself through racial discrimination, which refers to actions of the majority group that result in negative treatment of, or unequal resource distribution for, the racial minority group (Harrell, 2000). A consistent finding across studies is that the majority of African American adults, regardless of gender and social class, experience discrimination in their daily lives that leads to harmful psychological and physical effects (Kessler, Mickelson, & Williams, 1999; Klonoff, Landrine, & Ulman, 1999; Landrine & Klonoff, 1996; Utsey, Ponterotto, Reynolds, & Cancelli, 2000). In addition, when compared with other racial/ethnic minorities, African Americans report experiencing more stress related to racism than all other groups (Landrine, Klonoff, Corral, Fernandez, & Roesch, 2006; Utsey, Chae, Brown, & Kelley, 2002).

Perceived Racial Discrimination of African American Youth

Recent studies have revealed that perceived racial discrimination operates as a risk factor in adolescent development. The majority of African American children and adolescents surveyed, regardless of gender and socioeconomic class, report considerable numbers of racial hassles in their daily lives, which put them at risk for negative developmental outcomes (Brody et al., 2006; Caldwell, Kohn-Wood, Schmeelk-Cone, Chavous, & Zimmerman, 2004; Gibbons, Gerrard, Cleveland, Wills, & Brody, 2004; Sellers, Caldwell, Schmeelk-Cone, & Zimmerman, 2003; Sellers, Copeland-Linder, Martin, & Lewis, 2006; Simons et al., 2002). In a study with relatively affluent African American families, 50% to 70% of the adolescents (ages 11 to 17) reported having experienced each of the eight racial hassles surveyed, which included both overt (e.g., being insulted or called names) and covert (e.g., being ignored or treated suspiciously) discriminatory occurrences (Sellers et al., 2006). Similarly, preadolescents (ages 10 to 12) from less affluent families indicated that they had been insulted (67%), called racial slurs (46%), excluded from activities (47%), and threatened with physical harm (18%) because they were African American (Simons et al., 2002). In these two cross-sectional studies, results of regression analyses showed that, after controlling for demographic variables and ethnic/racial identity, the association of perceived racial discrimination to adolescents' depression and general stress was statistically significant (R^2 ranging from .10 to .19).

The adolescents in the Simons et al. (2002) study were the first-wave participants in the longitudinal Family Community Health Study (FACHS) that targeted African American families in rural, suburban, and metropolitan communities. Two follow-up studies with the FACHS youth cohort demonstrated long-term negative effects of discrimination in relation to depression, anxiety, substance use, and conduct problems (Brody et al., 2006; Gibbons et al., 2004). Results of structural equations modeling tests (Gibbons et al., 2004) indicated that perceptions of discrimination at Wave 1 (ages 10 to 12) predicted changes in the adolescents' level of psychological distress (anxiety and depression) over a 2-year period. In turn, distress mediated the relation of discrimination to substance use. Using latent growth curve modeling to examine within-person changes, Brody et al. (2006) demonstrated that in the span of 5 years, an increase in these youths' perceived discrimination was associated with increases in both conduct problems and depressive symptoms at each of the three times of measurement (ages 10 to 12, 12 to 14, and 15 to 17). These relations persisted even when three well-known protective factors in resilience research (nurturing-involved parenting, prosocial friends, and academic self-efficacy) were statistically controlled.

In correlational studies, it is difficult to determine to what extent the associations of perceived racial discrimination to negative outcomes such as depression are due primarily to method variance. It is possible that youth with problem behaviors or psychological distress are prone to perceive neutral or ambiguous situations as discriminatory. However, results of a cross-lagged analysis in the FACHS study showed that for both children and their parents, the relation of discrimination to psychological distress was not reciprocal. Perceived racial discrimination at time one predicted psychological distress 2 years later, but psychological distress at time one was not associated with subsequent perceived discrimination (Gibbons et al., 2004). Prospective studies with African American college students (Sellers & Shelton, 2003) and adults (Brown et al., 2000) have reported similar nonreciprocal relations of discrimination to psychological distress within the span of a year.

Racial Identity as a Protective Factor

Racial identity theories that describe the attitudes and beliefs African Americans hold about race have provided a framework for examining Blacks' understanding of themselves in the context of a racist society (Helms & Parham, 1996; Sellers, Smith, Shelton, Rowley, & Chavous, 1998). Researchers have hypothesized that feelings of attachment and positive identification with one's race are likely to counter the negative messages embedded in racial discrimination, reducing its negative impact on mental health outcomes. Sellers and colleagues' Multidimensional Model of Racial Identity (MMRI) captures the content of racial identity in terms of the significance and meaning that Black individuals attribute to race at a specific point in time. The four dimensions of the MMRI, operationalized through the Multidimensional Inventory of Black Identity (MIBI), include racial centrality, racial salience, racial ideology, and racial regard in both the public and private arenas (Sellers et al., 1998). Researchers have examined to what extent three of these dimensions—racial centrality (the degree to which race is a central component of an individual's identity), public regard (beliefs about how others feel about Blacks), and private regard (how the individual feels about being Black)—operate as compensatory and protective factors for African American youth in the face of racial discrimination (Caldwell et al., 2004; Sellers et al., 2003, 2006).

Two studies with African American young adults (ages 18 to 20) who had participated in a 6-year longitudinal study conducted in an urban setting, demonstrated the protective nature of racial centrality and public regard (Caldwell et al., 2004; Sellers et al., 2003). Consistent with the resilience model, these researchers first demonstrated that among these young adults racial discrimination predicted increases over time in psychological distress (anxiety and depression) and in self-reported involvement in violent behaviors (while controlling for school grades and violent behaviors in the ninth grade). The combined direct and indirect effect (mediated through general stress) of discrimination explained 29% of the variance in changes in psychological distress (Sellers et al., 2003). Results of interaction analyses showed that racial centrality and public regard moderated the relation of perceived discrimination to changes in psychological distress (Sellers et al., 2003) and involvement in violent behaviors (Caldwell et al., 2004). Having race as a central aspect of identity was protective because greater levels of perceived discrimination were associated with distress only for youth for whom race was a less central identity. Similarly, young men who believed that others have a negative view of Blacks (low racial public regard) were less likely to report involvement in violent behaviors compared with their peers who held more positive beliefs. Results of both studies also indicated that higher levels of racial centrality and lower levels of public regard predicted higher levels of subsequent perceived discrimination (Caldwell et al., 2004; Sellers et al., 2003).

In a cross-sectional study that included the three racial identity dimensions, Sellers et al. (2006) also found that low public regard (believing that others have a negative view of Blacks) was a protective factor in the relation of perceived discrimination to stress and depressive symptoms among a younger group of African American youth (11 to 17 years old). Private regard was associated with lower levels of stress and depression regardless of level of perceived discrimination, indicating that feeling good about being Black was a promotive (but not a protective) factor for positive mental health outcomes. Ethnic identity (a construct that overlaps with racial centrality and private regard; Phinney, 1992) also emerged as a protective factor among African American junior high school students in a relatively affluent and racially integrated suburban setting. A strong sense of ethnic identity tempered the negative association of school-based discrimination to changes in academic self-competence beliefs, school achievement, and involvement in problem behaviors, as students progressed from the beginning of seventh grade to the end of eighth grade (Eccles, Wong, & Peck, 2006; Wong, Eccles, & Sameroff, 2003).

The studies previously described provide evidence that perceived racial discrimination constitutes a risk factor that challenges the healthy development of African American children and adolescents in urban, suburban, and metropolitan contexts. Because of the prospective nature of many of the studies and the sophistication of the data-analytic procedures used, collectively these findings are consistent with a directional interpretation (although they do not unequivocally prove causality) of the relation of racial discrimination to psychological outcomes among African American youth. Findings showing that stress partially mediated the relation of perceived discrimination to psychological distress (Sellers et al., 2003) and of perceived discrimination to substance use (Gibbons et al., 2004) suggest that stress is one of the paths by which racial discrimination exerts a deleterious effect on adolescents' development.

Consistent with the resilience framework, findings also support the hypothesis that dimensions of racial identity counter the negative consequences of perceived racial discrimination on mental health outcomes. Paradoxically, youth with higher levels of racial centrality and lower levels of public regard appeared more sensitive to perceived racial discrimination, but at the same time seemed to suffer less from it. Taken together these findings suggest that awareness of racial discrimination may facilitate development of a more varied and sophisticated repertoire of coping skills to deal with discriminatory experiences (Caldwell et al., 2004; Sellers et al., 2003). Furthermore, for adolescents who endorse low levels of racial public regard, experiencing discrimination is probably expected because it is consistent with their racial worldview. In contrast, for those with a more idealistic view of racial relations, the incongruence between their beliefs and the experience of discrimination may lead to intrapsychic conflict, as predicted by cognitive dissonance theory (Aronson, 1997). The findings that among African American youth both racial centrality and racial private regard were associated with positive outcomes in the presence of racial discrimination, suggests that feeling good about and being connected to their racial heritage may prevent the internalization of negative messages embedded in racial discriminatory experiences, thus protecting the youth from discrimination's negative effects.

Research and Practice Implications

The existing literature has documented that racial discrimination is a pervasive experience that has deleterious mental health consequences in the lives of African American youth. Therefore, researchers should continue to explore factors that mitigate the negative impact of personal experiences of discrimination on developmental outcomes. In future studies, it may be instructive to assess racial identity from a developmental perspective to complement existing research that has focused on the significance and meaning that African Americans attribute to being Black at one point in time (Sellers et al., 1998).

Helms' and Parham's (1996) Racial Identity Attitudes Scale (RIAS-B) measures attitudes associated with four racial identity statuses (Pre-Encounter, Encounter, Immersion-Emersion, and Internalization) that capture the person's movement from an unhealthy perspective of devaluing their Blackness to an internalized, healthy Black racial identity that values their racial group membership. Even though researchers have noted some psychometric problems with the RIAS-B (Fischer & Moradi, 2001), Helms' model provides a developmental rather than a static view of racial identity.

Following the recent work of Seaton, Scottham, and Sellers (2006), researchers may also apply Phinney's (1992) ethnic identity model to examine the process of racial identity development among Black adolescents. Consistent with ego identity models, Phinney articulated four identity statuses (diffusion, foreclosure, moratorium, and achievement) characterized by levels of identity exploration and commitment, through which individuals progress toward a psychologically healthy resolution of ethnic identity issues. Seaton et al. (2006) successfully modified Phinney's (1992) Multigroup Measure of Ethnic Identity (MEIM) to assess these statuses in the progression toward developing a racial rather than an ethnic identity among Black adolescents. Using either the Helms or the Seaton et al.'s model to assess racial identity as a process will allow researchers to examine to what extent developmental changes in racial identity buffer the documented negative impact that perceived discrimination has on developmental trajectories.

The four studies reviewed in this section used the variable-focused approach to examine the association of perceived racial discrimination and racial identity to specific mental health outcomes (e.g., depressive and anxiety symptoms, substance use, academic motivation) utilizing regression models and multiitem scales to assess the constructs of interest. This methodology has allowed researchers to identify specific dimensions of racial identity that compensate for and buffer against the negative consequences of racial discrimination. However, the findings of these studies do not indicate to what extent statistically significant differences in mental health and behavioral outcomes between adolescents who differed in racial identity were clinically significant. Furthermore, it is impossible to know to what extent racial identity would confer similar benefits in relation to perceived discrimination for adolescents showing high levels of other risk circumstances such as poverty or parental mental illness. In the future, person-focused studies that compare at-risk youth experiencing clinically significant positive versus negative outcomes and that consider constellations of risk and protective factors could provide more nuanced information about the circumstances in which racial identity confers protection against racial discrimination.

The study of factors associated with resilient adaptation in the face of discrimination is relatively recent; therefore, the possibilities for further research are numerous. To mention just a few, future research can examine the pathways by which racial identity relates to mental health, the factors that predict racial identity development among youth, and other factors that may moderate the relation of perceived discrimination to mental health outcomes. In terms of pathways, Sellers et al. (2003) found that higher levels of racial centrality were associated with lower levels of general stress which, in turn, predicted lower distress. Cognitive appraisals of discriminatory experiences and racial coping may also mediate the relationship of racial identity to mental health in the presence of discrimination (Scott, 2003). Bandura's (1982) concept of collective self-efficacy, which refers to people's beliefs regarding to what extent the actions of their social group may lead to desired goals, may be useful in explaining how sociopolitical forces such as discrimination become internalized (Lent & Hackett, 1987). Future research may explore to what extent higher levels of collective self-efficacy among African Americans buffer the negative impact of perceived discrimination in mental health outcomes.

From an intervention perspective, it will be instructive to examine predictors of racial identity development such as racial socialization, which refers to the extent to which parents communicate with their children about their cultural/racial background and the existence of racial discrimination (McHale et al., 2006). Recent studies have indicated that racial socialization (Fischer & Shaw, 1999) as well as nurturing-involved parenting and prosocial friends (Brody et al., 2006) also moderate the relation of perceived discrimination to mental health among African American youth. As suggested by these studies, involved parents are likely to include racial issues in their socialization practices which, in turn, may lead to a secure racial identity and preparedness to deal with racial discrimination among their offspring—factors that seem to reduce the negative impact of racial discrimination on psychological and behavioral outcomes.

In terms of clinical practice, research findings suggest that interventions that serve to increase African American youths' racial centrality and private regard and develop realistic expectations about discrimination may be particularly effective in helping youth cope with the stress of racial discrimination. Moreover, the reality of racism and experience of racial discrimination is a pervasive and long-standing problem for African Americans. To that end, interventions aimed at buffering against discrimination's negative consequences are likely to be effective for promoting resilience. Rites of passage programs that emphasize a strong, positive connection to one's racial group have been shown to increase African American youths' self-esteem (Harvey & Hill, 2004) and academic motivation (Bass & Coleman, 1997). In addition, psychoeducational programs that inform African American youth about healthy, adaptive coping skills may reduce the negative outcomes of perceived racial discrimination (e.g., anxiety, depression, violence).

Luthar (2006) has suggested that resilience interventions include parental and community factors. Therefore, interventions aimed at promoting racial socialization through parents or nonparental adults in the community may prove to be effective. To the extent that racial socialization provides cultural knowledge and preparation for bias, this process may simultaneously increase race centrality in African American youth and convey realistic expectations about racism (low public regard attitudes).

CONCLUSION

Resilience research has identified a core of individual characteristics and support systems in the family and community that are associated with positive developmental outcomes in the midst of adversity. However, not much is known about how environmental factors interact with children's and adolescents' personality attributes in fostering resilience. Also, experimental work is needed to examine to what extent resilience, as a protective process, can be enhanced through education, prevention, and counseling interventions (Rolf & Johnson, 1999). Werner and Smith (2001) reported that the majority of the at-risk children and youth who as adults demonstrated resilient adaptation credited their families, teachers, and other adults in their informal community networks for their success, whereas more organized forms of help (e.g., community organizers, mental health professionals, social workers) were not mentioned as often. Therefore, they suggested that intervention programs should emphasize strengthening the already existing informal ties that at-risk children and adolescents have to individuals in their families and communities. From a policy perspective, the resilience framework emphasizes primary prevention to reduce or eliminate risk conditions and promote positive capabilities and supports rather than interventions to ameliorate youth problems.

REFERENCES

Anthony, E. J. (1974). The syndrome of the psychologically invulnerable child. In E. J. Anthony & C. Koupernik (Eds.), *The child and his family: Children at psychiatric risk* (Vol. 3, pp. 99–121). New York: Wiley.

Aronson, E. (1997). The theory of cognitive dissonance: The evolution and vicissitudes of an idea. In C. McGarty & S. A. Haslam (Eds.), *The message of social psychology: Perspectives on mind and society* (pp. 20–35). Oxford: Blackwell.

Bandura, A. (1982). Self-efficacy mechanisms in human agency. *American Psychologist, 37*, 122–147.

Bass, C. K., & Coleman, H. L. K. (1997). Enhancing the cultural identity of early adolescent male African Americans. *Professional School Counseling, 1*, 48–51.

Block, J. H., & Block, J. (1980). The role of ego-control and ego resiliency in the organization of behavior. In W. A. Collins (Ed.), *Minnesota Symposium on Child Psychology* (Vol. 13, pp. 39–101). Hillsdale, NJ: Erlbaum.

Brody, G. H., Cgen, Y., Murry, V. M., Ge, X., Simmons, R., Gibbons, F. X., et al. (2006). Perceived discrimination and the adjustment of African American youths: A 5-year longitudinal analysis with contextual moderation effects. *Child Development, 77*, 1170–1189.

Brooks-Gunn, J., & Duncan, G. J. (1997). The effects of poverty on children. *Future of Children, 7*, 55–71.

Brown, T. N., Williams, D. R., Jackson, J. S., Neighnors, H. W., Torres, M., Sellers, S. L., et al. (2000). "Being Black and feeling blue": The mental health consequences of racial discrimination. *Race and Society, 2*, 117–131.

Caldwell, C. H., Kohn-Wood, L. P., Schmeelk-Cone, K. H., Chavous, T. M., & Zimmerman, M. A. (2004). Racial discrimination and racial identity as risk or protective factors for violent behaviors in African American young adults. *American Journal of Community Psychology, 33*, 91–105.

Caldwell, C, H., Zimmerman, M. A., Bernat, D. H., Sellers, R. A., & Notaro, P. C. (2002). Racial identity, maternal support, and psychological distress among African American adolescents. *Child Development, 73*, 1322–1336.

Carter, R. T. (2007). Racism and psychological and emotional injury: Recognizing and assessing race-based traumatic stress. *Counseling Psychologist, 35*, 12–105.

Cauce, A. M., Stewart, A., Rodriguez, M. D., Cochran, B., & Ginzler, J. (2003). Overcoming the odds? Adolescent development in the context of urban poverty. In S. Luthar (Ed.), *Resilience and vulnerability: Adaptation in the context of childhood adversities* (pp. 343–363). Cambridge: Cambridge University Press.

Eccles, J. S., Wong, C., & Peck, S. C. (2006). Ethnicity as a social context for the development of African-American adolescents. *Journal of School Psychology, 44*, 407–426.

Fergus, S., & Zimmerman, M. A. (2005). Adolescent resilience: A framework for understanding healthy development in the face of risk. *Annual Review of Public Health, 26*, 399–419.

Fischer, A. R., & Moradi, B. (2001). Racial and ethnic identity: Recent developments and needed directions. In J. G. Ponterotto, J. M. Casas, L. A. Suzuki, & C. M. Alexander (Eds.), *Handbook of multicultural counseling* (2nd ed., pp. 341–370). Thousand Oaks, CA: Sage.

Fischer, A. R., & Shaw, C. M. (1999). African American's mental health and perceptions of racist discrimination: The moderating effects of racial socialization experiences and self-esteem. *Journal of Counseling Psychology, 46*, 395–407.

Garmezy, N., & Tellegen, A. (1984). Studies of stress-resistant children: Methods, variables, and preliminary findings. In F. Morrison, C. Lord, & D. Keating (Eds.), *Advances in applied developmental psychology* (Vol. 1, pp. 231–237). New York: Academic Press.

Gelso, C., & Fretz, B. (2001). *Counseling psychology* (2nd ed.). Fort Worth, TX: Harcourt Brace.

Gibbons, F. X., Gerrard, M., Cleveland, M. J., Wills, T. A., & Brody, G. (2004). Perceived discrimination and substance use in African American parents and their children: A panel study. *Journal of Personality and Social Psychology, 86*, 517–529.

Glantz, M. D., & Johnson, J. L. (1999). *Resilience and development: Positive life adaptations*. New York: Kluwer Academic/Plenum Press.

Gutman, L. M., Sameroff, A. J., & Eccles, J. S. (2002). The academic achievement of African-American students during early adolescence: An examination of multiple risk, promotive, and protective factors. *American Journal of Community Psychology, 30*, 367–399.

Hammen, C. (2003). Risk and protective factors for children of depressed parents. In S. L. Luthar (Ed.), *Resilience and vulnerability: Adaptation in the context of childhood adversities* (pp. 50–75). New York: Cambridge University Press.

Harrell, S. (2000). A multidimensional conceptualization of racism-related stress: Implications of the well being of people of color. *American Journal of Orthopsychiatry, 70*, 42–57.

Harvey, A. R., & Hill, R. B. (2004). Africentric youth and family rites of passage program: Promoting resilience among at-risk African American youths. *Social Work, 49*, 65–74.

Helms, J. E., & Parham, T. A. (1996). The Racial Identity Attitudes Scale. In R. L. Jones (Ed.), *Handbook of tests and measurements for Black populations* (Vol. 1, pp. 167–174). Hampton, VA: Cobb & Henry.

Kaplan, H. (1999). Toward an understanding of resilience: A critical review of definitions and models. In M. D. Glantz & J. L. Johnson (Eds.), *Resilience and development: Positive life adaptations* (pp. 17–84). New York: Kluwer Academic/Plenum Press.

Kessler, R. C., Mickelson, K. D., & Williams, D. R. (1999). The prevalence, distribution, and mental health correlates of perceived discrimination in the United States. *Journal of Health and Social Behavior, 40*, 208–230.

Klonoff, E. A., Landrine, H., & Ulman, J. D. (1999). Racial discrimination and psychiatric symptoms among Blacks. *Cultural Diversity and Ethnic Minority Psychology, 5*, 329–339.

Kumpfer, L. K. (1999). Factors and processes contributing to resilience: The resilience framework. In M. D. Glantz & J. L. Johnson (Eds.), *Resilience and development: Positive life adaptations* (pp. 179–224). New York: Kluwer Academic/Plenum Press.

Landrine, H., & Klonoff, E. A. (1996). The schedule of racist events: A measure of racial discrimination and a study of its negative physical and mental health consequences. *Journal of Black Psychology, 22*, 144–168.

Landrine, H., Klonoff, E. A., Corral, I., Fernandez, S., & Roesch, S. (2006). Conceptualizing and measuring ethnic discrimination in health research. *Journal of Behavioral Medicine, 29*, 79–94.

Laub, J. J., & Sapmson, R. J. (2003). *Shared beginnings, divergent lives: Delinquent boys to age 70.* Cambridge, MA: Harvard University Press.

Lent, R. W. (2004). Toward a unifying theoretical and practical perspective on well-being and psychosocial adjustment. *Journal of Counseling Psychology, 51*, 482–509.

Lent, R. W., & Hackett, G. (1987). Career self-efficacy: Empirical status and future directions [Monograph]. *Journal of Vocational Behavior, 30*, 347–382.

Luthar, S. S. (1991). Vulnerability and resilience: A study of high-risk adolescents. *Child Development, 62*, 600–616.

Luthar, S. S. (2006). Resilience in development: A synthesis of research across five decades. In D. Cicchetti & D. J. Cohen (Eds.), *Developmental psychopathology: Vol. 3. Risk, disorder, and adaptation* (2nd ed., pp. 739–795). Hoboken, NJ: Wiley.

Luthar, S. S., Cicchetti, D., & Becker, B. (2000). The construct of resilience: A critical evaluation and guidelines for future work. *Child Development, 71*, 543–562.

Luthar, S. S., & Cushing, G. (1999). Measurement issues in the empirical study of resilience: An overview. In M. D. Glantz & J. L. Johnson (Eds.), *Resilience and development: Positive life adaptations* (pp. 129–159). New York: Kluwer Academic/Plenum Press.

Luthar, S. S., & Goldstein, A. (2004). Children's exposure to community violence: Implications for understanding risk and resilience. *Journal of Clinical Child and Adolescent Psychology, 33*, 499–505.

Luthar, S. S., & Zelazo, L. B. (2003). Research on resilience: An integrative review. In S. L. Luthar (Ed.), *Resilience and vulnerability: Adaptation in the context of childhood adversities* (pp. 510–549). New York: Cambridge University Press.

Masten, A. S. (1994). Resilience in individual development: Successful adaptation despite risk and adversity. In M. C. Wang & E. W. Gordon (Eds.), *Educational resilience in inner city America: Challenges and prospects* (pp. 3–25). Hillsdale, NJ: Erlbaum.

Masten, A. S. (2001). Ordinary magic: Resilience processes in development. *American Psychologist, 56*, 227–238.

Masten, A. S., & Coatsworth, J. D. (1998). The development of competence in favourable and unfavorable environments. *American Psychologist, 53*, 205–220.

Masten, A. S., & Powell, J. L. (2003). A resilience framework for research, policy and practice. In S. Luthar (Ed.), *Resilience and vulnerability: Adaptation in the context of childhood adversities* (pp. 1–25). Cambridge: Cambridge University Press.

McHale, S. M., Crouter, A. C., Kim, J., Burton, L. M., Davis, K. D., Dotterer, A. M. et al. (2006). Mothers' and fathers' racial socialization in African American families: Implications for youth. *Child Development, 77*, 1387–1402.

Phinney, J. S. (1992). The Multigroup Ethnic Identity Measure: A new scale for use with diverse groups. *Journal of Adolescent Research, 7*(2), 156–176.

Rigsby, L. C. (1994). The Americanization of resilience: Deconstructing research practice. In M. C. Wang & E. W. Gordon (Eds.), *Educational resilience in inner city America: Challenges and prospects* (pp. 85–94). Hillsdale, NJ: Erlbaum.

Rolf, J. E., & Johnson, J. L. (1999). Opening doors to resilience interventions for prevention research. In M. D. Glantz & J. L. Johnson (Eds.), *Resilience and development: Positive life adaptations* (pp. 229–249). New York: Kluwer Academic/Plenum Press.

Rutter, M. (1987). Psychosocial resilience and protective mechanisms. *American Journal of Orthopsychiatry, 57*, 316–331.

Rutter, M. (2000). Resilience reconsidered: Conceptual considerations, empirical findings, and policy implications. In J. P. Shonkoff & S. J. Meisels (Eds.), *Handbook of early childhood interventions* (2nd ed., pp. 651–682). New York: Cambridge University Press.

Sameroff, A., Gutman, A. L., & Peck, S. C. (2003). Adaptation among youth facing multiple risks: Findings form a prospective study. In S. L. Luthar (Ed.), *Resilience and vulnerability: Adaptation in the context of childhood adversities* (pp. 364–391). New York: Cambridge University Press.

Scott, L. D. (2003). The relation of racial identity and racial socialization to coping with discrimination among African American adolescents. *Journal of Black Studies, 33*, 520–538.

Seaton, E. K., Scottham, K. M., & Sellers, R. M. (2006). The status model of racial development in African American adolescents: Evidence of structure, trajectories, and well-being. *Child Development, 77*, 1416–1426.

Seidman, E., & Pedersen, S. (2003). Holistic contextual perspectives on risk, protection, and competence among low-income urban adolescents. In M. D. Glantz & J. L. Johnson (Eds.), *Resilience and development: Positive life adaptations* (pp. 319–342). New York: Kluwer Academic/Plenum Press.

Seligman, M. E. P., & Csikszentmihalyi, M. (2000). Positive psychology: An introduction. *American Psychologist, 55*, 5–14.

Sellers, R. M., Caldwell, C. H., Schmeelk-Cone, K. H., & Zimmerman, M. A. (2003). Racial identity, racial discrimination, perceived stress, and psychological distress among African American young adults. *Journal of Health and Social Behavior, 43*, 302–317.

Sellers, R. M., Copeland-Linder, N., Martin, P. P., & Lewis, R. L. (2006). Racial identity matters: The relationship between racial discrimination and psychological functioning in African American adolescents. *Journal of Research on Adolescents, 16*, 187–216.

Sellers, R. M., & Shelton, J. N. (2003). The role of racial identity in perceived racial discrimination. *Journal of Personality and Social Psychology, 84*, 1079–1092.

Sellers, R. M., Smith, M. A., Shelton, J. N., Rowley, S. A. J., & Chavous, T. M. (1998). Multidimensional model of racial identity: A reconceptualization of African American racial identity. *Personality and Social Psychology Review 2*, 18–39. New York: Kluwer Academic/Plenum Press.

Simons, R. L., Murry, V., McLoyd, V., Lin, K., Cutrona, C., & Conger, R. (2002). Discrimination, crime, ethnic identity, and parenting correlates of depressive symptoms among African Americans: A multilevel analyses. *Development and Psychopathology, 14*, 371–393.

Smith, E. J. (2006). The strength-based counseling model. *Counseling Psychologist, 34*, 13–79.

Szalacha, L. A., Erkut, S., García-Coll, C., Fields, J. P., Alarcón, O., & Ceder, I. (2003). Perceived discrimination and resilience. In S. Luthar (Ed.), *Resilience and vulnerability: Adaptation in the context of childhood adversities* (pp. 414–435). Cambridge: Cambridge University Press.

Tolan, P. T. (1966). How resilient is the concept of resilience? *Community Psychologist, 29*, 12–15.

Utsey, S. O., Chae, M. H., Brown, C. F., & Kelley, D. (2002). Effect of ethnic group membership on ethnic identity, race-related stress, and quality of life. *Cultural Diversity and Ethnic Minority Psychology, 8*, 366–377.

Utsey, S. O., Ponterotto, J. G., Reynolds, A. L., & Cancelli, A. A. (2000). Racial discrimination, coping, life satisfaction, and self-esteem among African Americans. *Journal of Counseling and Development, 78*, 72–80.

Wang, M. C., & Gordon, E. W. (1999). *Educational resilience in inner city America: Challenges and prospects.* Hillsdale, NJ: Erlbaum.

Werner, E. E., & Smith, R. S. (2001). *Journeys from childhood to midlife: Risk, resilience and recovery.* New York: Cornell University Press.

Windle, M. (1999). Critical conceptual and measurement issues in the study of resilience. In M. D. Glantz & J. L. Johnson (Eds.), *Resilience and development: Positive life adaptations* (pp. 161–176). New York: Kluwer Academic/Plenum Press.

Wong, C. A., Eccles, J. S., & Sameroff, A. (2003). The influence of ethnic discrimination and ethnic identification on African American adolescents' school and socioemotional adjustment. *Journal of Personality, 71*, 1197–1232.

CHAPTER 29

Promoting Positive Development and Competency across the Life Span

STEVEN J. DANISH
TANYA FORNERIS

No mass disease or disorder afflicting humankind has ever been eliminated or brought under control by attempts at treating the affected individual. (Gordon, quoted by Albee in Kelly, 2003)

It is this perspective that guides our thinking in this chapter and it is in stark contrast to the way our society, in general, and counseling psychology, in particular, has tended to act. We are a society that likes to focus on fixing problems first, especially in times of emergencies. Such an orientation, while especially attractive to the media and individuals, is antithetical to enhancing development, or for that matter, prevention. The following fable illustrates this approach.

A woman is sitting on a riverbank enjoying a sunny day. All of a sudden she sees a child floating down the river struggling to stay afloat. Immediately she jumps into the water, pulls the child out, and performs mouth-to-mouth resuscitation. Just as the child is beginning to breathe normally, there is more yelling from the river. She turns around to see another child floating down the river in a similar state. Again she jumps into the river, pulls the child out, and performs mouth-to-mouth resuscitation. As the child regains her breathing, the woman is again startled by the screaming behind her. A third child is floating down the river.

This situation is repeated several more times. Each time the woman rescues a child she becomes more tired and frustrated. She wonders why children are falling into the water but is in a quandary. If she tries to go upstream to find out why the children are falling in and to try to prevent it from happening, she will be unable to help the children who are already in the river and floating downstream. However, if she does not go up stream, eventually she will be so tired and fatigued she will be unable to continue to pull children out. She feels helpless. What should she do? Should she direct her energies at the children in present need or at the community of children at large? If she chooses the latter, how should she intervene? Should she try to put up a temporary barrier to prevent children from falling in or teach the children how to swim and how to make effective decisions about what is appropriate risk taking?

This fable highlights two important issues: How prevalent are our concerns with fixing immediate problems, and if we decide to intervene at a community level, should we choose a prevention approach (e.g., keeping children from falling in by changing the environment to accommodate for a lack of competence) or a positive development approach (e.g., teaching competencies to the children that have utility in the present as well as in the future; Danish, Taylor, & Fazio, 2003)?

In this chapter, we explore positive developmental approaches to promoting human development. Although such approaches may ultimately lead to important preventive outcomes (e.g., reducing the incidences of depression or smoking and suicide rates in communities), they are distinguished from preventive interventions in that their primary goals are to enhance growth and promote positive outcomes rather than to facilitate adjustment and forestall the occurrence of negative outcomes. We approach this topic by addressing several important issues involved in developing and evaluating such interventions, including: (a) discussing appropriate participants for positive developmental interventions; (b) noting important competencies that might be promoted, (c) outlining the process for knowing when to intervene; (d) describing the rationale and methodology of the Life Development Intervention (LDI) approach to promoting positive development through the teaching of critical life skills; (e) highlighting the central role of dreams and goals in teaching life skills; (f) describing some well-researched and new LDI-based intervention programs; and (g) discussing issues related to program evaluation that need to be considered when designing and implementing programs.

APPROPRIATE PARTICIPANTS FOR LDI INTERVENTIONS

The Institute of Medicine (IOM; Mrazek & Haggerty, 1994) expanded on a prevention framework developed by Gordon (1987) that was based on a risk-benefit point of view (the risk of getting a disease must be weighed against the cost, risk, and discomfort of the intervention). The framework consists of three categories of interventions: universal, selective, and indicated.

Universal preventive interventions are ones that are desirable for everybody in an eligible population. In this category are all programs that can be advocated confidently for the general public and for all members of specific eligible groups, such as pregnant women, children, or the elderly. In many cases, universal preventive measures can be applied without professional advice or assistance because the benefits outweigh the cost and risk for everyone.

Selective preventive interventions are targeted to individuals or subgroups of a population whose risk of developing a disorder is above average. The subgroups may be distinguished by age, gender, occupation, family history, or other evident characteristics. Because of the increased risk of illness, the balance of benefits against risk and cost must be assessed.

Indicated preventive interventions apply to persons who are at high risk for developing the disorder in the future, especially if they show early symptoms of the disorder. The identification of persons for whom indicated preventive measures are advisable is the objective of screening programs. Indicated preventive measures are usually not totally benign to the subject nor are they minimal in cost.

Although the IOM considered promotion in a separate category, we feel this framework is applicable for both prevention and promotion interventions. In this chapter, we focus on universal interventions designed to promote positive outcomes by teaching life skills to members of eligible communities, regardless of the risk status of any individual participant. Universal interventions have advantages when the cost per individual is low, when the intervention is effective and acceptable to the population, and when it is considered to be low risk. Universal interventions also fit well with counseling psychology's emphasis on recognizing and promoting strengths in all individuals (Fretz, 1982; Watkins, 1983). As counseling psychologists, we have adopted a perspective that emphasizes positive development because we seek to promote and enhance the competencies of those with whom we work. Interventions that adopt a prevention orientation focus on the elimination of various behaviors, which the authors find limiting. We do not assess people in terms of problems or lack of problems, but in terms of their potential. Being problem-free is not the same as being competent or successful. Therefore, an important focus for interventions should be on defining and teaching individuals the skills, values, attitudes, and knowledge necessary to succeed in life (Danish, Forneris, & Wallace, 2005).

WHAT ARE IMPORTANT LIFE COMPETENCIES?

Many organizations have sought to define the competencies related to "positive youth development." In a series of reports, the Carnegie Council on Adolescent Development identified desired adolescent development outcomes. In 1989, the Council identified five desired outcomes: (1) to know how to process information from multiple sources and communicate clearly; (2) to be en route to a lifetime of meaningful work by learning how to learn and therefore to adapt to different educational and working environments; (3) to be a good citizen by participating in community activities and feeling concern for, and connection to, the well-being of others; (4) to be a caring and ethical individual by acting on one's convictions about right and wrong; and (5) to be a healthy person. In 1995, the Council identified other competencies associated with personal and social development. They include (a) finding a valued place in a constructive group; (b) learning how to form close and lasting relationships; (c) feeling a sense of worth; (d) achieving a reliable basis for informed decision making, especially on matters of large consequence; (e) being able to use available support systems; (f) having a positive future orientation; (g) learning respect (Carnegie Council, 1989, 1995). Although developed for youth, these competences seem as appropriate for adults as for adolescents.

A more parsimonious list of the competencies needed to be successful in life would be the ability to *work well, play well, love well, think well, serve well,* and *be well* (Bloom, 2000; Danish, 2000). This shortened list of competences serves as the basis for our intervention goals. Before describing our framework for promoting positive development and competency, it is helpful to consider how we decided which framework to use.

A PERSPECTIVE FOR CONSIDERING WHETHER AND HOW TO INTERVENE

When we help, we all want to make a difference. What are our motivations for wanting to do this; are they strictly professional or are there personal reasons as well? We can never be totally objective. Our own needs, feelings, values, experiences, and expectations affect the helping process. When asked why we help, we often give reasons, but rarely examine our *needs* or *motivations*. Whatever the motivation to help—and there are programs that can help us identify our needs and motivations (e.g., Danish, D'Augelli, & Hauer, 1980)—the goals we have for helping or making a difference should be the same as the goals of those who are seeking our help. When our goals are the same, we are working *with* the target group on making a difference rather than doing something *to* or *for* the group. We must also decide (a) whom we hope to help and (b) the level at which our intervention is targeted: the individual, family, group, institution, community, or society. Our own efforts have generally focused on promoting individual development, and the targets of our intervention have been the group, institution, or the community.

At this point, we must decide what kind of difference we want to make. In describing the difference between painting and sculpture, Leonardo da Vinci noted that in painting something is added, whereas in sculpture something is taken away. This distinction seems to parallel the difference between promotion and prevention. If we wish to promote development (painting), we should make sure we understand the dreams and goals of the individuals. If our focus is prevention (sculpting), such as reducing school truancy, it is important to keep in mind Ryan's (1971) concept of "blaming the victim." Ryan noted that when we assume that problems ranging from homelessness to educational failure are caused by deficits in the individual, we ignore the effect that the society and institutions within the society play in causing these problems. There are multiple levels or possible targets for interventions and when determining the type of intervention it is also important to determine at what level (e.g., individual, family, community, societal) we want to intervene.

Once we decide to make a difference, we must consider which framework to use to guide the intervention. Deciding on an intervention framework, however, does not necessarily determine how or where to intervene (individual, family, community, society). The following section describes the Life Development Intervention (LDI) approach used by the authors to implement programs designed to enhance development.

LIFE DEVELOPMENT INTERVENTION (LDI): A FRAMEWORK FOR ENHANCING DEVELOPMENT

Having an intervention framework is critical because it describes how to approach the task of enhancing development. Too often, we confuse strategies and frameworks. The LDI framework represents counseling psychology's unique and traditional approach and differentiates us from other psychological disciplines and helping professions. One of the main reasons LDI fits counseling psychology traditions is that it emphasizes making self-directed changes, being goal-directed, and focusing on the future, with an understanding of what needs to be done in the present to reach the best possible future.

Life development intervention (LDI) is based on a life span human development perspective (Danish & D'Augelli, 1983). The emphasis of the life development intervention is continuous growth and change, and since change is sequential, it is necessary to consider any stage of life within the context of what has happened in the past and what may happen in the future. The goal of LDI is to help develop capacity and competence in life planning that enables individuals to encounter and successfully manage both routine and unexpected life events (Danish, Kleiber, & Hall, 1987; Danish, Petitpas, & Hale, 1993). Although life events are often considered as discrete, they are really processes that commence prior to the event and continue well after the event. Life events, then, have histories, beginning from the time we anticipate them, through their occurrence, and lasting until the event's aftermath has been determined and assessed (Danish, Smyer, & Nowak, 1980).

Because change disrupts our routines and relationships with others and may result in stress, most of us try to avoid change. We like continuity and do not want to confront life decisions. The unexpected death of an individual will be a critical life event for one's spouse, children, circle of friends, the institution employing the individual, and depending on the roles the person played, the community and society. For this reason changes resulting from unexpected life situations have been called *critical life events*. Some have referred to these events as *crises*. Despite how we commonly interpret the meaning of the word "crisis," it is not synonymous with disaster. The origin of the word is Greek and it means *decision*. As defined by the Random House *Dictionary of the English Language,* crisis is "a stage in a sequence of events at which the trend of all future events, especially for better or for worse, is determined; turning point." We experience many critical life events throughout our lives. These events may result in stress and impaired functioning, little or no change in life circumstances, or may serve as a catalyst for growth.

Individuals' reactions to a critical life event depend on the resources they have prior to the event, the level of preparation for the event, and the past history in dealing with similar events. During the past decade, researchers have even examined the possibility of personal growth after trauma. In discussing the reaction to loss, Schaefer and Moos (2001) contend that personal growth after loss is possible and involves more than just adapting to a new lifestyle and experiencing less depression, anxiety, distress, and grief. Rather, it involves the enhancement of social resources, coping skills, and personal resources. Tedeschi, Park, and Calhoun (1998) examined a similar construct that they called "posttraumatic growth." From their perspective, posttraumatic growth is both a process and an outcome following a struggle with a traumatic event that may result in new strengths not evident before the event. These strengths may include enhanced relationships, a stronger sense of community, a gain in mastery, self-confidence, and self-efficacy, a willingness to strive and persevere for further successes, and an acquisition of an expanded philosophy of life with new directions and new priorities. What seems clear is that personal life circumstances may help individuals develop a meaning for their lives, a sense of coherence, and purpose. This meaning may result in the pursuit and attainment of worthwhile goals and an accompanying sense of fulfillment (Reker, 2000). Research conducted by Folkman and Moskowitz (2000) identified one form of coping as infusing ordinary events with positive meaning by taking ordinary daily life events and incorporating meaning into those events even during a stressful life circumstance or event.

Life Development Intervention is more than a conceptual framework for understanding the process of growth; it also represents a relatively unique intervention process. The intervention methodology, called a psychoeducational approach, adopts a skill-based teaching format to promote positive development. In discussing the psychoeducational model, Ivey (1980) distinguished between an illness or medical model (illness → diagnosis → prescription → therapy → cure) and a psychoeducational model (client dissatisfaction or ambition → goal setting → skill teaching → satisfaction or goal achievement) (p. 13).

Programs that focus on enhancing or promoting development can teach knowledge, skills, attitudes, and values. Although providing information is easy, it does not predictably produce the desired result. At best, information may augment other efforts because it describes *what* to do, but not *how* to do it. Moreover, it is reported that we remember only about 10% of what we are told, so information dissemination may be minimally effective (Chi, Bassok, Lewis, Reimann, & Glaser, 1989).

At the other extreme, teaching attitudes and values is hardest to do. Such qualities cannot be taught through lectures or by reading books about virtue, although these methods are often tried. Learning values is most likely to occur when an individual is continuously exposed to and taught these qualities by parents and other adults of social influence such as teachers, religious and community leaders during childhood and early adolescence, and peers during later adolescence. A better alternative is to teach skills. Skills can include the lessons of *how to* succeed in life, especially when combined with information about why such skills are important and when the use of the skills is reinforced in multiple settings (Danish, 2000).

The specific goal of LDI is to increase the likelihood of success by enhancing personal competence through the teaching of *life skills*. These are the skills that enable individuals to succeed in the different environments in which they live, such as school, home, and their neighborhoods. Life skills can be behavioral (communicating effectively), cognitive (making effective decisions), interpersonal (being assertive), or intrapersonal (setting goals).

The World Health Organization (1996) defines life skills as the abilities for adaptive and positive behavior that enable individuals to deal effectively with the demands and challenges of everyday life. Other researchers use different terms for achieving similar results such as social-emotional learning (Collaborative for Academic, Social, and Emotional Learning [CASEL], 2004), emotional intelligence (Goleman, 1995), positive psychology (Seligman & Csikszentmihalyi, 2000), resilience (Garmezy, 1991), and character education (Lickona, 1991). We chose the term life skills to emphasize that we teach skills. Additionally, we try to teach these skills in such a way that they are transferable across life domains.

The word *skills* emphasizes that learning life skills parallels the learning of any skill, whether it is throwing a ball, driving a car, or baking a cake. Learning a new skill entails explicitly describing, demonstrating, and practicing each component of the skill until it can be used consistently. For optimal learning, seven steps should take place:

1. The skill to be learned must be identified and defined.
2. The purpose or rationale for learning the skill must be described. Learning proceeds better when we know *why* it is important to learn something in addition to *what* is to be learned.
3. A level of skill attainment expected must be delineated. We must know what we are striving to achieve.
4. Demonstrations, examples, or models of the skill must be provided. It is useful to both *see* and *hear* the skill. Examples of good skill usage (high skill level) and poor skill usage (low skill level) should be provided to help learn the skill. Knowing what *not to do* is often helpful in learning what *to do*. When providing high and low skill level models, the differences should be clarified to the learner ahead of time.
5. Practice of the skill and feedback about the quality of the practice is necessary. A fact can be known immediately, but a skill calls for considerable practice. Practicing the skill correctly is the

most important part for effective learning. Practicing outside the training session, especially in the setting where the skill is to be used as well as during the training session, makes skill learning easier.

6. An assessment of whether the skill has been learned to the expected attainment level is necessary. We must have a way of judging how well we have learned the skill so that additional training can take place, if needed.

7. Opportunities for continuing practice and additional training should be provided (Danish & Hale, 1983; Weinberg & Gould, 2006, Chapter 11).

A key first step in teaching life skills is to assess what life skills are necessary to teach. Because environments vary from individual to individual, what is needed to succeed will differ across these individuals, as well as across environments. Individuals in the same environment are likely to be dissimilar from each other as a result of the life skills they have already mastered, their other resources, and their opportunities, real or perceived. For this reason, the needed life skills are likely to be different for individuals of different ages, ethnic and racial groups, or economic statuses. While it is necessary to be sensitive to these differences, it is also important to recognize that there is a core set of life skills that all individuals need to know and that they can effectively apply these skills learned in one environment to other environments as appropriate (Danish, 1997).

Gass (1985) identified strategies involved in implementation that can enhance the transfer of skills. These include designing conditions that enhance transfer of the skill at the beginning of the activity, creating similarities between the environment of the activity and the environment where the transfer is to occur, providing opportunities to practice transferring the skill during the activity, providing opportunities to reflect on the experiences, involving peers who have successfully completed the activity, and providing follow-up experiences to reinforce learning.

THE IMPORTANCE OF THE FUTURE: IMAGINING DREAMS AND SETTING GOALS

We view individuals as self-directing, proactive agents who are capable of shaping rather than solely responding to their environments. The capacity to be self-directing rests on the ability to conceptualize future potentialities and to bring them meaningfully into the present (Ford, 1987).

Previous researchers have found a relationship between problem behavior and aspects of future thinking. In a longitudinal study with adolescents, Newcomb, Bentler, and Collins (1986) found that dissatisfaction about perceived future opportunities and the "chances to be what you want" predicted increased alcohol use from adolescence to adulthood. For urban, low-income people of color, data from national surveys indicate that the future is characterized by such adversities as failure to graduate from high school, unemployment, and trouble with the law (U.S. Census Bureau, 2003). Transcending these conditions requires not "blaming the victim," but instead imagining future possibilities, finding positive role models, and being self-directed (Ford, 1987).

It has been suggested that individuals who are oriented toward goals that are highly valued by society, such as having a professional career, will be less involved in problem behavior and have higher school achievement (Nurmi, 1987). These goals may represent a commitment to conventional lines of action and a belief in the legitimacy of conventional society. On the one hand, individuals with positive expectations for their personal future may be at lower risk for developing problem behaviors and achieving poorly in school because they view participation in conventional society as having long-range rewards. As such, problem behavior may be seen as future-compromising and therefore as less attractive. On the other hand, individuals with negative future expectations subjectively have no future to ruin (Newcomb & Bentler, 1988).

Life success, then, seems to be tied to believing in a positive future and being goal directed. Many individuals do not know how to dream about their futures. They talk in generalities about what might be, but fail to identify their dreams. For this reason, we begin our life skills programs by teaching how to dream about the future, not any future, but *the best possible future*. Recently, we asked a group of 4-year-olds about their dreams for the future. The group mentioned wanting to be a princess, a train engineer, a builder, a fireman, a doctor, a cheerleader, a fish, a basketball coach, an artist, a ballerina, and a pirate. Where do these dreams go as the children become older?

Dreams are the outcomes or results we hope to have happen ("what we want"). Goals are actions that are totally under our control ("what we will do to get what we want"). We define a goal as a dream that one works hard to reach. Goals then are actions undertaken to reach some desired end, *not* the end itself. Goals are different from results.

In addition to having control over goals, three other elements are crucial for effective goal setting: (1) setting goals that the individual is motivated to attain; (2) making sure that the goal is stated in positive terms; and (3) having a goal that is specifically defined. Having individuals set goals for themselves is critical. If the goal is more important to others than it is to the individual, it is unlikely it will be achieved. When others set goals for individuals that they feel should or ought to be accomplished, there is generally a lower level of commitment to attain these goals compared with goals that the individual wants to attain. Therefore, to increase the likelihood that energy will be invested in goal attainment, it is important to ascertain whether the goal is a "should" or "want"; and if possible, change "should" goals to "want" goals (Bandura, 2004).

When goals are not positively stated, the focus is on the negative, and considerable energy is wasted trying *not* to do something. Setting a negative goal or having a negative image almost always produces a negative result. Goal statements or images that include words like "not," "avoid," "less than," and "limit" should be changed into positive statements so the image of the goal is something to be achieved and worked toward. Having a positive goal means identifying an action that must be done to reach the goal.

The goal should also be behaviorally stated or defined clearly. Goals that include vague statements such as "do better" or "improve" do not allow the individual the satisfaction of knowing whether the goal has been attained. When the individual cannot identify whether the goal has been reached, frustration and loss of motivation usually result, often leading to quitting. A rule of thumb when developing behaviorally stated goals is to answer the questions: How many times, when, and under what conditions will the action occur?

Setting a goal is one thing; reaching or attaining the goal is another. There are roadblocks to reaching goals regardless of the type. Most often when a goal is not attained, the individual is blamed for a lack of motivation. However, when individuals have determined that the goal is important to them, motivation is not the roadblock to goal attainment. Danish and D'Augelli (1983) have identified four major roadblocks: lack of knowledge, lack of skill, inability or fear to do appropriate risk taking, and lack of adequate social support.

A lack of knowledge means that the individual is missing some information necessary for goal attainment. It may be related to not knowing certain rules or what procedures to follow. By a lack of skills, we are referring to life skills such as not knowing how to relax, talk positively to oneself, concentrate, or be assertive. When individuals lack social support, they need to know what support they need, who can provide them the support (and who cannot), and how to ask for the support. There are two types of support; *tangible* support, such as advice or help, and *emotional* support, such as listening.

The final roadblock relates to risk taking. Many individuals live their lives in a comfort zone because they are afraid of failing. They believe it is better not to try to extend themselves to reach a goal than to try and fail. Risks are defined as the perceived benefits of an action minus the perceived costs. If the perceived costs outweigh the perceived benefits, individuals may abandon the goal; if the perceived benefits outweigh the perceived costs, individuals may choose to work toward the goal. To optimize risk taking, the benefits of an action must be increased and the costs decreased.

As part of the intervention, the roadblock(s) must be removed so that the individual may work toward the goal. Removing the roadblock(s) may become a goal in itself. Many LDI interventions involve learning to set goals, identifying and overcoming roadblocks, and reaching one's goals by developing new skills, acquiring new knowledge, learning to take risks, and developing effective social support systems.

As discussed, teaching life skills is an avenue through which we can help individuals and communities develop the personal competence that will enable them to engage in life planning and successfully manage various life events. The following is a description of different life skills programs based on the LDI framework that focus on positive growth and development. Life skills programming can lead to positive youth development, enhanced physical and psychological well-being, and enhanced sport experience and performance.

LIFE SKILLS PROGRAMS BASED ON THE LDI MODEL

Going for the Goal (GOAL)

Danish's (2002a) GOAL program focuses on teaching adolescents a sense of personal control and confidence about their future so that they can make better decisions and ultimately become better citizens. Consistent with a promotion perspective, this program is based on the belief that to be successful in life it is not enough to know what to avoid; one must also know how to succeed. For this reason, the focus is on teaching "what to say yes to" as opposed to "just say no."

GOAL is a 10-session, 10-hour program taught by well-trained high school students to middle school students, either during school or after school. Consistent with the life developmental intervention framework, this program is designed to teach youth life skills. The life skills taught in GOAL are how to (a) identify positive life goals, (b) focus on the process (not the outcome) of attaining these goals, (c) use a general problem-solving model, (d) identify health-compromising behaviors that can impede goal attainment, (e) identify health-promoting behaviors that can facilitate goal attainment, (f) seek and create social support, and (g) transfer these skills from one domain to another.

To learn these skills, 10 one-hour skill-based workshops are taught. After the first workshop, each subsequent session begins with a review of what has been taught in the previous workshop, followed by a brief skit introducing the material. Skits feature *Goal Seeker, Goal Buster, Goal Keeper,* and *Goal Shooter*. The participants assume the roles of the characters during the skits. The skits tell a story of a young person who has a dream to become a computer programmer. In each workshop, this protagonist faces some sort of obstacle to goal attainment; by using the skill taught in the workshop that day, goal attainment becomes more certain. The storyline of the skits, therefore, serves as a metaphor for how to transfer educational material to real-life situations. Following the skits, the skills are taught and practiced.

In the first workshop, *Dare to Dream,* the program and the leaders are introduced. Participants discuss the importance of dreams and learn to dream about their future. There are two major activities in this workshop: (1) participants are taken on a trip to their future and asked to identify their dreams and then write a brief story or draw a picture that depicts this future; and (2) they are asked to identify goal keepers in their lives, someone who serves as a role model to them, and goal busters, someone who tries to impede them from a positive future.

In the second workshop, *Setting Goals,* participants are taught that a goal is a dream they work hard to reach. They learn the value of goal setting and the importance of setting reachable goals. As noted, the four characteristics of a reachable goal are that it is stated positively, is specific, is important to the goal setter, and is under the goal setter's control. The major activity of this workshop is to learn how to distinguish goals that are reachable (have the essential four characteristics) from those that are not.

In the third workshop, *Making Your Goal Reachable,* participants apply what they learned in the second workshop. They are asked to write a reachable goal to be attained within the next month or two and to make sure that it meets the characteristics of a reachable goal. The participants discuss and evaluate in small groups each characteristic individually as it pertains to their goal statement and receive feedback from the leader and fellow participants on whether the goal is stated correctly. By the end of the session, participants develop a goal statement that meets the criteria and that they work with for the rest of the program.

In the fourth workshop, *Making a Goal Ladder,* participants learn how to make a plan to reach their goal. Participants put their goal at the top of the goal ladder, identify the steps (all of which must meet the characteristics of a reachable goal), and then place them in the order needed to reach the goal at the top of the ladder. Finally, they identify target dates by which each step or rung will be completed and sign a statement making a commitment to work hard to reach the goal.

In the fifth workshop, *Roadblocks to Reaching Goals,* participants learn how various roadblocks such as drug abuse, teen pregnancy, violence, dropping out of school, or lack of self-confidence can prevent them from reaching their goals in life. They read brief stories of others who encounter roadblocks, write stories about what happens to the characters in these stories, and identify some of their own possible roadblocks to their current goals.

In the sixth workshop, *Overcoming Roadblocks,* participants learn a problem-solving strategy called STAR (**s**top and take a deep breath, **t**hink of all your choices, **a**nticipate the consequences of each choice, and **r**espond with the best choice). They practice using STAR in simulated situations that they may encounter at school, after school, or at home.

In the seventh workshop, *Seeking Help from Others,* participants learn the importance of seeking social support to achieve goals. Two types of help, "doing" help and "caring" help, are described. Their activities include engaging in a game that requires helping each other, identifying a "dream team" of 10 individuals (family members, very close friends, good friends, and older friends and role models) who can help them reach their goals, and practicing how to ask for help in several simulated situations.

In the eighth workshop, *Rebounds and Rewards,* participants learn how to rebound when a goal or a step on the goal ladder becomes too difficult to reach. They are asked to respond to simulated letters that depict individuals who have not reached their goals and to suggest strategies to help them be successful. Participants also identify a rebound plan for themselves if they are having trouble reaching their goal. Finally, they are asked to share their accomplishments to date with the rest of the group and describe how they plan to reward themselves for these accomplishments.

In the ninth workshop, *Identifying and Building on Your Strengths,* participants identify their personal strengths, including those learned through the program, and delineate how they can develop these strengths. They then are asked to identify an area in which they want to improve and list ways they can undertake this improvement. In addition to ways they list, several additional steps based on other workshops in GOAL are suggested. This process is designed to help them transfer skills they have learned from one life domain to another.

In the tenth and final workshop, *Going for Your Goal,* participants play a game, "Know-It-All-Baseball," that provides an opportunity for them to integrate and apply the information covered in the nine other workshops (Danish, 1997).

There are several unique aspects in the design of GOAL. First, the focus is on skill learning because skills are concrete, easily taught and learned, and when directed toward areas of our everyday lives, empower us. Second, the teachers of GOAL are high school student leaders chosen by their schools for their academic performance, leadership qualities, and extracurricular involvement. They receive special training in how to teach the program. Following the training, the student leaders teach the skills during middle/junior high school (usually as part of the health curriculum) or in after-school programs. The ratio is approximately two to three high school student leaders to 15 middle/junior high school students. Successful high school students serve as concrete images of what early adolescents can become. Because these high school students have grown up in the same neighborhoods, attended the same schools, and confronted similar roadblocks, they can serve as important role models and thus are in an ideal position to be effective teachers (Danish, 1997).

Evaluations of GOAL indicated that participants learned the information the program taught, could achieve the goals they set, found the process easier than they expected, thought they had learned quite a bit about how to set goals, and thought the program was fun, useful, important, and something that would be helpful for their friends. They also had better school attendance (compared with a control group). In addition, boys did not report the same increase in health-compromising behaviors including getting drunk, smoking cigarettes, drinking beer, and drinking liquor as was found in the control group boys; they also reported a decrease in violent and other problem behaviors compared with control group boys who reported an increase in these behaviors (Danish, 1997).

Two subsequent studies of GOAL were conducted by O'Hearn and Gatz (1999, 2002). Both studies were conducted in multiethnic communities on the West Coast. The study design included an experimental group and wait-list control condition. The results showed that students gained in knowledge about the skills being taught, could attain the goals they set, and improved their problem-solving (means-end thinking) skills. In the first study, the results indicated that 79% of the students reached their goal, while 21% did not reach their goal. The second study, found that 56% of participants who stated appropriate goals reached their goal.

Hodge, Cresswell, Sherburn, and Dugdale (1999) also evaluated the effectiveness of the GOAL Program in changing intrinsic motivation for schoolwork and self-esteem for a group of New Zealand adolescents. The GOAL program was successful in developing self-esteem and intrinsic motivation for schoolwork among a group of at-risk 12-year-old children. There was a significant increase in both global and academic self-esteem for the GOAL group, but no change for the control group. In addition, there was a significantly greater increase in intrinsic motivation for both enjoyment and effort in schoolwork in the GOAL group versus the control group.

Sports United to Promote Education and Recreation (SUPER)

SUPER (Danish, 2002b) is a sports-based program that takes advantage of the clearly defined, contingency-dependent, closed environment of sport and uses it as a training ground for life. It consists of a series of 18 modules based on GOAL; 10 of the modules are the core modules of GOAL and focus on goal setting, problem solving, overcoming roadblocks, and seeking social support. The remaining 8 modules are designed as independent workshops whereby the school or community receiving the intervention plays a role in deciding which workshops they believe will be most beneficial to the target population.

The SUPER program is developed to be taught like sports clinics for middle school and high school students either during or after school. College student athletes are often the primary instructors. Participants are involved in three sets of activities: learning the physical skills related to a specific sport, learning life skills related to sports and life, and playing the sport. Participants are taught to recognize situations both in and out of sports requiring these skills, and then to apply them in sport and nonsport settings. The goals of the SUPER program are for each participant to leave the program with the understanding that (a) physical and mental skills are important for both sport and life, (b) it is important to set and attain goals in sport and in life, and (c) roadblocks to goals can be overcome.

SUPER has been implemented in many environments. In the United States, it has served as the basis of a summer camp conducted in conjunction with a national golf organization; it has also been conducted at neighborhood community centers and as part of university community service learning courses. A number of studies have been conducted to examine the effects of SUPER. Results from one evaluation of using SUPER showed that the program had a significant positive impact on adolescents' prosocial values and that, combined with a community service experience, positively affected adolescents' level of empathic concern and social responsibility compared with a control group. Results also showed moderate-to-large effect sizes for goal knowledge ($d = .34$), empathic concern ($d = .64$), and social responsibility ($d = .85$), suggesting that the average participant in SUPER gained an almost full standard deviation ($d = .85$) in social responsibility compared with the average control group participant (Brunelle, Danish, & Forneris, 2007).

Papacharisis, Goudas, Danish, and Theodorakis (2005) applied an abbreviated (eight-session) version of the SUPER program to soccer and volleyball with Greek schoolchildren, aged 10 to 12. Two pretest, posttest comparison group design evaluations were conducted. The first study involved 40 female volleyball players on two teams; the second study involved 32 male soccer players on two teams. In each study, in addition to practice time, one team received the intervention and the other team did not. In both studies, measures included assessments of physical skills, knowledge of the SUPER program, and self-beliefs about ability to set goals, problem-solve, and think positively. The results of both studies indicated that students who received the intervention indicated higher self-beliefs for personal goal setting ($ds = .66$ to 2.21), problem solving ($ds = .88$ to 2.08), and positive thinking ($ds = .70$ to 2.51) than did those on the control teams. In addition, the intervention group demonstrated an increase in program knowledge and improvement in physical skills compared with the control condition.

The *Hokowhitu Program* was a SUPER-based intervention program designed by New Zealand MÇori for their own community (Heke, 2001). The program used MÇori language and culture in program development, implementation, and evaluation. This approach was known as "Kaupapa MÇori Research" and appropriated MÇori-preferred learning and investigation styles. The aim of the Hokowhitu Program was to integrate both the life skills and *Kaupapa MÇori* ideologies so that a sport-based, life skills intervention could be developed that would prove effective with adolescent MÇori.

The Hokowhitu program involved 10, two-hour workshops taught by eight *TuÇkana*—16- to 18-year-old senior high school students— to 25 *Teina*, year 7 and year 8 junior students (Teina) aged between 10 and 13 years. There was no control group. The Hokowhitu program also recruited "Lifeskill coaches," or *Kaiwhakawaiwai,* who were employed by the Raukawa Trust Board (RTB) to train the *TuÇkana* in communication, group management, and the teaching skills necessary for running the Hokowhitu program.

The Hokowhitu program was evaluated using primarily qualitative methods. At the program's completion, a review by the Educational Review Office (Ministry of Education of New Zealand) was conducted at the intermediate school. They concluded:

> A selected group of students has benefited from involvement in an iwi-driven pilot program, Raukawa Hokowhitu. The *Tuakana-Teina* model of a group of trained Year 13 students mentoring Year Seven and Eight students has used the medium of sport to deliver an active preventative life skills program. The success of this program is largely due to using the preferred learning styles and protocols of Maori, delivered by Maori for Maori. Student self-esteem, attitude and focus have increased markedly and greater confidence is shown in planning for future career choices. It is hoped that the program becomes part of the national Health and Physical Education school curriculum. (Heke, 2001, p. 197)

Results also indicated that, at completion of the Hokowhitu program, there were improvements in coping with negative pressure, developing positive attitudes about future outcomes and learning to cope with peer pressure (Danish, Forneris, Hodge, & Heke, 2004; Heke, 2001).

Goals for Health (GFH)

This program, adapted from GOAL, is designed to enhance health and prevent cancer by teaching youth how to set and achieve health and life goals (GFH; Danish et al., 1999–2003). Youth learn about health behaviors and engage in some of these behaviors, such as eating healthy snacks. *Goals for Health* was a school-based randomized trial. Twenty-three schools in rural Virginia (16) and New York (8) received the intervention. Schools were randomly assigned to wait-list control or intervention groups in the state. Sixth graders ($n = 2,120$) received 12 classroom sessions taught by well-trained high school students that integrated health promotion and cancer prevention to achieve both short- and long-term goals in life. A short booster program was taught by teachers during the seventh grade.

Several evaluation strategies were used to investigate the impact of the intervention. The GFH intervention was implemented over a 2-year period for sixth graders and seventh graders. Evaluation by student surveys was conducted prior to (T1; $n = 2,120$) and immediately following (T2; $n = 1,830$) intervention, 1 year later (T3; $n = 1,410$), and 2 years later (T4; $n = 999$). Primary results included significant change patterns across the four assessment points (pre, post, 1-year, and 2-year follow-up) in the predicted direction for fat and fiber knowledge and diet-related self-efficacy. Effect sizes were small and ranged from .04 to .07. At the 2-year follow-up, measures decreased to baseline. No significant results were found at follow-up for fat, fiber, fruit, or vegetable food frequency (intake) scores.

A Bridge to Better Health (BRIDGE)

BRIDGE is a genealogy and health program that also uses the skills of goal setting to help youth increase health-enhancing behaviors (Danish, Fries, Westerberg, & Hoy, 2003–2005). The program is designed to teach participants to become their family's health historian as a means of sensitizing them to their own health risks, particularly breast and testicular cancer. The program is based on the belief that knowing one's family health history can influence participants' health behavior and become an empowering life skill.

The BRIDGE program has been implemented in seven schools in Virginia as part of the ongoing health curriculum. Preliminary results show that the BRIDGE program significantly influenced knowledge related to cancer, heart disease, genealogy, and family health history. There is also preliminary evidence suggesting increases in self-efficacy to engage in health-enhancing behaviors, behavioral intentions, competence, and the ability to correctly perform breast, testicular, and skin self-screening behaviors.

FREE 4 VETS

This is a new program directed at returning veterans who have served in Iraq or Afghanistan. To date, over 600,000 men and women have been deployed in either Operations Enduring Freedom (OEF) or Iraqi Freedom (OIF). Despite the best of intentions, the Veterans Administration (VA) cannot meet the needs of the large influx of veterans. It has been reported that 20% to 25% of those who have served in these recent conflicts return with posttraumatic stress disorder or some other form of psychopathology (Hoge et al., 2004). Caring for these returning veterans has stretched the VA to the limit. The VA is so focused on dealing with immediate needs that it is unable to do planning. A recent Government Accountability Office (GAO) report noted that $100 million meant for a mental health plan was not spent in 2005 and about a fifth of the $200 million allocated for 2006 to implement a mental health plan had not been spent by the end of September.

Additionally, in discussions with returning soldiers and VA staff, there seems to be a universal sense that soldiers and their families do not want to talk to mental health professionals because of the stigma involved with seeking professional help. Many vets seem also to feel that they are not being understood because most VA staff have neither served in a combat zone nor been removed from their family, career, and workplace for a year or more (Friedman, 2005). Finally, because so many returning veterans are from rural areas, access to professional help is difficult.

Although the prevalence of veterans needing professional mental health care is significant, not all returning veterans require such services. A large percentage of returning veterans (estimates are as many as 50%) have difficulties including, but not restricted to, family or relationship issues and interactions, work and employment difficulties, and a sense of a lack of focus or purpose in adjusting to their return home (Henderson, 2006). Available services for these veterans have been fragmented at best (Hoge et al., 2004). Moreover, the families of these veterans have had even less access to needed services.

What is unique about the veterans serving in these current conflicts is that approximately 40% are National Guard members and reservists. They are civilians not steeped in the culture of the military and who had not expected to be placed in a war zone. Their deployment, while stressful, is compounded by the stress of leaving their civilian lives. Deployment has disrupted their marriages and families, their employment, and their status in the community.

The FREE 4 VETS (**F**amily, **R**elationship, **E**ducation, and **E**mployment) program is designed to assist the readjustment process for veterans and their families. The program is psychoeducational rather than illness-oriented and builds on the soldiers' strengths rather than their problems. FREE 4 Vets has three components. The first is *Peer Coaching,* in which veterans from other wars will be trained to provide support as persons who have experienced similar situations. Second, in *Skills for Reintegration,* veterans and their families will be taught several skill-based resource components: Dealing with Stress, Repairing and Enhancing Families and Relationships, and "The Next Step." The latter involves having veterans/families identify their dreams and goals and the skills they possess to reach their goals. All these components are designed for them to do in the privacy of their own homes after receiving a short basic training session that will be later available on a DVD. A toll-free number will be available to help veterans or family members having problems implementing the resource components. The third component, *Re-entering the Work World,* is intended to help veterans who are interested in obtaining new jobs or careers or furthering their education. Many left jobs that are no longer available to them since deployment. Others had unsatisfying jobs and careers. Furthering their education or obtaining jobs that take advantage of their leadership experiences and other skills learned during combat should enable them to more successfully integrate into their communities. Because of this program's newness, it has not yet been evaluated.

EVALUATION OF LDI PROGRAMS

There is undoubtedly a great need for programs designed to promote competence and development. However, these programs often struggle to gain acceptance and widespread adoption. There are two main reasons for why this is true. First, there is a lack of rigorous evaluation. The funding available is often insufficient to allow for a comprehensive and rigorous evaluation. In addition, individuals who implement programs do not always have the experience to implement a rigorous evaluation. Second, if the program is evaluated, it often overlooks the importance of bridging the gap between science and practice. Researchers rarely take the time and effort to work with organizations to translate the findings into practice. As noted, if we want to be effective in developing and implementing programs to promote youth development, we need to work in collaboration with individuals, families, schools, and communities.

Several steps that can be taken to promote rigorous program evaluation that will allow for the continued improvement, acceptance, and widespread adoption of competency-based programs. First, researchers and program developers should redouble efforts to conduct evidence-based research and to communicate the results in ways that will help all involved. Often when there are evidence-based results, researchers are focused on writing the results for publication, rather than ensuring that the results are both relevant and applicable for use by the practitioner or community members involved in program development and implementation.

Second, researchers and practitioners must work together to reduce the gap between research and practice. One step is to help practitioners and community partners understand and incorporate strategies and practices related to competency building and development. The SUPER program provides opportunities to involve various community members so that they gain an understanding of the program and can build on the learning that has taken place for the youth who participate in the program. The result is that community members become part of participants' experiences and are better able to connect with the youth. In all our school-based programs, we meet with each school administration to explain the results of the study and to provide results specific to their school. Taking appropriate measures to involve community members in the process increases chances that programs will be sustainable in the communities in which they have been implemented.

Another important aspect of program evaluation is choosing the type of evaluation needed or desired. In recent years, there has been a growing emphasis on examining process variables in addition to outcomes (Dane & Schneider, 1998; Davis et al., 2000; Meyer, Nicholson, Danish, Fries, & Polk, 2000; Zins, Elias, Greenberg, & Pruett, 2000). Without measures of program implementation or an understanding of what components of a program are effective, conclusions drawn from outcomes may not be accurate and efforts to replicate the program may be stymied (Domitrovich & Greenberg, 2000). When counseling psychologists consider implementing a program, it is important that they do so accurately and successfully (Graczyk et al., 2000).

Researchers often are most interested in whether the program was associated with changes in attitudes, behavior, or knowledge. As a result, the only evaluation may be outcome evaluation. However, process evaluation is a valuable tool that can enhance understanding of outcome evaluation results (Graczyk et al., 2000). The purpose of process evaluation is to monitor the implementation process and the degree to which the program is being implemented as it was originally designed, to identify and address problems so that the quality of implementation can be maintained at a high level, and to document the implementation process to help in the interpretation of results from the outcome evaluation (Graczyk et al., 2000). If a program is implemented and the outcome evaluation shows weak support on various outcomes, without a process evaluation, it is difficult to determine whether the program overall is ineffective or if the implementation of the program was ineffective. Therefore, the level and quality of implementation should be examined with a process evaluation.

Process evaluation can take a number of forms. It can involve having independent observers randomly observe sessions, having instructors complete surveys after each session has been taught, or tracking the number of participants and conditions under which the program is implemented (e.g., determining whether the school/community is cooperative in providing enough time and space to effectively implement the program). To determine whether a program is effective both the implementation and evaluation are critical. Psychologists interested in implementing programs must ensure that they have the resources and support necessary to implement the program as it is designed to be implemented and to effectively evaluate the program by including both an outcome evaluation and a process evaluation.

Once decisions have been made regarding what type of evaluation will be conducted, it becomes important to determine how the evaluation will be carried out. It has been our experience that a mixed-methods approach that includes both quantitative and qualitative analysis is most useful. Quantitative measures, both self-report and behavioral indices, help determine the effect of the intervention on various outcome measures and process measures. They are cost-effective and can be used to evaluate large numbers of individuals in a relatively short period.

Qualitative measures are also important as they often allow researchers to gain an in-depth understanding of participants' experiences. They help researchers examine how the intervention or program is effective rather than just whether it is effective. One qualitative approach that we have found valuable is Interpersonal Phenomenological Analysis (IPA; Smith & Osborn, 2003). The IPA explores participants' own perceptions of their experiences (Willig, 2001).

FUTURE DIRECTIONS AND CONCLUSION

We have tried to highlight the value of interventions that promote development and competency throughout the life span. It is essential that developers of such interventions adopt a coherent framework before beginning and match the intervention methodology to that framework. We have presented examples so that readers can see how such programs can be developed and implemented. We have also stressed the importance of careful, rigorous evaluation, including process evaluation.

Many counseling psychologists still see the delivery of helping services as basically a one-on-one process in which the psychologist waits for the client to ask for help (Fitzgerald & Osipow, 1986; Watkins, 1983). This is unfortunate and outdated. First, many groups are unwilling to come for that kind of help. Waiting for them to seek help, and then being disappointed when they do not come in or do not continue seems to us to be a form of blaming the victim. In this case, we are blaming them for our failure to seek them out and offer help that will enhance their development and teach them skills that they can apply and transfer to multiple settings. Perhaps we need to assess, or at least reassess, our needs and motivations for helping.

Over 30 years ago, the first author (Danish, 1974) suggested that the future for counseling psychologists was to be indirect as opposed to direct providers—to provide training, develop programs, supervise others, evaluate programs, and administer programs. This prophecy has not come to pass. Perhaps as we understand how promoting development and competencies matches counseling psychology's values, we will decide that this future is now.

REFERENCES

Bandura, A. (2004). Health promotion by social cognitive means. *Health Education and Behavior, 31*(2), 143–164.

Bloom, M. (2000). The uses of theory in primary prevention practice: Evolving thoughts on sports and after-school activities as influences of social competence. In S. J. Danish & T. P. Gullotta (Eds.), *Developing competent youth and strong communities through after-school programming* (pp. 17–66). Washington, DC: CWLA Press.

Brunelle, J., Danish, S., & Forneris, T. (2007). The impact of a sport-based life skill program on adolescent prosocial values. *Applied Developmental Science, 11*(1), 43–55.

Carnegie Corporation of New York. (1989). *Turning points: Preparing American youth for the 21st century* (Reports of the Carnegie Council on Adolescent Development). Waldorf, MD: Author.

Carnegie Corporation of New York. (1995). *Great transitions: Preparing adolescents for a new century* (Reports of the Carnegie Council on Adolescent Development). Waldorf, MD: Author.

Chi, M. T. H., Bassok, M., Lewis, M. W., Reimann, P., & Glaser, R. (1989). Self-explanations: How students study and use examples in learning to solve problems. *Cognitive Science, 13*, 145–182.

Collaborative for Academic, Social, and Emotional Learning. (2004). *About SEL.* Retrieved January 15, 2005, from www.casel.org/about_sel/SELintro.php.

Dane, A. V., & Schneider, B. H. (1998). Program integrity in primary and early secondary prevention: Are implementation effects out of control? *Clinical Psychology Review, 18*(1), 23–45.

Danish, S., Fries, E., Meyer, A., Farrell, A., Donohue, T., & Buzzard, M. (1999–2003). *Cancer prevention in rural youth: Teaching health goals* (A five-year grant funded by the National Cancer Institute).

Danish, S., Fries, E., Westerberg, A. & Hoy, K. (2003–2005). *The BRIDGE Program: Bridging the Gap to Better Health.* (A two-year grant funded by the National Cancer Institute).

Danish, S. J. (1974). Counseling psychology and the Vail conference: An invited comment on training settings and patterns. *Counseling Psychologist, 4*, 68.

Danish, S. J. (1997). Going for the goal: A life skills program for adolescents. In T. Gullotta & G. Albee (Eds.), *Primary prevention works* (pp. 291–312). Newbury Park, CA: Sage.

Danish, S. J. (2000). Youth and community development: How after-school programming can make a difference. In S. J. Danish & T. P. Gullotta (Eds.), *Developing competent youth and strong communities through after-school programming* (pp. 275–302). Washington, DC: CWLA Press.

Danish, S. J. (2002a). *Going for the goal: Leader manual and student activity book* (4th ed.). Richmond: Virginia Commonwealth University, Life Skills Center.

Danish, S. J. (2002b). *SUPER (Sports United to Promote Education and Recreation) program: Leader manual and student activity book* (3rd ed.). Richmond: Virginia Commonwealth University, Life Skills Center.

Danish, S. J., & D'Augelli, A. R. (1983). *Helping skills: Vol. II. Life development intervention.* New York: Human Sciences Press.

Danish, S. J., D'Augelli, A. R., & Hauer, A. L. (1980). *Helping skills: A basic training program* (2nd ed.). New York: Human Sciences Press.

Danish, S. J., Forneris, T., Hodge, K., & Heke, I. (2004). Enhancing youth development through sport. *World Leisure, 46*(3), 38–49.

Danish, S. J., Forneris, T., & Wallace, I. (2005). Sport-based life skills programming in the schools. *Journal of Applied School Psychology, 21*(2), 41–62.

Danish, S. J. & Hale, B. D. (1983). Sport psychology: Teaching skills to athletes and coaches. *Journal of Physical Education, Recreation, and Dance, 54*(8), 11–13, 80–81.

Danish, S. J., Kleiber, D., & Hall, H. (1987). Developmental intervention and motivation enhancement in the context of sport. In M. L. Maehr & D. A. Kleiber (Eds.), *Advances in motivation and achievement: Vol. 5. Enhancing motivation* (pp. 211–238). Greenwich, CT: JAI Press.

Danish, S. J., Petitpas, A. L., & Hale, B. D. (1993). Life development intervention for athletes: Life skills through sports. *Counseling Psychologist (Major contribution), 21*(3), 352–385.

Danish, S. J., Smyer, M. A., & Nowak, C. A. (1980). Developmental intervention: Enhancing life-event processes. In P. B. Baltes & O. G. Brim Jr. (Eds.), *Life-span development and behavior* (Vol. 3, pp. 339–366). New York: Academic Press.

Danish, S. J., Taylor, T., & Fazio, R. (2003). Enhancing adolescent development through sport and leisure. In G. R. Adams & M. Berzonsky (Eds.), *Blackwell handbook on adolescence* (pp. 92–108). Malden, MA: Blackwell.

Davis, M., Baranowski, T., Resnicow, K., Baranowski, J., Doyle, C., Smith, M., et al. (2000). Gimme 5 fruit and vegetables for fun and health: Process evaluation. *Health Education and Behavior, 27*, 167–176.

Domitrovich, C. E., & Greenberg, M. T. (2000). The study of implementation: Current findings from effective programs that prevent mental disorders in school-aged children. *Journal of Educational and Psychological Consultation, 11*, 193–222.

Fitzgerald, L. F., & Osipow, S. H. (1986). An occupational analysis of counseling psychology: How special is the specialty? *American Psychologist, 41*(5), 535–544.

Folkman, S., & Moskowitz, J. T. (2000). Positive affect and the other side of coping. *American Psychologist, 55*(6), 647–654.

Ford, D. H. (1987). *Humans as self-constructing living systems: A developmental perspective on personality and behaviour.* Hillsdale, NJ: Erlbaum.

Fretz, B. (1982). Perspectives and definitions. *Counseling Psychologist, 10*(2), 15–19.

Friedman, M. (2005). Veteran's mental health in the wake of war. *New England Journal of Medicine, 352*, 1287–1290.

Garmezy, N. (1991). Resilience and vulnerability to adverse developmental outcomes associated with poverty. *Behavioral Scientist, 34*(4), 416–430.

Gass, M. (1985). Programming the transfer of learning in adventure education. *Journal of Experimental Education, 8*, 18–24.

Goleman, D. (1995). *Emotional intelligence.* New York: Bantam.

Gordon, R. (1987). An operational classification of disease prevention. In J. A. Steinberg & M. M. Silverman (Eds.), *Preventing mental disorders* (pp. 20–26). Rockville, MD: Department of Health and Human Services.

Graczyk, P. A., Weissberg, R. P., Payton, J. W., Elias, M. J., Greenberg, M. T., & Zins, J. E. (2000). Criteria for evaluating the quality of school-based social and emotional learning programs. In R. Bar-On & J. Parker (Eds.), *The handbook of emotional intelligence: Theory, development, assessment, and application at home, school, and in the workplace* (pp. 391–410). San Francisco: Jossey-Bass.

Heke, I. (2001). *The Hokowhitu program: Designing a sporting intervention to address alcohol and substance abuse in adolescent Maori.* Unpublished manuscript, University of Otago, Dunedin, New Zealand.

Henderson, K. (2006). *While they're at war.* Boston: Houghton Mifflin.

Hodge, K., Cresswell, S., Sherburn, D., & Dugdale, J. (1999). Physical activity-based lifeskills programmes: Pt. II. Example programmes. *Physical Education New Zealand Journal, 32*, 12–15.

Hoge, C., Castro, C., Messer, S., McGurk, D., Cotting, D., & Koffman, R. (2004). Combat duty in Iraq and Afghanistan, mental health problems, and barriers to care. *New England Journal of Medicine, 351*(1), 13–22.

Ivey, A. V. (1980). Counseling 2000: Time to take charge! *Counseling Psychologist, 8*(4), 12–16.

Kelly, J. G. (2003). Science and community psychology: Social norms for pluralistic inquiry. *American Journal of Community Psychology, 31*, 213–218.

Lickona, T. (1991). Moral development in the elementary school classroom. In W. M. Kurtines & J. L. Gerwirtz (Eds.), *Handbook of moral behavior and development* (pp. 143–161). Hillsdale, NJ: Erlbaum.

Meyer, A., Nicholson, R., Danish, S., Fries, E., & Polk, V. (2000). A model to measure program integrity of peer-led health promotion programs in rural middle schools: Assessing the implementation of the sixth grade Goals for Health program. *Journal of Educational and Psychological Consultation, 11*, 223–252.

Mrazek, P. J., & Haggerty, R. J. (1994). *Reducing risks for mental disorders: Frontiers for preventive intervention research.* Washington, DC: National Academy Press.

Newcomb, M. D., & Bentler, P. M. (1988). *Consequences of adolescent drug use*. Newbury Park, CA: Sage.

Newcomb, M. D., Bentler, P. M., & Collins, C. (1986). Influence of sensation seeking on general deviance and specific problem behaviors from adolescence to adulthood. *Journal of Personality and Social Psychology, 61*, 614–628.

Nurmi, J. (1987). Age, sex, social class, and quality of family interaction as determinants of adolescents' future orientation: A developmental task interpretation. *Adolescence, 88*, 977–991.

O'Hearn, T. C., & Gatz, M. (1999). Evaluating a psychosocial competence program for urban adolescents. *Journal of Primary Prevention, 20*(2), 119–144.

O'Hearn, T. C., & Gatz, M. (2002). Going for the goal: Improving youth problem solving skills through a school-based intervention. *Journal of Community Psychology, 30*, 281–303.

Papacharisis, V., Goudas, M., Danish, S., & Theodorakis, Y. (2005). The effectiveness of teaching a life skills program in a school-based sport context. *Journal of Applied Sport Psychology, 17*, 247–254.

Reker, G. T. (2000). Theoretical perspective, dimension, and measurement of existential meaning. In G. T. Reker & K. Chamberlain (Eds.), *Exploring existential meaning: Optimizing human development across the life span* (pp. 39–55). Thousand Oaks, CA: Sage.

Ryan, W. (1971). *Blaming the victim*. New York: Random House.

Schaefer, J. A., & Moos, R. H. (2001). Bereavement experiences and personal growth. In M. Stroebe, R. O. Hansson, W. Stroebe, & H. Schut (Eds.), *Handbook of bereavement research: Consequences, coping, and care* (pp. 145–167). Washington, DC: American Psychological Association.

Seligman, M., & Csikszentmihalyi, M. (2000). Positive psychology: An introduction. *American Psychologist, 55*(1), 5–14.

Smith, J. A., & Osborn, M. (2003). Interpretative phenomenological analysis. In J. A. Smith (Ed.), *Qualitative psychology: A practical guide to research methods* (pp. 51–80). London: Sage.

Tedeschi, R., Park, C., & Calhoun, L. (1998). *Posttraumatic growth: Positive changes in the aftermath of crisis*. London: Erlbaum.

U.S. Census Bureau. (2003). *The Black population in the United States: Population characteristics* (Publication No. P20-541). Washington, DC: U.S. Government Printing Office.

Watkins, C. E. (1983). Counseling psychology versus clinical psychology: Further explorations on a theme or once more around the "identity" maypole with gusto. *Counseling Psychologist, 11*(4), 76–92.

Weinberg, R., & Gould, D. (2006). *Foundations of sport and exercise psychology*. Champaign, IL: Human Kinetics.

Willig, C. (2001). *Introducing qualitative research in psychology*. Philadelphia: Open University Press.

World Health Organization. (1996). *Life skills education: Planning for research*. Geneva, Switzerland: Author.

Zins, J. E., Elias, M. J., Greenberg, M., & Pruett, M. K. (2000). Promoting quality implementation in prevention programs. *Journal of Educational and Psychological Consultation, 11*, 173–174.

CHAPTER 30

Promoting Health and Preventing and Reducing Disease

KATHLEEN CHWALISZ
EZEMENARI OBASI

Professional psychologists' earliest health-related roles involved helping patients and their families cope with the distress and disability associated with medical conditions. Such work was done from a traditional mental health perspective and involved a professional focus on psychopathology and remediation (Baum, Perry, & Tarbell, 2004). Advances in medical knowledge and technology have eliminated some life-threatening illnesses (e.g., polio, tuberculosis), but many chronic diseases and recurrent medical conditions remain, including heart disease, diabetes, stroke, and cancer. These chronic lifestyle illnesses necessitate new ways of conceptualizing and structuring health care as well as responding to their skyrocketing costs.

The shift in the nature of health problems has required the health care system to shift its focus from remediation alone to prevention and public health. Health science is also experiencing a shift from a purely biomedical model to a biopsychosocial conceptualization of health and illness (Suls & Rothman, 2004). More recently, social ecological theories have emerged that incorporate environmental and policy level factors in risky behavior and health (e.g., Sallis & Owen, 2002). Researchers are locating genes that identify those at risk for health problems, establishing that risk-related behaviors can be changed and health outcomes improved, and developing dissemination approaches to increase the impact of psychological interventions on health (Smith, Orleans, & Jenkins, 2004).

Demographic changes in the U.S. population are also affecting health psychology and health care, creating opportunities for counseling psychologists to contribute expertise in developmental, strength-based, positive psychology, and preventive domains. The average age of the population is going up as the baby boom generation ages, creating the need to modify health-related risk factors, given age-related increases in the prevalence of chronic diseases such as coronary heart disease, Type II diabetes, and cancer (Smith et al., 2004). The cultural diversity of U.S. society and greater recognition of culture-related health disparities and risk factors call for efforts to address issues specific to particular groups as well as those that cut across the American population (e.g., Yali & Revenson, 2004). Counseling psychologists are uniquely qualified to respond to health care and health psychology's calls for more extensive "contextual competency" (Yali & Revenson, 2004) as well as the demand by the health care system for larger numbers of culturally diverse health psychologists. Counseling psychologists can also contribute the theoretical background and methodological sophistication needed to test culturally relevant health behavior models and interventions, consider problems from life span developmental perspectives, and promote greater emphasis on subjective well-being and other quality-of -life outcomes (e.g., Smith et al., 2004).

In this chapter, we provide an overview of research findings and interventions in the realm of health promotion and disease prevention. In particular, we focus on a few of the leading health indicators— lifestyle-level health domains that have been associated with many of the major chronic diseases and are at the core of U.S. health policy.

WHAT IS HEALTH PROMOTION AND DISEASE PREVENTION?

Health promotion can best be viewed as an umbrella term that encompasses health education, public health, health protection, community development, and disease prevention (Evans & Kazarian, 2001). These activities increase public awareness of various dimensions of health and empower people to influence their environments, including systems and policies (Aboud, 1998). Health education involves individuals from various disciplines providing health-related information (e.g., knowledge, attitudes, practices) to voluntary audiences, with the goal of achieving specific health-related behavior change (Aboud, 1998). Health protection involves government activities to control health behavior and health outcomes either through legislation or fiscal policies (e.g., taxes and legal age for alcohol and tobacco use). Community development strategies empower and assist community leaders and members in developing programming to address a local health concern (e.g., a community-based walking program).

In 1957, the Commission on Chronic Illness defined disease prevention as involving three types of activities at different stages of disease risk. *Primary prevention* activities prevent the onset of an illness or injury (e.g., immunizations, stretching before exercise, genetic testing). *Secondary prevention* activities involve identifying and treating a disease or injury early to lessen its course or severity (e.g., regular mammograms, weight loss programs for persons with marginal indicators for Type II diabetes). *Tertiary prevention* activities decrease the residual negative outcomes or improve adjustment after disease or injury (e.g., postsurgical education, physical therapy, support groups). In addition to the traditional prevention focus on stage of disease risk, Smith et al. (2004) suggested that psychological researchers and practitioners should incorporate life span considerations and target all levels of influence (e.g., biological processes; individual psychological processes; family and small group processes; larger group, cultural, and environmental processes; institutional and public policy factors).

MAJOR DOMAINS OF HEALTH PROMOTION AND DISEASE PREVENTION: THE LEADING HEALTH INDICATORS

Health is determined by a complex interplay of biological, psychological, and social factors, and relevant processes can be considered at multiple levels (Smith et al., 2004; Suls & Rothman, 2004). In this section, we focus on several domains that may be particularly appropriate targets for health promotion and disease prevention activities. These domains represent some of the Leading Health Indicators targeted by the U.S. Department of Health and Human Services (USDHHS, 93) for the Healthy People 2010 national health initiative. They involve "'daily habits' (e.g., smoking, exercise and activity, diet, and alcohol use) and their immediate outcomes (e.g., obesity) [that] contribute to the development of virtually all of the major sources of morbidity and mortality in industrialized nations" (Smith et al., 2004, p. 126). Furthermore, these health behaviors affect individuals in all aspects of their lives, not just as they present for treatment in medical settings, and significantly affect quality of life.

Before discussing the specific leading indicators and health behavior domains, we briefly review general risk and protective factors that cut across health problems. We then turn to three of the leading health indicators, focusing on efforts to increase exercise, reduce obesity, and curtail risky sexual behavior. For each domain, we review incidence data, domain-specific risk and protective factors, conceptual models, and relevant psychological interventions. Although substance abuse is also an important leading health indicator, this topic is covered by Martens, Neighbors, and Lee (Chapter 32, this volume). We, therefore, refer readers to their chapter for a review of the substance abuse prevention literature.

General Risk and Protective Factors in Health, Illness, and Disability

Several factors have been found to predict or moderate health behaviors and immediate and long-term health outcomes; a few are considered here. It is important to be aware of and assess for individual and group differences in these risk and protective factors because the same factor that is protective for one person might increase health risk for another. Some general ideas about the risk and protective factors appear in this section, and specific findings are considered later in conjunction with the health indicators.

Cultural Beliefs, Values, and Practices

Although often relegated to physical objects like clothing, food, and art, there is also an intangible aspect of culture that can be defined as the complex constellation of mores, values, customs, traditions, and practices that provides an ethnic or otherwise defined cultural group with a general design for living and pattern for interpreting reality (Parham, White, & Ajamu, 1999). Culture evolves through an adaptive process that consolidates one's knowledge and skills related to frequently encountered problems (Hutchins, 1995). Since culture is transmitted from one generation to another through enculturation and socialization, it is constantly in flux, while simultaneously resistant to change. Culture influences conceptions of health and illness, affective aspects of health and illness involving health norms and values, health practices, and health roles and institutions (Mulato & Berry, 2001). Cultural dimensions affect both physical and psychological access to health care and interactions with health care professionals.

Ethnicity refers to the self-definition of any human social unit that has a shared culture that is generally linked to a common ancestral origin, history, worldview, language, tradition, religion, or spiritual system (Shiraev & Levy, 2004). An ethnic level of analysis is important, since it can enable scientists to identify the mutual influences of biological traits and learned cultural variables, and to distinguish genetically based characteristics from learned characteristics (Lieberman & Jackson, 1995). In contrast, a racial level analysis, as is typically reported in national survey data, is rooted in immutable constructs (e.g., skin tone, hair texture, bone structure) and ignores interethnic specificity (e.g., Chinese versus Vietnamese, Mexican versus Cuban).

Various dimensions of culture have been identified as protective factors for different cultural groups. For example, spirituality, religiosity, communalism, extended family, self-definition, African-centered philosophies, indigenous healing practices, improvisation, and an oral tradition have been found to be strong protective factors for African Americans (Belgrave & Allison, 2006). Additionally, "John Henryism" (the belief that obstacles can be overcome through heroic striving) has been a coping strategy useful to African Americans in the face of hardships. However, data also suggest that, despite its immediate coping benefits, John Henryism may be associated with negative long-term consequences (e.g., high blood pressure, increased stress, ignored physical and psychological symptom expression; Snowden, 2001). Cultural researchers are not suggesting that the aforementioned values are unique to each ethnic group, nor are they suggesting that each ethnic group is monolithic. It is critical to assess for individual differences, particularly worldview and acculturation, within ethnic groups.

Gender and sexual orientation are also associated with particular beliefs, values, experiences, and practices that affect health status. For example, women more frequently report all acute (except injuries) and most chronic illnesses. However, when men do report being ill it is more likely to be a serious or life-threatening illness, which may at least in part be attributable to gender role socialization (Mann, 1996). Lesbians and gay men have been found to have higher levels of stress and stress-related difficulties and to underuse health care services for such reasons as discrimination by providers and less insurance coverage (Mann, 1996).

Socioeconomic Status and Environment

Socioeconomic status (SES) is a multifaceted variable that describes individuals' or groups' relative social and economic position within a hierarchical social structure as influenced by educational attainment, occupation, wealth, and ownership. The relationship between SES, health (physical and mental), morbidity, and mortality has been widely documented (Pickett & Pearl, 2001). Moreover, SES has been implicated in the racial stratification of health (Hayward, Crimmins, Miles, & Yang, 2000).

More research is needed to articulate specific variables and processes that mediate the relationship between SES and health indicators. For example, lower SES is typically associated with poverty, inadequate educational facilities, poor employment opportunities, low income, segregated living conditions, poor recreational facilities, violence, crime, air pollution, water pollution, ambient noise, and hazardous waste (Hayward et al., 2000; Liu & Ali, Chapter 10, this volume). Such toxic conditions may negatively impact variables like stress, nutritional intake, physical activity, substance use, homelessness, prejudice, discrimination, social support, availability of health services, and help-seeking attitudes (e.g., Picket & Pearl, 2001).

Stress

Stress has been associated with both acute and chronic illnesses such as infectious diseases, cardiovascular disease, diabetes, cancer, asthma, and gastrointestinal disorders (Davis Martin & Brantley, 2004). Stress affects health through physiological mechanisms (e.g., metabolic activity, immune system changes) or changes in health behaviors. The behavioral effects of stress often involve some combination of using negative health behaviors to cope with the physical demands of the stressful situation (e.g., increased caffeine, nicotine, alcohol and drug use) or engaging in positive health behaviors less frequently (e.g., decreased exercise, poor diet, decreased sleep) due to more pressing priorities. These stress-related changes in health behavior, termed *lifestyle drift* (Chwalisz & Hanson, 2001), typically occur gradually and unconsciously, only coming into a person's awareness when a health problem (e.g., hypertension, diabetes) or other indicator of changing health status (e.g., weight gain, shortness of breath, pain) appears.

Stress is a complex phenomenon, and interventions typically involve strategies to improve clients' knowledge, skills, and behaviors related to the stressor and life in general (Davis Martin & Brantley, 2004). The most common technique employed in stress management programs is cognitive restructuring to change an individual's appraisals of stressors and coping resources. Techniques such as progressive relaxation, biofeedback, meditation, and yoga may also be incorporated to reduce the physiological arousal inherent in stress. Behavioral techniques may be incorporated to increase positive health behaviors or skills (e.g., exercise, assertiveness) or decrease negative health behaviors (e.g., smoking, excessive eating, anger). Stress management programs have been found to improve coping, decrease distress, and improve some physiological indicators for individuals with conditions such as HIV, diabetes, cancer, and asthma (Davis Martin & Brantley, 2004). A meta-analysis of various stress management programs conducted in occupational settings with adults revealed moderate effects for cognitive-behavioral ($d = .68$), relaxation ($d = .35$), and multimodal ($d = .51$) interventions (van der Klink, Blonk, Schene, & van Dijk, 2001).

Help-Seeking and Access to Health Care

A major factor in maintaining health is seeking and receiving health care services when it is necessary and appropriate to do so. A review by Martin and Leventhal (2004) revealed that fewer than half of symptomatic individuals seek health care, choosing instead to manage symptoms on their own, even when symptoms are potentially life-threatening. Once symptoms have been identified, individuals engage in strategies to correct the situation, which may or may not include self-referral for health care. In most cases, individuals consult with family and friends, referred to as the lay referral network, for information, comparison, and social support (Martin & Leventhal, 2004). The lay referral network may also encourage the patient to engage in self-care or network-based care for the symptoms rather than seeking professional health care, or it may engage in social sanctioning (e.g., nagging) of individuals deemed to be in need of professional services. The lay referral networks may also reflect cultural norms for interpretation of symptoms (e.g., expressing psychological distress in terms of physical symptoms, expectations of strength), self- and other-care practices, and expectations about professional services (Martin & Leventhal, 2004).

Access to quality health care is a particularly important factor in help-seeking behavior. Lack of insurance coverage is the most significant barrier to seeking medical care. Higher proportions of Hispanics (35%), American Indians (33%), African Americans (23%), and Asian Americans and Pacific Islanders (22%) under the age of 65 are uninsured compared with European Americans (13%) and have significantly greater reliance on public insurance (Institute of Medicine [IOM], 2003). These disparities in health care coverage affect the types of services that are available. African American (47%) and Hispanic (53%) adults under the age of 65 reported greater reliance on emergency rooms, outpatient departments, and community clinics for their health care compared with European Americans (30%) (IOM, 2003).

In addition to insurance coverage, low SES, cultural mistrust, culture-specific conceptions of illness and health, language barriers, perceived stigma, lack of knowledge about health care services, negative experiences of community members, administrative hurdles, long waits, and travel inconveniences have all been identified as potential barriers to help-seeking for minority group members (e.g., Johnson & Cameron, 2001; Vega & Lopez, 2001). Even when SES is controlled, ethnic minorities are more likely to receive care from lower quality facilities (IOM, 2003). They also experience a high rate of being misdiagnosed, receive treatment that often fails to meet practice guidelines, experience a high premature termination rate, and exhibit a low likelihood of adhering to the prescribed treatment regime (IOM, 2003).

Treatment Adherence

A critical factor in long-term health outcomes, particularly for individuals living with chronic illness, is adherence to treatment recommendations. One third of patients with acute illnesses fail to adequately follow provider recommendations (Bennett Johnson & Newman Carlson, 2004). Adherence figures for chronic health problems reveal that at least 50% of patients fail to follow prescribed regimens (e.g., Turk & Meichenbaum, 1991), whereas asymptomatic problems (e.g., hypertension) have been associated with 70% failed adherence (Sherbourne, Hays, Ordway, DiMatteo, & Kravitz, 1992). The adherence failure rate is 75% for provider-recommended lifestyle changes (Epstein & Cluss, 1982).

Adherence to medical recommendations is a complex process involving communication between patient and provider, patient recall of the details of the regimen, patient knowledge, and patient skills (Bennett Johnson & Newman Carlson, 2004). Many cases of nonadherence are inadvertent due to inaccurate recall of medical recommendations or knowledge-skill deficits (e.g., nutrition principles, medication dosing-administration). Physicians sometimes also contribute to reduced compliance via vague or poorly communicated medical advice, inappropriate prescriptions or unjustified changes to medication protocols, and noncompliance with health care procedures and practices (Bennett Johnson & Newman Carlson, 2004).

Barriers to treatment adherence, which vary by regimen and patient population, include longer disease duration (Brownbridge & Fielding, 1994), greater treatment regimen complexity (e.g., Kelly & Kalichman, 2002), and more negative side effects or negative beliefs about the side effects (Horne & Weinman, 1998). Psychological factors such as social support or comorbid disorders have also been found to affect adherence (Bennett Johnson & Newman Carlson, 2004). Adherence interventions are most likely to be effective if they combine education and skill training with behavioral strategies (e.g., goal setting, contracting, self-monitoring) within a health care organizational structure (e.g., access, continuity of care) that supports attention to both provider and patient behavior (Bennett Johnson & Newman Carlson, 2004).

Dietary Behavior and Obesity

Obesity is one of the most critical public health issues facing the United States, with an estimated prevalence rate of 31% in adults; an additional 34% are considered overweight (Smith West, Harvey-Berino, & Raczynski, 2004). Furthermore, rates of obesity among adults more than doubled between 1960 and 2000 and are expected to continue to increase (Flegal, Carroll, Ogden, & Johnson, 2002). In the

1999 to 2002 National Health and Nutrition Examination Survey, 16% of children and adolescents aged 6 to 19 were considered overweight or obese (Hedley et al., 2004), and the number of obese children and adolescents increased by 120% between 1986 and 1998 (Strauss & Pollack, 2001). Obesity is a prominent factor in many major medical conditions, the most prevalent being cardiovascular disease, hypertension, Type II diabetes, osteoarthritis, and most cancers (Smith West et al., 2004). Thus, factors related to obesity are important foci for health promotion and disease prevention activities.

Conceptualizing Dietary Behavior

Body weight is determined by the balance between energy consumed and energy expended. Genetic predispositions are thought to explain 25% to 40% of the variance in Body Mass Index (BMI)—weight in kilograms divided by height in meters squared, which is highly correlated with body fat content. Genetics also determine variables such as resting metabolic rate, weight gain with overfeeding, and body fat distribution (Wadden, Brownell, & Foster, 2002). Given that there have not been significant changes in the gene pool, the recent dramatic increases in obesity rates appear to be attributable to what has been referred to as a toxic environment, characterized by heavily advertised, easily accessible, inexpensive, and high-calorie foods, combined with an increasingly sedentary lifestyle that begins in childhood with excessive television and video game usage (Wadden et al., 2002).

If models are to capture the complexity of dietary behavior and its influence on obesity and health, they should include dimensions at various levels: (a) the food industry (e.g., product availability, consumer choices), (b) nutrition information (public and private sources), (c) background factors (e.g., cultural, social, psychosocial), (d) the food preparer (e.g., skills, methods), (e) individual dietary behavior (e.g., learned taste preferences, knowledge, attitudes), (f) physiology of food intake and energy metabolism (e.g., regulatory mechanisms, idiosyncratic sensitivities, genetic predispositions), and (g) individual chronic disease risk (Smith West et al., 2004). Furthermore, these dimensions interact and influence each other (e.g., sensitivities influence learned preferences, cultural background affects preferences and preparer skills), whereas most interventions have been focused on just one or two dimensions of dietary behavior.

Risk and Protective Factors in Obesity

There are well-documented ethnic group differences in obesity prevalence rates. African Americans exhibit the highest rates of obesity (45% versus 31% for Whites and 37% for Mexican Americans) and extreme obesity (11% versus 4% for Whites and 5% for Mexican Americans), with African American women being most affected (Ogden et al., 2006). Various factors have been considered as explanations for these ethnic differences in obesity. For example, there may be genetic differences that cause differential energy metabolism across ethnic groups (Zhang & Wang, 2004). Body image and attractiveness perceptions also vary by ethnic group (e.g., larger figures among African American women are considered attractive; Kumanyika, Wilson, & Guilford-Davenport, 1993).

Cultural norms and dietary preferences also appear to be relevant, given findings that increasing levels of acculturation to U.S. culture have been associated with greater weight gain, and groups whose diets traditionally contain greater proportions of fatty foods and carbohydrates have higher rates of obesity (Whitfield, Weidner, Clark, & Anderson, 2002). For example, high levels of adherence to traditional Hopi Indian culture were associated with a 40% less chance of obesity (Coe et al., 2004). Socioeconomic status appears to account for some variance in obesity and also interacts with ethnicity in predicting obesity. For African American and Mexican men, SES is positively associated with obesity, but SES is negatively associated with obesity among White men and women (Zhang & Wang, 2004). Whereas women are affected by obesity at higher rates, the negative health outcomes associated with obesity affect men to a greater degree, because men are more likely to store excess fact in the more dangerous abdominal area (Whitfield et al., 2002).

Stress has been associated with eating behavior and obesity. For example, poor decision making and emotional overeating under stress were positively associated with BMI (Davis, Levitan, Muglia, Bewell, & Kennedy, 2004). In mice, subordinate individuals ingested a higher fat diet and became heavier than mice in the dominant and control groups (Moles et al., 2006). Attention to factors affecting treatment adherence (gender, age, BMI, previous intervention participation) is particularly relevant to obesity treatment, given high rates of relapse and weight gain (Bautista-Castano, Molina-Cabrillana, Montoya-Alonso, & Serra-Majem, 2004).

Interventions

The majority of obesity interventions have been individual in nature, focused on dietary changes to produce weight loss, and based on behavioral or cognitive-behavioral theories such as social cognitive theory (Bandura, 1986). Most individual and group interventions involve decreasing consumption with the goal of weight loss, although some interventions target particular dietary elements such as fat or sodium. Strategies used in such interventions include self-monitoring of targeted behaviors, modeling of new dietary behaviors, stimulus control, psychoeducation to improve knowledge or skills, strategies to change attitudes or alter beliefs about dietary behaviors, problem-solving skills, relapse prevention, and social support (Smith West et al., 2004). Culturally relevant interventions also include attention to individual needs, food preferences, economic realities, food availability, and family and cultural dynamics (Whitfield et al., 2002). In general, effects for obesity interventions have been small and relapse rates high (Bautista-Castano et al., 2004). In a meta-analysis of obesity prevention programs, Stice, Shaw, and Marti (2006) reported an average intervention effect size (r) of .04, consistent with average effect sizes for other public health problems (e.g., HIV, smoking).

Interventions targeting physiological processes have the potential for greater effectiveness in terms of weight loss and maintenance, but the associated risks and side effects suggest that these interventions are recommended for individuals with BMI $\geq$ 30 (or BMI $\geq$ 27 with health complications). Pharmacotherapy interventions have yielded medium ($d = .45$) to large ($d = .91$) effect sizes, with greater weight loss associated with longer treatments (Haddock, Poston, Dill, Foreyt, & Ericsson, 2002). Surgical treatments such as gastric bypass or vertical banded gastroplasty may be appropriate treatments for individuals who are morbidly obese (BMI $\geq$ 40) and for whom other types of interventions have been unsuccessful (Wadden et al., 2002).

Attempts have also been made to intervene at the community and environmental levels, such as the "5-a-Day for Better Health" program to increase fruit and vegetable consumption, and efforts to manipulate the costs and availability of healthier foods in local supermarkets and cafeteria selections in schools. These have demonstrated some success, but the magnitude of the effects has been small (Smith West et al., 2004). For example, randomized clinical trials of the 5-a-Day intervention have revealed an average change in fruit and vegetable consumption of .68 servings per day (National Cancer Institute, 2006). McArthur's (1998) meta-analysis of school-based interventions for heart-healthy eating similarly revealed a small effect size ($d = .24$).

Physical Activity

Although physical activity can be related to obesity, physical activity has also been recognized by the American Heart Association as an independent factor in cardiovascular disease, and it has been identified as protective against other conditions such as hypertension, Type II diabetes, osteoporosis, colon cancer, depression, and anxiety (U.S. Department of Health and Human Services, USDHHS, 1996). Physical activity has also been found to affect health care utilization and health care costs. For example, moderately active retirees had significantly lower total health care costs over a 2-year period than did sedentary individuals (Wang, McDonald, Reffitt, & Edington, 2005).

Children are the most physically active segment of the population, but by the time they reach school age, activity levels start moving toward a more adult lifestyle (Dubbert, King, Marcus, & Sallis, 2004). The rates for meeting the National Association for Sport and Physical Education guideline of 60 minutes of moderate physical activity per day ranged from 100% for Grades 1 to 3 to 29% for Grades 10 to 12 (Pate et al., 2002), and only 25% of adults met the recommended 30 minutes per day of moderate activity (USDHHS, 1996).

Models of Physical Activity

Numerous theories have been used as the basis for interventions to promote physical activity. Dubbert et al. (2004) suggested that the most promising models are the social cognitive (Bandura, 1986), stages of change (Prochaska & DiClemente, 1992), and relapse prevention models (Marlatt & Gordon, 1985). However, they also noted that to date none of these models alone have been sufficient for understanding, predicting, and changing physical activity levels for health.

Risk and Protective Factors in Physical Activity

National surveys reveal that girls are less physically active than boys (Dubbert et al., 2004). Ethnic minority youth are less physically active than non-Hispanic White youth, but it is not clear whether this difference can be attributed to socioeconomic status or other cultural factors (USDHHS, 1996). Among African American women, intrapersonal (e.g., perceived functional ability, SES), interpersonal (e.g., social norms, social support), and environmental (e.g., safe facilities, organizational resources) factors have been identified as potential targets for physical activity research and interventions (Fleury & Lee, 2006). A number of barriers to exercise have been identified among youth, including gender stereotypes, program or facility barriers, family or relationship constraints on leisure time, and confidence or competence factors (Rees et al., 2006).

In a meta-analysis of international research examining media use and physical activity among children and youth, there were small but statistically significant relations of TV viewing ($r = -.13$) and video/computer game use ($r = -.14$) to physical activity (Marshall, Biddle, Gorely, Cameron, & Murdey, 2004). In adults, lower levels of physical activity have typically been associated with lower income, less education, older age, ethnic minority status, and less social support (Dubbert et al., 2004). Stress has not specifically been examined as a predictor in physical activity, although one might argue that exercise is one of the health behaviors that erode during the lifestyle drift that occurs in times of stress. Aerobic fitness has, however, been identified as a buffer against stress (Plante, Chizmar, & Owen, 1999).

Interventions to Increase Physical Activity

Physical activity interventions are typically age-specific. Most interventions with youth have been based in the school system and usually include a classroom component (Dubbert et al., 2004). A wide variety of intervention strategies have been tested with adults, involving individual face-to-face intervention, telehealth approaches, print-based interventions, health care counseling, and community-based strategies. A meta-analysis of the effects of physical activity interventions with older adults revealed small but significant effects for activity interventions ($d = .24$) on well-being, and the largest treatment effects were demonstrated for social cognitive outcomes such as self-efficacy, overall well-being, and view of self (Netz, Wu, Becker, & Tenenbaum, 2005).

A meta-analysis of physical activity intervention studies comparing treatment versus control conditions revealed an overall effect size of .26, with higher effect sizes found for various moderating conditions such as incorporating center-based exercise ($d = .49$), intense contact between participants and intervention personnel ($d = .40$), and recommending moderate intensity ($d = .58$) exercise (Conn,

Valentine, & Cooper, 2002). Dubbert et al. (2004) noted that most physical activity interventions are based on cognitive and behavioral theories. Dishman and Buckworth's (1996) meta-analysis of interventions to promote physical activity revealed that cognitive-behavioral treatment programs typically produced a 10% to 25% increase in physical activity frequency compared with no-treatment control conditions. However, more recent research testing interventions based on other theoretical models provides support for transtheoretical, social cognitive, and relapse prevention constructs (e.g., Lewis et al., 2006; Stetson et al., 2005), with moderate effect sizes ($d = .34$; Kosma, Cardinal, & McCubbin, 2005).

Environmental interventions to support physical activity appear to complement individual intervention strategies, making it easier for individuals of all ages to be active (Sallis & Owen, 2002). Examples of environmental interventions include improving access to recreational facilities and children's play areas, changing the aesthetic characteristics of neighborhoods to increase enjoyable scenery for exercisers, or planning neighborhoods so individuals may walk or cycle from residential areas to businesses. Relatively little research has been conducted to evaluate community-based physical activity interventions, and no meta-analyses have been conducted. A systematic review of workplace healthy lifestyle interventions revealed three studies with a physical activity component that yielded inconclusive results (Engbers, van Poppel, Chin A Paw, & van Mechelen, 2005).

Risky Sexual Behavior

Risky sexual behavior represents an important health issue for society in terms of both sexually transmitted diseases (STDs) and unintended pregnancies. Sexually risky behavior takes a toll on society directly through costs of treating STDs and indirectly through economic and societal consequences of morbidity and decreased social well-being associated with unintended births to teenagers and low-income single women (Clark, Rhodes, Rogers, & Liddon, 2004). An estimated 19 million STD infections occur each year, about half of them to people aged 15 to 24, with an estimated annual direct medical cost of about $14.1 billion annually (Centers for Disease Control and Prevention [CDC], 2006).

In 2001, 49% of the 6.4 million pregnancies in the United States were unintended, affecting roughly 5% of women ages 15 to 44 (Finer & Henshaw, 2006). Unintended births are associated with poorer child and maternal health outcomes, as women with unintended pregnancies are less likely to seek prenatal care and more likely to use alcohol and tobacco during pregnancy (e.g., Hellerstedt et al., 1998). The public cost of pregnancies to women under the age of 20 has been estimated to be $9.1 billion annually, factoring in effects on the mother, father, and child, such as costs associated with health care, child welfare, public assistance, and lost tax revenue associated with lower educational attainment (Hoffman, 2006).

Risky sexual behaviors include early onset of sexual intercourse, sex with multiple partners, unprotected intercourse (without use of condoms or other contraceptive methods), concurrent alcohol or drug use, anal intercourse, and intercourse with high-risk partners. Reviews of the psychological research on sexual risk behavior in HIV/AIDS revealed a consistent set of predictors of high-risk behaviors: (a) cognitive and attitude factors (e.g., incorrect beliefs about risk, negative attitudes toward condoms, low self-efficacy for safe sex behavior), (b) poor risk reduction skills (e.g., sexual negotiation, assertiveness, incorrect condom use), (c) relationship factors (e.g., safer sex behaviors in more casual relationships), (d) situational factors contributing to risk (e.g., concurrent substance abuse), and (e) limited social and peer support for risk-reducing behavior change (Kelly & Kalichman, 2002).

Risk and Protective Factors for Sexual Behavior

Sexually transmitted diseases (STDs) disproportionately affect adolescents and young adults. Factors implicated in those higher rates are that adolescents and young adults are more likely to have multiple sex partners, have partners from a population subgroup with a high rate of STDs, and have higher rates of unprotected sex (IOM, 1997). Adolescents experience more barriers to receiving health care and are less likely to seek health services. Adolescent sexually risky behavior, and other risk behaviors, might also be considered in the context of normal developmental processes involving experimentation with different behaviors and values and emancipation from parental dependency. However, the consequences of those risky behaviors can ultimately jeopardize other developmental tasks, such as the fulfillment of expected social roles and the acquisition of essential skills for young adulthood (Clark et al., 2004).

Some psychosocial factors in adolescent risky sexual behavior have been identified. Individual factors such as intelligence, trauma experience, substance use, and homelessness have been associated with earlier age of sexual initiation (Clark et al., 2004). Age of sexual initiation was also associated with mothers' history of sexual initiation and having sexually active peers (Mott, Fondell, Hu, Koweleski-Jones, & Menaghan, 1996). Length of the intimate relationship was also associated with initiation of sex and safe sex practices (Civic, 2000; Kelly & Kalichman, 2002). Condom use self-efficacy has been predicted by variables such as condom use attitudes, condom use barriers, satisfaction with sexual communication, anticipated numbers of sexual partners, one-time sexual encounters, and ethnic identity (Farmer & Meston, 2006).

Race and ethnicity are predictors of STD rates, with the highest rates among African American and American Indian/Alaska Native groups, followed by Hispanic/Latinos, Whites, and Asian Americans (CDC, 2006). Furthermore, risk reduction interventions were less consistently effective for African American women than women of other ethnic groups (Mize, Robinson, Bockting, & Scheltema, 2002). These disparities are not, however, simply the result of race/ethnicity but rather reflect the association between race/ethnicity and poverty, access to health care, drug use, and living in communities with high rates of STDs (Clark et al., 2004). Rates of unintended pregnancy were substantially higher for women who were younger (18 to 24), unmarried (particularly cohabitating), low-income, with less education, and who were members of racial/ethnic minority groups (Finer & Henshaw, 2006).

Researchers are beginning to identify specific cultural risk and protective factors. A comparison of cultural factors and risky sexual behavior revealed differences in the effects of cultural variables such as collectivism, which was negatively associated with risky behavior for Cambodian youth but not significantly associated with risky behavior among Lao/Mien youth (Le & Kato, 2006). Haubrich, Myers, Calzavara, Ryder, and Medved (2004) conducted a qualitative interview study in which they identified salient aspects of the bathhouse culture (e.g., moral conceptions of self and others, identity management) that have potential implications for safe sex practices in gay bathhouses.

Other psychosocial variables are also being considered with regard to sexual risk-taking. For example, stress, depression, and low levels of social support were associated with sexually risky behavior and STDs in a sample of 403 women, and the psychosocial variables were stronger predictors for adolescents (ages 14–19) versus young women (ages 20 to 25; Mazzaferro et al., 2006). Treatment adherence has been primarily focused on pharmacotherapy treatment. Factors that affect adherence to combination antiretroviral therapy include education, perceived treatment efficacy, and greater knowledge of HIV treatments and consequences of poor adherence (Wagner, Remien, Carballo-Dieguez, & Dolezal, 2002).

Interventions to Decrease Risky Sexual Behavior

A variety of face-to-face interventions have been tested with individuals, couples, and small groups. Such interventions have typically combined treatment components including education, exercises to change attitudes and beliefs about safer sex behaviors, behavioral skills training, communication/assertiveness training, risk-behavior self-management strategies, problem-solving training, and support for behavior change efforts (Kelly & Kalichman, 2002). Project RESPECT is one of the largest intervention trials, including nearly 6,000 men and women STD clinic patients, who were assigned to an education-only control condition, two-session skills training condition, or four-session intervention based on social cognitive theory and theory of reasoned action (Ajzen & Fishbein, 1980) principles. Relative risk (i.e., how much risk is reduced in a treatment group versus the control group) was calculated at 3-, 6-, 9-, and 12-month follow-ups. The intervention conditions showed significantly more participants reporting no unprotected intercourse (relative risk [RR] = 1.21 for advanced counseling; participants in the four-session counseling group were 1.21 times more likely to report no unprotected sex; RR = 1.15 for skills training) and significant reductions in STD infection rates (RR = .69 for advanced counseling, .71 for skills training) relative to control group participants (Kamb et al., 1998).

A meta-analysis of intervention studies involving Motivational Interviewing, a technique designed to move clients through the stages of change, revealed moderate effects ($d = .25$ to $.57$) compared to control conditions for alcohol, drugs, diet, and exercise, but such interventions were not efficacious for smoking or HIV-risk behavior (Burke, Arkowitz, & Menchola, 2003). In a meta-analysis of persuasive content of interventions, Albarracin et al. (2003) found that messages designed to teach behavioral skills had a greater effect on condom use ($d = .36$) versus those that did not ($d = .16$), and messages that had been the focus to date (i.e., risks of infection, increasing subjective experience of threat) did not have a positive effect on condom use.

Interventions have also been directed toward particular high-risk subpopulations such as adolescents, young men who have sex with men, injection drug users, sex workers, and individuals who are HIV seropositive (e.g., Clark et al., 2004; Kelly & Kalichman, 2002). A cultural adaptation of the Project RESPECT intervention was effective among female sex workers in China in increasing knowledge, consistent condom use (odds ratio [OR] = 2.23; that is, intervention participants were 2.23 times more likely to report increased condom use), and decreasing STD rates (OR = .44; i.e., .44 times less likely to report a newly diagnosed STD; Xiaoming et al., 2006). A meta-analysis of interventions with men who have sex with men revealed significant decreases in unprotected anal intercourse (OR = .77) and numbers of sexual partners (OR = .85), significant increases in condom use (OR = 1.61), and support for interventions based on the relapse prevention model (OR = .61) and diffusion of innovations theory (Rogers, 1962; OR = .62) (Herbst et al., 2005). OR is the ratio of the odds of an event occurring in one group to the odds of it occurring in another group; OR > 1.0 means that the odds for the treatment group have increased, while OR < 1.0 indicates a decrease. Based on a logistic model and used in case-control and cross-sectional designs, OR may exaggerate the effect size compared with relative risk (Schechtman, 2002). Furthermore, OR is dimensionless and does not approximate relative risk when the initial risk is high.

Risk reduction interventions provided as part of drug abuse treatment yielded small-to-moderate effect sizes for knowledge ($d = .31$), sexual behavior ($d = .26$), and risk-reduction skills ($d = .62$; Prendergast, Urada, & Podus, 2001). A meta-analysis of research on interventions to reduce adolescent unintended pregnancies unfortunately revealed no effects (odds ratios not significantly different than 1.0) on delay of first intercourse (OR = 1.12), use of birth control at every intercourse (OR = .95), or pregnancy rates (OR = 1.04; DiCenso, Guyatt, Willan, & Griffith, 2002). Examination of the effects of sexual risk reduction interventions on frequency of sexual behavior also revealed that interventions neither increased or decreased sexual frequency ($d = -.004$) or numbers of sexual partners ($d = .008$)— which may address conservative organizations' concerns that providing risk reduction programs in schools might inadvertently increase HIV rates by disinhibiting sexual contact (Smoak, Scott-Sheldon, Johnson, & Carey, 2006).

Interventions at the community level, involving role models and popular opinion leaders in the community, have yielded risk-behavior reductions as high as 30% (Kelly & Kalichman, 2002). Structural, policy, and environmental level interventions (e.g., condom availability programs, needle exchange programs) have also had positive effects on infection rates (Kelly & Kalichman, 2002). A meta-analysis of 10 studies involving needle exchange programs revealed a small but significant effect size ($d = .28$; Cross, Saunders, & Bartelli, 1998).

TERTIARY PREVENTION

Although the focus of this chapter has been on concepts and activities related to health promotion and disease prevention, counseling psychologists have for a long time made contributions to the health care system at the tertiary level of prevention; that is, after a disease has occurred. This includes remedial activities aimed at helping patients to manage or cope with illness and disability (e.g., see Peterson & Elliott, Chapter 13, this volume). "Practicing in medical and primary care settings provides a tremendous opportunity for psychologists to reduce psychological symptoms and hospital costs" (Robinson & James, 2005, p. 29).

Primary care consultation involves positioning psychologists in primary care settings to bring specialized psychological knowledge to bear on patients' health concerns and to provide support related to primary care activities and goals (Rowan & Runyan, 2005). As primary care consultants, psychologists provide assessment, brief intervention, and sometimes follow-up services to meet the immediate needs of medical patients. Psychologists working in medical settings might address issues such as psychological sequelae of medical conditions or disability (e.g., adjustment, family issues), psychophysiological disorders (e.g., migraine headaches, irritable bowel syndrome), lifestyle behavior change (e.g., smoking cessation, weight control), problems of health care providers and systems (e.g., physician-patient relationships, staff burnout), and psychological and behavioral aspects of stressful medical procedures (Papas, Belar, & Rozensky, 2004).

COMPETENCIES AND TRAINING FOR COUNSELING HEALTH PSYCHOLOGISTS

For a career as a professional health psychologist, the recommended training route is an American Psychological Association (APA)–accredited counseling or clinical psychology program, with eligibility for licensure as a professional psychologist and board certification (APA Division of Health Psychology, 2006), which can be achieved in such subdisciplines as health psychology, rehabilitation psychology, or neuropsychology. Although several individuals and organizations have made recommendations for health psychology training, no formal models have been developed and tested. The distinct knowledge base for professional practice in "clinical health psychology" is contained in the APA archival description of the specialty, which was recognized in 1997 (APA Council of Representatives, 1997).

In counseling psychology, attention to issues of training has not kept pace with student and professional interest in health psychology (D'Achiardi-Ressler, Zerth, Chwalisz, & Miller, 2006). Recommendations for counseling health psychology (CHP) training are consistent with the APA specialty description and include foundational training (e.g., scientific, methodological, and theoretical foundations for practice; professional, ethical, and legal aspects of practice; assessment and diagnosis; cultural and individual diversity), along with health care–specific training (e.g., biological and psychological bases of health systems and behavior, knowledge and skills regarding health policy and organizations, medical terminology, psychopharmacology, medical aspects of disability) (e.g., Alcorn, 1998). Practica involving supervised health psychology experiences in medical or community settings is critical for students to gain experience with health-related issues, clients who are experiencing such issues, structure and procedures of medical settings, and interactions with physicians and other health-related disciplines (Suls & Rothman, 2004). Health psychologists also need competencies relevant to the demands of managed care organizations: (a) brief therapy modalities and time-limited service delivery, (b) active/directive role in therapy, (c) patient advocacy, (d) interactions with staff and providers on behalf of patients, and (e) working within care plan limits (Papas et al., 2004).

A survey of doctoral programs in counseling psychology revealed that 82% of accredited programs either offered health psychology track training or could adapt training to suit students' interest in health psychology. Even programs that reported that they did not offer health psychology training for the most part had relevant coursework available to students, but lacked relevant practicum experiences (D'Achiardi et al., 2006). Interestingly, all counseling psychology programs, regardless of stated training focus, had students and faculty who were involved in research or other activities related to CHP.

In 2001, Kazarian and Evans concluded that health psychologists and other health care professionals had not received adequate training for culturally competent health research and practice and that lack of cultural competence posed major legal and ethical concerns for the professions. "Competence in cultural health psychology requires consideration of culture in health promotion and maintenance; prevention, treatment, and rehabilitation; advancement of etiological theories of illness; and health care system analysis and formulation" (Kazarian & Evans, 2001, p. 35). They suggested that multicultural health psychology competence also includes dimensions seen in the general multicultural counseling competence literature (e.g., awareness of own culture, awareness of other cultures, culturally relevant behavior and skills). Presumably all accredited counseling psychology programs provide training in multicultural psychology and develop students' multicultural counseling competencies, giving counseling psychology a "leg up" compared to other psychological disciplines in meeting the cultural demands of health psychology research and practice. Beyond basic multicultural counseling competence, training programs should include theory and research in multicultural health psychology (e.g., Whitfield et al., 2002).

CONCLUSION: COUNSELING PSYCHOLOGY AND HEALTH PROMOTION

Demographic, economic, and health care trends warrant increasing efforts toward health promotion and disease prevention in the United States. The biopsychosocial model, which is well supported within psychology and gaining increasing support in the medical community, provides many opportunities for science and practice in counseling health psychology. Furthermore, traditional counseling psychology work settings (e.g., college counseling centers, community mental health centers, Veteran's Administration facilities) are seeing increasing numbers of clients with health-related concerns such as obesity, eating disorders, substance abuse issues, and sexual health issues. Most counseling psychology training programs can gear up, with relatively few changes, to offer sufficient training for graduates to pursue a career in health psychology.

The training, philosophy, and identity of counseling psychology are perfectly suited to health promotion and disease prevention activities. Our holistic approach to conceptualizing client concerns maps nicely onto the biopsychosocial model. Counseling psychology's focus on strengths, consultation, and prevention can facilitate the development of health promotion and disease prevention activities. Perhaps most importantly, counseling psychologists have the theoretical, methodological, and practical knowledge in multicultural psychology needed to address the critical issue of health disparities. Thus, health promotion and disease prevention are professional activities that warrant additional attention by counseling psychologists.

REFERENCES

Aboud, F. E. (1998). *Health psychology in global perspective*. Thousand Oaks, CA: Sage.

Ajzen, I., & Fishbein, M. (1980). *Understanding attitudes and predicting social behavior*. Englewood Cliffs, NJ: Prentice-Hall.

Albarracin, D., McNatt, P. S., Klein, C. T., Ho, R. M., Michell, A. L., & Kumkale, G. T. (2003). Persuasive communications to change actions: An analysis of behavioral and cognitive impact in HIV prevention. *Health Psychology, 22*(2), 166–177.

Alcorn, J. D. (1998). Training for health settings. In S. L. Roth-Roemer, S. E. Robinson Kurpius, & C. Carmin (Eds.), *The emerging role of counseling psychology in health care* (pp. 30–54). Chicago: Norton Professional Books.

American Psychological Association Council of Representatives. (1997). Archival description of clinical health psychology as a specialty in professional psychology. *Minutes of the Council of Representatives Meeting, August 1997*. Washington, DC: Author.

American Psychological Association Division of Health Psychology. (2006). *What a health psychologist does and how to become one*. Washington, DC: Author. Retrieved December 1, 2006, from www.health-psych.org/articles/what_is.php on.

Bandura, A. (1986). *Social foundations of thought and action: A social cognitive theory*. Englewood Cliffs, NJ: Prentice-Hall.

Baum, A., Perry, N. W., Jr., & Tarbell, S. (2004). The development of psychology as a health science. In T. J. Boll, R. G. Frank, A. Baum, & J. L. Wallander (Eds.), *Handbook of clinical health psychology: Vol. 3. Models and perspectives in health psychology* (pp. 9–28). Washington, DC: American Psychological Association.

Bautista-Castano, I., Molina-Cabrillana, J., Montoya-Alonso, J. A., & Serra-Majem, L. (2004). Variables predictive of adherence to diet and physical activity recommendations in the treatment of obesity and overweight, in a group of Spanish subjects. *International Journal of Obesity, 28*(5), 697–705.

Belgrave, F. Z., & Allison, K. W. (2006). *African American psychology: From Africa to America*. Thousand Oaks, CA: Sage.

Bennett Johnson, S., & Newman Carlson, D. (2004). Medical regimen adherence: Concepts, assessment, and interventions. In T. J. Boll, J. M. Raczynski, & L. C. Leviton (Eds.), *Handbook of clinical health psychology: Vol. 2. Disorders of behavior and health* (pp. 329–354). Washington, DC: American Psychological Association.

Brownbridge, G., & Fielding, D. M. (1994). Psychosocial adjustment and adherence to dialysis treatment regimens. *Pediatric Nephrology, 8*, 744–749.

Burke, B., Arkowitz, H., & Menchola, H. (2003). The efficacy of motivational interviewing: A meta-analysis of controlled clinical trials. *Journal of Consulting and Clinical Psychology, 71*, 843–861.

Centers for Disease Control and Prevention. (2006). *Trends in reportable sexually transmitted diseases in the United States, 2005: National surveillance data for chlamydia, gonorrhea, and syphilis*. Atlanta, GA: U.S. Department of Health and Human Services, Centers for Disease Control and Prevention. Retrieved December 15, 2006, from http://www.cdc.gov/std/stats/05pdf/trends-2005.pdf.

Chwalisz, K., & Hanson, T. J. (2001, March). *Family caregivers: A population in need of counseling psychology's attention*. Poster presented at the National Counseling Psychology Conference, Houston, TX.

Civic, D. (2000). College students' reasons for nonuse of condoms within dating relationships. *Journal of Sexual and Marital Therapy, 26*(1), 95–105.

Clark, L. F., Rhodes, S. D., Rogers, W., & Liddon, N. (2004). The context of sexual risk behavior. In T. J. Boll, J. M. Raczynski, & L. C. Leviton (Eds.), *Handbook of clinical health psychology: Vol. 2. Disorders of behavior and health* (pp. 121–146). Washington, DC: American Psychological Association.

Coe, K., Attakai, A., Papenfuss, M., Giuliano, A., Martin, L., & Nuvayestewa, L. (2004). Traditionalism and its relationship to disease risk and protective behaviors of women living on the Hopi reservation. *Health Care for Women International, 25*(5), 391–410.

Commission on Chronic Illness. (1957). *Chronic illness in the United States* (Vol. 1). Cambridge, MA: Harvard University Press.

Conn, V. S., Valentine, J. C., & Cooper, H. M. (2002). Interventions to increase physical activity among aging adults: A meta-analysis. *Annals of Behavioral Medicine, 24*(3), 190–200.

Cross, J. E., Saunders, C. M., & Bartelli, D. (1998). The effectiveness of educational and needle exchange programs: A meta-analysis of HIV prevention strategies for injecting drug users. *Quality and Quantity, 32*(2), 165–180.

D'Achiardi-Ressler, C., Zerth, E. O., Chwalisz, K., & Miller, S. A. (2006). *Current training and research in counseling health psychology: A national survey*. Manuscript submitted for publication.

Davis, C., Levitan, R. D., Muglia, P., Bewell, C., & Kennedy, J. L. (2004). Decision-making deficits and overeating: A risk model for obesity. *Obesity Research, 12*(6), 929–935.

Davis Martin, P., & Brantley, P. J. (2004). Stress, coping, and social support in health and behavior. In T. J. Boll, J. M. Raczynski, & L. C. Leviton (Eds.), *Handbook of clinical health psychology: Vol. 2. Disorders of behavior and health* (pp. 233–267). Washington, DC: American Psychological Association.

DiCenso, A., Guyatt, G., Willan, A., & Griffith, L. (2002). Interventions to reduce unintended pregnancies among adolescents: A systematic review of randomized controlled trials. *British Medical Journal, 324*(7351), 1426–1430.

Dishman, R. K., & Buckworth, J. (1996). Increasing physical activity: A quantitative synthesis. *Medicine and Science in Sports and Exercise, 28*(6), 706–719.

Dubbert, P. M., King, A. C., Marcus, B. H., & Sallis, J. F. (2004). Promotion of physical activity through the life span. In T. J. Boll, J. M. Raczynski, & L. C. Leviton (Eds.), *Handbook of clinical health psychology: Vol. 2. Disorders of behavior and health* (pp. 147–181). Washington, DC: American Psychological Association.

Engbers, L. H., van Poppel, M. N. M., Chin A Paw, M. J. M., & van Mechelen, W. (2005). Worksite health promotion programs with environmental changes: A systematic review. *American Journal of Preventive Medicine, 29*(1), 61–70.

Epstein, L., & Cluss, P. (1982). A behavioral medicine perspective on adherence to long-term medical regimens. *Journal of Consulting and Clinical Psychology, 50*, 950–971.

Evans, D. R., & Kazarian, S. S. (2001). Health promotion, disease prevention, and quality of life. In S. S. Kazarian & D. R. Evans (Eds.), *Handbook of cultural health psychology* (pp. 85–112). San Diego: Academic Press.

Farmer, M. A., & Meston, C. M. (2006). Predictors of condom use self-efficacy in an ethnically diverse university sample. *Archives of Sexual Behavior, 35*(3), 313–326.

Finer, L. B., & Henshaw, S. K. (2006). Disparities in rates of unintended pregnancy in the United States, 1994 and 2001. *Perspectives on Sexual and Reproductive Health, 38*(2), 90–96.

Flegel, K. M., Carroll, M. D., Ogden, C. L., & Johnson, C. L. (2002). Prevalence and trends in obesity among U.S. adults, 1999–2000. *Journal of the American Medical Association, 288*, 1723–1727.

Fleury, J., & Lee, S. M. (2006). The social ecological model and physical activity in African American women. *American Journal of Community Psychology, 37*(1/2), 129–140.

Haddock, C. K., Poston, W. S. C., Dill, P. L., Foreyt, J. P., & Ericsson, M. (2002). Pharmacotherapy for obesity: A quantitative analysis of four decades of published randomized clinical trials. *International Journal of Obesity and Related Metabolic Disorders, 26*, 262–273.

Haubrich, D. J., Myers, T., Calzavara, L., Ryder, K., & Medved, W. (2004). Gay and bisexual men's experiences of bathhouse culture and sex: "Looking for love in all the wrong places." *Culture, Health, and Sexuality, 6*(1), 19–29.

Hayward, M. D., Crimmins, E. M., Miles, T. P., & Yang, Y. (2000). The significance of socioeconomic status in explaining the racial gap in chronic health conditions. *American Sociological Review, 64*, 910–930.

Hedley, A. A., Ogden, C. L., Johnson, C. L., Carroll, M. D., Curtin, L. R., & Flegal, K. M. (2004). Overweight and obesity among U.S. children, adolescents, and adults, 1999–2002. *Journal of the American Medical Association, 291*, 2847–2850.

Hellerstedt, W. L., Pirie, P. L., Lando, H. A., Curry, S. J., McBride, C. M., Grothaus, L. C., et al. (1998). Differences in preconceptional and prenatal behaviors in women with intended and unintended pregnancies. *American Journal of Public Health, 88*(4), 663–666.

Herbst, J. H., Sherba, R. T., Crepaz, N., DeLuca, J. B., Zohrabyan, L., Stall, R. D., et al. (2005). Sexual risk behavior of men who have sex with men. *Journal of Acquired Immune Deficiency Syndromes, 39*(2), 228–241.

Hoffman, S. D. (2006). *By the numbers: The public costs of teen childbearing.* Washington, DC: National Campaign to Prevent Teen Pregnancy. Retrieved December 12, 2006, from www.teenpregnancy.org/costs/pdf/report/BTN_National_Report.pdf.

Horne, R., & Weinman, J. (1998). Predicting treatment adherence: An overview of theoretical models. In L. Myers & K. Midence (Eds.), *Adherence to treatment in medical conditions* (pp. 25–50). New Delhi, India: Harwood Academic Press.

Hutchins, E. (1995). *Cognition in the wild.* Cambridge: MIT Press.

Institute of Medicine. (1997). *The hidden epidemic: Confronting sexually transmitted diseases.* Washington, DC: Committee on Prevention and Control of Sexually Transmitted Diseases, National Academy Press.

Institute of Medicine. (2003). *Unequal treatment: Confronting racial and ethnic disparities in healthcare.* Washington, DC: National Academies Press.

Johnson, J. L., & Cameron, M. C. (2001). Barriers to providing effective mental health services to American Indians. *Mental Health Services Research, 3*(4), 215–223.

Kamb, M. L., Fishbein, M., Douglas, J. M., Jr., Rhodes, F., Rogers, J., Bolan, G., et al. (1998). Efficacy of risk-reduction counseling to prevent human immunodeficiency virus and sexually transmitted diseases: A randomized controlled trial. *Journal of the American Medical Association, 280*(13), 1161–1167.

Kazarian, S. S., & Evans, D. R. (2001). Health psychology and culture: Embracing the 21st century. In S. S. Kazarian & D. R. Evans (Eds.), *Handbook of cultural health psychology* (pp. 3–43). San Diego: Academic Press.

Kelly, J. A., & Kalichman, S. C. (2002). Behavioral research in HIV/AIDS primary and secondary prevention: Recent advances and future directions. *Journal of Consulting and Clinical Psychology, 70*(3), 626–639.

Kosma, M., Cardinal, B. J., & McCubbin, J. A. (2005). A pilot study of a web-based physical activity motivational program for adults with physical disabilities. *Disability and Rehabilitation: An International Multidisciplinary Journal, 27*(23), 1435–1442.

Kumanyika, S., Wilson, J. F., & Guilford-Davenport, M. (1993). Weight-related attitudes and behaviors of Black women. *Journal of the American Dietetic Association, 93*(4), 416–422.

Le, T. N., & Kato, T. (2006). The role of peer, parent, and cultural in risky sexual behavior for Cambodian and Lao/Mien adolescents. *Journal of Adolescent Health, 38*(3), 288–296.

Lewis, B. A., Forsyth, L. H., Pinto, B. M., Bock, B. C., Roberts, M., & Marcus, B. H. (2006). Psychosocial mediators of physical activity in a randomized controlled intervention trial. *Journal of Sport and Exercise Psychology, 28*(2), 193–204.

Lieberman, L., & Jackson, F. L. C. (1995). Race and three models of human origin. *American Anthropologist, 97*(2), 231–242.

Mann, T. (1996). Why do we need a health psychology of gender or sexual orientation? In P. M. Kato & T. Mann (Eds.), *Handbook of diversity issues in health psychology* (pp. 187–198). New York: Plenum Press.

Marlatt, G. A., & Gordon, J. R. (1985). *Relapse prevention.* New York: Guilford Press.

Marshall, S. J., Biddle, S. J. H., Gorely, T., Cameron, N., & Murdey, I. (2004). Relationships between media use, body fatness, and physical activity in children and youth: A meta-analysis. *International Journal of Obesity, 28*(10), 1238–1246.

Martin, R., & Leventhal, H. (2004). Symptom perception and health care-seeking behavior. In T. J. Boll, J. M. Raczynski, & L. C. Leviton (Eds.), *Handbook of clinical health psychology: Vol. 2. Disorders of behavior and health* (pp. 299–328). Washington, DC: American Psychological Association.

Mazzaferro, K. E., Murray, P. J., Ness, R. B., Bass, D. C., Tyus, N., & Cook, R. L. (2006). Depression, stress, and social support as predictors of high-risk sexual behaviors and STIs in young women. *Journal of Adolescent Health, 39*(4), 601–603.

McArthur, D. B. (1998). Heart healthy eating behaviors of children following a school-based intervention: A meta-analysis. *Issues in Comprehensive Pediatric Nursing, 21*(1), 35–48.

Mize, S. J., Robinson, B. E., Bockting, W. O., & Scheltema, K. E. (2002). Meta-analysis of the effectiveness of HIV prevention interventions for women. *AIDS Care, 14*(2), 163–180.

Moles, A., Bartolomucci, A., Garbugino, L., Conti, R., Caprioli, A., Coccurello, R., et al. (2006). Psychosocial stress affects energy balance in mice: Modulation by social status. *Psychoneuroendocrinology, 31*(5), 623–633.

Mott, F. L., Fondell, M. M., Hu, P. N., Koweleski-Jones, L., & Menaghan, E. G. (1996). The determinants of first sex by age 14 in a high risk adolescent population. *Family Planning Perspectives, 28*(1), 13–18.

Mulato, M. S., & Berry, J. W. (2001). Health care practice in a multicultural context: Western and non-Western assumptions. In S. S. Kazarian & D. R. Evans (Eds.), *Handbook of cultural health psychology* (pp. 45–61). San Diego: Academic Press.

National Cancer Institute. (2006). *5 a Day for Better Health Program Evaluation Report: Evaluation.* Washington, DC: National Cancer Institute. Retrieved March 3, 2007, from www.cancercontrol.cancer.gov/5ad_6_eval.html.

Netz, Y., Wu, M., Becker, B. J., & Tenenbaum, G. (2005). Physical activity and psychological well-being in advanced age: A meta-analysis of intervention studies. *Psychology and Aging, 20*(2), 272–284.

Ogden, C. L., Carroll, M. D., Curtin, L. R., McDowell, M. A., Tabak, C. J., & Flegel, K. M. (2006). Prevalence of overweight and obesity in the United States, 1999–2004. *Journal of the American Medical Association, 295*(13), 1549–1555.

Papas, R. K., Belar, C. D., & Rozensky, R. H. (2004). The practice of clinical health psychology: Professional issues. In T. J. Boll, R. G. Frank, A. Baum, & J. L. Wallander (Eds.), *Handbook of clinical health psychology: Vol. 3. Models and perspectives in health psychology* (pp. 293–319). Washington, DC: American Psychological Association.

Parham, T. A., White, J. L., & Ajamu, A. (1999). *The psychology of Blacks: An African-centered perspective* (3rd ed.) Upper Saddle River, NJ: Prentice Hall.

Pate, R. R., Freedom, P. S., Sallis, J. F., Taylor, W. C., Sirand, J., Trost, S. G., et al. (2002). Compliance with physical activity guidelines: Prevalence in a population of children and youth. *Annals of Epidemiology, 12*(5), 303–308.

Pickett, K. E., & Pearl, M. (2001). Multilevel analyses of neighborhood socioeconomic context and health outcomes: A critical review. *Journal of Epidemiology and Community Health, 55*, 111–122.

Plante, T. G., Chizmar, L., & Owen, D. (1999). The contribution of perceived fitness to physiological and self-reported responses to laboratory stress. *International Journal of Stress Management, 6*(1), 5–19.

Prendergast, M. L., Urada, D., & Podus, D. (2001). Meta-analysis of HIV risk-reduction interventions within drug abuse treatment programs. *Journal of Consulting and Clinical Psychology, 69*(3), 389–405.

Prochaska, J. O., & DiClemente, C. C. (1992). *Stages of change in the modification of problem behaviors.* Newbury Park, CA: Sage.

Rees, R., Kavanagh, J., Harden, A., Shepherd, J., Brunton, G., Oliver, S., et al. (2006). Young people and physical activity: A systematic review matching their views to effective interventions. *Health Education Research, 21*(6), 806–825.

Robinson, J. D., & James, L. C. (2005). Assessing the patient's need for medical evaluation: A psychologist's guide. In L. C. James & R. A. Folen (Eds.), *The primary care consultant: The next frontier for psychologists in hospitals and clinics* (pp. 29–37). Washington, DC: American Psychological Association.

Rogers, E. M. (1962). *Diffusion of innovations.* New York: Free Press.

Rowen, A. B., & Runyan, C. N. (2005). A primer on the consultation model of primary care behavioral health integration. In L. C. James & R. A. Folen (Eds.), *The primary care consultant: The next frontier for psychologists in hospitals and clinics* (pp. 9–27). Washington, DC: American Psychological Association.

Sallis, J., & Owen, N. (2002). Ecological models of health behavior. In K. Glanz, B. K. Rimer, & F. M. Lewis (Eds.), *Health behavior and health education: Theory, research, and practice* (pp. 462–485). San Francisco: Jossey-Bass.

Schechtman, E. (2002). Odds ratio, relative risk, absolute risk reduction, and the number needed to treat: Which of these should we use? *Value in Health, 5*(5), 431–436.

Sherbourne, C. D., Hays, R. D., Ordway, L. D., DiMatteo, M. R., & Kravitz, R. L. (1992). Antecedents of adherence to medical recommendations: Results from the medical outcomes study. *Journal of Behavioral Medicine, 15*, 447–469.

Shiraev, E., & Levy, D. (2004). *Cross-cultural psychology: Critical thinking and contemporary applications.* Boston: Allyn & Bacon.

Smith, T. W., Orleans, C. T., & Jenkins, C. D. (2004). Prevention and health promotion: Decades of progress, new challenges, and an emerging agenda. *Health Psychology, 23*(2), 126–131.

Smith West, D., Harvey-Berino, J., & Raczynski, J. M. (2004). Behavioral aspects of obesity, dietary intake, and chronic disease. In T. J. Boll, J. M. Raczynski, & L. C. Leviton (Eds.), *Handbook of clinical health psychology: Vol. 2. Disorders of behavior and health* (pp. 9–41). Washington, DC: American Psychological Association.

Smoak, N. D., Scott-Sheldon, L. A. J., Johnson, B. T., & Carey, M. P. (2006). Sexual risk reduction interventions do not inadvertently increase the overall frequency of sexual behavior: A meta-analysis of 174 studies with 116,735 participants. *Journal of Acquired Immune Deficiency Syndromes, 41*(3), 374–384.

Snowden, L. R. (2001). Barriers to effective mental health services for African Americans. *Mental Health Services Research, 3*(4), 181–187.

Stetson, B. A., Beacham, A. O., Frommelt, S. J., Boutelle, K. N., Cole, J. D., Ziegler, C. H., et al. (2005). Exercise slips in high-risk situations and activity patterns in long-term exercisers: An application of the Relapse Prevention Model. *Annals of Behavioral Medicine, 30*(1), 25–35.

Stice, E., Shaw, H., & Marti, C. N. (2006). A meta-analytic review of obesity prevention programs for children and adolescents: The skinny on interventions that work. *Psychological Bulletin, 132*(5), 667–691.

Strauss, R. S., & Pollack, H. A. (2001). Epidemic increase in childhood overweight 1986-1998. *Journal of the American Medical Association, 286*, 2845–2848.

Suls, J., & Rothman, A. (2004). Evolution of the biopsychosocial model: Prospects and challenges for health psychology. *Health Psychology, 23*(2), 119–125.

Turk, D. C., & Meichenbaum, D. (1991). Adherence to self-care regimens: The patient's perspective. In J. Sweet, R. Rozensky, & S. Tovian (Eds.), *Handbook of clinical psychology in medical settings* (pp. 249–268). New York: Plenum Press.

U.S. Department of Health and Human Services. (1996). *Physical activity and health: A report of the surgeon general*. Atlanta, GA: Author, Centers for Disease Control and Prevention, National Center for Chronic Disease Prevention and Health Promotion.

U.S. Department of Health and Human Services (2000, November). *Healthy people 2010* (2nd ed.) with Understanding and Improving Health (Vols. 1–2). Washington, DC: U.S. Government Printing Office.

van der Klink, J. J. L., Blonk, R. W. B., Schene, A. H., & van Dijk, F. J. H. (2001). The benefits of interventions for work-related stress. *American Journal of Public Health, 91*(2), 270–276.

Vega, W. A., & Lopez, S. R. (2001). Priority issues in Latino mental health services research. *Mental Health Services Research, 3*(4), 189–200.

Wadden, T. A., Brownell, K. D., & Foster, G. D. (2002). Obesity: Responding to the global epidemic. *Journal of Consulting and Clinical Psychology, 70*(3), 510–525.

Wagner, G. J., Remien, R. H., Carballo-Dieguez, A., & Dolezal, C. (2002). Correlates of adherence to combination antiretroviral therapy among members of HIV-positive mixed status couples. *AIDS Care, 14*(1), 105–109.

Wang, F., McDonald, T., Reffitt, B., & Edington, D. W. (2005). BMI, physical activity, and health care utilization/costs among Medicare retirees. *Obesity Research, 13*(8), 1450–1457.

Whitfield, K. E., Weidner, G., Clark, R., & Anderson, N. B. (2002). Sociodemographic diversity and behavioral medicine. *Journal of Consulting and Clinical Psychology, 70*(3), 463–481.

Xiaoming, L., Wang, B., Fang, X., Zhao, R., Stanton, B., Hong, Y., et al. (2006). Short-term effect of a cultural adaptation of voluntary counseling and testing among female sex workers in China: A quasi-experimental trial. *AIDS Education and Prevention, 18*(5), 406–419.

Yali, A. M., & Revenson, T. A. (2004). How changes in population demographics will impact health psychology: Incorporating a broader notion of cultural competence into the field. *Health Psychology, 23*(2), 147–155.

Zhang, Q., & Wang, Y. (2004). Socioeconomic inequality of obesity in the United States: Do gender, age, and ethnicity matter? *Social Science and Medicine, 58*, 1171–1180.

CHAPTER 31

Suicide Prevention

JOHN S. WESTEFELD
LILLIAN M. RANGE
JAMES R. ROGERS
JENNIFER M. HILL

> The effective prevention of suicide and suicidal behaviors is in the best interest of all communities. Prevention efforts communicate that life is valued. It should make no difference whether that message is given to those suffering with cancer, with AIDS, with alcoholism, or with suicidal despair. Prevention efforts might actually save lives, provide years of productive life, and, in so doing, enhance protective factors that generalize across the spectrum of potential mental and public health problems. (Maris, Berman, & Silverman, 2000)

The prevention of suicide remains a major public health concern. In 2003, there were 31,484 completed suicides (American Association of Suicidology [AAS], 2006). That number represents 86 per day, approximately one every 17 minutes, or 9.1 suicides per 100,000 population (Centers for Disease Control and Prevention [CDC], 2006). Suicide is the 11th leading cause of death overall, and the third leading cause of death among young people aged 15 to 24. When suicide occurs, it is a devastating event for all concerned.

The importance of suicide prevention was underscored in 2001 when the U.S. Department of Health and Human Services, with leadership from the Surgeon General, established the National Strategy for Suicide Prevention. This strategy had a variety of critical goals, including increasing awareness about suicide as a preventable phenomenon, developing prevention programs nationwide, decreasing access to lethal means, and increasing research on suicide. Over the years, a variety of strategies and programs in addition to this one have been developed with the goal of preventing suicide.

This chapter addresses suicide prevention, beginning with a review of primary prevention (primarily community-level public health prevention) strategies, with examples of such strategies, and ideas about what a model program should resemble. Next, we discuss secondary prevention (typically aimed at individuals) strategies, including assessment techniques and treatment issues. The final section of the chapter deals with "postvention," highlighting its importance as a prevention strategy.

PRIMARY PREVENTION

Primary prevention in suicidology typically refers to systemic programs to reduce or eliminate suicidal risk prior to onset. It is a vital component to any comprehensive suicide prevention strategy.

The *Surgeon General's Call to Action to Prevent Suicide* (U.S. Department of Health & Human Services, 1994) identified needs in several areas, including increasing public awareness concerning suicide and its preventability, reducing the stigma associated with mental illness, increasing prevention strategy consultation between the public and private sectors, and generally increasing awareness, intervention, and research. This call may be the most comprehensively presented nationwide strategy for suicide prevention. Other comprehensive programs include those provided by AAS, the American Foundation for Suicide Prevention (www.afsp.org), and the Jed Foundation (jedfoundation.org, which focuses on preventing suicide among college students). Three examples of primary suicide prevention programs, described in the following sections, illustrate how such programs work in different settings.

Suicide Prevention in the Urban Community

The Los Angeles Area Suicide Prevention Center (SPC), part of the Didi Hirsch Community Mental Health Center, represents one of the oldest examples of a community-based prevention program. The first agency in the United States to establish a 24-hour suicide prevention crisis hotline, the SPC began in 1958 as the nation's first crisis hotline with a single phone line in an abandoned hospital ward. It is now the largest of approximately 70 suicide prevention centers and 700 crisis hotlines nationwide. Didi Hirch Suicide Prevention Center has a special hotline for gay, lesbian, and transgendered teens who are more likely to attempt suicide than their peers (Perina, 2001). According to their website (www.suicidepreventioncenter.org), the SPC uses more than 100 trained volunteers to offer crisis intervention annually via telephone to more than 18,000 persons who are contemplating suicide or are otherwise in severe psychological distress. Beginning in the 1980s and continuing today, SPC has also offered support groups for family members and friends who have lost a loved one to suicide. The SPC conducts prevention programs for schoolchildren and college students to teach warning signs and risk factors of suicidal behavior. Finally, SPC staff offer presentations to community and professional groups and media interviews many times annually. Thus, this agency serves multiple populations in multiple venues to maximize their goal of preventing suicide in their community.

The SPC reports that more than 50% of the persons who call their hotline are at moderate to high risk for suicide, and 10% have the means to complete suicide and are at high risk to do so within 48 hours of their call. Follow-up studies indicate that most suicidal callers report being helped after hotline calls and that they "no longer feel at risk for suicide" (www.suicidepreventioncenter.org). In addition, suicide rates in Los Angeles County have decreased from 14.5 per 100,000 in 1958 to 9.4 per 1,000,000 as of 1997. In comparison, the suicide rate of western states in 1990 to 1994, even after adjusting for age, race, ethnicity, and sex, was higher (14.7/100,000) than the overall national rate during that time period (12.0/100,000; CDC, 1997). These data are consistent with the assumption that the SPC reduces the rate of suicide though the uncontrolled nature of the findings needs to be noted.

The success of SPC in Los Angeles County offers implications for suicide prevention elsewhere. Notably, this program demonstrates that community members are interested in participating in training to provide crisis intervention and suggests they are successful in doing so. The use of volunteers in suicide prevention can drastically decrease costs of programming in communities. Although follow-up data collection from anonymous callers and programming interventions are difficult to gather, this program cites decreased suicide rates in their service area. While published data are not available, the decreased suicide rates imply that the availability of services and community outreach can reduce suicide rates.

Suicide Prevention in the University Community

The second example of a systemwide suicide prevention effort comes from a college campus. The Suicide Prevention Program at the university of Illinois Urbana-Champaign (UIUC) began in 1984 and is a joint effort between the University Counseling Center and the McKinley Health Center (www.couns.uiuc.edu/HelpPreventSuicide.html). Its foremost goal is to reduce the incidences of student suicide and overall suicide risk at UIUC. The program receives documentation from student affairs personnel any time a student threatens or attempts suicide (Joffe, 36). No other well-known university or primary prevention program requires documentation and screening of all community members who threaten or attempt suicide. Those students are then mandated by the University to attend four assessment sessions with a social worker or a psychologist. Compliance with ongoing assessment becomes a requirement to remain enrolled at the university. Paradoxically, UIUC personnel report that students who are at risk of ending their lives are typically motivated to stay enrolled in college classes and attend mandated assessment sessions.

In an 18-year span following the program's inception (1984 to 2001), suicides at UIUC decreased 55% with a 100% decline in women student deaths and a 44% decline in men student deaths by suicide (Joffe, 2003). During the first 19 years of the program, of the 1,670 students referred to the Suicide Prevention Program by university staff or faculty, none committed suicide while enrolled as a student (Chamberlain, 2003). Joffe (2003) reports that only one student involved with the Suicide Prevention Program was withdrawn from class by the university, although this student later returned and graduated. Nine percent of referees to the Suicide Prevention Program independently withdrew from the university. Although the suicide rate in the Big Ten increased by 9% between 1984 and 1990, the suicide rate at UIUC was dramatically lower during this same time period.

The data provided by the UIUC Suicide Prevention Program suggest that, when possible, mandating the continued assessment of suicide risk in those who have demonstrated suicidality may decrease the local rate of completed suicides. An implication is that other, community-based entities such as employers, schools, and government agencies may profitably mandate assessment for those demonstrating suicidal intent.

Suicide Prevention in the Military Community

The Air Force Suicide Prevention Program began in 1995 with the commissioning of a 75-member suicide prevention Integrated Product Team. The goals were to reduce the number of suicides by those on active duty with the Air Force, perpetuate a community approach to suicide prevention, and identify and alleviate factors that contribute to Air Force suicides (http://afspp.afms.mil/idc/groups/public/ documents/webcontent/knowledgejunction.hcst?functionalarea=AFSuicidePreventionPrgm&doctype= subpage&docname=CTB_018218&incbanner=0/). Many of the Air Force interventions were designed to increase feelings of social connectedness and community cohesion. The underlying theory is that increasing social support serves as a protective factor against suicide and other problems (Blakely & Campise, 2003). Specific changes implemented in the Air Force by the Suicide Prevention Program include promoting social support and help-seeking, educating personnel on suicide risk and awareness, tracking risk and protective factors, using critical incident stress management teams following potentially traumatizing events, and targeting attention to delivery of human services in individual communities (Litts, 2002).

When the Air Force Suicide Prevention Program (AFSPP) began, suicide was the second leading cause of death for Air Force members, occurring at an annual rate of 15.8 per 100,000 (Litts, 2002), second only to unintentional injury (Blakely & Campise, 2003). Over the first 3 years of the project, the suicide rate declined significantly and reached record lows in the first 6 months of 1999. Additional data concerning this program are as follows:

- In the 2005 fiscal year, there were 29 active duty suicides for a rate of 7.8 per 1,000,000 Air Force personnel, representing a 49% decrease over suicides in the 2004 fiscal year.

- There was a 33% overall reduction in Air Force suicides in the 6 years after implementation of AFSPP compared with the 6 years before its implementation. In addition to decreasing suicides in the Air Force, the AFSPP was also associated with decreased community risk for accidental death, homicide, and moderate and severe family violence (Knox, Litts, Talcott, Feig, & Caine, 2003).

- Among Air Force members, 80% have annual suicide prevention and awareness training. Supervisors, unit leaders, medical providers, attorneys, and chaplains receive concentrated training because their role in AFSPP is to refer persons at risk to available resources and agencies (CDC, 1999).

Litts (2002) highlighted some of the key similarities between the Air Force Suicide Prevention Program and civilian communities. Both have identifiable leaders who can influence community norms and practices, and both have complex systems within which agencies and organizations provide human services and health care. The hierarchical and concentrated nature of Air Force communities has likely sped the impact of their program and increased its effectiveness, but leveraging community leaders to promote change and increase social support should be "transportable to any civilian community with some minimal level of organization and cohesion" (p. 4). Therefore, civilian communities as well as military communities can streamline service provision and offer services to persons in need.

Summary—Primary Prevention

The people who lead the Los Angeles Program, the University of Illinois Program, and the Air Force Program are positive about their impact. Data on effectiveness of suicide prevention programs are mixed. In an analysis in the 1970s, communities with suicide prevention centers had fewer suicides than communities in general (Lester, 1997). In a meta-analysis in the late 1980s, crisis centers had no overall effect on community suicide rates (Dew, Bromet, Brent, & Greenhouse, 1987). In another meta-analysis in 1984, suicide hot lines were minimally effective in reducing suicidal behavior (Miller, Coombs, Leeper, & Barton, 1984). In one research project, independent raters judged suicidal callers significantly helped at the end of a call to a suicide crisis line, compared with the beginning of the call (King, Nurcombe, Bickman, Hides, & Reid, 2003). Overall, crisis centers appear to most help young European American women (Miller et al., 1984). It may be that the mixed results of community crisis centers are due to uneven quality. We therefore need more research to determine not only the overall effectiveness of primary prevention programs, but also why such programs are effective. Identifying helpful components would help with tailoring programs to particular populations and venues. Examining effective programs collectively, it appears that the following are good candidates for critical components of effective primary prevention programs: use of community members/volunteers, mandated assessment in certain venues, social support, education, and systematic tracking of risk factors.

SECONDARY PREVENTION

Secondary prevention activities are those that occur after identification of potentially suicidal individuals. The connection between primary and secondary prevention in this context is that one of the goals of suicide prevention programming is to identify those individuals for whom the idea of suicide is more than a passing thought or a philosophical enigma to ponder and to connect them with professionals who can provide individually focused prevention interventions. Therefore, this section of the chapter provides an overview of traditional and current perspectives on suicide risk assessment and treatment, along with directions for future research and practice.

Suicide Risk Assessment

In general, suicide risk assessment can be considered in terms of content and process. The content component focuses on *what* are the important variables to evaluate, and process focuses on *how* to conduct the risk assessment. Although there is not a generally accepted approach to the assessment of suicide risk, a consideration of commonly identified risk factors or correlates of suicide is the content cornerstone to the process. The most prominent risk factors are hopelessness, depression, environmental or situational stressors, and the lack of a supportive social network (Maris et al., 2000; Westefeld et al., 2000). Despite the identification of correlates of suicidal behavior, there seems to be little consensus on factors that can be considered *necessary and sufficient* for a comprehensive assessment of risk.

Content and Measurement Considerations

Content approaches to suicide risk assessment vary widely across clinicians and settings and may include checklists (e.g., *Clinical Instrument to Estimate Suicide Risk,* Motto, Heilbron, & Juster, 1985; *Suicide Assessment Checklist,* Rogers, Lewis, & Subich, 2002) and psychometrically constructed instruments (e.g., *Hopelessness Scale,* Beck, Weissman, Lester, & Trexler, 1974; *Suicidal Ideation Scale,* Rudd, 1989) as part of a clinical interview. Initially, the goal of instrument development was to construct actuarial-based prediction models that could be used in clinical practice to differentiate suicidal from nonsuicidal individuals (Maris, 1992). However, despite empirical evidence that actuarial prediction in general is more accurate than prediction based on clinical judgment (Ægisdóttir et al., 2006; Dawes, 1994; Meehl, 1986), evidence for the use of suicide risk assessment measures for prediction or for the superiority of actuarial over clinical prediction in this area has not been supportive.

Rothberg and Geer-Williams (1992) applied nine suicide risk prediction scales to five clinical cases that varied on risk for suicide to determine their ability to predict subsequent suicidal behavior. Applying the nine scales to the five cases resulted in a wide range of suicide risk estimates for each case with the exception of the low-risk case. For the low risk case, the scales uniformly predicted a low risk for suicide. Thus, with the exception of the low risk case, there was little consensus across the scales in terms of predicting risk level for the remaining cases. In conclusion, Rothberg and Geer-Williams suggested that the psychometric limitations of the scales were the primary obstacles to their use in statistical prediction.

Ægisdóttir et al. (2006) conducted a meta-analysis comparing the accuracy of clinical to actuarial predication across a wide array of clinical problems. While their results suggested a general 13% increase in accuracy using actuarial over clinical approaches, of the four studies they identified predicting suicide attempts specifically, only one indicated superiority for actuarial prediction ($d = .33$). For the remaining three studies, one indicated no difference between the two approaches ($d = .0$) and two studies found that clinical prediction outperformed statistical prediction with effect size estimates of .24 and .30. Thus, while their results supported claims for the efficacy of actuarial over clinical prediction approaches in general, parallel evidence for predicting suicide attempts was lacking.

In addition to the analyses provided by Rothberg and Geer-Williams (1992) and Ægisdóttir et al. (2006), several reviews of suicide risk assessment measures have appeared in the literature (e.g., Jobes, Eyman, & Yufit, 1995; Range, 2005; Range & Knott, 1997; Rogers & Oney, 2005; Westefeld et al., 2000). Common across these reviews has been the conclusion that suicide risk measures, in large part because they attempt to predict a very low base-rate behavior, cannot be developed to the levels of sensitivity, specificity, reliability, and validity necessary to allow clinicians to rely solely on their use for actuarial prediction (see also Maris, 1992).

The use of scores on suicide risk assessment measures to serve as predictors of subsequent suicidal behavior has not been supported in the extant data. In part, difficulties in the actuarial prediction of suicide behavior may reflect the complexity and multiplicity of trajectories toward suicide. Although there are commonalities in correlates of suicidal behavior, there seems to be no single, limited set of predictable correlates of suicide that would lead to accurate statistical prediction. According to a survey conducted by Jobes et al. (1995), the lack of empirical support for suicide risk assessment instruments as predictors of suicide has led to reluctance on the part of clinicians to use risk assessment measures in their clinical work. When measures are used, the resulting data are typically combined with additional information gleaned through the interview to inform clinical decision making about the client's probability or potential to engage in suicidal behaviors (Jobes, 2006; Jobes et al., 1995).

The mechanisms of integrating assessment data with clinical judgment of suicide risk are idiosyncratic and ill defined, which is a critical concern in developing empirically supported approaches to working with suicidal individuals. In the absence of standardized approaches, or at least some empirically grounded consensus, clinicians likely differentially assign weights to the various risk characteristics and clinical impressions based on their experience. The relative value of assessment data in relation to clinical impressions resulting from an interview is unknown. Because of the ambiguity of this process, the likelihood that two clinicians assessing the same client independently would arrive at the same treatment and disposition conclusions is a major concern when relying on clinical judgment.

Garb's (1998) review of clinical judgment research related to the prediction of suicide provides support for this concern about interrater reliability. In his review of the literature, Garb identified a range of interclass correlation coefficients of .22 to .90 as estimates of interrater reliability. These coefficients varied as a function of the source (direct interview versus case consultation), amount of information available to the clinicians, and the time period of prediction (short-term versus long-term prediction). Higher interclass correlation coefficients were observed for predicting suicidal behavior within a week and when clients were directly interviewed by the clinicians. Of even greater concern, however, in terms of a clinical decision-making approach is the accuracy of predictions. Here Garb's review of the literature has indicated that the clinical prediction of suicide, even when information from suicide risk assessment measures is combined with clinical judgment, is poor at best.

Thus, neither actuarial nor clinical predictions of suicidal behavior or a combination of those approaches have been supported in the empirical literature. Yet psychologists are routinely expected to assess clients for suicide potential and to make treatment or disposition decisions about the probability of their clients engaging in suicidal behavior in the future. In part because of concerns over this lack of empirical support, theory and research have begun to focus on the impact of process on suicide risk assessment.

Process Considerations

In terms of process, the most common model for a suicide risk assessment interview is derived from the crisis intervention model (Callahan, 1998; Leenaars, 1994; Rogers & Soyka, 2004; Westefeld et al., 2000). This approach typically includes an assessment of lethality or dangerousness, the identification of risk factors, identifying the underlying message, allowing for the expression of thoughts and feelings, engaging the client's support network, and developing follow-up plans. Despite its popularity both as a training model and in clinical practice, crisis intervention as an approach to suicide risk assessment is not universally accepted (e.g., Jobes & Drozd, 2004; Rogers & Soyka, 2004; Thomas & Leitner, 2005). In fact, empirical support for the effectiveness of using the crisis intervention model when working with suicidal individuals is lacking (Rogers & Soyka; Thomas & Leitner, 2005).

In their meta-analysis of 36 crisis intervention studies, Roberts and Everly (2006) found little support for the effectiveness of crisis intervention across presenting problems except in reducing child abuse in troubled families. A primary conclusion from their literature search, and one particularly relevant to crisis intervention with suicidal people, was their observation that crisis intervention programs were often implemented in the absence of evaluation based on relevant outcome criteria. Similarly, in a review sponsored by the World Health Organization, Guo and Harstall (2004) indicated that the available data do not provide evidence for the effectiveness of the crisis intervention approach to working with suicidal individuals.

Beyond the absence of empirical support, a major criticism of the model is that it is a top-down approach, placing the clinician in an "expert" position. Leenaars (1994) likened the application of the model to the approach of a cardiologist in a hospital emergency room. The key to this metaphor is that the clinician is active, assertive, and aggressive in attempting to resolve suicidal thoughts and feelings in the helpless and fragile client. Ellis (2004) and Rogers and Soyka (2004) have suggested that clients experience the "clinician as expert" position as disempowering and stigmatizing, and consequently disengage from a productive therapeutic alliance. This interpretation is supported in qualitative research (Michel et al., 2001; Thomas & Leitner, 2005) and case-study narratives (Rogers & Soyka, 2004), where interviewed clients have consistently reported dissatisfaction and negative reactions to this approach.

The therapist-as-expert position, however, is not the only possible approach to working with suicidal individuals. Following a review of the literature, Thomas and Leitner (2005) identified two additional response styles that can be derived from the crisis intervention model. Besides identifying a *fight* response style that is analogous to the therapist-as-expert approach, they also identified a *flight* and *ideal* mode. The flight mode is characterized by high anxiety on the part of the clinician that can result in avoidance of the topic of suicide, intellectualization, passive engagement, superficial reassurance of the client, and greater concern for personal ramifications (eliciting one's own existential concerns) than for the welfare of the client. As suggested by Shea (1999), this concern for personal ramifications or "forensic fears" (p. 113) can lead to major breaches in the therapeutic alliance, poor treatment adherence, and poor outcome.

The ideal mode, by contrast, is characterized by mutual respect, collaboration, empathy, a nonjudgmental attitude, and the viewing of suicide as a problem-solving strategy (although suicide may be the least desired option of those available to the client) as opposed to a symptom of mental illness. Based on their interviews with 39 clinicians and 20 clients, the typical response style of clinicians was the fight or expert position, although clients viewed the ideal style as most helpful (Thomas & Leitner, 2005). The relative disconnect between clients' perceptions of helpful approaches and the typical response of clinicians is also reflected in the work of Michel et al. (2001) as part of the *Aeschi Working Group,* an international group of clinicians focused on improving the therapeutic approach to working with suicidal people (www.aeschiconference.unibe.ch/meeting%20the%20suicidal.htm).

Another major criticism of the crisis intervention model for assessing suicide risk is that, although assessment most often occurs at a point when clients are vulnerable and most likely to become engaged in a therapeutic relationship (at the height of a suicidal crisis), a probable outcome of the process is referral to a different service provider. Rogers et al. (2002) have presented data indicating that as suicide risk ratings conducted in an emergency evaluation setting increase, so does the likelihood of a referral for inpatient treatment. Similarly, Callahan's (1998) integrative crisis intervention model includes an emergency intervention component that leads to a referral from the interviewing clinician to an inpatient setting when suicide risk is judged to be high. Thus, the model as typically applied almost guarantees discontinuity and disruption in the process by artificially disconnecting assessment from ongoing prevention or treatment efforts. Although most suicide risk assessments are grounded in the crisis intervention model, the lack of empirical support for its use with suicidal individuals, variability in the practical application of the model, and challenges that the model may create for developing a therapeutic alliance, are problematic. In fact, it is possible that a crisis intervention approach may exacerbate client noncompliance or diminish treatment persistence, although support for this conclusion is preliminary and mostly based on qualitative data (Michel et al., 2001; Rogers & Soyka, 2004; Thomas & Leitner, 2005).

Treatment

A variety of treatment approaches to prevent suicidal behavior have been identified (Maris et al., 2000). These include brief therapy, cognitive-behavioral therapy, dialectical behavior therapy, psychoanalytic and psychodynamic approaches, psychopharmacotherapy, electroconvulsive therapy, and various social system interventions including family therapy and group therapy. According to Maris et al., effectiveness research across these approaches is rare and the research that exists provides inconclusive results. Similarly, Rudd, Joiner, and Rajab (2001) identified 22 controlled or randomized treatment studies focused on the psychotherapeutic treatment of suicidality. Based on their critical review of the results, they suggested that only a few conclusions could be supported in the literature, including the following:

- Long-term intensive treatment following a suicide attempt is most appropriate and effective for high-risk clients.

- Short-term cognitive behavioral therapy with problem-solving skill training is effective for up to 1 year, but not for longer periods.

- Reducing suicide attempts requires long-term treatment focusing on emotional regulation, distress tolerance, anger difficulties, assertiveness, and characterological issues related to disturbed interpersonal relationships and self-image.

- High-risk clients can be treated on an outpatient basis if acute hospitalization is available as a backup.

These conclusions are limited and lack helpful specificity for psychologists working with suicidal individuals. Further, they demonstrate the mismatch between the treatment needs of suicidal clients and a mental health care system that dictates short-term treatment and limits hospitalization access (Jobes, 2006).

Current trends in treating suicidal individuals and thus preventing suicide are grounded in the literature on the curative nature of the therapeutic relationship (Wampold, 2001) and the identification of suicidality as the primary target problem rather than as a symptom of underlying pathology. This shift in focus is evident in the cognitive behavioral model of suicidality developed by Rudd et al. (2001) and the Collaborative Assessment and Management of Suicidality (CAMS) protocol developed by Jobes (2006).

Grounded in the work of Alford and Beck (1997), the model presented by Rudd et al. (2001) and Rudd (2004) revolves around conceptualizing the client's suicidality, identifying specific targets for crisis management and treatment, promoting client self-understanding and awareness, and identifying relevant outcome criteria. True to its cognitive-behavioral roots, this approach focuses on identifying the client's suicidal belief system and assessing the affective and behavioral components related to those beliefs. Once the client and clinician reach a shared understanding about the cognitive, affective, and behavioral modes as they relate to the client's current suicidality, they work together to develop a targeted treatment plan to address the suicide problem. Rudd et al. provide a treatment manual outlining their approach. This manual has the potential to encourage a more standardized approach to working with suicidal clients than is currently available.

An additional recent advance in assessment and intervention with suicidal clients is the CAMS model (Jobes, 2006). Unlike many approaches to assessment and intervention, this protocol is theoretically grounded, promotes collaboration and the therapeutic relationship, assesses both risk and protective factors from the client's perspective, and provides a clear link between assessment and treatment. Applying the CAMS model, clients and counselors collaboratively complete the *Suicide Status Form* which includes an assessment of risk and the development of a treatment plan. In addition to assessment and treatment planning, the protocol uses (a) a *Suicide Tracking Form* that is completed collaboratively during each counseling session until the resolution of the suicide problem and (b) a *Suicide Tracking Outcome* form that is completed at the resolution of the client's suicidality. Taken together, these forms, which are embedded in the CAMS protocol, provide a comprehensive, beginning to end, approach to working with suicidal clients.

Although research on these models is limited, they are relatively well articulated in both the content and process of treatment. Because of their articulation, attention to the therapeutic alliance, and specific focus on suicidality as the target problem, these models hold promise for the future of suicide prevention. Thus, we encourage readers to familiarize themselves with these two approaches to working with suicidal individuals and to consider their potential value in their clinical work.

Summary—Secondary Prevention

There is much work to be done related to the prevention of suicide and other suicidal behaviors through assessment and treatment activities. Current models of training and practice in the assessment and treatment of suicidal individuals have limited research support. Thus, advancement in the prevention of suicide and suicidal behaviors is more likely to come from new and creative initiatives in assessment and treatment than from a continued focus on crisis intervention and other generalized treatment perspectives.

An additional focus for future research is to continue to grow our understanding of the assessment and treatment processes from the perspective of clients. This line of research, exemplified by the work of the *Aeschi* group, considers suicidal individuals as the experts in their suicidality and in a position to provide valuable data related to their experiences of assessment and treatment. A greater understanding of suicidality and the assessment and treatment process from a phenomenological perspective, combined with targeted assessment and treatment protocols, may improve outcomes in the prevention of suicide.

POSTVENTION AS A PREVENTION STRATEGY

Postvention, a term coined by Shneidman (1972), is used to describe appropriate and helpful acts that come after a dire event. Postvention can focus on friends and family, those who knew the deceased person directly or indirectly, or the community at large. Suicidal contagion is of particular concern, and is the linkage between postvention and prevention; in fact, postvention may be a prevention strategy in and of itself.

Is Suicidal Bereavement Different?

A few research projects find no differences between those bereaved by suicide and those bereaved by other causes of death. Widows from suicide were similar to widows from other causes of death in terms of social adjustment (Demi, 1984), and parents bereaved from suicide were similar to those bereaved from other causes in physical health and emotional distress (Demi & Miles, 1988). In other research projects, suicide survivors were relatively similar to other bereavement groups, particularly survivors of sudden death (McIntosh, 1993), and differences between survivors due to cause of death were negligible after 2 years (Range & Niss, 1990). These findings suggest that grief is grief, no matter what the cause of death.

However, the bulk of research evidence indicates that suicidal deaths are especially difficult. Compared with persons bereaved from other causes, persons bereaved by suicide report more guilt, resentment (Demi, 1984), loneliness, depression, suicidality, complicated grief, insomnia (Hardison, Neimeyer, & Lichstein, 2005), need for professional help (de Groot, Keijser, & Neeleman, 2006), self-blame (Silverman, Range, & Overholser, 1994–1995), and struggles with making meaning of the death (Silverman et al., 1994–1995). A person's reaction to the suicide of a significant other may involve a wider repertoire of grief responses than those elicited after other modes of death (Ellenbogen & Gratton, 2001). Themes in grief following a suicidal death include more questions of meaning, higher feelings of self-responsibility, and heightened feelings of rejection or abandonment (Jordan, 2001).

Some aspects of a death by suicide can heighten or lessen impact. Seeing the body at the scene of death can be especially troublesome (Callahan, 2000), but viewing the body or at least being with the covered body at the funeral seems to help acknowledge the reality of the death and may prevent fantasies about its condition and possible trauma in the dying process (Clark, 2001). Having emotional support is especially protective (Callahan, 2000) and can help prevent self-blame and depression resulting from anger directed at the deceased, which bereaved individuals may consider wrong (Clark, 2001). Emotional support, however, is often unavailable in part as a function of such societal attitudes as the stigma associated with death by suicide.

Persons bereaved by suicide often report that others treat them differently. Suicidally bereaved individuals report feeling blamed and shunned by neighbors and family (Ness & Pfeffer, 1990). Not surprisingly, therefore, they frequently report less willingness to report the cause of death than individuals bereaved in other ways (Range & Calhoun, 1990). Potential comforters may not know how to respond and may perceive more social rules about what they *should not* do than what they *should* do (Calhoun, Abernathy, & Selby, 1986), and thus come across as clumsy or rejecting. Instead of empathizing, potential comforters may pressure the bereaved person to explain the cause of death (Range & Calhoun, 1990). Awkwardness often characterizes social interactions after a suicidal death. After death caused by suicide, bereaved family and loved ones may experience grief that is tinged with more anger than are deaths by other causes. However, there is no standard sequence or time line of what to expect.

Focus of Postvention Efforts

The unique stresses of bereavement from suicide and the likelihood of problems in the bereaved person's social network make the role of the counseling psychologist critical. In the case of suicide, psychologists may need to offer help more proactively than is usual in most health care systems (de Groot et al., 2006). In offering help, however, it is important to avoid naive optimism or banal platitudes (Leenaars & Wenckstern, 1998) and to use language that all can understand. The possibility of miscommunication is great, so the goals are simplicity and redundancy.

It may also be reasonable to conceptualize bereavement by suicide as a posttraumatic reaction. Therefore, it would be prudent for helping professionals to be conversant in helping people develop ways of coping with distressing flashbacks, visual images, or other horrific sensations and helping them confront painful, avoided memories (Callahan, 2000). Those involved in helping should keep in mind that suicide-bereaved individuals may develop posttraumatic stress disorder, and may become suicidal themselves. Thus, the concept of postvention as prevention is particularly relevant.

Other treatments include group therapy, journaling, and making meaning. Group approaches may be beneficial for those bereaved by suicide. In one study, widowers of spousal suicide received one of two group interventions (Constantino, Sekula, & Rubinstein, 2001). One intervention emphasized the 12 curative factors of group therapy as formulated by Yalom (1995). The other promoted the principle of socialization, recreation, and leisure as emphasized by Neulinger (1981). All groups consisted of 4 to 6 members, and met for 90 minutes once a week for 8 weeks. Immediate, 6-month, and 12-month follow-ups indicated that over time both group treatments lessened depression, decreased brief psychological symptoms, diminished grief, and improved social adjustment. The very process of interacting with a group of other survivors of suicide death helped, regardless of the focus of the group (Constantino et al., 2001). This study had no wait list control group, and did not report effect sizes (although it did adjust alpha levels to control for multiple testing). Nevertheless, one interpretation of these findings is that the opportunity to interact with others who have had similar experiences can help those bereaved by suicide.

Journaling may also be helpful for those who have suffered a trauma such as the suicidal death of a loved one. An Internet-based, twice-weekly journaling intervention focused on people suffering from complicated grief recruited from print and website announcements (Wagner, Knaevelsrud, & Maercker, 2006). Researchers asked 55 bereaved individuals, some of whom lost a loved one to suicide, to write for 45 minutes twice per week for 5 weeks on three topics. The first topic involved exposure to bereavement cues. Instructions included writing all their fears and thoughts about the event, focusing on sensory perceptions in as much detail as possible, writing in the present tense using the first person, and refraining from worrying about grammar, style, or logical chronology. The second involved concentrating on one moment that kept coming to mind intrusively, but that was so distressing that the individual could hardly bear thinking about it. The instructions encouraged respondents to use cognitive reappraisal and to write a supportive, encouraging letter to a hypothetical friend, reflecting on guilt feelings, challenging dysfunctional automatic thinking and behavior, and correcting unrealistic assumptions. The third topic emphasized recovery. Instructions were to think about rituals to remember the deceased, reaccess positive memories of the deceased, and activate resources such as social contacts, positive competencies, and experiences. The goal was that by reflecting on how the loss changed them and describing how they are going to cope now and in the future, bereaved individuals could integrate the death and restore their capacity to cope. Compared with those in a wait list control condition, at immediate and 3-month follow-up, those in the treatment condition had significantly less thought intrusion, avoidance, depression, and anxiety, and significantly better mental health and adaptation (better sleep, fewer problems with feeling worthless, lonely, empty, or having an altered sense of the future). Effect sizes were large to very large (Wagner et al., 2006), suggesting that an Internet-based approach is promising.

In another journaling study, 121 undergraduates screened for suicidality wrote for 20 minutes on 4 days about traumatic events/emotions or about innocuous topics. At pre-, post-, and 6-week follow-up, those who wrote about traumatic events did not differ from those who wrote about innocuous topics on outcome measures. Participants in both conditions reported about the same amount of suicidal thoughts, depression, and reasons for living at pretest and follow-up testing. Traumatic-writing condition participants reported fewer automatic negative thoughts, and higher self-regard, but more health center visits at follow-up (Kovac & Range, 2002). This study did not include a wait list control group and did not report effect sizes. Nevertheless, it is possible that journaling affects self-esteem more than suicidal thoughts. Another possibility is that demand characteristics and the attention of a researcher help reduce negative thoughts, regardless of the writing topic.

For young adults, high levels of the ability to make meaning consistently predict better grief outcomes during the first 2 years of bereavement (Neimeyer, Baldwin, & Gillies, 2006), with a small to medium-size effect. It may be that the ability to find some form of benefit or silver lining in the loss, to experience a progressive rather than regressive transformation of one's identity, and especially to make sense of the loss in personal, practical, existential, or spiritual terms helps to promote positive grief outcomes (Neimeyer et al., 2006). Thus, narrative strategies that promote meaning making about loss can mitigate bereavement complications (Neimeyer, 2001) and may be especially relevant when the circumstances of the death are violent.

An example of a narrative strategy is telling and retelling the story of the loss in the context of reviewing and revisiting life goals (Shear, Frank, Houck, & Reynolds, 2005). In one research project, the steps in the narrative included imagining a conversation with the deceased; completing a set of memories questions, mostly positive memories, about the deceased; defining life goals; considering what one would like for oneself if the grief was not so intense; identifying ways to know that one is working toward identified goals; making concrete plans to put goals into action; and reengaging in meaningful relationships. Improvement was measured by an independent evaluator and by participants' reports of their own symptoms of complicated grief. Bereaved individuals suffering from complicated grief responded more strongly and more quickly to this narrative strategy than to standard psychotherapy (effect sizes were in the middle range). By helping bereaved individuals make sense out of the death of their loved one, counseling psychologists can foster recovery and growth.

On the community level, potentially available interventions include crisis teams visiting family members within hours of the loss; structured interviews; critical incident stress debriefings; crisis intervention; self-help programs with the goal of fostering recognition and friendship; treatments involving sharing information, emotions, and support; and programs to educate bereaved individuals about working through grief. The format can be individual or group.

Successful programs typically address the needs of the specific community, which might be a specific geographic area, a single university or high school, or the community of people who frequent an Internet site. In Baton Rouge, Louisiana, a community team of crisis center staff members and paraprofessional survivor volunteers actually goes to the scenes of suicides to begin helping the survivors as close to the time of death or notification as possible (Campbell, Cataldie, McIntosh, & Millet, 2004). Team members communicate to survivors that they are not alone, provide immediate contact and support, describe available resources, and help instill hope. This team approach may permit the newly bereaved to have choices unavailable to those with no advocate. Team members support all the individuals at the scene (e.g., friends, neighbors, coworkers, distant family members, first responders) who might otherwise be overlooked. The relationship between team members and other first responders including law enforcement, emergency services, fire department, and funeral home representatives, enables this program to be tailored to the needs and opportunities available in this geographic area.

At Cornell University, staff developed Community Support Meetings to help students deal with a suicide on campus. These hour-long meetings included 12 specific steps: introduction (including comments on confidentiality), brief description of the death, clarification that the purpose of the meeting is to be a helpful, healing gathering for the community, an opening question that invites participants to share recollections of the deceased individual, reminiscing, a few brief comments about grief, discussion of "what ifs," helpful suggestions, wrap-up, community resources, and descriptions of memorial gatherings and staff availability (Meilman & Hall, 2006). Thus, the sharing occurred in a structured protocol. Leaders assert that this organic, intuitive program tailored to the specific university community provided a time-tested outline that helped group leaders anticipate and deal with myriad reactions. One step for the future would be to collect data about its efficacy.

Counseling psychologists might be called to address postvention at a high school as well. As is true for universities, prudence would recommend helping authorities plan in advance of a crisis. After a suicidal death, experts (Poland, 1989) recommend that school officials acknowledge the death, but downplay memorials and avoid glorifying the death in any way, continuing with normal procedures as much as possible to help people perceive school as going on as usual. Small classroom discussions, presentations, and announcements are seen as preferable to a large school assembly. It is reasonable that schools contact the parents, offering condolences and support and that school faculty and students attend the funeral following the same guidelines as for other causes of death. If possible, it is desirable for school officials to encourage the family to hold the funeral outside school hours (Poland, 1989).

The CDC recommends that school officials take care with media contact, appoint a media liaison, and keep media representatives from glorifying decedents or sensationalizing their deaths in any way (CDC, 1988). Recommendations for helping the community include school gatekeeper training; community gatekeeper training; school-based training for students on the warning signs for suicide, and on building self-esteem and coping skills; screening programs to identify those at high risk; peer support programs for high-risk youth; crisis centers and hotlines; and restriction of access to places (e.g., tall buildings) and instruments (especially guns) that make it easier to commit suicide (Kapusta, 2007). Counseling psychologists might be involved in all these activities.

The Internet provides an even broader definition of community and is yet another place where counseling psychologists may be called to offer postvention following a suicide. A comprehensive web-based program that deals with the experiences of adolescent suicide survivors (Hoffmann, 2006) includes several sections. In particular, the *survivor stories* section contains the edited narratives of persons who lost a significant other by suicide. The *experiences* section provides an extensive description of the wide array of emotions, thoughts, and behaviors that adolescents experience in the course of losing a loved one by suicide. The *resource* section provides suggestions for survivors and recommended reading. This program, designed for mental health professionals and adolescent suicide survivors, is based on a modern definition of community. It would be valuable to collect data about the efficacy of this program.

Due to the trauma of suicidal deaths, community efforts to help bereaved individuals must be prepared for the possibility of posttraumatic stress disorder. The opportunity to share feelings with individuals in a similar situation might be especially beneficial, as would efforts to help the bereaved individual make some meaning out of the experience.

In both individual-focused and community postvention efforts, counseling psychologists need to be sensitive to the possibility of suicidal contagion. This phenomenon represents one of the primary linkages between postvention and prevention. Suicidal contagion (also called behavioral contagion, suicide imitation, suicide epidemics, copycat effect, and the Werther effect) refers to the social or interpersonal transmission of suicidality. Vulnerable youth are susceptible to the influence of reports and portrayals of suicide in the mass media, particularly reports in the news media (Gould, Jamieson, & Romer, 2003). Many countries including the United States, New Zealand, Sri Lanka, the United Kingdom, Australia, Canada, and Hong Kong have media guidelines for reporting suicide. These guidelines are similar in content, emphasizing that descriptions should recognize the importance of role models, take the opportunity to educate the public and offer help to vulnerable readers or viewers, and avoid glamorizing, sensationalizing, or providing explicit descriptions (Pirkis, Blood, Beautrais, Burgess, & Skehan, 2006).

One case illustrates these recommendations in action. After the death of Kurt Cobain, a famous rock musician, in Seattle, the mental health community worked with the media to prevent future suicides. Public health and media officials worked together, expecting the media to view a suicidal death as newsworthy, but helping media professionals to point out that suicide is a complex problem. Cobain was a talented musician but a disturbed individual; the death was far from romantic; and the grief of family members was intense. These officials also pointed out how to identify high-risk persons, the role of treatment for depression, and agencies and resources where people could go for help (Jobes, Berman, O'Carroll, Eastgard, & Knickmeyer, 1996). There was no increase in the number of suicide deaths compared with before this suicide. Thus, the data from the Seattle King County area indicated that suicidal contagion did not occur. However, there was a significant increase in the number of suicide crisis calls compared with the time period before the death (Jobes et al., 1996). These researchers concluded that cooperation with the media can reduce the likelihood of suicidal contagion.

Summary—Postvention as Prevention

Postvention efforts may target individuals or communities. They may include specific techniques such as group therapy with like individuals, journaling, or meaning making. Across all efforts, postvention goals of promoting healing, preventing future problems, preventing future suicides, and encouraging new growth (Celotta, 1995), are consistent with the role of counseling psychologists. As was the case with primary prevention, postvention programs need to be researched empirically to see if and why they are effective so that the programs can be tailored to specific populations, situations, and venues.

CONCLUSION

In this chapter, we have reviewed primary prevention, secondary prevention, and postvention-as-prevention strategies. Though there are many models of primary prevention, the programs in Los Angeles, the University of Illinois, and the Air Force are especially promising and have some data to support their effectiveness. Empirical investigation should continue to assess specific outcomes. In terms of secondary prevention, there is much debate about the most efficacious models. We advocate examining some of the newer models, especially the CAMS model and the work of the *Aeschi* group. It is also of paramount importance that effective postvention strategies be developed, studied, and utilized as an additional means of preventing suicide.

We want to stress the importance of training in the area of suicide prevention (e.g., Westefeld et al., 2000) and suicidology generically. We advocate doing a better job in our counseling psychology doctoral programs of teaching students about suicide, how to treat suicidal individuals, and what suicide prevention programs exist. Didactic course work, practica, and the internship can provide students with experiences whereby they learn how to assess for suicide risk, strategies for intervening with suicidal people, and how to conduct a suicide prevention workshop (e.g., Kleespies, Penk, & Forsyth, 1993; Kleespies, Smith, & Becker, 1990; Westefeld et al., 2002).

In terms of all types of suicide prevention, we advocate that more empirical investigation be conducted to better determine what works and why. We also advocate doing more to understand both assessment and treatment from the client's perspective, and to understand that when it comes to preventing suicide, in many ways the client may be the expert of choice. Our clients have much to teach us in this complex area, and we need to listen to them.

The public health approach is consistent with many of the underpinnings of counseling psychology. Dr. Rodney Hammond, Director of the Division of Violence Prevention at CDC, wrote:

> The public health approach offers a guiding framework for continued exploration of the complex factors leading to suicidal behavior . . . widespread implementation of public health strategies holds promise for saving lives that might have been prematurely lost to suicide. (Hammond, 2001, p. 2)

We agree.

REFERENCES

Ægisdóttir, S., White, M. J., Spengler, P. M., Maugherman, A. S., Anderson, L. A., Cook, R. S., et al. (2006). The meta-analysis of clinical judgment project: Fifty-six years of accumulated research on clinical versus statistical prediction. *Counseling Psychologist, 34*, 341–382.

Alford, B. A., & Beck, A. T. (1997). *The integrative power of cognitive therapy.* New York: Guilford Press.

American Association of Suicidology. (2006). *Suicide statistics.* Retrieved September 25, 2006 from www .suicidology.org/associations.1045/files/203datapgv1.pdf.

Beck, A. T., Weissman, A., Lester, D., & Trexler, L. (1974). The measurement of pessimism: The Hopelessness Scale. *Journal of Consulting and Clinical Psychology, 42*, 861–865.

Blakely, K., & Campise, R. (2003). *High OPSTEMPO suicide prevention.* Retrieved September 28, 2006, from http://afspp.afms.mil.

Calhoun, L. G., Abernathy, C. B., & Selby, J. W. (1986). The rules of bereavement: Are suicidal deaths different? *Journal of Community Psychology, 14*, 213–218.

Callahan, J. (1998). Crisis in theory and crisis intervention in emergencies. In P. M. Kleepies (Ed.), *Emergencies in mental health practice* (pp. 22–40). New York: Guilford Press.

Callahan, J. (2000). Predictors and correlated of bereavement in suicide support group participants. *Suicide and Life-Threatening Behavior, 30*, 104–124.

Campbell, F. R., Cataldie, L., McIntosh, J., & Millet, K. (2004). An active postvention program. *Crisis: Journal of Crisis Intervention and Suicide Prevention, 25*, 30–32.

Celotta, B. (1995). The aftermath of suicide: Postvention in a school setting. *Journal of Mental Health Counseling, 17*, 397–412.

Centers for Disease Control and Prevention. (1988). CDC Recommendations for a Community Plan for the Prevention and Containment of Suicide Clusters. *Morbidity and Mortality Weekly Report, 37*(S-6), 1–12.

Centers for Disease Control and Prevention. (1997). Regional variations in suicide rates: United States, 1990–1994. *Morbidity and Mortality Weekly Report, 46*(34), 789.

Centers for Disease Control and Prevention. (1999). Suicide prevention among active duty air force personnel— United States, 1990–1999. *Morbidity and Mortality Weekly Report, 48*, 1053–1057.

Centers for Disease Control and Prevention. (2006). Homicides and suicides—National violent death reporting system, United States, 2003–2004, *Morbidity and Mortality Weekly Report, 55*(26), 721–724.

Chamberlain, C. (2003). *Mandatory counseling appears to reduce suicide rate by half.* Retrieved September 28, 2006, from University of Illinois at Urbana-Champaign News Bureau web site: www.news.uiuc.edu/gentips/ 03/08suicide.html.

Clark, S. (2001). Bereavement after suicide: How far have we come and where do we go from here? *Crisis: Journal of Crisis Intervention and Suicide Prevention, 22*, 102–108.

Constantino, R. E., Sekula, K., & Rubinstein, E. N. (2001). Group intervention for widowed survivors of suicide. *Suicide and Life-Threatening Behavior, 31*, 428–441.

Dawes, R. M. (1994). *House of cards: Psychology and psychotherapy built on myth.* New York: Free Press.

de Groot, M. H., Keijser, J., & Neeleman, J. (2006). Grief shortly after suicide and natural death: A comparative study among spouses and first-degree relatives. *Suicide and Life-Threatening Behavior, 36*, 418–431.

Demi, A. S. (1984). Social adjustment of widows after a sudden death: Suicide and non-suicide survivors compared. *Death Education, 8*(Suppl.), 91–111.

Demi, A. S., & Miles, M. S. (1988). Suicide bereaved parents: Emotional distress and physical health problems. *Death Studies, 12*, 297–307.

Dew, M. A., Bromet, E. J., Brent, D., & Greenhouse, J. B. (1987). A quantitative literature review of the effectiveness of suicide prevention centers. *Journal of Consulting and Clinical Psychology, 55*, 239–244.

Ellenbogen, S., & Gratton, F. (2001). Do they suffer more? Reflections on research comparing suicide survivors to other survivors. *Suicide and Life-Threatening Behavior, 31*, 83–90.

Ellis, T. E. (2004). Collaboration and a self-help orientation in therapy with suicidal clients. *Journal of Contemporary Psychotherapy, 34*, 41–57.

Garb, H. N. (1998). *Studying the clinician: Judgment research and psychological assessment.* Washington, DC: American Psychological Association.

Gould, M., Jamieson, P., & Romer, D. (2003). Media contagion and suicide among the young. *American Behavioral Scientist, 46*, 1269–1294.

Guo, B., & Harstall, C. (2004). *For which strategies of suicide prevention is there evidence of effectiveness?* Copenhagen, Denmark: WHO Regional Office for Europe (Health Evidence Network Report). Retreived December 23, 2006, from www.euro.who.int/Document/E83583.pdf.

Hammond, W. R. (2001). Suicide prevention: Broadening the field toward a public health approach. *Suicide and Life Threatening Behavior, 32*, 1–2.

Hardison, H. G., Neimeyer, R. A., & Lichstein, K. L. (2005). Insomnia and complicated grief systems in bereaved college students. *Behavioral Sleep Medicine, 3*, 99–111.

Help Prevent Suicide. (n.d.). Retrieved September 28, 2006, from www.couns.uiuc.edu/HelpPreventSuicide.html.

Hoffmann, W. A. (2006). Telematic technologies in mental health caring: A web-based psychoeducational program for adolescent suicide survivors. *Issues in Mental Health Nursing, 27*, 461–474.

Jobes, D. A. (2006). *Managing suicidal risk: A collaborative approach.* New York: Guilford Press.

Jobes, D. A., Berman, A. L., O'Carroll, P. W., Eastgard, S., & Knickmeyer, S. (1996). The Kurt Cobain suicide crisis: Perspectives from research, public health and the news media. *Suicide and Life-Threatening Behavior, 26*, 260–271.

Jobes, D. A., & Drozd, J. F. (2004). The CAMS approach to working with suicidal patients. *Journal of Contemporary Psychotherapy, 34*, 73–85.

Jobes, D. A., Eyman, J. R., & Yufit, R. I. (1995). How clinicians assess suicide risk in adolescents and adults. *Crisis Intervention and Time-Limited Treatment, 2*, 1–12.

Joffe, P. (2003, February). *An empirically supported program to prevent suicide among a college population.* Paper presented at Stetson College of Law, Twenty Fourth Annual National Conference on Law and Higher Education, Clearwater Beach, FL.

Jordan, J. R. (2001). Is suicide bereavement different? A reassessment of the literature. *Suicide and Life-Threatening Behavior, 31*, 91–102.

Kapusta, N. D. (2007). Firearm legislation reform in the European Union: Impact on firearm availability, firearm suicide, and homicide rates in Austria. *British Journal of Psychiatry, 191*, 253–257.

King, R., Nurcombe, B., Bickman, L., Hides, L., & Reid, W. (2003). Telephone counseling for adolescent suicide prevention: Changes in suicidality and mental state from beginning to end of a counselling session. *Suicide and Life-Threatening Behavior, 33*, 400–411.

Kleespies, P., Penk, W., & Forsyth, J. (1993). The stress of patient suicidal behavior during clinical training: Incidence, impact, and recovery. *Professional Psychology: Research and Practice, 24*, 293–303.

Kleespies, P., Smith, M., & Becker, B. (1990). Psychology interns as patient suicide survivors: Incidence, impact, and recovery. *Professional Psychology: Research and Practice, 21*, 257–263.

Knox, K. L., Litts, D. A., Talcottt, G. W., Feig, J. D., & Caine, E. D. (2003). Risk of suicide and related adverse outcomes after exposure to a suicide prevention programme in the U.S. air force: Cohort study. *British Medical Journal, 327*(7428), 1376–1378.

Kovac, S. H., & Range, L. M. (2002). Does writing about suicidal thoughts and feelings reduce them? *Suicide and Life-Threatening Behavior, 32*, 428–440.

Leenaars, A. A. (1994). Crisis intervention with highly lethal suicidal people. In A. A. Leenaars, J. T. Maltsberger, & R. A. Neimeyer (Eds.), *Treatment of suicidal people* (pp. 45–59). Washington, DC: Taylor & Francis.

Leenaars, A. A., & Wenckstern, S. (1998). Principles of postvention: Applications to suicide and trauma in schools. *Death Studies, 22*, 357–391.

Lester, D. (1997). The effectiveness of suicide prevention centers. A review. *Suicide and Life Threatening Behavior, 27*, 304–310.

Litts, D. A. (2002). *Best practice initiative from the assistant secretary for health: Air Force suicide prevention program.* Retrieved September 28, 2006, from http://phs.os.dhhs.gov/ophs/BestPractice/usaf.htm.

Maris, R. W. (1992). Overview of the study of suicide assessment and prediction. In R. W. Maris, A. L. Berman, J. T. Maltsberger, & R. I. Yufit (Eds.), *Assessment and prediction of suicide* (pp. 3–22). New York: Guilford Press.

Maris, R. W., Berman, A. L., & Silverman, M. M. (2000). *Comprehensive textbook of suicidology.* New York: Guilford Press.

McIntosh, J. L. (1993). Control group studies of suicide survivors: A review and critique. *Suicide and Life-Threatening Behavior, 23*, 146–161.

Meehl, P. E. (1986). Causes and effects of my disturbing little book. *Journal of Personality Assessment, 50*, 370–375.

Meilman, P. W., & Hall, T. M. (2006). Aftermath of tragic events: The development and use of community support meetings on a university campus. *Journal of American College Health, 54*, 382–384.

Michel, K., Leenaars, A. A., Jobes, D. A., Orbach, I., Valicj, L., Young, R. A., et al. (2001). *Meeting the suicidal person: New perspectives for the clinician.* Retrieved October 10, 2006, from http://aeschieconference.unibe.ch/index.html.

Miller, H. L., Coombs, D. W., Leeper, J. D., & Barton, S. N. (1984). An analysis of the effects of suicide prevention facilities on suicide rates in the United States. *American Journal of Public Health, 74*, 340–343.

Motto, J. R., Heilbron, D. C., & Juster, R. P. (1985). Development of a clinical instrument to estimate suicide risk. *American Journal of Psychiatry, 142*, 680–686.

Neimeyer, R. A. (2001). *Meaning reconstruction and the experience of loss.* Washington, DC: American Psychological Association.

Neimeyer, R. A., Baldwin, S. A., & Gillies, J. (2006). Continuing bonds and reconstructing meaning: Mitigating complications in bereavement. *Death Studies, 30*, 715–738.

Ness, D. E., & Pfeffer, C. R. (1990). Sequelae of bereavement resulting from suicide. *American Journal of Psychiatry, 147*, 279–285.

Neulinger, J. (1981). *To leisure: An introduction.* Boston: Allyn & Bacon.

Perina, K. (2001). Suicide watch. *Psychology Today, 43*, 14–15.

Pirkis, J., Blood, R. W., Beautrais, A., Burgess, P., & Skehan, J. (2006). Media guidelines on the reporting of suicide. *Crisis, 27*, 82–87.

Poland, S. (1989). *Suicide intervention in the schools.* New York: Guilford Press.

Range, L. M. (2005). The family of instruments that assess suicide risk. *Journal of Psychopathology and Behavioral Assessment, 27*, 133–140.

Range, L. M., & Calhoun, L. G. (1990). Responses following suicide and other types of death: The perspective of the bereaved. *Omega: Journal of Death and Dying, 21*, 311–320.

Range, L. M., & Knott, E. C. (1997). Twenty suicide assessment instruments: Evaluation and recommendations. *Death Studies, 21*, 25–58.

Range, L. M., & Niss, N. M. (1990). Long term bereavement from suicide, homicide, accidents, and natural deaths. *Death Studies, 14*, 423–433.

Roberts, A. R., & Everly, G. S., Jr. (2006). A meta-analysis of 36 crisis intervention studies. *Brief Treatment and Crisis Intervention, 6*, 10–21.

Rogers, J. R., Lewis, M. M., & Subich, L. M. (2002). Validity of the Suicide Assessment Checklist in an emergency crisis center. *Journal of Counseling and Development, 80*, 493–502.

Rogers, J. R., & Oney, K. M. (2005). The clinical use of suicide assessment scales: Enhancing reliability and validity through the therapeutic relationship. In R. Yufit & D. Lester (Eds.), *Assessment, treatment, and prevention of suicidal behavior.* Hoboken, NJ: Wiley.

Rogers, J. R., & Soyka, K. M. (2004). "One size fits all": An existential-constructivist perspective on the crisis intervention approach with suicidal individuals. *Journal of Contemporary Psychotherapy, 34*, 7–22.

Rothberg, J. M., & Geer-Williams, C. (1992). A comparison and review of suicide prediction scales. In R. W. Maris, A. L. Berman, J. T. Maltsberger, & R. I. Yufit (Eds.), *Assessment and prediction of suicide* (pp. 202–217). New York: Guilford Press.

Rudd, M. D. (1989). The prevalence of suicidal ideation among college students. *Suicide and Life-Threatening Behavior, 19*, 173–183.

Rudd, M. D. (2004). Cognitive therapy for suicidality: An integrative, comprehensive, and practical approach to conceptualization. *Journal of Contemporary Psychotherapy, 34*, 59–72.

Rudd, M. D., Joiner, T., & Rajab, M. H. (2001). *Treating suicidal behavior: An effective, time-limited approach.* New York: Guilford Press.

Shea, S. C. (1999). *The practical art of suicide assessment.* New York: Wiley.

Shear, K., Frank, E., Houck, P. R., & Reynolds, C. F. (2005). Treatment of complicated grief: A randomized controlled trial. *Journal of the American Medical Association, 293*, 2601–2608.

Silverman, E., Range, L., & Overholser, J. C. (1994–1995). Bereavement from suicide as compared to other forms of bereavement. *Omega: Journal of Death and Dying, 31*, 41–51.

Shneidman, E. S. (1972). Foreword. In A. C. Cain (Ed.), *Survivors of suicide* (pp. ix–xi). Springfield, IL: Charles C. Thomas.

Thomas, J. C., & Leitner, L. M. (2005). Styles of suicide intervention: Professionals' responses and clients' preferences. *Humanistic Psychologist, 33*, 145–165.

U.S. Department of Health and Human Services. (1999). *The Surgeon General's call to action to prevent suicide.* Washington: DC: Author.

Wagner, B., Knaevelsrud, C., & Maercker, A. (2006). Internet-based cognitive-behavioral therapy for complicated grief: A randomized controlled trial. *Death Studies, 30*, 429–453.

Wampold, B. (2001). *The great psychotherapy debate: Models, methods, and findings.* Mahwah, NJ: Erlbaum.

Westefeld, J. S., Range, L. M., Rogers, J. R., Maples, M. R., Bromley, J. L., & Alcorn, J. (2000). Suicide: An overview. *Counseling Psychologist, 28*, 445–510.

Yalom, I. D. (1995). *The theory of group psychotherapy* (4th ed.). New York: Basic Books.

CHAPTER 32

Substance Abuse Prevention and Treatment

MATTHEW P. MARTENS
CLAYTON NEIGHBORS
CHRISTINE M. LEE

Substance abuse disorders represent an important public health problem that impacts both individuals and society on many levels. National epidemiological studies have indicated that a considerable portion of people experience diagnosable substance abuse disorders. The most recent and comprehensive of these studies, the National Epidemiological Survey on Alcohol and Related Conditions (NESARC), completed the first wave of a longitudinal survey in the United States during 2001 to 2002 (see Grant, Moore, Shepard, & Kaplan, 2003). A nationally representative sample of 43,093 adults was surveyed through in-person interviews. Results from the NESARC survey have been included in several studies (e.g., Grant, Dawson, et al., 2004, Grant, Stinson, Dawson, Chou, Dufour, et al., 2004; Grant, Stinson, Dawson, Chou, Ruan, et al., 2004) and have indicated that of the approximately 220 million adults in the United States, almost 20 million (over 9%) experienced some type of substance use disorder in the past year. By far, the most commonly abused substance was alcohol, with 8.5% of the population reporting abuse or dependence in the past 12 months. Two percent of the population experienced illicit drug abuse or dependence, which may seem somewhat small unless one considers that this figure represents almost 4.5 million adults in the United States.

Prevalence data on substance use disorders among adolescents is not as comprehensive as the existing data on adults, although a recent study estimated a 12.2% lifetime prevalence rate of substance use disorders among adolescents (Costello, Mustillo, Erkanli, Keeler, & Angold, 2003). Comprehensive national studies have explored the substance use habits of adolescents (e.g., Johnston, O'Malley, Bachman, & Schulenberg, 2006). A recent survey among middle and high school students indicated that 6.0% of 8th graders, 17.6% of 10th graders, and 30.2% of 12th graders had been drunk at least once in the past 30 days, while past 30-day drug use ranged from 11.2% (8th grade students) to 24.2% (12th grade students; Johnston et al., 2006). Although this study did not provide specific information on diagnostic rates, one can assume that a sizable percentage of monthly drug and alcohol users were experiencing negative consequences as a result of their substance use.

In addition to the problems posed by substance use itself, research indicates that those with substance use disorders are more likely than others to experience a host of additional psychological problems. Studies from the NESARC database have shown that those with substance use disorders are considerably more likely than others to experience mood, anxiety, and personality disorders (Grant, Stinson, Dawson, Chou, Dufour, et al., 2004; Grant, Stinson, Dawson, Chou, Ruan, et al., 2004). Other studies have shown that women with substance abuse disorders are more likely than others to be diagnosed with an eating disorder (e.g., Dansky, Brewerton, & Kilpatrick, 2000). Although these studies do not infer specific causality, they do clearly indicate that experiencing a substance use disorder is a risk factor for additional psychological problems.

A final means of assessing the impact of substance use disorders is to calculate their overall costs to society. In addition to unmeasured costs such as increasing the likelihood that one's children will also experience a substance use disorder (e.g., Hawkins, Catalano, & Miller, 1992), researchers have estimated that the societal financial burden associated with substance use disorders is considerable. These disorders in the United States are thought to cost at least $300 billion annually (Harwood, 1998; Rice, 1999) through factors such as lost productivity, treatment services, and associated medical consequences.

Considering the prevalence, personal costs, and societal impact of substance abuse disorders, it is important that counseling psychologists work to help combat problems in this domain. Numerous preventive strategies and treatment approaches have been developed for addressing problems associated with substance abuse, although some approaches have stronger empirical and theoretical support than others. The main purpose of this chapter is to provide a broad overview of prevention and treatment strategies that have evidence of success in reducing substance abuse. We review universal prevention strategies, indicated approaches, and selective approaches that target particular high-risk groups, while also discussing the literature on effective treatment strategies for those already dealing with substance abuse disorders. Before delving into these topics, though, we should note three caveats to this chapter. First, we are focusing only on alcohol and illicit drug abuse, and excluding issues such as tobacco abuse. Second, the research and clinical literature on substance abuse is extensive, making a comprehensive review of all aspects of alcohol and drug prevention impossible. Third, we are only focusing on psychosocial, rather than pharmacological, interventions. We encourage those interested in pharmacological treatments of substance use disorders to consult existing literature summaries (e.g., C. P. O'Brien, 2005; Williams, 2005).

PREVENTION OVERVIEW

Prevention of alcohol and drug abuse has a long history in the United States. Early notable prevention efforts included the Temperance Movement in the late 1800s and Prohibition in the 1920s (Beck, 1998), while more recent popular efforts included the "Just Say No" and "War on Drugs" campaigns in the 1980s (White, 2002). Many prevention efforts have shifted pragmatically to reducing harms associated with use (Marlatt, 1996; Neighbors, Larimer, Lostutter, & Woods, 2006). Prevention efforts vary according to the specificity of those they target and include regulatory laws and policies, environmental interventions, school-based education, group-based programs, and individually focused interventions (Offord, 2000). The Institute of Medicine initiated a reconceptualization of prevention based on the specificity of the target population (Mrazek & Haggerty, 1994). Universal prevention strategies are presented to and are available to all members of a given population and do not target individuals or groups according to their level of risk or history of use. In contrast, both indicated and selective prevention strategies are targeted approaches. Indicated prevention usually refers to strategies for intervening with individuals who have begun to experience consequences associated with use but without yet meeting criteria for abuse or dependence. Selective prevention targets individuals presumed to be at risk for substance abuse based on the presence of characteristics associated with risk or based on their membership in groups identified as being at higher risk of abuse. The following three sections offer a brief overview of universal, indicated, and selective prevention approaches being conducted in the United States.

UNIVERSAL DRUG PREVENTION APPROACHES

Universal prevention strategies are designed for and target general populations with the aim of preventing the initiation of substance use, often focused on substances considered to be "gateway drugs" such as alcohol or marijuana. Current conceptualizations of these programs are designed to enhance protective factors and reduce risk factors associated with substance use (Hawkins et al., 1992). Universal prevention programs are typically attractive options for widespread application because they are less intensive than selective or indicated strategies, are less stigmatizing for individuals, can be delivered without prior screening or assessment, and are appropriate for non-treatment-seeking-individuals (Offord, 2000). Universal prevention programs typically target elementary and middle school youth, often between the ages of 10 and 16, prior to the initiation of substance use (Cuijpers, 2003).

Over the past 3 decades, several longitudinal studies have identified risk and protective factors that are related to adolescent substance use. Many of these factors are described and reviewed in Hawkins et al. (1992) and include individual/intrapersonal and contextual factors (e.g., individual, peer, family, school/academic, community/society) related to increased or decreased risk associated with substance use. Because many competing forces influence the developing child and adolescent, prevention programs often target one or more of these risk or protective factors. Universal prevention programs focusing on youth and adolescent substance use are typically delivered in schools, focusing on an entire school or grade, but universal programs can also be geared toward families or larger communities (Cuijpers, 2003). Although most of the programs evaluated have been school-based programs, universal family, media, and community programs have gained wider exposure.

School-Based Prevention Programs

Most of the published outcome literature on universal prevention programs focuses on school-based programs. Several reviews of universal school-based prevention programs have been conducted, with relatively consistent findings (e.g., Botvin, 2000; Cuijpers, 2002, 2003; Ennett et al., 2003; Tobler et al., 2000). Tobler and colleagues (2000) completed a comprehensive meta-analysis of universal school-based drug prevention programs. Over 200 studies were evaluated based on level of interaction among participants and core components of the program. Components were classified into seven content domains (knowledge, affect, drug refusal skills, generic skills, safety skills, extracurricular activities, and others) and four different levels of classroom interaction ranging from noninteraction (lecture/dyadic presentation and communication between student and teacher, but not among peers) to interactive (ranging from structured small group discussions encouraging peer interaction to almost entirely peer-led group interaction). Effects associated with different school-based programs are provided in the following subsections.

Knowledge and Affective-Based Approaches

As efficacy research and theoretical advances in prevention science continue, universal school-based prevention programs have been on a developmental trajectory toward increased interaction, with a focus on multicomponent domains and differing levels of influence (e.g., individuals, families, communities). Early prevention programs were primarily focused on providing knowledge about substance use and the associated risks and effects of use (Botvin, 2000; Cuijpers, 2003). Following these informational programs, programs were developed and implemented focusing on increasing affective insight into drug use. These programs addressed developing personal insight on thoughts, feelings, and behaviors and included factors such as self-esteem, values clarification, and decision making (Botvin, 2000; Cuijpers, 2003; Flay, 2000; Tobler et al., 2000). Most of these early programs were atheoretical and noninteractive and were shown not to be effective (Tobler et al., 2000). Results from Tobler et al.'s meta-analysis with studies of higher-quality research designs (a subset of the 207 studies that had characteristics such as randomized control group designs and posttesting at least 3 months after pretesting) showed that informational and affective programs did not differ significantly from control conditions on drug use measures and yielded only small effect sizes (mean ds of .11 and $-.04$ for informational and affective programs, respectively).

Social Influence–Based Approaches

Since the early 1980s, prevention programs have been more often based on psychosocial theories, particularly the social influence model (Botvin, 2000). The foundational theoretical tenet of these programs is that children and adolescents encounter both direct and indirect prodrug pressures that increase over time and with age. These approaches often provide information about the consequences of drug use, normative information about the prevalence of drug use (e.g., modifying and correcting normative misperceptions and expectancies about drug use), and behavioral skills training to resist pressures to use drugs (Botvin, 2000; Donaldson et al., 1996). These programs typically are interactive, giving opportunities for peer discussion and development and practice of resistance skills. Evidence suggests that social influence programs incorporating interactive delivery styles are efficacious (Botvin, 2000; Tobler et al., 2000). Tobler et al.'s review (2000) found a mean effect size for social influence programs to be .14 among higher-quality evaluations. Although the .14 mean effect size (d) obtained from these programs versus the .11 effect size for informational programs appears to be similar, the former emerged as statistically significant by conventional criteria but the latter did not. Several other studies have found social influence programs to be efficacious in reducing alcohol and marijuana initiation and use (Botvin, 2000; Hansen, 1992).

Comprehensive and Systemwide Programs

Comprehensive life skills and systemwide change programs (e.g., Botvin, Baker, Dusenbury, Tortu, & Botvin, 1990; Ellickson, McCaffrey, Ghosh-Dastidar, & Longshore, 2003; O'Donnell, Hawkins, Catalano, Abbot, & Day, 1995) are included under the category of interactive programs (Tobler et al., 2000). Comprehensive life skills (or competence enhancement approaches; Botvin, 2000) include the development of self-management, life, and social and refusal skills (e.g., goal setting, decision making, communication, assertiveness, coping) in addition to social influence factors (Botvin, 2000; Tobler et al., 2000). Systemwide (or community-wide) programs can be one of two types—those involving community, media, or families to support school-based interactive programs or those that implement change within the entire school system on multiple levels (e.g., encouraging student bonding to school or communication between parents and schools; Flay, 2000; Tobler et al., 2000). Tobler et al.'s review (2000) found that the mean effect size for comprehensive life skills and system-wide programs was .17 and .22, respectively, both significantly different from zero.

Family-Based Prevention Programs

A number of family interaction and parenting characteristics have been shown to be associated with risk for substance use (Hawkins et al., 1992). Several universal family-based prevention programs have been developed to promote positive family influences. Many of these programs are implemented with universal school-based programs or community programs. Family-based prevention programs focus on developing parental monitoring, promoting parenting skills, and providing communication training, parent drug education, and family relations/management training. Universal family-based interventions, such as Preparing for the Drug Free Years, have been found to increase positive parenting factors related to risk for substance use and reduce subsequent substance use compared with control groups (e.g., Kosterman, Hawkins, Spoth, Haggerty, & Zhu, 1997; Spoth, Redmond, & Shin, 1998). Spoth et al. (1998) found an intervention effect (d) of .45 on intervention-targeted parenting behaviors for Preparing for the Drug Free Years and .51 for the Iowa Strengthening Families Program, both conducted as universal family prevention programs.

Mass Media–Based Prevention Approaches

Universal media-based approaches, such as public service announcements, include targeting large populations of adolescents about drug messages through different media modalities including print, television, radio, and billboards (Derzon & Lipsey, 2002). There has been relatively little research evaluating the effectiveness of mass media–based approaches on reducing substance use or onset of use, and studies that have been conducted tend to have considerable methodological limitations (e.g., lack of control samples, inability to isolate specific mass media effects). Results from several meta-analytic studies have shown limited or inconclusive evidence (Cuijpers, 2003; Derzon & Lipsey, 2002). Derzon and Lipsey (2002) examined mass media influences on substance use behavior among 48 studies with media messages and 18 control studies and reported an average pre-post difference in substance use behavior of about .04 standard deviations between media and control studies. Number and dosage, sequencing, target recipient (e.g., youth versus parental attitudes), and delivery mode of media messages were suggested to be important variables in developing and examining mass media approaches, but more comprehensive research in the domain is needed.

Community-Based Prevention Programs

As mentioned, systemwide prevention using multiple targets is one of the more effective school-based programs (Tobler et al., 2000). Further, at the community level, universal prevention programs often involve multicomponent strategies focusing on both individual and environmental change and prevention (Wandersman & Florin, 2003). Community-based prevention programs often target multiple risk and protective factors in various ecological domains to impact substance use from a variety of levels (e.g., schools, families, community, and policy levels; Hawkins, Catalano, & Arthur, 2002; Wandersman & Florin, 2003). Often through community coalitions, different community stakeholders are mobilized to plan, implement, and participate in diverse prevention strategies, such as implementing school-based programs, incorporating parenting training, conducting mass media campaigns, and changing local policies about substances. Although several reviews of community-based prevention programs have revealed promising yet mixed results (e.g., Wandersman & Florin, 2003), there are documented successes in research-driven community based prevention programs in reducing adolescent substance use rates, such as Project Northland (Perry et al., 1996). This project was a multilevel, community program aimed to prevent and reduce risky alcohol use through individual and environmental change. It targeted one cohort of sixth-grade children and their families and communities over the course of 3 years in mostly rural northeast Minnesota communities. The program included developmentally appropriate components such as parent involvement/education programs, behavioral curricula, peer participation, and community task force activities. Efficacy trial results suggested that students in intervention school districts reported significantly less initiation and alcohol use, felt less pressure to use alcohol, and had better parent-child communication about alcohol compared with control school districts at the end of 3 years.

Characteristics of Effective Prevention

Nation and colleagues (2003) provided several key characteristics of efficacious prevention programs addressing multiple risk/protective factors and mediators of intervention efficacy. These mediators include interactive, hands-on experiences for students to develop skills; sufficient dosage and length of programming; being theoretically driven; developing positive relationships with adults and peers; being appropriately timed in the sequence of initiation and development of drug use; being culturally relevant; including appropriate outcome evaluations; and providing training (also see Dusenbury & Falco, 1995; Tobler et al., 2000). Other mediators include program size, type of leader (e.g., peer, teacher, clinician), and content/targeted drug (see Tobler et al., 2000; Tobler & Stratton, 1997). Tobler et al. (2000) estimated stronger weighted effect sizes for interactive programs with few participants compared with programs with more students (e.g., weighted effect sizes ranged from .35 for 30 participants to .15 with 1,000 participants). Although universal drug abuse prevention programs can be successful for targeting large numbers of people, one disadvantage is that the needs of high-risk individuals may not be met with universal prevention or they may need more targeted intensive intervention or treatments, such as those with indicated prevention programs.

Summary of Research on Universal Programs

School-based universal prevention programs have received considerable attention in the literature and have yielded several meta-analyses with important implications. In general, meta-analytic results suggest that purely informational and affective programs yield results that are both unimpressively small and not statistically significant. However, meta-analytic data provide much more support for the effectiveness of interactive social influence programs, including comprehensive and systems-based approaches in school settings. Finally, several family-based universal prevention programs and community based programs have yielded impressive outcomes and deserve more concerted research attention in the future.

INDICATED PREVENTION

Content and Format of Indicated Interventions

Indicated prevention strategies target individuals who have already initiated use and often have begun to experience consequences associated with use, but probably do not yet meet criteria for abuse or dependence. Indicated prevention overlaps considerably with treatment and brief, nonpharmacological therapeutic interventions. Strategies for indicated prevention typically include one or more components designed to provide education about the risks and consequences associated with use, address social influences associated with use, provide skills for eliminating or reducing use and associated risks, and enhance motivation for positive behavior change.

Individuals who are good candidates for indicated prevention interventions can be identified and referred through screening procedures in school or medical settings and can be individually referred by significant others including parents, teachers, employers, medical staff in primary care or other health care settings, friends, or courts. The scope and duration of indicated prevention interventions can vary within and across settings, typically ranging from a few minutes of brief advice in medical settings (e.g., Fleming, Barry, Manwell, Johnson, & London, 1997; Fleming et al., 2002) to one or more 45- to 90-minute sessions in some educational settings (e.g., Dimeff, Baer, Kivlahan, & Marlatt, 1999). Indicated prevention interventions often are delivered in Motivational Interviewing (MI) style (especially when delivered individually) and include multiple components designed to educate, provide skills, or enhance motivation to change. Such components include (a) review of behavior, (b) review of consequences, (c) social norms education and clarification, (d) review of risk factors, (e) substance use expectancies, (f) decisional balance, (g) risk reduction strategies, and (h) change plans.

Although all these components are commonly suggested to be critical ingredients for indicated programs, some data suggest that social norms and alcohol and drug expectancies may be especially critical in that both have been shown to be associated with reduced drinking rates. Using social norms as intervention components involves providing accurate normative information since substance users typically overestimate the prevalence of use among their peers (Baer, Stacy, & Larimer, 1991; Kilmer et al., 2006). Research evaluating indicated prevention has shown, at least with respect to alcohol use, successful reduction of normative misperceptions is associated with reduced subsequent use (Borsari & Carey, 2000; Neighbors, Larimer, & Lewis, 2004). Although provision of normative feedback has been largely limited to young adults, efforts to extend this approach to the general adult population also appear promising (Cunningham, Wild, Bondy, & Lin, 2001).

Alcohol and drug expectancies, when included as part of indicated interventions, involve changing expectancies about use. Several studies have demonstrated that expectancies about positive effects of alcohol can be experimentally manipulated (Darkes & Goldman, 1993 1998). Indicated prevention interventions often describe the results of these studies as a means of demonstrating that social effects of alcohol rely to some extent on alcohol expectancies (e.g., Dimeff et al., 1999). Films that portray interactions between individuals who have or have not consumed alcohol have also been incorporated in indicated prevention as a means of demonstrating expectancy effects of alcohol prevention strategies (Keillor, Perkins, & Horan, 1999). Moreover, indicated prevention interventions often include components designed to assess and challenge positive effects of substance use. In general, successfully changing substance use expectancies has shown promise in reducing subsequent use (Corbin, McNair, & Carter, 2001; Cruz & Dunn, 2003).

Indicated prevention interventions have been delivered in a variety of formats. Relatively little research has evaluated differential efficacy as a function of delivery formats, and much of this work has been limited to alcohol interventions among young adults. Delivery formats may vary according to whether they are administered to individuals or in small groups and whether they are delivered in person or by other means. In this context, personalized feedback about alcohol use has been relatively effective whether delivered in person (Carey, Carey, Maisto, & Henson, 2006; Marlatt et al., 1998), by mail (Collins, Carey, & Sliwinski, 2002; Cunningham et al., 2001), or by computer administration (Kypri et al., 2004; Neighbors et al., 2004). Moreover, little research has directly evaluated the extent to which feedback delivery format affects outcomes. This is a critical gap because there are notable feasibility and cost differences depending on whether feedback is provided by therapists, in person but not by therapists, by mail, or by the Web.

Outcomes Research on Indicated Interventions

Among the best documented empirically supported indicated prevention interventions that include many, if not all, of the previous components are those that have been evaluated in the context of college student drinking (see Larimer & Cronce, 2002, for a review) and in health care settings (e.g., Fleming et al., 1997). For example, Larimer and Cronce's review of indicated intervention studies found that seven out of the ten multicomponent interventions yielded reductions in college student alcohol use and/or alcohol-related problems, while all eight motivational-interviewing based interventions yielded positive effects. In health care settings, studies have indicated that brief physician advice (15 minutes or less) encouraging reduced use and identification of specific strategies and goals for reducing risks of use has been associated with reduced use, consequences, and health care costs (Fleming et al., 1997, 2002), while in emergency departments screening and brief interventions (40 to 60 minutes or less) incorporating feedback and motivational interviewing have also shown considerable promise (Gentilello, Ebel, Wickizer, Salkever, & Rivara, 2005; Longabaugh et al., 2001; Monti et al., 1999). Overall, effect sizes for these studies appear to be in the small to medium-size range. A meta-analysis of brief indicated interventions in primary care settings showed a 15% difference in alcohol reduction rates between intervention and control groups (Bertholet, Daeppen, Wietlisbach, Fleming, & Burnand, 2005). Finally, studies are beginning to support the efficacy of individual components of these interventions. A recent study (Neighbors et al., 2004) found that a personalized feedback intervention that included only information based on social norms was more effective than an assessment-only control group at reducing alcohol use in college students ($d = .35$ and $.36$ at 3 and 6 months, respectively).

Summary of Research on Indicated Prevention Programs

Research has generally suggested that brief, multicomponent indicated prevention programs are effective at reducing alcohol use and alcohol-related problems. Many of these programs are based on Motivational Interviewing principles. These programs have also been tested in a variety of formats, including in-person, online, and with mailed feedback. One limitation of this research is that the majority of studies have involved either college students or individuals in medical settings. A second limitation is that these studies have generally only addressed alcohol use. Finally, although some research suggests that certain intervention components may be particularly relevant to reduced alcohol use (e.g., social norms information, challenging alcohol expectancies), few studies have directly assessed the unique effects of these individual factors.

SELECTIVE PREVENTION: TARGETING SPECIFIC HIGH-RISK POPULATIONS

Selective prevention strategies typically target individuals at risk for substance abuse by virtue of group membership. Several groups have been identified as being good candidates for selective prevention, including members of fraternity and sorority organizations, mandated students or employees, homeless individuals, and athletes. Although by no means a comprehensive list, these populations illustrate representative factors relevant to selective prevention.

Fraternity and Sorority Members

Research has consistently found that fraternity and sorority members engage in substance use at higher levels than their peers (McCabe et al., 2005). This has been most widely documented for alcohol (Cashin, Presley, & Meilman, 1998; Larimer, Anderson, Baer, & Marlatt, 2000) but also appears to be true of other substances including marijuana (McCabe et al., 2005), ecstasy (Yacoubian, 2003), and nonmedical use of prescription drugs (McCabe, Teter, & Boyd, 2006). Overall, differences in substance use between fraternity and nonfraternity men appear to be larger than those between sorority and nonsorority women (Larimer et al., 2000; McCabe et al., 2005). Etiological explanations of the relationship between fraternity and sorority membership and substance use have focused on both selection and socialization effects, and both appear to be evident (McCabe et al., 2005; Read, Wood, Davidoff, McLacken, & Campbell, 2002; Sher, Bartholow, & Nanda, 2001). Prevention interventions directed specifically at fraternity or sorority members have included social norms marketing interventions (Carter & Kahnweiler, 2000; Trockel, Williams, & Reis, 2003) and brief individually delivered interventions as described earlier but modified for fraternity and sorority students (e.g., provision of house-specific norms; Larimer et al., 2001). Overall, the literature suggests that individually delivered interventions have been consistently found to be more effective than social norms marketing interventions, although direct comparisons of these approaches or related effect sizes are lacking (Larimer & Cronce, 2002).

Homeless Youth

Selective prevention approaches have begun to be implemented among homeless youth, whereas substance use among homeless adults tends to be addressed in the context of formal treatment. Youth without stable housing who spend a large proportion of their time "on the street" have much higher prevalence of use and problems related to alcohol and other drug use relative to other young adults (Forst, 1994; Peterson, Baer, Wells, Ginzler, & Garrett, 2006). Although social services are often available to these youth, brief interventions designed to reduce alcohol and other drug use have not yet been widely implemented in this population. Barriers to implementation of brief interventions with this group include that homeless youth are hard to find, hard to recruit, distrusting of authorities, and, given the salience of food and safety needs, unlikely to view substance use as a primary problem (Peterson et al., 2006).

As a noteworthy exception, Baer and colleagues described the implementation and evaluation of a brief motivational intervention in this population (Baer, Peterson, & Wells, 2004; Peterson et al., 2006). In this study, 285 homeless adolescents between 14 and 19 years of age were recruited and randomly assigned to receive a brief motivational intervention or assessment only condition. Intervention recipients did not reduce alcohol or marijuana use relative to control participants but they did significantly reduce the use of other illicit substances at 1-month follow-up ($d = .26$). Perhaps more importantly, this work demonstrates the feasibility of prevention interventions in this population and provides a valuable prototype.

Mandated Students

Virtually all United States colleges have policies in place regarding alcohol and other substance use. Policies often outline the consequences for violating substance use policies, which may include fines, community service, and "alcohol/drug education" (Wechsler, Lee, Nelson, & Kuo, 2002). Although the majority of campuses provide mandated intervention and education for policy violators, the content of these programs varies widely and relatively few have been empirically supported and evaluated by peer review. Barnett and Read (2005) conducted a systematic review of mandatory alcohol interventions in the college population and stressed the importance of evaluating programs that policy violators are required to attend.

It is perhaps not surprising that interventions tend to be less effective or not effective among students who are mandated to participate in prevention interventions relative to voluntary students (Barnett & Read, 2005). This population poses numerous challenges. Practical considerations and limited staff probably contribute to interventions in this population being most often group-based. Empirical support for individually focused interventions has been more widely documented in college students (e.g., Larimer & Cronce, 2002; Walters & Neighbors, 2005), and additional work is needed to evaluate relative efficacy and cost-benefits of group versus individual interventions in this context.

Participant resistance is among the challenges to prevention efforts for mandated individuals. At best, mandated individuals may be open-minded in considering behavior change. At worst, they may be angry and defensive about being required to attend an intervention. As noted, prevention efforts focusing only on education or lectures, or emphasizing only consequences of use, have not been effective and are unlikely to be effective in this context (Larimer & Cronce, 2002). Finally, efforts to evaluate prevention interventions among mandated students face several challenges. Some of these difficulties relate to ensuring confidentiality, meeting ethical requirements to provide active treatment control groups, and distinguishing between voluntary research participation and university-mandated sanctions (Barnett & Read, 2005).

Athletes

Large-scale, national research studies have shown that college athletes (those participating in a formal, sanctioned sport) are at greater risk for heavy alcohol use and subsequent negative consequences than their nonathlete peers (Leichliter, Meilman, Presley, & Cashin, 1998; Nelson & Wechsler, 2001). Studies among youth and adolescent athletes, elite athletes, and recreational athletes are not as comprehensive, but several studies report an association between participating in athletics and alcohol use (e.g., Gutgesell, Timmerman, & Keller, 1996; K. E. Miller et al., 2003; K. S. O'Brien, Blackie, & Hunter, 2005). In contrast, other studies have either shown no association between athletic participation and other illicit drug use, or that athletes were in fact less likely to use drugs than their counterparts (e.g., Naylor, Gardner, & Zaichkowsky, 2001; Wechsler, Davenport, Dowdall, Grossman, & Zanakos, 1997).

It is unclear why, compared with peers' illicit drug use, athletes seem to be more at risk than their counterparts for heavy alcohol use. Factors such as the societal link between athletics and alcohol, sport-related norms, and lack of awareness about the impact of alcohol on athletic performance play a role, but such possibilities have not been well-studied. Regardless of the reasons, selective prevention efforts with athletes seem warranted. Only a handful of studies have addressed prevention efforts specifically with athletes (e.g., Marcello, Danish, & Stolberg, 1989; Werch, Carlson, Pappas, Edgemon, & DiClemente, 2000), with results of such efforts modest, at best. Marcello et al. found no significant effects for a program developed specifically for college athletes, while Werch et al. found only modest effects on some of their drinking outcome variables for a program designed specifically for high school athletes ($\eta^2 = .02$). It is possible that modifying interventions for athletes to include approaches with well-established effectiveness (e.g., brief motivational or skills-based approaches: Larimer & Cronce, 2002) would boost their effectiveness with this group. Other modifications could include focusing on sport-specific pressures or environmental demands that result in alcohol use and addressing the impact of alcohol use on one's athletic training and performance.

Summary of Research on Selective Prevention Programs

Researchers and theorists have identified specific groups that may benefit from selective interventions, although, with some exceptions, research on prevention programs with these high-risk groups has been sparse. Although homeless youth and college athletes are demographic groups that are at-risk for heavy substance use, interventions targeted at these groups have not been well-studied. Prevention efforts targeted at other at-risk groups (e.g., fraternity/sorority members) have been shown to be effective at reducing alcohol use, suggesting that selective prevention efforts can be effective in this domain.

SUBSTANCE ABUSE TREATMENT

This section focuses on psychosocial treatments for those who already have identifiable substance abuse problems. In general, research indicates that substance abuse treatment works. W. R. Miller, Walters, and Bennett (2001) reviewed several multisite trials of alcoholism treatment and found that, among all clients, percentage days abstinent increased by 145% and drinking-related problems decreased by 60%. Similarly, Prendergast, Podus, Chang, and Urada (2002) conducted a meta-analysis of 78 studies comparing formal drug abuse treatment to either no-treatment or alternative-treatment controls, and reported statistically significant overall effect sizes (d) of .30 for reducing drug use and .13 for reducing criminal behavior. Although separate effect sizes were not provided for active treatment versus no-treatment comparisons, almost 80% of the studies used some type of active treatment for a comparison. Interestingly, several expected (e.g., degree of treatment implementation; researchers' allegiance to the treatment) and unexpected (e.g., lack of a theoretical foundation for the intervention) effect size moderators occurred. This section provides additional details on those types of treatments that have received particularly strong empirical support and addresses the issues of comparisons among different types of treatments and approaches that have been shown to be ineffective.

Motivational Interviewing

One of the most popular contemporary treatments for substance abuse involves Motivational Interviewing (MI)–based approaches. Briefly, MI is a client-centered, yet directive, approach that focuses on resolving client ambivalence and motivating clients to change their behaviors (W. R. Miller & Rollnick, 2002). Research has consistently demonstrated that MI-based treatments, often described as Motivational Enhancement Therapy (MET), are effective in treating substance abuse disorders (e.g., Burke, Arkowitz, & Menchola, 2003; W. R. Miller, Andrews, Wilbourne, & Bennett, 1998). A recent meta-analysis (Burke et al., 2003) incorporated 15 alcohol and four drug treatment studies across a diverse array of settings. Results indicated that when compared with no-treatment and placebo controls, MI approaches yielded effect sizes (d) between .25 and .56 in reducing various measures of alcohol and drug consumption (separate comparisons for MI versus the two control conditions were not conducted). Another recent multisite trial focusing on cannabis dependence treatment (Marijuana Treatment Project Research Group, 2004) reported that compared with a delayed treatment control group, MET decreased marijuana use ($d = .33$ and .60 for dependence symptoms and marijuana use per day, respectively). There is also some evidence that MI-based approaches are as effective as other approaches but in fewer numbers of sessions (e.g., Burke et al., 2003; Project MATCH Research Group, 1997), which is addressed in more detail in the following subsection.

Cognitive-Behavioral and Behavioral Treatment

Other psychosocial approaches that have been shown to be effective in reducing substance abuse are various cognitive-behavioral and behavioral treatments. Although many MI-based approaches incorporate cognitive-behavioral components, here we are referring to treatments that do not explicitly incorporate MI. Two broad reviews of the alcohol treatment literature both concluded that cognitive-behavioral and behavioral approaches were effective at reducing alcohol abuse (Finney & Moos, 1998; W. R. Miller et al., 1998). These reviews generally indicated that improving one's social skills, establishing more positive relationships, developing a social environment and relationships that reward refraining from alcohol use, and improving skills to manage one's drinking are effective alcohol treatment strategies. Similar findings have emerged in the drug treatment literature. The aforementioned multisite trial for cannabis dependence (Marijuana Treatment Project Research Group, 2004) reported that a nine-session cognitive-behavioral treatment demonstrated a considerable effect ($d = 1.14$) relative to a delayed treatment control condition at increasing abstinent days, and studies have also supported the efficacy of cognitive-behavioral approaches in treating cocaine dependence (e.g., Carroll et al., 2004). Finally, meta-analyses of behavioral strategies such as voucher-based treatments and contingency management strategies have supported their effectiveness at reducing substance use relative to controls (Griffith, Rowan-Szal, Roark, & Simpson, 2000; Lussier, Heil, Mongeon, Badger, & Higgins, 2006).

Marital and Family Therapy

A third group of psychosocial approaches that have been examined for their effectiveness at treating substance abuse problems are marital and family approaches. A meta-analysis of 15 randomized controlled trials found that, in general, matrial and family therapy was effective at treating drug abuse (Stanton & Shadish, 1997). Family therapy approaches retained more clients in treatment and yielded greater effects in reduced drug use ($d = .48$) than other types of treatment approaches (e.g., peer group treatment, individual counseling, treatment as usual), and results were consistent for both adults and adolescents. It was not possible, however, to determine the relative effectiveness of different types of family therapies. These studies generally did not compare family therapy to other treatments shown to be effective at treating substance abuse (e.g., MET, cognitive-behavioral social skills training). A recent study that did make such comparisons among adolescent marijuana users (Dennis et al., 2004) did not demonstrate superiority of a family therapy approach versus MI, cognitive-behavioral, and community reinforcement approaches.

Reviews of the effectiveness of marital and family therapy in treating alcohol abuse have indicated that although such approaches may be effective relative to control groups or other types of treatments, their impact may be somewhat modest. W. R. Miller et al.'s review (1998) provided overall support for the effectiveness of behavioral marital therapy approaches, although the efficacy was considerably less than approaches like MET and social skills training. Similarly, a meta-analysis by Edwards and Steinglass (1995) found support for the short-term effects of family systems treatments for alcoholism ($d = .75$ when compared with both no-treatment and alternative treatment control groups), but that the effects tended to dissipate at long-term follow-ups. They also found that studies testing community reinforcement approaches that included family members consistently yielded strong effects, but results from studies involving other forms of behavioral family therapy were not consistent. In general, though, various forms of marital and family therapy are effective at treating substance abuse disorders, but their effectiveness compared with other effective approaches is unclear.

Twelve-Step Approaches

Twelve-step groups are often part of inpatient, outpatient, and aftercare programs, and this approach is often foremost in the public mind because, in part, meetings are free and widely available. A fairly recent trend in the alcohol abuse treatment literature has involved assessing the effectiveness of standardized programs based on the 12-step model of addiction. The 12-step approach stems from self-help approaches such as Alcoholics Anonymous, and conceptualizes addiction as a lifelong disease with abstinence as the only treatment goal (McCrady, 1994). Treatment involves completing a series of steps, such as admitting powerlessness over one's alcoholism or addiction, turning over one's life over to a higher power, making amends to people whom one has harmed, and carrying one's message to others. Several trials of structured 12-step approaches have supported their effectiveness at treating alcohol-related problems. One large-scale trial (Project MATCH Research Group, 1997) found that a structured, manual-based 12-step approach was as effective as MET and cognitive-behavioral therapy in treating alcoholism, and another large trial of Veterans Administration clients found few differences between individuals treated in substance abuse programs classified as 12-step, cognitive-behavioral, or mixed (Ouimette, Finney, & Moos, 1997). At a 1-year follow-up, patients from 12-step programs were more likely than those from cognitive-behavioral programs to be abstinent and more likely to be employed than patients from both programs, but effect sizes were very small ($\eta^2 = .004$ to .005). Therefore, although these trials did not specifically compare 12-step approaches to no-treatment control groups, they did find that 12-step approaches were as effective as approaches that have been shown to be efficacious in the alcohol treatment literature.

Treatment Comparisons

One of the most controversial, yet important, issues in the general psychology treatment literature involves the effectiveness of different types of bona-fide treatments (e.g., Wampold, 2001). As one would expect, this is also the case in the substance abuse treatment literature. Several studies have addressed the issue of substance abuse treatment comparisons, but the results of these studies do not clearly answer the question of "which treatments are the best?"

Perhaps the most well-known study of comparative effectiveness was Project MATCH (Project MATCH Research Group, 1997). This study was conducted at nine different sites and included a total of 1,726 individuals receiving treatment for alcoholism via outpatient or inpatient aftercare services. Participants were randomly assigned to one of three treatment conditions: 4 sessions of MET, 12 sessions of cognitive-behavioral therapy (CBT), or 12 sessions of twelve-step facilitation (TSF) therapy. Follow-up data were collected over a 1-year period and yielded no significant differences in drinking outcomes among the three groups. Similarly, at a multisite trial involving 600 adolescents with marijuana use disorders (Dennis et al., 2004), results demonstrated that combinations of CBT and MET, CBT/MET combined with family support, community reinforcement therapy, and a multidimensional family therapy approach were equally effective at reducing marijuana use and dependence. Other studies in the literature have reported similar findings. Although the aforementioned Burke et al. (2003) meta-analysis found support for MI-based approaches relative to control groups, no significant differences emerged when MI interventions were compared with other "active" treatments ($d = .002$). Similarly, in a review of the cognitive-behavioral relapse prevention literature, Carroll (1996) concluded that this approach was as effective, but not superior to, other active treatments. Other studies have reported no treatment differences for those receiving CBT versus MI for marijuana dependence (Budney, Higgins, Radonovich, & Novy, 2000; Stephens, Roffman, & Curtin, 2000).

Before one concludes that different substance abuse treatments are equally effective, though, there are several important points to consider. First, although studies have often shown that MI-based approaches are equivalent in their effectiveness to other approaches, the MI interventions are generally delivered in a considerably shorter amount of time (e.g., Burke et al., 2003; Project MATCH Research Group, 1997; Stephens et al., 2000). Second, the finding that treatments are equivalent is by no means universal. A multisite trial for marijuana dependence found that CBT was more effective than MET at reducing marijuana use (Marijuana Treatment Project Research Group, 2004), although the MET condition was much briefer (2 versus 9 sessions). Other studies have demonstrated the enhanced effectiveness of combining behavioral approaches, such as contingency management, to other treatments across a variety of substances (e.g., Budney et al., 2000; Carroll et al., 2006). Finally, comprehensive reviews of the substance abuse treatment literature have consistently found the strongest support for certain types

564 SUBSTANCE ABUSE PREVENTION AND TREATMENT

of treatments, such as MET, behavioral approaches, and family-based treatments (e.g., Finney & Moos, 1998; W. R. Miller et al., 1998).

Questions about comparative treatment effectiveness, then, remain somewhat unanswered. There seems to be support that MI-based approaches can be as effective as other empirically supported approaches in a briefer amount of time, but this finding is not universal. Support does exist for certain treatments, such as family-based approaches and behavioral/CBT-based treatments, relative to other active interventions, but these approaches have often not been compared either with other empirically supported substance abuse treatments or with specific, well-defined alternative approaches (e.g., interpersonal therapy, brief dynamic therapy). It is noteworthy that when CBT has been compared with what might be considered a structured, alternative approach (12-step therapy), its effects were found to be equivalent (Project MATCH Research Group, 1997). Additional research focusing on comparisons between empirically supported substance abuse treatments and between such treatments and treatment shown to be effective in other domains may provide more satisfying answers to the question of comparative treatment effectiveness.

Ineffective Approaches

In addition to exploring what works in substance abuse treatment, researchers have documented that some commonly used approaches are generally ineffective. Educational lectures and confrontational approaches, although popular in treatment settings, have been consistently shown to be ineffective at treating substance abuse (Finney & Moos, 1998; W. R. Miller et al., 1998). This finding also occurs in the substance abuse prevention literature (e.g., Larimer & Cronce, 2002). Such findings suggest that (a) individuals do not abuse substances because of a lack of understanding about the potential harmful effects of the substances, and (b) vigorously confronting and challenging an individual about his or her substance abuse is generally not an effective treatment.

SUMMARY AND FUTURE DIRECTIONS

Substance abuse problems represent a considerable worldwide public health problem. In the past quarter century, the research literature in this domain has greatly expanded, addressing areas such as identifying particularly at-risk groups for substance abuse problems, developing and testing strategies to prevent substance abuse, and assessing the effectiveness of treatments for those already struggling with substance abuse disorders. In this chapter, we have provided a broad overview of the current state of the literature in these areas. We hope that this review will provide ideas and insights for counseling psychology practitioners working in the area of substance abuse.

Additionally, and considering that there is much yet to learn about successfully preventing and treating substance abuse disorders, we hope that counseling psychologists will be at the forefront of future research activities designed to answer many of the lingering questions about substance abuse prevention and treatment. For example, diversity-related issues have generally not been explicitly addressed in substance abuse intervention studies. Further, few studies have assessed the relative effects of common versus specific factors when comparing the effects of different interventions. Given the historical foundation of counseling psychology research in these domains, counseling psychologists may be especially suited to tackle such research questions. Other unanswered questions include determining the relative effectiveness of different aspects of multicomponent treatment and prevention programs, assessing mechanisms of change throughout the treatment process, and evaluating the feasibility of novel data collection techniques (e.g., web- or Palm pilot–based real-time data collection). Although substance abuse prevention and treatment has historically not been a research focus in the field, counseling psychology researchers are well positioned to answer these and other related questions.

REFERENCES

Baer, J. S., Peterson, P. L., & Wells, E. A. (2004). Rationale and design of a brief substance use intervention for homeless adolescents. *Addiction Research and Theory, 12*, 317–334.

Baer, J. S., Stacy, A., & Larimer, M. (1991). Biases in the perception of drinking norms among college students. *Journal of Studies on Alcohol, 52*, 580–586.

Barnett, N. P., & Read, J. P. (2005). Mandatory alcohol intervention for alcohol-abusing college students: A systematic review. *Journal of Substance Abuse Treatment, 29*, 147–158.

Beck, J. (1998). 100 years of "just say no" versus "just say know": Reevaluating drug education goals for the coming century. *Evaluation Review, 22*, 15–45.

Bertholet, N., Daeppen, J., Wietlisbach, V., Fleming, M., & Burnand, B. (2005). Reduction of alcohol consumption by brief alcohol intervention in primary care. *Archives of Internal Medicine, 165*, 986–995.

Borsari, B., & Carey, K. B. (2000). Effects of a brief motivational intervention with college student drinkers. *Journal of Consulting and Clinical Psychology, 68*, 728–733.

Botvin, G. J. (2000). Preventing drug abuse in schools: Social and competence enhancement approaches targeting individual-level etiologic factors. *Addictive Behaviors, 25*, 887–897.

Botvin, G. J., Baker, E., Dusenbury, L., Tortu, S., & Botvin, E. M. (1990). Preventing adolescent drug abuse through a multimodal cognitive-behavioral approach: Results of a 3-year study. *Journal of Consulting and Clinical Psychology, 58*, 437–446.

Budney, A. J., Higgins, S. T., Radonovich, K. J., & Novy, P. L. (2000). Adding voucher-based incentives to coping skills and motivational enhancement improves outcomes during treatment for marijuana dependence. *Journal of Consulting and Clinical Psychology, 68*, 1051–1061.

Burke, B. L., Arkowitz, H., & Menchola, M. (2003). The efficacy of motivational interviewing: A meta analysis of controlled clinical trials. *Journal of Consulting and Clinical Psychology, 71*, 843–861.

Carey, K. B., Carey, M. P., Maisto, S. A., & Henson, J. M. (2006). Brief motivational interventions for heavy college drinkers: A randomized controlled trial. *Journal of Consulting and Clinical Psychology, 74*, 943–954.

Carroll, K. M. (1996). Relapse prevention as a psychosocial treatment: A review of controlled clinical trials. *Experimental and Clinical Psychopharmacology, 4*, 46–54.

Carroll, K. M., Easton, C. J., Nich, C., Hunkele, K. A., Neavins, T. M., Sinha, R., et al. (2006). The use of contingency management and motivational/skills-building therapy to treat young adults with marijuana dependence. *Journal of Consulting and Clinical Psychology, 74*, 955–966.

Carroll, K. M., Fenton, L. R., Ball, S. A., Nich, C., Frankforter, T. L., Shi, J., et al. (2004). Efficacy of disulfiram and cognitive behavior therapy in cocaine-dependent outpatients. *Archives of General Psychiatry, 61*, 264–272.

Carter, C. A., & Kahnweiler, W. M. (2000). The efficacy of the social norms approach to substance abuse prevention applied to fraternity men. *Journal of American College Health, 49*, 66–71.

Cashin, J. R., Presley, C. A., & Meilman, P. W. (1998). Alcohol use in the Greek system: Follow the leader. *Journal of Studies on Alcohol, 59*, 63–70.

Collins, S. E., Carey, K. B., & Sliwinski, M. J. (2002). Mailed personalized normative feedback as a brief intervention for at-risk college drinkers. *Journal of Studies on Alcohol, 63*, 559–567.

Corbin, W. R., McNair, L. D., & Carter, J. A. (2001). Evaluation of a treatment-appropriate cognitive intervention for challenging alcohol outcome expectancies. *Addictive Behaviors, 26*, 475–488.

Costello, E. J., Mustillo, S., Erkanli, A., Keeler, G., & Angold, A. (2003). Prevalence and development of psychiatric disorders in childhood and adolescence. *Archives of General Psychiatry, 60*, 837–844.

Cruz, I. Y., & Dunn, M. E. (2003). Lowering risk for early alcohol use by challenging alcohol expectancies in elementary school children. *Journal of Consulting and Clinical Psychology, 71*, 493–503.

Cuijpers, P. (2002). Effective ingredients of school-based drug prevention programs: A systematic review. *Addictive Behaviors, 27*, 1009–1023.

Cuijpers, P. (2003). Three decades of drug prevention research. *Drugs: Education, Prevention and Policy, 10*, 7–20.

Cunningham, J. A., Wild, T. C., Bondy, S. J., & Lin, E. (2001). Impact of normative feedback on problem drinkers: A small-area population study. *Journal of Studies on Alcohol, 62*, 228–233.

Dansky, B. S., Brewerton, T. D., & Kilpatrick, D. G. (2000). Comorbidity of bulimia nervosa and alcohol use disorders: Results from the national women's study. *International Journal of Eating Disorders, 27*, 180–190.

Darkes, J., & Goldman, M. S. (1993). Expectancy challenge and drinking reduction: Experimental evidence for a mediational process. *Journal of Consulting and Clinical Psychology, 61*, 344–353.

Darkes, J., & Goldman, M. S. (1998). Expectancy challenge and drinking reduction: Process and structure in the alcohol expectancy network. *Experimental and Clinical Psychopharmacology, 6*, 64–76.

Dennis, M., Godley, S. H., Diamond, G., Tims, F. M., Babor, T., Donaldson, J., et al. (2004). The Cannabis Youth Treatment (CYT) study: Main findings from two randomized trials. *Journal of Substance Abuse Treatment, 27*, 197–213.

Derzon, J. H., & Lipsey, M. W. (2002). A meta-analysis of the effectiveness of mass-communication for changing substance-use knowledge, attitudes, and behavior. In W. Crano & M. Burgoon (Eds.), *Mass media and drug prevention: Classic and contemporary theories and research* (pp. 231–258). Mahwah, NJ: Erlbaum.

Dimeff, L. A., Baer, J. S., Kivlahan, D. R., & Marlatt, G. A. (1999). *Brief alcohol screening and intervention for college students.* New York: Guilford Press.

Donaldson, S. I., Sussman, S., MacKinnon, D. P., Severson, H. H., Glynn, T., Murray, D. M., et al. (1996). Drug abuse prevention programming: Do we know what content works? *American Behavioral Scientist, 39*, 868–883.

Dusenbury, L., & Falco, M. (1995). Eleven components of effective drug abuse prevention curricula. *Journal of School Health, 65*, 420–425.

Edwards, M. E., & Steinglass, P. (1995). Family therapy treatment outcomes for alcoholism. *Journal of Marital and Family Therapy, 21*, 475–509.

Ellickson, P. L., McCaffrey, D. F., Ghosh-Dastidar, B., & Longshore, D. L. (2003). New inroads in preventing adolescent drug use: Results from a large-scale trial of project ALERT in middle schools. *American Journal of Public Health, 93*, 1830–1836.

Ennett, S. T., Ringwalt, C. L., Thorne, J., Rohrbach, L. A., Vincus, A., Simons-Rudolph, A., et al. (2003). A comparison of current practice in school-based substance use prevention programs with meta-analysis findings. *Prevention Science, 4*, 1–14.

Finney, J. W., & Moos, R. H. (1998). Psychosocial treatments for alcohol use disorders. In P. E. Nathan & J. M. Gorman (Eds.), *A guide to treatments that work* (pp. 156–166). New York: Oxford University Press.

Flay, B. R. (2000). Approaches to substance use prevention utilizing school curriculum plus social environment change. *Addictive Behaviors, 25*, 861–885.

Fleming, M. F., Barry, K. L., Manwell, L. B., Johnson, K., & London, R. (1997). Brief physician advice for problem alcohol drinkers: A randomized controlled trial in community-based primary care practices. *Journal of the American Medical Association, 277*, 1039–1045.

Fleming, M. F., Mundt, M. P., French, M. T., Manwell, L. B., Stauffacher, E. A., & Barry, K. L. (2002). Brief physician advice for problem drinkers: Long-term efficacy and benefit-cost analysis. *Alcoholism: Clinical and Experimental Research, 26*, 36–43.

Forst, M. L. (1994). A substance use profile of delinquent and homeless youths. *Journal of Drug Education, 24*, 219–231.

Gentilello, L. M., Ebel, B. E., Wickizer, T. M., Salkever, D. S., & Rivara, F. P. (2005). Alcohol interventions for trauma patients treated in emergency departments and hospitals-A cost benefit analysis. *Annals of Surgery, 241*, 541–550.

Grant, B. F., Dawson, D. A., Stinson, F. S., Chou, S. P., Dufour, M. C., & Pickering, R. P. (2004). The 12-month prevalence and trends in DSM-IV alcohol abuse and dependence: United States, 1991–1992 and 2001–2002. *Drug and Alcohol Dependence, 74*, 223–234.

Grant, B. F., Moore, T. C., Shepard, J., & Kaplan, K. (2003). *Source and accuracy statement: Wave 1 National Epidemiologic Survey on Alcohol Abuse and Related Conditions (NESARC).* Bethesda, MD: National Institute on Alcohol Abuse and Alcoholism.

Grant, B. F., Stinson, F. S., Dawson, D. A., Chou, S. P., Dufour, M. C., Compton, W., et al. (2004). Prevalence and co-occurrence of substance use disorders and independent mood and anxiety disorders. *Archives of General Psychiatry, 61*, 807–816.

Grant, B. F., Stinson, F. S., Dawson, D. A., Chou, S. P., Ruan, W. J., & Pickering, R. P. (2004). Co-occurrence of 12-month alcohol and drug disorders and personality disorders in the United States. *Archives of General Psychiatry, 61*, 361–368.

Griffith, J. D., Rowan-Szal, G. A., Roark, R. R., & Simpson, D. D. (2000). Contingency management in outpatient methadone treatments: A meta-analysis. *Drug and Alcohol Dependence, 58*, 55–66.

Gutgesell, M. E., Timmerman, M., & Keller, A. (1996). Reported alcohol use and behavior in long-distance runners. *Medicine and Science in Sports and Exercise, 28*, 1063–1070.

Hansen, W. B. (1992). School-based substance abuse prevention: A review of the state of the art in curriculum, 1980–1990. *Health Education Research: Theory and Practice, 7*, 403–430.

Harwood, H. (1998). *Updating estimates of the economic costs of alcohol abuse in the United States: Estimates, update methods, and data* (NIH Publication No. 98–4327). Rockville, MD: National Institutes of Health.

Hawkins, J. D., Catalano, R. F., & Arthur, M. W. (2002). Promoting science-based prevention in communities. *Addictive Behaviors, 27*, 951–976.

Hawkins, J. D., Catalano, R. F., & Miller, J. Y. (1992). Risk and protective factors for alcohol and other drug problems in adolescence and early adulthood: Implications for substance abuse prevention. *Psychological Bulletin, 112*, 64–105.

Johnston, L. D., O'Malley, P. M., Bachman, J. G., & Schulenberg, J. E. (2006). *Monitoring the future national survey results on drug use, 1975–2005* (NIH Publication No. 06–5883). Bethesda, MD: National Institute on Drug Abuse.

Keillor, R. M., Perkins, W. B., & Horan, J. J. (1999). Effects of videotaped expectancy challenges on alcohol consumption of adjudicated students. *Journal of Cognitive Psychotherapy: An International Quarterly, 13*, 179–187.

Kilmer, J. R., Walker, D. D., Lee, C. M., Palmer, R. S., Mallett, K. A., Fabiano, P., et al. (2006). Misperceptions of college student marijuana use: Implications for prevention. *Journal of Studies on Alcohol, 67*, 277–281.

Kosterman, R., Hawkins, J. D., Spoth, R., Haggerty, K. P., & Zhu, K. (1997). Effects of a preventive parent-training intervention on observed family interactions: Proximal outcomes from preparing for the drug free years. *Journal of Community Psychology, 25*, 337–352.

Kypri, K., Saunders, J. B., Williams, S. M., McGee, R. O., Langley, J. D., Cashell-Smith, M. L., et al. (2004). Web-based screening and brief intervention for hazardous drinking: A double-blind randomized controlled trial. *Addiction, 99*, 1410–1417.

Larimer, M. E., Anderson, B. K., Baer, J. S., & Marlatt, G. A. (2000). An individual in context: Predictors of alcohol use and drinking problems among Greek and residence hall students. *Journal of Substance Abuse, 11*, 53–68.

Larimer, M. E., & Cronce, J. M. (2002). Identification, prevention, and treatment: A review of individual-focused strategies to reduce problematic alcohol consumption by college students. *Journal of Studies on Alcohol, 14S*, 148–163.

Larimer, M. E., Turner, A. P., Anderson, B. K., Fader, J. S., Kilmer, J. R., Palmer, R. S., et al. (2001). Evaluating a brief alcohol intervention with fraternities. *Journal of Studies on Alcohol, 62*, 370–380.

Leichliter, J. S., Meilman, P. W., Presley, C. A., & Cashin, J. R. (1998). Alcohol use and related consequences among students with varying levels of involvement with college athletics. *Journal of American College Health, 46*, 257–262.

Longabaugh, R., Woolard, R. F., Nirenberg, T. D., Minugh, A. P., Becker, B., Clifford, P. R., et al. (2001). Evaluating the effects of a brief motivational intervention for injured drinkers in the emergency department. *Journal of Studies on Alcohol, 62*, 806–816.

Lussier, J. P., Heil, S. H., Mongeon, J. A., Badger, G. J., & Higgins, S. T. (2006). A meta-analysis of voucher-based reinforcement therapy for substance use disorders. *Addiction, 101*, 192–203.

Marcello, R. J., Danish, S. J., & Stolberg, A. (1989). An evaluation of strategies developed to prevent substance abuse among student-athletes. *Sport Psychologist, 3*, 196–211.

Marijuana Treatment Project Research Group. (2004). Brief treatments for cannabis dependence: Findings from a randomized multisite trial. *Journal of Consulting and Clinical Psychology, 72*, 455–466.

Marlatt, G. A. (1996). Harm reduction: Come as you are. *Addictive Behaviors, 21*, 779–788.

Marlatt, G. A., Baer, J. S., Kivlahan, D. R., Dimeff, L. A., Larimer, M. E., Quigley, L. A., et al. (1998). Screening and brief intervention for high-risk college student drinkers: Results from a 2-year follow-up assessment. *Journal of Consulting and Clinical Psychology, 66*, 604–615.

McCabe, S. E., Schulenberg, J. E., Johnston, L. D., O'Malley, P. M., Bachman, J. G., & Kloska, D. D. (2005). Selection and socialization effects of fraternities and sororities on U.S. college student substance use: A multi-cohort national longitudinal study. *Addiction, 100*, 512–524.

McCabe, S. E., Teter, C. J., & Boyd, C. J. (2006). Medical use, illicit use and diversion of prescription stimulant medication. *Journal of Psychoactive Drugs, 38*, 43–56.

McCrady, B. S. (1994). Alcoholics anonymous and behavior therapy: Can habits be treated as diseases? Can diseases be treated as habits? *Journal of Consulting and Clinical Psychology, 62*, 1159–1166.

Miller, K. E., Hoffman, J. H., Barnes, G. M., Farrell, M. P., Sabo, D., & Melnick, M. J. (2003). Jocks, gender, race, and adolescent problem drinking. *Journal of Drug Education, 33*, 445–462.

Miller, W. R., Andrews, N. R., Wilbourne, P., & Bennett, M. E. (1998). A wealth of alternatives: Effective treatments for alcohol problems. In W. R. Miller & N. Heather (Eds.), *Treating addictive behaviors* (2nd ed., pp. 203–216). New York: Plenum Press.

Miller, W. R., & Rollnick, S. (2002). *Motivational interviewing: Preparing people to change addictive behavior* (2nd ed.). New York: Guilford Press.

Miller, W. R., Walters, S. T., & Bennett, M. E. (2001). How effective is alcoholism treatment in the United States? *Journal of Studies on Alcohol, 62*, 211–220.

Monti, P. M., Colby, S. M., Barnett, N. P., Spirito, A., Rohsenow, D. J., Myers, M., et al. (1999). Brief intervention for harm reduction with alcohol-positive older adolescents in a hospital emergency department. *Journal of Consulting and Clinical Psychology, 67*, 989–994.

Mrazek, P. J., & Haggerty, R. J. (1994). *Reducing risks for mental disorders: Frontiers for preventive intervention research*. Washington, DC: National Academy Press.

Nation, M., Crusto, C., Wandersman, A., Kumpfer, K. L., Seybolt, D., Morrissey-Kane, E., et al. (2003). What works in prevention: Principles of effective prevention programs. *American Psychologist, 58*, 449–456.

Naylor, A. H., Gardner, D., & Zaichkowsky, L. (2001). Drug use patterns among high school athletes and nonathletes. *Adolescence, 36*, 627–639.

Neighbors, C., Larimer, M. E., & Lewis, M. A. (2004). Targeting misperceptions of descriptive drinking norms: Efficacy of a computer-delivered personalized normative feedback intervention. *Journal of Consulting and Clinical Psychology, 72*, 434–447.

Neighbors, C., Larimer, M. E., Lostutter, T. W., & Woods, B. A. (2006). Harm reduction and individually focused alcohol prevention. *International Journal of Drug Policy, 17*, 304–309.

Nelson, T. F., & Wechsler, H. (2001). Alcohol and college athletes. *Medicine and Science in Sports and Exercise, 33*, 43–47.

O'Brien, C. P. (2005). Anticraving medications for relapse prevention: A possible new class of psychoactive medications. *American Journal of Psychiatry, 162*, 1423–1431.

O'Brien, K. S., Blackie, J. M., & Hunter, J. A. (2005). Hazardous drinking in elite New Zealand sportspeople. *Alcohol and Alcoholism, 40*, 239–241.

O'Donnell, J., Hawkins, J., Catalano, R., Abbott, R., & Day, L. (1995). Preventing school failure, delinquency among low-income children: Long-term intervention in elementary schools. *American Journal of Orthopsychiatry, 65*, 87–100.

Offord, D. R. (2000). Selection levels of prevention. *Addictive Behaviors, 25*, 833–842.

Ouimette, P. C., Finney, J. W., & Moos, R. H. (1997). Twelve-step and cognitive-behavioral treatment of substance abuse: A comparison of treatment effectiveness. *Journal of Consulting and Clinical Psychology, 65*, 230–240.

Perry, C. L., Williams, C. L., Veblen-Mortenson, S., Toomey, T. L., Komro, K. A., Anstine, P. S., et al. (1996). Project Northland: Outcomes of community-wide alcohol use prevention program during early adolescence. *American Journal of Public Health, 86*, 956–965.

Peterson, P. L., Baer, J. S., Wells, E. A., Ginzler, J. A., & Garrett, S. B. (2006). Short-term effects of a brief motivational intervention to reduce alcohol and drug use among homeless adolescents. *Psychology of Addictive Behaviors, 20*, 254–264.

Prendergast, M. L., Podus, D., Chang, E., & Urada, D. (2002). The effectiveness of drug abuse treatment: A meta analysis of comparison group studies. *Drug and Alcohol Dependence, 67*, 53–72.

Project MATCH Research Group. (1997). Matching alcoholism treatments to client heterogeneity: Project MATCH posttreatment drinking outcomes. *Journal of Studies on Alcohol, 58*, 7–29.

Read, J. P., Wood, M. D., Davidoff, O. J., McLacken, J., & Campbell, J. F. (2002). Making the transition from high school to college: The role of alcohol-related social influence factors in students' drinking. *Substance Abuse, 23*, 53–65.

Rice, D. P. (1999). Economic costs of substance abuse, 1995. *Proceedings of the Association of American Physicians, 111*, 119–125.

Sher, K. J., Bartholow, B. D., & Nanda, S. (2001). Short-and long-term effects of fraternity and sorority membership on heavy drinking: A social norms perspective. *Psychology of Addictive Behaviors, 15*, 42–51.

Spoth, R., Redmond, C., & Shin, C. (1998). Direct and indirect latent-variable parenting outcomes of two universal family-focused preventive interventions: Extending a public health-oriented research base. *Journal of Consulting and Clinical Psychology, 66*, 385–399.

Stanton, M. D., & Shadish, W. R. (1997). Outcome, attrition, and family-couples treatment for drug abuse: A meta-analysis and review of the controlled, comparative studies. *Psychological Bulletin, 122*, 170–191.

Stephens, R. S., Roffman, R. A., & Curtin, L. (2000). Comparison of extended versus brief treatments for marijuana use. *Journal of Consulting and Clinical Psychology, 68*, 898–908.

Tobler, N. S., Roona, M. R., Ochshorn, P., Marshall, D. G., Streke, A. V., & Stackpole, K. M. (2000). School-based adolescent drug prevention programs: 1998 meta-analysis. *Journal of Primary Prevention, 20*, 275–336.

Tobler, N. S., & Stratton, H. H. (1997). Effectiveness of school-based drug prevention programs: A meta-analysis of the research. *Journal of Primary Prevention, 18*, 71–128.

Trockel, M., Williams, S. S., & Reis, J. (2003). Considerations for more effective social norms based alcohol education on campus: An analysis of different theoretical conceptualizations in predicting drinking among fraternity men. *Journal of Studies on Alcohol, 64*, 50–59.

Walters, S. T., & Neighbors, C. (2005). Feedback interventions for college alcohol misuse: What, why, and for whom? *Addictive Behaviors, 30*, 1168–1182.

Wampold, B. E. (2001). *The great psychotherapy debate: Models, methods, and findings.* Mahwah, NJ: Erlbaum.

Wandersman, A., & Florin, P. (2003). Community interventions and effective prevention. *American Psychologist, 58*, 441–448.

Wechsler, H., Davenport, A. E., Dowdall, G. W., Grossman, S. J., & Zanakos, S. I. (1997). Binge drinking, tobacco, and illicit drug use and involvement in college athletics. *Journal of American College Health, 45*, 195–200.

Wechsler, H., Lee, J. E., Nelson, T. F., & Kuo, M. (2002). Underage college students' drinking behavior, access to alcohol, and the influence of deterrence policies. *Journal of American College Health, 50*, 203–217.

Werch, C. E., Carlson, J. M., Pappas, D. M., Edgemon, P., & DiClemente, C. C. (2000). Effects of a brief alcohol preventive intervention for youth attending school sports physical examinations. *Substance Use and Misuse, 35*, 421–432.

White, T. (2002). Controlling and policing substance users. *Substance Use and Misuse, 37*, 973–983.

Williams, S. H. (2005). Medications for treating alcohol dependence. *American Family Physician, 71*, 1775–1780.

Yacoubian, G. S. (2003). Correlates of ecstasy use among students surveyed through the 1997 College Alcohol Study. *Journal of Drug Education, 33*, 61–69.

CHAPTER 33

Preventing Eating and Weight-Related Disorders: Toward an Integrated Best Practices Approach

LAURIE B. MINTZ
EMILY HAMILTON
RASHANTA A. BLEDMAN
DEBRA L. FRANKO

The elevated incidence of eating disorders, their serious physical and psychological consequences, and the high costs of treatment have made development of effective prevention programs a critical research focus (Pearson, Goldklang, & Striegel-Moore, 2002). Eating disorders (EDs) are among the most prevalent psychological problems among females, affecting approximately 6% of women (Herzog & Delinsky, 2001; Hoek & van Hoeken, 2003). These disorders impair functioning and result in subjective distress; they also increase the risk of hospitalization, suicide attempts, and death (Franko et al., 2004; Keel et al., 2003). Moreover, EDs increase the risk for developing depressive disorders, anxiety disorders, substance abuse, and other health problems (Johnson, Cohen, Kasen, & Brook, 2002; Stice, Hayward, Cameron, Killen, & Taylor, 2000). Nevertheless, treatment is sought by less than one-third of individuals with EDs (Fairburn, Cooper, Doll, Norman, & O'Connor, 2000; Johnson et al., 2002). Among those who receive treatment, only 40% to 60% experience symptom remission (Agras, Walsh, Fairburn, Wilson, & Kraemer, 2000; Telch, Agras, & Linehan, 2001; Wilfley et al., 2002). In addition, for those who recover, relapse rates are alarmingly high (33% to 36%; Fairburn et al., 2000; Keel, Dorer, Franko, Jackson, & Herzog, 2005). Indisputably, this combination of high prevalence, slow rates of treatment seeking, minimal to moderate treatment success, and high relapse rates makes finding effective prevention a priority.

Not only are prevention efforts for full-syndrome EDs of great import, but so is preventing the full spectrum of eating and weight-related disorders. This spectrum includes negative body image, weight and shape concerns, and unhealthy, albeit not necessarily extreme, eating practices such as meal skipping and chronic dieting (Levine & Smolak, 2006; Neumark-Sztainer, 2005b). Concerns such as a negative body image and dieting are not only problematic in and of themselves, but they are also risk factors for the development of full-syndrome EDs (Striegel-Moore & Cachelin, 2001). Cash (2002) identified 19% of young adult females as suffering significant distress associated with body dissatisfaction. In a large study, over half of adolescent girls reported using unhealthy weight control behaviors during the previous year (Neumark-Sztainer, Story, Hannan, Perry, & Irving, 2002). Concerted prevention efforts for the full spectrum of eating and weight-related issues are greatly needed.

Although there is controversy about whether to include obesity in this spectrum, there is no doubt that obesity is a serious concern. Obesity has doubled in children and tripled in adolescents between 1976 to 1980 and 1999 to 2000 (National Center for Health Statistics, U.S. Department of Health and Human Services and Centers for Disease Control, 2004). In 2002, 15% of children and adolescents were overweight and another 15% were at risk for becoming overweight (Ogden, Flegal, Carroll, & Johnson, 2002). Obesity prevention has thus become a priority, as has developing prevention programs that simultaneously prevent EDs and obesity.

Counseling psychologists are uniquely suited to contribute to such prevention efforts. With our field's emphasis on developmental issues and prevention (Fretz & Simon, 1992; Heppner, Casas, Carter, & Stone, 2000), as well as the large number of counseling psychologists in educational settings (Metzler, 2006), we can work toward the prevention of EDs through training, research, and program development (Mussell, Binford, & Fulkerson, 2000). Likewise, our focus on understanding cultural influences on mental health makes us particularly suited for work in ED prevention. By ensuring that counseling psychologists-in-training gain knowledge about both EDs and research methodology for evaluating interventions, we can be future leaders in ED prevention and thus positively impact countless numbers of girls and women. We hope this chapter inspires and assists counseling psychologists to reach this lofty goal.

We begin our chapter by clarifying definitions and then review risk factors for EDs. Next is a discussion of the overlap between EDs and obesity, and a rationale for seeking interventions that prevent both. A targeted overview of prevention research is presented, followed by suggestions for research and practice. We conclude with a plea for societal intervention.

Two caveats are needed. Because females are predominantly affected by EDs, we focus the chapter here. While research is needed on males, the first priority is developing prevention programs for those most affected. In addition, although EDs are an "equal opportunity disorder" (Root, 2001, p. 754), we found no prevention research focused exclusively on ethnic minority women. Thus, we explicitly highlight studies that include ethnically diverse samples, and address this in our recommendations.

DEFINITIONS

Risk Factors

According to Striegel-Moore and Cachelin (2001), a *risk factor* is a variable that has been shown to precede a particular outcome (e.g., childhood abuse preceding the onset of an ED). If the risk factor cannot be changed, it is a *fixed marker* (e.g., sex). Conversely, a risk factor that is changeable is a *variable risk factor* (e.g., negative body image). If manipulation of the risk factor changes the risk of the outcome, then it is a *causal risk factor* (Jacobi, Hayward, de Zwaan, Kraemer, & Agras, 2004; Striegel-Moore & Cachelin, 2001).

Prevention Terms

Although varying terms are used, it is generally agreed that there are three categories of ED prevention. Munoz, Mrazek, and Haggerty (1996) define *universal* programs as those with the objective of strengthening protective factors in symptom-free individuals; such programs are directed toward an entire population irrespective of risk factors, with the goal of preventing the onset of EDs (Luce, Winzelberg, Zabinski, & Osborne, 2003). According to Stice and Shaw (2004), early ED prevention studies were universal, and more recent studies have been what Stice and Shaw (2004) term *targeted*, or what Luce et al. (2003) term *indicated*. These programs focus on individuals who do not yet have an ED, but who are at high risk because they have apparent precursors, such as a negative body image (Neumark-Sztainer et al., 2006). The goal of targeted programs is to modify risk factors (Franko et al., 2005), with the aim of preventing the onset of the disorder in high-risk individuals (Luce et al., 2003). An example would be an intervention conducted on women first identified through a large-scale screening as having poor body image but no eating disorder diagnosis. Finally, the third category is what Neumark-Sztainer et al. (2006) termed *universal-selected* programs, or what Luce et al. (2003) termed *selected* programs. These target subgroups are judged to be at increased risk for an ED because of a particular characteristic, such as age and gender, or due to participation in a sport for which low weight is emphasized. Examples include school-based interventions with adolescent girls, or interventions provided to elite dancers, a group found to be at increased risk across several studies (Luce et al., 2003). While a distinction is sometimes made between targeted (high risk due to a precursor) and selected (high risk due to a particular characteristic), we do not find this division to be useful and thus simply use the term targeted for interventions delivered to individuals at high risk.

Diagnostic Terms

The *Diagnostic and Statistical Manual of Mental Disorders* (*DSM-IV-TR*; American Psychiatric Association, 2000) lists three EDs: Anorexia Nervosa (AN), Bulimia Nervosa (BN), and Eating Disorder Not Otherwise Specified (EDNOS). AN is characterized by fear of gaining weight, refusal to maintain a normal weight, and a disturbed perception of body shape and size. BN is characterized by binge eating and compensatory behaviors aimed at preventing weight gain. Individuals diagnosed with BN consume an abnormally large amount of food during discrete periods of time, often followed by purging methods, and they do so at least twice a week for a period of 3 months. The diagnosis of EDNOS is given for EDs that do not meet the stringent criteria for AN or BN. The *DSM-IV-TR* lists six examples of EDNOS that can be thought of as atypical (a feature absent) or subthreshold (all features present but not at sufficient frequency) forms of AN or BN (Mintz, O'Halloran, Mulholland, & Schneider, 1997). The most commonly known EDNOS is Binge-Eating Disorder (BED; also included in the *DSM-IV-TR* Appendix B). When individuals have no diagnosable disorder but exhibit mild ED-related behaviors (e.g., occasional binge eating), they are considered to be symptomatic. Because these milder behaviors often precede the development of a full-blown eating disorder, symptomatic individuals are considered an at-risk group. Those who do not display symptomatic behaviors would be considered at low risk or no risk (Franko et al., 2005; Mintz et al., 1997).

BRIEF REVIEW OF RISK FACTORS

As should be apparent, the notion of risk is central to ED prevention work. Indeed, research identifying variable risk factors is needed to develop effective ED prevention interventions (Striegel-Moore & Cachelin, 2001; Neumark-Sztainer, Wall, Story, & Perry, 2003). Although a full review of etiological studies is beyond our scope, elucidating empirically suggested risk factors and risk factor models is critical to understanding ED prevention.

Risk Factor Research

In an outstanding review, Striegel-Moore and Cachelin (2001) divided ED risk factors into categories: (a) demographic, (b) familial and interpersonal, (c) constitutional vulnerability, (d) personal vulnerability, and (e) sociocultural. Among the demographic category is the fixed risk factor of gender. The female-to-male ratio is approximately 10:1 for AN and BN and 2.5:1 for BED (Jacobi et al., 2004). Age is another demographic risk factor: while risk factors often occur in childhood, the onset of EDs most often occurs during adolescence. Those at greatest risk for developing an eating disorder are adolescent girls between the ages of 15 and 19 (Lewinsohn, Striegel-Moore, & Seeley, 2000). Within the familial/interpersonal context, childhood sexual abuse, parental psychopathology, parental concern with eating and weight, familial ED, and being bullied in childhood are risk factors. In terms of constitutional vulnerability, childhood obesity is a risk factor, as is early menarche, premature birth, and severe childhood health problems. Personal vulnerability risk factors include, but are not limited to, negative affectivity, low self-esteem, poor body image, dieting, and internalization of the cultural thin-ideal. Finally, for the sociocultural category, Striegel-Moore and Cachelin state, "Risk factors unique to ethnic minority group status (e.g., acculturation, immigration-related stresses, discrimination) need to be considered in culturally sensitive models of risk" (p. 640), and a paucity of research examining these sociocultural factors renders conclusions premature.

Risk Factor Models

Although several risk factor models exist (e.g., Stice, Ziemba, Margolis, & Flick, 1996; Vohs, Bardone, Joiner, Abramson, & Heatherton, 1999), the dual pathway model of BN (Stice et al., 1996) has the most empirical support (Franko et al., 2005). This model proposes that sociocultural pressure to be thin leads to internalization of the thin ideal. This ideal is unattainable and, thus, body dissatisfaction results. Body mass also contributes to perceived sociocultural pressure and body dissatisfaction, which lead to dieting and negative affect. Dieting and negative affect increase the risk of developing ED behaviors; negative affect and dieting are the final proximal predictors of bulimic pathology and also mediate the effects of the other risk factors. This theory has been influential in the field of ED prevention in terms of intervention content and variables studied (e.g., Franko et al., 2005; Stice, Chase, Stormer, & Appel, 2001).

RATIONALE FOR PREVENTING ED AND OBESITY SIMULTANEOUSLY

Although ED prevention has traditionally focused on ED symptoms and risk, there is increasing interest in developing interventions to prevent EDs and obesity concurrently. Bolstering this attempt is research identifying factors that are precursors of both. Based on a review of this research, Haines and Neumark-Sztainer (2006) listed the following as shared risk factors between eating disorders and obesity: (a) media use and the internalization of media, (b) body dissatisfaction, (c) weight-related teasing, and (d) dieting. Regarding media use, Haines and Neumark-Szainter stated that most empirical evidence finds that television use heightens the risk for obesity by increasing dietary intake during viewing, often as a result of food advertising. Media use is also tied to EDs through advertising and other images portraying unrealistically thin images that are often internalized by women. Regarding body dissatisfaction, Haines and Neumark-Sztainer noted that body dissatisfaction is predictive of binge eating behavior and decreased physical activity (females who feel less positive about their bodies are less likely to engage in physical activity). Body dissatisfaction is also "one of the most consistent and robust risk factors for eating disorders" (Haines & Neumark-Sztainer, 2006, p. 775). These authors also stated that weight-related teasing has been found to be associated with both binge eating and other disordered eating behaviors, potentially increasing the risk for both obesity and eating disorders. A fourth shared risk factor, dieting, deserves special mention.

Haines and Neumark-Sztainer (2006) observed that dieting has been found to predict weight gain, and the majority of individuals with EDs indicate that they began dieting before disordered eating behaviors were initiated. Likewise, dieting is included in Stice et al.'s (1996) dual pathway model and was listed as a salient risk factor by Striegel-Moore and Cachelin (2001). However, recent experimental studies have found just the opposite—individuals randomly assigned to low-calorie diets showed decreased bulimic symptoms relative to wait list controls (Burton, Stice, Bearman, & Rohde, 2007; Groesz & Stice, 2007; Presnell & Stice, 2003). While the effect of dieting on subsequent EDs is yet to be resolved and may be related to the differing ways dieting is defined and measured in experimental versus risk factor studies, the vast majority of ED prevention research uses dieting as an outcome measure. Likewise, many researchers still tout dieting as a shared risk factor for ED and obesity, arguing that shared risk factors point to the feasibility of joint prevention programs (Haines & Neumark-Sztainer, 2006).

Shared risk factors are not the only reason for joint prevention efforts. First, obesity and EDs tend to co-occur. Project EAT, a study of nearly 5,000 adolescents, found that higher percentages of overweight youth engaged in binge eating and unhealthy weight control behaviors than did their nonoverweight peers (Neumark-Sztainer et al., 2002). Moreover, findings from Project EAT illustrate the crossover from one weight-related problem to another (Neumark-Sztainer, 2005a, 2005b). Given such crossover, addressing only one problem (e.g., obesity) has the potential for causing other problems (e.g., EDs): "We worry that more weightist prejudice, more widespread body dissatisfaction at all sizes, and more ED will be the collateral damages of a war on obesity that does not take into account the nature and the causes of the spectrum of negative body image and disordered eating" (Neumark-Sztainer et al., 2006, p. 274). Preventing obesity in our culture may have the inadvertent side effect of increasing EDs. Likewise, the focus of many ED prevention programs on discouraging restricted eating may have the unintentional effect of increasing weight gain and obesity (Zabinski, Celio, Wilfley, & Taylor, 2003). Another rationale for simultaneous prevention is economics: it is more cost-effective to prevent two disorders with one program (Neumark-Sztainer, 2005a). Neumark-Sztainer and colleagues (2006) noted that public health funding is focused heavily on preventing obesity rather than EDs, and they suggest targeting both through joint prevention efforts.

Our contention is that shared prevention efforts should be a priority. Dual-focused prevention programs would emphasize healthy weight management, healthy eating patterns, increased physical activity, enhanced media literacy, positive body image, and effective skills for coping with negative affect and stressors (Neumark-Sztainer et al., 2006). Our current environment does not promote body acceptance nor does it encourage healthy lifestyles and choices. Instead, individuals are exposed to a milieu in which unhealthy foods are made increasingly attractive and available, physical activity is viewed as not necessary and is not made accessible, and societal ideals for body size are stringent and unattainable. As stated by Battle and Brownell (1996), "It is difficult to envision an environment more effective than ours for producing nearly universal body dissatisfaction, preoccupation with eating and weight, clinical cases of ED, and obesity" (p. 761). There is a need to focus prevention on altering both this toxic environment and its collateral damage on girls and women. For truly effective far-reaching prevention, then, the most important question is: "Can we foster the development of physical and social environments that promote healthy eating and physical activity and promote the acceptance of diverse body shapes and sizes?" (Neumark-Sztainer, 2005a, p. 220).

EATING DISORDER PREVENTION RESEARCH

Given our recommendation for dual ED and obesity prevention, a central, although not exclusive, focus of our review is on programs that have effectively targeted both at once. Due to space constraints, we do not review studies focused solely on obesity prevention. Stice, Shaw, and Marti (2006) provided an excellent meta-analytical review of that literature. Likewise, not every ED prevention study is reviewed. Instead, we review findings from a 2004 meta-analysis (Stice & Shaw, 2004), followed by studies on two critical research trends that were not a focus of Stice and Shaw's meta-analysis: (a) computerized interventions and (b) the Cognitive Dissonance approach. We then highlight research that furthers the goal of developing broad-ranging prevention programs.

In the following review, we report effect sizes. While effect size statistics (e.g., d, r, n^2) varied across studies, we converted all to r for comparability. Despite d being better known in the counseling outcome research literature, we chose r because of its high frequency of use in the ED prevention literature and recommendations by ED researchers (Stice, Shaw, & Marti, 2006). Unfortunately, d to r conversions using standard formulas can yield rs that do not match conventional criteria for interpreting effect sizes. Cohen's (1988) standard conversion formula for a d of .80 would yield an r of .37. The former ($d = .80$) is considered a large effect by conventional criteria, whereas the latter ($r = .37$) would be interpreted as a moderate effect. Given these findings, McGrath and Meyer (2006) recommended using correlations of .10, .24, and .37 as the benchmarks for small, medium, and large effects, respectively. We, therefore, suggest that readers use these benchmarks when interpreting the effect sizes that we report in this chapter. In the following review, except in three specifically noted studies, all effect sizes are for intervention versus control or alternate intervention comparisons. In sum, even when unspecified, all effect sizes are *r* values, and except when otherwise noted, they refer to group comparisons

Stice and Shaw's (2004) Meta-Analysis

In reviewing ED prevention research, the logical starting point is Stice and Shaw's (2004) oft-cited meta-analysis. This article examined 51 prevention studies spanning 38 individual programs that were analyzed across 53 separate trials resulting in 60 separate effect sizes. Thus, we first provide a detailed review of this meta-analysis, followed by an overview of research trends subsequent to their study inclusion cutoff date of April 2003.

Prior to examining Stice and Shaw's (2004) findings, an overview of their methodology is instructive. First, they stated that to be optimally successful, a prevention program should reduce both risk factors and eating pathology, even if the intervention only focused on risk factors. Nevertheless, given the methods of existing studies, they included prevention trials that tested for effects on eating behaviors or risk factors alone. Second, they focused exclusively on programs evaluated in clinical trials, stating that the ideal design is to use random assignment to a minimal intervention or placebo control condition; however, they also included clinical trials that utilized matched controls, as well as wait list and assessment-only controls. Third, they only included studies that tested whether the change in outcomes was significantly greater in the intervention versus the control group. Finally, Stice and Shaw calculated effect sizes for eating pathology and for those risk factors examined in at least 10 trials. These are the same factors included in the dual pathway model of risk (Stice et al., 1996): thin-ideal internalization, body dissatisfaction, dieting, negative affect, and body mass. Knowledge about ED was also included as an outcome due to its widespread inclusion in prevention studies.

Stice and Shaw's (2004) overall findings were encouraging. Fifty-three percent of programs (*n* = 32) resulted in significant reductions in at least one risk factor, such as body dissatisfaction, and 25% of programs (*n* = 15) led to decreases in eating pathology. However, only six programs resulted in decreases in eating pathology that persisted at follow-up assessment (ranging from 1 to 24 months). Average effect sizes for the outcomes ranged from .11 to .29 at termination and .05 to .29 at follow-up. Stice and Shaw considered these findings encouraging given that early studies showed prevention efforts to be largely unsuccessful.

Stice and Shaw (2004) also examined factors that moderated effect sizes at both termination and follow-up. Moderators were chosen based on theory, research, and clinical experience, and included risk status of participants, participant sex, participant age, program format and content, number of sessions, and use of validated measures. Analyses indicated that selected programs provided to high-risk individuals produced larger average effect sizes (.18 to .27) on most outcomes than did universal programs provided to samples not at risk (.05 to .08). Indeed, 10 of the 15 programs that produced effects for eating pathology were selected programs (average *r* = .24). Average effect sizes were larger for interactive (.13 to .20) than for didactic programs (.02 to .08), with all the programs producing decreases in eating pathology being interactive (average *r* = .17). Average effect sizes were higher for interventions with participants who were 15 years or older (.17 to .26) than with younger participants (.06 to .13). Intervention effects were stronger for all-female (.15 to .23) than for mixed-sex groups (.05 to .07). Multisession programs were most effective (.12 to .14); no single-session program produced significant effects (−.03 to −.05). Intervention effects were stronger for trials using validated (.15 to .24) rather than unvalidated measures (.03 to .06). In summary, this meta-analysis supported the continued investigation of multisession, interactive programs conducted with targeted groups of at-risk 15+-year-old females, using validated measures in controlled trials. In parallel, these results pointed to the need to develop effective universal programs, interventions that could be effective with younger age groups, and programs whose effects could be sustained over time.

Surprisingly less definitive were Stice and Shaw's (2004) results for program content, leading to the conclusion that content may be less important than features of the participants (e.g., age, risk level)

and the program (e.g., interactive). The content of the 15 programs that resulted in reductions in eating pathology varied widely, suggesting that there may be multiple content paths to effective prevention. Nevertheless, Stice and Shaw observed that programs with the most promising effects included cognitive or behavioral interventions aimed at altering maladaptive attitudes (e.g., thin-ideal internalization) or behaviors (e.g., fasting).

Finally, Stice and Shaw (2004) reported that there was an inverse relationship between sociocultural pressures for thinness and body mass, or that "programs that reduce the impact of cultural pressures for thinness may have the unintended effect of condoning obesity" (Stice & Shaw, 2004, p. 221). In short, while not a focus of their meta-analysis, Stice and Shaw's findings underscore the benefit of interventions that prevent obesity and ED simultaneously.

Recent Trends

Computerized Interventions

With over 605 million Internet users worldwide (Zabinski et al., 2003), computers have become a medium for the dissemination of ED information. There are advantages (e.g., accessibility) and pitfalls (e.g., limitations in crisis situations) of computerized ED prevention interventions (for a review, see Luce et al., 2003). Still, computers offer promise for ED prevention.

Franko and colleagues (2005) designed a CD-ROM (*Food, Mood and Attitude; FMA*) ED prevention program to be suitable for both at-risk and low-risk college women. In a controlled trial, first-year college women were randomly assigned to the intervention or control conditions, so that half in each condition were at-risk and half were low-risk. The program was developed using the dual pathway risk model (Stice et al., 1996). Of note, the study was purposefully inclusive of ethnic minority women. Results indicated that *FMA* was safe and effective for both at-risk and low-risk college women. Franko et al. found that participants in the *FMA* condition improved on all risk factors (internalization of sociocultural attitudes about thinness, shape concerns, weight concerns) and eating behavior measures relative to controls, with at-risk participants in the intervention group improving on risk and eating behavior outcome measures to a greater extent than low-risk participants. At 3-month follow-up, significantly fewer women in the *FMA* group reported overeating and excessive exercise relative to controls. Effect sizes at posttreatment and follow-up ranged from .24 to .33. Although the low-risk women in the *FMA* group did not evidence change on the outcome variables, they did increase their knowledge of risk factors relative to controls at both postintervention and follow-up. Thus, *FMA* might serve as an effective psychoeducational prevention tool for low-risk women without inducing iatrogenic effects. Its effects on risk factors and eating behaviors for high-risk women were substantial.

A second computerized intervention, *Student Bodies*, is noteworthy in that research on it spans almost 10 years, with continual updates made based on study findings. *Student Bodies* was developed to decrease weight and shape concerns (risk factors for EDs) as well as unhealthy weight regulation behaviors (Zabinski et al., 2003). This 8- to 10-week program uses a self-help cognitive behavioral approach and focuses each week on (a) psychoeducational readings and reflection, covering media influences, nutrition and physical activity, and general ED information; (b) a cognitive-behavioral exercise; and (c) a web-based body image journal to monitor events that trigger body dissatisfaction. The program also includes discussion groups, which have varied in terms of being moderated or unmoderated and either synchronous (individuals chatting in real time) or asynchronous (individuals posting at different times to the discussion).

Initially, the asynchronous *Student Bodies* program was evaluated in controlled trials with college-age women (Celio et al., 2000; Winzelberg et al., 1998, 2000; Zabinski, Pung, et al., 2001), with the program being modified as studies progressed. Results of intervention versus control group comparisons (Celio et al., 2000; Winzelberg et al., 1998, 2000) and within group pre- to postcomparisons (Zabinski, Pung, et al., 2001) showed significant improvements in weight and shape concerns and eating attitudes and behaviors for participants in the *Student Bodies* intervention (effect sizes ranged from .11 to .26). Following the success with this asynchronous discussion version of the intervention, Zabinski, Wilfley, et al. (2001) adapted *Student Bodies* to include synchronous chats moderated by a discussion leader. A pilot study with four at-risk college women suggested that the intervention was effective in reducing body image concerns and eating disorder pathology and that participants reported high satisfaction. A subsequent controlled trial (Zabinski, Wilfley, Calfas, Winzelberg, & Taylor, 69) yielded similar results: 30 at-risk college women were assigned to either the synchronous version or a wait list control, with intervention participants also given access to an asynchronous support group. Women in the intervention evidenced greater improvement on measures of eating pathology and self-esteem than women in the control group. Effect sizes ranged from .24 to .34. The majority of the participants reported satisfaction with the synchronous medium, as well as preferring it to posting to the message board.

Low et al. (2006) compared a control group and three versions of *Student Bodies:* no discussion group, moderated discussion group, and an unmoderated discussion group. Approximately 8% of the participants were students of color. Compared with the control group, at 8- to 9-month follow-up, participation in all versions of the program prevented the onset of bulimic behaviors. Intervention versus control group effect sizes (K. Low, personal communication, November 15, 2006) were .12, .20, and .54 for the moderated, no discussion, and unmoderated formats, respectively. In terms of risk factors, at 8- to 9-month follow-up, those who received any version of the intervention fared better than the control group on drive for thinness (.27 for moderated, .36 for no discussion, and .51 for unmoderated), and those in the unmoderated discussion group fared better than controls on body dissatisfaction (.33) and weight/shape concerns (.22). Results thus suggest that moderation of discussion groups may not be essential for successful outcomes, mirroring Franko et al.'s (2005) findings that self-guided computer interventions can be effective.

Finally, in perhaps the most exciting ED prevention study to date, Taylor et al. (2006) evaluated the asynchronous, moderated chat version of *Student Bodies* in a sample of 480 at-risk college women. Outcome data were collected, via structured clinical interviews, at pretreatment and yearly over a 3-year follow-up interval. Results reinforced the efficacy of *Student Bodies* as an ED prevention: intervention versus control comparisons resulted in a .37 effect size for reductions in weight and shape concerns at postintervention, with differences remaining significant at 1-year follow-up ($r = .20$). Participation in the intervention was associated with a decrease in the onset of EDs in two subgroups: those with baseline compensatory behaviors (self-induced vomiting, laxative use, diuretic use, driven exercise) and elevated baseline weights. In fact, no overweight intervention participant subsequently developed an ED, while the rates of ED onset for control group participants with comparable weights were 4.7% at 1 year and 11.9% at 2 years. This is the only study to date to show that *DSM-IV* full-syndrome EDs can be prevented in high-risk groups.

While the preceding studies demonstrate the efficacy of *Student Bodies* with college students, two studies demonstrate its utility with adolescents. Brown, Winzelberg, Abascal, and Taylor (2004) provided *Student Bodies* to 153 high school sophomores. Sixty-nine parents (49 with daughters in the intervention and 20 in the control condition) also completed a parent version of *Student Bodies*. In the student sample, significant intervention versus control group changes in ED knowledge and eating behavior ($r = .14$) were found following the intervention, although changes were not maintained at 5-month follow-up. Further, parents in the intervention group showed significantly greater decreases in critical attitudes and behaviors toward others' weight, shape, or appearance than the control group parents, with r's ranging from .23 to .29. While there was no correlation between student and parent improvement, Brown et al. (2004) still concluded that "prospective studies might use the encouraging results from this study as a starting point for integrating student and parent prevention interventions" (p. 296).

Finally, in the *Student Bodies* study with the youngest age group to date, Abascal, Brown, Winzelberg, Dev, and Taylor (2004) evaluated the program with 13- to 16-year-old girls as part of their school curriculum. Participants were assessed prior to the start of the program on risk status (low/high) and motivation to improve body image (low/high). Two separate physical education classes were divided into two groups each: high risk–high motivation and low risk–low motivation. A third class was not split. In a pre- to post-score comparison, all groups improved on measures of eating-disordered attitudes and behaviors ($r = .15$ to .35). While this suggests benefit regardless of risk or motivation level, girls in the high risk–high motivation group reported experiencing more positive interactions and fewer negative comments about the program than did their counterparts in the combined group. Thus, these data suggest that it may be appropriate to separate high- and low-risk groups (to concurrently provide universal and targeted interventions) within a school setting.

The ability to provide universal and targeted interventions simultaneously is a unique benefit of computerized interventions. Recall that the Stice and Shaw (2004) meta-analysis found the largest effects for selected rather than universal interventions. However, the flexibility of computerized interventions allows for concurrent intervention with high- and low-risk groups. Abascal et al. (2004) capitalized on this flexibility, as did Franko et al. (2005), and both reported positive results. We hope the field will continue to take advantage of computerized methodology to provide targeted and universal interventions together.

Cognitive Dissonance (CD) Approach

Based on their finding that only 6 of 38 programs resulted in reductions in ED behaviors that persisted at follow-up, Stice and colleagues attempted to design an intervention to decrease bulimic behaviors that could be sustained over time, using both their own dual-pathway model (Stice et al., 1996) and cognitive dissonance (*CD*) theory (Festinger, 1957). The *CD* intervention attempts to reduce the extent of acceptance of the culturally prescribed ideal body image for women based on cognitive dissonance theory. The theory states that holding inconsistent cognitions creates psychological discomfort, which in turn motivates individuals to modify their thoughts to restore consistency. This intervention is based on the hypothesis that if females who had internalized the thin-ideal took a stance against it, they would reduce the degree to which they endorsed it. In accordance with the dual-pathway model, reducing thin-ideal internalization is thought to lead to decreases in body dissatisfaction, dieting, and negative affect, thereby leading to decreases in bulimic symptoms. The *CD* intervention occurs over three one-hour face-to-face sessions (see Stice, Chase, Stormer, & Appel, 2001).

Some studies using the *CD* approach with high-risk women (average ages 17 to 19) have met with success. In an initial pilot trial, Stice, Mazotti, Weibel, and Agras (2000) found that, when compared with a wait list control, *CD* resulted in significantly greater decreases in thin-ideal internalization, body dissatisfaction, negative affect, and bulimic symptoms, with all effects except negative affect holding at 1 month (r's $= .37$ to .46).

In a second *CD* study, this intervention was compared with a *Healthy Weight* (*HW*) control intervention, which promotes lasting decreases in caloric intake and increases in exercise to achieve a healthy weight and body satisfaction (Stice et al., 2001). In this trial, *CD* reduced thin-ideal internalization, body dissatisfaction, dieting, negative affect, and bulimic symptoms from baseline to termination, with the effects maintained at the 1-month follow-up. However, participants in the *HW* control condition also reported reductions in dieting, negative affect, and bulimic symptoms, which were not significantly different from those in the *CD* program; only effects for thin-ideal internalization were stronger for *CD* than *HW* (r of .30 at postintervention and .40 at 1-month follow-up). Because Stice and colleagues believed they may have unintentionally created an alternate effective prevention program *(HW)*, they conducted a follow-up trial in which both *CD* and *HW* were compared with a wait list control (Stice, Trost, & Chase, 2003). Both the *CD* and the *HW* interventions produced significantly greater reductions in negative affect and bulimic symptoms at both posttest and 1-month follow-up relative to wait-list control (*CD* effect sizes ranged from .21 to .27). The effects for *CD* were somewhat more pronounced than for *HW,* with the former showing greater reductions in thin-ideal internalization, body dissatisfaction, negative affect, and bulimic symptoms at posttest (r ranged from .23 to .27) and at 6-month follow-up for negative affect ($r = .20$).

Stice, Shaw, Burton, and Wade (2006) subsequently randomly assigned 481 adolescent girls (aged 14 to 18; 43% ethnic and racial minorities) with body dissatisfaction into *CD, HW,* an expressive writing placebo control group, and an assessment-only control group. The expressive writing placebo was used to isolate the effects of demand characteristics and expectancy effects from nonspecific factors (e.g., group social support); participants were told that body image concerns are linked to emotional issues and that writing about emotional issues helps resolve these issues. Both the *CD* and *HW* interventions resulted in reductions in eating disorder risk factors (e.g., thin-ideal internalization, dieting, body dissatisfaction, negative affect) and bulimic symptoms at posttest and follow-up (some results persisted for 6-month follow-up and some for 1-year follow-up) when compared with the active and the wait-list control conditions (r ranged from .13 to .38 for *CD* and .11 to .25 for *HW*). However, important differences were found between *CD* and *HW. CD* produced significantly greater decreases in thin-ideal internalization, body dissatisfaction, dieting, negative affect, and bulimic symptoms than *HW,* when compared immediately after the intervention ($r = .11$ to .26). Additionally, *CD* produced greater changes than *HW* in negative affect, when compared at both 6-month and 1-year follow-up (average $r = .11$). Conversely, *HW* was more effective in reducing risk for onset of binge eating, compensatory behaviors, and obesity than *CD*. At 1-year follow-up, as assessed by actual height and weight measurements, relative to the assessment-only control condition, *CD* produced a three-fold decrease in obesity onset and *HW* produced a 12-fold decrease, a finding the authors deem remarkable given that no obesity prevention programs have resulted in as large a decrease in obesity.

Three studies (Becker, Smith, & Ciao, 2005; Becker, Smith, & Ciao, 2006; Matusek, Wendt, & Wiseman, 2004) focus on the effectiveness of the *CD* intervention when delivered in natural settings by lay providers (e.g., teachers providing the intervention in schools). Matusek et al. (2004) compared one-session versions of *CD* and *HW* with a wait list control intervention (with primarily Asian American college women); health educators already working at the college provided the intervention. Compared with wait list controls, both interventions resulted in reductions in thin-ideal internalization and disturbed eating behavior (*CD* effect sizes $r = .30$ and .42), with no differences between *CD* and *HW.*

Using another shortened (two versus three sessions) version of *CD*, Becker et al. (2005) randomly assigned sorority members to *CD*, a media advocacy intervention (*MA*), or a wait list control condition. According to the authors, *MA* is similar to *CD* but replaces the dissonance activities of *CD* with videos targeting the role of the media in the maintenance of the thin ideal. Both interventions reduced dieting, eating pathology, and body-dissatisfaction at 1-month follow-up compared with wait-list controls (effect sizes for *CD* were .26 to .41), with *CD* also resulting in decreases in thin-ideal internalization relative to the waitlist control ($r = .22$). *MA* and *CD* did not differ significantly on any outcomes.

In a later study, *CD* and *MA* were compared when provided to new sorority members by peer leaders who had undergone training (Becker et al., 2006). Both *MA* and *CD* performed well, with both reducing bulimic pathology at 8-month follow-up, with no difference between the two. However, *CD* produced greater improvements in thin-ideal internalization, body dissatisfaction, and dieting when compared with *MA* ($r = .20$ to .26). In their interpretation, the authors speculated that while they attempted to design two distinct interventions, *MA* may actually be a slightly weaker version of *CD*. Most importantly, taken together, the Becker studies indicate that a shortened and independent (conducted by someone other than Stice) version of *CD* can be successful.

Research Furthering the Goal of Dual ED and Obesity Interventions

A vital priority is developing interventions that prevent obesity (or unhealthy weight gain) and EDs at once. As noted despite not initially being designed to do so, the *CD* intervention resulted in a three-fold decrease in obesity onset. Also, although originally designed only as a *CD* control condition, the *HW* intervention produced a 12-fold decrease in this same study (Stice, Shaw, Burton, et al., 2006). Stice,

Shaw, Burton, et al. (2006) thus concluded that both *CD* and *HW* have received enough empirical support to be termed efficacious according to the American Psychological Association Task Force on Psychological Intervention Guidelines (1995). However, they also stated that "given that obesity results in far greater morbidity and mortality than eating pathology and that the healthy weight intervention might be more easily integrated with universal prevention programs that promote healthy eating and exercise, the healthy weight intervention may have greater public health potential" (p. 273). Two other interventions have been found to successfully target obesity and EDs at once: a college class designed for this purpose and an obesity prevention program designed for adolescents.

Stice and Ragan (2002) designed a college class to prevent both EDs and overweight. The class ($N = 88$, 32% minority) met twice a week for 90 minutes during a 15-week semester and included guest speakers, readings, papers, and presentations. Course content focused on "descriptive pathology, epidemiology, etiologic models, empirically documented risk factors, preventive interventions, and treatments for eating disorders and obesity" (p. 162). Findings indicated that intervention participants, relative to controls in other college classes, demonstrated decreases in thin-ideal internalization, body dissatisfaction, dieting, eating disorder symptoms, and body mass over the 4-month study period. Effect sizes ranged from .24 to .38. Intervention students showed a 3% decrease in body mass, whereas the control students evidenced a 4% increase in body mass ($r = .32$). Participants who started at the highest body weight lost the most weight.

Stice, Orjada, and Tristen (2006) replicated this study, adding a 6-month follow-up. Effects were actually slightly larger at 6-month follow-up than at posttest (r's ranged .19 to .31). Stice, Orjada, et al. (2006) labeled these as "true prophylactic effects for thin-ideal internalization and weight gain" (p. 238), further noting "[the fact] that this intervention produced both a reduction in eating disorder symptoms and a weight gain prevention effect is novel, as most dedicated eating disorder and obesity prevention programs . . . have not produced these effects and virtually no other intervention has produced effects for both of these important outcomes" (p. 238).

While this college class intervention was designed for joint prevention, another intervention was intended initially for obesity prevention and later found to be successful in targeting both obesity and EDs among adolescent girls. *Planet Health* (*PH;* Gortmaker et al., 1999) is a school-based obesity prevention intervention for youth focused on behavioral changes, such as increasing fruit and vegetable intake, eating fat in moderation, being physically active every day, and limiting television and computer use. In an initial randomized clinical trial, Gortmaker et al. found that *PH*, provided within existing curricula by classroom teachers, could effectively reduce the risk of obesity in early adolescent girls across 2 school years. Subsequently, based on important linkages between EDs and overweight and the call for alliances between the fields of ED and obesity prevention research, Austin, Field, Wiecha, Peterson, and Gortmaker (2005) used data from 480 *PH* and control girls (average age = 11.5) to examine the impact of the intervention on risk of engaging in disordered weight-control behaviors at 21 months follow-up. The authors found that *PH* was effective in preventing the onset of purging behaviors and diet pill use, but only in girls who were not dieting at the start of the intervention. Among girls who reported dieting in the past 30 days at baseline, there was no difference between control and intervention in the odds of reporting disordered weight-control behaviors at follow-up. However, among baseline nondieters, girls in intervention schools were 12 times less likely than girls in control schools to report the use of purging or diet pills to control their weight at follow-up ($r = .15$). In addition, using a preventive factor calculation, these authors estimated that 59% of new cases of disordered weight-control behavior among girls in control schools might have been prevented had they received the *PH* intervention.

We end our review with an innovative development that holds promise for the continued success of joint prevention programs. Luce and colleagues (2005) provided an online assessment to 174 high-school sophomores and used a computer algorithm to sort them into one of four risk groups: no eating disorder/no overweight risk (NR), high eating disorder/no overweight risk (EDR), no eating disorder/high overweight risk (OR), and high eating disorder/high overweight risk (EDOR). Each group was provided with tailored feedback and options as follows. The NR group was told that their responses indicated that they had healthy feelings about their weight and shape and that their weight was within a healthy range. These participants engaged only in their required health curriculum, which included information on healthy eating, exercise, appearance concerns, and EDs. The EDR group was told that they were very worried about their weight and shape, although their weight was within a healthy range. They were told that they may be at risk of developing an ED, and were given the choice to participate in only the required curriculum or the required curriculum and a special additional body image curriculum (modeled after *Student Bodies*). Those in the OR group were informed that their weight was in the overweight range and were offered a specialized weight management curriculum that could be completed outside class (which included an online discussion group). Finally, those in the EDOR group were given the same feedback given to those in the OR and EDR groups, and asked if they were interested in participating in the same online body image program offered to those in the EDR group, as well as in the weight management program offered to those in the OR group. Twenty (56%) of the EDR and eight (50%) of the OR participants selected the recommended curricula. Among participants in the EDOR group, four (80%) chose to participate in both curricula programs. Although the sample size was very small, initial results of this combined universal/targeted prevention study were promising, with participants in all groups evidencing change in ED risk factors (e.g., weight and shape concerns, restrained eating) from pre- to postintervention ($r = .09$ to .35). Among the 11 participants who were engaging in self-induced vomiting or laxative use before the study, seven denied use at the close of the study and one had sought treatment. This initial study demonstrates that it may be feasible to use online screening to classify students within a school population by ED and overweight risk and to offer computer-based, targeted interventions accordingly. We hope that future studies will pursue this methodology in the quest for interventions that can simultaneously prevent the spectrum of eating and weight-related disorders. Integrating risk-level algorithms with promising programs (e.g., CD, *HW*) is a potentially useful direction.

SUGGESTIONS FOR RESEARCH AND PRACTICE IN ED PREVENTION

Methodological Suggestions

Stice and Shaw (2004) reached several methodological conclusions that we reiterate and expand on. Ideal ED prevention research includes the following: (a) testing for effects on both eating behaviors and risk factors; (b) using validated measures; (c) random assignment to intervention and control conditions; (d) appropriate statistics that assess whether the change in outcomes is significantly greater in the intervention versus the control group; and (e) reporting of effect sizes, including specification of which statistic was used. Regarding control groups, we recommend more studies that simultaneously use both passive controls (e.g., assessment only controls, wait list controls) in conjunction with controls that tease out demand characteristics and expectancy effects. In addition, we advocate the continued examination of both theory-driven and empirically validated risk factors (Franko et al., 2005; Stice & Shaw, 2004). Likewise, while acknowledging that not all researchers have the resources to do so, we especially endorse Taylor et al.'s (2006) methodology in which eating behaviors, risk factors, and importantly, ED diagnoses as assessed by a clinical interview were examined in a long-term follow-up. A follow-up assessment that demonstrates that an ED prevention program can actually decrease problematic eating behaviors or even better, the onset of EDs, is a central issue for researchers because short-term reduction of risk factors may be clinically meaningless in the absence of reduced long-term risk for problematic eating behaviors or disorders.

As noted, we suggest methodologies in which interventions are provided to low- and high-risk participants simultaneously and effects are compared across these groups. Another crucial issue is attention to ethnic minority status. We recommend the methodology of Franko et al. (2005): these researchers stratified participants into risk (low risk and at risk), and minority (minority and nonminority) categories yielding four groups: (1) low-risk nonminority, (2) at-risk nonminority, (3) low-risk minority, and (4) at-risk minority. They subsequently randomly selected participants so that students of color composed 25% of the total sample. They then randomly assigned participants in each group to the experimental conditions. Likewise, the computer algorithm methodology of Luce et al. (2005) could be used to accomplish the same goal, taking both minority and risk status into account.

A final methodological suggestion relates to the central call of this chapter. While we unequivocally recommend evaluations of interventions that target both EDs and obesity, we also implore researchers who evaluate interventions aimed only at EDs to include weight or weight status as an outcome variable. Such designs will at least allow us to ascertain if there are inadvertent effects (e.g., ED interventions increasing obesity) or if the intervention may have the added benefit of preventing obesity or overweight. We also make the parallel recommendation that obesity prevention researchers include ED behaviors or diagnoses as an outcome variable. As was the case with the *CD, HW,* and *Planet Health* interventions, the inclusion of such outcome variables may result in the discovery of an intervention that, while not originally designed as such, is capable of preventing both eating and weight-related issues together.

A Best Practices Approach to Research and Practice

ED prevention research and practice are inextricably intertwined. Specifically, ED prevention research is geared toward developing effective prevention practices. Likewise, ED prevention practice should continually be evaluated with sound research methodology to ascertain actual effectiveness. Nevertheless, two related problems plague ED prevention research and practice. First, many researchers spend time developing and evaluating new programs when several promising programs with positive effects already exist (Neumark-Sztainer et al., 2006); the result is a number of programs which show effectiveness in single-study evaluations. Second, many prevention programs with unknown effects are being used in schools and communities. The solution to both problems is a best-practices approach.

A best-practices approach entails prevention trials that build on the programs that have already demonstrated the most promising results, with each new study working to refine these interventions further or to expand them to other settings or providers. Expansion includes adapting programs found to be effective in one population (e.g., college students) to other populations (e.g., adolescents). A best-practices approach would also involve undertaking trials of effective programs in naturalistic settings with endogenous providers, as well as the study of effect size moderators, such as ethnic minority status (cf. Stice & Shaw, 2004). A best-practices approach necessitates forgoing single-study evaluations and focusing on improving interventions that have already demonstrated positive results. Such an approach involves the replication and study of various programs by multiple researchers in multiple labs. Likewise, a best-practices approach entails providing only such well-researched and proven interventions in schools, colleges, and communities. Based on our review, we recommend the following programs as best-practices: *Student Bodies, CD, HW,* and *PH.*

Student Bodies is deemed a best-practices approach based on multiple replications of positive findings, albeit within the same lab. *Student Bodies* has demonstrated positive outcomes across diverse age groups, including (a) high- and low-risk adolescents within a school setting (Abascal et al., 2004), (b) high school students and their parents (Brown et al., 2004), and (c) college students. The latter studies of college students have also included samples with a high percentage of students of color (Low et al., 2006). Notably, *Student Bodies* has been found to reduce bulimic behaviors at 9-month follow-up (Low et al., 2006) and actual onset of EDs, as assessed by clinical interviews, at 1-year follow-up with high-risk groups (Taylor et al., 2006). Controlled trials in independent labs are needed, as are longer-term studies with adolescent samples.

CD is deemed a best-practices approach due to both its positive results and replication in at least five independent labs (E. Stice, personal communication, November 21, 2006). *CD* has mainly demonstrated positive outcomes among high-risk college students, with one trial also finding positive effects in a racially and ethnically diverse sample of younger adolescents (Stice, Shaw, Burton, et al., 2006). *CD* has also demonstrated positive effects when provided in natural settings with endogenous providers (e.g., Becker and colleagues' studies) and has resulted in decreases in eating pathology that have persisted at follow-up across multiple trials (Stice et al., 2001, 2003; Stice, Shaw, Burton, et al., 2006). Additional controlled trials with younger age groups and lower risk samples are needed, as are longer follow-up periods. A study examining the *CD* approach in terms of actual ED onset, as assessed by clinical interviews, would be quite valuable.

HW is deemed a best-practices approach for similar reasons as those presented for *CD*. Also, because of *HW*'s demonstrated effects for reducing both obesity and eating pathology at 1-year follow-up among an ethnically and racially diverse sample of 14- to 18-year-old girls (Stice, Shaw, Burton, et al., 2006), we deem this a "best of the best" approach. Nevertheless, additional work is needed to replicate and extend these findings across multiple settings, risk groups, and ages.

PH is also deemed a "best of the best" approach due to its ability to prevent EDs and obesity (Austin et al., 2005) in young girls (10 to 14) at almost 2-year follow-up. Indeed, *PH* has filled a vital long-standing need in the prevention field: an effective program for younger age groups that can be provided by teachers in a school setting. Still, replication among diverse settings (different schools) and samples (age, ethnicity) is needed, as are refinements to increase the effectiveness of this program among those who start dieting prior to seventh or eighth grade.

In sum, programs now exist that can be effectively presented in universal and selected formats (e.g., *Student Bodies*) and with younger age groups (e.g., *PH, Student Bodies*). Importantly, all four of our designated best practices programs (*Student Bodies, CD, HW, Planet Health*) have proved effective in preventing problematic eating at long-term follow-up, and two have successfully combined the prevention of both ED symptomatology and obesity/overweight (*HW* and *PH*). The time is ripe for continued research using these promising approaches.

CONCLUSION—A PLEA FOR SOCIETAL CHANGE

While all the programs reviewed target individual changes, change on a larger scale is also necessary. The contribution of societal factors to body dissatisfaction, obesity, and disordered eating has been well established. Thus, in attempting to prevent the spectrum of eating and weight-related disorders, cultural change is essential.

One of the most prevalent purveyors of societal messages is the mass media. In fact, most of our best-practices approaches have at least some focus on fighting the effects of the media or the thin-ideal internalization that results from media messages. We suggest that there is a need for advocacy efforts to change the media messages rather than solely teaching individuals to be more critical of the media. We advocate changing the advertisements and media images to represent women of all body shapes and sizes. In short, a potent way to prevent EDs is to revolutionize current media messages.

Another aspect of the environment that warrants societal transformation is the food industry. Availability of unhealthy foods and large portions contribute to an environment that encourages overeating, while the booming diet industry promotes restricting food intake and the classification of foods into "good" and "bad" categories. Obviously, both are problematic and contribute to the development of risk factors for obesity and EDs. Therefore, we suggest the promotion of eating in response to physical hunger and reform of the diet industry as examples of modifications of societal norms that contribute to problematic eating behaviors.

Within this larger environmental context is the influential impact of the family, which is often the source of societal messages. Familial influence on eating and weight concern may include parental encouragement to diet, media use and weight-talk in the home, parental dieting, food availability, eating-out practices, family meals, parental support, parental physical activities, family communication, and parenting styles (Neumark-Sztainer, 2005b). Therefore, we also recommend that interventions include parents and focus on altering the home environment as a starting point for broader societal change.

To create change on an environmental level, we must collaborate with those in other fields, including public health professionals, school administrators, food manufacturers, and the fitness and fashion industries. We emphasize the immense importance of consensus-building with individuals within other spheres, as suggested by Neumark-Sztainer (2005a).

In closing, we repeat a question posed earlier: "Can we foster the development of physical and social environments that promote healthy eating and physical activity and promote the acceptance of diverse body shapes and sizes?" (Neumark-Sztainer, 2005a, p. 220). Sadly, we have not done so yet. While it is encouraging that effective prevention programs have been found, including some that can prevent EDs and obesity at once, our hope is that broad societal changes will someday render the need for prevention of eating problems obsolete. Who better than counseling psychologists to lead the charge?

REFERENCES

Abascal, L., Brown, J. B., Winzelberg, A. J., Dev, P., & Taylor, C. B. (2004). Combining universal and targeted prevention for school-based eating disorder programs. *International Journal of Eating Disorders, 35*, 1–9.

Agras, W. S., Walsh, B. T., Fairburn, C. G., Wilson, G. T., & Kraemer, H. C. (2000). A multicenter comparison of cognitive-behavioral therapy and interpersonal for bulimia nervosa. *Archives of General Psychiatry, 57*, 459–466.

American Psychiatric Association. (2000). *Diagnostic and statistical manual of mental disorders* (4th ed., text rev.). Washington, DC: Author.

American Psychological Association Task Force on Psychological Intervention Guidelines. (1995). *Template for developing guidelines: Interventions for mental disorders and psychological aspects of physical disorders.* Washington, DC: Author.

Austin, S. B., Field, A. E., Wiecha, J., Peterson, K. E., & Gortmaker, S. L., (2005). The impact of a school-based obesity prevention trial on disordered weight-control behaviors in early adolescent girls. *Archives of Pediatrics and Adolescent Medicine, 159*, 225–230.

Battle, E. K., & Brownell, K. D. (1996). Confronting a rising tide of eating disorders and obesity: Treatment vs. prevention and policy. *Addictive Behaviors, 21*, 755–765.

Becker, C. B., Smith, L., & Ciao, A. C. (2005). Reducing eating disorder risk factors in sorority members: A randomized trial. *Behavior Therapy, 36*, 245–254.

Becker, C. B., Smith, L., & Ciao, A. C. (2006). Peer-facilitated eating disorder prevention: A randomized effectiveness trial of cognitive dissonance and media advocacy. *Journal of Counseling Psychology, 53*, 550–555.

Brown, J. B., Winzelberg, A. J., Abascal, L. B., & Taylor, C. B. (2004). An evaluation of an internet-delivered eating disorder prevention program for adolescents and their parents. *Journal of Adolescent Health, 35*, 290–296.

Burton, E. M., Stice, E., Bearman, S. K., & Rohde, P. (2007). An experimental test of the affect-regulation model of bulimic symptoms and substance use: An affective intervention. *International Journal of Eating Disorders, 40*, 27–36.

Cash, T. F. (2002). The situational inventory of body-image dysphoria: Psychometric evidence and development of a short form. *International Journal of Eating Disorders, 32*, 362–366.

Celio, A. A., Winzelberg, A. J., Wilfley, D. E., Eppstein, D., Springer, E. A., Dev, P., et al. (2000). Reducing risk factors for eating disorders: Comparison of an internet and classroom delivered psychoeducational program. *Journal of Consulting and Clinical Psychology, 68*, 650–657.

Cohen, J. (1988). *Statistical power analysis for the behavioral sciences* (2nd ed.). Hillside, NJ: Erlbaum.

Fairburn, C. G., Cooper, Z., Doll, H. A., Norman, P. A., & O'Connor, M. E. (2000). The natural course of bulimia nervosa and binge eating disorder in young women. *Archives of General Psychiatry, 57*, 659–665.

Festinger, L. (1957). *A theory of cognitive dissonance.* Stanford, CA: Stanford University Press.

Franko, D. L., Keel, P. K., Dorer, D., Blais, M., Delinsky, S. S., Eddy, K. T., et al. (2004). What predicts suicide attempts in women with eating disorders? *Psychological Medicine, 34*, 843–853.

Franko, D. L., Mintz, L. B., Villapiano, M., Green, T. C., Mainelli, D., Folensbee, L., et al. (2005). Food, mood, and attitude: Reducing risk for eating disorders in college women. *Health Psychology, 24*, 567–578.

Fretz, B. R., & Simon, N. P. (1992). Professional issues in counseling psychology: Continuity, change, and challenge. In S. D. Brown & R. W. Lent (Eds.), *Handbook of counseling psychology* (2nd ed., pp. 3–36). New York: Wiley.

Gortmaker, S. L., Peterson, K., Wiecha, J., Sobol, A. M., Dixit, S., Fox, M. K., et al. (1999). Reducing obesity via a school-based interdisciplinary intervention among youth: Planet health. *Archives of Pediatric and Adolescent Medicine, 153*, 409–418.

Groesz, L. M., & Stice, E. (2007). An experimental test of the effects of dieting on bulimic symptoms: The impact of eating episode frequency. *Behaviour Research and Therapy, 45*, 49–62.

Haines, J., & Neumark-Sztainer, D. (2006). Prevention of obesity and eating disorders: A consideration of shared risk factors. *Health Education Research, 21*, 770–782.

Heppner, P. P., Casas, J. M., Carter, J., & Stone, G. L. (2000). The maturation of counseling psychology: Multi-faceted perspectives 1978–1998. In S. D. Brown & R. W. Lent (Eds.), *The handbook of counseling psychology* (pp. 3–49). New York: Wiley.

Herzog, D. B., & Delinsky, S. (2001). *Classification of eating disorders.* In R. H. Striegel-Moore & L. Smolak (Eds.), *Eating disorders: Innovations in research, treatment, and prevention* (pp. 31–50). Washington, DC: American Psychological Association.

Hoek, H. W., & van Hoeken, D. (2003). Review of the prevalence and incidence of eating disorders. *International Journal of Eating Disorders, 34*, 383–396.

Jacobi, C., Hayward, C., de Zwaan, M., Kraemer, H. C., & Agras, W. S. (2004). Coming to terms with risk factor for eating disorders: Application of risk terminology and suggestions for a general taxonomy. *Psychological Bulletin, 130*, 19–65.

Johnson, J. G., Cohen, P., Kasen, S., & Brook, J. S. (2002). Eating disorders during adolescence and the risk for physical and mental disorders during early adulthood. *Archives of General Psychiatry, 59*, 545–552.

Keel, P. K., Dorer, D. J., Eddy, K. T., Franko, D. L., Charatan, D. L., & Herzog, D. B. (2003). Predictors of mortality in eating disorders. *Archives of General Psychiatry, 60*, 179–183.

Keel, P. K., Dorer, D. J., Franko, D. L., Jackson, S. C., & Herzog, D. B. (2005). Post-remission predictors of relapse in eating disorders. *American Journal of Psychiatry, 162*, 2263–2268.

Levine, M. P., & Smolak, L. (2006). *The prevention of eating problems and eating disorders: Theory, research, and practice.* Mahwah, NJ: Erlbaum.

Lewinsohn, P. M., Striegel-Moore, R. H., & Seeley, J. R. (2000). Epidemiology and natural course of eating disorders in young women from adolescence to young adulthood. *Journal of the American Academy of Child and Adolescent Psychiatry, 39*, 1284–1292.

Low, K. G., Charanasomboon, S., Lesser, J., Reinhalter, K., Martin, R., Jones, H., et al. (2006). Effectiveness of a computer-based interactive eating disorders prevention program at long-term follow-up. *Eating Disorders: Journal of Treatment and Prevention, 14*, 17–30.

Luce, K. H., Osborne, M. I., Winzelberg, A. J., Das, S., Abascal, L. B., Celio, A. A., et al. (2005). Application of an algorithm-driven protocol to simultaneously provide universal and targeted prevention programs. *International Journal of Eating Disorders, 37*, 220–226.

Luce, K. H., Winzelberg, A. J., Zabinski, M. F., & Osborne, M. I. (2003). Internet-delivered psychological interventions for body image dissatisfaction and disordered eating. *Psychotherapy: Theory, Research, Practice, Training, 40*, 148–154.

Matusek, J. A., Wendt, S. J., & Wiseman, C. V. (2004). Dissonance thin-ideal and didactic healthy behavior eating disorder prevention programs: Results from a controlled trial. *International Journal of Eating Disorders, 36*, 376–388.

McGrath, R. E., & Meyer, G. J. (2006). When effect sizes disagree: The case of *r* and *d*. *Psychological Methods, 11*, 386–401.

Metzler, A. E. (2000, August). *Council of Counseling Psychology Training Programs survey of doctoral training programs.* Paper presented at the American Psychological Association Convention, Washington, DC.

Mintz, L. B., O'Halloran, S. M., Mulholland, A. M., & Schneider, P. A. (1997). Questionnaire for Eating Disorder Diagnoses: Reliability and validity of operationalizing DSM-IV criteria into a self-report format. *Journal of Counseling Psychology, 44*, 63–79.

Munoz, R. F., Mrazek, P. J., & Haggerty, R. J. (1996). Institute of Medicine Report on Prevention of Mental Disorders: Summary and commentary. *American Psychologist, 51*, 1116–1122.

Mussell, M. P., Binford, R. B., & Fulkerson, J. A. (2000). Eating disorders: Summary of risk factors, prevention programming, and prevention research. *Counseling Psychologist, 28*, 764–796.

National Center for Health Statistics, U.S. Department of Health and Human Services, & Centers for Disease Control. (2004, May). *Prevalence of overweight among children and adolescents: United States, 1999–2000.* Retrieved October 22, 2006, from www.cdc.gov/nchs/products/pubs/pubd/hestats/overwght99.htm.

Neumark-Sztainer, D. (2005a). Can we simultaneously work toward the prevention of obesity and eating disorders in children and adolescents? *International Journal of Eating Disorders, 38*, 220–227.

Neumark-Sztainer, D. (2005b). Preventing the broad spectrum of weight-related problems: Working with parents to help teens achieve a healthy weight and a positive body image. *Journal of Nutrition Education and Behavior, 37*, S133–S139.

Neumark-Sztainer, D., Levine, M. P., Paxton, S. J., Smolak, L., Piran, N., & Wertheim, E. H. (2006). Prevention of body dissatisfaction and disordered eating: What next? *Eating Disorders, 14*, 265–285.

Neumark-Sztainer, D., Story, M., Hannan, P. J., Perry, C. L., & Irving, L. M. (2002). Weight-related concerns and behaviors among overweight and non-overweight adolescents: Implications for preventing weight-related disorders. *Archives of Pediatrics and Adolescent Medicine 156*, 171–178.

Neumark-Sztainer, D., Wall, M. M., Story, M., & Perry, C. L. (2003). Correlates of unhealthy weight-control behaviors among adolescents. *Health Psychology, 22*, 88–98.

Ogden, C. L., Flegal, K. M., Carroll, M. D., & Johnson, D. L. (2002). Prevalence and trends in overweight among U.S. children and adolescents: 1999–2000. *Journal of the American Medical Association, 288*, 1728–1732.

Pearson, J., Goldklang, D., & Striegel-Moore, R. H. (2002). Prevention of eating disorders: Challenges and opportunities. *International Journal of Eating Disorders, 31*, 233–239.

Presnell, K., & Stice, E. (2003). An experimental test of the effect of weight-loss dieting on bulimic pathology: Tipping the scales in a different direction. *Journal of Abnormal Psychology, 112*, 166–170.

Root, M. P. P. (2001). Future considerations in research on eating disorders. *Counseling Psychologist, 29*, 754–762.

Stice, E., Chase, A., Stormer, S., & Appel, A. (2001). A randomized trial of a dissonance-based eating disorder prevention program. *International Journal of Eating Disorders, 29*, 247–262.

Stice, E., Hayward, C., Cameron, R., Killen, J. D., & Taylor, C. B. (2000). Body image and eating related factors predict onset of depression in female adolescents: A longitudinal study. *Journal of Abnormal Psychology, 109*, 438–444.

Stice, E., Mazotti, L., Weibel, D., & Agras, W. S. (2000). Dissonance prevention program decreases thin-ideal internalization, body dissatisfaction, dieting, negative affect, and bulimic symptoms: A preliminary experiment. *International Journal of Eating Disorders, 27*, 206–217.

Stice, E., Orjada, K., & Tristan, J. (2006). Trial of a psychoeducational eating disturbance intervention for college women: A replication and extension. *International Journal of Eating Disorders, 39*, 233–239.

Stice, E., & Ragan, J. (2002). A controlled evaluation of an eating disturbance psychoeducational intervention. *International Journal of Eating Disorders, 31*, 159–171.

Stice, E., & Shaw, H. (2004). Eating disorder prevention programs: A meta-analytic review. *Psychological Bulletin, 130*, 206–227.

Stice, E., Shaw, H., Burton, E., & Wade, E. (2006). Dissonance and healthy weight eating disorder prevention programs: A randomized efficacy trial. *Journal of Consulting and Clinical Psychology, 74*, 263–275.

Stice, E., Shaw, H., & Marti, C. N. (2006). A meta-analytic review of obesity prevention programs for children and adolescents: The skinny on interventions that work. *Psychological Bulletin, 132*, 667–691.

Stice, E., Trost, A., & Chase, A. (2003). Healthy weight control and dissonance-based eating disorder prevention programs: Results from a controlled trial. *International Journal of Eating Disorders, 33*, 10–21.

Stice, E., Ziemba, C., Margolis, J., & Flick, P. (1996). The dual pathway model differentiates bulimics, subclinical bulimics, and controls: Testing the continuity hypothesis. *Behavior Therapy, 27*, 531–549.

Striegel-Moore, R. H., & Cachelin, F. M. (2001). Etiology of eating disorders in women. *Counseling Psychologist, 29*, 635–661.

Taylor, C. B., Bryson, S., Luce, K. H., Cunning, D., Doyle, A. C., Abascal, L. B., et al. (2006). Prevention of eating disorders in at-risk college-age women. *Archives of General Psychiatry, 63*, 881–888.

Telch, C. F., Agras, W. S., & Linehan, M. M. (2001). Dialectical behavior therapy for binge eating disorder. *Journal of Consulting and Clinical Psychology, 69*, 1061–1065.

Vohs, K., Bardone, A., Joiner, T., Abramson, L., & Heatherton, T. (1999). Perfectionism, perceived weight status, and self-esteem interact to predict bulimic symptoms: A model of bulimic symptom development. *Journal of Abnormal Psychology, 108*, 695–700.

Wilfley, D. E., Welch, R. R., Stein, R. I., Spurrell, E. B., Cohen, L. R., Saelens, B. E., et al. (2002). A randomized comparison of group cognitive-behavioral therapy and group interpersonal psychotherapy for the treatment of overweight individuals with binge eating disorder. *Archives of General Psychiatry, 59*, 713–721.

Winzelberg, A. J., Eppstein, D., Eldredge, K. L., Wilfley, D., Dasmahapatra, R., Dev, P., et al. (2000). Effectiveness of an internet-based program for reducing risk factors for eating disorders. *Journal of Consulting and Clinical Psychology, 68*, 346–350.

Winzelberg, A. J., Taylor, C. B., Altman, T. M., Eldredge, K. L., Dev, P., & Constantinou, P. S. (1998). Evaluation of a computer-mediated eating disorder intervention program. *International Journal of Eating Disorders, 24*, 339–349.

Zabinski, M. F., Celio, A. A., Wilfley, D. E., & Taylor, C. B. (2003). Prevention of eating disorders and obesity via the internet. *Cognitive Behaviour Therapy, 32*, 137–150.

Zabinski, M. F., Pung, M. A., Wilfley, D. E., Eppstein, D. L., Winzelberg, A. J., Celio, A., et al. (2001). Reducing risk factors for eating disorders: Targeting at-risk women with a computerized psychoeducational program. *International Journal of Eating Disorders, 29*, 401–408.

Zabinski, M. F., Wilfley, D. E., Calfas, K. J., Winzelberg, A. J., & Taylor, C. B. (2002, April). *An interactive, computerized psychoeducational intervention for women at risk of developing an eating disorder*. Paper presented at the 23rd annual meeting of the Society for Behavioral Medicine, Washington, DC.

Zabinski, M. F., Wilfley, D. E., Pung, M. A., Winzelberg, A. J., Eldridge, K., & Taylor, C. B. (2001). An interactive internet-based intervention for women at risk of eating disorders: A pilot study. *International Journal of Eating Disorders, 30*, 129–137.

CHAPTER 34

School Violence and Bullying Prevention

From Research-Based Explanations to Empirically Based Solutions

DOROTHY L. ESPELAGE
ARTHUR M. HORNE

A major goal in the United States is to strengthen "the resource capacity of schools to serve as a key link to a comprehensive, seamless system of school- and community-based identification, assessment, and treatment services, to meet the needs of youth and their families" (U.S. Public Health Service, 2000, p. 6). Despite being a field with deep roots in education, counseling psychology has been slow to increase its presence in schools in recent years (B. L. Bernstein, Forrest, & Golston, 1994; Romano & Hage, 2000). Walsh, Galassi, Murphy, and Park-Taylor (2002) stated that, among all the applied subfields within psychology, school psychology *alone* has maintained an emphasis on K-12 education. Furthermore, the major journals in counseling psychology showed a decline in the percentage of articles related to schools between 1994 and 2000 (e.g., from 10% in 1994 to 1995 to 1% in 1999 to 2000 for the *Counseling Psychologist*).

An area that might be of particular interest to counseling psychologists is school violence and bullying, which is of great concern to school administrators, policymakers, and parents. Every child has the right to a safe school. Safe schools are not just settings where there is an absence of violence, but settings where children feel a sense of belonging and security that can help them develop to their full potential. Yet this inviting safe environment does not occur nearly as frequently as it should. Recent reports on the Youth Risk Behavior Survey (Centers for Disease Control and Prevention [CDC], 2006) provide troublesome findings. For 2005, 43% of boys and 28% of girls reported they were in a physical fight, and one-third of those fights occurred in school. Almost a third of all students had property stolen or deliberately damaged, and 6% of boys and girls avoided school because they thought it was unsafe.

High school students also reported high rates of dating violence, with more than 9% of both boys and girls being hit, slapped, or otherwise physically hurt by a dating partner; and more than 10% of girls and 4% of boys reported being forced to have sexual intercourse. A positive note is that weapon carrying among high school students is down from the 1990s, but the trend has been toward an increase in weapon carrying in recent years, and even during the best of reporting years, as many as 15% of students reported carrying a weapon to school (CDC, 2006). These are serious levels of aggressive behavior with damaging consequences for those who are the victims of the aggression, the perpetrators of the aggression, and the bystanders or witnesses.

This chapter focuses predominately on school bullying because of the pressure being placed on school administrators, faculty, and support staff to develop and evaluate schoolwide bullying prevention programs as a result of the many states that have either passed, or are considering, legislation to mandate policies toward bullying behaviors in the schools. First, definitions and prevalence of bullying are presented, a social-ecological framework is used to guide discussion of the risk and protective factors associated with bullying, and promising bullying prevention programs are described. Second, we discuss some less studied areas of school violence, including sexual harassment, dating violence, and homophobia bullying, with a focus on future research directions. The final section includes a detailed discussion of how counseling psychologists might move the school research agenda forward.

SCHOOL BULLYING

Bullying is defined as chronic physical or verbal teasing and threatening behaviors that have the potential to cause harm (Olweus, 2001). Bullying can include physical, verbal, and relational forms of aggression. It often involves an imbalance of strength and power between the bully and the target and is repetitive in nature. Many people experience isolated acts of aggression, but children who have been bullied live with the ongoing fear of the recurring abuse from the bully, which is usually more damaging than an isolated and unpredicted event. Sexual harassment refers to any unwelcome and unsolicited sexual advances, requests for sexual favors, or other verbal or physical conduct of a sexual nature and is considered by many to be an acute, focused form of bullying (Orpinas & Horne, 2006).

Bullying may be the most prevalent type of school violence (Batsche & Porter, 2006). Worldwide incidence rates for bullying in school-age youth range from 10% of secondary students to 27% of middle school students who report being bullied often (Whitney & Smith, 1993). Studies in the United States have yielded slightly higher rates of bullying, ranging from a low of 10% for "extreme victims" of bullying (Perry, Kusel, & Perry, 1988) to a high of 75% who reported being bullied at least one time during their school years (Hoover, Oliver, & Hazler, 1992). In a nationally representative study of American students in Grades 6 to 10, Nansel et al. (2001) reported that 17% had been bullied with some regularity (several times or more within the semester) and 19% had bullied others. Bullying is not part of normative development for young people and should be considered a precursor to more serious aggressive behaviors (Nansel et al., 2001). These statistics suggest that bullying is a prevalent problem that directly affects numerous school-age youth.

Recent conceptions of children involved in bullying have suggested a four-group classification scheme: (1) bullies (children who frequently bully others but are never victims), (2) bully victims (children who bully others and are victimized themselves), (3) victims (children who are victimized but do not resort to aggression against others), and (4) controls (children who have no significant history as aggressors or victims; Espelage & Holt, 2001). In a nationally representative study of 6th to 10th graders ($N = 15,686$) using self-report data, 13% were categorized as bullies, 11% as victims, and 6% as bully victims (Nansel et al., 2001). When peer, teacher, and self-reports were used to classify a sample of sixth graders ($N = 1,985$), the authors found 7% bullies, 9% victims, and 6% bully victims (Juvonen, Graham, & Schuster, 2003).

The discrimination between bully and bully victim groups has aroused particular interest because these subgroups appear to display different patterns of aggression. Bullies exhibit a more goal-oriented aggression, entailing more control and planning. In contrast, bully victims tend to display a more impulsive aggression with concurrent poor emotional and behavioral regulation, which is perceived as particularly aversive by their peers and contributes to their own victimization (Schwartz, Proctor, & Chien, 2001). In addition, bully victims are at risk for social maladjustment and have been found to experience victimization in other domains, including childhood sexual abuse and sexual harassment (Holt & Espelage, 2005).

Social-Ecological Framework of Bullying Perpetration and Victimization

Bronfenbrenner's (1979) ecological theory of development broke new ground in examining the complex interactions between the environment and the individual in shaping children's development. According to the social-ecological framework, the influence of various environmental systems is essential to understanding the child and to creating effective change (Bronfenbrenner, 1979). One system is the *microsystem,* which contains structures with which the child or adolescent has direct contact, including parents, siblings, peers, and schools. The *mesosysytem* comprises the interrelations among *microsystems,* such as an adolescent's family and peers. Social-ecological theory has been applied to the conceptualization of bullying and victimization (Garbarino & deLara, 2002; D. A. Newman, Horne, & Bartolomucci, 2000; Olweus, Limber, & Mihalic, 2000; Orpinas & Horne, 2006; Swearer & Espelage, 2004). It is clear from both theory and research that bullying and victimization unfold as a result of interactions among the many contexts that children encounter. A major task facing bullying researchers is how to empirically examine these reciprocal influences. Although it is beyond the scope of this chapter to study each area in depth, we provide a brief overview of selected social-ecological variables associated with bullying and victimization.

The correlates and causes of adolescent aggression and bullying have been addressed in research for decades. Some of the precursors include biological influences (Gottesman & Goldsmith, 1994; Miles & Carey, 1997), individual characteristics (Miles & Carey, 1997), cultural expectations (Tolan et al., 1995), peer influences (Espelage, Holt, & Henkel, 2003), parental factors (Eron, Huesmann, & Zell, 1991), lack of emotional competence (Berkowitz, 1993), and deficits in social skills (Nelson & Crick, 1999). Studies have found verbal and physical forms of aggression during childhood to be relatively stable and often predictive of violence and criminal behavior during adolescence and adulthood (Olweus, 1978; Zumkley, 1994). In 1960, Eron and Huesmann (1987) surveyed over 800 third graders in the Midwest and found that children who bullied their peers at the age of 8 were more likely to engage in similar behaviors as adults than students who did not bully at this age. In adulthood, childhood bullies were more likely to commit serious crimes, physically abuse their wives, and raise children who were bullies. Of the childhood bullies surveyed, 1 in 4 had a criminal record by the age of 30.

Individual Characteristics

Many individual influences might support or discourage bullying behaviors. Although it is generally accepted that boys engage in bullying behaviors to a greater degree and frequency than girls, gender differences in overt versus covert forms of bullying have not been well established (Espelage & Swearer, 2003). Some research has examined racial and ethnic issues in bullying. The consensus is that race and ethnicity are less of an issue per se than are the cultural norms in a given school (Juvonen & Graham, 2001). Bullying behaviors have been found to increase over the elementary school years, peak in middle school, and start to decline in high school (Nansel et al., 2001). It is likely that great heterogeneity exists in relation to the psychological makeup of bullies, victims, and bully victims. No consistent psychological profile representing these groups has emerged.

Bullying has serious consequences for both victims and bullies. These psychological outcomes place both groups at risk for continued involvement and can be seen as individual risk factors and outcomes. Victims display lower self-esteem (Olweus, 1978; Rigby & Slee, 1993), higher rates of depression (Craig, 1998; Swearer, Song, Cary, Eagle, & Mickelson, 2001), loneliness (Kochenderfer & Ladd, 1996), and anxiety (Craig, 1998; Rigby & Slee, 1993). Victims are more likely to avoid school (Kochenderfer & Ladd, 1996). Bullies, meanwhile, have been found to engage in other antisocial behaviors such as vandalism, fighting, theft (Olweus, 1993), drinking alcohol (Nansel et al., 2001; Olweus, 1993), smoking (Nansel et al., 2001), truancy (Byrne, 1994; Olweus, 1993), school dropout (Byrne, 1994), and gun carrying (Cunningham, Henggeler, Limber, Melton, & Nation, 2000).

Family Influences

Although much of the bullying and victimization reported by children and adolescents occurs in the schools, the families of bullies and victims have received some attention in the literature. Much of this research has focused on delineating how families of bullies differ from families of children and adolescents who do not bully. Greater attention has recently been paid to the *mesosystem* level of the social-ecological framework by examining how the family system influences interactions with peers in school. In considering the impact of family relationships on bullying, five areas of research are reviewed in this section: attachment style, parenting style, maltreatment, sibling relationships, and social support.

Attachment Theory

Attachment theory posits that the relationship between a caregiver and child functions as a model for the child's relationships with others. Thus, a child with an insecure attachment learns to expect inconsistent and insensitive interactions with others, whereas a child with a secure attachment style comes to expect consistent and sensitive interactions (Bowlby, 1969). In a widely cited study, Troy and Sroufe (1987) found that children who had insecure, anxious-avoidant, or anxious-resistant attachments at the age of 18 months were more likely than children with secure attachments to become involved in bullying at the age of four or five. In addition, Perry, Hodges, and Egan (2001) found that anxious/resistant children tend to cry easily, be manifestly anxious, and slow to explore their surroundings. All these characteristics may place them at heightened risk for being a target of bullying. Children and adolescents who have attachment problems with their parents also develop a self-concept that includes a sense of low self-worth, helplessness, and competence, again placing them at risk for being a target (Perry et al., 2001).

Parental Style

In addition to one's attachment style functioning as a template for future relationships, parenting styles or child-rearing behaviors also serve as models on which children base their expectations of future interactions with others. With respect to the family context, much more is known about families of children and adolescents who bully others than families of children who are chronically victimized (Finnegan, Hodges, & Perry, 1998; Rodkin & Hodges, 2003). Olweus (1993) found that caregivers of boys who develop an aggressive reaction pattern tend to lack involvement and warmth, use "power assertive" practices such as physical punishment and violent emotional outbursts, and demonstrate a high level of permissiveness. Bowers, Smith, and Binney (1994) found that family members of bullies often report higher needs for power than family members of children who do not bully. Bullies, victims, and bully victims have also been found to have relatively authoritarian versus authoritative or lenient parents (Baldry & Farrington, 2000).

Studies such as those by Bowers et al. (1994) suggest that differences across bully victim groups are more informative when quality of the parent-child relationship is explored with greater precision. Parents of bully victims often have what is referred to as an indifferent-uninvolved style, which is characterized by low warmth, abusive and inconsistent discipline, and absence of emotional support. In light of findings that bullying, or antisocial behavior in general, tends to occur when parents are absent or unaware of what their child is doing, Olweus (1993) highlighted the importance of parents monitoring their children's activities and peer associations outside school. High marital conflict between parents has also been found to influence the child's propensity toward aggressive behavior (Olweus, 1993).

McFadyen-Ketchum, Bates, Dodge, and Pettit (1996) found that aggressive children who experienced affectionate mother-child relations showed a significant decrease in their aggressive-disruptive behaviors. Furthermore, these positive parental connections appeared to buffer the long-term negative consequences of aggression. In contrast to the lack of warmth and involvement often demonstrated in families of bullies, victims' families have been characterized by overinvolved and overprotective mothers (Bowers et al., 1994). Olweus (1993) found that mothers who were positive but overly controlling inhibited their children's development of self-confidence, independence, and the ability to assert themselves. This lack of assertion then contributed to the child's difficulty in fostering and maintaining positive peer relations.

Maltreatment

Another risk factor for bullying perpetration and victimization in children is that of parental mal-treatment, including physical, sexual, and emotional abuse, and neglect. Shields and Cicchetti (2001) proposed that maltreatment is associated with emotional dysregulation, which then creates problems in negotiating interactions with peers and other individuals. Similarly, Schwartz, Dodge, Petit, and Bates (1997) found that bully victims were frequently exposed to violence in the home and were often targets of physical abuse. Although nonvictimized aggressive boys did not show the same experience of physical abuse, they received higher ratings for exposure to aggressive role models.

Sibling Aggression

There is a paucity of research examining the role sibling relationships play in bullying. Duncan (1999) surveyed 375 middle school students. Of the 336 children with siblings, 42% reported that they often bullied their siblings, 24% reported they often pushed or hit their brothers and sisters, and 11% stated that they often beat up their siblings. A smaller group (30%) reported that siblings frequently victimized them, with 22% stating they were often hit or pushed around and 8% reporting they were often beaten up by a sibling. As for concordance rates between bullying siblings and bullying peers at school, 57% of those who bullied their peers and 77% of bully victims reported also bullying their siblings. A previous study by Bowers et al. (1994) detected a similar pattern of relations, finding that bullies reported negative and ambivalent relationships with siblings and viewed their siblings as more powerful than themselves. The opposite was found for victims, who reported enmeshed and positive relationships with their siblings (Bowers et al., 1994).

Perceived Parental Support

Another area of investigation related to the potential influences of the family context includes studies of perceived social support. In a study of predominately Hispanic middle school students, those students classified as bullies and bully victims indicated receiving substantially less social support from parents than those students in the comparison group (Demaray & Malecki, 2003). Additionally, the researchers investigated the differences in perceptions of the *importance* of social support among the four groups and found the bully victim and victim groups rated total social support as more important relative to the bully and comparison groups.

Theories of Peer Influence on Aggression

Family dynamics play a role in the development of bullying perpetration and victimization. Peers also strongly influence aggression and bullying. There are several influential theories in this area, including the homophily hypothesis (Cairns & Cairns, 1994; Espelage et al., 2003), dominance theory (Pellegrini & Long, 2002), and attraction theory (Bukowski, Sippola, & Newcomb, 2000).

Homophily Hypothesis

Peer groups during early and late adolescence tend to include members of similar sex and race, who also engage in similar behaviors (e.g., delinquency; Cairns & Cairns, 1994; Leung, 1994). Group members have a strong influence on one another, and this within-group similarity is called *homophily* (Berndt, 1982; Kandel, 1978). Studies consistently report within-group similarity on aggression among peer social clusters; peers in the same friendship groups have similar levels of aggression (Gaines, Cairns, & Cairns, 36; Leung, 1993; Neckerman, 1992; Xie, 108). These studies also further supported the homophily hypothesis by demonstrating that nonaggressive peers who joined aggressive peer groups reported an increase in their aggression over time (Cairns, Leung, & Cairns, 1995). More recently, the hypothesis was evaluated separately for verbal and physical forms of aggression among middle school students (Espelage et al., 2003). Espelage and colleagues used social network analysis to identify peer networks and hierarchical linear modeling to determine the extent to which peers influenced each other to become aggressive over time. Overall, students tended to associate with others who bullied at similar rates, and students who hung out with kids who bullied others increased in self-reported bullying over the school year. Although these studies are informative, much more work needs to be conducted to understand the process by which aggression is transmitted from one peer group member to another.

Dominance Theory

Early adolescence is typically associated with an increase in aggressive behavior (Pellegrini, 2002a; P. K. Smith, Madsen, & Moody, 1999). A potential explanation for this increase is dominance theory. Dominance is viewed as a relationship factor in which individuals are arranged in a hierarchy in terms of their access to resources (Dunbar, 1988). Pellegrini (2002b) argued that the transition to middle school requires students to renegotiate previous relationships and to embark on new ones, and aggression is thought to be one strategy used to attain dominance within peer groups. Mouttapa, Valente, Gallaher, Rohrbach, and Unger (2004) argued that social dominance was at work in their sample of Latino and Asian sixth graders ($n = 1,368$) in which peers who were aggressive influenced bullies to become more aggressive or to target victims more often for bullying episodes.

Attraction Theory

Attraction theory posits that, in their need to separate from their parents, young adolescents become attracted to other youth who possess characteristics reflecting independence (e.g., delinquency, aggression, disobedience) and are less attracted to those who possess characteristics more descriptive of childhood (e.g., compliance, obedience; Bukowski et al., 2000; Moffitt, 1993). These authors argue that young adolescents manage the transition from primary to secondary schools through their attractions to peers who are aggressive. In a study of 217 boys and girls during this transition, Bukowski and colleagues found that girls' and boys' attraction to aggressive peers increased on entry to middle school. This increase was larger for girls, which is consistent with Pellegrini and Bartini's (2001) finding that at the end of middle school, girls nominated "dominant boys" as dates to a hypothetical party.

Classroom and School Factors

The school is one of the most salient and influential environments for children (Eccles et al., 1993). A tremendous amount of research has tied schooling to both academic and personal outcomes. School contextual factors have been linked to children's mental health, achievement, self-concept, and ability to form social relationships (Ringeisen, Henderson, & Hoagwood, 2003). Understanding the school environment is an essential part of understanding a child's behavior. In addition, educators have long seen the classroom as having an important impact on children's well-being. If a classroom does not meet the needs of a child, negative outcomes can occur and the child can be at risk for academic and social difficulties (Eccles et al., 1993).

Students involved in bullying reported more negative views of their school environment (Nansel et al., 2001), and positive school climate has been found to be vital to reducing bullying behaviors (Orpinas & Horne, 2006). Classroom practices and teachers' attitudes are also salient components of school climate that contribute to bullying prevalence. Aggression varies from classroom to classroom, and in some classrooms, aggression appears to be supported (Rodkin & Hodges, 2003). Bullying tends to be less prevalent in classrooms in which most children are included in activities (R. S. Newman, Murray, & Lussier, 2001), teachers display warmth and responsiveness to children (Olweus & Limber, 1999), teachers respond quickly and effectively to bullying incidents (Olweus, 1993), and parents are aware of their children's peer relationships (Roberts & Coursol, 1996). Hoover and Hazler (1994) noted that when school personnel tolerate, ignore, or dismiss bullying behaviors, they implicitly convey messages that students may internalize. Conversely, if staff members hold antibullying attitudes and translate those attitudes into behaviors, the school culture becomes less tolerant of bullying. Much more work needs to be conducted in this area to fully understand how to intervene with teachers, administrators, and school staff.

In summary, several risk and protective factors have been linked to bullying perpetration and victimization. These factors have been incorporated into prevention and intervention planning. Risk factors for bullying perpetration include individual characteristics such as being male, sibling bullying history, less empathy, anger disposition, and positive attitudes toward bullying; in some cases, perpetration is also associated with other forms of delinquency. Risk factors for victimization have included physical characteristics, overprotective parents, and prior experiences of victimization. Protective factors for perpetration and victimization include secure attachments with parents and teachers and positive social support. Peer group affiliation also plays an important role as members appear to socialize one another to bully others through group norms that support bullying perpetration. Teacher and school characteristics were also noted as both risk and protective factors of perpetration and victimization. Early efforts to work with families and schools to assist in the development of a culture of reduced aggression seem to be sorely needed. This may come about through an increased emphasis in community, school, and family educational programs informing parents and educators of the potential harm of ignoring the problem, combined with sharing information about the positive aspects of the prevention of bullying.

School-Wide Preventive Interventions

Educators and researchers have been charged by the 2001 No Child Left Behind Act (NCLB) to use data to guide the selection of programs and implementation methods. Although 300 violence prevention programs are available, less than one-fourth of these are empirically validated (K. A. Howard, Flora, & Griffin, 1999). What has been learned to date is that zero tolerance policies (policies that provide for punishment regardless of the basis of the problem behavior) are not effective in curbing aggressive behaviors (Casella, 2003), and expulsion appears to be equally ineffective (Morrison, Redding, Fisher, & Peterson, 2006). Thus, interventions that have been typically employed in school settings (group treatment, zero tolerance, and expulsion) are ineffective in dealing with bullying.

Whole-school preventive interventions for bullying have slowly been introduced over the past several decades following the introduction of the Norway-based *Olweus Bullying Prevention Program* (OBPP; Olweus, Limber, & Mihalic, 2000), which is discussed more completely later in this chapter. Since the introduction of this program in 1993, the U.S. Department of Health and Human Services launched its *Stop Bullying Now: Take a Stand, Lend a Hand* and provided schools and administrators with information on best practices in bullying prevention and intervention, which is available from their website (www.stopbullyingnow.hrsa.gov).

Programs to address problems of violence use two primary approaches: *universal* and *targeted*. A universal approach is provided to all people involved in the school and promotes the skills necessary to avoid developing problems. Like the addition of fluoride to the systemwide water supply, a universal bully prevention model includes programs that involve all students in the classroom or school. Such programs can be offered through classroom psychoeducational groups or school-wide presentations.

A targeted intervention involves specific groups of students identified as having a particular problem. Children identified as bullies would be targeted or selected for a more intensive intervention. A number of programs have been developed for each approach, but for the purposes of this chapter, we focus on universal programs that are provided in manual/standardized form and that have been more extensively evaluated.

Olweus Bullying Prevention Program (OBPP)

Numerous universal prevention programs have been developed, but the one most widely cited and evaluated is the *Olweus Bullying Prevention Program (OBPP)*. This comprehensive program was designated a Blueprints (model) program by the Office of Juvenile Justice and Delinquency Prevention (Olweus et al., 2000). The Blueprints designation means that this program has met rigorous standards and has demonstrated promising efficacy in reducing adolescent aggression. Data supporting this program's effectiveness include the Olweus et al. (2000) report that bullying is reduced by as much as 50% in 1 year of school program implementation. This comprehensive program aims to decrease bullying among elementary and middle school students by reducing bullying opportunities and the rewards that maintain bullying behavior. Consistent with data from the extant literature, teachers are trained to improve peer relations and create a positive school climate for all students. The intervention focuses on protecting victims, increasing awareness among students, teachers, and parents, and highlighting the need for clear and consistent guidelines or rules against bullying. Program ingredients are delivered at school, classroom, and individual levels.

At the *school level,* a student questionnaire is first administered to determine the extent of the problem. The findings are presented at a school conference day, ideally with teachers, administrators, counselors-psychologists, and parents present. A long-term plan of action for addressing the bullying problem is then developed. While plans vary across schools, research supports the inclusion of certain school-level interventions, and the program calls for attention to the density of supervisors during recess and breaks. Bullying occurs most often during lunchtime, recess, and passing periods. It is therefore necessary to have sufficient numbers of adult supervisors on hand to intervene quickly and decisively when bullying occurs. The intent is to send the message that "bullying is not tolerated." Supervisors communicate with each other about children who are consistently bullies or victims. In addition, many schools establish separate break times for older and younger students. Olweus et al. (2000) also recommend that schools have a contact telephone to respond to calls from students who are being bullied or parents who have concerns about bullying situations.

A general PTA meeting is also recommended to build collaboration between school faculty and parents in the community. In this meeting, the school faculty explicitly inform parents about the focus on minimizing bullying and social exclusion in their school. A plan of action is articulated and circulated to all parents, including those who did not attend the PTA meeting. Recognizing that teachers need support to embark on a bullying prevention program, Olweus encourages teachers to create a social milieu group in which 10 to 12 teachers meet on a regular basis to discuss efforts and challenges. The goal is to foster collegial support among small groups of teachers.

In the *classroom,* the teacher and students generate rules about bullying collaboratively. Olweus et al. (2000) recommend three basic rules: (1) We shall not bully other students; (2) We shall try to help students who are bullied; and (3) We shall make a point to include students who become easily left out. Students and teachers also generate sanctions for violating the rules. Possible sanctions include a serious individual talk with the student who breaks a rule, depriving the student of some privilege, and making the student stand next to the teacher during recess. Rules and sanctions are reviewed and evaluated in weekly class meetings in which students and teachers sit in a circle and discuss incidents of bullying. To promote a positive climate, teachers praise students when they do not engage in bullying behavior, foster collaboration among students by designing group activities, and encourage students to attend PTA meetings in which they report on their experiences with the bullying prevention program.

Finally, *individual interventions* are offered for bullies, victims, and their parents. Serious talks with bullies and victims are encouraged in this program. These talks occur quickly after incidents. Bullies are not allowed to make excuses or to blame others for their behavior. They are told that bullying will not be tolerated. Talks with victims need to guarantee them protection against harassment. Parents of victims are encouraged to consider seeking professional help for their child if the victimization has been going on for a long time. Parents of bullies are encouraged to create family rules at home against bullying and sanctions when these rules are broken.

Research by the program developer and colleagues in Norway (Olweus, 2005) has revealed a substantial correlation between more complete implementation of the program and the reduction of bully and victim problems. The program rests on the assumption that to reduce bullying, the social environment that supports this behavior has to be restructured. This program is based on the social-ecological approach to bully prevention, incorporates findings from the empirical literature, and has undergone systematic evaluation. Several outcome studies, both in the United States and worldwide, have demonstrated promising effectiveness. In a quasi-experimental study of 2,500 children in Bergen, Norway, the *OBPP* resulted in 50% to 70% reductions of bullying and victimization and increases in school satisfaction (Olweus, 1993). Implementation of this program with fourth through sixth graders ($n = 6,388$) in South Carolina resulted in reported significant reductions in self-reported bullying of approximately 25% (Melton et al., 1998). While this study was the first large-scale replication of the *OBPP* in the United States, it employed nonrandom assignment of matched pairs of school districts using 11 intervention schools and 28 control schools. Thus, the *OBPP* has demonstrated excellent results in other countries (Olweus, 2005) and appears to be a promising intervention among elementary schools in the United States; however, a randomized, controlled design is needed to rigorously evaluate the impact of the *OBPP*.

Bully Busters: A Teacher's Manual for Helping Bullies, Victims, and Bystanders

Although the Olweus program is a comprehensive approach to bully prevention programming, many schools do not have the resources to implement this program. Counselors, psychologists, and teachers often ask for a more focused and affordable approach. *Bully Busters* (D. A. Newman et al., 2000) is a program that might be implemented by schools with fewer resources. There are also data supporting this program. Teachers receiving the training program reported significantly higher levels of self-efficacy for managing bullying behavior, demonstrated greater knowledge of classroom behavior management, and had fewer classroom behavior problems and office referrals than comparison teachers (Newman-Carlson & Horne, 2004).

The program includes seven modules. The first is designed to increase awareness of bullying on the part of teachers and students. Teachers are encouraged to develop a definition of bullying collaboratively with students. Exercises facilitate a conversation among students about who is a bully, what is bullying, and where it happens. Students then participate in several activities to recognize how their words and actions can be hurtful, and they role-play more constructive ways of interacting. The second module includes a discussion with students about how bullying develops and the forms it can take. Activities in this module include viewing movies in which characters are victims or bullies. Students discuss both aggressive and passive forms of bullying, and differences between male and female bullying. This module ends with a focus on misconceptions about bullying.

Recognizing the victim is the topic of the third module. Students discuss the effects of victimization and challenge myths about victims. Students are encouraged to recognize different types of victim, including individuals who are passive, provocative, and bystanders. Bystander intervention is emphasized. The majority of students do not engage directly in bullying but their reluctance to intervene in a bully incident can promote this behavior in others. Students are encouraged to break the "code of silence" and create a safer climate for all students. The fourth module includes specific strategies for teachers to create a bully-free classroom. Similar to the classroom-level interventions of Olweus, teachers are given specific strategies (e.g., setting rules, acting quickly), along with empathy skills training, social skills training, and anger control training.

The fifth module expands on these skills by providing specific strategies for working with victims. Several activities are used to assist victims in becoming aware of their strengths, viewing themselves in a positive manner, and building skills and confidence in joining groups. The sixth module includes a discussion of the role of prevention. Activities are designed to educate teachers about the need for prevention and provide a basic introduction to prevention theory. Teachers are encouraged to identify how their attitudes and behaviors influence student behavior and how school-level factors relate to bullying. The final module focuses on teaching relaxation and coping skills to teachers. Finally, the manual includes a teacher inventory as well as additional activities.

Steps to Respect: A Bullying Prevention Program

This program was developed by the Committee for Children (www.cfchildren.org) and has empirical data suggesting promising outcomes (Hodges, Boivin, Vitaro, & Bukowskii, 1999). A fairly minimal intervention included having peers step in to tell bullies to stop the bullying, and more than 50% of the time it stopped within a few seconds. The foundation of this program includes creating a "safe, caring, and respectful" culture and targets students at three levels (Grades 3 and 4, 4 and 5, and 5 and 6). In the first phase, a school-wide framework is established before the curriculum is implemented. A program guide details the role of the principal or administrator as a supportive leader of the implementation and program evaluation. A steering committee is formed to facilitate this process, including teachers, administrators, and others who encounter students during the school day (e.g., bus drivers, nurses, secretaries). Steps of implementation are outlined and worksheets are used to guide the steering committee in their planning to increase the efficacy and sustainability of the program. Worksheets focus on challenges such as securing buy-in, capturing a school snapshot, developing an antibullying policy and procedures, assessing the school's physical features, planning for staff training, and rolling out the curriculum. The second phase involves training of all staff, curriculum orientation for classroom teachers, and then booster training for staff and faculty. The third phase of the program is implementation in classrooms and throughout the school environment. All staff involved in the school participate in immersing it in the antibullying campaign. The bully prevention lessons are incorporated into academic lessons so that learning of subject matter and skills development are complementary.

The Peaceful School Project

The *Peaceful Schools Project,* developed in 2000 (Twemlow, Fonagy, & Sacco, 2001; www .backoffbully.com), is a "philosophy, rather than a program" (Twemlow, Fonagy, & Sacco, 2005, p. 296). The goals include developing healthy relationships between all stakeholders in the educational setting and altering the school climate in permanent and meaningful ways. The *Project* includes five main components. First, schools embark on a positive climate campaign that includes counselor-led discussions and the creation of posters that help alter the language and the thinking of everyone in the school ("Back off, Bullies!" or "Stop Bullying Now"). All stakeholders in the school are flooded with an awareness of the bullying dynamic and bullying is described as a social relationship problem. Second, teachers are fully supported in classroom management techniques and are taught specific techniques to diffuse disruptive behavior from a relational perspective rather than from a punishment perspective. Third, peer and adult mentors help everyone in the school resolve problems without blame. These adult mentors are particularly important during times when adult supervision is minimal (in hallways and on the playground). The fourth component is called the "gentle warrior physical education program." It uses a combination of role-playing, relaxation, and defensive martial arts techniques to help students develop strategies to protect themselves and others. These are essentially confidence-building skills that support positive coping. Fifth, reflection time is included in the school schedule each day. Teachers and students talk for at least 10 minutes at the end of the day about bully, victim, and bystander behaviors. By engaging in this dialogue, language and thinking about bullying behaviors can be subtly altered (Twemlow et al., 2005).

The *Peaceful Schools Project* is a holistic philosophy that attempts to alter negative social relationships in schools, which in turn are hypothesized to reduce or eliminate bullying behaviors. In a recent study, it was found that elementary students whose schools participated in the *Peaceful Schools Project* had higher achievement scores than students from schools without the program; there were also significant reductions in suspensions for acting-out behavior in the treatment schools, whereas the comparison schools had a slight increase in suspensions for problem behavior (Fonagy, Twemlow, Vernberg, Sacco, & Little, 2005).

Summary of School Bullying Research and Prevention Efforts

Much research has been conducted internationally on the phenomenon of bullying in schools. Research is also emerging within the United States. Bullying is prevalent among children and young adolescents and has serious detrimental consequences for aggressors, victims, and bystanders. The onset of bullying is best understood from a social-ecological perspective in which individual characteristics of children interact with environmental factors to promote teasing and harassment. There is considerable debate in relation to the effectiveness of school-wide bullying prevention and intervention efforts. Although some evaluation efforts have offered promising findings, results of a recent meta-analytic study of 14 whole-school antibullying programs provide a more modest assessment (J. D. Smith, Schneider, Smith, & Ananiadou, 2004). This study included the *OBPP,* the *Peaceful Schools Project,* and the *Steps to Respect* program. Results indicated that there were moderate effect sizes on self-reported victimization that students experienced from bullies (e.g., being teased, called names, shoved or hit) and small to negligible effects on self-reported bullying perpetration (e.g., teasing, name calling, hitting or pushing others). The authors concluded that significant caution should be observed when implementing school-wide programs. At the same time, several programs have demonstrated positive impact, and future research is needed to identify the characteristics of those programs that have greater effects in order to build on their strengths.

SEXUAL HARASSMENT, DATING VIOLENCE, AND HOMOPHOBIC TEASING

Sexual Harassment

Two surveys conducted by the American Association of University Women (AAUW, 1993 2001) asked nationally representative samples of public school students about their experiences with sexual harassment at school. Sexual harassment was defined as "unwanted and unwelcome sexual behavior that interferes with your life. Sexual harassment is not behaviors that you like or want (for example, wanted kissing, touching, or flirting)" (AAUW, 2001, p. 2). Both surveys indicated that 81% of students had experienced some form of sexual harassment at some time during their school lives, with 59% occasionally and 27% often experiencing harassment. Seventy percent experienced nonphysical sexual harassment at some point in their school lives, and more than 50% experienced it often or occasionally. Physical sexual harassment was reported by 58% of students, and 32% experienced this form of sexual harassment often or occasionally.

Dating Violence

Rates of dating violence victimization are remarkably high for high school and college students (see Ely, Dulmus, & Wodarski, 2002). In dating relationships, 20% to 50% of college students have experienced violence (Bookwala, Frieze, Smith, & Ryan, 1992; Kuffel & Katz, 2002). A wide range of prevalence rates have been reported for high school students (e.g., 9% to 46%; Gray & Foshee, 1997; Katz, Kuffel, & Coblentz, 2002; Roscoe & Callahan, 1985). In a recent study of 7,824 female high school students, 9% of the adolescent girls reported experiencing physical dating violence (D. E. Howard & Wang, 2003). Higher rates emerged from a study of 526 eighth and ninth graders; 36% reported experiencing physical dating violence victimization, and 20% reported having perpetrated physical violence at some point in their lives (Arriaga & Foshee, 2004). As physical dating violence is often preceded by emotional and psychological abuse, these figures suggest that there is a great need to address dating violence among early adolescents. Research has indicated that less severe forms of physical violence (e.g., slapping) are more common than extreme forms (e.g., choking; Roscoe & Callahan, 1985).

Homophobic Aggression

Homophobia represents an emerging area of research on adolescence (Kimmel & Mahler, 2003). Homophobia includes negative beliefs, attitudes, stereotypes, and behaviors toward gays and lesbians (Wright, Adams, & Bernat, 1999). Examples of the behavioral component of homophobia include teasing, threats, harassment, and assault (including sexual assault). Reports of victimization of gays and lesbians are equally extreme. In their retrospective study of antigay/lesbian abuse in schools across the state of Pennsylvania, Gross, Aurand, and Adessa (1988) noted that 50% of the gay men who were surveyed and 12% of the lesbians had experienced some form of victimization in junior high school, rising to 59% for gay men and 21% for lesbians in high school. According to Berrill (1992), based on the evidence collated from various state and national task forces and coalitions, estimates of the prevalence of school-based victimization for gay and lesbian youth in the United States ranged from 33% to 49%. In the United Kingdom, in a national postal survey of 4,216 gays, lesbians, and bisexuals, Mason and Palmer (1996) found that, of those respondents under 18 years of age, 40% of all violent attacks had taken place at school, with 50% of those being perpetrated by same or similar-aged peers.

Pilkington and D'Augelli (1995) reported that 83% of gay and lesbian youth experienced some form of victimization, which included verbal insults, threats of violence, physical assault, and sexual assault. More recently, D'Augelli (2003) surveyed 542 lesbian, gay, and bisexual youth, ranging from 14 to 21 years of age. He found that 75% reported being verbally abused, and 15% reported being physically attacked, because of their sexual orientation. Greater levels of victimization were associated with more mental health symptoms. These forms of victimization parallel the behaviors associated with bullying as identified by bully researchers. Findings suggest that homophobic aggression contributes to shaping victimized gay, lesbian, and heterosexual students' negative perceptions of the school climate and, therefore, is an important factor to consider when examining students' social experiences. Peer groups and peer culture become increasingly influential as individuals approach and develop through adolescence, and a growing base of research suggests that homophobic behavior occurs frequently among peers (Plummer, 2001).

A recent investigation (Poteat & Espelage, in press) expands on the extant literature by looking beyond individual-level analyses to incorporate the peer group and social context in understanding and predicting homophobic behavior. Participants included 213 high school students (108 females, 105 males) in Grades 7 through 11. The sample was racially diverse (approximately 40% racial minorities). Participants completed a self-report survey that included indicators of behavioral homophobia, dominance, and support for violence. Students were also asked to nominate up to eight students (male or female) they considered as friends. Friendship nominations were subjected to social network analysis to identify peer groups. Hierarchical linear modeling was used to evaluate the relation of peer-level support for violence and dominance to individual-level homophobic behavior. As hypothesized, support for violence ($\gamma = .33$, $p < .001$) and dominance ($\gamma = .21$, $p < .001$) at the peer level were predictive of greater individual homophobic behavior. These relations were not moderated by sex, suggesting that students' own homophobic behaviors are influenced by attitudes toward violence and dominance within their primary peer group. The findings support the need for programs to address how peers encourage homophobic behavior among group members.

IMPLICATIONS FOR PREVENTION, INTERVENTION, AND TRAINING

Opportunities are increasing for collaborative, comprehensive school services that are tailored to individual needs and to the systems in which students function (Talley & Short, 1996). Schools are increasingly seeking the help of community providers to supplement the services of school-based staff and to implement and evaluate intervention programs. Counseling psychologists, with their strong developmental orientation and knowledge bases in prevention, are well positioned to assist schools in developing school-community partnerships. Walsh et al. (2002) noted that counseling psychologists' knowledge of multicultural issues is also an important asset, especially given the demographic changes in contemporary American schools.

Previously, intervention programs designed to combat bullying have tended to allocate more resources to identifying individual bullies and addressing their behavior than to developing universal interventions that address the entire student body. As presented in this chapter, more universal programs with school-wide prevention and early intervention goals are being developed and implemented. Furlong, Morrison, and Grief (2003) noted that despite the value of taking a relational approach to bullying, most formalized legislation addressing bullying and peer aggression in schools continues to emphasize taking action with bullies to the exclusion of addressing the needs of victims or addressing the larger school climate. A relational approach dictates that responses to bullies need to rely less on the traditional punitive approach, and more on targeting the patterns of behavior of both bullies and their victims, with attention to the noninvolved bystanders of the schools as well as the classroom-school climate (Furlong et al., 2003; Orpinas & Horne, 2006).

As we become increasingly knowledgeable about how bullying operates as a peer process, intervention strategies should consequently shift to a more comprehensive, universal approach, particularly with heightened emphasis on understanding the experiences of victims. Research has demonstrated that problem behaviors tend to be interrelated and share common risk factors, suggesting the need for prevention programs that implement a coordinated set of interventions to target and reduce overlapping risk factors rather than programs that focus on specific problems or separate disorders (Kenny, Waldo, Warter, & Barton, 2002).

As part of their training, counseling psychologists tend to have a strong knowledge base in family systems and group processes, as well as skills in consultation, grant writing, and interpersonal and intercultural communication (Kenny et al., 2002). These are all crucial elements to effective collaboration efforts with students, school staff, parents, and culturally diverse community organizations. Counseling psychology programs would do well to allocate more training in conducting systematic school-based interventions. Traditional practica and internship experiences focus on providing direct remedial services to clients. Therefore, students have limited opportunities to practice identifying organizational and systemtic constraints in planning and implementing interventions. Additionally, Furlong et al. (2003) point out the influence counseling psychologists can have in using their scientific knowledge to shape public policy through collaboration with legislators. Particularly in the area of bullying, many state laws and local policies have been limited in that they do not even properly define bullying and tend to vary greatly from state to state. Training experiences could provide more guidance on how counseling psychologists can seek out and fulfill these roles as advocates for public policy regarding school violence prevention. Improved training in how to collaborate with policymakers may foster more coherent, consistent, and effective services based on strong research.

REFERENCES

American Association of University Women Educational Foundation. (1993). *Hostile hallways: The AAUW survey on sexual harassment in America's schools* (No. 923012). Washington, DC: Harris/Scholastic Research.

American Association of University Women Educational Foundation. (2001). *Hostile hallways: Sexual harassment and bullying in schools*. Washington, DC: Harris/Scholastic Research.

Arriaga, X. B., & Foshee, V. A. (2004). Adolescent dating violence: Do adolescents follow in their friends' or their parents' footsteps? *Journal of Interpersonal Violence, 19*, 162–184.

Baldry, A. C., & Farrington, D. P. (2000). Bullies and delinquents: Personal characteristics and parental styles. *Journal of Community and Applied Social Psychology, 10*, 17–31.

Batsche, G. M., & Porter, L. J. (2006). Bullying. In G. G. Bear & K. M. Minke (Eds.), *Children's needs: Vol. III. Development, prevention, and intervention* (pp. 135–148). Washington, DC: National Association of School Psychologists.

Berkowitz, L. (1993). *Aggression: Its causes, consequences, and control*. New York: McGraw-Hill.

Berndt, T. J. (1982). The features and effects of friendship in early adolescence. *Child Development, 53*, 1447–1460.

Bernstein, B. L., Forrest, L., & Golston, S. S. (1994). Current practices of counseling psychology faculty in K-12 schools: A national survey. *Counseling Psychologist, 22*(4), 611–627.

Berrill, K. T. (1992). Anti-gay violence and victimization in the United States: An overview. In G. M. Herek & K. T. Berril (Eds.), *Hate crimes: Confronting violence against lesbians and gay men* (pp. 19–45). Thousand Oaks, CA: Sage.

Bookwala, J., Frieze, I. H., Smith, C., & Ryan, K. (1992). Predictors of dating violence: A multivariate analysis. *Violence and Victims, 7*, 297–309.

Bowers, L., Smith, P. K., & Binney, V. (1994). Perceived family relationships of bullies, victims, and bully/victims in middle childhood. *Journal of Social and Personal Relationships, 11*, 215–232.

Bowlby, J. (1969). *Attachment and loss: Vol. 1. Attachment*. New York: Basic Books.

Bronfenbrenner, U. (1979). *The ecology of human development*. Cambridge, MA: Harvard University Press.

Bukowski, W. M., Sippola, L. K., & Newcomb, A. F. (2000). Variations in patterns of attraction to same- and other-sex peers during early adolescence. *Developmental Psychology, 36*, 147–154.

Byrne, B. (1994). Bullies and victims in a school setting with reference to some Dublin schools. *Irish Journal of Psychology, 15*, 574–586.

Cairns, R. B., & Cairns, B. D. (1994). *Lifelines and risks: Pathways of youth in our time*. Cambridge: Cambridge University Press.

Cairns, R. B., Leung, M. C., & Cairns, B. D. (1995). Social networks over time and space in adolescence. In L. J. Crockett & A. C. Crouter (Eds.), *Pathways through adolescence: Individual development in relation to social contexts* (pp. 35–56). Hillsdale, NJ: Erlbaum.

Casella, R. (2003). Zero tolerance policy in schools: Rationale, consequences, and alternatives. *Teachers College Record, 105*, 872–892.

Centers for Disease Control and Prevention. (2006). *Youth risk behavior surveillance—United States 2005*. Complete report available as a pdf file from http://www.cdc.gov/mmwr/PDF/SS/SS5505.pdf or in table form from http://www.cdc.gov/HealthyYouth/yrbs/index.htm.

Craig, W. M. (1998). The relationship among bullying, victimization, depression, anxiety, and aggression in elementary school children. *Personality and Individual Differences, 24*, 123–130.

Cunningham, P. B., Henggeler, S. W., Limber, S. P., Melton, G. B., & Nation, M. A. (2000). Pattern and correlates of gun ownership among nonmetropolitan and rural middle school students. *Journal of Clinical Child Psychology, 29*, 432–442.

D'Augelli, A. R. (2003). Mental health problems among lesbian, gay, and bisexual youths ages 14 to 21. *Clinical Child Psychiatry and Psychiatry, 7*, 1359–1045.

Demaray, M. K., & Malecki, C. K. (2003). Perceptions of the frequency and importance of social support by students classified as victims, bullies, and bully/victims in an urban middle school. *School Psychology Review, 32*(3), 471–489.

Dunbar, R. I. M. (1988). *Primate social systems*. Ithaca, NY: Cornell University Press.

Duncan, R. D. (1999). Maltreatment by parents and peers: The relationship between child abuse, bullying victimization, and psychological distress. *Child Maltreatment, 4*, 45–55.

Eccles, J. S., Wigfield, A., Midgley, C., Reuman, D., Mac Iver, D., & Feldlaufer, H. (1993). Negative effects of traditional middle schools on students' motivation. *Elementary School Journal, 93*, 553–574.

Ely, G., Dulmus, C. N., & Wodarski, J. S. (2002). Adolescent dating violence. In L. A. Rapp-Paglicci, A. R. Roberts, & J. S. Wodarski (Eds.), *Handbook of violence* (pp. 34–53). Hoboken, NJ: Wiley.

Eron, L. D., & Huesmann, L. R. (1987). The stability of aggressive behavior in cross-national comparison. In C. Kagitcibasi (Ed.), *Growth and progress in cross-cultural psychology* (pp. 207–217). Berwyn, PA: Swets North America.

Eron, L. D., Huesmann, L. R., & Zell, A. (1991). The role of parental variables in the learning of aggression. In D. J. Pepler & K. H. Rubin (Eds.), *The development and treatment of childhood aggression* (pp. 169–189). Hillsdale, NJ: Erlbaum.

Espelage, D., & Holt, M. K. (2001). Bullying and victimization during early adolescence: Peer influences and psychosocial correlates. *Journal of Emotional Abuse, 2*, 123–142.

Espelage, D. L., Holt, M. K., & Henkel, R. R. (2003). Examination of peer-group contextual effects on aggression during early adolescence. *Child Development, 74*(1), 205–220.

Espelage, D. L., & Swearer, S. M. (2003). Research on bullying and victimization: What have we learned and where do we go from here? [Special issue]. *School Psychology Review, 32*(3), 365–383.

Finnegan, R. A., Hodges, E. V. E., & Perry, D. G. (1998). Victimization by peers: Associations with children's reports of mother-child interaction. *Journal of Personality and Social Psychology, 75*(4), 1076–1086.

Fonagy, P., Twemlow, S. W., Vernberg, E., Sacco, F., & Little, T. D. (2005). Creating a peaceful school learning environment: The impact of an antibullying program on educational attainment in elementary schools. *Medical Science Monitor, 11*, 317–325.

Furlong, M. J., Morrison, G. M., & Grief, J. L. (2003). Reaching an American consensus: Reactions to the special issue on school bullying. *School Psychology Review, 32*, 456–470.

Gaines, K. R. E., Cairns, R. B., & Cairns, B. D. (March, 1994). *Social networks and risk for school dropout.* Paper presented at the Society for Research on Adolescence, San Diego.

Garbarino, J. & deLara, E. (2002). *And words can hurt forever: How to protect adolescents from bullying, harassment, and emotional violence.* New York: Free Press.

Gottesman, I. I., & Goldsmith, H. H. (1994). Developmental psychopathology of antisocial behavior: Inserting genes into its ontogenesis and epigenesist. In C. A. Nelson (Ed.), *Threats to optimal development: Integrating biological, psychological, and social risk factors* (pp. 69–104). Hillsdale, NJ: Erlbaum.

Gray, H. M., & Foshee, V. A. (1997). Adolescent dating violence: Differences between one-sided and mutually violent profiles. *Journal of Interpersonal Violence, 12*, 126–141.

Gross, L., Aurand, S., & Adessa, R. (1988). *Violence and discrimination against lesbian and gay people in Philadelphia and the Commonwealth of Pennsylvania.* Unpublished report: Philadelphia Lesbian and Gay Task Force.

Hodges, E. V. E., Boivin, M., Vitaro, F., & Bukowski, W. M. (1999). The power of friendship: Protection against an escalating cycle of peer victimization. *Developmental Psychology, 35*, 94–101.

Holt, M., & Espelage, D. (2005). Multiple victimization of adolescents. In K. Kendall-Tackett & S. Giacomoni (Eds.), *Victimization of children and youth: Patterns of abuse, response strategies* (pp. 13-1–13-16). Kingston, NJ: Civic Research Institute.

Hoover, J. H., & Hazler, R. J. (1994). Bullies and victims. *Elementary School Guidance and Counseling, 25*, 212–220.

Hoover, J. H., Oliver, R., & Hazler, R. (1992). *Causal attributions: From cognitive processes to collective beliefs.* Oxford: Blackwell.

Howard, D. E., & Wang, M. Q. (2003). Risk profiles of U.S. adolescent girls who were victims of dating violence. *Adolescence, 38*, 1–14.

Howard, K. A., Flora, J., & Griffin, M. (1999). Violence-prevention programs in schools: State of the science and implications for future research. *Applied and Preventative Psychology, 8*, 197–215.

Juvonen, J., & Graham, S. (2001). *Peer harassment in school: The plight of the vulnerable and victimized.* New York: Guilford Press.

Juvonen, J., Graham, S., & Schuster, M. A. (2003). Bullying among young adolescents: The strong, the weak, and the troubled. *Pediatrics, 112*(6), 1231–1237.

Kandel, D. B. (1978). Homophily, selection, and socialization in adolescent friendships. *American Journal of Sociology, 84*, 427–436.

Katz, J., Kuffel, S. W., & Coblentz, A. (2002). Are there gender differences in sustaining domestic violence? An examination of frequency, severity, and relationship satisfaction. *Journal of Family Violence, 17*, 247–271.

Kenny, M. E., Waldo, M., Warter, E. H., & Barton, C. (2002). School-linked prevention: Theory, science and practice for enhancing the lives of children and youth. *Counseling Psychologist, 30*, 726–748.

Kimmel, M. S., & Mahler, M. (2003). Adolescent masculinity, homophobia, and violence. *American Behavioral Scientist, 465*, 1439–1458.

Kochenderfer, B. J., & Ladd, G. W. (1996). Peer victimization: Cause or consequence of school maladjustment? *Child Development, 67*, 1305–1317.

Kuffel, S. W., & Katz, J. (2002). Preventing physical, psychological, and sexual aggression in college dating relationships. *Journal of Primary Prevention, 22*, 361–374.

Leung, M. C. (1993). *Social cognition and social networks of Chinese schoolchildren in Hong Kong*. Unpublished doctoral dissertation, University of North Carolina at Chapel Hill.

Leung, M. C. (1994). Social cognition and social networks of Chinese schoolchildren in Hong Kong. *Dissertation Abstracts International, 54*(12-B).

Mason, A., & Palmer, A. (1996). *Queer bashing: A national survey of hate crimes against lesbians and gay men*. London: Stonewall.

McFadyen-Ketchum, S. A., Bates, J. E., Dodge, K. A., & Pettit, G. S. (1996). Patterns of change in early childhood aggressive-disruptive behavior: Gender differences in predictions from early coercive and affectionate mother-child interactions. *Child Development, 67*(5), 2417–2433.

Melton, G. B., Limber, S. P., Flerx, V., Cunningham, P., Osgood, D. W., Chambers, J., et al. (1998). *Violence among rural youth* (Final report, Grants 94-JN-CX-0005 and 96-MO-FX-0016). Clemson, SC: Office of Juvenile Justice and Delinquency Prevention.

Miles, D., & Carey, G. (1997). Genetic and environmental architecture of human aggression. *Journal of Personality and Social Psychology, 72*, 207–217.

Moffitt, T. E. (1993). Adolescent-limited and life-course-persistent anti-social behavior: A developmental taxonomy. *Psychological Review, 100*, 674–701.

Morrison, G. M., Redding, M., Fisher, E., & Peterson, R. (2006). Assessing school discipline. In S. R. Jimerson & M. Furlong, (Eds.), *Handbook of school violence and school safety: From research to practice* (pp. 211–220). Mahwah, NJ: Erlbaum.

Mouttapa, M., Valente, T., Gallaher, P., Rohrbach, L. A., & Unger, J. B. (2004). Social network predictors of bullying and victimization. *Source Adolescence, 39*(154), 315–335.

Nansel, T. R., Overpeck, M., Pilla, R. S., Ruan, W. J., Simons-Morton, B., & Scheidt, P. (2001). Bullying behaviors among U.S. youth: Prevalence and association with psychosocial adjustment. *Journal of the American Medical Association, 285*, 2094–2100.

Neckerman, H. J. (1992). *A longitudinal investigation of the stability and fluidity of social networks and peer relationships of children and adolescents*. Unpublished doctoral dissertation, University of North Carolina at Chapel Hill.

Nelson, D. A., & Crick, N. R. (1999). Rose-colored glasses: Examining the social information-processing of prosocial young adolescents. *Journal of Adolescence, 19*, 17–38.

Newman, D. A., Horne, A. M., & Bartolomucci, C. L. (2000). *Bully busters: A teacher's manual for helping bullies, victims, and bystanders*. Champaign, IL: Research Press.

Newman, R. S., Murray, B., & Lussier, C. (2001). Confrontation with aggressive peers at school: Students' reluctance to seek help from the teacher. *Journal of Educational Psychology, 93*(2), 398–410.

Newman-Carlson, D., & Horne, A. (2004). Bully-busters: A psychoeducational intervention for reducing bullying behavior in middle school students. *Journal of Counseling and Development, 82*, 259–267.

Olweus, D. (1978). *Aggression in the schools: Bullies and whipping boys*. Washington, DC: Hemisphere.

Olweus, D. (1993). Bully/victim problems among schoolchildren: Long-term consequences and an effective intervention program. In S. Hodgins (Ed.), *Mental disorder and crime* (pp. 317–349). Thousand Oaks, CA: Sage.

Olweus, D. (2001). Peer harassment: A critical analysis and some important issues. In S. Graham & J. Juvonen (Eds.), *Peer harassment in school: The plight of the vulnerable and victimized* (pp. 3–20). New York: Guilford Press.

Olweus, D. (2005). A useful evaluation design, *and effects of the Olweus Bullying Prevention Program. Psychology, Crime, and Law, 11*(4), 389–402.

Olweus, D., & Limber, S. (1999). *The Bullying-Prevention Program: Blueprints for violence prevention*. Boulder, CO: Center for the Study and Prevention of Violence.

Olweus, D., Limber, S. P., & Mihalic, S. (2000). *The Bullying Prevention Program: Blueprints for violence prevention* (Vol. 10). Boulder, CO: Center for the Study and Prevention of Violence.

Orpinas, P., & Horne, A. M. (2006). *Bullying prevention: Creating a positive school climate and developing social competence*. Washington, DC: American Psychological Association.

Pellegrini, A. D. (2002a). Affiliative and aggressive dimensions of dominance and possible functions during early adolescence. *Aggression and Violent Behavior, 7*(1), 21–31.

Pellegrini, A. D. (2002b). Bullying, victimization, and sexual harassment during the transition to middle school. *Educational Psychologist, 37*, 151–163.

Pellegrini, A. D., & Bartini, M. (2001). Dominance in early adolescent boys: Affiliative and aggressive dimensions and possible functions. *Merrill-Palmer Quarterly, 47*, 142–163.

Pellegrini, A. D., & Long, J. (2002). A longitudinal study of bullying, dominance, and victimization during the transition from primary to secondary school. *British Journal of Developmental Psychology, 20*, 259–280.

Perry, D. G., Hodges, E. V. E., & Egan, S. K. (2001). Determinants of chronic victimization by peers. In J. Juvonen & S. Graham (Eds.), *Peer harassment in schools: The plight of the vulnerable and victimized* (pp. 73–104). New York: Guilford Press.

Perry, D. G., Kusel, S. J., & Perry, C. L. (1988). Victims of peer aggression. *Developmental Psychology, 24*, 807–814.

Pilkington, N. W., & D'Augelli, A. R. (1995). Victimization of lesbian, gay, and bisexual youth in community settings. *Journal of Community Psychology, 23*, 34–56.

Plummer, D. C. (2001). The quest for modern manhood: Masculine stereotypes, peer culture, and the social significance of homophobia. *Journal of Adolescence, 24*, 15–23.

Poteat, P., & Espelage, D. L. (in press). Aggression, homophobia, and dominance among high school students. *Journal of Personality and Social Psychology.*

Rigby, K., & Slee, P. (1993). Dimensions of interpersonal relation among Australian children and implications for psychological well-being. *Journal of School Psychology, 133*, 33–42.

Ringeisen, H., Henderson, K., & Hoagwood, K. (2003). Context matters: Schools and the "research to practice gap" in children's mental health. *School Psychology Review, 32*, 153–168.

Roberts, W. B., & Coursol, D. H. (1996). Strategies for intervention with childhood and adolescent victims of bullying, teasing, and intimidation in school settings. *Elementary School Guidance and Counseling, 30*(3), 204–212.

Rodkin, P. C., & Hodges, E. V. (2003). Bullies and victims in the peer ecology: Four questions for psychologists and school professionals. *School Psychology Review, 32*(3), 384–400.

Romano, J. L., & Hage, S. M. (2000). Prevention and counseling psychology: Revitalizing commitments for the 21st century. *Counseling Psychologist, 28*, 733–763.

Roscoe, B., & Callahan, J. E. (1985). Adolescents' self-report of violence in families and dating relations. *Adolescence, 20*(79), 545–553.

Schwartz, D., Dodge, K. A., Petit, G. S., & Bates, J. E. (1997). The early socialization of aggressive victims of bullying. *Child Development, 68*, 665–675.

Schwartz, D., Proctor, L. J., & Chien, D. H. (2001). The aggressive victim of bullying, emotional and behavioral dysregulation as a pathway to victimization by peers. In J. Juvonen & S. Graham (Eds.), *Peer harassment in school: The plight of the vulnerable and victimized* (pp. 147–174). New York: Guilford Press.

Shields, A., & Cicchetti, D. (2001). Parental maltreatment and emotion dysregulation as risk factors for bullying and victimization in middle childhood. *Journal of Clinical Child Psychology, 30*, 349–363.

Smith, J. D., Schneider, B. H., Smith, P. K., & Ananiadou, K. (2004). The effectiveness of whole-school antibullying programs: A synthesis of evaluation research. *School Psychology Review, 33*(4), 547–560.

Smith, P. K., Madsen, K. C., & Moody, J. C. (1999). What causes the age decline in reports of being bullied at school? Toward a developmental analysis of risks of being bullied. *Educational Research, 41*, 267–285.

Swearer, S. M., & Espelage, D. L. (2004). Introduction: A social-ecological framework of bullying among youth. In D. L. Espelage & S. M. Swearer (Eds.), *Bullying in American schools: A social-ecological perspective on prevention and intervention* (pp. 1–12). Mahwah, NJ: Erlbaum.

Swearer, S. M., Song, S. Y., Cary, P. T., Eagle, J. W., & Mickelson, W. T. (2001). Psychosocial correlates in bullying and victimization: The relationship between depression, anxiety, and bully/victim status. *Journal of Emotional Abuse, 2*, 95–121.

Talley, R. C., & Short, R. J. (1996). Social reforms and the future of school practice: Implications for American psychology. *Professional Psychology: Research and Practice, 27*, 5–13.

Tolan, P., Kendall, P., Huessman, L., Eron, L., Acker, R. V., & Guerra, N. (1995). Stressful events and individual beliefs as correlates of economic disadvantage and aggression among urban children. *Journal of Consulting and Clinical Psychology, 63*, 518–528.

Troy, M., & Sroufe, L. A. (1987). Victimization among preschoolers: Role of attachment relationship history. *Journal of the American Academy of Child and Adolescent Psychiatry, 26*, 166–172.

Twemlow, S. W., Fonagy, P., & Sacco, F. C. (2001). An innovative psychodynamically influenced intervention to reduce school violence. *Journal of the American Academy of Child and Adolescent Psychiatry, 40*, 377–379.

Twemlow, S. W., Fonagy, P., & Sacco, F. C. (2005). A developmental approach to mentalizing communities: Pt. II. The peaceful schools experiment. *Bulletin of the Menninger Clinic, 69*, 282–304.

U.S. Public Health Service. (2000). *Report of the surgeon general's conference on children's mental health: A national action agenda.* Washington, DC: Department of Health and Human Services.

Walsh, M. E., Galassi, J. P., Murphy, J. A., & Park-Taylor, J. (2002). A conceptual framework for counseling psychologists in schools. *Counseling Psychologist, 30*, 682–704.

Whitney, I., & Smith, P. K. (1993). A survey of the nature and extent of bullying in junior/middle and secondary schools. *Educational Research, 35*, 3–25.

Wright, L. W., Adams, H. E., & Bernat, J. (1999). Development and validation of the homophobia scale. *Journal of Psychopathology and Behavioral Assessment, 21*, 337–347.

Xie, H. (1995, April). *Peer social networks of inner-city children and adolescents at school.* Paper presented at the biennial meeting of the Society for Research in Child Development, Indianapolis, IN.

Zumkley, H. (1994). The stability of aggressive behavior: A meta-analysis. *German Journal of Psychology, 18*, 273–281.

Author Index

Abascal, L. B., 577, 578, 580, 581, 582
Abbott, R., 555
Abeles, N., 7, 15
Aber, M. S., 166
Abernathy, C. B., 543
Abernathy, T. J., 166
Aboud, F. E., 518
Abrams, D., 251
Abramson, L., 573
Abramson, M., 313
Abreu, J. M., 146
Achenreiner, G. B., 164
Achter, J. A., 392
Acker, R. V., 590
Ackerling, S. J., 202
Ackerman, P. L., 383, 384
Ackerman, R. J., 179
Ackerman, S. J., 270
Acosta, F. X., 327, 330, 331
Acuff, C., 26
Adams, E. M., 202
Adams, H. E., 599
Adams, M., 430
Adams-Curtis, L. E., 178
Addis, M. E., 185, 186, 251, 253, 259
Adessa, R., 599
Adler, N. E., 159, 162, 168
Ægisdóttir, S., 71, 73, 76, 78, 80, 539
Agnew-Davies, R., 270, 279
Agras, W. S., 28, 257, 269, 270, 570, 571, 572, 578
Aguiar, L., 214
Aguilar-Gaxiola, S., 323
Ahadi, S., 382, 383
Ahn, H., 252, 253, 261, 326
Ahuvia, A., 94
Ajamu, A., 519
Ajzen, I., 527
Akerboom, S., 444
Akutsu, P., 329
Alarcón, O., 484, 489, 490, 492
Albarracin, D., 527
Albee, G. W., 55, 58
Alberts, G., 340
Alcorn, J., 33, 528, 538, 539, 540, 547
Alden, L. E., 304
Alexander, C. M., 71, 73, 81, 103, 123, 150, 151
Alexander, M. W., 46
Alford, B. A., 542
Ali, S. R., 159, 160, 165, 341, 362, 363, 364, 415
Alimohamed, S., 257, 449
Alleman, J. R., 39
Allen, G. J., 9
Allen, M., 178, 252, 258

Allen, R., 178
Allison, K. W., 519
Allison, R. D., 8
Altbach, P. G., 71
Altman, A., 340
Altman, T. M., 576
Altmann, R. A., 413, 444
Alva, L. A., 27
Alvarez, A. N., 152
Amanzio, M., 257
Ananiadou, K., 598
Anastasi, A., 106
Ancis, J. R., 341, 347
Anderson, A. K., 3, 14
Anderson, B. K., 559
Anderson, C., 412
Anderson, D. A., 177
Anderson, E., 89, 235
Anderson, J. R., 13
Anderson, K. G., 9, 10
Anderson, K. M., 180
Anderson, L. A., 539
Anderson, M. W., 306, 307
Anderson, M. Z., 199, 200, 201, 202, 203, 350, 380, 412
Anderson, N., 377
Anderson, N. B., 322, 522, 523, 529
Anderson, N. D., 312
Anderson, S. K., 7
Anderson, T., 29, 30, 251
Anderson, W. P., Jr., 449, 452, 454
Andréasson, S., 251
Andrew, M. E., 358, 359, 360
Andrews, N. R., 561, 562, 564
Angell, J. W., 364
Angold, A., 161, 162, 552
Angus, L., 294, 296
Anstine P .S., 556
Anthony, E. J., 483, 484
Antonuccio, D. O., 28
Appel, A., 573, 578, 583
Arabie, P., 380
Archambault, R. J., 13, 14
Archer, J., Jr., 40, 45
Arcinue, F., 9
Ardila, R., 71
Arganza, G. F., 142
Arguello, J., 168
Arkin, R. M., 164, 165
Arkowitz, H., 527, 561, 563
Armenia, A., 429
Armitage, S. H., 70
Armstrong, P., 358, 359, 380, 381, 383, 384, 385, 386, 411, 412, 419
Arnkoff, D. B., 260
Arnold, E., 180

Arnow, B. A., 257, 269, 270
Aron, L., 270
Aronson, E., 494
Arora, A. K., 127, 128
Arorash, T. J., 126, 128
Aros, J. R., 412
Arredondo, P., 7, 56, 64, 141, 152, 153
Arriaga, X. B., 598
Arsenau, J. R., 195, 196, 198
Arthur, M. W., 556
Asamen, J. K., 38
Asay, P. A., 148, 324, 329
Asay, T. P., 256
Asch, S. M., 166
Atkinson, D. R., 54, 105, 122, 123, 145, 147, 259, 325, 326, 327, 455
Atsma, N., 134
Attakai, A., 522
Au, M., 24
Auerbach, C. F., 182
Aurand, S., 599
Austin, J. A., 377, 382
Austin, J. T., 109, 420
Austin, R., 148
Austin, S. B., 580, 583
Austin, W., 327
Avis, N. E., 180
Ax, R. K., 29
Aycan, Z., 416, 418, 421
Ayoub, C., 233

Babladelis, G., 189
Babor, T., 562, 563
Bach, P., 29
Bachman, J. G., 552, 559
Bachmann, D., 45, 46
Bacigalupe, G., 94
Baden, A. L., 180
Badger, G. J., 562
Bae, S. W., 330, 331
Baehr, A. P., 311
Baer, J. S., 557, 558, 559
Baime, M., 313
Baker, E., 555
Baker, K. A., 303
Baker, K. D., 253
Baker, S., 59, 61, 251, 340
Baker, T. R., 12
Baldry, A. C., 591
Baldwin, S. A., 545
Baldwin, T. T., 466
Ball, S. A., 562
Balla, J. R., 109
Balsam, K. F., 193
Baltes, B. B., 413, 444
Baluch, S. P., 64

Bambling, M., 350
Bamossy, G., 164, 167
Banaji, M., 38, 46
Bandalos, D. L., 108, 110
Bandura, A., 91, 286, 361, 363, 364, 452, 468, 469, 470, 495, 506, 523, 524
Banerjee L., 324, 331
Banks, M. E., 179, 216
Barak, A., 39, 41, 42, 394
Barakett, M. D., 126, 128
Baranowski, J., 513
Baranowski, T., 513
Barbaranelli, C., 469
Barber, J. P., 269, 272, 287, 288, 297
Bard, C. C., 205
Bardash, R. J., 13, 14, 365, 386
Bardone, A., 573
Barends, A. W., 270
Barker-Hackett, L., 152
Barkham, M., 235, 295
Barley, D. E., 255, 256
Barling, J., 457, 467
Barnes, G. M., 560
Barnes, S. A., 452
Barnett, J. E., 5, 10, 11, 39
Barnett, N. P., 558, 560
Barnett, R., 176, 426, 430, 431, 434, 437
Barraclough, D. J., 414, 417
Barret, B., 5, 13
Barrett, A., 151
Barrett, K. A., 204
Barrick, M. R., 360, 376, 377, 378, 382, 385
Barry, K. L., 557, 558
Barsky, A. P., 360, 365, 465
Bartelli, D., 527
Bartholow, B. D., 559
Bartini, M., 593
Bartlett, J. E., II, 46
Bartolomucci, A., 523
Bartolomucci, C. L., 590, 596
Bartolucci, A., 225
Barton, C., 600
Barton, S. N., 538
Bashe, A., 7
Baskin, T. W., 252, 253, 260
Bass, C. K., 496
Bass, D. C., 526
Bassett, S. S., 215
Bassok, M., 504
Bates, J. E., 591, 592
Batsche, G. M., 589
Battle, E. K., 574
Baum, A., 517
Baumann, E., 292
Baumeister, R. F., 304
Baumgartner, H., 111, 112
Bauserman, R., 16
Bautista-Castano, I., 523
Baxter, W. J., 109
Beacham, A. O., 525
Bean, R. A., 331
Beard, K. W., 48
Bearman, S. K., 573
Beatty, J. E., 201
Beauchamp, T. L., 3, 46
Beautrais, A., 547
Beck, A. T., 306, 539, 542
Beck, J., 553
Beck, M., 307, 308, 310, 313, 349

Becker, B., 484, 485, 486, 489, 524, 547, 558
Becker, C. B., 579
Becker, D., 350
Becker-Blease, K. A., 47, 48, 49
Becker-Schutte, A., 106, 204
Beckstead, A., 207
Beckstead, D. J., 237
Bedi, R. P., 257
Beebe, K., 288
Beehr, T. A., 468
Behnke, S. H., 5
Beiser, M., 162
Belar, C. D., 22, 23, 25, 528
Belgrave, F. Z., 519
Bell, L. A., 55
Belland, J. C., 38
Bemak, F., 60, 64
Bempong, I., 15
Benbow, C. P., 378, 379, 386
Ben-David, M., 288
Benedetti, F., 257, 260
Benet-Martinez, V., 375, 376
Benjamin, D., 306
Benjamin, G. A. H., 13
Benjamin, L. T., 61
Benjamin, L., Jr., 22, 32
Bennet, B. E., 26
Bennett, J., 146, 148, 149
Bennett, M. E., 561, 562, 564
Bennett Johnson, S., 521
Benotsch, E. G., 48
Ben-Porath, Y. S., 38
Benson, K., 252, 261
Bent, R., 6, 7
Bentler, P. M., 108, 109, 115, 505
Berano, K. C., 348
Berg, C., 95
Berg, I. K., 326
Berger, T., 42, 43, 44, 298
Bergeron, L. R., 180
Bergin, A. E., 249
Berglund, M., 251
Bergman, S. J., 181
Bergvik, S., 43, 44
Berking, M., 245
Berkowitz, L., 590
Berman, A. L., 6, 535, 538, 541, 547
Berman, J., 6
Bernadelli, A., 288
Bernal, G., 147, 329
Bernal, M. E., 150
Bernard, J., 189, 431
Bernard, J. L., 10
Bernard, J. M., 8, 9, 342, 350
Bernat, D. H., 488
Bernat, J., 29, 599
Berndt, T. J., 592
Bernier, J. B., 141, 149, 153
Bernier, J. E., 333
Bernstein, B., 330, 588
Bernstein, J. H., 9, 10
Berrill, K. T., 599
Berry, J., 73, 76, 78, 79, 104, 123, 288, 295, 519
Bertholet, N., 558
Beruta, C., 377
Bess, J. M., 303
Bessenhoff, G. R., 178
Besser, A., 48
Betan, E. J., 10

Betancourt, H., 104
Betancourt, L., 166
Betz, N., 358, 359, 361, 362, 364, 365, 381, 382, 397, 398, 408, 409, 412
Beutler, L. E., 257, 270, 338, 449
Bewell, C., 523
Bhana, A., 166
Bhati, K. S., 252, 259, 260, 285
Bianchi, S. M., 430, 431, 432, 438
Bickenbach, J., 215, 217, 218, 226
Bickham, D. S., 178
Bickman, L., 538
Biddle, S. J. H., 524
Bidell, M. P., 206
Bieneck, S., 179
Bieschke, K. J., 194, 195, 197, 199, 202, 204, 205, 206, 207, 362, 363, 414
Bimrose, J., 452
Binder, J. L., 250, 254
Binford, R. B., 571
Binney, V., 582, 591
Birenbaum, A., 26
Bishop, M. J., 237
Bishop, S. R., 312
Bishop, T. A., 178
Bittman, M., 438
Bjorck-Akesson, E., 216
Blackie, J. M., 560
Blackmon, S. M., 126, 128
Blain, J., 438
Blair, K. L., 216
Blais, M., 570
Blake, D. D., 185
Blakely, K., 537
Blanchard, C. A., 368
Blanchard, E. B., 182
Blasey, C., 257, 269, 270
Blashfield, R. K., 9, 10
Blasko, K. A., 197, 204, 205, 206, 207
Blazina, C., 448
Bledsoe, M., 366, 367, 369, 452
Bleiberg, K. L., 259
Bloch, N., 39, 41, 42
Blocher, D. H., 68, 69
Block, J., 484
Block, S., 289
Blonk, R. W. B., 520
Blood, R. W., 547
Bloom, M., 502
Blustein, D., 15, 54, 56, 57, 71, 72, 76, 82, 165, 357, 366, 367, 368, 369, 409, 412, 415, 416, 418, 420, 421, 450
Boatwright, K. J., 202
Bobek, B. L., 45
Bock, B. C., 525
Bock, P. S., 23
Bockting, W. O., 526
Bodenreider, O., 226
Bogart, L. M., 162
Bögels, S. M., 304, 305, 313
Boggs, K., 394
Bohart, A., 261, 286, 297
Boivin, M., 597
Bolan, G., 527
Bolden, M. A., 64, 115
Bolduc, D., 177
Bollen, K. A., 108
Bolt, D. M., 251
Boma, H., 165
Bond, J. T., 427, 430

Bondas, T., 179
Bondy, S. J., 557, 558
Bongar, B., 6
Bonner, G., 312, 313
Bonner, R., 11, 12
Bono, J. E., 471, 472
Bontempo, D. E., 112, 113, 114, 115
Bookwala, J., 598
Booth, H., 289, 295
Borden, K. A., 7
Borders, L. D., 306, 307
Bordin, E. S., 269, 270, 342, 344, 345
Borgen, F., 57, 68, 358, 360, 362, 363,
     378, 379, 380, 381, 382, 386
Borgogni, L., 469
Borkovec, T. D., 285, 286
Bornstein, M. H., 432
Borquez, J., 165
Borsari, B., 557
Borzuchowska, B., 5
Bosacki, S. L., 177
Bosma, H., 162, 167
Bosnjak, M., 45
Boswell, J. F., 285, 286
Botvin, E. M., 555
Botvin, G. J., 554, 555
Bouchard, G., 431
Bouffard, B. B., 28, 29
Boumil, M. M., 182
Bound, J., 163
Boutelle, K. N., 525
Boven, L. V., 164
Bowers, K., 90, 91, 95
Bowers, L., 582, 591
Bowes, J. M., 430
Bowlby, J., 271, 591
Bowles, S. M., 358, 360
Bowman, J., 31
Bowman, S., 395, 396, 400
Boxley, R., 8, 9
Boyce, C., 16
Boyce, T., 166
Boyce, W. T., 162
Boyd, C. J., 7, 559
Brack, C. J., 306
Brack, G., 306, 307
Braddock, D., 226
Bradley, L. J., 350
Bradley, P., 89
Bradley, R., 182, 273
Brainard, G., 313
Branch, L. G., 214
Brannick, M. T., 464
Brannon, R., 181, 182, 185
Brantley, P. J., 520
Brayfield, A. H., 464
Brecheisen, B. K., 392, 449, 450, 453
Brecheisen, J., 452, 453
Brehm, S. S., 304
Breitkopf, C. R., 179
Brennan, R. T., 430
Brenner, B. R., 115, 200, 202, 324, 329,
     361, 362, 363, 364, 469, 470, 474
Brenock, K., 348
Brent, D., 538
Breuer, J., 268
Brewerton, T. D., 552
Bricklin, P., 26
Brickner, B. W., 182, 183
Brief, A. P., 462, 463, 466, 471, 472
Bright, J. I., 253

Brilman, E., 215
Brim, O. G., Jr., 165
Brinegar, M. G., 288
Brinkmann, U., 134, 135
Brislin, R., 104
Brittan-Powell, C. S., 345
Brobst, K., 126, 128, 130, 131, 132, 134,
     136, 146
Brodbeck, F., 134
Brodsky, N. L., 166
Brody, D. S., 23
Brody, G., 492, 493, 494, 495
Broido, E. M., 62
Broitman, J., 291, 297
Brokowski, A., 22
Bromet, E. J., 538
Bromley, J. L., 32, 33, 59, 538, 539, 540,
     547
Broneck, C. L., 414, 417
Bronfenbrenner, U., 159, 161, 163, 164,
     168, 170, 409, 589
Bronson, M. K., 350
Brook, J. S., 570
Brooks, D., 171
Brooks, G. R., 176, 181, 183, 184, 185,
     186, 187, 188
Brooks-Gunn, J., 485
Brossart, D. F., 127, 128, 289, 292
Brotman, M. A., 251, 252, 257
Brown, A., 341
Brown, C., 115, 329, 409, 492
Brown, D., 59, 60, 61
Brown, G. S., 235, 237
Brown, J. B., 577, 578, 582
Brown, K., 311
Brown, M. T., 159, 165, 409, 413, 415,
     419
Brown, S., 57, 164, 277, 359
Brown, S. D., 57, 73, 74, 93, 115, 116,
     164, 277, 357, 358, 359, 360, 361,
     362, 363, 364, 365, 369, 382, 392,
     393, 397, 400, 402, 403, 404, 412,
     413, 415, 418, 445, 446, 447, 448,
     449, 450, 451, 452, 453, 454, 455,
     456, 457, 458, 469, 470, 472, 473,
     476
Brown, S. P., 141, 153
Brown, T. N., 493
Brownbridge, G., 521
Browne, L., 106, 146
Brownell, K. D., 522, 523, 574
Brownson, C., 430
Brubaker, M., 48
Bruce, N., 257, 260
Brucker, B., 216
Bruckman, A., 38, 46
Brummett, B. R., 126, 128
Brun, C., 436
Brunelle, J., 510
Brunner, E., 165
Brunstein, J. C., 469, 470
Brunton, G., 524
Bruyère, S. M., 217
Bryant, F. B., 109
Bryant, R. M., 141
Bryk, A. S., 261
Bryson, S., 577, 581, 582
Bucci, W., 291, 297
Buchanan, A., 415
Buchanan, T., 38, 46
Buckingham, M., 88, 89

Buckworth, J., 525
Budd, J., 412
Budisin, I., 452, 453
Budney, A. J., 563
Bufka, L. F., 224
Buhle, M. J., 70
Buhrke, R. A., 4
Bui, K. T., 325
Bukowski, W. M., 592, 593, 597
Burchfield, C. M., 236
Burdette, H. L, 66
Burg, R., 48
Burgess, P., 547
Burggraf, K., 177, 178
Burgio, K. L., 305
Burkard, A. W., 146, 346
Burke, A., 313
Burke, B., 527, 561, 563
Burke, M. C., 206
Burke, R. J., 418
Burlew, A. K., 105
Burlingame, G. M., 236
Burnand, B., 558
Burns, C., 215
Burns, M. E., 90, 91, 95
Burns, P. B., 163
Burris, S., 5
Burroughs, J. E., 164
Burton, E., 573, 579, 580, 583
Burton, L., 307, 495
Bush, B., 225
Bush, J. W., 29, 30
Buss, A. H., 304, 307
Butcher, J. N., 38, 104
Butler, M., 292
Butler, S. F., 254
Button, C., 11, 12
Button, S. B., 201
Buzzard, M., 510
Byars, A., 362, 364
Byars-Winston, A. M., 414, 418
Byrne, B., 111, 112, 113, 114, 590

Cabassa, L., 323
Cable, D. M., 467, 468
Cabrera, N. J., 182
Cachelin, F. M., 570, 571, 572, 573
Cacioppo, J. T., 307
Caetano, R., 323
Cage, M., 48
Cahill, B. J., 202
Caine, E. D., 537
Cairns, B. D., 592, 593
Cairns, R. B., 592, 593
Calamari, J. E., 304
Caldwell, C. H., 488, 492, 493, 494, 495
Caldwell, M., 183
Caldwell, R., 313
Calfas, K. J., 577
Calhoun, K. S., 29
Calhoun, L., 503, 543, 544
Callahan, G. A., 398, 400
Callahan, J., 540, 541, 544, 598, 599
Calliotte, J. A., 396, 400, 401, 402, 403
Calzavara, L., 526
Cameron, M. C., 521
Cameron, N., 524
Cameron, R., 570
Campbell, B. W., 202
Campbell, C. D., 9
Campbell, D. P., 378, 379, 380, 386

Campbell, F. R., 545
Campbell, J. D., 304, 305
Campbell, J. F., 559
Campbell, R., 179
Campbell, W .K., 162
Campise, R., 537
Canary, D., 188
Cancelli, A. A., 492
Cancian, F. M., 438
Canel, D., 78
Cantarelli, E. A., 364
Canter, M., 26
Cantor, N., 469, 470
Capaldi, D., 366, 367
Caplan, P. J., 184, 185
Capobianco, J. A., 348
Caprara, G. V., 469
Caprioli, A., 523
Carballo-Dieguez, A., 526
Cardinal, B. J., 525
Carew, J., 146
Carey, B., 257
Carey, G., 590
Carey, J. C., 346
Carey, K. B., 557, 558
Carey, M. P., 527, 558
Carkhuff, R. R., 339
Carli, L. L., 428
Carlozzi, A. F., 127, 128
Carlson, J. M., 560
Carlson, L., 312
Carmody, J., 312
Carney, C. G., 394
Carney, P., 40
Carozzoni, P., 274, 310
Carr, A. N., 38
Carr, J. Z., 444, 467
Carranza, V. E., 81
Carroll, K., 251, 562, 563
Carroll, L., 10
Carroll, M., 350, 521, 522, 570
Carter, C. A., 559
Carter, J., 68, 71, 72, 81, 122, 268, 269,
   270, 276, 278, 279, 287, 291, 558,
   571
Carter, R. T., 103, 116, 153, 321, 324,
   326, 448, 484
Cartwright, B., 5, 148
Carver, C. S., 304, 305, 307
Cary, P. T., 590
Casares, M. T., 165, 409, 416, 420, 421
Casas, J. M., 56, 68, 71, 72, 81, 103, 122,
   123, 153, 571
Case, A., 166
Casella, R., 594
Cash, T. F., 570
Cashell-Smith, M. L., 558
Cashin, J. R., 559, 560
Caspar, F., 43, 298
Casper, W. J., 469
Caspi, A., 376, 382, 476
Cass, V. C., 196
Cassel, C. K., 214
Cassidy, K. W., 177
Castaneda, C. L., 76, 123
Castelino, P., 452, 453
Castelnuovo, G., 39
Castonguay, L. G., 254, 270, 284, 285,
   286, 296, 298
Castro, C., 511
Catalano, M., 358, 421

Catalano, R., 553, 554, 555, 556
Cataldie, L., 545
Cattani-Thompson, K., 454
Cattell, R. B., 89
Cauce, A. M., 490, 491
Cautela, J. R., 286
Cavett, A., 367
Ceballo, R., 165
Ceder, I., 484, 489, 490, 492
Ceja, M., 146
Celio, A., 574, 576, 580, 582
Celotta, B., 547
Cgen, Y., 492, 493, 495
Chae, M. H., 492
Chamberlain, C., 537
Chambers, J., 596
Chan, F., 215
Chan, W., 116
Chang, D., 320, 326, 329, 332
Chang, E., 561
Chang, L., 164, 165
Chang, R., 40
Chang, T., 40
Chang, V. Y., 313
Chao, C. M., 331
Chao, H. M., 79
Charanasomboon, S., 577, 582
Charatan, D. L., 570
Chartrand, J. M., 394, 396, 400, 401,
   402, 403, 453
Chase, A., 573, 578, 583
Chase, G. A., 215
Chatterji, S., 215, 217, 218, 226
Chauhan, R. V., 143
Chaves, A., 165, 366, 369, 409, 415,
   416, 418, 420, 421
Chavous, T. M., 492, 493, 494
Chen, E., 123, 153, 166, 167
Chen, G., 469
Chen, H., 305
Chen, Y., 225
Chesney, M., 162
Cheung, F. M., 71, 72, 76, 104
Cheung, G. W., 113, 114
Cheung, M., 327
Cheung, M. K., 327
Cheung, M. W. L., 116
Chi, M. T. H., 504
Chien, D. H., 589
Chien, W. W., 324, 331
Childress, C. A., 38
Childress, J. F., 3, 46
Chin A Paw, M. J. M., 525
Chisholm-Stockard, S., 293
Chittooran, M. M., 213
Chizmar, L., 524
Choi, B. C. K., 62
Choi, C., 226
Choi, N. G., 215
Chopra, S. B., 362, 363
Chou, C., 38
Chou, S. P., 552
Chrisler, J. C., 180
Christianso, J. B., 24
Christofferson, C., 238
Christopher, A. N., 164, 165
Christos, P. J., 259
Chrobot-Mason, D., 201
Chronister, K., 362, 363, 364, 415, 418,
   455
Chu, S., 453

Chun, C. A., 325
Chun, K. M., 324
Chung, J. Y., 171
Chung, R. C., 60, 64
Chung, R. H., 324
Chung, Y. B., 193, 195, 200, 201, 202,
   414, 417
Chur-Hansen, A., 346
Chute, C. G., 226
Chwalisz, K., 520, 528, 529
Ciao, A. C., 579
Ciarlo, J. A., 234
Cicchetti, D., 484, 485, 486, 489, 592
Cieza, A., 226
Cikanek, K. L., 43
Cislo, D., 289, 291
Civic, D., 526
Claiborn, C. D., 8, 255
Clair, J. A., 201
Claire, T., 159
Clark, L. A., 398
Clark, L. F., 525, 526, 527
Clark, M., 179
Clark, R., 322, 522, 523, 529
Clark, S., 543
Clark, V. R., 322
Clarke, G., 23
Claus, R. E., 5
Clay, D. L., 144, 147
Clay, R., 25
Cleveland, M. J., 492, 493, 494
Clifford, P. R., 558
Clifton, D. O., 88, 89
Clow, R. B., 367
Cluss, P., 521
Coan, J. A., 262
Coatsworth, J. D., 486, 487, 490, 491
Coblentz, A., 598
Coccurello, R., 523
Cochran, B., 490, 491
Cochran, S., 181, 186, 205
Cochrane, A. L., 333
Coe, K., 522
Coenen, A., 225
Coffin, T. K., 469
Cogar, M. M., 289
Cohen, B. B., 341
Cohen, D. A., 166
Cohen, G. E., 40
Cohen, H. J., 26
Cohen, J., 38, 46, 129, 164, 260, 290,
   340, 392, 446, 574
Cohen, L. R., 570
Cohen, P., 164, 570
Cohen, R. J., 304
Coker, A. L., 179
Coker, J. K., 44
Cokley, K., 123
Colby, S. M., 558
Cole, J. D., 525
Cole, N. S., 379
Coleman, E., 196
Coleman, H. L. K., 103, 147, 148, 152,
   153, 259, 496
Collin, A., 366, 409
Collins, C., 505
Collins, F. L., Jr., 7
Collins, J., 251
Collins, K. M., 430
Collins, N. M., 64, 448
Collins, S., 38, 43, 558

Collins, W. A., 432
Coltrane, S., 430, 433
Comas-Diaz, L., 323
Compton, S. N., 161, 162
Compton, W., 552
Condron, L., 38
Conger, J., 194
Conger, R., 165, 166, 492
Conn, V. S., 524, 525
Connerley, M. L., 125, 127, 128
Connolly, J. J., 465
Connolly Gibbons, M. B., 269, 270
Constantine, K., 366
Constantine, M., 94, 123, 126, 128, 141, 145, 146, 147, 148, 149, 150, 151, 152, 153, 341, 349, 415, 418
Constantino, M. J., 257, 260, 269, 270
Constantino, R. E., 544
Constantinou, P. S., 576
Conti, R., 523
Contreras-Tadych, D. A., 346
Cook, D. A., 55, 105
Cook, E. P., 404, 409, 410, 412, 421
Cook, J. E., 40
Cook, R. L., 526
Cook, R. S., 539
Cooke, K., 414, 417, 418
Coombs, D. W., 538
Cooney, N., 251
Cooper, A., 48, 297
Cooper, C. C., 26, 27
Cooper, H. M., 524, 525
Cooper, M. L., 180
Cooper, Z., 570
Copeland-Linder, N., 492, 493, 494
Corbett, M., 285, 287, 288, 348
Corbin, W. R., 29, 558
Cordeiro, B. L., 429
Corning, A., 63
Cornwell, J. M., 200
Corral, I., 492
Corrigan, J., 216
Cortese, J. R., 8
Cortina, L. M., 468
Cosgrove, L., 184, 185
Cossette, L., 177
Costa, C., 276, 277, 279
Costa, P. T., 130, 360, 400, 466
Costa-Wooford, C. I., 130, 131, 132, 134, 136
Costello, C. B., 179
Costello, E. J., 161, 162, 552
Coster, J. S., 303
Cotte, J., 165
Cotting, D., 511
Cottone, R. R., 5
Cottrol, C., 327
Couchman, C. E., 164
Couper, M., 38, 46
Coursol, D., 43, 594
Courtenay, W. H., 182, 183
Cover, S., 452
Cox, C. M., 167
Cozzarelli, C., 180
Crace, R. K., 451
Craig, W. M., 590
Craighead, L. W., 28
Crawford, C. E., 270
Crepaz, N., 527
Cresswell, S., 509
Crick, N. R., 590

Crimmings, A. M., 338
Crimmins, E. M., 519, 520
Cristo, M. H., 327
Crites, J. O., 365, 393
Crits-Christoph, P., 250, 257, 269, 270, 272, 287, 288, 291, 295, 297
Crocker, P., 269
Croizet, J. C., 159
Crombie, G., 412
Cron, E. A., 307
Cronce, J. M., 558, 559, 560, 564
Crook, R. E., 290
Crook-Lyon, R., 290, 292, 293, 295, 296, 297
Cropanzano, R., 466, 468, 470, 472, 473, 474, 475
Crosby, F. J., 190, 426, 427
Cross, J. E., 527
Croteau, J. M., 195, 199, 200, 201, 202, 203, 204, 205
Crouse, F. M., 61
Crouter, A., 432, 495
Cruet, D., 304
Crusto, C., 556
Crutchfield, L. B., 306
Cruz, I. Y., 558
Cruza-Guet, M. C., 358
Csikszentmihalyi, M., 87, 94, 309, 483, 504
Cudeck, R., 408
Cuellar, I., 122
Cuijpers, P., 554, 556
Cullen, E. A., 23, 29
Cummings, A. L., 289
Cummings, N. A., 22, 32
Cunning, D., 577, 581, 582
Cunningham, J. A., 557, 558
Cunningham, M., 4, 433
Cunningham, P., 590, 596
Cunningham, W. A., 110
Curran, P. J., 107, 108
Current, L. R., 434
Curry, S. J., 525
Curtin, L., 522, 563
Curtis, H., 291, 295
Curtis, J., 272, 291, 297
Curtis, N. T., 412
Cushing, G., 484, 485, 486, 487, 488, 489
Cushway, D., 289, 295
Cutler, R. L., 274
Cutrona, C., 492
Cypres, A., 25
Czitrom, D., 70

D'Achiardi, C., 411
D'Achiardi-Ressler, C., 528, 529
Daeppen, J., 558
Dages, P., 40
Dahlem, N. W., 239
Daiger, D. C., 396
Daley, M. C., 26
Dana, D. M., 259
Dana, R. H., 142, 328
D'Andrea, M., 54, 60, 146, 148, 330
Dane, A. V., 513
Daniels, J., 27, 54, 60, 146, 148, 330
Daniels, T. G., 340
Danish, S., 500, 501, 502, 503, 504, 505, 506, 507, 508, 509, 510, 511, 513, 514, 560

Dansereau, D. F., 328
Dansky, B. S., 552
Danton, W. G., 28
Darcy, M., 359, 380
Darden, E. E., 409
Darkes, J., 557
Darou, W. G., 15
Darrow, R., 367
Das, S., 580, 582
Dasmahapatra, R., 576
D'Augelli, A. R., 502, 503, 506, 599
Daus, C. S., 466, 469, 472
Dau-Schmidt, K. G., 436
Davenport, A. E., 560
Davenport, D. S., 9
Davey, F. H., 412
David, D., 181, 182, 185
Davidoff, O. J., 559
Davidov, B. J., 94
Davidson, R. J., 262
Davies, D. R., 305
Davies, J. B., 314
Davies, K., 176, 177, 179
Davis, C., 523
Davis, J., 75, 199, 201, 202, 203
Davis, K., 22
Davis, K. D., 495
Davis, K. M., 269
Davis, M., 513
Davis, R. A., 48
Davis, S. R., 25, 26
Davis, T., 269, 290, 362, 363
Davis Martin, P., 520
Dawes, R. M., 539
Dawis, R., 106, 212, 360, 361, 375, 376, 377, 378, 411, 462, 463, 464, 467, 475
Dawson, D. A., 552
Day, J. D., 3, 9
Day, L., 555
Day, M. A., 386
Day, S. X., 39, 40, 362, 380
Dayton, D. D., 244
Deaux, K., 176, 436
DeBar, L., 23
DeBell, C., 444, 456
DeBord, K. A., 194, 199, 207
de Chermont, K., 360, 365, 465
Deci, E. L., 467
Dees, S. M., 328
de Gregorio, A., 276, 308, 309, 310, 311
de Grijs, E., 131, 134
de Groot, M. H., 543, 544
De Jong, P. J., 304, 305, 313
de la Cruz, C., 269
deLara, E., 590
de las Fuentes, C., 7
DeLeon, P. H., 23, 28, 29, 30
Delgado-Romero, E. A., 103, 104
Delinsky, S., 570
Dellario, D., 224
Delmonico, D. L., 48
DeLuca, J. B., 527
Delworth, U., 342
Demarest, J., 17
Dematatis, A., 289, 292
Demi, A. S., 543
Dempsey, S. B., 177
DeNelsky, G. Y., 28
DeNisi, A. S., 376

Dennin, M. K., 349
Dennis, M., 562, 563
Denzin, N. K., 121
Der-Karabetian, A., 328
DeRubeis, R. J., 28, 251, 252, 257
DeRue, D. S., 467
Derzon J. H., 555, 556
DeShon, R. P., 444, 467
Desmarais, L. B., 376
Dessaulles, A., 288
de Stefano, J., 288
Detert, N. E., 295
Detrie, P. M., 206
Dev, P., 576, 577, 578, 582
DeVellis, R. F., 106
DeVoy, J., 165, 366, 367, 409, 416, 420, 421
Dew, B., 48
Dew, M. A., 538
de Waal, F. B. M., 262
DeWine, D., 366, 367
de Zwaan, M., 571, 572
Diamond, A. K., 8, 15, 121
Diamond, G., 350, 562, 563
Díaz-Lázaro, C., 341
DiCenso, A., 527
DiClemente, C. C., 524, 560
DiClementi, J. D., 201
DiCowden, M. A., 225
Diegelman, N. M., 365, 386
Diemer, M. A., 165, 409, 415, 416, 420, 421
Diemer, R., 275, 289, 290, 293, 310
Diener, E., 88, 164, 165, 382, 383, 464, 466, 470
Dies, R. R., 129
Dik, B. J., 378
Dill, P. L., 523
Dillon, F. R., 106, 198, 204, 206
DiMatteo, M. R., 521
Dimeff, L. A., 557, 558
Dimidjian, S., 251
Dindia, K., 177, 188
Dinehart, J. M., 151, 152
Dings, J. G., 149, 330
Dion, K. K., 432
Dion, K. L., 432
Dipoto, M. C., 409
Dishman, R. K., 525
Distefano, T. M., 199, 200, 201, 203
DiStephano, T. M., 201
Dixit, S., 580
Dixon, D. N., 325
Dixon, G., 260, 463
Doan, B.-T., 146
Dobson, K. S., 251, 253, 254, 262
Dodenhoff, J. T., 346
Dodge, K. A., 591, 592
Doehrman, M. J., 348
Doherty, W. J., 438
Dole, A. A., 307
Dolezal, C., 526
Doll, H. A., 570
Domitrovich, C. E., 513
Donaldson, J., 562, 563
Donaldson, S. I., 555
Donnay, D. A. C., 378, 381, 383, 384, 385, 386
Donnelly, P. C., 126, 128
Donner, S., 27
Donohue, T., 510

Donovan, D., 251
Dorer, D., 570
Dorsey, A. M., 306
Dotterer, A. M., 495
Douce, L. A., 74
Dougherty, T., 429, 436
Douglas, J. M., Jr., 527
Dowdall, G. W., 560
Doyle, A. C., 577, 581, 582
Doyle, C., 40, 513
Doyle, J., 177
Drew, C., 8, 9
Drozd, J. F., 540
Drummond, K., 164, 165
Du, N., 330
Dubbert, P. M., 524, 525
Duffy, R. D., 116
Dufour, M. C., 552
Dugan, K., 396, 401, 402, 403
Dugdale, J., 509
Dulmus, C. N., 598
Dunbar, R. I. M., 593
Duncan, B. L., 235, 263
Duncan, G. J., 159, 485
Duncan, R. D., 592
Dunivin, D. L., 29
Dunkle, J. H., 202
Dunn, J. E., 214
Dunn, M. E., 558
Dunn, T. W., 148, 151, 152
Dunston, K., 159, 160
Duran, G., 106, 146
Duran, M., 141, 149, 153
Durran, A., 333
Dusenbury, L., 555, 556
Duster, T., 16
Duval, S., 304, 305
Duval, T. S., 304, 305

Eagle, J. W., 590
Eagly, A. H., 428
Eastes, S. H., 380
Eastgard, S., 547
Eastman, K., 327
Easton, C. J., 563
Eastwood, J. D., 28, 29
Ebel, B. E., 558
Eberz, A. B., 205
Eccles, J. S., 488, 494, 593
Ecklund-Johnson, E. P., 40
Eddy, K. T., 570
Edelman, M. W., 163
Edelstein, B., 340
Edelstein, S., 288, 295
Edens, L., 452, 453
Edgemon, P., 560
Edington, D. W., 523
Edles, P. A., 126, 128
Edwards, J. K., 303
Edwards, J. R., 468
Edwards, L. M., 93, 94, 98
Edwards, M. E., 562
Edwardson, T. L., 24
Eells, T. D., 341
Egan, J., 184, 187
Egan, S. K., 591
Eggen, D., 179
Eggerth, D. E., 358, 359, 360, 463
Eggett, D., 237, 244
Ehrlich, F. M., 303
Eisenberg, M., 432

Eisenberg, N., 181
Eisenberger, R., 468
Eisman, E. J., 25, 26
Ekeberg, E., 467
Elder, G. H., Jr., 165, 166
Eldredge, K. L., 576
Eldridge, K., 577
Eldridge, N. S., 431
Elfrink, J., 45, 46
Elias, M. J., 513
Elkin, I., 251, 254, 257, 262
Ellenbogen, S., 543
Ellickson, P. L., 555
Elliott, R., 284, 289, 291, 293, 296
Elliott, T., 212, 216, 222, 225, 226
Ellis, A., 306
Ellis, C. A., 449, 454
Ellis, M. V., 307, 308, 310, 313, 345, 348, 349
Ellis, R. J., 313
Ellis, T. E., 540
Ellis-Kalton, C. A., 448, 454
Ellsworth, J. R., 237
Elman, N., 9, 15
Else-Quest, N., 179
Ely, G., 598
Emmelkamp, P. M. G., 251
Engbers, L. H., 525
England, G. W., 464
England, P., 438
Englar-Carlson, M., 186
Ennett, S. T., 554
Enns, C. Z., 185
Epperson, D., 33, 362, 363, 396, 402, 403
Eppstein, D., 576
Epstein, L., 273, 521
Ercolani, A. P., 131, 132, 134
Erez, M., 416, 418, 421
Erickson, C. D., 349
Erickson, M. F., 438
Erickson Cornish, J. A., 8
Ericsson, M., 523
Erikson, E., 432
Eriksson, K., 179
Erkanli, A., 552
Erkut, S., 484, 489, 490, 492
Eron, L., 590
Espelage, D., 589, 590, 592, 593, 599
Esposito, L., 16
Etaugh, C., 180
Ethington, C. A., 306
Eugser, S. L., 277
Euisman, E., 6, 7
Evans, C., 235
Evans, D. R., 518, 529
Evans, L., 176, 177, 330, 331
Evans, W. J., 38, 44
Everly, G. S., Jr., 540
Ewert, T., 226
Eyde, L. D., 129
Eyman, J. R., 539

Fabiano, P., 557
Fabrigar, L. R., 106, 107, 108, 395, 397
Fader, J. S., 559
Fagan, T. J., 29, 40
Fairburn, C. G., 570
Falco, M., 556
Falender, C. A., 8, 342
Falk, D. R., 290

Fang, X., 527
Faragher, J. M., 70
Farah, M. J., 166
Farber, B. A., 348
Farh, J.-l., 420
Farley, G. K., 239
Farmer, H. S., 408, 412
Farmer, M. A., 526
Farrar, J. T., 313
Farrell, A., 38, 510
Farrell, J., 116
Farrell, M. P., 560
Farrington, D. P., 591
Fassinger, R., 178, 194, 195, 196, 197,
    198, 200, 202, 206, 225, 274, 275,
    310, 361, 413, 414, 415, 417, 418,
    452
Fauth, J., 303, 308, 309, 310, 311, 312,
    313, 314
Fazio, R., 500
Feig, J. D., 537
Feinberg, L., 141, 149, 153, 333
Feiner, A. H., 273
Fejfar, M. C., 304
Feldlaufer, H., 593
Fenigstein, A., 304, 305, 313
Fenton, L. R., 562
Fergus, S., 487, 488, 489
Ferguson, A. D., 196
Fernandes, A., 447, 449
Fernandez, S., 492
Ferns, W., 171
Fertig, A., 166
Festinger, L., 578
Fiedler, F. E., 274
Field, A. E., 580, 583
Field, J. E., 59, 61
Fielding, D. M., 521
Fields, H. L., 260
Fields, J. P., 484, 489, 490, 492
Fields, S. A., 233
Finch, A. E., 237, 263, 350
Finch, B. K., 166
Finch, J. F., 107, 108
Fine, M. A., 10
Fineman, A. A., 429, 436
Finer, L. B., 525, 526
Finesinger, J. E., 285
Fink, P., 214
Finkelhor, D., 47, 48, 49
Finkelstein, D. M., 166
Finley, A., 429
Finn, S. E., 129
Finnegan, R. A., 591
Finney, J. W., 562, 563, 564
Finney, S. J., 108, 110
Fiorentine, R., 327, 328
Firth-Cozens, J., 289, 291, 293
Fischer, A. R., 105, 145, 203, 495
Fishbein, M., 527
Fisher, C. B., 3, 4, 14, 16, 41, 42
Fisher, E., 594
Fisher, G. M., 161
Fitzgerald, L. F., 408, 409, 513
Fivush, R., 177
Flay, B. R., 554, 555
Flegal, K. M., 521, 522, 570
Fleming, M., 557, 558
Flerx, V., 596
Fletcher, B., 305
Fletcher, J. K., 431

Flett, G. L., 48
Fleury, J., 524
Flick, P., 573, 575, 576, 578
Flora, J., 594
Flores, L., 362, 363, 364, 413, 417, 444,
    454
Flores, Y., 323
Florin, P., 556
Flouri, E., 167, 415
Flum, H., 366, 409, 415, 420
Folbre, N., 438
Folensbee, L., 571, 572, 573, 576, 577,
    578, 581
Foley, S., 429
Folkman, S., 162, 503
Folsom, B., 446, 450, 456
Folstein, M. F., 215
Foltz, C., 272
Fonagy, P., 597, 598
Fondell, M. M., 526
Fong, M. L., 306
Fong, S. C., 71
Fong-Beyette, M. L., 307
Fontana, A., 327
Forbes, G. B., 178
Forbes, M. R., 29
Ford, D. H., 505
Ford, J., 252, 444, 467
Ford, W. E., 25
Foreyt, J. P., 523
Forman, E. V., 235
Forneris, T., 501, 510
Forrest, L., 7, 9, 202, 588
Forst, M. L., 559
Förster, J., 314
Forsyth, J., 547
Forsyth, L. H., 525
Foshee, V. A., 598
Foster, G. D., 522, 523
Fouad, N., 15, 33, 54, 57, 58, 64, 68,
    152, 153, 159, 357, 359, 362, 367,
    380, 386, 408, 409, 412, 413, 414,
    415, 418, 419, 420, 448
Fouts, G., 177, 178
Fowers, B. J., 94
Fox, D., 54
Fox, M. D. R., 56, 58
Fox, M. K., 580
Fox, M. L., 468
Fox, R. E., 28, 29
Foy, D. W., 252
Frable, D. E. S., 159
Franck, J., 251
Franco, J. L., 190
Frank, D. A., 16
Frank, E., 545
Frank, J. B., 250, 251, 258, 259, 260,
    284
Frank, J. D., 250, 251, 252, 258, 259,
    260, 284
Frank, R. G., 216
Frankel, R. M., 306
Frankforter, T. L., 562
Franko, D. L., 570, 571, 572, 573, 576,
    577, 578, 581
Franks, R. P., 149, 153
Frazier, R., 142
Fredrickson, B. L., 87, 88, 95, 178
Freedom, P. S., 524
Freitas, G. F., 346
French, M. T., 557, 558

Fretter, P. B., 291, 297
Fretz, B., 34, 70, 86, 94, 447, 457, 483,
    501, 571
Freud, A., 276
Freud, S., 268, 271, 273, 285, 310
Fridman, A., 166
Fried, A. L., 41, 42
Friedlander, M. L., 8, 81, 342, 344, 345,
    347, 348
Friedman, J., 182
Friedman, M., 252, 511
Friedman, R. S., 314
Friedman, S., 273, 279
Friedman, S. C., 290, 295
Friedman, S. M., 275
Friedman, T. L., 71
Fries, E., 510, 511, 513
Frieze, I. H., 598
Frisco, M. L., 438
Fritz, J. J., 104
Fritz, S. P., 40
Fritzsche, B. A., 462, 463, 475
Frommelt, S. J., 525
Frone, M. R., 430, 444, 457
Frost, D. M., 61
Froyd, J. D., 234
Froyd, J. E., 234
Frydenberg, M., 214
Fryer, D., 378
Fuertes, J., 123, 125, 126, 128, 129, 146,
    148, 149, 153, 276, 277, 279, 321
Fuhrer, R., 165
Fujino, D. C., 327, 328, 329
Fujita, F., 470
Fukunaga, C., 9, 159, 165, 415, 419
Fukuyama, M. A., 196
Fulkerson, J. A., 571
Fulton, P. R., 314
Fuqua, D. R., 306, 307, 395, 396
Furlong, M. J., 600
Furner, S. E., 214
Furnham, A., 177

Gable, S. L., 87
Gadassi, R., 453
Gaggioli, A., 39
Gaines, K. R. E., 592
Gainor, K., 57, 365, 469, 470, 474
Galantino, M. L., 313
Galassi, J. P., 451, 588, 600
Galinsky, E., 427, 430, 432, 433
Gallagher, L., 165, 366, 369, 409, 415,
    416, 418, 420, 421
Gallaher, P., 593
Gallardo-Cooper, M., 153
Gallo, L. C., 162, 163, 166, 167
Gallop, R., 270
Gallor, S., 225
Galovski, T. E., 182
Galván, N., 103, 104
Gammon, D., 43, 44
Gamst, G., 328
Ganster, D. C., 468
Garb, H. N., 142, 540
Garbarino, J., 590
Garbugino, L., 523
Garcia, J. G., 5
García-Coll, C., 484, 489, 490, 492
Garcia-Vazquez, E., 152
Garcy, P. D., 215
Gardner, D., 560

Garfield, S. L., 249, 255, 256, 259
Garmezy, N., 483, 484, 504
Garner, J. D., 180
Garner, T. I., 161
Garnets, L. D., 196
Garrett, S. B., 559
Garrison, E. G., 16
Garske, J. P., 269
Gartin, B., 213
Gass, M., 505
Gasser, C. E., 381
Gaston, L., 269
Gatchel, R. J., 215
Gati, I., 380, 394, 449, 453
Gatz, M., 509
Gaudiano, B. A., 28
Gaw, A., 330
Gazda, G. M., 34
Gazes, P. C., 214
Ge, X., 165, 166, 492, 493, 495
Gee, D., 417
Geer-Williams, C., 539
Geis, G., 431
Gelfand, L. A., 28
Gelfand, M. J., 416, 418, 421
Gelso, C., 34, 80, 86, 94, 123, 124, 125,
    126, 136, 268, 269, 270, 271, 273,
    274, 275, 276, 277, 278, 279, 284,
    290, 294, 295, 296, 298, 310, 311,
    314, 321, 454, 483
Gendlin, E. T., 286
Gentilello, L. M., 558
Germer, C. K., 311, 312
Gernat, C. A., 347
Geronimus, A. T., 163
Gerrard, M., 492, 493, 494
Gerritsen, C. J., 28, 29
Gerson, K., 429, 430
Gerstein, L., 15, 54, 56, 57, 58, 64, 71,
    72, 73, 74, 76, 78, 80, 93
Gerstel, N., 429
Gervaize, P. A., 288
Getzelman, M. A., 9
Ghosh-Dastidar, B., 555
Giannetta, J. M., 166
Gibbons, C. J., 251, 252, 257
Gibbons, F. X., 304, 305, 492, 493, 494,
    495
Gibbons, M. B. C., 257, 287, 297
Gibbs, J. T., 321, 322
Gibson, D. E., 415
Gibson, W. M., 464
Giger, J., 225
Gilbert, L. A., 427, 430, 431, 432, 433
Gilbert, M. S., 202
Gill, M. M., 270
Gillies, J., 545
Gilroy, P. J., 10
Gim, R. H., 325
Ginnigan, F., 314
Ginzler, J., 490, 491, 559
Giuliano, A., 522
Gizara, S., 9
Gizinski, M. N., 267
Gladis, M., 269
Gladis, A. W., 159
Glantz, M. D., 489
Glascock, J., 177
Glaser, R., 504
Glasgow, N., 313
Glass, C. R., 260
Glass, G. V., 250, 261, 445

Glass, J., 429
Glass, R., 166
Glasscock, J. M. J., 409
Glaze, L. E., 12
Glazer, S., 468
Glenn, N., 437
Glick, M. J., 270, 279
Gloria, A. M., 149
Gloster, C. S., 115, 362, 363, 364
Glueckauf, R. L., 40, 42
Glynn, T., 555
Goates, M. K., 237, 290, 292, 293, 295,
    296
Goates-Jones, M., 292, 293, 296, 297
Goddard, M., 62
Goddard, T. G., 469
Godley, S. H., 562, 563
Godshall, F., 225
Goh, M., 70
Gold, J., 307, 448
Gold, R. G., 233
Goldberg, H., 183
Goldberg, J., 289
Goldberg, L. R., 382
Goldberg, M. E., 164, 167
Goldberg, S. G., 5
Goldfried, M. R., 254, 284, 286, 296
Goldklang, D., 570
Goldman, M. S., 557
Goldsmith, H. H., 590
Goldsmith, J. G., 23
Goldsmith, T. D., 47
Goldstein, A., 491
Goleman, D., 504
Gollan, K., 253
Golombok, S., 177
Golston, S. S., 588
Gomez, M., 274, 275, 285, 287, 288,
    310, 414, 417, 418
Gonzalez, A. Q., 177
Gonzalez, G., 329
Good, G. E., 10, 186, 259
Goode, M. R., 165
Goodman, E., 166
Goodman, J., 225
Goodman, L., 15, 54, 56, 64, 435, 436
Goodnow, J. J., 430
Goodyear, R., 8, 9, 21, 30, 32, 255, 346,
    350, 451
Goran, M. M., 23
Gordon, E. W., 146, 489, 490
Gordon, J. R., 524
Gordon, N. C., 260
Gordon, R., 501
Gore, P. A., 106, 108, 202, 357, 358, 359,
    362, 363, 456
Gore, P., Jr., 45, 49
Gorelick, P. B., 15
Gorely, T., 524
Gorn, G. J., 164, 167
Gorsuch, R. L., 106
Gortmaker, S. L., 580, 583
Gottesman, I. I., 590
Gottfredson, L., 368, 378
Gottfried, A. W., 159
Gottlieb, M., 6, 26, 27
Gottlieb, S. C., 54
Gottman, J., 433
Goudas, M., 510
Gough, H., 89
Gould, D., 505

Gould, M., 547
Gould, R. A., 28
Graczyk, P. A., 513
Graff, H., 273
Graham, S., 28, 589, 590
Granello, D. H., 45, 46
Grant, B. F., 552
Grant, J., 225
Grant, S. K., 54
Gratton, F., 543
Gray, G. V., 23, 237
Gray, H. M., 598
Gray, J., 176, 188, 437
Gray, L., 344, 347, 350
Greeley, A. T., 340
Green, B. L., 171
Green, T. C., 571, 572, 573, 576, 577,
    578, 581
Greenberg, J., 184, 270, 304, 313
Greenberg, L. S., 258, 270, 286, 288,
    296
Greenberg, M., 513
Greenberg, P. E., 214
Greenberg, R. P., 257, 260
Greene, B., 196
Greenfield, D. N., 47
Greenfield, P., 45
Greenhaus, J. H., 398, 400, 426, 430
Greenhouse, J. B., 538
Greenson, R. R., 267, 268, 269, 276
Greenstein, T. N., 431
Greenwald, M., 342
Greeson, J., 313
Grencavage, L. M., 255, 256
Gretchen, D., 125, 126, 128, 129, 143,
    148, 153
Grice, G. R., 44
Grief, J. L., 600
Grieger, I., 59, 150, 151, 341
Griffin, B., 361, 362, 367
Griffin, J. M., 165
Griffin, M., 594
Griffin, P., 201
Griffin-Shelley, E., 48
Griffith, J. D., 562
Griffith, K. H., 200
Griffith, L., 527
Griffiths, M., 38, 48
Grisso, T., 16
Grissom, G., 235
Grizzard, M. B., 308, 309, 310, 312
Groesz, L. M., 573
Gross, L., 599
Grossman, A., 366, 369
Grossman, J. M., 415, 418, 420
Grossman, S. J., 560
Grothaus, L. C., 525
Grzegorek, J. L., 204, 205, 206
Guerra, N., 590
Guerra, R. M., 204
Guilford-Davenport, M., 522
Guillen, A., 362, 448
Guilmino, A., 367
Guo, B., 540
Gupta, R., 360
Gupta, S., 358, 417
Gurin, P., 165
Gushue, G. V., 127, 128, 146, 364
Gustitus, C., 179
Gutgesell, M. E., 560
Gutkin, T. B., 148

Gutman, A. L., 485, 488, 491
Gutman, L. M., 488
Guyatt, G., 233, 527
Guzman, M., 81
Guzzardo, C. R., 8, 346
Gwilliam, L., 359
Gysbers, N. C., 448, 449, 454

Hackett, G., 57, 116, 123, 205, 360, 361, 362, 363, 364, 382, 404, 408, 412, 415, 418, 452, 456, 469, 470, 495
Hackman, J. R., 467
Haddock, C. K., 523
Haddock, S. A., 434
Hage, S., 56, 141, 588
Hagedorn, W. B., 303
Haggerty, K. P., 555
Haggerty, R. J., 501, 553, 571
Hahn, S., 314
Haidt, J., 87
Haines, J., 573
Hale, B .D., 503, 505
Hale, K. K., 307, 308, 310, 313
Haley, J. T., 11, 12
Hall, G. C. N., 322, 326, 332, 333
Hall, H., 503
Hall, M. L., 25
Hall, T., 166, 546
Hallberg, E. T., 289
Halpert, S. C., 205
Ham, J., 262
Ham, M. D., 324
Ham, T., 396, 401, 402, 403
Hamilton, M., 177
Hamilton, S., 236
Hammack, P. L., 432, 433
Hammar, L., 347
Hammen, C., 485, 486, 490
Hammer, A. L., 380
Hammond, M., 362
Hammond, W. R., 548
Handelsman, M. M., 4, 6
Haney, H., 350
Haney, M. R., 12
Hanisch, K. A., 377, 382
Hanna, F. J., 284
Hannan, C., 238, 246
Hannan, P. J., 570, 574
Hannöver, W., 235
Hansen, J. C., 357, 360, 378, 380, 386, 408, 411
Hansen, M., 182, 185, 214
Hansen, N., 68
Hansen, N. B., 235, 263, 350
Hansen, N. D., 5, 142
Hansen, S., 70
Hansen, W. B., 555
Hanson, T. J., 520
Harbach, R. L., 44
Harden, A., 524
Hardin, E., 366
Harding, R. K., 29, 30
Hardison, H. G., 543
Hardtke, K., 294, 296
Hardy, G., 270, 279, 289, 291, 293, 295
Hargrove, B. K., 341, 447
Haritos, C., 177
Harmon, C., 236, 238, 246
Harmon, L., 202, 358, 362, 380, 414, 417

Harmon, S. C., 236, 237, 239, 240, 242, 243
Harp, J. S., 274, 310
Harper, J. M., 331
Harrell, S., 492
Harris, G., 151
Harris, L. C., 122
Harris, Y., 15
Harris-Hodge, E., 448
Harstall, C., 540
Harter, J., 88, 89
Hartung, P., 365, 366, 367, 368, 411
Harvey, A. R., 496
Harvey-Berino, J., 521, 522, 523
Harway, M., 182, 185
Harwood, H., 553
Harwood, T. M., 257, 449
Hatanaka, H., 329
Hatch, A. L., 237
Hatcher, R., 8, 270
Hatfield, D., 236, 246
Hattie, J. A., 106
Hau, J. M., 152
Haubrich, D. J., 526
Hauenstein, A. L., 200
Hauer, A. L., 502
Hautle, I., 43
Hautzinger, M., 304
Haverkamp, B. E., 298
Hawkins, E. J., 36, 236, 238, 239, 240, 242, 243, 247
Hawkins, J., 553, 554, 555, 556
Hayden, G. F., 171
Haydin, B. M., 45, 46
Hayduk, L., 106
Hayes, J., 206, 268, 270, 271, 273, 274, 275, 276, 279, 298, 310, 311, 314, 545
Hayes, S. C., 29
Hays, D., 48
Hays, R. D., 521
Hayward, C., 178, 570, 571, 572
Hayward, M. D., 519, 520
Hazler, R. J., 594
Healy, C. C., 447, 449, 451, 454
Hearon, B., 257
Heatherton, T., 573
Heaton, K., 275, 289
Hebl, M. R., 200
Heck, R., 148, 330
Hecker, D. E., 375
Hedges, L. V., 445
Hedges, M., 39, 40
Hedley, A. A., 522
Hedlund, D. E., 70
Heerey, E., 293
Heesacker, M., 33
Heflin, C. M., 163
Heggestad, E. D., 376, 383, 384
Heiby, E. M., 29, 30
Heil, S. H., 562
Heilbron, D. C., 539
Heim, A., 273
Heim, D., 314
Heine, S. J., 76, 305
Heinemann, A., 225
Heke, I., 510
Helledy, K. I., 15
Heller, A., 55
Heller, D., 465, 466, 469, 470, 471, 472, 473, 474, 476

Hellerstedt, W. L., 525
Helms, J., 15, 54, 55, 56, 58, 64, 105, 122, 124, 321, 326, 329, 347, 413, 435, 436, 493, 494
Hemingway, H., 165
Hendelsman, M. M., 7
Henderson, D. J., 7
Henderson, G., 79
Henderson, K., 511, 593
Hendy, H. M., 179
Henggeler, S. W., 590
Henkel, R. R., 590, 592, 593
Henly, G. A., 412
Hennessy, K., 116
Henry, C., 448
Henry, W. P., 254, 273
Henshaw, S. K., 525, 526
Hensler-McGinnis, N., 225
Henson, J. M., 558
Henson, R. K., 125
Heppner, M., 78, 106, 179, 357, 396, 402, 403, 404, 409, 410, 412, 421, 444, 448, 449, 450, 454
Heppner, P. P., 68, 70, 71, 72, 73, 74, 76, 78, 80, 81, 82, 122, 396, 401, 402, 403, 450, 571
Herbst, J. H., 527
Herman, J. L., 185
Herman, K. C., 10
Hernandez, A., 148
Hernandez, J., 163, 166
Heron, A., 104
Herrett-Skjellum, J., 178
Herrick, S., 225
Hersh, M., 146, 148, 149
Hertlein, K. M., 38
Herzog, D. B., 570
Hesketh, B., 361, 362, 367
Hess, S., 277, 290, 292, 293, 295, 296, 297, 341
Hetherington, E. M., 432
Hewson, C. M., 45
Hezlett, S. A., 377
Hides, L., 538
Hiebert, B., 306
Higgins, C. A., 376, 377, 378, 382
Higgins, S. T., 562, 563
Hignite, M., 132, 134
Hill, C., 275, 277
Hill, C. A., 188, 444, 452
Hill, C. E., 268, 269, 274, 275, 284, 285, 287, 288, 289, 290, 291, 292, 293, 294, 295, 296, 297, 298, 300, 306, 307, 308, 309, 310, 312, 339, 340, 341, 346, 348, 448, 452, 454
Hill, C. L., 142, 143, 144
Hill, E. E., 185
Hill, R. B., 496
Hill, T., 292
Hillard, D., 10, 11
Hillemeier, M. M., 163
Hillhouse, M. P., 327, 328
Hilliard, R. B., 273
Hills, H. I., 150
Hilsenroth, M. J., 270
Hinkelman, J. M., 444, 454
Hitch, J., 357
Ho, M. R., 109, 110
Ho, R. M., 527
Hoagwood, K., 16, 593
Hoberman, H., 304

Hodge, K., 46, 509, 510
Hodge, R. W., 274
Hodges, E. V., 591, 593, 597
Hodges, T., 88, 89
Hoek, H. W., 570
Hofer, S. M., 112, 113, 114, 115
Hoffart, A., 295
Hofferth, S., 182
Hoffman, I. Z., 271
Hoffman, J. H., 560
Hoffman, L. W., 159
Hoffman, M., 150, 275, 289, 308, 309,
   310, 312, 340, 346, 452, 454
Hoffman, S. D., 525
Hoffmann, W. A., 546
Hofheinz, E., 148, 341
Hogan, R., 342, 376, 379, 382, 383
Hoge, C., 511
Hoglend, P., 457
Hoifodt, T. S., 43, 44
Holland, J. E., 393
Holland, J. L., 105, 358, 360, 379, 382,
   384, 387, 392, 393, 396, 463, 467
Holland, N. E., 177
Hollenweger, J., 216
Hollon, S. D., 28, 251
Holloway, E. L., 342, 343, 350
Holloway, J. D., 226
Holloway, P., 123, 124, 125, 126, 136
Holmbeck, G., 233
Holmes, J. G., 313
Holmes, S., 276, 277, 279, 346
Holmgren, K. M., 178
Holt, K., 313
Holt, M., 589, 590, 592, 593
Holtforth, M. G., 270, 285, 286
Hong, G. K., 324
Hong, Y., 527
Honos-Webb, L., 288
Hoover, J. H., 589, 594
Hopkins, N., 358
Hopps, J., 159, 160, 162
Horan, F. P., 235
Horan, J. J., 558
Horn, J. L., 111, 113, 115
Horne, A., 589, 590, 593, 596, 600
Horne, R., 521
Horowitz, L. M., 234
Horowitz, M. J., 234
Horvath, A. O., 257, 269, 270, 454
Hostetler, M., 395
Hotlib, I., 178
Hou, Z.-J., 420
Houck, P. R., 329, 545
House, C. J. C., 202
House, R. M., 342
Howard, D. E., 598
Howard, E., 340
Howard, G. S., 257, 259, 260
Howard, K. A., 594
Howard, K. I., 24, 235
Hoy, K., 511
Hoyle, R. H., 109, 304
Hsieh, C., 165
Hsieh, F. Y., 252
Hu, L., 109, 327, 328, 329
Hu, P. N., 526
Huang, L. N., 142, 321, 322
Huang, Y.-P., 417
Hubble, M. A., 263
Hubert, L., 358, 359, 380, 381, 419

Huessman, L., 590
Huff, D., 180
Huff, J. W., 413, 444
Hughes, D., 452
Hughes, F. M., 180
Hui, C. H., 359
Hulin, C. L., 464
Hull, J. G., 304
Hum, A., 15
Humphreys, L. G., 378
Hunkele, K. A., 563
Hunter, J. A., 560
Hunter, J. E., 116, 377
Hurley, K., 276, 308, 309, 310, 311
Hurst, R., 216, 217, 218, 222
Huston, A. C., 178
Huston, T. L., 431
Hutchins, E., 519
Hwang, K.-K., 417
Hyde, J. S., 176, 385, 386, 426, 430, 431,
   437
Hymer, S., 314
Hynan, M. T., 252, 258

Iacaboni, M., 262
Ilies, R., 462, 464, 465, 466, 469, 470,
   471, 472, 473, 474, 475, 476
Illfelder-Kaye, J., 7
Imber, S., 251
Imel, Z. E., 259, 260, 285
Inagami, S., 166
Inbar-Saban, N., 215
Ingram, K. M., 195, 200, 275, 310, 311,
   350
Ingram, R. E., 304, 305
Inman, A. G., 148, 150, 340, 341, 345,
   347
Innvaer, S., 62
Ironson, G. H., 464
Irvine, D. S., 180
Irving, L. M., 570, 574
Irwin, R., 463
Israel, T., 15, 54, 57, 64, 204, 205, 206,
   207
Ito, K. L., 328
Ivey, A. E., 33, 64, 104, 153, 331, 339
Ivey, A. V., 504

Jacewitz, M. M., 233
Jackson, C. L., 381
Jackson, F. L. C., 519
Jackson, J. S., 493
Jackson, M. L., 121, 122
Jackson, S. C., 570
Jackson, W. T., 226
Jacobi, C., 571, 572
Jacobs, H. E., 215
Jacobs, J. A., 429
Jacobs, T., 303
Jacobson, N. S., 236, 251, 253, 259
Jagers, R., 63
James, D. J., 12
James, E., 289, 291
James, J. B., 437
James, L. C., 528
James, R. M., 451
Jamieson, P., 547
Janowski, K., 98
Jara, C. S., 10
Jasso, R., 122
Jaya, A., 326

Jayaratne, T. E., 165
Jeanneret, P. R., 376
Jenal, S. T., 147
Jenkins, C. D., 517, 518
Jennings, L., 303
Jensen, M., 153
Jernigan, M., 413
Jerry, P., 38, 43
Jessell, J. C., 454
Jobes, D. A., 539, 540, 541, 542, 547
Joe, G. W., 328
Joffe, P., 536, 537
Johansson, C. B., 380
John, D. R., 164
Johns, M., 184
Johnson, A. J., 346
Johnson, A. W., 306, 307
Johnson, B. T., 527
Johnson, C. L., 521, 522
Johnson, D., 23, 125, 127, 128, 570
Johnson, E. C., 467, 468, 470
Johnson, J., 237, 413, 414, 415, 418, 452
Johnson, J. G., 570
Johnson, J. L., 489, 496, 521
Johnson, K., 557, 558
Johnson, P. J., 162
Johnson, R. G., 327
Johnson, R. T., 29
Johnson, R. W., 376, 378, 386
Johnson, W. B., 4, 9
Johnson-Jennings, M. D., 259, 260, 285
Johnston, L. C., 10, 11
Johnston, L. D., 552, 559
Joiner, T., 88, 541, 542, 573
Joinson, A., 46
Jolkovski, M. P., 275, 310
Jome, L. M., 105, 145, 413
Jones, A., 273, 279, 290, 295
Jones, H., 577, 582
Jones, J., 141, 153, 163
Jones, L. K., 394
Jones, N., 152
Jones, S. M., 177
Jones, W. P., 44
Jordan, D., 303
Jordan, J. R., 543
Jordan, J. V., 177, 181
Jöreskog, K., 108, 113
Juby, H. L., 448
Judge, A., 275, 308, 309, 310, 312, 340,
   376, 377, 378, 381, 382, 462, 464,
   465, 466, 471, 472, 474, 475
Jung, C. G., 124
Juntunen, C., 367, 414, 417, 444
Juster, R. P., 539
Juvonen, J., 589, 590

Kabat-Zinn, J., 313
Kadden, R., 251
Kagan, J., 164
Kagan, N., 339, 342
Kagawa-Singer, M., 325
Kahn, J., 106, 363, 364
Kahneman, D., 464
Kahnweiler, W. M., 559
Kakkad, D., 64
Kakouros, A., 285, 286
Kalichman, S., 48, 521, 525, 526, 527
Kalis, D., 142
Kallen, R. W., 178
Kamb, M. L., 527

Kammann, R., 463
Kamoie, B., 25
Kampa-Kokesh, S., 199, 200, 201, 203
Kandel, D. B., 592
Kandell, J. J., 47
Kane, E. W., 431
Kanitz, B., 152, 153, 285, 287, 288
Kanz, J. E., 38, 41, 42, 43, 44
Kaplan, A. G., 177, 181
Kaplan, H., 483, 485, 487
Kaplan, K., 552
Kaplan, R. M., 215
Kaplan, S. A., 360, 365, 465
Kapusta, N.D., 546
Karasek, R., 165
Kasen, S., 570
Kaslow, N. J., 7, 8, 152, 154
Kasper, L., 290
Kass, S. J., 49
Kasser, T., 164
Kasson, D., 116
Kato, T., 526
Katz, I. M., 305
Katz, J., 598
Kavanagh, J., 524
Kawachi, I., 166
Kay, G. G., 129
Kaye, N., 22
Kazarian, S. S., 518, 529
Kearney, L., 433
Keck, P. E., 47
Keefe, R. H., 25
Keel, P. K., 570
Keeler, G., 161, 162, 552
Keijser, J., 543, 544
Keil, J. E., 214
Keillor, R. M., 558
Kellem, I. S., 341
Kellems, I. S., 269
Keller, A., 560
Keller, B. K., 415
Keller, H. E., 38, 46
Keller, M., 164, 165
Kelley, D., 492
Kelley, F., 276, 277, 279, 290
Kelloway, E. K., 457
Kelly, E., 177
Kelly, J. A., 521, 525, 526, 527
Kelly, J. G., 500
Kelly, K. R., 393, 394, 395, 396, 400,
 403
Kelsey, J. L., 159
Kendall, L. M., 464
Kendall, P., 233, 237, 590
Kenna, A., 366, 367
Kennedy, B. P., 166
Kennedy, J. L., 523
Kennedy, S. H., 28
Kenny, M. E., 366, 367, 369, 415, 418,
 420, 452, 600
Kerewsky, S. D., 9
Kerr, B. A., 40
Kerr, D. L., 45, 46
Kerr, S. K., 204
Kessler, K. A., 27
Kessler, R. C., 214, 492
Ketterson, T. U., 42
Kettmenn, J. J., 11, 12
Ketz, K., 206
Ketzenberger, K., 202
Khosla, U. M., 47

Kidd, S. A., 16, 226
Kiesler, D., 274, 310
Kiger, G., 434
Killen, J. D., 570
Kilmer, J. R., 557, 559
Kilpatrick, D. G., 552
Kim, B. S. K., 106, 148, 152, 324, 329,
 455, 456
Kim, D., 251
Kim, E. Y. K., 331
Kim, H., 324
Kim, J., 324, 495
Kim, U., 79, 417
Kimerling, R., 179
Kimmel, M. S., 599
Kindaichi, M. M., 141, 418
King, A. C., 524, 525
King, D., 350
King, L., 88
King, R., 350, 538
Kirsch, I., 252, 258, 260
Kirschner, T., 452, 454
Kirshner, B., 233
Kiselica, M., 59, 186
Kitaoka, S. K., 148, 149
Kitchener, K. S., 3, 5, 14
Kivlahan, D. R., 557, 558
Kivlighan, D., 273, 279, 290
Kivlighan, D., Jr., 80
Kivlighan, D. M., 278, 279, 288, 289,
 290, 292, 294, 295
Kivlighan, D. M., Jr., 271, 272
Kjaersgaard, K. S., 180
Kleespies, P., 547
Klehe, U.-C., 367
Kleiber, D., 503
Kleiman, T., 453
Klein, C. T., 527
Klein, M. H., 293
Kleiner, A. J., 256, 257
Kleinman, A., 259
Klevansky, R., 7
Kline, F., 327
Kline, R. B., 108, 109
Kline, W. B., 306
Klitzke, M. J., 44
Klonoff, E. A., 492
Kloska, D. D., 559
Knaevelsrud, C., 544, 545
Knapp, S., 3, 5, 6, 13, 14, 26
Knickmeyer, S., 547
Knott, E. C., 539
Knowlton, B. J., 262
Knox, K. L., 537
Knox, S., 146, 277, 292, 293, 296, 297,
 341, 348
Kober, P. C., 16
Kochenderfer, B. J., 590
Kocsis, J. H., 259
Koehly, L. M., 447, 448
Koerner, K., 253
Koestner, R., 177
Koffman, R., 511
Kohatsu, E. L., 417
Kohlenberg, R. J., 251
Kohn-Wood, L. P., 492, 493, 494
Kohout, J., 25, 26, 151
Kokaly, M. L., 415
Kolchakian, M. R., 269, 290
Kolden, G. C., 293
Koltko-Rivera, M., 123

Komarraju, M., 420
Komro K. A., 556
Koocher, G. P., 5, 16, 38, 42
Kopecky, G., 182, 186
Kordy, H., 235, 237
Kosma, M., 525
Koss, M. P., 179, 182
Kostanjsek, N., 215, 217, 218, 226
Kosterman, R., 555
Kotler, R. M., 178
Kouneski, E. F., 438
Kovac, S. H., 545
Koweleski-Jones, L., 526
Kozlowski, J. M., 346
Kozol, J., 419
Kraemer, H. C., 570, 571, 572
Krahé, B., 179
Kral, M. J., 16, 226
Kramer, A. F., 314
Kramer, T., 328
Krane, N. E. R., 411
Kraus, D. R., 235
Krauskopf, C., 10
Krausz, M., 394
Kraut, R., 38, 46
Kravitz, R. L., 521
Krengel, M., 307, 308, 310, 313,
 349
Kreutzer, J. C., 104
Krieg, F. J., 22
Krieger, K. M., 43
Krieshok, T. S., 86, 94
Kristof-Brown, A. L., 467, 468,
 470
Kruczek, T., 71, 73, 81
Kruger, J., 245
Krumboltz, J. D., 40, 49
Krupnick, J., 171
Kruskal, J. B., 384
Kubany, E. S., 185
Kubzansky, L. D., 166
Kuffel, S. W., 598
Kuh, D., 178
Kumanyika, S., 522
Kumkale, G. T., 527
Kumpfer, K. L., 556
Kumpfer, L. K., 484
Kuncel, N. R., 377
Kung, W. W. M., 330, 331
Kuo, M., 560
Kuo, P. Y., 143
Kuppermann, M., 159, 168
Kurdek, L., 431
Kurpius, D. J., 306, 307
Kurtness, J., 15
Kurylo, M., 216
Kusel, S. J., 589
Kwok, O., 111, 112
Kypri, K., 558

LaBrie, R. A., 49
Lachman, M. E., 165
LaCost, H. A., 413, 444
Ladany, N., 8, 145, 148, 149, 150, 153,
 341, 342, 344, 345, 346, 347, 348,
 349, 350
Ladd, G. W., 590
LaFromboise, T. C., 148
Lam, R. W., 28
Lamb, M. E., 182
Lambert, L. S., 468

Lambert, M. J., 233, 234, 235, 236, 237, 238, 239, 240, 242, 243, 244, 246, 247, 255, 256, 263, 346, 350, 444, 454
Lambert, W., 104, 350
Lance, C. E., 112, 113, 114, 115
Lando, H. A., 525
Landrine, H., 492
Landsberg, G., 25
Lane, I. M., 462, 466
Langley, J. D., 558
Lapan, R., 365, 368, 396, 402, 403
LaPlante, D. A., 49
Larimer, M., 553, 557, 558, 559, 560, 564
Lark, J. S., 195, 204
La Roche, M. J., 323
Larson, L. M., 360, 363, 381, 382, 386, 396, 401, 402, 403
Lasoff, D. L., 445, 446, 447, 449, 453, 454, 456
Latta, R., 15, 54, 56, 64, 435, 436
Latts, M., 274, 275, 310
Lau, A. S. L., 325, 328, 329
Lau, M., 312
Laub, J. J., 490, 491
Laurent, D., 45
Lavallee, L. F., 305
Lavori, W., 252
Law, K. S., 420
Lazarus, A. A., 256
Le, T. N., 526
Leach, C., 235
Leahy, M., 215
Leal-Muniz, V., 415, 418
Leary, G. E., 151
Lease, S. H., 413
Lee, C. M., 557
Lee, D.-G., 78
Lee, D. Y., 306
Lee, J. E., 560
Lee, R., 106, 146
Lee, S., 38, 46, 417
Lee, S. H., 78, 80, 320, 326, 329, 331, 332, 333
Lee, S. M., 524
Lee, W. C., 393, 394, 395, 396, 400, 403
Lee, Y., 431
Leenaars, A. A., 540, 541, 544
Leeper, J. D., 538
Lees, J. L., 305
Lefley, H. P., 330, 331
Lehman, D. R., 76, 305
Lehn, L., 147
Lehr, R., 43
Lehrman-Waterman, D., 8, 345, 346, 349
Leibert, T., 39, 40, 45
Leichliter, J. S., 560
Leigh, W. A., 180
Leitner, L. M., 540, 541
Lent, R., 57, 73, 74, 93, 106, 115, 116, 137, 338, 339, 340, 341, 357, 360, 361, 362, 363, 364, 365, 369, 382, 404, 412, 413, 415, 418, 452, 456, 463, 464, 469, 470, 472, 473, 474, 483, 495
Lenz, J. G., 400
Leon, D. T., 49
Leonardi, M., 214, 215, 216, 217, 218
Leone, L., 131, 132, 134

Leong, F., 71, 72, 73, 76, 78, 80, 82, 94, 105, 123, 320, 321, 324, 325, 326, 328, 329, 331, 332, 333, 366, 417, 420
Lerner, J., 307
Lerner, M. J., 63
Lerner, R., 57, 409, 410
Lesh, T., 313
Leso, J. F., 451
Lesser, J., 577, 582
Lester, D., 538, 539
Leung, M. C., 592, 593
Leung, P., 212, 224, 226
Leung, S. A., 71, 73, 420
Leuwerke, W. C., 45, 49, 362
Lev, A. I., 196
Levant, R. F., 176, 180, 182, 186, 187
Leventhal, G., 8
Leventhal, H., 520
Levine, A., 177
Levine, J. A., 429
Levine, J. D., 260
Levine, M. P., 305, 313, 570, 571, 574, 582
Levinson, D. J., 379
Levitan, R. D., 523
Levitt, H., 292
Levy, A., 179, 182
Levy, D., 519
Lew, S., 122
Lewinsohn, P. M., 304, 572
Lewis, B. A., 525
Lewis, C., 126, 128
Lewis, J., 54, 448, 454
Lewis, L. S., 71
Lewis, M. A., 557, 558
Lewis, M. D., 54
Lewis, M. M., 539, 541
Lewis, M. W., 504
Lewis, R. L., 492, 493, 494
Li, L., 106, 142, 143, 144, 455, 456
Liang, B., 15, 54, 56, 64, 435, 436
Liang, C. T. H., 106, 324, 329, 455
Liao, Q., 142
Liberatos, P., 159
Liberman, R. P., 215
Lichstein, K. L., 543
Lichtenberg, J., 21, 30, 32, 33, 86, 94, 147, 154, 255, 368, 445
Lickona, T., 504
Lidderdale, M. A., 127, 128, 195, 199, 201, 202, 203
Liddle, B. J., 200
Liddle, H. A., 350
Liddon, N., 525, 526, 527
Lieberman, L., 519
Lieberman, M. A., 246
Lieberman, M. D., 262
Lightsey, R., 285, 287, 288
Ligiero, D., 275, 279, 314
Lilienfeld, S. O., 16
Lilly, R. L., 106, 146
Lim, B. K., 324
Lim, J., 104
Lim, L., 305
Lim, S., 324, 468
Limber, S., 590, 593, 594, 595, 596
Lin, E., 557, 558
Lin, K., 330, 492
Lin, V., 62
Lin, Y. J., 325

Lincoln, Y. S., 121
Lindeman, D. L., 452
Lindley, L. D., 362, 364, 386
Lindsey, E. W., 176
Linehan, M. M., 570
Link, B. G., 159
Linn, S. G., 413, 414, 415, 418, 452
Lippa, R., 386
Lipsey, M. W., 555, 556
Lisak, D., 181
Lish, J. D., 24
Liss, H. J., 40
Liss, M., 29
Litt, I. F., 178
Little, M., 10
Little, T. D., 110, 598
Littleton, H., 179
Litts, D. A., 537, 538
Liu, W., 103, 106, 123, 124, 125, 126, 136, 144, 159, 160, 161, 162, 163, 164, 166, 167, 168
Livne-Snir, S., 272
Llewelyn, S. P., 289, 291, 293, 295
Lobel, S. A., 429
Lobell, L. K., 290, 293
Locke, D. C., 141, 153
Locke, E. A., 462, 463, 464, 471, 472
Lockwood, P., 179
Lofquist, L., 212, 360, 378, 462, 463, 464
Loiselle, J., 180
Lollar, D., 216
Lombardo, T. W., 44
Lonborg, S. D., 200
London, P., 256
London, R., 557, 558
Lone, R., 125, 127, 128
Long, J., 592
Long, L., 380
Longabaugh, R., 38, 558
Longshore, D. L., 555
Lonner, W., 73, 76, 104
Lonsdale, C., 46
Loomis, J. S., 42
Lopez, S., 86, 87, 88, 89, 90, 91, 93, 94, 95, 98, 104, 333, 521
Lorenz, F. O., 165, 166
Lostutter, T. W., 553
Lott, B., 159
Low, K. G., 577, 582
Low, K. S. D., 378, 379
Lowe, S. M., 326
Lu, F. G., 330
Lubinski, D., 378, 379, 384, 385, 386, 392
Luborsky, L., 239, 253, 269, 272, 273, 291, 295, 297
Lucas, D., 314
Lucas, M. S., 396, 401, 402, 403, 448
Lucas, R. E., 464, 466
Luce, K. H., 571, 572, 576, 577, 580, 581, 582
Lucidi, F., 131, 132, 134
Lucock, M., 235
Lueger, R. J., 235
Luijters, K., 132, 135
Lumry, A., 304
Luna, J., 414, 417, 418
Lunnen, K. M., 237, 251
Luscher, K. A., 29
Lussier, C., 593

Lussier, J. P., 562
Lussier, Y., 431
Lusterman, D.-D., 176, 184, 185, 186, 187, 188
Luthar, S. S., 484, 485, 486, 487, 488, 489, 490, 491, 492, 496
Lutz, W., 235, 237, 245
Lux, J. B., 224
Luzzo, D., 200, 357, 386, 414
Lykken, D., 466, 469, 475
Lyles, J. S., 306
Lynch, F., 23
Lyons, H., 152, 200, 202, 361, 362, 363
Lyons, J. S., 24
Lyubomirsky, S., 87, 88, 313

MacCallum, R. C., 106, 107, 108, 109, 110, 395, 397
Maccoby, E. E., 176, 181, 432
MacConnell, J., 11, 12
Mac Iver, D., 593
Mackenbach, J. P., 162, 167
MacKinnon, D. P., 555
MacLean, T. L., 201
MacPhee, D., 104
MacQueen, G., 28
Madden, R., 226
Madsen, K. C., 593
Madson, M. B., 346
Maercker, A., 544, 545
Maes, S., 444
Magaletta, P. R., 40
Maggi, G., 257
Magnuson, S., 350
Magnusson, E., 433, 438
Magrath, C. P., 82
Maguire, M., 313
Magyar-Moe, J., 86, 93, 94, 98
Mahalik, J. R., 185, 186
Mahler, M., 599
Mahmood, A., 163
Mahrer, A., 287, 288, 289
Maier, G. W., 469, 470
Mainelli, D., 571, 572, 573, 576, 577, 578, 581
Maisto, S. A., 558
Major, B., 176, 180
Majors, R., 277
Mak, T., 177
Malcuit, G., 177
Maldonado, L. E., 290
Malik, M., 257, 449
Mallen, M. J., 24, 38, 39, 40, 41, 42
Mallett, K. A., 557
Mallinckrodt, B., 115, 270
Malta, L. S., 182
Maltzman, I. M., 251
Manese, J. E., 151
Manhal-Baugus, M., 39, 41
Mann, C. H., 287
Mann, J. H., 287
Mann, T., 519
Manolis, C., 167
Mantovani, F., 39
Manwell, L. B., 557, 558
Maples, M. R., 538, 539, 540, 547
Maramba, G. G., 328
Marcello, R. J., 560
Marchena, E., 433
Marci, C. D., 262
Marcos, L. R., 324

Marcus, B. H., 524, 525
Marecek, J., 429
Marek, P., 164, 165
Margavio, G. W., 132, 134
Margavio, T., 132, 134
Margison, F., 235
Margolis, J., 573, 575, 576, 578
Marin, G., 324
Maris, R. W., 535, 538, 539, 541
Markham, H., 433
Markin, R., 277
Markowitz, J. C., 259
Marlatt, G. A., 251, 524, 553, 557, 558, 559
Marmarosh, C., 276, 277, 279
Marmor, J., 259
Marmot, M., 165
Marrs-Garcia, A., 237
Marsella, A. J., 70, 71, 73, 76
Marsh, H. W., 109
Marshall, A., 306
Marshall, D. G., 554, 555, 556
Marshall, K., 165, 415, 416
Marshall, M., 142
Marshall, N. L., 430
Marshall, S. J., 524
Martens, A., 184
Martens, M. P., 106, 108, 109, 110
Marti, C. N., 523, 574
Martin, D. J., 269
Martin, D. W., 306
Martin, G. A., 451
Martin, J., 289, 306
Martin, L., 522
Martin, P. P., 492, 493, 494
Martin, R., 520, 577, 582
Martin, W., 306, 396, 400, 401, 402, 403
Martin-Baró, I., 55
Martinovich Z., 235
Martinuzzi, A., 216
Mascher, J., 413
Maschino, P., 103, 104
Maslow, A., 86
Mason, A., 599
Massel, H. K., 215
Masten, A. S., 483, 484, 485, 486, 487, 488, 489, 490, 491
Masters, K. S., 237
Matheson, G., 438
Mathy, R. M., 45, 46, 48
Maton, K. I., 151
Matthews, C., 202
Matthews, G., 305
Matthews, K. A., 162, 163, 166, 167
Matthews, L., 326
Mattison, M., 303
Matusek, J. A., 579
Mau, W., 447, 449
Mauery, D. R., 25
Maugherman, A. S., 539
Max, W., 214
Maxwell, S. E., 106, 108, 109, 110
Mayberg, H. S., 260
Mayer, T. G., 215
Mayers, R. E., 340
Mayo, N. E., 225
Mays, M., 23
Mays, V. M., 205
Mazotti, L., 578
Mazzaferro, K. E., 526
McArdle, J. J., 111, 113

McArthur, D. B., 523
McAuliffe, G. J., 396, 400, 401, 402, 403
McBride, C. M., 525
McCabe, S. E., 559
McCaffrey, D. F., 555
McCarn, S. R., 196, 197
McCartney, K., 62
McClanahan, M., 204, 205, 206, 274, 310
McClelland, D., 178
McClure, B. A., 274
McCormick, E. J., 376
McCracken, J. E., 274, 310
McCrady, B. S., 563
McCrae, R. R., 130, 360, 466
McCrea, L. G., 32, 33, 59
McCready, T., 289, 292
McCrone, P., 215
McCubbin, J. A., 525
McCullough, L., 38
McDaniel, M. A., 379
McDavis, R. J., 7, 61, 64, 141
McDonagh, A., 252
McDonald, P. A., 350
McDonald, R. P., 109, 110
McDonald, T., 523
McDowell, M. A., 522
McElroy, S. L., 47
McFadyen-Ketchum, S. A., 591
McFall, R. M., 27, 30
McFarlin, D. B., 430
McGee, R. O., 558
McGill, J., 225
McGinnies, E., 305
McGowan, J., 212
McGrath, R. E., 574
McGurk, D., 511
McHale, S. M., 495
McHugo, G., 252
McIntosh, J., 543, 545
McIntyre, R., 28
McLacken, J., 559
McLaren, L., 178
McLaughlin, C. J., 38
McLean, S., 346
McLeod, K. C., 179
McLoyd, V., 164, 165, 492
McMain, S., 269
McMullin, D., 179
McNair, L. D., 29, 558
McNally, C. J., 32, 33, 59
McNatt, P. S., 527
McNeill, B., 204, 342
McPartland, E., 363, 392, 393, 403, 404, 446, 455, 456, 457, 476
McPherson, R., 15, 21, 30, 32
McRae, R. R., 400
McWhirter, B. T., 204
McWhirter, E., 54, 56, 57, 165, 362, 363, 364, 367, 368, 414, 415, 418, 455
McWhirter, J. J., 70, 72, 73, 76
McWilliams, N., 27, 285
Mead, N. L., 165
Meara, N. M., 3, 9, 454
Mearns, J., 9
Mecham, R. C., 376
Mednick, M. T., 437
Medved, W., 526
Meehl, P. E., 246, 539
Meichenbaum, D., 306, 521

Meier, S. T., 25, 26
Meilman, P. W., 546, 559, 560
Meir, E. I., 358, 359, 421
Mejia, B., 414, 417, 418
Melincoff, D., 341, 345, 348
Meller, P. J., 142
Mellor-Clark, J., 235
Melnick, M. J., 560
Melton, G. B., 590, 596
Menaghan, E. G., 526
Menaker, E., 276
Menchola, H., 527
Menchola, M., 561, 563
Mendelsohn-Kacanski, J., 130, 131, 132, 134, 136
Mendoza, D. W., 152, 153
Meneades, L. M., 214
Mercer, S. O., 180
Meredith, W., 111, 112, 115
Merluzzi, T. V., 305
Mermis, B. J., 225
Messer, S., 285, 511
Meston, C. M., 526
Metzler, A. E., 571
Meulman, J., 380
Meyer, A., 510, 513
Meyer, G. J., 129, 574
Meyer, M., 306
Meyerson, D. E., 428
Meza, M., 341
Michaels, W. B., 428
Michaelson, S. D., 214, 215, 226
Michalak, E. E., 46
Michel, K., 540, 541
Michell, A. L., 527
Mickelson, K. D., 214, 492
Mickelson, W. T., 590
Midgley, C., 593
Mihalic, S., 590, 594, 595
Milbrath, C., 234
Milburn, L., 448
Mileham, B. L. A., 48
Miles, D., 590
Miles, M. S., 543
Miles, T. P., 519, 520
Milholland, K., 38
Milhouse, V. H., 79
Milkie, M. A., 430, 431, 438
Miller, B. A., 197
Miller, D. T., 63
Miller, H. L., 538
Miller, J. B., 177, 181
Miller, J. Y., 553, 554, 555
Miller, K., 349
Miller, K. E., 560
Miller, K. L., 38, 44
Miller, L., 412
Miller, M., 10, 104, 106, 110, 116, 392, 404, 452, 453
Miller, P. A., 181
Miller, S. A., 528, 529
Miller, S. D., 235, 263
Miller, S. M., 38, 44
Miller, T. I., 445
Miller, W. R., 251, 561, 562, 564
Millet, K., 545
Millsap, R. E., 111, 112
Milner, J. S., 233
Minami, T., 252, 253, 260
Mindes, E. J., 195
Mintz, J., 215

Mintz, L. B., 571, 572, 573, 576, 577, 578, 581
Minugh, A. P., 558
Mio, J. S., 152
Miranda, J., 147, 171
Mischel, W., 382
Mislowack, A., 146, 148, 149
Mislowack, C., 277
Mitchell, K. J., 47, 48, 49
Mitchell, S., 270, 274
Mitchell, T. R., 467, 469
Miville, M. L., 123, 124, 125, 126, 127, 128, 129, 136, 152
Mize, J., 176
Mize, S. J., 526
Mobley, M., 115, 144, 145, 147, 149, 153, 202
Modai, I., 215
Moffitt, T. E., 376, 382, 476, 593
Mohler, C. J., 386
Mohr, J., 125, 126, 128, 129, 198, 204, 275, 277, 447
Mokuau, N., 325
Mol, S., 132, 134, 135
Moldawsky, S., 26
Moles, A., 523
Molina, L. E., 151
Molina-Cabrillana, J., 523
Molinaro, M., 8, 345, 346, 349
Möller, I., 179
Molnar-Szakacs, I., 262
Mondin, G. W., 252, 261
Mongeon, J. A., 562
Monti, P., 251, 558
Montoya, J. A., 148, 151, 152
Montoya-Alonso, J. A., 523
Moody, J. C., 593
Moody, M., 252, 261
Moore, C., 177
Moore, T. C., 552
Moos, R. H., 503, 562, 563, 564
Mor, N., 304, 313
Moradi, B., 495
Moran, E., 262
Mordhorst, M. J., 147
Moreland, K. L., 129
Moreno, M. V., 149, 153
Morgan, K. S., 194
Morgan, R. D., 164, 165
Morgan, R. W., 291, 295
Morgan, S. P., 311
Morin, P. M., 414, 417
Mornitz, M., 262
Morran, D. K., 306, 307
Morray, E., 38, 42
Morrill, W. H., 394
Morrison, G. M., 594, 600
Morrissey-Kane, E., 556
Morrow, S. L., 76, 123, 202, 207
Morton, J. J., 236
Moses, D., 132, 134
Moskowitz, J. T., 503
Mott, F. L., 526
Motto, J. R., 539
Mount, M. K., 360, 382, 385, 465, 474
Mouttapa, M., 593
Mrazek, P. J., 501, 553, 571
Muchinsky, P. M., 396, 401, 402
Mudrack, P. E., 164
Mueser, K., 252
Muglia, P., 523

Muhlbauer, V., 180
Mulato, M. S., 519
Mulholland, A. M., 572
Mullen, B., 305
Multon, K., 272, 278, 288, 289, 292, 295, 362, 396, 402, 403, 448, 449, 454
Mundt, M. P., 557, 558
Munley, P. H., 127, 128
Munoz, R. F., 329, 571
Munson, J., 40, 45
Muran, J. C., 269, 270, 312, 313, 314
Muraven, M., 314
Murdey, I., 524
Murdick, N., 213
Murdock, N., 21, 30, 32, 33
Murphy, J. A., 588, 600
Murphy, J. W., 16
Murphy, K., 366, 367
Murphy, L. R., 413
Murphy, M., 10
Murra, J., 10
Murray, B., 593
Murray, D. M., 555
Murray, P., 269, 526
Murry, V., 492, 493, 495
Muse-Burke, J. L., 346, 349
Mussell, M. P., 571
Mustillo, S., 552
Muthén, B., 111, 112, 113, 114
Myers, D., 63, 279
Myers, J. E., 59
Myers, M., 558
Myers, T., 526

Nackel, J. G., 23
Nadler, W. P., 287, 288, 289
Nagel, D. P., 452
Nagel, J., 104
Nakamura, R., 147
Nakayama, E. Y., 269
Nanda, S., 559
Nansel, T. R., 589, 590, 593
Narducci, J., 270
Nasby, W., 305
Nash, J. M., 346
Nath, S. R., 237
Nation, M., 556, 590
Nauta, M., 202, 360, 362, 363, 364, 415
Navarro, R., 362, 363, 364, 413
Naylor, A. H., 560
Neavins, T. M., 563
Neckerman, H. J., 592
Necowitz, L. B., 109, 110
Neeleman, J., 543, 544
Neft, N., 177
Neighbors, C., 553, 557, 558, 560
Neighnors, H. W., 493
Neill, T. K., 350
Neimeyer, G. J., 8, 15, 31, 121, 146, 451
Neimeyer, R. A., 253, 543, 545
Nelson, D. A., 590
Nelson, G., 54, 55
Nelson, M., 8, 342, 344, 345, 347
Nelson, P., 6, 7, 89
Nelson, T. F., 560
Nemeroff, C. B., 251
Nepomuceno, C. A., 151
Nerdrum, P., 339, 340

Nerison, R. M., 194
Ness, D. E., 543
Ness, R. B., 526
Netz, Y., 524
Neukrug, E. S., 44
Neulinger, J., 544
Neumark-Sztainer, D., 570, 571, 572, 573, 574, 582, 584
Neville, H. A., 103, 106, 116, 144, 145, 146, 147, 153, 179
Nevitt, J., 106
Newcomb, A. F., 592, 593
Newcomb, M. D., 505
Newman, D. A., 590, 596
Newman, F. L., 234
Newman, J. L., 306, 307, 395, 396
Newman, R., 24, 29, 593
Newman-Carlson, D., 521, 596
Newnes, C., 289, 295
Ng, K., 81
Ng, P., 179
Nguyen, L., 142
Nich, C., 562, 563
Nicholas, J. P., 466, 469, 472
Nicholson, A. C., 165
Nicholson, R., 513
Nielsen, M. R., 431, 433, 434
Nielsen, S. L., 36, 236, 238, 239, 240, 242, 243, 244, 246, 247
Niles, S. G., 449, 452, 454
Nilsson, J., 60, 202, 350
Nirenberg, T. D., 558
Nishikawa-Lee, S., 325
Niss, N. M., 543
Nissenfeld, M., 307
Nitschke, J. B., 260
Noble, S., 257, 449
Nobles, W. W., 321
Nock, S. L., 431, 432
Noh, E. R., 104
Noldus, L. P., 44
Nolen-Hoeksema, S., 313
Noonan, B. M., 225
Norcross, J., 11, 39, 40, 249, 255, 256, 267, 303, 346
Norem, K., 350
Norfleet, M. A., 29
Norman, P. A., 570
Norsworthy, K. L., 72, 76
Nota, L., 73, 74, 362, 363, 364, 369
Notarius, C., 433
Notaro, P. C., 488
Novakovic, A., 448
Novotny, C. M., 250
Novy, P. L., 563
Nowak, C. A., 503
Nowak, T. M., 142, 144
Nowinski, J., 251
Nozick, R., 55
Nugent, F. A., 70
Null, U., 127, 128
Nunez, J., 322, 326, 332, 333
Nunnaly, J. C., 233
Nurcombe, B., 538
Nurmi, J., 505
Nutt, D. J., 28
Nutt, L., 348
Nutt, R. L., 72, 176, 179, 184, 185, 186, 187, 188
Nutter, K. J., 394
Nutt-Williams, E., 275, 307, 312

Nuvayestewa, L., 522

Oakes, J. M., 159, 160
Oakman, J. M., 38
O'Brien, C. P., 553
O'Brien, K., 57, 276, 308, 309, 310, 311, 339, 361
O'Brien, K. M., 180, 341, 348, 363, 364, 404, 409, 410, 412, 417, 421, 444, 447, 452, 454
O'Brien, K. S., 560
O'Brien, M. E., 304
O'Byne, K. K., 30
O'Byrne, K. K., 21, 32, 33, 59
O'Carroll, P. W., 547
Ochshorn, P., 554, 555, 556
O'Conner, B. P., 107
O'Connor, L. E., 288, 295
O'Connor, M. E., 570
O'Connor, R., 314
O'Connor Pennuto, T., 6
O'Donnell, J., 555
O'Donovan, C., 28
O'Farrell, M. K., 287, 291
Offord, D. R., 553, 554
Ogden, C. L., 521, 522, 570
Ogles, B. M., 233, 235, 237, 243, 244, 246, 251, 255, 346, 454
O'Grady, K. E., 306
Oh, E., 179
O'Halloran, S. M., 572
O'Hearn, T. C., 509
Ojeda, L., 417
Öjehagen, A., 251
Okawa, Y., 216
Okazaki, S., 329
Okiishi, J. C., 236, 244
Okin, S. M., 429, 438
Oldehinkel, T., 215
Oldham, G. R., 467
Olivares, S., 27
Oliver, L. W., 444, 445, 449, 453, 454, 457
Oliver, M. N. I., 9, 10
Oliver, R., 589
Oliver, S., 524
Olkin, I., 445
Olkin, R., 216, 224, 226
Olmsted, M., 254, 262
Olson, J., 38, 46
Olweus, D., 589, 590, 591, 593, 594, 595, 596
O'Mahoney, M. T., 24
O'Malley, P. M., 552, 559
O'Neil, J. M., 184, 187
Ones, D. S., 377
Oney, K. M., 539
Oravec, J. A., 41, 42, 44
Orbach, I., 540, 541
Ordway, L. D., 521
Oren, C. Z., 9
Organista, K. C., 329
Organista, P. B., 324
Orjada, K., 580
Orleans, C. T., 517, 518
Orlinsky, D. E., 257, 259, 260
Ormel, J., 215
Orpinas, P., 589, 590, 593, 600
Orr, S. P., 262
Orth, U., 245
Orthwein, J., 6

Orton, M., 452
Osatuke, K., 270, 279
Osborn, D. S., 453
Osborn, M., 513
Osborne, M. I., 571, 572, 576, 580, 582
Osgood, D. W., 596
Osipow, S., 31, 32, 394, 395, 366, 409, 513
Öst, L., 252
Ostby, S., 224
Ostrove, J. M., 159, 168
Otten, S., 132, 135
Otto, M. W., 28
Ouellette, S. C., 61
Ouimette, P. C., 563
Overholser, J. C., 10, 342, 543
Overpeck, M., 589, 590, 593
Owen, D., 524
Owen, N., 517, 525
Owens, J. A., 185
Oxhoj, M. L., 214
Ozer, D. J., 375, 376

Packard, T., 8
Packman, W. L., 6
Padgett, M. Y., 466
Pager, D., 413
Palesh, O., 313
Palfai, T. P., 304
Palma, T. V., 409
Palmer, A., 599
Palmer, R. S., 557, 559
Paludi, M. A., 177, 179, 182, 192
Panayiotou, G., 305
Pang, T., 62
Pannu, R., 123, 124, 125, 126, 136, 345
Papacharisis, V., 510
Papas, R. K., 528
Papenfuss, M., 522
Pappas, D. M., 560
Parham, T. A., 61, 321, 493, 494, 519
Parikh, S., 28
Park, C., 503
Park, H.-J., 78
Park, J., 204, 205, 206
Park, K., 180
Park, N., 90, 92, 93, 95
Park, S., 329
Parker, C. P., 413, 444
Parker, L., 162
Parker, R. M., 216
Parks, A. C., 90, 92, 93, 95
Park-Taylor, J., 588, 600
Parrish, T. J., 462, 463, 475
Parsons, F., 54, 57, 357, 411, 451
Pascual-Leone, A., 286
Pate, R. R., 524
Pate-Carolan, L., 344, 347, 350
Patterson, C. J., 188
Patterson, J. B., 216
Pattillo, M., 163
Patton, J., 203, 347
Patton, M. J., 272, 278, 288, 295, 454
Patton, S., 291
Paul, K. B., 464
Paul, P. L., 197, 204, 205, 206, 207
Pavela, G., 12
Pawlik, K., 75
Paxson, C., 166
Paxton, S. J., 571, 574, 582
Payton, J. W., 513

Pearce, K., 304
Pearce, M. S., 162
Pearl, M., 519, 520
Pearson, J., 570
Pearson, S. M., 414
Peck, S. C., 485, 488, 491, 494
Pedersen, P., 68, 71, 72, 76, 104, 123, 130, 136, 137, 141, 149, 153, 212, 331, 333
Pedersen, S., 486
Pedrotti, J. T., 93, 94, 98
Pellegrini, A. D., 592, 593
Pelletier, J. R., 224
Pendery, M. L., 251
Penk, W., 547
Peplau, L., 183
Peracchio, L. A., 164, 167
Percevic, R., 237
Perel, J. M., 329
Perez, P., 56
Perez, R. M., 194, 199, 207
Perina, K., 536
Perkins, W. B., 558
Perrone, K. M., 432
Perry, C. L., 556, 570, 572, 574, 589
Perry, D. G., 589, 591
Perry, J., 54, 56, 57, 185, 367, 368
Perry, N. W., Jr., 517
Perry-Jenkins, M., 432
Perugini, M., 131, 132, 134
Petersen, D. A., 292, 341, 348
Petersen, S. E., 86, 94
Peterson, C., 86, 87, 88, 89, 90, 92, 93, 95
Peterson, D., 214, 215, 216, 217, 224, 226, 277
Peterson, G. W., 400, 453
Peterson, K., 580, 583
Peterson, P. L., 559
Peterson, R., 380, 594
Petit, G. S., 592
Petitpas, A. L., 503
Petren, S., 21, 30, 32
Pettit, G. S., 591
Petty, R. E., 307
Peyrot, M. F., 40
Pfeffer, C. R., 543
Phelan, M., 215
Phelps, R., 25, 26, 29
Phillips, J. C., 195, 203
Phillips, J. M., 200
Phillips, S. D., 400
Phillips, S. T., 124
Philpot, C. L., 176, 184, 185, 186, 187, 188
Phinney, J. S., 494, 495
Pickering, J. W., 396, 400, 401, 402, 403
Pickering, R. P., 552
Pickett, K. E., 161, 519, 520
Pickett, T., 159
Pickett, T., Jr., 159, 160
Pickett, T. C., 42
Piekstra, J., 131, 134, 135
Pierce, C., 146
Pierce-Gonzalez, D., 146
Piercy, F. P., 38
Pieterse, A. L., 64, 324
Pilkington, N. W., 599
Pilkonis, P. A., 234
Pilla, R. S., 589, 590, 593
Pinto, B. M., 525

Pipes, R. B., 4
Piran, N., 571, 574, 582
Pirie, P. L., 525
Pirkis, J., 547
Pittinsky, T. L., 429
Pittman, F., 184, 186, 187
Pitts, J. H., 306
Plante, T. G., 524
Pleck, J. H., 180, 430
Pledger, C., 216, 224
Plummer, D., 183, 599
Ploszaj, A., 362, 363, 364
Plummer, D., 183, 599
Podus, D., 527, 561
Poland, S., 546
Polatin, P. B., 215
Polk, V., 513
Pollack, H. A., 522
Pollack, M. H., 28
Pollack, W. S., 177, 186
Pollo, A., 257
Polster, D., 308, 309, 310, 312
Pomales, J., 326
Pomerantz, A. M., 4
Pomerleau, A., 177
Ponce, F. Q., 326
Ponterotto, J., 59, 71, 72, 73, 76, 81, 103, 122, 123, 126, 128, 130, 131, 132, 134, 136, 137, 142, 143, 148, 150, 151, 153, 341, 492
Pope, M., 199
Pope-Davis, D. B., 103, 106, 149, 160, 330
Porfeli, E., 366, 367, 368
Porter, J. R., 428
Porter, L. J., 589
Porter, T., 212
Poston, W. S. C., 523
Poteat, P., 599
Potoczniak, D. J., 196, 197
Potvin, L., 180
Powell, G. N., 426, 430
Powell, J. L., 483, 484, 489
Power, P. G., 396
Prediger, D. J., 376, 378, 379, 382, 383, 386
Predragovich, K. S., 409
Prendergast, M. L., 527, 561
Presaghi, F., 131, 132, 134
Presley, C. A., 559, 560
Presnell, K., 573
Preston, S. D., 262
Preston-Schreck, C., 177
Price, S. W., 164
Prieto, L. R., 350
Prilleltensky, I., 16, 54, 55, 56
Prilleltensky, O., 56
Prochaska, J. O., 39, 40, 524
Proctor, L. J., 589
Prosser, J., 413, 414, 415, 417, 418, 452
Pruett, M. K., 513
Pruitt, N. T., 346
Pryor, J. B., 305
Pugh, R. H., 114
Pung, M. A., 576, 577
Puska, P., 62
Pyszczynski, T., 304, 313

Quigley, L. A., 558
Quillian, L., 413
Quilty, L. C., 38
Quinn, D. M., 178

Quintana, S. M., 78, 106, 108, 109, 110, 150

Rabinowitz, F., 181, 186
Rabinowitz, J., 215
Racker, H., 274
Raczynski, J. M., 521, 522, 523
Radonovich, K. J., 563
Ragan, J., 580
Raghunathan, R., 448
Ragins, B. R., 200, 201
Ragusea, A. S., 40, 41, 42
Rahardja, D., 452
Rain, J. S., 462, 466
Rainey, J. A., 142, 144
Rainey, L. M., 306
Rainey, S. E., 39, 41, 42
Raingruber, B., 292
Rajab, M. H., 541, 542
Rakhsha, G., 76, 123
Ralston, C. A., 381
Ram, G., 449
Ramirez, M., III, 55, 129
Ramos-Sanchez, L., 326
Randazzo, K. V., 142
Range, L., 538, 539, 540, 543, 544, 545, 547
Rangel, D., 8, 9
Rapee, R. M., 305
Rappaport, J., 54, 436, 437
Rashid, T., 90, 92, 93, 95
Rasmussen, A., 166
Rattay, A., 180
Raudenbush, S. W., 261, 430
Raue, P., 254, 350
Rawls, J., 55
Raz, A., 272
Read, J. P., 559, 560
Real, T., 181
Reardon, R., 387, 400, 446, 450, 453, 456
Reason, J., 314
Rector, C. C., 397
Recupero, P. R., 39, 41, 42
Redding, M., 594
Redmond, C., 555
Reed, C. A., 387
Reed, G. M., 38, 224
Reed, J. H., 452
Rees, R., 524
Reese, H. E., 28
Reeve, C. L., 376
Reffitt, B., 523
Regier, D. A., 215
Rehm, L., 6, 7
Reibel, D., 313
Reibstein, J., 289
Reich, A., 311
Reid, J. R., 285
Reid, P. T., 177
Reid, R. C., 236
Reid, S. L., 325
Reid, W., 538
Reimann, P., 504
Reimschuessel, C., 289, 291
Reinhalter, K., 577, 582
Reinhardt, B., 205
Reis, J., 559
Reise, S. P., 111, 113, 114
Reker, G. T., 503
Remer, P., 184, 185

Remien, R. H., 526
Rempel, V., 367
Rensvold, R. B., 113, 114
Renzetti, C. M., 179
Repetti, R., 432
Resnick, R. J., 29
Resnicow, K., 513
Reuman, D., 593
Revenson, T. A., 517
Revicki, D. A., 171
Reynolds, A. L., 492
Reynolds, C. F., 545
Reynolds, L., 45
Rhoades, L., 468
Rhodes, F., 427, 527
Rhodes, R., 275
Rhodes, S. D., 525, 526, 527
Rice, D. P., 214, 553
Rice, J. K., 179
Rice, K. G., 115
Rice, R. W., 430
Rich, B. L., 381
Richard, M., 235
Richards, C., 180
Richards, J. M., Jr., 379
Richardson, B., 306
Richardson, M. S., 366
Richer, C., 431
Richie, B. S., 413, 414, 415, 418, 452
Richie, M. H., 284
Richmond, M. S., 23
Rickard-Figueroa, K., 122
Ridley, C. R., 142, 143, 144, 146, 152,
    153, 256, 257
Rieger, B. P., 148
Rieger, B. T., 151
Rigby, K., 590
Riger, S., 185, 437
Rigsby, L. C., 484
Rijsemus, W., 304, 305, 313
Riker, J. R., 275, 310, 311
Riley, P. J., 434
Rimmer, J. H., 226
Rind, B., 16
Rindfleisch, A., 164
Ringeisen, H., 593
Ringwalt, C. L., 554
Rios, P., 285, 287, 288
Rios-Ellis, B., 323
Risco, C., 197
Risinger, R., 412
Risko, E. F., 38
Ritchie, P., 6, 7
Ritchie, R., 165
Ritter, K. Y., 198
Riva, G., 38, 39
Rivara, F. P., 558
Rivera, P., 216, 222
Rivers, C., 176, 430, 431, 434, 437
Roark, R. R., 562
Robbins, S. B., 45, 275, 310, 358, 359,
    394, 396, 400, 401, 402, 403
Roberts, A. R., 540
Roberts, B., 376, 378, 382, 383, 476
Roberts, J. A., 167
Roberts, M., 9, 10, 525
Roberts, R. K., 413
Roberts, T., 178
Roberts, W. B., 594
Robinson, B. E., 526
Robinson, J. D., 528

Robinson, J. P., 430, 431, 438
Robinson, M., 59, 164, 165
Robinson, S., 413, 414, 415, 418, 452
Robitschek, C., 91
Roche, V., 342
Rochlen, A., 24, 38, 39, 40, 41, 42, 275,
    277, 289, 292, 447, 448
Rockenbaugh, J., 308, 309, 310, 312
Rodkin, P. C., 591, 593
Rodolfa, E., 6, 7
Rodriguez, B. F., 304, 305
Rodriguez, C., 322
Rodriguez, M. D., 490, 491
Roesch, S., 492
Roffman, M., 290, 292, 293, 295
Roffman, R. A., 563
Roger, P. R., 126, 128
Rogers, C., 69, 286, 339
Rogers, E. M., 527
Rogers, J., 13, 14, 527, 538, 539, 540,
    541, 547
Rogers, M. R., 150, 151
Rogers, S. E., 224
Rogers, W., 525, 526, 527
Rohde, P., 573
Rohrbach, L. A., 554, 593
Rohsenow, D. J., 558
Rojewski, J. W., 396, 402, 403
Rolf, J. E., 496
Rollnick, S., 251, 561
Rollock, D., 146
Romano, J., 43, 70, 588
Romans, J. S. C., 125, 127, 128
Romer, D., 547
Rønnestad, M. H., 339, 340
Roona, M. R., 554, 555, 556
Rooney, S. C., 204
Root, M. P. P., 571
Roscoe, B., 598, 599
Rose, E. A., 46
Rose, S. M., 180
Rosenbaum, S., 25
Rosenberg, J. I., 9
Rosenberger, E. W., 275, 279, 311
Rosenheck, R., 327
Rosenmann, A., 48
Rosenthal, D., 216, 217, 224, 226, 252
Rosenthal, R., 62, 446
Rosenthal, S. L., 5
Rosenzweig, M. R., 75
Rosenzweig, S., 255, 313
Ross, J., 464, 476
Rossello, J., 329
Rossi, P. H., 59, 160
Rotella, S., 412
Rothbaum, B. O., 38
Rothberg, J. M., 539
Rothblum, E. D., 194
Rothe, H. F., 464
Rotheram-Borus, M. J., 171
Rothman, A., 517, 518, 528
Rothman, A., 517, 518, 528
Rotunda, R. J., 49
Rounds, J., 358, 359, 378, 379, 380, 381,
    382, 383, 384, 385, 386, 397, 411,
    419, 448, 457
Rowan-Szal, G. A., 562
Rowen, A. B., 528
Rowland, M., 103, 104
Rowley, S. A. J., 493, 494

Roysircar, G., 7, 15, 54, 57, 64, 142, 143,
    152, 303
Roysircar-Sodowsky, G., 143
Rozee, P. D., 179, 182
Rozensky, R. H., 42, 528
Roznowski, M., 109, 110
Ruan, W. J., 552, 589, 590, 593
Rubin, D. B., 446
Rubin, S., 303
Rubinstein, E. N., 544
Rudberg, M. A., 214
Rudd, M. D., 539, 541, 542
Rude, S. S., 34
Rudestam, K. E., 43
Ruelas, S. R., 326
Ruiz de Esparza, C., 413
Runyan, C. N., 528
Rusalem, H., 212
Russell, D. W., 115
Russell, G. L., 327
Russell, J. T., 377
Russell, R. R., 338
Russo, N. F., 180
Rust, P. F., 214
Rutter, M., 483, 484, 488, 489
Ryan, K., 598
Ryan, N., 403, 450, 451, 452, 476
Ryan, R., 164, 311, 467
Ryan, V. L., 267
Ryan, W., 502
Ryan Krane, N., 392, 397, 400, 404, 445,
    446, 447, 448, 449, 450, 451, 452,
    453, 454, 455, 456, 458
Ryder, J., 86, 93, 94
Ryder, K., 526

Sabattini, L., 426, 427
Sabattini, S., 190
Sabo, D., 560
Sabourin, M., 82
Sabourin, S., 431
Sacco, D., 329
Sacco, F., 597, 598
Sack, N., 289, 291
Sackett, P. R., 376
Sacks, M., 259
Saelens, B. E., 570
Safir, M. P., 48
Safran, J. D., 269, 270, 312, 313, 314
Saginak, K. A., 438
Saginak, M. A., 438
St.-Denis, M., 180
Saka, N., 453
Sakata, R., 224
Salaspuro, M., 251
Salgado, J. F., 377
Salkever, D. S., 558
Sallis, J., 517, 524, 525
Salomone, P. R., 393, 395, 398
Salovey, P., 304
Salvi, L. M., 288
Sam, D. L., 123
Sameroff, A., 164, 485, 488, 491, 494
Sammons, M. T., 29
Sampson, H., 272
Sampson, J. P., Jr., 400, 450, 453
Samstag, L. W., 269, 270
Samuels, P., 15
Sanchez, C. M., 151
Sanchez, J., 141, 153
Sanchez, L., 32, 431

Sanchez-Hucles, J., 152
Sanderson, C. A., 469, 470
Sandil, R., 11, 12
Santiago-Rivera, A., 73, 153
Sapmson, R. J., 490, 491
Sapolsky, R., 165, 166
Sapp, M., 93
Sarason, S. B., 54
Sarinopoulos, I., 260
Satcher D., 21
Satorra, A., 108, 115
Saucier, A. M., 202
Saunders, C. M., 527
Saunders, J. B., 558
Saunders, J. L., 364
Savage, J. H., 166
Savickas, M., 69, 76, 357, 365, 366, 367, 369, 397, 409, 456, 462
Savoy, H. B., 198, 204
Sawyerr, O. O., 127, 128
Sayama, M., 22
Sayer, A., 430
Sayer, L., 432, 438
Scales, J. E., 448
Scanlon, C. R., 448
Scantlin, R. M., 178
Scarr, S., 432
Schaalje, B. G., 237
Schacht, T. E., 254
Schaefer, H. S., 262
Schaefer, J. A., 503
Schamberger, M., 270, 287, 297
Schara, S. L., 127, 128
Schaub, M., 360, 364, 369
Schaubroeck, J., 468
Schechtman, E., 527
Scheetz, K., 39
Scheidt, P., 589, 590, 593
Scheier, M. F., 304, 305, 307
Scheinholtz, J., 130, 131, 132, 134, 136
Scheltema, K. E., 526
Schene, A. H., 520
Scher, M., 185
Scherer, M., 216, 226
Schienholtz, J., 146, 148, 149
Schimel, J., 184
Schkade, D., 87
Schmaling, K. B., 251
Schmeelk-Cone, K. H., 492, 493, 494, 495
Schmidt, A. M., 444, 467
Schmidt, C., 60, 202
Schmidt, F. L., 116, 377
Schmidt, J., 115, 362, 363, 364, 474
Schmidt, L. C., 474
Schmidt, L. D., 3, 9
Schneider, B., 430, 513, 598
Schneider, K. L., 293
Schneider, M., 217, 226
Schneider, P. A., 572
Schneider, P. L., 40
Schnurr, P. P., 252
Schoener, G. R., 9
Schoepke, J., 224
Schraedley, P. D., 178
Schreiner, L., 89
Schroeder, D. J., 304
Schroeder, M., 207
Schuck, K., 200
Schulberg, H. C., 329

Schulenberg, J., 57, 395, 409, 410, 552, 559
Schulman, C. E., 41
Schultheiss, D., 366, 409, 415, 420
Schürch, E., 237
Schuster, M. A., 589
Schwartz, A., 142
Schwartz, D., 589, 592
Schwartz, G., 312, 313
Schwartz, R. H., 171
Schwebel, M., 303
Schweitzer, R., 350
Scott, B. A., 381
Scott, C. W., 68
Scott, K. J., 350
Scott, L. D., 495
Scottham, K. M., 495
Scott-Sheldon, L. A. J., 527
Scullen, S. M., 382, 385
Seaton, E. K., 495
Sedlacek, W., 125, 126, 127, 128, 129, 137, 204
Seeley, J. R., 572
Seeman, T., 287
Segal, S. P., 215
Segal, Z. V., 270
Segall, M. H., 73, 76
Seguin, L., 180
Seibel, G. A., 414, 417
Seidman, E., 436, 437, 486
Seiffge-Krenke, I., 185
Sekaran, U., 420
Sekula, K., 544
Selby, J. W., 543
Seligman, M., 86, 87, 88, 89, 90, 92, 93, 94, 95, 483, 504
Sellers, R. A., 488
Sellers, R. M., 492, 493, 494, 495
Sellers, S. L., 493
Sengupta, A., 252
Serafica, F., 78, 331, 366
Serling, D. A., 397, 398
Serra-Majem, L., 523
Seta, C. E., 180
Severson, H. H., 555
Sexton, H., 293, 294, 295, 296
Sexton, T. L., 256, 257, 445, 446, 447, 449, 453, 454, 456
Seybolt, D., 556
Shadish, W. R., 116, 562
Shaffer, H. J., 49
Shafranske, E. P., 342
Shahar, G., 110
Shapira, N. A., 47
Shapiro, A. K., 252, 258
Shapiro, D., 250
Shapiro, D. A., 250, 270, 279, 289, 291, 293
Shapiro, D. E., 41
Shapiro, E., 252, 258
Shapiro, S., 312, 313
Shapiro, S. J., 260
Shapiro, S. L., 311
Sharpe, M., 180
Shaughnessy, P., 10, 279
Shavelson, R. J., 111, 112, 113, 114
Shaw, B. F., 254, 262
Shaw, C. M., 495
Shaw, H., 39, 41, 42, 523, 571, 574, 575, 576, 578, 579, 580, 581, 582, 583
Shaw, J. B., 376

Shaw, J. C., 381
Shaw, J. D., 430
Shaw, S. F., 39, 41, 42
Shayne, L., 45
Shea, M., 234, 251, 252
Shea, S. C., 541
Shear, K., 545
Shechtman, Z., 288
Sheldon, D., 383
Sheldon, K. M., 87, 164
Sheldrick, R. C., 237
Shelton, J. N., 493, 494
Shelton, M. C., 409
Shemesh, N., 453
Shepard, J., 552
Shepherd, J., 524
Sher, K. J., 559
Shera, D. M., 166
Sherba, R. T., 527
Sherbourne, C. D., 521
Sherburn, D., 509
Sherman, G., 62
Sherman, M. D., 10
Sherry, A., 203, 347
Sheu, H., 115, 106, 116, 362, 363, 364, 469, 470, 474
Shi, J., 562
Shidlo, A., 207
Shields, A., 592
Shields, S. A., 432, 437
Shimizu, K., 395
Shimokawa, K., 238, 246
Shin, C., 555
Shipp, A. J., 468
Shiraev, E., 519
Shivy, V. A., 447, 448
Shneidman, E. S., 543
Shore, L. M., 468
Shore, P., 213
Shore, T. H., 468
Short, K. S., 161
Short, R. J., 599
Short, S. J., 260
Shovel, G-A., 277
Shulman, J. L., 206
Siddique, J., 171
Sieber, J. E., 16
Sieber, W., 304
Siegel, S. M., 348
Silberschatz, G., 272, 291, 297
Silverman, E., 543
Silverman, M. M., 535, 538, 541
Silverstein, L. B., 176, 182
Silvia, P. J., 304, 305, 313, 364
Sim, W., 292, 293, 296, 297, 300
Simeonsson, R. J., 216
Simmons, R., 492, 493, 495
Simon, N. P., 571
Simons, A. D., 28
Simons, R. L., 165, 166, 492
Simons-Morton, B., 589, 590, 593
Simons-Rudolph, A., 554
Simpson, D. D., 328, 562
Singer, E., 285
Singer, M. S., 469
Singley, D., 125, 127, 128, 137, 469, 470, 474
Sinha, D., 79
Sinha, R., 563
Sippola, L. K., 592, 593
Siqueland, L., 269

Sirand, J., 524
Sirin, S., 165, 415, 416
Skehan, J., 547
Skilbeck, W. M., 331
Skovholt, T. M., 70, 303
Slack, A. K., 466
Slade, K., 236, 238, 239, 240, 242, 243
Slane, S., 467
Slaney, R. B., 115, 202
Slee, P., 590
Slemon, A., 289, 306
Sliwinski, M. J., 558
Sloan, D. M., 304
Sloan, T., 57
Smahel, D., 45
Smallwood, J., 314
Smallwood, S., 427
Smart, D. W., 36, 236, 238, 239, 240, 242, 243, 246, 247
Smart, J., 216
Smith, C., 598
Smith, E., 90, 91, 95, 141, 149, 153, 333
Smith, E. E., 260
Smith, E. J., 408, 483
Smith, H. L., 464, 466
Smith, J., 362, 363, 364
Smith, J. A., 513
Smith, J. D., 598
Smith, K., 430
Smith, L., 159, 160, 579
Smith, M., 513, 547
Smith, M. A., 250, 261, 493, 494
Smith, M. L., 445
Smith, N. G., 195, 200, 350
Smith, P., 362
Smith, P. C., 464
Smith, P. K., 582, 589, 591, 593, 598
Smith, P. L., 420
Smith, R. C., 306
Smith, R. D., 350
Smith, R. S., 483, 486, 489, 490, 491, 496
Smith, T. B., 148, 151, 152
Smith, T. J., 383, 384, 385
Smith, T. W., 167, 304, 517, 518
Smith West, D., 521, 522, 523
Smits, J. A. J., 28
Smoak, N. D., 527
Smolak, L., 570, 571, 574, 582
Smyer, M. A., 503
Snell, A. F., 379
Snowden, L. R., 327, 519
Snyder, C. R., 86, 87, 91, 94, 95, 98
Snyder, W. U., 287
Sobell, L. C., 251
Sobell, M. B., 251
Sobol, A. M., 580
Sodowsky, G. R., 148
Soisson, E. L., 5
Solberg, E. G., 164, 165
Soleck, G., 159, 160
Solomon, J., 291, 295
Solórzano, D., 146
Sommers-Flanagan, J., 256
Sommers-Flanagan, R., 256
Song, S. Y., 590
Sonnenberg, R. T., 185
Sophie, J., 196
Sörbom, D., 108, 113
Soresi, S., 73, 74, 362, 363, 364, 369
Sorlie, T., 43, 44

Sorrell, R., 235
Soth, A. M., 149, 153
Sotsky, S., 251
Sox-Harris, A., 86
Soyka, K. M., 540, 541
Spangler, P., 300
Spanierman, L., 106, 146, 179
Sparks, E., 15, 54, 56, 64, 435, 436
Sparks, R., 151
Spear, J., 224
Spearman, C., 106
Spector, P. E., 462, 463, 466
Speight, S., 54
Speight, S., 8, 15, 54, 55, 56, 62, 161
Speisman, J. C., 297
Spelke, E. S., 386
Spelliscy, D., 130, 131, 132, 134, 136
Spellman, M., 25
Spengler, P. M., 450, 539
Sperber Richie, B., 206
Sperry, L., 187
Spiegel, A. D., 22, 24
Spiegel, S. B., 297
Spielmans, G. I., 237
Spigner-Littles, D., 79
Spirito, A., 558
Spofford, M., 23
Spokane, A., 357, 358, 421, 444, 445, 449, 453, 454, 457
Spoth, R., 555
Springer, E. A., 576
Spruell, M., 225
Spurrell, E. B., 570
Sroufe, L. A., 591
Stackpole, K. M., 554, 555, 556
Stacy, A., 557
Stahl, J., 290, 292, 293, 295, 300
Stalikas, A., 288
Stall, R. D., 527
Stankov, L., 314
Stanley, B., 16
Stanley, S., 433
Stansfeld, S. A., 165
Stanton, A. L., 10
Stanton, B., 527
Stanton, M. D., 562
Staples, P. A., 44
Stark, S., 224
Stauffacher, E. A., 557, 558
Stavans, l., 323
Staw, B. M., 464, 476
Stead, G. B., 395, 396
Stebbins, L. F., 428, 430
Steca, P., 469
Steen, T. A., 90, 92, 93, 95
Steenkamp, J. E. M., 111, 112
Steil, J. M., 430, 433, 438
Stein, R. I., 570
Steinberg, L., 432
Steiner, D. D., 462, 466
Steinglass, P., 562
Stelmaczonek, K., 289
Stemmler, M., 185
Stephens, J., 392, 449, 450, 453
Stephens, R. S., 563
Stephenson, B. O., 309
Stern, D., 271
Sterner, I., 288
Stetson, B. A., 525
Stevens, C., 269
Stevens, D., 434

Stevens, E., 54
Stevens, S. E., 252, 258
Stevens, S. S., 105
Stevenson, J. F., 346
Stewart, A., 29, 31, 490, 491
Stewart, E. A., 29
Stewart, S. H., 28
Stice, E., 523, 570, 571, 573, 574, 575, 576, 578, 579, 580, 581, 582, 583
Stich, F., 252, 261
Stiles, W. B., 270, 279, 284, 288, 291, 293, 295, 296
Stinson, C. H., 234
Stinson, F. S., 552
Stinson, R., 163
Stiver, I. P., 177, 181
Stockton, R., 43
Stohler, C. S., 260
Stokes, G. S., 359
Stolberg, A., 560
Stoltenberg, C., 33, 307, 308, 310, 313, 342, 350
Stone, A. J., 179
Stone, G. L., 68, 71, 72, 81, 122, 306, 571
Stone, K. V. W., 429
Stormer, S., 573, 578, 583
Story, M., 570, 572, 574
Stracizzi, T. I., 146, 148, 149
Strahan, E. J., 106, 107, 395, 397
Stratton, H. H., 556
Stratton, J. S., 350
Strauman, T. J., 293
Strauss, J., 125, 127, 128
Strauss, R. S., 522
Streke, A. V., 554, 555, 556
Strickland, B. R., 15
Striegel-Moore, R. H., 570, 571, 572, 573
Strong, E. K., 380, 469
Strong, S. R., 303
Stronkhorst, R., 134
Strozier, A. L., 150
Strupp, H. H., 234, 250, 254, 273
Stucki, G., 226
Stulz, N., 237
Sturza, M. L., 179
Subich, L., 165, 364, 365, 386, 412, 420, 539, 541
Subrahmanyam, K., 45
Sudberry, M., 314
Sue, D., 7, 64, 72, 82, 94, 103, 104, 105, 123, 141, 149, 153, 160, 170, 324, 331, 333
Sue, S., 147, 322, 326, 327, 328, 329, 332, 333
Suh, E. M., 464, 466
Suinn, R. M., 122
Suler, J. R., 39
Sullivan, B. A., 360
Sullivan, C., 300
Sullivan, J. G., 205
Suls, J., 305, 517, 518, 528
Sung, L. H., 259
Super, D., 86, 93, 365
Surko, M., 288
Suro, R., 323
Surrey, J. L., 177, 181
Sussman, S., 555
Sutherland, S. E., 214
Sutton, M. A., 49

Suzuki, L. A., 103, 123, 142
Swanberg, J. E., 427, 430
Swaney, K., 380
Swanson, J., 357, 411, 444, 456, 457
Swanson, N. G., 413
Swearer, S. M., 590
Sweeney, T. J., 59
Sykes, C., 226
Syme, L., 162
Symonds, B., 269, 454
Szabo, A., 46
Szalacha, L. A., 484, 489, 490, 492
Szapary, P., 313
Szymanski, D. M., 193, 347
Szymanski, E. M., 216

Tabak, C. J., 522
Taffe, R. C., 148
Tait, M., 466
Takeuchi, D. T., 325, 327, 328, 329
Talbert, F. S., 4
Talcottt, G. W., 537
Talebi, H., 257
Talley, R. C., 599
Talleyrand, R., 64, 362, 363
Tallman, K., 261
Tamis-LeMonda, C. S., 182
Tan, J. A., 149, 153
Tang, M., 78, 105, 331, 420
Tang, T. Z., 28
Tanner, J. F., Jr., 167
Tanney, F., 31, 32
Tarbell, S., 517
Tarvydas, V. M., 214, 215, 226
Tashiro, T., 298
Tata, S. P., 325
Tatum, B., 428, 435
Taylor, C. B., 570, 574, 576, 577, 578,
    581, 582
Taylor, G., 78
Taylor, H. C., 377
Taylor, K., 164
Taylor, T., 500
Taylor, W. C., 524
Tedeschi, R., 503
Tee, K., 304
Telch, C. F., 570
Tellegen, A., 404, 466, 469, 475, 483,
    484
Tenenbaum, G., 524
Tepper, C. A., 177
Teri, L., 304
Terndrup, A. I., 198
Terry, S., 448
Teschuk, M., 304
Teter, C. J., 559
Teyber, E., 274, 300
Thase, M. E., 28
Thelander, S., 251
Thelen, M. H., 10
Theodorakis, Y., 510
Theorell, T., 165
Thiagarajan, M., 127, 128
Thoits, P. A., 430
Thomas, J. C., 540, 541
Thomas, K., 70, 260
Thombs, B., 126, 128
Thompson, A. S., 86
Thompson, B., 125, 275, 308
Thompson, C. E., 54, 122, 146, 147, 327
Thompson, E. H., 183

Thompson, L., 429, 431
Thompson, M. N., 165
Thompson, R. L., 127, 128
Thompson-Brenner, H., 250
Thoresen, C., 86, 360, 365, 376, 377,
    378, 382, 465
Thoreson, R., 10
Thorne, J., 554
Threats, T., 224
Throop, C. J., 262
Tien, H. S., 394
Tierney, S. C., 252, 253, 260
Tiffin, P. A., 162
Timmerman, M., 560
Timmers, P. H., 44
Tims, F. M., 562, 563
Tinsley, H. E., 325, 359, 395, 396, 397,
    400, 453
Tinsley, T. J., 448, 457
Tirre, W. C., 411
Tobler, N. S., 554, 555, 556
Tokar, D., 360, 364, 369, 413
Tolan, P., 483, 590
Tomlinson, M., 202
Toohey, M. J., 205
Toomey T. L., 556
Toporek, R., 15, 54, 57, 58, 64, 103, 106,
    141, 153
Torres, M., 493
Torrey, E. F., 259
Tortu, S., 555
Touradji, P., 123, 124, 125, 126, 136
Tovar-Murray, D., 199, 201, 202, 203
Tozer, E., 204, 205, 206
Trabin, T., 234
Tracey, T., 73, 74, 255, 358, 359, 363,
    364, 366, 369, 380, 417
Tranberg, M., 467
Trapnell, P. D., 304, 305
Trask, C., 224
Tree, H., 90, 91, 95
Treistman, D., 362, 363, 469, 470, 474
Trexler, L., 539
Triandis, H., 104, 323
Tristan, J., 580
Trockel, M., 559
Trommald, M., 62
Tromovitch, P., 16
Trost, A., 578, 583
Trost, S. G., 524
Troy, M., 591
Troyano, N., 78
Truax, P., 236, 253
Trude, S., 24
Truell, A. D., 46
Trupin, L., 214
Trusty, J., 59, 60, 61
Tsabari, O., 359
Tschitsaz, A., 237
Tseng, W. S., 331
Tulkin, S. R., 164
Tunick, R. H., 358, 360
Turk, D. C., 521
Turkson, M. A., 290
Turner, A. P., 559
Turner, N., 467
Turner, R. J., 162
Turner, S. L., 365
Turner, S. M., 32
Tuten, T. L., 45
Tuttle, K., 236, 239, 240, 242, 243

Twemlow, S. W., 597, 598
Twenge, J. M., 162, 178
Tyler, L. E., 357
Tynes, B., 45
Tyroler, H. A., 214
Tyus, N., 526
Tziner, A., 359

Uchino, B. N., 108
Ueda, M., 127, 128
Ueda, S., 216
Uffelman, R., 86, 365, 386
Uhlemann, M. R., 303, 306
Ulman, J. D., 492
Umemoto, D., 9, 159, 165, 415, 419
Unger, J. B., 593
Urada, D., 527, 561
Urbina, S., 106
Üstün, T., 215, 217, 218, 226
Utsey, S. O., 115, 123, 130, 136, 137,
    148, 347, 492

Vacha-Haase, T., 9
Valach, L., 409
Valente, T., 593
Valentine, J. C., 524, 525
Valicj, L., 540, 541
Vallis, T. M., 254, 262
van Balen, R., 286
VandeCreek, L., 3, 5, 13, 14, 40, 41, 42
Vandell, K., 177
Van de Loo, E. L., 44
van de Mheen, H. D., 162, 167
Vandenberg, R. J., 112, 113, 114, 115
VandenBos, G. R., 41
vanden Brink, W., 215
van der Klink, J. J. L., 520
van der Kolk, B. A., 185
VanderWal, B. L., 199, 201, 202
Van der Zee, K., 123, 130, 131, 132, 134,
    135, 136
Vandewater, E. A., 178
van Dijk, F. J. H., 520
Vandiver, B. J., 195
van Hoeken, D., 570
van Mechelen, W., 525
Van Oudenhoven, J. P., 123, 130, 131,
    132, 134, 135, 136
van Poppel, M. N. M., 525
Van Wagoner, S., 275, 310
Vargas, M. J., 287
Vargo-Moncier, C. L., 454
Vazquez, L. A., 152
Vazzana, G., 45, 46
Veach, P., 347, 348
Veblen-Mortenson S., 556
Veenhoven, R., 466
Vega, W. A., 521
Velicer, W. F., 107
Velozo, C. A., 225
Vera, E., 8, 15, 54, 55, 56, 62, 161
Verduin, T., 233
Vermeersch, D. A., 36, 236, 237, 238,
    239, 240, 242, 243, 244, 247
Vermeulen, M., 166
Vernaglia, E. R., 198
Vernberg, E., 598
Vernick, S. H., 387, 450
Versland, S., 295
Victor, T. L., 15
Vigil, P., 122

Villapiano, M., 571, 572, 573, 576, 577, 578, 581
Vincus, A., 554
Vinokurov, A., 151
Vinson, T. S., 146
Vist, J., 62
Viswesvaran, C., 465
Vitanza, S. A., 350
Vitaro, F., 597
Vivino, B. L, 290, 293
Vogel, C. M., 45
Vogel, D. L., 24, 29, 38, 39, 40, 41, 42
Vohs, K., 165, 573
Vondracek, F., 57, 366, 367, 368, 395, 409, 410
Vontress, C. E., 124
Vrana, R. S., 305
Vranceanu, A. M., 162

Wachtel, P. L., 271
Wadden, T. A., 522, 523
Wade, E., 579, 580, 583
Wade, J., 126, 128, 150
Wade, K. A., 32, 33, 59
Wade, P., 330
Waehler, C. A., 147
Wager, T. D., 260
Wagner, B., 544, 545
Wagner, G J., 526
Wagner, K. S., 365, 386
Wahler, C. A., 445
Waidmann, T. A., 163
Waite, L. J., 430
Waldo, C. R., 200
Waldo, M., 600
Walfish, S., 31
Walitt, B., 25
Walker, A. J., 429, 431
Walker, C. M., 359, 412, 419
Walker, D. D., 557
Walker, J., 344, 345, 347, 350
Walker, J. A., 342, 347, 349
Walker, J. U., 171
Walker, W. R., 204
Walkup, J., 214
Wall, M. M., 572
Wallace, B. C., 418
Wallace, I., 501
Wallace, R. L., 451
Walser, R. D., 29
Walsh, B. T., 570
Walsh, M. E., 588, 600
Walsh, R., 311
Walsh, W. B., 94, 357, 453, 462, 463
Walters, G D., 29
Walters, S. T., 560, 561
Wampold, B., 80, 147, 153, 249, 250, 251, 252, 253, 255, 257, 258, 259, 260, 261, 270, 277, 285, 326, 445, 542, 563
Wan, C. M., 448
Wanberg, C. R., 396, 401, 402
Wandersman, A., 556
Wandrop, J., 412
Wang, B., 527
Wang, F., 523
Wang, L. F., 78, 79
Wang, M. C., 489, 490
Wang, M. Q., 598
Wang, P. S., 214
Wang, Y., 78, 325, 522

Ward, C. C., 342
Wardrop, J. L., 412
Warner, D. A., 204
Warr, P., 467
Warren, C. R., 360, 365, 465
Warter, E. H., 600
Washburn, M., 366
Washington, A. E., 159, 168
Watanabe, S., 466
Watkins, C. E., 501, 513
Watkins, J., 251
Watson, D., 398, 404, 466, 469, 470, 471, 472, 473, 474, 476
Watson, J. C., 258
Watson, J. J., 164
Watson, M. B., 395, 396
Watts, R., 63
Wayne, J. H., 429
Weaver, M., 225
Weaver, S. L., 165
Webster, G., 166
Wechsler, H., 49, 560
Wegener, D. T., 106, 107, 108, 395, 397
Wegener, J. H., 216
Wei, M., 115
Weibel, D., 578
Weidner, G., 522, 523, 529
Weinberg, R., 505
Weinberger, J., 257
Weinman, J., 521
Weinshenker, M. N., 433
Weintraub, R. M., 272
Weintraub, S., 15, , 54, 56, 64, 435, 436
Weis, D., 307
Weisman, H., 272
Weiss, D. J., 464
Weiss, H. M., 462, 463, 466, 468, 469, 470, 472, 473, 474, 475
Weiss, J., 272, 288, 295
Weissberg, M., 34
Weissberg, R. P., 513
Weissman, A., 539
Welch, R. R., 570
Welfel, E. R., 13
Wellisch, D., 325
Wellisch, M., 325
Wells, E. A., 559
Wells, M., 346
Wenckstern, S., 544
Wendt, S. J., 579
Werch, C. E., 560
Werner, E. E., 483, 486, 489, 490, 491, 496
Werth, J. L., Jr., 13, 14
Wertheim, E. H., 571, 574, 582
West, L. J., 251
West, S. G., 107, 108
Westbrook, F. D., 121
Westefeld, J. S., 11, 12, 538, 539, 540, 547
Westen, D., 250, 272, 273
Westerberg, A., 511
Westling, B. E., 252
Weston, R., 106, 108
Westra, H. A., 28, 29
Wethington, E., 437
Wexler, M. M., 289
Whaley, A. L., 116
Whearty, P. M., 183
Wheaton, J. E., 45, 46

Wheeler, S., 350
Whilde, M. R., 203, 347
Whipple, J. L., 36, 236, 237, 238, 240, 242, 247
Whiston, S. C., 392, 409, 415, 445, 446, 447, 449, 450, 452, 453, 454, 456, 457
Whitaker, R. C., 166
White, J. L., 519
White, J. W., 179
White, K. B., 178
White, M. J., 539
White, M. V., 288
White, T., 553
Whiteley, J. M., 31, 69
Whiteley, S., 325
Whitely, J. M., 212
Whitfield, K. E., 522, 523, 529
Whitney, D. R., 379
Whitney, I., 589
Whitson, M. L., 364
Whittaker, T. A., 106
Whitton, S., 433
Whitty, M. T., 38
Wicherski, M., 151
Wicker, L., 9, 159, 165, 415, 419
Wickizer, T. M., 558
Wicklund, R. A., 304, 305, 309
Widaman, K. F., 110, 111, 113, 114
Wiecha, J., 580, 583
Wiesner, M., 366, 367
Wietlisbach, V., 558
Wigfield, A., 593
Wight, V. R., 179
Wilbourne, P., 561, 562, 564
Wilcox, W. B., 431, 432
Wild, T. C., 557, 558
Wiley, M. O., 180
Wilfley, D., 570, 574, 576, 577
Wilk, S. L., 376
Wilkinson, R. G., 161
Wilkinson, S., 277
Willan, A., 527
Williams, C. L., 556
Williams, C. M., 364, 412
Williams, D. R., 322, 492, 493
Williams, E., 24, 275, 276, 303, 308, 309, 310, 311, 312, 313, 340
Williams, K., 346, 438
Williams, N. C., 63
Williams, S., 41
Williams, S. H., 553
Williams, S. M., 558
Williams, S. S., 559
Williams, V., 326
Williamson, E. G., 69, 393
Williamson, I. O., 468
Willig, C., 513
Willis, D., 146
Willmuth, M. E., 7
Wills, T. A., 492, 493, 494
Wilson, G. T., 570
Wilson, J. F., 522
Wilson, L. A., 285, 286
Wilson, W., 56
Windle, M., 486
Wine, B., 273, 279, 290, 295
Winquist, J., 304, 313
Winrow, S. A., 414, 417
Winston, A., 270
Winston, S. M., 5

Winzelberg, A. J., 571, 572, 576, 577, 578, 580, 582
Wisch, A. F., 186
Wise, S. L., 148
Wiseman, C. V., 579
Wiser, S., 254
Wish, M., 384
Witty, T., 225
Wodarski, J. S., 598
Wolfe, J., 179
Wolfe, N., 177
Wolgast, B., 8, 345, 346, 349
Wonell, T. L., 269
Wong, C., 494
Wong, E., 449
Wong, J., 90, 95
Wong, P., 94
Wonnell, T., 289
Wood, D., 166
Wood, G. H., 54
Wood, M., 164, 559
Woodard, L. E., 202
Woods, B. A., 553
Woods, J. D., 201
Woody, S. R., 304, 305
Woolard, R. F., 558
Worell, J., 184, 185
Worrall, L., 224
Worthington, E. L., 432
Worthington, R., 106, 146, 147, 149, 153, 198, 204, 206, 259, 327, 367, 413
Wrenn, C. G., 68, 69
Wright, J., 178, 431
Wright, K. S., 13, 14
Wright, L. W., 599
Wu, J. T., 151
Wu, M., 524

Xiaoming, L., 527

Xie, H., 592

Yacoubian, G. S., 559
Yali, A. M., 517
Yalom, I. D., 124, 246, 262, 286, 544
Yam, I., 272
Yamaguchi, J., 254, 262
Yamamoto, J., 330, 331
Yamini-Diouf, Y., 413
Yan, J., 127, 128
Yang, K.-S., 417
Yang, K. U., 79
Yang, W., 359
Yang, Y., 519, 520
Yao, G., 378
Yap, L., 28
Yarrow, C., 7
Yates, B. T., 305
Yatham, L. N., 28
Yeh, C. J., 40, 127, 128, 324, 325
Yeh, M., 327
Yep, G. A., 325
Yoon, M., 378
York, D. C., 395, 396, 400
York, G., 40, 45
Yosso, T., 146
Young, I. M., 55
Young, J., 342
Young, K., 39, 47, 322, 326, 329, 332, 333
Young, R., 366, 409, 540, 541
Young, S. A., 413, 444
Yuen, R. K., 325
Yufit, R. I., 539

Zaal, J. N., 131, 134, 135
Zabinski, M. F., 571, 572, 574, 576, 577

Zacharatos, A., 467
Zack, J., 275, 277, 289, 292, 453
Zaichkowsky, L., 560
Zakai, A., 453
Zakalik, R. A., 115
Zamostny, K. P., 180
Zanakos, S. I., 560
Zane, N., 322, 326, 327, 328, 329, 332, 333
Zao, K. E., 362
Zax, M., 164
Zelazo, L. B., 484, 485, 486, 487, 488, 489, 490
Zell, A., 590
Zerth, E. O., 528, 529
Zetzel, E. R., 269
Zhang, N., 325
Zhang, Q., 522
Zhao, R., 527
Zhu, K., 555
Ziegler, C. H., 525
Ziemba, C., 573, 575, 576, 578
Ziemba, S., 434
Zikic, J., 367
Ziller, R. C., 124
Zimet, G. D., 239
Zimet, S. G., 239
Zimmerman, M. A., 487, 488, 489, 492, 493, 494, 495
Zimmerman, R. D., 467, 468, 470
Zimmerman, T. S., 434
Zins, J. E., 513
Zohrabyan, L., 527
Zook, C., 448, 449, 454
Zubek, J., 180
Zuber-Skerritt, O., 342
Zubieta, J., 260
Zumkley, H., 590
Zwick, W. R., 107

Subject Index

Advocacy and social justice, 59–61
    competencies, 60–61
    dispositions, 60
    forms of, 59
    knowledge-based competencies, 61
    lobbyists, 59–60
    public policy, 61–62
    research on, 60
    skills-based competencies, 61
    training/education, 59–60, 61
African Americans:
    attitudes and preferences, 322
    career decision making, 423, 414
    client-therapist match, 327
    effectiveness of psychotherapy, 329
    ethnic identity, strong sense of, 494
    health insurance and, 521
    John Henryism, 519
    literature review of counseling and psychotherapy, 331–332
    Multidimensional Inventory of Black Identity, 493
    obesity rates, 522
    personalities and values, 321–322
    physical activity, 524
    race/ethnicity of therapist, 321, 326, 327
    racial discrimination of youth, perceived, 492–493
    racial identity as protective factor, 493–494
    racism against, 496
    research and practice implications for racial discrimination
        and identity, 494–496
    sexually transmitted diseases, 526
    stress and racism against, 492, 494
    Whites approach to therapy versus, 322
Alcohol. *See also* Substance abuse prevention and treatment
    abuse statistics, 552
    Alcoholics Anonymous, 562
    college athletes abuse of, 560
    community-based prevention programs, 556
    fraternity and sorority members and abuse of, 559
    indicated interventions for abuse, 557–558
    marital and family therapy in treating abuse of, 562
    social norms as abuse intervention, 557, 558
American Counseling Association (ACA):
    on advocacy competencies, 61
    on social justice research, 63
    on terminally ill patients, 14
American Psychiatric Association:
    on homosexuality not a mental disorder, 194
    on need for prescriptive authority, 29
American Psychological Association:
    accredited counseling or clinical psychology program, 528
    Association of Lesbian and Gay Psychologists, 194
    Committee on Accreditation, 33
    Committee on Legal Issues, 15
    Committee on Lesbian, Gay, and Bisexual Concerns, 194
    on conversion (sexual) therapy, 207
    documentation and, 4–5

electronic communications and Ethics Code, 41
Ethics Code, 3, 4, 11, 14
Guidelines on Multicultural Education, Training, Research,
    Practice, and Organization Change, 103
on homosexuality, 194
*International Classification of Functioning Disability, and
    Health* and, 224
interrogation and Ethics Code, 12
on labels used by counseling psychologists, 32
on lack of psychiatrists, 29
membership, 21
multiculturalism and, 8
Multiculturalism Guidelines, 153
on obesity, 580
online counseling and, 40
on positive psychology initiative, 87
on prescriptive privileges, 30, 34
professional confidence and, 10
Resolution on Poverty and Socioeconomic Status, 418–419
Task Force on Psychological Intervention Guidelines, 580
on terminally ill patients, 14
test data versus test materials and Ethics Code, 14–15
on torture, 11
Anxiety disorders treatment differences, 251–252
APA. *See* American Psychological Association
Asian Americans:
    acculturation, 324–325
    acculturation and job satisfaction, 417
    career counseling and, 455–456
    client preferences, 326
    client-therapist match, 328, 329
    coping mechanisms, 325
    counseling expectation, 325
    diversity of group, 323
    effectiveness of psychotherapy, 329
    experiences of psychological distress, 325
    family, 324, 331
    health insurance and, 521
    help-seeking attitudes, 325
    language, 324
    literature review of counseling and psychotherapy, 323, 325
    personality characteristics, 324
    race and ethnicity of therapist, 326
Assessing and promoting strengths, 86–99
    broadening individuals thought-action repertoire, 87–88
    Clifton StrenghtsFinder, 88–89, 90, 91, 92, 94, 95
    closing remarks, 95
    cultural nuances in strength-based scholarship and practice,
        accounting for, 93–94
    depression treatment by capitalizing on strengths, 92–93
    developing and evaluating strengths-based practices, 90–93
    future research and practice, 93–95
    human strengths assessment, 88–90
    positive psychology, 86–88, 92–93
    positive psychology definitions, 86–87
    positive psychotherapy (PPT), 90, 92–93, 95

Assessing and promoting strengths (*Continued*)
  positive traits and emotions, 87–88
  promoting strengths in pursuit of happiness, 92
  signature strengths, 92, 93
  skills enhancement, 96–97
  strength-based practices, 90
  strengths-based counseling (SBC) for adolescents, 91
  strengths-centered therapy (SCT), 90, 91
  strengths discovery and enhancement and positive emotions
    link, 94–95
  strengths enhancement imagery and interaction, 95–97
  strengths imagery, 95–96
  strengths mentoring (SM), 91–92
  Values in Action Classification of Strengths, 89–90
Association of Counseling Center Training Agencies
  (ACCTA), 81
Association of Psychology Postdoctoral and Internship Centers (APPIC):
  Competencies Conference, 8
  on defining competence, 7
  training, 33

Behavioral problems associated with Internet use, 47–49
  gaming, gambling, and role playing, 49
  infidelity, 48
  overuse of Internet, general, 47
  pornography and sexual exploitation, 48
  summary and recommendations, 49
Bullying, school. *See* School bullying

Career development and vocational psychology, 355–480
Challenge to profession. *See* Social justice challenge to profession
Changing landscape of professional practice, 21–37
  expanding practice roles, 31–33
  factors affecting choice of new roles and settings, 31–32
  managed care (*see* Managed care)
  possibilities, sense of broad, 31–32
  prescriptive authority (*see* Prescriptive authority)
  scientist-practitioner training, 32
  summary, 33–34
  training as barrier, 32–33
Characteristics of professional psychologists, essential, 9
Child abuse and confidentiality, 13
Classism. *See* Social class and classism
Clifton StrengthsFinder, 88–89, 90, 91, 92, 94
Common factors approach in psychology. *See* Treatment and
  science of common factors in psychology, importance of
Competence, 6–11
  defining, 7
  ethics, 7
  faculty and supervisor, 8
  graduate students with problems of, 9–10
  multicultural, 7–9
  people with problems of, 8–9
  professional, 10
  self-care, 10–11
Contextual factors in vocational psychology, 408–425
  acculturation, 417, 420, 421
  context definition, 408
  culture of origin, 416–417
  developmental-contextualism model, 409
  differences from mainstream culture, 417–418
  discrimination, 417–418, 421
  ecological development model, 409–410
  families and career choice, 420
  gender and influences, 412–413
  group level influences, 412–416
  group and societal intersections, 421
  individual, group, and societal intersection, 421
individual and group intersections, 419–420

  individual influences, 410, 411
individual and societal intersections, 420–421
  intersections: implications for research and practice,
    419–421
  mainstream culture, influences from, 418–419
  multiple levels of influence, 409
  opportunity structures, 418, 419
  person-environment matching model, 411
  proposed model, 410, 411
  race and ethnicity influences, 413–414
  relational and familial influences, 415
  social class influences, 415–416
  Social Cognitive Career Theory, 412
  societal level influences, 416–419
  summary, 421–422
  work as moving target, 408
Council of Counseling Psychology Training Programs
  (CCPTP), 33, 81
Counseling psychologist term origin, 212
Counseling and supervision, 231–354
Crisis definition, 503
Culture definition, 104
Culture and race in counseling and psychotherapy literature
  review, 320–337
  African Americans (*see* African Americans)
  Asian Americans (*see* Asian Americans)
  client preferences, 326
  client preferences and client-therapist matching research,
    326–328
  client-therapist match, 327–328
  client variables, 321–325
  competency and appropriateness of treatment, cultural,
    330–331
  conclusions, 334
  counselor's bias, 330
  cultural accommodation model, 331, 332, 333
  future research needs and recommendations, 332–333
  Hispanic/Latino Americans (*see* Hispanic/Latino Ameri-
    cans)
  process and outcome with ethnic minority clients, counsel-
    ing, 328–329
  sensitivity and training, cultural, 330–331
  theories and models of cross-cultural counseling, 331–332
  training bias, 330

Dating violence, 598–599
Depression treatment differences, severe, 251
Development and prevention, 481–605
Developments in counseling skills training and supervision.
  See Skills training and supervision developments, counseling
Disability, advances in conceptualizing and studying, 212–230
  biopsychosocial model, 216–217
  causes and costs, 214
  challenge of defining disability, 214
  conclusions, 226
  foundational models of disability, 214–216
  impairment, 219
  implications, 224–226
  increases in disability rates, 213
  *International Classification of Functioning, Disability, and
    Health* (*see International Classification of Function-
    ing, Disability, and Health*)
  measurement and assessment, 224–225
  medical model, 215–216, 222, 223–224
  prevalence of disability, 213–214
  services and policy development, 225–226
  social-constructionist views of disability, 226
  social model, 216
  universe of well-being, 218, 219
Diversity and multicultural psychology, 101–230

Dual-earner families. *See* Work, family, and dual-earner couples
Duty to protect, 13–14

Eating and weight-related disorders, preventing, 570–587
  age where risk highest, 572
  anorexia nervosa definition, 572
  best practices approach to research and practice, 582–583
  binge-eating disorder, 572
  body dissatisfaction, 573, 574
  bulimia nervosa definition, 572
  cognitive dissonance approach, 578–579, 582–583
  components of research, ideal, 581
  computerized interventions, 576–578, 581
  conclusions, 583–584
  definitions, 571–572
  diagnostic terms, 572
  dieting, 573
  duty to protect and, 14
  familial influence, 583–584
  Food, Mood and Attitude CD-ROM, 576
  food industry impact, 583
  goal of dual eating disorders and obesity interventions, research furthering, 579–581
  Healthy Weight control intervention, 578–579, 580, 582, 583
  media advocacy intervention, 579
  media contributing to disorders, 573, 583
  methodological research and practice suggestions, 581–582
  Planet Health prevention intervention, 580, 582, 583
  prevention research for eating disorders, 574–581
  prevention terms, 571–572
  rationale for preventing eating disorders and obesity simultaneously, 573–574
  relapse rates, 570
  research suggestions for prevention, 581–583
  risk factor models, 573
  risk factor research, 572–573
  risk factors definitions, 571
  risk factors review, brief, 573–573
  societal change, plea for, 583–584
  statistics, 570
  Stice and Shaw's (2004) meta analysis, 575–576, 578
  Student Bodies computerized intervention program, 576–578, 581, 582, 583
  trends, recent, 576–579
  universal programs, 571
Ethical issues. *See* Legal and ethical issues
Ethical Principles of Psychologists and Code of Conduct, 3
Ethics competence, 7

Faculty and supervisor competence, 8
Female psychology. *See* Gender, psychology of
Forces of counseling psychology, 86

Gender, psychology of, 176–193
  appearance for females, 178
  bias in assessment, theory, and diagnosis for females, 184–185
  biological issues for females, 178
  changing paradigms of comparing women and men, 436–437
  context and interventions for females, 185
  counselor attitudes and beliefs for males, 186
  counselor awareness of stereotypes for females, 184
  customizing interventions to diverse masculinities, 187
  dark side of masculinity, 182
  emotion socialization for males, 180–181
  fatherhood, 182
  gender broker, 184, 186
  homophobia, male friendships, and social isolation, 183
  impact of gender socialization on boys and men, 180–183
  impact of gender socialization on girls and women, 178–180
  implications for practice with boys and men, 185–187
  implications for practice with couples and families, 187–188
  implications for practice with girls and women, 183–185
  late-life issues for men, 183
  marriage for males, 181–182
  men's health, 182–183
  relationships for males, 181
  reproduction and childbirth for females, 179–180
  socialization across life span, 176–183
  socialization for media, 177–178
  socialization for parents, 176–177
  socialization for school systems, 177
  socialization into sexuality for males, 181
  summary and conclusions, 188–189
  therapist skills and males, 186–187
  viewing men's presenting problems in gender context, 186
  violence and abuse for males, 181
  women and aging, 180
  women and workplace, 179–180
  work and career for males, 181
Gender differences and career development, 385–387

Health Insurance Portability and Accountability Act (HIPAA), 3
  access to records and, 5
  APA's Ethics Code and, 15
  informed consent and, 4
Health promotion and preventing and reducing disease, 517–534
  competencies and training for counseling health psychologists, 528–529
  conceptualizing dietary behavior, 522
  conclusions, 529
  counseling psychologists role in, 517
  cultural beliefs, values, and practices, 519
  defining, 518
  dietary behavior and obesity, 521–523
  dietary behavior and obesity interventions, 523
  domains of, major, 518–527
  help-seeking and access to health care, 520–521
  HIV/AIDS, 525, 527
  indicators, leading health, 518–527
  interventions to decrease risky sexual behavior, 526–527
  interventions to increase physical activity, 524–525
  lay referral network, 520
  models of physical activity, 524
  physical activity, 523–525
  risk and protective factors, general, 518–521
  risk and protective factors in obesity, 522–523
  risk and protective factors in physical activity, 524
  risk and protective factors for sexual behavior, 525–526
  sexual behavior, risky, 525–527
  socioeconomic status and environment, 519–520
  stress, 520, 523
  tertiary prevention, 528
  treatment adherence, 521
Hispanic/Latino Americans:
  acculturation and immigration, 322–323, 326
  career decision making, 413, 414, 417
  client preferences, 326
  client-therapist match, 327–328
  effectiveness of psychotherapy, 329
  family ties, 323
  health insurance, 521
  language importance, 327
  literature view of counseling and psychotherapy, 322–323
  parental support and school bullying, 592
  physical activity and, 524
  race/ethnicity of therapist, 326

Hispanic/Latino Americans (*Continued*)
  self-orientation, 323
  training Latino therapist, 331
  women's earnings, 428
  worldview, 323
Homosexuality. *See* Sexual orientation

Implications for research, training, and practice. *See* Technological Advances
Implications for research and practice in work, family, and dual-earner couples. *See* Work, family, and dual-earner couples
Informed consent, 4
Insight in counseling and psychotherapy, facilitating, 284–302
  attainment of insight, 296–297
  association between insight and other therapeutic outcomes, 294–295
  categories of insight, 289
  changes in insight as outcome of therapy, 290–291
  client contributions to insight attainment, 293
  coding insight as client verbal behavior in therapy sessions, 287–288
  cognitive/behavioral therapy, 286
  conclusions and new directions, 295–298
  definitions of insight, 284–285, 286
  dreams focus and insight, 290, 291, 292, 293, 295
  empirical studies, 287–295
  evidence for insight in therapy, 287–291
  facilitators of insight, 291–294
  helpful event in therapy, insight as, 289
  humanistic/experiential therapy, 286
  Insight Rating Scale, 288, 295
  measurement of insight, 296
  patterns of interaction between therapists and clients associated with insight gains, 293–294
  post-session self-report measures, 289–290
  psychoanalytic/psychodynamic therapy, 285–286
  purpose of insight, 287
  role of therapist interpretation in client insight acquisition, 297–298
  synonyms for insight, 285
  theoretical perspectives, 285–287
  therapist interventions associated with insight attainment, 291–293
  therapist versus client generation of insight, 297
  transference, 294–295
  value of insight, 298
Interdisciplinary connections and future directions. *See* Self-awareness, therapist
International Association for Cross-Cultural Psychology (IACCP), 75
International Association of Applied Psychology (IAAP), 75, 76
International Classification of Functioning, Disability, and Health (IFC), 213, 214, 217–226
  activities and participation, and capacity and performance, 220, 222
  activity definition by, 222
  body functions and structures, 220, 223
  by-product of, one, 224
  chapters in, summary of, 221
  classification levels, 220
  components, 220
  components interaction diagram, 218
  context, 219–220
  contextual factors, 222, 223
  definition, 217
  developing services and policy, 225–226
  disability defined by, 218
  environmental factors, 222
  framework, conceptual, 218

impairment definition by, 217, 219
  implications for counseling psychology, 224–226
  individual, 219
  measurement and assessment, 225–226
  medical model versus, 222, 223–224
  overview, 223
  participation definition by, 222
  personal factors, 222, 225
  promise of, 217
  structure, 219–222
  universe of well-being, 218, 219
  versions, 219
International Council of Psychologists (ICP), 75
Internationalization growth, 68–85
  categories of influence on, 69
  challenges and opportunities, 76–82
  collaboration among counseling organizations, 81–82
  collaborations, international, 73–74
  conclusions, 82
  cross-cultural competence, enhancing, 77
  cross-national collaborations, 73–74
  cross-national research collaboration, promoting, 80
  cultural accommodation model (CAM), 78
  culturally valid practice around globe, promoting, 80
  cultures pervasive role in United States, 71–73
  early efforts, 69–70
  education, enhancing and promotion, 80–81
  ethnocentrism, overcoming, 76–77
  history of efforts in United States, 69–74
  indigenous psychologies, supporting and extending, 79
  integration of multicultural and cross-cultural foci, promoting, 79
  initiatives with professional organizations, 74
  journal articles encouraged for international colleagues, 72
  Minnesota International Counseling Institute, 70
  obstacles to, 72–73
  professions global growth, 74–76
  theory development-cultural sensitivity versus imposed etics, 77–79
  university environments changes, 70–71
International Journal for the Advancement of Counseling (IJAC), 69–70
International Society for Mental Health Online (ISMHO), 40, 41
International Union of Psychological Sciences (UUPsyS), 75
Internet used for conduction research, 44–47
  benefits and risks, 45–46
  ethical and legal issues, 46
  informed consent, 46
  representation of population issue, 45
  social communication behavior studying, 45
  summary and recommendations, 46–47
  surveys, 45, 46
Intersections of individual, group, and societal dimensions. *See* Contextual factors in vocational psychology

Job satisfaction. *See* Work satisfaction, understanding and promoting
Journal of Counseling and Development (JCD) on multiculturalism, 71
Journal of Counseling Psychology (JCP)
  disability articles, 212–213
  on sexual orientation, 195

Legal and ethical issues, 3–20
  challenging ethical situations, 11–16
  characteristics of professional psychologists, essential, 9
  child abuse, 13
  competence. *See* Competence
  conclusions, 16–17
  conflicts, ethical, 11–13

duty to protect, 13–14
eating disorders, 14
ethical decision-making models, 5–6
informed consent, 4
interrogation, 12
maintenance of integrity of assessment situation, 14–15
managed care and difficulties with, 26
online counseling and, 40–42
risk management. *See* Risk management
socially sensitive topics and action research, 15–16
suicide, 6, 12
Lesbian, gay, bisexual, and transgender (LGBT). *See* Sexual orientation; Vocational psychology and lesbians, gays, bisexuals, and transgenders
Life development intervention (LDI). *See* Positive development and competency across life span, promoting

Male psychology. *See* Gender, psychology of
Managed behavioral health care organizations (MBHOs), 23
Managed care (MC), 21–28
    accountability emphasis, 23–24
    administrative costs increase, 26
    agency hardships, 27
    challenges and opportunities of, 25–28
    cost containment strategies, 22
    cost increases reasons, 22
    cost obsession, 25
    de-emphasis on psychiatric hospitalization, 27
    effects of, 25–28
    ethical and legal difficulties, 26
    evidence-based practice (EBP), 25
    evolution of, 22–23
    freedom of choice legislations, 21–22
    health maintenance organizations (HMOs), 22
    imposition of medical model, 25
    inadequate health care, 26–27
    integration of health services, greater, 23
    International Classification of Functioning, Disability, and Health and, 226
    paperwork increase, 26
    point of service plans (POS), 22
    positive aspects, 27–28
    preferred provider organizations (PPOs), 22
    prototypic, 22
    psychotherapy factory, 27
    roles outside of, 31
    service types and who delivers them, 25
    training opportunities and emphases, 27
    trends, 22–23
Minnesota International Counseling Institute (MICI), 70
Minnesota Multiphasic Personality Inventory (MMPI), 104, 233, 234, 236
Multicultural competence in practice and training, 7–8, 141–158
    assessment, 142
    assessment considerations, 142–144
    clinician bias, 142–143
    colorblind racial attitudes, 146
    conceptualizations of assessment, 143–144
    counseling considerations, 144–148
    counseling processes and attention to racial and cultural issues in treatment, 145–147
    critiques on status of training, 152
    Cross-Cultural Counseling Inventory, 148
    cultural nuances in strength-based scholarship and practice, accounting for, 93–94
    dimensions, 145
    ecological model, 144–145, 147, 153
    empathy, 145–146
    evidence-based practice, 147–148
    implications and future research directions, 152–154

measurement of competence, 148–149
models of counseling, 144–145
Multicultural Awareness-Knowledge Skills Survey, 148, 149
Multicultural Competency Checklist, 150
Multicultural Counseling Inventory, 148, 149
Multicultural Counseling Knowledge and Awareness Scale, 148–149
racial microaggressions, 146, 147, 153
racism, 146
students of color, 151
training, 149–152
tripartite model, 141, 148
youth assessment, 144
Multicultural counseling and psychology. *See* Theoretical and empirical advances in multicultural counseling and psychology
Multicultural counseling and social justice, 55–56
Multicultural personality (MP) development, 129–136
    components, 130
    definitions, 129–130
    factor structure and reliability summary, 131, 132–133
    in international adult worker samples, 135
    measuring, 130–131
    questionnaire (MPQ), 130–131, 132–135, 136, 137
    recommendations for research, 136
    research review, 131, 134
    studies summary using MPQ, 132–133
    summary, 135–136
    in university and high school student samples, 134–135
Multicultural psychology research, conceptual and measurement issues in, 103–120
    assessment of model fit, 109
    confirmatory factor analysis (CFA), 108–111, 113, 115, 125
    considerations, 108
    exploratory factor analysis, 106–107, 110
    exploratory factor analysis strategy appropriateness, 107
    extraction method for factor analysis, 107
    factor analysis use, 105–111
    factorial invariance, 112
    factor retention, 107
    factor rotation, 107
    implementation of exploratory and confirmatory factor analysis in development literature, 110–111
    implementation of measurement equivalence, 115–116
    item parceling, 110
    measurement invariance approaches, 111–116
    meta-analysis to integrate findings and test models, 116–117
    model modification, 109–110
    multivariate normality, 108–109
    principal components analysis, 107
    reporting model parameters, 109
    structural invariance, 114
    summary, 117
    terminology review of measurement equivalence, 111–112
    types of invariance, 113–114
    universality versus specificity, 104–105
    what/whom is multicultural question, 104

National Association of School Counselors (NASC):
    on advocacy, 60
    on social justice research, 63
National Board for Certified Counselors and online counseling, 41

Online counseling, 39–42
    benefits and risks, 39
    components, 39
    confidentiality of, 41
    face-to-face versus, 40, 42
    legal and ethical issues associated with, 40–42

Online counseling (*Continued*)
  National Board for Certified Counselors and, 41
  nonverbal clues absence with, 41
  prisoners and videoconference sessions, 40
  research on, 40
  state licensure laws and, 42
  summary and recommendations, 42
  text-based, 39
  videoconferencing, 40
Outcome Questionnaire psychotherapy quality management
    system, 236–244
  categories based on observed change, 237
  classification of signal-alarm clients example, 244
  clinical support tool problem-solving decision tree example,
    239
  computer software for, 240, 241, 246
  defining positive and negative outcome, 236–237
  domain assessed, 236
  feedback and clinical support tools, provision of, 238–240,
    241
  feedback messages, 238, 240
  impact of feedback on client outcome, 240, 241–244
  other measurement scores correlated with, 236
  prediction of treatment failure, 237–238
  signal-alarm system, 238, 241, 242, 245
  therapists effects and improving outcomes, 244
Outcome in routine practice of psychotherapy, measuring and
    improving, 233–248
  advantage of outcome management, major, 235
  barrier to testing outcomes, 246
  defining positive and negative outcome, 236–237
  discriminative measures, 233
  evaluative measure, 233
  from measuring and monitoring to management of outcome,
    235–236
  Minnesota Multiphase Personality Inventory, 233,
    234
  Outcome Questionnaire psychotherapy quality management
    system. *See* Outcome Questionnaire psychotherapy
    quality management system
  prediction of treatment failure, 237–238
  predictive measure, 233
  psychological measures, 233–234
  selection criteria, 234
  summary and conclusions, 244–246

Positive and counseling psychology interfacing. *See* Assessing
    and Promoting Strengths
Positive development and competency across life span, pro-
    moting, 500–516
  bridge to better health program, 511
  critical life events, 503
  evaluation of life development intervention programs,
    512–513
  evaluations of GOAL, 509
  Family, Relationship, Education, and Employment (FREE)
    4 VETS program, 511–512
  framework for enhancing development, 503–505
  future, importance of, 505–507
  future directions and conclusions, 513–514
  goal of life development intervention, 503, 504
  GOAL program, 507–509
  goal setting elements, 506
  GOAL's ten workshops, 507–508
  imaging dreams and setting goals, 505–507
  indicated prevention interventions, 501
  intervening consideration perspective, 502
  interventions focus, 501
  life competencies question, important, 501–502
  life development intervention (LDI), 503–505
  life skills definition, 504

  life skills programs based on life development intervention
    model, 509–511
  participants for Life Development Interventions, appropri-
    ate, 501
  personal growth after loss, 503
  posttraumatic growth, 503
  psychoeducational model, 504, 511–512
  roadblocks to attaining goals, 506–507
  selective prevention interventions, 501
  sports united to promote education and recreation (SUPER),
    509–510, 512
  steps in learning a skill, 504–505
  teaching attitudes, values, and/or skills, 504–505
  universal preventive interventions, 501
Prescriptive authority, 28–31
  benefits of medication, 28
  to prescribe or not question, 28–30
  states that grant, 34
  training, 29
  training levels proposed, 30–31
Prison inmates and ethical conflicts, 12
Professional and scientific issues, 1–99
Psychological impact of poverty and inequality, understand-
    ing. *See* Social class and classism
Psychology in United States as white middle-class enterprise,
    71

Risk management, 4–6
  consultation, 5
  documentation, 4–5
  ethical decision-making models, 5–6
  example, 6
  informed consent, 4
  suicide and, 6
Risk and resilience, 483–499
  assessing risk in resilience, 485
  competence definition, 486
  competence and resilience, 486–487
  conclusions, 496
  definition and measurement of resilience-related constructs,
    484–488
  ego resiliency versus resilience, 484
  environmental risk factors and IQ levels, 490, 491
  indicator of risk, 485
  measuring risk, 485
  measurement of competence, 486–487
  person-focused approach, 488, 489, 491
  protective and vulnerability factors, 487–488
  quality relationships, 490
  racial discrimination and racial identity, 492–496
  racial discrimination of African American youth, perceived,
    492–493
  racial identity as protective factor, 493–494
  racial socialization, 495–496
  research and practice implications for racial discrimination
    and identity, 494–496
  resilience definitions, 483, 484
  strategies in resilience research, 488–489
  themes in resilience research, 489–492
  variable-focused approach, 488, 489, 491

School bullying:
  antisocial behavior of bullies, 590
  attachment theory, 591
  attraction theory, 593
  Bully Busters, 596–597
  causes, 590
  characteristics, individual, 590
  classification of, 589
  classroom and school factors, 593–594
  definition, 589

dominance theory, 593
emotions of victims, 590
family influences, 590–592
gender differences in, 590
homophily hypothesis, 592–593
implications for prevention, intervention, and training, 600
maltreatment, parental, 591
Olweus Bullying Prevention Program, 594, 595–596
parental style, 591
Peaceful School Project, 597–598
peer influence on aggression theories, 592–593
perceived parental support, 592
prevention program, 597
program approaches to address problems, 594
school-wide prevention information, 594–598
sibling aggression, 592
social-ecological framework of perpetration and victimization, 589–590
statistics on, 589
steps to respect program, 597, 598
summary, 598
teachers manual for helping bullies, victims, and bystanders, 596–597
School violence and bullying prevention, 588–605
bullying (*see* School bullying)
dating violence, 598–599
homophobic aggression, 599
implications for prevention, intervention, and training, 599–600
sexual harassment, 598
sexual harassment definition, 589
Youth Risk Behavior Survey, 588
Scientist-practitioner training, 32
Self-awareness, therapist, 303–319
alternative definitions, 303, 312
attention flexibility, 314
conclusions, 314
confusion over meaning of self-awareness, 303–304
Counselor Self-Talk Inventory, 306–307
definitions, theories, and empirical findings from outside counseling psychology, 303–306
future research, 312–314
importance of, 303
mindfulness in management of countertransference, 311–312, 313–314
novices, 308, 309
objective self-awareness theory, 304
in psychotherapy literature, 306–312
scope, 313
self-absorption paradox, 305
Self-Awareness and Management Strategies Scales for Therapists, 308
Self-Care/Self-Reflection and Cognitive/Relaxation Techniques, 309
self-evaluation, 305
self-focus, 307
self-insight in management of countertransference, 310–311, 312
self-talk, 306–307
task performance, 305
Sexual orientation, 194–211
affirmative counseling competencies recent developments, 206
affirmative training, state of, 203–204
American Psychological Association on, 194
aspects of professional training, specific, 204–205
career development, choice, and assessment, 202–203
conclusions, 207
conversion therapy, 206–207
curing homosexuality focus, 194
dual trajectory lesbian and gay identity model, 197–198

gender-transgressive identity enactment, 198–199
heterosexual identity models, 198
history and current status of lesbian, gay, bisexual, and transgender affirmative perspectives, 195–196
homophobia aggression, 599
journal articles on, 195
Lesbian, Gay, and Bisexual Affirmative Counseling Self-Efficacy Inventory, 206
Lesbian, Gay, Bisexual, and Transgendered Climate Inventory, 200
phases, 197
professional training and education, 203–205
religious beliefs and, 196
scholarship and research on lesbian, gay, bisexual, and transgender, affirmative, 196–205
sexual identity management, 200–202
sexual identity theory, 196–197
sexual minority clients and counseling practice, 205–207
Sexual Orientation Counselor Scale, 206
trainee attitudes and clinical judgments, 204
vocational psychology and lesbians, gays, bisexuals, and transgenders (*see*
Vocational psychology and lesbians, gays, bisexuals, and transgenders)
workplace climate, 200
Workplace Heterosexism Experiences Questionnaire (WHEQ), 200
Workplace Sexual Identity Model, 201, 202
Skills training and supervision developments counseling, 338–354
areas for future investigation, 340–341
components in evaluation by supervisors, 346
conclusions, 350
conflicts in supervision, 347–348
countertransference supervisor, 349–350
covert processes, 348
critical events in supervision, 343–344
criticism of skills training, major, 340–341
ethics, supervision, 349
evaluation of supervisory research, 345–356
feedback, supervisory, 345–346
gender issues in supervision and research, 347
helping skills training models, 339, 340
Hill's helping skills model, 339, 341
human relations training or integrated didactic experiential training, 339, 340, 341
integrated development model, 342–343
interpersonal process recall, 339, 340
meta-analytic finds, 340
microcounseling skills training, 339, 340
multicultural issues in supervision research, 346–347
parallel process, 348
research, supervision, 344–348
research on counseling skills, 339–341
research to practice and practices to research linkages, 348–350
self-supervision, 344
specialization areas of supervision, 350
supervisee development, 348
supervisee sexual attraction toward clients and use of supervision, 348–349
supervision and client outcome, 350
supervisor training, 350
supervisory relationship research, 344–345
supervisory self-disclosure, 349
systems approach to supervision, 343
taping supervisees, 349
theories, supervision, 342–344
Social class and classism, 159–175
career decision making and, 415–416, 420
conclusions, 170–171

Social class and classism (*Continued*)
defining, 159–163
defining world view, 168
development of mental health problems, 164–167
downward classism, 160
ecological theory and impact of poverty, 163–164
economic cultures, 168, 170
effects on person's life of, 159
exosystems, 163, 165–166
gradients and mental health, defining, 162–163
income, asking about, 159
internalized classism, 160, 168
interventions, 169–170
lateral classism, 160
macrosystems, 163, 164–165
materialistic value orientation, 164, 165
mesosystems, 163, 166, 168
microsystems, 163, 166–167, 168
poverty and inequality, defining, 161
practicing world view model, 167–170
reverse capacity theory, 162–163
socioeconomic status and, 160
upward classism, 160
using world view, 168–170
world view model, 160, 168
Social cognitive career theory (SCCT), 361–365
commingling studies with, 369
diverse groups, 364
environmental and contextual influences, 363
hypothesis testing, 362–363
interventions, 364–365
measurement issues, 362
men's versus women's lower self-efficacy, 364
outcome expectations, 361, 362, 363, 365
personal goals, 361
satisfaction factors, 365
self-efficacy expectations, 361, 362, 363, 365
self-efficacy and interests relationships, 363–364, 382
summary, 365
Social justice challenge to profession, 54–67
advocacy (*see* Advocacy and social justice)
barriers, 58
communitarian model of justice, 55
conclusions, 65
current state of, 58–59
defining social justice, 54–55
evolution of, 54
future directions, 62–65
Handbook of Social Justice in Counseling Psychology, 57
Liberal Reformist approach, 55
Libertarian model, 55
marginalization, 55
multicultural counseling, 55–56
public policy, 61–62
research, 62–64
Socialist approach, 55
training, 56, 64
vocational psychology, 56–57
Society for the Science of Clinical Psychology (SSCP) on prescribing privileges, 29
Society of Counseling Psychology (SCP)
establishment of, 69
international issues, 74
on labels used by counseling psychologist, 32
membership, 21
multiculturalism survey and, 94
on prescriptive privileges, 30, 34
Section on Lesbian/Gay/Bisexual Awareness, 195
training programs, 33

Society of Vocational Psychology (SVP), 74
Strengths. *See* Assessing and promoting strengths
Substance abuse prevention and treatment, 552–569
athletes, 560
characteristics of effective prevention, 556
cognitive-behavioral and behavioral treatment, 561–562, 563, 564
in combination with additional psychological problems, 552
community-based prevention programs, 556
comparisons of treatments, 563–564
comprehensive and systemwide school-based programs, 555
content and format of indicated interventions, 557–558
costs to society of abuse, 552–553
family-based prevention programs, 555
fraternity and sorority members, 559
homeless youth, 559
indicated prevention, 557–558
ineffective approaches, 564
knowledge and affective-based approaches to school-based programs, 554
mandated students, 559–560
marital and family therapy, 562
mass media-based prevention approaches, 555–556
motivational interviewing, 561, 562, 563, 564
outcomes research on indicated interventions, 558
prevention overview, 553
school-based prevention programs, 554–555
selective prevention, 559–561
social influence-based approaches to school-based programs, 554–555
statistics on abuse, 552
summary and future directions, 564
summary of research on indicated prevention programs, 558
targeting specific high-risk populations, 559–561
treatment, 561–564
twelve-step approaches, 562–563
universal drug prevention approaches, 553–557
Suicide prevention, 535–551
Air Force Suicide Prevention Program, 537–538
bereavement difference question, suicidal, 543–544
clinical judgments, 539–540
Collaborative Assessment and Management of Suicidality model, 542
conclusions, 547–548
content and measurement consideration, 539–540
crisis intervention model, 540, 541, 543
focus of postvention efforts, 544–547
group therapy for bereaved ones, 544
journaling for bereaved ones, 544–545
meaning making bereavement process, 544, 545
media coverage of suicide, 546–547
in military community, 537–538
National Strategy for Suicide Prevention, 535
number of suicides (2003), 535
post-traumatic stress disorder of suicide-bereaved individuals, 544, 546
postvention places for counseling psychologists, 546
postvention as prevention strategy, 543–547
primary prevention, 535–538
process considerations, 540–541
risk assessment, 538
secondary prevention, 538–543
Suicide Prevention Center, Los Angeles Area, 536, 538
Suicide Prevention Program at University of Illinois Urbana-Champaign, 536–537, 538
treatment, 541–542
in university community, 536–537
urban community, 536
Suicide and risk management, 6

Supervision. *See* Skills training and supervisor developments, counseling

Technological advances, 38–53
  behavioral problems associated with Internet use (*see* Behavioral problems associated with Internet use)
  conclusions, 49–50
  Internet used for conducting research (*see* Internet used for conduction research)
  online counseling (*see* Online counseling)
  prisoners and videoconference sessions, 40
  surveys conducted on Internet, 45, 46
  training and supervision (*see* Training and supervision online)
Theoretical and empirical advances in multicultural counseling and psychology, 121–140
  beyond borders and disciplines (2000-present), 123
  birth of movement (1960s and 1970s), 122
  gaining momentum and establishing a specialty (1980s), 122
  historical developments, 121–123
  implications for practice, 136–137
  maturation and expansion of a specialty (1990s), 122–123
  neglect (pre-1960s), benign, 121–122
  personality development (*see* Multicultural personality development)
  universal-diverse orientation (*see* Universal-diverse orientation)
Therapeutic relationship, tripartite model of, 267–283
  assumption, 267
  Core Conflictual Relationship Theme method, 272
  countertransference definitions, 273–274
  countertransference double helix, 273–276
  countertransference interaction hypothesis, 275
  countertransference management and outcome, 275–276
  countertransference occurrence, origins, and manifestations, 274–275
  countertransference and working alliance mutually influence on one another, 279
  current status and future directions, 278–280
  defined, 267–268
  empirical beginnings in study of interacting components, 278–280
  empirical efforts to study real relationship, 277–278
  empirical findings on countertransference, 275–276
  empirical perspectives on transference, 271–273
  Freud on countertransference, Sigmund, 273
  measuring real relationship, 277–278
  others names for working alliance, 269
  Plan Formulation Method, 272
  psychotherapy's hidden dimension, 276–278
  real relationship defined, 276–278
  real relationships and working alliance mutually influence on another, 279
  research on working alliance, 269–270
  transference definitions, 271, 272
  as transference or real relationship to foreground other recedes to background, 279–280
  transference and theoretical and empirical perspectives, 270–273
  transference types per Sigmund Freud, 271
  transference and working alliance mutually influence one another, 278
  Working Alliance Inventory, 270
  working alliance rupture and repair, 268–270
  working alliance theory, 268–269
Training. *See also* Multicultural competence in practice and training
  advocacy, 59–60, 61
  Association of Psychology Postdoctoral and Internship Centers and, 33
  for counseling health psychologists, 528–529

  cultural, 330–331
  cultural bias in, 330
  developing counseling skills (*see* Skills training and supervisor development, counseling)
  International Classification of Functioning, Disability, and Health for assistance in, 225
  lesbian, gay, bisexual, and transgender counseling and, 203–205
  managed care and, 27
  multicultural counseling competence, 149–152
  scientist-practitioner, 32
  social justice and, 56, 64
Training and supervision online, 42–44
  benefits and risks, 43–44
  face-to-face versus, 44
  programs examples, 42–43
  research on, 44
  summary and recommendations, 44
Treatment and science of common factors in psychotherapy, importance of, 249–266
  adherence, 253–254, 261
  alcohol use disorders, 251
  anxiety disorders, 251–252
  centrality of coherent treatment, 258–259
  common factor models emergence, 254–260
  common factors perspective overview, 255–256
  component designs, 253
  controls, common factor, 252–253
  criticism, 256–258
  criticisms clarifications and elaboration, 258–260
  depressive, severe, 251
  differences, treatment, 250–252
  expectation as common mechanism of change, 260
  implications for research practice summary, 262–263
  implications for research summary, 261–262
  integrated theoretical models, 259–260
  mechanisms of change, common, 260
  medical model, 249–250, 257–258
  medical model versus common factors model, 250–252, 258, 261
  outcome research findings, 250–254
  Rogerian therapy, 258–259
  scientific question of common factors, 257–258
  specificity as essence of medical model, 249, 250
  strategy of common factors proponents, 255
  techniques dismissal of common factors, need for, 256
  theory-specific mediators of outcome, 252–254
  warm relationship equals common factors, 256–257

Universal-diverse orientation (UDO), 123–129
  components, 124
  definition, 123
  factor structure and reliability summary, 125, 128
  links, 124
  measuring, 124–128
  Miville-Guzman Universality-Diversity Scale, 124–125, 126–127, 128
  recommendations for research, 129, 136
  research review, 128–129
  studies summary, 126–127
  summary, 129

Values in Action (VIA) Classification of Strengths, 89–90, 94
Vocational counseling process and outcome, 444–461
  building support, attention to, 452–453
  career assessments and technology-based interventions, 453
  career counseling definition, 444
  client factors and input variables, 447
  computer-assisted career decision-making system, 453, 457
  conclusions, 457–458
  conclusions about input factors, 450

Vocational counseling process and outcome (*Continued*)
  conclusions about process factors, 455
  counselor factors in career interventions, 449
  diagnosis and distress, 448
  dose effect of career counseling, 454
  effectiveness of career interventions question, 445–446
  future research, 463–464
  gender and input variables, 447–448
  importance of work in people's lives, 444
  individualized interpretation and feedback, 451
  ingredients to achieve best results, critical, 450–451
  input variables influence outcome question, 447–450
  modalities of input variables, 449–450
  modeling as critical ingredient, 452
  negative effects, 454
  number of sessions effect, 454
  occupational information, 451–452
  processes producing best results question, 450–455
  race and ethnicity and intervention outcomes, 448
  variance by outcome question, career intervention effectiveness, 446–447
  what works for whom under what circumstance question, 455–456
  working alliance, 453–454
  written exercises as critical ingredient, 451, 455
Vocational decision making, conceptualizing and diagnosing problems in, 392–407
  Career Decision Difficulties Questionnaire, 394, 395, 400, 405
  Career Decision Profile, 394, 395, 396, 398, 400, 401, 405
  Career Decision Scale, 394–395, 396, 400, 402, 405
  Career Factors Inventory, 394, 395, 396, 398, 400, 405
  chronic indecisiveness, 401–402
  cluster analytic studies, 396–397, 402, 403
  correlational and factor analytic research, 395–396
  factor interpretation of four factor model, 398, 400–401
  four factor model of vocational indecision, 397–404
  indecisiveness/trait negative affect factor, 398, 404, 405
  information deficits, 403
  interpersonal conflicts and barriers, 403–404
  measurement of vocational indecision, 394–395
  methods and results of our factor model, 397–398, 399
  reasons to seek vocational counseling, 392, 393
  recommendations and conclusions, 404–405
  reconceptualization of cluster analytic data, 401–404
  research on past career indecision, 393–397
  summary factor pattern matrix, 399
  unreadiness, 402
  unready indecisives, 402–403
Vocational psychology, contextual factors in. *See* Contextual factors in vocational psychology
Vocational psychology and individual differences, 375–391
  ACT Interest Inventory, 380
  applications of individual differences, 375–376
  career counseling goal, 386
  career success, defining, 376
  cognitive and noncognitive measures, 376–382
  cognitive predictors of career-related outcomes, 377–378, 387
  ethnics and Holland's mode, various, 380, 381
  extrinsic career success, 376, 382, 387
  gender differences and career development, 385–387
  General Mental Ability, 377, 378, 381, 382, 385
  Holland's RIASEC model, 379, 380, 382, 383, 384, 387, 467
  individual differences and counseling psychology, 375–376
  integrative models of individual differences, 383–385
  integrated models and other future directions, 382–387
  interests and self-efficacy, 381–382
  intrinsic career success, 376, 382, 387

  multiple indicators and prediction of career-related outcomes, 382–383
  noncognitive predicators of career-related outcomes, 378–382, 387
  People-Things dimensions of interests, 379, 386
  role for vocational psychologist, critical, 375
  Strong Interest Inventory, 380, 381
  Strong Ring, 384, 385
  Strong Vocational Interest Blank, 380
  summary and conclusions, 387
  trait complexes, 383, 384
Vocational psychology and lesbians, gays, bisexuals, and transgenders, 199–203
  career development, choice, and assessment, 202–203
  Lesbian, Gay, Bisexual, and Transgendered Climate Inventory, 200
  sexual identity management, 200–202
  workplace climate, 200
  Workplace Heterosexism Experiences Questionnaire, 200
  Workplace Sexual Identity Model, 201, 202
Vocational psychology and social justice, 56–57
Vocational theories advances, 357–374
  career definition, 366
  career stages, Super's, 366–367
  commingling studies, 369
  conclusions, 369
  development theories, 365–368
  environmental and contextual influences, 363
  Gottfredson's theory, 368
  hallmarks for theory, 357
  Holland's theory, 358–360, 362, 369, 379, 380, 382, 383, 384, 387, 413, 421
  hypothesis testing, 362–363
  integrating measures of personality and Holland's theory, 360
  interest structure and individual differences, 359
  outcome expectations, 361, 362, 363
  outcomes of congruence, 358–359
  personal goals, 361
  self-efficacy expectations, 361, 362, 262
  self-efficacy and interests relationships, 363–364
  social cognitive career theory (*see* Social cognitive career theory)
  from stages to communities, 367
  steps in career choices, 357
  tests of congruence hypotheses, 360
  theory of work adjustment, 360–361
  trait-factor theories, 357–361

Weight-related disorders. *See* Eating and weight-related disorders, preventing
Work, family, and dual-earner couples, 426–443
  achieving work-life balance, 433–435
  additional areas for future research, 435–439
  belief systems, families, 428–429
  case example of fairness issue, 434
  changing paradigms for comparing women and men, 436–437
  communication, mutuality, and spousal support, 434–435
  conclusions, 439
  conditions for relationship stability and satisfaction, 431, 432
  demographics, 427
  education, 427–428
  employment, 427
  helping counseling psychologists be social justice agents, 435–436
  income, 428
  interface between paid work and spouse/partner relationships, 430–433
  parenting of adolescents, 432–433

relational work and mutuality of partners support, 431–432

social problems, defining, 436

societal context of family and work relations, 427–429

socioeconomic factors framing family and work relations, 428–429

studying power and equity, 438–439

therapist intervention, 434

views of fairness in work-life balance, 433–434

work-family convergence, 430–431, 437, 438

working fathers visibility, 437–438

workplace practices and policies of dual–earner families, 429

Workplace climate and lesbians, gays, bisexuals, and transgenders, 200

Work satisfaction, understanding and promoting, 462–480

affective events theory, 472–473

characteristics as mediator of personality and objective conditions, perceived job, 471

conclusions, 477

consideration of job and life satisfaction simultaneously, 471–472

definitions and measures of job satisfaction, 463–465

future inquiry and practice directions, 474–477

genetic influence on job satisfaction, 465

global versus facet job satisfaction, 464

goal and efficacy-relevant environmental supports and barriers, 470

goals and goal-directed behavior, 468–469

implications for intervention, 475–476

integrated views of work satisfaction, 470

job characteristics, conditions, and outcome/values, general, 467

job satisfaction fascination, psychology's, 462–463

life satisfaction and relation to, 466

multiple sources of job satisfaction, 465–470

organizational support and role stressors perceived, 468

outcome expectations, 469

personality and affective traits, 465–466, 476

person-environment fit forms, 467–468, 470

person-environment fit and work conditions, 466–468

self-efficacy, 469

social cognitive model of work satisfaction, 472, 473–474

social cognitive variables, 468–470

subjective well-being, 464, 469

temporal considerations, 464